1868

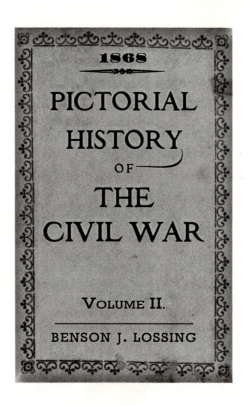

PICTORIAL HISTORY OF THE CIVIL WAR

VOLUME II.

BENSON J. LOSSING

APPLEWOOD BOOKS
Carlisle, Massachusetts

Pictorial History of the Civil War Vol. II
was originally published in 1868

ISBN: 978-1-4290-2032-9

Thank you for purchasing an Applewood book.
Applewood reprints America's lively classics—books from the past
that are still of interest to modern readers.

Our mission is to build a picture of the past through primary sources.
We do not change a word of the editions we reissue, believing that it is
important to present the past without editing it. Sometimes words, thoughts,
images or ideas from the past may seem inappropriate to the
modern reader. We apologize for any discomfort this may bring.
We believe in the value of bringing the past back, just as it was,
for the purposes of informing the present and future.

This facsimile was printed using many new technologies together
to bring our tradition-bound mission to you. Applewood's facsimile
edition of this work may include library stamps, scribbles, and margin notes
as they exist in the original book. These interesting historical artifacts
celebrate the place the book was read or the person who read the book.
In addition to these artifacts, the work may have additional errors
that were either in the original, in the digital scans,
or introduced as we prepared the book for printing.
If you believe the work has such errors, please let us know
by writing to us at the address below.

For a free copy of our current print catalog
featuring our bestselling books, write to:

APPLEWOOD BOOKS
P.O. Box 27
Carlisle, MA 01741

For more complete listings, visit us on the web at:
www.awb.com

Prepared for publishing by HP

A. Lincoln

PICTORIAL HISTORY

OF

THE CIVIL WAR

IN THE

UNITED STATES OF AMERICA.

By BENSON J. LOSSING.

ILLUSTRATED BY MANY HUNDRED ENGRAVINGS ON WOOD, BY LOSSING AND BARRITT, FROM SKETCHES BY THE AUTHOR AND OTHERS.

VOLUME II.

HARTFORD:
T. BELKNAP, PUBLISHER.
1868.

PREFACE.

THE peculiar circumstances under which this work has been prepared, caused a much longer interval between the appearance of the first and second volumes than was expected; but the delay has been an advantage to the book, because it has enabled the author to procure and use more authentic and valuable materials than could have been obtained earlier, especially from Confederate sources.

An essential part of the original plan of the writer, and which has been carried out, was to make a personal visit to the principal battle-fields and other places of interest connected with the Civil War. This could not be done within the Confederate lines during the war, and it was difficult to do so in many places for several months after the conflict had ceased. As much as possible of this labor was accomplished before the completion of the first volume, in which the events of the conflict, civil and military, to the close of the first battle of Bull's Run, are recorded.

After the first volume was completed, in the spring of 1866, the writer made a journey of several thousand miles in visiting the historical localities within the bounds of the Confederacy, observing the topography of battle-fields and the region of the movements of the great armies, making sketches, conversing with actors in the scenes, procuring documents, and in every possible way gathering valuable materials for the work. The writer bore a cordial letter of introduction from General Grant to any officer commanding a military post within the late Slave-labor States, asking him to afford the bearer every facility in his power. To General O. O. Howard the writer was also indebted for a similar letter, directed to any agent of the Freedmen's Bureau. These, and the kind services everywhere proffered by, and received from, persons who had been in the Confederate armies, procured for the author extraordinary facilities for gathering historical materials, and he was enabled to send and bring home a large amount of valuable matter. This had to be carefully examined and collated. In this and kindred labor, and in the construction of small illustrative maps, and the preparation of the sketches for the engraver, all by his own hands, months were consumed, and the delay in the appearance of the second volume was the consequence.

The interval between the appearance of the second and third volumes will be much shorter. The latter (which will conclude the work) will be ready for publication, it is believed, early in the ensuing spring. The present volume includes the record of the war eastward of the Alleghany Mountains to the close of the battle of Fredericksburg, in the operations of the Army of the Potomac; the beginning of the siege of Charleston; the movements of the armies of the Ohio and of the Cumberland to the close of the battle of Murfreesboro', and of the armies of Tennessee, Missouri, and the Gulf, to the fall of Vicksburg and Port Hudson.

Since the appearance of the first volume, George W. Childs has relinquished the publication of the work, and it has been assumed by Thomas Belknap. Mr. Childs relinquished it because his entire attention was needed in the business of publishing the *Public Ledger* newspaper, of Philadelphia, of which he became proprietor just before the first volume of this work was finished. Mr. Belknap will relax no efforts in giving it every excellence in its publication promised by Mr. Childs.

B. J. L.

POUGHKEEPSIE, N. Y., *September*, 1867.

Contents

VOLUME II.

CHAPTER I.

EFFECT OF THE BATTLE OF BULL'S RUN.—REORGANIZATION OF THE ARMY OF THE POTOMAC.—CONGRESS AND THE COUNCIL OF THE CONSPIRATORS.—EAST TENNESSEE.

CHAPTER II.

CIVIL AND MILITARY OPERATIONS IN MISSOURI.

CHAPTER III.

MILITARY OPERATIONS IN MISSOURI AND KENTUCKY.

CHAPTER IV.

MILITARY OPERATIONS IN WESTERN VIRGINIA AND ON THE SEACOAST.

CHAPTER V.

MILITARY AND NAVAL OPERATIONS ON THE COAST OF SOUTH CAROLINA.—MILITARY OPERATIONS ON THE LINE OF THE POTOMAC RIVER.

CHAPTER VI.

THE ARMY OF THE POTOMAC.—THE TRENT AFFAIR.—CAPTURE OF ROANOKE ISLAND.

CHAPTER VII.

MILITARY OPERATIONS IN MISSOURI, NEW MEXICO, AND KENTUCKY.—CAPTURE OF FORT HENRY.

CHAPTER VIII.

SIEGE AND CAPTURE OF FORT DONELSON.

CHAPTER IX.

EVENTS AT NASHVILLE, COLUMBUS, NEW MADRID, ISLAND NUMBER TEN, AND PEA RIDGE.

CHAPTER X.

GENERAL MITCHEL'S INVASION OF ALABAMA.—THE BATTLE OF SHILOH.

CHAPTER XI.

OPERATIONS IN SOUTHERN TENNESSEE AND NORTHERN MISSISSIPPI AND ALABAMA.

CHAPTER XII.

OPERATIONS ON THE COAST OF THE ATLANTIC AND THE GULF OF MEXICO.

CHAPTER XIII.

THE CAPTURE OF NEW ORLEANS.

CHAPTER XIV.

MOVEMENTS OF THE ARMY OF THE POTOMAC.—THE MONITOR AND MERRIMACK.

CHAPTER XV.

THE ARMY OF THE POTOMAC ON THE VIRGINIA PENINSULA.

CHAPTER XVI.

THE ARMY OF THE POTOMAC BEFORE RICHMOND.

CHAPTER XVII.

POPE'S CAMPAIGN IN VIRGINIA.

CHAPTER XVIII.

LEE'S INVASION OF MARYLAND AND HIS RETREAT TOWARD RICHMOND.

CHAPTER XIX.

EVENTS IN KENTUCKY AND NORTHERN MISSISSIPPI.

CHAPTER XX.

EVENTS WEST OF THE MISSISSIPPI AND IN MIDDLE TENNESSEE.

CHAPTER XXI.

SLAVERY AND EMANCIPATION.—AFFAIRS IN THE SOUTHWEST.

CHAPTER XXII.

THE SIEGE OF VICKSBURG.

CHAPTER XXIII.

SIEGE AND CAPTURE OF VICKSBURG AND PORT HUDSON.

VOLUME II.

THE CIVIL WAR.

CHAPTER I.

EFFECT OF THE BATTLE OF BULL'S RUN.—REORGANIZATION OF THE ARMY OF THE POTOMAC.—CONGRESS, AND THE COUNCIL OF THE CONSPIRATORS.—EAST TENNESSEE.

THE Battle of Bull's Run, so disastrous to the National Arms, and yet so little profitable, as a military event, to the Confederates, was in its immediate effects a profound enigma to the people of the whole country. They could not understand it. The Confederates held the field, yet they did not seek profit from the panic and flight of their opponents, by a pursuit. The Nationals were beaten and dispersed; yet, after the first paralysis of defeat, they instantly recovered their faith and elasticity. There had been marches, and bivouacs, and skirmishes, and a fierce battle, within the space of a week; and at the end of twenty-four hours after the close of the conflict, the respective parties in the contest were occupying almost the same geographical position which they did before the stout encounter.

The people at home, in both sections, were excited by the wildest tales of overwhelming defeat and disgrace on one side, and the most complete and advantageous victory on the other. It was said, and believed, that fifteen thousand Confederates had easily and utterly routed and dispersed thirty-five thousand National troops,[1] and smitten, beyond hope of recovery,

[1] See Jefferson Davis's dispatch to the "Confederate Congress," volume I., page 603. On the 28th of July, Generals Johnston and Beauregard issued a joint address to their soldiers, which was full of exultation. "One week ago," they said, "a countless host of men, organized into an army, with all the appointments which modern art and practiced skill could devise, invaded the soil of Virginia. Their people sounded their approach with triumph and displays of anticipated victory. Their generals came in almost regal state. Their Ministers, Senators, and women came to witness the immolation of this army, and the subjugation of our people, and to celebrate them with wild revelry." After speaking of the battles, the capture of nearly every thing belonging to the National army, "together with thousands of prisoners," they said, "Thus the Northern hosts were driven by you from Virginia. . . . . We congratulate you on an event which insures the liberty of our country. We congratulate every man of you whose privilege it was to participate in this triumph of courage and truth, to

the Army of the Potomac charged with the duty of seizing the Capital of the insurgents, driving them from Virginia, and relieving the City of Washington from all danger of capture.

Whilst one section of the Republic was resonant with shouts of exultation, the other was silent because of the inaction of despondency. Whilst the Confederates were elated beyond measure by the seeming evidence given by the battle, of their own superior skill and valor and the cowardice of their opponents, and thousands flocked to the standard of revolt from all parts of the Southern States, the Loyalists were stunned by the great disaster, and the seventy-five thousand three-months men, whose terms of service were about expiring, were, for the moment, made eager to leave the field and retire to their homes. Whilst in Richmond, now become the Capital of the Confederation, the bells were ringing out merry peals of joy; and "the city seemed lifted up, and every one seemed to walk on air," and "the men in place felt that now they held their offices for life;"[1] where Jefferson Davis said to the multitude, when referring to the vanquished Nationals, with bitter scorn, "Never be haughty to the humble;" where all believed that Walker's prediction would that day be fulfilled, and the banner of Rebellion be unfurled from the dome of the Capitol in Washington,[2] and that the "tide of war would roll from that day northward into the enemy's country"[3]—the fertile fields and rich cities of the Free-labor States—there was terror and anguish, and the most gloomy visions of a ruined Republic at the seat of the National Government, and men in place there were not certain of filling their offices for an hour. Whilst the streets of Richmond were populous with prisoners from the vanquished army, and eager volunteers pressing on toward the camp of the victors at Manassas, the streets of Washington were crowded with discomfited and disheartened soldiery, without leaders, and without organization—the personification of the crushed hopes of the loyal people.

Such was the sad picture of the situation of the Republic and of the relative character of the contending parties, much exaggerated, which was presented to Europe in the month of August.[a] The first account of the battle, the panic that seized some of the National troops, and the confused flight of soldiers and civilians back to Washington, was given to the Elder World through the London *Times*, the assumed and accredited exponent of the political and social opinions of the ruling class in England, by the pen of Dr. Russell,[4] who did not see the conflict, and who was one of the most speedy and persevering of the civilians in

[a] 1861.

---

fight in the battle of Manassas. You have created an epoch in the history of liberty, and unborn nations will rise up and call you blessed. Continue this noble devotion, looking always to the protection of a just God, and, before time grows much older, we will be hailed as the deliverers of a nation of ten millions of people. Comrades, our brothers who have fallen have earned undying renown, and their blood, shed in our holy cause, is a precious and acceptable sacrifice to the Father of truth and right. Their graves are beside the tomb of Washington; their spirits have joined his in eternal commune."

Jefferson Davis addressed the people on his arrival at Richmond, on the evening of the 23d, and boldly declared that his troops had captured "every thing the enemy had in the field," including "provisions enough to feed an army of 50,000 men for twelve months."—Richmond papers, July 24. Davis's exaggeration is made plain by the statement that it would require more than 12,000 wagons to transport that amount of food.

1 *A Rebel War Clerk's Diary at the Confederate States Capital*, page 65.

2 See volume I., page 339.

3 *A Rebel War Clerk's Diary*, page 65.

4 See note 3, page 91, volume I.

their eager flight from the suspected dangers of an imaginary pursuit of Confederate cavalry. His was, in a great degree, a tale of the imagination, "founded on fact," and well served the conspirators for a brief season.[1] It excited among the ruling classes in Europe a derision of the loyal people and the Government of the United States, and the desires of the enemies of republicanism and the sovereignty of the people were gratified. The ruin of the Great Republic of the West seemed to them almost as certain as a fact accomplished. English statesmen and journalists dogmatically asserted it, and deplored the folly and wickedness of the President and Congress, in "waging war upon Sovereign States," in vindication of an idea and a principle, and attempting to hold in union, by force, a people who had the right and the desire to withdraw from a hated fellowship. It was declared that "the bubble of Democracy had burst." There was joyful wailing over "the late United States;" and one of England's poets was constrained to write—

"Alas for America's glory!
  Ichabod—vanished outright;
And all the magnificent story
  Told as a dream of the night!
Alas for the Heroes and Sages,
  Saddened, in Hades, to know
That what they had built for all ages,
  Melts like a palace of snow!"

This relative condition of the parties was temporary. The loyal people instantly recovered from the stunning blow,[2] and in that recovery awakened from the delusive dream that their armies were invincible, that the Confederates were only passionate and not strong, and that the rebellion could be crushed in ninety days, as the hopeful Secretary of State had predicted, and continued to predict. It was evident that the battle just fought was only the beginning of a desperate struggle with the enemies of the Republic, who had made thorough preparation for the conflict, and had resolved to win the prize at all hazards. With this conviction of danger added to the sting of mortified national pride, the patriotism of the Loyalists was intensely exercised.

The Government, which had been lulled into feelings of security by the song of its own egotism, and had hesitated when urged to engage more troops, "for three years or the war," was now also aroused to a painful sense of danger and the penalties of misjudgment; and the Secretary of War, who had refused to sanction a call for a larger body of Pennsylvania volunteers

---

[1] Although nearly disabled by weariness of mind and body, Dr. Russell wrote his famous dispatch to the *Times* during the night succeeding his flight from Centreville, that it might go to England by the next Boston steamer. "The pen went flying about the paper," he says, "as if the spirits were playing tricks with it. When I screwed up my utmost resolution, the 'y's' would still run into long streaks, and the letters combine most curiously, and my eyes closed, and my pen slipped." After a brief nap, he was aroused by a messenger from Lord Lyons, to inquire after him, and invite him to supper. "I resumed my seat," he says, "haunted by the memory of the Boston mail, which would be closed in a few hours, and I had much to tell, although I had not seen the battle." On the testimony thus given, the *Times* said (August 10, 1861): "It is evident that the whole volunteer army of the Northern States is worthless as a military organization . . . . a screaming crowd;" and spoke of it as a collection of "New York rowdies and Boston abolitionists, desolating the villages of Virginia."

[2] Five days after the Battle of Bull's Run, the Secretary of State wrote to Mr. Adams, the American Minister in London, saying: "Our Army of the Potomac, on Sunday last, met a reverse equally severe and unexpected. For a day or two the panic which had produced the result was followed by a panic that seemed to threaten to demoralize the country. But that evil has ceased already. The result is already seen in a vigorous reconstruction upon a scale of greater magnitude and increased enthusiasm."

than its prescribed quota, stating that "it was more important to reduce than to enlarge the number,"[1] was now glad to receive all that might be offered from every quarter. Then it was that the Pennsylvania Reserves, called into existence by Governor Curtin, were so speedily transferred from Harrisburg to Washington,[2] and gave security to the National Capital. Everywhere the people flew to arms with a feeling of devotion to their country, deeper, because born of serious contemplation, than when Fort Sumter was attacked. There was another grand uprising; and within a fortnight after the Battle of Bull's Run, when the terms of service of the seventy-five thousand three-months men had expired, more than an equal number were in camps or in the field, engaged "for three years or the war." Among them were a large portion of the three-months men, who had re-enlisted. Nine-tenths of the non-combatants shared in the fervor and the faith of those who took up arms, and the people of the Free-labor States presented to the world a sublime spectacle difficult to comprehend. That terrible crisis in the life of the nation was promptly met, and the salvation of the Republic was assured.

In the mean time, the Confederates, flushed with victory, and satisfied that their so-called attorney-general (Benjamin) had predicted wisely, that pacification through recognition by France or England, or both, would occur "in ninety days," and their independence be secured, were wasting golden moments in celebrating their own valor.[3] Yet, in the manner of that unthriftiness of time and opportunity, there was a potential force that gave amazing strength to the Confederacy. There was a prestige in that battle, and the celebration of the triumph, which almost silenced opposition to the war; for multitudes, who had loved the Union supremely, and had no faith in the success of the conspirators, now thought they saw a great revolution nearly accomplished, and themselves made part of a new nation carved suddenly by the sword out of the Republic, with whose fortunes it was their duty and their interest to link themselves. They had already suffered much from the despotism established by the conspirators; and now, by an act of the "Congress,"[a] threatened with banishment and confiscation, they were utterly helpless, and sought peace and reconciliation by a display of zeal in what was dignified by the name of a war for independence.[4] That "united South" which the conspirators had falsely

[a] Aug. 8 and 30, 1861.

---

[1] General Patterson's *Narrative of the Campaign in the Shenandoah Valley.*

[2] See note 2, page 520, volume I.

[3] It is reported that General Buckner, captured at Fort Donelson several months afterward, while on his way to Fort Warren, at Boston, as a prisoner of war, said to a gentleman in Albany: "The effect of that battle was to inspire the Southerners with a blind confidence, and lull them into false security. The effect upon the Northerners, on the other hand, was to arouse, madden, and exasperate."

[4] The pressure brought to bear on the Union men was terrible, and the youth of that class were driven into the army by thousands, because of the social proscription to which they were subjected. The zeal of the women in the cause of rebellion was unbounded, and their influence was extremely potential. Young men who hesitated when asked to enlist, or even waited to be asked, were shunned and sneered at by the young women; and many were the articles of woman's apparel which were sent, as significant gifts, to these laggards at home. Men who still dared to stand firm in their true allegiance, were denounced as "traitors to their country," and treated as such; and the proscription and the persecution became so general and fiery, that Millie Mayfield was justified in singing, with scornful lips—

"Union men! O thrice-fooled fools!
As well might ye hope to bind
The desert sands with a silken thread,
When tossed by the whirling wind,

declared months before, now became a fact, and the terrible strife instantly assumed the proportions and the vigor of a civil war of unparalleled magnitude. Almost the entire resources of the inhabitants of the States in which rebellion existed were devoted to the cause, and with wonderful energy on both sides, the great conflict went on. During that conflict, while weaker men were in practical sympathy with the conspirators, there were thousands of the best men of the South, imbued with the martyr-spirit which reverences principle, who could not be made to yield to the terrible pressure, but maintained their integrity throughout. These unconditional Unionists suffered intensely in person and property, and large numbers perished. But the survivors were many, and offered to the nation, at the close of the war, the proper instrumentalities for co-operation with the Government in the reorganization of the disordered Union on a basis of justice, which should secure for the Republic, for all time, tranquillity and prosperity.

When the shouts of triumph had died away, and the smoke of battle was dissipated, and the people of the Confederacy saw their victorious army immovable at Manassas and indisposed to follow up their victory, they were uneasy, and many a lip queried why "President" Davis, the chief of the army, returned so quickly to Richmond, and spent time in public boastings of the achievements of the present and in predictions of the future, instead of directing Johnston and Beauregard to press on after the fugitives and capture Washington City, the great and coveted prize? The immobility of their army was an enigma. It was an incubus on the spirits of the people. While their tongues were jubilant, their hearts were misgiving.

Johnston and Beauregard desired to press on, but the wisdom and the prudence of the first-named officer restrained his own impatience and the folly and rashness of the Creole; and the perilous movement was delayed until it was too late to hope for success. Johnston knew that it would be madness to follow the retreating Nationals, and hurl his wearied troops against the strong defenses of Washington, behind which they were resting, supported by fresh soldiers. But he was anxious to carry out his original plan of crossing the Potomac above the National Capital, cut off that city's communications with the North, and capture it by a vigorous movement in the rear. But for a pursuit, or this grand flank movement, there were two essential requisites lacking—namely, a sufficient cavalry force, and means of subsistence, for which lack Confederate experts hold Davis responsible. It is agreed that he always seemed to take a delight in thwarting the wishes of others; and with a most mischievous obstinacy he followed the dictates of his own will, passions, and caprice, rather than the counsels of judicious advisers. This disposition was conspicuous in his appointment to important offices of his incapable personal and political friends; and the best of the Confederate army officers declare that, by his interference in details, he was a

---

Or to blend the shattered waves that lash
  The feet of the cleaving rock,
When the tempest walks the face of the deep,
  And the water-spirits mock,
As the sacred chain to reunite
  In a peaceful link again:
On our burning homesteads ye may write,
  'We found no Union men.'"

marplot in the way of military affairs throughout the war. At the beginning he appointed an incompetent and vicious companion-in-arms at a former period, named Northrop, to the vitally important post of Chief of Subsistence. This was done in the face of earnest protests; and now, at the first momentous trial, this Chief Commissary's incapacity was fatally conspicuous. Under the sanction, if not at the command of Davis, he refused to allow his subordinates to purchase supplies for the army at Manassas in the fertile country adjacent, but sent others to gather them in the rear of the army, and forward them in daily doles, at heavy expense, by the Orange and Alexandria Railway, exposed to the vicissitudes of war. He allowed no deposits of supplies to be established near the army; and on the day of the battle, Beauregard had only a single day's rations for his troops.[1] For weeks afterward this state of things continued, and it was impossible for the army to move forward with safety, under such circumstances.[2] There it lay at Manassas for many weeks, its officers chafing with impatience, whilst an immense National army was gathering and organizing, and drilling in front of Washington City. Johnston made his head-quarters at Grigsby's house in Centreville.[3] He was compelled to content himself with sending out scouting and foraging parties, and guerrilla bands, who sometimes approached within cannon-shot of the National defenses on Arlington Heights.

GRIGSBY'S HOUSE, CENTREVILLE.

The physical disabilities of the Confederates alluded to, were, probably, not the only reasons for the immobility of their army after the battle. Davis and his associates at Richmond well knew the strength of the lion of the North, which their wickedness had aroused. They had promised their dupes "peaceable secession," because they thought that strength would not be put forth. They found themselves mistaken, and their cause in great peril; and they well knew, that if they should push on to the extremity of seizing Washington at that time, it would so consolidate and invoke to terrible action the power of the North, that the conspirators would not hold the National Capital ten days, nor prevent the utter extermination of the insurgent armies, and the desolation of their territories by an exasperated people. This moral effect they dreaded; so they were content to have the vanity of their followers gratified by the accident of a victory at Bull's Run, and hoped to accomplish, by negotiation and compromise, what they could not expect to win by arms.

---

[1] Statement of General Thomas Jordan, then chief of Beauregard's staff, in *Harper's Magazine*, xxxi. 610. Jordan says: "Flour bought by speculators in the Valley and Loudon was carried to Richmond, sold to the Subsistence Bureau, and transported back to Manassas."

[2] Late in August, Johnston wrote to Beauregard: "It is impossible, as the affairs of the commissariat are now managed, to think of any other military course than a strictly defensive base."

[3] From a photograph by Alexander Gardiner, of Washington City.

The National Government now acted with decision and energy. General McClellan, who, with able subordinates and brave troops, had made a brilliant and successful campaign in Western Virginia, was summoned to Washington on the day after the Battle of Bull's Run,[a] and, with the approbation of the people, who were loudly sounding his praises, he was placed in command of the shattered army at and near the seat of Government. General McDowell, like a true soldier, gracefully withdrew, and on the 25th of July, the Adjutant-General announced the creation of a Geographical Division, formed of the *Departments of Washington* and of *Northeastern Virginia*, under the young chieftain, with head-quarters at Washington City.

[a] July 22, 1861.

Other changes had already been determined upon. On the 19th,[b] an order was issued from the War Department for the honorable discharge from the service of Major-General Robert Patterson, on the 27th, when his term of duty would expire; and General N. P. Banks, then in command at Baltimore, was directed to take his place in charge of the *Department of the Shenandoah*, he being relieved by General John A. Dix. There was a new arrangement of Military Departments,[1] and Lieutenant-General Scott, who was the General-in-Chief of the armies, greatly disabled by increasing infirmities, was, at his own suggestion, relieved from active duties.

[b] July.

General McClellan turned over the command of the army in Western Virginia to Brigadier-General Rosecrans, and entered with zeal and vigor upon the arduous task of reorganizing the army, of which he took charge on the 27th of July. He brought to the service, youth, a spotless moral character, robust health, a sound theoretical military education with some practical experience, untiring industry, the prestige of recent success in the field, and the unlimited confidence of the loyal people. He found at his disposal about fifty thousand infantry, less than one thousand cavalry, six hundred and fifty artillerymen, and thirty pieces of cannon.[2] He found, in the men, excellent materials out of which to fashion a fine army, but in a disorganized and comparatively crude condition. His first care was to effect a moral improvement by thorough discipline; and then, under the sanction of a recent Act of Congress, to winnow the officers of all the volunteer regiments, and dismiss all incompetents. By this process no less than three hundred officers were compelled to leave the service in the course of a few months.

Having laid the moral foundations for an efficient army organization, McClellan proceeded with skill and vigor to mold his materials into perfect symmetry. He made the regiment a unit. Four regiments composed a brigade, and three brigades a division. Each division had four batteries: three served by volunteers and one by regulars; the captain of the latter commanding the entire artillery of the division. With the assistance of Majors William F. Barry and J. G. Barnard, he organized artillery and engineering establishments; and the dragoons, mounted riflemen, and cavalry

---

[1] The counties of Washington and Alleghany, in Maryland, were added to the *Department of the Shenandoah*, created on the 19th of July, with head-quarters in the field; and the remainder of Maryland, and all of Pennsylvania and Delaware, constituted the *Department of Pennsylvania*, head-quarters at Baltimore. A Board was also established at this time for the examination of all officers of volunteer regiments.

[2] General McClellan's Report to the Secretary of War, August 4, 1863.

were all reorganized under the general name of cavalry. To Major Barry were intrusted the details of the artillery establishment; and Major Barnard was directed to construct a system of defenses for Washington City, on both sides of the Potomac. In the course of a few months every considerable eminence in the vicinity of the National Capital was crowned with a fort or redoubt well mounted. Early in the following year the number of these works was fifty-two, whose names and locations are indicated on the accompanying map.[1] This system of works was so complete, that at no time afterward, during the war, did the Confederates ever seriously attempt to assail them. At no time was the Capital in danger from external foes.

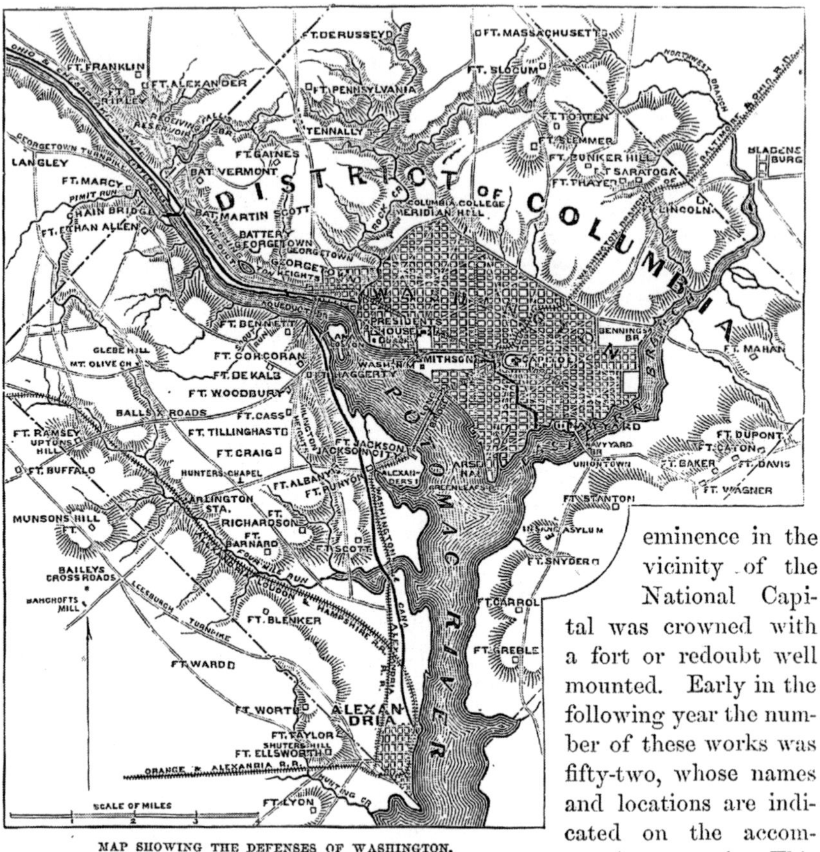

MAP SHOWING THE DEFENSES OF WASHINGTON.

The work of organization was performed with such energy, that in the place of a raw and disorganized army of about fifty thousand men, in and around Washington City, at the close of July,[a] there was, at the end of fifty days, a force of at least one hundred thousand men, well organized and officered, equipped and disciplined. Of these, full seventy-five thousand were then in a condition to be placed in column for active operations. The entire force under McClellan's command, at that time, including those under Dix, at Baltimore, was one hundred and fifty-two thou-

[a] 1861.

---

[1] According to General Orders issued by McClellan on the 30th of September, 1861, in which the names and locations of these forts were designated, thirty-two of them were then completed. At the beginning of December forty-eight were finished.

sand men, of whom between eight and nine thousand were sick or absent. This number was continually increased, until, on the first of March, 1862, when the army was put in motion, its grand total was two hundred and twenty-two thousand, of whom about thirty thousand were sick or absent.[1] Such was the force with which General McClellan was furnished for the first campaign in Virginia after the Battle of Bull's Run. It was known as the GRAND ARMY OF THE POTOMAC, whose existence was a wonder.[2]

One of the most serious difficulties encountered by the Government, at the beginning of the war, was a lack of arms. We have seen how Secretary Floyd stripped the arsenals and armories in the Free-labor States, and filled those of the Slave-labor States, when preparations were making for rebellion.[3] The armories at Harper's Ferry and Springfield were the principal ones on which the Government could rely for the manufacture of small arms. The former was destroyed in April, and the latter could not supply a tithe of the demand. It was necessary to send to Europe for arms; and Colonel George L. Schuyler was appointed an agent for the purpose,[a] with specific instructions from the Secretary of War. He purchased 116,000 rifles, 10,000 revolvers, 10,000 cavalry carbines, and 21,000 sabers, at an aggregate cost of $2,044,931.[4] It was not long before the private and National armories of the United States were able to meet all demands. The loss of over two thousand cannon at the Gosport Navy Yard[5] was a serious one; but the foundries of the country soon supplied the Government with all that were required.

[a] July 29, 1861.

Of the "absent" soldiers alluded to, more than two thousand were, at the time in question, in the loathsome prisons of the Confederates, and suffering intensely from cruel treatment and privations of every kind. A large portion of these prisoners were captured at the Battle of Bull's Run. These were taken by railway to Richmond on the 23d and 24th of July. Among the first who arrived there was Alfred Ely, member of Congress from the State of New York,[6] and Calvin Huson, his rival can-

---

[1] In a "Memorandum" which General McClellan submitted to the President, on the 4th of August, 1861, he said: "For the main army of operations, I urge the following composition:—

250 regiments of infantry, say	225,000	men.
100 field batteries, 600 guns	15,000	"
28 regiments of cavalry	25,500	"
5 regiments engineer roops	7,500	"
Total	273,000	men."

[2] "The creation of such an army," said General McClellan, "in so short a time, will hereafter be regarded as one of the highest glories of the Administration and the nation." In this organization of that army, and the discipline which it received during the seven months that it remained at Washington City and in the vicinity, we may fairly look for the groundwork of those successes which it achieved long afterward, to the "glory of the Administration and the nation."

[3] See volume I., page 121.

[4] Colonel Schuyler could not procure arms in England and France on his arrival, and a greater portion of them were purchased Germany. He bought 70,000 rifles in Vienna, and 27,000 in Dresden. Of the "Small-arms Association," in England, he procured 15,000 Enfield rifles. The revolvers were purchased in France and Belgium; also 10,000 cavalry carbines; and the sabers were bought in Germany. Through the interference of Confederate agents in France, the French Government would not allow any arms to be taken, by either party, from its arsenals.—See Report of Colonel Schuyler to the Secretary of War, April 8, 1862.

[5] See volume I., page 397.

[6] Mr. Ely was one of the civilians, mentioned in the first volume of this work (page 605), who went out as a spectator of the Battle of Bull's Run. He was captured by some South Carolina troops, who ascertained his name and position, and conducted him to their colonel, E. B. C. Cash, of South Carolina. That officer was excited by liquor, and, drawing his pistol, was about to shoot the prisoner, when the others interfered. Mr. Ely

didate for the same office, accompanied by Colonel Michael Corcoran and forty other officers, and a large number of private soldiers. It was at about ten o'clock, on a moonlit evening, when they reached the city, where an immense crowd had assembled. Amid the scoffs and sometimes curses of the populace, they were marched three-fourths of a mile to Harwood's large tobacco factory, on Main Street, near Twenty-fifth Street. It was a brick building, hastily prepared for the occasion. Into it officers and men were thrust, to the number of more than six hundred;[1] and they were so closely huddled that it was difficult for any one to lie down. No doubt this was the best arrangement that could be made immediately for the unexpected captives.

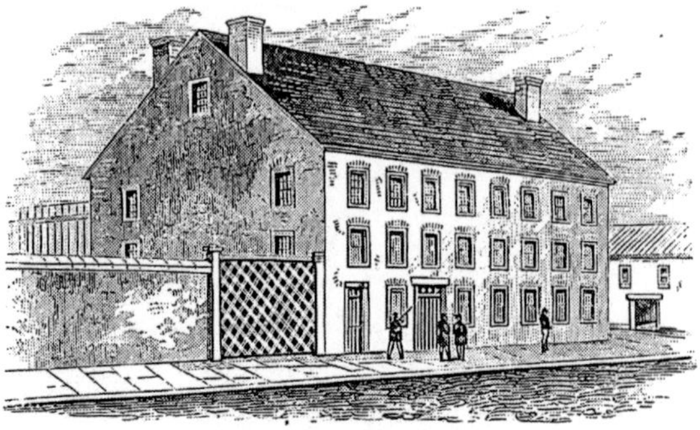

TOBACCO WAREHOUSE PRISON.

On the following morning the officers were waited upon by John H. Winder, a stout, gray-haired man, from Maryland, and lately a lieutenant-colonel, by brevet, in the National Army. He was now a Confederate brigadier-general, in command of the post at Richmond, and appeared for the first time on the theater of the Rebellion as Commissary-General of prisoners, in which capacity he acted throughout the war, and gained for himself the most unenviable notoriety. He promised the prisoners better quarters, and on that day the officers were removed to an adjoining building, where they had a little more room, light, and air; but neither chair nor bench to sit upon, nor bed to lie upon. For a short time they entertained hopes of a speedy release;[2] and a considerable number of men, somewhat distinguished in the political world, visited Mr. Ely, and made abundant promises of aid, which they never fulfilled.[3] Yet there were a few persons

JOHN H. WINDER.

was compelled to walk to the railway, at Manassas, about seven miles; and near Beauregard's head-quarters, he, with Corcoran and several officers, spent the night in an old barn, from which they were marched to the railway station and sent to Richmond.

[1] In the Appendix to Mr. Ely's *Journal*, kept during his imprisonment, may be found a complete list of all the Bull's Run prisoners who were confined with him.

[2] On the day after his arrival in Richmond, Mr. Ely, at the request of his fellow-prisoners, prepared a petition to the President, requesting immediate steps to be taken by the Government for their release. It was signed by the officers, and was forwarded.

[3] Among these were Messrs. Keitt and Boyce, of South Carolina, and Pryor and Bocock, of Virginia, who were Mr Ely's fellow-members in the Thirty-sixth Congress, and were now occupying seats in the so-called Confederate Congress.

in Richmond who did not only promise, but afforded all the aid in their power to the Union prisoners, at this time and ever afterwards.[1]

The prisoners in Richmond were soon convinced that the tobacco warehouse would be their home for some time. As the days wore wearily away, their sufferings increased, for their treatment became less humane. Yet they did not yield to melancholy. There were some irrepressibly buoyant spirits among them, and every thing possible to be done to render their situation endurable, was employed. They formed a club called *The Richmond Prison Association*, of which Mr. Ely was made President,[a] and at their first meeting, held on the day of organization, they were enlivened by speeches, songs, and toasts.[2] This was the more agreeable beginning of that terrible prison-life to which tens of thousands of the National troops were exposed during the war, of which more will be recorded hereafter.

[a] July 26, 1861.

The Thirty-seventh Congress had been in session more than a fortnight when the battle of Bull's Run was fought, and they had already made several enactments preparatory to the vigorous prosecution of the war.[3] Yet they were not unmindful of their obligations to humanity, to endeavor to secure peace by any just and honorable means. As we have observed,[4] a resolution was introduced into the House of Representatives,[b] by Mr. Crittenden, declaring the sole object of the Government in waging war to be the preservation of the Union and the vindication of the National authority. It was "laid over until Monday," the 22d, and in the mean time the battle at Bull's Run was fought. Notwithstanding the National Capital was filled with fugitives from a shattered army, and it

[b] July 19.

---

[1] Distinguished among these benefactors were Mrs. John Van Lew and her daughter. Mrs. Van Lew was an aged and wealthy widow, who lived in a fine mansion on Church Hill. Warmly devoted to the Union, and animated by the most generous impulses of humanity, these women continued, throughout the war, merciful ministrations for the comfort of the National soldiers starving and freezing in Libby prison and on Belle Isle. They suffered the most withering social proscription, and received the most vulgar abuse from the politicians and the press of Richmond. They were branded as "Southern women with Northern sympathies;" and one of the Richmond papers, with characteristic coarseness and ill-breeding, said: "If such people do not wish to be exposed and dealt with as alien enemies to their country, they would do well to cut stick while they can do so with safety to their worthless carcasses." In the same paper was a eulogy of "Southern chivalry and refinement." On the lips of many a dying prisoner lingered a blessing for those "honorable women."

[2] For a full account of prison-life in this Richmond tobacco warehouse, see Ely's *Journal;* Lieutenant Harris's *Prison Life in Richmond; Five Months in Rebeldom, or Notes from the Diary of a Bull's Run Prisoner;* and *General Corcoran's Captivity.* Among the early prisoners was Lieutenant Isaac W. Hart, of Indiana, whose praise was on the lips of all his fellow-captives, because of his overflowing spirits, vivacity, and wit. He told funny stories and sung good songs. One composed by himself, always provoked hopeful feelings when he sang it. It was entitled "The Prisoner's Song," and its burden was the prospect of a speedy exchange. Its concluding words were:—

"And when we arrive in the Land of the Free,
They will smile and welcome us joyfully;
And when we think of the Rebel band,
We'll repeat our motto—'*Bite and be damned.*'"

PRISON ASSOCIATION SEAL.

This motto was on the seal of the Prison Association, which was drawn with a pen, and attached to each certificate of membership. The annexed copy is from a book containing the autographs of a number of the officers who were captives at that time. It may here be mentioned that Mr. Huson, who experienced the kind hospitality of Mrs. Van Lew and her family, died while in prison. Mr. Ely was afterward exchanged for Charles James Faulkner, who was the resident Minister of the Republic at the French Court when Buchanan retired from office, and who, on his return to the United States, was arrested and imprisoned under a charge of complicity in the schemes of the conspirators.

[3] See chapter xxiv., volume I.

[4] See volume I., page 573.

was believed by many that the seat of Government was at the mercy of its enemies, Congress, on Monday, deliberated as calmly as if assured of perfect safety. Mr. Crittenden's resolution was adopted by a vote of 117 to 2; and two days afterwards,[a] one identical with it passed the Senate by a vote almost as decisive.[1] It was such a solemn declaration of the Government that the conspirators were speaking falsely when charging that Government with waging war for the subjugation of the Southern States, the emancipation of the slaves, and the confiscation of property, that it was not allowed to be published within the bounds of the Confederacy. The writer was so informed by Southern men of intelligence, and that they never heard of the resolution until the war had ceased; also that, had its declarations been known, multitudes would have paused in their rebellious career, and the terrible desolation of the South might have been prevented. This was what the conspirators, who had resolved on rule or ruin, justly feared.

[a] July 24, 1861.

On the same day[b] the House of Representatives, by an almost unanimous vote, anticipated the wishes of the loyal people by declaring that "the maintenance of the Constitution, the preservation of the Union, and the enforcement of the laws are sacred trusts which must be executed; that no disaster shall discourage us from the most ample performance of this high duty; and that we pledge to the country and the world the employment of every resource, national and individual, for the suppression, overthrow, and punishment of Rebels in arms."

[b] July 22.

On the same sad day a bill, reported by the Judiciary Committee on the 20th, providing for the confiscation of property used for insurrectionary purposes, was considered in the Senate, to which Mr. Trumbull, of Illinois, the chairman of that committee, offered an amendment, providing that the master of any slave who should employ him for such purpose should forfeit all right to his service or labor thereafter. It was adopted by a vote of 33 against 6. When this bill reached the Lower House, on the 2d of August, it met with strenuous opposition, especially Trumbull's amendment, from Crittenden and Burnet, of Kentucky, Vallandigham, Pendleton, and Cox, of Ohio, and Diven, of New York, chiefly on the ground that it would confirm the belief of the slaveholders that the war was waged for the emancipation of their slaves, and, as a consequence, would produce great exasperation, and increase the rigors of war without increasing the means for the success of the army. Mr. Crittenden was opposed to the passage of any penal laws. "Shall we send forward to the field," he asked, "a whole catalogue of penal laws to fight this battle with? Arms more impotent were never resorted to. They are beneath the dignity of our great cause. They are outside of the policy which ought to control this Government, and lead us on to success in the war we are now fighting. If you hold up before your enemies this cloud of penal laws, they will say, 'War is better than peace: war is comparative repose.' They will say when they are subdued, or if they choose now to submit, 'What next? Have we peace, or is this new army

---

[1] The negatives were Breckinridge and Powell, of Kentucky; Johnson and Polk, of Missouri; and Trumbull, of Illinois. The latter opposed it because of the particular wording of the first clause, and said, "the revolt was occasioned, in my opinion, by people who are not here, nor in this vicinity. It was started in South Carolina. I think the resolution limits it to a class of persons [those 'in arms around the Capital'] who were not the originators of this Rebellion."

of penal laws then to come into action? Are these penal laws to inflict upon us a long agony of prosecution and forfeiture?' No, gentlemen, it is not by such means that we are to achieve the great object of establishing our Union and reuniting the country. Sir, these laws will have no efficacy in war. Their only effect will be to stimulate your adversaries to still more desperate measures. That will be the effect of this army of penal laws."

Mr. Stevens, of Pennsylvania, strenuously advocated the bill, and especially Mr. Trumbull's amendment concerning the freedom of slaves employed for insurrectionary purposes; and, in reply to the assertions that the insurgents would never submit, that they could not be conquered, that they would "suffer themselves to be slaughtered and their whole country to be laid waste," he said, "Sir, war is a grievous thing at best, and civil war more than any other; but if they hold this language, and the means which they have suggested must be resorted to, if their whole country must be laid waste and made a desert in order to save this Union from destruction, so let it be. I would rather, sir, reduce them to a condition where their whole country is to be peopled by a band of freemen than to see them perpetrate the destruction of this people through our agency. . . . . I warn Southern gentlemen that if this war is to continue, there will be a time when my friend from New York [Mr. Diven] will see it declared by this free nation that every bondsman in the South—belonging to a rebel, recollect; I confine it to them—shall be called upon to aid us in war against their masters, and to restore this Union."[1] The bill was recommitted to the Committee on the Judiciary, and on the following day[a] it was reported back with Trumbull's amendment so modified as to include only those slaves whose labor for insurrectionary purposes was employed in "any military or naval service against the Government and authority of the United States." With the amendment so modified, the bill was passed by a vote of 60 against 48. When it was returned to the Senate, it was concurred in, on motion of Mr. Trumbull, and was passed[b] by a vote of 24 against 11. The President's signature to it made it law on the same day. This was the first act of Congress, after the beginning of the war, concerning the emancipation of slaves and the confiscation of property.

[a] Aug. 3, 1861.

[b] Aug. 6.

We have already observed the peace propositions of Vallandigham, of Ohio, and Wood, of New York.[2] These were followed, later in the session, after Clarke, of New Hampshire, had asked and obtained leave of the Senate to offer a joint resolution declaratory of the determination of Congress to maintain the supremacy of the Government and integrity of the Union, by propositions for securing peace and reconciliation by friendly measures. One of these, offered in the House of Representatives by S. S. Cox, of Ohio, proposed the appointment of a committee, composed of one member of Congress from each State, who should report to the House, at the next session, such amendments to the National Constitution as should "assuage all grievances and bring about a reconstruction of the national unity;" also the appointment of a committee for the purpose of preparing such adjustment, and a conference

---

[1] *Congressional Globe*, Aug. 2, 1861; *History of the Anti-slavery Measures of the Thirty-seventh and Thirty-eighth Congresses*, by Senator Henry Wilson, chapter I.

[2] Volume I., page 573.

requisite for that purpose, composed of seven citizens, whom he named,[1] who should request the appointment of a similar committee "from the so-called Confederate States," the two commissions to meet at Louisville, Kentucky, on the first Monday in September following. This was followed by a proposition from W. P. Johnson, of Missouri, to recommend the Governors of the several States to convene the respective legislatures for the purpose of calling an election to select two delegates from each Congressional district, to meet in convention at Louisville on the same day, "to devise measures for the restoration of peace to our country." These, and all other propositions of like nature, Congress refused to entertain, for they were satisfied that the conspirators, who had appealed to the arbitrament of the sword, would not listen to the voice of patriotism. The judgment of the majority was in consonance with a resolution which Mr. Diven, of New York, proposed to offer, namely: "That, at a time when an armed rebellion is threatening the integrity of the Union and the overthrow of the Government, any and all resolutions or recommendations designed to make terms with armed rebels are either cowardly or treasonable." They recognized war as existing in all its hideousness in the bosom of the nation, and legislated accordingly.

Acting upon the recommendation of the Secretary of the Treasury (Mr. Chase), Congress authorized a loan of $250,000,000, for which bonds and Treasury-notes were to be issued. The bonds were to be irredeemable for twenty years, and to bear interest not exceeding seven per cent. per annum; while the Treasury notes of fifty dollars and upwards were to be payable three years after date, with annual interest at the rate of seven and three-tenths per cent. per annum. For greater convenience in the disbursements of the Government, and the payment of revenue, Treasury notes were authorized in denominations not less than five dollars, and to the extent of fifty millions of dollars. The Government was allowed to deposit its funds with solvent banks, instead of confining these deposits to the National Sub-treasury. This measure, together with the issue of the bills receivable for specie, relieved the financial pressure at a time when it threatened serious embarrassments.

SEAL OF THE TREASURY DEPARTMENT.

To provide for the payment of the interest on this debt, and to meet other demands, an act[2] was passed[a] for the increase of revenues from imports, by which new duties were imposed upon foreign articles of luxury and necessity. By a provision of the same act, a direct tax of twenty millions of dollars was to be laid upon the real estate of the country, in which the amount to be raised in each State was specified, not excepting those in which rebellion existed. Provision was also made for levying a tax on the excess of all incomes above eight hundred dollars; but

[a] August 5, 1861.

---

[1] Edward Everett, of Massachusetts; Franklin Pierce, of New Hampshire; Millard Fillmore, of New York; Reverdy Johnson, of Maryland; Martin Van Buren, of New York; Thomas Ewing, of Ohio; and James Guthrie, of Kentucky.

[2] See No. 40 of the Acts and Resolutions passed during the First Session of the Thirty-seventh Congress.

Mr. Chase's suggestion concerning excise duties, and other taxes on special articles of personal property, legacies, &c., were not adopted at that time. Indeed, this system of taxation was not put in operation until after it was modified at the next session of Congress; for the President, who was invested with power to appoint officers to carry it out, was not allowed by the act to exercise it until the following February.[1]

In the month of September, Mr. Chase sent forth a patriotic appeal to the people, in behalf of the subscription to the authorized loan.[2] He called for purchasers at par of one hundred and fifty millions of Treasury notes, bearing seven and three-tenths per cent. interest, and met with a cordial response from individuals and banking institutions. The obvious advantages of the loan caused the first and second issues, of fifty millions each, to be generally absorbed for investment; and this mark of confidence in the Government and the financial system of the Secretary filled the hearts of the loyal people with gladness. We shall, as occasion offers, hereafter notice the working of the Treasury Department under the management of Mr. Chase.

When Congress had finished the business for which they were called together, they adjourned on the 6th of August, after a session of thirty-three days. They had worked earnestly and industriously, and the product of their labors consisted of the passage of sixty-one public and seven private acts, and five joint resolutions. They had made ample provisions for sustaining the contest against the enemies of the Republic; and, on the day before the adjournment, in a joint resolution, they requested the President to "recommend a day of public humiliaiton, prayer, and fasting, to be observed by the people of the United States with religious solemnity, and the offering of fervent supplications to Almighty God for the safety and welfare of these States, his blessings on their arms, and a speedy restoration of peace."[3]

Whilst the National Congress was in session at Washington, and armies were contending along the borders of Bull's Run, the Third Session of the so-called "Provisional Congress" of the conspirators (who, as we have seen, had left the Senate-Chamber of the Capitol of Alabama, at Montgomery,[a] wherein their Confederacy was formed) was commenced in the Capitol of Virginia, at Richmond, on the 20th of July.[4] There was a full attendance. The members assembled at noon, and were called to order by Howell Cobb, when the Rev. S. K. Tallmadge, of Georgia, made a prayer. At half-past twelve o'clock, Col. Josselyn, the private secretary of Jefferson Davis, appeared, and delivered to "Congress" a communi-

[a] May 21, 1861.

---

[1] It was estimated by the Secretary of the Treasury, that the real and personal values in the United States, at that time, reached the vast aggregate of $16,000,000,000, of which $11,000,000,000 were in the loyal States. It was also estimated that the yearly surplus earnings of the loyal people amounted to over $400,000,000.

[2] "The war," said Mr. Chase, "made necessary by insurrection, and reluctantly accepted by the Government, must be prosecuted with all possible vigor, until the restoration of the just authority of the Union shall insure permanent peace. The same Providence which conducted our fathers through the difficulties and dangers which beset the formation of the Union, has graciously strengthened our hands for the work of its preservation. The crops of the year are ample. Granaries and barns are everywhere full. The capitalists of the country come cheerfully forward to sustain the credit of the Government. Already, also, even in advance of this appeal, men of all occupations seek to share the honors and the advantages of the loan. Never, except because of the temporary depression caused by the rebellion, and the derangement of business occasioned by it, were the people of the United States in a better condition to sustain a great contest than now."

[3] The President, by proclamation on the 12th of August, appointed the last Thursday in September to be observed as a day of fasting, humiliation, and prayer.

[4] See page 547, volume I.

THE SENATE-CHAMBER AT MONTGOMERY.[1]

cation from that chief leader of the Rebellion. In that "message," Davis congratulated his confederates on the accession of States to their league. He assured them that the National Government had now revealed its intentions to subjugate them by a war "whose folly" was "equaled by its wickedness," and whose "dire calamities would fall with double severity" on the loyal people themselves. He charged the President with "a violation of an armistice" concerning Fort Sumter,[2] and declared the assertion that the insurgents commenced hostilities, to be "an unfounded pretense." He argued that the Confederacy was "a great and powerful nation," because the Government had made such extensive preparations for its overthrow; also that the nationality of the leagued insurgents had been recognized by the Government, by its establishment of "blockades by sea and land;" also that the idea that the inhabitants of the "Confederate States" were citizens of the United States was repudiated by the Government, in making war upon them "with a savage ferocity unknown to modern civilization."

With the same disregard of candor which characterized Beauregard's proclamation at Manassas, in June, and with the same evident intention to "fire the Southern heart,"[3] Davis said of the warfare of the Nationals: "Rapine is the rule; private residences, in peaceful rural districts, are bombarded and burnt," and pains taken to have "a brutal soldiery completely destroy every article of use or ornament in private houses." "Mankind will shudder," he continued, "to hear the tales of outrages committed on defenseless females, by soldiers of the United States now invading our homes." He

---

[1] This picture is from a sketch made by the author, while on a visit to Montgomery, early in April, 1866. The mahogany furniture was the same as that used by the conspirators at the formation of their Confederacy.

[2] See pages 305 to 309, inclusive, volume I. [3] See page 550, volume I.

charged the Government with making "special war" on the South, including the women and the children, "by carefully devised measures to prevent their obtaining medicines necessary for their cure," with "cool and deliberate malignity, under pretext of suppressing an insurrection." He spoke of "other savage practices which have been resorted to by the Government of the United States," and cited the case of the prisoners taken with the pirate-ship *Savannah*, already referred to in this work.[1] After speaking of the annunciation at the seat of Government, that the States were subordinate to the National authority and had no right to secede, and that the President was authorized to suspend the privilege of the writ of Habeas Corpus, "when," as the Constitution says, "in cases of rebellion or invasion the public safety may require it," he said: "We may well rejoice that we have severed all connection with a Government which thus tramples on all the principles of constitutional liberty, and with a people in whose presence such avowals could be hazarded." He then spoke of the enthusiasm of the Southern people, their abundant offers of aid to the Confederacy, and the "almost unquestioning confidence which they display in their government during the impending struggle;" and he concluded his communication by saying: "To speak of subjugating such a people, so united and determined, is to speak in language incomprehensible to them. To resist attacks on their rights or their liberties, is with them an instinct. Whether this war shall last one, or three, or five years, is a problem they leave to be solved by the enemy alone; it will last till the enemy shall have withdrawn from their borders—till their political rights, their altars, and their homes, are freed from invasion. Then, and then only, will they rest from this struggle, to enjoy in peace the blessings which, with the favor of Providence, they have secured by the aid of their own strong hearts and sturdy arms."

With a determination such as Davis expressed, the "Congress" made provision for the contest, and for creating that "United South" which had been proclaimed to the world. For the latter purpose it passed an act[a] which authorized the banishment from the limits of the "Confederate States" of every masculine citizen of the United States (with some exceptions named[2]) over fourteen years of age, who adhered to his Government and acknowledged its authority. The act prescribed as the duty of all courts of justice to cause the arrest of all Union men who did not proclaim their allegiance to the conspirators or leave the Confederacy within forty days, and to treat them as "alien enemies." Another act[b] authorized the confiscation of every species of property within the limits of the Confederacy belonging to such "alien enemies" or absent citizens of the United States, with the exceptions mentioned. Various measures were adopted for the increase and efficiency of the army and navy, and for carrying on the immense financial operations of the so-called government.[3] It was officially reported that there were two hundred

[a] Aug. 8, 1861.

[b] Aug. 31.

[1] See page 557, volume I.

[2] The citizens of Delaware, Maryland, Kentucky, Missouri, the Territories of New Mexico, Arizona, and the Indian Territory south of Kansas, and the District of Columbia, were excepted.

[3] Further issues of Treasury notes were authorized, and provision was made for a war-tax, for the creation of means for their redemption, to the amount of fifty cents upon each one hundred dollars in value of real estate, slaves, merchandise, stocks of corporations, money at interest or invested in various securities, excepting Confederate bonds, money in hand or in bank, live stock, gold watches, gold and silver plate, pianos, horses, and pleasure carriages.

thousand soldiers in the field; and Davis was authorized to increase this force by an addition of four hundred thousand volunteers, to serve for not less than twelve months or more than three years. He was authorized to send additional commissioners to Europe; and on the last day of the session[a] an act was passed giving him authority to inflict retaliation upon the persons of prisoners of war. This measure had special reference to the captives of the pirate-ship *Savannah*, concerning whom, as we have observed,[1] Davis had already sent a threatening letter to the President, to which no reply was given.[2] Under the provisions of that act, Colonel Corcoran and other officers were closely confined as hostages, and treated worse than the pirates were.[3] The latter, as we have observed, were, for the sake of humanity, treated as prisoners of war, and in due time the hostages were exchanged.

[a] Aug. 31, 1861.

On the establishment of the so-called government at Richmond, Davis's committee of advisers, whom he dignified with the title of "Cabinet," was reorganized. R. M. T. Hunter, of Virginia, had become his "Secretary of State." Judah P. Benjamin, his law officer, was made "Secretary of War," and was succeeded in his office by ex-Governor Thomas Bragg, of North Carolina. The other members of the "Cabinet" were the same as those first appointed.[4] In every phase of its organization, the "new government" was modeled after the rejected one; and in form, and numbers, and operations, the Confederacy presented to the world the outward aspect of a respectable nation. Seals were devised for the use of the several "Departments;" and on that made for the "Department of State," which, more than others, might be seen abroad, was the significant legend, in indifferent Latin, NULLA PATRIA AMICTÆ FIDEI, meaning, No country, no fatherland, that does not keep faith, or where faith is covered up—that is to say, We reject the National Government because it is faithless.[5] With this feeling they set about the establishment of a new empire, with wonderful energy, and called forth all of the industrial resources of the region under their control, with results the most

---

[1] See page 557, volume I.

[2] This letter was taken by Captain Thomas H. Taylor, with a flag of truce, to the head-quarters of General McDowell, at Arlington House, when the bearer was conducted to the quarters of General Scott, in Washington City, where the letter was delivered.

[3] See note 2, page 557, volume I. The trial of the officers and crew of the *Savannah* occurred at New York, in October, 1861. It continued seven days, when, the jury disagreeing, the prisoners were remanded to the custody of the marshals. In the mean time, William Smith, another Confederate privateersman, had been tried in Philadelphia, and found guilty of piracy, the penalty for which was death by hanging. Now was afforded an opportunity for the exercise of that system of retaliation which the Confederate "Congress" had authorized. Accordingly, on the 9th of November, 1861, Judah P. Benjamin, the Confederate "Secretary of War," instructed General Winder to select by lot "from among the prisoners of war of the highest rank" one who was to be confined in a cell appropriated to convicted felons, to be a hostage for Captain Smith, of the *Savannah*, and to be executed if he should suffer death. Also to select in the same way thirteen other prisoners of war, the highest in rank, to be confined in cells used for convicted felons, and to be treated as such so long as the National Government so treated a "like number of prisoners of war captured by them at sea." This order was read by General Winder, in the presence of seventy-five captive officers, in the old Tobacco Warehouse, in Richmond, on the 10th of November. He had six slips of paper, each containing the name of one of the six colonels of the National Army then held as prisoners. These were handed to Colonel W. R. Lee, of the 20th Massachusetts Regiment, recently captured at Ball's Bluff, who was directed to place them in a deep tin case provided for the purpose, when Mr. Ely was directed to draw one out, the officer whose name it should bear "to be held as hostage for William Smith, convicted of piracy." The lot fell upon Colonel Corcoran, then a prisoner in Castle Pinckney, in Charleston harbor. The names of the other thirteen hostages were drawn in the same way. They were: Colonels Lee, Wilcox, Cogswell, Wood, and Woodruff; Lieutenant-Colonels Bowman and Neff; Majors Potter, Revere, and Vogdes; and Captains Rockwood, Bowman, and Keffer.—*Journal* of Alfred Ely, Nov. 10, 1861, pages 210 to 216, inclusive.

[4] See page 258.

[5] See engraving on page 35.

astonishing. The blockade becoming more and more stringent every day, they perceived the necessity of relying upon their own ingenuity and industry for the materials of war; and forges, and foundries, and powder manufactories soon appeared in various parts of the Confederacy, while those already established were taxed to their utmost capacity in responding to orders. Of these the great Tredegar Iron Works, at Richmond (see page 36), was the most extensive of its kind within the limits of the Slave-labor States, and some of the most effective heavy ordnance used by the Confederate Army, and projectiles of various kinds, were made there, directly under the eye of the so-called government. The labors of this establishment in the cause of the rebellion made its name and deeds familiar to every American.

CONFEDERATE "STATE DEPARTMENT" SEAL.[1]

Jefferson Davis was quick to act upon the authority of the decree of the Confederate "Congress" concerning the banishment of Union men. He issued a proclamation on the 14th of August, in accordance with the intent of that decree; and then commenced those terrible persecutions of loyal inhabitants within the limits of the "Confederate States," under the sanction of law, which made that reign of terror in those regions tenfold more dreadful than before. This, and the Confiscation Act, put the seal of silence upon the lips of nearly all Union men. Few could leave, for obstacles were cast in their way. To remain was to acquiesce in the new order of things, or suffer

---

[1] This delineation of the seal is from a pass which the "Secretary of State" of the Confederacy issued in the following form:—

"CONFEDERATE STATES OF AMERICA.

"*To all to whom these presents shall come, Greeting:*

"I, the undersigned, Secretary of State of the Confederate States of America, hereby request all whom it may concern, to permit safely and freely to pass, A—— B——, a citizen of the Confederate States of America, and in case of need to give him all lawful aid and protection.

"Given under my hand and the impression of the seal of the Department of State, at the City of [SEAL.] Montgomery, May 20, 1861.

"ROBERT TOOMBS, *Secretary of State.*"

While on a visit to Fort Fisher, North Carolina, in the spring of 1866, the writer met a resident of Wilmington and a native of North Carolina, who had been employed in the secret service of the National Government during a portion of the war, with the commission of colonel, and in command of a regiment of 850 spies, who were scattered over the Confederacy. He also entered the service of the Confederacy as a spy, in order that he might work more efficiently for his Government, and was furnished with a pass like the above, on the margin of which, it should have been mentioned, was an exact description of the person to whom it was given. He desired to furnish each of his spies with such a pass. Through some of them in Richmond, he procured a large number of blank passes. These required the impression of the seal of the "State Department." He went to Richmond, and through spies there, professedly in the service of the Confederates, he was introduced to Judah P. Benjamin, then "Secretary of State," and visited his office daily for about a fortnight, endeavoring to ascertain where the seal of the "Department" was kept. He was finally successful. One day, when no one was in the office but a boy, he sent him on an errand, and then going boldly to the place where the seal was kept, he made an impression of it in wax. He then started with his own pass to "go into the Yankee lines." He hastened to Washington, and thence to New York, where he had a seal cut in steel precisely like the original." With this he stamped the blank passes, which he properly filled up and signed successfully with the forged name of Benjamin. With these he furnished his spies with passes, and they performed essential service by gaining information in the camps and at the Capital, and in communicating with the blockading squadrons. The commander of this regiment of spies was arrested several times on suspicion, but was never implicated by sufficient proof.

intensely. Then, for the same reason that gave truth to the proclamation of the despot—"Order reigns in Warsaw"—there was a "United South" in

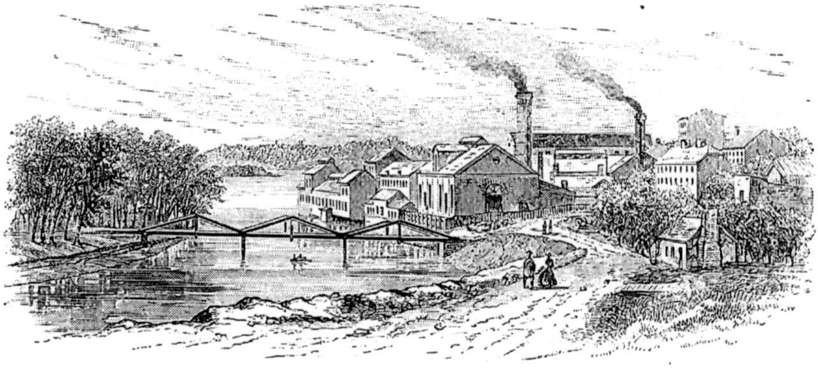

THE TREDEGAR IRON WORKS, AT RICHMOND, VIRGINIA.[1]

favor of the conspirators. Under their subordinate officers, civil and military, almost unbounded license was exercised, and no man's life, liberty, and property were secure from violence.

In districts of the Confederacy, such as East Tennessee, where the blight of slavery was but little known, where a greater portion of the inhabitants were loyal to their Government, and where the Confederates held sway, the keenest cruelties were exercised. Those who, in East Tennessee, had voted for the Union at the election of which Governor Harris made fraudulent returns,[2] were continually persecuted. Good and peaceable citizens were taken before magistrates without cause, and imprisoned without mercy. They were arrested by the authority of processes issued by J. Crozier Ramsey, the Confederate district attorney, who was assisted in the work of crushing the Unionists in that region by R. B. Reynolds, a Confederate commissioner, and W. B. Wood, a Methodist clergyman from Alabama, who bore the commission of a Confederate colonel. Under the direction and assistance of these men, loyalists were hunted, arrested, taken to camps and prisons, and insulted and abused by mobs. Confederate cavalry, as well as infantry, scoured the country, offering every indignity to men and women, destroying the crops of the rich and poor alike, turning their horses to feed into fields of growing corn, burning barns and stacks of hay, and plundering the people of provisions. The jails were soon filled with loyalists, and an extensive disarming of the people was accomplished. So thoroughly were they under the control of the Confederates, that in November[a] Colonel Wood was able to write to Benjamin, at Richmond, "The rebellion [resistance to Confederate outrages] in East Tennessee has been put down in some of the counties, and will be effectually suppressed in less than two weeks in all the counties. Their camps in Sevier and Hamilton Counties," he continued, "have been broken up, and a large number of them have been made prisoners. . . . . It is a mere farce to arrest them and turn them

[a] 1861.

[1] This view is from the ruins of the Virginia State Arsenal. The works are on the left bank of the James River, nearly opposite Mayo's Island.

[2] See pages 388–389, volume I.

over to the courts. . . . . They really deserve the gallows, and, if consistent with the laws, ought speedily to receive their deserts." With the spirit of this Alabama clergyman, the Loyalists were everywhere ill-treated, and no measures seemed to be considered too cruel to be employed in crushing them.[1]

Among the most prominent of the East Tennessee Loyalists, who suffered persecution, were Andrew Johnson and Horace Maynard, members of Congress, and Rev. W. G. Brownlow, D. D., a Methodist preacher, and editor of the *Knoxville Whig*.[2] Brownlow's fearless spirit, caustic pen, social position, and public relations through the press and the pulpit, made him intensely hated by the conspirators and their friends, and much feared. They thirsted for his life, and finally the false charge was made, that he was accessory to the burning of several railway-bridges in East Tennessee,[3] to cut off communication between that region and Virginia. His life had been daily threatened by Confederate soldiers; and, at the urgent solicitations of his family, he left his home in the autumn, and went into another district of his State. While he was absent, several railway-bridges were burned. Brownlow was accused of being in complicity with their destroyers, and Colonel Wood sent out cavalry in search of him, with instructions, publicly given in the street, at Knoxville, not to take him prisoner, but to shoot him at once.[4]

Brownlow was informed of his peril, and, with other loyal men, he secreted himself in the Smoky Mountains, on the borders of North Carolina, where they were fed by Loyalists. It was finally resolved by the Confederates to rid themselves of so dangerous an enemy, by giving Brownlow a pass to go into Kentucky, under a military escort. The "Secretary of War" at Richmond (Benjamin) was asked for one. He would not give it himself. He said he greatly preferred seeing Brownlow "on the other side of the lines, as an avowed enemy;"[5] and instructed General Crittenden, then in command at Knoxville, to give him a pass. General Crittenden sent for Brownlow to come to Knoxville to receive it. He did so, and was on the point of departure for the Union lines, when he was arrested[a] for treason, on the authority of a warrant issued by "Commissioner" Reynolds, on the affidavit of Attorney Ramsey. He was refused

[a] December 6, 1861.

---

[1] Notwithstanding the Loyalists were disarmed, the hatred and cruel passions of the Secessionists were not appeased. Two Confederate officers had the following advertisement printed in the *Memphis Appeal:*

"Bloodhounds Wanted.—We, the undersigned, will pay five dollars per pair for fifty pairs of well-bred hounds, and fifty dollars for one pair of thoroughbred bloodhounds, that will take the track of a man. The purpose for which these dogs are wanted, is to chase the infernal, cowardly Lincoln bushwhackers of East Tennessee and Kentucky (who have taken advantage of the bush to kill and cripple many good soldiers) to their haunts and capture them. The said hounds must be delivered at Captain Hammer's livery-stable by the 10th of December next, where a mustering officer will be present to muster and inspect them.

"F. N. McNairy.
"H. H. Harris.

"Camp Comfort, Campbell Co., Tenn., Nov. 16."

BLOODHOUND.

[2] See page 38, volume I.

[3] So eager were the Confederates to implicate Brownlow in these transactions, that they offered men under sentence of death their lives and liberty, if they would testify to that effect. The latter spurned the bribe, and would not sacrifice truth and honor even for the sake of life.

[4] *Sketches of the Rise, Progress, and Decline of Secession.* By W. G. Brownlow.

[5] Letter of J. P. Benjamin to Major-General Crittenden, Nov. 20th, 1861.

a hearing or bail, but was cast into the county prison at Knoxville, from which appeals to the honor and good faith of Crittenden and his superiors were made in vain. There, in a room so crowded that not all could lie down, and not a chair, bench, stool, table, or other article of furniture, excepting a wooden bucket and tin cup, was to be seen, he and his associates, some of them among the best men in the land, were kept a long time, subjected to the vile ribaldry of soldiers and guards, and threats of being hung. Nor were these threats idle; for, from time to time, prisoners were taken out and hung—men as innocent of crime as infants. These were citizens, charged with burning the railway-bridges. The alleged crimes of these men and other Loyalists were set forth by Colonel Wood in a letter to Benjamin,[a] in which he declared that the sentiment of the inhabitants in East Tennessee was "hostile to the Confederate government," and that the people were slaves to Andrew Johnson and Horace Maynard. "To release the prisoners," he said, "is ruinous. To convict them before a court is next to an impossibility. The bridge-burners and spies ought to be tried at once."

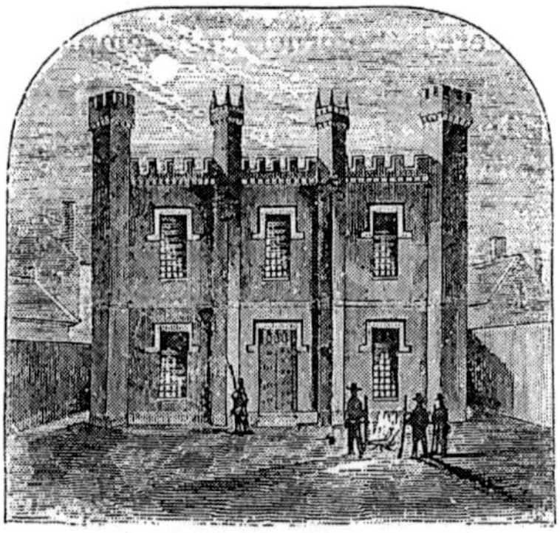

THE COUNTY JAIL AT KNOXVILLE.[1]

[a] Nov. 20, 1861.

This letter excited the brutal instincts of Benjamin, and he wrote back instantly[b] from Richmond, saying, "All such as can be identified in having been engaged in bridge-burning, are to be tried summarily by drum-head court-martial, and, if found guilty, executed on the spot by hanging. *It would be well to leave their bodies hanging in the vicinity of the burned bridges.*" He ordered the seizure of all arms that were "concentrated by these traitors," and said, "In no case is one of the men, known to have been up in arms against the government, to be released on any pledge or oath of allegiance. The time for such measures is past. They are all to be held as prisoners of war, and held in jail to the end of the war."

[b] Nov. 25.

Acting upon these suggestions, some of those who were *charged* with bridge-burning, but not found guilty, were hung under circumstances of great cruelty. In compliance with Benjamin's savage instructions, they were left hanging in public places, to receive the indignities of a brutal mob. Such was the case with the bodies of two victims (Hensie and Fry), who were hanged together upon the limb of an oak tree, near the railway-station, at Greenville, Tennessee, by the hands of Colonel Leadbetter, already mentioned.[2] He ordered their bodies to hang there four days and nights; and when the trains upon the road passed by, they were detained long enough to allow the passengers to go up and offer insults to the lifeless remains.

---

[1] This picture is from a sketch made by the author in May, 1866, and shows the front of the prison. The window that lighted the room on the lower floor, in which Brownlow was confined, is seen on the right of the door. In the upper story are two immense iron cages, into which the worst criminals are put, and in these some of the most obnoxious Loyalists were confined. Out of this loathsome place several were taken to the gallows.

[2] See page 174, volume I. This man, who was guilty of enormous crimes, it is said, during the war, and fled to Upper Canada at its close, died at Clifton, in that province, of apoplexy, on the 25th of September, 1866.

This was done, especially by Confederate soldiers on their way to Virginia, in view of many of the loyal inhabitants of Greenville.

In the midst of these fiery trials, the intrepid Brownlow remained firm, and exercised the greatest boldness of speech. They dared not hang him without legal conviction, and they well knew that he had done nothing worthy of death. He was not only bold, but defiant. They offered him life and liberty if he would take the oath of allegiance to the Confederacy. He scorned the proposition, saying: "Rather than stultify myself, and disgrace my family by such an oath, I agree to die. I never could sanction this government, and I trust no child of mine will ever do it." Whilst suffering in the Knoxville jail, and almost daily menaced with death, he wrote to Benjamin a characteristic letter,[a] in which he said, "You are reported to have said to a gentleman in Richmond, that I am a bad man, and dangerous to the Confederacy, and that you desire me out of it. Just give me my passports, and I will do for your Confederacy more than the devil has ever done—I will quit the country!"

[a] December 16, 1861.

THE GALLOWS-TREE.[1]

This letter, and a visit from General Crittenden (who felt sensitive on this point), brought one from Benjamin[b] to the authorities at Knoxville, indicating his wish that Brownlow should be sent out of the Confederacy, and regretting the circumstances of his arrest and imprisonment; "only," as he said, because "color is given to the suspicion that he has been entrapped." He was finally released and sent to Nashville (then in possession of National troops) early in March. Dr. Brownlow was a type of the Loyalists of the mountain regions of that State, who suffered terribly during a great portion of the war. A minute record of the faithful and fearless patriotism of the people of East Tennessee during the struggle, and the cruel wrongs and sufferings which they endured a greater portion of that time, would make one of the most glorious and yet revolting chapters in the history of the late fierce conflict. Incidents of that patriotism and suffering will be observed, as we proceed in our narrative.

[b] December 22.

Let us return a moment to the consideration of the other measure of the Confederate Congress, designed to force loyal men into a support of the rebellion, namely, the Confiscation Act.[2] From the "Department of Justice," at the head of which was Judah P. Benjamin, went out instructions that *all*

---

[1] This is from a sketch made by the author, in May, 1866. The tree was a vigorous red oak, standing on a slope overlooking the town, a few rods northeastward of the Greenville Station. Some person commenced cutting it down a while after the execution, but was restrained by the consideration offered, that it might serve the purpose of a gallows for the punishment of some of those who were engaged in the murder of the men who were hanged there. Near the root of the gallows limb (from which a rope is seen suspended) we observed a scar made by the passage of a Confederate cannon-ball through the tree. Its place is marked by a black spot, in the picture.

[2] See page 545, volume I., and page 33, volume II.

persons, Americans or Europeans, having a domicile in the "Confederate States, and carrying on business or traffic within the States at war with the Confederacy," were alien enemies; that the property, of every kind, of these persons should be seized and held, and that the receivers of the same should apply to the clerk of courts for writs of garnishment,[1] commanding persons suspected of holding in trust the property of an alien enemy to appear and answer such questions, under oath, touching such custody, as might be propounded. The authorized persons making the seizures were furnished with a formula of questions for the garnishees, which implied the establishment of a court of inquisition of the most despotic kind.

The citizen was asked, first, whether he held in trust any property belonging to an alien enemy; secondly, what was the character of such property, and what disposition had been made of any profit, interest, or rent accruing from the use thereof; thirdly, whether the citizen so questioned had, since the 21st day of May, 1861, been indebted to such alien enemy or enemies, and if so to what amount, and to what extent the debts had been discharged, and also to give the names of the creditors; fourthly, whether he knew of any property or interest belonging to such alien enemies, and if so to tell where it might be found. The citizen was warned that it was his duty, according to the law, to answer all of these questions, under penalty of indictment for a high misdemeanor, punishable by heavy fines and imprisonment.

Under this searching sequestration act a vast amount of property belonging to owners in the loyal States was seized, swelling the entire loss to the inhabitants of those States by the repudiation of, or inability to pay, honest debts by the business men of the South, to about three hundred millions of dollars. It was one of the strong arms of the despotism established by the conspirators, and few men had the boldness to oppose its operations. Yet the constitutionality of the act was questioned in the Confederate courts; and in that of the district of Charleston, over which Judge Magrath[2] presided, it was opposed in open court by that stanch loyalist J. L. Pettigru, who, from the beginning of the rebellion until his death, defied the conspirators and their instruments. He was served with a writ of garnishment, and refused to obey it, telling the court plainly that such proceedings were no better than those which made the English Star Chamber and the Spanish Inquisition odious to every lover of liberty. "Was there ever a law like this endured, practiced, or heard of?" he asked. "It certainly is not found among the people from whom we derive the common law. No English monarch or Parliament has ever sanc-

JAMES LOUIS PETTIGRU.

[1] A writ of garnishment in English law is a warning or notice for a person to appear in court, or give information of any kind required. The person named was called a garnishee.

[2] See page 49, volume I.

tioned or undertaken such a thing. It is no more a part of the law of war than it is a part of the law of peace." The inquisitors quailed in the presence of the honest old patriot, and his example and his words blunted the keen edge of the law.[1] Its enforcement gradually declined, and it became almost a dead letter during the later period of the war.

At the close of August, Congress and the chief council of the conspirators at Richmond had each finished its session, and both parties to the contest were preparing to put forth their utmost strength. Let us leave the consideration of these preparations, and whilst General McClellan is preparing the grand Army of the Potomac for a campaign, let us return to the observation of the performances on the theater of war westward of the Alleghany Mountains.

---

[1] Mr. Pettigru's boldness, and fidelity to principle while the terrible insanity of rebellion afflicted the people of his State, was most remarkable. He never deviated a line, in word or act, from the high stand of opposition to the madmen, which he had taken at the beginning of the raving mania. And the respect which his courage and honesty wrung from those whose course he so pointedly condemned was quite as remarkable. The Legislature of South Carolina, during that period of wild tumult, elected him to the most important trust and the largest salary in their gift, namely, to codify the State laws.

William J. Grayson, a life-long friend of Pettigru, and who died during the siege of Charleston, at the age of seventy-five years, left, in manuscript, an interesting biographical study of his friend. Concerning Mr. Pettigru's action at the period we are considering, he wrote:

"To induce the simple people to plunge into the volcanic fires of the revolution and war, they were told that the act of dissolution would produce no opposition of a serious nature; that not a drop of blood would be spilled; that no man's flocks, or herds, or negroes, or houses, or lands would be plundered or destroyed; that unbroken prosperity would follow the Ordinance of Secession; that cotton would control all Europe, and secure open ports and boundless commerce with the whole world for the Southern States. To such views Mr. Pettigru was unalterably opposed. He was convinced that war, anarchy, military despotism would inevitably follow a dissolution of the Union; that secession would impart to the abolition party a power over slavery that nothing else could give them—a power to make war on Southern institutions, to proclaim freedom to the negroes, to invoke and command the sympathy and aid of the whole world in carrying on a crusade on the Southern States."

"Mr. Pettigru saw that bankruptcy would follow war; that public fraud would find advocates in Richmond as well as in Washington. He opposed these schemes of disorder which have desolated the South. Their projectors professed to protect her from possible evils, and involved her in present and terrible disasters. The people were discontented at seeing rats infesting the granaries of Southern industry, and were urged to set fire to the four corners of every Southern barn to get rid of the vermin. They were alarmed at attacks on slavery by such men as John Brown and his banditti, and proposed as a remedy to rush into war with the armed hordes of the whole world. For a bare future contingency, they proposed to encounter an enormous immediate evil."

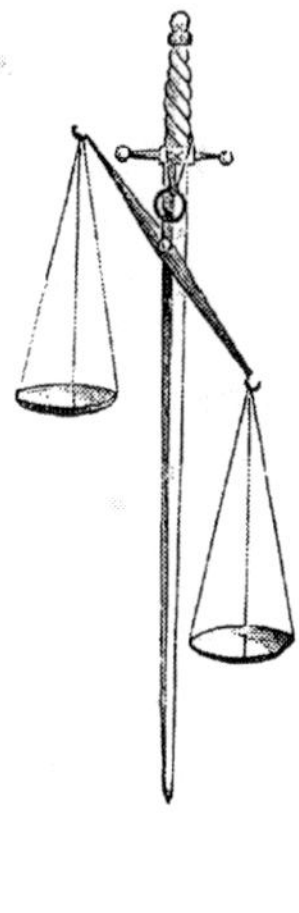

CHAPTER II.

CIVIL AND MILITARY OPERATIONS IN MISSOURI.

WE left General Lyon in possession of Booneville, Missouri,[1] from which he had driven the Confederates under Price and Jackson, on the 18th of June.[a] These leaders, as we have observed, were satisfied that the northern part of the State was lost to the cause of Secession, for the time, and they endeavored to concentrate their troops with Ben McCulloch's more southern men, in the southwestern part of the Commonwealth. We also left Colonel Franz Sigel in the vicinity of Rolla, pushing with eager Missouri loyalists toward the Confederate camps, on the borders of Kansas and Arkansas.[2]

[a] 1861.

Colonel Sigel arrived at Springfield on the 23d of June, where he was informed that the Confederates, under Governor Jackson, were making their way from the Osage River in a southwesterly direction. He pushed on to Sarcoxie, a post-village in Jackson County, where he arrived toward the evening of the 28th, and learned that General Price, with about nine hundred troops, was encamped at Pool's Prairie, a few miles north of Neosho, the capital of Newton County, and that other State troops, under Jackson and Rains, were making their way in the same direction. It was important to prevent their junction. Sigel resolved to march first on Price, and capture or disperse his force, and then, turning northward, attack the other troops, and so open a communication with General Lyon, who, he had been informed (but incorrectly), had been fighting with the Confederates on the banks of the Little Osage.

Sigel's march from Sarcoxie had just commenced, when a scout brought him word that Price had fled from Pool's Prairie to Elk Mills, thirty miles south of Neosho. He at once turned his attention to the troops north of him, who he supposed were endeavoring to make their way into Arkansas. He sent forward a detachment of two companies, under Captain Grone, with two field-pieces, toward Cedar Creek and Grand Falls, on the Neosho, to occupy a road in this supposed route of the Confederates, and to gain information, while he pushed on with the remainder of his command to Neosho, receiving greetings of welcome from the inhabitants on the way, who had been pillaged by the insurgents. He had already summoned Colonel Salomon, with his Missouri battalion, to join him at Neosho, and with this addi-

[1] See page 542, volume I. [2] See page 543, volume I.

tion to his force, he went forward to meet his foe, leaving a single rifle company, under Captain Conrad, to protect the loyal inhabitants there, with orders to retreat to Sarcoxie if necessary.

Sigel encamped close by the south fork of the Spring River, southeast of Carthage, the capital of Jasper County, on the evening of the 4th of July, after a march of twenty-five miles, where he was informed that Jackson was nine or ten miles distant, in the direction of Lamar, the county seat of Barton County, with four or five thousand men. Sigel's force consisted of about five hundred and fifty men of the Third (his own) Missouri Regiment, and four hundred of the Fifth (Salomon's) Regiment, with two batteries of artillery, each consisting of four field-pieces—in all about fifteen hundred men. With these troops, and with his baggage-train three miles in the rear, he slowly advanced to find his foe on the morning of the 5th, his skirmishers driving before them large numbers of mounted riflemen, who seemed to be simply gathering information. Six miles northward of Carthage they passed the Dry Fork Creek, and, after a brisk march of three miles farther, they came upon the Confederates, under Governor Jackson, assisted by Brigadier-Generals Rains, Clark, Parsons, and Slack. They had been marching that morning in search of Sigel, and were now drawn up in battle order on the crown of a gentle ascent.

Sigel was soon convinced that his foe was vastly his superior, not only in numbers, but in cavalry, but was deficient in artillery. They had but a few old pieces, which were charged with trace-chains, bits of iron, and other missiles. Sigel therefore determined to make his own cannon play an important part, for they were his chief reliance for success.

The battle commenced at a little past ten o'clock by Sigel's field-pieces, under Major Bischoff, and, after a desultory contest of over three hours, it was observed that the Confederate cavalry under Rains were outflanking the Nationals, on the right and left. Sigel's baggage-train at the Dry Fork Creek was in danger, and he fell back to secure it. His antagonist slowly followed, but was kept at a respectful distance by the National cannon, two of which were on each flank, and four in the rear, of the little Union army. The retreat was made in perfect order, and was but little interrupted by fighting, excepting at the bluffs at Dry Fork Creek, through which the road passed. There the Confederate cavalry massed on Sigel's front and tried to impede his progress. These were quickly dispersed by his guns, and by a vigorous charge of his infantry.

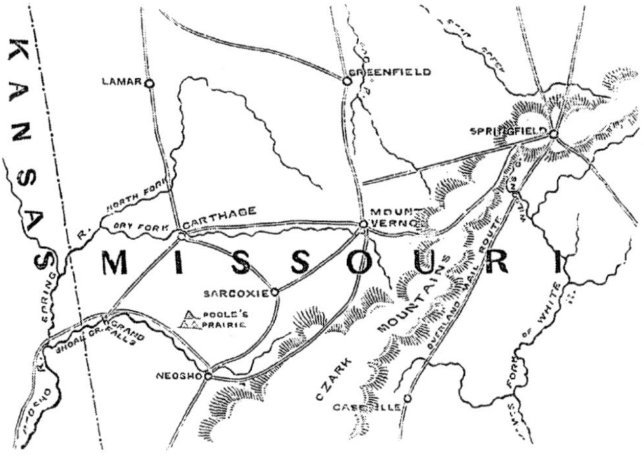

SIGEL'S FIELD OF OPERATIONS.

Finding the presence of an overwhelming force (estimated at full five thousand men, including a heavy reserve) too great to be long borne with safety, Sigel continued his orderly retreat to the heights near Carthage, having been engaged in a running fight nearly all the way. The Confederates still pressed him sorely. He attempted to give his troops rest at the village, but the cavalry of his enemy, crossing Spring River at various points, hung so threateningly on his flank, and so menaced the Springfield road, that he continued his retreat to Sarcoxie without much molestation, the Confederates relinquishing the pursuit a few miles from Carthage. The Nationals had lost in the battle thirteen killed and thirty-one wounded, all of whom were borne away by their friends. They also lost nine horses, a battery of four cannon, and one baggage wagon. In the mean time, Captain Conrad and his company of ninety men, who were left in Neosho, had been captured by the Confederates.[1] The loss of the insurgents, according to their own account, was from thirty to forty killed, and from one hundred and twenty-five to one hundred and fifty wounded.[2] They also lost forty-five men made prisoners, eighty horses, and a considerable number of shot-guns, with which Jackson's cavalry were armed.

Being outnumbered by the Confederates, more than three to one, Colonel Sigel did not tarry at Sarcoxie, but continued his retreat by Mount Vernon to Springfield, where he was joined by General Lyon on the 13th,[a] who took the chief command. It was a fortunate movement for Sigel; for within twelve hours after the battle, Jackson was re-enforced by Generals Price and Ben McCulloch, who came with several thousand Missouri, Arkansas, and Texas troops.

[a] July, 1861.

General Lyon had left Booneville in pursuit of the fugitive Confederates on the 3d of July, with a little army numbering about twenty-seven hundred men, with four pieces of artillery and a long baggage-train. The day was intensely hot. The commander was mounted on an iron-gray horse, accompanied by his body-guard, composed of ten German butchers of St. Louis, who were noted for their size, strength, and horsemanship, and were all well mounted and heavily armed with pistols and sabers. He reached an important ferry on the Grand River, a branch of the Osage, in Henry County, on the 7th,[b] where he was joined by three thousand troops from Kansas, under Major Sturgis. The whole force crossed the river, by means of a single scow, by ten o'clock on the 8th. In the mean time, two companies of cavalry, who crossed on the evening of the 7th, had pushed forward to gain the ferry on the Osage, twenty-two miles ahead. Near that point, in the midst of a dense forest, the main army reached the river in the afternoon of the 9th, when they were stirred by intense excitement, produced by intelligence of Colonel Sigel's fight near Carthage.

[b] July.

Lyon was now eighty miles from Springfield. Satisfied of Sigel's peril, he decided to change his course, and to hasten to the relief of that officer, by forced marches. Early on the morning of the 10th, regardless of the intense heat and lack of sleep, the army moved from the south bank of the

---

[1] Report of Colonel Sigel to Brigadier-General Sweeney, dated Springfield, July 11th, 1861.

[2] Pollard's *First Year of the War*, page 133. It is believed that the entire loss of the Confederates was at least 300 men.

Osage, and soon striking a dense forest, sometimes pathless and dark, they were compelled to make their way among steep hills, deep gorges, swiftly running streams, miry morasses, ugly gullies washed by the rains, jagged rocks, and fallen timbers. At three o'clock in the afternoon, when the army halted for dinner, they were twenty-seven miles from their starting-place in the morning. The march was resumed at sunset, and was continued until three o'clock on the morning of the 11th, when the commander ordered a halt. For forty-eight hours, most of the men had not closed their eyes in sleep. Within ten minutes after the order to halt was given, nine-tenths of the wearied soldiers were slumbering. They did not stop to unroll their blankets, or select a good spot for resting; but officers and privates dropped upon the ground in deep sleep. They had marched over a horrible road, during twenty-four hours, almost fifty miles. Early the next morning a courier brought intelligence of Sigel's safety in Springfield, and the remainder of the march of thirty miles was made leisurely during the space of the next two days.[1]

Lyon encamped near Springfield,[a] and then prepared to contend with the overwhelming and continually increasing number of his enemies. Within the period of a few weeks, the Confederates had been driven into the southwestern corner of Missouri, on the border of Kansas and Arkansas. Now they were making vigorous preparations to regain the territory they had lost. They had been largely re-enforced, and were especially strong in cavalry. At Cassville, the capital of Barry County, near the Arkansas line, on the great overland mail route, they established a general rendezvous; and there, on the 29th of July, four Southern armies, under the respective commands of Generals Price, McCulloch, Pearce, and McBride, effected a junction.

[a] July 13 1861.

At that time General Lyon, with his little force daily diminishing by the expiration of the terms of enlistment, was confined in a defensive attitude to the immediate vicinity of Springfield. He had called repeatedly for re-enforcements, to which no response was given. He waited for them long, but they did not come. Every day his position had become more perilous, and now the Confederates were weaving around him a strong web of real danger; yet he resolved to hold the position at all hazards.[2]

At the close of July, Lyon was informed that the Confederates were marching upon Springfield in two columns (in the aggregate, more than twenty thousand strong); one from Cassville, on the south, and the other from Sarcoxie, on the west, for the purpose of investing the National camp and the town. He determined to go out and meet them; and, late in the afternoon of the 1st of August, his entire army (5,500 foot, 400 horse, and 18 guns), led by himself, moved toward Cassville, with the exception of a small force left behind to guard the city.[3] They bivouacked that night on Cave

---

[1] *Life of General Nathaniel Lyon.* By Ashbel Woodward, M. D.

[2] On the 31st of July, Lyon wrote, saying: "I fear the enemy may become emboldened by our want of activity. I have constant rumors of a very large force below, and of threats to attack us with overwhelming numbers. I should have a much larger force than I have, and be much better supplied."

[3] Lyon's force at this time consisted of five companies of the First and Second Regulars, under Major Sturgis; five companies of the First Missouri Volunteers, Lieutenant-Colonel Andrews; two companies of the Second Missouri, Major Osterhaus; three companies of the Third Missouri, Colonel Sigel; Fifth Missouri, Colonel Salomon; First Iowa, Colonel Bates; First Kansas, Colonel Deitzler; Second Kansas, Colonel Mitchell; two com-

Creek, ten miles south of Springfield, and moved forward at an early hour in the morning, excessively annoyed by heat and dust, and intense thirst, for most of the wells and streams were dry. At Dug Springs, nineteen miles southwest of Springfield, they halted. They were in an oblong valley, five miles in length, and broken by projecting spurs of the hills, which formed wooded ridges. Soon after halting, they discovered, by clouds of dust at the other extremity of the valley, that a large body of men were there and in motion. These were Confederates, under General Rains. A battle-line was formed by the Nationals, and in that order the little army moved forward toward the enemy, led by a company of Regular Infantry, under Captain Steele, supported by another of the Fourth Regular Cavalry, under Captain Stanley, which held the advanced position on the left. Owing to the ridges in the valley, the real force of each party was easily concealed from the other, and afforded opportunities for surprises. And so it happened. While the vanguard of the Nationals was moving cautiously forward, followed by the main body, and skirmishers were exchanging shots briskly, a large force of Confederates suddenly emerged from the woods, to cut off Steele's infantry from Stanley's cavalry. The latter (about a hundred and fifty strong) immediately drew up his men in proper order, and when the foe was within the range of their Sharp's carbines, they opened a deadly fire upon them. The latter numbered nearly five hundred. They returned the fire, and a regular battle seemed about to open, when a subordinate officer in Stanley's command shouted "Charge!" and twenty-five horsemen dashed in among the Confederate infantry, hewing them down with their sabers with fearful slaughter. Stanley could do nothing better than sustain the irregular order; but before he could reach the heroic little band with re-enforcements, the Confederates had broken and fled in the wildest confusion. "Are these men or devils—they fight so?" asked some of the wounded of the vanquished, when the conflict was over.

When this body of Confederate infantry fled, a large force of their cavalry appeared emerging from the woods. Captain Totten brought two of his guns to bear upon them from a commanding eminence with such precision, that his shells fell among and scattered them in great disorder, for their frightened horses became unmanageable. The whole column of the Confederates now withdrew, leaving the valley in possession of the National troops. Thus ended THE BATTLE OF DUG SPRINGS. Lyon's loss was eight men killed and thirty wounded, and that of the Confederates was about forty killed and as many wounded.

The Nationals moved forward the next morning in search of foes, but were disappointed. They encamped at Curran, in Stone County, twenty-six miles from Springfield, and remained in that vicinity until the next day, when General Lyon called a council of officers,[1] and it was determined to return to Springfield. The army moved in that direction on the following morning,[a] and reached Springfield on the 6th.[2]

[a] August 4, 1861.

---

panies First Regular Cavalry, Captains Stanley and Carr; three companies First Regular Cavalry (recruits). Lieutenant Lathrop; Captain Totten's Battery, Regular Artillery, six guns, 6 and 12-pounders; Lieutenant Du Bois' Battery, Regular Artillery, four guns, 6 and 12-pounders; Captain Schaeffer's Battery, Missouri Volunteer Artillery, six guns, 6 and 12-pounders. General Lyon gave the most important secondary commands to Brigadier-General Sweeney, Colonel Sigel, and Major Sturgis.

[1] The officers called into the council were Brigadier-General Sweeney, Colonel Sigel, Majors Schofield, Shepherd, Conant, and Sturgis, and Captains Totten and Schaeffer.

[2] Correspondence of the New York *World* and *Herald*; *Life of General Lyon*, by Dr. Woodward, pages 297 to 301, inclusive.

The events of the past few days had given great encouragement to both officers and men.

The affair at Dug Springs impressed General McCulloch (a part of whose column it was that had been so smitten there) with the importance of great circumspection, and, after consultation with some of his officers, he fell back, and moving westward, formed a junction with the weaker force under Price, then advancing from Sarcoxie. Information reached them at Cane Creek that Lyon's force was immensely superior, and McCulloch counseled a retrograde movement. Price entertained a different opinion, and favored an immediate advance. His officers agreed with him, and he asked McCulloch to loan him arms, that his destitute Missouri soldiers, who were willing to fight, might be allowed to do so. McCulloch refused. So the matter stood, when, on the same evening,[a] an order was received by McCulloch, from Major-General Polk,[1] ordering an advance upon Lyon. He called a council of his officers, exhibited the order to Price, and offered to march immediately on Springfield, upon condition that he should have the chief command of the army. Price, anxious to drive the Nationals out of Missouri, yielded to the Texan, saying he was "not fighting for distinction but for the defense of the liberties of his country. He was willing to surrender his command and his life, if necessary, as a sacrifice to the cause."[2]

[a] August 4, 1861.

On taking chief command, General McCulloch issued an order,[b] directing all unarmed men to remain in camp, and all others to put their arms in order, provide themselves with fifty rounds of ammunition each, and be in readiness for marching at midnight. He divided the army into three columns; the first commanded by himself, the second by General Pearce, of Arkansas, and the third by General Price; and at the appointed hour the whole force, full twenty thousand strong, in fine spirits, moved toward Springfield, expecting to meet Lyon eight miles distant from their camp, where there were strong natural defenses. They approached the position cautiously, at sunrise, but were disappointed. They pushed forward, unmindful of the intense heat, the stifling dust, and the lack of water; and on the night of the 10th the wearied army encamped at Big Spring, a mile and a half from Wilson's Creek, and about ten and a half miles south of Springfield. They were in a sad plight. Their baggage-train was far behind, and so were their beef cattle. The troops had not eaten any thing for twenty-four hours, and for ten days previously they had received only half rations. They satisfied the cravings of hunger by eating green corn on the way, but without a particle of salt or a mouthful of meat. They had no blankets, nor tents, nor clothes, excepting what they had on their backs, and four-fifths of them were barefooted. "Billy Barlow's dress at a circus," wrote one of their number, "would be decent in comparison with that of almost any one, from the major-general down to the humblest private."

[b] August 7.

On the 9th, the whole Confederate army moved to Wilson's Creek, at a point southwest of Springfield, where that stream flows through a narrow valley, inclosed on each side by gentle sloping hills covered with patches of

[1] See page 540, volume I.

[2] Pollard's *First Year of the War*, page 135.

low trees and fields of corn and wheat. They encamped on both sides of the creek, and for nearly two days subsisted wholly upon green corn. Their effective force, according to the best estimates, was about fifteen thousand men, of whom six thousand were horsemen. The latter were indifferently armed with flint-lock muskets, rifles, and shot-guns; and there were many mounted men not armed at all. They had fifteen pieces of artillery.[1] General Price reported the number of Missouri State troops at five thousand two hundred and twenty-one. The entire number of Confederates encamped on Wilson's Creek appears to have been about twenty-three thousand.

General Lyon had now only a little more than five thousand effective men, and prudence seemed to dictate a retreat northward rather than risk a battle under such disadvantages. But he knew that a retreat at that time would ruin the Union cause in Missouri, and he was willing to risk every thing for that cause. He was conscious of the extreme peril by which his little army was surrounded, but he had reason to hope for success, for he was in command of good officers, and brave and well-armed men. Yet, in a council of war, which he called on the 9th, these officers, with great unanimity, favored the evacuation of Springfield, in order to save the troops; but General T. W. Sweeney vehemently opposed it, and urged making a stand where they were, and withdrawing from Springfield only on compulsion.[2] On the same day[a] each party in the contest prepared to advance upon the other within twenty-four hours.

[a] August 9, 1861.

Necessity compelled Lyon to go out and meet his foe, for Springfield, situated on an open plain, could not be made defensible by means at his command. Every avenue leading from it would soon be closed by the overwhelming numbers of the Confederates, and the loss of his whole command might be the consequence. Every thing now depended upon secrecy and skill of movement, and he resolved to march out at night, surprise his enemy, and by a bold stroke scatter his forces. Twice already he had appointed the hour for such a movement to begin, but each time prudence compelled him to postpone it. Finally, on Friday, the 9th of August, he prepared to execute his plan that night. He divided his little army into two columns, and made dispositions to strike the Confederate camp at two points simultaneously.[3]

At the same time, as we have observed, the Confederates were preparing for a similar movement. They were divided into four columns, and ordered to march at nine o'clock on the night of the 9th,[b] so as to surround Springfield and attack the National Army at dawn the next morning. On account of a gathering storm and the intense darkness, McCul-

[b] August.

---

[1] Pollard's *First Year of the War*, page 136.

[2] Woodruff's *Life of Lyon*, page 303. General Sweeney had been in Springfield some time, from which place he had issued a proclamation, on the 4th of July, commanding all disloyalists to cease their opposition to the Government and to take an oath of allegiance.

[3] Lyon's column consisted of three brigades, commanded respectively by Major S. D. Sturgis, Lieutenant-Colonel Andrews, and Colonel Deitzler. Major Sturgis's brigade was composed of a battalion of Regular Infantry, under Captain Plummer, Captain Totten's light battery of six pieces, a battalion of Missouri Volunteers, under Major Osterhaus, Captain Wood's company of mounted Kansas Volunteers, and a company of Regular Cavalry, under Lieutenant Canfield. Lieutenant-Colonel Andrews's brigade consisted of Captain Steele's battalion of Regulars, Lieutenant Du Bois' light battery of four pieces, and the First Missouri Volunteers. Deitzler's brigade was composed of the First and Second Kansas and First Iowa Volunteers, and two hundred mounted Missouri Home Guards. Sigel's column consisted of the Third and Fifth Missouri Volunteers, one company of cavalry, under Captain Carr, another of dragoons, under Lieutenant Farrand, of the First Infantry, and a company of recruits, with a light battery of six guns, under Lieutenant Lothrop.

loch countermanded the order, and his army, wearied with waiting and watching, was still in camp on Wilson's Creek on the morning of the 10th.[1] This was a fortunate circumstance for Lyon. He had moved at the appointed hour; and as McCulloch, in anticipation of his march upon Springfield, had withdrawn his advanced pickets, and, feeling no apprehensions of an attack by Lyon with his small force, had not thrown them out again, the Nationals were afforded an opportunity for a complete surprise of their foe.

The two columns of the National Army were led respectively by Lyon and Sigel. The former, with Major Sturgis as his second in command, marched from Springfield with the main body, at five o'clock in the afternoon of the 9th,[a] to fall upon the Confederates in front, leaving Sigel, with twelve hundred men and six guns, to gain their rear by their right. Lyon's force arrived within sight of the Confederate guard-fires at one o'clock in the morning, where they lay on their arms until dawn. Sigel in the mean time had left his position a little south of Springfield, and was in the Confederate rear at the appointed time, ready to strike the meditated blow.

[a] August, 1861.

Lyon formed a line of battle at five o'clock,[b] and moved forward to attack the extreme northern point of the Confederate camp, occupied by General Rains, closely followed by Totten's Battery, which was supported by a strong reserve. The Confederate pickets were driven in by Lyon's skirmishers, and the Nationals were within musket-range of the hostile camp in front of Rains before the latter was aware of their approach. Rains immediately communicated the astounding fact to General Price. He told him truly, that the main body of the National Army was close upon him, and he called earnestly for re-enforcements. McCulloch was at Price's quarters when the alarming news arrived, and he hastened at once to his own, to make dispositions for battle.

[b] Aug. 10.

General Lyon pushed on with vigor when the Confederate camp pickets were driven in. The mounted Home Guards and Captain Plummer's battalion were thrown across Wilson's Creek, near a sharp bend, and moved on a line with the advance of the main body, for the purpose of preventing the left flank of the Nationals being turned. Steadily onward the main column marched along a ravine, when, on ascending a ridge, it confronted a large force of Confederate foot-soldiers, composed of the infantry and artillery of Price's command, under Generals W. Y. Slack, J. H. McBride, J. B. Clark, and M. M. Parsons. These were all Missouri State Guards. Dispositions for a contest were at once made by both parties. The battalions of Major Osterhaus, and two companies of the First Missouri Volunteers, under Captains Yates and Cavender, of the Nationals, deployed as skirmishers. At the same time the left section of Captain Totten's Battery, under Lieutenant Sokalski, fired upon their foe. A few moments afterward, the remainder of the battery, planted on an eminence more to the right and front, opened with such destructive effect, that the Confederates broke, and were driven by Lyon's infantry to the hills overlooking their camp.

To seize and occupy the crest of the hills from which the Confederates

[1] Report of General Price to Governor Jackson, August 12th, 1861. Pollard, in his *First Year of the War*, page 137, says, that after receiving orders to march, on the evening of the 9th, the troops made preparation, and got up a dance before their camp-fires. This dance was kept up until a late hour.

had been driven was most desirable, and for that purpose the First Missouri, First Kansas, and First Iowa, with Totten's Battery, pushed forward, Major Osterhaus's battalion being on the extreme right, his own right resting on the side of an abrupt ravine. A line of battle was immediately formed on the hill, with the Missouri troops in front, the Kansas troops sixty yards to the left, on the opposite side of a ravine, and the Iowa troops still farther to the left. Totten's Battery was planted on an eminence, between the Missouri and Kansas troops; and Dubois's Battery, supported by Steele's battalion, was placed about eighty yards to the left and rear of it, in a position to play upon a concealed Confederate battery on the crest of a ridge across the creek, which swept the position of the Nationals. In the mean time, Totten attacked a masked battery on the left bank of the creek, whose position could only be known by the flash and smoke of its guns. Directly in front, under Totten's guns, lay the camp of General Rains, entirely deserted.

The battle now became general. A very severe contest was raging on the right, where the First Missouri was fighting in thick underwood. It was a contest involving a struggle between superior arms well used, and overwhelming numbers. As the ranks of the Confederates were penetrated and gaps were made, they were immediately filled; and in this terrible conflict the line of the Missourians was sadly thinned. Totten was ordered up to their support, and his canister-shot made awful lanes through a large body of Confederates, who, by the trick of carrying a Union flag, approached quite near for the purpose of capturing his cannon. The deception was discovered in time to allow Totten to punish them severely, and full half an hour his and Dubois's Battery made a continual roar. In the mean time, Plummer's battalion, in the bend of the stream, was encountering a large body of infantry in a corn-field. The fight there was terrific for a while, when over two thousand Confederates came pouring into the open field from the woods like a torrent, threatening to overwhelm and annihilate the Nationals in an instant. The latter, perceiving their peril, retreated in good order, while shells from Dubois's Battery, thrown with precision, fell among the pursuers with such fearful effect, that they turned and fled. The Confederates had been struggling vigorously and bravely to turn the left flank of the Nationals; but now, after such fearful loss and demoralization, they abandoned the attempt.

Whilst Lyon was thus carrying on the battle on the Confederate front, Sigel, whose assigned duty was to turn their right, by the rear, had opened fire. With his twelve hundred men, and battery of six cannon, he had reached a position within a mile of their camp at dawn. He had moved with great skill and caution, and his alert little force had cut off several squads of their enemy in such a way that no intelligence of his approach could reach the Confederate Army. Almost the first intimation given them of his presence was the bursting of his shells over their tents near the middle of their encampment, at the moment when the booming of Lyon's heavy guns was heard in another part of the field. The dismayed Confederates, composed of the regiment of Colonel Churchill, Greer's Texan Rangers, and nearly seven hundred mounted Missourians, commanded by Colonel Brown, fled, leaving every thing behind them; when Sigel's men rushed across the creek, traversed the desolate camp, and formed almost in its center. The

Confederates immediately reappeared in strong force of infantry and cavalry, when Sigel brought his artillery into a commanding position, and with it drove his foes into the woods.

Hearing the continued roar of Lyon's heavy guns, Sigel now pressed forward to attack the Confederate line of battle in the rear. He had passed along the Fayetteville road, as far as Sharp's farm, with about a hundred prisoners whom he had captured, when the firing at the northward almost ceased. Seeing at the same time large numbers of the Confederates moving southward, he believed that Lyon had won a victory; and that belief was strengthened, when it was reported to him that National soldiers were approaching his line. Orders were given not to fire in that direction, and flags of friendly greeting were waved, when suddenly the advancing troops raised the Confederate banner, and two batteries, directly in front of Sigel's force, opened a heavy and destructive fire upon the Nationals. The Confederates, strong in numbers, and dressed like Sigel's men, had so deceived that commander, that they were allowed to approach within less than musket-shot distance before the trick was discovered. The consternation in his ranks was terrible, and every arm seemed paralyzed for a moment. In the sudden confusion the Confederates rushed forward, killed the artillery horses, and, turning the flanks of the infantry, caused them to fly in the wildest disorder. They rushed into bushes and by-roads, incessantly attacked by large numbers of Arkansas and Texas cavalry. The entire battery was captured; and, in the course of a few minutes, of his twelve hundred men, Sigel had only about three hundred left. He saved these and one of his cannon,[1] but lost his regimental flag. Such now composed the entire remnant of Lyon's second column.[2]

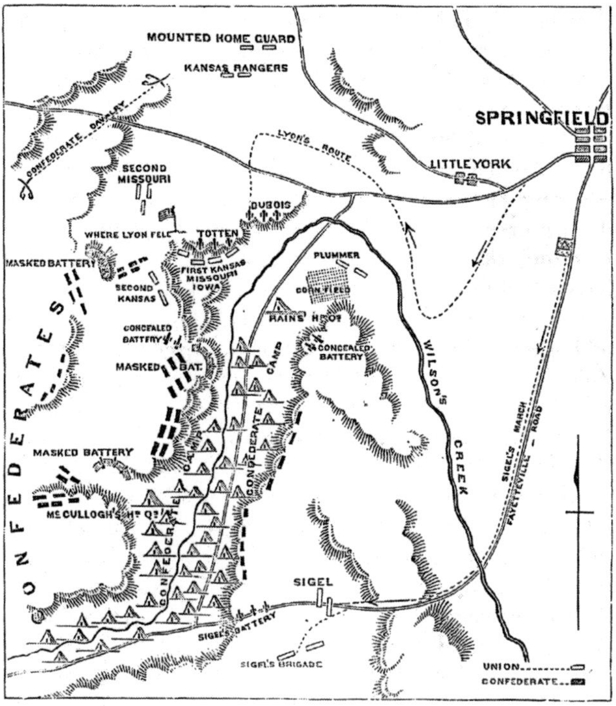

PLAN OF THE BATTLE OF WILSON'S CREEK.

[1] Captain Flagg fastened ropes to this gun, and made some of the Confederate prisoners draw it off the field.

[2] The composition of Sigel's corps was not well fitted for a trying position. The term of service of the Fifth Missouri had expired, and the engagement to remain eight days longer ended on the day before the battle.

There had been a lull in the tempest of war, when this successful stratagem of the Confederates was performed. Now the storm burst with increased fury, and the fight was terrific all along the line, as we shall observe presently.

We left Lyon's column contending with the Confederates in front, when each party in turn had been compelled to give way, but, equally brave and determined, had renewed the contest with vigor. At length, as we have seen, when Sigel was pushing along the Fayetteville road, to strike the Confederate rear, the firing had ceased along almost the entire line. The exception was on the extreme right of the National forces, where the First Missouri, assisted by the First Iowa and Kansas regiments, were valiantly beating back the foe, in their attempts to turn that flank. They were patiently carrying on an unequal contest with a superior force, though decimated, during over four hours' hard fighting. They were almost fainting with weariness and thirst, after having repeatedly driven back their enemy, when a heavy body of fresh Confederates were seen hurrying forward to give them a crushing blow. The quick eye and judgment of General Lyon saw the peril of his comrades, and he ordered the Second Kansas to their support. He rode forward himself, and perceiving the danger greater than he apprehended, ordered Totten to send aid from his battery for the right of the contending Nationals. Lieutenant Sokalski was immediately ordered forward with a section, and prompt relief was afforded by his skillful use of his guns.

A new danger to the Nationals now appeared. Eight hundred Confederate cavalry had formed a line of battle, unobserved, behind a ridge, and suddenly dashed toward the National rear, where some Kansas troops were guarding ambulances for the wounded. Volleys from infantry did not check their movement; but when they were within two hundred yards of Totten's Battery, that officer suddenly wheeled his guns, turned them upon the horsemen, and opened such a deadly fire that they and their beasts fell in heaps. The effect was marvelous. Those mounted men, who had just been prouldy scorning all opposition, and feeling sure of turning the tide of victory in favor of the Confederates with very little more fighting, were now suddenly scattered in confusion. The check immediately became a rout, and every man in the saddle sought the shelter of the woods or intervening ridges. Meanwhile the support of Steele's Battery was transferred from Dubois's to Totten's. These had just formed in battle line when a very heavy body of Confederates came pouring out of the woods on Lyon's front and flank. Instantly the hurricane of war was again in full career over that hard-fought field. Backward and forward the contending lines swayed, their fronts often within a few yards of each other. Every effective man in Lyon's column was now engaged. For an hour the conflict was terrible, and all that time it seemed as if a feather's weight would turn the scale in favor of one or the other. Lyon was seen continually moving along the lines wherever the storm raged most furiously, encouraging his men by brave words and braver deeds. Very early in this fierce engagement his horse was shot. Then he received a wound in the leg; another in the head soon

The men serving the cannon were taken from the infantry, and were mostly recruits. Many officers had left, and a greater portion of the men of the Third Regiment were imperfectly drilled, and had never been under fire before.

followed, when, partially stunned, he walked a few paces to the rear and said to Major Schofield, despondingly, "I fear the day is lost."—"No, General, let us try once more," was the reply. The commander soon rallied, and, regardless of the blood still flowing from his wounds, he mounted the horse of one of Major Sturgis's orderlies, and placing himself in front of the Second Kansas, who were led by the gallant Colonel Mitchell, he swung his hat over his head, and calling loudly for the troops to follow, dashed forward with a desperate determination to gain the victory. Mitchell fell severely wounded, and his troops asked, "Who shall lead us?"—"I will lead you," said the chief; "come on, brave men!" In a few moments afterward a rifle-ball entered his left side and passed through his body near the heart. He fell in the arms of his body-servant, Albert Lehman, saying: "Lehman, I am going," and expired a few seconds afterward.

It was about nine o'clock in the morning when General Lyon fell, and the command devolved upon Major Sturgis. The Confederates had just been repulsed along the whole line, and for twenty minutes there was another lull in the storm. Taking advantage of this respite, Sturgis consulted with his officers. The little army was dreadfully shattered, and its beloved leader was slain. In its front were at least twenty thousand men, of whom two-thirds were effective soldiers. The Nationals had then been without water nearly thirty hours, and a supply could be had only at Springfield, twelve miles distant. Certain defeat seemed to await the little band. The loss of Sigel's column was not then known. His silence was ominous. If he had retreated, nothing was left for Sturgis to do but to follow his example. The great question to be decided was, "Is retreat possible?" It was under consideration when the council was suddenly broken up by the appearance of a heavy body of infantry advancing from the hill on which Sigel's guns had been heard. Above them was seen waving the banner of the Union. Preparations were made to form a junction with them, and they had approached to a covered position within a short distance of Sturgis's line, when a battery upon a hill in the rear opened a heavy fire upon the Nationals, and the approaching troops displayed the Confederate flag.

For the third time during the battle the Union soldiers had been deceived by this stratagem. In this case the Confederates came, having an appearance exactly like Sigel's men, and the battery with which they announced their true character was composed of Sigel's captured guns! Their voice was the signal for a renewal of the conflict, and they were speedily silenced by Dubois, supported by Osterhaus and a remnant of the First Missouri. The battle raged fiercely for a time. Totten's Battery, supported by Iowa and Regular troops, in the center of the National line, was the special object of attack. The two armies were sometimes within a few feet of each other, and faces were scorched by the flash of a foeman's gun. The Union column stood like a rock in the midst of turbulent waves, dashing them into foam. Its opponents were vastly its superior in numbers. At length its line, pressed by an enormous weight, began to bend. At that critical moment Captain Granger dashed forward from the rear with the support of Dubois's Battery, consisting of portions of the First Kansas, First Missouri, and First Iowa Regiments. These poured upon the Confederates a volley so destructive that their right wing recoiled, leaving the earth strewn with their dead and wounded. The confusion caused by this disaster spread over the entire Confederate line, and in broken masses they fell back to the shelter of the woods. At the same time, their wagon-train was on fire, its huge columns of black smoke in the distance giving heart to the Nationals by its seeming indications of a design on the part of the enemy to fly. But this they did not do. They held the field.

[a] August 10, 1861.

Thus ended, at eleven o'clock in the morning,[a] the BATTLE OF WILSON'S CREEK,[1] after a struggle of five or six hours, which was not surpassed in intensity and prowess, on both sides, during the great war that followed.[2] The National loss was between twelve and thirteen hundred, and that of the Confederates was, according to the most careful estimate, full three thousand.[3] The shattered National troops were in no condition to follow up the advantage which they had gained in the closing contest. Their strength and their ammunition were nearly exhausted, and nothing remained for them to do but to fall back to Springfield. The order for that movement was given at the close of the battle, and the little army, joined on the way by a portion of the remnant of Sigel's column, reached the old camp, still under the protection of a body of Home Guards, at five o'clock in the afternoon. In the hurry of retreat, the body of General Lyon was left behind, but it was subsequently recovered.[4]

[b] August 11.

Under the general command of Colonel Sigel, the entire Union force left Springfield the next morning[b] at three o'clock, and in good order retreated to Rolla, one hundred and twenty-five miles distant, in the direction of St. Louis, safely conducting a Government train, five miles in length, and valued at one million five hundred thousand dollars.

---

[1] The Confederates called this the *Battle of Oak Hill.*

[2] The example of Lyon in the campaign, which for him ended at Springfield, inspired all of his followers with the most soldierly qualities, and they were eminently displayed afterward. From his little army a large number of commanders emanated, and were conspicuous, especially in the West. Two years afterward, a writer in the Detroit *Tribune* said: "There was present at Wilson's Creek the usual complement of officers for a force of five thousand men. From them have been made six major-generals, and thirteen brigadiers; colonels, lieutenant-colonels, and majors by the score have sprung from those who were then either line or non-commissioned officers. From one company of the First Iowa Infantry thirty-seven commissioned officers are now in the service. Similarly, one company of the First Missouri has contributed thirty-two. It is a curious fact, that, of the officers who survived the battle of Wilson's Creek, not one has been killed in battle, and only one has died from disease. In every battle for the Union the heroes of this terrible contest are found, and nowhere have they disgraced their old record. 'Is it not worth ten years of life to be able to say, I was in the campaign with Lyon?'"

A poet of the day, apostrophizing the Spirit of Lyon as a terror to the conspirators, wrote:

"For wheresoe'er thy comrades stand
To face the traitors, as of yore,
Thy prescient spirit shall command,
And lead the charge once more."

[3] See reports of Major Sturgis, August 20th, 1861; of Colonel Sigel, August 18th, 1861, and of the subordinate officers of Lyon's army; also, reports of Generals Price and McCulloch and their subordinate officers. The National loss was reported at 223 killed, 721 wounded, and 292 missing. McCulloch reported the Confederate loss at 265 killed, 800 wounded, and 30 missing. At the same time, he reported the National loss to be over 2,000. He had previously said to a National officer, who was with a party at his quarters, under a flag of truce, "Your loss was very great, but ours was four times yours." See *Report of the Committee on the Conduct of the War.*

General Price, in his report (August 12th, 1861), says the loss of his command was nearly 700, or nearly one-fifth of his entire force.

[4] Lyon's body was placed in an ambulance to be moved from the field, but in the hurry of departure it was left. From Springfield, a surgeon with attendants was sent back for it, and General Price sent it to the town in his own wagon. In the confusion of abandoning Springfield, the next morning, it was again left behind, when, after being carefully prepared for burial by two members of Brigadier-General Clark's staff, it was delivered to the care of Mrs. Phelps (wife of J. S. Phelps, a former member of Congress from Missouri, and a stanch Union man), who caused it to be buried. A few days afterward it was disinterred and sent to St. Louis, and from there it was conveyed to its final resting-place in a churchyard at East Hartford, in Connecticut.

The Confederates, so greatly superior in numbers, did not follow, thereby acknowledging the groundlessness of their claim to a victory, which was so exultingly made.[1] Indeed, McCulloch, in his first official report, only said of the Nationals, "They have met with a signal repulse." It was not even that.

The Union forces reached Rolla, a point of railway communication with St. Louis, on the 19th of August, where "Camp Good Hope" was established. The southern portion of Missouri was now left open to the sway of the Confederates, and they were securing important footholds in the vicinity of the Mississippi River. In the mean time, Harris, one of Governor Jackson's brigadiers, had been making a formidable display of power in Northeastern Missouri. He had rallied a considerable force at Paris, and commenced the work of destroying the Hannibal and St. Joseph Railway. He was driven away by loyal forces under Colonel Smith, when he organized guerrilla parties to harass and plunder the Union people. Finally, with twenty-seven hundred men, he joined General Price before Lexington.

Other organized bands of Secessionists had been operating in Northeastern Missouri at the same time, and had compelled the Unionists to organize and arm themselves for defense. The latter, under Colonel Moore, formed a camp at Athens. The Secessionists also organized; and on the 5th of August, nearly fifteen hundred of them, led by Martin Green, and furnished with three pieces of cannon, fell upon Moore's force, of about four hundred in number, in the village of Athens, where the assailants were repulsed and utterly routed. The Unionists now flocked to Moore's victorious standard; and these being aided by General Pope, the Secessionists north of the Missouri River were soon made to behave very circumspectly.

In the mean time, the loyal civil authorities of Missouri were making efforts to keep the State from the vortex of secession. The popular Convention, which had taken a stand in favor of the Union, as we have observed,[2] reassembled at Jefferson City on the 22d of July, and proceeded to reorganize civil government for the State, which had been broken up by the flight of the Executive and other officers, and the dispersion of the legislators, many of whom were in the ranks of the enemies of the Government. The Convention declared the offices of Governor, Lieutenant-Governor, and Secretary of State, to be vacant, by a vote of fifty-six to twenty-five. They also declared the seats of the members of the General Assembly vacant, by a vote of fifty-two to twenty-eight.[a] On the following day they proceeded to the election of officers for a provisional government,[3] and appointed the first Monday in November following as the time for the people

[a] July 30, 1861.

[1] McCulloch telegraphed to L. Pope Walker, at Richmond: "We have gained a great victory over the enemy." General Price spoke of it as "a brilliant victory," "achieved upon a hard-fought field," and said the Confederates had "scattered far and wide the well-appointed army which the usurper at Washington" had been for more than six months gathering. The Confederate "Congress," at Richmond, on the 21st of August, in the preamble to a resolution of thanks tendered to McCulloch and his men, declared that it had "pleased Almighty God to vouchsafe to the arms of the Confederate States another glorious and important victory;" while the newspaper press exhibited the greatest jubilation. "The next word will be," shouted the New Orleans *Picayune* of the 17th of August, "'On to St. Louis!' That taken, the power of Lincolnism is broken in the whole West; and instead of shouting 'Ho! for Richmond!' and 'Ho! for New Orleans!' there will be hurrying to and fro, among the frightened magnates at Washington, and anxious inquiries of what they shall do to save themselves from the vengeance to come."

[2] See page 462, volume I.

[3] Hamilton R. Gamble, Provisional Governor; Willard P. Hall, Lieutenant-Governor; and Mordecai Oliver, Secretary of State.

to elect persons to fill the same offices. After transacting other necessary business, the Convention issued an Address to the people, in which the state of public affairs was clearly set forth, and the dangers to the State, in consequence of the hostile movements of the Secessionists within its borders and invaders from without, were as plainly portrayed. The treason of the Governor and his associates was exposed, whereby the action of the Convention in organizing a provisional government was justified.

On the 3d of August, the Provisional Governor issued a proclamation to the people, calculated to allay their apprehension concerning one of their special interests. "No countenance," he said, "will be afforded to any scheme, or to any conduct, calculated in any degree to interfere with the institution of slavery existing in the State. To the very utmost extent of executive power that institution will be protected." This assurance was a mordant for the loyalty of the Union-loving slaveholders, and the new provisional government received the confidence and support of the majority of the people. Large numbers of the disaffected inhabitants took an oath of allegiance,[1] and the friends of order were greatly encouraged.

Whilst the loyal State Convention and the provisional government were laboring to bring order out of chaos in Missouri, the leaders in rebellion there were making the strongest efforts to secure the absolute control of the Commonwealth. On the day when the Convention sent forth its address, the disloyal Lieutenant-Governor (Thomas C. Reynolds), then at New Madrid, on the Mississippi River, issued a proclamation to the people of the State, in which he declared that, acting as Chief Magistrate during the temporary absence of Governor Jackson, he had returned to proclaim, under the provisions of an act of the disloyal legislature, the absolute severance of Missouri from the Union. "Disregarding forms, and looking to realities," he said, "I view any ordinance for the separation from the North, and union with the Confederate States, as a mere outward ceremony to give notice to others of an act already consummated in the hearts of her people," and that, consequently, "no authority of the United States will hereafter be permitted in Missouri." With such views of the political rights of the people, it was natural for him to consign them to the inflictions of a military despotism; so, in the same proclamation, he announced that, by invitation of Governor Jackson, General Pillow, commander of the Tennessee troops in the Confederate service, had entered Missouri,[2] and that he was empowered "to make

---

[1] The following is a copy of the oath which the Confederate leaders had compelled the citizens to take:—

"Know all men, that I, ——, of the County of ——, State of Missouri, do solemnly swear that I will bear true allegiance to the State of Missouri, and support the Constitution of the State, and that I will not give aid, comfort, information, protection, or encouragement to the enemies or opposers of the Missouri State Guard, or of their allies, the Armies of the Confederate States, upon the penalty of death for treason."

[2] General Pillow landed with his troops at New Madrid, at near the close of July. His first order issued there was on the 28th, prohibiting the sale of intoxicating liquors to his soldiers. He had suggested this movement into Missouri at an early period, as one of vast importance in his plans for seizing Bird's Point and Cairo. Whilst engaged in strongly fortifying Memphis, Randolph, and one or two other points on the Tennessee shore of the Mississippi, he earnestly recommended the occupation of New Madrid and Island No. 10 by his troops, and the erection of strong fortifications there, for the twofold purpose of making New Madrid his base of operations against Bird's Point and Cairo, and of preventing armed vessels descending the river, it being evident early in June that preparations were being made for that purpose. At the middle of June he was ready to move forward, and only awaited a compliance of Governor Harris, with a requisition of Pillow for additional troops from Middle Tennessee. The threatening aspect of affairs in loyal East Tennessee at that time so alarmed Harris that he hesitated, and telegraphed to Pillow on the 22d of June, as follows: "I still approve, but cannot send troops from here until matters in East Tennessee are settled." Pillow was disappointed and annoyed, and

and enforce such civil police regulations as he may deem necessary for the security of his forces, the preservation of order and discipline in his camp, and the protection of the lives and property of the citizens;" in other words, martial law was established within indefinite limits by this avowed usurper of the rights of the people. He clothed M. Jeff. Thompson,[1] one of Jackson's Missouri brigadiers, with the same power; and he and Pillow, and W. J. Hardee (who had abandoned his flag, joined the insurgents, and was commissioned a brigadier in the Confederate Army), now held military possession of the southeastern districts of the Commonwealth, and made vigorous preparations to co-operate with Price and his associates in "expelling the enemy from the State." Pillow assumed the pompous title of "*Liberator of Missouri*," and his orders and dispatches were commenced, "Head-Quarters Army of Liberation."

Governor Jackson, who had been to Richmond to make arrangements for

---

on the following day he wrote to the Governor, saying: "I think it exceedingly unfortunate that you have *suspended* the movements *forward* against Bird's Point and Cairo for the relief of Missouri. The main body of the force at these two points has been withdrawn, in consequence of the pressure in the East and the rising up of Missouri, and the work of taking these *points* would now be of comparatively easy accomplishment. If my movements are to be suspended until East Tennessee ceases to *sulk* and becomes loyal, it will defer my action to a period when I cannot assume the *offensive state*. In my judgment, two, three, or four regiments is a force sufficient for any probable contingency in view of the position of East Tennessee. Without aid from the forces of Middle Tennessee I have not the means of advancing, nor will I attempt it. In ten days the enemy will, in all probability, increase his force at Cairo, and will have his three gunboats, mounting 30 guns, at Cairo, and then it would be madness to attempt a *dislodgment*."

Then, and for some time afterward, the great want of the Army of Tennessee was arms. In July, Pillow issued an order directing the gathering up of all the rifles in private hands in Western Tennessee, for the purpose of having them made of uniform bore and devoted to the public use.

In his appeal to the people, he said: "Seventy thousand additional troops must be raised to protect the country. These troops can be armed only by the country rifles being procured, and thus converted. . . These rifles will give you no protection when scattered over the country in your houses. Nothing will save the country from being overrun and devastated by a more than savage foe, but arms in the hands of organized and drilled troops." Workshops for the purpose of changing these arms were employed at Memphis, under Captain Hunt. Agents were appointed to collect the rifles, who were authorized to give certificates of purchase, the weapons to be afterwards paid for by the Confederate government.—*Pillow's MS. Order Book.*

Among a mass of autograph letters before me is one from General S. R. Anderson to General Pillow, dated May 18th, 1861, in which he makes an important disclosure concerning evident preparations for revolt having been made by the authorities of Tennessee, several months before the election of Mr. Lincoln. He says: "I am using every effort to collect together *the arms of the State issued to volunteer companies, raised for political purposes and otherwise*, and now disbanded; and in looking over the bonds given for arms, as found in the Secretary of State's office, I find that *on the 4th of July last* [1860], there was issued to W. J. Hendricks, J. E. Crowder, R. E. Moody, and R. Winslow, of Lagrange, West Tenn., the following arms: 64 swords and 128 pistols. These arms are worth looking after, and I would respectfully suggest to you to have them looked after and gathered up, if not in the hands of such men as are going to take the field."

[1] Thompson, who became a notorious guerrilla chief, like Pillow, seemed fond of issuing proclamations and writing letters, in both of which he indulged much in hyperbole. Many of the latter, written at the period we are now considering, are before me. The day after Reynolds issued his proclamation, Thompson sent forth the following manifesto to the people of Missouri, which is a fair specimen of his style:—

"Come, now, strike while the iron is hot! Our enemies are whipped in Virginia. They have been whipped in Missouri. General Hardee advances in the center, General Pillow on the right, and General McCulloch on the left, with 20,000 brave Southern hearts, to our aid. So leave your plows in the furrow, and your oxen in the yoke, and rush like a tornado upon our invaders and foes, to sweep them from the face of the earth, or force them from the soil of our State! Brave sons of the Ninth District, come and join us! We have plenty of ammunition, and the cattle on ten thousand hills are ours. We have forty thousand Belgian muskets coming; but bring your guns and muskets with you, if you have them; if not, come without them. We will strike your foes like a Southern thunderbolt, and soon our camp-fires will illuminate the Merrimac and Missouri. Come, turn out.

"JEFF. THOMPSON, *Brig.-General Comd'g*."

Many Missourians who had fled from the State, late in May and early in June, had entered the Tennessee Army. It was desirable to have these and other exiled citizens of that State organized for home duty, and Thompson was sent to Memphis for that purpose. There, on the 14th of June, a meeting of Missourians was held, and in a series of resolutions they asked Pillow for quarters and subsistence, and the release from service in the Tennessee Army, such Missourians as had been enlisted. The autograph letter to Pillow inclosing these resolutions is before me, and is signed by M. Jeff. Thompson, B. Newton Hart, Thomas P. Hoy, N. J. McArthur, James George, and Lewis H. Kennerly.

military aid, and the annexation of Missouri to the Confederacy, had just returned, and from New Madrid he also issued a proclamation.[a] It was in the form of a provisional declaration of the independence of the State, in which he gave reasons which, he said, "justified" a separation from the Union. These "reasons" consisted of the usual misrepresentations concerning the National Government, in forms already familiar to the reader, and were followed by a formal declaration that Missouri was "a sovereign, free, and independent republic." On the 20th of the same month, the Confederate "Congress" at Richmond passed an act to "aid the State of Missouri in repelling invasion by the United States, and to authorize the admission of said State as a member of the Confederate States of America." Jefferson Davis was authorized to "muster into the service of the Confederate States" such Missouri troops as might volunteer to serve in the Confederate Army; the officers to be commissioned by Davis, who was also empowered to appoint all field officers for the same. Missouri was to be admitted into the Confederacy on an equal footing with the other States, when the Constitution of the "Confederate States" should be "adopted and ratified by the properly and legally constituted authorities of said State;" in other words, when the disloyal fugitive Governor, Jackson, and his friends, and not the *people* of Missouri, should so adopt and ratify that unholy league.

[a] Aug. 5, 1861.

M. JEFF. THOMPSON.

By the same act the government of Missouri, of which Jackson was recognized as the chief magistrate, was declared to be "the legally elected and constituted government of the people and State of Missouri."[1] Measures were speedily adopted for the consummation of the alliance, and, during a greater portion of the war, men claiming to represent the people of Missouri occupied seats in the Confederate "Congress" at Richmond.[2]

At this critical juncture of public affairs in Missouri, John C. Fremont, who had been brought prominently before the American people in 1856, as

---

[1] See *Acts and Resolutions of the Provisional Congress of the Confederate States*, Third Session, No. 225.

[2] By proclamation, in September, Jackson called a session of the disloyal members of the General Assembly of Missouri, at Neosho, on the 21st of October. In his message to that body, on the 28th of October, he recommended, 1st, the passage of an ordinance of secession; 2d, of an "act of provisional union with the Confederate States;" 3d, the appointment of "three commissioners to the Provisional Congress of the Confederate States;" 4th, the passage of a law empowering the Governor to cause an election to be held for Senators and Representatives to the "Confederate States Congress" as soon as practicable after Missouri should become a member of the league; and, 5th, the passage of an act empowering the Governor to issue bonds of the State of Missouri. The pliant instruments of the Governor responded cheerfully to his recommendations. An Ordinance of Secession was passed the same day (October 28th, 1861), and an "Act to provide for the defense of the State of Missouri" was adopted on the 1st of November. It authorized the issue of what were termed "Defense Bonds," to the amount of $10,000,000, all of which, of the denomination of $5 and upwards, should bear interest at the rate of ten per cent. per annum. They were to be issued in denominations not less than $1, and not greater than $500, payable in three, five, and seven years. They were made a legal tender for all dues. Such was the currency offered to the people of Missouri as members of the Confederacy. See *Journals of the Senate, &c.*, noticed at the close of note 1, page 464, volume I.

the candidate of the newly formed Republican party for the Presidency of the United States, assumed the command of the *Western Department*. He was in Europe when the war broke out, and on the 14th of May, 1861, he was commissioned a major-general of Volunteers. On receiving notice of his appointment, he left his private affairs abroad in the hands of others, and hastened home. He arrived at Boston on the 27th of June,[a] bringing with him an assortment of arms for his Government, and on the 6th of July he was appointed to the important command in the West just mentioned.[1] He remained a short time in New York, where he made arrangements for over twenty thousand stand of arms, with munitions of war, to be sent to his Department. On hearing of the disaster at Bull's Run, he left for the West, and arrived at St. Louis on the 26th of July, where Colonel Harding, Lyon's Adjutant-General, was in command. Fremont had already issued orders for General John Pope to proceed from Alton, in Illinois, with troops to suppress the armed Secessionists in Northern Missouri, who, as we have observed, had commenced the destruction of railways, and depredations upon the Unionists.

[a] 1861.

JOHN C. FREMONT.

Fremont made his head-quarters in St. Louis at the house of the late Colonel Brant, an elegant and splendid mansion, and proceeded at once with great vigor in the performance of his duties. He found disorder everywhere prevailing. The terms of enlistment of the Home Guards, or three-months men, were expiring; and these, being composed chiefly of working-men, with dependent families, and having been some time without pay, were unwilling to re-enlist—in fact, some yet in the service were in a state of mutiny on that account. Fremont was embarrassed. He had very little money at his disposal to meet the just demands of these soldiers; neither had he arms for new recruits, who were now coming into St. Louis in considerable numbers, and were compelled to remain there in idleness for lack of weapons, when he was anxious to send them to the aid of Lyon, and to points exposed to capture. The guns ordered at New York were detained for the use of the Army of the Potomac. Indeed, the National authorities were so absorbed in

FREMONT'S HEAD-QUARTERS IN ST. LOUIS.

[1] The *Western Department* was created on the 6th of July, and comprised the State of Illinois, and the States and Territories west of the Mississippi and east of the Rocky Mountains, including New Mexico. Head-quarters at St. Louis.

taking measures for the defense of Washington City, that the care of the Government was little felt in the West, for a time.

Fremont perceived that he could be useful only by assuming grave responsibilities, and he resolved upon that course, with the belief that he would be sustained by his Government. Funds were indispensable, and he applied to the National Sub-Treasurer at St. Louis for a supply. That officer had three hundred thousand dollars in his hands, but he refused to let the General have a dime without an order from the Secretary of the Treasury. So Fremont prepared to seize one hundred thousand dollars of it by military force, when the custodian yielded.[1] With these funds he secured the re-enlistment of many of the three-months men.

With vigor and secrecy, Fremont prepared for offensive and defensive action. He strongly fortified St. Louis against external and internal foes, and prepared to place Cairo in a condition of absolute security; for upon the holding of these points rested, in a great degree, the salvation of the North-west from invasion and desolation. He was compelled to choose between securing the safety of these places, or re-enforcing Lyon; and wisely, it seems, he decided upon the former course. Kentucky, professedly neutral, and with doors closed against Union troops from other States, was giving shelter and welcome to large bodies of Confederate soldiers in its western districts. Already full 12,000 Confederate troops were within a circle of fifty miles around Cairo, in Kentucky and Missouri. Pillow, as we have seen,[2] had invaded the latter State at its southeastern extremity with a large number of troops, preparatory to an immediate advance upon Bird's Point and Cairo, while Hardee, with a considerable force, was pushing into the interior to menace Lyon's flank and rear. At the same time Liutenant-Governor Reynolds, in his proclamation at New Madrid,[a] taking advantage of the joy of the secessionists, and the depression of the loyalists, on account of the sad news from Virginia, had said, in connection with his announcement of the presence of Pillow with Tennessee troops, "The sun which shone in its full midday splendor at Manassas is about to rise in Missouri." Every thing at that moment seemed to justify the prediction. Lyon, with the only considerable National force in the field, was surrounded with the greatest peril, as we have seen; every county in the Commonwealth was in a state of insurrection, and every post held by the Unionists—even St. Louis itself—was menaced with real danger.

[a] July 31 1861.

To avert the perils threatening Bird's Point and Cairo, Fremont secretly and quickly prepared an expedition to strengthen the latter post; for General Prentiss, its commander, had not more than twelve hundred men in

[1] Fremont laid a brief statement of the condition of affairs in Missouri, and his needs, before the President, in a letter on the 30th of July. He said: "We have not an hour for delay. There are three courses open for me. One, to let the enemy possess himself of some of the strongest points in the State and threaten St. Louis, which is insurrectionary; second, to force a loan from secession banks here; third, to use the money belonging to the Government which is in the Treasury here. Of course I will not lose the State, nor permit the enemy a foot of advantage. I have infused energy and activity into the Department, and there is a thoroughly good spirit in officers and men. This morning I will order the Treasurer to deliver the money in his possession to General Andrews, and will send a force to the Treasury to take the money, and will direct sub-payments, as the exigency requires." The President made no reply; and this silence, with a dispatch received four days before from a Cabinet minister (Postmaster-General Blair), saying, "You will have to do the best you can, and take all needful responsibility to defend and protect the people over whom you are specially set," justified his course, to his judgment.

[2] See page 56.

garrison there at the close of July. Mustering about thirty-eight hundred troops on board of eight steamers,[1] at St. Louis, on the night of the 30th of July, he left that city at noon the next day with the entire squadron, and making a most imposing display. Nobody but himself knew the real strength of the expedition, and the most exaggerated rumors concerning it went abroad. The loyal people and the insurgents believed that these vessels contained at least twelve thousand men. The deception had its desired effect. Cairo was re-enforced without opposition. Other points were strengthened. Pillow, who had advanced some troops, and, with Thompson, was preparing to seize Cape Girardeau, Bird's Point, and Cairo, and overrun Southern Illinois, fell back, and became very discreet in action; and Hardee, with his independent command, was checked in his movements into the interior of Missouri.

Pillow, notwithstanding he had about twenty thousand troops at his command, alarmed by rumors of an immense National force on his front, sent a dispatch[a] to Hardee, then supposed to be at Greenville, urging the necessity for a junction of their forces, before an attempt might be safely made to march on Commerce and Cape Girardeau. "Having a good deal of work before us," he said, "we should be careful not to so cripple our forces as to be unable to go forward. . . . I ought to have your support before engaging the enemy on my front. . . . . Without the co-operation of your force, I doubt if I can reach you at Ironton, except in a very critical condition. We ought to unite at Benton."[2] He informed Hardee that General Thompson, Governor Jackson, and Lieutenant-Governor Reynolds were with him, and that they all regarded the union of the two forces as essential. On the same day General Polk wrote to Pillow, urging him to "put his troops in the trenches," and strongly fortify New Madrid, near which it was proposed to stretch a chain, to obstruct the navigation of the Mississippi.[3] Polk was then gathering

[a] August 5, 1861.

---

[1] *Empress*, *War Eagle*, *Jennie Dean*, *Warsaw*, *City of Alton*, *Louisiana*, *January*, and *Graham*. General Fremont and Staff were on the *City of Alton*. The squadron was in charge of Captain B. Able.

[2] Autograph letter of General Pillow, dated, "Head-quarters Army of Liberation, August 5th, 1861."

[3] At that time there were various plans proposed for barricading the Mississippi against the "invaders." The stretching of a chain across was a favorite one, and materials for the purpose were sent up from New Orleans to Memphis. An anonymous writer, whose autograph letter is before me, dated "New Orleans, July 3d, 1861," proposed a plan, by which, he said, "steamboats of the enemy could be as effectually prevented from descending the Mississippi, as from steaming across the Alleghany Mountains." The letter contained the annexed illustrative diagram.

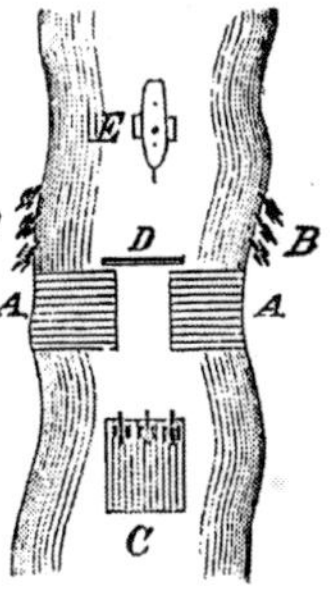

STEAMBOAT OBSTRUCTIONS.

Thomas J. Spear, of New Orleans, in a letter dated the 31st of July, proposed a species of torpedo for the same purpose, which might also be of use in battle on land. His accompanying diagram, which is annexed, represents the manner of using the torpedo in the river. It was to be attached to the end of a long rod, projecting, under water, from the bow of the vessel, and fixed by a tube filled with gunpowder. These plans were not tried; but other obstructions, in the way of sunken vessels, *chevaux de frise* of various kinds, and a great variety of torpedoes, were used during the war. Spear proposed to place his torpedoes on land, at "shooting distance in front of a chosen place of battle, or in roads over which the enemy would travel, a few inches underground, with wires attached, so as to explode them by means of electricity." The plan was to fall back as the enemy approached, and when they were above the torpedoes to explode them. The illustrations of this note may be explained as follows:—

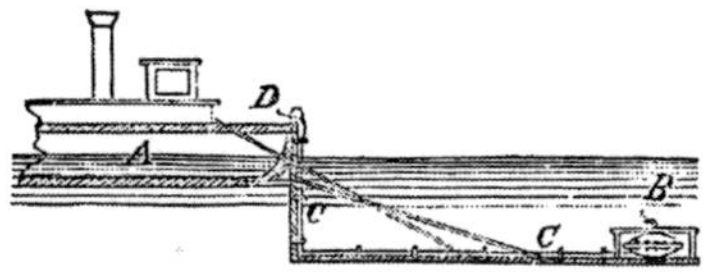

SPEAR'S TORPEDO.

STEAMBOAT OBSTRUCTIONS.—A A, rafts anchored between the shore and the channel. B B, batteries

strength at Randolph and Fort Pillow, on the Tennessee side of the Mississippi. He had prohibited all steamboats from going above New Madrid, had pressed into the service several Cincinnati pilots, and had ordered up two gunboats from New Orleans, to operate between New Madrid and Cairo.[1]

Fremont returned to St. Louis on the 4th of August, having accomplished the immediate objects of his undertaking. He had spread great alarm among the Confederates immediately confronting him, who were somewhat distracted by divided commanders. Polk was chief;[2] and from his

[a] August 7, 1861.

head-quarters at Memphis he ordered[a] Pillow to evacuate New Madrid, and, with his men and heavy guns, hasten to Randolph and Fort Pillow, on the Tennessee shore. The ink of that dispatch was scarcely dry, when he countermanded the order, for he had heard glad tidings from McCulloch, in front of Lyon. Again, on the 15th, he was so alarmed by rumors from above, that he again ordered Pillow to abandon New Madrid, and cross to Tennessee with his troops and armament immediately. The ambitious Pillow, evidently anxious to win renown by seizing Cape Girardeau, and with that victory to gain possession of Bird's Point and Cairo, was tardy in his obedience, and the result was, that he kept his head-quarters at New Madrid until early in September, as we shall hereafter observe.[3]

---

on the shore. C, raft with heavy battery in the channel. D, floating boom to allow friendly vessels to pass through. E, steamer descending the river Such rafts were constructed at several places on the Mississippi, in the form seen in the annexed engraving, being held by chains, attached to anchors, passing over them lengthwise. They were inefficient, and were soon abandoned.

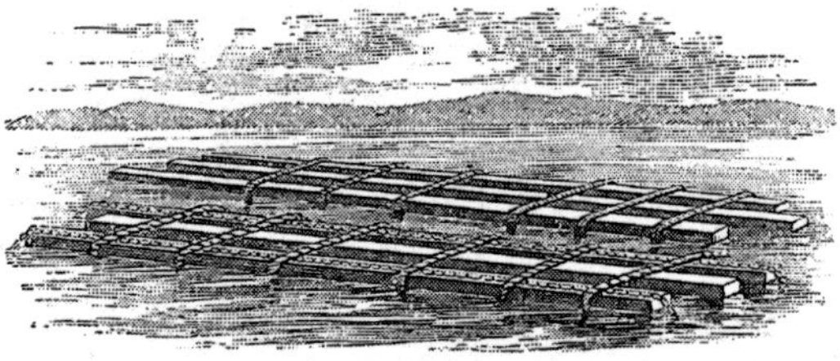

RAFT ANCHORED IN THE MISSISSIPPI.

SPEAR'S TORPEDO.—A, bow of torpedo vessel. B, torpedo. C C, tube filled with gunpowder, supported by a strong framework, to which the torpedo is attached. D, end of tube to which the match is applied.

[1] Autograph letter of Leonidas Polk to Gideon J Pillow, dated at Memphis, August 5th, 1861.

[2] General Polk, as we have observed, was Bishop of the Diocese of Louisiana, of the Protestant Episcopal Church, when the war broke out. A correspondent of the New Orleans *Picayune*, writing from Richmond on the day of Polk's appointment as major-general in the Confederate service, related the secret history of his laying aside the crook of the bishop for the sword of the soldier. He had been urged to take the appointment, his military education at the West Point Academy being thought sufficient to promise a successful career in the field. He finally visited Bishop Meade, of Virginia, the senior bishop of the church in the United States, to consult with him about it. The result was in his case, as in that of General Joseph E. Johnston (who also consulted Bishop Meade as to what was his duty in a similar emergency); he received the approval of the prelate, and joined the army. It seems that Polk had satisfied himself that he ought to accept the commission, before he visited Bishop Meade; for the writer says, that when the latter suggested that the Diocesan of Louisiana was already holding a commission in a very different army, to which he owed allegiance, the great slave-holding bishop replied: "I know that very well, and I do not intend to resign it. On the contrary, I shall only prove the more faithful to it by doing all that in me lies to bring this unhallowed and unnatural war to a speedy and happy close. We, of the Confederate States, are the last bulwarks of civil and religious liberty; we fight for our hearthstones and our altars; above all, we fight for a race that has been, by Divine Providence, intrusted to our most sacred keeping. When I accept a commission in the Confederate Army, therefore, I not only perform the duties of a good citizen, *but contend for the principles which lie at the foundation of our social, political, and religious polity.*"

[3] Pillow had always been restive under the restraints imposed by the transfer of the Tennessee Army to the service of the Confederate authorities, and he never obeyed the commands of General Polk with alacrity. Thompson was under the command of Governor Jackson; and Hardee, who was at Greenville, some distance in the interior of Missouri, early in August was operating with independence, in a measure, of both Pillow and Polk. Pillow and Thompson had set their hearts on the seizure of Cape Girardeau and Bird's Point, whilst Hardee was aiming at a similar result in a different way. Polk, at Memphis, alarmed by rumor of an immense arma-

News of the Battle of Wilson's Creek,[1] and the death of Lyon, reached Fremont on the 13th of August. The secessionists in St. Louis were made jubilant and bold by it. This disposition was promptly met by the Commander-in-Chief. Martial law was declared,[a] and General McKinstry was appointed Provost-Marshal. Some of the most active secessionists were arrested, and the publication of newspapers charged with disloyalty was suspended.[2] So tight was held the curb of restraint in the city that an outbreak was prevented. More free to act in the rural districts, the armed secessionists began again to distress the loyal people. In bands they moved over the country, plundering and destroying. Almost daily, collisions between them and the Home Guards occurred. One of the most severe of these conflicts took place at Charleston, west of Bird's Point, on the 19th,[b] when three hundred Illinois Volunteers, under Colonel Dougherty, put twelve hundred Confederates to flight. Two days afterward, a battery planted by Thompson, at Commerce, was captured by National troops sent out from Cape Girardeau; and everywhere the loyalists were successful in this sort of warfare. But the condition of public affairs in Missouri was becoming daily more alarming. The provisional government was almost powerless, and Governor Gamble, by a mistaken policy, seriously injured the public service at that critical time by refusing to commission military officers appointed by Fremont. The President commissioned them himself, and the work of organizing a force for the

[a] August 14, 1861.

[b] August.

---

ment about to descend the Mississippi and attack that place, was anxious to strengthen it and the supporting posts above it on the Tennessee shore, and hence his order for Pillow[c] to evacuate New Madrid and hasten with his troops and heavy guns to Randolph and Fort Pillow. Pillow demurred, and charged Polk, by implication, with keeping back re-enforcements, and thwarting his well-laid plans for the liberation of Missouri. Polk retorted, and intimated that Pillow's neglecting to fortify New Madrid, as he had been ordered to do, before the Nationals were ready for an offensive movement, was a blunder that now made the evacuation of that post a necessity. In his dispatch revoking the order for the evacuation of New Madrid, Polk directed Pillow to break up his base there, send his heavy cannon to Randolph and Fort Pillow, and, marching by the way of Pleasanton, join his forces with those of Hardee at Greenville. This was also distasteful to the Tennessee commander. He reported that he had tried the path and had been compelled to fall back to New Madrid on account of unsafe bridges; also, that he intended to move on Cape Girardeau by the river road. Polk, was annoyed, and wrote him a long letter on the 16th of August, in its tone deprecatory of Pillow's course; whilst the restless Thompson, who was now with Hardee, and now with Pillow, was eagerly urging a forward movement "I would like very much," he wrote on the 16th of August, "to have your permission to advance, as I am sure that I can take Cape Girardeau without firing a gun, by marching these moonlight nights and taking them by surprise. Every one gives me the credit of at least 7,000 men, and I have them frightened nearly to death." The following day he wrote to Pillow, saying, "If you wish a legal excuse for advancing, withdraw your control over me for a few hours, and then come to my rescue. We must not lose the *moon;* the weather may change, and the swamps become impassable."

[c] August 7, 1861.

Hardee, on the contrary, who desired, as a preliminary movement against Cape Girardeau, to seize the post at Ironton, the then terminus of the railway running southward from St. Louis, did not seem disposed to aid Pillow in his designs; whilst Polk, according to a letter from Lewis G. De Russey, his aid-de-camp, dated at Fort Pillow on the 17th of August, was anxious for Pillow and Hardee to join their forces at Benton, and march upon St. Louis. In this undecided state, the question concerning offensive movements in Missouri remained until the close of August, when the National forces at Ironton, the Cape, and Bird's Point, had been so increased, that any forward movement of the Confederates would have been extremely perilous. "We can take the Cape, but what would we do with it?" Pillow asked significantly on the 29th. Hardee, an old and experienced officer, had positively refused to go forward, and Pillow and Polk would not risk such a movement without his concurrence. The conduct of the ambitious Pillow in this connnection became so insubordinate, that General Polk submitted a statement of it to the "War Department," at Richmond, on the 20th of August. "Considering you have usurped an authority not properly your own," wrote De Russey, in behalf of Polk, "by which you have thwarted and embarrassed his arrangements and operations for the general defense, he feels it his duty to submit to the War Department the position you have thought proper to assume." Events during the few succeeding days changed all plans.—*Autograph Letters of Polk, Hardee, Pillow, Thompson*, and others, from the close of July to the close of August, 1861.

[1] The Confederates, as we have observed, call it the Battle of Oak Hill.

[2] *Morning Herald*, *Evening Missourian*, and *War Bulletin*.

purpose of sweeping the insurgents out of the State, and clearing the banks of the Mississippi of all blockading obstructions to free navigation from St. Louis to New Orleans, went steadily on.

Satisfied that nothing but martial law and the most stringent measures toward the secessionists would secure peace and quiet to Missouri, and safety to the cause, Fremont took the administration of public affairs there into his own hands, and on the 31st of August he issued a proclamation, in which he declared that martial law was thereby established throughout Missouri, and that the lines of the Army of Occupation in that State extended, for the present, from Leavenworth, in Kansas, by way of the posts of Jefferson City, Rolla, and Ironton, to Cape Girardeau on the Mississippi River. He declared that all persons within those lines taken with arms in their hands should be tried by court-martial, and, if found guilty, should be shot;[1] that the property, real and personal, of all persons in Missouri, who should be proven to have taken an active part with the enemies of the Government, in the field, should be confiscated to the public use, and their slaves, if they had any, should be thereafter free men; and that all persons engaged in the destruction of bridges, railway tracks, and telegraphs, should suffer the extreme penalty of the law. All persons who, by speech or correspondence, should be found guilty of giving aid to the insurgents in any way, were warned of ill consequences to themselves; and all who had been seduced from their allegiance to the National Government were required to return to their homes forthwith. The declared object of the proclamation was to place in the hands of the military authorities the power to give instantaneous effect to existing laws, while ordinary civil authority would not be suspended, where the law should be administered in the usual manner.[2]

General Fremont acted promptly in accordance with his proclamation, and the greatest consternation began to prevail among the insurgents of Missouri, when his hand was stayed. He was most bitterly assailed by the enemies of the Administration, especially because of that portion of his proclamation which related to emancipation and confiscation. In the border Slave-labor States there arose a storm of indignation which alarmed the Government; and the President, anxious to placate the rebellious spirit in those States, requested Fremont to modify his proclamation concerning the confiscation of property and the liberation of the slaves, so as to strictly conform to an act of Congress passed on the 6th of August.[3] Fremont declined to do so, and asked the President to openly direct him to make that modification, for his judgment and self-respect would not

---

[1] M. Jeff. Thompson, already mentioned, and who became the terror of all law-abiding citizens in Missouri, issued a proclamation on the 2d of September, declaring that he was intrusted by Acting Governor Reynolds not only with the commission of brigadier-general, but also with "certain police powers," and said: "I do most solemnly promise that, for every member of the Missouri State Guard or soldier of our allies, the armies of the Confederate States, who shall be put to death in pursuance of the said order of General Fremont, I will *hang*, *draw*, and *quarter* a minion of said Abraham Lincoln."

[2] Fremont specified, as reasons for his assuming the administrative powers of the State, the fact that "its disorganized condition, the helplessness of the civil authority, the total insecurity of life, and the devastation of property by bands of murderers and marauders," who infested nearly every county in the State, and availed themselves of the public misfortunes and the vicinity of a hostile force, to gratify private and neighborhood vengeance, and who found an enemy wherever they found plunder, demanded the severest measures to suppress these disorders, to maintain the public peace, and "to give security and protection to the persons and property of loyal citizens."

[3] See page 29.

allow him to do it himself.[1] The President accordingly issued an order to that effect,[a] and a most powerful war measure, which was adopted by the Government less than a year later, and which now promised, as such, the most efficient aid to the National cause, was made almost inoperative. Only those slaves who were actually employed in the military service of the Confederates were to be declared free by the President's order. So cautiously did the Government move at this time, in the matter of slaves, that special orders were issued to commanders in other Departments on the subject, all having a tendency to calm the apprehensions that a general emancipation of the bondsmen was contemplated.[2]

[a] Sept. 11, 1861.

---

[1] "If I were to retract of my own accord," said Fremont, "it would imply that I myself thought it wrong, and that I acted without the reflection which the gravity of the point demanded. But I did not. I acted with full deliberation, and with the certain conviction that it was a measure right and necessary; and I think so still."

[2] The conservative attitude of the Government in relation to slavery, at that time, however expedient it may have been as a soothing policy toward the border Slave-labor States, was a disappointment to its friends abroad, who well understood the object of the conspirators to be the formation of a great empire whose political and industrial system should be founded on human slavery. In Western Europe, the long controversy on that subject in our National Legislature had been watched with great interest; and the more enlightened observers, when the war broke out, believed and hoped that the prediction of a distinguished member of Congress (Joshua R. Giddings), made in that body in 1848, when members from Slave-labor States insolently threatened to dissolve the Union if their wishes were not gratified, would be fulfilled. He said that when that contest should come, "the *lovers* of our race will then stand forth and exert the legitimate powers of this Government for freedom. We shall then have constitutional power to act for the good of our country and to do justice to the slave. We will then strike off the shackles from his limbs. The Government will then have power to act between slavery and freedom, and it can then make peace by giving liberty to its slaves."—See *Giddings's History of the Rebellion*, page 431.

They were disappointed when, in Mr. Seward's carefully written dispatch to Minister Dayton, on the 22d of April, 1861, they were assured that the majority of the people of the Republic were willing to let the system of slavery alone, and that whatever might be the result of the war then kindling, it would receive no damage. "The condition of slavery in the several States," he said, "will remain just the same, whether it succeed or fail. There is not even a pretext for the complaint that the disaffected States are to be conquered by the United States if the revolution fail; for the rights of the States, and the condition of every human being in them, will remain subject to exactly the same laws and forms of administration, whether the revolution shall succeed or whether it shall fail. In the one case the States would be federally connected with the new confederacy; in the other, they would, as now, be members of the United States; but their constitutions and laws, customs, habits, and institutions, in either case will remain the same. It is hardly necessary to add to this incontestable statement the further fact that the new President, as well as the citizens through whose suffrages he has come into the administration, has always repudiated all designs, whatever and wherever imputed to him and them, of disturbing the system of slavery as it is existing under the Constitution and the laws."

The prediction of Mr. Giddings was fulfilled, while those of his friend and co-worker in the anti-slavery movement, contained in his official assurances, were not. They only served to inflict moral injury upon the cause of the Government, and discourage the friends of humanity; and such also was the effect of the conservative action of the Government on the subject of slavery during the earlier period of the war. It was not until the President issued his Emancipation Proclamation, sixteen months later, that the warmest sympathies of the lovers of liberty and the rights of man, in the Old World, were manifested for the cause of the Government.

CHAPTER III

MILITARY OPERATIONS IN MISSOURI AND KENTUCKY.

CONTRARY to general expectation, the Confederates did not pursue the shattered little army that was led by Sigel, from Springfield to Rolla.[1] McCulloch contented himself with issuing a proclamation to the people of Missouri,[a] telling them that he had come, on the invitation of their Governor, "to assist in driving the National forces out of the State, and in restoring to the people their just rights." He assured them that *he* had driven the enemy from among them, and that the Union troops were then in full flight, after defeat. He called upon the people to act promptly in co-operation with him, saying, "Missouri must be allowed to choose her own destiny—*no oaths binding your consciences.*" This was all that the Texan did in the way of "driving the enemy out of the State," after the battle of Wilson's Creek. His assumptions and deportment were offensive to Price and his soldiers. Alienation ensued, and McCulloch soon abandoned the fortunes of the Missouri leader for the moment, and, with his army, left the State.

[a] Aug. 12, 1861.

Price now called upon the secessionists to fill his shattered ranks. They responded with alacrity, and at the middle of August he moved northward toward the Missouri River, in the direction of Lexington, in a curve that bent far toward the eastern frontier of Kansas, from which Unionists were advancing under General James H. Lane. With these he had some skirmishing on the 7th of September, at Drywood Creek, about fifteen miles east of the border. He drove them across the line, and pursued them to Fort Scott, which he found abandoned. Leaving a small force there, he resumed his march, and reached Warrensburg, in Johnson County, on the 11th.[b] In the mean time, he had issued a proclamation to the inhabitants of Missouri,[c] dated at Jefferson City, the capital of the State, in which he spoke of a great victory at Wilson's Creek, and gave the peaceable citizens assurance of full protection in person and property.

[b] September.

[c] Aug. 28.

Lexington,[2] a town on the southern bank of the Missouri River, three hundred miles, by its course, above St. Louis, and occupying an important frontier position, was now brought into great prominence as the theatre of a desperate struggle. It commanded the approach to Fort Leavenworth by water; and when Fremont was apprised of Price's northward movement, and the increasing boldness of the secessionists in that region, he sent a

---

1 See page 54.

2 Capital of Lafayette County, Missouri, and then containing about five thousand inhabitants.

small force to Lexington to take charge of the money in the bank there, and to protect the loyal inhabitants. This little force was increased from time to time, until early in September, when Price was approaching Warrensburg, the number of Union troops at Lexington was nearly twenty-eight hundred,[1] commanded by Colonel James A. Mulligan, of the "Irish Brigade" of Chicago, Illinois. Mulligan, with his men, reached Lexington on the 9th of September, after a march of nine days from Jefferson City, and, being the senior officer, he assumed the chief command. Peabody's regiment had come in, on the following day, in full retreat from Warrensburg, having been driven away by the approach of the overwhelming forces of Price.[2]

Satisfied that Price would speedily attack the post, Colonel Mulligan took position on Masonic Hill, northeastward of the city, which comprised about fifteen acres, and on which was a substantial brick building erected for a college. He proceeded at once to cast up strong intrenchments on the eminence, in compass sufficient to accommodate within their area ten thousand men. His first line of works was in front of the college building. Outside of his embankments was a broad ditch, and beyond this were skillfully arranged pits, into which assailants, foot or horse, might fall. The ground was also mined outside of the fortifications, with a good supply of gunpowder and suitable trains. But the troops, unfortunately, had only about forty rounds of ammunition each, and six small brass cannon and two howitzers. The latter were useless, because there were no shells. Hourly expecting re-enforcements, Mulligan resolved to defy his enemy with the means at hand.

On the morning of the 11th of September, after a violent storm that had raged for several hours, Price moved from Warrensburg toward Lexington, and that night encamped two or three miles from the city. There he rested until dawn,[a] when he drove in the National pickets, and opened a cannonade, with the batteries of Bledsoe and Parsons, upon Mulligan's intrenched camp from four different points. Their fire was at first concentrated upon the stronger works at the college building. Some outworks were captured, and the Nationals were driven within their intrenchments; not, however, until several fierce struggles had

[a] Sept. 12, 1861.

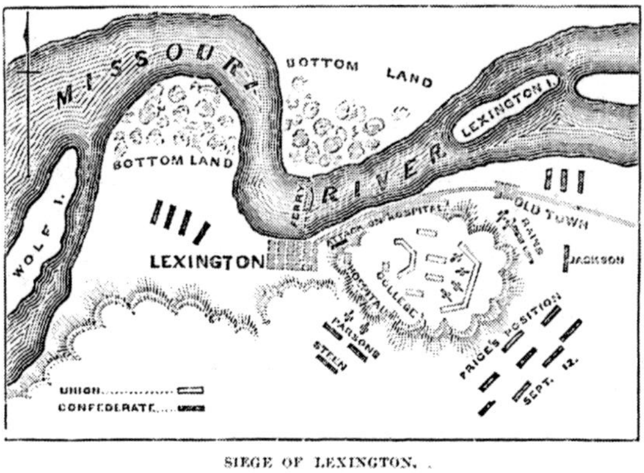

SIEGE OF LEXINGTON.

[1] These troops were composed of the Thirteenth Missouri, Colonel Peabody; First Illinois Regiment of Cavalry, Colonel Marshall; five hundred Missouri Home Guards, and the Twenty-third Illinois, of the Irish Brigade, Colonel Mulligan.

[2] These troops had been sent from Lexington to Warrensburg, to secure about $100,000 in money. Price was informed of this movement, and had hurried forward, by forced marches, to seize the treasure before the National troops could reach there. He was too late, and to his disappointment was added great indignation, because of caricatures which some of the German officers, who were clever artists, had left behind, illustrative of the distress of the Confederates when they should find the treasure gone.

been endured. The defense was bravely kept up during the whole day, when Price, finding his ammunition and his famished men[1] nearly exhausted, withdrew, at sunset, to the Fair-grounds, to await the arrival of his wagon-train and re-enforcements. Mulligan's men immediately resorted to the trenches, to complete their preparations for a siege.

Mulligan now anxiously looked for expected re-enforcements, while his men worked night and day in strengthening the fortifications. He was disappointed. His courier, sent with supplications for aid to Jefferson City, was captured on the way.[2] Hour after hour and day after day went by, and no relief appeared. Yet bravely and hopefully his little band worked on, until, on the morning of the 17th, General Price, who had been re-enforced, and now had in hand over twenty-five thousand troops, including a large number of recruits who had come with their rifles and shot-guns, cut off the communication of the besieged with the city, upon which they chiefly relied for water, and on the following day[a] took possession of the town, closed in upon the garrison, and began a siege in earnest. The Confederates had already seized a steamboat well laden with stores for the National troops; and, under every disadvantage, the latter conducted a most gallant defense.

[a] Sept. 18, 1861.

General Rains's division occupied a strong position on the east and north-east of the fortifications, from which an effective cannonade was opened at nine o'clock, and kept up by Bledsoe's Battery, commanded by Captain Emmit McDonald, and another directed by Captain C. Clark, of St. Louis. General Parsons took a position southwest of the works, from which his battery, under Captain Guibor, poured a steady fire upon the garrison. Near Rains, the division of Colonel Congreve Jackson was posted as a reserve; and near Parsons, a part of General Steen's division performed the same service, whilst sharpshooters were sent forward to harass and fatigue the beleaguered troops, who were not allowed a moment's repose.

General Harris (who, as we have seen,[3] came down from Northeastern Missouri and joined Price at Lexington) and General McBride, scorning all rules of Christian warfare, stormed a bluff on which was situated the house of Colonel Anderson, and then used as a hospital, capturing it with its inmates, while a yellow flag, the insignia of its character, was waving over it. It was retaken by the Montgomery Guards, Captain Gleason, of the "Irish Brigade," eighty strong, who charged, in the face of the hot fire of the foe, a distance of eight hundred yards up a slope, driving the Confederates from the building and far down the hill beyond. The fight was desperate, and some of the sick were killed in their beds. The Guards were finally repulsed. Captain Gleason came back with a bullet through his cheek and another through his arm, and with only fifty of his eighty men. "This charge," said Colonel Mulligan, in his official report, "was one of the most brilliant and reckless in all history."

---

[1] In consequence of a forced march to Lexington, a large number of Price's soldiers had neither eaten nor slept for thirty-six hours.—Price's Report to Governor Jackson, September 23, 1861.

[2] On the 10th he sent Lieutenant Rains, of his "Irish Brigade," with 12 men, on the steamer *Sunshine*, on this errand. The distance to Jefferson City from Lexington is 160 miles. Forty miles below Lexington the steamer was captured, and those on board were made prisoners.

[3] See page 55.

For seventy-two hours Mulligan's little band maintained the contest without cessation, fighting and laboring on the works alternately beneath a scorching sun by day and a scarcely less debilitating heat by night, under a cloudless moon, choked with the smoke of gunpowder, their tongues parched with thirst from which there was little relief, and at last with ammunition and provisions completely exhausted. During that time, Colonel Mulligan was seen at all points where danger was most imminent; and there were deeds of courage and skill performed on the part of the besieged that baffle the imagination of the romancer to conceive. At length, at two o'clock in the afternoon of the 20th,[a] the Confederates, who had constructed movable breastworks of bales of hemp, two deep, wetted so as to resist hot shot, pressed up to within ten rods of the works, along a line forty yards in length. Further resistance would have been madness. Retreat was impossible, for the ferry-boats had been seized, and these being in possession of the Confederates, re-enforcements could not reach the garrison. No water could be had excepting that which came from the clouds in little showers, and was caught in blankets and wrung into camp dishes. The stench of horses and mules killed within the intrenchments was intolerable.[1] The scant amount of artillery ammunition was of poor quality, and the firearms of the Illinois cavalry (who composed one-sixth of Mulligan's command) consisted of pistols only. Major Becker, of the Eighth Missouri Home Guards (whose colonel, White, had been killed), now, for the second time and without authority, raised a white flag from the center of the fortifications, and the SIEGE OF LEXINGTON ceased.[2]

[a] September, 1861.

Colonel Mulligan, who had been twice wounded, now called a council of officers, and it was decided that the garrison must surrender. That act was performed. The officers were held as prisoners of war,[3] whilst the private soldiers, for whom Price had no food to spare, were paroled. The victor held all arms and equipments as lawful prize.[4] The National loss in men had been forty killed, and one hundred and twenty wounded. Price reported his loss at twenty-five killed and seventy-five wounded. Colonel Mulligan was soon exchanged, and for his gallant services was rewarded with the

---

[1] There were about 3,000 horses and mules within the intrenchments. These were a burden of much weight, under the circumstances. In the center of the encampment, wagons were knocked into pieces, stores were scattered and destroyed, and the ground was strewed with dead horses and mules.—Correspondence of the Chicago *Tribune*.

[2] The Home Guards seem to have become discouraged early in the siege, and on the morning of the 20th, after Mulligan had replied to Price's summons to surrender, by saying, "If you want us, you must take us," Major Becker, their commander, raised a white flag. Mulligan sent the Jackson Guard, of Detroit, Captain McDermott, to take it down. After a severe contest that soon afterward ensued, the Home Guards retreated to the inner line of the intrenchments, and refused to fight any longer. Then Becker again raised the white flag, for he was satisfied that resistance was utterly vain, to which conclusion Mulligan and his officers speedily arrived.

[3] These were Colonels Mulligan, Marshall, White, Peabody, and Grover, and Major Van Horn, and 118 other commissioned officers.

[4] The spoils were 6 cannon, 2 mortars, over 3,000 stand of infantry arms, a large number of sabers, about 750 horses, many sets of cavalry equipments, wagons, teams, ammunition, and $100,000 worth of commissary stores.—See General Price's Report to Governor Jackson, September 24th, 1861. "In addition to all this," Price said, "I obtained the restoration of the great seal of the State, and the public records, which had been stolen from their proper custodian, and about $900,000 in money, of which the bank at this place had been robbed, and which I have caused to be returned to it."

The disloyal State Legislature, with Governor Jackson, had held a session in the court-house at Lexington only a week before the arrival of Colonel Mulligan. They fled so hastily that they left behind them the State seal and $800,000 in gold coin, deposited in the vault of the bank there. These treasures, with the magazine, were in the cellar of the college, which was the head-quarters of Mulligan.

offer of the commission of a brigadier-general, the thanks of Congress, and the plaudits of the loyal people. Congress gave the Twenty-third Illinois Regiment (which was now called "Mulligan's Brigade") authority to wear on its colors the name of LEXINGTON. Mulligan declined the commission of brigadier, because he preferred to remain with his regiment.

General Fremont was censured for his failing to re-enforce the garrison at Lexington. The public knew little of his embarrassments at that time. His forces were largely over-estimated,[1] and he was receiving calls for help from every quarter. Pressing demands for re-enforcements came from General Ulysses S. Grant, at Paducah, for the Confederates, then in possession of Columbus, in Kentucky, were threatening an immediate march upon that place, so as to flank and capture Cairo. General Robert Anderson, commanding in Kentucky, was imploring him to send troops to save Louisville from the Confederates; and a peremptory order was sent by Lieutenant-General Scott[a] to forward five thousand "well-armed infantry to Washington City, without a moment's delay." There were at that time seventy thousand men under General McClellan in camp near the National Capital, while Fremont's total force was only about fifty-six thousand men, scattered over his Department, and menaced at many points by large bodies, or by guerrilla bands of armed insurgents. He had only about seven thousand men at St. Louis; the remainder were at distant points. When he heard[b] of Mulligan's arrival at Lexington, and of General Price's movements in that direction with continually increasing strength, he did not doubt that General Jefferson C. Davis, commanding nearly ten thousand men at Jefferson City, and keeping a vigilant eye upon the Confederate leader, would give him immediate aid. He had reason to believe that a large portion of General Pope's five thousand men in Northern Missouri, sent for the purpose under General Sturgis,[2] would co-operate with the forces of General Lane on the frontier of Kansas, over two thousand strong, and those of Davis at Jefferson City, in giving all needed relief to Mulligan.[3] So confident was he that Price would be driven from Lexington by these combined forces, that he telegraphed to General Davis on the 18th, directing him to send five thousand men to the South Fork of La Mine River, in Cooper County, where it is crossed by the Pacific Railway, there to intercept the expected retreat of the Confederates to the Osage River.

[a] Sept. 14, 1861.

[b] Sept. 13.

In these reasonable calculations Fremont was disappointed. Whilst expecting tidings of success, he received from Pope[c] the sad news of Mulligan's surrender. The active and vigilant Price, with a force of more than twenty-five thousand men, had been enabled

[c] Sept. 22.

---

[1] Fremont's force in St. Louis alone, at that time, was estimated at 20,000. A week before the fall of Lexington, Schuyler Colfax, Representative in Congress from Indiana, visited him, and urged him to send forward a part of that force to confront Price. Fremont informed him how few were his troops in St. Louis then, and the importance of allowing the false impression of their number to remain. His muster-roll was laid before Colfax, and it showed that within a circuit of seven miles around the city, the whole number of troops, including the Home Guards, was less than 8,000. The official returns to the War Department at that date gives the number in the City of St. Louis at 6,890, including the Home Guards.—Speech of Schuyler Colfax, March 7, 1862, cited by Abbott in his *Civil War in America*; 282.

[2] Major Sturgis had been commissioned a brigadier-general for his gallant service at the *Battle of Wilson's Creek*, on the 10th of August.

[3] General Pope telegraphed to General Fremont on the 16th, saying: "The troops I sent to Lexington will be there the day after to-morrow [the day when the assault on Mulligan commenced], and consist of two full

to beat back re-enforcements for the garrison and to keep the way open for recruits for his own army.[1] In this work a severe fight occurred at Blue Mills, on the Missouri, thirty miles above Lexington, on the 17th,[a] in which the insurgents, commanded by General David R. Atchinson,[2] were victorious; and on the 19th, General Sturgis, with a large body of cavalry, appeared opposite Lexington, but finding no boats for transportation, and being confronted by two thousand men under General Parsons, he was compelled to make a hasty retreat northward.

[a] Sept., 1861.

The fall of Lexington was a discouraging blow to the Union cause in Missouri. Fremont was violently assailed with charges of incapacity, extravagance in expenditure, and a score of faults calculated to weaken his hold upon the confidence of the people, and the troops in his Department. The disasters at Wilson's Creek and Lexington were attributed to his remissness in forwarding re-enforcements; and he perceived the necessity for prompt action in the way of repairing his damaged character. In a brief electrograph to the Adjutant-General on the 23d,[b] announcing the fall of Lexington, he said he was ready to take the field himself, with a hope of speedily destroying the enemy, before McCulloch, who was gathering strength in Arkansas to return to Missouri, should rejoin Price. Believing the latter would follow up his success at Lexington, and march in the direction of Jefferson City or establish himself somewhere on the Missouri River, he immediately pepared to proceed with a large force in the direction of the insurgents. On the 27th of September he put in motion an army of more than twenty thousand men, of whom nearly five thousand were cavalry, arranged in five divisions under the respective commands of Generals David Hunter, John Pope, Franz Sigel, J. A. McKinstry, and H. Asboth, and accompanied by eighty-six pieces of artillery, many of them rifled cannon. While this formidable force is moving forward cautiously, let us observe the course of events on the borders of the Mississippi, and in Kentucky, bearing upon the fortunes of war in Fremont's Department.

[b] September.

During the few weeks preceding the fall of Lexington, General Pillow, as we have seen, had been making great efforts to secure the possession of Cairo by military operations in Missouri. In this effort, as he alleged, he had been thwarted by a lack of hearty co-operation on the part of Generals Polk and Hardee,[3] and he now turned his attention to a plan which he had proposed at an early day, in which it is probable he had the active sympathies of the disloyal Governor of Kentucky, namely, the occupation and intrenching of Columbus, in Kentucky, from which he believed he could flank the position at Cairo, take it in reverse, and, turning its guns upon Bird's Point, drive out and disperse its force.[4] So early as the 13th of May,[c] he had asked the consent of Governor Magoffin to take possession of and fortify Columbus; and in reporting the fact to his "Secretary of War,"

[c] 1861.

---

regiments of infantry, four pieces of artillery, and 150 regular horse. These, with two Ohio regiments, which will reach there on Thursday [19th], will make a re-enforcement of 4,000 men and four pieces of artillery."

[1] Martin Green, already mentioned (see page 55), was at about that time operating successfully in Northeastern Missouri with 3,000 men. They were effectually broken up by General Pope.

[2] Atchinson was at one time a member of the United States Senate, and was conspicuous as a leader of the Missourians called "Border Ruffians," who played a prominent part in the politics of Kansas a few years before.

[3] Autograph letter of General Pillow to L. Pope Walker, "Secretary of War," Sept. 6, 1861.

[4] Autograph letter of General Pillow to L. Pope Walker, Sept. 1, 1861.

he exhibited his contempt for the neutrality of Kentucky, by saying: "If he (Magoffin) should withhold his consent, my present impression is that I shall go forward and occupy the position, upon the ground of its necessity to protect Tennessee."[1] The action of the people and the Legislature of Kentucky made Magoffin very circumspect. At the election in June, for members of Congress, there appeared a Union majority of over fifty-five thousand, and the Governor saw no other way to aid his southern friends than by insisting upon the strict neutrality of his State in outward form, in which its politicians had placed it. He had sent Buckner to confer with General McClellan (then[a] in command at Cincinnati) on the subject, who reported that he had consummated an agreement officially with that officer, for a thorough support of that neutrality. He declared that McClellan agreed that his Government should respect it, even though Confederate troops should enter the State, until it should be seen that Kentucky forces could not expel them; and then, before troops should be marched into its borders, timely notice of such intended movement should be given to the Governor; also, that, in case United States troops were compelled to enter Kentucky to expel Confederate troops, the moment that work should be accomplished the National forces should be withdrawn. McClellan promptly denied ever making any such agreement with Buckner.[2] Yet Magoffin insisted upon acting as if such an agreement had been actually entered into by the National Government; and Governor Harris, of Tennessee, to whom Buckner was directed by Magoffin to make an oral report of his conference with McClellan, determined to aid Kentucky in preserving that neutrality, because it promised his own State the best protection against the power of the Government troops.[3]

[a] June 10, 1861.

While Magoffin endeavored to enforce neutrality as against National troops, he seems to have given every encouragement to the secessionists that common prudence would allow. They were permitted to form themselves into military organizations and enter the service of Tennessee or of the Confederate States;[4] and recruiting for the latter went on openly. The Unionists soon followed the example, and "Camp Joe Holt" was established near Louisville, at an early day, as a military rendezvous for loyal citizens. This was chiefly the work of Lovell H. Rousseau, a loyal State Senator who, when he left the hall of legislation, prepared for the inevitable conflict for the National life. At about the same time, William Nelson, another loyal

---

[1] Autograph letter of General Pillow to L. Pope Walker, May 15, 1861. He appealed to Walker for arms, and promised him, if he should comply with his request, that he would have 25,000 of the best fighting men in the world in the field in twenty days. "If we cannot get arms," he said, "it is idle to indulge the hope of successfully resisting the bodies of Northern barbarians of a tyrant who has trampled the Constitution under his feet." The Mayor of Columbus, B. W. Sharpe, seems to have been in complicity with Pillow in his designs for invading Kentucky. On the first of June he informed him by letter, that the citizens there were preparing to mount heavy guns and to collect military stores.

[2] Letter to Captain Wilson, of the United States Navy, June 26, 1861.

[3] Autograph letter of Isham G. Harris to General Pillow, June 13, 1861.

[4] Many young men joined the Tennessee troops under Pillow, and with his army were transferred to the Confederate service. So early as the middle of May, organizations for the purpose had been commenced in Kentucky. On the 17th of that month, William Preston Johnston, a son of General A. Sidney Johnston, of the Confederate Army, in a letter to Governor Harris, from Louisville, said: "Many gentlemen, impatient of the position of Kentucky, and desirous of joining the Southern cause, have urged me to organize a regiment, or at least a battalion, for that purpose." He offered such regiment or battalion to Governor Harris, on certain conditions, and suggested the formation of a camp for Kentucky volunteers, at Clarkesville or Gallatin, in Tennessee. This was one of many offers of the kind received from Kentucky by Governor Harris.

Kentuckian, established a similar rendezvous in Garrard County, in Eastern Kentucky, called "Camp Dick Robinson." Both of these men were afterward major-generals in the National Volunteer service. The Government encouraged these Union movements. All Kentucky, within a hundred miles south of the Ohio River, had been made a military department, at the head of which was placed Robert Anderson, the hero of Fort Sumter, who, on the 14th of May, had been commissioned a brigadier-general of Volunteers.

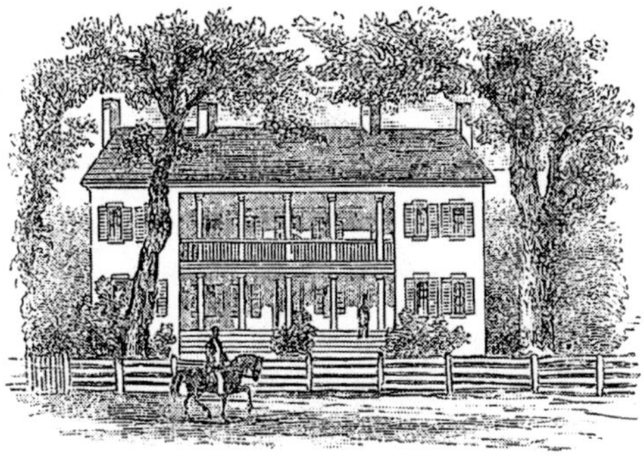
HEAD-QUARTERS AT CAMP DICK ROBINSON.

When Union camps were formed in Kentucky, Magoffin became concerned about the violated neutrality of his State, and he finally wrote to the President,[a] by the hands of a committee, urging him to remove from the limits of Kentucky the forces organized in camps and mustered into the National service. The President not only refused compliance with his request, but gave him a rebuke[b] so severe that he did not venture to repeat his wishes.[1] A similar letter was sent by the Governor to Jefferson Davis, softened with Magoffin's assurance that he had no belief that the Confederates would think of violating the neutrality of Kentucky. Davis, thus made apparently unmindful of the fact that his "Congress" at Richmond had authorized[c] enlistments for the Confederate armies in Kentucky; that his officers were organizing bands of Volunteers on its soil, and that already Tennessee troops in his employ had invaded the State, and carried away six cannon and a thousand stand of arms, replied that his "government" had scrupulously respected the neutrality of Kentucky, and would as scrupulously maintain that respect "so long as her people will maintain it themselves."

[a] Aug. 19, 1861.

[b] Aug. 24.

[c] Aug. 7.

The loyal Legislature of Kentucky assembled at Frankfort on the 2d of September. Its action was feared by the conspirators;[2] and under the pretext of an expectation that National troops were about to invade the State, General Polk, with the sanction of Davis, and Governor Harris, of Tennessee, and the full knowledge, it is believed, of Governor Magoffin, proceeded to carry out General Pillow's favorite plan of scorning Kentucky's neutrality, and seizing Columbus. On the 30th of August, Polk telegraphed to Pillow, saying: "I shall myself be at New Madrid to-morrow to arrange for the future;" and on the 3d of September, De Russey, Polk's aid-de-camp, telegraphed to the same officer, that "the general-commanding determines, with troops now at Union City, to fall at once upon Columbus;" and directed Pillow

[1] The President said that, taking all means within his reach for forming a judgment, he did not believe it was the popular wish of Kentucky that the Union troops should be removed, and added: "It is with regret I search, and cannot find, in your not very short letter, any declaration or intimation that you entertain any desire for the preservation of the Federal Union."

[2] In the Senate were 27 Union and 11 Secession members, and in the Lower House 76 Union and 24 Secession representatives.

to take his whole command immediately to Island No. 10. This was done, and on the 4th[a] Polk seized Hickman and Columbus, and commenced the erection of batteries on the bluff near the latter place.[1] He immediately telegraphed the fact to Davis, at Richmond, and to

[a] Sept., 1861.

THE BLUFF, AND POLK'S HEAD-QUARTERS, NEAR COLUMBUS.

Governor Harris, at Nashville.[2] Then followed some transparent chicanery

[1] Columbus is in Hickman County, about twenty miles below the mouth of the Ohio River.

[2] On the same day General Polk issued a proclamation, in which he gave as a reason for his violation of the neutrality of Kentucky, that the National Government had done so by establishing camp depots for its armies, by organizing military companies within its territory, and by making evident preparations, on the Missouri shore of the Mississippi, for the seizure of Columbus. It was, therefore, "a military necessity, for the defense of the territory of the Confederate States, that a Confederate force should occupy Columbus in advance."

When General Fremont heard of this movement, he wrote a private letter to the President, dated the 8th of September, in which he set forth a plan for expelling the Confederates from Kentucky and Tennessee.* The President urged its immediate adoption, but was overruled by his counsellors. Experts say, that had Fremont's plan been promptly acted upon, the war that so long desolated Kentucky and Tennessee might have been averted.

* The following is a copy of Fremont's letter:—

HEAD-QUARTERS WESTERN DEPARTMENT, September 8, 1861.

To the President:—

MY DEAR SIR:—I send, by another hand, what I ask you to consider in respect to the subject of the note by your special messenger.

In this, I desire to ask your attention to the position of affairs in Kentucky. As the rebel troops, driven out of Missouri, had invaded Kentucky in considerable force, and by occupying Union City, Hickman, and Columbus, were preparing to seize Paducah and Cairo, I judged it impossible, without losing important advantages, to defer any longer a forward movement. For this purpose I have drawn from the Missouri side a part of the force stationed at Bird's Point, Cairo, and Cape Girardeau, to Fort Holt and Paducah, of which places we have taken possession. As the rebel forces outnumber ours, and the counties of Kentucky, between the Mississippi and Tennessee Rivers, as well as those along the Cumberland, are strongly Secessionist, it becomes imperatively necessary to have the co-operation of the Union forces under Generals Anderson and Nelson, as well as those already encamped opposite Louisville, under Colonel Rousseau. I have re-enforced, yesterday, Paducah with two regiments, and will continue to strengthen the position with men and artillery. As soon as General Smith, who commands there, is re-enforced sufficiently for him to spread his forces, he will have to take and hold Mayfield and Lovelaceville, to be in the rear and flank of Columbus, and to occupy Smithland, controlling in its way both the Tennessee and Cumberland Rivers. At the same time Colonel Rousseau should bring his force, increased, if possible, by two Ohio regiments, in boats, to Henderson, and taking the Henderson and Nashville Railroad, occupy Hopkinsville, while General Nelson should go, with a force of 5,000, by railroad to Louisville, and from there to Bowling Green. As the population in all the counties through which the above railroads pass are loyal, this movement could be made without delay or molestation to the troops. Meanwhile, General Grant would take possession of the entire Cairo and Fulton Railroad, Piketon, New Madrid, and the shore of the Mississippi opposite Hickman and Columbus. The foregoing disposition having been effected, a combined attack will be made on Columbus, and, if successful in that, upon Hickman, while Rousseau and Nelson will move in concert, by railroad, to Nashville, occupying the State capital, and, with adequate force, New Providence. The conclusion of this movement would be a combined advance towards Memphis, on the Mississippi, as well as the Ohio and Memphis Railroad, and I trust the result would be a glorious one to the country. In a reply to a letter from General Sherman, by the hand of Judge Williams, in relation to the vast importance of securing possession, in advance, of the country lying between the Ohio, Tennessee, and Mississippi, I have to-day suggested the first part of the plan. By extending my command to Indiana, Tennessee, and Kentucky, you would enable me to attempt the accomplishment of this all-important result, and in order to secure the secrecy necessary to its success, I shall not extend the communication I have made to General Sherman, or repeat it to any one else.

With high respect and regard, I am very truly yours,

J. C. FREMONT.

on the part of the conspirators, to deceive the people and defend Confederate honor. Walker, the "Secretary of War," ordered Polk to withdraw his troops from Kentucky, while Davis, his superior, telegraphed to the same officer in approval of his movement—"The necessity justifies the act."[1] When the authorities of Kentucky demanded from Governor Harris, of Tennessee, an explanation of the movement, that functionary replied with the false assertion that it had been done without his knowledge or consent; "and I am confident," he said, "without the consent of the President. I have telegraphed President Davis," he continued, "requesting their immediate withdrawal."

FELIX K. ZOLLICOFFER.

On the day after Polk invaded Kentucky on the west, and General Felix K. Zollicoffer, formerly a member of Congress, with a considerable force had passed from East Tennessee, through the Cumberland Mountains, and entered the State on its eastern border, Magoffin laid a message before the Legislature, in which he made special complaint of Union military organizations within the State, and asked for the passage of a law for maintaining for the Commonwealth an armed neutrality; also to request the National Government to order the immediate disbanding of such organizations. The Legislature responded by directing the Governor to order, by proclamation, all the Confederate troops within the State to leave it immediately. An attempt to have the Union troops included in the order was promptly voted down. The Legislature did more. They passed a series of resolutions, by an overwhelming vote,[2] declaring that the peace and neutrality of Kentucky had been wantonly violated, its soil invaded, and the rights of its citizens grossly injured "by the so-called Southern forces;" and, therefore, by special act, the Governor was requested to call out the military force of the State, "to expel and drive out the invaders." It was further resolved that the National Government should be asked for aid and assistance in that business; that General Anderson be requested "to enter immediately upon the discharge of his duties" in that military district, and that they appealed to the people to assist in expelling and driving out "the lawless invaders of the soil."

---

[1] This was denied by some of the partisans of Davis. I have before me an autograph letter, written by Nash H. Burt to Governor Harris, dated at Nashville, September 6, 1861, in which he says: "The following dispatch is received this morning, dated Union City, 12 P. M., Sept. 5, 1861," directed to Governor Harris:—

"On last evening I had the honor of telegraphing to you the necessity I had been under, of seizing the town of Columbus in advance of the enemy, who had already taken all the preparatory measures to do so. On this evening I received from his honor the Secretary of War, an order to withdraw the troops from Kentucky; but while issuing the appropriate orders to that effect, had the gratification to receive from the President the following dispatch, viz.: 'GENERAL POLK, Union City—Your telegram received. *The necessity must justify the act.* Signed, JEFFERSON DAVIS.'

"LEONIDAS POLK, *Major-General.*"

General Polk sent a dispatch to Governor Magoffin, announcing to him that military necessity had compelled him to take possession of Columbus, and that, in reporting to Davis, his reply was, "the necessity justified the action." That dispatch is before me.

[2] In the House, 68 to 26; and in the Senate, 26 to 8.

Magoffin vetoed these resolutions, and they were promptly passed over his negative by a large majority.[1] In the mean time, the invasion of Kentucky by Tennessee troops had brought in a National force, under Major-General Ulysses S. Grant, then in command of the district around Cairo. He took military possession of Paducah,[a] at the mouth of the Tennessee River, where he found Secession flags flying in different parts of the town in expectation of the arrival of a Confederate army, nearly four thousand strong, reported to be within sixteen miles of that place. He seized property there prepared for the Confederates, and he issued a proclamation declaring that he had come solely for the purpose of defending the State from the aggression of rebels, and to protect the rights of all citizens, promising that when it should be manifest that they were able to maintain the authority of the Government themselves, he should withdraw the forces under his command.

[a] Sept. 6, 1861.

Thus ended the neutrality of Kentucky, in which its politicians had unfortunately placed it.[2] That neutrality had suppressed the practical loyalty of the State, given freedom to the growth of its opposite, and allowed Confederate troops to make such a lodgment on its soil, that large National armies were required to oppose them, and war in its most horrid aspects filled all its borders with misery. But for that neutrality, Tennessee, whose disloyal authorities had espoused the Confederate cause, would probably have been the frontier battle-ground, and the blood and treasure of Kentucky, so largely spent in the war, would have been spared. Too late to avoid the penalties of remissness in duty, Kentucky, five months after the war was begun in Charleston harbor, took a positive stand for the Union.

Encouraged by the new attitude of Kentucky, the National Government determined to take vigorous measures for securing its loyalty against the wiles of dangerous men. Ex-Governor Morehead, who was reported to be an active traitor to his country, was arrested at his residence, near Louisville, and sent as a State prisoner to Fort Lafayette, at the entrance to the harbor of New York. Others of like sympathies took the alarm and fled, some to the Confederate armies or the more southern States, and others to Canada. Among them was John C. Breckinridge, late Vice-President of the Republic, and member of the National Senate, also William Preston, late American Minister to Spain; James B. Clay, a son of Henry Clay; Humphrey Marshall, lately a member of Congress, and a life-long politician; Captain John Morgan, Judge Thomas Monroe, and others of less note.

HUMPHREY MARSHALL.

[1] Compelled to issue a proclamation by order of the Legislature, Magoffin put forth one on the 13th as mild as possible, simply saying that he was instructed to declare that "Kentucky expects the Confederate or Tennessee troops to withdraw from her soil immediately."

[2] See page 458, volume I.

Breckinridge, Marshall, and Morgan entered the military service of the Confederates. The first two were commissioned brigadier-generals, and the latter became a conspicuous guerrilla chief.

Breckinridge became a zealous servant of the Confederates. He issued an address, in which he announced his resignation of his seat in the United States Senate, and in bitter language spoke of the dissolution of the Union, and the atrocious despotism which he alleged had been established at Washington; and he charged his own State Legislature with abject "submission to every demand o Federal despotism, and woeful neglect of every right of the Kentucky citizens." It is well suggested that "Mr. Breckinridge, in his exodus from Kentucky, perpetrated a serious blunder;"[1] for, had he, like other "friends of the South," remained in Congress, he might have served the cause of the conspirators more efficiently. He was an able and adroit politician and legislator, but was an indifferent soldier.

Vigorous military action in Kentucky, besides the seizure of Columbus and Hickman, speedily followed that act. Simon B. Buckner, the corrupter of the patriotism of large numbers of the young men of Kentucky,[2] bearing the commission of brigadier-general in the Confederate service, had established a camp on the Nashville and Louisville Railway, just below the Kentucky line. Soon after the seizure of Columbus, he left his camp with a considerable force, with the intention of moving quickly upon Louisville, by the railway, seizing that city, and establishing a Confederate post on the Ohio at that important point. The telegraph wires were cut, and he was far on his way before any intimation was given of his approach. The trains due at Louisville did not arrive, and the managers sent out an engine to ascertain the cause. It, like a train before it, was seized by Buckner. A fireman escaped, and, procuring a hand-car, soon returned to Louisville with the startling news.

General Anderson immediately ordered General Rousseau to move out on the road with his little force at Camp Joe Holt,[3] and some Louisville Home Guards. These were his only available forces at that moment. The order was obeyed with alacrity, and very soon a considerable force, under the chief command of General William T. Sherman, Anderson's lieutenant, were on their way to repel the invaders—the latter, who was in delicate health, remaining in Louisville to forward re-enforcements. Fortunately, Buckner had been delayed, near Bowling Green, by the patriotic act of a young man of that place, who went quietly up the road and displaced a rail, by which the engine of the invaders' train was thrown from the track. But for this, Buckner might have reached Louisville before Anderson could have put any forces in motion. As it was, he penetrated the county as far as Elizabethtown, forty miles from that city, when he heard of the approaching troops. He thought proper to fall back to Bowling Green, where he established an intrenched camp, and issued a proclamation[a] to his "fellow-citizens of Kentucky,"[4] and where he remained for several months. At the same time, Sherman established a camp and general rendez-

[a] Sept. 18, 1861.

[1] Greeley's *American Conflict*, i. 615. [2] See page 458, volume I. [3] See page 72.

[4] That proclamation abused the National Government and the loyal Legislature of Kentucky. He declared in it that Confederate troops occupied "a defensive position" in that State, "on the invitation of the people of Kentucky;" that he returned to his native State with peaceful intentions, "at the head of a force, the advance of

vous on Muldraugh's Hill, not far from Elizabethtown, and there laid the foundation of that notable organization afterward known as the *Army of the Cumberland.* On account of Anderson's feeble health, General Sherman was placed in chief command of the Department of the Cumberland (which included the States of Kentucky and Tennessee) early in October, when, with a forecast not then appreciated, he declared that an army of two hundred thousand men would be necessary to expel the Confederates from Kentucky and Tennessee, and carry the National banner victoriously to the Gulf. Because of that assertion, whose wisdom was speedily vindicated, he was called insane, and for a time he was overshadowed by a cloud of neglect.

Let us now return to a consideration of affairs in Missouri.

We left General Fremont, with a strong force, moving toward the interior of Missouri. He had strengthened the forces in Eastern Missouri and at Cairo, that they might keep the Confederates so well employed in that region, that they could not give aid to Price, nor seriously menace St. Louis. In this service, as we have seen, they were successful. Hardee dared not advance much from Greenville; Pillow was kept in the neighborhood of New Madrid, without courage to move far toward Bird's Point and Cape Girardeau; and Jeff. Thompson, the guerrilla, contented himself with eccentric raids and "scaring the Federals to death," as he foolishly supposed and declared.

Fremont went forward, and on the 28th of September he was at Jefferson City, the State capital, where he adopted vigorous measures for driving Price from the State. The latter had cause for serious alarm. McCulloch, as we have seen, had left him and gone to Arkansas, and Pillow and Hardee had abandoned Southeastern Missouri, and taken position in Kentucky and Tennessee. McCulloch, who had promised an escort for an ammunition train to be sent from Arkansas to Price, not only withheld that promised aid, but arrested the progress of the train, with the pretext that it would be unsafe in Missouri.

These adverse circumstances compelled Price to retreat toward Arkansas. [a] 1861. He abandoned Lexington on the 30th of September,[a] leaving a guard of five hundred men there in defense of National prisoners. A squadron of cavalry, called the "Prairie Scouts," one hundred and eighty strong, under Major Frank J. White, surprised this party by a bold [b] October 16. dash,[b] dispersed them, made nearly seventy of them prisoners, released the Union captives, and, bearing away with them the Secession State flag, joined Fremont's forces, which were then on the Osage River, at Warsaw, in pursuit of Price. Fremont, with his splendid body-guard of cavalry, under Major Charles Zagonyi, a Hungarian,[1] had arrived [c] October. there on the 16th,[c] after encountering a severe rain storm. Gen-

---

which is composed entirely of Kentuckians," whom he had seduced by false representations from their homes and their national allegiance; and that the Legislature of Kentucky was "faithless to the will of the people." He assured the people that his forces at Bowling Green would be used in aiding Kentucky in maintaining its strict neutrality, and "to enforce it against the two belligerents alike."

General Anderson issued a counter-proclamation, in which he said that he, a native of Kentucky, had "come to enforce, not to make laws," and to protect the lives and property of the people of the Commonwealth. He called upon the citizens to arm in their might and drive the invader from their soil. "The leader of the hostile force," he said, "who now approaches, is, I regret to say, a Kentuckian, making war on Kentucky and Kentuckians." He called them to "rally around the flag our fathers loved," and bade them trust in God and do their duty.

[1] Zagonyi had been a soldier in his native land, under General Bem. He came to America as an exile. Offering his services to Fremont at St. Louis, he was charged with the duty of recruiting a body of cavalry as

eral Sigel, who led the advance, had already crossed his force over the rapidly swelling stream by means of a single flatboat and the swimming of his horses; but its banks were now filled to the brim with the recent rains, and could not be forded, nor were boats or lumber for their construction to be had there. The ax was soon heard in the surrounding forest, and in the course of five days a rude strong bridge was constructed, under the direction of Captain Pike, of the engineers, over which the whole army, now thirty thousand strong, with eighty-six heavy guns, safely passed, and moved on in the direction of Springfield, by the way of Bolivar. The commander was full of confidence in the success of his plans, yet fearful of official interference with them by the Secretary of War (Cameron) and the Adjutant-General (Thomas), then in pursuit of him, as he had been informed.[1] That plan was to capture or disperse the forces of Price, and seizing Little Rock, the capital of Arkansas, so completely turn the position of the Confederate forces under Polk, Pillow, Thompson, and Hardee, as to cut off their supplies from that region, and compel them to retreat, when a flotilla of gunboats then in preparation near St. Louis, in command of Captain Foote, could easily descend the river and assist in military operations against Memphis, which, if successful, would allow the Army and Navy to push on and take possession of New Orleans. "My plan is New Orleans straight," he wrote on the 11th of October, from his camp near Tipton. "It would precipitate the war forward, and end it soon and victoriously."[2]

SIGEL CROSSING THE OSAGE.

When Fremont's army was at the *Pomme de Terre* River, fifty-one miles north of Springfield,[a] he sent the combined cavalry forces of Zagonyi and Major White (led by the former), to reconnoiter the position of the Confederates at the latter place, with instructions to attempt its capture if circumstances should promise success. The whole force did not exceed three hundred men. When within a few miles of Springfield,[b] on the highest point of the Ozark Mountains, they fell in with some foragers and captured them; and there a Union

[a] Oct. 23, 1861.

[b] Oct. 24.

a body-guard for the General. He selected for this purpose young men, and formed them into three companies, one of which were nearly all Kentuckians. There were very few foreigners in the guard, and all the officers were Americans excepting three, one Hollander and two Hungarians, the latter being Major Zagonyi and Lieutenant Majthenyi. The Guard was mounted on well-equipped blooded bay horses. Each man was armed with two of Colt's six-barrel navy revolvers, one five-barrel rifle, and a saber.

[1] See letters to his wife in Mrs. Fremont's *Story of the Guard*.

[2] Letter of General Fremont to his wife, October 11th, 1861. Mrs. Fremont, daughter of the late Senator Benton of Missouri, was then at Jefferson City. Her husband had long been in the habit of referring all manner of work and duties to her as acting principal in his absence, and in that capacity she was now at Jefferson City and gave him efficient aid. See note on page 88 of *The Story of the Guard: a Chronicle of the War*. By Jessie Benton Fremont.

farmer told Zagonyi that the Confederate force in the town was full two thousand in number. He was not daunted by this information, but pushed forward. One of the foragers who escaped had heralded his coming, and when he approached the suburbs of the village, on the Mount Vernon road, at a little past four o'clock in the afternoon, he found twelve hundred infantry and four hundred cavalry well prepared, on the brow of a hill in front of sheltering woods, to receive him. Zagonyi was still undaunted. Notwithstanding White's Prairie Scouts had been separated from the Guard, Zagonyi was determined to fight. Turning to his officers, he said: "Follow me and do like me!" And to his little band of followers he spoke a few hurried words, saying: "Comrades! the hour of danger has come; your first battle is before you. The enemy is two thousand strong, and we are but one hundred and fifty. It is possible no man will come back. If any of you would turn back, you can do so now!" Not a man moved.

Zagonyi was delighted. "I will lead you!" he exclaimed. "Let the watchword be, '*The Union and Fremont!*' Draw sabers! By the right flank—quick trot—*march!*" and away dashed the bold leader and his comrades with a shout down a narrow lane fringed with concealed sharp-shooters, with a miry brook and a stout rail fence ahead to oppose them. These were all passed in a few minutes, while the fire from the infantry in their front was terrible. On an eminence nearer stood the Confederate cavalry, ready to engage in the fray. Already the lane had been strewn with the fallen men and horses of the Guard, and yet Zagonyi's troops had not struck a blow. The moment for dealing that blow was now at hand. The word is given, and Lieutenant Majthenyi, with thirty men, dashed madly upon the center of the Confederate cavalry, breaking their line, and scattering the whole body in confusion over the adjoining corn-fields. Then Zagonyi shouts to the impatient soldiers he is holding in leashes, as it were, "In open order—*charge!*" and with the impetuosity of a whirlwind they sweep up the slope in the face of bullets that fly thick as hail. At the same moment fifty Irish dragoons of Major White's squadron, led by Captain McNaughton, fall upon the foe, and away scampers almost the entire body of Confederate infantry in wild search for safety. The remnant of the Guard, led by Zagonyi, follow the fugitive horsemen and smite them fearfully, chase them into the town, and fight them fiercely in detail in the streets and in the public square of Springfield, whilst Union women, undismayed by the dangers, come out, and, waving their handkerchiefs, cheer on the victors. When the conflict ended, the Confederates were utterly routed; and of the one hundred and fifty of Zagonyi's Guard, eighty-four were dead or wounded.[1] The action had lasted an hour and a half; and in the dim twilight of that bright October evening, the National flag was raised in triumph over the court-house.

At a little past midnight, Zagonyi, with a captured Confederate flag and only seventy of his Guard, and a few released prisoners, rode proudly but sadly out of Springfield, because it was unsafe for them to remain. They

[1] Dispatch of Major Zagonyi to General Fremont, October 25, 1861. Report of Major Zagonyi to Colonel J. H. Eaton, Assistant Adjutant-General, October 28, 1861. Letter of Major Zagonyi to Mrs. Fremont, quoted in her *Story of the Guard*. Narrative of Major Dorsheimer, of Fremont's staff, in the *Atlantic Monthly*. The number of the Guard killed was 15; mortally wounded, 2; the remainder were wounded or made prisoners. Zagonyi said, "Of the wounded not one will lose a finger." The prisoners were released, and the actual loss to the Guard was only 17. So Zagonyi said in a letter to Mrs. Fremont, October 23, 1861.

fell back until they met Sigel's advance, between Springfield and Bolivar. The report of this brilliant charge and victory, which had preceded them, filled the whole army with delight and enthusiasm. "This was really a Balaklava charge," wrote Fremont. "The Guard numbered only one hundred and fifty. You notice that Zagonyi says he has seen charges, but never such a one. Their war-cry, he says, sounded like thunder. This action is a noble example to the army."[1] There had been other noble examples for the army during its advance in Missouri.[2]

Fremont's army arrived at Springfield at the beginning of November, inspirited by news of recent successes in the Department, and the prospect of speedily ridding Missouri of insurgents. While it had been moving forward, Lane and Montgomery, who, we have seen, had been driven back into Kansas by Price,[3] had crossed into Missouri again, to cut off or embarrass the Confederates in their retreat from Lexington. Montgomery pushed on to the town of Osceola, the capital of St. Clair County, on the Osage, but was too late to intercept Price. The armed Confederates at that place, after a brief skirmish,[a] were driven away, and the village was laid in ashes, with no other excuse for the cruel measure than the fact that it was a rendezvous for the foe, and its inhabitants were all disloyal.

[a] Sept. 20, 1861.

A month later the National troops gained a signal victory over the guerrilla chief, Thompson (who was called the "Swamp Fox," and his command, the "Swamp Fox Brigade"), at Fredericktown, the capital of Madison County, in Southeastern Missouri. General Grant was in command at Cape Girardeau at that time. General Thompson and Colonel Lowe had been roaming at will over the region between New Madrid and Pilot Knob. Thompson, with six hundred men, had captured the guard at the Big River Bridge, near Potosi, and destroyed that structure on the 15th of October, and on the following day he and Lowe were at the head of a thousand men near Ironton, threatening that place, where they were defeated by Major Gavitt's Indiana cavalry, and a part of Colonel Alexander's Twenty-first Illinois cavalry, with a loss of thirty-six killed and wounded. Grant determined to put an end to the career of these marauders, if possible. Informed that they were near Fredericktown, he sent out a considerable force under Colonel Plummer,[4] to strike them from the East, while Captain Hawkins, with Missouri cavalry, was ordered up from Pilot Knob on the Northeast, followed by Colonel Carlin with a body of infantry as a support,[5] to engage and occupy Thomp-

[1] An accident occurred to Major White and prevented his being in this action. He had sickened on the way and been compelled to lag behind. When attempting to overtake his troops, he was made a prisoner, but escaped and reached Springfield on the morning after the fight, with a few Home Guards. Stationing 22 of his 24 men as pickets, he deceived the Confederates in the town with the belief that he had a considerable force with him. After receiving a flag of truce, and permitting them to bury their dead, he prudently fell back to meet the advancing army.

[2] Other detachments of cavalry from Fremont's army, besides those of White and Zagonyi, had been operating against the Confederates during the march of the main body. One of them, under Major Clark Wright, routed and dispersed a body of Confederates near Lebanon, in Laclede County, on the 13th of October; and on the following day the same forces captured the village of Lynn Creek. In the former engagement, after a charge, and a running fight for a mile and a half, there were about 60 Confederates killed and wounded, while the Union loss was only one man killed.—Report of Major Wright, October 13, 1861.

[3] See page 66.

[4] They consisted of the Eleventh, Seventeenth, and Twentieth Illinois, and 400 cavalry.

[5] These consisted of parts of the Twenty-first, Twenty-third, and Twenty-eighth Illinois, the Eighth Wisconsin, Colonel Baker's Indiana cavalry, and Major Schofield's Battery.

son until Plummer's arrival. They formed a junction at Fredericktown, with Plummer in chief command, and, starting in pursuit of the Confederates, who they supposed were in full flight, found them about one thousand strong, well posted and ready for battle, partly in an open field and partly in the woods, only a mile from the village, with four iron 18-pounders in position. Schofield opened the battle with his heavy guns. A general engagement ensued, and, after two hours' hard fighting, the Confederates fled, hotly pursued by the Indiana cavalry for twenty miles. The Confederate Colonel Lowe was killed early in the action. Their loss was large—how large is not known. The loss of the Nationals was ten killed and twenty wounded. This defeat and dispersion completely broke up Thompson's guerrilla organization for a time, which was composed almost wholly of disloyal and deluded Missourians. They had fought bravely with inferior arms against superior numbers.[1]

We have observed that General Fremont had anticipated an interference with his plans when he heard that the Secretary of War and the Adjutant-General were in pursuit of him. They had overtaken him on the 13th,[a] at Tipton, the then Western terminus of the Pacific Railway, about thirty miles south of Jefferson City. The interview of the officials was courteous and honorable. The Secretary frankly told him that their errand was to make personal observations of his army, and of affairs in his Department. Complaints concerning his administration of those affairs had filled the mind of the President with painful apprehensions, and the Secretary of War bore with him an order, relieving him of his command, with discretionary powers to use it or not. The Secretary carried it back to Washington, and the Adjutant-General made a report highly unfavorable to the commanding general in Missouri. This was published, and had the two-fold effect of prejudicing the public mind against Fremont, and revealing to the enemy secrets which the highest interests of the country at that time required to be hidden.[2]

[a] Oct., 1861.

The assertion was publicly made, after the return of the Government officials, that the campaign in Missouri was a failure; and the prediction was confidently uttered that Fremont's army could never cross the Osage, much less reach Springfield. The fallacy of this prophecy was proven in less than a fortnight, when that army lay on the Ozark hills and on the plain around Springfield; and the campaign failed only, it is believed, because its progress was suddenly checked when the most reasonable promises of abundant success were presented. That check was given on the morning of the 2d of November, when a courier arrived at head-quarters with an order from General Scott, directing General Fremont to turn over his command to General

---

[1] More than half of their fire-arms were old flint-lock squirrel guns. "Of the dead," wrote an eye-witness, "not a single one that I saw was dressed in any kind of uniform, the cloth being generally home-made, and butter-nut colored."

[2] This report was in the form of a journal, and contained a great amount of gossip and scandal, gathered from subalterns and Fremont's political enemies, which subsequent information showed to be unworthy of credit. It is due to the Adjutant-General to say that he disclaimed any intention to make that journal public. It is said that a copy of it was surreptitiously obtained and given to a newspaper reporter, and suspicion at the time pointed to the Postmaster-General (whose brother, an officer in the army, it was known had quarrelled with Fremont), as the one on whom the responsibility of the publication should rest. Fremont afterward published a vindication of his administration in the Department of Missouri, which almost wholly removed from the public mind the unfavorable impression made by that journal.

David Hunter, then some distance in the rear. This order came when the army was excited by the prospect of a battle almost immediately. Price had at first fled to Neosho,[1] when, finding Fremont still in pursuit, he pushed on to Pineville, in the extreme Southwestern part of Missouri. Further than that his "State-Guard" were not disposed to go. He was unwilling to leave Missouri without measuring strength and powers with Fremont, so he changed front and prepared to receive him. This attitude gave rise to startling rumors in Fremont's camp, and, at the moment when he was relieved of command, it was reported that Price was marching on Springfield, and that his vanguard had reached Wilson's Creek, ten miles distant, prepared to give battle on the ground where Lyon was killed three months before. McCulloch was reported to be at Dug Springs;[2] and the number of the combined armies was estimated at forty thousand men.[3]

DAVID HUNTER.

Hunter had not yet arrived, and Fremont, who had made his troops exceedingly sorrowful by the announcement in a formal address that he was about to leave them,[4] was implored by one hundred and ten of his officers to lead his army against the foe. He promised compliance with their wishes, if his successor should not reach them by sunset.[5] Hunter failed to do so, and at eight o'clock in the evening Fremont issued the order of battle, and the entire camp was alive with enthusiasm. Lyon's plan for surrounding and capturing the Confederates was substantially adopted. They were to be assailed simultaneously by Generals Pope and McKinstry in the front, by Generals Sigel and Lane in the rear, and by General Asboth on the east, from the Fayetteville road.

---

1 There Jackson and the disloyal Legislature of Missouri met, as we have observed (note 2, page 57), under Price's protection.

2 See page 45.

3 General Asboth's report to General Fremont, Nov. 3, 1866.

4 The following is a copy of his address: "SOLDIERS OF THE MISSISSIPPI ARMY: Agreeable to orders this day received, I take leave of you. Although our army has been of sudden growth, we have grown up together, and I have become familiar with the brave and generous spirit which you bring to the defense of your country, and which makes me anticipate for you a brilliant career. Continue as you have begun, and give to my successor the same cordial and enthusiastic support with which you have encouraged me. Emulate the splendid example which you have already before you, and let me remain, as I am, proud of the noble army which I had thus far labored to bring together. Soldiers! I regret to leave you. Most sincerely I thank you for the regard and confidence you have invariably shown to me. I deeply regret that I shall not have the honor to lead you to the victory which you are just about to win; but I shall claim to share with you in the joy of every triumph, and trust always to be fraternally remembered by my companions in arms."

5 "The intelligence of this determination of the commanding general," wrote an eye-witness, "was at once communicated from camp to camp, and the greatest enthusiasm prevailed. Every five minutes during the succeeding two and a half hours, the wildest cheering could be heard from some portion of the army as the information was carried to the various regiments. A dozen bands at once proceeded to the head-quarters and serenaded the General. Crowds of officers gathered in front of his quarters, and greeted him with loud and prolonged cheering; and, had the battle occurred according to arrangements, the troops would have fought in the most determined manner."

General Hunter arrived at head-quarters at midnight, and Fremont, after informing him of the position of affairs, laid before him all his plans. The order for battle was countermanded,[1] and nine days afterward Major-General H. W. Halleck was appointed to the command of the Missouri Department.

FREMONT'S SWORD.

On the morning of the 4th, Fremont and his Staff left the army for St. Louis. The parting with his devoted soldiers was very touching, and his reception in St. Louis[a] was an ovation like that given to a victor. Crowds of citizens greeted him at the railway station and escorted him to his head-quarters. An immense torch-light procession passed through the streets that night in honor of his arrival;[2] and at an assemblage of the citizens, resolutions of confidence and sympathy, and an address, were adopted. Afterward he was presented with an elegant sword in token of profound regard, which was inscribed with these words:—"TO THE PATHFINDER, BY THE MEN OF THE WEST."[3]

[a] Nov. 8, 1861.

Disappointed and disheartened, the National army commenced a retrograde march from Springfield toward St. Louis at the middle of November, followed by a long train of vehicles filled with Union refugees. The women of Springfield, who had welcomed Zagonyi, and the Union men everywhere throughout

---

[1] Price seems not to have moved his army from Pineville, but his scouts penetrated to the front of the National troops, and thus caused the alarm.

[2] "The General was to have been at home by nine in the morning; but the management of the train being in other hands, they were delayed until nearly that hour in the evening. But patient crowds had kept their watch through the long day, and by night it was a sea of heads in all the open spaces around our house. The door-posts were garlanded, and the very steps covered with flowers—touching and graceful offerings from the Germans. China-asters and dahlias, with late roses and regular bouquets of geraniums, beautified the entrance and perfumed the air; and when the General did make his way at last through the magnificent assemblage, it was to be met by the wives and children of the German officers he had left at Springfield. Unknown to me, they had come to speak their hearts to him, but they had more tears than words. Touched to the heart already, the General was not prepared for the arrival of citizens—American as well as German—who came to thank him for past services, and ask to stand by him in the hour of disgrace. Meantime, the unceasing cheers and shouts of the vast crowd without sounded like the tide after a high wind. I could not stand it; I went far up to the top of the house, and in the cold night air tried to still the contending emotions, when I saw a sight that added to the throbbing of my heart. Far down the wide avenue the serried crowd was parting, its dark, restless masses glowing in the lurid, wavering torchlight, looking literally like waves; and passing through them came horsemen, stamped with the splendid signet of battle, their wounded horses and bullet-torn uniforms bringing cries of love and thanks from those for whom they had been battling. When they halted before the door, and the sudden ring and flash of their drawn sabers added new beauty to the picture, I think only the heart of a Haman could have failed to respond to the truth and beauty of the whole scene. Were not these men for the king to delight to honor? Who could have foreseen what was the official recognition already preparing for them?"*—Mrs. Fremont, in her *Story of the Guard*, page 201.

[3] Fremont had long before been called *The Pathfinder*, because of his wonderful explorations among the Rocky Mountains. The blade of the sword now presented to him was made at Solingen, on the Rhine. The scabbard was of silver, with a design near its upper part, four inches in length. In its center was a bust of Fremont sculptured out of gold, in high relief, with a rich border of diamonds, and on each side a sculptured figure of fame. In the rear of the hilt was a hollow, arched at the top so as to form a canopy for a figure of America, at the foot of which, in the midst of appropriate surroundings, was a medallion of blue enamel, bearing the initials J. C. F. in diamonds. The cost of the sword was $1,000.

---

* "The official recognition" referred to by Mrs. Fremont is indicated in the following electrographs:—

ST. LOUIS, MISSOURI, November 11, 1861.

Maj.-Gen. GEORGE B. MCCLELLAN, Commanding-in-Chief, Washington, D. C.:—

I would regard it as an act of personal courtesy and kindness to me, if you will order my Body-Guard to remain with me, subject to no orders in this department but my own. It is composed of educated and intelligent young men, to whom the country and I owe more than the usual co sideration accorded to the rank and file of the army.

J. C. FREMONT, *Maj.-Gen. U. S. A.*

HEAD-QUARTERS OF THE ARMY, WASHINGTON, Nov. 11, 1861.

Maj.-Gen. J. C. FREMONT:—

Before receiving your dispatch, I had given instructions that the cavalry corps, known as your Body-Guard, should be otherwise disposed of. Official information had reached this city that members of that body had at Springfield expressed sentiments rendering their

that region who had received Fremont as a liberator, dared not remain, for they expected, what really happened, that General Price would follow up the receding army, and they would be made to suffer for their loyalty. Price did follow, with more than fifteen thousand men, in three columns; and all South-western Missouri below the Osage was soon delivered into the power of the Confederates.

When at the point of being deprived of his command, Fremont sent an order to General Grant at Cairo, directing him to make some co-operating movements. That officer, as we have observed, had taken possession of Paducah, in Kentucky,[a] on hearing of the invasion of that State by General Polk. He had proceeded to strengthen the position by casting up fortifications there; and by order of General Fremont, an immense pontoon bridge was thrown across the Ohio, half a mile below the

[a] Sept. 6, 1861.

PONTOON BRIDGE AT PADUCAH.

town.[1] He also seized and occupied Smithland, not far from the mouth of the Cumberland River, and thus closed two important gateways of supply for the Confederates in the interior of Kentucky and Tennessee, from the Ohio.

When Fremont's order for co-operation reached Grant, and was followed the next day by a dispatch,[b] saying, "Jeff. Thompson is at Indian Ford of the St. François River, twenty-five miles below Greenville, with about three thousand men, and Colonel Carlin has started with a force from Pilot Knob; send a force from Cape Girardeau and Bird's Point, to assist Carlin in driving Thompson into Arkansas," he was ready to move quickly and effectively. Grant had already sent Colonel

[b] Nov. 2.

---

[1] A pontoon bridge is a portable structure made to float on boat-shaped buoys, and used by an army on its march for the purpose of crossing rivers where bridges may have been destroyed, or a fordable river made impassable by rains. The more modern boats used for the purpose are made of vulcanized india-rubber, and consist of cylinders peaked at each end, so as to offer very little resistance to a current.

The river at Paducah is 3,600 feet across. The bridge was constructed of coal-barges, strongly braced together, and otherwise connected by trestle-work planked over. It was capable of bearing the heaviest ordnance and thousands of men.

---

continuance in the service of doubtful expediency. With every desire to gratify your wishes, I do not see exactly how I can violate every rule of military propriety. Please reply.

GEO. B. MCCLELLAN, *Com.-in-Chief.*

General Fremont tried to find out what were the offensive sentiments that had been expressed by members of his Guard, which had caused this harsh official action toward them; but to his application for a reconsideration of their case, in order that the truth might be discovered, General McClellan made no reply. The Guard was mustered out of service on the 28th of November, 1861. It is said that the offensive sentiments alluded to were those of Fremont's emancipation proclamation. It was well known that some of the Guard were outspoken against the slave system, whose supporters had commenced the war against the Government.

Oglesby to Commerce and Sikeston, to pursue Thompson in conjunction with some troops from Ironton, and had been informed that Polk was sending re-enforcements to Price from Columbus. In this situation of affairs, he determined to threaten Columbus by attacking Belmont, a little village and landing-place on the Missouri shore opposite, and break up the connection between Polk and Price. Oglesby's force was deflected toward New Madrid, and Colonel W. H. L. Wallace, of Illinois, was sent from Cairo to re-enforce him. The movement on Belmont would keep Polk from interfering with Grant's troops in pursuit of Thompson.

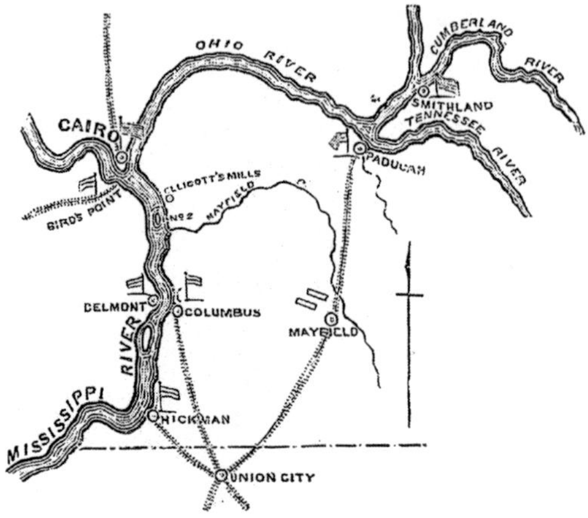

FIELD OF OPERATIONS AGAINST BELMONT.

General Charles F. Smith, a soldier of rare qualities, was now in command at Paducah. Grant requested him to make a demonstration toward Columbus, to attract the attention of Polk, and at the same time he sent a force down the Kentucky shore to Ellicott's Mills, about twelve miles above Columbus. When these deceptive movements were put in operation, Grant went down the Mississippi from Cairo,[a] with about three thousand troops, mostly Illinois Volunteers,[1] in four steam transports, convoyed by the wooden gunboats *Tyler* and *Lexington*, commanded respectively by Captains Walke and Stemble. They lay at Island No. 1, eleven miles above Columbus, that night. There Grant received information that Polk was sending troops across to Belmont, to cut off Colonel Oglesby. At dawn the next morning, he pressed forward and landed his forces at Hunter's Point, on the Missouri shore, three miles above Belmont, where a battalion was left to guard the transports from an attack by land, whilst the remainder pushed on and formed a line of battle two miles from the village. In the mean time, the gunboats had moved down and opened fire upon the Confederate batteries on the Iron Banks, a short distance above Columbus, on the Kentucky shore, and two hundred feet above the river, where twenty heavy guns were planted. Colonel Fouke took command of the center of the attacking column, Colonel Buford of the right, and Colonel Logan of the left. Polk was surprised. He was looking for an attack only in the rear, for General Smith was threatening him at Mayfield. He at once sent over three regiments, under General Pillow, to re-enforce the regiments of Russell and Tappen (the former acting as brigade commander), then holding Belmont.

[a] Nov. 6, 1861.

[1] These consisted of a part of General John A. McClernand's Brigade, composed of the Twenty-seventh, Thirtieth, and Thirty-first Illinois, commanded respectively by Colonels N. B. Buford, Philip B. Fouke, and John A. Logan; and a company of cavalry led by Captain J. J. Dollins. To these were added another company of cavalry under Lieutenant J. R. Catlin, and Captain Ezra Taylor's Chicago Light Artillery of six pieces and 114 men, all Illinois Volunteers. Also the Twenty-second Illinois, Colonel H. Dougherty, and the Seventh Iowa, Colonel Lauman.

Grant moved forward, with Dollins' cavalry scouring the woods to the right, and, deploying his whole force as skirmishers, he fought from tree to tree, and drove back the foe to their intrenched camp, which was protected by a strong *abatis* of slashed trees.[1] Behind these, opposing Grant's left, lay the Thirteenth Arkansas and Ninth Tennessee; and opposite his left was a battery of seven guns, commanded by Colonel Beltzhoover, and Colonel Wright's Tennessee regiment. Against these the Nationals charged over the fallen timber, captured the battery, and drove the Confederates back across the low level ground to the river, and some of them to their boats. In this movement Pillow's line was broken into a confused mass of men. The powder of the Confederates was nearly exhausted. The victory was complete; but the ground being commanded by the heavy guns on the bluffs at and near Columbus, it was untenable. The victors gave three cheers for the Union, set fire to the Confederate camp (having no wagons, in which to carry away property), and fell back with captured men, horses, and artillery, toward their landing-place in the morning.

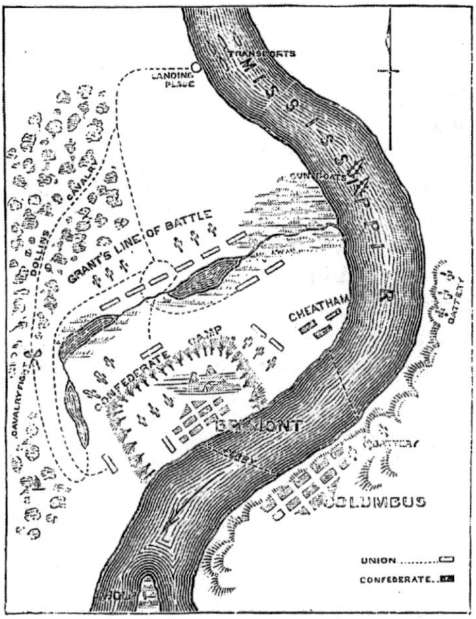

BATTLE OF BELMONT.

Polk determined not to allow Grant to escape with his victory and booty. He opened upon him with some of his heaviest guns, and sent General Cheatham with three regiments to cross the river above, and land between Grant and his flotilla. At the same time the chief crossed, at the head of two regiments, to aid Pillow in his chase of the Nationals. The Confederates now were not less than five thousand strong, and pressing hard. There was desperate fighting for a short time. Grant pushed on in good order toward his landing-place, under fire of the Confederate batteries on the Iron Banks, turning once to punish severely some of Cheatham's troops on his flank, and once again to send back in confusion some of Pillow's men, under Colonel Marks, who had endeavored to cut him off from his boats. He finally reached his landing-place, and embarked, after suffering severely. The fight had been gallant on both sides.[2] The gun-boats had performed most efficient service in

[1] *Abatis* is a French word for rows of felled trees, having their smaller branches cut off and the larger ones sharpened, and placed with their ends toward the approach of assailants, either in front of a fort or an intrenched camp. Sometimes the smaller branches are left, and so intertwined as to make it extremely difficult to penetrate the mass, excepting by cannon-balls.

[2] In a general order, Nov. 8th, General Grant said: "It has been my fortune to have been in all the battles fought in Mexico by Generals Scott and Taylor, save Buena Vista, and I never saw one more hotly contested, or where troops behaved with more gallantry." In his report on the 12th, he spoke in highest terms of General McClernand, as being in the midst of danger throughout the engagement, displaying coolness and judgment,

engaging the Confederate batteries, protecting the transports, and covering the re-embarkation. Indeed, to Captains Walke and Stemble, who managed their craft with the greatest skill and efficiency, the country was mostly indebted for the salvation of that little army from destruction or capture.[1] At five o'clock in the afternoon, the flotilla, with the entire force, was on its way back to Cairo, carrying away two of Beltzhoover's heavy guns, the others having been recaptured. Grant had lost four hundred and eighty-five men,[2] and Polk six hundred and thirty-two.[3] Cotemporaries and eye-witnesses on both sides related many deeds of special daring by individuals.

The repulse of Grant did not relieve the Confederates of a sense of impending great danger, for intelligence was continually reaching Columbus of the increase of National forces on the Ohio border. General Mansfield Lovell, then in command at New Orleans, was solicited to send up re-enforcements; and Governor Pettus, of Mississippi, and Governor Rector, of Arkansas, were implored for aid. But these men perceived the peril threatened by the land and water campaign commanded by Fremont, which events had sufficiently developed to make it fully suspected by the Confederates, and they dared not spare a man. Lovell answered that he had no more troops than were necessary to defend New Orleans, whilst both Pettus and Rector considered themselves deficient in strength for the expected conflict.[4] Governor Harris, of Tennessee, was urged to increase his efforts in raising volunteers. He had telegraphed to Pillow,[a] saying: "I congratulate you and our gallant volunteers upon their bloody but brilliant and glorious victory;" and a week later he added, "I am organizing, as rapidly as possible, thirty thousand volunteers and militia, armed with country guns." The hope thus held out was fallacious, for nearly all the troops that Harris could then muster, by force or persuasion, were soon needed in the interior of his State, in keeping in check the Loyalists of East

[a] Nov. 14, 1861.

---

and having had his horse shot three times. Grant's horse was also shot under him. Colonel Dougherty, of the Twenty-second Illinois, was three times wounded, and finally taken prisoner. Major McClurken, of the Thirtieth Illinois, and Colonel Lauman, of the Seventh Iowa, were badly wounded. Among the killed were Colonel Wentz, of the Seventh Iowa, Captains Brolaski and Markle, and Lieutenant Dougherty. The Twenty-second Illinois lost 23 killed and 74 wounded; and the Seventh Iowa had 26 killed and 80 wounded, including nearly all of its field officers. The loss of property was estimated at 25 baggage wagons, 100 horses, 1,000 overcoats, and 1,000 blankets. One man was killed and two wounded on the gunboats.

Among the Confederates killed was Colonel John V. Wright, of the Thirteenth Tennessee, and Major Butler, of the Eleventh Louisiana. Wright was a Democratic Congressman, and an intimate friend of Colonel Philip B. Fouke, of the Illinois Volunteers. "When they parted at the close of the session of 1860-61," says Mr. Greeley, (*American Conflict*, i. 597), Wright said to his friend, 'Phil, I expect the next time we meet it will be on the battle-field.' Their next meeting was in this bloody struggle."

[1] After the transports had departed from before Columbus, and gone some distance up the river, followed by the gunboats, Captain Walke was informed that some of the troops had been left behind. He returned with the *Tyler*, and met detached parties along the banks. He succeeded in rescuing nearly all of the stragglers from capture.

[2] Eighty-five killed, 301 wounded, and 99 missing. General Pillow, whose performances on this occasion were the least creditable, with his usual bombast and exaggerations, spoke in his report of his "small Spartan army" withstanding the constant fire of three times their number for four hours.—Pollard's *First Year of the War*, 203.

[3] Official reports of Grant and Polk, and their subordinate officers; private letter of General Grant to his father, Nov. 8th, 1861; Grant's Revised Report, June 26th, 1865; Pollard's *First Year of the War*. The latter gives the Confederate loss as it is above recorded. MS. Reports of Acting Brigadier-General R. M. Russell, Nov. 9, and of Colonels E. Ricketts, Jr., and T. H. Bell, Nov. 11, 1861.

[4] A little later, Governor Pettus changed his views, and, in a special message to the Mississippi Legislature, he suggested to that body the propriety of sending such troops as could "be immediately raised and armed, to assist in the defense of the important post of Columbus. I deem the safety of our position and forces at Columbus as of such vital importance to this State," he said, "as to claim the prompt and decisive action of all the State authorities."

Tennessee; in aiding Zollicoffer in his invasion of Southeastern Kentucky, already alluded to;[1] and in supporting Buckner in his treasonable operations in his native State. Zollicoffer had advanced to Barboursville, the capital of Knox County, so early as the 19th of September, where he dispersed an armed band of Kentucky Unionists, and captured their camp. He proclaimed peace and security in person and property for all Kentuckians, excepting those who should be found in arms for the Union; but his soldiers could not be restrained, and the inhabitants of that region were mercilessly plundered by them.

Zollicoffer's invasion aroused the Unionists of Eastern Kentucky, and they flew to arms. A large number of them were mustering and organizing under Colonel Garrard, a plain, earnest, and loyal Kentuckian, at a point among the Rock Castle Hills known as Camp Wild Cat. It was in a most picturesque region of one of the spurs of the Cumberland Mountains, on the direct road from Cumberland Gap toward the rich "blue-grass region" of Kentucky. Upon this camp Zollicoffer advanced on the 18th of October, with seven regiments and a light battery. When intelligence of his approach was received, Colonel Garrard had only about six hundred effective men to oppose him. Others in sufficient numbers to insure a successful resistance were too remote to be available, for the invader moved swiftly, swooping down from the mountains like an eagle on its prey. Yet when he came, on the morning of the 21st,[a] he found at Camp Wild Cat, besides Garrard's three regiments, a part of Colonel Coburn's Thirty-third Indiana, and Colonel Connell's Seventeenth Ohio regiments, and two hundred and fifty Kentucky cavalry, under Colonel Woolford, ready to resist him. With the latter came General Schoepf, an officer of foreign birth and military education, who assumed the chief command.

[a] October, 1861.

The position of the Unionists was strong. Zollicoffer with his Tennesseans and a body of Mississippi "Tigers" boldly attacked them, and was twice repulsed. The first attack was in the morning, the second in the afternoon. The latter was final. The contests had been very sharp, and the latter was decisive. The camp-fires of Zollicoffer's invaders were seen that evening in a sweet little valley two or three miles away from the battleground. Promptly and efficiently had Garrard's call for help been responded to, for toward the close of the second attack a portion of Colonel Steadman's Fourteenth Ohio also came upon the field to aid the Kentuckians, Indianians, and Ohioians already there; and when the invaders had withdrawn, others were seen dragging cannon wearily up the hill for the defense of Camp Wild Cat.

A little later a trial of strategy and skill occurred in the most eastern

[1] Zollicoffer, like Polk, made necessity the pretext for scorning the neutrality of Kentucky. On the 14th of September he telegraphed to Governor Magoffin, informing him of his occupation of three mountain ranges in Kentucky, because it was evident that the Unionists in Eastern Kentucky were about to invade East Tennessee, to destroy the great railway and its bridges. He said, apologetically, that he had delayed that "precautionary movement," until it was evident that "the despotic Government at Washington" had determined to subjugate first Kentucky and then Tennessee, whom he regarded as twin sisters. With the old plea of the unrighteous, that "the end justifies the means," he declared that he felt a "religious respect for Kentucky's neutrality," and would continue to feel it, so long as the safety of the Confederate cause would permit. He issued an order at the same time, setting forth that he entered Kentucky to defend "the soil of a sister State against an invading foe."

portion of Kentucky, between about three thousand loyalists, under General William Nelson, and a little more than a thousand insurgents, under Colonel John S. Williams. The latter were at Piketon, the capital of Pike County, and were marched against by General Nelson's force from Prestonburg, on the Big Sandy River. He sent[a] Colonel Sill, with nearly one-half of that force,[1] to march by way of John's Creek to gain the rear of Williams at Piketon, whilst with the remainder he should move forward and attack his front, so bringing him between two fires, and compelling him to surrender. Some one, counting positively on success, telegraphed to Washington that this result had been accomplished, and that a thousand prisoners had surrendered. The whole country was thrilled by the good news, for it seemed as if a way was about to be opened for the relief and the arming of the suffering loyalists in East Tennessee.

WILLIAM NELSON.

[a] November, 1861.

Truth soon told a different story. Nelson had moved on the 9th with his main column[2] directly toward Pikeville, twenty-eight miles distant, a battalion of Kentucky volunteers, under Colonel C. A. Marshall, in advance. They met picket-guards eight miles from that village. The road now lay along a narrow shelf cut in a high mountain side, ending in a steep ridge at Ivy Creek, which bent around it. There lay the Confederates in ambush, and did not fire until Marshall's battalion was close upon them. Then a volley was poured upon his men, and a sharp skirmish ensued. Confederates on the opposite side of the creek joined in the attack; but, after a contest of almost an hour and a half, all the insurgents fled, leaving thirty of their comrades dead on the field. How much greater was their loss was not ascertained. Nelson's loss was six killed and twenty-four wounded. He did not pursue far, and, as he had no cavalry, Williams escaped. The latter was too watchful and discreet to be caught in the trap laid for him by Nelson. Seeing his danger, he fled to the fastnesses of the mountains at Pound Gap, carrying with him a large amount of cattle and other spoils.

General Nelson entered Pikeville on the 10th, where he found Colonel Sill and his division, who, after fighting on the way, had arrived the previous evening, and given Williams's troops a few shot and shell when they departed. On the same day Nelson had the pleasure of saying to his troops, in an order issued from "Camp Hopeless Chase," that "In a campaign of twenty days,

[1] Sill's troops for this occasion were the Thirty-third Ohio (his own regiment), a light battalion, under Major Hart, composed of portions of the Second, Thirty-third, and Fifty-ninth Ohio, and two Kentucky companies; one hundred and forty-two mounted men, mostly teamsters, commanded by Colonel Metcalf; thirty-six volunteers, under Colonel Apperson, and a section of artillery (two rifled 6-pounders), under Colonel Roher Vacher.

[2] This was composed of the greater portions of the Second, Twenty-first, and Fifty-ninth Ohio Volunteers, under Colonels Harris, Norton, and Tyffe; a battalion of Kentucky volunteers, commanded by Colonel C. A. Marshall, and two sections of artillery, in charge of Captain Konkle.

you have driven the rebels from Eastern Kentucky, and given repose to that portion of the State." He alluded to their privations, and then said: "For your constancy and courage, I thank you, and, with the qualities which you have shown that you possess, I expect great things from you in the future."

The East Tennessee patriots were compelled to wait and suffer longer. Bright hopes had been excited among them by the repulse of Zollicoffer at Camp Wild-Cat; and many from the great valley between the Allegheny and Cumberland ranges, had made their way to the camps of the Unionists in Kentucky, fully persuaded that they would soon return with a victorious host as liberators of East Tennessee. It might have been so, had not General Schoepf been deceived by false reports concerning the strength of the insurgents at the mountain gaps, and the movements of others who were occupying Bowling Green, in the heart of Kentucky, under General Buckner, and who at that time were too weak to make any aggressions. Startled by a report that a large force from Bowling Green was marching to strike his flank, Schoepf fell back hastily toward the Ohio, making two days' forced marches, and leaving behind him and along the road ample evidence of a precipitate and rather disastrous flight. Not a platoon of soldiers had gone out from Buckner's camp in that direction. That retrograde movement of Schoepf extinguished the hope of speedy relief in the hearts of the East Tennesseans.

Now, at the middle of November, the Confederates had obtained a firm foothold in Tennessee, and occupied a considerable portion of Southern Kentucky, from the mountains to the Mississippi River; also a greater portion of Missouri south of the Missouri River. At the same time the National authorities were making vigorous preparations to drive them southward. At this interesting point, let us leave the consideration of events westward of the Alleghenies for a time, and glance at stirring scenes eastward of that lofty range of mountains, and on the sea-coast.

CHAPTER IV.

MILITARY OPERATIONS IN WESTERN VIRGINIA, AND ON THE SEA-COAST

IN the autumn of 1861, the Confederates made a severe struggle for the possession of West Virginia. They hoped, by the employment of other commanders than those who had failed there, to recover all that had been lost in the summer by the dispersion of Garnett's forces at Carricksford,[1] and the pushing of the incompetent Wise out of the Kanawha Valley, as we have observed.[2] General Robert E. Lee was sent with re-enforcements to take command of the troops left by Garnett and Pegram in Northern Virginia. He made his head-quarters at Huntersville, in Pocahontas County. His entire force, early in August, numbered full sixteen thousand men. He placed a strong guard on Buffalo Mountain, at the crossing of the Staunton turnpike, and extended his line northward from the Warm Springs, in Greenbrier County. General Floyd, the late Secretary of War,[3] had, in the mean time, taken chief command of his own and Wise's troops, in the region of the Gauley River.[4] With these two armies acting simultaneously, it was intended to expel the National troops from Western Virginia, and menace Ohio. Floyd was to sweep down the Kanawha Valley, and drive General Cox, of Ohio, beyond the border, while Lee should scatter the Union army, under General Rosecrans (McClellan's successor),[5] in Northern Virginia, and, planting the Confederate flag at Wheeling, threaten Western Pennsylvania.

Floyd took a strong position between Cox and Rosecrans, at Carnifex Ferry,[6] on the Gauley River, just below Meadow Creek, and eight miles from Summersville, the capital of Nicholas County. He left Wise with his force, called "Wise's Legion," at Pickett's Mills, to prevent a flank movement from Hawksnest, a mountain on the southern side of the Gauley, near which, on

---

1 See page 534, volume I. 2 See page 537, volume I. 3 See page 145, volume I.

4 Wise was so great a boaster, and so poor a performer, that his signal failures as a military leader on all occasions caused him to be much ridiculed. The following is a specimen of some of the shafts of wit that were cast at him through the newspapers of the day—

"There was a man of Accomac,
And he was bully Wise;
He jumped into Kanawha's bush,
And scratched out both his eyes;
And, when he saw he lost his eyes,
With all his might and main,
From Kanawha he quickly flies,
To brag, and—run again."

5 See page 537, volume I. 6 *Carnifex* is a Latin word, signifying a villain, or villainous.

the New River, Cox's main force was then stationed. Floyd had just settled his command at Carnifex Ferry, when he received intelligence that some National troops were approaching from the direction of Summersville, north of him. These were the Seventh Ohio, under Colonel E. B. Tyler, who, as a fur-trader, had made himself well acquainted with that region. Floyd had been placed in a perilous position in passing over the Gauley, by the capsizing of a ferry-boat. His command was severed; most of his cavalry and four pieces of artillery being on the southern side of the river, whilst his infantry and a small portion of his cavalry were on the opposite shore. Tyler had information of this affair, and hoped to strike Floyd before he could reunite his troops. But he was a little too late. He was encamped at Cross Lanes, not far from Summersville, on the night of the 25th of August, and, while at breakfast the next morning,[a] his command was surprised by a force of Virginians sent out stealthily by Floyd, severely handled, and dispersed with the loss of about fifty men.

[a] Aug. 26, 1861.

General Rosecrans, soon after this defeat of Tyler, marched to the aid of Cox against Floyd. He issued a stirring proclamation to the loyal inhabitants of Western Virginia, and promised them ample protection. General Cox, of Ohio, in the mean time, had advanced from Charleston to the site of Gauley bridge, which Wise, in his hasty flight, had burnt; and, at the junction of New River with the Gauley,[1] he had reported to Governor Pierpont, on the 29th of July, that the Kanawha Valley was "free from the Secession troops," and that the inhabitants were denouncing Wise "for his vandalism." He had moved up the Kanawha, by land and water, having under his control a number of steamboats. His whole force proceeded cautiously, for masked batteries were dreaded. His scouting parties were very active. One of these, under Colonel Guthrie, composed of the First Kentucky cavalry, routed a Confederate troop at Cissonville. Others were driven from their camps, and as Cox moved steadily onward, Wise, as we have observed, becoming alarmed,[2] abandoned his strong intrenchments at Charleston, and fled up the river, burning the bridges over the streams in his rear. When approaching the abandoned town, Cox captured a Confederate steamer, and on the 25th of July he entered the village, just after the Confederate rear-guard had left. He found the fine suspension bridge over the Elk River in ruins, and Wise beyond his reach; so he fortified his position there, and, with some of his troops, followed his fugitive foe as far as the confluence of the New and Gauley Rivers, and took position, as we have observed, in the region between them.

JOSEPH J. REYNOLDS.

[1] New River rises among the spurs of the Blue Ridge, in North Carolina, and, uniting with the Gauley, forms the Great Kanawha.

[2] See page 537, volume I.

General Rosecrans had organized a strong column of nearly ten thousand men at Clarksburg, on the Baltimore and Ohio Railway; and early in September he marched southward, with several of his best Western regiments, to attack Floyd, wherever he might be found, leaving the remainder of his force under General Reynolds, who was in command of the Cheat Mountain division, to watch and oppose Lee. He soon ascertained that Floyd was at or near Carnifex Ferry, and he pushed forward in that direction, through Lewis, Braxton, and Nicholas Counties, by way of Weston, Jacksonville, and Braxton Court House, to Summersville. His route lay along some of the wildest of the mountain roads, over the western spurs of the Alleghenies, and among the most charming and picturesque scenery of Western Virginia. Sometimes his troops thridded deep and gloomy ravines, and narrow defiles, and then climbed the steepest hillsides; at times along slippery winding paths, among beetling crags, catching here and there, at some sharp angle, glimpses of distant mountain groups, and fertile valleys covered with corn.[1] Especially rugged was the Gauley mountain range, over which the army climbed, after leaving Suttonsville, on the Elk, and the valley of its tributary, the Big Birch Creek.

ASCENT OF GAULEY MOUNTAIN.

Rosecrans reached the summit of the mountain at noon, on the 9th,[a] when a magnificent panorama of lofty wooded ranges met the eye. On that height, near Muddlethy Bottom, they began to feel the foe. He had an advanced camp in the vicinity, and there picket-firing commenced. Union cavalry dashed forward, and Floyd's vedettes were soon seen scampering toward Summersville, with information of the approach of the National troops. The latter passed through that town with General Benham's brigade in the advance, on the morning of the 10th, a few hours after the Thirty-sixth Virginia had left it and fled to Floyd's intrenchments at the Ferry.

[a] Sept., 1861.

The little army moved cautiously forward from Summersville, properly

[1] The ascent of one of these steep mountain pathways by a portion of the Twelfth Ohio Regiment was described by an eyewitness as presenting a singularly picturesque appearance. This was accomplished a short time before the march of the army now under consideration, when those troops were making their way over the mountains south of the Gauley, to reconnoiter Floyd's position. A part of the ascent was made at night, in the light of torches. The troops were compelled to go in single file, sometimes crawling on their hands and knees, and at midnight they reached the summit. The sketch given in the text is from the pencil of one who accompanied the army.

fearing an ambuscade. The Tenth Ohio, under Colonel Lytle, led the way; and, at about two o'clock in the afternoon, the vanguard came in sight of Floyd's works, a mile distant, beyond a deep wooded valley. These occupied a bald eminence on the north side of the Gauley River, which here swept in a curve, so that each flank of the Confederate intrenchments rested on the stream. Over that eminence, and through these works, passed the road to Carnifex Ferry, a passage of the river just below Meadow Creek, and a battery of twelve guns was so placed upon the hill as to sweep this road back for full a mile, in the face of Rosecrans' approach.

HENRY W. BENHAM.

Placing his entire force in proper order for conflict, the commander ordered Benham to advance with his brigade and make a reconnoissance, in force. That brigade was composed of three Ohio regiments and two batteries.[1] The order was promptly obeyed. The Tenth Ohio still led, and at half-past three o'clock in the afternoon, when Lytle's skirmishers emerged from the woods into an open field of corn, they found themselves near some of the Confederate works. Musket firing immediately commenced, first lightly, but soon it was a perfect storm of lead from the entire Confederate front. The remainder of the regiment was ordered forward to the aid of the skirmishers, and the colors were placed in front, with the intention of attacking the main Confederate battery. This drew upon them the concentrated fire of the foe. The storm was so heavy that the line recoiled and broke, but it was soon rallied, and the batteries of Schneider and McMullen were ordered up to the support of the smitten regiment.

Benham was now satisfied that Floyd's weakest point was on his right wing, and he resolved to attack him there. He ordered the Twelfth and Thirteenth Ohio to advance, pass the deep valley on his left, and under cover of the woods make the attack. While this movement was in progress, Colonel Lytle dashed up the hill with his regiment, to assail the intrenchments in the center. He was so warmly received that he was compelled to direct his men to seek shelter from the storm. He had received a severe wound in his leg, and his horse was fatally shot. He took refuge in a deserted house between the two fires, and lay there until the conflict ceased. His regiment, discouraged at the loss of their Colonel, became somewhat scattered in the woods, but kept up an incessant firing.

Colonel Smith, in the mean time, had opened upon Floyd's right, and Colonel Lowe with the Twelfth Ohio was led by Adjutant-General Hartsuff into the woods, in a position to work his way up under cover and form on

[1] These were the Tenth, under Colonel Lytle, the Twelfth, under Colonel Lowe, and the Thirteenth, under Colonel Smith. A battery of two rifled 6-pounders was commanded by Captain Schneider, and another of four mountain howitzers was in charge of Captain McMullen.

Smith's right, so as to threaten more positively the extreme right flank of the Confederates. Lowe was pushing rapidly forward, when he was instantly killed by a musket-ball that pierced his forehead and entered his brain. Hartsuff hurried McMullen's battery into a position to play effectively on the principal redoubt, whilst Schneider's on the right of the road completely commanded the entire front of the Confederate works. Two of Floyd's guns were soon silenced, and the fire of the others became weaker.

In the mean time Rosecrans was busy on the hill to the right of the road, exposed to the hottest of the fire, in forming Colonel Robert L. McCook's Brigade—the Third, Ninth (his own regiment), and Twenty-eighth Ohio—for co-operation in the movement, with Scammon's Brigade a little in the rear as a reserve. McCook's Regiment was composed mostly of Germans, and these were to lead the column. When they were ready for an advance, Adjutant-General Hartsuff was sent to bring the brigade forward. McCook, who had been restive in inactivity while the battle had been raging for nearly an hour, now glowed with delight. He was acting as brigadier, and was eager for usefulness and renown. He dashed up and down his line like a weaver's shuttle, distinguished from other officers by his citizen's dress and slouched hat. He told his men what was to be done, and what was expected of them, and asked them if they were ready to do it. He was answered by cheers that smothered the roar of battle on the left. Then standing high in his stirrups, and snatching his hat from his head, he waved it in the air, and shouted, "Forward, my bully Dutch! We will go over the intrenchments if every man dies on the other side!" Another volley of cheers broke from the column as it moved forward at the double quick to storm the intrenchments, with the calm Hartsuff at their head. Down into the densely wooded ravine they plunged, and McCook's Ninth and Colonel Mohr's Twenty-eighth Ohio were already feeling the severe storm from the intrenchments, and fighting bravely, when they were suddenly checked by an order from Rosecrans to halt. The General had more minutely examined the plan (which Hartsuff had submitted and begged permission to carry out) for storming the works in front, and perceiving, as he thought, too much peril to his troops involved in it, he countermanded the order when the movement was in mid career, and at the moment when Colonel Smith, with the Thirteenth Ohio, was at the point, apparently, of successfully carrying the works on Floyd's right. The troops were all recalled from the assault, after fighting between three and four hours.

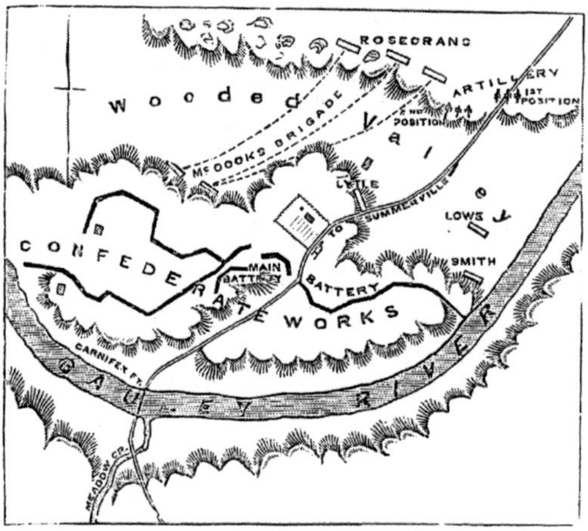

PLAN OF THE BATTLE OF CARNIFEX FERRY.

It was near the end of twilight when this conflict, known as the BATTLE of Carnifex Ferry, ceased. Rosecrans intended to renew it in the morning, and his troops lay on their arms all night, some of them within a hundred yards of the intrenchments. When day dawned,[a] Floyd, who had been wounded in the arm, had fled. Terrified by the fury of the assault on the previous day, he had stolen softly away in the dark, leaving a large amount of ammunition, arms, stores, and equipage behind. He crossed the Gauley over a hastily constructed bridge of logs, which he broke down behind him, destroyed the ferry-boat, and hastened to Dogwood Gap, and thence to a secure spot on the summit of Big Sewell Mountain, near New River, thirty miles distant from the battle-field. After resting there a few days, he pushed on to Meadow Bluff, whilst Wise, who had refused to send him re-enforcements at the Ferry, and now refused to follow him,[1] strengthened the position on Big Sewell Mountain, and called it "Camp Defiance."

[a] Sept. 11, 1861.

The Battle of Carnifex Ferry was regarded as a decided victory for the Nationals, and an excellent test of the quality of the soldiers. These troops, with the exception of the cavalry of Stewart, of Indiana, and Schaumberg, of Chicago, were all from Ohio. They went into the battle after a hard march of seventeen miles, not more than four thousand strong, and fought nearly two thousand men, behind intrenchments,[2] for three or four hours, losing fifteen killed, and seventy wounded. The Confederates reported their loss at one killed and ten wounded.[3]

ROBERT E. LEE.

The expulsion of Floyd from Carnifex Ferry was soon followed by a conflict between the forces of General Reynolds, of the National army, and those of General Lee, of the Confederate army, at important posts among the mountains farther to the northward. Reynolds's troops, forming the first brigade of Rosecrans's Army of Occupation in Western Virginia, consisted of the Thirteenth, Fourteenth, and Fifteenth Indiana Regi-

---

[1] Wise could not reconcile his pride and duty. The former prevailed, and made him insubordinate. He refused to send re-enforcements to Floyd, at Carnifex Ferry, and the latter declared to his superiors at Richmond that the failure to receive them was a capital reason for his inability to hold that position. Wise, at that time, according to Pollard, was endeavoring to win laurels exclusively for himself in another direction; but, as usual, he failed. He was quick to follow Floyd in his retreat before danger; but, as soon as that danger seemed remote, he again became insubordinate, and, as we have observed in the text, remained on the summit of Big Sewell Mountain, and established "Camp Defiance" there. There, on the 18th, he made a speech to his Legion, in which he told them that hitherto he had never retreated, excepting in obedience to superior orders, and that there he was determined to make a stand, notwithstanding his own troops numbered only 1,700, while those of his foe were reported by Floyd to be 15,000. He did not believe this statement; "nevertheless, they must be prepared to fight great odds, front and rear, for successive days."

[2] Pollard, in his *First Year of the War*, page 165, says: "The force of General Floyd's command was 1,740 men. Others put it at a much higher number. It was probably about 2,000."

[3] Report of General Rosecrans to Adjutant-General Townsend, September 11th; of General Benham to General Rosecrans, September 13th; of Colonels Lytle and Smith, and Lieutenant-Colonel White, September 11th, 1861; and of General Floyd, to the Confederate "Secretary of War," September 12th; also army correspondence of the *Cincinnati Gazette* and *Lynchburg* (Va.) *Republican*.

ments, the Third and Sixth Ohio, detachments of the First and Second Virginia, Burdsall's Ohio, and Bracken's Indiana cavalry, and Loomis's Michigan Battery. With these forces he held the roads and passes of the more westerly ranges of the great Allegheny chain, from Webster, on the Baltimore and Ohio Railway, to the head waters of the Gauley, among the spurs of the Greenbrier Mountains. His head-quarters, at the time of Rosecrans's movement from Clarksburg, were at Cheat Mountain Pass (Crouch's), at the western foot of the hills over which goes the highway from Huttonsville to Staunton. There he had the Thirteenth Indiana, Colonel Sullivan, with two pieces of artillery, and a small cavalry force. These were disposed along the approaches to the Pass, to guard against surprise. On the Summit of the Cheat, as we have observed, General McClellan had left Colonel Kimball with the Fourteenth Indiana as an outpost,[1] which that officer had strengthened, and where he now had the aid of about forty cavalrymen.

General Lee's head-quarters, at this time, were at Huntersville, in Pocahontas County. His scouts were active everywhere, and so were those of Reynolds. The adventures of these men during several weeks furnish material for the wildest romances. The opposing parties frequently met, and engaged in sharp conflicts; and scarcely a day passed that the sound of the desultory firing of small-arms was not heard among those solitary hills. Scouting became a most exciting pleasure to many who were engaged in it; but time and circumstances soon brought about more sober work.

It was evident, from the movements of Lee's scouts on the mountains, early in September, that he was contemplating an expedition against some of Reynolds's important posts, for the purpose of capturing his army in detail, or of breaking through and severing his lines of communication, and marching to the Ohio; or, possibly, for the interception of Rosecrans in his march toward the Gauley. He was watched with sleepless vigilance, and on the day after Floyd's retreat from Carnifex Ferry, it was evident that he was moving against the post on the Summit, and another at Elk Water, at the western foot of the mountain, seven miles from the former by a bridle-path over the hills, and eighteen by the road. His object was to secure the great Cheat Mountain Pass, and have free communication with the Shenandoah Valley at Staunton. For this purpose he marched from Huntersville on the night of the 11th of September,[a] with nine thousand men, and nearly a dozen pieces of artillery. He had succeeded, with great difficulty, in placing his troops to make a simultaneous attack upon the Summit, Elk Water, and the Pass. A storm was sweeping over the mountains, and favored the expedition. At midnight the telegraph wires between Kimball, at the Summit, and head-quarters, were cut, and all communication ceased. The last message to the Colonel from General Reynolds was one from Elk Water, warning him of impending danger. It was heeded, and promptly acted upon. The bridle-path between the Summit and Elk Water was immediately picketed, and, on the morning of the 12th, a horseman was sent down the mountain with dispatches for Reynolds. He met some wagons without horses or men. It was a supply-train, that had been moving

[a] 1861.

[1] See page 536, volume I.

up under the escort of the Twenty-fifth Ohio, and had been cut off. He hastened back with the news, when Colonel Kimball, at the head of the Fourteenth Indiana and twelve dragoons, hurrieed to the spot, near which they met the Confederates in force, and drove them. Kimball then detailed one hundred men, under Captain Higgins, to re-enforce Captain Coons, who was closely invested on a ridge near the Pass. They fought their way down, and found Coons stubbornly holding his position, having repelled every assault. In a short time the Confederates in that vicinity, driven at several points by the men of the Thirteenth and Fourteenth Indiana, and Twenty-fourth and Twenty-fifth Ohio, were discomfited and dispersed, and in their flight cast away every thing that might encumber them. So the attempt to reach the rear of the National works on the Summit was foiled, and another portion of the Confederate troops, which appeared on and near the Cheat River, on the front and flank of Kimball's position, were at about this time routed by a few Indiana and Ohio troops, under Captain Foote, of the Fourteenth Indiana. The Confederates engaged in this attempt upon the Summit and the Pass were nearly five thousand in number, and were led in person by General Anderson, of Tennessee.[1] The troops that opposed them did not number more than six hundred.

General Reynolds, who had hastened around to Elk Water, was ignorant of these important movements on the mountain. He arrived there toward evening,[a] and found a large force of Confederates, under General Lee, threatening the position. They were kept at a respectful distance by the Parrot guns of Loomis's battery, and all was silent at the gathering of darkness on the evening of the 12th. Reynolds was satisfied that Kimball had performed all that could be done in defense of his post, yet he was determined to open communication with him. He ordered Colonel Sullivan to take his Thirteenth Indiana, and cut his way, if necessary, by the main road; and Colonels Morrow and Moss were ordered to do the same by the bridle-path. These troops left at three o'clock on the morning of the 13th;[b] the former from the Pass, and the latter from Elk Water. They found their prescribed work already performed. They secured the provision train, and reached the Summit at dawn. At the same time Lee advanced in heavy force upon Elk Water, with the apparent intention of making a direct attack. Reynolds's pickets were driven in, when a 10-pounder Parrot gun of Loomis's battery was pushed about three-fourths of a mile to the front, and did such execution that the Confederates withdrew. In that position both armies remained until night, when Lee withdrew still farther under cover of the darkness, and on the following day took post along the slopes of the Greenbrier Mountains, about ten miles from Elk Water. He attempted a flank movement on the Cheat Summit, on the 15th, but was driven away. The repulse of Anderson on the mountain had satisfied Lee that his grand strategic plan for severing and destroying Reynolds's army, and pushing on to the Ohio, had failed. In the encounters during these two or three days, the Nationals lost ten

[a] Sept. 12, 1861.

[b] Sept.

[1] General Anderson's brigade consisted chiefly of Tennessee and Arkansas troops, with some Virginians. Those employed against the Summit and the Pass were the Twenty-third, Twenty-fifth, Thirty-first, and Thirty-seventh Virginia Regiments, a Virginia battery under Colonels Talliafero and Heck, and the First, Seventh, and Fourteenth Tennessee, under Colonel Manly.

killed, fourteen wounded, and sixty-four prisoners. The Confederate loss was about one hundred killed[1] and wounded, and ninety prisoners.[2]

Lee, having failed in his designs against Reynolds, withdrew from the Cheat Mountain region with a greater part of his force, and joined Floyd at Meadow Bluff, at the close of September.[a] He had left General H. R. Jackson, of Georgia, with about three thousand men, on the Greenbrier River, at the foot of Cheat Mountain, and a small force at Huntersville, to watch Reynolds. He now proceeded to fortify Wise's position on Big Sewell Mountain, which confronted the Nationals on and near the Gauley River and New River, and there, as the senior officer, he concentrated his own forces, and those of Floyd and Wise, and found himself in command of an army of at least twenty thousand men.[3]

[a] Sept. 20, 1861.

Reynolds now resolved to act on the offensive. At the beginning of October he moved with about five thousand men upon Jackson's intrenched camp, on the Greenbrier, near a noted tavern, called "Travelers' Repose," on the Staunton pike. His forces, composed of Indiana, Ohio, Michigan, and Virginia troops, left the summit of Cheat Mountain at a little before midnight,[b] for "an armed reconnoissance," as he termed it. They reached the front of the Confederates, twelve miles distant, at dawn, when the Ninth Indiana, under Colonel Milroy, drove in the advance pickets. Kimball's Fourteenth Indiana took position directly in front, and Loomis's battery was planted within seven hundred yards of the works, where it opened fire. Howe, of the Fourth Regular Artillery, and Daum, also in command of artillery, brought their guns into position at about the same distance. Three of the Confederate cannon were disabled, when heavy re-enforcements for the garrison were reported to be near. The Nationals were eager to storm the works before these should arrive, but the General would not permit it. They were allowed to make a flank movement on the Confederate right, and attempt a dislodgment. The Confederates, perceiving their design, were prepared at that point, and with a terrible storm of grape and canister they repulsed the assailants. Reynolds lost ten killed and thirty-two wounded. Jackson's loss in the picket-firing and in the trenches was estimated at over two hundred. The engagement had lasted about seven hours. Reynolds fell back to Elk Water.

[b] Oct. 2.

[1] Among the killed was Lieutenant-Colonel John A. Washington, of General Lee's staff. He was the former owner of the mansion and mansion-farm of the estate of Mount Vernon, which he sold to the Ladies' Mount Vernon Association a few years before the war broke out. He was out on the evening of the 13th, with two other officers, reconnoitering the works at Elk Water, when he was shot dead by three Minié balls, from a picket post of the Seventeenth Indiana. These penetrated his breast, which was covered by a rich white satin vest. In his pocket was found a complete description of the works at Elk Water. His remains were tenderly cared for, and sent to General Lee the next morning. Washington was about forty years of age.

[2] Report of General J. J. Reynolds to Assistant Adjutant-General George L. Hartsuff, September 17th, 1861; of General Robert E. Lee to L. Pope Walker, September 18th, 1861; *The Cheat Mountain Campaign*, in Stevenson's *Indiana Roll of Honor;* Pollard's *First Year of the War*. Whilst evidently giving Lee full credit for rare abilities as an engineer, Pollard regarded him as incompetent to execute well. He says: "There is reason to believe that, if General Lee had not allowed the immaterial part of his plan to control his action, a glorious success would have resulted, opening the whole northwestern country to us, and enabling Floyd and Wise to drive Cox with ease out of the Kanawha Valley. Regrets, however, were unavailing now. General Lee's plan, finished drawings of which were sent to the War Department at Richmond, was said to have been one of the best-laid plans that ever illustrated the consummation of the rules of strategy, or ever went awry on account of practical failures in its execution."

[3] When Lee arrived at Floyd's camp at Meadow Bluff, he wrote to Wise, advising him to fall back without delay. Wise hesitated, and invited General Lee to visit him, and inspect his position. Lee did so, and, satisfied that it was the most advantageous place of the two, ordered him to remain. This tacit approval of Wise's insubordination offended Floyd; but the concentration of all the forces under Lee prevented any ill consequences.

Lee's position on Big Sewell Mountain was directly in front of that of Rosecrans, who occupied the country in the crotch formed by the Gauley River and New River. His main camp was on New River, and his lines extended down to the Gauley. The breach between Wise and Floyd widened, and, late in September,[a] the former was recalled to Richmond by the Confederate "Secretary of War." Lee held Wise's position on Big Sewell for about three weeks, in sight of Rosecrans, who had been re-enforced;[1] but did not venture to attack him. The latter then fell back, without Lee's knowledge, and concentrated his forces near the junction of the rivers. Lee, too, was then recalled to Richmond,[2] and was soon afterward sent to take charge of the coast defenses of South Carolina and Georgia.[3] Floyd and Rosecrans were once more competitors for the possession of the Kanawha Valley. The former, late in October, took position on the left bank of New River, and erected batteries there a little above its junction with the Gauley, and on the first of November he opened an annoying fire on the National camp. Already very troublesome raids had been made by small parties of Confederates, and on one occasion they had approached within twelve miles of Charleston.

[a] Sept. 24, 1861.

Floyd's batteries now commanded the road over which Rosecrans's supplies had to pass to his camp at the junction, and it was resolved to dislodge or capture him. Troops were thrown across for that purpose. An attempt of General Schenck to cross behind Fayetteville, and strike Floyd's rear, was frustrated by a sudden flood in New River, and the Confederates were struck only in the front, opposite the mouth of the Gauley, by the First Kentucky, under Major Leeper. This was gallantly performed,[b] and Floyd recoiled. General Benham had crossed below the mouth

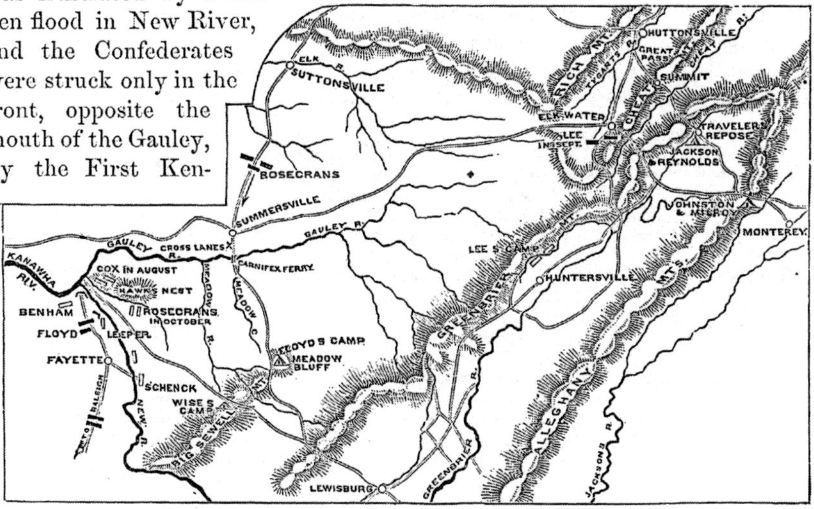

REGION OF MILITARY OPERATIONS IN WESTERN VIRGINIA.

[b] Nov. 12.

[1] His army now numbered about 10,000 men, composed of the brigades of Generals Cox, Benham, and Schenck, the latter having been transferred from the Army of the Potomac.

[2] Lee's campaign in Western Virginia was a failure, and the hopes centered on him were signally disappointed. The Confederate historian of the war, Pollard, commenting on Lee's failure to attack Rosecrans, says (i. 171): "Thus the second opportunity of a decisive battle in Western Virginia was blindly lost, General Lee making no attempt to follow up the enemy, who had so skillfully eluded him; the excuse alleged for his not doing so being mud, swollen streams, and the leanness of his artillery horses."

[3] See Lee's letter of resignation, note 3, page 421, volume I.

of New River, with his brigade. Rosecrans, fearing Floyd would retreat, ordered Benham to push forward at once to Cassidy's Mills, on his flank and rear, to intercept him. This was not accomplished in time, and Floyd fled precipitately, strewing the way with tents, tent-poles, working utensils, and ammunition, in his efforts to lighten his wagons. Benham pressed his rear heavily through Fayetteville, and on the road toward Raleigh; and near the latter place he struck the Confederate rear-guard of four hundred cavalry, under Colonel Croghan,[1] who was mortally wounded.

Onward Floyd sped, with Benham close at his heels; but the pursuit was ended near Raleigh, after a thirty miles' race, by the recall of Benham, and the fugitive escaped to Peterston, full fifty miles southward from his point of departure. He soon afterward took leave of his army, in a stirring proclamation, praising his men for their courage and fidelity, and reminding them that for five months "hard contested battles and skirmishes were matters of almost daily occurrence." General Rosecrans also issued an address to his troops, in which he recapitulated their services, and implored them to prepare for greater deeds in the future.[2] Thus ended the campaign in the Kanawha Valley.[3]

But little more effort was needed to rid Western Virginia of the insurgents. Already General Kelly, who had behaved so gallantly at Philippi in June,[4] had struck them a severe blow on the spot where Colonel Wallace first smote them a few months before.[5] Kelly had recovered from his severe wound, and, with the commission of Brigadier-General, was in command of troops in the autumn, guarding the Baltimore and Ohio Railway along its course through West Virginia. Ascertaining that a considerable insurgent force, consisting of cavalry, under Colonel Angus McDonald, and militia under Colonel Monroe, was at Romney, preparing

---

[1] St. George Croghan was a son of the eminent Colonel George Croghan, who so gallantly defended Fort Stephenson, at lower Sandusky, in the War of 1812. His family were residing in Newburgh, on the Hudson River, at this time.

[2] Rosecrans said: "When our gallant young commander was called from us, after the disaster of Bull's Run, this department was left with less than 15,000 men to guard 300 miles of railroad, and 300 miles of frontier, exposed to bushwhackers, and the forces of Generals Floyd, Wise, and Jackson. The northwestern pass into it was fortified and held, Cheat Mountain secured, the rebel assaults there victoriously repelled, and the Kanawha Valley occupied. A march of 112 miles, over bad roads, brought you upon Floyd's intrenched position, whence the rebels were dislodged and chased to Sewell. Finally, your patience and watchings put the traitor Floyd within your reach, and though, by a precipitate retreat, he escaped your grasp, you have the substantial fruits of victory. Western Virginia belongs to herself, and the invader is expelled from her soil. In the name of our Commander-in-Chief, and in my own, I thank you."

[3] On the 10th of November, a most unhappy event occurred in the extreme southwestern portion of Virginia. The village of Guyandotte, on the Ohio River, near the Kentucky line, was held by a small Union force under R. V. Whaley, a loyal Virginian, commanding the Ninth Virginia Regiment, who had a recruiting station there. At eight o'clock in the evening, a guerrilla chief, named Albert G. Jenkins, who, with his mounted men, had been for some time carrying on a distressing warfare in that region, dashed into the little village, surprised the Union force, and made over 100 of them prisoners. They killed every man who resisted. With prisoners and plunder, Jenkins fled the next morning. It was reported that the Secessionists in the village had entrapped many of the Union soldiers in the coils of social enjoyments, and then gave Jenkins notice that he could easily win a prize. This so exasperated Colonel John J. Zeigler, a loyal citizen of Wayne County, who was in command of the Fifth Virginia, and who entered the town the next morning, that he ordered the houses of the disloyalists to be burned. Almost the whole village was laid in ashes. Jenkins had represented his section of Virginia in Congress.

The guerrilla bands who infested portions of Virginia during the whole war, were composed of the disloyal citizens of that State. Some of them gave themselves names significant of their character and intentions. A portion of one of these bands, composed of residents of Flat Top Mountain, in Mercer County, were captured near Raleigh, in Western Virginia, by Colonel (afterward General) Rutherford B. Hays, of Ohio, and he found by papers in their possession, that their organization was known as "The Flat Top Copperheads," their avowed object being the destruction of the lives and property of Union men.

[4] See page 496, volume I. [5] See page 518, volume I.

for a descent on the railway, he led about twenty-five hundred Ohio and Virginia troops against them, from the New Creek Station, along the route first traversed by Wallace. He came upon the insurgents a few miles from Romney, at three o'clock in the afternoon of the 26th of October, drove in their outposts, and, after a severe contest of about two hours, completely routed them, capturing their three cannon, much of their camp equipage, a large number of prisoners, besides killing and wounding between thirty and forty in the fray. This victory paralyzed the rebellion in that region for a time. It was followed by a proclamation from General Kelly, assuring the inhabitants that full protection should be given to those who were peaceable, at the same time telling them that, if they joined in guerrilla warfare, they should be treated as enemies. He required all who had taken up arms against the Government to lay them down immediately, and take an oath of allegiance to the National Government. For a while that region of the State enjoyed repose.

Soon after Reynolds's attack on Jackson, at "Travelers' Rest," a large portion of the Cheat Mountain troops were sent to Kentucky, and Colonel Robert H. Milroy, who had been commissioned a Brigadier-General,[a] was kept with a single brigade to hold the mountain passes. Reynolds was ordered to report in person to General Rosecrans, who at the close of the Kanawha campaign had retired to Wheeling, and, in December, Milroy succeeded to the command of the Cheat Mountain division of the army. Milroy had at first established his head-quarters on Cheat Summit, and vigorously scouted the hills in that region, making the beautiful little Greenbrier Valley lively with frequent skirmishing. Jackson had withdrawn from Camp Bartow at "Travelers' Rest," and, being ordered to Georgia, had left his command of twelve hundred Confederates and about eight hundred Virginians with Colonel Edward Johnston of Georgia, to confront Milroy. He made his head-quarters at Allegheny Summit; and Milroy, when he took chief command, established his at Huttonsville, in Tygart's Valley.

[a] Sept. 3, 1861.

ROBERT H. MILROY.

Milroy determined to attack Johnston, and for that purpose moved a little over three thousand men on the 12th of December. He directed Colonel Moody of the Ninth Indiana to lead his regiment, with a detachment of the Second Virginia, around to make a flank movement, and charge and capture a battery on a bluff commanding the Staunton pike. At the same time the Twenty-fifth Ohio, Colonel Jones, with detachments of the Thirteenth Indiana, and Thirty-second Ohio, was to assault Johnston's front. This was done, but Colonel Moody did not arrive in time to co-operate with Jones. The fight was continued, but Jones was not successful. The Confederates became the aggressors, and they in turn were discomfited. Milroy had lost about one hundred and fifty men when Moody commenced his flank attack. This, too, was unsuccessful, and the whole force retired in good order, unpursued by the Confederates. The losses on both sides appear to have been about equal, and amounted to very nearly two hundred men each. Both parties had fought with the most commendable valor.

Milroy was not discouraged by his failure on the Allegheny Summit. Late in December he sent a force to break up a Confederate post at Huntersville, and capture or destroy military stores there. The main expedition consisted of a battalion of the Twenty-fifth Ohio, and a detachment of the Second Virginia, with Bracken's cavalry, and was commanded by Major Webster, of the first-named regiment. Other troops were sent to co-operate with these. The expedition was successful. After a weary march of about fifty miles, the ground covered with snow, the post was attacked, the Confederates were dispersed, a large amount of stores were burned, and the jail, which was used for the confinement of Union prisoners, was partially destroyed. This event closed the campaign of 1861 in Western Virginia, and armed rebellion in that region was effectually crushed.

Whilst the scenes we have just recorded were transpiring in the Middle Mississippi Valley, and in West Virginia, others even more remarkable, and quite as important in their relations to the great contest, were occurring on the sea-coast. Let us see what official records and narratives of eye-witnesses reveal to us on this subject.

In a previous chapter,[1] we have considered some stirring events at and near Fortress Monroe, in Southeastern Virginia. In Hampton Roads, in front of that fortress, a great land and naval armament was seen in August, 1861, destined to strike a severe blow at the rebellion farther down the coast. It had been collected there while the smoke of the once pleasant village of Hampton, near, was yet making the air of Old Point Comfort murky with its density. Let us see how that village, whose ruins have already been depicted in this work,[2] came to destruction.

We have observed that, after the disastrous *Battle of Bull's Run*, General Butler, in command at Fortress Monroe, was compelled to reduce the garrison at Newport-Newce, and to abandon the village of Hampton, the latter movement causing a general exodus of the colored people living there,[a] who flocked into the Union lines. The whole country between Old Point Comfort and Yorktown was now left open to Confederate rule; and General Magruder, commanding at the latter post, moved down the peninsula with about five thousand men, infantry, cavalry, and artillery, to menace Newport-Newce, and take position at or near Hampton, for the close investment of Fortress Monroe. A deserter[3] had swum across Hampton Creek, and given General Butler such timely notice of the movement that preparations were made at both posts for Magruder's warm reception.

[a] July 26, 1861.

Camp Hamilton, commanded by Colonel Max Weber, was soon alive with preparations for battle, and a force stationed at the redoubt at Hamp-

[1] Chapter XXI., volume I.

[2] See pages 511, 512, and 514, volume I.

[3] Mr. Mahew, of the State of Maine. He was in Georgia when the war broke out, and had been pressed into the Confederate service.

ton Bridge[1] were ordered to oppose the passage of the foe at all hazards. These were attacked late in the evening, and repulsed,[a] and soon afterward the town was set on fire in several places. This was done, as it afterward appeared, by order of General Magruder, whose judgment and feelings were at that time in subjection to his passions, excited by the too free use of intoxicating drinks. It was at about midnight when the town was fired, and before dawn it was almost entirely in ashes, with a greater portion of the bridge. The Confederates ran wildly about the village with blazing firebrands, spreading destruction in all directions. Even the venerable parish church, built in colonial times, and standing out of danger from the conflagration of the village, was not spared; it having been fired, according to testimony subsequently given, by the special order of the drunken Magruder.[2] The cruelty of this destruction was at first charged upon the Union troops, but the truth was soon known, and the odium fixed where it belonged. Magruder contented himself with this performance, and withdrew his forces to Big Bethel and Yorktown.

a Aug. 7, 1861.

BURNING OF HAMPTON.

It was at about this time that General Butler was relieved of his command at Fortress Monroe, and Major-General John E. Wool was put in his place. Butler was not assigned to any other duty; but he was not long idle. The generous and sagacious Wool gave him the command of all the volunteer troops outside of the fortress. This service was a temporary one. Weeks before, a Union prisoner (Daniel Campbell, of Maine), who had escaped from Hatteras Inlet, brought information to Commodore Stringham, commanding in Hampton Roads, that through that pass English blockade-runners were continually carrying in supplies of

SILAS H. STRINGHAM.

[1] See page 514, volume I.

[2] The troops employed for the purpose were all Virginians, under the respective commands of Captains Goode, Phillips, Sullivan, and Curtis; the whole under the control of Colonel J. J. Hodges. Many of these troops were citizens of Hampton, and set fire to their own property, to prevent, as they said, its "being occupied by Northern Vandals."

arms, ammunition, and clothing for the Confederates, and that two forts guarded the Inlet. Stringham informed General Butler of these facts, and the latter sent the report to Washington, with suggestions that land and naval forces should be sent to capture the forts at the Inlet, and close up the passage. The suggestion was acted upon, and, at the time we are considering, a small squadron of vessels was in Hampton Roads for the purpose, on which were to be borne nine hundred land troops. Butler volunteered to command these troops. His offer was accepted, and on Monday, the 26th of August,[a] at one o'clock P. M., the expedition departed, the squadron being under the command of Commodore Silas H. Stringham.[1] General Butler took passage in the flag-ship (the *Minnesota*), and his troops were on the transports *George Peabody* and *Adelaide*.[2] The frigate *Cumberland* was ordered to join the squadron. The expedition rendezvoused off the Hatteras inlet to Pamlico Sound (at the western end of Hatteras Island, and about eighteen miles from the Cape) at five o'clock on Tuesday afternoon,[b] when preparations were immediately made for landing the troops in the morning, twelve hours later.

[a] 1861.

[b] Aug. 27.

Two forts, named respectively Hatteras and Clark, occupied the western end of Hatteras Island. The troops were to be landed a short distance up the beach, to attack them in the rear, while the vessels should assail them in front. The *Pawnee*, *Monticello*, and *Harriet Lane* were to be sent forward to cover the landing of the forces, and take position, at first, about two miles from the forts. These movements began at the appointed hour.[c] Breakfast was served at four o'clock. The *Cumberland* (sailing vessel) was there, and was taken in tow by the *Wabash*. Dragging her charge to a proper position, the *Wabash* opened fire on the forts at a quarter to ten o'clock, and the *Cumberland* joined in the work. The flag-ship (*Minnesota*) was near, and soon passed inside the other two and engaged in the fight. The *Susquehanna*, which had joined the expedition, came up at eleven o'clock, and at once opened fire. In the mean time a few of the troops had landed near a wreck, about two miles up the beach, under the direction of General Butler, who, with the marines, had gone on board the *Harriet Lane*. A heavy surf made the landing very difficult, and it was effected by only a little over three hundred men, who were completely covered by the guns of the *Monticello* and *Harriet Lane*.

[c] Aug. 28.

The assault on the Confederate works had continued for more than four hours, when the firing ceased on both sides. The flags of the forts were down, and the men from the smaller work had fled to the greater, which was Fort Hatteras. Some of the Coast Guard, under Mr. Weigel, of Colonel Weber's command, who had landed, took possession of the former, and raised the Union flag over it; and it was believed that both works were about to

---

[1] The vessels composing the squadron were the *Minnesota*, Captain G. A. Van Brune; *Wabash*, Captain Samuel Mercer; *Monticello*, Commander John P. Gillis; *Pawnee*, Commander S. C. Rowan; *Harriet Lane*, Captain John Faunce; chartered steamer *Adelaide*, Commander H. S. Stellwagen; *George Peabody*, Lieutenant R. P. Lowry; and tug *Fanny*, Lieutenant Pierce Crosby. The *Minnesota* was the flag-ship. The transport, *Service*, was in charge of Commander Stellwagen, who had made the preparations.

[2] These troops consisted of 500 of the Twentieth New York, Colonel Weber; 220 of the Ninth New York, Colonel Hawkins; 100 of the Union Coast Guard, Captain Nixon; and 60 of the Second United States Artillery, Lieutenant Larned.

be surrendered. The *Monticello* was ordered to go cautiously into the Inlet, followed by the *Harriet Lane*, and take possession of them; but it had proceeded only a short distance, when fire was opened upon it from Fort Hatteras, and at the same time a tug-steamer was seen approaching, having in tow a schooner filled with troops, for the relief of the fort. The *Minnesota*, *Susquehanna*, and *Pawnee* immediately reopened fire on the fort, and the attack

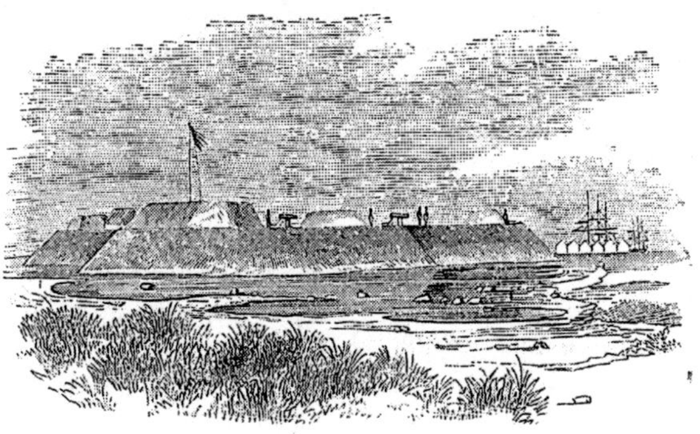

FORT HATTERAS.[1]

was kept up until half-past six, when the whole squadron, excepting the *Pawnee* and the *Harriet Lane*, hauled off for the night. The *Monticello* was much exposed during the fight, and, at one time, her capture or destruction seemed inevitable; but she was finally taken out of range of the heavy guns of the fort, without much damage.

Early on the morning of the 29th the contest was renewed. During the preceding evening, Major W. S. G. Andrews, the commander of the two forts (who had been absent on the main), accompanied by Samuel Barron, who was in command of a little Confederate navy in charge of the defenses of Virginia and North Carolina, and then lying in Pamlico Sound, not far from the Inlet, arrived at Fort Hatteras. They found Colonel Martin, who had conducted the defense during the day, completely prostrated by fatigue, and it was agreed that Barron should assume the chief command of the fort, which he did. Guns were speedily brought to bear on Fort Clark, then supposed to be held by the Nationals, and the batteries were placed in charge of fresh troops. But Fort Clark was not held by Butler's troops. They were well and cautiously handled by their commander, Colonel Weber, and had been withdrawn toward the landing-place. Not far from the fort they had placed in battery during the night two howitzers and a rifled 6-pounder cannon, landed from the fleet. These were very serviceable in the hands of Lieutenant Johnson, of the Coast Guard, who, early in the morning, beat off the Confederate steamer *Winslow*, commanded by Arthur Sinclair (who had abandoned his country's flag), which was filled with re-enforcements

---

[1] Fort Hatteras was the principal work, and mounted ten guns. Fort Clark was a square redoubt, about 750 yards northward of it, and mounting seven guns. The former occupied a point on a sandy beach, and was almost surrounded by water. It could only be approached on the land side by a march of 500 yards circuitously over a long neck of land, within half musket-shot of its embankments, and over a narrow causeway, only a few feet in width, which was commanded by two 32-pounder guns loaded with grape and canister shot. The parapet was nearly octagon in form, and inclosed about three-fourths of an acre of ground, with several sufficient traverses.

Mr. Fiske, acting aid-de-camp of General Butler, performed a gallant feat. When Fort Clark was abandoned, he swam ashore, through quite heavy breakers, with orders from Butler to Colonel Weber. He entered the fort, and found books and papers there containing much valuable information. He formed them into a package, strapped them on his shoulders, and swam back with them to the general. After the capitulation, the Confederate officers expressed their surprise at the accuracy of Butler's information on the previous day, being ignorant that their own documents had furnished it.

for the garrison. The *Harriet Lane*, in the mean time, had run in shore to assist the land forces who had moved up to Johnson's battery.

The *Susquehanna* was the first of the squadron to open fire on the fort on the second day. The *Wabash* and *Minnesota* followed, and a little later the *Cumberland* sailed in and took part in the fight. The *Harriet Lane* also came up and became a participant. The pounding of the fort was too severe to be borne long, and Barron attempted the trick of hauling down his flag, and assuming the attitude of the vanquished; but the Nationals were not deceived a second time. At almost eleven o'clock a white flag appeared over the fort, and the firing ceased. The tug *Fanny*, with General Butler on board, moved into the Inlet to take possession of the works. The Confederate vessels in the Sound, with troops on board, fled at her approach. The *Harriet Lane* and the transport *Adelaide* followed the *Fanny* in, and both grounded,[1] but they were finally hauled off. The forts were formally surrendered, under a capitulation signed by the respective commanders.[2] "No one of the fleet or army was in the least degree injured," said Butler, in his report to General Wool. He added, that the loss of the Confederates was "twelve or fifteen killed and thirty-five wounded."[3]

The capture of the forts at Hatteras Inlet was a severe blow to the Confederates, and opened the way to most important results, beneficial to the National cause, as we shall observe hereafter.[4] General Butler had been ordered to destroy the forts, and not attempt to hold them. He was so impressed with the importance of preserving them, that, after consultation with Stringham and Stellwagen, he returned immediately to Fortress Monroe, and hastened to Washington with the first news of the victory, to explain his views to the Government in person. It was determined to hold them, and the troops, which had only been provisioned for five days, were immediately supplied. Butler was now commissioned by the Secretary of War[a] to go to New England and "raise, arm, uniform, and equip a volunteer force for the war." He did so. What was done with them will be revealed when we come to consider events at Ship Island, in the Gulf of Mexico, and at New Orleans.

[a] September, 1861.

Colonel Hawkins was left, with the portion of his Ninth New York (Zouaves) that had joined the expedition, to garrison the post at Hatteras

---

[1] This was an anxious moment for the Unionists, for, by these accidents, a valuable ship of war and a transport filled with troops were under the guns of the fort, and within the power of the Confederates.

[2] The capitulation was signed on board the flag ship *Minnesota*, August 29th, 1861, by "S. H. Stringham, Flag Officer Atlantic Blockading Squadron," and "Benjamin F. Butler, Major-General U. S. Army, commanding," on one part, and "S. Barron, Flag Officer C. S. Navy, commanding naval forces, Virginia and North Carolina," "William F. Martin, Colonel Seventh Light Infantry, N. C. Volunteers," and "W. S. G. Andrews, Major, commanding Forts Hatteras and Clark." It was agreed that commanders, men, forts, and munitions of war should be immediately surrendered to the Government of the United States, in terms of full capitulation, "the officers and men to receive the treatment of prisoners of war." Barron had proposed that the officers and men should "retire" (in other words, not be detained as prisoners), the former to go out with their side-arms. The proposition was rejected. The prisoners were taken to New York, and afterward exchanged.

[3] Reports of General Butler, August 30th, and of Commodore Stringham, August 30th and September 1st, 1861, and other subordinate officers; also of "Commodore" Barron and Major Andrews, of the Confederate service, September 1st, 1861. The number of troops surrendered, including the officers, was 715, and with them 1,000 stand of arms, 5 stand of colors, 31 pieces of cannon, vessels with cotton and stores, and 75 kegs of gunpowder. One of the flags was new, and had been presented, within a week, by the women of New Berne, North Carolina, to the "North Carolina Defenders."—General Wool's *General Order*, No. 8, August 31st, 1861.

[4] General Wool issued a stirring order, announcing the victory, and Secretary Welles congratulated Stringham and his men for the "brilliant achievement accomplished without the loss of a man on the Union side."

and hold the Island and Inlet. Late in September he was re-enforced by Colonel Brown and his Twentieth Indiana regiment. In the mean time an expedition had been secretly prepared for following up the victory at Hatteras, by seizing and holding the whole coast of North Carolina washed by the waters of Pamlico and Albemarle Sounds, and threatening Norfolk, still held by the Confederates, in the rear.[1]

The first object was to close the passages to these Sounds from the sea. Accordingly, a little naval force was sent[a] to break up a Confederate post at Ocracoke Inlet, a few miles down the coast from Hatteras. Commodore Rowan sent Lieutenant J. T. Maxwell to perform this service. He went in the tug *Fanny*, with a detachment of mariners and soldiers of the Naval Brigade which had been organized in Hampton Roads. The tug towed a launch, and the *Susquehanna* accompanied them. An earthwork, little inferior to Fort Hatteras, was found on Beacon Island, commanding the Inlet; but this, called Fort Ocracoke, and older Fort Morgan near, were abandoned. They were disabled by Maxwell.

[a] Sept. 17, 1861.

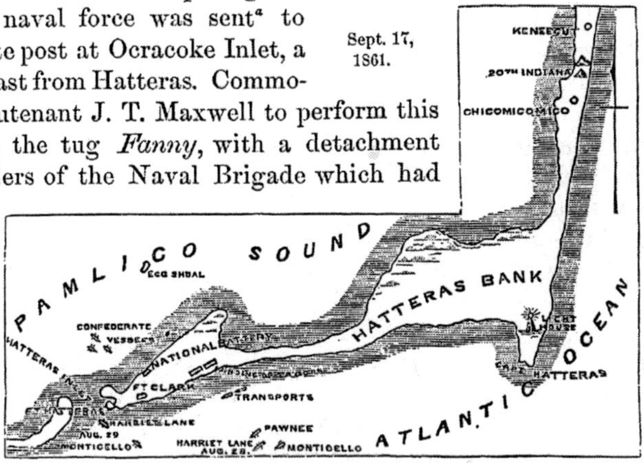

OPERATIONS NEAR CAPE HATTERAS.

In the meantime the Confederates were evidently preparing to throw a force on to Roanoke Island, to the northward of Hatteras, with the intention of recovering their losses at the Inlet, and keeping open two small inlets to Pamlico, above Cape Hatteras. Hawkins sent Colonel Brown,[b] with his Twentieth Indiana, up the island to a hamlet called Chicomicocomico, partly to defend the professedly loyal inhabitants there, but more particularly to watch the Confederates, and, if possible, prevent their gaining possession of Roanoke. The regiment was landed in small boats,[c] with very scant supplies. The *Fanny* was sent with stores,[d] but was captured by the Confederates, who thus obtained property of the value of one hundred and fifty thousand dollars. The most important loss was the camp equipage, provisions, and intrenching tools of Brown's regiment. It defeated his undertaking; for when, on the 4th of October, a squadron of five or six Confederate steamers, bearing over two thousand men, composed of North Carolinians and Georgians, who had taken possession of Roanoke Island, bore down from Croatan Sound, with the evident intention of attacking him, he was compelled to retreat. Troops were landed from the steamers at Kenéekut and Chicomicocomico, above and below Brown's Camp, under cover of shells thrown from the armed vessels. The Indianians succeeded in escaping to Cape Hatteras, where they were met by five hundred of Hawkins's Zouaves, supported by the *Susquehanna* and *Monticello*. They had lost about fifty men, most of whom were cap-

[b] Sept. 29.
[c] Sept. 30.
[d] Oct. 1.

[1] See page 397, volume I.

tured while straggling.[1] A number of the islanders had followed them; and all had suffered much from hunger, thirst, and fatigue, during that exciting march of twenty-eight miles. The Confederate vessels were a part of the little fleet in that region, under the command of Lieutenant Lynch, who had lately abandoned his flag and joined the insurgents. The assailants fled back to Roanoke, and after that left Hatteras in the undisputed possession of the National forces. General Mansfield was sent from Washington with five hundred troops, to still further strengthen the position. He was soon relieved by Brigadier-General Thomas S. Williams, of the Regular Army.

While these events were transpiring, Colonel Hawkins, in pursuance of the humane and conciliatory policy of the Government toward misguided and misinformed inhabitants, issued a proclamation to the people of North Carolina, in which he exposed the misrepresentations of the intentions of the Government put forth by the conspirators and their allies, assuring them that the war was waged only against traitors and rebels (who were called to lay down their arms and have peace), and that the troops had come to give back to the people law, order, and the Constitution, and all their legitimate rights. To this there was a public response by the inhabitants in the immediate vicinity of Hatteras, who professed to be loyal. A convention of the citizens of Hyde County was held,[a] which, by resolutions, offered the loyalty of its members to the National Government. A committee was appointed to draw up a statement of grievances, and a declaration of independence of Confederate rule was put forth, in form and style like that issued in 1776.[2] A more important convention was held at Hatteras a month later,[b] in which appeared representatives from forty-five counties in North Carolina. That body assumed the prerogatives of the State, and by a strong ordinance provided for the government of North Carolina in allegiance to the National Constitution. This promise of good was so hopeful that the President, by proclamation, ordered an election to be held in the First Congressional District of North Carolina. The people complied, and elected a representative[c] (Charles Henry Foster), but he was not admitted to Congress,[3] because of some technical objection. This leaven of loyalty, that promised to affect the whole State, was soon destroyed by the strong arm of the Confederates in power.

[a] Oct. 12, 1861.

[b] Nov. 18.

[c] Nov. 27.

---

[1] The Indiana Regiment was peculiarly unfortunate at Hatteras. In the affair near Chicomicocomico, it had lost its stock of winter clothing. This disaster was followed by a fearful storm on the night of the 2d of November, which swept along the coast, and bringing the sea in with such violence that it submerged Hatteras Island between the forts, threatening instant destruction to Fort Clark, the smaller one, occupied by the regiment. Its sick were much distressed by removal for safety; and nearly one-half of its new supply of winter clothing was swept away.

[2] This Declaration bore the signatures of Rev. Marble Nash Taylor, of the North Carolina Methodist Conference, Caleb B. Stowe, and William O'Neal.

[3] This movement was brought prominently before the citizens of New York by Mr. Taylor, one of the signers of the Declaration of Independence, at a meeting over which Mr. Bancroft, the historian, presided, in which he said that "some 4,000 of the inhabitants living on the narrow strip of land on the coast had, on the first arrival of the troops, flocked to take the oath of allegiance, and this had cut them off from their scanty resources of traffic with the interior. They were a poor race," he said, "living principally by fishing and gathering of yoakum, an evergreen of spontaneous growth, which they dried and exchanged for corn." The yoakum is a plant which is extensively used in that region as a substitute for tea.

The appeal of Mr. Taylor in behalf of these people was nobly responded to by generous gifts of money, food, and clothing.

Whilst the stirring events just mentioned were occurring on the coast of North Carolina, the vicinity of Fort Pickens, on the waters of the Gulf of Mexico, had again become the theater of conflict. We have observed how that fortress was saved from seizure by the insurgents at Pensacola in the spring of 1861, and the arrival in June, at Santa Rosa Island (on which the fort stands), of the New York Sixth, known as Wilson's Zouaves.[1] These troops and a small blockading squadron, with a garrison in the fort, were stationed there for the purpose of securing from capture by the Confederates that fortress, whose possession was so much coveted by them. Although no serious hostilities occurred between these forces and the insurgents on the main, who threatened them, the former were not inert, but dispelled the uneasiness of camp and deck life by an occasional disturbance of the quiet of their foe, sometimes by threatening a descent on the coast, and at others by firing on some supply-vessel of the Confederates, moving in Pensacola Bay. On the night of the 2d of September,[a] a party from Fort Pickens, under Lieutenant Shepley, burned the Dry Dock at the Navy Yard at Warrington; and, on the night of the 13th of the same month, about one hundred men, under Lieutenant John H. Russell, of Commodore Merwin's flagship *Colorado*, crossed over to the Navy Yard, and before daylight boarded a large schooner (the *Judah*), which was being fitted out as a privateer, and lying at the wharf there. They spiked a ten-inch columbiad, with which she was armed, and burnt her to the water's edge. By the use of muffled oars they eluded the vigilance of the sentinels until it was too late for useful resistance.[2] This was a most daring feat, for at the Navy Yard near by there were at least a thousand Confederate soldiers. "They were led by an officer with the courage of forty Numidian lions, and their success was perfect," said an account of the affair written by an officer at the Navy Yard.

[a] 1861.

The Confederates soon became the aggressors. Early in October, they made an attempt to surprise and capture Wilson's troops on Santa Rosa Island. About fourteen hundred picked men, chosen mostly from Georgia troops and from some Irish volunteers, and commanded by General Anderson, assisted by General Ruggles, crossed Pensacola Bay in the evening on several steamers, and at two o'clock in the morning[b] landed at Deer Point, on Santa Rosa Island, four or five miles eastward of the encampment of the Zouaves. Anderson divided his force into three columns, and in this order marched upon the camp, wherein there was no suspicion of danger near. The pickets were suddenly driven in, and the Zouaves were completely surprised.

[b] October 9.

The Confederate war-cry was, "Death to Wilson! no quarter!"[3] The Zouaves fought desperately in the intense darkness, while being driven back by superior numbers to the cover of batteries Lincoln and Totten, situated

---

[1] See chapter XV., volume I.

[2] Lieutenant Russell lost three men killed and twelve wounded. The planning and fitting out of the expedition was intrusted to Captain Bailey, of the *Colorado*. Lieutenant Russell was promoted to Commander on the 4th of October.

[3] Common report had given to Wilson's men the character of being mostly New York "roughs," and the people of the South were taught to believe that they were selected for the purpose of plunder and rapine. It was on that account that the troops at Pensacola hated them, and resolved to give them no quarter. Wilson, in a characteristic letter to General Arthur, of New York, reporting the affair, says, alluding to wild rumors on

one on each side of the island, and about four hundred yards from Fort Pickens. They numbered only one hundred and thirty-three effective men. They were met in their retreat by two companies, under Major Vogdes, sent out of the fort by Colonel Harvey Brown, its commander, to aid them. Two other companies, under Major Arnold, immediately followed, and the combined force returned and charged upon the Confederates. The latter had already plundered and burnt the camp,[1] and were in a disorganized state. In this condition they were driven in great confusion to their vessels, terribly galled by the weapons of their pursuers. As the vessels moved off with the retreating assailants, several volleys of musketry were poured upon them, and one of the launches, loaded with men, was so riddled by bullets that it sank. In this affair the Nationals lost, in killed, wounded, and prisoners, sixty-four men. Among the latter was Major Vogdes. The Confederates lost about one hundred and fifty,[2] including those who were drowned. Such was the confusion in which they fled to their boats, that, according to the statement of one of their officers, they shot down their own friends in numbers. "Night skirmishing is a dangerous business," he said, "especially in an unknown country, as was the Island of Santa Rosa." So ended THE BATTLE OF SANTA ROSA ISLAND.

Fort Pickens had been silent during the entire summer and autumn of 1861, until late in November, when its thunders were heard for miles along the coast, mingling with those of some vessels of war there, in a combined attack upon the forts and batteries of the Confederates on the main. The garrison at Fort Pickens then numbered about thirteen hundred men, under Colonel Brown. The number of the Confederates, whose works stretched along the shore, from the Navy Yard to Fort McRee, in a curve for about four miles, was about seven thousand, commanded, as in the spring,[3] by General Braxton Bragg. His defenses consisted of Forts McRee and Barrancas, and fourteen separate batteries, mounting from one to four guns each, many of which were ten-inch columbiads, and several thirteen-inch sea-coast mortars.

Having determined to attack Bragg's works, Colonel Brown invited flag-officer McKean, who was in command of the little blockading squadron there (composed of the *Niagara*, *Richmond*, and *Montgomery*), to join him. McKean prepared to do so, and at a little before ten o'clock, on the morning of the 22d of November,[c] the heavy guns of Fort Pickens opened upon some transports at the Navy Yard. This was the signal for McKean to act. The *Niagara* was run in as near Fort McRee as the depth of water would allow, accompanied by the *Richmond*, Captain Ellison. The latter became instantly engaged in a hot contest with the fort and the water

c 1861.

---

the main after the fight, "They are exhibiting my head and hair in Pensacola—the reward is already claimed; also an old flag which I nailed to a flagstaff on the 4th of July, which has been hanging there ever since: nothing left, however, but the stars. The leaders have cut it up in pieces, and have pinned it on their bosoms as a trophy. Every one in Pensacola has my sword and uniform. I must have a large quantity of hair, and plenty of swords and uniforms. They say if I was to be taken alive, I was to be put in a cage and exhibited."

[1] This camp was on the sea-side of the island, a short mile from Fort Pickens. The tents were arranged in parallel lines, forming pleasant avenues, and each was sheltered by a canopy of boughs and shrubs, to protect it from the hot sun. Santa Rosa Island is a long and narrow sand-bank, with an average width of about half a mile.

[2] Report of Colonel Harvey Brown to Adjutant-General E. D. Townsend, October 11th, 1861; also of Colonel Wm. Wilson to General Arthur, October 14th, 1861; Correspondents of the Atlantic *Intelligencer* and Augusta *Constitutionalist*. See map of Pensacola Bay and vicinity, on page 368, volume I.

[3] See page 371, volume I.

battery, and was soon joined in the fight by the *Niagara.* The guns of Fort Pickens were also brought to bear upon Fort McRee; and at noon the artillery of the former and of Battery Scott, and also of the two vessels, were playing upon the devoted fortress and the surrounding batteries. The guns of McRee were all speedily silenced but one. Those of Barrancas were soon reduced to feeble efforts; and from those at the Navy Yard, and one or two other batteries, there was no response for some time before the close of the day.

The bombardment from Fort Pickens was resumed early the next morning,[a] but, owing to the shallowness of the water, the vessels could not get within range of Fort McRee. The fire of Pickens was less rapid, but more effective than the day before. McRee made no response, and the other forts and the batteries answered feebly. At three o'clock in the afternoon, a dense smoke arose from the village of Warrington, on the west of the Navy Yard, and at about the same time buildings in Wolcott, at the north of the yard, were in flames. These villages were fired by the missiles from the fort, and large portions of them, as well as of the Navy Yard, were laid in ashes. The bombardment was kept up until two o'clock the next morning, when it ceased.[1]

[a] Nov. 23, 1861.

After this bombardment of two days, there was quiet on Pensacola Bay until the first day of the year,[b] when another artillery duel occurred, lasting nearly twelve hours, but doing very little damage to either party.

[b] January 1, 1862.

Looking farther westward, along the Gulf of Mexico, we observe little sparks of war threatening a conflagration at several points, at about the time when the events we have just considered were occurring on the shores of Pensacola Bay. One of the most notable of these minor hostilities was exhibited at the mouth of the Mississippi River, on the 12th of October, and was first announced by Captain Hollins, an old officer of the National navy, whose merits were much below his pretensions, as the Confederates, to whom he offered his services when he abandoned his flag, in May, 1861, soon learned to their cost. Hollins startled the public with a telegraphic dispatch to his employers at Richmond, boasting of a successful attack on the National blockading fleet at the Southwest Pass of the Mississippi. He claimed to have driven all the vessels aground on the bar there, sinking one of them and "peppering well" the others.[2] The official account of this affair showed the following facts:

J. S. Hollins was placed in command of a peculiarly shaped iron-clad vessel called a "ram," and named *Manassas.* At about four o'clock in the morning[c] this ram was seen approaching the little blockading squadron, consisting of the war steamer *Richmond*, sloops-of-war *Vincennes* and *Preble*, and steam-tender *Water-Witch*, all under the

[c] October 12, 1861.

---

[1] Report of Colonel Brown, November 24th, 1861; also of Commodore McKean to Secretary Welles, November 25th, 1861; report of General Bragg to Samuel Cooper, November 27th, 1861.

[2] The following is a copy of the dispatch, dated at Fort Jackson, below New Orleans, October 12th, 1861: "Last night I attacked the blockaders with my little fleet. I succeeded, after a very short struggle, in driving them *all* aground on the Southwest Pass bar, except the *Preble, which I sunk.*

"I captured a prize from them, and after they were fast in sand I peppered them well. There were no casualties on our side. It was a complete success.—Hollins."

command of Captain John Pope.[1] The *Manassas* was close to the *Richmond* before she was discovered, and by the time the watch could give the alarm, her iron prow had struck the vessel "abreast the port fore-channels," tearing a coal schooner that was alongside from her fastenings, and staving a hole in the ship's side, about five inches in circumference, two feet below the water-line. The ram then drew off, and, passing aft, made an ineffectual attempt to breach the *Richmond's* stern. The crew of the assailed vessel had promptly hastened to quarters at the first alarm, and, as the monster passed abreast of the ship in the darkness, had given it a volley from the port battery, but with what effect was not known until some time afterward.

J. S. HOLLINS.

A signal of danger had been given to the other vessels. They at once slipped their cables and got under way, with orders to run down to the Pass, while the *Richmond* should cover their retreat. This was done at five o'clock. In an attempt to pass the bar, the *Richmond* and *Vincennes* grounded, at about eight o'clock, in the morning, where they were bombarded for a while by the *Manassas*, and some fire-rafts were sent down to burn them. A little later, Commander Robert Handy, of the *Vincennes*, mistaking the meaning of a signal from Pope, abandoned his ship, placed a slow match at the magazine, and with his officers and crew fled, some to the *Richmond* and some to the *Water-Witch*. Happily, the fire of the match expired, and Handy and his men returned to the ship and saved her. The fire-rafts sent down by Hollins were harmless, and at ten o'clock the Confederate "Commodore" withdrew and ran up to Fort Jackson, to send news of his great "victory" to Richmond. The only damages inflicted by Hollins were slight bruises on the coal schooner, sinking a large boat, and staving Captain Pope's gig. When his dispatch and the facts were considered together, they produced great merriment throughout the country at the expense of the weak Confederate "Commodore."

The *Manassas* would have been a formidable enemy to the blockaders at the mouth of the Mississippi, in the hands of a competent officer. It was so considered by the Government; and the apprehension that others of like character might be speedily fitted out at New Orleans, hastened the preparations already commenced for sending an expedition to the Lower Mississippi, for the purpose of controlling it and its connecting waters, and taking possession of the great commercial city on its banks. This expedition and its results will be hereafter considered.

---

[1] This squadron had been placed there by Flag-officer McKean, commander of the squadron off Pensacola, for the purpose of guarding the several entrances to the Mississippi, and erecting a battery at the head of the passes, which would command the entire navigation of the river.

CHAPTER V.

MILITARY AND NAVAL OPERATIONS ON THE COAST OF SOUTH CAROLINA.—MILITARY OPERATIONS ON THE LINE OF THE POTOMAC RIVER.

HAMPTON ROADS presented a spectacle, in October, similar to that, late in August, of the Hatteras expedition; but more imposing. It was a land and naval armament, fitted out for a descent upon the borders of lower South Carolina, among the coast islands between Charleston harbor and the Savannah River.

The want of some harbors under the control of the Government in that region, as stations, and as places of refuge of the blockading vessels during the storms of autumn and winter, had caused the Government to take action on the subject even before the meeting of Congress in July. So early as June, a Board of army and navy officers was convened at Washington City.[1] The Board, after careful investigations, made elaborate reports, and, in accordance with their recommendations, expeditions were planned. The Secretary of the Navy, with the help of his energetic assistant, Mr. Fox, had so far matured an expedition for the Southern coast, that, early in October, rumors of it began to attract public attention. It became tangible when in Hampton Roads a large squadron was seen gathering, and at Annapolis a considerable land force was collecting, which, it was said, was to form a part of the expedition. Whither it was to go was a mystery to the public, and its destination was so uncertain to the popular mind, that it was placed by conjecture at almost every point of interest between Cape Hatteras and Galveston, in Texas. Even in official circles its destination was generally unknown when it sailed, so well had the secret been kept.

The land forces of the expedition, which assembled at Annapolis, in Maryland, about fifteen thousand in number, were placed in charge of Brigadier-General T. W. Sherman, acting as major-general. The naval portion of the expedition was placed under the command of Captain S. F. Dupont, who had served as chairman of the Board of Inquiry just mentioned. The fleet was composed of fifty war vessels and transports, with twenty-five coal vessels under convoy of the *Vandalia*. These, with the troops, left Hampton Roads and proceeded to sea on a most lovely October morning,[a] having been summoned to the movement at dawn by the booming of a gun on the *Wabash*, the Commodore's flag-ship. The destination of the expedition was not generally known by the partici-

[a] Oct. 29, 1861.

[1] This Board was composed of Major John G. Barnard, of the Engineer Corps of the army, Professor Alexander Bache, of the Coast Survey, and Captains Samuel F. Dupont and Charles H. Davis, of the Navy.

pants in it until it was well out to sea, when, under peculiar circumstances, as we shall observe, it was announced to be Port Royal entrance and harbor, and the coast islands of South Carolina.

S. F. DUPONT.

The army under Sherman was divided into three brigades, commanded respectively by Brigadier-Generals Egbert S. Viele, Isaac J. Stevens, and Horatio G. Wright; all of them, including the chief, being graduates of the West Point Military Academy. The transports which bore these troops were about thirty-five in number, and included some powerful steamships.[1]

The *Wabash* led the way out to sea, and its followers, moving in three parallel lines, and occupying a space of about twelve miles each way, made a most imposing appearance. The war-vessels and transports were judiciously intermingled, so that the latter might be safely convoyed.[2] During a greater portion of the day of departure, they moved down the coast toward stormy Cape Hatteras, most of the vessels in sight of the shore of North Carolina, and all hearts cheered with promises of fine weather. That night was glorious. The next day was fair. The second night was calm and beautiful. There was no moon visible; but the stars were brilliant. The dreaded Cape Hatteras was passed in the dimness with such calmness of sea, that on the following morning a passenger on the *Atlantic* counted no less than thirty-eight of the fifty vessels in sight from her deck. But, on that evening, the aspect of the heavens changed, and the terrible storm, already mentioned, which swept over Hatteras so fearfully at the beginning of November, was soon encountered, and the expedition was really "scattered to the winds." So complete was the dispersion, that, on the morning of the 2d of November, only a single vessel might be seen from the deck of the *Wabash*. Fortunately, there were sealed orders on board of each vessel. These were opened, and the

---

[1] The *Atlantic* and *Baltic*, each carrying a full regiment of men and a vast amount of provisions and stores, were of the larger class. Among the other more notable vessels may be named the *Vanderbilt*, *Ocean Queen*, *Ericsson*, *Empire City*, *Daniel Webster*, and *Great Republic*, the latter having been employed in the British service for the same purpose during a part of the Crimean war. Among the lesser vessels were five or six ferry-boats, calculated, on account of their capacity and light draught, for landing troops in shallow and still waters. The entire tonnage of the transports was estimated at about 40,000 tons.

[2] The vessels moved in the following order and connection: The *Wabash* was flanked by the gunboats *Pawnee*, *Ottawa*, *Curlew*, *Isaac P. Smith*, *Seneca*, *Pembina*, *Unadilla*, *Penguin*, and *R. B. Forbes*. The *Baltic*, towing the *Ocean Express*, led the column on the left, and was supported by the *Pocahontas*. The *Illinois* towed the *Golden Eagle*, and was followed by the *Locust Point*, *Star of the South*, *Parkersburg*, *Belvidere*, *Alabama*, *Coatzacoalcas*, *Marion*, *Governor*, and *Mohican*.

The *Atlantic* led the central line, and was followed by the *Vanderbilt*, towing the *Great Republic*; the *Ocean Queen*, towing the *Zenas Coffin*; and these were followed by the *Winfield Scott*, *Potomac*, *Cahawba*, *Oriental Union*, *R. B. Forbes*, *Vixen*, and *O. M. Petit*.

The *Empire City* led the right, followed by the *Ericsson*, *Philadelphia*, *Ben De Ford*, *Florida*, *Roanoke*, *Matanzas*, *Daniel Webster*, *Augusta*, *Mayflower*, *Peerless*, *Ariel*, *Mercury*, *Osceola*, and two ferry-boats. The twenty-five coal-barges, convoyed by the *Vandalia*, had been sent out the day before, with instructions to rendezvous off the Savannah River, so as to mislead as to the real destination of the expedition.

place of rendezvous, off Port Royal, was made known. In that fearful storm four transport vessels were lost,[1] but not a dozen persons perished. It was most remarkable how small was the aggregate amount of disaster suffered by so large a number of vessels in company, by a storm so severe that at times it was a hurricane. Some were compelled to part with freight, in order to insure salvation. The gunboat *Mercury* lost one of her two rifled guns, thrown overboard to lighten her; and the *Isaac P. Smith* was saved by parting with eight 8-inch guns in the same way. The side-wheel steamer *Florida*, carrying nine guns, was disabled, and put back in distress; and the *Belvidere* and two New York ferry-boats (*Ethan Allen* and *Commodore Perry*) were compelled to go back to Fortress Monroe, where they gave the first public notice of the storm and the dispersion of the fleet.

The sad news disturbed the loyal people with alarm and distress until the small amount of disaster was known, while the Confederate newspapers were jubilant with the expressed idea that the elements were in league with them in destroying their enemies. "The stars in their courses fought against Sisera," one of them quoted, and added, "So the winds of heaven fight for the good cause of Southern independence. Let the Deborahs of the South sing a song of deliverance." That joyous song was very brief, for, whilst it was swelling in full chorus, a voice of wailing went over the Southern land, such as had not been heard since its wicked betrayers had raised their arms for the destruction of the Republic and the liberties of the people.

On Sunday morning[a] the storm began to abate, and the vessels of the expedition to reassemble around the flag-ship. When passing Charleston harbor, Commodore Dupont sent in Captain Lardner with the *Seneca* to direct the *Susquehanna*, on blockading duty there, to proceed to Port Royal; and on the following morning, at eight o'clock, the *Wabash* anchored off Port Royal Bar in company with twenty-five vessels, whilst many others were continually heaving in sight in the dim offing.

[a] Nov. 3, 1861.

The expedition was now on the threshold of a theater of great and important events, with many difficulties and dangers still before it. The awful perils of the sea had been passed, but there were others, no less fearful, to be encountered in the works of man before it. There were also grave dangers beneath the waters on which that armada floated, for the insurgents had, as we have observed,[2] removed lighthouses, beacons, buoys, and every help to navigation all along the Southern coasts. Yet a remedy for this evil was found in the person of Commander Charles H. Davis (the fleet captain, and chief of Dupont's staff), and Mr. Boutelle, of the Coast Survey, a man of

---

[1] The lost vessels were the *Governor*, *Peerless*, *Osceola*, and *Union*. The *Governor*, Captain Litchfield, was a steam transport. It foundered on Sunday (Nov. 3), having on board a battalion of marines, numbering 350. All were saved by the frigate *Sabine* (see page 366, volume I.), Captain Ringold, excepting a corporal and six men, who were drowned, or crushed between the vessels; nearly all the arms and half of the accouterments of the marines were saved, and about 10,000 rounds of cartridges. The *Peerless* was a small Lake Ontario steamer, loaded with beef cattle. Its officers and crew were saved by the gunboat *Mohican*, Captain Gordon. The propeller *Osceola*, Captain Morrell, also loaded with beef cattle, was wrecked on North Island, near Georgetown, S. C., and its people, 20 in number, were made prisoners. The *Union*, Captain Sawin, was a new and stanch steamer, and went ashore off Beaufort, N. C., with a large quantity of stores, which were lost. Its crew and passengers, and a few soldiers, in all 73 persons, were captured and taken into the interior. The stanch steamer *Winfield Scott*, with 500 men of the Fiftieth Pennsylvania regiment, barely escaped destruction.

[2] See page 453, volume I.

great scientific skill, who had recently been engaged in making a minute examination of this coast. By these well-informed men the channel entrance to Port Royal Sound was found, and so well buoyed in the course of a few hours that the fleet might enter with perfect safety. At three o'clock in the afternoon Commodore Dupont was informed that all of his gun-boats and transports drawing less than eighteen feet water might go forward without danger. The movement commenced at once, and at twilight these vessels were all anchored in the roadstead of Port Royal.

To oppose the further progress of the expedition, the Confederates had earthworks on each side of Port Royal entrance. The one on the northern side, at Bay Point, Phillip's Island, was named Fort Beauregard, and that on the southern side, near Hilton Head, Hilton Head Island, was called Fort Walker. The latter was a strong regular work, with twenty-four guns; and the former, though inferior to it in every respect, was formidable, being armed with twenty guns.

Fort Walker was manned, when the expedition arrived, by six hundred and twenty men,[1] under General T. F. Drayton, a wealthy land-owner, whose mansion was not more than a mile distant from it, standing a few yards from the beach, and overlooking a beautiful expanse of land and water. He was a brother of Captain Percival Drayton, commander of the *Pocahontas*, of this expedition. On the beach at Camp Lookout, six miles from Fort Walker, were sixty-five men of Scriven's guerrillas, who acted as scouts and couriers for the commander. These forces were increased, before the battle commenced, to one thousand eight hundred and thirty-seven men.[2] The force on Bay Point was six hundred and forty men, commanded by Colonel R. G. M. Dunovant.[3] Of these, one hundred and forty-nine, consisting of the Beaufort Volunteer Artillery, garrisoned Fort Beauregard, under the immediate command of Captain Stephen Elliott, Jr., of Beaufort. Dunovant's infantry force was stationed so as to protect the eastern portion of Phillip's Island, and the entrance to Trenchard's Inlet.

T. F. DRAYTON.

In addition to these land forces, there was a little squadron called the "Musquito Fleet," under Commodore Josiah Tatnall, a brave old veteran of the National navy, who served with distinction in the war of 1812, but who had been seduced from his allegiance and his flag by the siren song of supreme State sovereignty. He had followed the politicians of his native

---

[1] Two companies of Wagner's South Carolina First Regiment of Artillery, three companies of Hayward's Ninth South Carolina Volunteers, and four companies of Dunovant's Twelfth South Carolina Volunteers, under Major Jones.

[2] The re-enforcements were composed of 450 infantry from Georgia, under command of Captain Berry; Captain Reed's battery of two 10-pounder howitzers and 50 men, and Colonel De Saussure's Fifteenth South Carolina Volunteers, numbering 650 men.

[3] See page 138, volume I.

Georgia in the wicked ways of treason, and in the course of a few months he had fallen from his high position of an honored commander, kindly placed by his Government in a retreat of ease and comfort, at the naval station at Sackett's Harbor, on Lake Ontario, in New York, to be the chief manager of a little flotilla of eight small armed steamers that had been employed in navigating the shallow waters among the Coast Islands, and losing, by lack of success, even the respect of those whose bad cause he had consented to serve. His achievements on the occasion we are now considering consisted of a harmless show of opposition to the fleet when it anchored in Port Royal roadstead; a successful retreat from danger when a few shots were hurled at his vessels; assisting in the flight of the Confederate land forces upon Hilton Head Island, and in the destruction of his own flotilla to prevent its capture by his late brothers in the National navy.

On Tuesday, the 5th,[a] Commander John Rogers, a passenger with Dupont, on his way to his own ship, the *Flag*, accompanied by General Wright, made a reconnoissance in force of the Confederate works in the *Ottawa*, supported by the *Curlew*, *Seneca*, and *Smith*. The forts on both shores opened upon them, as they desired they should, and an engagement of about three-quarters of an hour ensued, by which the strength and character of those works were fairly tested. In the mean time, the great *Wabash* had passed safely over the bar, and every thing was now ready for an attack. It was delayed by an ugly wind off shore, and meanwhile the Confederates were re-enforced and their works were strengthened.

[a] Nov., 1861.

Thursday, the 7th, dawned gloriously. The transports were all in sight, and in the light of the morning sun a grand spectacle was speedily presented. It had been ascertained by Rogers and Wright that Fort Walker, on Hilton Head, was by far the most powerful of the defenses, and upon it the bolts of the fleet were chiefly hurled. The order of battle "comprised a main squadron ranged, in a line ahead, and a flanking squadron, which was to be thrown off on the northern section of the harbor, to engage the enemy's flotilla (Tatnall's), and prevent them taking the rear ships of the main line when it turned to the southward, or cutting off a disabled vessel."[1] That flotilla was then lying at a safe distance between Hilton Head and Paris Islands.

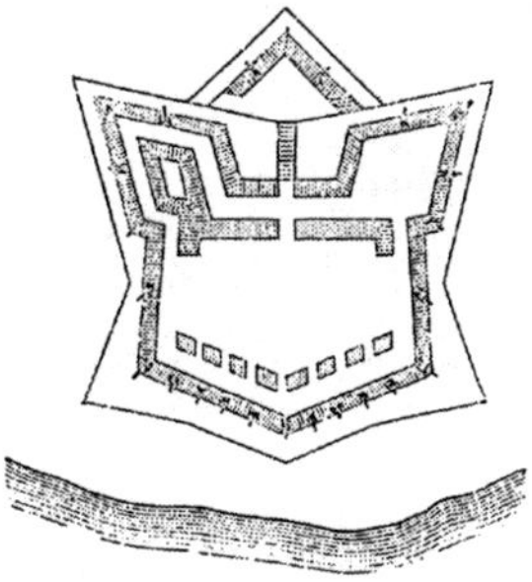

FORT WALKER, HILTON HEAD.

The plan of attack was to pass up midway between Forts Walker and Beauregard (which were about two miles apart), receiving and returning the fire of both; and at the distance of two and a half miles northward of the latter, round by the west, and closing in with the former, attack it on

[1] Report of Commodore Dupont to the Secretary of the Navy, November 11th, 1861. The main squadron consisted of the *Wabash*, Commander C. R. P. Rogers, leading; frigate *Susquehanna*, Captain J. L. Lardner; sloop *Mohican*, Commander L. W. Gordon; sloop *Seminole*, Commander J. P. Gillis; sloop *Pawnee*, Lieutenant commanding T. H. Stevens; gunboat *Pembina*, Lieutenant commanding J. P. Bankhead; sailing sloop *Vandalia*, towed by the *Isaac P. Smith*, Lieutenant commanding J. W. A. Nicholson. The flanking squadron consisted of the gunboats *Bienville*, Commander Charles Steedman, leading; *Seneca*, Lieutenant commanding Daniel Ammen; *Curlew*, Lieutenant commanding P. G. Watmough; *Penguin*, Lieutenant commanding F. A. Budd; and *Augusta*, Commander E. G. Parrott.

its weakest flank, and enfilade its two water faces.[1] The vessels were to pass abreast of the fort very slowly, in the order of battle, and each avoid becoming a fixed mark for the Confederate guns. On reaching the shoal ground making off from the extremity of Hilton Head, the line was to turn to the north by the east, and, passing to the northward, to engage Fort Walker with the port battery nearer than when first on the same course. These evolutions were to be repeated. The captains of the vessels were called on board the *Wabash*, and fully instructed in the manner of proceeding; and this plan of pursuing a series of elliptical movements was strictly followed in the engagement that ensued.

The signal to get under way was given at eight o'clock in the morning,[a] and the action commenced at about half-past nine, by a gun at Fort Walker, which was instantly followed by one at Fort Beauregard. The *Wabash* immediately responded, and was followed by the *Susquehanna*. After the first prescribed turn, the signal for closer action was given, at a quarter past ten, the *Wabash* passing Fort Walker at a distance, when abreast, of eight hundred yards. In the designated order the fight went on. At half-past eleven the flag of Fort Walker was shot away, and the heavy guns of the *Wabash* and *Susquehanna* had so "discomforted the enemy," as Dupont reported, and the shells from the smaller vessels were falling so thickly upon them at the enfilading point,[2] that their fire became sensibly weaker and weaker, until their guns ceased altogether to reply. At a quarter past one P. M., the *Ottawa* signalled that the fort was abandoned.

[a] Nov. 7, 1861.

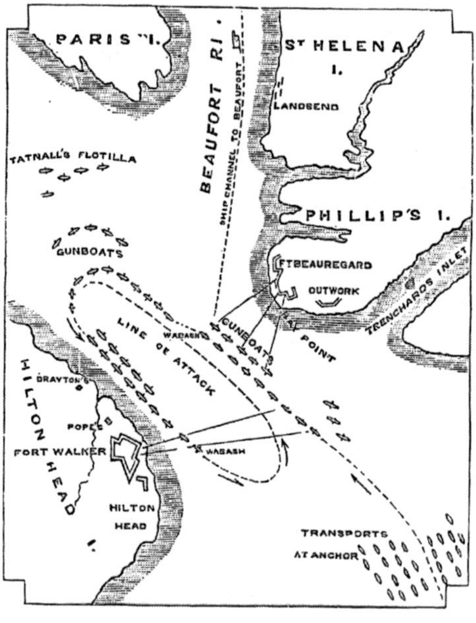

PLAN OF BATTLE AT PORT ROYAL ENTRANCE.

Fort Beauregard was also silent and abandoned. The garrisons of both had fled for their lives. According to the official and unofficial reports of the Confederate officers and correspondents, Fort Walker had become the scene of utter desolation, at noon. Dismounted cannon lay in all directions, and the dead and dying were seen on every side. The place had become utterly untenable, yet it was a perilous thing

---

[1] Dupont's Report.

[2] Commander John Rogers, in a letter to a friend, said:

"During the action I looked carefully at the fort with a powerful spy-glass. Shell fell in it, not twenty-eight in a minute, but as fast as a horse's feet beat the ground in a gallop. The resistance was heroic; but what could flesh and blood do against such a fire? . . . . . .

"The *Wabash* was a destroying angel, hugging the shore, calling the soundings with cold indifference, slowing the engine so as only to give steerage-way, signalling to the vessels their various evolutions, and at the same time raining shells, as with target practice, too fast to count."

to leave it. An open space of a mile, directly in range of the National guns, lay between the fort and a thick wood to which they must go for shelter. Across this they ran, each man for himself, divested of every thing that might make him a laggard. Each of the wounded was placed in a blanket and borne away by four men, but the dead were left. The garrison, with their commander, ran six miles across the island, to Seabrook, where they embarked for Savannah.

So too at Fort Beauregard the retreat had been hasty. General Drayton had vainly endeavored to send over re-enforcements to the little garrison there, that fought bravely and well. Seeing danger of being cut off from retreat, Colonel Dunovant ordered them to flee while there was a chance for safety. Leaving an infernal machine in Fort Beauregard for a murderous purpose,[1] and a note for Commodore Dupont,[2] Captain Elliott and his command retreated with the rest of the troops, first to St. Helen's, then to Port Royal Island, and then to the main, with all possible haste, for the Charleston and Savannah Railway.

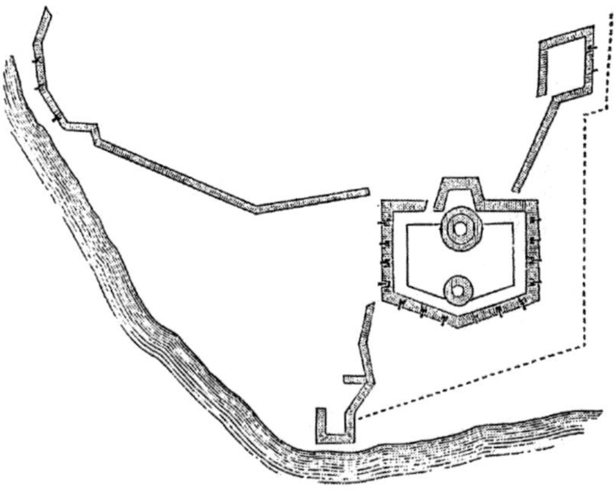
PLAN OF FORT BEAUREGARD.

The loss on board the fleet during the action was very slight.[3] Dupont reported it at thirty-one, of whom eight were killed. The Confederate officers reported their loss in both forts at fifty, of whom ten were killed in Fort Walker, but none in Fort Beauregard. On the evening succeeding the battle, a procession of seventeen boats, from the *Wabash*, conducted the remains of the dead to their burial-place on Hilton Head, near Pope's man-

---

1 The fair fame of Captain (afterwards General) Elliott as a humane man and honorable soldier received an unerasable blemish by an act at this time perfectly consistent with the fiendish spirit of the conspirators, but not at all so with what common report says was his own. He left the Confederate flag flying, and its halliards so connected with a percussion-cap apparatus, that when the victors should enter the fort and attempt to pull down the ensign of treason, a mine of gunpowder beneath would be exploded. Fortunately, the arrangement was so defective that no life was lost by a partial explosion that occurred.

2 The following is a copy of Elliott's note to Dupont:—

"Bay Point, Nov. 7th, 1861.

"We are compelled to leave two wounded men. Treat them kindly, according to the poet's saying—'*Haud ignara mali miseris succurrere disco.*' We abandon our untenable position that we may do the cause of the Confederate States better service elsewhere. Respectfully,

"STEPHEN ELLIOTT, JR."

The Latin quotation in the above is a line from Virgil's Æneid, in which Dido, remembering her own misfortunes, pities the errors of Æneas. It says, "Not unacquainted with misfortune, I have learned to succor the distresses of others." I am indebted to the Rev. John Woart (who was chaplain at the U. S. General Hospital at Hilton Head when I visited that post in April, 1866) for a copy of Elliott's note, taken from the original by Captain Law, of the *New Hampshire*, then in that harbor. The humane injunction of Elliott was in a spirit directly opposed to his act in the matter of the infernal machine. He doubtless acted under the orders of his superiors. Captain Elliott became a brigadier-general, and commanded Fort Sumter during a greater portion of the siege of that fortress. He was blown up by the explosion of the mine at Petersburg, when one of his arms was broken. He died at Aiken, South Carolina, in March, 1866.

3 The vessels engaged were all more or less injured by the Confederate cannon. The *Wabash* was struck thirty-four times. Its mainmast was injured beyond hope of repair, its rigging was cut, and it was made to leak badly.

sion, in a grove of palm and orange trees, not far from the fort; and on the following day,[a] Dupont issued a stirring general order, in which, after speaking in praise of his officers and men, he said: "The flag-officer fully sympathizes with the officers and men of the squadron, in the satisfaction they must feel at seeing the ensign of the Union once more in the State of South Carolina, which has been the chief promoter of the wicked and unprovoked rebellion they have been called upon to suppress." The flags captured at the forts were sent to the Navy Department, where they were put to a better use as curtains for a window.

[a] Nov. 8, 1861.

STEPHEN ELLIOTT, JR.

Up to the time when the forts were silenced, the land forces were only spectators of the conflict; then it was their turn to act, and promptly they performed their duty. The transports containing them at once moved forward, the launches were prepared, and a flag of truce was sent ashore to ask whether the garrison had surrendered. There was no one there to respond. The Union flag was hoisted by Commander Rogers,[1] amid the greetings of cheers from the fleet and transports; and very soon the surface of the water was dark with a swarm of troops in boats made specially for such occasions. Early in the evening, the brigades of Generals Wright and Stevens had landed on the beach, which was so flat that the water is always shallow a long distance out. Wright's men landed first, close by Fort Walker; and so eager were they to tread the soil of South Carolina, that many of them leaped from the boats and waded ashore. Fort Walker was formally taken possession of, and General Wright made his head-quarters near it, at the abandoned mansion of William Pope, and the only dwelling-house at that point. It had been the head-quarters of General Drayton.

POPE'S HOUSE, HILTON HEAD.

General Stevens's brigade, consisting of the Seventy-ninth New York and Eighth Michigan, crossed over to Bay Point the next morning, and took possession of Fort Beauregard. The victory was now complete, and the universal joy which it created in the Free-labor States found public expression in many places; for it seemed as if the hand of

[1] "Commodore Dupont," Rogers wrote to a friend, "had kindly made me his aid. I stood by him, and I did little things which I suppose gained me credit. So, when a boat was sent on shore to ask whether they had surrendered, I was sent. I carried the Stars and Stripes. I found the ramparts utterly desolate, and I planted the American flag upon those ramparts with my own hands—first to take possession, in the majesty of the United States, of the rebel soil of South Carolina."

retributive justice, so long withheld, was about to be laid heavily upon the chief offender, South Carolina.[1]

> "A thrill pervaded the loyal land
> When the gladdening tidings came to hand;
> Each heart felt joy's emotion!
> The clouds of gloom and doubt dispersed,
> The sun of hope through the darkness burst,
> And the zeal the patriot's heart had nursed
> Burned with a warm devotion."

The joy of the Loyalists was equaled in intensity by the sadness of the Secessionists everywhere. The latter perceived that an irreparable blow had been dealt against their cause, and throughout the Confederacy there was much wailing, lamentation, and bitter recriminations. It was believed that Charleston and Savannah would soon be in possession of the National forces, and that Forts Sumter and Pulaski would be "repossessed" by the Government.

General R. S. Ripley, an old army officer who had abandoned his flag, was the Confederate commander of that sea-coast district,[2] having his head-quarters at Charleston. He had arrived on Hilton Head just before the action commenced, but retired to Coosawhatchie, on the main, satisfied that no glory was to be achieved in a fight so hopeless on the part of his friends. It was under his advice that the Confederate troops abandoned that region to the occupation of the National forces. The latter fact was officially announced by General Sherman, in a proclamation to the people of South Carolina on the day after the battle. Unfortunately, a portion of that proclamation was couched in such terms, that neither the personal pride nor the political pretensions of the rebellious leaders was offended. It was so lacking in positiveness that they regarded it with perfect indifference.[3] Indeed, it was difficult to get them to notice it at all.

R. S. RIPLEY.

---

[1] In all the cities and towns in the Free Labor States flags were flung out, and in many places salvos of cannon were fired. The chimes of Trinity church, in the city of New York, beneath its great flag that floated from its spire, rang out two changes on eight bells, and twelve airs, under the direction of Mr. Ayliffe, the celebrated chimist. The airs were as follows: Hail Columbia; Yankee Doodle; Air from "Child of the Regiment;" Home, Sweet Home; Last Rose of Summer; Evening Bells; Star Spangled Banner Airs by De Beriot; Airs from "Fra Diavolo;" Columbia, the Gem of the Ocean; Hail Columbia; and Yankee Doodle.

The Secretaries of War and of the Navy publicly tendered to the commanders of the expedition and to their men thanks, and the latter issued a General Order on the 16th of November, in which it was directed that a national salute should be fired from each navy-yard at meridian on the day after the reception, to commemorate the signal victory.

[2] See page 311, volume I.

[3] He acknowledged their pretensions to State sovereignty by speaking of "the dictates of a duty" which he owed "to a great sovereign State;" and he flattered them by speaking of them as "a proud and hospitable people, among whom he had passed some of the pleasantest days of his life." Then he assured them that they were in a state of active rebellion against the laws of their own country, and that the civilized world stood amazed at their course, and appalled by the crime they were committing against their "own mother." He narrated some

Messengers were sent with it, under a flag of truce, first to Port Royal Island, and thence to the main. The Confederate officers they met told them there were no "loyal" citizens in South Carolina, and that no others wanted it, and advised them to turn back with their bundle of proclamations. They acted upon this recommendation, and so ended the attempt to conciliate the South Carolinians.

General Sherman set vigorously to work to strengthen his position on Hilton Head, for it was to be made a depot of supplies. Mechanics and lumber had been brought out in the transports. Buildings were speedily erected; also an immense wharf; and in a short time the place assumed the outward appearance of a mart of commerce. Meanwhile, Dupont sent his armed vessels in various directions among the islands and up the rivers of the coast of South Carolina, in the direction of Charleston; and before the close of November, every soldier occupying earthworks found here and there, and nearly every white inhabitant, had abandoned those islands and fled to the main, leaving the negroes, who refused to accompany them, to occupy their plantations and houses. Everywhere, evidences of panic and hasty departure were seen; and it is now believed that, had the victory at Port Royal been immediately followed up, by attacks on Charleston and Savannah, both cities might have been an easy prey to the National forces. Beaufort, a delightful city on Port Royal Island, where the most aristocratic portion of South Carolina society had summer residences, was entered,[a] and its arms and munitions of war seized, without the least resistance,[1] there being, it was reported, only one white man there, named Allen (who was of Northern birth), and who was too much overcome with fear or strong drink to give any intelligible account of affairs there.[2] The negroes everywhere evinced the greatest delight at the advent of the "Yankees," about whom their masters had told them fearful tales; and it was a most touching sight to see them—men, women, and children—flocking to the island shores when the vessels appeared, carrying little bundles containing all their worldly goods, and with perfect faith that the invader was their

[a] Nov. 9, 1861.

of their crimes, implored them to pause, and warned them that they would bring great evils upon their State. He assured them that he and his troops would respect any constitutional obligations to them, and begged them to believe that if, in the performance of their duty in enforcing the National authority, some of those obligations should be neglected, such neglect came only because of the "necessities of the case." The general had been specially instructed by the War Department to treat all slaves as General Butler had been authorized to treat them at Fortress Monroe, and to assure all loyal masters that Congress would provide just compensation to them for the loss of the labor of their slaves taken into the public service.

CANNON CAPTURED AT BEAUFORT.

[1] Among the trophies secured at Beaufort, and now (1867) preserved at the Washington Navy Yard, was a 6-pounder brass cannon, which had been captured from the British while marauding on the coast of South Carolina during the war of 1812. It was deposited in the trophy room of the National Arsenal, at Charleston, and there it remained until the conspirators in that city seized it, with the other public property, and appropriated it to their use. According to their code of ethics, the act of seizure conferred the right of ownership, and so they had the name of "South Carolina" engraved upon the cannon. It also bore the date of its construction, "1803." Its carriage was modern, having been made after its capture from the British. It, too, was of brass, and was decorated with stars.

[2] Report of Lieutenant Sproston, of the *Seneca*, who was the first to land at Beaufort. He says that while he was talking with Mr. Allen, at his store in Beaufort, an intelligent mulatto boy dismounted from a horse, and said, "The whole country have left, sir, and all the soldiers gone to Port Royal Ferry. They did not think that you could do it, sir." He informed him that there were then about 1,000 soldiers at the ferry, a portion of whom were the Beaufort Artillery, under Captain Elliott.

deliverer, expressing a desire to go on board the ships, evidently fearing that their masters would return.[1] The latter had used great exertions, by persuasion, threats, and violence, to induce their slaves to accompany them in their flight to the interior, but with very little success.[2]

With equal ease Dupont took possession of Big Tybee Island, at the mouth of the Savannah River, from which Fort Pulaski, which was within easy mortar distance, might be assailed, and the harbor of Savannah perfectly sealed against blockade runners. On the approach of the National gunboats, the defenses, which consisted of a strong martello tower erected there during the war of 1812, and a battery at its base, were abandoned, and on the 25th[a] Dupont wrote to the Secretary of War: "The flag of the United States is flying over the territory of the State of Georgia."[4]

[a] Nov., 1861.

MARTELLO TOWER ON TYBEE ISLAND.[3]

Before the close of the year the National authority was supreme from Wassaw Sound, below the mouth of the Savannah, to the North Edisto River. Every fort on the islands in that region had been abandoned, and there was nothing to make serious opposition to National authority.[5] But at the close of November, and in the month of December, over the curious net-work of creeks and rivers on that coast hung the black clouds of extensive conflagrations, evincing intense hostility to that authority by the South Carolinians. Vast quantities of cotton were on the islands when the National forces came; and, when the first panic had

---

[1] Nowhere in the South were the negroes so shut out from all knowledge of the world as among these coast islands. Their masters assured them that the "Yankees" were coming to steal them and sell them into bondage in Cuba; and some described the "Northerners" as monsters who would devour them, or kill and bury them in the sand. But most of these simple people did not believe a word of these tales; on the contrary, they believed the Lord had sent the "Yankees" to take them out of bondage. This faith and hope was most remarkable.

[2] When the National forces reached Beaufort, the negroes, finding themselves sole occupants of the place and property, had begun to pillage. They reported that their masters, before their departure, had tried to drive them back into the woods, in the direction of the main, and numbers of them had been shot and killed. Commander Rogers, in a letter to a friend (Nov. 9th), said: "A boat which came off to the *Seneca* said one man (giving his name) shot six of the negroes."

[3] This was the appearance of the tower when I sketched it, in April, 1866. Its height had been somewhat diminished by demolishing a portion of its upper part, on which rested a roof. Such towers had been erected early in the present century along the British coasts, as a defense against an expected invasion by Bonaparte. The lower story was used for stores, and the upper, being bomb-proof, as secure quarters for the men. The walls terminated in a parapet, behind which cannon were placed. The tower at Tybee was built of solid masonry, like the best of those on the British coast.

[4] Besides those on Hilton Head, and at Bay Point on Phillip's Island, there were five other fortifications on these islands, namely, on Botany Bay Island, North Edisto; on Otter Island, St. Helena's Sound; on Fenwick's Island; on Bay Point, on the South Edisto River; and on Sam's Point, on the Coosaw River. The little sketch here given of the fort on Bay Point, South Edisto, conveys an idea of the general form of these works, which were constructed of loose earth, and blocks of tough marsh sod.

FORT ON BAY POINT.

[5] See map on page 126.

passed by, planters returned stealthily and applied the torch to that which was gathered and ungathered, that it should not fall into the hands of the invaders.[1]

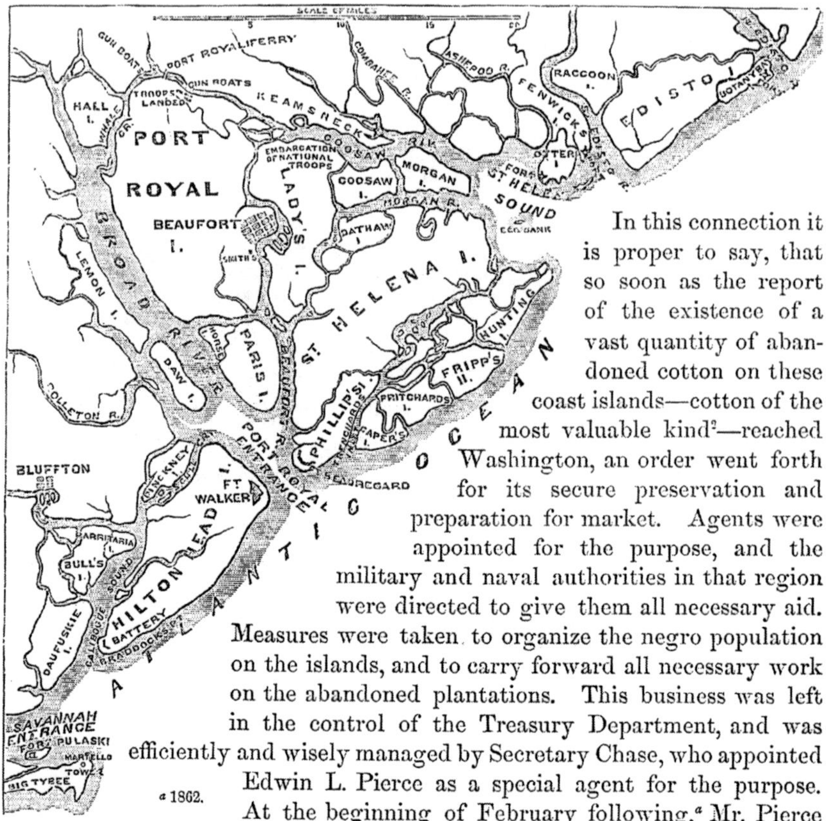

COAST ISLANDS.

In this connection it is proper to say, that so soon as the report of the existence of a vast quantity of abandoned cotton on these coast islands—cotton of the most valuable kind[2]—reached Washington, an order went forth for its secure preservation and preparation for market. Agents were appointed for the purpose, and the military and naval authorities in that region were directed to give them all necessary aid. Measures were taken to organize the negro population on the islands, and to carry forward all necessary work on the abandoned plantations. This business was left in the control of the Treasury Department, and was efficiently and wisely managed by Secretary Chase, who appointed Edwin L. Pierce as a special agent for the purpose. At the beginning of February following,[a] Mr. Pierce reported that about two hundred plantations on fifteen of the South Carolina coast islands were occupied, or under the control of the

[a] 1862.

---

[1] The *Charleston Mercury* of Nov. 30th, 1861, said: "The heavens to the southwest were brilliantly illuminated with the patriotic flames ascending from burning cotton. As the spectators witnessed it, they involuntarily burst forth with cheer after cheer, and each heart was warmed as with a new pulse. Such a people can never be subjugated. Let the holy flames continue to ascend, and let the demons of hell who come here on their diabolical errand learn a lesson and tremble. Let the torch be applied wherever the invader pollutes our soil, and let him find, as is meet, that our people will welcome him only with devastation and ruin. Our people are in earnest, men, women, and children, and their sacrifice will ascend as a sacred holocaust to God, crying aloud for vengeance against the fiends in human shape who are disgracing humanity, trampling down civilization, and would blot out Christianity. Patriotic planters on the seaboard are hourly applying the torch to their crops of cotton and rice. Some are authorized by military authorities to destroy their crops, to prevent ravages by the enemy. Plantations on North Edisto and in the neighborhood, and elsewhere on the coast of South Carolina, are one sheet of flames and smoke. The commanding officers of all the exposed points on our coast have received positive instructions to burn or destroy all property which cannot be conveniently taken away and is likely to be seized by the enemy."

[2] The "Sea Island Cotton" of commerce is the product of a narrow belt of coast islands along the shores of South Carolina, and in the vicinity of the mouth of the Savannah River. The seed was obtained from the Bahama Islands, and the first successful crop raised in South Carolina was on Hilton Head Island, in 1790. It is of the arborescent kind, and noted for its long fiber, adapted to the manufacture of the finest fabrics and the best thread. It always brought a very high price. Just before the war, when the common cotton brought an average of ten or twelve cents a pound, a bale sent from South Edisto Island brought, in Liverpool, one dollar and thirty-five cents a pound.

Union forces, and that upon them there was an aggregate negro population of about eight thousand, exclusive of several thousand colored refugees at and around Hilton Head. The industrial operations in this region under the control of the Government will be further considered hereafter.

The only stand made by the Confederate forces in defense of the South Carolina coast islands, after the battle of the 7th of November, was at Port Royal Ferry, on the Coosaw, at the close of the year. They had a fortified position there, and a force estimated at eight thousand strong, under Generals Gregg and Pope, from which it was determined to expel them. A joint land and naval expedition against this post was undertaken, the former commanded by Brigadier-General Stevens, and the latter by Commander C. R. P. Rogers. The troops employed by Stevens were Colonel Frazier's Forty-seventh and Colonel Perry's Forty-eighth New York regiments, and the Seventy-ninth New York Highlanders, Major Morrison; Fiftieth Pennsylvania, Colonel Crist; Eighth Michigan, Colonel Fenton; and the One Hundredth Pennsylvania ("Round Heads"), Colonel Leasure, of Stevens's brigade; in all about four thousand five hundred men. The naval force assembled at Beaufort for the purpose was composed of the gun-boats *Ottawa*, *Pembina*, *Hale*, and *Seneca*, ferry-boat *Ellen*, and four large boats belonging to the *Wabash*, each of them carrying a 12-pounder howitzer, under the respective commands of Lieutenants Upshur, Luce, and Irwin, and Acting Master Kempff.

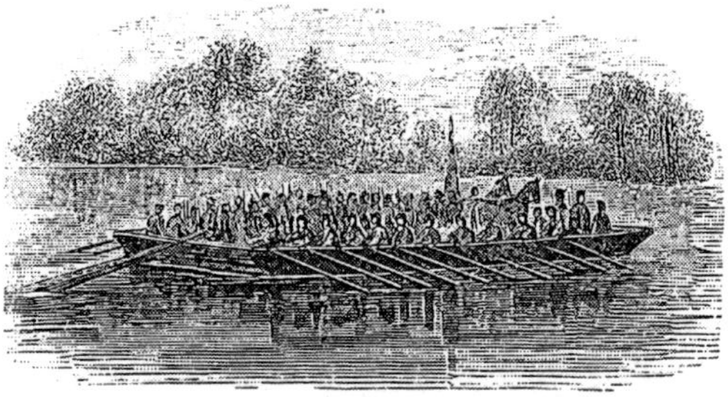

FLAT BOATS USED FOR LANDING TROOPS.

The expedition moved in the evening of the 31st of December.[a] A large portion of the vessels went up the Broad River, on the westerly side of Port Royal Island, to approach the Ferry by Whale Creek; and at the same time General Stevens's forces made their way to a point where the Brick Yard Creek, a continuation of the Beaufort River, unites with the Coosaw. There he was met by Commander Rogers, with launches, and his troops were embarked on large flat boats, at an early hour in the morning.[b] The *Ottawa*, *Pembina*, and *Hale* soon afterward entered the Coosaw, and at Adams's plantation, about three miles below the Ferry, the land and naval forces pressed forward to the attack, two of the howitzers of the *Wabash* accompanying the former, under Lieutenant Irwin.

[a] 1861.

[b] Jan. 1, 1862.

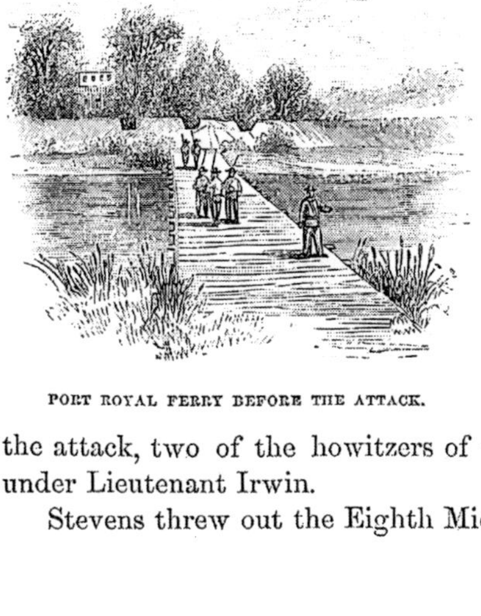

PORT ROYAL FERRY BEFORE THE ATTACK.

Stevens threw out the Eighth Michigan as skirmishers, and the gun-boats opened a brisk fire into the woods in their front. The Seventy-ninth New York led. Very soon a concealed battery near the Ferry was encountered. It opened upon them with grape and canister, but was soon silenced by a close encounter, in which the Eighth Michigan bore the brunt. The Fiftieth Pennsylvania pressed forward to the support of these and the Highlanders, but very little fighting occurred after the first onset. The Confederates, seeing the gun-boats *Seneca*, *Ellen*, *Pembina*, and *Ottawa* coming forward, abandoned their works and fled, and the Pennsylvania "Round Heads" passed over the Ferry and occupied them. At four o'clock in the afternoon, General Stevens joined them. The works were demolished, and the houses in the vicinity were burned. General Stevens's loss was nine wounded, one of them (Major Watson, of the Eighth Michigan) mortally.

While the National forces were thus gaining absolute control of the South Carolina coast islands, and the blockading ships, continually multiplying on the Atlantic and on the Gulf, were watching every avenue of ingress or egress for violators of the law, the Government, profiting by the hint given by the insurgents themselves, several months before, in sinking obstructions in the channel leading up to Norfolk,[1] proceeded to close, in like manner, the main entrances to the harbors of Charleston and Savannah. For that purpose a number of condemned merchant vessels, chiefly whalers, were found in New England harbors, and purchased by order of the Secretary of the Navy. Twenty-five of them, each of three or four hundred tons burden, were stripped of their copper bottoms, and were as heavily laden as their strength would permit, with blocks of granite, for the purpose of closing up Charleston harbor. In their sides, below water-mark, holes were bored, in which movable plugs were inserted, so that when these vessels reached their destination these might be drawn, and the water allowed to pour in.

THE CHANNELS OF CHARLESTON HARBOR.

This "stone fleet," as it was called, reached the blockading squadron off Charleston at the middle of December, and on the 20th, sixteen of the vessels,[2] from New Bedford and New London, were sunk on the bar at the entrance of the Main Ship channel,[3] six miles in a direct southern line from Fort Sumter. This was done under the superintendence of Fleet-captain Charles H. Davis. They were placed at intervals, checkerwise, so as to form

---

[1] See page 398, volume I.

[2] One of these vessels was named *Ceres*. It had been an armed store-ship of the British navy, and as such was in Long Island Sound during the old war for Independence, when it was captured by the Americans.

[3] There are four channels leading out from Charleston harbor. The Main Ship channel runs southward along Morris Island. Maffitt's channel, on the northern side of the entrance, is along the south side of Sullivan's Island. Between these are the North channel and the Swash channel, the former having eight, and the latter nine feet of water on the bar. The Main Ship channel had fifteen feet, and Maffitt's channel eleven.

disturbing currents that would perplex but not destroy the navigation. Indeed, the affair was intended by the Government, and expected by those acquainted with the nature of the coast, the currents, and the harbor, to be only a temporary interference with navigation, as a war measure, and these experts laughed at the folly of those who asserted, as did a writer who accompanied the fleet, that "Charleston Bar is paved with granite, and the harbor is a thing of the past."[1] The idea that such was the case was fostered by the Confederates, in order to "fire the Southern heart;" and their newspapers teemed with denunciations of the "barbarous act," and frantic calls upon commercial nations to protest by cannon, if necessary, against this "violation of the rights of the civilized world." The British press and British statesmen sympathizing with the insurgents joined in the outcry, and the British Minister at Washington (Lord Lyons) made it the subject of diplomatic remonstrance. He was assured that the obstructions would be temporary, and he was referred to the fact that, since they had been placed there, a British ship, in violation of the blockade, had run into Charleston harbor with safety, carrying supplies for the enemies of the Government.

The work of the "stone fleet" was a failure,[2] and the expected disaster to Charleston, from its operations, did not occur. But a fearful one did fall upon that city at the very time when this "stone fleet" was approaching. A conflagration commenced on the night of the 14th of December, and continued the following day, devouring churches and public buildings, with several hundred stores, dwellings, manufactories, and warehouses, valued, with their contents, at millions of dollars.

Let us now turn from the sea-coast, and observe events at the National capital and in its vicinity, especially along the line of the Potomac River.

We left the Confederate army, after the Battle of Bull's Run, lying in comparative inactivity in the vicinity of its victory, with General Joseph E. Johnston as its chief commander, having his head-quarters at Centreville.[3] We left the Army of the Potomac in a formative state,[4] under General McClellan, whose head-quarters were in Washington City, on Pennsylvania Avenue, opposite the southeast corner of President Square. He was busily engaged, not only in perfecting its physical organization, but in making a solid improvement in its moral character. He issued orders that commended themselves to all good citizens, among the most notable of which was one[a] which enjoined "more perfect respect for the Sabbath." He won "golden opinions" continually, and with the return of every morning he found himself more and more securely intrenched in the faith and affections of the people, who were lavish of both.

[a] Sept. 6, 1861.

General McClellan's moral strength at this time was prodigious. The soldiers and the people believed in him with the most earnest faith. His short campaign in Western Virginia had been successful. He had promised, on taking command of the Army of the Potomac, that the war should be "short, sharp, and decisive;" and he said to some of his followers,[b] while the President and Secretary of War were standing by,

[b] Sept. 10.

[1] Special correspondence of the New York *Tribune*, Dec. 26th, 1861.

[2] A similar attempt had been made to close Ocracoke Inlet, in September, but with the same lack of success, the old hulks being either carried to sea by the strong currents, or so deeply imbedded in the sand as to be harmless.

[3] See page 22.

[4] See page 25.

"Soldiers! We have had our last retreat. We have seen our last defeat. You stand by me, and I will stand by you, and henceforth victory will crown our efforts."[1] These words found a ready response from the soldiers and the people, and they were pondered with hope, and repeated with praise. In them were promises of the exercise of that promptness and energy of action, in the use of the resources of the country, that would speedily bring peace. In the hearts of the people still rang the cry of "On to Richmond!" while their lips, taught circumspection by the recent disaster at Bull's Run, were modestly silent. The soldiers, eager to wipe out the disgrace of that disaster, were ready to obey with alacrity, at any moment, an order to march on Richmond. And it was evidently the determination of the commander, all through the earlier weeks of autumn, to strike the foe at Manassas, as quickly as possible, and march triumphantly on the Confederate capital.[2] But the retirement of Lieutenant-General Scott from the chief command of the National Army,[a][3] and the appointment of McClellan to fill his place, imposed new duties and responsibilities upon the latter, and his plan of campaign against the insurgents in Virginia was changed.

[a] Nov. 1.

The new organization of the Army of the Potomac was perfected at the middle of October, when at least seventy-five thousand well-armed and fairly disciplined troops were in a condition to be placed in column for active operations against the Confederates in front of Washington. At that time the National city was almost circumvallated by earth-works, there being no

---

[1] This little speech was on the occasion when Governor Curtin, accompanied by the President and Secretary of War, presented a set of flags to the Pennsylvania Brigade of General McCall, on Arlington Heights.

[2] Mr. Swinton, in his *History of the Campaigns of the Army of the Potomac* (note on page 69), says: "Though General McClellan used to keep his own counsel, yet General McDowell tells me he was wont, in their rides over the country south of the Potomac, to point toward the flank of Manassas, and say, '*We shall strike them there.*'"

[3] General Scott was then in the 76th year of his age, having been born in June, 1786. He had been for some time suffering from physical and mental infirmities, and was incapable of performing, in any degree of efficiency, the duties of his office at that important time. His voluntary retirement from active military duty was a fortunate circumstance for the country and his own reputation, and he descended into the quiet of private life after a most distinguished military career of more than fifty years' duration, followed by the benedictions of a grateful people. It was on his recommendation that General McClellan, his junior by forty years, was made the Commander-in-chief of all the armies of the Republic.—See *General Orders*, No. 94, dated Washington, November 1st, 1861.*

General Scott left Washington city immediately after he retired from active command, accompanied by his staff, the Secretaries of War and the Treasury, and other distinguished officials. General McClellan bade him an affectionate farewell at the Washington railway-station, and the veteran was conveyed easily on a couch fitted up for his use. He was everywhere greeted by the people with the most earnest demonstrations of respect. In New York, a committee of the Chamber of Commerce and the Union Defense Committee made formal calls upon him, tendering him addresses, to which he replied in the most feeling manner. He expressed confidence in the ultimate success of the National cause, and spoke in highest terms of President Lincoln, to whom he was politically opposed. "I had no part nor lot in his election," he said. "I confess that he has agreeably disappointed me. He is a man of great ability, fidelity, and patriotism."

On the 9th of November, General Scott departed for Havre, in the steamship *Arago*, his heart cheered by intelligence, by way of Richmond, of the victory of Dupont at Port Royal, and the capture of Beaufort.

---

* The following letter of the President was embodied in the order:

"Executive Mansion,
"*Washington, November 1st*, 1861.

"On the 1st day of November, A. D. 1861, upon his own application to the President of the United States, Brevet Lieutenant-General Winfield Scott is ordered to be placed, and hereby is placed upon the list of retired officers of the Army of the United States, without reduction in his current pay, subsistence, or allowance.

"The American people will hear with sadness and deep emotion that General Scott has withdrawn from the active control of the army, while the President and a unanimous Cabinet express their own and the nation's sympathy in his personal affliction, and their profound sense of the important public services rendered by him to his country during his long and brilliant career, among which will ever be gratefully distinguished his faithful devotion to the Constitution, the Union, and the Flag, when assailed by parricidal rebellion.

"ABRAHAM LINCOLN."

less than thirty-two forts completed and armed for its defense, and to these sixteen were added in the course of six weeks.[1] Provisions, stores, ammunition, and clothing, were on hand in the greatest abundance, and the chief commander was furnished with numerous and efficient staff officers,[2] among whom were two French Princes of the House of Orleans, who had just arrived at the capital, with their uncle, the Prince de Joinville, son of the late Louis Philippe, King of the French. These were the Count of Paris and the Duke of Chartres, sons of the late Duke of Orleans, who wished to acquire military experience in the operations of so large a force as was there in arms.

A prominent member of the then reigning family in France, whose head was considered a usurper by the Orleans family, had just left this country for his own. It was the Prince Jerome Bonaparte, a cousin of the Emperor Napoleon the Third, who, with his wife, had arrived in New York in the preceding July, in his private steam yacht. He went to Washington, where he was entertained by the President, and visited the Houses of Congress and the army on Arlington Heights and vicinity. He passed through the lines and visited the Confederate forces under Beauregard, at Manassas. Returning to New York, he started on a tour to Niagara, Canada, and the Western prairies, with the princess. At the middle of September, he went from New York to Boston and Halifax in his yacht, and so homeward.

It was only a few days before Prince Jerome's departure from New York that the Prince de Joinville arrived there, with members of his family. He came to place his son, the Duke of Penthievre (then sixteen years of age), in the Naval School at Newport. He brought with him his two nephews above named, who offered their services to the Government, with the stipulation on their part that they should receive no pay. Each was commissioned a captain, and assigned to the staff of General McClellan. They remained in the service until the close of the Peninsula campaign, in July, 1862, and acquitted themselves well.

---

[1] See map and foot-note on page 24 of this volume. On the 7th of December, Chief Engineer Barnard reported that the defenses of Washington city consisted of about forty-eight works, mounting over 300 guns, some of which were of very large size, and added, "that the actual defensive perimeter occupied is about thirty-five miles, exceeding the length of the famous, and hitherto the most extensive—fortified by extemporized field-works—lines of Torres Vedras by several miles."

Concerning the creation and use of heavy ordnance at that time, Swinton says: "The task of forming an artillery establishment was facilitated by the fact that the country possessed, in the regular service, a body of accomplished and energetic artillery officers. As a basis of organization, it was decided to form field-batteries of six guns (never less than four guns, and the guns of each battery to be of uniform caliber), and these were assigned to divisions, not to brigades, in the proportion of four batteries to each division; one of which was to be a battery of regulars, and the captain of the regular battery was in each case appointed commandant of the artillery of the division. In addition, it was determined to create an artillery reserve of a hundred guns, and a siege-train of fifty pieces. This work was pushed forward with so much energy, that whereas, when General McClellan took command of the army, the entire artillery establishment consisted of nine imperfectly equipped batteries of thirty guns, before it took the field this service had reached the colossal proportions of ninety-two batteries of five hundred and twenty guns, served by twelve thousand five hundred men, and in full readiness for active field duty."—*Campaigns of the Army of the Potomac*, page 65.

[2] The following officers composed the staff of General McClellan soon after taking the command of the Army of the Potomac: "Major S. Williams, Assistant Adjutant-General; Captain Albert V. Colburn, Assistant Adjutant-General; Colonel R. B. Marcy, Inspector-General; Colonel T. M. Key, Aid-de-Camp; Captain N. B. Sweitser, 1st Cavalry, Aid-de-Camp; Captain Edward McK. Hudson, 14th Infantry, Aid-de-Camp; Captain L. A. Williams, 10th Infantry, Aid-de-Camp; Major A. J. Myer, Signal Officer; Major Stewart Van Vliet, Chief Quartermaster; Captain H. F. Clarke, Chief Commissary; Surgeon C. S. Tripler, Medical Director; Major J. G. Barnard, Chief Engineer; Major J. N. Macomb, Chief Topographical Engineer; Captain Charles P. Kingsbury, Chief of Ordnance; Brigadier-General George Stoneman, Volunteer Service, Chief of Cavalry; Brigadier-General W. F. Barry, Volunteer Service, Chief of Artillery."

McClellan had organized every necessary department thoroughly, and had endeavored to place at the head of each the best men in the service.[1] These had been active co-workers with him, and their several departments were in the best possible condition for effective service. The main body of the army was now[a] judiciously posted, for offense or defense, in the immediate vicinity of Washington City, with detachments on the left bank of the Potomac as far up as Williamsport, above Harper's Ferry, and as far down as Liverpool Point, in Maryland, nearly opposite Acquia Creek.[2]

[a] Oct. 15, 1861.

At the close of September a grand review had been held, when seventy

---

[1] The *Engineers*, as we have observed, were placed in charge of Major J. G. Barnard, and the *Artillery* under the chief command of Major William F. Barry. The *Topographical Engineers* were commanded by Lieutenant-Colonel John N. Macomb, and a *Signal Corps*, formed by Major Albert J. Myer, the inventor of a most efficient system of signalling, was placed in charge of that officer. This system was first practically tested during the organization of the Army of the Potomac, and, as we shall observe hereafter, it performed the most essential and important service on land and water, in reconnoitering and in directing the fire of artillery, where objects, such as hills or woods on land, or bluffs or wooded points on the shores of rivers, intervened between the belligerents. The value of that service during the war cannot be estimated. A full explanation of its operations, with illustrations, may be found in another part of this work.

The *Telegraphic* operations of the army were intrusted to Major Thomas J. Eckert. In this connection, T. S. C. Lowe, a distinguished aeronaut, was employed, and for some time balloons were used with great efficiency in reconnoitering, but later in the progress of the war they fell into disuse. Mr. Lowe made experiments with his balloon in connection with the telegraph so early as June, 1861, and by perfect success demonstrated the feasibility of the joint use of the balloon and telegraph in reconnoitering. At the height of full five hundred feet above Arlington Heights, Mr. Lowe telegraphed to the President, at Washington, as follows:

"SIR:—From this point of observation we command an extent of country nearly fifty miles in diameter. I have pleasure in sending you this first telegram ever dispatched from an aerial station, and acknowledging indebtedness to your encouragement for the opportunity of demonstrating the availability of the science of aeronautics in the service of the country.

"I am your Excellency's humble servant,

"T. S. C. LOWE."

War-balloons were first regularly used by Louis Napoleon in the Italian War, in 1859. Their success there commended their introduction into the National army, and the attention of the military authorities was early called to the subject. On receiving the above dispatch, Mr. Lincoln invited Mr. Lowe to the Executive mansion. He introduced him to General Scott, and he was soon afterward employed as an aeronaut in the military service. When in use, the balloon is kept under control by strong cords in the hands of men on the ground, who, when the reconnoissance is ended, draw it down to the place of departure.

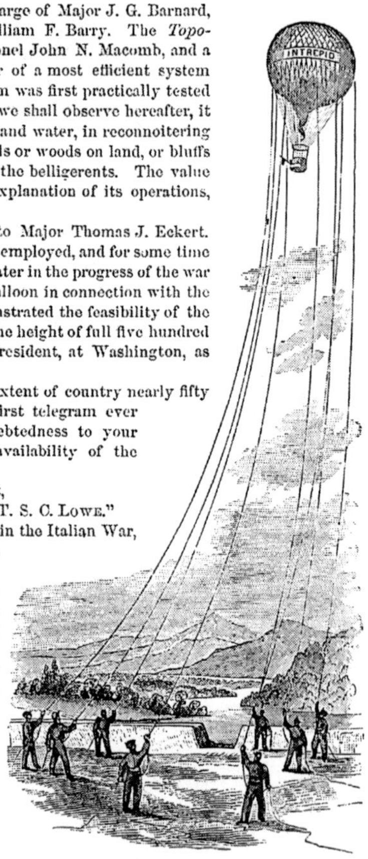

WAR BALLOON.

The *Medical Department* of the army was placed in charge of Surgeons Charles S. Tripler and Jonathan Letterman, who in turn performed the duties of Medical Director. The *Quartermaster's Department* was intrusted to Major S. Van Vliet. The *Subsistence Department* was placed in charge of Captain H. F. Clarke; and to the control of the *Ordnance Department* was assigned Captain C. P. Kingsbury. Colonel Andrew Porter was made *Provost-Marshal General* of the Army of the Potomac; and Colonel Thomas G. Garrett, of the General's staff, was made *Judge Advocate*.—See General McClellan's Report on the *Organization of the Army of the Potomac, and its Campaigns in Virginia and Maryland.*

[2] The different divisions were posted as follows: "Hooker at Budd's Ferry, Lower Potomac; Heintzelman at Fort Lyon and vicinity; Franklin near the Theological Seminary; Blenker near Hunter's Chapel; McDowell at Upton's Hill and Arlington; F. J. Porter at Hall's and Miner's Hills; Smith at Mackall's Hill; McCall at Langley; Buell at Tenallytown, Meridian Hill, Emory's Chapel, &c., on the left bank of the river; Casey at Washington; Stoneman's cavalry at Washington; Hunt's artillery at Washington; Banks at Darnestown, with detachments at Point of Rocks, Sandy Hook, Williamsport, &c.; Stone at Poolesville; and Dix at Baltimore, with detachments on the Eastern shore."

thousand men of all arms[a] were assembled and maneuvered. It was the largest military force ever gathered on the American Continent, and gave the loyal people assurance of the safety of the Republic. And to these troops, regiment after regiment, at the rate of two thousand men each day, and battery after battery, was continually added from the teeming population and immense resources of the Free-labor States. A little later,[a] there was another imposing review. It was of artillery and cavalry alone; when six thousand horsemen, and one hundred and twelve heavy guns, appeared before President Lincoln, the Secretary of State, Prince de Joinville, and other distinguished men. Their evolutions were conducted over an area of about two hundred acres: the cavalry under the direction of General Palmer, and the artillery under the command of General Barry. The whole review was conducted by General Stoneman.

[a] Oct. 1861.

But drills, parades, and reviews were not the only exhibitions of war near the Potomac during these earlier days of autumn. There was some real though not heavy fighting between the opposing forces there. The audacity of the Confederates was amazing. Soon after the Battle of Bull's Run, General Johnston had advanced his outposts from Centreville and Fairfax Court House to Munson's Hill, only six miles in an air-line from Washington City, where the Confederate flag was flaunted for weeks, in full view of the National Capitol. At other points above the city, his scouts pressed up almost to the Potomac, and he was at the same time taking measures for erecting batteries at points below the Occoquan Creek, for the purpose of obstructing the passage of supplies up that river, for the National army around Washington. The probability of such a movement had been perceived at an early day by vigilant and expert men.

FAIRFAX COURT HOUSE.[1]

So early as June, the Navy Department had called the attention of the Secretary of War (Mr. Cameron) to the importance, in view of the possible danger, of seizing and holding Matthias Point, in order to secure the navigation of the river. At different times afterward,[2] the attention of the President, General Scott, and General McClellan was called to the matter by the same Department, but nothing was done until toward the close of September, when Confederate batteries were actually planted there.[3] Then it was proposed to send a land force down the Maryland side of the river, and crossing in boats, covered by the Potomac flotilla, take possession of the shore just above Matthias Point. The Secretary of the Navy, having

[1] This is a view of one of the most frequently mentioned buildings in the records of the Civil War. It is from a sketch made by the author in 1866. It gives the name to the village around it, which is the shiretown of the county. The village was much injured during the war.

[2] July 1st, August 20th, and August 31st.

[3] It appears by an autograph letter before me, written by Colonel Wade Hampton, at Freestone Point, between Occoquan and Dumfries, and dated September 24th, 1861, that a battery was completed at that place, and

use for the Potomac flotilla elsewhere, was anxious that the movement should take place at once.[1] Preparations were accordingly made to send four thousand of Hooker's division for the purpose. The Navy Department furnished transportation, and Captain Craven, the commander of the flotilla, gathered his vessels in the vicinity of Matthias Point, to co-operate in an attack on the batteries there. In the mean time the chief engineer (Major Barnard) reported adversely,[2] and the project was abandoned.

On the assurance of sufficient aid from the Navy Department, it was agreed that a land force should march down the right bank of the Potomac, capture all batteries found there, and take permanent possession of that region. This project was also abandoned, because McClellan believed that the movement might bring on a general engagement, for which he did not feel prepared. No attempt was afterward made to interfere with the Confederates in their mischievous work, and early in October Captain Craven officially announced that the navigation of the Potomac was closed, and the National capital blockaded in that important direction. Craven was so mortified because of the anticipated reproach of the public for the supposed inefficiency of his command, that he made a request to be assigned to duty elsewhere. The President, who had warmly seconded the Navy Department in urging McClellan to take measures for keeping the navigation of the river open, was exceedingly annoyed; whilst the nation at large, unable to understand the cause of this new disaster, and feeling deeply mortified and humiliated, severely censured the Government.[3] That blockade, so disgraceful to the Government, was continued until the Confederates voluntarily evacuated their position in front of Washington, in March following.

---

was ready for action at that date. His letter was addressed to Colonel Thomas Jordan, Beauregard's Assistant Adjutant-General. He says the works were constructed under Captain Lee, whose battery and a long 32-pounder rifled gun were there. The latter had been sent there by General Trimble, a Maryland traitor, then in the Confederate army. He reported that he had every thing in readiness to open fire the previous evening. A fringe of trees had been left standing on the point, to conceal the troops while erecting the works. These were cut down on the night of the 23d.

[1] At that time (late in September) there were in the Potomac the *Pawnee*, *Pocahontas*, and *Seminole*, three heavily armed vessels, and the *R. B. Forbes*, with two very formidable guns on board. These vessels had been detailed to go with Dupont's expedition to Port Royal, and it was urged by the Navy Department that they should first be employed in destroying the Confederate batteries on the river, and assisting the Army of the Potomac in taking possession of their positions.

[2] He referred to the fact that High Point, Freestone Point, and Cock-pit Point, and thence down to Chapawausic Creek, opposite Hooker's quarters at Budd's Ferry, were eligible places for batteries, and considered it unwise to attempt the capture of any already completed, unless a campaign was about to be opened in that direction. He concluded that the best way to prevent the erection of batteries, and to keep open navigation, was to have a sufficient naval force patrolling the Potomac. See McClellan's Report, page 59. In a review of the Peninsula Campaign, Major (then General) Barnard, alluding to this project, says (page 16), if it had been attempted "a Ball's Bluff affair, ten times intensified, would have been the certain result."

[3] General McClellan, in his report to the Secretary of War of the operations of the Army of the Potomac while under his command, made in August, 1863 (nearly two years after the events here recorded), attributed the failure to keep the navigation of the Potomac open, at this time, to the remissness of the Navy Department in not furnishing a sufficient number of armed vessels for the purpose. G. V. Fox, the Assistant Secretary of the Navy, in his testimony before the *Committee on the Conduct of the War* (i. page 239), attributes that failure partly to the remissness of the War Department, under the management of Cameron, but chiefly to the failure of General McClellan to furnish a force from his immense army in time to have taken and held possession of the Virginia shore of the river. The *Committee on the Conduct of the War*, in their summary of the testimony of both Mr. Fox and General McClellan, says: "After repeated efforts, General McClellan promised that 4,000 men should be ready, at a time named, to proceed down the river. The Navy Department provided the necessary transports for the troops, and Captain Craven, commanding the Potomac flotilla, upon being notified to that effect, collected at Matthias Point all the boats of his flotilla at the time named. The troops did not arrive, and the Navy Department was informed of the fact by Captain Craven. Assistant Secretary Fox, upon inquiring of General McClellan why the troops had not been sent, according to agreement, was informed by him that his engineers were of the opinion that so large a body of troops could not be landed, and therefore he had concluded not to send them. Captain Fox replied that the landing of the troops was a matter of which the Navy Depart-

As the Army of the Potomac rapidly increased in numbers and equipment in Virginia in front of Washington, it required more space than the narrow strip between the river and the advance posts of the Confederates, and early in September it was determined to acquire that space by pushing back the intruders. Already there had been several little skirmishes between the pickets and the outposts of the confronting contestants. On the 5th of August, a detachment of the Twenty-eighth New York, under Captain Brush, mostly firemen, attacked a squad of Confederate cavalry in Virginia, opposite the Point of Rocks, killing and wounding eight men, and capturing nine prisoners and twenty horses; and on the 12th a detachment of the Tenth New York, under Captain Kennedy, crossed the Potomac from Sandy Hook, and attacked and routed some Virginia cavalry at Lovettsville.

On the 12th of September,[a] a reconnoissance was made toward Lewinsville, four or five miles from Camp Advance, at the Chain Bridge, by about two thousand men, under the command of General William F. Smith,[1] in charge of a brigade at that post. They had accomplished a topographical survey, for which purpose they were chiefly sent, and were returning, when they were attacked by a body of Virginians,[2] under the command of Colonel J. E. B. Stuart, afterward the famous general leader of cavalry in the Confederate army. Stuart opened heavily with his cannon, which at first disconcerted the National troops. The latter were kept steady until Griffin's Battery was placed in position, when its guns soon silenced those of the Virginians, and scattered their cavalry. Then the National troops, having accomplished their object, returned to their post near the Chain Bridge "in perfect order and excellent spirits," with a loss of two killed and ten wounded.[3]

[a] 1861.

---

ment had charge; that they had provided the necessary means to accomplish the landing successfully; that no inquiry had been made of them in regard to that matter, and no notification that the troops were not to be sent. It was then agreed that the troops should be sent the next night. Captain Craven was again notified, and again had his flotilla in readiness for the arrival of the troops; but no troops were sent down at that time, nor were any ever sent down for that purpose. Captain Fox, in answer to the inquiry of the Committee, as to what reason was assigned for not sending the troops according to the second agreement, replied that the only reason, so far as he could ascertain, was that General McClellan feared that it might bring on a general engagement. The President, who had united with the Navy Department in urging its proposition, first upon General Scott and then upon General McClellan, manifested great disappointment when he learned that the plan had failed in consequence of the troops not being sent. And Captain Craven threw up his command on the Potomac, and applied to be sent to sea, saying that, by remaining here and doing nothing, he was but losing his own reputation, as the blame for permitting the Potomac to be blockaded would be imputed to him and the flotilla under his command."

As the reports of the Committee may be frequently referred to in this work, it is proper to say that it was a joint committee of both Houses of Congress, appointed in December, 1861, consisting of three members of the Senate and four members of the House of Representatives, with instructions to inquire into the conduct of the war. The Committee consisted of B. F. Wade, Z. Chandler, and Andrew Johnson, of the Senate, and D. W. Gooch, John Covode, G. W. Julian, and M. F. Odell, of the House of Representatives. They constituted a permanent court of inquiry, with power to send for persons and papers. When Senator Johnson was appointed Military Governor of Tennessee, his place on the Committee was supplied by Joseph A. Wright, of Indiana.

[1] These troops consisted of the Seventy-ninth (Highlanders) New York Militia; battalions of Vermont and Indiana Volunteers, and of the First United States Chasseurs; a Cavalry company, and Griffin's West Point Battery.

[2] These were the Thirteenth Virginia Volunteers, Rosser's Battery of the Washington Artillery, and a detachment of cavalry.

[3] Reports of Lieutenant-Colonel Shaler and Adjutant Ireland, and dispatch of General McClellan, all dated September 11th, 1861. General McClellan joined the column at the close of the affair. Colonel Stuart (Confederate) gave a glowing account of the confusion into which the Nationals were thrown by his first attack, and gave the affair the aspect of a great victory for himself. He reported "fearful havoc in the ranks of the enemy." "Our loss," he said, "was not a scratch to man or horse."—Stuart's Report, Sept. 11, 1861.

Stuart appears to have been accused of rashness on this occasion, in exposing his cannon to the danger of capture. In an autograph letter before me, dated at Munson's Hill, September 14th, and addressed to General Longstreet, he repels the accusation, and declares that at no time was a piece of his cannon "in a position that it

Three days after the affair near Lewinsville, the pickets on the right of the command of Colonel John W. Geary, of the Twenty-eighth Pennsylvania, stationed three miles above Darnestown, in Maryland, were attacked[a] by four hundred and fifty Virginians, who had boldly crossed the Potomac. A spirited skirmish for about two hours ensued, resulting in a loss to the assailants of eight or ten killed, and several wounded, and their utter repulse. Geary's loss was one killed; and his gain was great animation for the troops under his command, who were charged with holding the country opposite Harper's Ferry. A little later, National troops permanently occupied Lewinsville,[b] Vienna,[c] and Fairfax Court House,[d] the Confederates falling back to Centreville without firing a shot. They had evacuated Munson's Hill on the 28th of September, when the position was formally taken possession of by the Nationals, who had been for some time looking upon it from Bailey's Crossroads with much respect, because of its apparently formidable works and heavy armament. These had been reconnoitered with great caution, and pronounced to be alarmingly strong, when the fort was really a slight earthwork, running irregularly around about four acres on the brow of the hill, without ditch or glacis, "in every respect a squirming piece of work," as an eye-witness wrote. Its armament consisted of one stove-pipe and two logs, the latter with a black disc painted on the middle of the sawed end of each, giving them the appearance, at a distance, of the muzzles of 100-pound Parrott guns. These "Quaker Guns," like similar ones at Manassas a few months later, had, for six weeks, defied the Army of the Potomac. In a house near the fort (which was soon made into a strong regular work), Brigadier-General James Wadsworth, who was placed in command, there made his head-quarters; and on the roof he caused a signal-station to be erected, from which there was an interchange of intelligence with another station on the dome of the capitol at Washington. There the writer visited General Wadsworth, late in November, 1861, and found that ardent and devoted patriot, who had left all the ease and enjoyments which great wealth and a charming domestic circle bestow, and for the sake of his endangered country was enduring all the privations incident to an arduous camp life. His quarters were humble, and in no respect did his arrangements for comfort differ from those of his brother officers.

[a] Sept. 15, 1861.

[b] Oct. 9.

[c] Oct. 16.

[d] Oct. 17.

QUAKER GUN AT MANASSAS.[1]

On the day of the grand review of the cavalry and artillery of the Army

could not have safely retreated from before an army of 10,000 advancing at the double-quick." Longstreet sent Stuart's letter to General Johnson, with an indorsement, testifying to the judicious disposition of the cannon in the engagement.

[1] This is from a photograph by Gardner, of Washington City, and represents one of the logs in the form of a cannon, and painted black, that was found in an embrasure at Manassas, after the Confederates withdrew from that post, in the spring of 1862.

of the Potomac,[1] there was an important movement in the vicinity of Harper's Ferry, which led to a still more important one a week later. On that day,[a] Major J. P. Gould, of the Thirteenth Massachusetts, was sent across the river to some mills a short distance above Harper's Ferry, to seize some wheat there belonging to the Confederates.[2] The movement was made known to General Evans,[3] commanding in the vicinity, and quite a heavy force was sent to oppose them.[4] Geary was called upon for re-enforcements. He promptly responded by crossing the river with about six hundred men and four pieces of cannon, the latter under the respective commands of Captain Tompkins of the Rhode Island Battery, and Lieutenant Martin of the Ninth New York Battery.[5] The wheat was secured and made into flour; and Geary was about to recross the river with his booty, on the morning of the 16th, when his pickets, on Bolivar Heights, two and a half miles west of Harper's Ferry, and extending from the Potomac to the Shenandoah, were attacked by Confederates in three columns, consisting of infantry and cavalry, and supported by artillery. The pickets were driven into the town of Bolivar. Geary, who, with his main body, was on Camp Heights,[6] an eminence around the foot of which nestles the village of Harper's Ferry, rallied them, and a general fight ensued. In his front, on Bolivar Heights, were a large body of troops and three heavy guns, and suddenly there appeared on Loudon Heights on his left, across the Shenandoah River, another large body of men, with four pieces of cannon, which with plunging shot might terribly smite the little National force, and command the ferry on the Potomac.

[a] Oct. 8, 1861.

GEARY'S HEAD-QUARTERS ON CAMP HEIGHTS.

Geary sent a company of the Thirteenth Massachusetts, under Captain Schriber, to guard the fords of the Shenandoah, and prevent troops crossing there and joining those on Bolivar Heights. He then had only four hundred and fifty men left to fight his foe on his front. With these he repelled three

[1] See page 132.

[2] His force consisted of three companies of the Third Wisconsin, and a section of Captain Tompkins's Rhode Island Battery.

[3] This was Colonel Evans, who commanded the extreme left of the Confederates at the stone bridge, at the opening of the battle of Bull's Run, on the morning of the 21st July, 1861. See page 590, volume I.

[4] This force consisted of the Thirteenth and Nineteenth Mississippi, Eighth Virginia, Ashby's Virginia Regiment of cavalry, and Rogers's Richmond Battery of six pieces, the whole commanded by General Evans in person.

[5] The remainder of Geary's force consisted of four companies of the Twenty-eighth Pennsylvania and three of the Third Wisconsin.

[6] Geary's quarters were at the large Government house on Camp Heights, delineated in the engraving, in which Generals Kenley, Banks, and Miles were afterward quartered. It was in a terribly dilapidated condition when the writer visited and sketched it, early in October, 1866, its outer walls scarred by shot and shell, and its interior almost a ruin. On the left of the picture is seen the western slope of Loudon Heights, across the Shenandoah.

fierce charges of Ashby's cavalry, and withstood the storm of bullets from a long line of infantry on Bolivar Heights, until joined, at eleven o'clock, by Lieutenant Martin, with one rifled cannon, with which he had crossed the Potomac Ferry under a galling fire of riflemen on Loudon Heights. These two companies of the Twenty-eighth Pennsylvania turned the Confederate left near the Potomac, and gained a portion of the Heights. At the same time, Martin opened a telling fire on the Confederate cannon in front, and Tompkins silenced two guns on Loudon Heights. The main body moved forward at this crisis, charged the foe, and in a few minutes were in possession of Bolivar Heights from river to river. It was now half-past one o'clock in the afternoon. The Confederates fled, and were driven up the valley in the direction of Halltown. They did not cease their flight until they reached Charlestown, on the line of the railway between Harper's Ferry and Winchester, a distance of six miles.

Major Tyndale arrived from Point of Rocks with five companies of Geary's regiment immediately after the capture of the Heights. He brought with him the standard of the Twenty-eighth Pennsylvania. It was immediately unfurled, "and under its folds," wrote the victor, "we directed the fire of our artillery against the batteries and forces on Loudon Heights, and soon succeeded in silencing every gun and driving away every rebel that could be seen. The victory was now complete."[1] Geary's troops rested until evening, when, there being no military necessity for holding Bolivar Heights at that time, he crossed the Ferry with his whole command and resumed his position in Maryland. His loss was four killed, seven wounded, and two taken prisoners. The loss fell chiefly on the Wisconsin troops.[2] The loss of the Confederates is unknown.

Still more important movements were made on the line of the Potomac River as the beautiful month of October was passing away. At that time Major-General Banks was in command of troops holding the Maryland side of the river from Darnestown to Williamsport. Brigadier-General Charles P. Stone (who had been assigned to the command of a special corps of observation on the right flank of the Army of the Potomac), with a considerable body of troops, then had his head-quarters at Poolesville, a short distance from Conrad's and Edwards's Ferries, on the Potomac River. These ferries were not far from Leesburg, the capital of Loudon County, Virginia, where it was reported that the Confederate left, under General N. G. Evans, was strong in numbers. The troops under Stone confronted this left wing, and commanded the approaches to Leesburg, a village at the terminus of the Alexandria, Loudon, and Hampshire railway, and which was the key to the upper interior communication with the Valley of the Shenandoah. Between the two ferries just named (which were four or five miles apart) was Harrison's Island, three miles in length and very narrow and nearly equally dividing the river.

[1] Report of Colonel John W. Geary, October 18th, 1861. In that report Colonel Geary mentioned the fact that the Honorable Daniel McCook (father of the several McCooks who served the Union cause as general officers so well throughout the war) was in the engagement, gun in hand, as an "amateur soldier."

[2] In his report General Geary said: "The four men who were killed were afterward charged upon by the cavalry and stabbed through the body, stripped of all their clothing, not excepting shoes and stockings, and left in perfect nudity. One was laid out in the form of crucifixion, with his hands spread and cut through the palms with a dull knife. This inhuman treatment incensed our troops exceedingly, and I fear its consequences may be shown in retaliating hereafter."

On the 17th of October it was reported (erroneously) that the Confederates had evacuated Leesburg. General McClellan then determined to make a thorough reconnoissance of the Confederate left, to ascertain their strength, and to cover the operations of his topographical engineers in making a map of that region. He accordingly ordered[a] General McCall, who held the advanced command in Virginia on the right of the National line, to move forward and occupy Drainsville, about half way between the Chain Bridge and Leesburg. He did so, and pushed his scouts forward to Goose Creek, within four miles of the latter place.

[a] Oct. 19, 1861.

On the following morning,[b] General Banks telegraphed to General McClellan from Darnestown, saying, "The signal station at Sugar Loaf telegraphs that the enemy have moved away from Leesburg." McCall had also reported to McClellan the previous evening that he had not encountered any opposition, and that it was reported that the Confederates had abandoned the town. On the strength of Banks's dispatch, and without waiting for later information from Drainsville, McClellan notified[c] General Stone of the movement of McCall. He assured him that "heavy reconnoissances" would be sent out that day "in all directions" from Drainsville, and desired him to keep "a good lookout on Leesburg," to see if it had the effect to drive the Confederates away, adding, "Perhaps a slight demonstration on your part would have the effect to move them." This dispatch reached Stone before noon. He acted promptly, and at evening he telegraphed to the Chief that he had made a feint of crossing the river, during the afternoon, at two places, and had sent out a reconnoitering party toward Leesburg, from Harrison's Island, adding, "I have means of crossing one hundred and twenty-five men once in ten minutes at each of two points." To this dispatch he received no reply.

[b] Oct. 20.

[c] Oct. 20.

The feint had been made at the ferries of Edwards and Conrad, already mentioned. The brigade of General Gorman, Seventh Michigan, two troops of the Van Alen cavalry, and the Putnam Rangers were sent to the former, where a section of Bunting's New York Battery was on duty. To the latter Stone sent a battalion of the Twentieth Massachusetts, under its commander, Colonel Lee, a section of Vaughan's Rhode Island Battery, and Colonel Cogswell's New York (Tammany) Regiment. The ferry was at that time defended by a section of Ricketts's Battery. Colonel Devens was sent to Harrison's Island in two flat-boats from the Chesapeake and Ohio Canal, bearing four companies of his Massachusetts Fifteenth. One company of the same regiment was already there. A reserve, numbering about three thousand men, was held in readiness to co-operate, should a battle ensue. With this reserve was the fine body of Pennsylvanians known as the First California regiment, commanded by Colonel E. D. Baker, then a representative of the State of Oregon in the National Senate. These movements, at first designed as a feint, resulted in a battle.

McCall had made a reconnoissance on Sunday, the 20th,[d] which had evidently caused an opposing movement on the part of the Confederates. An infantry regiment of these had been observed marching from Leesburg and taking shelter behind a hill, about a mile and a half from the position of the Nationals at Edwards's Ferry. In order to disperse or intimidate these, General Gorman was ordered to deploy his forces in their

[d] October.

view. Three flat-boats, filled with troops, were maneuvered as if crossing, and shot and shell were cast into the place where the foe was concealed. This demonstration caused the Confederates to retire, and at twilight Gorman's force returned to camp.

In the mean time, a scouting party of about twenty men had been sent out from Harrison's Island under Captain Philbrick, of the Fifteenth Massachusetts. They ascended the steep bank on the Virginia side, opposite the island, known as Ball's Bluff, which rises about one hundred and fifty feet above the Potomac. Philbrick went a short distance toward Leesburg, when he discovered, as he supposed, a small camp of Confederates, apparently not well guarded. Upon receiving information of this fact, General Stone, who supposed that McCall was near to assist, if necessary, sent orders to Colonel Devens to cross from Harrison's Island with five companies of his regiment, and proceed at dawn to surprise that camp. Colonel Lee was also ordered to cross from the Maryland shore with four companies of his regiment and a four-oared boat, to occupy the island after Devens's departure, and to send one company to the Virginia shore, to take position on the heights there, and cover his return. Two mountain howitzers were also to be sent stealthily up the tow-path of the canal, and carried over to the opposite side of the island, so as to command the Virginia shore. These orders were promptly obeyed. Devens advanced at dawn, but the reported camp could not be found. It proved that other objects had been mistaken for tents. He marched cautiously on to within a mile of Leesburg, without discovering scarcely a trace of a foe. There he halted in a wood, and sent a courier to General Stone for further orders.

Devens had been watched by vigilant Confederates.[1] Evans and his main force lay on Goose Creek. Riflemen and cavalry were hovering near, and waiting a favorable opportunity to strike Devens. He had a slight skirmish with the former, in which one of his men was killed and nine were wounded, when he fell back in safety and in perfect order toward the bluff, at about eight o'clock in the morning, and halted within a mile of the little band under Colonel Lee. While tarrying in an open field of about eight acres, he received a message from General Stone, directing him to remain there until support could be sent to him. The remainder of Devens's regiment had been brought over by Lieutenant-Colonel Ward. His entire force consisted of only six hundred and twenty-five men.

In the mean time, Colonel Baker, who was acting as brigadier-general, in command of the reserves, had been ordered to have the California Regiment, under Lieutenant-Colonel Wistar, at Conrad's Ferry at sunrise, and the remainder of his command ready to move early. In order to divert attention from Devens's movement, Colonel Gorman was directed to send two companies of the First Minnesota Regiment, Colonel Dana, across the river at Edwards's Ferry, under cover of Ricketts's cannon, to make a recon-

---

[1] "An English Combatant" in the Confederate service, in a volume entitled *Battle-fields of the South, from Bull's Run to Gettysburg* (page 80), says that there were several Marylanders in Evans's camp who were employed as spies. Among these was a wealthy young farmer named Elijah White, who resided near Poolesville. He belonged to a company of Confederate cavalry, and often crossed the Potomac by swimming his horse, and gathered valuable information for the insurgents. He sometimes went even to Baltimore, where he held conference with the secessionists, and always returned with assurances that ninety-nine of every hundred of the Marylanders were rebels.

noissance toward Leesburg; and a party of the Van Alen cavalry, led by Major Mix, were ordered to scour the country in the direction of that town, and after gaining all possible information concerning its topography, and the position of the Confederates, to hasten back to the cover of the Minnesota skirmishers. These movements were well performed. The scouts came suddenly upon a Mississippi regiment, when shots were exchanged without much harm to either party.

At a little past noon, Devens and his band were assailed by Confederates under Colonels Jenifer and Hunton, in the woods that skirted the open field in which they had halted. Infantry attacked the main body on their left, and cavalry fell upon the skirmishers in front. His men stood their ground firmly; but, being pressed by overwhelming numbers, and re-enforcements not arriving, they fell back about sixty paces, to foil an attempt to flank them. This was accomplished, and they took a position about half a mile in front of Colonel Lee.

In the mean time Colonel Baker had been pressing forward from Conrad's Ferry, to the relief of the assailed troops. Ranking Devens, he had been ordered to Harrison's Island to take the chief command, with full discretionary powers to re-enforce the party on the Virginia shore, or to withdraw all of the troops to the Maryland shore. He was cautioned to be careful with the artillery under his control, and not to become engaged with greatly superior numbers.

E. D. BAKER.

When Baker found that Devens had been attacked, he decided to re-enforce him. It was an unfortunate decision, under the circumstances, and yet it then seemed to be the only proper one. The task was a most difficult and perilous one. The river had been made full by recent rains, and the currents in the channels on each side were very swift. The means for transportation were entirely inadequate. There had been no expectation of such movement, and no provision had been made for it. There was only one scow, or flat-boat, for the service, between the Maryland shore and Harrison's Island, and at first only two skiffs and a Francis metallic life-boat were on the opposite side. To these were soon added one scow; and these four little vessels composed the entire means of transportation of several hundred troops and munitions of war.

McClellan had not ordered more than a "demonstration" by a small portion of Stone's troops, in conjunction with those of McCall; but Stone, to whom the chief had not intimated his object in ordering "heavy reconnoissances in all directions" in that vicinity, and who knew that there were forty thousand troops within easy call of his position, naturally considered that they were to complete the expulsion of the Confederates from the Potomac. He therefore made what disposition he might to assist in the movement, in conjunction with McCall, and, as he supposed, with the division of General Smith, known to be within supporting distance.[1] He was ignorant of the very important fact that, on the previous evening, General McClellan had ordered McCall to fall back from Drainesville. It was so. At the very time when Baker was preparing to pass over the reserves in force, McCall, by order of McClellan, was marching back to his camp near the Chain Bridge, and Smith was without orders to do any thing in particular, thus making the peril that threatened the Nationals at Ball's Bluff much greater for want of this support.

Colonel Baker, like General Stone, was ignorant of this damaging movement, and was pressing on in high spirits, with the most wearisome and perplexing toil in slowly passing his troops in three scows,[2] when, hearing the sound of battle on the Virginia shore, he hastened over in a small skiff, leaving instructions to forward the artillery as quickly as possible. His California regiment had already crossed and joined Devens and Lee. A rifled 6-pounder of Bunting's Rhode Island Battery, under Lieutenant Bramhall, followed them. Two howitzers under Lieutenant French were already there; and, just before Baker reached the Bluff, a detachment of Cogswell's Tammany Regiment had climbed the winding path leading up from the river. Baker now took command of all the forces on the Bluff, numbering nineteen hundred.[3] These were immediately formed in battle order, and awaited attack.

The ground on which the Nationals were compelled to give battle was unfavorable for them. It was an open field, surrounded on three sides by a dense forest, and terminating on the fourth at the brow of the high bluff at the river. With their backs to the stream, the Union forces were prepared for the contest, which was begun at three o'clock in the afternoon, by General Evans, who hurled the Eighteenth Mississippi, under Colonel Burt, upon Baker's left flank, and the commands of Jenifer and Hunton upon his front.[4] These came from the woods, that swarmed with Confederates, and were received with the most determined spirit. The battle instantly became general and severe. Colonel Featherston, with the Seventeenth Mississippi, joined in the fray. Bramhall and French soon brought their heavy guns to bear, and were doing good execution, when both officers were borne wounded away, and their pieces were hauled to the rear, to prevent their falling into the hands of their foe. A greater calamity speedily followed. The gallant Baker was seen here and there in the thickest of the fight, encouraging his men by words and deeds, and when the battle had lasted nearly two hours he fell dead, pierced with many bullets.[5]

---

[1] See page 135.

[2] The current was so strong and deep that it could be navigated by the scows only by dragging them up the Maryland shore above the island, and letting them float diagonally across the stream until they touched the island. The voyage from the latter to the Virginia shore was accomplished in the same way. The operation was very slow, and the passage of the few troops occupied about three hours.

[3] Baker's entire force consisted of the California Regiment, Lieutenant-Colonel Wistar, 570; the New York Tammany Regiment, Colonel Milton Cogswell, 360; and portions of the Fifteenth Massachusetts, Colonel Devens, 653 and of the Twentieth, Colonel Lee, 318—total, 1,901.

[4] The attacking troops were Evans's brigade, composed of the Eighth Virginia, and Thirteenth, Seventeenth, and Eighteenth Mississippi.

[5] Colonel Baker was probably killed instantly. Eye-witnesses say that a tall, red-haired man appeared emerging from the smoke, and approaching to within five feet of the commander, fired into his body the contents of a self-cocking revolver pistol. At the same moment a bullet entered his skull behind his ear, and a

The immediate command now devolved upon Colonel Lee, but Cogswell, his superior, soon took the control of affairs. Seeing the desperate situation of the troops, with an overwhelming force on their front and flanks, and a deep and turbulent river in their rear, Cogswell ordered them to move to the left, and attempt to cut their way through to Edwards's Ferry, about three miles distant, where they might receive the aid of the force there under General Stone. This movement was about to take place, when the Tammany Regiment, deceived by the beckoning of a Confederate officer, whom they mistook for a National one, dashed off on a charge in the direction indicated by the deceiver, carrying with them the rest of the line. Then a destructive fire at close distance was poured upon the whole column by the Thirteenth Mississippi Regiment, Colonel William Barksdale, which advanced from the direction of the ferry. Cogswell's plan was frustrated, and he gave orders for his whole force to retire immediately to Harrison's Island, and thence to the Maryland shore.

That retreat almost instantly became a rout. Down the steep declivity the Nationals hurried, in wild disorder, to reach the boats, while the Confederates, who had followed them up to the brow of the bluff with ball and bayonet, fired into the straggling mass below with murderous effect. The fugitives huddled on the shore, formed in some order at first, and kept up the hopeless fight for a time, while endeavoring to cross the flood to Harrison's Island. Only one large flat-boat was there, and that, with an over-load of wounded and others, at the beginning of its first voyage, was riddled with bullets, and sunk. The smaller vessels had disappeared in the gloom, and there was no means of escape for the Unionists but by swimming. This was attempted by some. Several of them were shot in the water,[1] and others, swept away by the current in the darkness, were drowned.[2] A little more than one-fourth of the whole of Cogswell's

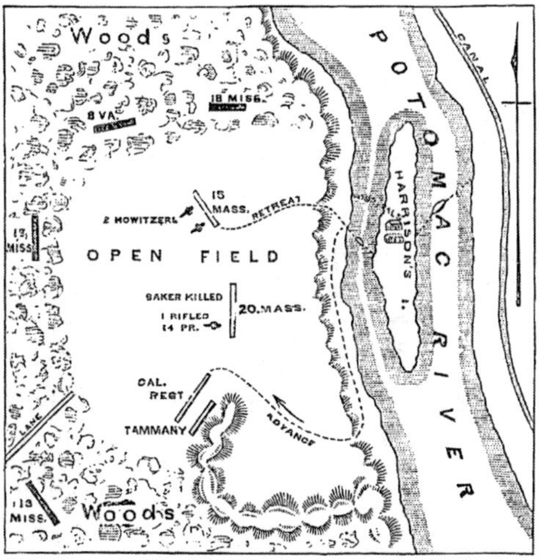

MAP OF THE BATTLE OF BALL'S BLUFF.

sling from a Mississippi Yager wounded his arm and made a terrible opening in his side. Captain Beirel, of the California regiment, who was close by Baker, caught the slayer of his friend by the throat, just as he was stooping to seize the colonel's sword, and with his pistol blew out his brains. Baker had enjoined many of his California regiment that if he should fall in battle, not to let the Confederates get possession of his body. Beirel, the avenger, and the brave leader of company G of that regiment, acting upon these instructions, raised the precious burden in his arms and bore it away amid a shower of bullets, and delivered it to Major Young, who conveyed it safely to the river and took it across.

[1] Pollard says (i. 181) that after the Nationals had surrendered, "the Confederates kept up their fire upon those who tried to cross, and many not drowned in the river were shot in the act of swimming."

[2] The gallant Captain Beirel was among the last who left the shore and swam across the river. He was compelled to drop his sword midway, in order to save his life. Many of the men, before they surrendered, threw their arms into the river. Bramhall's gun had been spiked and completely disabled. It was brought to the bluff and tumbled over, with the intention of having it go into the river.

command, including himself and Colonel Lee, were made prisoners, and marched off to Leesburg, whilst Colonel Devens escaped on his horse, that swam across the turbulent Potomac. A few were saved from captivity by stealing along under the banks, and making their way to Gorman's camp below.

While the contest was raging at Ball's Bluff, General Stone, who was at Edwards's Ferry with about seven thousand troops, had been sending over the remainder of Gorman's brigade to co-operate with Baker, all the while unsuspicious of the perilous condition of the troops of that commander. He had received information from time to time that Baker was perfectly able to hold his position, if not to advance; and, believing that he would repulse and drive his assailants, he was prepared to push Colonel Gorman forward to strike the retreating forces on their flank. He felt anxious, however, and at four o'clock telegraphed to General Banks for a brigade of his division, to place on the Maryland shore, in support of the troops on Harrison's Island and the severely pressed combatants on Ball's Bluff.[1]

BANKS'S HEAD-QUARTERS AT EDWARDS'S FERRY.

A little while afterward, the sad news of Baker's death was received, and Stone hastened forward to take command in person. On his way he was met by some of the fugitives, with the tale that the Confederates were ten thousand strong, and that all was lost. Still ignorant of the position of McCall, he left orders to hold Harrison's Island, and then hastened back to Edwards's Ferry, to secure the safety of the twenty-five hundred troops that he had sent across the river. There he was joined by General Banks,

a Oct. 22, 1861. at three o'clock in the morning,[a] who took the chief command. Orders arrived at about the same time, from General McClellan, to hold the Island and the Virginia shore at all hazards, and intimating that re-enforcements would be sent.[2]

So ended the BATTLE OF BALL'S BLUFF,[3] in disaster to the National arms. In the camps of the Unionists, in the vicinity of the battle, on that gloomy night of the 21st of October, there was darkness and woe, while the little

---

[1] Stone had kept McClellan advised of the progress of affairs at Ball's Bluff during the afternoon, and the latter commander, toward evening, ordered General Banks to send one brigade to the support of the troops on Harrison's Island, and to move with the other two to Seneca Mills, ready to support General Stone, at Edwards's Ferry.—See McClellan's Report, page 34.

[2] Reports of General Charles P. Stone and his subordinates, October 28th, 1861, and of General N. G. Evans, the Confederate commander, October 25th, 1861. The latter report was, in several respects, marred by misrepresentations. It represented the Confederate force at only 1,709, omitting to state the fact that there was a strong reserve of Mississippi troops, with six guns, posted so as to repel any troops that might approach from Edwards's Ferry. From the best information since obtained, it is agreed that Evans's force numbered 4,000. His report also claimed that, with his small force of 1,700, eight thousand Nationals were fought and beaten, and that the Confederates killed and captured a greater number than their whole force engaged. It also declared that long-range cannon were fired upon the Confederates from the Maryland side of the river, when there were no heavy guns there at the time of the battle.

[3] This is called the Battle of Leesburg by Confederate writers.

village of Leesburg, near by, whither the captives were taken, was brilliantly illuminated, and the Confederates there were wild with joy. The Union loss was about one thousand men and three cannon. Nearly three hundred men were killed, and over five hundred were made prisoners and taken to Richmond.[1] The Confederate loss was about three hundred. According to General Evans's report, he had one hundred and fifty-three killed, including Colonel E. R. Burt, of the Eighteenth Mississippi, and two taken prisoners. He did not mention the number of his wounded, which was reported to be large.

The death of Senator Baker was felt as a national calamity.[2] He was one of the ablest men of his time as a statesman and orator. Thoroughly comprehending the great issue, and the horrible crime of the conspirators, he had eagerly left the halls of legislation (where he had combated the friends of the criminals with eloquent words, and voted for abundant means to crush the rebellion) to lead his countrymen into battle for the right. The achievements of his little band at Ball's Bluff, who composed a part of the Army of the Potomac, assisted greatly in effacing from the escutcheon of that army the stain it received at the battle of Bull's Run.

Again, as in the case of the battle of Bull's Run, the grieved, and disappointed, and mortified loyal people demanded an explanation of the catastrophe. To the most inexpert there appeared evidence of fatal mismanagement. General McClellan, General Stone, and Colonel Baker all received censure at different times, and by different persons; the first, for remissness in duty in not informing Stone of the retrograde movement of McCall, and sending re-enforcements; the second, for sending troops across the river without adequate transportation for a larger body at a time; and the third, for rashness in crossing at all and engaging the Confederates, double his own in numbers.

There was a natural clamor for investigation, and, on the assembling of Congress, the House of Representatives passed a resolution asking the

---

[1] Twenty-four of the prisoners were officers, namely, two colonels, one major, one adjutant, one assistant-surgeon, seven captains, and twelve lieutenants. The colonels were M. Cogswell (Captain of the Eighth U. S. Infantry), of the Forty-second New York Volunteers, and W. Raymond Lee, of the Twentieth Massachusetts Volunteers. The major was P. J. Rivers, of the latter regiment. At Leesburg, General Evans (who was represented as a tall, strong man, of unusual length of limb, and in manners courteous and dignified) offered the captains a parole on the condition that they should not, unless exchanged, again "bear arms against the Southern Confederacy." They refused to accept it, and were sent to Richmond by way of Manassas, arriving there at nine o'clock in the morning of the 24th of October, where they were greeted with many jeers from an immense crowd, such as "I say, Yanks, how do you feel?" The captains were confined in the tobacco warehouse, already mentioned on page 26, where they were soon brought under the petty tyranny of the notorious General Winder. A full account of the experience of the captains may be found in a little volume entitled "*Prison Life in the Tobacco Warehouse at Richmond*," by Lieutenant William C. Harris, of Baker's California regiment.

[2] In a general order issued by McClellan, on the day after the battle, he announced the death of Baker, and spoke of him as one having "many titles to honor," as a patriot "zealous for the honor of his adopted country" (he was born in England), cut off "in the fullness of his power as a statesman, and in the course of a brilliant career as a soldier distinguished in two wars." When Congress met, in December, the Senate appointed a day (the 11th of that month) for the consideration of the death of this distinguished member. The President was there to participate in the mournful proceedings. Most touching eulogies were pronounced by the dead hero's compatriots of the Senate. From that body went resolutions to the House of Representatives, where like proceedings were held; and all over the country there was general grief because of the fall of that noble man. In California, which had been his chosen residence for a long time, the news of his death created a profound sensation. It reached San Francisco a few days after the battle, the line of telegraph between the Atlantic and Pacific oceans having been just completed. That line was opened for messages on the 25th of October, when a communication (the first) was sent by Judge Field to President Lincoln. While they were preparing in San Francisco, on the following day, to fire a salute in honor of this important event, a dispatch from the East announced the death of Baker. Rejoicing was changed into mourning, and the celebration was deferred.

Secretary of War "whether any, and, if any, what measures had been taken to ascertain who was responsible for the disastrous movement of
[a] Dec. 16, 1861. the National troops at Ball's Bluff." It was answered[a] that General McClellan was of the opinion that "an inquiry on the subject of the resolution would, at that time, be injurious to the public service." But General McClellan had already answered that inquiry, so far as one of the commanders was concerned. He was at Stone's head-quarters, at Poolesville, twenty-four hours after the disaster, and from there had telegraphed to the President, saying, "I have investigated this matter, and General Stone is without blame. Had his orders been followed, there could (or would) have been no disaster."[1] This was unknown to the public. They were dissatisfied with the apparent desire on the part of the General-in-chief to stifle investigation, and more than ever he was held to be personally responsible for the disaster.

For a time there were warm discussions in Congress on the subject. Finally a victim appeared to propitiate the public feeling, in the
[b] Feb. 8, 1862. person of General Stone, who was arrested[b] by order of the War Department and sent to Fort Lafayette, at the entrance to New York Bay, and then used for the confinement of political prisoners. There he was detained until the following August, when, without trial, or any public proceedings whatever, he was released. That fortress being a place of durance for men charged with treasonable acts, this gallant and truly patriotic officer suffered patiently and silently, for a greater portion of the war, under the imputations of disloyalty. He was imprisoned without public accusation, was held a prisoner about six months, in profound ignorance of any charges against him, and was released without comment by the power that closed the prison doors upon him.[2]

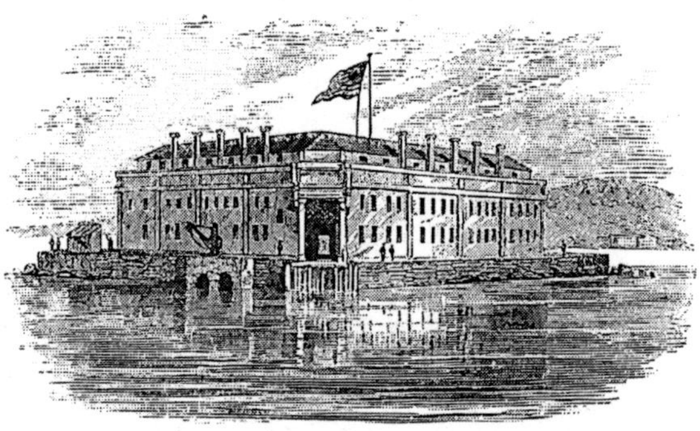

FORT LAFAYETTE.

But little more remains to be said concerning affairs at Ball's Bluff.

---

[1] Dispatch to President Lincoln, Tuesday evening, October 22d, 1861. General Stone well knew that the public would naturally blame him for the disaster, he being in chief command there, and he had suggested to General McClellan that he should desire a court of inquiry, when that officer showed him the above satisfactory vindication by the highest authority.

[2] The proceedings in this case were extraordinary. So full was the acquittal of all blame accorded by General McClellan to General Stone, in his dispatch to the President, that Stone was not only retained in command, but his force was increased to the number of 12,000 men. For about a hundred days Stone was busily engaged in his duties, and had just submitted to McClellan a plan for the capture of General D. H. Hill and his force of 4,500 men, lying opposite his camp, when he was ordered to Washington, and placed before the Committee on the Conduct of the War, to answer charges against his loyalty. His explanations were such that the Committee simply reported to the Secretary of War that, on the points to which his attention had been called, "the testimony was conflicting."

General Stone heard nothing more of the matter until the night of the 8th of February, when, after being engaged at Willard's hotel, in Washington, in the examination of maps until almost midnight, he was retiring to his residence, he found General Sykes, an old friend, and then commander of the city guard, waiting for him.

Supposing all the troops to be on the Virginia side of the Potomac, McClellan telegraphed to Stone to intrench himself there, and to hold his position, at all hazards, until re-enforcements should arrive. At the same time he ordered Banks to remove the remainder of his division to Edwards's Ferry, and send over as many men as possible to re-enforce Stone. These orders were promptly obeyed. Intrenchments were thrown up; large numbers of

with orders from General McClellan for his arrest, and immediate departure for Fort Lafayette.* He exchanged his military for citizen's dress, said a few consoling words to his wife, and departed for Sykes's quarters. where he was kept until morning, and then sent under a guard to Fort Hamilton, near Fort Lafayette. Before leaving he had written to the Adjutant-General, asking for information concerning his arrest, not doubting that there was some strange misunderstanding in the matter. On the 10th he was in the custody of Colonel Burke, at Fort Hamilton, and was then taken over to Fort Lafayette in a boat. There he was confined in a casemate fifty-four days, receiving the most kind treatment. There he again wrote to the Adjutant-General, requesting a copy of charges, and a trial, but, as before, was denied any response.

In the mean time, General Stone's friends had unsuccessfully endeavored to obtain justice for him at Washington. When his brother-in-law, on his way thither, stopped in New York, to consult with Lieutenant-General Scott, the astonished veteran, who had not till then heard of his arrest, indignantly exclaimed, "Colonel Stone a traitor! Why, if he is a traitor, I am a traitor, and we are all traitors. While holding Washington last year, he was my right hand, and I do not hesitate to say that I could not have held the place without him."†

After the lapse of fifty-four days, General Stone was transferred to Fort Hamilton, where he had larger liberty. He was released on the 16th of August, by an order from the War Department, sent by telegraph. He immediately applied for orders to active duty; and on returning to Washington he searched in vain in the office of the Adjutant-General and of the War Department for the order for his arrest; the law requiring the officer issuing such order to give a statement in writing, signed with his own name, and noting the offense, within twenty-four hours. Halleck, then General-in-Chief, knew nothing about it. Stone then went to the President, who said he knew nothing about the matter, but kindly remarked, "I could never be made to believe General Stone was a traitor." In endeavors to give to his country his active services in the war he was thwarted, and it was not until May, 1863, that he was allowed to enter again upon duty in the field, when he was ordered to report to General Banks, then the commander of the Department of the Gulf. He served faithfully during the remainder of the war, until prostrated by malarious fever before Petersburg, when the service lost a meritorious and patriotic officer.

In this connection, the following letter, written to the author by the Superintendent of the Metropolitan Police of the City of New York, may be appropriately given. It furnishes interesting additions to the history of Mr. Lincoln's journey from Philadelphia to Washington, in February, 1861, given in the first volume of this work.

"Office of the Superintendent of Metropolitan Police,
"300 Mulberry Street.
"*New York, August 13th,* 1866.

"Benson J. Lossing, Esq.,
"Poughkeepsie, New York.

"Dear Sir:—On reading your description of the manner in which the late President Lincoln was induced to change his route in going to the City of Washington, in February, 1861, I was impressed with the faithfulness, so far as the narrative goes, but regretted that it was not more full in showing how and to whom the country is indebted for the safety of his valuable life at that important period.

"It will be remembered that there was much uncertainty at the beginning of the late rebellion as to what course the conspirators designed taking to carry out their plans; and, with the view of ascertaining their purpose, in the latter part of December, 1860, I detailed two of my most intelligent detectives to proceed to Washington, with instructions to endeavor to discover the secret plans of the conspirators, if they had any, for taking possession of the seat of Government, and to communicate with Senator Grimes, of Iowa, on the subject. I did not know the Senator personally at that time, but I had a reputation of him that justified me in confiding in him.

"On Friday, January 4th, 1861, I received a note from Hon. Schuyler Colfax, requesting me to send a number of detectives to Washington, for the same purpose that I had already dispatched the two alluded to. I then

* In the report of the Committee on the Conduct of the War (Part II., page 18) is a statement of General McClellan, that on the day of the arrest he received information from a refugee from Leesburg, which, in his mind, "tended to corroborate some of the charges made against General Stone," which he reported to the Secretary of War, and received orders to arrest the General and send him immediately to Fort Lafayette. What those charges were, neither the Committee on the Conduct of the War nor General McClellan ever made public.

† When, late in 1860, General Stone, who had left the army (in which he held the commission of captain by brevet, awarded for meritorious services in Mexico), was in Washington City, General Scott desired him to rally around him the loyal men of the District of Columbia. He complied, and on the 1st of January, 1861, he was made Inspector-general of the District. He at once commenced organizing and instructing volunteers and when Fort Sumter was attacked he had under him no less than 3,000 well-organized troops fit for service. He was the first man mustered into the service for the defense of the Capital. That was done on the 2d day of January, 1861. He was in command of the troops in Washington during the dark days at the close of April, when that city was cut off from the loyal people. During those seven days, he slept but three hours in his bed, all other rest being taken in his military cloak. All the outposts around Washington were under his command until the passage of a portion of the army into Virginia, in May (see pages 480, 481, and 482, volume I.), and some of his troops were the first to encounter the pickets of the insurgents.

troops were crossed, and active preparations were in progress for moving strongly upon the Confederates, when, on Tuesday night,[a] General McClellan arrived at Poolesville. Then, as he says, he "learned, for the first time, the full details of the affair." The preparations for a forward movement, which promised the most important results for the National cause, were immediately suspended, and orders were

[a] Oct. 23, 1861.

---

determined to go that night myself, and take with me another of my men. I purposed looking the field over, with the view of ascertaining the probability of such an attempt being made. In the morning of Saturday I found a want of harmony among the friends of the Union—scarcely any two looked at the crisis through the same medium. Mr. Colfax invited me to attend a meeting of a sort of committee of members of both houses of Congress, at the residence of Senator Trumbull, that morning. It numbered about a dozen persons, and there were about twelve different opinions among them as to the ultimate designs of the conspirators. The extreme views were entertained by Senator Trumbull and Rep. E. B. Washburn. One of these gentlemen regarded the 'matter as nothing more than the usual Southern vaunting; that the South had been badly defeated, and the secession talk meant nothing but braggadocio; that they had had things so long their own way, it could not be expected of them to quietly submit to defeat; a few weeks and all would be peaceful again.' The other gentleman was of opinion 'that the Southern men meant every word they uttered; that they had been preparing for this thing since 1832; that he was convinced they had selected this time because they think themselves ready, while we are not; that they have made preparations which we know nothing about; that their plan was to destroy the Government and to start one of their own; and that to take possession of Washington was more than half the battle.'

"None of the remaining gentlemen agreed with either of these, nor with themselves.

"While at this meeting, I learned that a large number of detectives had been sent for to all the larger cities, East, North, and West, and among these it was mentioned that Marshal Kane, of Baltimore, had been applied to, and had promised to send ten detectives. I told the gentlemen plainly the Marshal would betray them; that his sympathies were with the South in any movement they would make; that but a few weeks before he had declined an invitation to exchange a detective of his for one of mine, on the ground that he had but *one* in his force, and consequently he could not now furnish them with ten. In reply, I was informed that Mr. Corwin had confidence in Marshal Kane, and they also had confidence in Mr. Corwin. So, as they decided to hold on to the Marshal and his bogus detectives, I concluded not to act with them.

"I then called on a number of other members of Congress, without finding much improvement; the exceptional case was Senator Grimes. One distinguished Senator informed me that he was in counsel with Jefferson Davis, and that in a day or two *they* would be able to adjust all apparent differences.

"After that I went among the people, and soon found that Mr. Washburn was nearer right than any other member of Congress I had talked with. I also found that the safety of the country depended on Lieutenant-General Scott, and I determined to consult with him; but I feared the General could not spare sufficient time to talk with me as fully as I desired, and then concluded to see one of his confidential officers. On inquiring, I learned that two of General Scott's family had great influence with him, Col. Robt. E. Lee and Capt. Chas. P. Stone. I do not know what induced me to select Captain Stone in preference to Col. Lee, but I did so, and called on the Captain at his quarters. We conversed freely in regard to the impending trouble, and especially of the danger in which Washington stood. I informed him I would leave three of my detectives in the city, and, at his request, agreed to instruct them to report to him verbally any things of importance they should discover.

"I stopped in Baltimore that night on my way home, and ascertained from Marshal Kane himself the plan by which Maryland was to be precipitated out of the Union, against the efforts of Govr. Hicks to keep it there; and with Maryland also the District of Columbia. He told me Maryland would wait for the action of Virginia, and that action would take place within a month; and 'that when Virginia seceded through a convention, Maryland would secede by gravitation.' It was at this interview I ascertained Fort McHenry to be garrisoned by a corporal's guard, consisting of one man, and that the Baltimore police were keeping guard on the outside, to prevent the roughs from capturing it prematurely. I communicated the facts to Captain Stone, and on the following Wednesday, January 9th, troops from Washington took possession of the fort, under orders from General Scott.

"At a subsequent visit to Washington I called, of course, on Captain Stone, and informed him of the purposes contemplated in Baltimore. He then requested me to put some of my men on duty there, and instruct them to report to him in person, by word of mouth, and not by mail, as he could not trust the mails. I had previously placed two men there, and on my return selected a third, whom I sent directly to Captain Stone for special instructions. Under these instructions, this officer, David S. Bookstaver, remained at Baltimore until February 23d, when I relieved him. During that period, while apparently occupied as a music agent, Bookstaver gave particular attention to the sayings and doings of the better class of citizens and strangers who frequent music, variety, and book stores, while the other two detectives had joined an organization of rebel roughs, destined to go South or elsewhere, whenever their services should be required.

"It was on the evening of Wednesday, February 20th, that Bookstaver obtained the information that made it necessary for him to take the first train for Washington. Before going, he posted a letter to me, briefly stating the condition of things, and of his intention to go on the four o'clock morning train and report. I shall complete this narrative with an extract from a letter written by Captain Stone on the subject.

"'It is impossible, with the time now at my disposal, to give you any thing like a detailed history of the information derived from your men, and from dozens of letters and reports from other sources, addressed some-

given for the entire force to recross the river to the Maryland side. Generals Banks and Stone, and the troops under their commands, were disappointed and mortified, for they knew of no serious impediments then in the way of an advance. General McClellan subsequently said, that "a few days afterward," he "received information which seemed to be authentic, to the effect that large bodies of the enemy had been ordered from Manassas to Leesburg, to cut off our troops on the Virginia side;" and that their "timely withdrawal had probably prevented a still more serious disaster."[1] Plain people inquired whether sufficient re-enforcements for the Nationals, to counteract the movement from Manassas, might not have been spared from the almost one hundred thousand troops then lying at ease around Washington, only a few miles distant. Plain people were answered by the question, What do you know about war?

---

times to the General-in-Chief and sometimes to myself, which served to convince both of us that there was imminent danger that Mr. Lincoln's life would be sacrificed, should he attempt to pass through Baltimore at the time and in the manner published in the newspapers as the programme of his journey.

"'The closing piece of information on the subject was brought by one of your men, Bookstaver. He had for weeks been stationed in Baltimore, and on the morning of Thursday (two days before the intended passage of Mr. Lincoln through Baltimore) he arrived by the early train and reported to me. His information was entirely corroborative of that already in our possession; and at the time of making my morning report to the General-in-Chief, I communicated *that*. General Scott had received from other sources urgent warnings also, and he stated to me that it was almost a certainty that Mr. Lincoln could not pass Baltimore alive by the train on the day fixed. "But," said the General, "while you and I know this, we cannot convince these gentlemen that Mr. Lincoln is not coming to Washington to be inaugurated as quietly as any previous President."

"'I recommended that Mr. Lincoln should be officially warned; and suggested that it would be altogether best that he should take the train of that evening from Philadelphia, and so reach Washington early the next day. General Scott said that Mr. Lincoln's personal dignity would revolt at the idea of changing the programme of his journey on account of danger to his life. I replied to this, that it appeared to me that Mr. Lincoln's personal dignity was of small account in comparison with the destruction, or, at least, dangerous disorganization of the United States Government, which would be the inevitable result of his death by violence in Baltimore; that in a few days more the term of Mr. Buchanan would end, and there would (in case of Mr. Lincoln's death) be no elected President to assume the office; that the Northern cities would, on learning of the violent death of the President-elect, pour masses of excited people upon Baltimore, which would be destroyed, and we should find ourselves in the worst form of civil war, with the Government utterly unprepared for it.

"'General Scott, after asking me how the details could be arranged in so short a time, and receiving my suggestion that Mr. Lincoln should be advised quietly to take the evening train, and that it would do him no harm to have the telegraph wires cut for a few hours, he directed me to seek Mr. W. H. Seward, to whom he wrote a few lines, which he handed me.

"'It was already ten o'clock, and when I reached Mr. Seward's house he had left: I followed him to the Capitol, but did not succeed in finding him until after 12 M. I handed him the General's note; he listened attentively to what I said, and asked me to write down my information and suggestions, and then, taking the paper I had written, he hastily left.

"'The note I wrote was what Mr. Frederick Seward carried to Mr. Lincoln in Philadelphia. Mr. Lincoln has stated that it was this note which induced him to change his journey as he did. The stories of *disguise* are all nonsense; Mr. Lincoln merely took the sleeping-car in the night train. I know nothing of any connection of Mr. Pinkerton with the matter.'

"The letter from which the above extract is made was sent to me by General Stone, in reply to an inquiry of mine, made in consequence of having seen an article in a newspaper which gave the whole credit of the movement to a person who I supposed had little to do with it. My opportunity for knowing who the parties were that rendered this service to the country was very good, but I thought it advisable to have the testimony of one of the most active in it to sustain my views. For obvious reasons, I have not called on either of the other living parties to the matter, regarding the above sufficient to satisfy all reasonable persons that the assassination consummated in April, 1865, would have taken place in February of 1861 had it not been for the timely efforts of Lieutenant-General Scott, Brigadier-General Stone, Hon. Wm. H. Seward, Frederick W. Seward, Esq., and David S. Bookstaver, of the Metropolitan Police of New York.

"I am, very respectfully, yours, &c.,

"JOHN A. KENNEDY."

[1] See General McClellan's Report, page 34.

CHAPTER VI.

THE ARMY OF THE POTOMAC.—THE TRENT AFFAIR.—CAPTURE OF ROANOKE ISLAND.

FOR the space of nearly two months after the disaster at Ball's Bluff, the public ear was daily teased with the unsatisfactory report, "All is quiet on the Potomac!" The roads leading toward the Confederate camps, near Bull's Run, were never in better condition. The weather was perfect in serenity. The entire autumn in Virginia was unusually magnificent in all its features. Much of the time, until near Christmas, the atmosphere was very much like that of the soft Indian summer time. Regiment after regiment was rapidly swelling the ranks of the Army of the Potomac to the number of two hundred thousand men, thoroughly equipped and fairly disciplined; while at no time did any reliable report make that of the Confederates in front of it over sixty thousand. Plain people wondered why so few, whom politicians called "ragamuffins" and "a mob," could so tightly hold the National Capital in a state of siege, while the "bravest and best men of the North," fully armed and provisioned, were in and around it, and Nature and Patriotism invited them to walk out and disperse the besiegers, lying not two days' march from that Capital. But what did plain people know about war? Therefore so it was that they were satisfied, or tried to be satisfied, with a very little of it from time to time, though paying at enormous rates in gold and muscle for that little. And so it was that when, just before Christmas, the "quiet on the Potomac" was slightly broken by an event we are about to consider, the people, having learned to expect little, were greatly delighted by it. Let us see what happened.

FORAGERS AT WORK.

When McCall fell back from Drainsville, the Confederates reoccupied it. His main encampment was at Langley, and Prospect Hill, near the Leesburg road, and only a few miles above the Chain Bridge, on the Virginia side. The Confederates became very bold after their victory at the Bluff, and pushing their picket-guards far up toward the National lines, they made many incursions in search of forage, despoiling Union men, and distressing the country in general. With

McClellan's permission, McCall prepared to strike these Confederates a blow that should make them more circumspect, and stop their incursions. He had observed that on such occasions they generally left a strong reserve at Drainsville, and he determined to attempt their capture when an opportunity should offer. Later in December the opportunity occurred, and he ordered Brigadier-General E. O. C. Ord to attempt the achievement; and at the same time to gather forage from the farms of the secessionists.

E. O. C. ORD.

Ord, with his brigade,[1] undertook the enterprise on the 20th.[a] McCall ordered Brigadier-General Reynolds to move forward with his brigade toward Leesburg, as far as Difficult Creek, to support Ord, if required. When the force of the latter was within two miles of Drainsville, and his foragers were loading their wagons, the troops were attacked by twenty-five hundred Confederates, under General J. E. B. Stuart,[2] who came up the road from the direction of Centreville. A severe fight ensued. The Confederates were greatly outnumbered, and were soon so beaten that they fled in haste, carrying in their wagons little else than their wounded men. The brunt of the battle had fallen on the Sixth and Ninth Pennsylvania, the Rifles, and Easton's Battery. The National loss consisted of seven killed and sixty wounded; and their gain was a victory, and "sixteen wagon-loads of excellent hay, and twenty-two of corn." Stuart reported his loss at forty-three killed and one hundred and forty-three wounded.[3] He had been induced to attack superior numbers by the foolish boast of Evans, that he had encountered and whipped four to his one; and he tried to console his followers by calling this affair a victory for them, because McCall did not choose to hold the battle-field, but leisurely withdrew to his encampment. This little victory greatly inspired the loyal people, for it gave them the assurance that the troops of the Army of the Potomac were ready and able to fight bravely, whenever they were allowed the privilege.

[a] Dec., 1861.

While the friends of the Government were anxiously waiting for the almost daily promised movement of the Grand Army toward Richmond, as the year was drawing to a close, and hearts were growing sick with hopes deferred, two events, each having an important bearing on the war, were in

---

[1] His brigade was composed of Pennsylvania regiments, and consisted of the Ninth, Colonel Jackson; Tenth, Colonel McCalmont; Twelfth, Colonel Taggart; Bucktail Rifles, Lieutenant-Colonel T. L. Kane; a battalion of the Sixth; two squadrons of cavalry, and Easton's Battery—in all about 4,000 men.

[2] His troops consisted of the Eleventh Virginia, Colonel Garland; Sixth South Carolina, Lieutenant-Colonel Seagrist; Tenth Alabama, Colonel Harvey; First Kentucky, Colonel T. H. Taylor; the Sumter Flying Artillery, four pieces, Captain Cutts; and detachments from two North Carolina cavalry regiments, 1,000 in number, under Major Gordon. Stuart was also on a foraging expedition, and had about 200 wagons with him.

[3] Report of General McCall, December 20, 1861; also, General Stuart to General Beauregard, December 21, 1861.

progress; one directly affecting the issue, and the other affecting it incidentally, but powerfully. One was the expedition that made a permanent lodgment of the National power on the coast of North Carolina; and the other was intimately connected with the foreign relations of the Government. Let us first consider the latter event. The incidents were few and simple, but they concerned the law and the policy of nations.

We have already noticed the fact that the conspirators, at an early period of their confederation against the Government, had sent representatives to Europe, for the purpose of obtaining from foreign powers a recognition of the league as an actual government.[1] These men were active, and found swarms of sympathizers among the ruling and privileged classes of Europe, and especially in Great Britain. There was an evident anxiety among those classes in the latter country to give all possible aid to the conspirators, so that the power of the Republic of the West, the hated nursery of democratic ideas, might be destroyed by disintegration resulting from civil dissensions.[2]

Fortunately for the Republic, the men who had been sent abroad by the conspirators were not such as the diplomats of Europe could feel a pro-

---

[1] See page 259, volume I.

[2] We have already observed the "precipitate and unprecedented" proceedings, as Mr. Adams termed it, of the British Government, and the leaders of public opinion in England, in allowing to the insurgents the privileges of belligerents. [Chapter XXIV., volume I.] In Parliament and out of it, no favorable occasion was omitted, by many leading men, to speak not only disparagingly, but often very offensively, of the Government and people of the Republic. The enemies of free institutions and supporters of privileged classes acted upon the old maxim of political craft, "Divide and Govern," and they exerted all their powers to widen the breach between the people of the Free and Slave-labor States. Sir Edward Bulwer Lytton, the author, who had received the honors of knighthood, which allied him to the aristocratic class in Great Britain, appeared among the willing prophets of evil for the Republic. He declared in an address before an Agricultural Society, on the 25th of September, 1861, that he had "long foreseen and foretold to be inevitable" a dissolution of the American Union; and then again, mounting the Delphic stool, he solemnly said: "I venture to predict that the younger men here present will live to see not two, but at least four, and probably more than four, separate and sovereign Commonwealths arising out of those populations which a year ago united their legislature under one President, and carried their merchandise under one flag." He rejoiced in the prospect that so gladdened his vision, and said: "I believe that such separation will be attended with happy results to the safety of Europe, and the development of American civilization." The desire for such separation was evidently engendered in the speaker's mind by an unpleasant horoscope of the future of the Great Republic. "If it could have been possible," he said, "that, as population and wealth increased, all the vast continent of America, with her mighty seaboard, and the fleets which her increasing ambition as well as her extending commerce would have formed and armed, could have remained under one form of government, in which the executive has little or no control over a populace exceedingly adventurous and excitable, why, then, America would have hung over Europe like a gathering and destructive thunder-cloud. No single kingdom in Europe could have been strong enough to maintain itself against a nation that had once consolidated the gigantic resources of a quarter of the globe."

A little later, Earl Russell, the Minister for Foreign Affairs, in an after-dinner speech at Newcastle-upon-Tyne, declared that the struggle in America was "on the one side for empire, and on the other for power," and not for the great principles of human liberty, and for the life of the Republic, for which the Government was really contending. A little later still, the Earl of Shrewsbury, speaking with hope for his class, at the old city of Worcester, said that he saw in America the trial of Democracy, and its failure. He believed the dissolution of the Union to be inevitable, and that men there before him would live to "see an aristocracy established in America." In the same hour, Sir John Pakington, formerly a cabinet minister, and then a member of Parliament, told the same hearers, that, "from President Lincoln, downward, there was not a man in America who would venture to tell them that he really thought it possible that by the force of circumstances the North could hope to compel the South to again join them in constituting the United States." Sir John Bowring, an eminent English scholar, in a kindly letter to an American friend in England, expressed his solemn conviction of the utter separation of the States, and intimated that the Government lacked the sympathy of Englishmen because it had not "shown any disposition to put down slavery." Overlooking the fact that the fathers of the Republic fought for the establishment of liberty for all, and that the conspirators were fighting for the establishment of the slavery of the many for the benefit of the few, he made a comparison, and said, "It does not appear to me that you are justified in calling the Southerners rebels. Our statesmen of the time of George III. called Washington and Franklin by that name." Lord Stanley, who had traveled in the United States a dozen years before, and better understood American affairs, said, in a speech early in November, that a Southern Confederacy would be established. "He did not think it reasonable to blame the Federal Government for declining to give up half their territory without striking a blow in its defense;" but the real difficulty in this case, in his mind, was

found respect for;[1] and at the beginning of the autumn of 1861 it was painfully evident to their employers that they were making no progress toward obtaining the coveted good of recognition. It was therefore determined to send men of more ability to vindicate and advocate their cause at the two most powerful Courts of Europe, namely, Great Britain and France. For these missions, James Murray Mason[2] and John Slidell[3] were appointed. They were original conspirators. The former was a native of Virginia, and the latter of New York, but long a resident of Louisiana. The former was accredited to the Court of St. James, and the latter to the Court of St. Cloud. Both had been prominent members of the Senate of the United States, and both were somewhat known in Europe. Mason was justly supposed to possess a sufficiency of that duplicity (which unfortunately too often characterizes a diplomatist), to cover up the real objects of the conspirators and win for them the good offices of confiding English statesmen. Slidell (whose wife was an accomplished French Creole of Louisiana) was well versed in the French language and habits; and for adroit trickery and reckless disregard of truth, honor, or justice, he was rightly supposed to be a match for the most wily employé of the Emperor of France, honest or dishonest. These men were duly commissioned as "Ambassadors" for the "Confederate States of America," and their proposed work was regarded as of vital importance to the interests of the Confederacy.

The blockade of the Southern ports of the Republic was then very stringent, and it was some time before these men found an opportunity to leave the country. They finally went to sea on the 12th of October,[a] in the small steamship *Theodore*, which left Charleston harbor at a little past midnight, while rain was falling copiously, and in the darkness escaped the notice of the blockading fleet. Mason was accompanied by his secretary (Mr. McFarland), and Slidell by his wife and four children, and his secretary (Mr. Eustis) and his wife, who was a daughter of Corcoran, the eminent banker of Washington City. The *Theodore* touched first at

[a] 1861.

---

involved in the question, "If they conquer the Southern States, what will they do with them when they have got them?" He pictured to himself the need of the establishment of a powerful military government to keep them in subjection. He wisely recommended great caution in judging of American affairs.

Mr. Gladstone, the Chancellor of the Exchequer, in a speech at Edinburgh, in January, 1862, expressed there the opinion that the National Government could never succeed in putting down the Rebellion, and if it should, he said, it "would only be the preface and introduction of political difficulties far greater than even the military difficulties of the war itself." This speech was delivered just after the surrender of Mason and Slidell to the British Government; and Mr. Gladstone, evidently unmindful of the true greatness of fixed principles of action as inseparable from mere worldly interests, was ungenerous enough to make that display of honor, honesty, and consistency on the part of our National Government an occasion for disparaging that Government and the people, by charging them with instability of purpose, if not cowardice. He tauntingly said: "Let us look back to the moment when the Prince of Wales appeared in the United States of America, and when men by the thousand, by tens of thousands, and by hundreds of thousands, trooped together from all parts to give him welcome as enthusiastic, and as obviously proceeding from the depths of the heart, as if those vast countries had still been a portion of the dominions of our Queen. Let us look to the fact that they are of necessity a people subject to quick and violent action of opinion, and liable to great public excitement, intensely agreed on the subject of the war in which they were engaged, until aroused to a high pitch of expectation by hearing that one of their vessels of war had laid hold on the Commissioners of the Southern States, whom they regarded simply as rebels. Let us look to the fact that in the midst of that exultation, and in a country where the principles of popular government and democracy are carried to extremes—that even, however, in this struggle of life and death, as they think it to be—that even while ebullitions were taking place all over the country of joy and exultation at this capture—that even there this popular and democratic Government has, under a demand of a foreign Power, written these words, for they are the closing words in the dispatch of Mr. Seward: 'The four Commissioners will be cheerfully liberated.'"

[1] See page 260, volume I. [2] See page 384, volume I. [3] See page 231, volume I.

Nassau, New Providence, a British port, where blockade-runners and Confederate pirate-ships always found a welcome and shelter during the war, and thence went to Cuba. At Havana, the "Ambassadors" were greeted with the most friendly expressions and acts, by the British Consul and other sympathizers, and there they took passage for St. Thomas,[a] in the British mail-steamer *Trent*, Captain Moir, intending to leave for England in the next regular packet from that island to Southampton.

CHARLES WILKES.

[a] Nov. 7, 1861.

The National Government heard of the departure of Mason and Slidell, and armed vessels were sent in pursuit. None of these won the prize. That achievement was left for Captain Charles Wilkes, of the navy, to perform, an officer of world-wide fame, as the commander of the American Exploring Expedition to the South Seas, a quarter of a century before. At that time he was on his way home from the coast of Africa, in command of the National steam sloop-of-war *San Jacinto*, mounting thirteen guns. He put into the port of St. Thomas, and there hearing of the movements of the pirate ship *Sumter*, he departed on a cruise in the Gulf of Mexico and among the West India Islands in search of it. At Havana he was informed of the presence and intentions of the Confederate "Ambassadors," and after satisfying himself that the law of nations, and especially the settled British interpretation of the law concerning neutrals and belligerents, would justify his interception of the *Trent*, and the seizure on board of it of the two "Ambassadors," he went out[b] in the track of that vessel in the Bahama Channel, two hundred and forty miles from Havana, and awaited its appearance. He was gratified with that apparition toward noon on the 8th of November, when off Paredon del Grande, on the north side of Cuba, and less than a dozen miles distant.

[b] Nov. 2.

On the appearance of the *Trent*, all hands were called to quarters on the *San Jacinto*, and Lieutenant D. M. Fairfax, a kinsman of Mason by marriage, was ordered to have two boats in readiness, well manned and armed, to board the British steamer, and seize and bring away the "Ambassadors" and their secretaries. When the *Trent* was within hailing distance, a request was made for it to heave to. It kept on its course, when a shell fired across its bow made a demand that was heeded. Fairfax was sent on board of the *Trent*, but found he could do nothing in the matter of his errand without the use of physical force. Captain Moir had declined to show his papers and his passenger-list, and the "Ambassadors" had treated with scorn the summons to go on board the *San Jacinto*, which, like all the other acts of Fairfax, had been done with the greatest courtesy and propriety.[1] A proper force was

[1] The appearance of Lieutenant Fairfax on board the *Trent*, with a warrant for the arrest of Mason and

sent, and Mason and Slidell, compelled to yield to circumstances, went quietly on board the *San Jacinto* with their secretaries. The *Trent*, with the families of Slidell and Eustis on board, and its large number of passengers, was permitted to proceed on its voyage, after a detention of only little more than two hours. The captives were conveyed first to New York and then to Boston Harbor, where they were furnished with quarters in Fort Warren,[1] then used as a prison for political offenders, under the charge of Captain Dimick, the defender of Fortress Monroe against the Virginia insurgents.[2]

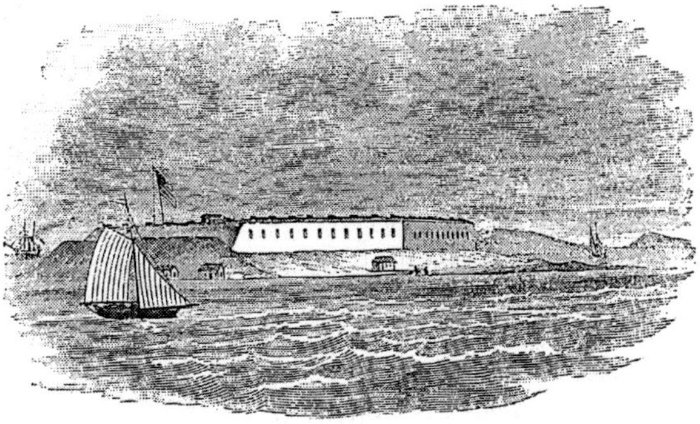

FORT WARREN.

The act of Captain Wilkes was universally applauded by loyal men, and filled the land with rejoicings because two of the worst of the conspirators were in the custody of the Government. For the moment men did not stop to consider either the law or the expediency involved in the act. Public honors were tendered to Commander Wilkes,[3] and resolutions of thanks were passed by public bodies. He partook of a public dinner in Boston. The New York Historical Society, while he was present at a stated meeting,[a] elected him an honorary member of that body, by acclamation. Two days afterward, he was publicly received by

[a] Dec. 3, 1861.

Slidell, and their secretaries, produced great excitement. The Captain was asked to show his passenger-list. He refused to do so. Fairfax then said that the vessel would not be allowed to proceed until he was satisfied whether the men he was seeking were on board or not. These, hearing their names mentioned, came forward. They protested against arrest, and in this act they were joined by Captain Moir, and by the Mail Agent, Captain Williams, of the Royal Navy, who said he was the "representative of Her Majesty."

The "Ambassadors" refused to leave the *Trent*, except by force. Fairfax called to his aid Lieutenant Greer, who came on board with a few marines. The Lieutenant then took Mason by the shoulder, and, with another officer on the opposite side, conducted him to the gangway of the steamer, and handed him over to Greer. He then returned for Slidell, who gave him to understand that a good deal of force would be required to make him go. The passengers gathered around in great commotion, making contemptuous remarks, with threats of violence, and one cried out, "Shoot him!" The wife and daughter of Slidell joined in vehement protests, and the latter struck Fairfax in the face, according to the testimony of Capt. Williams, who told the story of this cabin scene in an after-dinner speech at Plymouth. "Some of the public papers," he said, "have described her as having slapped Mr. Fairfax's face. [Here his audience cried out, 'Served him right if she did,' and 'Bravo.'] She did strike Mr. Fairfax," he continued, and the audience gave cheers in her honor. "But she did not do it with the vulgarity of gesture which has been attributed to her. Miss Slidell was with her father in the cabin, with her arm encircling his neck, and she wished to be taken to prison with her father. (Hear, hear.) Mr. Fairfax attempted to get into the cabin—I do not say forcibly, for I do not say a word against Mr. Fairfax, so far as his manner is concerned—he attempted to get her away by inducements. In her agony, then, she did strike him in the face three times. I wish that Miss Slidell's little knuckles had struck me in the face. I should like to have the mark forever." Exclamations of "Oh!" and laughter followed this assertion.

The marines were called in, and Slidell was compelled to go. McFarland and Eustis went quietly, under protest.

[1] Fort Warren is on George's Island, and commands the main entrance to Boston Harbor. It is a strong work of masonry, with five fronts, the southern, eastern, and northern ones being seen in the little sketch. Around the main work is a ditch 30 feet in width. The entire circuit of the fort is 3,136 feet. Against the south front is an outwork of much strength, which is seen in the sketch.

[2] See page 498, volume I.

[3] The crew of the *San Jacinto* presented to Lieutenant Fairfax, on board that vessel, in Boston Harbor, a beautiful silver goblet, with national, naval, and military devices on it, and the inscription,—"Presented to Lieutenant Fairfax, by the crew of the *San Jacinto*, as a slight token of their esteem and love."

the authorities of the City of New York; and on his arrival in Washington City, toward the middle of December, he was made the recipient of special honors. Already the Secretary of the Navy had written to him[a] a congratulatory letter on the "great public service" he had rendered "in capturing the rebel emissaries, Mason and Slidell," who, the Secretary said, "have been conspicuous in the conspiracy to dissolve the Union; and it is well known that, when seized by you, they were on a mission hostile to the Government and the country." He assured him that his conduct had "the emphatic approval of the Department." In his annual report, submitted to Congress three days afterward, the Secretary as emphatically approved Wilkes's course, and at the same time remarked that his generous forbearance in not capturing the *Trent* must not be "permitted to constitute a precedent hereafter for the treatment of any case of similar infraction of neutral obligations by foreign vessels engaged in commerce or the carrying trade."

[a] Nov. 30, 1861.

On the first day of the Session of Congress,[b] the House of Representatives, on motion of Mr. Lovejoy, of Illinois, tendered "the thanks of Congress to Captain Wilkes, for his arrest of the traitors Slidell and Mason." By a further resolution, the President was requested, in retaliation for the outrageous treatment of Colonel Corcoran, then a prisoner in the hands of the Confederates, in confining him in the cell of a convicted felon, to subject Mason to like treatment in Fort Warren.[1]

[b] Dec. 2.

By most of the writers on international law in the United States, instructed by the doctrines and practices of Great Britain, the essays of British publicists, the decisions of British courts, and by the law as laid down by the Queen's recent proclamation,[2] the act of Captain Wilkes was decided to be abundantly justified. But there was one thoughtful man, in whom was vested the tremendous executive power of the nation at that time, and whose vision was constantly endeavoring to explore the mysteries of the near future, who had indulged calmer and wiser thoughts than most men at that moment, because his feelings were kept in subjection to his judgment by a sense of heavy responsibility. That man was Abraham Lincoln. The author was in Washington city when the news reached there of the capture of the conspirators, and he was in the office of the Secretary of War when the electrograph containing it was brought in and read. He can never forget the scene that ensued. Led by the Secretary, who was followed by Governor Andrew of Massachusetts, and others, cheer after cheer was given by the company, with a will. Later in the day, the writer, accompanied by the late Elisha Whittlesey, First Comptroller of the Treasury, was favored with a brief interview with the President, when the clear judgment of that far-seeing and sagacious statesman uttered through his lips the words which formed the key-note to the judicious action of the Secretary of State afterward. "I fear the traitors will prove to be white elephants," said Mr. Lincoln. "We must stick to American principles concerning the rights of neutrals. We fought Great Britain for insisting, by theory and practice, on the right to do

[1] Report of the Proceedings of Congress in the *Congressional Globe*, Dec. 2d, 1861.

[2] See page 567, volume I. of this work. In that proclamation, after enumerating many acts that would be a violation of the duty of neutrals, the Queen specified that of "carrying *officers*, soldiers, dispatches," et cetera. Mason and Slidell were civil officers of the Confederacy, and were themselves living *dispatches*.

precisely what Captain Wilkes has done. If Great Britain shall now protest against the act, and demands their release, we must give them up, apologize for the act as a violation of our doctrines, and thus forever bind her over to keep the peace in relation to neutrals, and so acknowledge that she has been wrong for sixty years."[1]

That demand speedily came. When intelligence of the affair on board the *Trent* reached England, and details were given by "Captain Williams, R. N.," in a public communication dated at sea, November 9th (and also in his after-dinner speech already mentioned), in which he so highly colored a few facts that the courteous acts of Lieutenant Fairfax were made to appear

---

[1] For more than a hundred years Great Britain had denied the sanctity of a neutral ship, when her interests seemed to require its violation. That Power had acquired full supremacy of the seas at the middle of the last century, and Thompson had written that offering to British pride, the song of "Rule Britannia," boastingly asserting that—

> When Britain first, at Heaven's command,
> Arose from out the azure main,
> This was the charter of the land,
> And guardian angels sung the strain—
> Rule Britannia! Britannia rules the waves!
> Britons never shall be slaves!"

Conscious of its might, Great Britain made a new law of nations, for its own benefit, in 1756. Frederick the Great of Prussia had declared that the goods of an enemy cannot be taken from on board the ships of a friend. A British order in Council was immediately issued, declaring the reverse of this to be "the law of nations," and forbidding neutral vessels to carry merchandise belonging to those with whom she might be at war. So violative of the golden rule was this order, that the publicists of Great Britain found it necessary, out of respect for the opinions of mankind, to put forth specious sophistries to prove that England was not ambitious!

Under what was called "The Rule of 1756," the British navy began to depredate upon the commerce of the world. The solemn treaty made by Great Britain with Holland, eighty-two years before, in which it was expressly stipulated that free ships should make free goods—that a neutral flag should protect a neutral bottom—that the contraband of war should be strictly limited "to arms, artillery, and horses, and to include naval materials," was wantonly violated by the possession of might. The vessels of Holland were not only prohibited from carrying naval stores, but were seized, and their cargoes used for the benefit of the English war-marine. From that time until the present, Great Britain has steadily adhered to "The Rule of 1756," excepting in a few instances, when it suited her interests to make a temporary change in her policy. So injuriously did this "Rule," practically enforced, operate upon the commerce of the world for England's benefit, that in 1780 the northern powers of Europe—Russia, Sweden, Denmark, and Holland—formed a treaty of alliance, called the "Armed Neutrality," to resist the pretensions and evil practices of Great Britain. The doctrine of the league was that of Frederick, but much enlarged. Armaments were prepared to sustain the doctrine, but Great Britain's naval strength was too great, and the effort failed.

In 1793, when Great Britain was at war with France, "The Rule of 1756" was again put into active operation. By an order in Council, it was directed that "all vessels laden with goods, the produce of any colony of France, or carrying provisions or supplies for such colony, should be seized and brought in for adjudication." This was aimed at American commerce, which was then exciting the envy of the British. To that commerce France had then opened all her West India ports. The order was secretly circulated among the British cruisers, and captures were made under it before its existence was known in London! For that treachery, English statesmen and publicists offered the selfish excuse that it was "British policy to maintain for that power the supremacy of the seas," that its children might continue to sing "Rule Britannia! Britannia rules the waves."

These aggressions were soon followed by more serious outrages against the rights of friends, or neutrals. Great Britain declared its right to search any vessel on the high seas, and take therefrom any subject of hers found there. This was a "new law of nations," promulgated by Great Britain to suit her necessities. Her cruisers roamed the seas, and held no flag to be an absolute protection of what was beneath it. Seamen were continually dragged from American vessels and placed in the British navy. The British cruisers were not very particular when they wanted seamen, and under the pretext of claiming the subjects of His Majesty, about 14,000 American citizens were forced into the British service in the course of twelve or fifteen years. This practice was one of the chief causes of the war declared against Great Britain by the United States in 1812. In the midst of that war, when overtures for peace on righteous terms were offered by the Americans, the right of search and impressment was insisted upon by a carefully prepared manifesto of the acting head of the British Government, in which it was declared that "if America, by demanding this preliminary concession, intends to deny the validity of that right, in that denial Great Britain cannot acquiesce, nor will she give countenance to such pretensions by acceding to its suspension, much less to its abandonment, as a basis on which to treat." The war went on, and when it was ended Great Britain yet maintained the doctrine laid down in "The Rule of 1756," and continued to insist, until 1861, upon the right of a nation at war to enter the ship of a neutral power in search and for the seizure of its subjects, or articles contraband of war, or things intended to be injurious to the British nation. In doctrine and practice, Great Britain justified the act of Captain Wilkes.

like rude outrages, a storm of indignation was raised. The most violent and coarse abuse of Americans was uttered by a portion of the British press; and the most absurd threats of vengeance on the offending nation were put forth. Of the courteous and accomplished gentleman, Captain Wilkes, the London *Times*, the accredited exponent of the opinions of the Government and the ruling class, said: "He is unfortunately but too faithful a type of the people in whose foul mission he is engaged. He is an ideal Yankee. Swagger and ferocity, built up on a foundation of vulgarity and cowardice—these are his characteristics, and these are the most prominent marks by which his countrymen, generally speaking, are known all over the world. To bully the weak, to triumph over the helpless, to trample on every law of country and custom, willfully to violate all the most sacred interests of human nature, to defy as long as danger does not appear, and, as soon as real peril shows itself, to sneak aside and run away—these are the virtues of the race which presumes to announce itself as the leader of civilization and the prophet of human progress in these latter days. By Captain Wilkes let the Yankee breed be judged."

Other publications, of higher and lower character than the *Times*, used equally offensive language;[1] and the Government itself, without waiting to hear a word from the United States on the subject, at once assumed a belligerent position, and made energetic preparations for war. So urgent seemed the necessity, that not an hour of procrastination was permitted. All through Sunday, the 1st of December (immediately after the arrival of the passengers of the *Trent*), men were engaged in the Tower of London in packing twenty-five thousand muskets to be sent to Canada. On the 4th,[a] a royal proclamation was issued, prohibiting the exportation of arms and munitions of war; and the shipment of saltpeter was stopped. A general panic prevailed in business circles. Visions of British privateers sweeping American commerce from the seas floated before the English mind, and no insurance on American vessels could be obtained. American securities dropped amazingly, and large fortunes were made by wise ones, under the shadow of high places, who purchased and held them for a "rise"! Orders were issued for a large increase in the naval squadrons on the North American and West India stations, and powerful transports were called for. The great steam-packet *Persia* was taken from the mail-service, to be employed in carrying troops to Canada. The immense iron-clad *Warrior*, supposed to be invincible, was fitted out for service in haste. Armstrong and Whitworth cannon were purchased by the score; and preparations were made for sending various conspicuous batteries and regiments

[a] December, 1861.

---

[1] The *Saturday Review*, conducted chiefly by members of the British aristocracy, said with a bitter sneer, "The American Government is in the position of the rude boor, conscious of infinite powers of annoyance, destitute alike of scruples and of shame, recognizing only the arbitration of the strong arm, which repudiates the appeal to codes, and presuming, not without reason, that more scrupulous States will avoid or defer such an arbitration as long as ever they can." The London *Punch* gave, in one of its cartoons, a picture representing the relative position of the two Governments at that crisis. America appeared as a diminutive blusterer, in the form of a slave-driver, and carrying an American flag. Before him is a huge English sailor, impersonating Great Britain, who says to the little American, "You do what's right, my son, or I'll blow you out of the water."—"Now, mind you, sir," says the Briton, to a most uncouth American Commodore—"no shuffling—an ample apology—or I will put the matter into the hands of my lawyers, Messrs. Whitworth and Armstrong," alluding to the popular cannon invented by men of that name, and then extensively manufactured in England, and afterward furnished in considerable numbers to the Confederates.

to the expected "seat of war." It seemed, from the action of the British Government, and the tone of the utterances of many of the British writers and speakers, that the time had come when the calamity of civil war that had overtaken the Republic of the West was considered England's opportunity to humble her rival. And it was with infinite delight that the conspirators at Richmond contemplated the probability of war between the two countries, for in that event they felt sure of achieving the independence of the Confederacy, and procuring its recognition as a nation by the powers of Europe.

Yet all Englishmen were not so ungenerous and mad. The great mass of the *people*—the *governed* class of Great Britain—continued to feel kindly toward the Americans,[1] and there were leading men, who, in the qualities of head and heart, towered above the common level of all society in England as Chimborazo rises above the common height of the Andes, who comprehended the character of our Government, the causes of the rebellion, and the war it was making upon the rights of man; and with a true catholic and Christian spirit they rebuked the selfishness of the ruling class. Among these, John Bright, the Quaker, and eminent British statesman, stood most conspicuous. In the midst of the tumultuous surges of popular excitement that rocked the British islands in December and January, his voice, in unison with that of Richard Cobden, was heard calmly speaking of righteousness and counseling peace. He appeared as the champion of the Republic against all its enemies, and his persuasions and warnings were heard and heeded by thousands of his countrymen. All through the war, John Bright in England, and Count de Gasparin in France,[2] stood forth conspicuously as the representatives of the true democracy in America, and for their beneficent labors they now receive the benedictions of the good in all lands.

JOHN BRIGHT.

There were other men in Great Britain who had an intelligent conception of the machinery of our Government, and who could not be deceived by the sophistries of the disciples of Calhoun into a belief that the armed enemies of the Republic were any less rebels against sovereign authority than would a like band of insurgents be in Lancashire, or any county of England, arrayed

---

[1] In a speech in Parliament on the 17th of February, 1862, when appropriations for the army expenses in the contemplated war with the United States were under consideration, John Bright said: "A large portion of the people of this country see in it a Government, a real Government; not a Government ruled by a mob, and not a Government disregarding law. They believe it is a Government struggling for the integrity of a great country. They believe it is a country which is the home of every man who wants a home, and moreover they believe this—that the greatest of all crimes which any people in the history of the world has ever been connected with—the keeping in slavery four millions of human beings—is, in the providence of a Power very much higher than that of the Prime Minister of England, or of the President of the United States, marching on, as I believe, to its entire abolition."

[2] See note 4, page 569, volume I.

against the Crown. They well understood that if the American insurgents, whose fathers helped to form the Republic which they were trying to destroy, and who had perfect equality in public affairs with the whole nation, could be justified in rebelling against it, the Irish people—a conquered nation, and made a part of Great Britain against their will—had the fullest warrant for rebelling against their English conquerors at any and at all times. Among these men we find the names of John Stuart Mill, Professors Goldwin Smith and J. E. Cairnes, Rev. Baptist Noel, Henry Vincent, Layard, the eminent Eastern traveler, the eloquent young O'Donoughue,[1] and others less conspicuous; while Lord Brougham, who for sixty years was an opponent of slavery, and was known to be thoroughly conversant with the structure of our Government, and an admirer of its practical workings, following the lead of the spirit of his class, took sides with the slaveholders, and said most unkind words. Kinglake, the eminent author and member of Parliament, announced, as a principle which he "had always enforced," that "in the policy of states a sentiment never can govern;" that ideas of right, justice, philanthropy, or common humanity should have no influence in the dealings of one nation with another, "because they are almost always governed by their great interests," which he thought to be a sound principle; while Thomas Carlyle, the cold Gothicizer of the English language, dismissed the whole matter with an unintelligible sneer.

The British Government, acting upon *ex parte* and, as was afterward found to be, unreliable testimony in the person of Captain Williams, treated the proceedings on board of the *Trent* as "an act of violence which was an affront to the British flag and a violation of international law;" and as soon as the law officers of the Crown had formally pronounced it so, Lord John Russell, the Foreign Secretary, sent a letter,[a] by a special Queen's messenger (Captain Seymour), to Lord Lyons, the British Ambassador at Washington, authorizing his Lordship to demand from the Government of the United States the liberation of the captives and their restoration to the protection of the British flag, and "a suitable apology for the aggressions which had been committed," at the same time expressing a hope that that Government would, of its own accord, offer such redress, "which alone could satisfy the British nation."[2]

[a] Nov. 30, 1861.

On the same day when Earl Russell dated his dispatch to Lord Lyons,[b] Mr. Seward, the Secretary of State, in a confidential note to Mr. Adams, the American Minister in London,[3] alluded to the affair, and

[b] Nov. 30.

---

[1] "The O'Donoughue," as he was called, was of one of the most ancient families in Ireland. He was less than thirty years of age at that time, of great beauty in form and feature, polished in manners, eloquent in speech, of proven courage, and a man of the people in his instincts. In the great Rotunda in Dublin, this man boldly declared to an audience of 5,000 persons, after the reception of the news of the *Trent* affair, that if war should come, *Ireland would be found on the side of America.* This declaration was received with the most vehement applause.

[2] Lord John Russell sent with his dispatch the following private note to Lord Lyons: "Should Mr. Seward ask for delay, in order that this grave and painful matter should be deliberately considered, you will consent to a delay not exceeding seven days. If at the end of that time no answer is given, or if any other answer is given except that of a compliance with the demands of Her Majesty's Government, your lordship is instructed to leave Washington, with all the members of your legation, bringing with you the archives of the legation, and to repair immediately to London; if, however, you should be of opinion that the requirements of Her Majesty's Government are substantially complied with, you may report the facts to Her Majesty's Government for their consideration, and remain at your post till you receive further orders."

[3] See page 567, volume I.

mentioned the fact that no words on the subject had passed between himself and the British minister, and that he should say nothing until advised of the action of the British Government in the matter. At the same time he called Mr. Adams's attention to the fact that Captain Wilkes did not act under instructions from his Government, and therefore the subject was free from much embarrassment. Mr. Seward expressed a hope that the British Government would consider the subject in a friendly temper, and declared that it might expect the best disposition on the part of the Government of the United States. He gave Mr. Adams leave to read his note, so indicative of a desire to preserve a good understanding with the Cabinet of St. James, to Earl Russell and Lord Palmerston (the Prime Minister), if he should deem it expedient. Mr. Adams did so,[a] and yet the British Government, with this voluntary assurance that a satisfactory arrangement of the difficulties might be made, continued to press on its warlike measures with vigor, to the alarm and distress of the people.[1] The fact that such assurance had reached the Government was not only suppressed, but, when rumors of it were whispered, it was semi-officially denied.[2] And when the fact could no longer be concealed, it was, by the same authority, affirmed, without a shadow of justice, that Mr. Adams had suppressed it, at the same time suggesting, as a reason, that the minister might profit by the purchase of American stocks at panic prices.[3] The most absurd stories concerning the

[a] Dec. 19, 1861.

---

[1] Lieutenant-General Scott was in Paris at the time of the arrival of the news of the capture of the conspirators. He wrote and published a very judicious letter (Dec. 3), in which he gave assurance of friendly feeling toward Great Britain on the part of the Government of the United States. But this semi-official declaration from so high a source was not allowed to have any weight.

[2] Letter of Charles Francis Adams to Mr. Seward, January 17th, 1862.

[3] Letter of Charles Francis Adams to Mr. Seward, January 17th, 1862. An incident occurred on this side of the Atlantic in connection with the *Trent* affair, and stock speculations, which gave rise to much comment. Dr. Russell, the correspondent of the London *Times* (see page 358, volume I.), was then in Washington City, and remained there for some time. He had so persistently disparaged the National Government and its supporters, and predicted success for the rebellion with an earnestness which indicated the wish that is "father to the thought," that the confiding courtesy which had been shown him by the National authorities was withdrawn. He was now, it was said, in daily and intimate intercourse with Lord Lyons. On the 26th of December, Secretary Seward communicated to that Minister his letter announcing that Mason and Slidell would be given up to the British Government. The fact was intended to be kept in most profound secrecy from the public for the moment; but on the following day Russell, possessed of the secret, was allowed to telegraph to a stock speculator in New York: "Act as though you heard some very good news for yourself and for me, as soon as you get this." At that time, operations in New York, in Government stocks, were active and remunerative. Those stocks had been depressed by the menaces of war. Words that would give assurance of peace would send them up. These had been spoken in secret; and the first man who was allowed to profit by them pecuniarily was a British subject, a representative of the British journal in the interest of the Crown, most abusive of the American people, and who was then in intimate relations with the British embassy. What is still more strange is the fact that, in violation of a positive order to the Censor of the Press and Telegraph at Washington, to suppress *all* communication concerning the *Trent* affair, this dispatch, so palpably burdened with contraband information, was allowed to be sent forty-five minutes after the order for suppression was received. Still more strange is the fact that, while the reporters of the Press were not allowed to send *any* dispatches, for all of which they were ready to pay, on the back of the favored Dr. Russell's message (the original is now before the author) were these words, written in pencil: "Mr. Russell's messages are free, by order of Mr. Sanford," who was the Censor. For a further elucidation of this subject, see the *Report of the Judiciary Committee of the House of Representatives*, on the Censorship of the Press at Washington.

With words calculated to keep up the excitement and alarm, and warlike measures on the other side of the Atlantic, and still further to depress the stocks of the United States, Russell wrote to the London *Times*, on the day when his profitable dispatch was sent to New York free, saying: "As I write there is a rumor that Messrs. Slidell and Mason are to be surrendered. If it be true, this Government is broken up. There is so much violence of spirit among the lower orders of the people, and they are so ignorant of every thing except their own politics and passions, so saturated with pride and vanity, that any honorable concession, even in this hour of extremity, would prove fatal to its authors. It would certainly render them so unpopular that it would damage them in the conduct of this civil war." He had already ventured to make many predictions of evil to the Republic. So early as the previous April he had said to Europe, through the *Times*, "The Union is gone forever, and no serious attempt will be made by the North to save it." In August he had said, "General bankruptcy is

temper of the American Government, calculated to inflame the public mind and excite a warlike spirit, were put forth, such as the following, paraded conspicuously in the columns of the London *Times:*

"During the visit of the Prince of Wales to America, Mr. Seward took advantage of an entertainment to the Prince to tell the Duke of Newcastle he was likely to occupy a high office; that when he did so it would become his duty to insult England, and he should insult her accordingly."

In the mean time, Earl Russell's demand was communicated to the Government at Washington. It produced much indignation in the public mind, and there was a general disposition to give a flat refusal. The legality of Captain Wilkes's act was not doubted by experts in international law. British precedents were all in favor of it; and even a writer in the London *Times*, two days before the date of Earl Russell's dispatch, admitted this fact, and complained only of the informality of Captain Wilkes, in taking the "Ambassadors" out of the *Trent*, instead of taking the ship itself with all on board into port, to have the case adjudicated in a court of admiralty. Such was a feature of the decision in the case, of the law officers of the crown, in alluding to which Mr. Adams said, "In other words, Great Britain would have been less offended if the United States had insulted her more."[1]

In opposition to popular feeling and opinion, the Government decided to restore Mason and Slidell to the protection of the British flag; and the Secretary of State, in a very able letter to Mr. Adams, for the ear of the British Government, discussed the subject in the light in which the President had viewed it from the beginning. He corrected the misrepresentations of Captain Williams as to the facts of the capture, declaring that Captain Wilkes was not acting under instructions from his Government, but only "upon his own suggestions of duty;"[2] "that no orders had been given to any one for the arrest of the four persons named," and that the United States had no purpose or thought of doing any thing "which could affect in any way the sensibilities of the British nation."

Then, with the Queen's proclamation in mind, Mr. Seward spoke of the captives as pretended "Ministers Plenipotentiary, under a pretended commission from Jefferson Davis, who had assumed to be president of the insurrectionary party in the United States," and so publicly avowed by him, and argued that it was fair to presume that they had carried papers known in law as dispatches.[3] He also stated that it was asserted by competent authority that such dispatches, having escaped the search, were actually carried to England, and delivered to the emissaries of the conspirators there;[4] also,

inevitable, and Agrarian and Socialist riots may be expected pretty soon." He had declared, so late as Dec. 23d, that Mr. Seward would "refuse, on the part of his Government, to surrender Mason and Slidell and their secretaries;" and in the first days of 1862, he said, "The fate of the American Government will be sealed if January passes without some great victory."

[1] Mr. Adams to Mr. Seward, Nov. 29th, 1861.

[2] Captain Wilkes said in a second dispatch to the Secretary of the Navy, that he carefully examined all the authorities on international law at hand—Kent, Wheaton, Vattel, and the decisions of British judges in the admiralty courts—which bore upon the rights and responsibilities of neutrals. Knowing that the Governments of Great Britain, France, Spain, and Portugal had acknowledged the Confederates as belligerents, and that the ports of these powers were open to their vessels, and aid and protection were given them, he believed that the *Trent*, bearing agents of that so-called belligerent, came under the operations of the law of the right of search.

[3] See note 2, page 156.

[4] This service for the Confederates was performed, it is said, by Captain Williams, R. N., Her Majesty's only representative on the *Trent*.

that the assumed characters and purposes of Mason and Slidell were well known to the officers of the *Trent*, including Captain Williams.

Having prepared the way for argument, the Secretary entered upon it by a consideration of the inquiries: "*First*, Were the persons named and their supposed dispatches contraband of war? *Second*, Might Captain Wilkes lawfully stop and search the *Trent* for these contraband persons and dispatches? *Third*, Did he exercise that right in a lawful and proper manner? *Fourth*, Having found the contraband persons on board, and in personal possession of the contraband dispatches, had he a right to capture the persons? *Fifth*, Did he exercise the right of capture in the manner allowed and recognized by the law of nations? If all these inquiries shall be resolved in the affirmative," said the Secretary, "the British Government will have no claim for reparation."

These questions, excepting the last, were affirmatively argued by the Secretary, with the assumption that the British doctrine was correct. The conclusion from his reasoning was inevitable, that every thing had been done in strict conformity to the law on the subject of neutrals, as expounded by British authority, excepting the failure of Captain Wilkes to exercise the right of capture in the manner allowed and recognized by the law of nations. Here the Secretary frankly admitted that there had been a fatal irregularity. To meet the requirements of law, Wilkes should have been less generous and humane.[1] It was his business to capture lawfully, but it was that of a court of admiralty to decide upon the question of holding the vessel or its contents as a lawful prize. It was not for the captor to determine the matter on the deck of his vessel.

Having concluded his argument, which British jurists and publicists, and the practice of the British Government, admitted was unanswerable, the Secretary, after briefly summing up in an interrogatory the iniquitous features of the "right of search," so strictly maintained by the British, said: "If I decide this case in favor of my own Government, I must disallow its most cherished principles, and reverse and forever abandon its essential policy. The country cannot afford the sacrifice. If I maintain these principles and adhere to that policy, I must surrender the case itself. It will be seen, therefore, that this Government could not deny the justice of the claims presented to us in this respect, upon its merits. *We are asked to do to the British nation just what we have always insisted all nations ought to do unto us.*" The Secretary added that, if the safety of the Union required the detention of the conspirators, it would be the duty of the Government to detain them; but the condition of the rebellion, "as well as the comparative unimportance of the captured persons themselves," he said, happily forbade him from resorting to that defense. He continued by delicately alluding to the injuries inflicted on his countrymen by the British in the past, when exercising power in the manner they now complained of, and said: "It would

---

[1] In his dispatch to the Secretary of the Navy, Captain Wilkes said it was his determination to take possession of the *Trent*, and send her to Key West as a prize, for resisting the search, and carrying those "Ambassadors, whom he considered as 'the embodiment of dispatches;'" but the reduced number of his officers and crew, and the large number of passengers on board bound to Europe, who would be put to great inconvenience in not being able to join the steamer from St. Thomas to Europe, "decided him to allow them to proceed." This weak point in the proceedings was noticed by the Secretary of the Navy, both in his congratulatory letter to Captain Wilkes and his Annual Report.

tell little for our claims to the character of a just and magnanimous people, if we should so far consent to be guided by the law of retaliation as to lift up buried injuries from their graves to oppose against what national consistency and the national conscience compel us to regard as a claim intrinsically right. Putting behind me all suggestions of this kind, I prefer to express my satisfaction that, by the adjustment of the present case upon principles confessed to be American, and yet, as I trust, mutually satisfactory to both of the nations concerned, a question is finally and rightly settled between them which heretofore, exhausting not only all forms of peaceful discussion, but also the arbitrament of war itself, for more than half a century alienated the two countries from each other, and perplexed with fears and apprehensions all other nations."

The Secretary then announced that the four persons confined at Fort Warren would be "cheerfully liberated," and requested Lord Lyons to indicate the time and place for receiving them. The latter ordered the British gun-boat *Rinaldo* to proceed to Provincetown, Massachusetts, for that purpose, where, on the 1st of January, 1862, the prisoners were delivered to the protection of the British flag. They were conveyed first to Bermuda, and then to St. Thomas, where they embarked for England, and arrived at Southampton on the 29th of the same month.[1]

LORD LYONS.

So began and ended, in the space of eighty-three days, the event known as "the *Trent* affair," which cost Great Britain ten millions of dollars for unnecessary warlike preparations, and the people of the two nations concerned four times that amount, in consequence of the derangement of their industrial operations. While the result was full of promise of good for the two nations, it was pregnant with promises of disaster to the conspirators and their cause. It was so unexpected and discouraging to them and their sympathizers in America and Great Britain, who hoped for and confidently expected a war between the two Governments that would redound to the

[1] When the captives could no longer serve a political purpose for the ruling class in Great Britain, they sank into their proper insignificance, and, as a general rule, Mason was treated with courteous contempt by the public authorities and cultivated people everywhere. The Liverpool *Post*, imitating the severer example of the London *Times*,* gave the following contemptuous notice of their arrival, on which occasion they were almost unnoticed: "Messrs. Mason and Slidell have arrived. Already the seven weeks' heroes have shrunk to their natural dimensions, and the apprehensions expressed by the London *Times*, by ourselves, and by other journals, lest they should have a triumphal reception, already seems absurd."

* The *Times*, in an editorial, said they were "about the most worthless booty" it would be possible to extract from the jaws of the American lion, for it recognized in them the leading revilers of Great Britain for many years, and the promoters of discord between the two Governments, hoping thereby to bring on war, when the opportunity for the conspirators against the Republic would be presented. The *Times* hoped Englishmen would let the "fellows," as it called them, alone. "England would have done just as much," it said, "for two negroes." This language produced both indignation and alarm throughout the Confederacy, for it was significant of a policy on the part of Great Britain in favor of entire non-interference. The *Richmond Enquirer* said, "England may dishonor herself if she will. She may prove false to her duty if she choose. Thank Heaven, we are not dependent upon her, and her course will not affect ours. . . . John Bull is a surly animal, we know, but such gratuitous rudeness shows a want of practical sense as well as good manners."

benefit of the insurgents, that they could not conceal their chagrin and disappointment. They had tried to fan the flame of discord between the Cabinets of Washington and London. In England, Liverpool was the focus of efforts in aid of the rebellion. There the friends of the conspirators held a meeting,[a][1] which was presided over by James Spence, who, for a time, was the fiscal agent of the Confederates and a bitter enemy of the Republic. [a] Nov. 28, 1861. On that occasion the act of Wilkes was denounced as a gross violation of the honor of the British flag, for which, according to a resolution offered by Spence, the most ample reparation should be demanded. In concert with these expressions, a sympathizing friend in the American Congress (C. L. Vallandigham, of Ohio) offered a resolution[b] in the House of Representatives, in which the President was enjoined to maintain the position of approval and adoption by the Government (already assumed by the House) of the act of Captain Wilkes, "in spite of any menace or demand of the British Government," and declaring that "this House pledges its full support in upholding now the honor and vindicating the courage of the Government and people of the United States against a foreign power." "We have heard the first growl of the British lion," said the author of the resolution, "and now let us see who will cower. The time has now come for the firmness of this House to be practically tested, and I hope there will be no shrinking."[2] [b] Dec. 16.

Fortunately, better counsels prevailed in Congress, and out of it.[3] The loyal people acquiesced in the wise decision of the Government, and soon rejoiced that it had sustained American principles in a case so tempting to a different course, for thereby the nation was amazingly strengthened. This act of the Government was warmly commended by the best men in Europe, and gratified those powers who, like the United States, had been in vain endeavoring to persuade England to a righteous and unselfish course concerning the sacred rights of neutrals. M. Thouvenal, the French Minister for Foreign Affairs, had expressed, in a confidential note to Count Mercier, the representative of France at Washington, a desire that the captives might be delivered up, in accordance with the liberal

COUNT MERCIER.

[1] The meeting was called by the following placard, posted all over the town: "OUTRAGE ON THE BRITISH FLAG—THE SOUTHERN COMMISSIONERS FORCIBLY REMOVED FROM A BRITISH MAIL STEAMER. A public meeting will be held in the Cotton Salesroom at three o'clock."

[2] Proceedings of Congress, reported in the Congressional *Globe*, December 16, 1861. The resolution, by a vote of 109 to 16, was quietly disposed of by being referred to the Committee on Foreign Relations. The 16 who voted against laying the resolution on the table were: Messrs. Allen, G. H. Brown, F. A. Conckling, Cox, Cravens, Haight, Holman, Morris, Noble, Nugen, Pendleton, Shier, T. B. Steele, Vallandigham, Vandaver, and C. A. White.

[3] The Chairman of the Senate Committee on Foreign Relations (Charles Sumner) approved the action of the Government, and made it the occasion of an elaborate speech in that body. He declared that in the dispute Great Britain was "armed with American principles, which throughout our history have been constantly, deliberately, and solemnly rejected." Speaking of the release of the prisoners, he said: "Let the rebels go. . . .

principles of the Republic; and the Prussian and Austrian Governments, through their respective Ministers, had also given their views of the policy of releasing the prisoners, in deference to the principles to which the Americans were so firmly pledged. To their communications, which were read to Secretary Seward, that Minister made the most friendly responses; and from that time, during the entire war, there was never any serious danger of the recognition of the independence of the so-called "Confederate States" by France and England, however much their respective Governments may have wished for a reasonable excuse to do so. This the conspirators, and their chief supporters North and South, well knew; yet they continued to deceive the people within the Confederacy with false hopes of foreign aid, while they were being robbed of life, liberty, and property by their pretended friends. So persuaded was the Secretary of State that war would certainly be averted, that, with a playful exhibition of his consciousness of the strength of the Republic, he telegraphed[a] to the British Consul at Portland, Maine, that British troops that must be sent over to fight the Americans might pass through the United States territory, whilst on their way to Canada to prepare for hostilities!

[a] Jan. 12, 1862.

The public mind was just becoming tranquil after the excitement caused by the *Trent* affair, when its attention was keenly fixed on another expedition to the coast of North Carolina, already alluded to. The land and naval armaments of which it was composed were assembled in Hampton Roads early in January, 1862, ready for departure, after a preparation of only two months. Over a hundred steam and sailing vessels, consisting of gun-boats, transports, and tugs, and about sixteen thousand troops, mostly recruited in New England, composed the expedition. General Ambrose Everett Burnside, an Indianian by birth, a West Point graduate,[b] and a resident of Rhode Island when the war broke out, was appointed the commander-in-chief, and the naval operations were intrusted to Flag-Officer Louis M. Goldsborough, then the commander of the North Atlantic Naval Squadron.

[b] 1847.

LOUIS M. GOLDSBOROUGH.

Prison doors are opened; but principles are established which will help to free other men and to open the gates of the sea. Never before in her active history has Great Britain ranged herself on this side. Such an event is an epoch. *Novus sæclorum nascitur ordo.* To the liberties of the sea this Power is now committed. To a certain extent this course is now under her tutelary care. If the immunities of passengers, not in the military or naval service, as well as of sailors, are not directly recognized, they are at least implied; while the whole pretension of impressment, so long the pest of neutral commerce, and operating only through the lawless adjudication of a quarter-deck, is made absolutely impossible. Thus is the freedom of the sea enlarged, not only by limiting the number of persons who are exposed to the penalties of war, but by driving from it the most offensive pretension that ever stalked upon its waves. To such conclusion Great Britain is irrevocably pledged. Nor treaty nor bond was needed. It is sufficient that her late appeal can be vindicated only by a renunciation of early, long-continued tyranny. Let her bear the rebels back. The consideration is ample, for the sea became free as this altered Power went forth upon it, steering westward with the sun on an errand of liberation."

The military force which, like Butler's,[1] had been gathered at Annapolis, was composed of fifteen regiments and a battalion of infantry, a battery of artillery, and a large number of gunners for the armed vessels, who were able to render service on land if required. The whole force was divided into three brigades, commanded respectively by Generals John G. Foster, of Fort Sumter fame, Jesse L. Reno, and John G. Parke.[2] The fleet was divided into two columns for active service, intrusted respectively to the charge of commanders S. F. Hazard and Stephen C. Rowan.[3] Every thing necessary for the peculiar service assigned to the expedition was furnished and arranged. The fleet guns were equipped with ship and field carriages, that they might be used on land or water; and the cannon were mostly of the newest construction. A well-organized signal corps accompanied the expedition, and there were two extensive pontoon trains. Fully equipped in every way, the expedition, whose destination had been kept a profound secret, left Hampton Roads on Sunday, the 11th of January,[a] and went to sea.

[a] 1862.

When it was known that the expedition had actually gone out upon the Atlantic at that inclement season, there was great anxiety in the public mind. The storm of November, by which Dupont's fleet had been scattered, was vivid in memory, and awakened forebodings of like evil. They were well founded. A portion of Goldsborough's fleet now met with a similar fate off tempestuous Cape Hatteras. Its destination was Pamlico Sound, which was to be reached through Hatteras Inlet. The voyage had been lengthened by a heavy fog on Sunday,[b] and on Monday night those vessels of the fleet which had not reached the stiller waters of the Inlet were smitten and scattered by a terrible tempest. Four transports, a gun-boat, and a floating battery were wrecked. Among these was the fine steamer *City of New York*, Captain Nye. It went down in sight of the shore,[c] with four hundred barrels of gunpowder, one thousand five hundred rifles, eight hundred

STEPHEN C. ROWAN.

[b] Jan. 11.

[c] Jan. 12.

---

[1] See page 106.

[2] The first brigade (Foster's) was composed of the Twenty-third, Twenty-fourth, Twenty-fifth, and Twenty-seventh Massachusetts regiments, and the Tenth Connecticut. The second (Reno's) consisted of the Twenty-first Massachusetts, Fifty-first Pennsylvania, Fifty-first New York, Ninth New Jersey, and Sixth New Hampshire. The third (Parke's) was composed of the Fourth and a battalion of the Fifth Rhode Island, the Eighth and Eleventh Connecticut, the Fifty-third and Eighty-ninth New York, and Belgier's Rhode Island Battery of 106 men, 120 horses, four 10-pounder Parrott guns, and two 12-pounder field howitzers.

[3] The fleet consisted of thirty-one gun-boats, with an aggregate armament of ninety-four guns. These were the *Brickner*, commanded by J. C. Giddings; *Ceres*, S. A. McDermaid; *Chasseur*, John West; *Com. Barney*, R. D. Renshaw; *Com. Perry*, C. H. Flusser; *Delaware*, S. P. Quackenbush; *Granite*, E. Boomer; *Granite*, W. B. Avery; *Gen. Putnam*, W. J. Hoskiss; *Huzzar*, Fred. Crocker; *Hunchback*, E. R. Calhoun; *Hetzel*, H. K. Davenport; *J. N. Seymour*, F. S. Welles; *Louisiana*, Hooker; *Lockwood*, S. L. Graves; *Lancer*, B. Morley; *Morse*, Peter Hayes; *Philadelphia*, Silas Reynolds; *Pioneer*, C. S. Baker; *Picket*, T. P. Ives; *Rocket*, James Lake; *Ranger*, J. B. Childs; *Stars and Stripes*, Reed Werden; *Southfield*, Behm; *Shawsheen*, T. S. Woodward; *Shrapnel*, Ed. Staples; *Underwriter*, Jeffers; *Valley City*, J. C. Chaplin; *Vidette*, —— ———; *Whitehead*, French; *Young Rover*, I. B. Studley.

shells, and other stores and supplies; but no human life perished with it. Nor was any man lost in the other vessels that were wrecked; but of a party who went ashore from one of the transports[a] yet outside, three were drowned by the upsetting of their boat on its return. These were Colonel J. W. Allen, of Burlington, New Jersey, commander of the Ninth Regiment from that State; the surgeon, F. S. Weller; and the mate of the transport.

[a] Jan. 14, 1862.

It was several days before all of the surviving vessels of the expedition entered the Inlet. The weather continued boisterous. Many of them drew too much water to allow them to cross the bars; and the remainder of the month of January was spent in overcoming the difficulties of that perilous passage, and in making full preparations for moving forward over the still waters of Pamlico Sound.

General Burnside (whose head-quarters were on the *S. R. Spaulding*) with his officers and men had been unwearied in their assistance of the seamen. Time was precious. Delay was very injurious, for the Confederates, accurately divining the destination of the fleet that was worrying its way through that "perilous gut," as Goldsborough called it, had made preparations for its reception. The newspapers of the North had not yet learned to be as discreet as those of the South,[1] but vied with each other in giving early revelations of military and naval movements. Through these channels the Confederates had obtained very accurate knowledge of the force that was coming. With the logic furnished by the nature of the coasts and waters of Pamlico and Albemarle Sounds, and the points in their vicinity which it was evident the Nationals intended to seize, they correctly argued that Roanoke Island, about thirty miles from Hatteras Inlet, would be the first object of attack. It is situated between Pamlico and Albemarle Sounds, with a narrow channel on each side, called respectively Roanoke Sound and Croatan Sound. This island, well fortified and manned, presented the only effectual barrier to an invasion from the sea of the entire north-eastern coast of North Carolina, and the rear approaches to Norfolk and Portsmouth in Virginia. In some respects it was almost as important as Fortress Monroe, and deserved the special attention of the Confederates.

AMBROSE E. BURNSIDE.

At the time of the approach of Burnside's expedition, Roanoke Island

[1] At a very early period of the war, a censorship of the press was established by the conspirators, which was extremely rigid from the beginning. No contraband intelligence was allowed to be given; and as the contest progressed, and the despotism at Richmond became more and more absolute, even the *opinions* of the conductors of the press in general were in complete subjection to that despotism. That control was really of essential service in carrying on the war, for the National authorities could never find any reliable information concerning the Confederate forces in the Southern newspapers. So early as May, 1861, General Lee requested the press of Virginia to keep silent on the subject of military movements.

and its vicinity were under the command of Brigadier-General H. A. Wise, the Department commander being Major-General Benjamin Huger, of South Carolina, whose head-quarters were at Norfolk. Owing to the illness of General Wise, who was at Nag's Head, on a narrow strip of sand lying between Roanoke Sound and the sea, that stretches down from the main far above, Colonel H. M. Shaw, of the Eighth North Carolina Regiment, was in chief command of the forces on the island. These consisted of his own regiment; the Thirty-first North Carolina Volunteers, under Colonel J. V. Jordan; three companies of the Seventeenth North Carolina, under Major G. H. Hill. and four hundred and fifty men, under Lieutenant-Colonel Anderson.

BENJAMIN HUGER.

Several batteries had been erected on prominent points of the shores of Roanoke, which commanded the Sounds on its eastern and western sides; and upon its narrowest part, between Shallowbag Bay and Croatan Sound, was a strong redoubt and intrenched camp, extending across the road that traversed the middle of the island. These several fortifications mounted about forty heavy guns. There were batteries also on the main, commanding the channels of Croatan Sound.

Vessels had been sunk in the main channel of Croatan Sound, and heavy stakes had been driven in its waters from the main to the island, to obstruct the passage of vessels. Above these obstructions was a flotilla of small gun-boats—a sort of "Musquito fleet" like that of Tatnall at Port Royal—eight in number, and carrying eleven guns. These were commanded by Lieutenant W. F. Lynch, late of the National navy, who had abandoned his flag, received a commodore's commission from the conspirators, and was now charged with the defense of the coast of North Carolina.

After a reconnoissance, Commodore Goldsborough slowly moved his fleet of seventy vessels, formed on the morning of the 5th of February,[a] toward Croatan Sound, fifteen of the gun-boats leading, under the immediate command of Rowan, and followed by the armed transports. On the following day Lynch sent the *Curlew*, Captain Hunter, to reconnoiter the approaching fleet, and her commander reported it at anchor six miles below Roanoke Island. That evening was dark and misty, and the morning of the 7th was lowery for a time. At length the sun broke forth in splendor, and at about ten o'clock Goldsborough, hoisting the signal, "This day our country expects every man to do his duty," advanced his gun-boats in three columns, the first being led by the *Stars and Stripes*, Lieutenant Werden; the second by the *Louisiana*, Commander Alexander Murray; and the third by the *Hetzel*, Lieutenant H. R. Davenport. Goldsborough made the *Southfield* his flag-ship.

[a] 1862.

At eleven o'clock, a bombardment was opened upon Fort Bartow, on Pork

Point, toward the northern end of the island, and, within thirty minutes afterward, a general engagement between the gun-boats and the batteries on Croatan Sound ensued. The Confederate flotilla joined in the fight, but was soon driven beyond the range of the National guns, with the *Curlew*, its largest steamer, so badly disabled, that it began to sink, and was soon afterward beached, under cover of the guns of Fort Forrest, on Redstone Point.[1] These vessels disposed of, Goldsborough concentrated his fire upon Fort Bartow, at a range of about three-fourths of a mile. Its flagstaff was soon shot away, the barracks were set on fire, its guns began to give feeble responses, and its walls of sand to fall into a confused mass, under the weight of shot and shell hurled upon them.

The army transports now came up, and preparations were made for landing them on the island at Ashby's Harbor, about two miles below Fort Bartow. They were confronted by two thousand men, and a battery of three pieces in the neighboring woods; but these were soon dispersed by a storm of shells from the gun-boats. Meanwhile the Confederate flotilla had returned to the attack, and, after an engagement for bout an hour. had been compelled again to retire, considerably damaged.

[a] Feb. 7-8, 1862.

At midnight,[a] in the midst of a cold rain-storm, eleven thousand troops were safely put on shore.[2] They were without shelter, and at an early hour the next morning they moved forward to attack the intrenchments in the interior of the island, to which all of the Confederate forces out of the other redoubts had now repaired. The advancing column was under the command of General Foster, who was next in rank to Burnside. These works were about five miles from the landing-place at Ashby's Harbor,[3] and were situated on land flanked on both sides by a morass. They occupied a line a greater portion of the way across the narrower part of the island. The main work to be attacked could be reached only by a narrow causeway, which was well protected by a battery of three guns, mounted on an earthwork. Within the intrenchments to be assailed were about twenty-five hundred troops, under the command of Colonel Shaw.

Foster led the way with his brigade, which was accompanied by a battery of six 12-pounder boat howitzers, brought from the naval launches, and commanded by Midshipman B. F. Porter. The brigades of Reno and Parke followed. The road being swampy and fringed with woods, the march was slow and cautious. The first pickets encountered fired their pieces and ran for their lives. Foster pressed on, and soon coming in sight of the Confederate works, he disposed his troops for action by placing the Twenty-fifth Massachusetts, Colonel Upton, in line, with the Twenty-third Massachusetts,

---

[1] Lynch, who was a man of very moderate ability and courage, was disheartened. He wrote to Mallory that he should endeavor to get the guns from the *Curlew*, and with the squadron proceed to Elizabeth City, from which he would send an express to Norfolk for ammunition. There he would make a final stand, and would blow up the vessels rather than they should fall into the hands of his enemy.

[2] The water was so shallow that the launches and other small boats could not get very near the shore, and the soldiers were compelled to wade several hundred feet through the water, sometimes sinking deeply into the cold ooze.

[3] Much valuable information concerning Roanoke Island, the position of the Confederates, and the best place for landing was obtained from a colored boy named Thomas R. Robinson, the slave of J. M. Daniel, of Roanoke, who ten days before had escaped to Hatteras. He was taken with the expedition.

Colonel Kurtz, for a support. With musketry and cannon he opened the battle, and was hotly answered by musketry and cannon. The fight was severe, and soon the Twenty-seventh Massachusetts, Colonel Lee, came to the aid of their fellow New Englanders, by falling upon the sharpshooters in the woods, on the left of the Confederate line. To relieve the Twenty-third Massachusetts, the Tenth Connecticut, Colonel Russell, came up to the support of the Twenty-fifth, from the former State.

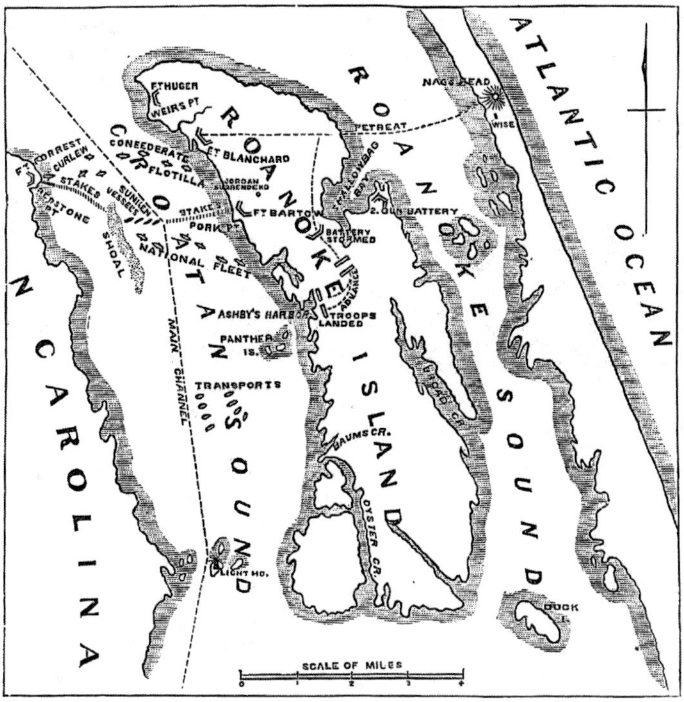

THE ATTACK ON ROANOKE ISLAND.

The Confederates made a gallant defense; and the fight raged fiercely. Reno brought up his brigade to the help of Foster's. These were the Twenty-first Massachusetts, Colonel Maggi; Fifty-first New York, Colonel Ferrero; Fifty-first Pennsylvania, Colonel Hartrauf, and Ninth New Jersey. He pushed through the tangled swamps and took a position on Foster's right, with the intention of turning the Confederate left flank, where Lieutenant-Colonel Frank Anderson was in command of a battalion of "Wise's Legion." The fight in that direction soon became warm, while it continued to rage fiercely in the front. Massachusetts, Connecticut, New York, and New Jersey troops were zealous rivals in deeds of daring, fortitude, courage, and generosity. They continually gained advantages, but at the cost of heavy work. Parke came up with his Fourth Rhode Island, Colonel Rodman; the first battalion Fifth Rhode Island; the Eighth Connecticut; and Ninth New York, Colonel Hawkins, and gave timely aid to the Twenty-third and Twenty-seventh Massachusetts.

With all this pressure of overwhelming numbers, the Confederates still held out. At length the artillery ammunition of the Nationals began to fail, and they were suffering very severely in killed and wounded. Victory could now be won only by a charge. That movement was resolved upon. Major E. A. Kimball, of Hawkins's (Ninth New York) Zouaves (a hero of the Mexican war, who fought gallantly in every battle, from Vera Cruz to the City of Mexico), perceiving the necessity, and eager to serve his country (for whose cause he finally gave his life), offered to lead the charge across the causeway against the main battery, with the bayonet. The delighted Foster said, "You are the man, the Ninth the regiment, and this is the moment! Zouaves, storm the battery!" he shouted—"Forward!" In an instant they were on the run across the causeway, yelling fearfully, and cheered by their admiring comrades on every side, who cried out, "Make way for the red-caps! They are the boys!" Colonel Hawkins, who was leading two companies in a flank movement on the left, seeing his men rushing to the perilous performance, could not resist his impulses, and, joining them, pressed forward the whole battalion, shouting, "Zou! Zou! Zou!" and closely followed by the Tenth Connecticut. The frightened Confederates, after firing once, had fled, and into the battery the Zouaves rushed, with none to oppose them, almost simultaneously with the Fifty-first New York and Twenty-first Massachusetts, who had attacked the Confederates on their right. The colors of the Fifty-first, being at the head of the regiment, were first planted on the captured battery, and at the same time the State flag of the Massachusetts Twenty-first was triumphantly displayed. The fugitives, in their haste, had left every thing behind them. There lay their dead and wounded as they had fallen. Their heavy guns were in perfect order, and the knapsacks and blankets of the routed soldiers were strewn about the works.

JOHN G. FOSTER.

General Foster, who had skillfully directed these successful movements in person, now re-formed his brigade, whilst Reno, with the Twenty-first Massachusetts and Ninth New York, started in pursuit. Foster soon followed and overtook Reno, who was maneuvering to cut off the retreat of about eight or nine hundred Confederates on the left, near Weir's Point. With a part of his force, Reno pushed on in that direction. Hawkins, with his Zouaves, hurried toward Shallowbag Bay, where, it was said, the Confederates had a two-gun battery. Foster pressed forward with an adequate force, and was on the heels of the fugitives, after a chase of five or six miles, when he was met by a flag of truce, borne by Colonel Pool, of the Eighth North Carolina, carrying a message from Colonel Shaw, who, as we have observed, was the senior acting officer in command on the Island, asking what terms of capitulation would be granted. "Unconditional surrender!"

was Foster's reply. These were accepted, and two thousand Confederates soon laid down their arms as prisoners of war.

In the mean time, General Reno had received the surrender of about eight hundred Confederates, under Colonel Jordan; and Colonel Hawkins, after taking possession of the deserted battery on Shallowbag Bay, captured about two hundred Confederates, who were seeking a chance to escape from the island to Nag's Head. Among these was Captain O. Jennings Wise, son of the General in command, and editor of one of the bitterest of the rebellious journals in Richmond, who had been severely wounded while fighting gallantly.[1]

To complete the conquest of the Island, General Foster sent a force to capture Fort Bartow, which Goldsborough had been bombarding while the land battle had been going on. Its inmates had retired, and at a little past four o'clock in the afternoon the National flag was unfurled over its walls, when Goldsborough signalled to his fleet, "The fort is ours." This was followed by the most joyous cheers. In the mean time the Confederate steamer *Curlew*, which, as we have observed, had been beached under the guns of a battery on Redstone Point, on the main, had been fired by the insurgents, together with the barracks at that place, and the remainder of the flotilla had fled up Albemarle Sound. So ended, in triumph for the National cause, the conflict known as THE BATTLE OF ROANOKE.[2] It disappointed the prophets of evil at home and abroad, and spread consternation throughout the Confederacy. There, on Roanoke Island, where the first germ of a privileged aristocracy had been planted in America,[3] the first deadening blow had been given to the hopes of an oligarchy, fighting for the establishment of such a social system. The "Government" at Richmond (and especially Jefferson Davis and his "Secretary of War," Benjamin) were severely censured for alleged neglect in making Roanoke Island and its approaches impregnable. Davis, in a "message to Congress," cast reflections upon the troops there; but a committee of that body, appointed to investigate the matter, declared that the battle was "one of the most gallant and brilliant actions of the war," and laid the blame, if any existed, on Huger and Benjamin, especially on the latter, who, it was said, had positively refused to put the Island in a state of defense.[4]

---

[1] His father, who, as we have observed, was ill, had remained with a part of the "Legion" at Nag's Head. The wounded son had been placed in a boat to be sent to his camp, when it was fired upon, and compelled to return. He was tenderly cared for by Colonel Hawkins and his officers, but died toward noon on the following day.

[2] Report of General Burnside to General McClellan, Feb'y 10th, 1862; of Generals Foster, Reno, and Parke; of Commodore Goldsborough to Secretary Welles, Feb'y 9th, 1862; of Commander Lynch to R. S. Mallory, Feb'y 7th, 1862; and accounts by other officers and eye-witnesses on both sides.

[3] There, in the year 1587, Manteo, a native chief, who had been kind to colonists sent to that coast by Sir Walter Raleigh, was, by that baronet's command, and with the approval of Queen Elizabeth, invested with the title of *Lord of Roanoke*, the first and last peerage created in America. Nearly a hundred years later, an attempt was made to found in North Carolina an aristocratic government, with the nominal appendages of royalty, it being designed to have orders of nobility and other privileged classes in exact imitation of English society of that period.

[4] Pollard, the Confederate historian of the war, says, that records showed that Wise, who assumed the command there on the 7th of January, had "pressed upon the Government the importance of Roanoke Island to Norfolk." In a report to Benjamin, on the 13th of that month, he said the canals and railroads connecting with Norfolk "were utterly defenseless." Later he reported that "a force at Hatteras, independent of the Burnside expedition, was amply sufficient to capture or pass Roanoke Island in twenty-four hours." Wise also asked for re-enforcements from Huger's fifteen thousand men, lying idle around Norfolk. He was answered by a peremptory order, when Burnside's expedition was passing into Pamlico Sound, to proceed immediately to Roanoke Island and

The conquest was complete, and Burnside, taking up his quarters at a house near Fort Bartow, prepared at once for other aggressive movements on the coast. In his report, he generously said, "I owe every thing to Generals Foster, Reno, and Parke," and sadly gave the names of Colonel Charles S. Russell and Lieutenant-Colonel Vigeur de Monteuil[1] as among the killed. The number of his prisoners amounted to about three thousand. Many of the troops on the Island escaped to Nag's Head, and thence, accompanied by General Wise and the remainder of his Legion, they fled up the coast toward Norfolk.[2] The spoils of victory were forty-two heavy guns, most of them of large caliber, three being 100-pounders.[3]

BURNSIDE'S HEAD-QUARTERS.

The Confederate flotilla was immediately followed[a] by Captain Rowan. It had gone up Albemarle Sound thirty or forty miles, and into the Pasquotank River, toward Elizabeth City, not far southeast of the Great Dismal Swamp. Rowan's fleet consisted of fourteen vessels, the *Delaware* being his flag-ship. On the morning of the 10th it was in the river near Elizabeth City, and confronting seven steamers and a schooner armed with two 32-pounders, and a four-gun battery on the shore, and one heavy gun in the town in front. The whole force was in charge of Commander Lynch.

[a] Feb. 9, 1862.

Rowan opened fire upon flotilla and batteries at about nine o'clock. After a short but very severe engagement, Lynch, who was on shore, signalled for the abandonment of the vessels, when they were run aground

---

defend it. The neglect of Benjamin was so notorious, that the Committee held him responsible. The public indignation was intense, and yet, in the face of all this, Davis, assuming the attitude of a Dictator, as he really was, with his usual haughty disregard of the opinions of others and the wishes of the people, promoted Benjamin to the position of "Secretary of State." The insult was keenly felt, but the despotism of the conspirators was too powerful to allow much complaint from the outraged people.

In his report to General Huger, Wise said Roanoke Island was the key to all the defenses of Norfolk It unlocked two sounds—Albemarle and Currituck; eight rivers—the North, West, Pasquotank, Perquimmons, Little, Chowan, Roanoke, and Alligator; four canals—the Albemarle and Chesapeake, Dismal Swamp, Northwest, and Suffolk; two railways—the Petersburg and Norfolk, and Seaboard and Roanoke. At the same time it guarded four-fifths of the supplies for Norfolk. Its fall, Wise said, gave lodgment to the Nationals in a safe harbor from storms, and a command of the seaboard from Oregon Inlet to Cape Henry, at the entrance of Chesapeake Bay. "It should have been defended," he said, "at the expense of twenty thousand men, and many millions of dollars."

[1] The entire National loss in the capture of Roanoke was about 50 killed and 222 wounded. That of the Confederates, according to Pollard (i. 231), was 23 killed, 58 wounded, and 62 missing. Colonel Monteuil was the commander of a regiment of New York Volunteers, known as the D'Epineuil Zouaves. These had accompanied the expedition as far as Hatteras, when, for the want of transportation, they were sent back to Fortress Monroe. Their Lieutenant-Colonel remained with the army, and in the battle he served as a volunteer. With a Sharp's rifle he fought gallantly in the ranks of Hawkins's Zouaves, was shot through the head while urging these forward in the notable charge, with the words "Charge, *mes enfans!* Charge, Zouaves!" In honor of this brave and devoted soldier, General Burnside named one of the captured batteries Fort de Monteuil.

[2] On the 13th of February, Wise issued a characteristic "Special Order No. 1," from "Canal Bridge, Currituck County, N. C.," informing the public that the flag of Captain O. Jennings Wise would be raised for true men to rally around.

[3] New names were given to the forts. Fort Bartow was changed to Fort Foster; Fort Huger to Fort Reno; and Fort Blanchard to Fort Parke.

and set on fire. Then the Confederates fled, and Lynch, retiring to the interior of North Carolina, was not heard of again during the war until he reappeared at Smithville, when Fort Fisher was captured, early in 1865.

Shortly after the flight of the Confederates, Acting Master's-Mate J. H. Raymond planted the National flag on the shore battery, and thus proclaimed the first conquest achieved by the Nationals on the main of North Carolina. The battle had lasted only forty minutes, and Rowan's loss was only two killed and five or six wounded.[1] The number lost by the Confederates was

---

[1] An extraordinary example of heroism was exhibited during this engagement by John Davis, a Finlander, who was a gunner's mate on board the *Valley City*. A shell entered that vessel, and, exploding in the magazine, set fire to some wood-work. Davis was there, and, seeing the imminent danger to the vessel and all on board, because of an open barrel of gunpowder from which he had been serving, he seated himself upon it and so remained until the flames were extinguished. For this brave act the Secretary of the Navy rewarded him with the appointment of acting-gunner in the navy (March 11, 1862), by which his salary was raised from $300 to $1,000 a year. Admiring citizens of New York raised and presented to him $1,100. The Secretary of the Navy, by authority of an act of Congress, approved Dec. 21, 1861, presented him with a *Medal of Honor*, on which are inscribed the following words: "PERSONAL VALOR—JOHN DAVIS, GUNNER'S MATE, U. S. S. VALLEY CITY, Albemarle Sound, February 10th, 1862." Such medals were afterward presented to a considerable number of gallant men in subordinate stations, for acts of special bravery "before the enemy." Davis was the first recipient.

The act of Congress authorized the Secretary to cause two hundred of these *Medals of Honor* to be prepared, and to be bestowed by him upon "such petty officers, others of inferior rating, and marines, as should most distinguish themselves by their gallantry in action and other commendable qualities during the present war." These were made of bronze, in the form of a star of five rays, with a device emblematic of Union crushing the monster Rebellion, around which is a circle of thirty-three smaller stars, representing the thirty-three States then (1861) composing the Union. The medal is suspended from the flukes of an anchor, which in turn is attached to a buckle and ribbon. The Secretary directed that the medal should be worn suspended from the left breast, by a ribbon all blue at top for half an inch downward, and thirteen vertical stripes, alternate red and white for eight-tenths of an inch. The name of the recipient to be engraved on the back, with his rating, the name of the vessel in which he was serving, and the place where, and the date when, his meritorious act was performed. The picture here given of the medal—an American "Legion of Honor"—is the exact size of the original. For fuller particulars concerning the MEDAL OF HONOR, see *Regulations for the Government of the United States Navy*, 1865, page 140.

The following is a list of the names (320 in number) of those to whom medals were awarded: James McCloud, Louis Richards, Thomas Flood, James Buck, Oscar E. Peck, Thomas Gehegan, Edward Farrel, Peter Williams, Benjamin Sevearer, John Davis, Charles Kenyon, Jeremiah Regan, Alexander Hood, John Kelley, Daniel Lakin, John Williams, John Breese, Alfred Patterson, Thomas C. Barton, Edwin Smith, Daniel Harrington, John Williams, J. B. Frisbee, Thomas Bourne, William McKnight, William Martin, John Greene, John McGowan, Amos Bradley, George Hollat, Charles Florence, William Young, William Parker, Edward Wright, Charles Bradley, Timothy Sullivan, James Byrnes, John McDonald, Charles Robinson, Pierre Leno, Peter Colton, Charles W. Morton, William Martin, Robert Williams, George Bell, William Thompson, John Williams, Matthew Arthur, John Mackie, Matthew McClelland, Joseph E. Vantine, John Rush, John Hickman, Robert Anderson, Peter Howard, Andrew Brinn, P. R. Vaughn, Samuel Woods, Henry Thielberg, Robert B. Wood, Robert Jordan, Thomas W. Hamilton, Frank Bois, Thomas Jenkins, Martin McHugh, Thomas E. Corcoran, Henry Dow, John Woon, Christ. Brennen, Edward Ringgold, James K. L. Dun-

NAVAL MEDAL OF HONOR.

large, but was never ascertained. Only one of the Confederate vessels (the *Ellis*) was saved from destruction; and it was with difficulty that the town was preserved, for the insurgents, when they abandoned their vessels, set fire to it in several places. It was a most barbarous act, for only a few defenseless women and children remained in the town. These at once experienced the humanity of the Nationals, who showed them every kindness, when, on the following day,[a] they took possession of the place.

[a] Feb. 11, 1862.

This success was followed up by other movements for securing the control of Albemarle Sound and the adjacent country, as well as the waters through which communication was held with Norfolk. To this end, Rowan sent Lieutenant A. Maury, with a part of his fleet, to take possession of Edenton, near the western end of the Sound. This was easily done on the day after the capture of Elizabeth City,[b] a body of flying artillery stationed there having left it precipitately without firing a shot. Maury destroyed a schooner on the stocks and eight cannon, and then passed on, capturing vessels on the Sound. On the following day,[c] Lieutenant Jeffers, with some of the fleet, proceeded to the Chesapeake and Albemarle Canal, that traverses the Dismal Swamp on its way from the Elizabeth River to the Pasquotank, for the purpose of

C. F. LYNCH.

[b] Feb. 12, 1862.

[c] Feb. 13.

---

can, Hugh Melloy, William P. Johnson, Bartlett Laffey, Richard Seward, Christopher Nugent, James Brown, William Moore, William P. Brownell, William Talbot, Richard Stout, George W. Leland, Horatio N. Young, Michael Huskey, John Dorman, William Farley, J. Henry Denig, Michael Hudson, William M. Smith, Miles M. Oviatt, Barnett Kenna, William Halsted, Joseph Brown, Joseph Irlam, Edward Price, Alexander Mack, William Nichols, John Lawson, Martin Freeman, William Dinsmore, Adam Duncan, Charles Deakin, Cornelius Cronin, William Wells, Hendrick Sharp, Walter B. Smith, George Parks, Thomas Hayes, Lebbeus Simkins, Oloff Smith, Alexander H. Truett, Robert Brown, John H. James, Thomas Cripps, John Brazell, James H. Morgan, John Smith, James B. Chandler, William Jones, William Doolen, James Smith, Hugh Hamilton, James McIntosh, William M. Carr, Thomas Atkinson, David Sprowle, Andrew Miller, James Martin, William Phinney, John Smith, Samuel W. Kinnard, Patrick Dougherty, Michael Cassidy, George Taylor, Louis G. Chaput, James Ward, Daniel Whitfield, John M. Burns, John Edwards, Adam McCulloch, James Sheridan, John E. Jones, William Gardner, John Preston, William Newland, David Naylor, Charles B. Woram, Thomas Kendrick, James S. Roantree, Andrew Jones, James Seanor, William C. Connor, Martin Howard, James Tallentine, Robert Graham, Henry Brutsche, Patrick Colbert, James Haley, John F. Bickford, Charles A. Read, William Smith, William Bond, Charles Moore, George H. Harrison, Thomas Perry, John Hayes, George E. Read, Robert Strahan, James H. Lee. Joachim Pease (colored), William B. Poole, Michael Aheam, Mark G. Ham, John W. Loyd, Charles Baldwin. Alexander Crawford, John Laverty, Benjamin Loyd, David Warren, William Wright, John Sullivan, Robert T. Clifford, Thomas Harding, Perry Wilkes, John Hyland, Michael McCórmick, Timothy O'Donohue, George Butts, Charles Asten, John Ortega, Maurice Wagg, R. H. King, —— Wilkes, —— Demming, Bernard Harley, William Smith, Richard Hamilton, Edward J. Houghton, Oliver O'Brien, Frank Lucas, William Garvin, Charles J. Bibber, John Neil, Robert Montgomery, James Roberts, Charles Hawkins, Dennis Conlan, James Sullivan, William Hinnegan, Charles Rice, John Cooper, Patrick Mullin, James Saunders, James Horton, James Rountry, John H. Ferrell, John Ditzenbach, Thomas Taylor, Patrick Mullin. Aaron Anderson or Sanderson (colored), Charles H. Smith, Hugh Logan, Lewis A. Horton, George Moore, Luke M. Griswold, John Jones, George Pyne, Thomas Smith, Charles Reed, John S. Lann, George Schutt, John Mack, John H. Nibbe, Othniel Tripp, John Griffiths, Edward Swatton, John Swatson, Phillip Bazaar, George Province, Augustus Williams, Auzella Savage, John Jackson, Robert M. Blair, Anthony Williams, James W. Verney, Asa Bettram, John P. Ericson, Clement Dees,

disabling it. They found Confederates engaged in the same work, who fled on the approach of the Nationals. The latter sunk two schooners in the canal and departed. Finally, on the 19th, the combined fleet set out from Edenton on a reconnoissance, which extended up the Chowan River as far as Winton (which was partially destroyed), and the Roanoke to Plymouth. The *Perry*, bearing Colonel Hawkins and a company of his Zouaves, received a volley of musketry from the high bank near the latter place, when Rowan ordered the town to be shelled. It was nearly all destroyed excepting the church.

HAWKINS ZOUAVE.

The power of the Government was so fully displayed in this region, while its justice and clemency were proclaimed by Burnside and Goldsborough conjointly, in an address to the people of North Carolina, issued on the 18th, that the great bulk of the inhabitants, naturally inclined to loyalty, were anxious to render full submission. The proclamation assured them that the expedition was not there for the purpose of invading any of their rights. On the contrary, it came to protect them under the rightful authority of the National Government, and to close the desolating war which their wicked leaders had commenced. They were admonished of the truth, that those leaders were imposing upon their credulity, deceiving them by fictions about the intentions of the Government, such as destroying their property, injuring their women, and liberating their slaves. "We are Christians as well as yourselves," they said, "and we profess to know well and to feel profoundly the sacred obligations of the character. No apprehensions need be entertained that the demands of humanity or justice will be disregarded." . . . "We invite you, in the name of the Constitution, and in that of virtuous loyalty and civilization, to separate yourselves at once from these malign influences, to return to your allegiance,

---

George W. McWilliams, John Angling, William Dunn, Robert Summers, Joseph B. Hayden, Isaac N. Fry, Edward R. Bowman, William Shipman, William G. Taylor, George Prance, Thomas Jones, William Campbell, Charles Mills, Thomas Connor, David L. Bass, Franklin L. Wilcox, Thomas Harcourt, Gurdon H. Barter, John Rannahan, John Shivers, Henry Thompson, Henry S. Webster, A. J. Tomlin, Albert Burton, L. C. Shepard, Charles H. Foy, James Barnum, John Dempster, Edmund Haffee, Nicholas Lear, Daniel S. Milliken, Richard Willis, Joseph White, Thomas English, Charles Robinson, John Martin, Thomas Jordan, Edward B. Young, Edward Martin, John G. Morrison, William B. Stacy, Henry Shutes, John Taylor, John Harris, Henry Baker, James Avery, John Donnelly, John Noble, John Brown, Richard Bates, Thomas Burke, Thomas Robinson, Nicholas Irwin, John Cooper, John Brown, John Irving, William Blagdeen, William Madden, James Machon, William H. Brown, James Mifflin, James E Sterling, Richard Dennis, Samuel W. Davis, Samuel Todd, Thomas Fitzpatrick, Charles Melville, William A. Stanley, William Pelham, John McFarland, James G. Garrison, Thomas O. Connell, Wilson Brown.

The following named persons, having had Medals of Honor awarded to them for distinguished service in battle, and having again performed acts which, if they had not received that distinction, would have entitled them to it, were authorized to wear a bar attached to the ribbon by which the medal is suspended: John Cooper, Patrick Mullen.

The following persons, whose names appear on the above list, forfeited their medals by bad conduct: Joseph Brown, John Brazell, Frank Lucas, John Jackson, Clement Dees, Charles Robinson, John Martin, Richard Bates.

and not compel us to resort further to the force under our control. The Government asks only that its authority may be recognized; and, we repeat, in no manner or way does it desire to interfere with your laws, constitutionally established, your institutions of any kind whatever, your property of any sort, or your usages in any respect."

This appeal alarmed the Confederate leaders in that State, and the Governor, Henry T. Clark, issued a counter-proclamation a few days afterward,[a] in which he denounced the expedition as an attempt to deprive the inhabitants of liberty, property, and all they held "most dear as a self-governing and free people." He called upon them to supply the requisitions just made by Jefferson Davis for troops to repel the enemy. "We must resist him," he said, "at all hazards, and by every means in our power. He wages a war for our subjugation—a war forced upon us in wrong, and prosecuted without right, and in a spirit of vengeful wickedness, without a parallel in the history of warfare among civilized nations." He assured them that the Government was increasing its efforts "and straining every nerve" not to regain its rightful authority, but to overrun the country and subjugate the people to its domination, its "avarice and ambition." "I call upon the brave and patriotic men of our State to volunteer," he said, "from the mountains to the sea."

[a] Feb. 22, 1862.

Such was the opposing spirit of the Government, and the conspirators against its life. The former was anxious for peace, the latter were zealous for war. The former, battling for right, justice, and the perpetuity of free institutions, and conscious of the righteousness of its cause, was firm but mild, patient, and persuasive; the latter, battling for wrong, injustice, and the perpetuation of slavery for the negro, and serfdom for the poor white man, with no warrant for their acts but selfishness, were bitter, vehement, and uncompromising; continually appealing to the passions of the people rather than to their reason and judgment, and by fraud and violence dragging them into the vortex of rebellion, in which their prosperity and happiness were sadly wrecked.

Here we will leave the National forces for a while in the waters of North Carolina, preparing for another important victory, which they achieved a month later, and observe the progress of military events westward of the Alleghanies during the later days of autumn, and the winter of 1861–62.

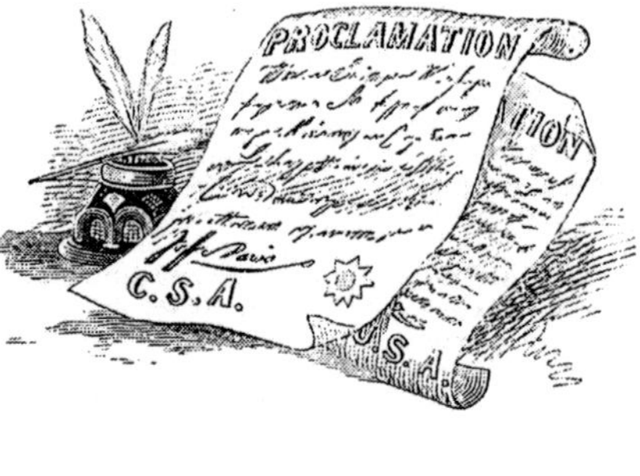

CHAPTER VII.

MILITARY OPERATIONS IN MISSOURI, NEW MEXICO, AND EASTERN KENTUCKY—CAPTURE OF FORT HENRY.

TOWARD the close of the autumn of 1861, the attitude of the contending parties, civil and military, in the great basin of the central Mississippi Valley was exceedingly interesting. We left the National army in Southern Missouri, at the middle of November, dispirited by the removal of their favorite leader, slowly making their way toward St. Louis under their temporary commander, General Hunter, while the energetic Confederate leader, General Price, was advancing, and reoccupying the region which the Nationals abandoned.[1] We left Southern Kentucky, from the mountains to the Mississippi River, in possession of the Confederates. Polk was holding the western portion, with his head-quarters at Columbus; General Buckner, with a strongly intrenched camp at Bowling Green, was holding the center; and Generals Zollicoffer and Marshall and others were keeping watch and ward on its mountain flanks. Back of these, and between them and the region where the rebellion had no serious opposition, was Tennessee, firmly held by the Confederates, excepting in its mountain region, where the most determined loyalty still prevailed.

On the 9th of November, 1861, General Henry Wager Halleck, who had been called from California by the President to take an active part in the war, was appointed to the command of the new Department of Missouri.[2] He had arrived in Washington on the 5th,[a] and on the 19th took the command, with Brigadier-General George W. Cullum, an eminent engineer officer, as his chief of staff, and Brigadier-General Schuyler Hamilton as assistant chief. Both officers had been on the staff of General Scott. The head-quarters were at St. Louis. General Hunter, whom Halleck superseded, was assigned to the command of the Department of Kansas.[3] General Don Carlos Buell had superseded General Sherman, and was appointed commander of the Department of the Ohio;[4] and the Department of Mexico, which included only the territory of New Mexico, was intrusted to Colonel E. R. S. Canby. Such was the arrangement of the military divisions of the territory westward of the Alleghanies late in 1861.

[a] Nov., 1861.

---

[1] See page 84.

[2] It included Missouri, Iowa, Minnesota, Wisconsin, Illinois, Arkansas, and that portion of Kentucky lying west of the Cumberland River.

[3] This included the State of Kansas, the Indian Territory, most of Arkansas, and the Territories of Nebraska, Colorado, and Dakota.

[4] This included the State of Ohio, and the portion of Kentucky lying eastward of the Cumberland River, which had formed a part of Sherman's Department of the Cumberland.

General Halleck was then in the prime of life, and he entered upon his duties with zeal and vigor. He was possessed of large mental and physical energy, and much was expected of him. He carefully considered the plan arranged by Fremont for clearing the States of Kentucky, Tennessee, Missouri, and Arkansas of armed insurgents, and securing the navigation of the Mississippi by sweeping its banks of obstructions, from Cairo to New Orleans.[1] Approving of it in general, he pushed on the great enterprise with strong hopes of success.

HENRY WAGER HALLECK.

Halleck's first care was to establish the most perfect discipline in his army, to overawe the secessionists, and to relieve the loyal people of Missouri of the effects of the dreadful tyranny inflicted by the latter, many of whom were engaged in armed bands in plundering the inhabitants, desolating the property of Union men, and destroying railways and bridges. Refugees were then crowding into the Union lines by thousands. Their miseries cannot be described. Men, women, and children were stripped, plundered, and made homeless. Naked and starving, they sought refuge and relief in St. Louis. Seeing this, the commander determined to apply an effectual remedy. In a general order, he directed the Provost-Marshal of St. Louis (Brigadier-General Curtis) to inquire into the condition of these refugees, and to take measures for quartering them "in the houses of avowed secessionists," and for feeding and clothing them at the expense of that class of citizens, or others known to have been guilty of giving "assistance and encouragement to the enemy." He also further ordered[a] wealthy secessionists to contribute for the support of these refugees, and that all who should not voluntarily do so should be subjected to a levy, either in money, food, clothing, or quarters, to the amount of ten thousand dollars each. This order was rigidly enforced, and many wealthy citizens were made to pay liberal sums. One prominent merchant, named Engel, who ventured to resist the order by appealing to the civil courts, was ordered out of the Department. This was the last appeal of that kind.

[a] Dec. 12, 1861.

Determined to put a stop to the continual outflowing of information to the Confederates from within his lines, Halleck issued some very stringent orders. The earliest of these was Order No. 3,[b] which forbade fugitives entering or remaining within his lines, it having been represented to him that they conveyed contraband information out of them.[2] This order was a subject of much comment, because of its seeming tenderness for the rebellious slaveholder, and cruelty toward the bondman seeking

[b] Nov. 20.

---

[1] See page 79.

[2] "In order to remedy this evil," ran the order, "it is directed that no such person be hereafter permitted to enter the lines of any camp, or of any forces on the march, and that any now within such lines be immediately excluded therefrom."

freedom. That it was a mistake, subsequent experience fully demonstrated; for throughout the war the negro, whether bond or free, was uniformly the friend and helper of the National cause. General Halleck had been misinformed, and upon that misinformation he acted with the best intentions, one of which was to prevent the betrayal of the secret of his camps, and another that he might keep clear of the questions relating to masters and slaves,[1] in which Fremont had been entangled, to his hurt.

In the order of the 4th of December, concerning the treatment of avowed secessionists, Halleck further directed that all rebels found within his lines in the disguise of pretended loyalty, or other false pretenses, or found giving information to the insurgents, should be "arrested, tried, and, if condemned, shot as spies." This and all other orders, concerning the disloyalists by whom he was surrounded, were enforced; and he directed that any one attempting to resist the execution of them should be arrested and imprisoned, to be tried by a military commission. Many offenders being women, it was declared that "the laws of war make no distinction of sex."

To enforce these laws, it was necessary to use military power, especially in the suppression of the bands of marauders who were then sweeping over the country. He accordingly sent General John Pope, who, as we have already observed, had been active in that Department, to disperse the encampments of these guerrillas in Western Missouri. Pope had been acting with vigor during the latter part of summer and the early autumn. The people of a district where outrages were committed had been held responsible for them. He had quartered his troops on such inhabitants, and required from them contributions of horses, mules, provisions, and other necessaries. He had organized Committees of Safety, on which were placed prominent secessionists, charged to preserve the peace; and in a short time comparative good order was restored. Now Pope was charged with similar duties. On the 7th of December, he was assigned to the command of all the National troops between the Missouri and Osage Rivers, which included a considerable portion of Fremont's army that fell back from Springfield. Price was advancing. He had made a most stirring appeal by proclamation to the Missourians to come and help him, and so help themselves to freedom and independence. The Governor (Jackson), he said, had called for fifty thousand men, but only five thousand had responded. "Where are those fifty thousand men?" he asked. "Are Missourians no longer true to themselves? Are they a timid, time-serving race, fit only for subjugation to a despot? Awake! my countrymen," he cried, "to a sense of what constitutes the dignity of the true greatness of a people. . . . . Come to us, brave sons of the Missouri Valley! Rally to our standard! I must have the fifty thousand men. . . . . Do you stay at home for protection? More men have been murdered at home than I have lost in five successive battles. Do you stay at home to secure terms with the enemy? Then I warn you the day soon may come when you will be surrendered to the mercies of that enemy, and your substance given to the Hessians and the Jayhawkers.[2] . . . Leave

---

[1] Letter of General Halleck to General Asboth, December 20, 1861.

[2] A name given to certain rangers or guerrilla bands of Kansas and especially those under Colonel Jennison, who was active against the insurgents.

your property to take care of itself. Come to the Army of Missouri, not for a week or a month, but to free your country.

'Strike till each armed foe expires!
Strike for your country's altar fires!
Strike for the green graves of your sires,
God and your native land!'

Be yours the office to choose between the glory of a free country and a just government, or the bondage of your children. I, at least, will never see the chains fastened upon my country. I will ask for six and a half feet of Missouri soil in which to repose, for I will not live to see my people enslaved."

This appeal aroused the disaffected Missourians, and at the time when Pope was ordered to his new field of operations, about five thousand recruits, it was said, were marching from the Missouri River and beyond to join Price. To prevent this combination was Pope's chief desire. He encamped thirty or forty miles southwest from Booneville, at the middle of December, and after sending out some of the First Missouri cavalry, under Major Hubbard, to watch Price, who was then at Osceola with about eight thousand men, and to prevent a reconnoissance of the main column of the Nationals, he moved his whole body[a] westward and took position in the country between Clinton and Warrensburg, in Henry and Johnson counties. There were two thousand Confederates then near his lines, and against these Lieutenant-Colonel Brown, of the Seventh Missouri, was sent with a considerable cavalry force that scattered them. Having accomplished this, Brown returned to the main army,[b] which was moving on Warrensburg.

[a] Dec. 16, 1861

[b] Dec. 18.

Informed that a Confederate force was on the Blackwater, at or near Milford, North of him, Pope sent Colonel Jefferson C. Davis and Major Merrill to flank them, while the main body should be in a position to give immediate aid, if necessary. Davis found them in a wooded bottom on the west side of the Blackwater, opposite the mouth of Clear Creek. His forces were on the east side, and a bridge that spanned the Blackwater between them was strongly guarded. This was carried by assault, by two companies of the Fourth Regular Cavalry, under Lieutenants Gordon and Amory, supported by five companies of the First Iowa cavalry. Gordon led the charge in person, and received several balls through his cap. The Confederates were driven, the bridge was crossed, and a pursuit was pressed. Unable to escape, the fugitives, commanded by Colonels Robinson, Alexander, and Magoffin (the latter a brother of the Governor of Kentucky), surrendered. The captives were one thousand three hundred in number, infantry and cavalry; and with them the Nationals gained as spoils about eight hundred horses and mules, a thousand stand of arms, and over seventy wagons loaded with tents, baggage, ammunition, and supplies of every kind.

At about midnight the prisoners and spoils were taken into Pope's camp, and the next day the victors and the vanquished moved back in the direction of Sedalia, Pope's starting-place. In the space of five days the infantry had marched more than one hundred miles, and the cavalry double that distance. During that time they had captured nearly fifteen hundred prisoners, with the arms and supplies just mentioned. They had swept the whole country west of Sedalia, in the direction of Kansas, far enough to foil the attempts of recruits to reach Price in any considerable numbers, and to compel him to withdraw, in search of safety and subsistence, toward the borders of Arkansas.

Among the captured on the Blackwater, were many wealthy and influential citizens of Missouri. This event dealt a stunning blow to secession in that State for the moment, and Pope's short campaign gave great satisfaction to all loyal people. Halleck complimented him on his "brilliant success," and feeling strengthened there by, he pressed forward with more vigorous measures for the complete suppression of the rebellion in his Department westward of the Mississippi River. On the 23d of December he declared martial law in St. Louis; and by proclamation on the 25th this system of rule was extended to all railroads and their vicinities.[1] At about the same time General Price, who had found himself relieved from immediate danger, and encouraged by a promise of re-enforcements from Arkansas, under General McIntosh, concentrated about twelve thousand men at Springfield, where he put his army in comfortable huts, with the intention of remaining all winter, and pushed his picket-guards fifteen or twenty miles northward. This demonstration caused Halleck to concentrate his troops at Lebanon, the capital of Laclede County, northeastward of Springfield, early in February, under the chief command of General (late Colonel) S. R. Curtis. These were composed of the troops of Generals Asboth, Sigel, Davis, and Prentiss.

In the midst of storms and floods, over heavy roads and swollen streams, the combined forces moved on Springfield[a] in three columns, the right under General Davis, the center under General Sigel, and the left under Colonel (soon afterward General) Carr. On the same day they met some of Price's advance, and skirmishing ensued; and on the following day about three hundred Confederates attacked Curtis's picket-guards, but were repulsed. This feint of offering battle was made by Price to enable him to effect a retreat. On the night of the 12th and 13th[b] he fled from Springfield with his whole force. Not a man of them was to be seen when Curtis's vanguard, the Fourth Iowa, entered the town at dawn the next morning. There stood their huts, in capacity sufficient to accommodate ten thousand men. The camp attested a hasty departure, for remains of supper and half-dressed sheep and hogs, that had been slain the previous evening, were found.

[a] Feb. 11, 1862.

[b] February.

Price retreated to Cassville, closely pursued by Curtis. Still southward he hastened, and was more closely followed, his rear and flanks continually harassed during four days, while making his way across the Arkansas border to Cross Hollows.[2] Having been re-enforced by Ben McCulloch, near a range of hills called Boston Mountains, he made a stand at Sugar Creek, where, in a brief engagement, he was defeated,[c] and was again compelled to fly. He halted at Cove Creek, where, on the 25th, he reported

[c] Feb. 20.

[1] The proclamation of the 25th was issued in consequence of the destruction or disability, on the 20th, of about one hundred miles of the Missouri railroad, by some men returned from Price's army, assisted by inhabitants along the line of the road, acting by pre-concert. On the 23d, Halleck issued an order, fixing the penalty of death for that crime, and requiring the towns and counties along the line of any railway thus destroyed, to repair the damages and pay the expenses.

[2] During the operations of this forward movement of the National troops, Brigadier-General Price, son of the chief, was captured at Warsaw, together with several officers of the elder Price's staff, and about 500 recruits.

to his wandering chief, Jackson, saying, "Governor, we are confident of the future." General Halleck, quite as "confident of the future," was now able to report to his Government that Missouri was effectually cleared of the armed forces of insurgents who had so long infested it, and that the National flag was waving in triumph over the soil of Arkansas. In accomplishing this good work, no less than sixty battles and skirmishes, commencing with Booneville at the middle of June,[1] and ending at the middle of the succeeding February,[a] had been fought on Missouri soil, resulting in an aggregate loss to both parties, in killed, wounded, and prisoners, of about eleven thousand men.[2]

[a] 1862.

While Halleck was thus purging Missouri, Hunter, with his head-quarters at Fort Leavenworth, was vigorously at work in Kansas, on the west of it.[3] The general plan of his treatment of the rebellion, which was rife on the Missouri border, was set forth in a few words addressed to the Trustees of Platte City,[b] concerning an outlaw named Gordon, who, with a guerrilla band, was committing depredations and outrages of every kind in that region. Hunter said, "Gentlemen, I give you notice, that unless you seize and deliver the said Gordon to me at these head-quarters within ten days from this date, or drive him out of the country, I shall send a force to your city with orders to reduce it to ashes, and to burn the house of every secessionist in your county, and to carry away every negro. Colonel Jennison's regiment will be intrusted with the execution of this order." Jennison, who was the commander of the First Kansas cavalry, was well known to the people as an ardent anti-slavery champion during the civil war in Kansas in 1855,[4] and a man ready to execute any orders of the kind. That letter, the power given to Jennison, and a proclamation issued by the latter a short time before,[5] made the secessionists very circumspect for a while, and "all quiet in Kansas" was a frequent report in the Spring of 1862.

[b] Dec. 2, 1861.

Active and armed rebellion was at this time co-extensive with the slave-labor States. Colonel Canby found it ready to meet him even in the remote region of New Mexico, in the shape of invaders from Texas. Like Halleck and Hunter, he attacked the monster quickly and manfully.

---

[1] See page 540, volume I.

[2] Several of these skirmishes were so light, and so unimportant in their bearings upon the great issues, that the narrative of this general history has not been unduly extended by a record of them. Such record belongs to a strictly statistical and military history of the war. During the last fortnight of the month of December, 1861, the Nationals in Missouri captured 2,500 prisoners, including 70 commissioned officers; 1,200 horses and mules; 1,100 stand of arms; 2 tons of powder; 100 wagons, and a large amount of stores and camp equipage.

[3] Preparations had been made for organizing an army in Kansas to go through the Indian Territory and a portion of Southwestern Arkansas and so on to New Orleans, to co-operate with the forces that were to sweep down the Mississippi and along its borders. James H. Lane, then a member of the United States Senate, was to command that army. Owing to some difficulties, arising from misapprehension, the expedition was abandoned, and Lane took his seat in the Senate at Washington.

[4] See note 2, page 181.

[5] Jennison had said to the inhabitants of Lafayette, Cass, Johnson, and Pettis Counties, in Missouri: "For four months our armies have marched through your country. Your professed friendship has been a fraud; your oaths of allegiance have been shams and perjuries. You feed the rebel army, you act as spies while claiming to be true to the Union. . . . . Neutrality is ended. If you are patriots, you must fight; if you are traitors, you must be punished." . . . . He told them that the rights and property of Union men would be everywhere respected, but "traitors," he said, "will everywhere be treated as outlaws—enemies of God and men, too base to hold any description of property, and having no rights which loyal men are bound to respect. The last dollar and the last slave of rebels will be taken and turned over to the General Government. Playing war is played out, and whenever Union troops are fired upon the answer will boom from cannon, and desolation will follow."

We have seen the loyal people of Texas bound hand and foot by a civil and military despotism after the treason of General Twiggs.[1] The conspirators and their friends had attempted to play a similar game for attaching New Mexico to the intended Confederacy, and to aid Twiggs in giving over Texas to the rule of the Confederates. So early as 1860, Secretary Floyd sent Colonel W. H. Loring, of North Carolina (who appears to have been an instrument of the traitor), to command the Department of New Mexico, while Colonel George B. Crittenden, an unworthy son of the venerable Kentucky senator, who had been sent out for the same wicked purpose as Loring, was appointed by the latter, commander of an expedition against the Apaches, which was to start from Fort Staunton in the Spring of 1861. It was the business of these men to attempt the corruption of the patriotism of the officers under them, and to induce them to lead their men into Texas and give them to the service of the rebellion. One of these officers (Lieutenant-Colonel B. S. Roberts, of Vermont), who had joined Crittenden at Fort Staunton, perceiving the intentions of his commander, refused to obey any orders that savored of a treasonable purpose, and procuring a furlough, he hastened to Sante Fé, the head-quarters of the Department, and denounced Crittenden to Colonel Loring. He was astonished when, instead of thanks for his patriotic service, he received a reproof for meddling with other people's business, and discovered that Loring was also playing the game of treason. Roberts was ordered back to Fort Staunton, but found an opportunity to warn Captain Hatch, the commander at Albuquerque, and Captain Morris, who held Fort Craig (both on the Rio Grande), as well as other loyal officers, of the treachery of their superiors. The iniquity of Loring and Crittenden soon became known to the little army under them, and they found it necessary to leave suddenly and unattended. Of the twelve hundred regular troops in New Mexico, not one proved treacherous to his country.

Loring and Crittenden made their way to Fort Fillmore, not far from El Paso and the Texas border, then commanded by Major Isaac Lynde, of Vermont. They found a greater portion of the officers there ready to engage in the work of treason. Major Lynde professed to be loyal, but, if so, he was too inefficient to be intrusted with command. Late in July, while leading about five hundred of the seven hundred troops under his control toward the village of Mesilla, he fell in with a few Texas insurgents, and, after a slight skirmish, fled back to the fort. He was ordered to evacuate it, and march his command to Albuquerque. Strange to say, the soldiers were allowed to fill their canteens with whisky and drink when they pleased. A large portion of them were drunken before they had marched ten miles, and then, as if by previous arrangement, a Texas force appeared on their flank.[a] The soldiers who were not prostrated by intoxication wished to fight, but, by order of a council of officers, with Lynde at their head, they were directed to lay down their arms as prisoners of war. Lynde's commissary, Captain A. H. Plummer, who held seventeen thousand dollars in Government drafts, which he might have saved, handed them over to Baylor, the commander of the insurgents. For this cowardice or treachery, Lynde was simply dismissed from the army, and Plummer was reprimanded

[a] July 27, 1861.

[1] See chapter XI., volume I.

and suspended from duty for six months. Thus, at one sweep, nearly one-half of the Government troops in New Mexico were lost to its service. The prisoners were paroled, and then permitted to go on to Albuquerque. Their sufferings from thirst on that march were terrible; some of them seeking to quench it by opening veins and drinking their own blood!

It was now thought that New Mexico would be an easy prey to the Texas insurgents. Miguel A. Otero, its delegate in the National Congress, had endeavored, by a published address,[a] to incite the inhabitants of New Mexico to rebellion, while Governor Abraham Rencher, of North Carolina, took measures to defend the Territory against the insurgents. His successor, Henry Connolly, was equally loyal. So also were the people; and when, at this juncture of affairs, Colonel Canby arrived as Commander of the Department, he was met with almost universal sympathy. He successfully appealed for a regiment of volunteers to the Governor of the neighboring Territory of Colorado, and these, with his few regular troops and New Mexico levies, made quite a respectable force in numbers, when Canby was informed that Colonel Henry H. Sibley, a major by brevet in the National army, and a Louisianian, who had abandoned his flag and put himself at the head of a band of insurgents known as Texas Rangers, some of them of the worst sort, was invading the Territory. His force was formidable in numbers (twenty-three hundred) and in experience, many of them having been in successive expeditions against the Indians.

[a] Feb. 16, 1861.

HENRY H. SIBLEY.

Sibley issued a proclamation to the people of New Mexico, in which he denounced the National Government and demanded from the inhabitants aid for and allegiance to his marauders. Confident of success, he moved slowly, by way of Fort Thorn, and found Canby at Fort Craig, on the Rio Grande,[b] prepared to meet him. A reconnoissance satisfied him that, with his light field-pieces, an assault on the fort would be foolish. He could not retreat or remain with safety, and his military knowledge warned him that it would be very hazardous to leave a well-garrisoned fort behind him. So he forded the Rio Grande at a point below Fort Craig, and out of reach of its guns, for the purpose of drawing Canby out. In this he was successful. Canby at once threw a force across the river,[1] to occupy a position on an eminence commanding the fort, which it was thought Sibley might attempt to gain.

[b] Feb. 19, 1862.

In the afternoon of the following day, some cavalry, under Captain Duncan, and a battery were sent across, and drew a heavy cannonade from the Texans. The infantry were nearly all thrown into confusion, excepting

[1] These consisted of the Fifth, Seventh, and Tenth Regular Infantry, under Captains Selden and Wingate, and the volunteer regiments of Colonels Carson and Pine.

Colonel Kit Carson's regiment. The panic was so great that Canby ordered a return of all the forces to the fort. That night the exhausted mules of the Texans became unmanageable, on account of thirst, and scampered in every direction. The National scouts captured a large number of these, and also wagons, by which Sibley was greatly crippled in the matter of transportation.

At eight o'clock the next morning,[a] Canby sent Lieutenant-Colonel Roberts, with cavalry, artillery, and infantry,[1] across the Rio Grande; and at Valverde, about seven miles north of the fort, they confronted the vanguard of the Texans under Major Pyron, who were making their way toward the river. The batteries opened upon Pyron, and he recoiled. Desultory fighting, mostly with artillery, was kept up until some time past noon, when Canby came upon the field, and took command in person. In the mean time, Sibley, who was quite ill, had turned over his command to Colonel Thomas Green, of the Fifth Texas regiment. Canby, considering victory certain for his troops, was preparing to make a general advance, when a thousand or more Texans, foot and horse, under Colonel Steele, who had gathered in concealment in a thick wood and behind sand-hills, armed with carbines, revolvers, and bowie-knives, suddenly rushed forward and charged furiously upon the batteries of McRea and Hall. The Texas cavalry, under Major Raguet, charged upon Hall's battery, and were easily repulsed; but those on foot, who made for McRea's battery, could not be checked. His grape and canister shot made fearful lanes in their ranks, but they did not recoil. They captured the battery, but not without encountering the most desperate defenders of the guns in McRea and his artillerists, a large number of whom, with their commander, were killed. McRea actually sat upon his gun, fighting his foe with his pistol until he was shot. The remainder of the Nationals, with the exception of Kit Carson's men and a few others, panic-stricken by the fierce charge of the Texans, fled like sheep before wolves, and refused to obey the commands of officers who tried to rally them. That flight was one of the most disgraceful scenes of the war, and Canby was compelled to see victory snatched from his hand when it seemed secure. The surviving Nationals took refuge in Fort Craig. Their loss was sixty-two killed and one hundred and forty-two wounded. The loss of the Texans was about the same.

[a] Feb. 21, 1862.

ONE OF SIBLEY'S TEXAS RANGERS.[2]

Sibley well comprehended the situation. The fort could not be taken,

[1] These were composed of a portion of Roberts's and Colonel Valdez's cavalry; Carson's volunteers; the Fifth, Seventh, and Tenth Regulars, and two batteries, commanded respectively by Captain McRea and Lieutenant Hall.

[2] These Rangers who went into the rebellion were described as being, many of them, a desperate set of fellows, having no higher motive than plunder and adventure. They were half savage, and each was mounted on a mustang horse. Each man carried a rifle, a tomahawk, a bowie-knife, a pair of Colt's revolvers, and a lasso for catching and throwing the horses of a flying foe. The above picture is from a sketch by one of Colonel Canby's subalterns.

and the spirit shown by a large portion of Canby's troops satisfied him that, notwithstanding his loss of transportation by the capture of his mules and wagons, he need not fear a pursuit. So, passing on and leaving his wounded at Socorro, thirty miles above Fort Craig, Sibley pressed forward to Albuquerque, fifty miles farther, which was at once surrendered. His destination was Santa Fé, and he was marching with perfect confidence of success there, when his vanguard, under W. R. Scurry, was met near Fort Union, in the Cañon Glorietta, or Apache Pass, fifteen miles from the capital of New Mexico, by about thirteen hundred National troops, under Colonel John P. Slough. These were mostly Colorado Volunteers, with a few regulars. A greater part of these had just traversed the mountain wilderness from Denver, and during the latter part of their journey, after hearing of Sibley's approach to Santa Fé, they had marched at the rate of forty miles a day. In that narrow defile, where flanking was out of the question, a very severe fight between the infantry and artillery of both parties occurred,[a] in which the Texans were victorious, after a loss of thirty-six killed and sixty wounded. The National loss was twenty-three killed and fifty wounded.[1]

[a] March 24, 1862.

Sibley entered Santa Fé without further resistance. His army was greatly crippled, and the people were either indifferent or actively opposed to him. He seized whatever property might be useful to him, and hoped to hold his position; but a month had not elapsed before he was compelled to fly back to Albuquerque, which he had made his depot of supplies, for these were threatened by the forces of Colonel Canby, approaching from below. He accomplished that purpose, but was so satisfied that he could not hold New Mexico, that he evacuated Albuquerque on the 12th of April,[b] leaving his sick and wounded in hospitals there and at Santa Fé. After skirmishing with his opponents along the river, each party moving on opposite sides of the stream, and perceiving imminent danger to his whole command, Sibley fled under cover of the night to the mountains, with his scanty provisions on pack mules, dragging his cannon over rugged spurs and along fearful precipices, for ten days. Then he again struck the Rio Grande at a point where he had ordered supplies to meet him. He then made his way to Fort Bliss,[2] in Texas,[c] a wiser if not a happier man. Canby did not follow him over the mountains, but returned to Santa Fé, and reported to the Secretary of War that Sibley, who had been compelled to evacuate New Mexico, had left behind him, "in dead and wounded, and in sick and prisoners, one-half of his original force."

[b] 1862.

[c] May 4.

Let us now observe events eastward of the Mississippi River, within the Departments of Generals Halleck[3] and Buell,[4] having a connection with the

[1] On the previous morning, in a skirmish with Pyron's Cavalry, Colonel Slough took fifty-seven prisoners, but losing fifteen of his own men. In the fight just recorded, Major Chivington, with four Colorado companies, gained the rear of the Texans, and was inflicting serious injury upon them, when he heard of Slough's defeat, and was compelled to withdraw.

[2] At Albuquerque, according to Sibley's report, the brothers Raphael and Manuel Armijo were so warmly interested in the Confederate cause that they placed at his disposal stores valued at $200,000. They fled over the mountains with Sibley. Their generosity and sacrifices so touched his heart, that he expressed a hope that they might not be forgotten by the "Confederate Government" in the final settlement.

[3] See page 179.

[4] See page 179.

grand plan for expelling the Confederates from Kentucky, and liberating Tennessee from their grasp.

We have seen how the loyalists in the Kentucky Legislature foiled the efforts of the Governor and his political friends to link the fortunes of that State with those of the "Southern Confederacy." These efforts were met, as we have observed, by the occupation of the whole southern portion of the commonwealth by Confederate troops, all of which were within the Department commanded by General Albert Sidney Johnston. That officer had been an able veteran in the army of the Republic, and was then about sixty years of age. He was a Kentuckian by birth, and his sympathies were with the conspirators. He was on duty in California when the war was kindling, and was making preparations, with other conspirators there, to array that State on the side of the Confederacy,[1] when he was superseded in command by Lieutenant-Colonel E. V. Sumner, of Massachusetts. Johnston then abandoned his flag, joined the conspirators in active rebellion, and was appointed by Jefferson Davis to the command of the "Western Department," with his head-quarters at Nashville.

ALBERT SIDNEY JOHNSTON.

Under the shadow of Johnston's protection, and behind the cordon of Confederate troops stretched across the State, the disloyal politicians of Kentucky proceeded to organize an independent government for the commonwealth. They met at Russellville, the capital of Logan County, in the southern part of the State, on the 29th of October. They drew up a manifesto, in which the grievances of Kentucky were recounted, and the action of its Legislature denounced. They then called upon the people of the State to choose, "in any manner" they might see fit, "delegates to attend a 'Sovereignty convention,'" at Russellville, on the 18th of November. At the appointed time, about two hundred men from fifty-one counties, not elected by the people, assembled, and with difficult gravity adopted a "Declaration of Independence," and an "Ordinance of Secession,"[a] and then proceeded to organize a "Provisional Government," by choosing a governor, a legislative council of ten, a treasurer, and an auditor.[2] Bowling Green was selected as the new capital of the State. Commissioners were appointed to treat with the "Confederate Government," for the admission of Kentucky into the league;[3] and before the close of December the arrangement was made, and so-called

[a] Nov. 20, 1861.

[1] Annual Cyclopædia for 1862. Article—A. S. Johnston.

[2] George W. Johnson, of Scott County, was chosen Governor. The ministers of the Legislative Council were: William B. Machin, John W. Crockett, James P. Bates, James S. Critman, Philander R. Thompson, J. P. Burnside, H. W. Bruce, J. W. Moore, E. M. Bruce, and George B. Hodge.

[3] The Commissioners were: Henry C. Burnett, W. E. Simons, and William Preston.

representatives of that great commonwealth were chosen by the "Legislative Council"[a] to seats in the "Congress" at Richmond.[1] The *people* had nothing to do with the matter, and the ridiculous farce did not end here. All through the war, disloyal Kentuckians pretended to represent their noble old State in the supreme council of the conspirators, where they were chosen only, a great portion of that time, by the few Kentuckians in the military service of Jefferson Davis.

[a] Dec. 16, 1861.

While these political events in Kentucky were in progress, military movements in that quarter were assuming very important features. General Johnston concentrated troops at Bowling Green, and General Hardee was called from Southeastern Missouri, to supersede General Buckner in command there. The forces under General Polk at Columbus were strengthened, and Zollicoffer, having secured the important position of Cumberland Gap, proceeded to occupy the rich mineral and agricultural districts around the upper waters of the Cumberland River. He issued a proclamation[b] to the people of Southeastern Kentucky, declaring, in the set phrases used by all the instruments of the conspirators, when about to plant the heel of military despotism upon a community, that he came as their "liberator from the Lincoln despotism" and the ravages of "Northern hordes," who were "attempting the subjugation of a sister Southern State."

[b] Dec. 16.

In the mean time, General Buell had organized a large force at Louisville, with which he was enabled to strengthen various advanced posts, and throw forward, along the line of the railway toward Bowling Green, about forty thousand men, under General Alexander McD. McCook. As this strong body advanced, the vanguard of the Confederates, under General Hindman (late member of Congress from Arkansas), fell back to the southern bank of the Green River, at Mumfordsville, where that stream was spanned by one of the most costly iron bridges in the country.[3] This was partially destroyed, in order to impede the march of their pursuers. The latter soon constructed a temporary one. For this purpose, a greater portion of Colonel Auguste Willich's German regiment (the Thirty-second Indiana), forming McCook's vanguard, were thrown across the river, where they were attacked,[c] at Rowlett Station, by a regiment of mounted Texas Rangers, under Colonel Terry, supported by two

BUELL'S HEAD-QUARTERS AT LOUISVILLE.[2]

[c] Dec. 17.

[1] These were: Henry C. Burnett, John Thomas, Thomas L. Burnett, S. H. Ford, Thomas B. Johnson, George W. Ewing. Dr. D. V. White, John M. Elliott, Thomas B. Monroe, and George B. Hodge. On the day when these men were chosen by the "Council," two of them—Henry C. Burnett and Thomas Monroe—were sworn in at Richmond as members of the Confederate Senate. Of such usurpers of the political rights of the people, the "Confederate Congress," so called, was composed.

[2] This is a view of General Buell's head-quarters on Fourth Street, between Green and Walnut Streets, in the most aristocratic portion of the city of St. Louis.

[3] See page 351, volume I.

regiments of infantry and a battery of six guns. The Nationals, though greatly outnumbered, and attacked chiefly by cavalry and artillery, repulsed the assailants with ball and bayonet, killing Terry and thirty-two others, wounding about fifty, and losing eight killed and ten wounded themselves.[1] In this work they were aided by a battery on the north side of the river. Seeing re-enforcements crossing, the Confederates withdrew toward Bowling Green, slowly followed by the Nationals.

THOMAS C. HINDMAN IN 1858.

In the mean time, stirring scenes were in progress in the extreme eastern part of Kentucky, and movements there caused a brief diversion of a part of Buell's army from the business of pushing on in the direction of Tennessee. Humphry Marshall was again in the field, at the head of about twenty-five hundred insurgents, and at the beginning of January was intrenched in the neighborhood of Paintsville, in Johnston County, on the main branch of the Big Sandy River, that forms the boundary between Kentucky and Virginia. Colonel James A. Garfield, one of the most energetic young men of Ohio, was sent with the Forty-second Ohio and Fourteenth Kentucky regiments, and three hundred of the Second Virginia cavalry, to dislodge him. Garfield followed the course of the river in a march of greatest difficulty and danger, at an inclement season. When Marshall heard of his approach, he fled in alarm up the river toward Prestonburg. Garfield's cavalry pursued, and, in an encounter with those of Marshall,[a] at the mouth of Jennis's Creek, they killed some, and drove the others several miles. On the following day, Garfield also set out with about eleven hundred of his force in pursuit, and overtaking Marshall in the forks of Middle Creek, three miles above Prestonburg, where he was strongly posted with three cannon on a hill, he gave battle, fought him from one o'clock in the afternoon until dark, and drove him from all his positions. Garfield, having been re-enforced by seven hundred men from Paintsville, was enabled to make the victory for the Unionists at the BATTLE OF PRESTONBURG, as it is called, complete. The National loss was two killed and twenty-five wounded. That of the insurgents was estimated at sixty killed, and about one hundred wounded or made prisoners.[2] The ponderous Marshall was not heard of afterward as a military leader. Because of his services on this occasion, Garfield was commissioned[b] a brigadier-general of volunteers.

[a] Jan. 7, 1862.

[b] Jan. 11.

---

[1] Report of General Buell to General McClellan, December 18, 1861. General Hindman, in his report on the 19th, said General Terry and three of his regiment were killed, three others slightly wounded, and only six missing. As they left a much larger number dead on the field, Hindman's report must have been incorrect.

[2] Garfield, in his report, says that twenty-seven dead insurgents were found on the field the next morning. The Richmond papers reported the battle as a success for the insurgents, in which they lost only nine killed and the same number wounded; while the loss of the Nationals was "from 400 to 500 killed, and about the same number wounded!" Such was the usual character of the reports in the Confederate newspapers, under the

This victory on the Big Sandy was soon followed by another of the greatest importance, on the borders of the Cumberland River, farther westward. Zollicoffer, as we have observed, had established himself in the region of the upper waters of the Cumberland. At the close of the year[a] he was strongly intrenched at Beech Grove, on the north side of that river, opposite Mill Spring, in Pulaski County, at the bend of the stream where it receives the White Oak Creek. On a range of hills that rise several hundred feet above the river, and with water on three sides of him, he had constructed a series of fortifications; and on the opposite, or south side of the Cumberland he had also erected supporting works. There he had gathered a large part of his force, composed of infantry, cavalry, and artillery; and there, early in January,[b] he was joined by Major-General George B. Crittenden, already mentioned,[1] who had been discharged from the National army because of his intemperance, and had espoused the cause of the conspirators, while a brother was in the military service of the Government, in the same State. He ranked Zollicoffer, and assumed the chief command.[c] On the same day he inflicted a long and bombastic proclamation on the "people of Kentucky," closing with the appeal, "Will you join in the moving columns of the South, or is the spirit of Kentucky dead?"

[a] 1861. [b] 1862. [c] Jan. 6.

At this time General Buell had under his command about one hundred and fourteen thousand men, composed chiefly of citizens of Ohio, Indiana, Illinois, Michigan, Wisconsin, Minnesota, Pennsylvania, and loyalists of Kentucky and Tennessee, with about one hundred and twenty-six pieces of artillery.[2] This large army was divided into four grand divisions, commanded respectively by Brigadier-Generals Alexander McDowell McCook, Ormsby M. Mitchel, George H. Thomas, and Thomas L. Crittenden, acting as major-generals, aided by twenty brigade commanders. These divisions occupied a line across the State, nearly parallel to that held by the Confederates. McCook's, as we have observed, was in the vicinity of Mumfordsville. Brigadier-General William Nelson was

DON CARLOS BUELL.

eye of the conspirators at Richmond. With the most absurd mendacity, they made the deceived people believe that in every fight the Confederates won a victory over vastly superior numbers, killing, wounding, and capturing the Nationals by hundreds and thousands. These false reports were made on purpose to deceive the people, so as to draw men into the army, and money from the pockets of the dupes of the conspirators.

[1] See page 185.

[2] The contributions of these States to Buell's army were as follows: Ohio, thirty regiments of infantry, two and a half of cavalry, and eight batteries of artillery; Indiana, twenty-seven regiments of infantry, one and a half regiment of cavalry, and five batteries of artillery; Illinois, three regiments of infantry; Kentucky, twenty-four regiments of infantry, four of cavalry, and two batteries of artillery; Pennsylvania, three regiments of infantry, two of cavalry, and one battery of artillery; Michigan, three regiments of infantry, and one battery of artillery: Wisconsin, three regiments of infantry; Minnesota, two regiments of infantry and one battery of artillery; Tennessee, two regiments of infantry.

about ten miles farther east, with a considerable force, and Mitchel's was held as a reserve to aid McCook in his contemplated attack on Hindman, at Cave City. General Thomas was at Columbia, midway between Bowling Green on the west, and Somerset on the east, and Crittenden was in the extreme eastern part of the State, in the direction of Cumberland Gap.

To General Thomas was assigned the duty of attacking the Confederates at Beech Grove and Mill Spring, where, at the middle of January, there were about ten thousand effective men, with nearly twenty pieces of artillery. If successful there, Thomas was to push on over the Cumberland Mountains into the great valley of East Tennessee, seize the railway that traversed that region, and afforded quick communication between the Confederate armies in the West and in Virginia, and liberate the East Tennesseeans from their terrible thrall. It was a great work to be performed, and Thomas was precisely the man for the task. He entered upon it with alacrity. He divided his force, giving a smaller portion to the care of General Schoepf at Somerset, while he led the remainder in person, in a flank movement from Columbia, by way of Jamestown. He reached Logan's Cross Roads, ten miles from Beech Grove, on the 17th,[a] where, during the prevalence of a heavy rain-storm, he gathered his troops and made disposition for an immediate attack. In the mean time the Confederates had left their intrenchments, and had marched to meet him. General Crittenden, satisfied that Zollicoffer's position was untenable against superior numbers,[1] had determined to take the offensive. The Fishing Creek, which lay between the forces of Thomas and Schoepf, was so swollen by the rain that he hoped to strike the Nationals before these divisions could unite. He called a council of war on the evening of the 18th, when it was unanimously agreed to make the attack.[2] Zollicoffer was immediately ordered to lead the column. He started at midnight, Carroll's Brigade following his.[3] Following these as a reserve were the Sixteenth Alabama, Colonel Wood, and Branner's and McClellan's battalions of cavalry. The whole force was between four and five thousand strong. At early dawn, Zollicoffer's advance met the Union pickets.

[a] January, 1862.

General Thomas had been advised of this movement. He had made dispositions accordingly, and the pickets, encountered by the Confederate vanguard, were of Woolford's cavalry. These fell slowly back, and Woolford reported to Colonel M. D. Manson, of the Tenth Indiana, who was in command of the Second Brigade, stationed in advance of the main body. That officer formed his own and the Fourth Kentucky (Colonel S. S. Fry) in battle order, at the junction of the Somerset and Mill Spring Roads,

---

[1] The line of intrenchments was so extensive that the force was not sufficient to defend it thoroughly. The face of the country was such that there was bad range for artillery. At the same time, the country around the post could not furnish adequate subsistence for the army. At the time in question, the troops were reduced to a single ration of beef and a half ration of corn a day, the latter being parched, and not issued as meal.

[2] Correspondence of the *Louisville Courier*, by an eye-witness, January 25th, 1862.

[3] Zollicoffer's Brigade was composed of the Fifteenth Mississippi, and the Tennessee regiments of Colonels Cummings, Battle, and Stanton, marching in the order here named, with four guns commanded by Captain Rutledge, immediately in the rear of the Mississippians. Carroll's troops were composed of the Tennessee regiments of Colonels Newman, Murray, and Powell, with two guns commanded by Captain McClung, marching in the order named. Colonel Wood's Sixteenth Alabama was in reserve. Cavalry battalions in the rear; Colonel Branner on the right, and Colonel McClellan on the left. Independent companies in front of the advance regiments. Following the whole were ambulances, and ammunition and other wagons.

about five miles from the latter place, to await attack, and then sent a courier to inform Thomas of the situation. The commanding general hastened forward to view the position, when he found the Confederates advancing through a corn-field, to flank the Fourth Kentucky. He immediately ordered up the Tennessee brigade and a section of artillery, and sent orders for Colonel R. L. McCook to advance with his two regiments (Ninth Ohio, Major Kæmmerling, and Second Minnesota, Colonel H. P. Van Cleve) to the support of the vanguard.

The battle was opened at about six o'clock by the Kentucky and Ohio regiments, and Captain Kinney's Battery, stationed on the edge of the field, to the left of the Fourth Kentucky. It was becoming very warm when McCook's reserves came up to the support of the Nationals. Then the Confederates opened a most galling fire upon the little line, which made it waver. At that moment it was strengthened by the arrival of the Twelfth Kentucky, Colonel W. A. Hoskins, and the Tennessee Brigade, who joined in the fight. The conflict became very severe, and for a time it was doubtful which side would bear off the palm of victory. The Nationals had fallen back, and were hotly contesting the possession of a commanding hill, with Zollicoffer's Brigade, when that General, who was at the head of his column, and near the crest with Colonel Battle's regiment, was killed. The Confederate General Crittenden immediately took his place, and, with the assistance of Carroll's Brigade, continued the struggle for the hill for almost two hours. But the galling fire of the Second Minnesota, and a heavy charge of the Ninth Ohio with bayonets on the Confederate flank, compelled the latter to give way, and they retreated toward their camp at Beech Grove, in great confusion, pursued by the victorious Nationals to the summit of Moulden's Hill. From that commanding point Standart's and Wetmore's Batteries could sweep the Confederate works, while Kinney's Battery, stationed near Russell's house on the extreme left, opened fire upon the ferry, to prevent the Confederates from escaping across the Cumberland.

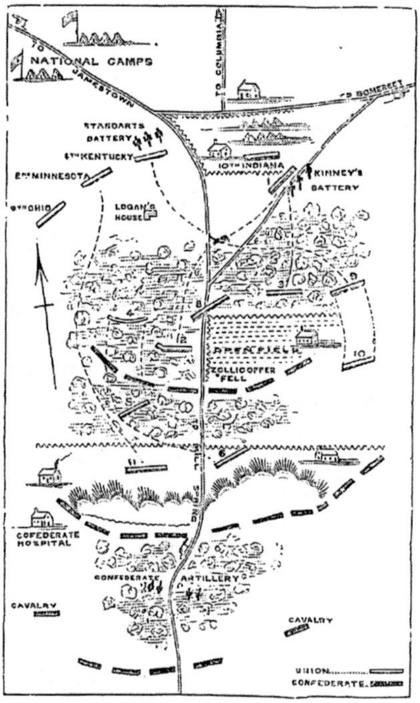

MAP OF THE BATTLE OF MILL SPRING.[1]

Such was the situation on Sunday evening,[a] at the close of the battle, when Thomas was joined by the Fourteenth Ohio, Colonel Stedman, and the Tenth Kentucky, Colonel Harlan; also by General

[a] Jan. 19, 1862.

[1] REFERENCES.—The figures 1, 2, 3, 4, 5, and 6, refer to the first and succeeding positions of the Tenth Indiana Regiment in the battle; 8, denotes the second position of the Fourth Kentucky; 9, the second position of the Second Minnesota; 10, the third position of the same; and 11, the second position of the Ninth Ohio.

Schoepf, with the Seventeenth, Thirty-first, and Thirty-eighth Ohio. Disposition was made early the next morning to assault the Confederate intrenchments, when it was ascertained that the works were abandoned. The beleaguered troops had fled in silence across the river, under cover of the darkness, abandoning every thing in their camp, and destroying the steamer *Noble Ellis* (which had come up the river with supplies), and three flat-boats, which had carried them safely over the stream.[1] Destitute of provisions and forage, the sadly-smitten Confederates were partially dispersed among the hills on the borders of Kentucky and Tennessee, while seeking both. Crittenden retreated first to Monticello, and then continued his flight until he reached Livingston and Gainesborough, in the direction of Nashville, in order to be in open communication with head-quarters at the latter place, and to guard the Cumberland as far above it as possible.

Thus ended the BATTLE OF MILL SPRING (which has been also called the Battle of Beech Grove, Fishing Creek, and Somerset), with a loss to the Nationals of two hundred and forty-seven, of whom thirty-nine were killed, and two hundred and eight were wounded; and to the Confederates of three hundred and forty-nine, of whom one hundred and ninety-two were killed, sixty-two were wounded, and eighty-nine were made prisoners. Among the killed, as we have seen, was General Zollicoffer, whose loss, at that time, was irreparable.[2] The spoils of victory for Thomas were twelve pieces of artillery, with three caissons packed, two army forges,[3] one battery wagon, a large amount of ammunition and small arms, more than a thousand horses and mules, wagons, commissary stores, intrenching tools,

ARMY FORGE.

[1] Some accounts say that the *Ellis* was set on fire by the shells of the Nationals, but the preponderance of testimony is in favor of the statement in the text. The Confederates hoped to prevent immediate pursuit by leaving nothing on which their foe could cross the river.

The Confederates suffered terribly in their retreat. "Since Saturday night," wrote one of their officers, "we had but an hour of sleep, and scarcely a morsel of food. For a whole week we have been marching under a bare subsistence, and I have at length approached that point in a soldier's career when a handful of parched corn may be considered a first-class dinner. We marched the first few days through a barren region, where supplies could not be obtained. I have more than once seen the men kill a porker with their guns, cut and quarter it, and broil it on the coals, and then eat it without bread or salt. The suffering of the men from the want of the necessaries of life, of clothing, and of repose, has been most intense, and a more melancholy spectacle than this solemn, hungry, and weary procession, could scarcely be imagined."

[2] Zollicoffer was killed by Colonel Fry, of the Fourth Kentucky. That officer, according to his own statement in a letter to his wife, was leading his regiment in a charge upon the Mississippians, when he was mistaken for a Confederate officer by Zollicoffer. The latter rode up to Fry, saying, as he pointed toward the Mississippians, "You are not going to fight your friends, are you?" At that instant Zollicoffer's aid, Major Henry M. Fogg, of Nashville, fired at Fry, wounding his horse. Fry turned and fired, killing Zollicoffer, not knowing at the time his person or his rank. He was covered in a white rubber coat, and on the previous evening had his beard shaved off, so as not to be easily recognized. The aid of Zollicoffer was mortally wounded at the same time. Zollicoffer's body was taken to Mumfordsville, and sent by a flag of truce to General Hindman. It was honored with a funeral salute at the National camp when it was carried over Green River.

[3] The army forge is a part of the equipment of a corps of artillery or cavalry in the field, and is portable. It consists of a four-wheeled carriage, with compartments in which a blacksmith's outfit of fuel and implements may be carried, and may be made ready for use in the course of half an hour. The fore and the hind wheels of the carriage may be separated—"unlimbered"—the same as those of a cannon. Attached to the fore wheels are

and camp equipage. The men in their flight left almost every thing behind them, except the clothing on their persons.[1]

This victory was considered one of the most important that had yet been achieved by the National arms. It broke the line of the Confederates in Kentucky, opened a door of deliverance for East Tennessee, and prepared the way for that series of successful operations by which very soon afterward the invaders were expelled from both States. The Government and the loyal people hailed the tidings of the triumph with great joy. The Secretary of War, by order of the President, issued an order announcing the event, and publicly thanking the officers and soldiers who had achieved the victory. He declared the purpose of the war to be "to pursue and destroy a rebellious enemy, and to deliver the country from danger;" and concluded by saying, "In the prompt and spirited movements and daring at Mill Spring, the nation will realize its hopes," and "delight to honor its brave soldiers."

The defeat was severely felt by the Confederates; for they were wise enough to understand its significance, prophesying, as it truly did, of further melancholy disasters to their cause. The conspirators perceived the urgent necessity for a bold, able, and dashing commander in the West, and believing Beauregard to be such an one, he was ordered to Johnston's Department,[a] and General G. W. Smith, who had been an active democratic politician in New York city, was appointed to succeed him at Manassas.[2] Crittenden was handled without mercy by the critics. He was accused of treachery by some, and others, more charitable, charged the loss of the battle to his drunkenness. All were compelled to acknowledge a serious disaster, and from it drew the most gloomy conclusions. Their despondency was deepened by the blow received by the Confederate cause at Roanoke Island soon afterward;[3] and the feeling became one of almost despair, when, a few days later, events of still greater importance, and more withering to their hopes, which we are about to consider, occurred on the Tennessee and Cumberland Rivers.[4]

[a] Jan. 27, 1862.

So active and skillful had Johnston been in his Department, in strengthening his irregular line of posts and fortifications for nearly four hundred

the boxes for supplies and tools, and to the rear wheels the bellows and forge, as seen in the engraving. When needed for use, the anvil is taken out and placed on a block made from any neighboring tree, and the work may be speedily begun.

[1] Report of General Thomas to General Buell, dated at Somerset, Kentucky, Jan. 31, 1862; also the reports of his subordinate officers.

[2] On leaving the army at Manassas, Beauregard issued a characteristic address to them, telling them he hoped soon to be back among them. "I am anxious," he said, "that my brave countrymen here in arms, fronting the haughty array and muster of Northern mercenaries, should thoroughly appreciate the exigency." Alluding to their disquietude because of long inaction, and the disposition to give up, he said it was no time for the men of the Potomac army "to stack their arms, and furl, even for a brief period, the standards they had made glorious by their manhood."

[3] See page 173.

[4] These are remarkable rivers. The Tennessee rises in the rugged valleys of Southwestern Virginia, between the Alleghany and Cumberland Mountains, having tributaries coming out of North Carolina and Georgia. It sweeps in an immense curve through Northern Alabama for nearly three hundred miles, from its northeast to its northwest corner, and then entering Tennessee, passes through it in a due north course, when, bending a little near the Kentucky border, it traverses that State in a northwesterly direction, and falls into the Ohio seventy miles above its mouth. It drains an area of forty thousand square miles, and is navigable for small vessels to Knoxville, five hundred miles from its mouth.

The Cumberland River rises on the western slopes of the Cumberland Mountains, in Eastern Kentucky, sweeps around into Middle Tennessee, and turning northward, in a course generally parallel to the Tennessee River, falls into the Ohio. It is navigable for large steamboats two hundred and fifty miles, and for smaller ones, at high water, nearly three hundred miles farther.

miles across Southern Kentucky, and within the Tennessee border from Cumberland Gap to Columbus on the Mississippi, that when General Thomas had accomplished the first part of the work he was sent to perform, it was thought expedient not to push farther, seriously, in the direction of East Tennessee just at that time. It was evident that the Confederates were preparing to make an effort to seize Louisville, Paducah, Smithville, and Cairo, on the Ohio, in order to command the most important land and water highways in Kentucky, so as to make it the chief battle-ground in the West, as Virginia was in the East, and keep the horrors of war from the soil of the more Southern States. As Charleston was defended on the

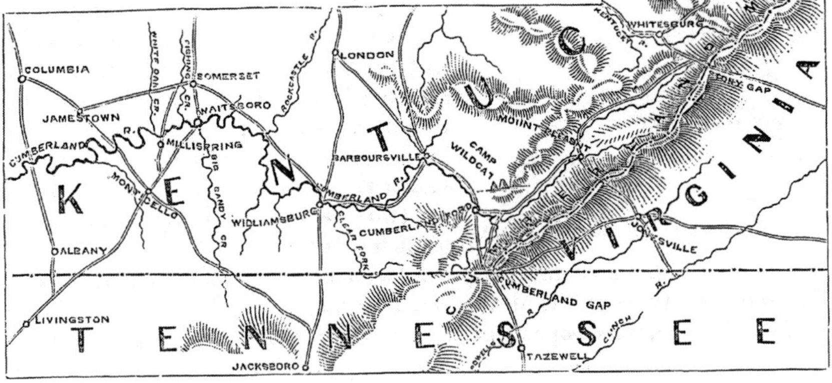

REGION OF MILITARY MOVEMENTS IN EASTERN KENTUCKY.[1]

Potomac, so New Orleans was to be defended by carrying the war up to the banks of the Ohio. Looking at a map of Kentucky and Virginia, and considering the attitude of the contending forces in each at that time, the reader may make a striking parallelism which a careful writer on the subject has pointed out.[2]

Governed by a military necessity, which changing circumstances had created, it was determined to concentrate the forces of Halleck and Buell in a grand forward movement against the main bodies and fortifications of the Confederates. Thomas's victory at Mill Spring had so paralyzed that line eastward of Bowling Green, that it was practically shortened at least one-half. Crittenden, as we have observed, had made his way toward Nashville, and left the Cumberland almost unguarded above that city; yet so mountainous was that region, and so barren of subsistence, that a flank move-

---

1 For an account of other movements in Eastern Kentucky, see Chapter III. of this volume.

2 "If Washington was threatened in the one quarter, Louisville was the object of attack on the other. As Fortress Monroe was a great basis of operations at one extremity, furnishing men and arms, so was Cairo on the west; and as the one had a menacing neighbor in Norfolk, so had the other in Columbus. What the line of the Kanawha was to Northern Virginia, penetrating the mountainous region, the Big Sandy, with its tributaries emptying also in the Ohio, was to the defiles of Eastern Kentucky. What Manassas or Richmond was, in one quarter, to the foe, Bowling Green, a great railway center, was to the other. As Virginia was pierced on the east by the James and the Rappahannock and the York, so was Kentucky on the west by the Cumberland and Tennessee; and as the Unionists held Newport News [Newport-Newce], a point of great strategic importance at the mouth of one of these streams, so were they in possession of Paducah, a place of equal or greater advantage, at the entrance to another."—*History of the War for the Union*, by E. A. Duyckinck.

ment in that direction would have been performed with much difficulty and danger.

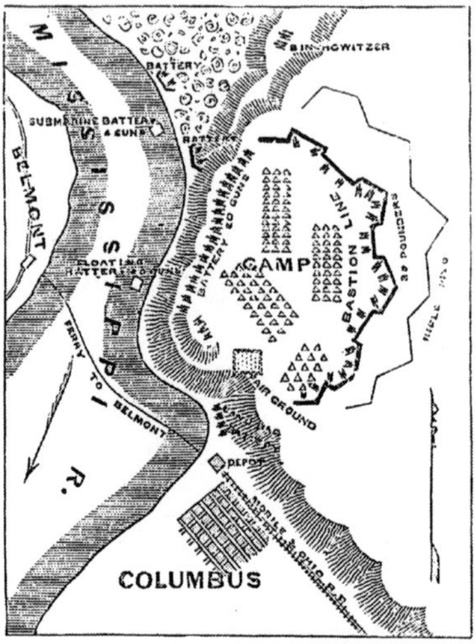

PLAN OF THE FORTIFICATIONS AT COLUMBUS.

The great body of the Confederate troops, and their chief fortifications, were between Nashville and Bowling Green and the Mississippi River, and upon these the combined armies of Halleck and Buell prepared to move. These fortifications had been constructed with skill, as to location and form, under the direction of General Polk, and chiefly by the labor of slaves. The principal works were redoubts on Island No. 10, in the Mississippi River, and at Columbus, on its eastern bank; Fort Henry, on the Tennessee River, and Fort Donelson, on the Cumberland River. The two latter were in Tennessee, not far below the line dividing it from Kentucky, at points where the two rivers approach within a few miles of each other.

During the autumn and early winter, a naval armament, projected by Fremont for service on the Mississippi River, had been in preparation at St. Louis and Cairo, for co-operation with the military forces in the West. It consisted, at the close of January,[a] of twelve gun-boats (some new and others made of river steamers), carrying one hundred and twenty-six heavy cannon and some lighter guns,[1] the whole commanded by Flag-officer Andrew Hull Foote, of the National navy. Seven of these boats were covered with iron plates, and were built very wide in proportion to their length, so that on the still river waters they might have almost the steadiness of stationary land batteries when discharging their heavy guns. The sides of these armored vessels were made sloping upward and downward from the water-line, at an angle of forty-five degrees, so as to ward off shot and shell; and they were so constructed that, in action, they could be kept "bow on," or the bow toward the enemy. Their hulls were made of heavy oak timber, with triple strength at the bows, and sheathed with wrought-iron plates two and a half inches in thickness. Their engines were very powerful, so as to facilitate movements in action; and each boat carried a mortar of 13-inch caliber.[2]

[a] 1862.

These vessels, although originally constructed for service on the Mississippi River, were found to be of sufficiently light draft to allow them to navigate the Cumberland and Tennessee Rivers, into whose waters they were speedily summoned, to assist an army which General Halleck had placed under the command of General Grant, in an expedition against Forts

[1] None of the cannon were less in metal than 32-pounders. Some were 42-pounders; some were nine and ten-inch Navy Columbiads, and the bow guns were rifled 84-pounders.

[2] The larger of these vessels were of the proportion of about 175 feet to 50 feet, and drawing, when armed and laden, about five feet of water. They were manned by Western boatmen and Eastern volunteers who had been navigators, commanded by officers of the National navy.

Henry and Donelson. Notwithstanding repeated assurances had been given to Mallory—the Confederate Secretary of the Navy—that these forts would be, in a great degree, at the mercy of the National gun-boats abuilding, that conspirator, who was remarkable for his obtuseness, slow method, and indifferent intellect, and whose ignorance, even of the geography of Kentucky and Tennessee, had been broadly travestied in "Congress,"[1] paid no attention to these warnings, but left both rivers open, without placing a single floating battery upon either. This omission was observed and taken advantage of by the Nationals, and early in February a large force that had moved from the Ohio River was pressing toward the doomed forts, whose

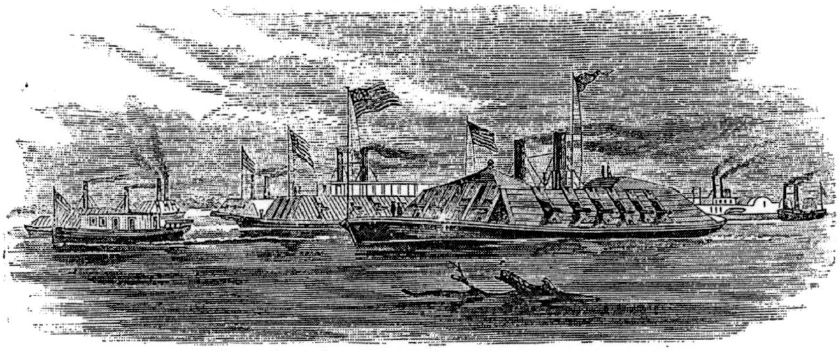

FOOTE'S FLOTILLA.

capture would make the way easy to the rear of Bowling Green. By that movement the Confederate line would be broken, and the immediate evacuation of Kentucky by the invaders would be made an inexorable necessity.

Preliminary to this grand advance, and for the double purpose of studying the topography of the country, and for deceiving the Confederates concerning the real designs of the Nationals, several reconnoissances, in considerable force, were made on both sides of the Mississippi River, toward the reputed impregnable stronghold at Columbus. One of these minor expeditions, composed of about seven thousand men, was commanded by General McClernand, who left Cairo for Fort Jefferson, and other places below, in river transports, on the 10th of January.[a] From that point he penetrated Kentucky far toward the Tennessee line, threatening Columbus and the country in its rear. At the same time, General Paine marched with nearly an equal force from Bird's Point, on the Missouri side of the Mississippi, in the direction of Charleston, for the purpose of supporting McClernand, menacing New Madrid, and reconnoitering Columbus; while a third party, six thousand strong, under General C. F. Smith, moved from Paducah to Mayfield, in the direction of Columbus. Still another force moved eastward to Smithland, between the Tennessee and Cumberland Rivers; and at the same time gun-boats were patrolling the waters of the Ohio and Mississippi, those on the latter threatening Columbus. These reconnoitering

[a] 1862.

[1] Pollard's *First Year of the War*, page 237.

parties all returned to their respective starting places preparatory to the grand movement.

These operations alarmed and perplexed the Confederates, and so puzzled the newspaper correspondents with the armies, that the wildest speculations about the intentions of Halleck and Buell, and the most ridiculous criticisms of their doings, filled the public journals. These speculations were made more unsatisfactory and absurd by the movements of General Thomas, immediately after the Battle of Mill Spring, who, it was then believed by the uninformed, was to be the immediate liberator of East Tennessee. He had crossed the Cumberland River in force, after the battle of Mill Spring, at the head of navigation at Waitsboro, and had pushed a column on toward Cumberland Gap. Predictions of glorious events in the great valley between the Alleghany and Cumberland Mountains were freely offered and believed; but the hopes created by these were speedily blasted. The movement was only a feint to deceive the Confederates, and was successful. To save East Tennessee from the grasp of Thomas, Johnston sent a large body of troops by railway from Bowling Green by way of Nashville and Chattanooga to Knoxville, and when the Confederate force was thus weakened in front of Buell, Thomas was recalled. The latter turned back, marched westward, and joined Nelson at Glassgow, in Barren County, on Hardee's right flank. In the mean time, Mitchel, with his reserves that formed Buell's center, had moved toward the Green River in the direction of Bowling Green. These developments satisfied Johnston that Buell was concentrating his forces to attack his front, so he called in his outlying posts as far as prudence would allow, and prepared[a] for the shock of battle, that now seemed inevitable.

[a] January, 1862.

The combined movements of the army and navy against Forts Henry and Donelson, arranged by Generals Grant and C. F. Smith,[1] and Commodore Foote, and approved by General Halleck, were now commenced. The chief object was to break the line of the Confederates, which, as we have observed, had been established with care and skill across the country from the Great River to the mountains; also to gain possession of their strongholds, and to flank those at Columbus and Bowling Green, in the movement for clearing the Mississippi River and valley of all warlike obstructions. Fort Henry, lying on a low bottom land on the eastern or righ tbank of the Tennessee River, in Stewart County, Tennessee, was to be the first object of attack. It lay at a bend of that stream, and its guns commanded a reach of the river below it toward Panther Island, for about two miles, in a direct line. The fort was an irregular field-work, with five bastions, the embrasures revetted with sand-bags. It was armed with seventeen heavy guns, twelve of which commanded the river. Both above and below the fort was a

[1] General Smith seems to have been fully instructed by Fremont with the plan of his Mississippi Valley campaign. An officer under Smith's command (General Lewis Wallace), in a letter to the author, says: "One evening General Smith sent for me. At his head-quarters, before a cozy fire, he opened his map on the table, and with fingers now on his map, then twirling his great white moustache, and his gray eyes all the time as bright as the flames in his grate, he painted glowingly the whole Tennessee River campaign. I recollect distinctly his stopping at Corinth, and saying emphatically, 'Here will be the decisive battle.' He finished the conversation by saying that the time was come. The troops at Cairo, strongly re-enforced, and those at Paducah would very shortly embark. In the mean time I was to go to Smithland, at the mouth of the Cumberland River, and get the regiments there in condition to march. He handed me an order to that effect, and I executed it."

creek defended by rifle-pits, and around it was swampy land with backwater in the rear. It was strong in itself, and so admirably situated for defense, that the Confederates were confident that it could not be captured. At the time we are considering, the garrison in the fort and the troops in camp within the outer works, consisting of less than three thousand men,[2] were commanded by Brigadier-General Loyd Tilghman, a Marylander, and graduate of West Point Academy, and it was supplied with barracks and tents sufficient for an army fifteen thousand strong.

PLAN OF FORT HENRY.[1]

General Halleck, as we have seen, had divided his large Department into military districts, and he had given the command over that of Cairo to General Grant. This was enlarged late in December,[a] so as to include all of Southern Illinois, Kentucky west of the Cumberland River, and the counties of Eastern Missouri south of Cape Girardeau. Grant was therefore commander of all the land forces to be engaged in the expedition against Fort Henry.[3] To that end he collected his troops at the close of the reconnoissance just mentioned, chiefly at Cairo and Paducah, and had directed General Smith to gain what information he could concerning the two Tennessee forts. Accordingly, on his return, that officer struck the Tennessee River about twenty miles below Fort Henry, where he found the gun-boat *Lexington* patrolling its waters. In that vessel he approached the fort so near as to draw its fire, and he reported to Grant that it might easily be taken, if attacked soon. The latter sent the report to General Halleck.

[a] Dec. 20, 1861.

Hearing nothing from their chief for several days afterward, Grant and Foote united, in a letter to Halleck,[b] in asking permission to storm Fort Henry, and hold it as a base for other operations. On the following day Grant wrote an urgent letter to his commander setting forth the advantages to be expected from the proposed movement, and on the 30th an order came for its prosecution.[4] The enterprise was

[b] Jan. 28, 1862.

---

[1] REFERENCES.—The A's denote the position of twelve 32-pounders; B, a 24-pounder barbette gun; C, a 12-inch Columbiad; D, 24-pounder siege-gun; E E, [illegible]pounder siege-guns; F, Flag-staff; H, Draw-bridge; K, Well; M, Magazine; O, Ordnance Stores; P, Adjutant's Quarters; Q, Head-quarters; R, Officers' Quarters.

[2] These were divided into two brigades—the first, under Colonel A. Hieman, was composed of the Tenth Tennessee (his own), consisting of about 800 Irish volunteers, under Lieutenant-Colonel McGavock; Twenty-seventh Alabama, Colonel Hughes; Forty-eighth Tennessee, Colonel Voorhies; Tennessee battalion of cavalry, Lieutenant-Colonel Gantt; and a light battery of four pieces, commanded by Captain Culbertson. The Second Brigade, under Colonel Joseph Drake, of the Fourth Mississippi Regiment, was composed of his own troops under Major Adair; Fifteenth Arkansas, Colonel Gee; Fifty-first Tennessee, Colonel Browder; Alabama battalion, Major Garvin; light battery of three pieces, Captain Clare; Alabama battalion of cavalry; an independent company of horse, under Captain Milner; Captain Padgett's Spy Company, and a detachment of Rangers, commanded by Captain Melton. The heavy artillery manned the guns of the fort, and were in charge of Captain Jesse Taylor.—Report of General Tilghman to Colonel Mackall, Johnston's Assistant Adjutant-General, Feb. 12, 1862.

[3] The number of troops—officers and men—under General Grant's command, who were fit for duty at the middle of January, 1862, was 24,608.

[4] *Grant and his Campaigns*, by Henry Coppée, pages 39 and 40.

immediately begun, and on Monday morning, the 2d of February,[a] Flag-officer Foote left Cairo with a little flotilla of seven gun-boats[1] (four of them armored), moved up the Ohio to Paducah, and on that evening was in the Tennessee River. He went up that stream cautiously, because of information that there were torpedoes in it, and on Tuesday morning,[b] at dawn, he was a few miles below Fort Henry.

[a] 1862.

[b] Feb. 3.

ANDREW H. FOOTE.

Grant's army, composed of the divisions of Generals McClernand and C. F. Smith, had, in the mean time, embarked in transports, which were convoyed by the flotilla. These landed a few miles below the fort, and soon afterward the armored gun-boats (*Essex*, *St. Louis*, *Carondelet*, and *Cincinnati*) were sent forward by Grant, with orders to move slowly and shell the woods on each side of the river, in order to discover concealed batteries, if they existed. At the same time the *Conestoga* and *Tyler* were successfully engaged, under the direction of Lieutenant Phelps, in fishing up torpedoes.[2]

---

[1] These were the armored gun-boats *Cincinnati* (flag-ship), Commander Stembel; *Carondelet*, Commander Walke; *Essex*, Commander W. D. Porter; and *St. Louis*, Lieutenant Commanding Paulding; and the wooden gun-boats *Lexington*, Lieutenant Commanding Shirk; *Tyler*, Lieutenant Commanding Givin; and *Conestoga*, Lieutenant Commanding Phelps.

[2] Information concerning these had been given by a woman living near the banks of the river. The "Jessie Scouts," a daring corps of young men in Grant's army, went into a farm-house wherein a large number of women were gathered for safety. When their fears were allayed, one of the women said that her husband was a soldier in Fort Henry. "By to-morrow night, madam," said one of the scouts, "there will be no Fort Henry—our gun-boats will dispose of it."—"Not a bit of it," was the reply; "they will all be blown up before they get past the Island"—meaning Panther Island. The scouts threatened to carry her away a prisoner if she did not tell all she knew about them, when she told them that torpedoes had been planted all along the channels near the island, and gave them directions as to their locations. Acting upon this information, these little floating mines were searched for, and eight of them were found. They were cylinders of sheet iron, five feet and a half long, pointed at each end, each containing, in a canvas bag, seventy-five pounds of gunpowder, with a simple apparatus for exploding it by means of a percussion cap, to be operated upon by means of a lever, extending to the outside, and moved by its striking a vessel. These were anchored in the river, a little below the surface. The rise in the river at this time had made them harmless, and it was found that moisture had ruined the powder.

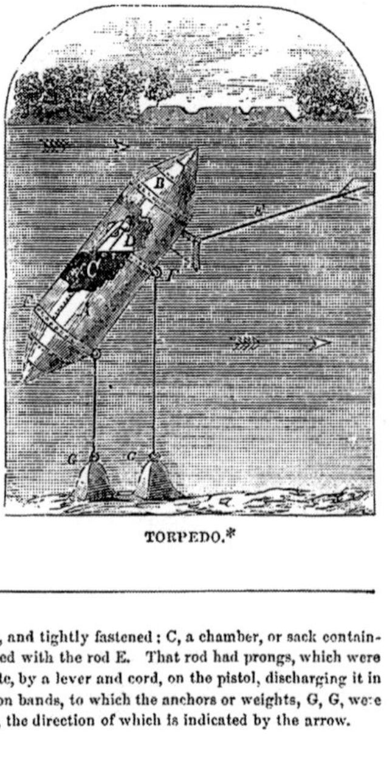

TORPEDO.*

---

* EXPLANATION.—A, the shell of the Torpedo; B, air chamber, made of sheet zinc, and tightly fastened; C, a chamber, or sack containing gunpowder; D, a pistol with the muzzle in the powder, having its trigger connected with the rod E. That rod had prongs, which were designed to strike the bottom of a vessel in motion in such a way that it would operate, by a lever and cord, on the pistol, discharging it in the powder, and so exploding the torpedo under the bow of the vessel. E, F, heavy iron bands, to which the anchors or weights, G, G, were attached. The torpedo was anchored so as to meet a vessel going against the current, the direction of which is indicated by the arrow.

By the morning of the 6th, every thing was in readiness for the attack, which was to be made simultaneously on land and water. McClernand's division[1] moved first, up the eastern side of the Tennessee, to get in a position between Forts Henry and Donelson, and be in readiness to storm the former from the rear, or intercept the retreat of the Confederates, while two brigades of Smith's division,[2] that were to make the attack, marched up the west side of the river to assail and capture half-finished Fort Hieman,[3] situated upon a great hill, and from that commanding point bring artillery to bear upon Fort Henry.

There had been a tremendous thunder-storm during the night, which made the roads very heavy, and caused the river to rise rapidly. The consequence was, that the gun-boats were in position and commenced the attack some time before the troops, who had been ordered to march at eleven o'clock in the morning, arrived. The little streams were so swollen that they had to build bridges for the passage of the artillery; and so slow was the march that they were compelled to hear the stirring sounds of battle without being allowed to participate in it.[4]

It was at half-past twelve o'clock at noon when the gun-boats opened fire. The flotilla had passed Panther Island by the western channel, and the

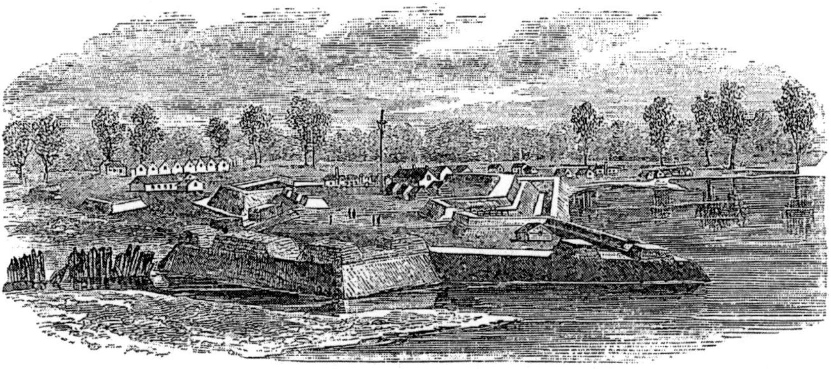

INTERIOR OF FORT HENRY.

armored vessels had taken position diagonally across the river, with the unarmored gun-boats *Tyler*, *Lexington*, and *Conestoga*, in reserve. The fort warmly responded to the assault at the beginning (which was made at a distance of six hundred yards from the batteries), but the storm from the

---

[1] This was the First division, and consisted of two brigades, composed of the Eighth, Eleventh, Eighteenth, Twentieth, Twenty-seventh, Twenty-ninth, Thirtieth, Thirty-first, Forty-fifth, and Forty-eighth Illinois Regiments; with one Illinois cavalry regiment, and four independent cavalry companies, and four batteries of artillery.

[2] This, the Second division, comprised the Seventh, Ninth, Twelfth, Twenty-eighth, and Forty-first Illinois Regiments, the Eleventh Indiana, the Seventh and Twelfth Iowa, the Eighth and Thirtieth Missouri, with a considerable body of cavalry and artillery.

[3] So named in honor of Colonel A. Hieman, of Tilghman's command, who was at the head of a regiment of Irish volunteers. Hieman was a German, and a resident of Nashville. He was an architect, and a man of taste, culture, and fortune.

[4] General Lewis Wallace, who commanded one of the brigades that marched upon Fort Hieman, in a letter to the author soon after the affair, said: "The whole march was an exciting one. When we started from our bivouac, no doubt was entertained of our being able to make the five miles, take up position, and be ready for

flotilla was so severe, that very soon the garrison became panic-stricken. Seven of the guns were dismounted, and made useless; the flag-staff was shot away; and a heavy rifled cannon in the fort had bursted, killing three men. The troops in the camp outside the fort fled, most of them by the upper Dover road, leading to Fort Donelson, and others on a steamer lying just above Fort Henry. General Tilghman and less than one hundred artillerists in the fort were all that remained to surrender to the victorious Foote.[1]

The Confederate commander had behaved most soldierly throughout, at times doing a private's duty at the guns. His gallantry, Foote said in his report, "was worthy of a better cause." Before two o'clock he hauled down his flag and sent up a white one, and the BATTLE OF FORT HENRY ceased,[a] after a severe conflict of little more than an hour.[2] It was all over before the land troops arrived, and neither those on the Fort Henry side of the river, nor they who moved against Fort Hieman, on the other bank of the stream, had an opportunity to fight. The occupants of the latter had fled at the approach of the Nationals without firing a shot, and had done what damage they could by fire, at the moment of their departure.

[a] Feb. 6, 1862.

"A few minutes before the surrender," says Pollard, "the scene in and around the fort exhibited a spectacle of fierce grandeur. Many of the cabins in and around the fort were in flames. Added to the scene were the smoke from the burning timber, and the curling but dense wreaths of smoke from the guns; the constantly recurring, spattering, and whizzing of fragments of crashing and bursting shells; the deafening roar of artillery; the black sides of five or six gun-boats, belching fire at every port-hole; the volumes of smoke settled in dense masses along the surrounding back-waters; and up and over that fog, on the heights, the army of General Grant (10,000), deploying around our small army, attempting to cut off its retreat. In the

---

the assault at the appointed hour. Never men worked harder. The guns of the fleet opened while we were yet quite a mile from our objective. Our line of march was nearly parallel with the line of fire to and from the gun-boats. Not more than seven hundred yards separated us from the great shells, in their roaring, fiery passage. Without suffering from their effect, we had the full benefit of their indescribable and terrible noise. Several times I heard the shot from the fort crash against the iron sides of the boats. You can imagine the excitement and martial furor the circumstances were calculated to inspire our men with. I was all eagerness to push on with my brigade, but General Smith rode, like the veteran he was, laughing at my impatience, and refusing all my entreaties. He was too good a soldier *to divide his* column."

[1] Report of Commander Foote to the Secretary of the Navy, February 6, 1862. Commander Stembel and Lieutenant-Commander Phelps were sent to hoist the Union flag over the fort, and to invite General Tilghman on board the commodore's flag-ship. When, an hour later, Grant arrived, the fort and all the spoils of victory were turned over to him. General Tilghman, and Captain Jesse Taylor of Tennessee, who was the commander of the fort, with ten other commissioned officers, with subordinates and privates in the fort, were made prisoners. It was said that the General and some of his officers attempted to escape, but were confronted by sentinels who had been pressed into the service, and who now retaliated by doing their duty strictly. They refused to let them pass the line, such being their orders, and threatened to shoot the first man who should attempt it.

[2] The National loss was two killed and thirty-eight wounded, and the Confederates had five killed and ten wounded. Of the Nationals, twenty-nine were wounded and scalded on the gun-boat *Essex*, Captain W. D. Porter; some of them mortally. This calamity was caused by a 32-pound shot entering the boiler of the *Essex*. It had passed through the edge of a bow port, through a bulkhead, into the boiler, in which, fortunately, there was only about sixty pounds of steam. In its passage it took off a portion of the head of Lieutenant S. B. Brittain, Jr., one of Porter's aids. He was a son of the Rev. S. B. Brittain, of New York, and a very promising youth, not quite seventeen years of age. He was standing very near Commander Porter at the time, with one hand on that officer's shoulder, and the other on his own cutlass. Captain Porter was badly scalded by the steam that escaped, but recovered. That officer was a son of Commodore David Porter, famous in American annals as the commander of the *Essex* in the war of 1812; and he inherited his father's bravery and patriotism. The gun-boat placed under his command was named *Essex*, in honor of his father's memory.

midst of the storm of shot and shell, the small force outside of the fort had succeeded in gaining the upper road, the gun-boats having failed to notice their movements until they were out of reach. To give them further time, the gallant Tilghman, exhausted and begrimed with powder and smoke, stood erect at the middle battery, and pointed gun after gun. It was clear, however, that the fort could not hold out much longer. A white flag was raised by the order of General Tilghman, who remarked, 'It is vain to fight longer. Our gunners are disabled—our guns dismounted; we can't hold out five minutes longer.' As soon as the token of submission was hoisted, the gun-boats came alongside the fort and took possession of it, their crews giving three cheers for the Union. General Tilghman and the small garrison of forty were taken prisoners."[1]

The capture of Fort Henry was a naval victory of great importance, not only because of its immediate effect, but because it proved the efficiency of gun-boats on the narrow rivers of the West, in co-operating with land troops. On this account, and because of its promises of greater achievements near, the fall of Fort Henry caused the most profound satisfaction among the loyal people. Halleck announced the fact to McClellan with the stirring words, "Fort Henry is ours! The flag of the Union is re-established on the soil of Tennessee. It will never be removed." Foote's report, brief and clear, was received and read in both Houses of Congress, in open session; and the Secretary of the Navy wrote to him, "The country appreciates your gallant deeds, and this Department desires to convey to you and your brave associates its profound thanks for the service you have rendered."

The moral effect of the victory on the Confederates was dismal, and drew forth the most serious complaints against the authorities at Richmond, and especially against Mallory, the so-called "Secretary of the Navy." Painful apprehensions of future calamities were awakened; for it was felt that, if Fort Donelson should now fall, the Confederate cause in Kentucky, Tennessee, and Missouri must be ruined. The first great step toward that event had been taken. The National troops were now firmly planted in the rear of Columbus, on the Mississippi, and were only about ten miles by land from the bridge over which was the railway connection between that post and Bowling Green. There was also nothing left to obstruct the passage of gun-boats up the Tennessee to the fertile regions of Northern Alabama, and carrying the flag of the Republic far toward the heart of the Confederacy.

---

[1] *First Year of the War*, page 238.

CHAPTER VIII.

THE SIEGE AND CAPTURE OF FORT DONELSON.

THE fall of Fort Henry was followed by immediate preparations for an attack on Fort Donelson, on the Cumberland River. Preparatory to this was a reconnoissance up the Tennessee River. Lieutenant-Commander S. L. Phelps was sent up that river on the evening of the day of battle,[a] with a detachment of Foote's flotilla, consisting of the *Conestoga*, *Tyler*, and *Lexington*, to reconnoiter the borders of the stream as far toward its upper waters as possible. When he reached the bridge of the railway between Memphis and Bowling Green, he found the draw closed, its machinery disabled, and some Confederate transports just above it, escaping up the river. A portion of the bridge was then hastily destroyed, and the work of demolition was completed the following day by Commander Walke, of the *Carondelet*, who was sent up by General Grant for the purpose. The fugitive transports were so closely pursued that those in charge of them abandoned all, and burned two that were laden with military stores.[1] In this flight an officer left papers behind him which gave an important official history of the Confederate naval preparations on the western rivers.

[a] Feb. 6, 1862.

Onward the little flotilla went, seizing Confederate vessels and destroying Confederate public property as far up as Florence, in Alabama, at the foot of the Muscle Shoals. When Phelps appeared in sight of that town, three Confederate steamers there, loaded with supplies, were set on fire, but a part of their contents, with other property on shore, was saved. A delegation of citizens waited upon the commander to ask for kind treatment for their families, and the salvation of the bridge that spanned the Tennessee there. He assured them that women and children would not be disturbed, as he and his men were not savages; and as to the bridge, being of no military account, it should be saved.

Returning, Lieutenant Phelps recruited a number of loyal Tennesseeans, seized arms and other Confederate property in several places, and caused the

[1] "The first one fired," says Lieutenant Phelps, in his report to Commodore Foote, "had on board a quantity of submarine batteries; the second one was freighted with powder, cannon-shot, grape, balls, &c. Fearing an explosion from the fired boats, I had stopped at the distance of a thousand yards; but even there our skylights were broken by the concussion." The boat was otherwise injured; and he said, "the whole river for half a mile round about was completely beaten up by the falling fragments and the shower of shot, grape, balls, &c." He also said that the house of a reported Unionist was blown to pieces. It was believed that the vessels were fired in front of it for the purpose of destroying it.

flight of a considerable number of troops from Savannah, on the eastern bank of the river, which he had prepared to attack. His reconnoissance was a perfect success. It discovered the real weakness of the Confederacy in that direction, the feasibility of marching an army into the heart of the Confederacy, and, better than all, it developed the most gratifying evidences of genuine Union feeling in Tennessee, Mississippi, and Alabama. The river banks in places were crowded with men, women, and children, who greeted the old flag with the greatest enthusiasm. "I was assured at Savannah," he said, "that, of the several hundred troops there, more than one-half, had we gone to the attack in time, would have hailed us as deliverers, and gladly enlisted with the National forces." Over and over again he was assured that nothing but the dreadful reign of terror then prevailing kept thousands from openly expressing their attachment to the old flag. "Bring us a small organized force, with arms and ammunition," they said, "and we can maintain our position."[1]

The report of this reconnoissance was very cheering, and it was determined to capture Fort Donelson as speedily as possible, and then, with a heavy force, march across Tennessee and penetrate Alabama. Foote had already hurried back to Cairo with the *Cincinnati*, *Essex*, and *St. Louis*, to prepare mortar-boats for the new enterprise, leaving Commander Walke, of the *Carondelet*, in charge of a portion of his flotilla at Fort Henry. With the spirit of the old Puritans (from whom he was descended[2]), who were everr eady to fight or pray, as circumstances might require, he went into the pulpit of the Presbyterian church at Cairo, on the Sunday after the capture of Fort Henry,[3] and preached a stirring sermon from the words of Jesus—"Let not your hearts be troubled. Ye believe in God; believe also in me." He poured forth eloquent sentences in humble thanks to Almighty God for the recent victory, and inspired all who heard him with burning zeal in the National cause.

A MORTAR-BOAT.[4]

General Grant, at the same time, was making vigorous preparations for attacking Fort Donelson.[5] Re-enforcements were arriving in Cairo, where

---

[1] Report of Commodore Foote, Feb. 6th, 1862.

[2] He was a son of Senator Samuel Foote, of Connecticut, whose resolution concerning the public lands occasioned the famous debate in the Senate of the United States between Daniel Webster and Robert Y. Hayne.

[3] The congregation were disappointed by the non-appearance of their pastor at the proper time, and Foote was invited to conduct the religious services of the occasion.

[4] This represents a mortar-boat. They were constructed for strength and steadiness of position. On a broad float were walls of wood, about eight feet in height, plated with iron on the outside, and sloping, so as to more easily ward off shot. In each was a single heavy mortar, with ammunition below water-mark, a tent for shelter, and other conveniences.

[5] The following named officers composed General Grant's personal Staff at this time: Colonel J. D. Webster, Chief of Staff; Colonel J. Riggin, Jr., Volunteer Aid; Captain J. A. Rawlins, Assistant Adjutant-General; Captains C. B. Logan and W. S. Hillyer, Aids; and Lieutenant-Colonel V. B. McPherson, Chief Engineer. According to the report of the Adjutant-General, Grant had under him in the district of Cairo, on the 10th of January, 1862, 26,875 men, officers and privates.

they were rapidly gathering. He reorganized his army, with McClernand and Smith at the head of the principal divisions, as before, while a third division was formed of small proportions at first, but destined to be enlarged by six regiments sent around by water. The latter division was under the command of Lewis Wallace, of the famous Eleventh Indiana Zouave Regiment,[1] who was promoted to be a brigadier-general on the day of the capture of Fort Henry.[2] With McClernand's division were the field batteries of Schwartz, Taylor, Dresser, and McAllister; and with Smith's were the heavy batteries of Richardson, Stone, and Walker, the whole under the command of Major Cavender, chief of artillery.

On the 11th, General Grant called a council of war, which was composed of his division commanders and several acting brigadiers. "Shall we march on Donelson, or wait for further re-enforcements?" was the question considered. Information that heavy re-enforcements were hastening toward that stronghold carried a decision in favor of an immediate march against it; and in general field orders the next morning,[a] Grant directed one of McClernand's brigades to move at once by the telegraph road directly upon Fort Donelson, and to halt within two miles of it; his other three brigades to march by the Dover Ridge road, to within the same distance, to unite with the first in forming the right wing in the investment of the fort. Two of Smith's Brigades were to follow by the Dover Road, and these were to be followed, in turn, by the troops on the left bank of the river, then occupying Fort Hieman, as soon as they could be sent forward. Smith was directed to occupy the little village of Dover, on the river bank, a short mile above the fort, if possible, and thus cut off the retreat of the Confederates up the stream.

[a] Feb. 12, 1862.

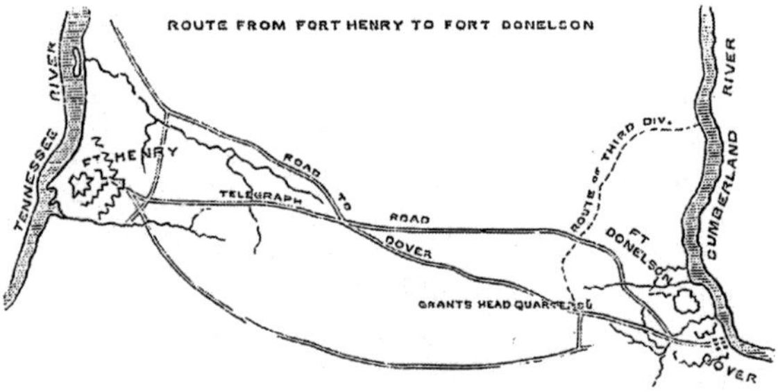

Let us observe the character and strength of the works to be assailed, called Fort Donelson.

In the center of Stewart County, in Tennessee, was its shire town of Dover, situated on the left bank of the Cumberland River, where that stream, running nearly due north, makes an abrupt turn to the westward, and, after flowing about half a mile, as suddenly turns to the northward. At this turn, about a mile below Dover, Fort Donelson was constructed, with two water batteries near the river's edge, and all so arranged as to have a large number of guns trained directly down the stream. The country in that vicinity is broken into a singular conglomerate of hills and knolls, divided by deep valleys and ravines, rendering possession easy, and attack very difficult. Upon one of these hills, terminating at the river, and broken by hollows, Fort Donelson was built. Its lines were irregular, and inclosed almost one hundred acres of land. Below it was Hickman's Creek,

[1] See page 516, volume I.

[2] His commission was dated September 3d, 1861.

a sort of back-water of the Tennessee, seldom fordable, excepting at the distance of a mile or more from the river. Just above the fort, and between it and Dover, was a small creek, flowing through a ravine.

The water batteries were admirably planted for commanding the river approaches from below. They had strong epaulments, or side works, and

LOWER WATER BATTERY.

their embrasures were revetted with coffee-sacks filled with sand. The lower or principal battery was armed with eight 32-pounders, and one 10-inch Columbiad; and the other bore a heavy rifled cannon that carried a 128-pound bolt, flanked by two 32-pound carronades.[1] The only guns in the fort (which was at a mean elevation above the river of nearly one hundred feet) were four light siege-guns, a 12-pound howitzer, two 24-pounders, and one 64-pound howitzer. Back of the fort the forest was cut down, and supporting field works were erected for the use of infantry and artillery. Still farther back, at the mean distance of a mile from the fort, was an irregular and detached line of light intrenchments for riflemen, fronting landward, with a parapet of logs and earth, which commenced at Hickman's Creek, and extended to a back-water on Hysmith's farm, above Dover, thus completely surrounding the fort and the town landward. In front of these intrenchments was a row of slashed timber, forming strong *abatis*. Altogether, the post seemed to have been made by nature and art almost impregnable. And within these intrenchments, when Grant appeared before them to make an assault, were more than twenty thousand effective men.[2] It was expected

[1] A carronade is a short piece of ordnance, having a large caliber, and a chamber for the powder like a mortar. It is similar to the howitzer. Its name is derived from Carron, a place in Scotland, where it was first manufactured.

[2] These consisted of thirteen regiments of Tennessee troops, two of Kentucky, six of Mississippi, one of Texas, two of Alabama, four of Virginia, two independent battalions of Tennessee infantry, and a regiment of cavalry, under the afterward famous leader Colonel A. B. Forest. With these were artillerymen for manning six batteries of light cannon, and seventeen heavy guns.

that this force behind fortifications would check the further advance of the Nationals up the Cumberland, and thus secure the safety of Nashville. Johnston clearly perceived the importance of the post, and when it was threatened by the attack on Fort Henry, which was only twelve miles distant, he gave it all the re-enforcements in his power. "I determined," he said, "to fight for Nashville at Donelson, and have the best part of my army to do it," and so he sent sixteen thousand troops there, retaining only fourteen thousand men to cover his front at Bowling Green.[1]

It is difficult to conceive how a veteran soldier like Johnston could have intrusted a business so important as the command of so large a force, on so momentous an occasion, to such weak men as Gideon J. Pillow and John B. Floyd, who were successively placed in chief command of Fort Donelson, at that time. But so it was. Pillow had arrived there on the 10th of the month,[a] and with the aid of Major Gilmer, General Johnston's chief engineer, had worked diligently in strengthening the defenses. On the 13th he was superseded by Floyd, who, as we have observed, had fled from Virginia with his followers.[2] He had been ordered from Cumberland City by General Johnston, to hasten to Fort Donelson, and take chief command. He arrived there, with Virginia troops, on the morning of the 13th. General Simon B. Buckner was there at the head of re-enforcements from Bowling Green, and he was the only one of the three possessed of sufficient ability and military knowledge to conduct the defense with any hope of success; yet he was subordinate to the other two, until, as we shall observe presently, their fears overcame their honor, and in the hour of extreme necessity they invested him with the chief command, and deserted him.

[a] Feb., 1862.

BERGE'S SHARP-SHOOTER.

The morning of the 12th[b] was like one in spring, so warm and balmy was the atmosphere. At an early hour, the divisions of McClernand and Smith, preceded by cavalry, in all about fifteen thousand men, began their march over the hilly country toward Fort Donelson, leaving behind them a brigade at Fort Hieman, under General Wallace, who was placed in command of that post and Fort Henry. At the same time, Foote was moving up the Cumberland with his gun-boats, convoying transports filled with troops that were to constitute Wallace's Third Division. The columns, commanded respectively by Colonels Oglesby and W. H. L. Wallace, of the First division, and Colonels Cook and Lauman, of the Second division (who were acting brigadiers), while moving across the wooded country between the two rivers, met with no armed men; and early in

[b] Feb.

[1] Letter of General Johnston to "Congressman" Barksdale, at Richmond, March 18, 1862.
[2] See page 102.

the afternoon they came in sight of the fort, drove in the pickets, and proceeded, with some severe skirmishing, to take their prescribed positions, as nearly as possible. Every thing was in readiness for battle before morning, and at dawn[a] the attack was commenced by the sharp-shooters of Colonel Berge (Sixty-sixth Illinois Regiment[1]), who advanced upon the Confederate pickets, and thus disclosed the position of the Nationals. The batteries of the Confederates, on the land side, were at once opened, while the water batteries engaged the *Carondelet*, a solitary iron-clad gun-boat in the river. During a desultory fire from the Confederates, Grant rapidly posted his troops for the most vigorous work. McClernand was placed on the right, with Oglesby's Brigade at the extreme, and Smith's was posted on the left, opposite the northwest portion of the fort. The light artillery was planted, with proper infantry supports, upon the various roads, to repel approaching columns, while the heavier guns, under the direction of Major Cavender, were brought to bear upon those of the fort.

[a] Feb. 13, 1862.

With this general disposition of his troops along a line nearly four miles in length, Grant, who had made the house of Mrs. Crisp, about two miles from Dover, at the head of Hickman's Creek, his head-quarters, refrained from a general attack, while waiting for the arrival of the gun-boats and Wallace's Third Division. Yet heavy artillery firing and brisk skirmishing were kept up all the forenoon, and Berge's sharpshooters, concealed behind logs and trees, spread terror among the Confederate gunners, who were rapidly picked off by them. Finally, with a determination to make a lodgment upon the Confederate intrenchments, McClernand, at about noon, ordered Colonel Wallace to capture a formidable battery, known as the Middle Redoubt, on a hill west of a valley, which separated the right wing under Buckner from the right center commanded by Colonel Hieman. The troops employed for this purpose were Illinois regiments—the Seventeenth, Major Smith, commanding; the Forty-eighth, Colonel Hayne; and the Forty-ninth, Colonel Morrison—covered by McAllister's battery. They were placed under Hayne, who was the senior colonel. Dashing across the intervening knolls and ravines, and up toward the battery, with great spirit, they found themselves confronted by superior numbers. Their line not being long enough to envelope the works, the Forty-fifth Illinois, Colonel Smith, were

GRANT'S HEAD-QUARTERS, FORT DONELSON.

[1] This regiment, armed with the Henry rifle, were organized as sharp-shooters by General Fremont. Each man was chosen because of his skill as a marksman. The regiment first appeared in action in the siege now under consideration. They were afterward conspicuous at the battle of Shiloh, and the siege of Corinth. They were also in active service in Sherman's Campaign in 1864, where they were highly complimented by Generals McPherson and Logan, for having held a ridge at Resaca against a brigade of Confederates. I am indebted to Lieutenant A. W. Bill, of the regiment, for the sketch from which the engraving on page 210 was made.

sent to their support on the right. They, too, displayed great courage in the face of a galling fire. The Confederates were concentrated in defense of the position with two supporting field batteries, and soon began to show strength in front of Oglesby's brigade. Schwartz's battery was first advanced to meet this new danger, and then Taylor was directed to throw forward two sections of his battery to that position. The fight for a little while was severe and stubborn, when the Nationals were repulsed. Similar movements on the left by a portion of Colonel Lauman's brigade were equally unsuccessful, and in both cases the National loss was heavy. The troops, somewhat discouraged, fell back to the position they occupied in the morning, and anxiously awaited the arrival of the gun-boats and expected re-enforcements.

That night the National troops were terribly smitten by an unexpected enemy. The spring-like morning, during which many of them, in expectation of a battle, had laid aside their overcoats and blankets, was succeeded by clouds and chilliness in the afternoon, heavy rain in the evening, and sleet and snow and severe frost at midnight, the mercury having rapidly fallen at that hour to only ten degrees above zero. The besiegers were bivouacked without tents, and dared not light a fire, because it immediately became a mark for the guns of the besieged. Their food was scant, and some were without any; and in that keen wintry air, the ground like iron, and mailed in ice, with insufficient clothing, no shelter, and half starved, the weary, worn, and intensely-suffering troops sadly and anxiously awaited the dawn and the expected re-enforcements. The Confederates, who lay upon their arms all night in the trenches, were equal sufferers.

Conscious of the peril of his situation, Grant had sent a courier to General Wallace at Fort Henry, to bring over the garrison there immediately. The order reached that officer at about midnight. At dawn[a] he marched for Fort Donelson, with the Eleventh Indiana, the Eighth Missouri, and his battery in charge of Company A, Chicago Artillery. A crust of sleet and snow covered the ground, and the air was full of drifting frost. With cheering, and singing of songs, and sounding of bugles these troops pressed on, and at noon the general reported at Grant's head-quarters, and dined with him on crackers and coffee.

[a] Feb. 14, 1862.

In the mean time the gunboats and transports had arrived, and with them the re-enforcements that were to form the Third Division. The advent of the latter was most timely. They were landed with their artillery three miles below the fort, and, rapidly clearing the woods before them, were standing around Grant's head-quarters soon after Wallace's arrival there. He was at once placed in command of them,[1] and posted between McClernand and Smith, thereby (with two of Smith's regiments, under McArthur, posted on McClernand's extreme right) completing the absolute investment of the fort and its outworks. He was ordered by Grant to hold that position, and to prevent

[1] This division consisted of two brigades, commanded respectively by Colonels Cruft and John M. Thayer. The first brigade (Cruft's) was composed of the Thirty-first Indiana, Colonel Osborn; Seventeenth Kentucky Colonel McHenry; Forty-fourth Indiana, Colonel Reed; and Twenty-fifth Kentucky, Colonel Shackelford. The second brigade (Thayer's) was composed of the First Nebraska, Colonel McCord; Seventy-sixth Ohio, Colonel Woods; and Fifty-eighth Ohio, Colonel Steadman. Three regiments (Forty-sixth Illinois, Colonel Davis; Fifty-seventh Illinois, Colonel Baldwin; and Fifty-eighth Illinois, Colonel Lynch) came up the next day during the action, and were attached to Colonel Thayer's command.

the enemy from escaping in that direction; in other words, to repel any sally from the fort. Rations that had been brought forward were now issued to the half-starved men of the line, and all the preparations for a general assault were soon completed.

The gun-boat *Carondelet*, Commander Walke, which had arrived two days before, and made a diversion in favor of Grant[1] on the 13th, had the honor of opening the assault on Fort Donelson, at three o'clock in the afternoon of Friday, the 14th,[a] and was immediately joined by the armored vessels *St. Louis*, *Pittsburg*, and *Louisville*. These formed the first line. The second line was composed of the unarmored gun-boats *Conestoga*, *Tyler*, and *Lexington*. The whole were under the personal command of Commodore Foote, who had not been able to get his mortar-boats in readiness to accompany the expedition.

[a] February, 1862.

The flotilla made direct war upon the water-batteries, with the intention of silencing and passing them, so as to gain a position to enfilade the faces of the fort with broadsides. The fight was severe. Never was a little squadron exposed to so terrible a fire. Twenty heavy guns were trained upon it, those from the hill-side hurling plunging shot with awful precision and effect, while only twelve boat-guns could reply. Yet, in the face of this terrific storm, Foote, with his flag-ship (*St. Louis*) and the other armored boats, slowly moved nearer and nearer in the desperate struggle, until he was only four hundred yards from the batteries. Very soon the upper one of four guns was silenced, the men were flying from both to the fort above, and the victorious vessels were on the point of shooting by, when the *Louisville*, assailed by flying missiles and a cross fire, was disabled by a shot which cut away her rudder-chains. Utterly helpless, she drifted away with the current of the narrow river. The flag-ship was very soon in a similar condition, and the commodore was severely wounded in the foot by a falling piece of timber. The other two armored vessels were terribly wounded, and a heavy rifled cannon on the *Carondelet* was bursted during the engagement.

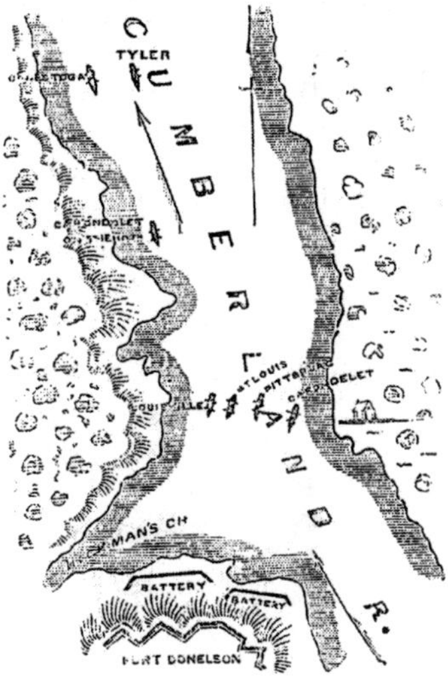

POSITION OF THE GUN-BOATS IN THE ATTACK ON FORT DONELSON.[2]

For more than an hour the tempest of iron had been beating furiously

---

[1] That diversion was more in the form of a reconnoissance, and the operations of the gun-boat were extremely useful. The *Carondelet* lay behind a jutting promontory, secure from the heavier shots from the shore, and hurled shot and shell into the fort and on the water batteries with great effect. The commander of these batteries afterward declared that the fire of the *Carondelet* did more actual damage to his guns than the heavy bombardment on the following day. A shot from the *Carondelet*, on the morning of the 13th, killed Captain Dixon, one of the best of the Confederate engineers, and that vessel was specially singled out for injury on the 14th, for, as a Confederate officer (Paymaster Nixon) said, "She was the object of our hatred;" and added, "Many a gun was leveled at her alone."

[2] I am indebted to the courtesy of Commander Walke, of the *Carondelet*, for the above sketch showing the position of the flotilla at the beginning of the attack on the water batteries.

upon the four armored vessels, and so perilous became the condition of them all, that Foote ordered them to withdraw. Then the fugitives from the shore batteries ran back to their guns, and gave the retiring flotilla some deadly parting blows. The four vessels received during the action, in the aggregate, no less than one hundred and forty-one wounds from the Confederate shot and shell,[1] and lost fifty-four men killed and maimed.

After consultation with General Grant and his own officers, Foote set out for Cairo, for the purpose of having the damages to his flotilla repaired, and to bring up a competent naval force to assist in carrying on the siege with greater vigor.[2] Grant resolved to wait for his return and for large re-enforcements, meanwhile strengthening his own weak points, holding the Confederates tightly in their intrenchments, and cutting off their supplies, with a possibility of starving them into a surrender. The besieged were conscious of their peril, which would increase with every hour of delay. The officers of divisions and brigades held a council of war on the evening of the 14th,[a] over which Floyd, the chief commander, presided. He gave it as his opinion that the fort was untenable with less than fifty thousand men to defend it, and proposed, for the purpose of saving the garrison, to make a sortie next morning, with half his army and Forrest's cavalry, upon McClernand's division on Grant's right, crush it, or throw it back upon Wallace, and by a succeeding movement on the center, by Buckner, cast the whole beleaguering army into confusion, or rout and destroy it, when the liberated troops might easily pass out into the open country around Nashville. This plan, promising success, was agreed to by unanimous consent, and preparations were made accordingly.

[a] February, 1862.

The troops designated for the grand sortie, about ten thousand in number, were under the command of Generals Pillow and Bushrod R. Johnston, the former being chief. They were put in motion from Dover at five o'clock on Saturday morning;[b] Colonel Baldwin's brigade of three regiments of Mississippi and Tennessee troops in advance, followed by four Virginia regiments, under Colonels Wharton and McCausland, and several more under Colonels Davidson, Drake, and others. These were accompanied by Forest's cavalry and thirty heavy guns, with a full complement of artillerists. This main body were directed to attack McClernand's troops, who occupied the heights that reached to the river, just above Dover. Buckner was directed to strike Wallace's division, which lay across the Wynne's

[b] Feb. 15.

BUSHROD R. JOHNSTON.

[1] Fifty-nine shot struck the *St. Louis*, thirty-six hit the *Louisville*, twenty-six wounded the *Carondelet*, and twenty shot were received by the *Pittsburg*.

[2] Report of Commodore Foote to the Secretary of the Navy, on board his flag-ship, Feb. 15th, 1862.

Ferry road, at about the same time, so that it should not be in a condition to aid McClernand. Pillow expected, he said, "to roll the enemy in full retreat over upon General Buckner, when, by his attack in flank and rear," they "could cut up the enemy and put him completely to rout."[1]

McClernand's division was well posted to resist the assailants, had they been on the alert; but the movement of the Confederates appears not to have been even suspected. Reveillé was just sounding, and the troops were not under arms; and so sudden and vigorous was Pillow's attack, that the whole of Grant's right wing was seriously menaced within twenty minutes after the presence of the Confederates was observed. Then vigor and skill marked every movement, and Pillow's attempt to throw cavalry in the rear of McArthur, on Oglesby's extreme right, was thwarted.

The attack was quick, furious, and heavy. Oglesby's brigade had received the first shock of the battle, and gallantly withstood it until their ammunition began to fail. Colonel W. H. L. Wallace's brigade hastened to their relief, but the pressure was so tremendous that Oglesby's line all gave way, excepting the extreme left, held by the Thirty-first Illinois, whose commander, Colonel John A. Logan, inspired his troops with such courage and faith by his own acts, that they stood like a wall opposed to the foe, and prevented a panic and a rout. In the mean time the light batteries under Taylor, McAllister, and Dresser, shifting positions and continually sending heavy volleys of grape and canister shot, made the line of the assailants recoil again and again. But the fresh troops continually pressing forward in greater numbers kept its strength unimpaired, and very soon the whole of McClernand's division was in such a perilous situation, that at about eight o'clock he sent to General Lewis Wallace, commanding the Third Division, for immediate assistance. As the latter was assigned to the special duty of preventing the escape of the Confederates, he applied to head-quarters for instructions. Grant was away in conference with Commodore Foote. Again McClernand sent for assistance, saying substantially that his flank was turned, and his whole command was endangered. Wallace took the responsibility of immediately ordering Colonel Cruft to move his brigade on to the right, and report to McClernand. An incompetent guide took Cruft too far to the right, where he was fiercely assailed by a greatly superior force, and compelled to bear the brunt of battle for a time. He struggled gallantly with an equally gallant foe, charging and receiving charges with varied fortunes, until his antagonists gave up the fight.

JOHN A. McCLERNAND.

In the mean time General Buckner had made his appearance, in consider-

[1] Pillow's report to Captain Clarence Derrick, "Assistant Adjutant-General," written at his home in Columbia, Tennessee, on the 18th of February, 1862.

able force, to attack the left of the center of Grant's line, and produce the confusion as directed in Floyd's programme. There seemed to be much peril to the National troops in this movement, and the danger seemed more imminent when some frightened fugitives from the battle came crowding up the hill in the rear of Wallace's Division, and a mounted officer dashed along, shouting, "We are cut to pieces!" It was here that the whole of McClernand's line, including Cruft's men, was rapidly falling back. Colonels Logan, Lawler, and Ransom were wounded, and a large number of subalterns had been killed, yet there was no confusion in that line. This was the crisis of the battle, and it was promptly met. To prevent a panic in his own brigade, Wallace ordered Colonel Thayer to move on by the right flank. Riding at the front, he met the retiring troops, moving in good order and calling for ammunition, the want of which had been the chief cause of their misfortune. He saw that every thing depended upon prompt action. There was no time to wait for orders, so he thrust his third brigade (Colonel Thayer commanding) between the retiring troops and the flushed Confederates, who were rapidly following, formed a new line of battle across the road, with the Chicago artillery, Lieutenant Wood, in the center, and the First Nebraska, Fifty-eighth Illinois, Fifty-eighth Ohio, and a company of the Thirty-second Illinois on its right and left. Back of these was a reserve, composed of the Seventy-sixth Ohio, and Forty-sixth and Fifty-seventh Illinois. In this position they awaited attack, while McClernand's retiring troops, halting near, supplied themselves with ammunition from wagons which Wallace had ordered up.

These preparations were just completed when the Confederates (the forces of Pillow and Buckner combined[1]) fell heavily upon the battery and First Nebraska, and were cast back by them as the rock throws back the billows. "To say they did well," said Wallace, "is not enough; their conduct was splendid. They alone repelled the charge;"[2] and the Confederates, after a severe contest, retired to their works in confusion. "They withdrew," said Buckner, "without panic, but in some confusion, to the trenches."[3] This was the last sally from the fort, for, by the timely and effectual interposition of the Third Division, the plans of the Confederates were frustrated. "*I speak advisedly*," wrote Captain W. S. Hillyer (Grant's Aid-de-camp) to General Wallace the next day, on a slip of paper with pencil, "God bless you! you did save the day on the right!" Poor Pillow, with his usual shallowness, had sent an aid, when McClernand's line gave way, to telegraph to Johnston, that "on the honor of a soldier" the day was theirs;[4] and he foolishly persisisted in saying, in his first report, a few days afterward, that the Confederates had accomplished their object, when it was known to all that they had utterly failed.

It was at about noon when the Confederates were driven back to their trenches. General Grant seemed doubtful of his ability to make a successful assault upon their works with his present force, and at about three o'clock in the afternoon he called McClernand and Wallace aside for consultation.

---

[1] General Pillow's first Report [2] Report of General Wallace. [3] Report of General Buckner.

[4] On the strength of this, Johnston sent a dispatch to Richmond, announcing a great victory, and on Monday the *Richmond Enquirer* said: "This splendid feat of arms and glorious victory to our cause will send a thrill of joy over the whole Confederacy."

They were all on horseback. Grant held some dispatches in his hand. He spoke of the seeming necessity of falling back and intrenching, so as to stand on the defensive, until re-enforcements and Foote's flotilla should arrive. His words were few, as usual, and his face was flushed by strong emotions of the mind, while he turned his eyes nervously now and then on the dispatches. It was suggested that McClernand's defeat uncovered the road by which the enemy might escape to Clarksville. In an instant the General's countenance changed from cloudiness to sunshine. A new thought took possession of him and he acted instantly on its suggestions. Grasping the dispatches more firmly, he ordered McClernand to retake the hill he had lost, while Smith should make a simultaneous attack on the Confederate right.[1]

The new movement was immediately begun. McClernand requested Wallace to retake the ground lost in the morning. A column of attack was soon formed, with the Eighth Missouri, Colonel Morgan L. Smith, and the Eleventh Indiana (Wallace's old regiment), Colonel George McGinnis (both led by the former as a brigade), moving at the head. Two Ohio regiments, under Colonel Ross, formed a supporting column. At the same time, Colonel Cruft formed a line of battle at the foot of the hill.

The Eighth Missouri led the van, closely followed by the Eleventh Indiana; and when about half way up the hill, they received a volley from its summit. The ground was broken, rough, and partly wooded. The Nationals pressed on, and the struggle was fierce and unyielding for more than an hour. Gradually the Confederates were pushed back, and their assailants soon cleared the hill. They drove the insurgents to their intrenchments, and would have assailed them there had not an order reached Wallace, when he was only one hundred and fifty yards off the works, to halt and retire his column, as a new plan of operations was in contemplation for the next day. That commander was astonished and perplexed. He was satisfied that Grant was not informed of the entire success of his movement. He was also satisfied that if he should fall back and give up the hill (it was then five o'clock in the evening) the way would be opened for the Confederates to escape under cover of approaching darkness. So he assumed the responsibility of disobeying the order, and he bivouacked on the field of victory. All of that keen wintry night his wearied troops were busy in ministering to the wants of the wounded, and in burying the many Illi-

THE GRAVES OF THE ILLINOIS TROOPS.[2]

[1] General Sherman says that General Grant told him that, at a certain period of the battle, "he saw that either side was ready to give way if the other showed a bold front, and he determined to do that very thing, to advance on the enemy, when, as he prognosticated, the enemy surrendered."—Sherman's Letter to the Editor of the *United States Service Magazine*, January, 1865.

[2] This is from a sketch made by the author early in May, 1866. This burial-place, surrounded by a rude wattling fence, was in Hysmith's old field, in the edge of a wood, near where McArthur's troops were posted. The trees and shrubbery in the adjoining wood showed hundreds of marks of the severe battle.

nois troops who had fallen in the conflict of the morning. They also made preparations for storming the Confederate works at an early hour on the following day.

While Wallace was carrying on the successful movement on the Confederate left, Smith was assailing their intrenchments on their right. He posted Cavender's heavy guns so as to pour a murderous fire upon these and the fort. Lauman's Brigade formed the attacking column, while Cook's Brigade, posted on the left, was ordered to make a feigned attack.

Lauman was directed to carry the heights on the left of the position that had been assailed on Thursday. He placed the Second Iowa, Colonel Tuttle, in the van. These were followed by the Fifty-sixth Indiana as a support. These, in turn, were closely followed by the Twenty-fifth Indiana and Seventh and Fourteenth Iowa, while Berge's sharp-shooters were deployed as skirmishers on the extreme right and left of the column. When all were in readiness, General Smith rode along the line, told the troops he would lead them, and directed them to clear the rifle-pits with the bayonet alone. At a given signal, the column moved, under cover of Captain Stone's Missouri Battery; and Smith, with a color-bearer at his side, rode in advance, his commanding figure, flowing gray hair, and courageous example, inspiring the men with the greatest admiration.

Very soon the column was swept by a terrible fire from the Confederate artillery. It wavered for a moment, but the words and acts of the General soon restored its steadiness, and it moved on rapidly. When Tuttle was within range of the Confederate muskets, he placed himself at the head of his men and shouted "Forward!" Without firing a gun, they charged upon the Confederates with the bayonet, driving them from their intrenchments, and, in the midst of cheers from a thousand voices, the National standard was planted upon them. When darkness fell, General Grant knew that his plan, so suddenly conceived in a moment of anxiety, had secured a solid triumph—that the rich fruit of victory was ripe and ready to fall into his lap. There was joy in the National camp that night, while terror brooded over the imprisoned Confederates.

"How shall we escape?" was the important question anxiously considered by the Confederate leaders that night, especially by Floyd and Pillow; the former terror-stricken, because of the danger of falling into the hands of the Government, against which he had committed such fearful crimes; and the latter suffering unnecessarily for the same reason, his vanity magnifying his own importance much beyond its true proportions. A Council of War was held at Pillow's head-quarters, in Dover, at midnight, to consider the matter. There were criminations and recriminations, and Floyd and Pillow seemed to think of little else than the salvation of themselves from the power of their injured Government. Buckner, too, desired to escape, and it was resolved to effect it, if possible, by cutting their way through the supposed weak right of the National lines, at five o'clock in the morning, and press on toward Nashville.

Colonel Forest was ordered, at about two o'clock, to ascertain the position of the Nationals, and the practicability of escaping by the river road. He reported, that the position from which the Confederates had been driven by Wallace in the afternoon, on the left, by which lay their projected course of escape, was held by a large body of troops, and that the back-water above Dover could not be crossed except by cavalry. Again the council deliberated, when is was agreed that the cost of an attempt to cut their way out would probably be the loss of the lives of three-fourths of the troops. "No commander," said Buckner, "has a right to make such a sacrifice." Floyd agreed with him, and quickly said, "Then we will have to capitulate; but, gentlemen," he added, nervously, "*I* cannot surrender; you know my position with the Federals: it wouldn't do, it wouldn't do." Pillow then said to Floyd, "I will not surrender myself nor the command; *will die first.*"—"Then," said Buckner, coolly, "I suppose, gentlemen, the surrender will devolve upon me." The terrified Floyd quickly asked, "General, if you are put in command, will you allow me to take out, by the river, my brigade?"—"If you move before I shall offer to surrender," Buckner replied. "Then, sir," said Floyd, "I surrender the command." Pillow, who was next in rank, and to whom Floyd offered to transfer the command, quickly exclaimed, "I will not accept it—I will never surrender." While speaking, he turned toward Buckner, who said, "I will accept, and share the fate of my command."[1]

When the capitulation was determined upon, Floyd and Pillow, who, it has been justly remarked, had already disgraced the name of American citizens, proceeded to disgrace the character of a soldier also,[2] by stealing away under cover of the night, deserting, in the most cowardly manner, the soldierly Buckner and the brave men who had defended the post. In order to aid their flight, the latter allowed Forest to attempt to cut his way out with his cavalry. In too much haste to save himself, Floyd did not wait for all of his Virginians to get ready to escape with him, but with a few of them, hastily collected, he embarked on a steamer at Dover, followed by the curses and hisses of thousands on the shore, and fled to Nashville.[3] Pillow sneaked away in the darkness, and, in perfect safety at his home in Columbia, in Middle Tennessee, he sat down a few days afterward to write a report to his indignant superiors. Forest and his horsemen, about eight hundred in number, also escaped. There is not in all history a meaner picture of the conduct of traitors than that afforded by the Council of War at Dover, on Sunday morning, the 16th of February, 1862.

That Sunday morning dawned brightly upon the Union army. At day-break, Wallace prepared to storm the Confederate intrenchments, and while making dispositions for that purpose, a bugle in the direction of the fort sounded a parley. Dimly seen in the morning twilight was an officer with the bugler, bearing a white flag, and at the same time a similar flag was seen waving over the fort, in token of a willingness to surrender. Wallace immediately rode to Buckner's quarters. The latter had posted a letter to Grant, asking for the appointment of commissioners to agree upon terms of

---

[1] Sworn statements of Colonel Forest, Major Gustavus A. Henry, Major W. H. Haynes, and Hunter Nicholson, who were present at the council.

[2] Coppée's *Grant and his Campaigns*, page 66.

[3] An epigrammatist of the day wrote concerning Floyd's escape, saying:—

"The thief is a coward by nature's law;
Who betrays the State, to no one is true;
And the brave foe at Fort Donelson saw
Their light-fingered Floyd was light-footed too.

capitulation, and suggesting an armistice until noon. Wallace immediately sent word to Grant that Dover was surrendered, and his troops were in possession of the town. This made Grant's reply to Buckner short and explicit. He considered Buckner and his troops as simply rebels in arms, with no right to ask any terms excepting such as humanity required, so he said, "No terms other than unconditional and immediate surrender can be accepted. I propose to move immediately upon your works."

Grant's reply irritated the helpless Buckner, and, with folly equal to his chagrin, he answered, "The distribution of the forces under my command, incident to an unexpected change of commanders, and the overwhelming force under your command, compel me, notwithstanding the brilliant success

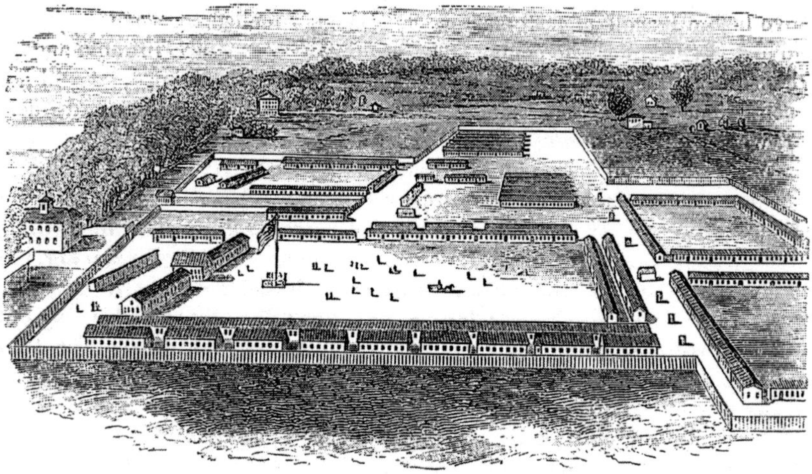

CAMP DOUGLAS.

of the Confederate arms yesterday, to accept the ungenerous and unchivalrous terms which you propose." This was followed by the speedy surrender of the fort, with thirteen thousand five hundred men, as prisoners of war (including the sick and wounded), a large proportion of whom were sent to Camp Douglas, near Chicago;[1] also three thousand horses, forty-eight field-

[1] Generals Buckner and Tilghman, who were captured at Fort Henry, were sent to Fort Warren, in Boston Harbor. Leading Unionists of Kentucky asked for the surrender of Buckner to the civil authorities of that State, to be tried for treason against that commonwealth. The application was refused, and he was afterward exchanged.

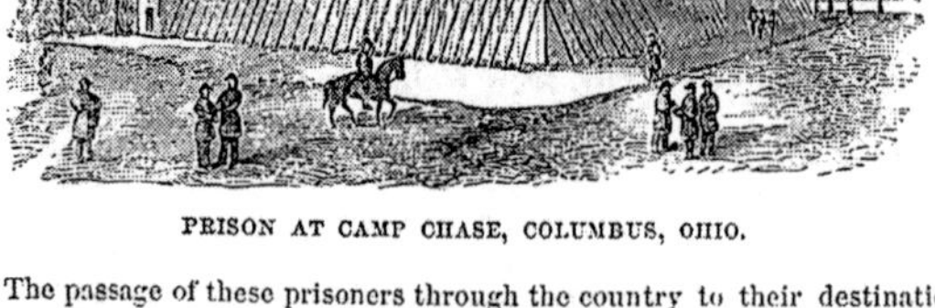

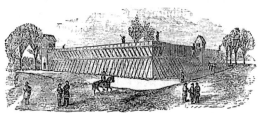

PRISON AT CAMP CHASE, COLUMBUS, OHIO.

Camp Douglas was so named in honor of Senator Douglas, and was situated on land that had belonged to him. In this camp many of the Western regiments, that performed such signal service, were drilled. It was converted into a prison, and early in April, 1862, after the battle of Shiloh, it contained full 8,000 captives, most of whom were from Alabama, Mississippi, and Texas. The passage of these prisoners through the country to their destinatiog produced a profound sensation. A St. Louis journal mentioned the arrival there of ten thousand of them, on ten steamers.

A large number of the captives at Forts Henry and Donelson were also sent to Camp Chase, at Columbus,

pieces, seventeen heavy guns, twenty thousand muskets, and a great quantity of military stores.[1] On the following day, two regiments of Tennessee

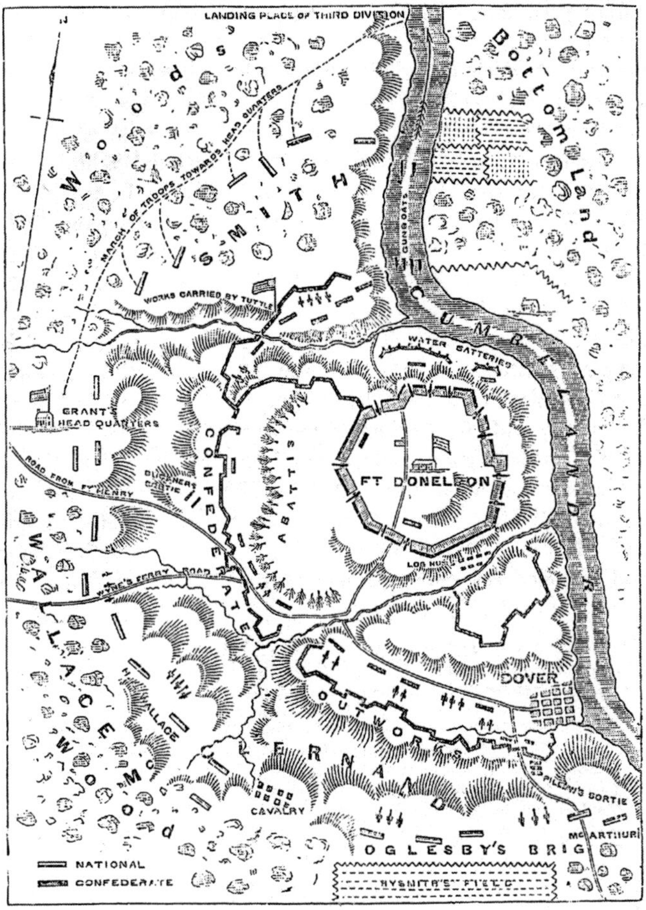

PLAN OF THE SIEGE OF FORT DONELSON.

troops, that came up to re-enforce the garrison, in ignorance of the surrender, were also made prisoners. During the siege, the Confederates had lost, it

Ohio, which was so named in honor of the Secretary of the Treasury. The prison there was in the southeast corner of the camp. The strong inclosure was about sixteen feet in height, built of two-inch pine plank, with scantling well bolted and braced. The picture shows the exterior of the prison and the guard-houses.

[1] A participant in the scenes at Fort Donelson wrote as follows concerning the surrender: "One of the grandest sights in the whole siege, and one which comes only once in a century, was the triumphal entry into the Fort on Sunday morning. . . . The sight from the highest point in the fort, commanding a view of both river and camp, was imposing. There were on one side regiment after regiment pouring in, their flags floating gayly in the wind; some of them which had been rent and faded on the fields of Mexico, and others with 'Springfield' emblazoned on their folds; one magnificent brass band pouring out the melodies of 'Hail Columbia,' 'Star Spangled Banner,' 'Yankee Doodle,' etc., in such style as the gazing captives had never heard, even in the palmy days of peace. On the other was a spectacle which surpasses all description. The narrow Cumberland seemed alive with steamers. First came the gun-boats, firing salutes; then came little black tugs, snorting their acclamations; and after them the vast fleet of transports, pouring out volumes of black smoke, their banners floating gayly in the breeze, firing salutes, their decks covered with people sending deafening shouts in response to those from the shore. The scene was sublime, impressive, and will not easily be forgotten."

was estimated, two hundred and thirty-seven killed, and one thousand and seven wounded. The National loss was estimated at four hundred and forty-six killed, one thousand seven hundred and forty-five wounded, and one hundred and fifty prisoners. The latter had been sent across the river, and were not re-captured.[1]

The victory at Fort Donelson was of the greatest importance to the National cause, and the official announcement of it,[2] spreading with speed of lightning over the land, produced intense joy in every loyal bosom. Cities were illuminated, heavy guns thundered forth National salutes; and everywhere the flag of the Republic was flung to the breeze, in token of profound satisfaction. The news filled the conspirators with despair, and terribly depressed the spirits of the soldiers of the Confederate army. By it Europe was made to doubt the success of the rebellion; and at some courts it produced the first serious thoughts of abandoning the cause of the conspirators. Its effect, in all relations, was similar to that of the capture of Burgoyne and his army at Saratoga, in 1777. So powerful was the impression, that the Confederate Commissioners abroad felt compelled to do all in their power to belittle the event, and, by taking advantage of the general deficiency of knowledge of American geography,[3] to satisfy the ruling class that it was of no military importance whatever. In that effort the Commissioners failed.

At Richmond the fall of Fort Donelson caused emotions of mingled anger and dismay. The loss of Roanoke Island, a few days before, had greatly alarmed and irritated the conspirators; and now the chief of the Confede-

---

[1] Reports of Generals Grant, McClernand, Wallace, and subordinate officers; and of Floyd, Pillow, and Buckner, and their subordinates. Also written and oral statements to the author by participants in the action.

[2] Commander Walke, in the *Carondelet*, carried the first news of the victory to Cairo, from which it was telegraphed to General McClellan by General George W. Cullum, Halleck's Chief of Staff, then at Cairo, saying: "The Union flag floats over Donelson. The *Carondelet*, Captain Walke, brings the glorious intelligence. The fort surrendered at nine o'clock yesterday (Sunday) morning. Generals Buckner, Bushrod R. Johnston, and 15,000 prisoners, and a large amount of materials of war, are the trophies of the victory. Loss heavy on both sides. Floyd, the thief, stole away during the night previous with 5,000 men, and is denounced by the rebels as a traitor." He then spoke of the good conduct of Commodore Foote, and announced the fact that, notwithstanding his sufferings from the wound in his foot, he would immediately make an attack on Clarksville, an important post about forty miles above. He concluded by saying, "We are now firing a National salute from Fort Cairo, General Grant's late post, in honor of the glorious achievement."

The women of St. Louis, desirous of testifying their admiration of General Halleck, in whose Department and by whose troops these victories had been achieved (and because of his energy in suppressing secession in Missouri), ordered an elegant sword to be made by Tiffany & Co., of New York, to be presented to him in their name. This was done in the parlor of the Planters' Hotel, in St. Louis, on the evening of the 17th of March, 1862, by Mrs. Helen Budd, who spoke in behalf of the donors. In his brief reply, General Halleck assured the women of St. Louis that it should be "used in defense of their happiness, their rights, and their honor, and solely in behalf of justice." The weapon was an elegant one, richly ornamented with classical designs.

HALLECK'S SWORD.

[3] The amazing territorial extent of the United States is but little comprehended in Europe, and the relative position of places mentioned in connection with the war seemed to be very little understood, even by some of the best informed writers and speakers. This lack of exact information led writers on American affairs into the most absurd speculations as well as serious blunders. An illustrative example was found in the summary of war news from America in the Paris *Moniteur*, at about the time we are considering. Speaking of the capture of Roanoke Island, and of Elizabeth City, in Eastern North Carolina,[a] the writer observed: "The Federal army landed, and proceeded toward Elizabeth City, which it found evacuated and burned by the Southern troops. *From there a detachment advanced as far as the Tennessee River*, and thus occupies the principal road between Memphis and Columbus. This movement establishes the troops of General Burnside in the rear of the great army of the Potomac." Elizabeth City, on the Atlantic coast, and the Tennessee River, at the point indicated, are fully 750 miles apart, in an air line, and at least 1,200 miles by any route troops might be taken.

[a] Feb., 1862.

rates, with as much dignity as possible, commented seriously on their calamities in a message to his "Congress." Official information had not reached him. "Enough is known," he said, "of the surrender of Roanoke Island to make us feel that it was deeply humiliating." Of the disaster at Fort Donelson, he said: "I am not only unwilling but unable to believe that a large army of our people has surrendered without a desperate effort to cut its way through the investing forces, whatever may have been their numbers, and to endeavor to make a junction with other divisions of the army."[1] A little later, in transmitting to his "Congress" the reports of Floyd and Pillow, he said they were "incomplete and unsatisfactory. It is not stated," he said, "that re-enforcements were at any time asked for; nor is it demonstrated to have been impossible to have saved the troops by evacuating the position; nor is it known by what means it was found practicable to withdraw a part of the garrison, leaving the remainder to surrender; nor upon what authority or principle of action the senior generals abandoned responsibility by transferring the command to a junior officer." Notwithstanding General Johnston attempted to gloss the cowardice of Floyd and Pillow,[2] Davis, in the communication we are considering, said: "I have directed, upon the exhibition of the case *as presented by the two senior* Generals, that they should be relieved from command, to await further orders, whenever a reliable judgment can be rendered on the merits of the case."[3]

Davis himself, it has been charged since the close of the rebellion (for all spoke of him during the war with bated breath), was continually interfering in military affairs, and with the action of skillful commanders most mischievously.[4]

Generals Grant, McClernand, and Wallace[5] issued orders congratulating their victorious troops;[6] and General Halleck, who had drawn from General

---

[1] Message of Jefferson Davis to the Confederate Congress, Feb. 28th, 1862.

[2] General Johnston said in a private letter to Jefferson Davis: "Although the command was irregularly transferred, it was not apparently to avoid any just responsibility, or from any lack of personal or moral intrepidity." Johnston could not have been aware of the disgraceful scene in the midnight council at Pillow's quarters in Dover, when he wrote that apology. The temper of the Conspirators in Richmond was in no mood to receive an apology. They had been elated beyond measure by Pillow's premature boast of victory, and now the disappointment was of corresponding force.

[3] Jefferson Davis's message to his "Congress," March 11th, 1862.

[4] So say military experts, and those most intimately acquainted with his official conduct. "Twenty years hence," says a politician of Mississippi, who was a fellow-worker in rebellion with Davis in Richmond, "no one will be heard to deny that to the *direct* and unwise interferences in great military movements, on the part of Davis, are to be attributed nearly all the principal disasters of the war. In the gross mismanagement of the War Department, under the supervision and control of Mr. Davis himself, may safely be charged the calamitous occurrences at Forts Donelson and Henry, and at Roanoke Island."—*War of the Rebellion*, by Henry S. Foote.

[5] For their services in the siege of Fort Donelson, Generals Grant, McClernand, and Wallace were each promoted to Major-General of volunteers, the commission of the former bearing the date of the surrender (February 16, 1862), and the other two of March 21st, 1862.

[6] Grant said (February 17th), after congratulating his troops on their "triumph over the rebellion, gained by their valor," that "for four successive nights, without shelter during the most inclement weather known in this latitude, they faced an enemy in large force in a position chosen by himself. Though strongly fortified by nature, all the additional safeguards suggested by science were added. Without a murmur this was borne, prepared at all times to receive an attack, and with continuous skirmishing by day, resulting ultimately in forcing the enemy to surrender without conditions. The victory achieved is not only great in the effect it will have in breaking down rebellion, but has secured the greatest number of prisoners of war ever taken in any battle on this continent. Fort Donelson will hereafter be marked in capitals on the map of our united country, and the men who fought the battle will live in the memory of a grateful people."

McClernand, in a field-order (February 18th), said: "You have continually led the way in the Valley of the Lower Mississippi, the Tennessee, and the Cumberland. You have carried the flag of the Union farther South than any other land forces, marching from the interior toward the sea-board.

"Being the first division to enter Fort Henry, you also pursued the enemy for miles, capturing from him,

Hunter's Kansas Department some of the re-enforcements which he had sent to Grant, said, in a letter to him,[a] "To you, more than to any other man out of this Department, are we indebted for our success at Fort Donelson. In my strait for troops to re-enforce General Grant, I applied to you. You responded nobly, placing your forces at my disposition." The Secretaries of War and of the Navy also issued congratulatory orders. The Government and people were satisfied that a withering blow had been given to the rebellion, and that henceforth its proportions would be less, and its malignity not so dangerous to the life of the Republic.

[a] Feb. 19, 1862.

At Forts Henry and Donelson was successfully begun that army mail-service which was so admirably organized and so efficiently executed during the war by Colonel A. H. Markland. It was suggested to General Grant by Colonel Markland, who was the special agent of the National Post-office Department. It was immediately adopted, and was ever afterward warmly cherished by that sagacious commander; and to him is justly due much of the credit of making it practically effective in blessing the officers and soldiers of the armies of the Republic during the great struggle. The perfection of the system was exhibited even so early as at the capture of Forts Henry and Donelson, and it never failed to give ample satisfaction to all, until the end of the war.[1]

The peculiar army mail-service organized under the auspices of General Grant was finally extended to all Departments, and was managed by Colonel Markland, who was made the general superintendent of the mails of the armies of the Republic. Soldiers in camp or on the march, and even under the fire of the enemy, received letters from home with as much regularity as if they had been residents of a large city. That system was not introduced into the Army of the Potomac while McClellan commanded it. One much less perfect and efficient, which he found in operation, was continued. That was established when the troops under the first call began to assemble around Washington, in April and May, 1861. The chaplain of each regiment was recognized as "regimental post-master," and he usually called at the Washington City Post-office for the army mail. When the army was increased

---

in his flight, six field-pieces, many of his standards and flags, a number of prisoners, and a great quantity of military stores. Following the enemy to this place, you were the first to encounter him outside of his intrenchments, and drive him within them." After recounting their exploits, he said: "The battle-field testifies to your valor and constancy. Even the magnanimity of the enemy accords to you an unsurpassed heroism, and an enviable and brilliant share in the hardest-fought battle and most decisive victory ever fought and won on the American continent." . . . . . "The death-knell of rebellion is sounded; an army has been annihilated; and the way to Nashville and Memphis is opened."

[1] The origin and general efficiency of that service is stated in the following letter to the author, dated, "Head-quarters Armies of the United States, Washington, D. C., July 30th, 1866:"—

"DEAR SIR:—Among the subjects that occupied my mind when I assumed command at Cairo, in the fall of 1861, was the regular supply of mails to and from the troops; not only those in garrison, but those on the march when active movements should begin. When I commenced the movement on Fort Henry, on Jan. 7, 1862, a plan was proposed by which the mails should promptly follow, and as promptly be sent from the army. So perfect was the organization, that the mails were delivered to the army immediately upon its occupation of the fort. Within one hour after the troops began to march into Fort Donelson, the mail was being distributed to them from the mail wagons. The same promptness was always observed in the armies under my command, up to the period of the final disbandment. It is a source of congratulation that the postal service was so conducted, that officers and men were in constant communication with kindred and friends at home, and with as much regularity as the most favored in the large cities of the Union. The postal system of the army, so far as I know, was not attended with any additional expense to the service. The system adopted by me was suggested and ably superintended by A. H. Markland, special agent of the Post-office Department.

"Respectfully, &c.,

"U. S. GRANT, General."

and fully organized, the commanding officer of each regiment selected a reliable man from the non-commissioned officers or privates to act as mail messenger, and that system was continued until the troops were called to the field in the spring of 1862. Then the mails were "brigaded," placed in canvas bags, labeled and addressed to the brigade, and forwarded to their destination by steamer or railway, under military authority. The Post-office Department had no further control of the army mail after it left the post-office at Washington City

During the Peninsula campaign, the mail for the Army of the Potomac was forwarded from Washington by way of Baltimore and Old Point Comfort, the Potomac being blockaded by shore batteries. At the same time, the troops in the Shenandoah Valley were supplied with a mail service by way of Harper's Ferry, the mails being sent under military control to that place, over the Baltimore and Ohio railway, and there furnished to the brigades when called for. Owing to the peculiar condition of affairs in that region, much of the time there was very little regularity in the delivery of the mails, and communication between the army and home was at times very uncertain.

The mails for these armies, and also for the Army of the James, were all distributed in the Post-office at Washington City, where they were assorted into regiments, batteries, and independent commands. Rosters, for the guidance of the postmaster at Washington, were furnished when troops changed localities. In his office boxes were prepared and labeled for the respective regiments; and at one time no less than eight hundred regiments and batteries, which extended over the seaboard to New Orleans, and the entire Shenandoah Valley, had the mail matter for them thus prepared for distribution. After being thus sorted, these mails were delivered to authorized military agents, who attended to their transmission. In this way hundreds of thousands of letters passed to and from the army daily.[1]

The regularity with which the great armies of Grant, Sherman, Thomas, and others in the West were supplied with mails, under the general superintendence of Colonel Markland, was marvelous. He and his assistants seemed to be almost ubiquitous. No danger was so appalling, and no obstructions were so apparently insurmountable as to deter these messengers of good. They endured all that the army endured—perils, fatigues, and privations. The mail was nearly always in advance of the armies, or moving in a direction to meet them, and yet Colonel Markland never lost one, by capture, over which he had personal control. When Sherman reached tide-water, after his march for the sea, the mail for his army was in readiness for distribution; and the

[1] "For months," says Mr. S. J Bowen, the postmaster of Washington City, in a letter to the author, on the 22d of July, 1866, "we received and sent an average of 250,000 military letters per day. It is believed that this number was exceeded after General Sherman's army reached Savannah, and up to the time of the review of the troops in this city in the month of May, 1865."

"Taking into consideration," continues Mr. Bowen, "the quantity of mail matter, consisting of letters, newspapers, packages of clothing, and other articles of every conceivable kind that passed through this office to and from our armies. it is surprising that so few losses occurred. Almost every package reached the person to whom it was addressed, and the failure of letters to find their owners in 'due course of mail' was extremely rare. Indeed, I think the armies were provided with mails with just about as much certainty as people are in large cities, and with about as little delay.

"The only loss of any moment that occurred to the Post-office Department, on account of this heavy mail service, was in mail-bags. It is estimated that at least thirty thousand of these were sent out which never found their way back to this office, although every effort was made by us to have them returned."

first vessel to reach King's Bridge, on the Ogeechee River, was the mail steamer. Subsequently, when Sherman marched through the Carolinas, and after the hard-fought battle of Bentonville, he met the mail for his army on the evening of the day of that battle.[1]

That army mail-service presents to the contemplation of those who comprehend its extent and usefulness, one of the moral wonders of the great conflict; and in its salutary influence and value seems second only to the Sanitary Commission or the Christian Commission. It kept entire armies in continual communion, as far as possible, with home and kindred—a circumstance of incalculable benefit to the soldier and the service. It prevented that terrible home-sickness with which raw troops are often prostrated. It also exercised the affections, and, in a remarkable degree, brought the sweet influences of the domestic circle to bear most powerfully in strengthening the men against the multiform temptations of the camp, and the yearnings for family joys which so often seduce the less favored soldier to desert; while courage and patriotism were continually stimulated by heroic words from patient and loving ones at home.

The writer visited the theater of events recorded in this chapter, early in May, 1866. He left Nashville in the steamer *Tyrone*, toward the evening of the 5th. Most of his fellow-passengers, as far as Clarksville, sixty miles down the Cumberland River, consisted of about two hundred colored soldiers, who had just been paid off and discharged from the service. The few white passengers on board, and the officers and crew of the *Tyrone*, who were mostly secessionists, were greatly relieved when these soldiers debarked at midnight, for the fearful massacre of negroes at Memphis had just occurred, and they did not know what might be the temper of these troops on that account. They were in dread of personal danger. But there was no occasion for alarm. The preparations made for surrendering the steamer to the soldiers, on demand, and taking the women and children ashore in the yawl-boat, as well as the more belligerent one for giving the negroes a shower of hot water from the boiler, in the event of an uprising, were quite unnecessary. The writer, who mingled among and conversed with many of the soldiers, never saw a more orderly and well-disposed company of men, just loosed from military discipline, than they. There was only one intoxicated man among them. They were too full of joy to think of mischief. The shores of the Cumberland resounded with their songs and laughter, for

---

[1] Letter to the author by General Markland, August 20, 1866. In a letter to Colonel Markland, written in May, 1865, General O. O. Howard says: "For more than a year the Army of the Tennessee has been campaigning in the interior of the Southern States, a great portion of the time far separated from depots of supplies, and connected with home and friends only by a long and uncertain line of railroad, that was, for the most part, overworked to supply provisions, or, moving off without base or lines of communication, the army only touched at points not always previously designated. During all this time, from Chattanooga to Atlanta, from Atlanta to Savannah, and in the homeward campaign across the Carolinas, you, my dear Colonel, have received the warmest thanks from officers and men for your interest, energy, and uniform success in bringing to them the mail, often immense from accumulation, forwarding it promptly, by sea or by land, for distribution. During the campaign of four months against Atlanta, the mail was received with great regularity. On the 13th December, the very day our communication was opened on the Ogeechee River with Admiral Dahlgren's fleet, the mail-boat, with your personal charge, was the first to pass the obstructions and greet the Army of the Tennessee. When our army arrived at Goldsborough, having been marching 500 miles without communication, it found letters from home in waiting, and you were there to welcome us again. From this time till we left Raleigh, *en route* for Washington, all mail matter was regularly received, and you still provided for us while the army was encamped in sight of the capital."

General Sherman, in a letter to General Markland, bore similar testimony.

they were all happy in the thought of money in their pockets, and the greetings of friends at home.

The *Tyrone* lay at Clarksville until daylight, when the writer had the opportunity to make a sketch of Fort Bruce and its vicinity, events at which will be considered presently. We left there while breakfasting; and nearly all of that beautiful day we were voyaging on that winding and picturesque river, whose bosom and shores have been made historical by great events. At about two o'clock in the afternoon we passed the ruins of the Cumberland Iron Works, and at three o'clock we landed at the site of Dover. The little village, with its church, court-house, and almost one hundred dwellings and stores, when Fort Donelson[1] was built, had disappeared. The public buildings and most of the private ones had been laid in ashes during the war, and only a few dilapidated structures remained.

At Cooley's tavern, near the landing-place (in which General Tilghman had quartered), the writer was introduced to Captain James P. Flood, the commander of the famous Flood's Second Illinois Battery, who performed gallant service at Dover, in repelling an attack by the cavalry of Forest and Wheeler. He had settled there as a lawyer, and was familiar with every foot of the battle-ground. He kindly offered to accompany the writer to the points of interest in connection with the battle, and took him to the house of G. M. Stewart, near the fort, an old and leading citizen of Stewart County, who had been faithful to the old flag, and had suffered much for its sake during the war. Mr. Stewart and his son (who had been in the Union service) kindly offered to go over the field of conflict with us. He furnished saddle-horses for the whole company, and at twilight we had traversed the entire line of works, in front of which the divisions of McClernand and Wallace fought, and visited the head-quarters of General Grant. Near McClernand's extreme right, in Hysmith's old field, we found the grave-yard of the Illinois troops, delineated on page 217. We followed the lines toward the center in their devious way through the woods, and clearings covered with sprouting oaks, and came to the burial-place of the dead of the Eleventh Illinois Regiment, similar in appearance to the other, and having a board in the center with the names of the killed upon it. Everywhere the trees were terribly scarred by bullets, and cannon-shot and shell, giving evidence of the severity of the battle. All through these woods and openings, we found the detached lines of the Confederate intrenchments half concealed by the already rank growth of grass, and bushes shoulder high, and blackberry shrubs and vines, then white with blossoms. Nature was rapidly hiding from view these evidences of man's iniquity.

Grant's head-quarters, as we have observed, were at the house of Mrs. Crisp, a short distance from the road leading from Dover to Fort Henry. Mrs. Crisp, a stout, kind-hearted, good-natured old lady, was still there, and refreshed us with a draught of the finest spring water. She did not approve of National troops in general, but had most pleasant recollections of General Grant and his staff. She committed to our keeping kind

---

[1] This fort was so named in honor of Andrew Jackson Donelson, the adopted son of President Jackson, and who at that time was occupying the "Hermitage," a few miles from Nashville. He warmly espoused the cause of the conspirators.

compliments to the General, and then, at almost sunset, we bade her farewell and galloped back toward Dover, diverging to the left to visit Fort Donelson, and sketch the scene of the battle on the river between the armed vessels and the water-batteries. The sun was just setting behind some thin clouds when we arrived there, and it was soon too dark to allow the use of the pencil. So we rode to Dover, supped with Mr. Stewart, and lodged at Cooley's.

Wishing to take passage on the first steamer that should pass up the Cumberland the next morning, the writer arose at dawn, and found Mr. Stewart, as previously arranged, ready, with two saddle-horses, to visit the fort. We breakfasted before sunrise, and then rode over the lines of the famous stronghold on which the Confederates had spent so much labor, and placed so much dependence. These, too, were half hidden by shrubbery and vines, and in the course of a very few years it will be difficult to trace the

VIEW AT FORT DONELSON.[1]

outlines of these fortifications. Between these and Dover, we visited a strong work on a commanding eminence, built by the National troops under the direction of Captain Flood and others, but which was never made use of. From the hill overlooking the water batteries I made the accompanying sketch, and had just finished it when a steamer came in sight below, at the point where Foote's armored vessels, ranged in a line, assailed the Confederate works. Remounting our horses, we hurried back to Dover, reaching

[1] This is a view looking down the river, in which the remains of the upper water battery are seen in the foreground. In the distance, on the left, near which is seen a steamboat, is the promontory behind which the *Carondelet* lay while bombarding the Confederate works on the 13th. The fort lay on the top of the hill on the extreme left. Across the river is seen the shore to which Pillow escaped when he stole out of the fort.

there just as the steamer was moored at the gravelly bank. It was the *Emma Floyd*, one of the most agreeable boats on the Cumberland, and with its intelligent pilots, John and Oliver Kirkpatrick, and their wives and children, the writer spent most of the day in the pilot-house, listening to the stories of the adventures of these men while they were acting as pilots in the fleets of Farragut and Porter, during those marvelous expeditions on the Mississippi, its tributaries, and its mysterious bayous, carried on in connection with the armies of Grant and Banks. After a delightful voyage of twenty-four hours, we arrived at Nashville, where the writer was joined by his former traveling companions, Messrs. Dreer and Greble, of Philadelphia, with whom he afterward journeyed for six weeks upon the pathways and battle-fields of the great armies in Tennessee, Georgia, and Virginia.

The aspect of Nashville, and especially its surroundings, had materially changed since the author was there in 1861. The storm of war had swept over the country in its vicinity with fearful effect. The city itself had not suffered bombardment, yet at times it had been in imminent danger of such calamity; first on the approach of the forces of Grant and Buell, and afterward when it was held by the National troops and was threatened by the Confederates. The hills had been stripped of their forests, pleasure-grounds had been robbed of their shade-trees, and places of pleasant resort had been scarred by trenches or disfigured by breastworks. Buildings had been shattered by shot and shell or laid in ruins by fire; and at every approach to the city were populous cemeteries of soldiers who had fallen in defense of their country.

In the Capitol were stores of correspondence and other papers captured from Pillow and his fellow-traitors, and these were placed at the disposal of the author, who also had the good fortune to meet in Nashville General Ewell, one of the most estimable of the Confederates who took up arms against the Government, as a man and as a military leader. He kindly allowed him to make abstracts of his later reports, in manuscript, concerning operations in the Shenandoah Valley, in which he and "Stonewall Jackson" were associated, and also furnished him with information relative to the evacuation of Richmond, and the destruction of a great portion of it by fire immediately succeeding that event, when Ewell was in command of the post. That subject will be considered hereafter.

CHAPTER IX.

EVENTS AT NASHVILLE, COLUMBUS, NEW MADRID, ISLAND NUMBER TEN, AND PEA RIDGE.

WHEN Fort Donelson fell, Kentucky and Missouri, and all of northern and middle Tennessee were lost to the Confederates, and the more Southern States, whose inhabitants expected to have the battles for their defense fought in the border Slave-labor States, were exposed to the inroads of the National armies.

The terror inspired all along the Confederate line by the fall of Fort Henry, and the forward movement of General Mitchel, of Buell's army, from his camp at Bacon's Creek, across the Green River at Mumfordsville, toward Bowling Green, simultaneously with Grant's investment of Fort Donelson,[a] caused that line, which seemed so strong almost to invincibility a few weeks before, to crumble into fragments and suddenly disappear as a mist. General Johnston clearly perceived that both Bowling Green and Columbus were now untenable, and that the salvation of his troops at each required the immediate evacuation of these posts. He issued orders accordingly, and when Mitchel, having marched forty-two miles in thirty-two hours, reached the northern bank of the Barren River, on whose southern border Bowling Green[1] stood, the main body of Johnston's troops, seven or eight thousand strong, had left it and fled southward. Mitchel found the bridges on that stream all destroyed; and when, on the same night, Colonel Turchin crossed it below the village, with his brigade, the heavens were illuminated by the flames of the burning railway station-house, and Confederate stores in the

[a] Feb. 11, 1862.

BOWLING GREEN AFTER THE EVACUATION.

[1] Bowling Green is about 74 miles from Nashville, and contained a little less than 3,000 inhabitants when the war broke out. Around it are numerous little hills or "knobs," on which the insurgents planted batteries and made the post very strong. Our litle picture shows the appearance of Bowling Green, in the vicinity of the railway station, on the day after the evacuation.

center of the town. These had been fired by Texas Rangers, left behind for the purpose, and who were then just moving off on a railway train. Mitchel's troops were exhausted by their forced march in the keen frosty air, and the labor of removing trees from the roads which the Confederates had cut down; and the water in the stream being too high to ford, his army did not cross until the next day, when they found Bowling Green to be almost barren of spoils. Half a million dollars' worth of property had been destroyed, and only a brass 6-pounder, and commissary stores valued at five thousand dollars, remained. The Confederates had also removed, during the preceding four days, a large quantity of provisions and stores to Nashville.

Imminent danger now impended over Nashville. Johnston, as we have seen, had declared that he fought for that city at Fort Donelson. When the latter fell, Nashville was doomed, and its disloyal inhabitants were pale with terror.

On the day of the surrender, the intelligence of the sad event reached the city just as the people were comfortably seated in the churches, for it was the Christian Sabbath. Pillow's foolish boast[1] and dispatch founded upon it[2] had allayed all fears; now these were awakened with ten-fold intensity. The churches were instantly emptied, and each citizen seemed to have no other thought but for personal safety.[3] That the town would be speedily occupied by the Government troops, no one doubted. Grant's vigor had been tested. It had been observed that he did not stop when a victory was gained, but pushed forward to reap in full all of its advantages. So they gave up all as lost. The public stores were thrown wide open, and everybody was allowed to carry off provisions and clothing without hindrance.

The panic among the Secessionists was fearful. Governor Harris, the worst criminal of them all, was crazy with alarm. He rode through the streets with his horse at full speed, crying out that the papers in the capital must be removed.[4] He well knew what evidence of his treason was among them. He and his guilty legislature gathered as many of the archives as possible, and fled by railway to Memphis,[5] while the officers of banks, bear-

---

[1] See page 216. This boast had so assured the citizens that all was safe, that they felt no apprehensions of evil. Indeed, they had indulged in rejoicings over the victory of the Confederates at Fort Donelson. For this reason, the astounding news that now reached them was more appalling.

[2] The dispatch was headed in large letters—ENEMY RETREATING!—GLORIOUS RESULT!!—OUR BOYS FOLLOWING AND PEPPERING THEIR REAR!!—A COMPLETE VICTORY!!

[3] "An earthquake," says Pollard (i. 247), "could not have shocked the city more. The congregations at the churches were broken up in confusion and dismay; women and children rushed into the streets, wailing with terror; trunks were thrown from three-story windows in the haste of the fugitives, and thousands hastened to leave their beautiful city in the midst of the most distressing scenes of terror, confusion, and plundering by the mob."

The panic of the people was natural. They had been deceived and misled, by false teachers in their midst, into the belief that the people of the North were half savages. Among these teachers, who should be held responsible for much of the sufferings inflicted by the war, was W. E. Ward, a clergyman who, in his paper, called *The Banner of Peace*, published at Nashville, had just said: "We have felt too secure, we have been too blind to the consequence of Federal success. If they succeed, we shall see plunder, insult to old and young, male and female, murder of innocents, release of slaves, and causing them to drive and insult their masters and mistresses in the most menial services, the land laid waste, houses burned, banks and private coffers robbed, cotton and every valuable taken away before our eyes, and a brutal, drunken soldiery turned loose upon us. Who wants to see this? If you do not believe, you will see it; look at Missouri."

[4] Nashville correspondent of the *Richmond Dispatch*, Feb. 17, 1862.

[5] At Memphis, on the 19th, Governor Harris issued a proclamation, in which he deplored the loss of Fort Donelson, and the danger that threatened the capital, and told the people that henceforth Tennessee was to become the battle-field in which her inhabitants would show to the world that they were worthy to be—weat they had solemnly declared themselves to be—"freemen." He encouraged, or discouraged them by the announcement that he would take the field at their head; and then in turgid phrases he tried to arouse them

ing away specie from the vaults, and citizens encumbered with their most valuable effects that were portable, crowded the stations of the railways leading to Decatur and to Chattanooga. Every vehicle was brought into requisition, and hack-hire was raised to twenty-five dollars an hour. This fearful panic was increased when a portion of the troops, flying from Bowling Green, came rushing into the city across the railway and the Suspension bridges, and a rumor spread over the town that the victors at Fort Donelson were making their way rapidly up the Cumberland.

The rumor was true. On the evening of the day after the surrender of Fort Donelson,[a] Commodore Foote sent the *St. Louis* up the Cumberland to the Tennessee Iron Works, six or seven miles above Dover. These belonged, in part, to John Bell, the candidate of the "Constitutional Union Party" for President, in 1860,[1] who, as we have observed, had early espoused the cause of the conspirators.[2] There appeared to be sufficient evidence of these works having been employed in the interest of the rebellion to warrant their destruction, and they were laid in ashes. Nothing remained of them, when the writer passed by the spot in the spring of 1866, but three tall chimneys, ruined machinery, and heaps of brick.

[a] Feb. 16, 1862.

On the 19th, the commodore, with the gun-boats *Cairo*, Lieutenant-commanding Bryant, and *Conestoga*, Lieutenant-commanding Phelps, ascended

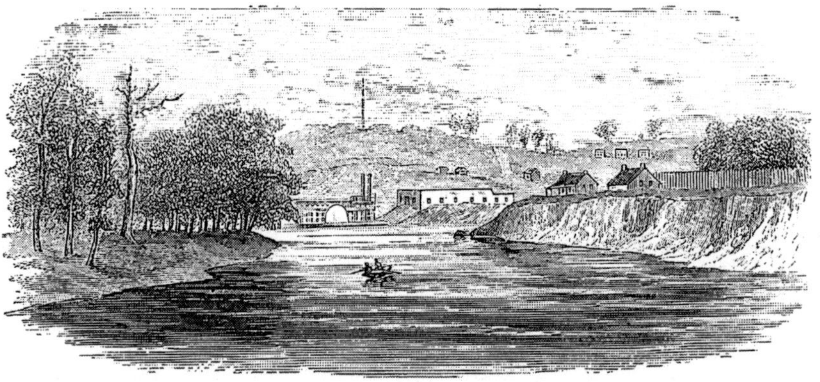

FORT BRUCE AND ITS VICINITY.[3]

the river to Clarkesville (a city on its right bank, of about two thousand inhabitants before the war, and the capital of Montgomery County), with the intention of attacking an unfinished fort there, which the Confederates

---

to resist the Union armies. He had, he said, in a message to the Legislature on the 20th, organized and put into the field since May, 1861, "for the Confederate service, fifty-nine regiments of infantry, one of cavalry, eleven cavalry battalions, and over twenty independent companies, mostly of artillery." Fifteen thousand of these troops, he said, had been armed by the "Confederate Government," and to arm the remainder he called for "the sporting guns" of the citizens.

[1] See page 30, volume I.

[2] See page 374, volume I.

[3] The National troops completed the work and named it Fort Bruce, in honor of the loyal Colonel Bruce, of Nashville. The engraving shows its situation at the bend of the Cumberland, about half a mile below Clarksville. It commanded the river up and down. The mouth of the Red River is seen at the center of the picture, near a storehouse. On the Clarksville side of that stream was a small redoubt, called the Mud Fort, it being overflowed and covered with sediment at high water. This sketch was made by the writer from the deck of the *Emma Floyd*, while lying at Clarksville, looking down the river.

were erecting on the high bluff at the mouth of the Red River, a small stream that enters the Cumberland just below the town. The garrison, startled by the general panic, fled, and, in defiance of the wishes and remonstrances of the citizens of Clarkesville, set fire to the fine railway bridge that spanned the river at that place. Colonel Webster, Grant's chief of staff, and Lieutenant Phelps, immediately went ashore and hoisted the National flag over the fort. Two-thirds of the terrified citizens of Clarkesville had fled when Foote arrived. At the suggestion of the late venerable Cave Johnson, and one or two others, he proclaimed full protection to all peaceable citizens, at the same time warning them not to display any secession flags or other evidence of rebellious feeling.

General Smith, with the advance of the National army, marched up to Clarkesville and took command there; while Foote returned to Cairo for more gun-boats, for the purpose of attacking Nashville. In the mean time General Johnston and his forces from Bowling Green had continued their flight southward as far as Murfreesboro, twenty-five miles on the way toward Chattanooga,[1] leaving General Floyd, the fugitive from Fort Donelson, with a few troops to secure the immense amount of stores and provisions in Nashville. Pillow, the other fugitive from Fort Donelson, and Hardee, who had come down from Bowling Green, were directed to assist Floyd in the business. The assignment to the perilous duty of remaining nearest the dreaded Nationals seemed like punishment inflicted on Floyd and Pillow by Johnston for their cowardice. If so, it was successful; yet it was injurious to the Confederate cause, for these men, unwilling to risk their persons again, suffered terribly from fear, and counseled flight, as before. Floyd, on hearing that Foote's gun-boats were coming, gave orders on Monday[a] for the Confederate stores to be thrown open to the public; two steam-packets, which were being changed into gun-boats, to be burned; and the two bridges[2] at Nashville to be destroyed. Against the last act the citizens most vehemently protested, and it was postponed until Tuesday night, when they were both burned by Floyd's order; and he and Pillow literally scampered away southward by

[a] Feb. 17, 1862.

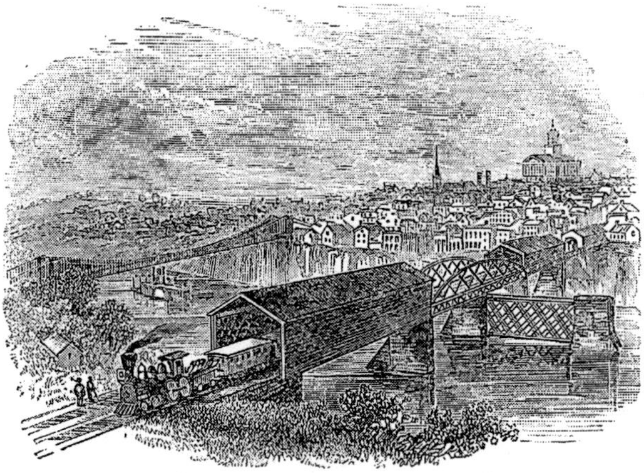

NASHVILLE AND ITS BRIDGES

[1] It was supposed by the Confederates that the Nationals would push on toward East Tennessee, and it was for the purpose of confronting such movement that Johnston took position at Murfreesboro.

[2] The wire suspension-bridge was a beautiful structure, and cost about $150,000. A large portion of the stock belonged to the slain General Zollicoffer, and was the chief reliance for support, of his orphaned daughters. But Floyd and Pillow wished to put a gulf between themselves and the Nationals, that they might save their own worthless persons; and so the claims of orphans and the prayers of citizens were of no avail.

the light of the conflagration.[1] The troops that remained longest in Nashville were Forest's cavalry, led by that brave captain.

During the remainder of the week, Nashville was the theater of the wildest anarchy, and neither public nor private property was safe for an hour. Happily for the well-disposed inhabitants, Colonel Kenner, of the Fourth Ohio cavalry, of Mitchel's division, entered the city on Sunday evening, the 23d, and endeavored to restore order. He was immediately followed by the remainder of his commander's force, who encamped at Edgefield, opposite Nashville, and there awaited the arrival of General Buell. That officer came on the 25th, and on the same morning the *Conestoga* arrived from Clarkesville, as a convoy to transports bearing a considerable body of troops, under General Nelson. These had not been opposed in their passage up the river, for the only battery on its banks between the two cities was Fort Zollicoffer, on a bluff, four or five miles below Nashville, which was unfinished, and was then abandoned. The citizens of Nashville, believing General Johnston would make a stand there, had commenced this fort on the south or left bank of the Cumberland, and were much incensed by its sudden abandonment.

Pursuant to previous arrangement, the mayor of Nashville (R. B. Cheatham) and a small delegation of citizens crossed over to Buell's quarters at Edgefield, and there made a formal surrender of the city.[a] General Buell at once issued an order congratulating the troops "that it had been their privilege to restore the National banner to the Capitol of Tennessee."[2] He expressed a belief that the hearts of a greater portion of the people of that State would be rejoiced by the fact; and he assured the inhabitants that the rights of person and property should be respected. On the following day, General Grant and staff arrived, and he and General Buell held a consultation about future movements. Colonel Stanley Matthews, of the Fifty-first Ohio Volunteers, was appointed Provost-Marshal, and order was speedily re-

[a] Feb. 26, 1862.

CAPITOL AT NASHVILLE.

[1] A greater portion of the cannon at Nashville were spiked, and many of them were placed upon the bridges before they were fired, and when these perished in the flames, the cannon went to the bottom of the Cumberland.

[2] The Capitol of the State of Tennessee is one of the finest of its kind in the United States. It is in the center of four acres of ground in the midst of the city, and crowns a hill that rises 197 feet above the Cumberland River. It is composed of fossilated limestone, taken from quarries near the city, and its style is of the most beautiful of the Grecian orders, with four porticoes, whose columns are 33 feet in height. It is a parallelogram in form, 140 by 270 feet in size, and is surrounded by a terrace 17 feet in width and six in height. The pinnacle

stored. Railroad connection with Louisville was soon opened, and the inhabitants were invited to resume their avocations.

The capture of Nashville, the flight of the Governor and Legislature of Tennessee from the State capital, and the virtual dissolution of civil government in that Commonwealth, imposed upon the National authorities the duty of providing a substitute for the people. It was resolved to appoint a military governor to administer the public affairs of the State under martial law; and Andrew Johnson, formerly a chief magistrate of that Commonwealth, and then one of its representatives in the United States Senate, was appointed[a] to that responsible position, with the military rank of Brigadier-General.[1] He reached Nashville on the 12th of March, and, in a speech to the citizens assembled that evening, he promised friendship and protection to the loyal, and gave them to understand that "intelligent and conscious treason in high places" would be punished.

[a] March 4, 1862.

Another bloodless victory soon followed the capture of Nashville. Six days after the formal surrender of that city, General Halleck telegraphed to General McClellan from St. Louis,[b] "Columbus, the Gibraltar of the West, is ours, and Kentucky is free, thanks to the brilliant strategy of the campaign by which the enemy's center was pierced at Forts Henry and Donelson, his wings isolated from each other and turned, compelling thus the evacuation of his stronghold of Bowling Green first, and now Columbus."

[b] March 4.

The history of the latter event may be told in few words. When it was evident to the conspirators at Richmond that the "Gibraltar" was untenable, the so-called Secretary of War instructed Polk, through Beauregard, "to evacuate Columbus, and select a defensive position below." Polk chose that section of the Mississippi and its shores which embraces Island Number Ten, the main land in Madrid Bend on the Kentucky shore, and New Madrid. Defensive works had been thrown up at the two latter places during the preceding autumn, and now measures were immediately taken for strongly fortifying Island Number Ten.

So early as the 25th of February, Polk ordered the removal of the sick from Columbus, as a preparatory step toward the evacuation of that post, and assigned the command of the river defenses at the position chosen to General I. P. McCown, whose division was ordered thither on the 27th. The remainder of the troops, excepting the cavalry, left Columbus on the 1st of March. General Stuart's brigade went by steamer to New Madrid, and the remainder marched by land to Union City, in Tennessee,[2] under General Cheatham. The removal of special articles of value to Jackson, Tennessee,

---

of its cupola is 200 feet from the ground. In compliance with the request of Mr. Strickland, its architect, his remains are inclosed in its walls, with a proper inscription on the outside; and so that imposing pile has become his monument. The cost of the building was over $1,000,000. The population of Nashville, at the time we are considering, was about 24,000 souls.

In our little sketch is seen a cabin in front of the Capitol. It was used by the architects during the erection of the great; building and in it Governor Harris was living, it is said, in a very frugal manner, when he was summoned to fly from Nashville.

[1] See page 226, volume I.

[2] This is at the intersection of the Nashville and Northwestern and the Mobile and Ohio Railways; the former leading directly to Hickman, on the Mississippi River.

had been accomplished at that time. Then the cavalry set fire to the military buildings of the post, and, accompanied by Polk and his staff, followed the retiring columns, at three o'clock in the afternoon of the 2d.[a][1]

[a] March, 1862.

In the mean time preparations had been made to capture Columbus, with its troops and munitions of war. When Foote returned to Cairo from Clarkesville, he collected a flotilla of six gun-boats, commanded respectively by Captains Davis, Walke, and Stembel, and Lieutenants-commanding Paulding, Thompson, and Shirk; four mortar-boats, under the general command of Lieutenant-commanding Phelps, assisted by Lieutenant Ford, of the Ordnance Corps, and Captain George Johnson, of Cincinnati; and three transports. The latter bore a small land force of little more than two thousand men,[2] commanded by Brigadier-General W. T. Sherman (who was in command at Paducah), accompanied by General Cullum, of Halleck's staff. The flotilla left Cairo before daylight on the morning of the 4th,[b] and at sunrise was in sight of the fortified bluffs at Columbus. Preparations were made for attack. Rumor had declared that the fort had been evacuated. It was cautiously approached, even after a farmer, a professedly Union man, had assured the commodore that the troops had fled. At length the National flag was dimly seen waving over the Confederate works. It might be a trick. Colonel Buford and a detachment of the Twenty-seventh Illinois were landed to reconnoiter. They were soon clambering up the steep bluffs with shouts of triumph. Troops were in the fortifications, but they were friends. A detachment of the Second Illinois cavalry, under Lieutenant Hogg, two hundred and fifty strong, who had been sent out as scouts from Paducah, had entered the place at five o'clock the day before, and hoisted the Stars and Stripes over the main work of that stronghold.[3] They found the town deserted by nearly all of its disloyal inhabitants.[4] There was evidence of great haste in the evacuation, "considering," says General Cullum, "the quantities of ordnance and ordnance stores, and number of anchors, and the remnant of the chain which was once stretched over the river,[5] and a large

[b] March.

---

[1] Report of Major-General Leonidas Polk to Colonel Thomas Jordan, March 18th, 1862. "In five days," said Polk, in his report, "we removed the accumulation of six months, taking with us all our commissary and quartermaster stores—an amount sufficient to supply my whole command for eight months; all our powder and other ammunition and ordnance stores (excepting a few shot, and gun-carriages), and every heavy gun in the fort. Two 32-pounders in a remote outwork were the only valuable guns left." These, with some smaller ones, were spiked. "The whole number of pieces of artillery comprising our armament," he continued, "was one hundred and fifty." General Cullum's report contradicts that of Polk concerning the removal of nearly all that was valuable, for a large quantity of ordnance and ordnance stores, he says, was found there.

[2] These were composed of Colonel Buford's Twenty-seventh Illinois, and a battalion each of the Fifty-fourth and Seventy-fourth Ohio, and Fifty-fifth Illinois regiments, commanded by Majors Andrews and Sawyer.

[3] Report of Commodore Foote to the Secretary of the Navy, March 4, 1862; also of General Cullum to General McClellan, on the same day.

General Polk, in his report, says, "The enemy's cavalry, the first of his forces to arrive after the evacuation, reached Columbus in the afternoon of the next day [March 3], twenty-four hours after the last of our troops had left."

[4] A correspondent of the *Cincinnati Gazette*, who accompanied Commodore Foote, mentioned "Mrs. Sharpe, wife of the ex-mayor of Columbus," as the only woman he met with in his rambles through the town. She said she had stuck up for the Union cause while the secessionists threatened to pull her house down. Her husband, she said, had been "forcibly carried off by the rebels."—See notice of Sharpe's letter to General Pillow, note 1, page 72.

[5] This was a contrivance of General Pillow, and, like most of his military operations, was a failure. It was a huge affair, stretching down from the bluffs into the Mississippi, with its Missouri shore end loose, and the most of it lying at the bottom of the river.

supply of torpedoes remaining.[1] Desolation was visible everywhere—huts, tents, and barricades presenting but their blackened remains." A number of heavy cannon had been spiked and rolled off the bluff into the river. A train on fire, connected with both ends of a magazine, was cut, and safety was soon secured. A garrison of a little over two thousand men, including four hundred cavalry, was left to hold the post.

We have observed that Polk and his confederates, on retiring from Columbus, took position on the Mississippi shores and Island Number Ten

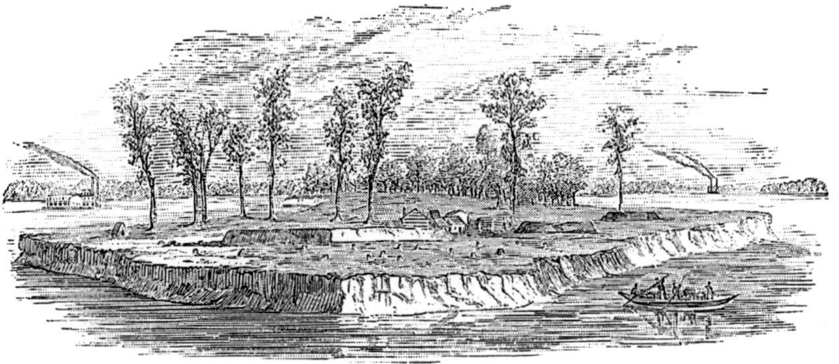

ISLAND NUMBER TEN.[2]

below. New Madrid, on the Missouri side of the river,[3] to which many of the troops went, had been much strengthened by Jeff. Thompson,[4] who had occupied it for some time, and had strong military works there, one of which was

---

[1] These torpedoes were numerous and formidable, and, had men been there to fire those in the river, by the electrical batteries on the shore, there might have been much damage done to Foote's flotilla, had it gone near. These, and "infernal machines," found in mines in the bluff, attested the great danger to which the National forces would have been exposed in an assault upon the Confederate works, which were of immense strength from the water to the table-land above. In the bluff near the grand battery above Columbus a cavern was discovered, in which were found electrical machines, having a connection by wires with portable mines in several directions, so arranged as to destroy troops that might be gathered above them. These mines were iron casks, something of a pear shape, about three feet in height, with an iron cap, fastened with eight screws. In each was a 4-pound shell, with grape and canister shot, "surrounded by about two bushels of coarse powder," wrote an eye-witness. On the bottom of each cask was a wooden box, to which, and entering the powder, were fastened insulated wires, connecting with the electrical machines in the cavern. Several other caverns were found with these machines connecting with mines, to the number, it was supposed, of nearly one hundred. The torpedoes found in the river and on the shore were pointed cylinders, about three feet in length, containing fifty or sixty pounds of powder, which was to be ignited by electricity. The electrical machines were very much like those used in telegraph offices.

TORPEDOES.

INFERNAL MACHINE.

[2] This was the appearance of Island Number Ten, to the eye of the author, from a Mississippi steamer in April, 1866. It lies in a sharp bend of the Mississippi, about 40 miles below Columbus, and within the limits of Kentucky.

[3] New Madrid is the capital of New Madrid County, Missouri, 79 miles below Cairo, and 947 miles above New Orleans, by the winding river. Island Number Ten is about ten miles above it. The islands in the Mississippi, from the mouth of the Ohio River downward, are distinguished by numbers, this, as its name implies, being the tenth.

[4] See page 58.

called Fort Thompson.[1] The post was now in charge of General Gantt, of Arkansas. The town was at the junction of a bayou and the Mississippi, at a sharp turn of that stream, and was naturally an eligible position to repel an enemy approaching by water, from above or below. In addition to its land defenses, it was now guarded by a flotilla of six gun-boats, carrying from four to eight heavy guns each, which had been sent up from New Orleans, under the command of the incompetent Hollins.[2] The country around New Madrid being flat, and the water in the river, at the time we are considering, very high, the cannon of the flotilla commanded the land approaches to the town for a long distance. This post, although about a thousand miles away from New Orleans, was, with Island Number Ten, a few miles above, regarded as the key to the lower Mississippi, and the metropolitan city on its banks, and therefore an object of great importance to both parties.

When the garrison at New Madrid was re-enforced from Columbus, it was placed under the charge of General McCown, while the troops on Island Number Ten were commanded by General Beauregard.[3] These officers had scarcely established their quarters at their respective posts, when they were disturbed by the thunder of the Union troops, who were bent upon the redemption of the navigation of the Mississippi from the control of rebel cannon and vessels. It was confidently expected at Richmond, however, that, at this great bend in the river, they might say to the National

---

[1] This was an irregular bastioned work, mounting fourteen heavy guns, and situated about half a mile below New Madrid. There was another similar, but smaller work at the upper end of the town, mounting seven heavy guns. Between them was a continuous line of intrenchments and defensive works.

[2] See page 114.

[3] Beauregard, who had just been appointed to the command of the Department of Mississippi, was in immediate command of the troops, and the property at Jackson, Tennessee, after the evacuation of Columbus; and, inspired by an appeal from the Ordnance Department at Richmond,* he there indulged in his favorite amusement of issuing sensation orders. He sent forth one dated the 8th of March, addressed "To the Planters of the Mississippi Valley," telling them that more than once a people fighting with an enemy less ruthless than theirs, for "imperiled rights not more dear and sacred," for "homes and a land not more worthy of resolute and unconquerable men," and for "interests of far less magnitude than theirs, had not hesitated to melt and mould into cannon the precious bells surmounting their houses of God, which had called generations to prayer. The priesthood," he told them, "had ever sanctioned and consecrated the conversion, in the hour of their country's need, as one holy and acceptable in the sight of God. We want cannon," he continued, "as greatly as any people who ever, as history tells you, melted their church bells to supply them;" so he, their General, called upon them to send their "plantation bells to the nearest railroad depot," subject to his order, "to be melted into cannon for the defense of their plantations." There was a liberal response to this call, and not only "plantation bells" but church bells were offered for the purpose. "In some cities," wrote a soldier in the Confederate army, "every church gave up its bell. Court-houses, factories, public institutions, and plantations, sent theirs. And the people furnished large quantities of old brass of every description—andirons, candlesticks, gas-fixtures, and even door-knobs. I have seen wagon-loads of these lying at depots, waiting shipment to the foundries."—See *Thirteen Months in the Rebel Army*, by an impressed New Yorker (William G. Stevens), page 84.

These brazen contributions were all sent to New Orleans, where they were found by General Butler, who sent the bells to Boston, to be used for a more peaceful purpose. They were sold at auction there in August following, by Colonel N. A. Thompson, who prefaced the sale by a patriotic speech.

Ten days before Beauregard's appeal for bell-metal, his Surgeon-General, Dr. Choppin, whom he had sent to New Orleans, after the fall of Fort Donelson, for the purpose, issued in that city the following characteristic address to his Creole brethren:

"SOLDIERS OF NEW ORLEANS: You are aware of the disasters which have befallen our arms in the West. *Greater disasters still are staring us in the face.* General Beauregard—the man to whom we must look as the saviour of our country—sends me among you to summon you to a great duty and noble deeds—invoking and inspired by the sacred love of country and of priceless liberty, he has taken the deathless resolution *de les venger ou de les suivre.* And, with the immortal confidence and holy fervor of a soul willing, if need be, to meet martyrdom, he calls upon you to join him, in order that he may restore to our country what she has lost,

---

* Tin, an essential article in the manufacture of brass cannon, was so scarce within the bounds of the Confederacy, that the Ordnance Department solicited the people to contribute bells for the purpose. It is said that sufficient bell-metal was sent to Richmond, from Fredericksburg alone, to make two light batteries.

forces, "Thus far shalt thou go, and no farther;" but, like most of their calculations, this one signally failed.

While Johnston was pressing southward through Nashville with his fugitive army from Bowling Green, and Polk was trembling in his menaced works at Columbus, Halleck was giving impetus to a force destined to strike a fatal blow at the Confederates at New Madrid. He dispatched General Pope from St. Louis on the 22d of February, with a considerable body of troops, chiefly from Ohio and Illinois, to attack that post. Pope went down the Mississippi in transports, and landed at Commerce, in Missouri, on the 24th. He marched from there on the 27th, and three days afterward two companies of the Seventh Illinois cavalry, under Captain Webster, and a company of independent cavalry, under Captain Noleman, encountered the guerrilla chief M. Jeff. Thompson with about two hundred mounted men. These were routed, and pursued with great vigor to Thompson's lines at New Madrid, losing in their flight three pieces of artillery, and throwing away guns and every thing else that might lessen their speed. In the mean time Pope's main column moved on, traversed with the greatest difficulty overflowed miry swamps,[1] and on the day when the National standard was unfurled at Columbus[a] it appeared before New Madrid. Pope found the post occupied by five regiments of infantry and several companies of artillery, with Hollins's flotilla on the river. Satisfied that he could accomplish very little with his light artillery, he encamped out of range of the gun-boats, and sent Colonel Bissell, of the Engineer Corps, to Cairo for heavy cannon.

[a] March 3, 1862.

While Pope was waiting for his siege-guns, the Confederates were strengthening New Madrid by re-enforcements from Island Number Ten; and on the 12th, when the cannon from Cairo arrived, there were about nine thousand infantry, besides artillery, within the works in front of Pope, commanded by Generals McCown, Stuart, and Gantt. Meanwhile, three gun-boats had been added to Hollins's flotilla.

POPE'S HEAD-QUARTERS NEAR NEW MADRID.

Fearing the Confederates might be re-enforced from below, Pope sent Colonel J. B. Plummer, of the Eleventh Missouri, to Point Pleasant, ten or twelve miles down the river, to plant a battery, and blockade it at that

and lead you on to glory and independence. *In tones rigid and sullen as the tollings of the funeral knell*, but with clarion accents that should send a quiver through every heart, and string the nerves of every man, he cries out the final refrain of that immortal hymn—

"'Aux armes citoyens! formez vos bataillons,
Marchons!
Marchons
Qu'un sang impur abreuve nos sillons!'

"'Creoles of Louisiana, on to the work!'"

[1] "The men," said a newspaper correspondent, "waded in mud, ate in it, slept in it, were surrounded by it, as St. Helena is by the ocean."

point. He took with him three regiments of infantry, three companies of cavalry, and a field battery of 10-pound Parrott guns. He formed rifle-pits for a thousand men, and planted his cannon in sunken batteries below them. This was done with perfect success in the face of cannonading from the Confederate gun-boats. This position commanded the passage of the river in the rear of Island Number Ten, and prevented supplies being furnished to that post across the peninsula formed by Reel Foot Lake and Madrid Bend.

[a] March 12, 1862.

Pope's four siege-guns (three 32-pounders and an 8-inch mortar) arrived at near sunset,[a] and at dawn the next morning (thirty-five hours after they left Bird's Point, on the Cairo and Fulton Railway) they were in position, within half a mile of Fort Thompson.[1] On that work and Hollins's flotilla he at once opened a vigorous cannonade and bombardment.[b] They replied with equal vigor, but in the course of a few hours three of the cannon in the fort were dismounted, and three of the gun-boats were disabled. The fierce artillery duel continued throughout the whole day,[2] the Nationals continually extending their trenches, for the purpose of pushing their heavy batteries to the river bank during the night. General Paine, in the mean time, was making demonstrations against intrenchments on the Confederate right, supported by General Palmer's division. The Confederate pickets were driven in, and when night fell the entire insurgent force at New Madrid, on land and water, were in a perilous position. Their commanders perceived this, and during a furious thunder-storm, at about midnight, while the Twenty-seventh and Thirty-ninth Ohio and Tenth and Sixteenth Illinois were on duty guarding the rifle-pits and batteries, they evacuated the post and fled to Island Number Ten, leaving almost every thing behind them.[4] So precipitate was their flight that their suppers and lighted candles were in their tents, and their dead were left unburied. New Madrid presented a most pitiable spectacle. The original inhabitants had fled, and it had evidently been sacked and plundered by its Confederate occupants, for household articles were scattered in every direction. The human loss of the Confederates in this quick, sharp siege is not known. One hundred new graves and many bodies left unburied showed it to have been severe on the land. That of the Nationals was fifty-one killed and wounded.[5]

[b] March 13.

A CANNON TRUCK.[3]

---

[1] These guns were carried twenty miles by railway, and dragged on trucks (such as is delineated in the engraving) twenty miles farther, over a miry road most of the way.

[2] The heavy guns were handled by companies A and H, of the First U. S. Regular Infantry, under Captain Mower.

[3] See page 583, volume I.

[4] They left thirty-three cannon, several thousand stand of small arms, a magazine full of fixed ammunition, several hundred boxes of musket cartridges, tents for an army of ten thousand men, intrenching tools, and a large number of horses, mules, and wagons.

[5] Report of General John Pope to General Cullum, March 14, 1862; and statements to the author by eye-witnesses.

Just before daylight on the morning after the siege, Brigadier-General David S. Stanley, whose command had been in the trenches all night, was relieved by Major-General Schuyler Hamilton; and, a little after dawn, a flag of truce appeared with information that the place was abandoned. When the fact was certified, Hamilton sent Captain Mower and his artillerists to plant the national flag on Fort Thompson. At almost the same hour,[a] Commodore Foote left Cairo with a powerful fleet, composed of seven armored gun-boats, one not armored, and ten mortar-boats,[1] for the purpose of co-operating with General Pope. At Columbus he was joined by the Twenty-seventh Illinois, Colonel Buford, and some other troops,[b] and moving down to Hickman, on the same shore of the Mississippi, he took possession of that place.[2] He did not tarry, but, pressing forward, his fleet appeared in sight of Island Number Ten the next day,[c] when he carefully reconnoitered the Confederate position and prepared for a siege.

[a] March 14, 1862.

[b] March 14.

[c] March 15.

Under the skillful and energetic management of General Beauregard, Island Number Ten had been made the most impregnable to assault of all the posts in the Mississippi valley. On the day of his arrival there,[d] he had assumed the command of the Department of the Mississippi, to which, as we have observed, he had recently been appointed, and had called General Bragg from Pensacola to his aid. He issued a stirring order, from Jackson, Tennessee,[e] addressed to the inhabitants of his department, announcing his assumption of the command, and calling upon the men to arouse in defense of their "mothers, wives, sisters, and children." If high-sounding words and good engineering could have made Island Number Ten impregnable, it would have been so.

[d] March 5.

[e] March 5.

On Saturday night,[f] Commodore Foote was prepared for action, and on Sunday morning he commenced the siege with a bombardment by the rifled guns of the *Benton*, his flag-ship. This was followed by the mortar-boats, moored at proper points along the river shore, from which these immense pieces of ordnance hurled tons of iron upon the devoted island[3]

[f] March 15.

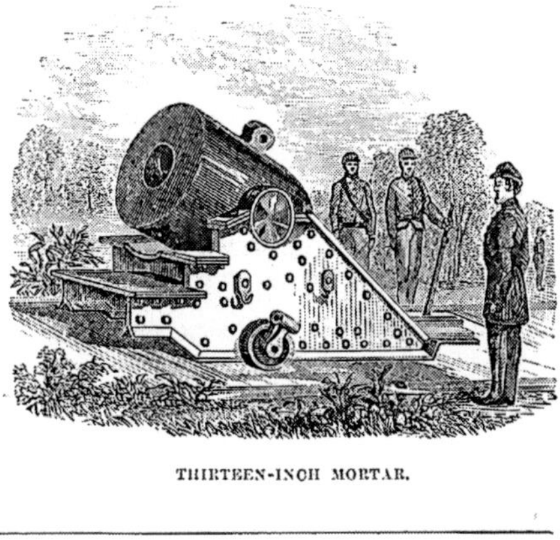

THIRTEEN-INCH MORTAR.

[1] The fleet consisted of the gun-boats *Benton*, Lieutenant Phelps acting flag-captain; *Cincinnati*, Commander Stembel; *Carondelet*, Commander Walke; *Mound City*, Commander Kelley; *Louisville*, Commander Dove; *Pittsburg*, Lieutenant Thompson; *St. Louis*, Lieutenant Paulding; and *Conestoga* (not armored), Lieutenant Blodgett. The mortar-boats were in charge of Captain H. E. Maynadier, commander of the squadron; Captain E. B. Pike, assistant commander; and Sailing-Masters Glassford, Gregory, Simonds, and Johnson.

[2] Hickman had been visited by National gun-boats once before. On the day when it was first occupied by the Confederates,[a] the *Tyler* and *Lexington* approached that place, where they encountered a Confederate gun-boat called *The Yankee*. With this, and a masked battery of four rifled cannon on the shore, just above Hickman, the *Tyler* and *Lexington* fought about an hour, driving *The Yankee* to Hickman, silencing the shore battery, burning the tents near it with hot shot, and scattering the insurgents.

[a] Sept. 4, 1861.

[3] The *mortar* was one of the earliest forms of cannon, being in use in Europe as early as 1435. Its name is derived from its form, which resembles the apothecaries' utensil of that name. The more ancient form is seen

and the batteries on the Kentucky shore opposite. All day long the bombardment was kept up, and vigorous responses were made, with very little injury to either party.[1]

Meanwhile a battery of the Second Illinois artillery was landed on the Missouri shore, in a position to assail the Confederate fleet near the island.

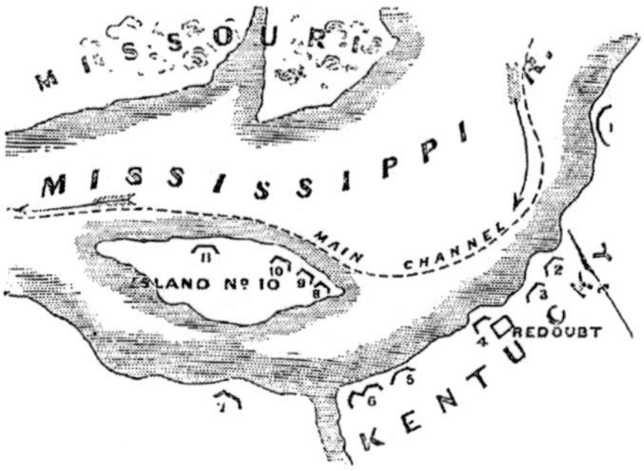

ISLAND NUMBER TEN AND ITS DEFENSES.[2]

This battery was active and effectual, and did excellent service the next day, when a most deadly attack was made on the Confederate works, after meridian, by a floating battery of ten guns, formed of the gun-boats *Cincinnati*, *Benton*, and *St. Louis*, lashed side by side, followed by the *Carondelet*, *Pittsburg*, and *Mound City*. They went nearer to the works, and pounded them severely. Heavy blows were given in return, and the second day of the siege was as barren of decisive results as the first.

[a] March 19, 1862.

"Island Number Ten," said Commodore Foote to the Secretary of the Navy,[a] "is harder to conquer than Columbus, as the island

---

in the little engraving on page 247. The great mortars used in sieges on land and water, during the late war, were truly monster-weapons for destruction. Our picture shows one used on land, mounted and worked precisely as were those on the mortar-boats. It is what is technically termed a 13-inch mortar, that is to say, it will receive a bomb-shell thirteen inches in diameter. Its weight was 17,000 pounds. It was discharged by means of a cord attached to a percussion lock. The immense balls or shells used for these mortars were so heavy (weighing over two hundred pounds), that one man could not handle one of them, and they were carried from the magazine to the mortar by the method delineated in the engraving. In the river-service, during the late war, the mortar-boats were firmly moored to the bank, and a derrick was set up on the shore in a position to drop the shell into the mouth of the monster after a bag full of powder had gone down its throat.

METHOD OF CARRYING A SHELL.

A correspondent of the *Chicago Times*, who was at the bombardment of Island Number Ten, thus graphically describes the manner of using these immense cannon: "The operation of firing the mortars, which was conducted while we were near by, is interesting and rather stunning. The charge is from fifteen to twenty-two pounds. The shell weighs 230 pounds, and is thirteen inches in diameter. For a familiar illustration, it is about the size of a large soup-plate, so your readers may imagine, when they sit down to dinner, the emotions they would experience if they happened to see a ball of iron of those dimensions coming toward them at the rate of a thousand miles a minute. The boat is moored alongside the shore, so as to withstand the shock firmly, and the men go ashore when the mortar is to be fired. A pull of the string does the work, and the whole vicinity is shaken with the concussion. The report is deafening, and the most enthusiastic person gets enough of it with one or two discharges. There is no sound from the shell at this point of observation, and no indication to mark the course it is taking, but in a few seconds the attentive observer, with a good glass, will see the cloud of smoke that follows its explosion, and then the report comes back with a dull boom. If it has done execution, the enemy may be seen carrying off their killed and wounded."

1 During the bombardment of this day, Commodore Foote was informed of the death, at New Haven, Connecticut, of his second son, a promising boy thirteen years of age. It was so unexpected that, for a moment, the brave warrior was overcome. He soon rallied, and pushed on the combat with great vigor, making private sorrow subordinate to public duty.

2 The figures on this map denote the numbers of the batteries, as given by the Confederates. It will be seen that the channel of the river was completely covered by them at the approaches of the island from above.

shores are lined with forts, each fort commanding the one above it." And so the siege went on, with varying fortunes, until the first week in April, when Foote's flotilla was yet above Island Number Ten, and Beauregard telegraphed[a] to Richmond that the National guns had "thrown three thousand shells and burned fifty tons of gun-powder" without damaging his batteries, and killing only one of his men. The public began to be impatient, but victory was near.[1]

[a] April 5, 1862.

While Commodore Foote was pounding away at Island Number Ten and its seven supporting shore-batteries, General Pope was chafing at New Madrid with impatience for decisive action. His guns easily blockaded the river, but he wished to do more. He desired to cross it to the peninsula and attack the island in the rear, a movement that would insure its capture with its dependencies, their garrisons and munitions of war. The river there was about a mile in width, and with a current then flowing at the speed of seven or eight miles an hour. The opposite shore was lined with batteries garnished with guns of heavy caliber. Until these could be silenced, it would be madness to attempt to cross the river with any means at Pope's command. He tried to induce Foote to allow some of his armed vessels to run the batteries of Island Number Ten, and, after silencing these Tennessee shore-batteries, transport the troops across. Foote would not incur the risk, and Pope was at his wit's end, when General Hamilton came to his relief with a most extraordinary proposition. It was the construction of a canal from the bend of the Mississippi, near Island Number Eight, across the neck of a swampy peninsula, to the vicinity of New Madrid, of sufficient capacity to allow the passage of gun-boats and transports, and thereby effectually flank Number Ten and insure its capture. He offered to undertake the task with his division, and to execute the work in the space of two weeks, under the general direction of Lieutenant Henry B. Gaw, of the Engineers.

SCHUYLER HAMILTON.

General Pope favored General Hamilton's proposition, and directed Colonel Bissell to perform the task, with the plans so modified as to allow only transports and barges to pass through. Bissell set about it with his regi-

---

1 While Foote was carrying on this siege, Colonel Buford with the Twenty-seventh Illinois, Colonel Hogg with the Fifteenth Missouri, and Colonel Foster with a battalion of the Twenty-second Missouri, accompanied by a battery of six rifled cannon, under Captain Spatsmon, of the Second Illinois artillery, and 200 of the Second Illinois cavalry, went to Hickman on the gun-boat *Louisville*. They landed quietly, and soon afterward pushed on toward Union City, an important point at the junction of railways south of Columbus, occupied by a Confederate force composed of the Twenty-first Tennessee infantry and a battalion of cavalry, in all about 1,000 men. Their way led through a densely wooded country. Their march was rapid, and they fell suddenly upon their enemies and scattered them at the first onset. After burning their camp, and effectually purging Union City of armed insurgents, the Nationals returned to Hickman and re-embarked for Island Number Ten.

ment, with great vigor, assisted by some of Buford's command. Four light-kraft steamers and two or three gun-barges were sent down from Cairo for use in the work; and, after nineteen days of the most fatiguing labor, a canal twelve miles long, one-half the distance through a growth of heavy timber,[1] was completed;[a] a wonderful monument to the engineering skill and indomitable perseverance of the Americans.[2] In the mean time Foote had not been idle, as Beauregard's electrograph attested. The upper (Rucker's Battery) or number one of the seven forts on the Kentucky shore had received his special attention, and on the night of the 1st of April an expedition to take it by storm was set in motion under the command of Colonel Roberts, of the Forty-second Illinois, who was accompanied by only forty of his men. They went in five boats manned by armed crews picked from the steamers *Benton*, *St. Louis*, *Cincinnati*, *Pittsburg*, and *Mound City*—a hundred men in all, seamen and soldiers—and, pulling directly for the face of the battery, met with no other opposition than the fire of two sentinels, who scampered away. The six guns of the battery were spiked, and thus one of Foote's most formidable opponents was silenced.

[a] April 4, 1862.

CONSTRUCTING THE CANAL.[3]

This daring feat was followed on the night of the 3d[b] by another. Pope had frequently implored Foote to send a gun-boat to his assistance. At length the gallant Captain Walke obtained permission of the commander to undertake to run by the Confederate batteries with the *Carondelet.* This perilous feat was successfully performed at midnight, during a tremendous thunder-storm. The flashes of lightning revealed her to the Confederates, and she was compelled to run the gantlet of a heavy fire from all of the batteries. She did not return a shot; and Foote was soon rejoiced by hearing the booming of three signal-guns from her deck, which was to be his assurance of her safety.[4] She was received at New

[b] April.

[1] Through this timber a way, at an average of fifty feet in width, was cut by sawing off trees, in some places four feet under water.

[2] Report of General Pope to General Halleck, April 9, 1862. Statement of General Hamilton to the author, June 7, 1863.

[3] In this picture the accompanying gun-barges are seen to the right and left of the steamer.

[4] The weak sides of the *Carondelet*, where the iron plates did not cover them, were protected by bales of

Madrid with the wildest demonstrations of delight, the soldiers catching up in their arms the sailors who rowed Walke's gig ashore, and passing them from one to another. The *Carondelet* was the first vessel that ran the Confederate blockade on the Mississippi River; and her brave commander and his men received the special thanks of the Secretary of the Navy,[a] for his courageous and important act. On the following morning,[b] the *Benton*, *Cincinnati*, and *Pittsburg*, with three boats, opened a heavy fire upon a huge floating battery of sixteen guns, which the Confederates had moored at Island Number Ten.[1] Unable to defend it, the Confederates imperfectly scuttled the monster, and cut it loose. It drifted down the river and lodged a short distance above Point Pleasant. So one by one advantages were gained by the Nationals.

[a] April 12, 1862.

[b] April 4.

THE CARONDELET.

The impatient Pope, satisfied that he could not rely upon the flotilla for much aid on his side of Island Number Ten, had caused several floating batteries to be constructed of coal-barges, at the upper end of the canal, with which he intended to silence the guns on the Kentucky shore, opposite his position, and cover the passage across of his troops.[2] These were completed when the canal was finished, and on the 5th of April they, with four steamers and some barges, were brought through that channel into the bayou which empties into the Mississippi at New Madrid. There all were kept concealed until every thing was in readiness for a forward movement.

On the morning of the 6th, Pope sent the *Carondelet* down the river toward Tiptonville, with General Granger, Colonel Smith, of the Forty-third Ohio, and Captain L. B. Marshall, of his staff, to reconnoiter the stream below. They found the whole Kentucky and Tennessee shore for fifteen miles lined with heavy guns, at intervals in no case more than a mile apart, and between these intrenchments for infantry were thrown up. On their

hay, lashed firmly together. She was cast loose at ten o'clock, and very soon afterward the furious thunder-storm commenced. The thunder above and the artillery below kept up a continual and fearful roar. The vessel was about half an hour passing the batteries, and in that time forty-seven shot were fired at her, but not one touched her.—Statement of Captain Walke to the author.

[1] This was formerly the "Pelican Floating Dock," in New Orleans, and had been towed up the river over nine hundred miles.

[2] Each battery was constructed of three heavy coal-barges, lashed together and bolted with iron. The middle one carried the men and the guns, and was bulk-headed all around so as to give four feet of thickness of solid timber, sides and ends. The outside barges had a layer of empty water-tight barrels securely lashed, then layers of dry cotton-wood rails and cotton, closely packed, so that a shot before reaching the middle barge must pass through twenty feet of rails and cotton. The empty barrels were intended as floats, in the event of the outer barges being pierced by shot below water-mark. Each battery had three heavy guns protected by traverses of sand-bags, and carried eighty sharp-shooters.

return, the *Carondelet* silenced a battery opposite Point Pleasant, and Captain Marshall, with a few men, landed and spiked its guns.

That night, at the urgent request of Pope, Foote ordered the *Pittsburg*, Lieutenant Thompson, to run the blockade. It was done, and she arrived at New Madrid at dawn on the 7th, when Captain Walke went down the river with the two gun-boats to silence batteries near Watson's Landing, below Tiptonville (Tennessee), where Pope intended to disembark his troops (then on the steamers that had passed through the canal), on the Tennessee shore, in the rear of Island Number Ten. A few days before, he had established batteries of 32-pounders, under Captain Williams, of the First Regular Infantry, opposite that point.

The troops on the steamers comprised General Paine's division, and consisted of the Tenth, Sixteenth, Twenty-second, and Fifty-first Illinois regiments, with Houghtailing's Battery. A heavy rain-storm was sweeping over the country, but it did not impede the movement. Captain Walke performed his assigned duty admirably, and struck the final blow that secured a victory for the Nationals. At noon he signaled to Pope that the batteries were silenced. The steamers with the troops immediately moved forward, and when they commenced crossing the broad river (which Pope said was the most magnificent spectacle he had ever seen), it was ascertained that the Confederates were abandoning their batteries along that portion of the Tennessee and Kentucky shore. Walke's victory assured the latter that all was lost, and their only thought was concerning safety in flight. There was now equal commotion on Island Number Ten. Positive information concerning the flanking canal had been given at Confederate head-quarters there, but the story was not believed until the steamers were seen emerging from the bayou at New Madrid, when hope forsook them. Sinking their gun-boat, *Grampus*, and six transports in the river between the island and New Madrid, so as to form, as they supposed, effectual obstructions to navigation, they abandoned every thing and fled.

SUNKEN VESSELS IN THE MISSISSIPPI.

It was important to capture the fugitives, and for that purpose Pope directed Stanley and Hamilton, who had come down by land, to cross their divisions. He pushed his troops on toward Tiptonville as fast as they were landed. They met and drove back the Confederates, who were attempting to fly toward Union City. These were joined at Tiptonville that night by many fugitives from Island Number Ten. The wildest confusion prevailed among them. They were driven to the swamps by Pope's advancing forces, and, at four o'clock in the morning,[a] hemmed in on all sides, and finding it impossible to escape, they sur-

[a] April 8, 1862.

rendered unconditionally, laid down their arms, and received each his parole.

At almost the same hour, Commodore Foote received a flag of truce from Island Number Ten, with an offer to surrender the island to him. Up to that time, the Confederates on the island had been ignorant of the disaster that Walke and Pope had inflicted upon their friends below, and those who had fled in that direction expected to find shelter behind the batteries near Tiptonville. There had been grave doubts in the minds of the commanders on the island concerning their ability to hold it, ever since the *Carondelet* ran the blockade,[a] and Beauregard's quick perceptions were satisfied that the siege must soon end in disaster and perhaps disgrace. So, on the morning after the passage of that vessel,[b] he turned over the command on the island to General McCall, leaving McCown in charge of the troops on the Tennessee and Kentucky shores, and, with a considerable body of the best troops, departed for Corinth, in Upper Mississippi, there to prepare to check a formidable movement of the Nationals toward Alabama and Mississippi, by way of Middle Tennessee and the Tennessee River, which we shall consider presently.

[a] April 4, 1862.

[b] April 5.

On assuming command, McCall issued a flaming order announcing it,[1] and within thirty-six hours afterward he, too, satisfied of imminent danger, ordered his infantry and Stewart's battery to the Tennessee shore, in a position favorable to escape, leaving only the artillerists on the island. The latter was the force that offered to surrender to Foote, and the entire number of his prisoners was only seventeen officers, three hundred and sixty-eight private soldiers, four hundred sick, and one hundred men employed on the Confederate vessels. The number of prisoners taken by Pope and Foote together was seven thousand two hundred and seventy-three, including three generals and two hundred and seventy-three field and company officers. The spoils of victory were nearly twenty batteries, with one hundred and twenty-three cannon and mortars,[2] the former varying from 32 to 100-pounders; seven thousand small arms; an immense amount of ammunition on the island and in magazines at points

MAGAZINE OPPOSITE ISLAND NUMBER TEN.

[1] The following is a copy of the order which was found at the Confederate head-quarters on the island:

"SOLDIERS,—We are strangers, commander and commanded, each to the other. Let me tell you who I am. I am a general made by Beauregard—a general selected by Beauregard and Bragg for this command, when they knew it was in peril. They have known me for twenty years; together we have stood on the fields of Mexico. Give them your confidence now; give it to me when I have earned it. Soldiers! the Mississippi valley is intrusted to your courage, to your discipline, to your patience. Exhibit the vigilance and coolness of last night and hold it."

[2] Among the mortars on the island was an ancient one, already alluded to, made of bronze and bearing the name of George the Second of England, which fact declared that it was more than one hundred years old. It was formerly in Jackson Square, New Orleans, where it was regarded as a precious trophy, it having been captured by the Americans from the British during the battle near that city, at the close of 1814 and the beginning of 1815. Many of the cannon were from the Navy Yard at Norfolk. See page 397, volume I.

ANCIENT MORTAR.

along the Kentucky and Tennessee shores; many hundred horses and mules with wagons, et cetera, and four steamers afloat.

Never was a victory more complete and decisive, for very few men escaped and very little property was destroyed.[1] During the whole of his operations in the siege, Pope did not lose a man, nor meet with an accident; and the casualties in the fleet were very few. There did not seem to be evidence of much loss of life on the part of the Confederates; but everywhere, from Beauregard's and McCall's head-quarters on the island to the smallest tent, there were proofs of the greatest haste in leaving. Among other things found at head-quarters was a bundle of important official papers, one of them containing a drawing of Fort Pillow on the river below.

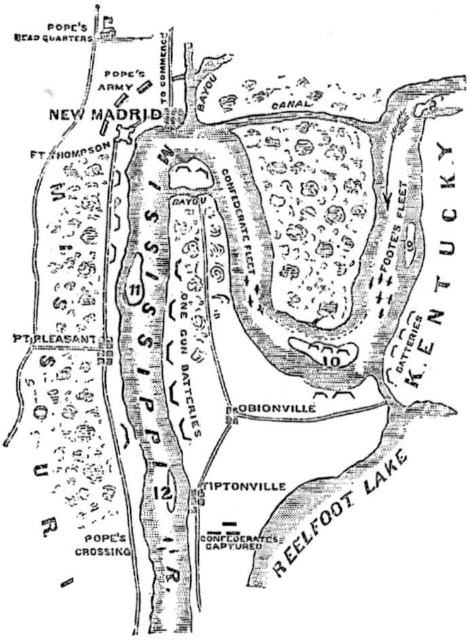

MAP OF THE OPERATIONS OF POPE AND FOOTE.[2]

The victory at Island Number Ten produced the most profound sensation throughout the entire republic. Its importance to each party in the conflict could scarcely be estimated. The announcement of it went over the land simultaneously with that of the hard-won triumph at Shiloh on the Tennessee River,[a] which we shall consider presently, and was followed, a few days afterward, by that of the capture of Fort Pulaski, at the mouth of the Savannah River. Every loyal heart was filled with joy and hope, and Government securities, which were at two and a half and three per cent. below par, immediately commanded a premium. The Confederates almost despaired. It was probable that Memphis, one of their strongholds on the Mississippi, where they had immense workshops and armories, would soon share the fate of Columbus. It was probable that the great river would speedily be patrolled from Cairo to New Orleans by the almost invincible armored vessels of the Government, and the rich supply-country west of that stream be separated from the rest of the confederacy. They also apprehended that the great line of railway running almost parallel with the Mississippi, between Southwestern Tennessee and New Orleans, would be seized

[a] April 7, 1862.

CONFEDERATE HEAD-QUARTERS, ISLAND NUMBER TEN.[3]

1 The value of the captured property was estimated at over a million of dollars. The steamers that were sunk were easily raised.

2 The figures on this map refer to the numbers of the islands.

3 In this little picture is seen a representation of one of the "plantation bells" that Beauregard called for.

by National troops. Panic everywhere prevailed along the "Father of Waters" below Island Number Ten. Martial law was proclaimed in Memphis, and the specie of the banks there was removed to places of supposed safety. Many inhabitants fled; and the troops that "guarded the city," and secessionists that remained, proposed to lay it in ashes if it could not be saved from "northern invaders;" but the mayor somewhat allayed the panic caused by this proposition by publicly proclaiming ("not as magistrate," he said, "but as John Park"), that "he who attempted to fire his neighbor's house, or even his own, whereby it endangers his neighbor's, regardless of judge, jury, or the benefit of clergy, I will have him hung to the first lamp-post, tree, or awning."

The disloyal inhabitants of New Orleans were also filled with the most dreadful apprehensions. The Governor of Louisiana (Moore), who had been chiefly instrumental in that State in bringing on the war, issued a despairing appeal to the people;[1] while in Richmond, the head-quarters of the conspirators, the most gloomy apprehensions were entertained by them and by the disloyal inhabitants. "The trepidations and murmurings, the croakings and prophesyings of doom that have possessed many of the citizens of Richmond during the past week," wrote a resident of that city, "would be enough to make us despair of the republic, if we could suppose the masses of the people of the Confederate States were equally timorous and irresolute."[2]

There were reasons for despondency, for upon every breeze of intelligence from the West, for several weeks preceding, were borne to Richmond

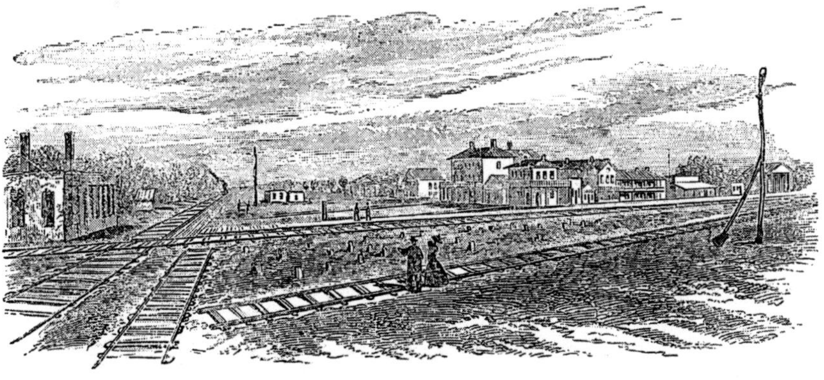

GRAND JUNCTION, MISSISSIPPI.

tidings of disaster to the Confederate cause. There were desperate reasons why the most vigorous efforts should be put forth to stay the southern march of the Nationals; and conscriptions and impressments were commenced.

---

1 "This is not the hour for vain regrets or despondency," said Moore. "No, not even for hesitation. An insolent and powerful foe is already at the castle gate. The current of the mighty river speaks to us of his fleets advancing for our destruction, and the telegraph wires tremble with the news of his advancing columns. In the name of all most dear to us, I entreat you to go and meet him." But there was little disposition to comply with the Government's wishes. When a letter from General Beauregard, which he sent by his Surgeon-General, Dr. Choppin (see note 3, page 238), making an urgent demand for New Orleans to send 5,000 troops to him at once, "to save the city," and it was read by the Surgeon to the First and Second City Brigades, who were called out, their reply was, "We decline to go."

2 Richmond correspondent of the *Memphis Appeal*.

Jackson, in Tennessee, and Grand Junction,[1] on the southern border of that State; Corinth, in Mississippi, and Decatur, in Alabama, all of them along the line of the Charleston and Memphis Railway, that stretches from the Mississippi to the Atlantic seaboard—were made places for the rendezvous of troops from Louisiana, Mississippi, and Alabama. And while Johnston was fleeing southward before the followers of the energetic Mitchel, to join his forces to those of Beauregard, the latter was gathering an army at Corinth to confront a most serious movement of the Nationals up the Tennessee River, already alluded to.

While Grant and Foote were pulling down the strongholds of rebellion in Middle Tennessee and Western Kentucky, the National troops, under Generals Curtis, Sigel, and others, were carrying the standard of the Republic, in triumph into Arkansas, in the grand movement down the Mississippi Valley toward the Gulf. We have observed how Price was expelled from Missouri and driven into Arkansas. He was closely followed by the National forces under the chief command of General Samuel R. Curtis, of Iowa, who crossed the line on the 18th of February, his troops cheering with delight as they saw the old flag waving in triumph over the soil of another of the so-called Confederate States. On the same day, General Halleck sent a thrill of joy to every loyal heart, by telegraphing to General McClellan, "The flag of the Union is floating in Arkansas. . . . The army of the Southwest is doing its duty nobly."

SAMUEL R. CURTIS.

Curtis pushed on, notwithstanding his effective fighting force was continually diminishing, by the planting of guards along his extended line of communication with his sources of supply and re-enforcements. He captured here and there squads of Missouri recruits for Price's army; fought the halting Confederates at the strong positions of Sugar Creek,[2] the Cross Hollows, and other places in mountain defiles; and his cavalry penetrated as far as Fayetteville, the capital of Washington County, near the northwestern border of the State. The Confederates fled so hastily from Cross Hollows that they left behind them their sick and wounded, and stores that they could not take away. They burned their extensive barracks there, left poisoned provisions

---

[1] Grand Junction was a very important point, being at the junction of the Charleston and Memphis Railway and the railway from New Orleans to Jackson, in Tennessee. It was only about two miles northward of the State of Mississippi. During all the time that the Confederates held that section of the country, Grand Junction was the scene of large gatherings of troops. See page 348, volume I.

[2] Here, on the 20th of February, some of Curtis's cavalry, under Colonel Ellis, and Majors McConnell, Wright, and Bolivar, made a desperate charge on a brigade of Louisianians, under Colonel Hubert. Two regiments of infantry, under Colonels Phelps and Heron, and Captain Hayden, with his Dubuque Battery, followed in support of the National cavalry. There was a sharp but short fight, and the Confederates were dispersed. The loss of the Nationals was nineteen, killed and wounded.

in the pathway of their flight,[1] and, setting fire to Confederate stores and buildings at Fayetteville when they left it, went over the range of hills known as the Boston Mountains, in much confusion. This march of the Nationals was one of the most extraordinary of the war. The little army had moved at the rate of twenty miles a day, often fighting, and enduring great privations from inclement weather and insufficient food.

General Price, meanwhile, had been joined by Ben McCulloch, with Texas, Louisiana, and Arkansas troops, and his force had become fully equal in numbers to that of Curtis. The latter, glancing back over his long line of communications, and reflecting on the fact that his troops had been subsisting mostly upon what had been taken from the Confederates since he had entered Arkansas, considered it prudent to retrace his steps, and take a stronger position nearer the Missouri border. He accordingly fell back from Fayetteville to Sugar Creek, not far from Bentonville, the capital of Benton County, Arkansas. On the 1st of March he issued an address to the inhabitants of Arkansas, who had fled from their homes on his approach, to remove from their minds the false impressions which the Confederates had given them of the character of his army and the object of its presence in their State. He assured all peaceable citizens of safety and protection in person and property, and he called upon the deluded ones who had taken up arms to lay them down at once and take an oath of allegiance to their common country.

Curtis did not wait for a response to his friendly communication. He was aware that his foe was rapidly increasing in numbers, and behind the sheltering hills was preparing to strike a heavy blow. Suddenly came the startling intelligence that Price and McCulloch had been joined by General Earl Van Dorn,[a] one of the most dashing and energetic of the Confederate officers, who had lately been appointed[b] commander of the Trans-Mississippi Department;[2] also by General Albert Pike,[3] at the head of a considerable body of half-civilized Indians, making the whole Confederate force, including large numbers of Arkansas compulsory recruits, about twenty-five thousand strong.[4] These were in and near Boston Mountains at the beginning of March. Van Dorn, the senior officer, was in chief command, and he was

[a] March 2, 1862.

[b] Jan. 29.

EARL VAN DORN.

---

[1] They left poisoned provisions at a place called Mud Town, of which forty-two of the officers and soldiers of the Fifth Missouri cavalry partook. Several of them died, and all suffered much.—Halleck's dispatch to McClellan, Feb. 27, 1862.

[2] He had come from Richmond with instructions from Davis to stop the march of the National troops southward.

[3] See page 475, volume I.

[4] Arkansas, Louisiana, and Texas troops under McCulloch, 13,000. Choctaw, Cherokee, Chickasaw, and other Indians, with two white regiments under Pike, about 4,000; and Missouri troops under Price, about 8,000.

rallying the whole Confederate army in that quarter, to drive Curtis back into Missouri. The forces of the latter, of all arms, did not at that time exceed eleven thousand men, with forty-nine pieces of artillery, including a mountain howitzer. Satisfied that he must soon fight a greatly superior force, he at once prepared for the encounter by so arranging his troops as best to present a strong front to the foe from whatever point he might approach. His head-quarters were near Cross Hollows, on the main road and telegraph line from Fayetteville to Springfield.[1]

The advent of General Van Dorn in the Confederate camp was a cause for great rejoicing. Forty heavy guns thundered a welcome, and the chief harangued his troops in a boastful and grandiloquent style.[2] For the purpose of encouraging the people to take up arms, he caused telegraphic dispatches to be published, falsely proclaiming a great battle at Columbus, in which the Nationals had lost three gun-boats and twenty thousand men; and he told his dupes that the way was now opened to drive the invaders from the soil of Arkansas, and give a final and successful blow for a Southern Confederacy.[3] Van Dorn's preliminaries were followed by vigorous measures. Two days afterward his troops were in motion for offensive action, and animated by a full expectation of gaining a victory whenever they should meet the Nationals.

---

[1] The following was the disposition of the National forces on the 4th of March. The First and Second Divisions, under General Sigel and Colonel Asboth, were at Cooper's farm, near Osage Springs, four miles southwest of Bentonville, the capital of Benton County, under general orders to move round to Sugar Creek, about fourteen miles eastward. The Third Division, under General Jefferson C. Davis (acting major-general), was at Sugar Creek; and the Fourth Division, under Colonel E. A. Carr (acting brigadier-general), was near Cross Hollows, about twelve miles from Sugar Creek. Large detachments were out for forage and information, under Colonel Vandever, Major Conrad, and others, and some of them were too distant to engage in the battle that speedily ensued.*

[2] "Soldiers," he cried, "behold your leader! He comes to show you the way to glory and immortal renown. He comes to hurl back the minions of the despots at Washington, whose ignorance, licentiousness, and brutality are equaled only by their craven natures. They come to free your slaves, lay waste your plantations, burn your villages, and abuse your loving wives and beautiful daughters." Van Dorn had sent forth a characteristic address to "the young men of Arkansas, Texas, and Northern Louisiana." "We have voted to be free," he said. "We must now fight to be free, or present to the world the humiliating spectacle of a nation of braggarts, more contemptible than the tyrants who seek to enslave us. The flag of our country is waving on the southern borders of Missouri—planted there by my hands, under authority from our chief magistrate. It represents all that is dear to us in life. Shall it wave there in melancholy loneliness, as a fall leaf in our primeval forests, or shall its beautiful field and bright stars flaunt in the breeze over the bright battalions of Arkansas, of Texas, and of Louisiana, as they are marshaling to do battle with Missouri for victory, for honor, and for independence? Awake, young men of Arkansas, and arm! Beautiful maidens of Louisiana, smile not upon the craven youth who may linger by your hearth when the rude blast of war is sounding in your ears! Texas chivalry, to arms! Hardships and hunger, disease and death are preferable to slavish subjugation; and a nation with a bright page in history and a glorious epitaph is better than a vassaled land with honor lost, and a people sunk in infamy."

[3] General Curtis's second report to General Halleck.

---

* The following was the composition of General Curtis's army at this time:—

First Division, commanded by Colonel Peter J. Osterhaus, consisted of the Thirty-sixth Illinois, Twelfth and Seventeenth Missouri, a battalion of the Third Missouri; the Twenty-fifth and Twenty-fourth Illinois, under Colonel Coler, two battalions of Illinois cavalry, and batteries A and B, twelve guns. There was also a brigade of two regiments under Colonel Greasel.

The Second Division, commanded by Colonel (acting Brigadier-General) Asboth, consisted of two brigades, the first commanded by Colonel Schaeffer, and composed of the Second Missouri and Second Ohio Battery, six guns, under Lieutenant Chapman. The Second Brigade, Colonel Joliet, was composed of the Fifteenth Missouri; the Sixth and a battalion of the Fourth Missouri cavalry; and a flying battery of six guns, under Captain Elbert. These two divisions were commanded by General Sigel.

The Third Division, under Brigadier-General J. C. Davis, consisted of two brigades; the first composed of the Eighth, Eighteenth, and Twenty-second Indiana; and an Indiana battery of six guns was commanded by Colonel Barton. The second, commanded by Colonel White, was composed of the Thirty-seventh Illinois and Ninth Missouri, and the First Missouri cavalry, with a battery of four guns.

The Fourth Division, under Colonel Eugene A. Carr, was composed of two brigades. The first, under Colonel Dodge, consisting of the Fourth Iowa, Thirty-fifth Illinois, and an Iowa battery under Captain Jones. The Second Brigade, under Colonel Vandever, was composed of the Ninth Iowa, Twenty-fifth Missouri, Third Illinois Cavalry, and a Dubuque battery of six guns under Captain Hayden. There were also two battalions of the Third Iowa cavalry under Captain Bussey, and a battery of four mountain howitzers under Captain Stevens, that were not brigaded. There was also a battalion of cavalry under Major Bowen, acting as General Curtis's body-guard.

The morning of the 5th[a] (when Van Dorn moved) was blustery, and snow covered the ground. Curtis was unsuspicious of the movements of his enemy until two o'clock in the afternoon, when scouts and fugitive citizens came hurrying to his tent, in which he was writing, with the startling intelligence that the Confederates were approaching in large force from the direction of Fayetteville, that their artillery had already passed that place, and that their cavalry would be at Elm Springs, not more than twelve miles from head-quarters, that night. Curtis at once determined to concentrate his forces in Sugar Creek Valley, not far from Mottsville, and a short distance south of Pea Ridge, a portion of a spur of the Ozark Mountains, on the highway between Fayetteville and Springfield, where there was a good point for defense and an abundance of water, and where General Davis had already thrown up intrenchments.[1] He gave orders accordingly, and there, on the morning of the 6th of March,[b] the greater portion of his troops were gathered, excepting those under General Sigel and a few who were yet abroad. Sigel had moved his camp[c] from Osage Springs to a point nearer Bentonville, to secure a better position for obtaining forage. He now found his command, and a train of two hundred wagons, placed in a perilous position by Van Dorn's sudden and unexpected advance; but, as we shall observe presently, he extricated them with small loss.

[a] March, 1862.

[b] 1862.

[c] March 1.

Van Dorn had marched rapidly from his camp near the Boston Mountains, in the edge of the Indian Country, about fifty miles from Pea Ridge, accompanied by Generals Price, McCulloch, McIntosh, and Pike. Informed of the strength of Curtis's position in front, he left the direct road at Fayetteville, and, marching more westward through Bentonville, struck the highway near the State line, about eight miles north of Sugar Creek, in the rear of the Nationals, thereby, as he thought, cutting off Curtis's supplies and re-enforcements, and securing him and his army as captives. It was while he was on that march from Fayetteville that his approach was made known.[d] He encamped that night at Cross Hollows,[2] which Carr had left; and Sigel, by a skillful movement in sending cavalry to Osage Springs to cover his right flank, safely conducted his train from McKissick's farm, west of Bentonville, to the latter place, and secured it from the grasp of the Confederates. Leaving a rear-guard (Thirty-sixth Illinois and a portion of the Second Missouri) at Bentonville, he sent his train forward toward Sugar Creek. Mistaking an order, Colonel Schaeffer with the Second Missouri also went forward, leaving only about six hundred men and five pieces of light artillery behind. These were surrounded by a battalion of cavalry forming Price's body-guard, and Louisiana infantry. Fortunately, Sigel had remained with his rear-guard, and he handled his little band so skillfully and bravely that they cut their way through, and, changing front, they fought and fell

[d] March 5.

---

[1] That valley is low, and from a quarter to half a mile wide. The hills are high on both sides, and the main road from Fayetteville, by Cross Hollows to Keitsville, intercepts the valley nearly at right angles. The road from Fayetteville, by Bentonville, to Keitsville is quite a détour, but it also comes up the Sugar Creek Valley.—General Sturgis's Second Report.

[2] This is a place at the head waters of the Osage Creek, and not far from those of Sugar Creek. It was so named because three hollows, or ravines, from 75 to 100 feet wide, there cross each other. It was to this strong position that General Price fled when he left Missouri, and from which Curtis drove him in the march to Fayetteville.

back alternately along the cross road leading through Leetown to the Elkhorn Tavern, until they were met by re-enforcements sent out by Curtis, when the pursuit ended. In this gallant affair Sigel lost twenty-eight killed and wounded and about fifty made prisoners.[1] The latter were chiefly Schaeffer's men, who had fallen into an ambuscade. The remainder joined the forces of Davis and Carr at the west end of Pea Ridge, an elevated table-land broken by ravines, and inclosed in a large bend of Sugar Creek.

Van Dorn completed his flank movement on the night of the 6th,[a] and proceeded to attack the Nationals early the following morning. He left a small force to make a feint on their front, while Pike, with his Indian followers, took position about two miles to their right, to divert their attention from the main point of attack in their rear. Price occupied the main road not far from the Elkhorn Tavern, north of Curtis's camp, and McCulloch and McIntosh lay north of Sigel and Davis, after the National army had changed position, as we shall observe presently. In the mean time Curtis had been busy in felling trees to block the avenues of approach to his camp, and the roads running parallel to the main highway. Breastworks had been speedily constructed at important points, and a battery had been planted and masked near the passage of the main road across Sugar Creek, under the direction of General Davis. His position was strong.

[a] March. 1862.

On the morning of the 7th, Curtis was first informed of Van Dorn's flank movement, which seriously threatened the communication between his camp and his resources. The peril was extreme, and prompt action was necessary. He at once changed his front to rear, bringing his line of battle across Pea Ridge, and prepared to fight. The number of his foes was more than double that of his own, but there was no alternative. He must either fight or make a perilous flight. His ample preparations to receive Van Dorn in his front were now useless, and he was compelled to meet the skillful Mississippian on a field of the latter's own choosing. In that change of front, the First and Second divisions, under Sigel and Asboth, were on his left, the Third, under Davis, composed his center, and Carr's Fourth division formed his right. His line of battle stretched between three and four miles, from Sugar Creek to Elkhorn Tavern. Confronting this was the Confederate line, with Price and his Missourians on their right, McIntosh in the center, and McCulloch on their left. A broad and deep ravine called Cross Timber Hollow, covered with fallen trees, intersected the lines of both armies, and made maneuvering very difficult.

ALEXANDER ASBOTH.

At about half-past ten in the

[1] Congratulating his troops on the 15th of March, Sigel said of this affair—"On the retreat from Bentonville to Sugar Creek, a distance of ten miles, you cut your way through an enemy at least five times stronger than yourselves."

morning,[a] Colonel Osterhaus was sent out with a detachment of the Third Iowa cavalry and some light artillery (Davidson's Peoria Battery), supported by the First Missouri cavalry, Colonel Ellis, and Twenty-second Indiana, Colonel Hendricks, to fall upon Van Dorn's center before he could fully form in battle order. Just as this movement had commenced, and Curtis was giving instructions to division commanders at Asboth's tent, word came to him that his pickets, under Major Weston (Twenty-fourth Missouri), on his extreme right, near Elkhorn Tavern, had been heavily attacked. Colonel Carr was at once sent to the support of Weston, and a severe battle ensued. Thus opened the fight on that eventful morning. Meanwhile Osterhaus had advanced about a mile beyond Leetown, and attacked what seemed to be a small body of Confederates in the edge of a wood and shrub-oak thicket. He brought three cannon (Davidson's Battery) to bear upon them, and they were apparently dispersed. Then he moved forward with the Iowa cavalry, to clear the woods of any insurgents that might be left, when he fell into a trap which had been laid for him. The woods swarmed with Confederates. The charge of the cavalry was broken, and they were driven back in disorder upon their supports, hotly pursued by Van Dorn's horse and foot. Two guns were captured by the latter, and a total rout and dispersion of the attacking column seemed inevitable, when General Davis and his division, who had bivouacked on the alert all the night before, came to the rescue, with General Sigel, who appeared on the Confederate flank. Curtis had at first ordered Davis to the relief of Carr on his extreme right, but, deeming the peril to Osterhaus the most imminent, he directed him to hasten to his aid. Davis changed his march skillfully under fire, and advancing through Leetown his Second brigade,[1] commanded by Colonel Julius White, he was soon fighting heavily with McCulloch and McIntosh, and Pike's Indians, under himself and Ross. The battle was fierce and destructive. The Confederates were continually re-enforced. Davis and Osterhaus recoiled and recovered alternately; and the line of battle swayed like a pendulum. The issue of the strife seemed doubtful, when the Eighteenth Indiana, who had been ordered to attack the Confederate flank and rear, performed the duty so vigorously with ball and bayonet that they drove them from that part of the field, strewed it with the dead and wounded bodies of Texans and Indians, and recaptured the two cannon which, amid the shouts of the victors, were instantly trained upon their foe. That regiment and the Twenty-second (Colonel H. D. Washburn), from the same State, were conspicuous for their gallantry on the occasion. The latter had engaged a large force of Arkansas troops and Indians, and put them to flight.

[a] March 7, 1862.

The Confederates had now become fugitives in turn. In their flight they left their dead and wounded on the field, among whom were Generals McCulloch and McIntosh, mortally hurt. The insurgents tried to re-form at their former position on the Bentonville road, but the arrival, at about this time, of Sigel with two batteries of heavy artillery (18-pounders) settled the issue of the day. After a brief but sharp artillery duel, the Confederates were driven back, and Sigel's heavy guns, with Osterhaus's command, were

---

[1] See sub-note, page 252.

moved toward the right to assist Colonel Carr, if necessary. The day was fast wearing away, and, there being no indications of a disposition on the part of the Confederates to renew the fight, Davis's command bivouacked on the field they had so nobly assisted in winning.[1]

While the battle was raging in the center, Curtis's right wing was heavily pressed. Colonel Carr had moved up the main road toward Elkhorn Tavern; Colonel Dodge's brigade filing off to the road leading from that place to Bentonville, where Captain Jones, of the Iowa Battery, opened upon the Confederates, and a smart artillery fight ensued, in which infantry were engaged. Colonel Vandever's brigade passed about half a mile beyond the tavern, and Captain Hayden's Dubuque battery at about nine o'clock also opened upon the Confederates.[2] Very soon there was fighting along the whole line of Carr's division, and one of the guns of the Dubuque battery was captured by the foe. So fierce and heavy was the work of the Confederates, that Carr was driven back a short distance after an hour's hard fighting. Still hard pressed, he fought on. He sent for re-enforcements, but all Curtis could spare were a few cavalry, his body-guard, and a little mountain howitzer, under Major Bowen. He told the gallant Colonel to stand firm, and he did so. Again, when Carr thought he could hold out no longer, Curtis sent him word to "persevere" and he should receive succor. He did so at a fearful cost—how fearful, the records of the sad havoc made in the ranks of the Fourth and Ninth Iowa, and Twenty-fourth and Twenty-fifth Missouri, bear witness. A little later, when Curtis was satisfied that his left and center were safe, he sent first some artillery and a battalion of infantry to Carr's aid. Then he ordered General Asboth to move to the right with his division, by the Fayetteville road, and take position at the Elkhorn Tavern, while Sigel should re-enforce Davis, and, if proper, press toward the Elkhorn also. Asboth was accompanied by the Commanding General, who arrived at Carr's position at about five o'clock, and found him severely wounded in the arm, but fighting bravely. Many of his officers were disabled, and his dead and maimed, composing nearly one-fourth of his entire command, strewed the ground, over which he had been pushed back about a mile. For seven hours he had contested the field inch by inch, under a continuous fire.

The re-enforcements were timely, and prevented more severe disaster. General Asboth planted his cannon in the road and opened a heavy fire at short range, but was soon severely wounded, while his guns became silenced for want of ammunition. The fight, for a time, was very fierce. The Second Missouri regiment became hotly engaged; and the Fourth Iowa, who were falling back in good order, after exhausting their ammunition, quickly obeyed a command to make a bayonet charge, and so recovered the field they had abandoned. One of Curtis's body-guard was shot dead, and an orderly near the General was hit with a bullet. The pressure on his line was yet heavy

---

1 This has been called The Battle of Leetown, it having been fought near that village.

2 Colonel Vandever had been to Huntsville, in Madison County, for the purpose of capturing a regiment of insurgents there. These had left two days before. On receiving a message from General Curtis, announcing the approach of Van Dorn, Vandever made a forced march of forty-one miles to the National camp, making only three halts, of fifteen minutes each, during the entire distance. The infantry consisted of the Ninth Iowa and Twenty-fifth Missouri. Vandever arrived on the evening of the 6th, and went into the fight refreshed. Another expedition under Major Conrad, consisting of about six hundred infantry, a section of artillery, and a battalion of cavalry which had been sent toward the borders of the Indian Nation, did not return in time to engage in the battle.

and unabated, and Asboth had directed his now useless cannon to be taken back to a place of safety, when a courier came from Sigel to herald his near approach. Animated by these tidings, the Nationals stood firm until their ammunition was entirely exhausted and night fell. The Confederates fired the last shot, but the Nationals held the field.[1] The wearied Union troops slept that night on their arms. Their right had suffered disaster, but their center had driven the Confederates from the battle-ground, and their left was untouched. In such condition (the lacking being supplied with ammunition), they awaited the dawn to renew the conflict. Their foe, severely smitten and disheartened by the loss of two generals and scores of maimed and slaughtered comrades, were quite willing to have an opportunity for repose. Both armies lay among the dead and dying during that gloomy night.

Van Dorn, who had been a greater part of the day in command of the troops that fought Carr, now concentrated his whole available force on Curtis's right. He lodged at the Elkhorn Tavern that night, and made preparations to open the battle in the morning. Curtis was vigilant, and easily penetrated his enemy's designs; so, notwithstanding the weariness of his troops, he effected a change of front during the darkness. At two o'clock in the morning he was joined by Sigel and his command, who had been compelled to make a wide circuit in order to reach that position, and at a little after sunrise the Nationals were almost ready for battle, the whole four divisions so posted as to fight Van Dorn with vigor.

Curtis and his troops were in fine spirits, and felt confident of victory. The silence of the Confederates so late in the morning seemed ominous of weakness, and when a stir was observed among them, the General, fearing they might be moving off, did not wait for Asboth and Sigel to get into position, but ordered Davis, who occupied the center in the new line, to open the battle. Davis at once deployed Colonel Pattison's brigade a few hundred yards to the right of the Fayetteville road, to support Klaus's First Indiana battery, which was placed at the edge of an open field, between the hills at Elkhorn Tavern and the National camp. Davidson's battery was placed in a similar position on the left of the road, supported by White's brigade. These batteries opened fire briskly, and were responded to with terrible energy from batteries which the Confederates had planted during the night, some of their heavy guns sending raking shot, and compelling the National right to fall back to avoid them.

The battle-line was soon perfected, with Asboth and Sigel a little to the rear of the remainder. Curtis well knew the ground and the relative position of his foe. He ordered his right to move forward to a position occupied the night before, while the left was so extended as to command Pea Ridge and make a flank movement on that wing almost impossible. Upon an elevation on the extreme right, which commanded Van Dorn's center and left, he planted the Dubuque battery, with orders for the right wing to support it, and very soon its commander, Hayden, opened a galling fire on the Confederates. Captain Davidson, with his First Iowa battery, also opened fire on their center, and thus skirmishing was kept up until Sigel's command on the left was in perfect readiness, when the decisive action commenced.

[1] This was called by the Confederates the Battle of Elkhorn.

Sigel first ordered Colonel Coler to post his Twenty-fifth Illinois along a fence in open view of the Confederate batteries, which immediately opened fire on them. At the same time, Sigel placed a battery of six guns on a rise of ground in their rear. Then the Twelfth Missouri wheeled into line on the right of Coler's regiment, and another battery of heavy guns was planted in a similar position behind these. Then other regiments and other batteries were brought into line; and, when all were in readiness, the infantry lay down in front of the heavy guns, and a terrible cannonade was opened. Battery after battery of the Confederates was silenced in the course of two hours, and so horrible was the tempest of iron that fell upon Van Dorn and his followers that they were compelled to fly to the shelter of the ravines of Cross-Timber Hollow. Sigel's infantry at the same time crept steadily forward, and the troops of the center and right pressed onward and joined in the fight. When the Confederates fled, Sigel's whole division were seen climbing up and occupying the rugged hills from which the insurgents had been driven.[1]

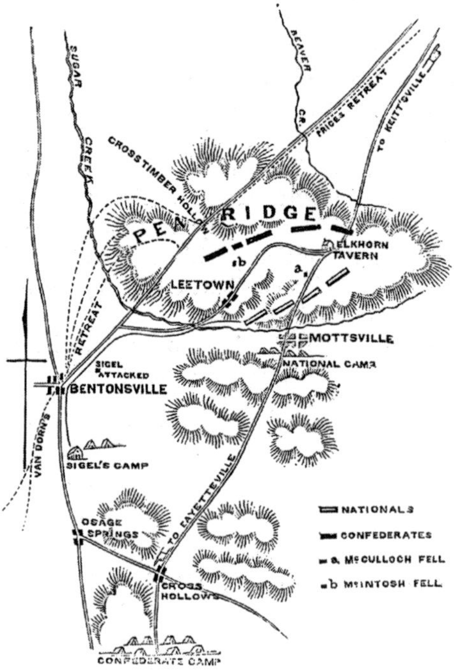

BATTLE-FIELD OF PEA RIDGE.

The flight of Van Dorn's troops was so sudden, rapid, and scattering, that it was difficult for Curtis to determine which way to follow them with the best effect.[2] General Sigel pushed forward along the main road toward Keitsville, where General Price had been posted. He too had fled, and the Confederate army, so strong and so confident of victory twenty-four hours before, was broken into fragments.[3]

---

[1] "The upward movement of the gallant Thirty-sixth Illinois," said Curtis, in his report, "with its dark-blue line of men and its gleaming bayonets, steadily rose from base to summit, when it dashed forward into the forest, driving and scattering the rebels from these commanding heights. The Twelfth Missouri, far in advance of others, rushed into the enemy's lines, bearing off a flag and two pieces of artillery. Everywhere our line moved forward and the foe as gradually withdrew. The roar of cannon and small arms was continuous, and no force could then withstand the converging line and concentrated cross-fire of our gallant troops. Our guns continued some time after the rebel fire ceased, and the rebels had gone down into the deep caverns through which they had begun their precipitate flight. Finally, our firing ceased. The enemy suddenly vanished."

[2] "Following down the main road, which enters a deep cañon, I saw some straggling teams and men running in great trepidation through the gorges of the mountain. I directed a battery to move forward, which threw a few shots at them, followed by a pursuit of cavalry, comprised of the Benton Hussars, and my escort from Bowen's battalion, which was all the cavalry convenient at the time. General Sigel also followed in pursuit toward Keitsville, while I returned, trying to check a movement which led my forces north, where I was confident a frightened foe was not likely to go. I soon found the rebel forces had divided and gone in every direction, but it was several hours before I learned that the main force, after entering the cañon, had turned short to the right, following ravines which led into the Huntsville road in a due south direction. General Sigel followed, some miles north, toward Keitsville, firing on the retreating force that ran away; Colonel Bussy, with cavalry and the little howitzers, followed beyond Bentonville; I camped on the field, and made provision for burying the dead and care of the wounded."—General Curtis, in his official report.

[3] Reports of General Curtis and his subordinate officers; also of Generals Van Dorn and Price.

The hard struggle during those early days of Spring,[a] in the extreme northwestern corner of Arkansas, called by the general name of the BATTLE OF PEA RIDGE,[1] notwithstanding its magnitude, was not of very great importance in its bearing upon the results of the war. There was heavy loss incurred by both parties.[2] Although victory was awarded to the Nationals, the spoils that fell into their hands were of inconsiderable consequence, for Van Dorn managed very skillfully in carrying away nearly all of his artillery and baggage. Indeed, his whole design in giving battle on the morning of the 8th was to blind Curtis to the fact that he was withdrawing his troops and materials of war. His army was not captured, nor was it more than temporarily dispersed. There was great gallantry displayed on both sides, sufficient to receive the highest praise from, and give the greatest satisfaction to, the friends of each,[3] but a stain that cannot be effaced tarnishes the glory of all the achievements of the Confederates on that occasion, because of their employment of Indians in that campaign, whose savage atrocities on the field of Pea Ridge are too well authenticated to be denied.[4]

[a] March 6, 7, 8, 1862.

Both parties tacitly agreed to fight no more in that exhausted section of the State, and both soon disappeared from the scene of this conflict. Van Dorn collected his scattered forces on the road between the Elkhorn Tavern and Bentonville, about eight miles from the battle-field, made an arrange-

---

1 The Confederates gave it the general title of Battle of Elkhorn.

2 General Curtis reported his loss at 1.351 killed, wounded, and missing, of whom more than one-half (701) were of Colonel Carr's division. Among the slain was Colonel Hendricks. The loss of the Confederates was never reported. It could not have been less than that of the Nationals. Pollard (i. 277) says Van Dorn estimated his entire loss at "about 600."

3 Van Dorn wrote to his superiors at Richmond, saying, "During the whole of this engagement I was with the Missourians under Price, and I have never seen better fighters than these Missouri troops, or more gallant leaders than General Price and his officers. From the first to the last shot, they continually rushed on, and never yielded an inch they had won; and when at last they had orders to fall back, they retired steadily and with cheers."

In a stirring address to his troops from "Camp Pea Ridge," a week after the battle, Sigel said: "You may look with pride on the few days just passed, during which you have so gloriously defended the flag of the Union. From two o'clock on the morning of the sixth, when you left McKissick's farm, until four o'clock in the afternoon of the ninth, when you arrived from Keitsville in the common encampment, you marched fifty miles, fought three battles, took not only a battery and a flag from the enemy, but more than one hundred and fifty prisoners. . . . You have done your duty, and you can justly claim your share in the common glory of this victory. But let us not be partial, unjust, or haughty. Let us not forget that alone we were too weak to perform the great work before us. Let us acknowledge the great services done by all the brave soldiers of the Third and Fourth divisions, and always keep in mind that 'united we stand, divided we fall.' Let us hold out and push the work through—not by mere words and great clamor—but by good marches, by hardships and fatigues, by strict discipline and effective battles.

"Columbus has fallen, Memphis will follow, and if you do in future as you have done in these days of trial, the time will soon come when you will pitch your tents on the beautiful shores of the Arkansas River, and there meet our own iron-clad propellers at Little Rock and Fort Smith. Therefore keep alert, my friends, and look forward with confidence."

4 According to the statement of eye-witnesses, and a correspondence between Generals Curtis and Van Dorn, commenced when the latter asked (March 9th) the privilege of burying his dead, the Indians, under Pike and Ross, tomahawked, scalped, and shamefully mangled the bodies of National soldiers. These Indians, many of whom claimed to be civilized, were maddened with liquor, it is said, before the battle of the 7th, that they might allow the savage nature of their race to have unchecked development. In their fury they respected none of the usages of war, but scalped the helpless wounded, and committed atrocities too horrible to mention. When Curtis made the charge against these allies of the insurgents, Van Dorn did not deny it, but sought to break its force by accusing the Germans in Curtis's army of murdering prisoners of war.

We have already observed (pages 474 to 477, inclusive, volume I.) how the conspirators had tampered with the civilized and half-civilized Indians in the regions bordering on Kansas and Texas, and how in August, 1861. the Cherokees tendered their support to the Confederate cause. That was after the battle of Wilson's Creek, which the emissaries of the Confederates made the Indians believe was an overwhelming defeat to the Unionists, and utter destruction of the National power in Missouri. The battle of Bull's Run was represented as a complete discomfiture of the Government; and the flight of the Union army from that field, and the death of Lyon,

ment with Curtis for burying the Confederate dead, and, after accomplishing that humane object, withdrew; Curtis gave his army ample rest on the field of his victory, and finding no foe to fight in that section of Arkansas, he marched in a southeasterly direction to Batesville, the capital of Independence County, on the White River, where he arrived on the 6th of May.

---

and the falling back of the Union troops in Missouri after the battle of Wilson's Creek, fixed the impression on the minds of the Indians that henceforth the Confederate "Government" would be the only legitimate and powerful one on which they could rely.

While Chief Ross and his associates were perplexed by indecision, Ben. McCulloch and his Texans, who, as we have seen, abandoned Price in Missouri, marched to the Indian border, and required the Creeks and Cherokees to decide immediately to which cause they would adhere, on penalty of having their country ravaged by 20,000 Texas and Arkansas troops. This produced the council at Tahlequah on the 20th of August, and the message of Chief Ross, printed on page 476, volume I. A large minority of both nations, led by the Creek Chief Opothleyolo, resisted the Confederates and their Indian adherents. Between these and the Indian insurgents a battle was fought on the 9th of December, 1861, on Bushy Creek, 180 miles west of Fort Smith, when Opothleyolo and his followers, as we have observed, were driven into Kansas. The Indian Territory was then left in the undisputed possession of the Confederates; and there it was that Pike collected about 4,000 warriors, who appeared in the Battle of Pea Ridge. This was the only battle in the war in which any considerable number of Indians were engaged; and it was agreed by the Confederate officers that they damaged their cause more than they aided it. Pike and his Indians soon afterward disappeared from the stage, and were not again summoned to action. In his official report, General Van Dorn does not mention that any assistance was derived from the plumed Pike and his dusky followers. That degenerate Bostonian (see note 1, page 475, volume I.) soon took off his Indian costume and was hidden in the shadows of obscurity until the close of the war, when he re-appeared for a moment as a suppliant for mercy, and was granted a full pardon by President Johnson.

CHAPTER X.

GENERAL MITCHEL'S INVASION OF ALABAMA.—THE BATTLES OF SHILOH.

ET us return to Tennessee, and observe what Generals Grant and Buell did immediately after the fall of Fort Donelson, and the flight of the Confederates, civil and military, from Nashville.

We left General Grant at the Tennessee capital, in consultation with General Buell.[a] His praise was upon every loyal lip. His sphere of action had just been enlarged. On hearing of his glorious victory at Fort Donelson, General Halleck had assigned[b] him to the command of the new District of West Tennessee, which embraced the territory from Cairo, between the Mississippi and Cumberland Rivers, to the northern borders of the State of Mississippi, with his headquarters in the field. It was a wide and important stage for action, and he did not rest on the laurels he had won on the Tennessee and Cumberland, but at once turned his attention to the business of moving vigorously forward in the execution of his part of the grand scheme for expelling the armed Confederates from the Mississippi valley. For that purpose he made his headquarters temporarily at Fort Henry, where General Lewis Wallace was in command, and began a new organization of his forces for further and important achievements. Foote's flotilla was withdrawn from the Cumberland, and a part of it was sent up the Tennessee River, while its commander, as we have observed, went down the Mississippi with a more powerful naval armament to co-operate with the land troops against Columbus, Hickman, Island Number Ten, and New Madrid.

[a] Feb. 27, 1862.

[b] Feb. 14.

An important objective was Corinth, in Northern Mississippi, at the intersection of the Charleston and Memphis and Mobile and Ohio railroads, and the seizure of that point, as a strategic position of vital importance, was Grant's design. It would give the National forces control of the great railway communications between the Mississippi and the East, and the border slave-labor States and the Gulf of Mexico. It would also facilitate the capture of Memphis by forces about to move down the Mississippi, and would give aid to the important movement of General Curtis in Arkansas. Grant was taking vigorous measures to accomplish this desirable end, when an order came from General Halleck,[c] directing him to turn over his forces to his junior in rank, General C. F. Smith, and to remain himself at Fort Henry. Grant was astonished and mortified. He was unconscious of acts deserving of the displeasure of his superior, and he requested Halleck

[c] March 4.

to relieve him entirely from duty. That officer, made satisfied that no fault could justly be found with Grant, wrote a letter to head-quarters that removed all misconception, and on the 14th of March the latter was restored to the chief command.[1] This satisfied the loyal people, who were becoming impatient because of seeming injustice toward a successful commander.

Meanwhile the troops that gathered at Fort Henry had been sent up the Tennessee in transports. The unarmored gun-boats *Tyler* and *Lexington* had gone forward as far as Pittsburg Landing, at the termination of a road

CHARLES FERGUSON SMITH.[3]

from Corinth, and about twenty miles from that place. There they were assailed by a six-gun battery, which, after a mutual cannonade, was silenced. When the report of this success reached General Smith, sixty-nine transports, with over thirty thousand troops, were moved up the river.[2] The advance (Forty-sixth Ohio, Colonel Worthington) landed at Savannah,[a] the capital of Hardin County, on the eastern bank of the stream, and took military possession of the place. General Smith, whose head-quarters were on the steamer *Leonora*, immediately sent out scouts in the direction of Corinth, where Beauregard was straining every nerve to concentrate an army to oppose this formidable movement. Their reports satisfied him that the Confederates were not then more than ten thousand strong in his front, and that their capture or dispersion would be an easy matter. He hoped to be allowed to move upon them at once, and, as a preparatory measure, he ordered General Lewis Wallace, with his division, to Crump's Landing on the west side of the river, four miles above Savannah, and thence sixteen miles westward to Purdy, a village on the railway between Humbolt, in Tennessee, and Corinth, to destroy portions of the road and important bridges in that vicinity, and especially one with extended trestle-work at each end, a few miles south of Purdy. This was a hazardous undertaking, for General Cheatham, with a large force of the Confederates, was lying near, in the direction of Pittsburg Landing. But it was successfully accomplished by a battalion of Ohio cavalry, under Major Hayes, in the midst of a series of heavy thunder-

[a] March 10, 1862.

---

[1] It seems that some malignant or jealous person had made Grant's consultation with Buell at Nashville seem like an offense against General Halleck, his immediate chief; and the march of General Smith's forces up the Cumberland from Fort Donelson was condemned as a military blunder. Grant's inability, on account of sufficient reasons, to report the exact condition of his forces at that time was also a cause of complaint; and, without inquiry, he was suspended from the chief command for ten days.—See Coppée's *Grant and his Campaigns*. Note on page 81.

[2] "It is difficult to conceive any thing more orderly and beautiful," wrote General Wallace to the author, soon afterward, "than the movement of this army up the river. The transports of each division were assembled together in the order of march. At a signal, they put out in line, loaded to their utmost capacity with soldiers and materials. Cannon fired, regiments cheered, bands played. Looking up the river, after the boats had one by one taken their places, a great dense column of smoke, extending far as the eye could reach, marked the sinuosities of the stream and hung in the air like a pall. It was, indeed, a sight never to be forgotten."

[3] From a photograph by Brady, taken before the war.

showers. A train, crowded with Confederate troops, came down while the bridge and trestle-work were burning, and escaped capture by reversing the engine and fleeing at railway speed.

PITTSBURG LANDING, IN 1866.

General Sherman's division was sent farther up the river to Tyler's Landing,[a] at the mouth of Yellow Creek, just within the borders of Mississippi, to strike the Charleston and Memphis railway at Burnsville, a little east of Corinth. Floods prevented his reaching the railway, when, by order of General Smith, he turned back and disembarked at Pittsburg Landing, and took post in the vicinity of Shiloh Meeting-house, a little log-building in the forest, about two miles from the Tennessee River, that belonged to the Methodists. General Stephen A. Hurlbut took possession of Pittsburg Landing[1] without opposition, and held it in quiet until the night of the 20th,[b] when a scouting party, composed of detachments of the Fourth Illinois and Fifth Ohio cavalry, three hundred and fifty strong, and nearly one hundred infantry, all under Lieutenant-Colonel Heath, went out in the direction of the railway, near

[a] March 14, 1862.

[b] March.

SHILOH MEETING-HOUSE.

1 Pittsburg Landing was the projected site of a commercial river-town, to rival Savannah, below it, and Hamburg, above it. The only buildings there were a store-house on a terrace, at the mouth of a ravine near the shore, and a dwelling-house, on the high bank above, which served as a post-office. When the writer visited the Landing, in April, 1866, only a few scattered bricks and some charred wood were to be seen on the site of the buildings. In the view here given, the spectator is looking down the Tennessee River from across the ravine and creek, at the mouth of which, as we shall hereafter observe, the gun-boats *Tyler* and *Lexington* lay on Sunday night, April 6th and 7th. The river had been made brim full by recent rains at the time of the author's visit.

Iuka. These encountered, and, in a skirmish in Black Jack Forest, dispersed, six hundred Confederate horsemen, on their way to surprise and attack Hurlbut's encampment.[1] These had come from Beauregard's army at Corinth.

While the movement up the Tennessee was going on, General Buell's army was slowly making preparations to march southward overland and join Grant's at Savannah. It was not until the 28th of March, when Grant's position had become a perilous one, as we shall observe, that Buell left Nashville. A part of his force, under General Mitchel, went in the direction of Huntsville, in northern Alabama, to seize and hold the Memphis and Charleston railway at that place, while the main body under Buell, composed of the division of Generals Thomas, McCook, Nelson, Crittenden, and T. J. Wood, moved more to the westward by way of Columbia, at which place they left the railway.

General James S. Negley was left in command of reserves at Nashville, where he immediately commenced casting up strong fortifications on the surrounding heights for its defense. Among these, Fort Negley was the most formidable and conspicuous. It was erected on the most commanding hill near the city; and on other eminences redoubts and block-houses were soon built.

JAMES S. NEGLEY.

The Confederates under Johnston, as we have observed, hastened from Nashville to Murfreesboro, twenty-five miles below, on the railway leading to Chattanooga.[2] From that point they went across the country in a southwesterly direction, to form a junction with the

---

[1] This skirmish was maintained by the advanced company of Illinois cavalry, under Captain George Dodge.

[2] It was at about this time that John Morgan, the famous guerrilla chief, first became conspicuous. The Confederate Congress had given its sanction to what the Spaniards call guerrilla warfare, which was carried on in small bands by troops not under any brigade-commanders, roaming at pleasure, with power to take any thing from foes or neutrals, but generally responsible to the major-general commanding in their department. They became, in many instances, mere roving bands of marauders and plunderers, equally terrible to all parties. Among the most noted of these was Morgan, a young man about thirty-five years of age, six feet in height, well made, strong, agile, and perfect master of himself. He had a keen, bluish-gray eye, a light complexion, sandy hair, and generally wore a moustache. Before the war he was known as a generous and jolly horse-loving and horse-racing Kentuckian, and he had great influence over his associates. He was an admirable horseman and precise marksman. He was an inexorable disciplinarian, and demanded implicit obedience. He once ordered one of his troopers to perform some perilous act in battle. The man did not move. "Do you understand my orders?" asked the chief. "Yes, Captain, but I cannot obey," was the answer. "Then good by," said Morgan, and shot him dead. Turning to his men, he said, "Such be the fate of every man disobeying orders in the face of an enemy." After that, no man waited for a second order.

We shall meet this bold rider frequently westward of the mountains and in East Tennessee. Here we will notice a single act of his, at about the time we are considering, which illustrates his coolness and daring. It is said to have been performed just after Johnston had fled from Nashville, and Morgan was scouting and foraging in his rear. He went into the city dressed as a farmer, with a load of meal, which he gave to the National Commissary, saying that there were some Union men out in his region, but they had to be careful to avoid the rebel cavalry. He dined at the St Cloud hotel, and, at the table, sat by the side of General McCook, who was so cruelly murdered afterward. He was pointed out as the generous Union farmer who had made the gift to the commissary, and he was persuaded to take the value of it in gold. Then he secretly informed the general that a band of Morgan's cavalry was camping near his residence, and that if one or two hundred horsemen would come to his house he would show them how to capture the noted rough-rider. They were sent, and were all captured by Morgan.—See *Thirteen Months in the Rebel Army, by an impressed New Yorker.*

forces of Beauregard at Corinth. This was effected on the 1st of April, and the united armies lay upon the line of the Mobile and Ohio railway from Corinth south to Bethel, and on the Memphis and Charleston railway, from Corinth east to Iuka. They were joined by several regiments from Louisiana; two divisions from Columbus, under General Polk; and a fine corps from Mobile and Pensacola, commanded by General Bragg. "In numbers, in discipline, in the galaxy of the distinguished names of its commanders, and in every article of merit and display, the Confederate army in the vicinity of Corinth was one of the most magnificent ever assembled by the South on a single battle-field."[2] The whole number of effective troops was about forty-five thousand. It was this army that Grant and Buell were speedily called upon to fight near the banks of the Tennessee.

FORT NEGLEY.[1]

General Mitchel performed his part of the grand movement southward with the most wonderful vigor and success. With the engines and cars captured at Bowling Green, his troops had entered Nashville. He was sent forward, and occupied Murfreesboro' when the Confederates abandoned it in March. After he parted with the more cautious Buell at that place, on the moving of the army southward at the close of March,[a] his own judgment was his guide, and his was practically an independent command. Before him the insurgents had destroyed the bridges, and these he was compelled to rebuild for the passage of his troops and munitions of war. This work was done so promptly, that his army was seldom even halted in waiting. On the 4th of April he was at Shelbyville, the capital of Bedford County, Tennessee, at the terminus of a short railway branching from that which connects Nashville with Chattanooga. This was almost sixty miles from Nashville, and there he made his deposit of supplies. At that point he

ORMSBY M. MITCHEL.

[a] March 28, 1862.

[1] This is a view of the front of Fort Negley, or the face toward the country, commanding the southern approaches to Nashville, as it appeared when sketched by the author in May, 1866

[2] Pollard's *First Year of the War*, page 295.

struck across the country with a supply-train, sufficient for only two days' provisions, in the direction of Huntsville, making forced marches all the way.

[a] April, 1862.

On the 10th[a] he left Fayetteville, in Lincoln County, Tennessee, crossed the State line the same day, and entered Northern Alabama, somewhat depressed in spirits by a rumor that Grant had been terribly defeated in a battle near Pittsburg Landing. Mitchel had passed through a very hostile region, but now began to perceive some signs of loyalty among the inhabitants,[1] and before midnight he was cheered by another rumor that Grant had been victorious and that Beauregard was in flight toward Corinth. Both rumors were true, as we shall observe presently.

Mitchel had pushed on with his cavalry to within eight miles of Huntsville, the capture of which and the seizure of the Memphis and Charleston railway there was the chief objective of his rapid march. There he halted for his artillery and infantry to come up, that he might prepare for striking a decisive blow. His entire march had been so rapid and well masked that the Confederate leaders were puzzled. They could obtain no positive information of his whereabouts or his destination. It was only known that he was moving southward with the apparent fleetness of a northern gale, and was spreading consternation among the inhabitants into whose midst his armed hosts suddenly appeared.

[b] April 11.

At this last halting-place no tents were pitched, for work was to be done before the dawn. The weary troops slumbered around their camp-fires in the evening, and when the half-moon went down, at a little past two o'clock in the morning,[b] they were summoned to their feet by the shrill notes of a bugle. They were soon in motion toward Huntsville, with one hundred and fifty of Kenner's Ohio cavalry and a section of Captain Simonson's battery, in advance, supported by Turchin's brigade, the whole commanded by Colonel Kenner, who, as we have observed, was the first to enter deserted Nashville. What force might meet them, none could conjecture. Every thing must be developed by action. Two working parties, well supported by troops, were sent with picks and crowbars to tear up the railway at the east and west of the town, while the cavalry moved directly upon the city and the railway station.

[c] April 11.

Never was a surprise more complete. It was accomplished at a little before dawn,[c] while the inhabitants were yet in bed. "The clattering noise of the cavalry," wrote a spectator, "aroused them from their slumbers in the dawn of the morning, and they flocked to door and window, exclaiming, with blanched cheek and faltering tongue, 'They come! they come! the Yankees come!' Men rushed into the streets almost naked, the women fainted, the children screamed, the darkies laughed, and for a time a scene of perfect terror reigned." Seventeen locomotives, more than one hundred passenger cars, a large amount of supplies of every kind, and about one hundred and sixty prisoners were the spoils of this bloodless victory.

---

1 On this day's march, Mitchel's army passed the extensive estate of L. Pope Walker, the Confederate "Secretary of State," which stretched along the road for miles. The mansion had been deserted, and the furniture removed; but a host of slaves remained who gave the "Yankees" a cordial welcome. One of the slaves had a heavy iron ring and bolt fastened to one of his legs, which he said he had worn for three months.

General Mitchel did not tarry long at Huntsville. Appointing Colonel Gazeley, of the Thirty-seventh Indiana, Provost-Marshal, and finding himself in possession of an ample supply of rolling stock on the railway, he immediately organized two expeditions to operate along its line each way from Huntsville. One, under Colonel Sill, went eastward as far as Stevenson, at the junction of the roads leading to Chattanooga and to Nashville, where five locomotives and a considerable amount of other rolling stock were captured. The other, under Colonel Turchin, went westward to Decatur[1] and Tuscumbia, south of Florence, from which an expedition was sent southward as far as Russellville, the capital of Franklin County, Alabama. Neither of these expeditions encountered any serious opposition, and on the 16th[a] Mitchel said to his soldiers, "You have struck blow after blow with a rapidity unparalleled. Stevenson fell, sixty miles to the east of Huntsville. Decatur and Tuscumbia have been in like manner seized, and are now occupied. In three days you have extended your front of operations more than one hundred miles, and your morning guns at Tuscumbia may now be heard by your comrades on the battle-field made glorious by their victory before Corinth."[2] He had placed his army midway between Corinth and Nashville, opened communication with Buell, and controlled the navigation of the Tennessee for more than one hundred miles. For these achievements, accomplished without the loss of a single life, Mitchel was commissioned a Major-General of Volunteers, and, with orders to report to the War Department directly, his force was constituted an independent corps.

[a] April, 1862.

Let us turn again to the banks of the Tennessee, and see what was occurring there.

General Grant arrived at Savannah on the 17th of March, and made his head-quarters at the house of Mr. Cherry, eight or nine miles below Pittsburg Landing, which General Smith had chosen for his own. The latter had already selected the position of the army in the vicinity of Pittsburg Landing. On its right was Snake Creek, and on its left Lick Creek, streams which formed good natural flank defenses against approach. The whole country for miles around was mostly covered with woods, in some parts filled with undergrowth, and at others presenting a beautiful open forest, composed of large red oak trees. Pittsburg Landing, the post on the river nearest to the Confederates, was protected by the gun-boats *Tyler* and *Lexington*. Sherman's division formed a sort of outlying picket, while those ot McClernand and Prentiss were the real line of battle, with General C. F. Smith's, commanded by W. H. L. Wallace, in support of the right wing, and Hurlbut on the left.[3] Lewis Wallace's division was detached and stationed at Crump's Landing, to observe any movements of the Confederates at Purdy, and to cover the river communications between Pittsburg Landing and Savannah. The latter was made the depot of stores, to which point General Halleck at St. Louis continually forwarded supplies of every kind.

---

[1] Here the railway southward from Nashville connects with the Memphis and Charleston road.

[2] General Mitchel's thanks to his soldiers, Camp Taylor, Huntsville, April 16th, 1862.

[3] Letter of General Sherman to the Editor of the *United States Service Magazine*, January, 1865. "The ground was well chosen," General Sherman wrote: "On any other we surely would have been overwhelmed, as both Lick and Snake Creeks forced the enemy to confine his movements to a direct front attack, which new troops are better qualified to resist than when the flanks are exposed to real or chimerical danger."

From the time of Grant's arrival at Savannah[a] until the first week in April, very little of interest occurred. The commander-in-chief continued his head-quarters at Savannah; and there seemed to be very little apprehension of any attack from the Confederates. No breastworks were thrown up, or *abatis* formed in front of the National army, at whose rear lay the broad and deep Tennessee River. The greater portion

[a] March 17, 1862.

RUINS OF SHILOH MEETING-HOUSE.

of General Sherman's division was then lying just behind Shiloh Meeting-house.[1] General Prentiss's division was encamped across the direct road to Corinth, and General McClernand's was behind his right. These three divisions formed the advanced line. In the rear of this, between it and the Landing, lay General Hurlbut's division, and that of General Smith, under General W. H. L. Wallace.[2] General David Stuart's brigade, of Sherman's division, lay on the Hamburg road, near its crossing of Lick Creek, on the extreme left. General Lewis Wallace's division was still at Crump's Landing.

Such was the disposition of Grant's army on the eventful Sunday morning, April 6, 1862. Nearly four miles intervened between parts of Sher-

[1] The meeting-house (see page 263) was destroyed after the battle there, early in April. Near it some of the severest of that struggle occurred. The above picture shows the appearance of its site when the author visited it, four years after the contest. Nothing remained but a few logs of which it was built. Several had been carried away, to be manufactured into canes.

[2] General Smith was then so ill at his head-quarters at Savannah that he could not take the field. In passing from General Lewis Wallace's head-quarters on a steam-boat, two or three weeks before, he fell from the guard into his yawl, and abraded his leg between his knee and his foot. The hurt disabled him, and it resulted in a fever, which, in connection with chronic dysentery, contracted while serving in Mexico, proved fatal. He died at the house of Mr. Cherry, on the 25th of April, 1862.

man's division; and large gaps existed between the divisions of McClernand and Prentiss. The extreme left of the line was commanded by unguarded heights, overlooking Lick Creek, which were easily approached from Corinth. The eleven thousand men at Corinth three weeks before had increased to over forty thousand, and the skillful Johnston and active Beauregard were at their head. Re-enforcements had been continually arriving there, while General Buell was making easy marches across Tennessee, to the assistance of Grant, and great uncertainty existed as to the time when he might be expected.

On the first of April, Johnston was informed that Van Dorn and Price were making their way toward Memphis from Central Arkansas, with thirty thousand troops, and would join him within a week. A day or two afterward he heard of the approach of Buell, and at once prepared for an advance upon Grant. His right, under General John C. Breckinridge,[1] eleven thousand strong, rested at Burnsville, ten miles east of Corinth; his center, more than twenty thousand in number, under Generals Hardee and Bragg, were massed at Corinth; and his left, under Generals Polk and Hindman, about ten thousand, extended northward from the Memphis and Charleston road. His cavalry pickets were continually scouring the country in all directions, and were surprised and gratified by never falling in with a scout or vedette from the National lines, though sometimes approaching within a mile and a half of them. Informed of this fact, and made fully acquainted, by spies and resident informers, of the position and number of his opponent's army, Johnston was about to move forward on the 5th,[a] to attempt to penetrate its center, divide it, and cut it up in detail, when information reached him that the troops from the west would certainly join him the next morning.

BRAXTON BRAGG.

[a] April, 1862.

The Confederate forces were now within four miles of the National camp. They had moved silently forward by separate routes, in a heavy rain-storm, toward Shiloh, as the region around Shiloh Meeting-house was called, and on the morning of the 5th these divisions had joined on the range of rugged hills on which stood the little hamlet of Monterey, seven or eight miles from Corinth. Cautiously and silently they had moved still farther on, and halted near the intersection of the roads leading to Hamburg and Pittsburg Landing, and there it was resolved to wait for Van Dorn and Price. Yet there was peril in delay. If Buell should arrive, Johnston's golden opportunity might be lost. Becoming satisfied that evening that his forward movement was unknown to Grant, the chief commander called a council of war at eight

[1] See page 76.

o'clock, and, after a deliberation of two hours, it was resolved to strike their enemy a blow before the dawn. Pointing toward the Union camp, at the close of the council, Beauregard said: "Gentlemen, we sleep in the enemy's camp to-morrow night."[1]

The greatest precautions were now taken by the Confederates to prevent any knowledge of their presence reaching the Nationals. No one was permitted to leave the camp, and no fires were allowed, excepting in holes in the ground. It was a chilly and cheerless night, and many of the soldiers lay down in the gloom supperless. At three o'clock in the morning[a] the whole army was in marching order, in three lines of battle, the first and second extending from Owl Creek on the left to Lick Creek on the right, a distance of about three miles, supported by the third and a reserve. The first line was commanded by General Hardee, and was composed of his own corps and Gladden's brigade of Bragg's corps, with artillery following by the main road to Pittsburg Landing. The cavalry was in the rear and on the wings. Bragg's corps, composing the second line, followed in the same order, at the distance of five hundred yards. At the distance of about eight hundred yards behind Bragg was Polk's corps, in lines of brigades, deployed with their batteries in rear of each brigade, also moving on the Pittsburg Landing road, supported by cavalry on the left wing. The reserves, commanded by Breckinridge, closely followed Polk's (third) line, its right wing supported by cavalry.

[a] April 6, 1862.

W. J. HARDEE.

In this order the Confederate army was slowly advancing to battle early on Sunday morning, the 6th of April,[2] over the rolling wooded country, while the Nationals were reposing in fancied security. It was one of the most delightful of those spring mornings, which so often give exquisite pleasure to the dwellers in that region; and he who in the gray dawn of that eventful day should have stood at the house of the widow Rey, on a branch of the Owl Creek, within the sound of voices of Sherman's camp near the Shiloh Meeting-house, would not have believed a prophecy that within an hour that Sabbath stillness would be broken by the tumult of battle, and those quiet woods just robed in the most delicate green, and enlivened by the songs of birds, would within sixty minutes be filled with sulphureous smoke, and all the hideous sounds

---

[1] Statement of "An impressed New Yorker" (*Thirteen Months in the Rebel Army*, page 147), who was on Breckinridge's staff, and was present at the council.

[2] General Johnston issued a stirring order to his troops when they were about to move, saying: "I have put you in motion to offer battle to the invaders of your country. With resolution and disciplined valor, becoming men fighting as you are, for all that is worth living or dying for, you can but march to decisive victory over the agrarian mercenaries who have been sent to despoil you of your liberties, your property, and your honor." He told them that the eyes and hopes of eight millions of people were resting upon them, and assured them that their generals would lead them to victory.

and images of infernal war. So it was. Hardee's advance first touched heavily and destructively Sherman's left,[1] and glancing off from that commander's skillful foil, fell with crushing force upon Prentiss's division.[2] The pickets of each and five companies under Colonel Moore, sent out by Prentiss to reconnoiter, were driven in at daylight, and the advancing foe reached the camp of the Nationals almost as soon as did the assailed out-lying troops. It was a complete surprise. Many of the officers were yet slumbering; others were dressing; others were washing or cooking, and others were eating breakfast. Their guns were unloaded, and accouterments were strewn around without order. Many of the troops were without a sufficient supply of ammunition. The first intimation that the Confederates were close upon them in force, was the wild cry of the flying pickets rushing into the camps, and the scream and crash of shells, and the whistle of bullets as they flew on deadly errands through the tents and the forest. A few minutes afterward, Hardee's eager troops were pouring like a flood into the camps of the bewildered Nationals, fighting desperately here, driving half-dressed or half-armed fugitives there, and dealing death and terror on every hand. It was an unexpected assault, followed by the most fearful results.

PICKETS ON DUTY.[3]

Hildebrand's brigade of Sherman's corps, which was the first attacked, was lying near Shiloh Meeting-house, at which point Sherman's artillery, under Captain Ezra Taylor, was stationed. Ruggles's division of Bragg's corps, with Hodgson's battery, made the direct assault, and Hildebrand's brigade, composed largely of comparatively raw troops, was driven from its camp almost without a struggle, for a panic seized some of the companies at the first onslaught. Buckland's and McDowell's had just time to fly to arms and form in battle order, when they, too, were attacked by the brigades of Pond and Anderson, of Ruggles's division, with a heavy artillery fire. For a

1 The troops here attacked were those of the brigade of Colonel Hildebrand, composed of the Fifty-third, Fifty-ninth, and Seventy-seventh Ohio, and Fifty-third Illinois; Colonel Buckland's brigade, composed of the Forty-eighth, Seventieth, and Seventy-second Ohio; and Colonel McDowell's brigade, composed of the Sixth Iowa, Fortieth Illinois, and Forty-sixth Ohio.

2 This was composed of the Twelfth Michigan. Sixteenth and Eighteenth Wisconsin, Eighteenth, Twenty-third, and Twenty-fifth Missouri, and Sixty-first Illinois.

3 This is from a sketch by W. Homer, published in *Harper's Weekly*, showing the manner of watching for an enemy by out-lying pickets in the woods.

while the conflict raged fiercely along the whole of Sherman's line. That gallant officer was seen in the thickest of the fight, exposing his life to quick destruction every moment, in encouraging his men to resist the tremendous assault, and escaping with only the hurt of a bullet passing through his hand. He tried in vain to rally Hildebrand's brigade, but he kept those of Buckland and McDowell steady for some time, while Taylor's heavy guns did admirable execution. These, heavily pressed, were soon compelled to fall back to an eminence across a ravine, where they made a gallant stand for a while.

In the mean time, McClernand, who lay in the rear of Sherman,[1] and at first supposed the firing to be only picket skirmishing, had thrown forward his left to the support of the smitten Hildebrand, and these troops for a while bore the shock of battle. This was at about seven in the morning, and before nine o'clock a greater part of Sherman's division was virtually out of the fight. His flanks had been rolled up by fresh troops under Bragg; and Polk, with the third Confederate line, was soon moving toward Sherman's rear, endangering his communication with the rest of the army and with the river. He collected and reorganized his broken columns, keeping up a desultory fight until, in the afternoon, he formed a new battle-line on a ridge in advance of a bridge over Snake Creek, by which General Lewis Wallace's division, ordered up from Crump's Landing, had been expected.

Turned by the steadiness of a portion of Sherman's division, and the troops of McClernand, the Confederates threw nearly their whole weight upon Prentiss. Only his first brigade, under Colonel Peabody,[2] was there to receive them, the second brigade being near the landing. These men, though surprised and bewildered, fought obstinately for a while, but in vain. The foe was in their midst, and a wall of living men, strong with ball and bayonet, was closing around them, ready to crush them out and make an open way for the Confederates to the river. Prentiss had asked Hurlbut for help. Veatch's brigade was sent, but it was not sufficient. Then the brigades of Williams and Lauman were ordered to his assistance, when back upon these Prentiss was pushed by Wither's division of Bragg's corps. At that perilous moment seeming relief came, but it was only a mockery. McArthur's brigade of W. H. L. Wallace's division had been sent to the aid of Stuart's brigade of Sherman's division, on the

B. M. PRENTISS.

[1] McClernand's division was composed of three brigades. The first, commanded by Colonel Hare, was composed of the Eighth and Eighteenth Illinois, and Eleventh and Thirteenth Iowa. The second brigade, commanded by Colonel C. C. Marsh, consisted of the Eleventh, Twentieth, Forty-fifth, and Forty-eighth Illinois. The third brigade was led by Colonel Raith, and was composed of the Seventeenth, Twenty-ninth, Forty-third, and Forty-ninth Illinois. Attached to this division were the fine batteries of Schwartz, Dresser, McAllister, and Waterhouse.

[2] The Twenty-fifth Missouri, Sixteenth Wisconsin, and Twelfth Michigan.

extreme left, which was in danger of being cut off if Prentiss's hard-pressed troops should perish. McArthur took a wrong road, and came directly upon Withers. He engaged him gallantly, and for a time there seemed to be a prospect of salvation for the environed troops. But McArthur was soon compelled to fall back. Prentiss's second division was hurried up, but it was too late. In the struggle, Peabody had been killed, Prentiss had become separated from a greater portion of his division, and it fell into the wildest confusion. By ten o'clock in the morning, it had practically disappeared. Fragments of brigades and regiments continued to fight as opportunity offered, and a large number of the division drifted behind new-formed lines, particularly those of Hurlbut. Prentiss and three of his regiments, over two thousand in number, maintained an unassailed position until late in the afternoon, when they were captured, sent to the rear of the Confederate army, and then marched in triumph to Corinth, as prisoners of war.

We have seen how McClernand's left hastened to the support of Hildebrand. As Sherman's line fell back, McClernand was compelled to bring in the remainder of his brigades to the protection of his left; for against that the Confederates, elated by their success in demolishing Prentiss, now hurled themselves with great force. McClernand's whole division formed a front along the Corinth and Pittsburg Landing road, with his batteries in good position, and there, until ten o'clock, he foiled every attempt of his foe to gain that road. Very soon a new peril appeared. The falling back of Sherman gave the Confederates a chance to flank McClernand's right, and quickly they seized the advantage. They dashed through the abandoned camps and pressed onward until driven back by Dresser's rifled cannon, which had smitten them fearfully. But reserves and fresh regiments pressing up toward the same point, with great determination and overwhelming numbers, compelled McClernand to fall back. His batteries were broken up,[1] many of his officers were wounded, and a large number of his men lay dead or mutilated on the field. The division fell slowly back, fighting gallantly, and by eleven o'clock it was in a line with Hurlbut's, that covered Pittsburg Landing.

We have alluded to the perilous position of the brigade of Stuart, of Sherman's division, on the extreme left of the National line,[2] to whose assistance General W. H. L. Wallace sent McArthur. It was posted about two miles from Pittsburg Landing on the Hamburg road, near the crossing of Lick Creek. Its position was isolated, and could be easily reached by the foe by a good road from Corinth; but, as it was intended to land Buell's forces at Hamburg, it was thought the brigade might be safely left there until that event. But the Confederates did not wait for the arrival of Buell; and now, when they were thundering away at the front of Sherman, McClernand, and Prentiss, his advance was more than half a day's usual march away. The isolated brigade was, therefore, placed in great peril. So isolated was it, that the first intimation its commander had of disaster on

[1] Dresser had lost several of his rifled cannon, three caissons, and eighteen horses. Schwartz had lost half of his guns and sixteen horses; and McAllister had lost half of his 24-pound howitzers.

[2] David L. Stuart was a resident of Chicago, and was then, as colonel of a regiment from Illinois, acting brigadier-general, in command of a brigade composed of the Fifty-fifth Illinois, and Fifty-fourth (Zouaves) and Seventy-first Ohio regiments.

the right was the cessation of firing in that direction, the scream of a shell in its passage among the branches above him, and in the apparition of a Confederate column of cavalry and infantry bearing down upon him by the forest road from Corinth to Hamburg. That column was mostly composed of Breckinridge's reserves. He had planted batteries on heights near the ford, and under cover of these his troops rushed to the attack. For ten minutes a desperate conflict ensued, when Stuart fell back and sent to Wallace for aid. It was furnished, as we have seen, but missed its aim. McArthur, however, so vigorously fought the Confederates that Stuart's force was saved from capture, and was enabled to retreat to a place of comparative safety, where its shattered members were brought into order.

It was now twelve o'clock at noon.[a] The Confederates had full possession of the ground on which lay the first line of the National army in the morning, and of the camps of Sherman, McClernand, Prentiss, and Stuart. Three of the five divisions of that army on the field had been thoroughly routed, and all were hemmed within a narrow strip of ground between the triumphant Confederate line and the broad and rapid Tennessee River. General Grant, who was at his head-quarters at Cherry's, eight miles away when the battle commenced,[1] had hastened to the field at the summons of the cannon's roar. He reached it at about eight o'clock, and at ten was with Sherman, when the battle was hottest. He comprehended the peril that threatened his whole army, and he took vigorous measures to avert it by re-forming the shattered brigades, re-establishing batteries and new lines, and ordering General Lewis Wallace, at Crump's Landing, to hasten to the field of strife with his fresh division. Buell's advance was at Savannah, but could not come in time, perhaps, to assist in the struggle, and he believed that he must win or lose the battle without them.

[a] April 6, 1862.

ULYSSES S. GRANT.

The gap made by the demolition of Prentiss's brigade and Stuart's retreat, through which the Confederates expected to rush upon Hurlbut and push him into the Tennessee River, was speedily closed by General W. H. L. Wallace, who marched with his remaining brigades and joined McArthur, taking with him the Missouri batteries of Stone, Richardson, and Webber, which were all under the command of Major Cavender. Hurlbut had been stationed in open fields; now he fell back to the thick woods between his camp and

[1] There was some disposition to censure General Grant for having his head-quarters so far away from the bulk of his army. It is proper to remember that Savannah was the point toward which his expected re-enforcements, under Buell, were to join him; and it was essential for him to be where he could, at the earliest moment, confer with that commander, after he should reach the Tennessee. Grant spent most of each day with his main army, returning to his quarters in a steamer at evening.

the river, and there, from ten o'clock in the morning until between three and four o'clock in the afternoon, he and Wallace held the Confederates in check, fighting a greater part of the time, and hurling back tremendous charges by the massed foe. On both sides death had been reaping a bountiful harvest. The brave General Wallace had fallen, mortally wounded, and been carried on a litter from the field. General Gladden, of the Confederate army, had been killed, and their Commander-in-chief, General A. S. Johnston, who had almost recklessly exposed himself, had also been mortally hurt at about half-past two o'clock.[1]

A HAND-LITTER.[2]

The superior force of the Confederates pressed Hurlbut further toward the river at four o'clock. At that time the gallant Wallace fell, and the command devolved on General McArthur. His division, animated by his words and deeds, had been fighting hopefully, but they too were now compelled to retreat, to avoid being flanked and surrounded, as Prentiss had been. They took position in a line with Hurlbut's men, about half a mile from the river, having lost only a single heavy gun, which was afterward recovered.

The day was now fairly lost. The victorious Confederates occupied the camps of all the Union divisions on the field excepting Wallace's,[3] and just in the rear of that the broken and terribly smitten army had now gathered in a space of not more than four hundred acres on a rolling plateau, very near the high banks at Pittsburg Landing, below which four or five thousand fugitives from the battle-field, chiefly inexperienced troops, were ignobly sheltering themselves from the storm of war. The army could fall back no farther. Its next retrograde movement could only be into the flood of the Tennessee, for there were not transports enough there to carry over it a single division.[4]

---

[1] Johnston was hit by a piece of a shell that burst near him. It struck his thigh, half way between his hip and knee, cutting a wide path, and severing the femoral artery. Governor Harris, of Tennessee (his brother-in-law), who was his chief of staff, was at his side. Ten minutes after he was lifted from his horse he died. Johnston was one of the bravest and most accomplished officers in the Confederate army. His death was concealed from his troops at that time, and it was not publicly made known until the army had returned to Corinth. Johnston's body was left on the field when the Confederates fled the next day, and was buried there. In January, 1867, his remains were taken to Austin, in Texas, for re-interment. The disloyal mayor and other citizens of Galveston asked permission of General Sheridan, the military commander of that district, to honor the remains by a public demonstration of respect in that city, to which Sheridan replied, in a note to the mayor:—

"SIR:—I respectfully decline to grant your request. I have too much regard for the memory of the brave men who died to preserve our Government to authorize Confederate demonstrations over the remains of any one who attempted to destroy it.

"P. H. SHERIDAN,
"Major-Gen. U. S. A."

[2] This shows the manner of carrying the wounded from the field when unable to walk. These litters are made as portable as proper strength will allow, and so constructed as to fold up. They are composed of two poles with a canvas stretched between, and strap yokes for the bearers.

[3] The Nationals had lost a division commander (Prentiss), a large number of field officers, and about three thousand men as prisoners, besides many killed and wounded, together with a great portion of their artillery, about twenty flags, colors, and standards, thousands of small arms, and a large supply of forage, subsistence, and munitions of war.

[4] It is related that Buell, when talking with Grant about the peril of giving battle with a deep river so nearly at his back, inquired, "What would you have done had you been pressed once more on Sunday evening?"—"Put

The only hope of salvation seemed to be in the co-operation of the gunboats, which now might give them aid in fighting, or the help of Buell's vanguard, then on the opposite shore, or the advent of Lewis Wallace with his fine division,[1] who had been anxiously expected all the afternoon. As the columns were pushed back from one position to another, Grant anxiously listened for the noise of Wallace's cannon thundering on the flank of the Confederates. Early in the morning he had sent him word to hold his troops in readiness to march at a moment's warning, "certainly not later than eleven o'clock." At half-past eleven Wallace received an order from his chief to move up and take position "on the right of the army, and form a line of battle at a right angle with the river." Time passed on; the Confederates were pressing hard; the disorganized brigades were in great confusion and falling back toward the river's brink. Yet Wallace did not come. Grant sent one of his staff to hurry him up. He did not come. Then he sent his adjutant-general (Captain Rawlins) to urge him forward, and yet he did not appear. Night had fallen, and the discomfited army lay huddled in great peril on the banks of the Tennessee, when the seemingly tardy General arrived. He was afterward censured for the delay, for the impression went abroad that, had he promptly responded to Grant's call, victory for the National army might have been achieved on that day, for he was a skillful commander, and his men, fresh and spirited, had been well tried, and found sufficient in all things. A few words of explanation, afterward given, made the record of that prompt and gallant officer clear to the apprehension of his chief and the people, and showed that the whole delay had occurred in consequence of a blunder of omission committed by Grant's messenger who bore the order for his advance.[2]

STEPHEN A. HURLBUT.

my troops across the river," was Grant's reply. "But you had not transportation sufficient," answered Buell. "Plenty," responded Grant, "to take over all that would have been left when we had done fighting."

[1] Wallace's division was composed of three brigades, stationed on the road from Crump's Landing to Purdy, the first at the Landing, the second two miles out, and the third two miles and a half farther, at Adamsville. Owing to the pushing back of an Ohio brigade, that had been sent out to reconnoiter in the direction of Purdy, his division marched as far as Adamsville in a drenching rain, on Friday night (April 4), and there a brigade was left. The first brigade, commanded by Colonel Morgan L. Smith, was composed of the Eleventh and Twenty-fourth Indiana and Eighth Missouri. The second, commanded by Colonel John M. Thayer, was composed of the First Nebraska, Twenty-third Indiana, and the Fifty-sixth and Fifty-eighth Ohio. The third brigade, under Colonel Charles Whittlesy, was composed of the Twentieth, Sixty-eighth, Seventy-sixth, and Seventy-eighth Ohio. To the division were attached Thurber's Missouri and Thompson's Indiana Batteries; also the third battalion of the Fifth Ohio, and third battalion of the Eleventh Illinois cavalry.

[2] General Grant, as we have seen, had ordered General Wallace to place his division "on the right of the army." That position in the morning was about four miles from Pittsburg Landing. The messenger who bore the order not only omitted to inform Wallace that the "right" had been beaten back, and was thus much nearer Pittsburg Landing, but had told him (as he doubtless supposed truly) that the Confederates were being repulsed at all points. Believing it to be yet in its morning position at the right of Shiloh Meeting-house, Wallace promptly put his whole division (excepting two regiments left at Crump's Landing) in motion half an hour after receiving the order, by the nearest route to the supposed "right of the army." When he had proceeded, as rapidly as the miry roads would allow, for about six miles, the roar of battle quickening the steps of his soldiers,

By the side of a little log house which had lately been the post-office of Pittsburg Landing, and constituted the "village," General Grant and his staff were grouped at sunset on that fearful Sunday evening, while there was a lull in the storm of war. They were in continual expectation of another attack, but Grant felt confident of final victory.[1] Buell's vanguard was in sight, and Wallace was expected to appear at every moment. If the assailants could be kept at bay a few hours, all would be well. Preparations to withstand them were hastily made. The quiet time was improved, and in a semicircle around the army, half a mile back from the bluff, slight earthworks of half-moon form were quickly thrown up, and twenty-two heavy guns were mounted on them, under the direction of Colonel Webster, Grant's chief of staff, and manned by artillerists selected from all the batteries.

These guns were scarcely in position, toward the close of twilight, when a lurid glare lighted up the surrounding forests, and shot and shell from Confederate cannon on the left and center of the Nationals came crashing through the trees in the direction of the Landing, but falling short of the intended victims. These were quickly answered by Grant's guns, when the Confederate brigades in full force pressed forward from their new line, that stretched between the positions of Stuart and Hurlbut in the morning, from Lick Creek across the Corinth road, and tried to cross a ravine that separated them from the Nationals, in order to give a final and crushing blow to the latter. This force was large, composed of Chalmers on the right, with Breckinridge in the rear; and ranging to the left, the reduced brigades of Withers, Cheatham, Ruggles, Anderson, Stuart, Pond, and Stevens were engaged. They were bravely met by the National infantry, composed of portions of all the brigades, and by the well-directed artillery,[2] and were kept at bay until a force that had not yet been brought into action was placed in position and commenced work. This was composed of the gun-boats *Tyler* and *Lexington*, under the general command of Lieutenant William Gwin. They came up to the mouth of the little creek that traverses a short ravine at Pittsburg Landing, and were soon hurling 7-inch shells and 64-pound shot up that hollow in the bluff, in curves that dropped them in the midst of the Confederates. General Nelson, who led Buell's advance, had crossed the river with Ammon's brigade, and bore an important part in repelling the assailants. The crushing blow which the latter expected to give was foiled, and the palm of victory, which they confidently expected to hold before midnight, eluded their grasp. Three hours before that midnight, the roar of battle, which had been kept up during the evening, had ceased, and Beau-

---

he was overtaken by Captain Rawlins and another, and from them first learned that the National troops had been beaten back toward the river. His route would take him to an isolated and dangerous position in the rear of the Confederates, so he retraced his steps, crossed over to the river road near Snake Creek, by the nearest possible route, passed that stream over a bridge, and took his assigned position on the right of the army. He had marched and countermarched, in consequence of misinformation and lack of information, about sixteen miles, which had consumed the whole afternoon.

[1] A remark made by General Prentiss seems to have been the cause of Beauregard not pressing an attack that night. That general asked Prentiss if the Nationals had any fortifications at the river, to which he replied, "You must consider us poor soldiers, general, if you suppose we would have neglected so plain a duty." The truth was, the Nationals had not a single fortification anywhere on or near that battle-field until after Beauregard ceased to fight on Sunday evening. Had he pressed forward, he might have captured the entire army.

[2] Among these pieces were two long 32-pound siege guns, but there seemed to be no one to work them, when Dr. Cornyn, surgeon of the old First Missouri artillery, offered his services for the purpose. They were accepted, and the guns were worked most efficiently.

regard, who succeeded the slain Johnston in supreme command, ignorant of the arrival of Buell, and feeling confident of victory in the morning, was writing a glowing dispatch to Adjutant-General Cooper from his quarters in Shiloh Meeting-house, announcing a complete victory.[1]

We have observed that the vanguard of Buell's army,[2] composed of Nelson's division, made its appearance, opposite Pittsburg Landing, toward Sunday evening.[a] It had reached the Tennessee River, at Savannah, on the previous day; and, on the same evening, the commanding General arrived there. On the following morning, hearing the sound of heavy guns up the river, Buell hastened to Grant's head-quarters, at Cherry's, for information. The latter had just started for Pittsburg Landing in a steamer, having left orders for Nelson's division to be sent up at once. It started early in the afternoon, leaving its cannon to be forwarded by water, on account of bad roads, and arrived opposite the Landing, as we have observed, toward sunset. Buell reached there at about the same time, and requested Grant to send vessels down to bring up Crittenden's division, which had just arrived at Savannah. These, and the remainder of Nelson's division, and Wallace's, from Crump's Landing, had taken positions before midnight, and were preparing, in the midst of a drenching rain, to renew the conflict in the morning. All night long Buell's troops were arriving by land and water; and, at intervals of ten or fifteen minutes, the gun-boats were hurling a heavy shell into the camps of the Confederates, wearying and worrying them with watching and unceasing alarm. By these they were compelled to fall back from their position, from which they intended to spring upon the Nationals during the night, and they lost more than half the ground they had gained by the retreat of the Unionists on Sunday afternoon.

[a] April 6, 1862.

The morning of the 7th dawned gloomily upon the battle-field, which was overshadowed by heavy clouds, distilling a drizzling rain. Before sunrise the conflict was opened by General Lewis Wallace, whose division had been disposed in battle order at a little past midnight, and formed the extreme right of the newly established line of the army. Captain Thompson's field

---

[1] The following is a copy of the dispatch, dated "Battle-field of Shiloh, April 6, 1862: We have this morning attacked the enemy in a strong position in front of Pittsburg, and after a severe battle of ten hours, thanks to Almighty God, gained a complete victory, driving the enemy from every position. The loss on both sides is heavy, including our commander-in-chief, General Albert Sidney Johnston, who fell gallantly leading his troops into the thickest of the fight."

[2] Buell's forces, that reached the field of action in time to participate in its events, consisted of three divisions, commanded respectively by Generals William Nelson, Thomas T. Crittenden, and Alexander McDowell McCook. Nelson's division was composed of three brigades: the first, commanded by Colonel Ammon, consisted of the Sixth and Twenty-fourth Ohio, and Thirty-sixth Indiana; the second, Colonel Bruce, consisted of the First, Second, and Twentieth Kentucky; the third, Colonel Hazen, was composed of the Forty-first Ohio, Sixth Kentucky, and Ninth Indiana.

General Crittenden's division consisted of three brigades: the first, commanded by General Boyle, was composed of the Nineteenth and Fifty-ninth Ohio, and Ninth and Thirteenth Kentucky; the second, Colonel William L. Smith, consisted of the Thirteenth Ohio, and Eleventh and Twenty-sixth Kentucky, with Mendenhall's regular and Bartlett's Ohio batteries.

General McCook's division was composed of three brigades: the first, General Rousseau, consisted of the First Ohio, Sixth Indiana, Third Kentucky (Louisville Legion), and battalions of the Fifteenth, Sixteenth, and Nineteenth regulars; the second brigade, General Johnson, consisted of the Thirty-second and Thirty-ninth Indiana, and Forty-ninth Ohio; the third brigade, Colonel Kirk, was composed of the Thirty-fourth Illinois, Thirteenth and Twenty-ninth Indiana, and Seventy-first Pennsylvania.

The division of General T. J. Wood was too far in the rear to reach the scene of action in time to participate in the battle. That of General Thomas was still farther in the rear.

guns first awakened the echoes of the forest and brought both armies to their feet. These shelled the Confederates, who were strongly posted, with artillery, upon a bluff across a stream and a deep wooded ravine in front of Wallace. The response was vigorous, and Thurber came to Thompson's aid. The conflict was brief. One of the rifled guns of the Confederates was speedily silenced, and its supporters were falling back. At that moment General Grant arrived, and directed Wallace to press forward and attack the Confederate left, commanded by General Bragg in person, and consisting of the division of General Ruggles, and the brigade of Colonel Wobue, of Breckinridge's reserves. This was done with his brigades *en èchelon*, his line at right angles with the river. The Confederates were soon driven from the hill, and their places were occupied by Wallace's victorious troops. There a halt was made for Sherman's division, which lay to the left, to come up in support.

Wallace was now on the edge of an open field, and a wood and low swampy grounds, along Snake Creek, formed an impassable flank defense. Perceiving this, and that the left flank of the Confederates was exposed by the falling back of the force on the bluff, he attempted to turn it. To do so, it was necessary to change his front. This was skillfully done by a left half-wheel of the whole division, leaving a gap between it and Sherman's right, which was expected to move forward at once.

While this movement was in progress, a heavy column of the foe was seen in the woods, across an open field, making rapidly toward their endangered left, evidently for the purpose of turning Wallace's right. Buell's veterans had made Grant's left too strong for Beauregard to hope to win his expected victory there, and he was now seeking it on the National right. But there he found as determined a foe. Wallace ordered up Thompson's battery, which played upon the moving column with terrible effect until its ammunition was exhausted, when Thurber's was sent forward and continued the work most effectually. The flank movement was checked, and then Confederate cavalry attempted to take the battery. They were driven back by the skirmishers of the Eighth Missouri. Then a heavy column of infantry, with Watson's Louisiana Battery of destructive steel rifled cannon moved against Wallace's advance, when his first brigade, Colonel M. L. Smith, easily repelled them. For an hour and a half the contest went on, the bulk of Wallace's division all the while enduring a furious cannonade, but well sheltered, as they lay in wooded hollows, waiting for Sherman to come up.

While Wallace was holding the Confederates in check, Sherman, who had been waiting to hear the thunders of Buell's cannon advancing along the main Corinth road, moved forward with a resolution to obey Grant's command to retake the camp, lost the day before. At the same time Wallace ordered his division to advance. The first brigade led the way from the woods into and across an open field, beyond which, on a thickly wooded ridge, not far from Shiloh Meeting-house, the foe was posted. The division moved steadily on under an ordinary fire down into a slight hollow, and up a gentle slope toward their foe, when suddenly the woods were all ablaze with musketry, and the destructive Louisiana Battery hurled its bolts with fearful effect. Sherman's advance recoiled, when Wallace, whose flank was thereby exposed, ordered a halt.

Let us see what has been doing on the left meanwhile. Buell's forces on the field lay near Pittsburg Landing, and composed the center and left wing of Grant's new line of battle, upon which it was expected the Confederates would fall in the morning. Only the divisions of Nelson and Crittenden were well in hand at dawn. The former had quietly called up his men at four o'clock, and soon afterward he notified his general of his readiness for motion. Crittenden was ready at the same time, and when the booming of Wallace's heavy guns on the right was heard, they both moved forward, Nelson's division leading, with Ammon's brigade on the extreme left, Bruce's in the center, and Hazen's on the right. Nelson's artillery, which was to be sent up by water, had not yet arrived, but the battery of Mendenhall, of the regular service, and Bartlett's Ohio Battery, were on the field. McCook, who had been moving all night, so as to be a participant in the impending battle, had just arrived at Pittsburg Landing with his division when Nelson and Crittenden began their march, at half-past five in the morning.[a]

[a] April 7, 1862.

Nelson moved forward through the open woods and some cleared fields over the rolling plateau for about a mile before encountering the Confederates in force, when, at six o'clock, he was assailed by their artillery, and halted. Mendenhall's battery was brought into action, and Crittenden took a commanding position on the right of Nelson, with Bartlett's battery posted at his center. A contest was maintained for some time, when McCook's division arrived on the ground, accompanied by General Buell, who assumed the direction of affairs. McCook's forces were formed on Crittenden's right, and some straggling troops that were on the field the day before were placed on McCook's right, making Buell's entire line about a mile in length, extending from a point southeastward of the Hamburg road, and across the Corinth road, so as to touch Hurlbut on the left and at the rear of McClernand. The entire National line formed an irregular curve.

While Buell's force was getting into position, Mendenhall and Bartlett fought three batteries of the Confederates in front of Nelson and Crittenden. The foe was evidently in strong force. A little to the rear of his left was the high, open wooded ridge on which Sherman and McClernand were encamped on the morning of the 6th, and this was an objective, according to Grant's order already alluded to. Forward Buell's column moved, and Nelson's division first felt the shock of battle, which soon became general along the whole line. Colonel Hazen, with his brigade, made a gallant charge and seized one of the Confederate batteries, but was driven back by superior numbers thrown into the woods on Crittenden's left, and a cross-fire of artillery, sustaining a heavy loss. Colonel Smith's brigade of Crittenden's division then advanced into the woods and repulsed the Confederates, and at the same time Terrell's Regular Battery of 24-pound howitzers was brought on the field and advanced to Nelson's left, near the Hamburg road, then heavily pressed by great numbers. Its effect was most salutary, for it soon silenced the right battery of the Confederates; but Terrell was speedily forced back, with Ammon's brigade, when a regiment from Boyle's brigade re-enforced Nelson's left, and it again moved forward and drove the foe. This exposed the Confederates at their second and third batteries, from which they were soon driven by the concentrated fire of Mendenhall and Terrell, with a loss of several of their cannon.

Meanwhile McCook's division had been fighting the Confederate center, pushing it back step by step, until it was driven from its position. The action of that division was commenced by General Rousseau's, which was well supported by Generals Kirk and Gibson, Willich's regiment, and two regiments of Hurlbut's division.[1] After expending its ammunition, and marching to the rear for a supply, it was seen moving "in splendid order, and steadily to the front, sweeping every thing before it,"[2] smiting the foe so severely that he was driven from his position, and lost one of his batteries at the first onset.[3] It was in front of this division that the Confederates, commanded by Beauregard in person, assisted by Bragg, Polk, and Breckinridge, made their last decided stand, in the woods beyond Sherman's old camp, near Shiloh Meeting-house, where we left that officer and Wallace confronting them. Two brigades of General T. J. Wood's division had just reached the field, but not in time to participate in the engagement. But they relieved the weary fighters, and sealed the doom of the Confederates, who now abandoned all hope of conquering the National left, and concentrated on their right, as we have observed.

It was now long past noon. Wallace had again changed his front for attack, with Sherman on his left as a support. Again his first brigade had moved forward, when a squadron of Confederate cavalry dashed out of the woods toward his temporarily exposed flank. These were repulsed by the Twenty-third Indiana, aided by an oblique fire by the First Nebraska. But a greater peril was menacing Wallace's whole division, at that moment. Sherman's forces, touching his left, had again given way, and were followed by a heavy mass of desperate Confederates, who were eagerly pushing forward to isolate Wallace from the rest of the National army. The situation of the gallant Indianian was extremely critical for a while. He immediately ordered up Colonel Charles R. Woods, of the reserves, with his Seventy-eighth Ohio. These, with a regiment sent by General McClernand, and the Eleventh Indiana, Colonel McGinniss, whose front and flank had been attacked, stoutly held the ground, with the gallant Thurber ready to act with his artillery if required, until Colonel August Willich, with his splendid Thirty-second Indiana, of McCook's division, dashed against the Confederates, and drove them back.[4] Meanwhile Sherman had recovered his line, and the brigade of the wounded Colonel Stuart (now commanded by the skillful Colonel T. Kilby Smith) and that of Colonel Buckland, supported by two 24-pound howitzers of McAllister's battery, moved forward abreast of Rousseau's Kentucky brigade. Wallace's troops, who had entered the woods, also

---

[1] Hurlbut's shattered division, which had fought on the previous day, was held in reserve much of the time at the rear and left of McClernand.

[2] See General Sherman's report.

[3] General Rousseau had the honor of retaking General McClernand's head-quarters on Sunday morning. At the outer edge of that encampment the dead body of General A. S. Johnston was found.

[4] Speaking of this movement in his report, General Sherman said: "Here I saw Willich's regiment advance upon a point of water-oaks and thicket, behind which I knew the enemy was in great strength, and enter it in beautiful style. Then arose the severest musketry-fire I ever heard, and lasted twenty minutes, when this splendid regiment had to fall back. This green point of timber is about five hundred yards east of Shiloh Meeting-house, and it was evident here was to be the struggle."

pressed steadily forward, while "step by step, from tree to tree, position to position," said that officer, "the rebel lines went back, never stopping again—infantry, horses, and artillery—all went back. The firing was grand and terrific. Before us was the Crescent regiment of New Orleans; shelling us on the right was the Washington artillery, of Manassas renown, whose last stand was in front of Colonel Whittlesey's command. To and fro, now in my front, then in Sherman's, rode General Beauregard, inciting his troops, and fighting for his fading prestige of invincibility. The desperation of the struggle may be

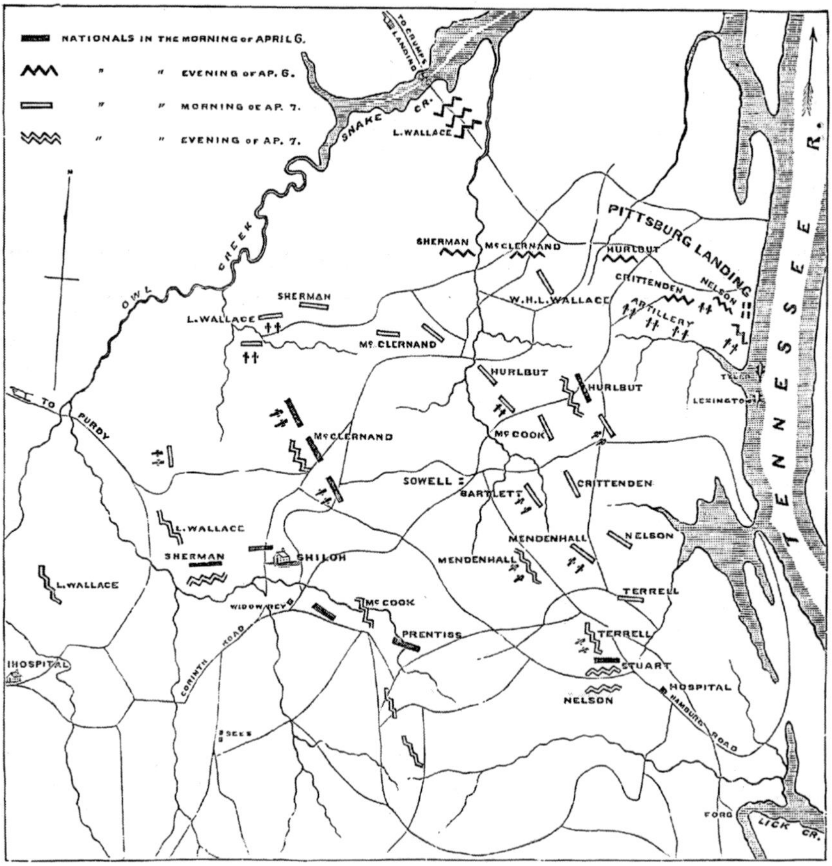

POSITION OF THE NATIONAL TROOPS IN THE BATTLES OF SHILOH.[1]

easily imagined. While this was in progress, far along the lines to the left the contest was raging with equal obstinacy. As indicated by the sounds, however, the enemy seemed retiring everywhere. Cheer after cheer rang through the woods, and each man felt the day was ours."[2]

And so it was. Heavily pressed on all sides, the Confederates gave way,

---

[1] The general position of the Confederates may be understood, by considering that on both days their lines were parallel to those of the Nationals.

[2] Wallace's report.

and flying through the National camps of Sunday morning, they burned their own, and with a powerful rear-guard under Breckinridge,[1] they hurried, in a cold, drizzly rain that soon changed to hail, with their sick and wounded in every conceivable conveyance,[2] to the heights of Monterey that night, far on the road toward Corinth, but happily pursued by the conquerors only as far as the bluffs and swamps of Lick Creek. They were astonished at the fact that they were not more vigorously followed,[3] for Breckinridge, it was thought, could easily have been separated from the remainder of the Confederate army and captured, and Beauregard's whole force might have been dispersed or made prisoners.[5] Thus ended THE BATTLE OF SHILOH.[6]

MULES CARRYING WOUNDED MEN.[4]

Although the Confederates had utterly failed in their intentions, and were thoroughly vanquished and driven from the field, with an acknowledged loss of nearly eleven thousand men,[7] Beauregard telegraphed to Richmond

---

1 Breckinridge's command was strengthened by the cavalry regiments of Forest, Adams, and the Texas Rangers, making the effective force of the rear-guard about 12,000 men.

2 That retreat must have been a terrible experience for the sick and wounded. "Here," wrote an eye-witness, "was a long line of wagons loaded with wounded, piled in like bags of grain, groaning and cursing, while the mules plunged on in mud and water, belly deep, the water sometimes coming into the wagons. Next came a straggling regiment of infantry, pressing on past the train of wagons; then a stretcher borne upon the shoulders of four men, carrying a wounded officer; then soldiers staggering along, with an arm broken and hanging down, or other fearful wounds which were enough to destroy life. . . . . I passed long wagon-trains, filled with wounded and dying soldiers, without even a blanket to shield them from the driving sleet and hail, which fell in stones as large as partridge-eggs, until it lay on the ground two inches deep. Some three hundred men died during that awful retreat, and their bodies were thrown out to make room for others, who, although wounded, had struggled on through the storm, hoping to find shelter, rest, and medical care."

3 Beauregard expected a vigorous, and possibly disastrous pursuit, and said to Breckinridge, "*This retreat must not be a rout!* You must hold the enemy back, if it requires the loss of your last man."—"Your orders shall be executed to the letter," was the reported reply.—See Pollard's *First Year of the War*, page 302.

4 The picture shows the method of carrying sick and wounded on mules, which was in practice at the earlier periods of the war by both parties. The horse-litter, on which men who could not sit up were carried, is shown in the front figure; and the *Cacolet*, in which men wounded in the upper extremities were carried sitting, is seen in the figure behind. When good ambulances came into use, these methods were abandoned or became rare exceptions.

5 A rapid and persistent pursuit would have created a complete rout of the now weary, broken, and dispirited rebels. Two hours more of such fighting as Buell's fresh men could have made would have demoralized and destroyed Beauregard's army.—*Thirteen Months in the Rebel Army, by an impressed New Yorker*, page 169.

6 See reports of Generals Grant and Buell and their subordinate commanders; also of General Beauregard and his division commanders. A very spirited, and, it is said, correct account was given in the *Cincinnati Gazette*, written by its army correspondent "Agate" (Whitelaw Reid), who was an eye-witness of the battles. The author has been favored with the written and oral statements of participants in the battle on both sides.

7 Beauregard reported his loss at 1,728 killed, 8,012 wounded, and 957 missing; total, 10,697. General Grant reported his entire loss, including about 4,000 prisoners, 1,735 killed, 7,882 wounded, and 3,956 prisoners; total, 13,573. It was probably about 15,000, and there is reason to believe that Beauregard's was not less. Among the killed in the Confederate army, on Monday, was George W. Johnston, "Provisional Governor of Kentucky" (see page 189), who was with the Kentucky troops in the action. His horse was shot under him on Sunday, and on Monday he was in the ranks. General Hindman had a very narrow escape, just before the retreat, on Monday evening. While leading his men, in a fearful struggle, a small shell entered the breast of his horse and exploded in his body. The horse was blown into fragments, and his rider, with his saddle, was lifted about ten feet in the air. His staff-officers near supposed he was killed, and one of them exclaimed, "General Hind-

from Corinth, almost twenty miles from the battle-field, twenty-four hours after his flight,[a] "We have gained a great and glorious victory. Eight to ten thousand prisoners, and thirty-six pieces of cannon."[1] Conscious that his misrepresentations would be exposed by facts in a few days, he added: "Buell re-enforced Grant, and we retired to our intrenchments at Corinth, which we can hold." He had sent a flag of truce that morning from Monterey, where he had a hospital, asking Grant to allow him to send mounted men to the battle-field, to bury his dead. Grant refused. He informed him that, owing to the warmth of the weather, that office of humanity had already been attended to by his own army. "I shall always be glad," wrote Grant in his reply, "to extend any courtesy consistent with duty, especially so when dictated by humanity."[2] There was also a sanitary consideration in this matter. It was important for the health of the National army, which might remain some time in that vicinity, that the bodies of men and horses should be removed from the surface of the ground. The former were buried and the latter were burned.

[a] April 8, 1862.

BURNING HORSES NEAR PITTSBURG LANDING.

The writer visited the battle-field of Shiloh late in April, 1866. At seven o'clock in the evening of the 23d, he left Meridian in Mississippi, for a journey of about two hundred miles on the Mobile and Ohio railway to Corinth, near the northern borders of the State. It was a cool moonlit night, and the topography of the country through which that railway passed, and over which Grierson had raided and Confederate troops and National prisoners of war had been conveyed, might be easily discerned. At twenty miles from Meridian it was a rolling prairie, with patches of forest here and there, and broad cotton-fields, stretching in every direction as far as the eye could comprehend. That character it maintained all the

man is blown to pieces." At that instant Hindman sprang to his feet and shouted, "Shut up there! I'm worth two dead men yet. Get another horse." In a few moments he was again in the saddle, but he was so much shocked that he was unable to take the field the next day.

[1] In this number Beauregard evidently ncluded all the cannon he had captured on Sunday, but did not mention the fact that on Monday he had lost nearly as many.

[2] Most of the prisoners taken at Shiloh were sent to Camp Douglass at Chicago. They were generally in a most miserable condition when captured. A lady at Chicago, writing to a friend, said: "But I have not told you how awfully they were dressed. They had old carpets, new carpets, and rag carpets—old bed-quilts, new bed-quilts, and ladies' quilts, for blankets. They had slouch hats, children's hats, little girls' hats, and not one soldier cap on their heads. One man had two old hats tied to his feet instead of shoes. They were the most ragged, torn and worn, and weary-looking set I ever saw. Every one felt sorry for them, and no one was disposed to speak unkindly to them. Some of them looked careless and happy enough, and some looked very sad, and others would be very good-looking if they were well dressed and in good company. Even the officers were the most forsaken looking set of men I ever dreamed of. We have sent them newspapers and books, but we find that very few of them can read."

way to a more hilly country within thirty or forty miles of Corinth. With an interesting traveling companion (John Yerger, of Jackson, Mississippi), the night passed pleasantly away. We arrived at the reviving village of Corinth, which had been nearly destroyed during the war, at about half-past eight o'clock in the morning,[a] where we breakfasted. The writer spent the time until past noon in sketching the head-quarters of officers, National and Confederate, around the village, and then started for Pittsburg Landing, about twenty miles distant, in a light wagon drawn by a powerful horse driven by an intelligent young man, a brother of the owner of the conveyance. He was a native of that region, and had been in the Confederate army. He was acquainted with all the roads in the direction of the Landing, and with most of the localities of interest connected with the great battle. With his knowledge, and the assistance of an official map of the battle, very little difficulty was found in identifying them.

[a] April 24, 1866.

We first visited the principal fortifications around Corinth. About two and a half miles northward of the village, we passed out through the inner line of Confederate works, and were soon beyond the desolated region that had been stripped of its trees by the army, and riding through magnificent red oak forests, whose leaves were yet too tiny to give much shelter from the sun, then shining with great warmth. For nearly nine miles the country was gently rolling, and well watered with little streams, when, approaching Pea Ridge, it became hilly and very picturesque. On that ridge we came to the site of the once pretty little hamlet of Monterey, where the only building that remained was a store-house, which the Confederates had used for a hospital. Near it was a ruined house, around which were the remains of what had doubtless been a fine flower-garden.

CONFEDERATE HOSPITAL AT MONTEREY.

From Monterey to some distance beyond Lick Creek the country was hilly, very little cleared, and less cultivated, dotted here and there with miserable log-houses, and mostly covered with woods. Half-way between Monterey and Shiloh Meeting-house we crossed the recently overflowed Lick Creek Bottom, partly upon a log causeway built by the National army when moving on Corinth, and partly in the deep mud. Driftwood had been floated into barricades on the causeway in many places, and a more difficult journey cannot well be conceived. A horse less powerful than ours could not have dragged us through the sloughs. It gave us a vivid impression of the difficulties experienced by the armies in taking their artillery and wagon-trains through that region. Happily, our journey over that wooded and tangled "bottom" did not exceed half a mile in distance, when we forded clear and pebbly Lick Creek, climbed the hills on its opposite side, and, just at sunset, crossed a little tributary of Owl Creek, and halted in perplexity at the forks of the road, near the ruins of a house in open fields. It was the site of poor widow Rey's, not far from that of Shiloh Meeting-house, near which Hardee formed his forces for assault on the morning of the 6th.[1] We were, as we soon ascertained, at the parting of the ways for Hamburg and Pittsburg Landings. While deliberating which to take, and considering seriously where we might obtain supper and lodging, for the gloom of twilight was gathering in the woods, the questions were settled by a woman (Mrs. Sowell) on a gaunt gray horse, with her little boy, about six years of age, striding the animal's back behind her. She kindly consented to give us such entertainment as she could. "It is but little I have," she said, in a pleasant, plaintive voice, and we expressed our willingness to be content therewith. So we followed her through the woods and a few open fields for nearly a mile in the direction of Pittsburg Landing, and at dark were at her home, not far from McClernand's camp on Sunday morning, where the battle raged with so much fury. All around it were the marks of war in scarred, decapitated, and shattered trees, and the remains of clothing and accouterments strewing the ground.

OUR HOSTESS AT SHILOH

Our hostess was a widow, with six children. Her husband was dying with consumption when the battle commenced. She did not leave him, but remained in the house with her children throughout that terrible storm of war. A heavy shell went

OUR LODGING-PLACE ON THE FIELD OF SHILOH.

through her house, and several trees standing near it were cut off or shattered by them. "The Lord was with me," she piously said, as we sat at her humble table, lighted by a lamp composed of wick and melted lard in a tin dish, and supping upon hoe-cake without butter, just baked in the ashes, some fried bacon, and coffee without milk or sugar. "My husband died, but my children were spared," she said; "but God only knows what will become of them in this desolated country, without a school or a church." We had just

[1] See page 270.

come in from the enjoyment of the bright moonlight, and balmy April air, and the burden of the whippowil, and felt that peace and serenity imparted by nature in repose, that inclines one to forgive as we hope to be forgiven. The sweet spell was broken when, in that dingy and battered cabin, lighted by a few blazing fagots and the primitive lamp, with only one half-bottomed chair and a rude box or two to sit upon, we looked upon that lonely, suffering, educated woman, with her six really pretty and intelligent boys and girls, half clad, but clean, struggling for the right to live—an example of like misery in thousands of households, once prosperous and happy, thus crushed into poverty by the wickedness of a few ambitious men. In that presence, the Rebellion seemed doubly infernal, and the spirit of forgiveness departed.

We slept soundly in one of the log houses, with our horse stabled in an adjoining room, nailed up for the night, to keep him from the clutches of prowling bushwhackers, and the pigs grunting under our open floor; and at dawn we went out, while the cuckoo's song was sweetest and the mocking-bird's varied carols were loudest, and rambled far over the battle-field, meeting here a tree cut down by shot near its base, there a huge one split by a shell that passed through it and plunged deeply into another beyond, and everywhere little hillocks covering the remains of the slain. After an early breakfast we rode to Pittsburg Landing, and made the sketch seen on page 263, and then, riding along the greater portion of the lines of battle from Lick Creek to Owl Creek, we visited the site of Shiloh Meeting-house, made a drawing of it, and again striking the Corinth road at the ruins of widow Rey's house, returned to that village by way of Farmington, where Paine and Marmaduke had a skirmish,[1] in time to take the afternoon train to the scene of another battle, Iuka Springs, twenty miles eastward.

EFFECTS OF A SHOT NEAR SHILOH MEETING-HOUSE.

[1] See page 292.

CHAPTER XI.

OPERATIONS IN SOUTHERN TENNESSEE AND NORTHERN MISSISSIPPI AND ALABAMA.

VIEWING events in the light of fair analysis and comparison, it seems clear that a prompt and vigorous pursuit of the Confederates from Shiloh would have resulted in their capture or dispersion, and that the campaign in the Mississippi Valley might have ended within thirty days after the battle we have just considered. Within a few days afterward, the Lower Mississippi, with the great city of New Orleans on its banks, was in the absolute possession of the National forces. Mitchel was holding a line of unbroken communication across Northern Alabama, from Florence to the confines of East Tennessee; and the National gun-boats on the Mississippi were preparing, though at points almost a thousand miles apart, to sweep victoriously over its waters, brush away obstructions to navigation, and meet, perhaps, at Vicksburg, the next "Gibraltar" of the Valley. Little was to be feared from troops coming from the East. They could not be spared, for at that time General McClellan was threatening Richmond with an immense force, and the National troops were assailing the strongholds of the Confederates all along the Atlantic coast and the waters of the Gulf of Mexico.

BEAUREGARD'S HEAD-QUARTERS AT CORINTH.[2]

Beauregard's army was terribly smitten and demoralized, and he had sent an imploring cry to Richmond for immediate help.[1] The way seemed wide open for his immediate destruction; but the judgment of General Halleck, the commander of both

[1] On the day after his arrival at Corinth, Beauregard forwarded a dispatch, written in cipher, to General Cooper, at Richmond, saying he could not then number over 35,000 effective men, but that Van Dorn might join him in a few days with about 15,000. He asked for re-enforcements, for, he said, "if defeated here, we lose the Mississippi Valley, and probably our cause." This dispatch was intercepted by General Mitchel, at Huntsville, and gave, doubtless, a correct view of Beauregard's extreme weakness thirty-six hours after he fled from Shiloh.

[2] This was the dwelling of Mr. Ford when the writer visited Corinth, late in April, 1866. It stood upon the brow of a gentle slope in the northwestern suburbs of the village.

Grant and Buell, counseled against pursuit, and for about three weeks the combined armies of the Tennessee and Ohio, not far from seventy-five thousand strong, rested among the graves of the loyal and the disloyal (who fought with equal gallantry) on the field of Shiloh, while Beauregard, encouraged by this inaction, was calling to his standard large re-enforcements, and was casting up around the important post of Corinth a line of fortifications not less than fifteen miles in extent.

Meanwhile the people everywhere had become acquainted with the true outline history of the great battle of Shiloh, and began to perceive its significance. Jefferson Davis, who, on the reception of Beauregard's dispatch of Sunday evening,[a] had sent an exultant message to the Confederate "Senate,"[1] had reason to change his tone of triumph; while the orders that went out from the War and Navy Departments at Washington[2] on the 9th,[b] for demonstrations of thanksgiving and joy throughout the army and navy for the victories gained at Pea Ridge, New Madrid, Island Number Ten, and Shiloh, and the proclamation from the Executive Department recommending the same in the houses of public worship throughout the land, were not stripped of their power by the fingers of truth. They were substantial and most important victories for the Government, over which the loyal people had reason to rejoice. Yet the latter battle was a victory that carried terrible grief to the hearts of thousands, for in the fields and forests around Shiloh hundreds of loved ones were buried, and the hospital vessels that went down the Tennessee with their human freight, carried scores of sick and wounded soldiers who never reached their homes alive.

[a] April 6, 1862.

[b] April.

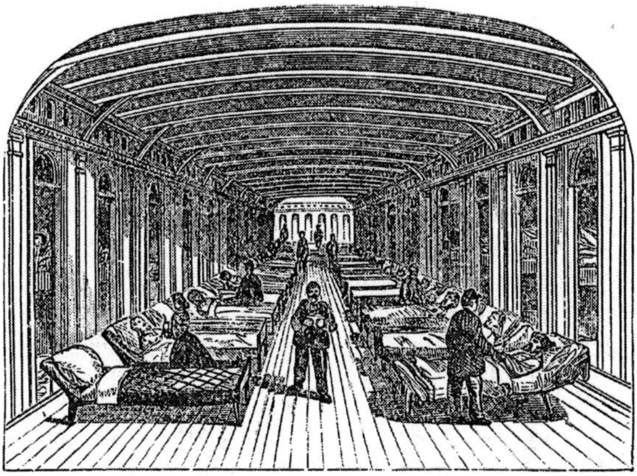

CABIN OF A HOSPITAL STEAMER ON THE TENNESSEE RIVER.

General Halleck arrived from St. Louis, his head-quarters, on the 12th of April,[c] and took command in person of the armies near Pittsburg Landing. He found General Grant busily engaged in prepa-

[c] 1862.

[1] He told them that, from "official dispatches received from official sources," he was able to announce, "with entire confidence," that it had "pleased Almighty God to crown the Confederate arms with a glorious and decisive victory, after a hard-fought battle of ten hours." He spoke in feeling terms of the death of Johnston, and of his loss as "irreparable."

[2] The order from each Department directed that, on the Sunday next after receiving it, chaplains should offer in each behalf a prayer, "giving thanks to the Lord of Hosts for the recent manifestations of His power, in the overthrow of rebels and traitors," and invoking a continuance of His aid in delivering the nation, "by arms, from the horrors of treason, rebellion, and civil war."

The President recommended (April 10) to the people, at their "next weekly assemblage in their accustomed places of public worship" which should occur after notice of his proclamation should be received, to especially acknowledge and render thanks to "our Heavenly Father for the inestimable blessings He had bestowed, and to implore His continuance of the same;" also to implore Him to hasten the establishment of fraternal relations at home, and "among all the countries of the earth."

rations for an advance upon Corinth while Beauregard was comparatively weak and disheartened, not doubting that it would be ordered on the arrival of his chief. He had sent Sherman out in that direction with a body of cavalry on the day after the battle, who skirmished some with horsemen of Breckinridge's rear-guard and drove them, and who found a general hospital with nearly three hundred sick and wounded in it. The roads, made miry by the recent rains, were strewn with abandoned articles of every kind, testifying to the precipitancy of the retreat. Sherman returned the same night, and was sent up the Tennessee, accompanied by the gun-boats as far as Eastport, to destroy the Memphis and Charleston railway over Big Bear Creek, between Iuka and Tuscumbia, and cut off Corinth from the latter place, where Colonel Turchin had large supplies. This expedition was arranged before Halleck arrived, and was successfully carried out, after which such demonstrations ceased for a while. No movement of importance was again made toward Corinth until about the first of May, when Monterey, nine or ten miles in that direction, was occupied by National troops. General Pope had arrived in the mean time,[a] with the Army of Missouri, twenty-five thousand strong, and these, with some regiments from Curtis, in Arkansas, made Halleck's forces a little over one hundred thousand in number.

[a] April 22, 1862.

General Mitchel, in the mean time, with his few troops and the cordial assistance of the negroes, who acted as spies and informers,[1] had been holding a hundred miles of the Memphis and Charleston railway, on Beauregard's most important flank, tightly in his grasp. Turchin held Tuscumbia,[2] at the western end of his line, until the 24th of April, when a Confederate force advanced from Corinth, for the purpose of seizing his stores (one hundred thousand rations, which had been sent to him by way of Florence), in such strength that he was compelled to fly; but he carried away the coveted property and fell back to Decatur, skirmishing on the way. He was yet hard pressed, so, burning a part of his provisions (forty thousand rations), he fled across the Tennessee River[b] at Decatur, his rear-guard under Colonel Lytle firing the magnificent railway bridge that spanned the stream at that place.[3] It was the only bridge over the Tennessee between Florence and Chattanooga, excepting one at Bridgeport, eastward of Stevenson, which was then the eastern extremity of Mitchel's occupation of the railway.

[b] April 27.

At this time Mitchel's left was threatened by a considerable force under General E. Kirby Smith, that came up from Chattanooga; and the Confederates were collecting here and there in his rear in alarming numbers. His chief objective was now Chattanooga, from which point he might operate

[1] General Mitchel informed the writer, late in the summer of that year, that he could not have held the railway from Tuscumbia to Stevenson so long as he did, had it not been for the assistance of the negroes. He found, near Huntsville, an intelligent one who was a carpenter. Having worked at his trade along the whole line of the railway then held, he knew trusty slaves on plantations all along its course, and of the Tennessee River. He employed this man to organize, among his fellow-slaves, a band of informers, who should watch the river and the railway, and report to him any hostile movements of the Confederates. To every man who should give important information he offered freedom from slavery, among the rewards. They were faithful, and he often checked incipient movements against his posts, in consequence of information received from these slaves.

[2] See page 267.

[3] That bridge, lying upon massive stone piers, was one of the finest of the kind in the South. It was not yet rebuilt when the writer visited Decatur and crossed the Tennessee in a ferry-boat, late in April, 1866.

against the great system of railways which connected the eastern and western portions of the Confederacy, and by their destruction or control to isolate the active body of that organization beyond the mountains from the scheming head at Richmond, and so paralyze its whole vitality. Mitchel proposed to reach out from Chattanooga a helping hand to East Tennessee in destroying the Confederate forces at Knoxville, Greenville, and Cumberland Gap; and another, as a destructive one, smiting the great founderies of the Confederates at Rome, and breaking up the railway connection between Chattanooga and Atlanta. Already a secret expedition for the latter purpose had been set on foot; and it was more important for Mitchel to extend his conquests to Chattanooga than to hold the posts at Decatur and Tuscumbia. Accordingly, when Colonel Turchin was driven from the latter place, Colonel Sill, at Stevenson, was ordered to Bridgeport, in the direction of Chattanooga, at which point a fine railway bridge crossed the Tennessee River.

When Turchin fled from Decatur, he was ordered to the support of Sill. Lytle's brigade of Ohioans joined that leader on the 28th, between Stevenson and Bridgeport, and, four miles from the latter place, a severe skirmish occurred the next day.[a] Mitchel, on hearing of the danger to his left, had hastened thither to take command in person. The skirmish resulted favorably to the Nationals. The Confederates were driven beyond the Tennessee, at Bridgeport, with a loss of sixty-three killed, many wounded, and two pieces of cannon. They attempted to destroy the great bridge[1] there, but failed. A detachment of Mitchel's troops crossed it in pursuit, captured two cannon on the eastern side, and, pushing on as far as Shellmound station, destroyed a Confederate saltpeter manufactory in Nickajack Cave, at the base of the mountain, half a mile southward of the railway.[2] Having secured the post at Bridgeport, Mitchel wrote to the Secretary of War on the first of May,[b] "The campaign is ended, and I now occupy Huntsville in perfect security, while in all Alabama north of the Tennessee River floats no flag but that of the Union."

[a] April 29, 1862.

[b] 1862.

Let us now return to a consideration of events in the vicinity of Corinth.

General Halleck's army commenced a cautious forward movement on the 27th of April,[c] and on the 3d of May his advance, under Sherman, was in the vicinity of Monterey, within six or seven miles of Beauregard's lines. It had been re-organized with the title of the *Grand Army of the Tennessee*, and Grant was made his second in command. That General's army was placed in charge of General George H. Thomas, and composed the right wing. General Pope commanded the left, and General Buell the center. The reserves, composed of his own and Wallace's divisions, were in charge of General McClernand. The whole force now slowly approaching Corinth, and cautiously casting up breastworks, numbered about one hundred and eight thousand men.

[c] 1862.

Beauregard prepared to meet Halleck. He too had been re-enforced, and his army was re-organized. Price and Van Dorn had arrived with a large

---

[1] The river is there divided by an island, and the bridge was a long and important one, as it continued at a considerable elevation over the island.

[2] This is a most remarkable cave, and has been explored for more than a mile. For some distance from its mouth it is spacious enough for a man to ride on horseback. This opening in the mountain is plainly visible from the railway near Shellmound station.

body of Missouri and Arkansas troops; and General Mansfield Lovell, who had fled from New Orleans when Butler's troops and the National gun-boats approached that city,[a] had just arrived with his retreating force. In addition to these, the army had been largely increased by militia who had been sent forward from Alabama, Mississippi, and Louisiana, the States immediately threatened with invasion. The organization of the corps of Hardee, Polk, Breckinridge, and Bragg, was continued. The whole number of Beauregard's troops was about sixty-five thousand. Most of them were the best drilled and best tried fighting men in the Confederacy. Bragg was Beauregard's second in rank, and commanded the *Army of the Mississippi.* Van Dorn was placed at the head of the re-enforcements, and Breckinridge of the reserves. The whole force was within intrenched lines.[1] Such was the condition and position of the contending armies on the 3d of May.[b]

[a] April 28, 1862.

[b] 1862.

On that day General Pope sent out Generals Paine and Palmer with detachments[2] on a reconnoissance in force toward the hamlet of Farmington, an outpost of the Confederates, about five miles northwest of Corinth, and then in command of General Marmaduke, of Missouri.[3] His troops, about forty-five thousand strong, were in the woods around the little log meeting-house near the hamlet. Marmaduke made very little resistance when attacked, but fled to the lines at Corinth, leaving as spoils for the victors about thirty of his command slain and a hundred wounded; also his camp, with all its supplies, and two hundred prisoners. The National loss was two killed and eleven wounded. The cavalry and artillery pushed on to Glendale, a little east of Corinth, and destroyed the railway track and two important trestle-bridges there. In the mean time, General Wallace had sent out[c] Colonel Morgan L. Smith, with three battalions of cavalry and a brigade of infantry, upon the Mobile and Ohio railway, who fought the Confederates in a wood, and destroyed an important bridge and the track not far from Purdy, by which supplies and re-enforcements for Beauregard, at Jackson, Tennessee, were cut off.[4]

FARMINGTON MEETING-HOUSE.

[c] April 30.

[1] These defenses were mostly along the brows of the first ridges outside of the village of Corinth, extending from the Memphis and Charleston railway on the east, and sweeping around northward, crossed the Mobile and Ohio railway to the former road, about three miles westward of Corinth. See map of the battle-field, on page 294. At every road-crossing there was a redoubt, or a battery with massive epaulements. Outside of these works on the north were deep lines of *abatis*.

[2] These troops were composed of the Tenth, Sixteenth, Twenty-second, Twenty-seventh, Forty-second, and Fifty-first Illinois volunteers; the Tenth and Sixteenth Michigan volunteers; Yates's Illinois sharp-shooters; Houghtailing's Illinois and Hezcock's Ohio batteries; and the Second Michigan cavalry.

[3] See page 540, volume I.

[4] This was a timely movement, for, while the bridge was burning, an engine that had been sent up from Corinth to help through three trains heavily laden with troops from Memphis, and hurrying forward by the longer way of Humbolt and Jackson, because the direct road was of insufficient capacity at that time, came thundering on. The Nationals, who lay in ambush, captured it, and ran it off at full speed into the ravine under the burning bridge. The re-enforcements for Beauregard were thus effectually cut off.

Pope left a brigade to hold Farmington and menace Beauregard's right. Twenty thousand men, under Van Dorn, fell upon them on the 9th,[a] and drove them back. Eight days afterward, Pope re-occupied the post with his whole force, and, at the same time, Sherman moved forward and menaced the Confederate left. On the 20th, Halleck's whole army was engaged in regular siege-operations, casting up field-work after field-work, so as to invest and approach Corinth, and at the same time engaging in skirmishing with all arms, in force equal to that employed in battles at the beginning of the war. Steadily the army moved on, and, on the 28th, it was at an average distance of thirteen hundred yards from Beauregard's works, with heavy siege-guns in position, and reconnoissances in great force in operation on flanks and center. In these the Confederates were driven back. On the following day, Pope expelled them from their advance batteries, and Sherman planted heavy guns within a thousand yards of Beauregard's left.

Halleck expected a sanguinary battle the next morning,[b] and prepared for it. He felt confident of success, and quite sure of capturing or dispersing the whole Confederate army, for he had a greatly superior force; had cut Beauregard's railway communications on the north and east of Corinth, and had sent Colonel Elliott on the night of the 27th to strike the Mobile and Ohio railway in his rear.

Halleck's expectations were not realized. All night the vigilant ears of his pickets and sentinels heard the continuous roar of moving cars at Corinth, and reported accordingly. At dawn skirmishers were thrown out, but no foe appeared. How strange! Then the earth was shaken by a series of explosions, and very soon heavy smoke rolled up from Corinth. What did all this mean? "I cannot explain it," said Halleck to an inquiry by Sherman; and then ordered that officer to advance and "feel the enemy if still in his front." This was done, but no enemy was found. Beauregard

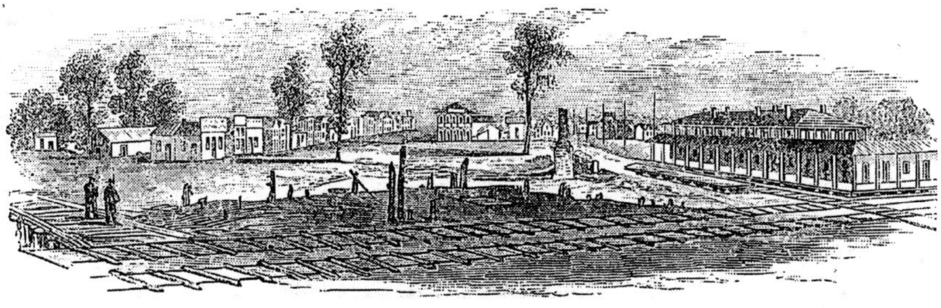

CORINTH AFTER THE EVACUATION.

had entirely evacuated Corinth during the night. For two or three days he had been sending toward Mobile his sick and his most valuable stores; and twenty-four hours before, he had sent away in the same direction a part of his effective force, with nearly all of his ordnance. The rear-guard had left for the south and west during the night, allowing many pickets, unsuspicious of the movement, to be captured. They had blown up the magazines, and fired the town, store-houses, and railway station; and when the Nationals entered[c] they found the smoldering ruins of many

[a] May, 1862.

[b] May 30.

[c] May 30.

dwellings, and warehouses filled with Confederate stores. Thus ended The Siege of Corinth; and thus the boastful Beauregard, whose performances generally fell far short of his promises, was utterly discomfited.[1] He staggered at Shiloh and fell at Corinth.

The fugitives were pursued by the brave Gordon Granger from Farmington to Guntown, on the Mobile and Ohio railway, a little more than forty miles south of Corinth, and there the chase ended. Few captures were made, excepting of stragglers. The expedition of Colonel Elliott, with his Iowa cavalry, had not materially intercepted Beauregard in his flight, for he did not strike the road until two o'clock on the morning of the 30th, when the Confederates were pressing southward in force. He destroyed much property at Boonville, and produced a panic, but the raid had little to do with the great result, except to expedite it.[2]

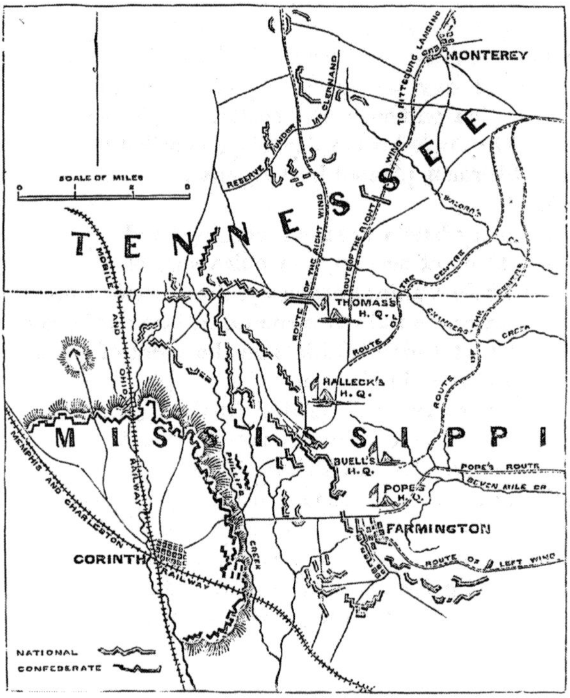

THE SIEGE OF CORINTH.

Beauregard collected his scattered troops at Tupelo, on a tributary of the Tombigbee, in a strong position, and on the 13th of June reported to head-quarters at Richmond that he was "doing all practicable to organize for defensive operations." He soon afterward turned over his army temporarily to General Bragg, and sought

[1] Beauregard had issued the following address to his combined army on the 8th of May: "*Soldiers of Shiloh and Elkhorn:** We are about to meet once more in the shock of battle the invaders of our soil, the despoilers of our homes, the disturbers of our family ties, face to face, hand to hand. We are to decide whether we are freemen, or vile slaves of those who are only free in name, and who but yesterday were vanquished, although in largely superior numbers, in their own encampments, on the ever-memorable field of Shiloh. Let the impending battle decide our fate, and add a more illustrious page to the history of our revolution—one to which our children will point with noble pride, saying, 'Our fathers were at the battle of Corinth.' I congratulate you on your timely junction. With our mingled banners, for the first time during the war, we shall meet our foe in strength that should give us victory. Soldiers, can the result be doubtful? Shall we not drive back to Tennessee the presumptuous mercenaries collected for our subjugation? One more manly effort, and, trusting in God and the justness of our cause, we shall recover more than we lately lost. Let the sound of our victorious guns be re-echoed by those of Virginia on the historic battle-field at Yorktown."†

[2] Colonel Elliott's movement, without doubt, hastened Beauregard's departure. When it became known to that General, a train of box and flat cars, with flying artillery and 5,000 infantry, were kept running up and down the road continually, to prevent Elliott's reaching it. He struck it at Boonville, at a little past midnight on the

* The Confederates, as we have observed, called the conflict between Curtis and Van Dorn, at Pea Ridge, the Battle of Elkhorn.

† It so happened that the Confederates had fled from Yorktown, before McClellan, on the day this address was issued.

repose and health for a few days at Bladen Springs, in Alabama. Jefferson Davis, whose will was law in the Confederacy, on hearing of this, directed Bragg, his favorite, to take permanent command of that army, and he "passionately declared" that Beauregard should not be reinstated, "though all the world should urge him to the measure."[1] This was a fortunate circumstance for the National cause.

Although the possession of Corinth was of great military importance, and the news of it was hailed with delight by the loyalists, it could not be considered a victory, in its proper sense. The Confederate army had escaped, with its cannon and most of its stores, thereby frustrating and deranging the plans of Halleck; and it was soon again ready for offensive operations. This result was charged to Halleck's tardiness; and experts declared their belief that, if he had remained in St. Louis a week longer, Grant, left free to act, would have captured Beauregard's army, supplies, and munitions of war.

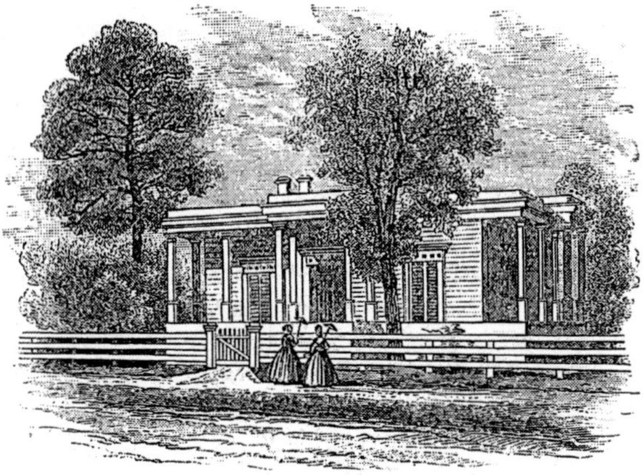

HALLECK'S HEAD-QUARTERS AT CORINTH.[2]

After the evacuation of Corinth, no military operations of importance were undertaken by the Grand Army of the Tennessee while General Halleck was in personal command of it. The Confederate fortifications at Corinth were much weaker than Halleck supposed, and were indeed unworthy of Beauregard, whose skill as an engineer was acknowledged by all. These Halleck proceeded to strengthen for defense, and as the heat of summer would make the Tennessee River too shallow for transportation for his supplies, the railways leading to Columbus from Corinth were put in order. A portion of the army was picketed along the railway between Iuka and Memphis; and General Buell was sent with the Army of the Ohio toward Chattanooga, where the active Mitchel was keeping General E. Kirby Smith, the Confederate commander in East Tennessee, in a state of continual alarm for the safety of his department. Mitchel begged Buell to march the combined forces into East Tennessee, but the more cautious General declined to do so.[3]

30th, destroyed the switch, track, depot, locomotives, twenty-six cars filled with supplies, 10,000 small arms, three pieces of artillery, and a large quantity of clothing and ammunition. He also captured and paroled 2,000 sick and convalescent soldiers, whom he found in a very suffering condition.

[1] Notes of an interview of a "Congressional Committee" with Davis, who requested the restoration of Beauregard, cited by General Jordan, in *Harper's Magazine*, xxxi., 616. While Beauregard was at Bladen, he wrote a letter to the Confederate General Martin, in which he expressed a coincidence of opinion with "Stonewall Jackson," that the time had come for raising the black flag—in other words, giving no quarter—but killing every foe, armed or disarmed, in battle. "I believe," he said, "it is the only thing that will prevent recruiting at the North."—See *The Weekly Register*, Lynchburg, Virginia, April 16, 1864.

[2] This was the dwelling of Mr. Symington when the writer visited Corinth, late in April, 1866. It was one of the houses in the suburbs of the village that survived the war.

[3] Oral statement of General Mitchel to the author, in August, 1862.

McClernand's reserve corps, employed in keeping open communication with the Tennessee River, was now broken up, and General Wallace was sent to preserve and protect the Memphis and Ohio railway between Humbolt and the City of Memphis. He made his head-quarters at the latter place; and very soon afterward Halleck was called to Washington, to occupy the important position of General-in-Chief of all the armies of the Republic in the place of McClellan, leaving General Thomas at Corinth, and General Grant again in command of his old army, and with enlarged powers.

We have just observed that Wallace made his head-quarters in Memphis. How came that city, one of the Confederate strongholds, and most important posts, to be in possession of the Nationals? Let us see.

We left Commodore Foote and his fleet, after the capture of Island Number Ten, ready, at New Madrid,[1] for an advance down the Mississippi River. This was soon begun, with General Pope's army on transports. Memphis was the main object of the expedition; but above it were several formidable fortifications to be passed.[2] The first of these that was encountered was Fort Wright (then named Fort Pillow), on the first Chickasaw bluff, about eighty miles above Memphis, and then in command of General Villepigue, a creole of New Orleans, who was educated at West Point as an engineer. He was regarded as second only to Beauregard. His fort was a very strong one, and the entire works occupied a line of seven miles in circumference. There Memphis was to be defended from invasion by the river from above. Jeff. Thompson was there, with about three thousand troops, and Hollins had collected there a considerable flotilla of gun-boats.

The siege of Fort Pillow was begun by Foote with his mortar-boats on the 14th of April, and he soon drove Hollins to shelter below the fort. General Pope, whose troops had landed on the Arkansas shore, was unable to co-operate, because the country was overflowed; and, being soon called by Halleck to Shiloh, Foote was left to prosecute the work alone. Finally, on the 9th of May, the painfulness of his ankle, because of the wound received at Fort Donelson, compelled him to leave duty, and he was succeeded in command by Captain C. H. Davis, whose important services with Dupont at Port Royal we have already observed.[3]

Hollins, meanwhile, had reformed his flotilla, and early in the morning of the 10th[a] he swept around Point Craighead, on the Arkansas shore, with armored steamers. Several of them were fitted with strong bows, plated with iron, for pushing, and were called "rams." Davis's vessels were then tied up at the river banks, three on the eastern and four on the western side of the stream.

[a] May, 1862.

Hollins's largest gun-boat (*McRea*), finished with a sharp iron prow, started for the mortar-boat No. 16, when its commander, Acting-master Gregory, made a gallant fight, firing his single mortar no less than eleven times.[4] The gun-boats *Cincinnati* and *Mound City*, lying not far off, came

---

[1] See page 248.

[2] These were Fort Osceola, on Plum Point, on the Arkansas shore; Fort Wright, on the first Chickasaw bluff; Fort Harris, nearly opposite Island Number Forty, and Fort Pillow, just above Memphis. Fort Pillow was named in honor of the Confederate General; Fort Wright in honor of Colonel Wright, of the Tennessee troops, who cast up fortifications there a year before; and Fort Harris after the fugitive Governor of Tennessee.

[3] See page 117.

[4] The engines of the *McRea* were protected by railway iron, and other parts were shielded by bales of

to his assistance. The *McRea* then turned upon the former with great fury, striking her port quarter, and making a large hole. The *Cincinnati* gave the ram a broadside, when the latter drew off, struck the gun-boat again on her starboard side, making an ugly wound. The assailed vessel gave its antagonist another broadside, when the ram *Van Dorn*, that now came up, struck her in the stern. The *Mound City* hastened to help her companion, and as she bore down she hurled a heavy shot at the *McRea*, which dismounted its bow gun, which was about to be discharged at her. Seeing this, another ram (the *Sumter*) hastened to the support of the *McRea*, and, in spite of two broadsides from the *Mound City*, she pressed on and struck the bow of the latter vessel with such force, that a breach was made in her through which the water poured in large streams. The *Sumter* was about to strike its victim again, when the gun-boat *Benton* gave her a broadside with telling effect.

The Confederate gun-boats were lying on the Tennessee shore, meanwhile, and firing at the National vessels every few minutes, while the howitzers of Fort Pillow were throwing shells, but without effect. Finally, the *Benton* sent a shell that pierced the *McRea.* Hot steam instantly enveloped the vessel, killing and scalding many of its people, and causing its flag to be struck in token of surrender. The conflict, which had continued for an hour, now ceased. The *McRea* floated away and escaped; the *Cincinnati* and *Mound City* were too much injured to give chase, and the former soon sunk to the bottom of the Mississippi. The Union loss in the engagement was four men wounded. That of the Confederates was said to have been heavy, especially on the *McRea*, by the steam. Among the wounded was Captain Stembel, of the *Cincinnati*, very severely, a ball having entered his body at the right shoulder, and passing out at his throat.

For more than three weeks the two flotillas lay off Fort Pillow, watching each other, and in the mean time that of Davis had been re-enforced by a "ram" squadron under Colonel Charles Ellet, Jr., the eminent civil engineer, who built the Niagara Suspension Bridge. He had recommended the use of such vessels, and had been constructing them under the authority of the Secretary of War.[1] But when, with this addition, the National fleet was ready for another trial of strength, at the beginning of June, there was no foe to encounter at Fort Pillow. The flight

CHARLES ELLET.

cotton, behind which there was a large number of Jeff. Thompson's sharp-shooters, to pick off the officers of the National vessels. The "rams" proper were protected by cotton and filled with sharp-shooters, yet it was seldom that a man appeared on their decks.

[1] These vessels were river boats, some with stern wheels and some with side wheels, whose bows were strengthened by the addition of heavy timber, and covered with plates of iron. Their chief business was to destroy vessels by powerful collision. Their average cost to the Government was between $25,000 and $30,000 each.

of Beauregard from Corinth had filled the garrison with alarm, and on the night of the 4th[a] they evacuated that post in great haste, leaving every thing behind them, blowing up their magazines, and burning their barracks and stores. The National standard was hoisted over the works the next morning. The fugitives went down the river in transports, accompanied by the Confederate fleet. Fort Randolph was also evacuated, and Colonel Ellet, whose ram fleet was in advance of the now pursuing flotilla, raised the flag over that stronghold likewise.[b] The same evening the flotilla of gun-boats[1] anchored at about a mile and a half above Memphis, and the ram fleet[2] a little farther up the river. The Confederate fleet,[3] now commanded by "Commodore" Montgomery, in place of Hollins, was then lying on the Arkansas shore, opposite Memphis, with steam up, and ready for action.

[a] June, 1862.

[b] June 5.

At dawn on the morning of the 6th,[c] the National vessels, with the *Cairo* in the advance, moved slowly toward the Confederate fleet, in battle order. When within long range, the *Little Rebel* hurled a shot from her rifled cannon at the *Cairo*, to which the latter answered by a broadside. So the conflict was opened in front of the populous city of Memphis, whose inhabitants, suddenly aroused from repose, quickly covered the bluffs and roofs as most anxious spectators of what soon became a severe naval battle. This was waged for a time between the gun-boats, when two of the Confederate rams (*Beauregard* and *Price*) pushed swiftly forward to engage in the affray. The watchful Colonel Ellet saw this movement, and instantly took a position in front of the gun-boats with his flag-vessel, the ram *Queen of the West*, followed by the ram *Monarch*, Captain Dryden. They both made for the two Confederate rams, when the latter, unwilling to fight, tried to get away. The *Queen* dashed first at the *Beauregard* (which opened fire), and missed her, but was more successful in chasing the *Price*. She struck the wheel-house of that vessel with her iron prow, crushing it, and so damaging the hull that she was compelled to run for the Arkansas shore, to avoid sinking in deep water. The *Beauregard* now turned furiously upon the *Queen*, when both vessels rushed toward each other at full speed. The skillful pilot of the former so managed his vessel as to avoid a blow from the latter, but gave one to the *Queen* so heavily that she was disabled. Her consort, the *Monarch*, hastened to her relief. Dashing at the *Beauregard*, she stove in her bow, and caused her to sink in the space of a few minutes, but in water so shallow that her upper works were above it. A white flag waved over the ruined vessel, and the fight of the terrible rams ceased. The *Monarch* found the *Queen* in the midst of the smoke, badly wounded, and towed her to a place of safety at the shore.

[c] June.

The National gun-boats continued pressing hard upon those of the Confederates, which were steadily falling back. A conquering blow was soon given by the *Benton*, whose 50-pound rifled Parrott gun hurled a ball at the

---

[1] *Benton*, Captain Phelps; *Carondelet*, Captain Walke; *St. Louis*, Lieutenant-commanding McGonigle; *Louisville*, Captain Dove; *Cairo*, Lieutenant Bryant.

[2] These consisted of the *Monarch Queen of the West*, *Lioness*, *Switzerland*, *Mingo*, *Lancaster No. 3*, *Fulton*, *Hornet*, and *Samson*, all under the general command of Colonel Ellet.

[3] It consisted of the *General Van Dorn* (Hollins's flagship), *General Price*, *General Bragg*, *General Lovell*, *Little Rebel*, *Jeff. Thompson*, *Sumter*, and *General Beauregard*.

Lovell with such precision and effect that she was made a wreck in an instant, and began to sink. In less than four minutes she went to the bottom of the Mississippi, where the water was seventy-five feet in depth. A greater portion of the officers and crew of the *Lovell* went down with her, or were drowned before help could reach them. The battle continued only a short time after this, when the Confederates, having only four vessels afloat (*Thompson*, *Bragg*, *Sumter*, and *Van Dorn*), and these badly injured, made for the shore, where they abandoned all their craft but one, and fled for life and liberty. The *Van Dorn* escaped down the river, the sole survivor of the Confederate fleet. Not a man had been killed on board the National gun-boats during the action. What the Confederate loss was, in killed and wounded, is not known. About one hundred of them were made captives.

Jeff. Thompson, then in command in Memphis, after providing for the safe flight of his troops, had stood upon the bluff and watched the strange naval battle. When he saw his friends vanquished, he galloped away and joined his retreating troops.

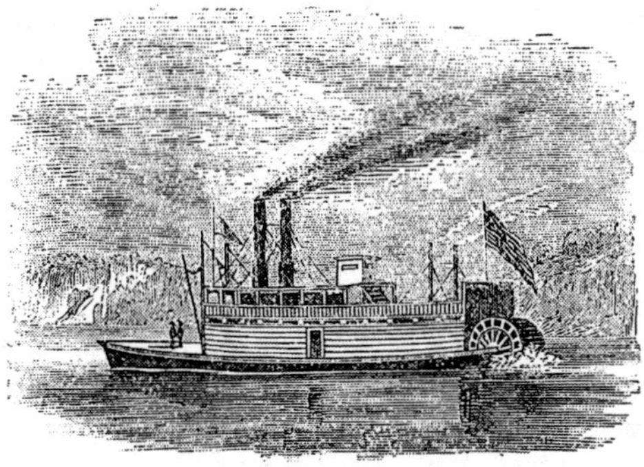

ELLET'S STERN-WHEEL RAM.

The National fleet was now drawn up in front of Memphis, and Commodore Davis sent a request to the Mayor of the city to surrender it. That officer (John Park[1]) replied, that, as the civil authorities had no means for defense, the city was in his hands. The National flag had already been raised there. Colonel Ellet, at the conclusion of the ram fight, informed that a white flag was waving in the city, approached the shore on his vessel, and sent his son, Charles R. Ellet, with a message to the Mayor, saying, that the bearer would place the National ensign on the Custom-house and Post-office, "as evidence of the return of the city to the care and protection of the Constitution." The Mayor made a reply to this note, substantially the same as that to Commodore Davis; and young Ellet, with Lieutenant Crankell, of the Fifty-ninth Illinois, and two men of the boat-guard, unfurled the Stripes and Stars over the Post-office, in the midst of an excited and threatening populace.

Immediate military possession of Memphis followed the reply of Mayor Park to Commodore Davis, and Colonel Fitch, of the Forty-sixth Indiana, was appointed Provost-marshal. So it was that General Wallace, of Grant's army, was permitted to enter and occupy Memphis without resistance. His advent was hailed with joy by the Indiana regiment there and the Union citizens, for they were not strong enough to repress the secessionists, or guard the city against the incursions of Jeff. Thompson's guerrillas.

All Kentucky, Western Tennessee, and Northern Mississippi and Alabama were now in the possession of the National authorities, and it was confidently expected that East Tennessee would almost immediately be in the same

[1] See page 249.

position. When General Buell joined Mitchel, after the close of the siege of Corinth, the latter, as we have observed, urged that officer to march directly into the great valley between the Cumberland and Alleghany Mountains, by way of Chattanooga and Cleveland, for it then seemed an easy matter to do so. Buell would not consent, and again East Tennessee, made confident of speedy liberation by so large an army on its borders, was doomed to bitter disappointment, and the endurance of still greater afflictions than it had yet suffered.

[a] May 1, 1862.

Although Mitchel had assured the Secretary of War[a] that his campaign was ended,[1] and that he occupied Huntsville in perfect security, he was not idle nor less vigilant than before. He not only watched, but worked, and scouts and raiders were continually out on special duties, the chief object being to keep danger from his rear, and the door open into East Tennessee and Northern Georgia. Colonels Turchin and Lytle were sent northward along the line of the Nashville and Decatur railway, while General Negley was operating in that vicinity, and farther eastward, dispersing the Confederate forces at various points. On the 13th of May, the latter went out from Pulaski on that railway, and, supported by Colonel Lytle, at Athens below, drove a gathering force of Confederates from Rogersville, in Alabama, across the Tennessee River.[2]

[b] June 4.

Later, Colonel Turchin, who was at Athens, was attacked by Confederates[b] and driven away. In the assault and pursuit, many of the citizens of that village joined. With re-enforcements Turchin returned, and drove the Confederate troops out of the town, when his exasperated soldiers sacked and pillaged the houses of secessionists there, because of their active complicity in the hostile movements. For this Colonel Turchin was tried by a court martial, and acquitted. He was promoted to brigadier-general while the investigation was going on.

[c] June 4.

On the same day,[c] General Negley, who, in a forced march of twenty miles, had climbed over an almost impassable mountain, northeastward of Stevenson, surprised a Confederate camp of cavalry under General Adams at its foot, at a place called Sweeden's Cove, on the road between Winchester and Jasper, and drove them from it. After a very severe skirmish near Jasper, in which Colonel Hambright led the Nationals, the Confederates were routed and dispersed, leaving as spoils their ammunition and commissary wagons with supplies; also arms scattered along the pathway of their flight, and twelve prisoners. Adams escaped without his hat, sword, or horse, borrowing one of the latter from a negro on which to fly. Negley lost two killed and seven wounded.[3]

But one of the most important of the expeditions sent out by Mitchel, and, indeed, one of the most daring of the war, was the secret one, already alluded to, sent to break up the railway between Chattanooga and Atlanta. This expedition was composed of twenty-two picked men,[4] led by J. J. Andrews, who had been for several months in the secret service under

---

[1] See page 291.
[2] Reports of Generals Mitchel and Negley, May 14th and 18th, 1862.
[3] Report of General Negley to General Mitchel, June 4, 1862.
[4] Two of these (Andrews and Campbell) were civilians, and citizens of Kentucky; the remainder were soldiers, selected from the Second, Twenty-first, and Thirty-third Ohio regiments of volunteers, Sill's brigade. Their names were as follows: J. J. Andrews, William Campbell, George D. Wilson, Marion A. Ross, Perry G.

General Buell. He had proposed the expedition to Buell at Nashville, and that officer directed General Mitchel, then at Murfreesboro, to furnish him with the means for carrying it out.[1] Mitchel did so with alacrity, for it promised to be of vast service to him in executing his designs against the Confederates beyond the Tennessee River; and that band of young men left in detachments on their perilous errand at about the time when that daring general commenced his march for Alabama. They passed within the Confederate lines at Wartrace, on the Nashville and Chattanooga railway, thirteen miles from Murfreesboro, traveling on foot as Confederate citizens making their way from oppression in Kentucky to freedom in Georgia. In this disguise they went over the rugged Cumberland mountains. Most of them met at Chattanooga, on the day that Mitchel took possession of Huntsville.[a] Some, who had arrived sooner, had gone by railway to Marietta, in Georgia, the final rendezvous of the party before commencing operations. On the same evening the whole party were at the latter place.

[a] April 11, 1862.

The designated point at which to begin their bold raid on the Georgia State road was at Big Shanty, eight miles above Marietta, and a short distance from the foot of the Great Kenesaw Mountain, where several regiments of Confederate troops were stationed. With an early train the next morning, all but two of the party, who were accidentally left behind, started for that place. While the conductor and engineer were at breakfast, the raiders uncoupled the engine and three empty box-cars from the passenger cars, and started at full speed up the road,[2] leaving behind them wonderers who could scarcely believe the testimony of their own eyes. On they went with the fleetness of the wind, answering all questions satisfactorily, where they were compelled to stop, with the assurance that it was a powder-train for Beauregard. After going five miles on their journey, they cut the telegraph wires and picked up about fifty cross-ties. Before reaching Adamsville, at a curve on the summit of a high embankment, they tore up the rails of the road, and placed some of the ties in such position on the bank that a passing train was hurled off and down the precipice. At this point Andrews said, exultingly, "Only one more train to pass, boys, and then we will put our engine to full speed, burn the bridges after us, dash through Chattanooga, and on to Mitchel at Huntsville."

But more than one train had to be passed before they could commence their destructive work; and just as they had begun it, well up toward Calhoun, they were made to desist and flee by the sound of the whistle of a pursuing train. When this came to the break in the road just mentioned, the engineer of the train they had passed, made acquainted with the circumstances, reversed his engine, and it became a pursuer. Then occurred one of the most thrilling races on record. Both engines were put at full speed, and away they went, thundering along, to the amazement of the inhabitants,

---

Shadrack, Samuel Slavens, Samuel Robinson, John Scott, W. W. Brown, William Knight, J. R. Porter, Mark Wood, J. A. Wilson, M. J. Hawkins, John Wollam, D. A. Dorsey, Jacob Parrott, Robert Buffum, William Bensinger, William Reddick, E. H. Mason, William Pettinger.

[1] Letter of General Buell to the adjutant-general, August, 1863.

[2] Andrews, the leader, W. W. Brown, and William Knight, had taken position on the locomotive; Brown being the engineer, while J. A. Wilson, mounted on one of the box-cars, acted as brakesman.

who had no conception of the urgency of the errand of both. That of the pursued, having the less burden, was fleetest, but its time was consumed by stopping to cut telegraph wires and tear up rails. The latter, and also ties, were cast upon the track; but very soon the pursuers were too close to allow the pursued to do this, or to allow them to take in a supply of fuel and water. Their lubricating oil became exhausted; and, such was the speed of the machine, that the brass journals on which the axles revolved were melted. Fuel failing, the fugitives despaired; and, when within fifteen miles of Chattanooga, Andrews ordered them to leave the train, and every man to seek his own safety. They jumped from the train while it was in motion, and fled for shelter to the tangled forests of Georgia, around the sinuous Chickamauga Creek.[a]

[a] April 12, 1862.

Notice of this chase had been telegraphed to Chattanooga, and produced great consternation. A stupendous man-hunt was at once organized. Rewards were offered; every ford, ferry, cross-road, and mountain pass was picketed; and thousands of horsemen and foot soldiers and citizens, and several blood-hounds, scoured the country in all directions. The whole party were finally captured and imprisoned; and thus ended one of the most adventurous incidents in history.[1] Twelve of them, after being confined at Chattanooga, were taken to Knoxville for trial, and kept in the iron cages there in which Brownlow and his friends had suffered, in the county jail.[2] Andrews, the leader, soon afterward escaped from the prison at Chattanooga, but, after intense suffering on the shores and little islands of the Tennessee River, was re-captured, taken to Atlanta with eight of his comrades, and was there hanged without trial. Seven of those who were taken to Knoxville had been tried by a court-martial as spies, when the cannon of General Mitchel, thundering near Chattanooga, broke up the court, and the prisoners, against whom there was not a particle of evidence to support the charge, were soon afterward conveyed to Atlanta. After a brief confinement, the seven who had been arraigned at Knoxville were taken out and hanged. Eight of those bold and patriotic young men thus gave their lives to their country.[3] Eight of their companions afterward escaped from confinement, and six were exchanged as prisoners of war in March, 1863. To each of the survivors of that raid, the Secretary of War afterward presented a medal of honor.[4] When the writer visited the National cemetery at Chatta-

ENTRANCE TO THE CAVE.

[1] The adventure commanded the admiration of both parties. "It was the deepest laid scheme, and on the grandest scale," said an Atlanta newspaper, on the 15th of April, "that ever emanated from the brains of any number of Yankees." Judge Holt, in an official report, said: "The expedition, in the daring of its conception, had the wildness of a romance, while, in the gigantic and overwhelming results it sought, and was likely to accomplish, it was absolutely sublime."

[2] See page 37.

[3] These were, Andrews, Campbell, G. D. Wilson, Ross, Shadrack, Stevens, Robinson, and Scott.

[4] This medal was precisely like that presented to naval heroes. Instead of an anchor at the connective between the medal and the ribbon, there was an eagle surmounting crossed cannon, and some balls.

nooga, in May, 1866, he saw, in the cave that forms the receiving vault,[1] seven coffins, containing the remains of the seven young men who were hanged at Atlanta, and which had lately been brought from that city for re-interment.[2]

Before General Buell's arrival, General Mitchel had made an effort to seize Chattanooga. His force was too small to effect it, for Kirby Smith, commanding the Confederates in East Tennessee; was skillful, active, and watchful. Mitchel had asked for re-enforcements, but they were not afforded. Finally, General Negley, three days after his successful attack on Adams, near Jasper, having made his way rapidly over the rugged ranges of the Cumberland Mountains, suddenly appeared opposite Chattanooga. It was on the morning of the 7th of June when he arrived. Toward evening he had heavy guns in position; and for two hours he cannonaded the town and the Confederate works on Cameron's Hill and at its base. The guns of his enemy were silenced; and that night the inhabitants fled from the town. During the darkness Smith was re-enforced, and some of his infantry took positions to annoy Negley greatly. The latter opened his batteries again at nine o'clock, and before noon the Confederates had all been driven from the town and their works, and had commenced burning railway bridges, eastward of Chattanooga, to impede a pursuit. Considering the inferiority of his numbers, and the approach of re-enforcements for Smith, Negley prudently withdrew. Reporting to the military governor of Tennessee, he said, "The Union people in East Tennessee are wild with joy."

Here, it now seems, was presented a golden moment in which to accomplish great results, but it was not improved. With a few more regiments, Negley might have captured and held Chattanooga; and Buell and Mitchel could doubtless have marched into East Tennessee with very little resistance, and so firmly established the National power there that it might not have been broken during the remainder of the war. But General Buell would not consent to such movement, even when the thunder of Negley's cannon at Chattanooga made the Confederates in all that region so fearful, that they were ready to abandon every thing at the first intimation of an advance of their adversary. See how precipitately they fled from Cumberland Gap, their "Gibraltar of the mountains," and the fortified heights around it, when, ten days after the assault on Chattanooga, General George W. Morgan, with a few Ohio and Kentucky troops, marched against it[a] from Powell's Valley. Twenty miles his soldiers traveled that day, climbing the Cumberland Mountains, dragging their cannon up the precipices by block and tackle, and skirmishing all the way without losing a man. They were cheered by rumors that the foe had fled. At sunset they were at the main works, and the flags of the Sixteenth Ohio and Twenty-second Kentucky were floating over those fortifications in the twilight. The Confederate rear-guard had departed four hours before; and the whole force had fled so hastily that they left almost every thing behind them. They had been supplied with food chiefly by plunderers of the Union

[a] Jan. 18, 1862.

---

[1] This cave and the National cemetery will be considered hereafter.

[2] For a minute account of the daring adventures of Andrews and his party of young soldiers, see a well-written volume from the pen of one of them (Lieutenant William Pettinger, of the Second Ohio), entitled, *Daring and Suffering: A History of the Great Railroad Adventure.*

people. They saw a prospect of a sudden cessation of that supply, so they fled while a way of escape was yet open.

The cautious Buell and the fiery Mitchel did not work well together, and the latter was soon called to Washington City and assigned to the command of the Department of the South, with his head-quarters at Hilton Head, leaving his troops in the West in charge of General Rousseau. For a short

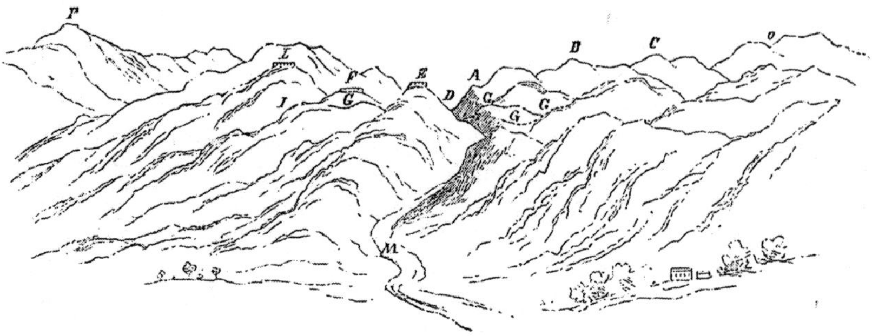

CUMBERLAND GAP AND ITS DEPENDENCIES.[1]

time afterward there was a lull in the storm of war westward of the Alleghany Mountains, but it was the precursor of a more furious tempest. During that lull, let us observe and consider events on the Atlantic coast, along the northern shores of the Gulf of Mexico, and on the Lower Mississippi.

---

[1] Cumberland Gap is a cleft in the Cumberland Mountains, five hundred feet in depth, and only wide enough at the bottom in some places for a roadway. It forms the principal door of entrance to southeastern Kentucky from the great valley of East Tennessee, and during the war was a position of great military importance. It was very strongly fortified by the Confederates at the beginning of the contest, and supporting works were constructed on all of the neighboring heights. The relative position of these, their names, and a general outline of the mountains at the Gap, and in the vicinity, are seen in the above topographical sketch, by Dr. B. Howard, of the United States Army, from the western side. A small force, well provisioned, might have held the Gap against an immense army.

EXPLANATION.—A, Fort State corner; B, a fort not named; C, Fort Colonel Churchill; D, the Gap; E, Fort Colonel Rains; F, Fort Colonel Mallory; G, G, G, G, stockades and rifle-pits; I, Lewis's Gap; L, Fort Colonel Hunter; M, Kentucky road through the Gap; O, Baptists' Gap; P, Earthworks then recently constructed.

CHAPTER XII.

OPERATIONS ON THE COASTS OF THE ATLANTIC AND THE GULF OF MEXICO.

WE left General Burnside in Albemarle Sound, after the capture of Roanoke Island and the operations at Elizabeth City, Edenton, and Plymouth,[1] preparing for other conquests on the North Carolina coast. For that purpose he concentrated his forces, with the fleet now in command of Commodore Rowan (Goldsborough having been ordered to Hampton Roads), at Hatteras Inlet. New Berne, the capital of Craven County, at the confluence of the rivers Trent and Neuse, was his first object of attack.[2]

The land and naval forces left Hatteras Inlet on the morning of the 12th of March,[a] and at sunset the gun-boats and transports anchored off the mouth of Slocum's Creek, about eighteen miles from New Berne, where Burnside had determined to make a landing. His troops numbered about fifteen thousand. The landing was begun at seven o'clock the next morning,[b] under cover of the gun-boats; and so eager were the men to get ashore, that many, too impatient to wait for the boats, leaped into the water, waist deep, and waded to the land. Then they pushed on in the direction of New Berne, in a copious rain, dragging their heavy cannon,[3] with great difficulty and fatigue, through the wet clay, into which men often sank knee deep. The head of the column was within a mile and a half of the Confederate works at sunset, when it halted and bivouacked. During the night the remainder of the army came up in detachments hour after hour, meeting no resistance. The gun-boats meanwhile had moved up the river abreast the army, the flag-ship *Delaware* leading. A shore-battery opened upon her at four o'clock in the afternoon, but was soon quieted by her reply.

[a] 1862.

[b] March 13.

The main body of the Confederates, under the command of General Branch, consisted of eight regiments of infantry and five hundred cavalry, with three batteries of field-artillery of six guns each. These occupied a line of intrenchments extending more than a mile from near the river across the railway, supported by another line, on the inland flank, of rifle-pits and detached intrenchments in the form of curvettes and redans, for more than a mile, and terminating in a two-gun redoubt. On the river-bank and cover-

---

[1] See Chapter VI. pages 170 to 175, inclusive.

[2] New Berne was a point of much military importance. It was near the head of an extensive and navigable arm of the sea, and was connected by railway with Beaufort harbor at Morehead City, and Raleigh, the capital of the State.

[3] Among them were six naval howitzers that Rowan put ashore, under Lieutenant R. S. McCook, to assist in the attack.

ing their left was Fort Thompson, four miles from New Berne, armed with thirteen heavy guns; and other works and appliances, prepared by good engineering skill, for the defense of the river-channel against the passage of gun-boats, were numerous.[1]

[a] March, 1862.

At daylight on the morning of the 14th,[a] the army moved forward in three columns, under Generals Foster, Reno, and Parke. A heavy fog lay for a short time upon the land and water, but it was soon dissipated. Foster, with the first brigade, marched up the main country road to attack Fort Thompson and the Confederate left. Reno, with the second brigade, followed nearer the line of the railway, to fall upon their right; and Parke, with the third brigade, kept such position that he might attack their front or assist the other two brigades.

Foster began battle at eight o'clock.[2] At the same time Reno pushed on toward the Confederate right flank, while Parke took position on their front. Foster was supported on his left by the boat-howitzers, manned by Lieutenants McCook, Hammond, Daniels, and Tillotson, with marines and a detachment of the Union Coast Guard. Before the Confederate center was placed a 12-pounder steel cannon, under Captain Bennett, of the *Cossack*, who was assisted in its management by twenty of that ship's crew; and on the left of the insurgents was Captain Dayton's battery, from the transport *Highlander*.

Foster's brigade bore the brunt of the battle for about four hours. In response to his first gun, the assailed ran up the Confederate flag with a shout, and opened a brisk fire which soon became most severe. There was a hard struggle for the position where their intrenchments crossed the railway, and in this the Second Massachusetts and Tenth Connecticut were conspicuous. General Parke gave support to Foster until it was evident that the latter could sustain himself, when the former, with his whole brigade excepting the Eleventh Connecticut, Colonel Mathews, went to the support of Reno in his flank movement, which that officer was carrying on with success. After he had fought about an hour, he ordered the Twenty-first Massachusetts, Colonel Clark, to charge a portion of the Confederate works. It dashed forward at the double-quick, accompanied by General Reno in person, and in a few moments was within the intrenchments, from which it was as speedily driven by two of Branch's regiments. This was followed by a charge of the Fourth Rhode Island upon a battery of five guns in its front, supported by rifle-pits. The battery was captured, the National flag was unfurled over it, and its occupants and supporters were driven pell-mell far away

---

[1] A little below Fort Thompson was Fort Dixie, four guns. Between Fort Thompson and the city were Forts Brown, Ellis, and Lane, each mounting eight guns; and a mile from New Berne was Union Point Battery, of two guns, manned by a company of public singers. In the channel of the Neuse were twenty-four sunken vessels, several torpedoes,* and submerged iron-pointed spars, planted so as to pierce the bottoms of vessels ascending the river. On the left bank of the Neuse was a succession of redoubts, over half a mile in extent, in the midst of woods and swamps, for riflemen and field-pieces.

[2] His troops consisted of the Twenty-third, Twenty-fourth, Twenty-fifth, and Twenty-seventh Massachusetts, commanded respectively by Colonels Kurtz, Stevenson, Upton, and Lee; and the Tenth Connecticut, Colonel Drake.

---

* These torpedoes consisted of a cylinder of iron, about ten inches in diameter, into which fitted a heavily loaded bomb-shell, resting on springs. The torpedo was placed on the point of heavy timber, in the form and position of *chevaux-de-frise*, held firmly at the bottom of the river by stones in a box, and lying at an angle of forty-five degrees in the direction of an approaching vessel. The shell was so arranged, that when a vessel should strike the cylinder on the point of the timber, a percussion cap would be discharged and the shell exploded. These were very formidable missiles, but the gun-boats did not go near them.

from their lost guns and breast-works. The victory was made complete by the aid of the Fifth Rhode Island and Eighth and Eleventh Connecticut.

All this while, Reno was losing heavily from the effects of another battery. So he called up his reserve regiment (the Fifty-first Pennsylvania, Colonel Hartrauft), and ordered it to charge the work. It was done gallantly, and the Fifty-first New York, Twenty-first Massachusetts, and Ninth New Jersey participated in the achievement and the triumph. Foster, meanwhile, hearing the shouts on the left when the order to charge was given, had directed his brigade to advance along the whole line. Pressed at all points, on front and flank, the Confederates abandoned every thing and fled, pursued by Foster to the verge of the Trent. The fugitives were more fleet than he, and, burning the railway and turnpike bridges behind them that spanned the Trent (the first by sending a raft of flaming turpentine and cotton against it), they escaped. So ended the BATTLE OF NEW BERNE.[1]

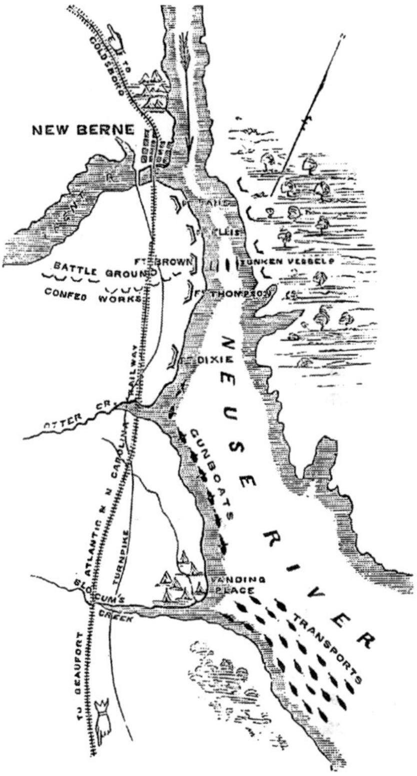

OPERATIONS NEAR NEW BERNE.

The National squadron, in the mean time, had co-operated with the army in the attack on Fort Thompson, and in driving the Confederates from the other batteries on the shore. When these were evacuated, the gun-boats passed the obstructions and went up to the city. The Confederate troops had fired it in seven places, and then hurried to Tuscarora, about ten miles from New Berne, where they halted. Large numbers of the terrified citizens had abandoned their homes and fled to the interior. No less than seven railway trains, crowded to overflowing with men, women, and children, left New Berne for Goldsboro' on the day of the battle. "The town of New Berne," says Pollard, "originally contained twelve hundred people; when occupied by the enemy, it contained one hundred people, male and female, of the old population." Pollard did not count the large number of colored loyalists who remained as "people."

General Foster's brigade was taken over the Trent and to the city wharves by some of Rowan's boats, and took military possession of New Berne. General Burnside made the fine old mansion of the Stanley family,

---

[1] See reports of General Burnside and his subordinate officers, and of Commodore Rowan.

in the suburbs of the town, his head-quarters, and there, on the following day, he issued an order, appointing General Foster military governor of the city, and directing the places of public worship to be opened on Sunday, the 16th, at a suitable hour, in order that the chaplains of the different regiments might hold divine service in them; the bells to be rung as usual. On the same day Burnside issued an order, congratulating his troops on account of the "brilliant and hard-won victory," and directed each regiment engaged in it to place the name of *New Berne* on its banner. In his report, he spoke in the highest terms of the courage and fidelity of his troops, and gave to the general-in-chief (McClellan) the credit of planning the expedition.[1]

BURNSIDE'S HEAD-QUARTERS, NEW BERNE.

In this battle the Nationals lost about one hundred in killed and four hundred and ninety-eight in wounded. Among the former were Lieutenant-Colonel Henry Merritt, of the Twenty-third Massachusetts, and other gallant officers and men. The loss of the Confederates was much less in killed and wounded, but two hundred of them were made prisoners.[2] The spoils of victory were many and important,;[3] and the possession of the town of New Berne, by which the Wilmington and Weldon Railway, the great line of travel between the North and the South, was exposed, gave to the National cause in that region an almost incalculable advantage. Its moral effect was prodigious, and greatly disheartened the enemies of the Government, who saw in it "a subject of keen mortification to the South."[4]

In the midst of the horrors of war at New Berne, and almost before the smoke of battle was dissipated, the Christian spirit of the friends of the Government was made conspicuous in acts of benevolence by the generous deeds of Vincent Colyer, a well-known citizen of New York, and the originator of the CHRISTIAN COMMISSION of the army, whose holy ministrations, nearly co-extensive with those of the UNITED STATES SANITARY COMMISSION, in the camp, the field, and the hospital, throughout almost the entire period of the war, will be considered hereafter. Mr. Colyer was with Burnside's

---

1 "I beg to say to the general commanding the army," he wrote, "that I have endeavored to carry out the very minute instructions given me by him before leaving Annapolis, and thus far events have been singularly coincident with his anticipations."

2 They reported their loss at 64 killed, 101 wounded, and 413 missing.

3 These were the important town and harbor of New Berne; eight batteries mounting forty-six heavy guns: three batteries of light artillery of six guns each; two steamboats; a number of sailing vessels; wagons, horses, and mules; a large quantity of ammunition and army supplies; the entire camp equipage of the Confederates; and much turpentine, rosin, and cotton,

4 Pollard's *First Year of the War*, i. 288.

expedition for the two-fold purpose of distributing to the sick and wounded the generous contributions of patriotic and charitable citizens, and to exercise a fostering care of the poor and ignorant colored people, from whose limbs the hand of the loyal victor had just unloosed the shackles of hopeless slavery.

Mr. Colyer began his blessed work on Roanoke Island in February, and now, at the middle of March, he was made busy in the same high vocation at New Berne. When his labors in the hospitals were finished, he was placed in charge of the helpless of that town of every kind, by an order issued by Burnside,[a] which read thus: "Mr. Vincent Colyer is hereby appointed Superintendent of the Poor, and will be obeyed and respected accordingly."[1] Mr. Colyer took for his head-quarters a respectable dwelling in the town, and at once began the exercise of the most commendable form of benevolence, in finding remunerative employment for the healthy destitute.[2] He opened evening schools for the education of the colored people, in which over eight hundred of the most eager pupils were nightly seen, some of General Foster's New England soldiers acting as teachers. But this promising, benevolent work was suddenly stopped by Edward Stanley, who had been appointed[b] by the President military governor of North Carolina, and whose policy was that of a large class of Unionists in border slave-labor States, namely, to preserve slavery, and, if possible, the Union. The closing of the schools was the first administrative act of the new governor, in conformity with the barbarous laws of North Carolina, which made it, he said, "a criminal offense to teach the blacks to read." He also returned fugitive slaves to their masters; and the hopes of that down-trodden race in that region, which were so delightfully given in promises, were suddenly extinguished.[3]

[a] March 30, 1862.

[b] May.

COLYER'S HEAD-QUARTERS.

Having taken possession of New Berne, Burnside proceeded at once to further carry out the instructions of General McClellan by leading a force

---

[1] On the 24th of April, General Foster issued an order that all passes given to negroes by Mr. Colyer to go *out* of the lines be respected at the outposts, and that all persons outside, inquiring for him, be sent to him unquestioned.

[2] Mr. Colyer gave employment to every able-bodied man that could be found; and in the course of the four months that he administered the duties of his office under Burnside there, colored men built three first-class earthwork forts: one at New Berne, another on Roanoke Island, and a third at Washington, North Carolina. They also performed much labor as carpenters and blacksmiths, and were made useful in loading and discharging cargoes for about three hundred Government vessels, serving as crews on about twenty steamers, and as gangs of laborers in several departments. More than fifty of them were employed in the perilous duty of spies, going sometimes three hundred miles within the Confederate lines, and bringing back the most reliable information, because the negroes were uniformly loyal to the National cause.

During the four months that Mr. Colyer was in New Berne, he and his assistants cared for and kept from want and suffering over eight hundred people.

[3] When this fact was told to President Lincoln, he said, with great earnestness, "Well, this I have always maintained and shall insist on, that no slave who once comes within our lines a fugitive from a rebel shall ever be returned to his master. For my part, I have hated slavery from my childhood." This was said at about the time when he had written a proclamation of emancipation, which, by the advice of the Secretary of State, was

against Fort Macon, that commanded the important harbor of Beaufort, North Carolina, and Bogue Sound.[1] That fort, with others, it will be remembered, was seized by Governor Ellis, early in 1861,[2] before the so-called secession of the State. Its possession by the Government would secure the use of another fine harbor on the Atlantic coast to the National vessels engaged in the blockading and other service, an object of great importance. It stands upon a long spit or ridge of sand, cast up by the waves, called Bogue Island, and separated from the main by Bogue Sound, which is navigable for small vessels. At the head of the deeper part of Beaufort harbor, and at the terminus of the railway from New Berne, is Morehead City, thirty-six miles from the former; and on the northern side of the harbor is Beaufort, the capital of Carteret County, and an old and pleasant town, which was a popular place of resort for the North Carolinians in the summer. Into that harbor blockade-runners had for some time been carrying supplies for the Confederates.[3]

General Burnside intrusted the expedition against Fort Macon to the command of General Parke, at the same time sending General Reno to make further demonstrations in the rear of Norfolk. Parke's forces were transferred by water to Slocum's Creek, from which point they marched across the country and invested Morehead City, nine days after the fall of New Berne.[a] The latter place was evacuated. On the 25th, a detachment, composed of the Fourth Rhode Island and Eighth Connecticut, took possession of Beaufort without opposition, for there was no military force there.

[a] March 23, 1862.

In the mean time a flag had been sent to Fort Macon with a demand for its surrender. It was refused, the commander, Colonel Moses T. White (nephew of Jefferson Davis), declaring that he would not yield until he had eaten his last biscuit and slain his last horse. Vigorous preparations were at once made to capture it, and on the 11th of April General Parke made a reconnoissance in force on Bogue Spit, drove in the Confederate pickets, and selected good points for the planting of siege-guns. At that time regular siege operations commenced, and the garrison was confined within the limits of the fort, closely watched, for it was expected that in their supposed des-

---

withheld for some months, for prudential reasons.—See Mr. Colyer's *Report of the Christian Mission to the United States Army*, from August, 1861, to August, 1862. In that report may be found most interesting details of work and experience among the freedmen on the Atlantic coast.

[1] "Having gained possession of which [New Berne], and the railroad passing through it, you will at once throw a sufficient force upon Beaufort, and take the steps necessary to reduce Fort Macon and open that port."—McClellan's Instructions, January 7th, 1862.

[2] See page 161, volume I.

[3] The Confederates owned a war steamer called the *Nashville*, commanded by Captain R. P. Pegram. At the beginning of February, 1862, she was lying in the harbor of Southampton, England, with a cargo of stores valued at $3,000,000. Near her was the United States gun-boat *Tuscarora*, Captain Craven, carrying nine heavy guns, which had been sent over for the special purpose of watching the *Nashville*, and capturing her when she should put to sea. The British authorities, sympathizing with the Confederates, notified Captain Craven that the *Tuscarora* would not be allowed to leave the port until twenty-four hours after the *Nashville* should depart. The British war-ship *Dauntless* lay near, ready to enforce the order, and the armored ship *Warrior* was within call, if necessity should require its presence. The result was, that on the 3d of February the *Nashville* left Southampton, eluded the chase of the *Tuscarora*, that commenced twenty-four hours afterward, and ran the blockade into Beaufort harbor on the 28th of the same month, with her valuable cargo. She had coaled on the way at the friendly English port of Bermuda, where, on the 22d of February, an order was promulgated prohibiting the use of that port as a coal dépôt by the United States. This was one of many similar exhibitions of the professed neutrality of Great Britain during the war. The *Nashville* remained in Beaufort until the night of the 17th of March, when she again ran the blockade, and went to sea to depredate upon American merchant-vessels.

perate strait they might make a sudden and fierce sortie, but there was only some picket skirmishing occasionally. Ordnance and ordnance stores were rafted over from a wooded point near Carolina City by General Parke, and batteries were constructed behind sand dunes on Bogue Spit. Gun-boats

VIEW AT THE LANDING AT MOREHEAD CITY.[1]

were co-operating with them, and the garrison, composed of about five hundred North Carolinians, was cut off from all communication by sea and land.[2]

Three siege batteries were erected on Bogue Spit behind sand-hills, the sides and front being formed by sand-bags. The most distant, under Lieutenant Flagler, of the New York Third Artillery, was in the borders of a marsh, about fourteen hundred yards from the fort, and mounted four ten-

[1] This is a view looking westward of the causeway, on which lies the railway track from the main at Morehead City to the wharf at deep water. Morehead City is seen in the distance, and Bogue Sound and Spit appear on the left, where the vessels are seen. The single bird indicates the place of Morehead City; the two birds, the site of a fort erected by the Nationals; the three birds, the wooded point at Carolina City from which ordnance and supplies were sent over to the Spit; and the four birds show the position of the landing-place on the Spit from which the siege-guns were taken to their proper places. The picture is from a sketch made by the writer from the deck of the *Ben Deford*, in December, 1864.

[2] Two of the companies in the fort were young men from Beaufort, and there, in sight of their homes, they were really prisoners. They resorted to various devices to keep up communication with their friends. Among others, they would send out tiny vessels, with sails all set, to drift across the bay, around the marshes, to Beaufort, carrying letters or other kinds of messages. On a thin board, thus set afloat on the 20th of April, was inscribed the following message: "*To the Ladys of Beaufort,*—we are still induring the privations of War, with unexosted Hopes if this vessil due reach hur port of destiny you will find that we are still well and alive and will not leeve till we sea the ruins of theas old Walls we have had several scurmish fights with the Yankee Piket Gard, the old topsail gards sends there best Respects to all there Lady friends of Beaufort and surrounding country."

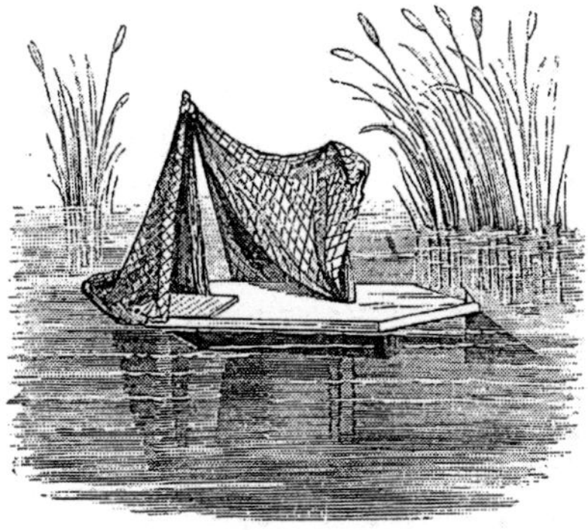

NEWSPAPER-BOAT AT FREDERICKSBURG.

Such contrivances for communication were used elsewhere. While the contending armies were on the Rappahannock, the pickets of both sides would send newspapers backward and forward across the stream in that way. Our little picture shows one in the possession of Lieutenant C. A. Alvord, Jr., of General Caldwell's staff, which he brought from the Rappahannock. It is made of a piece of thin board, about twenty-three inches in length, with a strip of the same for a keel, and a rudder of tin. Two small sticks formed masts, and the sails were made of checked cotton cloth. On it a newspaper was sent over by the insurgents from the Fredericksburg side of the river.

inch mortars. The second was about two hundred yards in front of it, under Captain Morris, of the First Regular Artillery, and mounted three long 30-pound Parrott guns; and the third was one hundred yards still nearer the fort, composed of four 8-inch mortars, and commanded by Lieutenant Prouty, of the Third New York Artillery. When these batteries were completed, the gun-boats *Daylight* (flag-ship); *State of Georgia*, Commander Armstrong; and *Chippewa*, Lieutenant Bryson, and the barque *Gemsbok*, Lieutenant Cavendish, took position for battle outside the Spit, within range of the fort. Burnside came down from New Berne, and passed over to the batteries; and at six o'clock, on the morning of the 25th of April,[a] Flagler opened fire with his 10-inch mortars, directed by Lieutenant Andrews of the Signal Corps, and his accomplished young assistant, Lieutenant Wait.[1] The other batteries followed, and in the course of ten minutes the fort replied with a shot from Captain Manney's 24-pounder battery on the terreplein. The heavy columbiads and 32-pounders *en barbette* joined in the cannonade, and at eight o'clock the fort, belching fire and smoke like an active volcano, was sending a shot every minute. The National batteries were responding with equal vigor, and the war vessels were doing good service, maneuvering in an elliptical course, like Dupont's at Port Royal Entrance, and throwing heavy shot and shell upon the fortress. But the roughness of the sea, caused by a southwest wind, compelled them to withdraw after fighting an hour and a quarter. The land batteries kept at work until four o'clock in the afternoon, when a white flag, displayed on Fort Macon, caused their firing to cease. Captain Guion, of the garrison, came out with a proposition from Colonel White to surrender; and before ten o'clock the next morning[b] the fort was in the possession of the National forces, with about five hundred prisoners of war.[2] Burnside was present, and had the pleasure of seeing the ensign of the

[a] 1862.

[b] April 26.

---

[1] In cases like this, where the mortars and guns were so situated behind obstructions to vision that the range could not be precisely known, nor the effects of missiles sent determined, the services of the members of the Signal Corps were most important. As an illustrative example, I quote from the report of Lieutenant Andrews on this occasion: "I was the only [Signal] officer on duty on Beaufort station, until Lieutenant Marvin Wait reported for duty. My station was at a right angle with the line of fire, so that I was enabled to judge with accuracy the distance over or short a shot fell. The 10-inch shell were falling, almost without exception, more than three hundred yards beyond the fort. Lieutenant Wait and myself continued to signal to the officer in charge until the correct range was obtained. The 8-inch shell were falling short—we signaled to the officer in charge of that battery with the same effect. The same was the case with the battery of Parrott guns, which was too much elevated. From the position of our batteries, it was impossible for the officers in charge to *see* how their shots fell, but owing to the observations made by Lieutenant Wait and myself, and signaled to them from time to time, an accurate range was obtained by all the batteries, and was not lost during the day. *After* 12 *M.*, *every shot fired from our batteries fell in or on the fort.*"

Lieutenant Wait (son of John Q. Wait, of Norwich, Connecticut) was then only a little more than nineteen years of age. He had acquired great skill in signaling, and, for his services on this occasion, Major Myer, the chief of the Signal Department, presented him with a very beautiful battle-flag. A few months later he gave his young life to his country, while gallantly battling with his regiment (Eighth Connecticut) on the field of Antietam.

[2] The capitulation was signed by Colonel M. T. White, General J. G. Parke, and Commodore Samuel Lockwood. The troops of the garrison were held as prisoners of war on parole until duly exchanged. The officers were allowed to retain their side-arms; and both officers and men had the privilege of saving their private effects. In this conflict the Nationals lost only one man killed and two wounded. The Confederates lost seven killed and eighteen wounded. The fruits for the victors were—the important fort; the command of Beaufort Harbor; 20,000 pounds of powder; 150 10-inch shells; 250 32-pound shot; 150 8-inch shot, and 400 stand of arms.—See Reports of General Burnside and Commodore Lockwood, April 27, 1862.

On the day after the surrender Burnside issued a congratulatory order, in which he said he took particular pleasure "in thanking General Parke and his brave command for the patient labor, fortitude, and courage displayed in the investment and reduction of Fort Macon," and declared that the troops had "earned the right to wear upon their colors and guidons the words, 'FORT MACON, April 25, 1862.'"

Republic, and the new colors of the Fifth Rhode Island battalion, which had just been presented to it by the women of Providence, unfurled over the fort.[1]

The writer visited and sketched Fort Macon in December, 1864, while accompanying the expedition under General Butler against Fort Fisher. The transports bearing his troops, and the *Ben Deford*, his head-quarters ship, had been furnished with water and fuel for only ten days. Having waited three days at the place of rendezvous, twenty-five miles at sea, off Fort Fisher, for the arrival of the war-vessels that were to co-operate with the soldiers, it was necessary to run up the coast seventy miles to Beaufort for a new supply of fuel and water. This gave the writer a wished for opportunity to visit Beaufort Harbor and its surroundings. We entered it during one of the heaviest gales known on that coast for thirty years, and were detained there four days, during which time we visited the old town of Beaufort, the more modern Morehead City, Carolina City, the Bogue Banks or Spit, and Fort Macon. The latter is at the eastern point of the Spit, upon an elevation above the common level, composed of a huge mound of sand thrown up for the purpose. The fort was built of brick and stone,

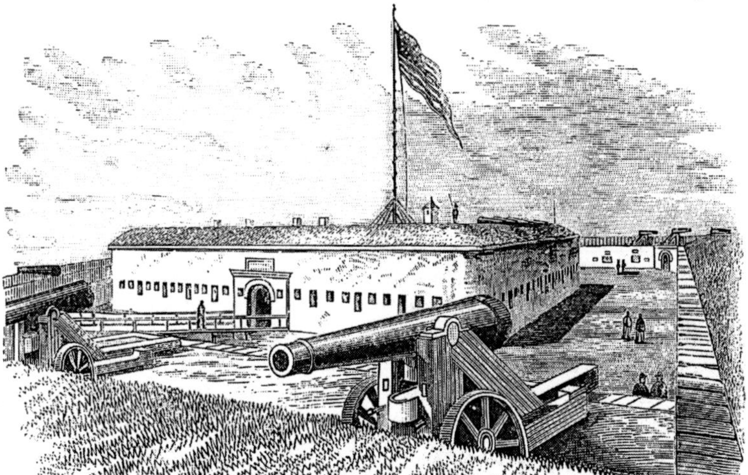

FORT MACON IN 1864.[2]

and named in honor of Nathaniel Macon, a distinguished statesman of North Carolina. Built for defense against a foreign foe, its principal strength in

[1] The Confederate flag that was displaced by the National banner was made of the old United States flag that was over the fort when the insurgents seized it, more than a year before. The red and white stripes had been ripped apart, and then put together so as to form the broad bars of the Confederate flag. The superfluous stars had been cut out, and the holes thus made were left.

[2] This view is from the ramparts, near the sally-port, looking seaward. The lower and the upper terreplein, on which forty-nine heavy guns and some mortars were then mounted, *en barbette*, are seen, the first being a part of the outer works, and the second the surmounting of the walls of the citadel (eighteen feet in height), which were casemated, covered with turf, and surrounded a large parade. In the foreground is seen an iron 32-pounder.

masonry and guns was toward the sea, and it perfectly commanded the narrow ship channel at the entrance to the harbor.

We found Fort Macon very much in the condition in which Burnside observed it when he entered it, excepting the absence of fragments of shot and shell and cannon and carriages, made by the National missiles. On its wall, landward (seen in shadow in the engraving), that bore the brunt of the bombardment, were the broad wounds made by shot and shell; and here and there the remains of furrows made by them were seen on the parades, the ramparts, and the glacis. After passing half an hour pleasantly with Captain King, the commandant, and other officers of the garrison, and making the sketch on the preceding page, we departed for the *Ben Deford* in the tug that took us from it and on the following day left the harbor for the waters in front of Fort Fisher.

While Parke and Lockwood were operating at Beaufort Harbor, troops under General Reno were quietly taking possession of important places on the waters of Albemarle Sound, and threatening Norfolk in the rear. The movement was partly for the purpose of assisting Parke in his siege of Fort Macon, and partly to gain some substantial advantages on the Sounds.

Reno's force consisted of the Twenty-first Massachusetts, Fifty-first Pennsylvania, the Sixth New Hampshire, and a part of the Ninth and Eighty-ninth New York. They advanced in transports up the Pasquotank to within three miles of Elizabeth City, and, landing cautiously in the night,[a] a part of them under Colonel Hawkins were pushed forward to surprise and intercept a body of Confederates known to be about leaving that place for Norfolk. Hawkins took with him portions of the Ninth and Eighty-ninth New York, and Sixth New Hampshire; and a few hours later he was followed by General Reno and the remainder of the troops.

[a] April 19, 1862.

Hawkins was misled by a treacherous or incompetent guide, and, marching ten miles out of his way, lost so much time that in retracing his steps he came in behind General Reno. Meanwhile the Confederates had been apprised of the movement, and when the Nationals were within a mile and a half of South Mills, near Camden Court-house, they were assailed with grape and canister shot from the foe, who were in a good position with artillery, having a dense forest in their rear for a protection and cover, and swamps on their flanks. The attack was bravely met. Reno's superior numbers soon flanked the Confederates, and the latter hastily withdrew. A gunboat under Captain Flusser had, in the mean time, driven the foe out of the woods along the river-banks. Hawkins's Zouaves had made a gallant charge, but were repulsed, and in this the chief loss to the Nationals occurred. They had fifteen killed, ninety-six wounded, and two made prisoners. The loss of the Confederates is not known. They left thirty killed and wounded on the field. This engagement is called THE BATTLE OF SOUTH MILLS. The defeat of the Third Georgia regiment in the fight produced much consternation in Norfolk.

General Reno allowed his wearied troops to rest on the battle-field about six hours, when they returned to the boats. For want of transportation, he was compelled to leave some of his killed and wounded behind.

Winton, at the head of the Chowan; Plymouth, at the mouth of the

Roanoke; and Washington, at the head of the Pamlico River, were all quietly occupied by the National forces.[1] This occupation so widely dispersed Burnside's troops, which at no time numbered more than sixteen thousand, that he could no longer make aggressive movements. The Government had no troops to spare to re-enforce him; and matters remained comparatively quiet in his department until the middle of July, when he was hastily summoned to Fortress Monroe[a] with all the forces he could collect; for the Army of the Potomac, on the Virginia Peninsula, under General McClellan, was then apparently in great danger. General Burnside promptly obeyed the summons, leaving General Foster in command of the department. During the four months of his campaign in that region, Burnside had exhibited those traits of character that marked him as an energetic, sagacious, and judicious commander, and led to his appointment to more important posts of duty.

[a] July 17, 1862.

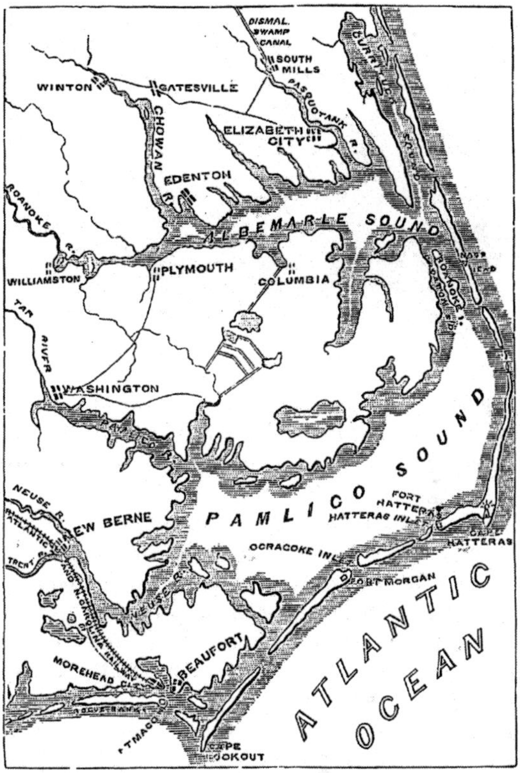

OPERATIONS IN BURNSIDE'S DEPARTMENT.

For the remainder of the year, the coasts of North Carolina were in the possession of the National troops. Its ports were closed, either by actual occupation or by blockading vessels, and its commerce ceased entirely, excepting such as was carried on by British blockade-runners. These, in spite of the greatest vigilance of the blockading squadrons cruising off its entrances, constantly entered the Cape Fear River, with military supplies and necessaries for the Confederates, until the fall of Fort Fisher, at the beginning of 1865. These blockade-runners were steamships, built expressly

[1] At about this time, an expedition under Commodore Rowan was sent to obstruct the Dismal Swamp Canal, in the rear of Norfolk. Rowan left Elizabeth City on the 23d of April, with the *Lockwood*, *Whitehead*, and *Putnam*, each with an officer and a detachment of troops. In the afternoon he landed one hundred men (fifty on each bank), and then, with a launch on the canal carrying a heavy 12-pounder, went forward about two miles. They sunk a schooner in the canal, and filled the stream, for about fifty yards above it, with stumps and trunks of trees, brush, vines, and earth. In this work they met with no opposition. In fact, the Confederates themselves had evidently abandoned the use of the canal, for they had obstructed it farther on toward Norfolk.

for the purpose, and were remarkable for strength and speed. They drew but little water, and had raking smoke-stacks. Every part of them was painted a gray color, so that they could not be seen even in a very light fog. Their achievements in supplying the Confederates with arms, ammunition, and the necessaries and luxuries of life, will be considered hereafter.

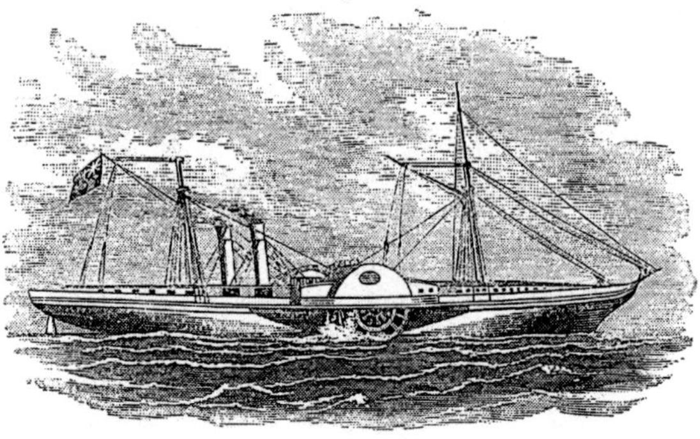

A BLOCKADE-RUNNER.

While Burnside and Rowan were operating on the coast of North Carolina, Sherman and Dupont were engaged in movements on the coasts of South Carolina and Georgia, having for their first object the capture of Fort Pulaski, and ultimately other important points and posts between the Savannah River and St. Augustine in Florida.

We have seen that at the close of 1861 the National authority was supreme along the coast from Wassaw Sound, below the Savannah River, to the North Edisto, well up toward Charleston.[1] National troops were stationed as far down as Daufuskie Island; and so early as the close of December, General Sherman had directed General Quincy A. Gillmore, his Chief Engineer, to reconnoiter Fort Pulaski and report upon the feasibility of a bombardment of it. Gillmore's reply was, that it might be reduced by batteries of rifled guns and mortars placed on Big Tybee Island, southeast of Cockspur Island, on which the fort stood, and across the narrower channel of the Savannah; and that aid might be given from a battery on Venus Point of Jones's Island, two miles from Cockspur, in the opposite direction. While waiting orders from Washington on the subject, the Forty-sixth New York, Colonel Rosa, was sent to occupy Big Tybee.

At about this time[a] explorations were made by the Nationals for the purpose of finding some channel by which gun-boats might get in the rear of Fort Pulaski. Lieutenant J. H. Wilson, of the Topographical Engineers, had received information from negro pilots that convinced him that such channel might be found, connecting Calibogue Sound with the Savannah River. General Sherman directed him to explore in search of it. Taking with him, at about the first of January, 1862, seventy Rhode Island soldiers, in two boats managed by negro crews and pilots, he thridded the intricate passages between the low, oozy islands and mud-banks in that region (always under cover of night, for the Confederates had watchful pickets at every approach to the fort), and found a way into the Savannah River above the fort, partly through an artificial channel called Wall's Cut, which had for several years connected Wright's and New Rivers. He

[a] Jan., 1862.

[1] See page 125.

reported accordingly, when Captain John Rogers made another reconnoissance at night, and so satisfied himself that gun-boats could navigate the way, that he offered to command an expedition that might attempt it. Sherman and Dupont at once organized one for the purpose. The land troops were placed in charge of General Viele,[1] and the gun-boats were commanded by Rogers. Another mixed force, under General H. G. Wright[2] and Fleet-

OBSTRUCTIONS IN THE SAVANNAH RIVER.[3]

captain Davis, was sent to pass up to the Savannah River, in rear of Fort Pulaski, by way of Wassaw Sound, Wilmington River, and St. Augustine Creek. The latter expedition found obstructions in St. Augustine Creek; but the gunboats were able to co-operate with those of Rogers in an attack[a] on the little flotilla of five gun-boats of Commodore Tatnall, which attempted to escape down the river from inevitable blockade. Tatnall was driven back with two of his vessels, but the others escaped.

[a] Jan. 28, 1862.

The expedition, having accomplished its object of observation, returned to Hilton Head, and the citizens of Savannah believed that designs against that city and Fort Pulaski were abandoned. Yet the Confederates multiplied the obstructions in the river in the form of piles, sunken vessels, and regular *chevaux-de-frise;* and upon the oozy islands and the main land on the right bank of the river they built heavy earthworks, and greatly enlarged and strengthened Fort Jackson, about four miles below the city. Among the most formidable of the new earthworks was Fort Lee, built under the direction of Robert E. Lee, after his recall from Western Virginia, in the autumn of 1861.

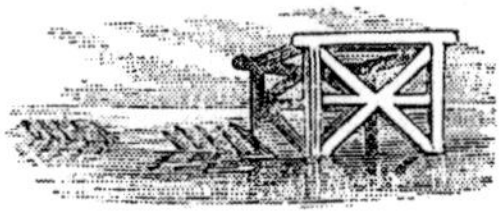

CHEVAUX-DE-FRISE.

Soon after the heavy reconnoissance of Rogers and Wright, the Nationals made a lodgment on Jones's Island, and proceeded, under the immediate direction of General Viele, to erect an earthwork on Venus Point, which was named Battery Vulcan. This was completed on the 11th of February, after very great labor,[4] and with a little battery on Bird Island, opposite

---

[1] These troops consisted of the Forty-eighth New York; two companies of New York volunteer engineers, and two companies of Rhode Island volunteer artillery with twenty heavy guns.

[2] Wright's troops consisted of the Fourth New Hampshire, Colonel Whipple; Sixth Connecticut, Colonel Chatfield; and Ninety-seventh Pennsylvania, Colonel Guess.

[3] This is from a sketch made by the author from the deck of a steam-tug, just at sunset in April, 1866. These were only the remains of the formidable obstructions, those from the main channel having been removed. The scene is near Fort Jackson. On the right are seen earthworks on a small island, and on the left the shore of the main land, while in the distance is the City of Savannah.

[4] A causeway was built across the island, chiefly by the Forty-eighth New York, over which heavy mortars

(Battery Hamilton), effectually closed the Savannah River in the rear of Fort Pulaski. That fortress, as we have already observed,[1] was a strong one on Cockspur Island, which is wholly a marsh. Its walls, twenty-five feet in height above high water, presented five faces, and were casemated on all sides, and mounted one tier of guns in embrasures and one *en barbette*.

QUINCY A. GILLMORE.

The absolute blockade of Fort Pulaski may be dated from the 22d of February. Preparations were then made on Tybee Island to bombard it. Nearly all of the work had to be done in the night, and it was of the same laborious nature as that performed on Jones's Island. It took about two hundred and fifty men to move a single heavy gun, with a sling-cart, over the quaking mud jelly of which Tybee Island is composed; and it was often with the greatest difficulty that it was kept from going down twelve feet to the bottom of the morass, when, as sometimes it happened, it slipped from the causeway or a platform.[2] Patiently the work was carried on under the supervision of General Gillmore, who was in chief command, and on the 9th of April eleven batteries, containing an aggregate of thirty-six guns, were in readiness to open fire on the fort.[3] On that day the commanding General

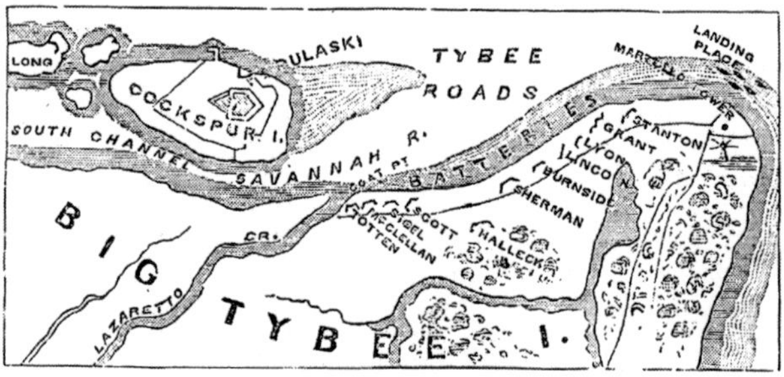

SIEGE OF FORT PULASKI.

were dragged. The islands near the mouth of the Savannah are formed of mud, of jelly consistency, from four to twelve feet in depth, and resting on half liquid clay. The surface is covered with a light turf of matted grass-roots. Over this the causeway was built, of poles covered with loose planks; and upon this road mortars weighing more than eight tons were dragged, and placed in battery on heavy plank platforms. This labor was all performed at night.

[1] See page 179, volume I.

[2] "No one," said Gillmore in his report, "can form any but a faint conception of the Herculean labor by which mortars of eight and a half tons weight, and columbiads but a trifle lighter, were moved in the dead of night over a narrow causeway bordered by swamps on each side, and liable at any moment to be overturned, and buried in the mud beyond reach."

[3] These were batteries *Stanton* and *Grant*, three 10-inch mortars each; *Lyon* and *Lincoln*, three columbiads each; *Burnside*, one heavy mortar; *Sherman*, three heavy mortars; *Halleck*, two heavy mortars; *Scott*, four columbiads; *Sigel*, five 30-pounder Parrott, and one 48-pounder James; *McClellan*, two 84-pounders and two 64-pounders James; *Totten*, four 10-inch siege mortars. *Totten* and *McClellan* were only 1,650 yards from the fort; *Stanton* was 3,400 yards distant. Each battery had a service magazine for two days' supply of ammunition, and a depot powder magazine of 3,000 barrels capacity was constructed near the Martello tower, printed on page 125, which was the landing-place for all supplies on Tybee.

issued minute orders for the working of the batteries, which was to commence at daybreak the next morning.[1]

General David Hunter, who had just succeeded General Sherman[a] in the command of the Department, arrived at Tybee on the evening of the 8th, accompanied by General Benham as district commander. At sunrise on the morning of the 10th, Hunter sent Lieutenant J. H. Wilson to the fort, with a summons to the commander of the garrison (Colonel Charles H. Olmstead, of the First Georgia Volunteers) to surrender. It was refused, the commander saying, "I am here to defend this fort, not to surrender it," and at a quarter past eight o'clock the batteries opened upon it. They did not cease firing until night, when five of the guns of the fortress were silenced, and the responses of the others were becoming feeble. All night long, four of Gillmore's guns fired at intervals of fifteen or twenty minutes; and at sunrise the next morning[b] the batteries commenced afresh, and with the greatest vigor. It was soon evident that the fort, at the point on which the missiles from the three breaching batteries (Sigel, Scott, and McClellan) fell, was crumbling. A yawning breach was visible; and yet the fort kept up the fight gallantly until two o'clock in the afternoon, when preparations were made to storm it. Then a white flag displayed from its walls caused the firing to cease, and the siege to end in its surrender. Ten of its guns were dismounted; and so destructive of masonry had been the Parrott projectiles (some of which went through the six or seven feet of brick walls) that there was imminent danger of their piercing the magazine and exposing it to explosion.[3] The Nationals, who were under the immediate command of General Viele, had only one killed. The Confederates had one killed and several wounded. It was a very hard fought but almost bloodless battle. The spoils of victory were the fort, forty-seven

[a] March 31, 1862.

[b] April 11.

BREACH IN FORT PULASKI.[2]

---

[1] See the report of General Gillmore, dated April 30, 1862.

[2] This is a view of the angle of the fort where the great breach was made. It was copied by permission, from a drawing that accompanied General Gillmore's report, published by D. Vanostrand, New York. It was sketched on the morning after the battle. When the writer visited Fort Pulaski, in April, 1866, this breach was repaired, but the casemates within it were still in ruins.

[3] Gillmore's breaching batteries had been ordered to assail the eastern half of the pancoupé, covering the south and southeast faces, so as to take in reverse, through the opening formed by them, the powder magazine. These batteries were established at the mean distance of 1,700 yards from the scarp walls of the fort.

heavy guns, a large supply of fixed ammunition, forty thousand pounds of gunpowder, and a large quantity of commissary stores. Three hundred men were made prisoners.[1] By this victory, won on the first anniversary of the fall of Fort Sumter,[a] the port of Savannah was sealed against blockade-runners. The capture of Fort Jackson above, and of the city, would have been of little advantage to the Nationals then, for the forces necessary to hold them were needed in more important work farther down the coast.

[a] April 12, 1862.

While Gillmore and Viele were besieging Fort Pulaski, Commodore Dupont and General Wright were making easy conquests on the coast of Florida. Dupont left Port Royal on the 28th of February,[b] in the *Wabash*, with twenty armed vessels, and six transports bearing land forces, and on the 1st of March arrived in St. Andrew's Sound, north of Cumberland and St. Andrew's Islands. Leaving the *Wabash*, Dupont raised his flag on the smaller war vessel *Mohican*, and, at ten o'clock on the 2d, the fleet anchored in Cumberland Sound, between Cumberland Island and the Georgia main. Its destination was Fort Clinch,[2] on the

[b] 1862.

FORT CLINCH.

northern extremity of Amelia Island, a strong regular work, and prepared by great labor for making a vigorous defense. Outside of it, along the shores, were heavy batteries, well sheltered and concealed behind sand-hills on their front, while on the southern extremity of Cumberland Island was a battery of four guns. These, with the heavy armament of Fort Clinch, perfectly commanded the waters in the vicinity.

Dupont had expected vigorous resistance at Fort Clinch, and he was incredulous when told by a fugitive slave, picked up on the waters, that the troops had abandoned it, and were fleeing from Amelia Island. The rumor was confirmed, and Dupont immediately sent forward Commander Drayton, of the *Pawnee*, with several gun-boats, to save the public property there and prevent outrages. He then returned to the *Wabash*, and, going outside, went down to the main entrance to Fernandina harbor. There he was detained until the next morning. Meanwhile Drayton had sent Lieutenant White, of the *Ottawa*, to hoist the National flag over Fort Clinch. This

[1] Report of General Hunter, April 13; of General Benham, April 12, and of General Gillmore, April 30, 1862.

[2] So named in honor of Brigadier-General Clinch, who was active in the war of 1812. He was the father-in-law of General Robert Anderson.

was the first of the old National forts which was "repossessed" by the Government.

The Confederates fled from the village of Fernandina,[1] near the fort, and also from the village of St. Mary's, a short distance up the St. Mary's River. These were at once occupied by National forces. Fort Clinch was garrisoned by a few of General Wright's troops, and Commander C. R. P. Rogers, with some launches, captured the Confederate steamer *Darlington*, lying in the adjacent waters. The insurgent force was utterly broken up. "We captured Port Royal," Dupont wrote to the Secretary of the Navy,[a] "but Fernandina and Fort Clinch have been given to us."

[a] March 4, 1862.

News reached Dupont that the Confederates were abandoning every post along the Florida coast, and he took measures to occupy them or hold them in durance. Commander Gordon was sent with three gun-boats to Brunswick, the terminus of the Brunswick and Pensacola railway. He took possession of it on the 9th of March. The next day he held the batteries on the islands of St. Simon and Jekyl, and on the 13th he proceeded with the *Potomska* and *Pocahontas* through the inland passage from St. Simon's Sound to Darien, on the Altamaha River, in Georgia. This place, like Brunswick, was deserted, and nearly all of the inhabitants on St. Simon's and neighboring islands had fled to the main. In the mean time Dupont sent a small flotilla, under a judicious officer, Lieutenant Thomas Holdup Stevens, consisting of the gun-boats *Ottawa*, *Seneca*, *Pembina*, and *Huron*, with the transports *I. P. Smith* and *Ellen*, to enter the St. John's River, twenty-five miles farther down the coast, and push on to Jacksonville, and even to Pilatka, if possible. Stevens approached Jacksonville on the evening of the 11th of March,[b] and saw large fires in that direction; and on the following day he appeared before the town, which was abandoned by the Confederate soldiers.[2] The fires had been kindled by order of General Trapier, the insurgent commander of that district, who directed the houses, stores, mills, and other property of persons suspected of being in favor of the Union, to be burnt. Under that order, eight immense saw-mills and a vast amount of valuable lumber were burned by guerrillas. On the appearance of Stevens's flotilla, the corporate authorities of the town, with S. L. Burritt at their head, went on board his vessel (the *Ottawa*) and formally surrendered the place. The Fourth New Hampshire, Colonel Whipple, landed and took possession, and it was hailed with joy by the Union people who remained there.

[b] 1862.

Two days before Jacksonville was surrendered to Stevens, Fort Marion and the ancient city of St. Augustine, still farther down the coast,[3] were surrendered to Commander C. R. P. Rogers, who had crossed[c]

[c] March 11.

---

[1] Fernandina was the eastern terminus of the Cedar Keys and Fernandina Railway, that crossed from the island to the main on trestle-work. A train was just starting on the arrival of Drayton. In the *Ottawa* he pursued it about two miles, firing several shots at the locomotive, but without doing much damage.

[2] So large a number of Northern people inhabited Jacksonville at the beginning of the war, that it was called by the natives a "Yankee town." But many of them were secessionists, and of 400 families who were there when Dupont arrived on the coast, only 70 remained when Stevens appeared. Jacksonville was one of the most beautiful, as well as the most flourishing and important cities in Florida; but this beginning of misery for the inhabitants did not end until it was nearly all destroyed during the war.

[3] St. Augustine is the capital of St. John's County, Florida, and is situated on an estuary of the Atlantic, called North River, and two miles from the ocean. It is upon a plain a few feet above the sea. It is the oldest town in the United States founded by Europeans. The Spaniards built a fort there in 1565.

the bar in the *Wabash*. With a flag of truce, and accompanied by Mr. Dennis, of the Coast Survey, he landed, and was soon met by the Mayor of the town, who conducted him to the City Hall, where he was received by the Common Council. He was informed that two Florida companies, who had garrisoned the fort, had left the place on the previous evening, and that the city had no means for resistance, if there was a disposition to fight. On assuring the authorities of the kind intentions of his Government toward all peaceful citizens, they formally resigned St. Augustine into his hands. Fort Marion, a decayed castle of heavy walls, built by the Spaniards early in the last century (and which was seized by the insurgents early in 1861[1]), with its dependencies, passed into the hands of the Nationals. On the top of the broad walls of the fort, huts and tents were soon erected.

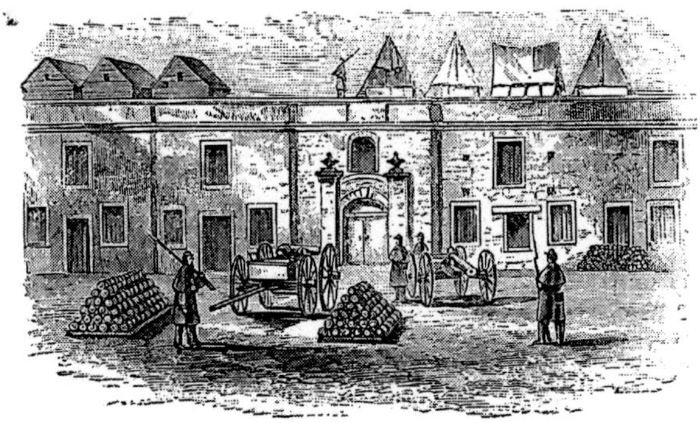

FORT MARION.

The capture of St. Augustine was followed by a visit of National gunboats to Musquito Inlet, fifty miles farther down the Florida coast, into which it was reported light-draft vessels were carrying English arms and other supplies for the Confederates, which had been transhipped from the British port of Nassau. The boats were the *Penguin*, Lieutenant Budd, who commanded the expedition, and the *Henry Andrew*, Acting-master Mather. On their arrival, a small boat expedition, composed of forty-three men, under Budd and Mather, was organized for a visit to Musquito Lagoon.

While returning, the two commanders, who were in one boat, landed at an abandoned earthwork and dense grove of live oaks. There they were fired upon by the concealed foe. Budd and Mather, and three of the five men composing the boat's crew, were killed, and the remaining two were wounded and made prisoners. The other boats were fired upon when they came up, and their passengers suffered much; but under the cover of night they escaped.

In this expedition the Nationals lost five killed and eleven wounded. Had it been entirely successful, all Florida might have been brought under the control of the National forces for a time, for there was panic everywhere in that region after the fall of Fort Pulaski. Pensacola was soon afterward evacuated[a] by the Confederate General, T. N. Jones, who burnt every thing that he could at the navy yard, at the hospital, and in Forts McRee and Barrancas, and retreated toward the interior. But, as events proved, the Nationals could not have held Florida at that time. Because of their weakness in numbers, their conquests resulted, apparently, in more harm than good to the Union cause. At first, the hopes

[a] May 9 and 10, 1862.

[1] See page 170, volume I.

they inspired in the breasts of the Union people developed quite a widespread loyalty. A Union convention was called to assemble at Jacksonville on the 10th of April, to organize a loyal State Government, when, to the dismay of those engaged in the matter, General Wright prepared to withdraw his forces, two days before the time when the convention was to meet. General Trapier would of course return, so the leaders were compelled to fly for their lives with the National troops, instead of attempting to re-establish a loyal government. In consequence of a sense of insecurity caused by this event, very little Union feeling was manifested in Florida during the remainder of the war.

Dupont returned to Port Royal on the 27th of March, leaving a small force at different points to watch the posts recovered. He found Skiddaway and Greene Islands abandoned by the Confederates, and the important Wassaw and Ossabaw Sounds and the Vernon and Wilmington Rivers entirely open to the occupation of National forces. So early as the 11th of February, General Sherman, with the Forty-seventh New York, had taken quiet possession of Edisto Island, from which all the white inhabitants had fled, burning their cotton on their departure. By this movement the National flag was carried more than half way to Charleston from Beaufort. And so it was, that on the first anniversary of the attack on Fort Sumter, the entire Atlantic and Gulf coast, from Cape Hatteras to Perdido Bay, excepting the harbor of Charleston and its immediate surroundings, had been abandoned by the insurgents, and the National power was supreme. To Dupont and the new Commander of the Department of the South (General Hunter) Charleston was now a coveted prize, and they made preparations to attempt its capture. That movement we will consider hereafter.

Turning again to Hampton Roads, we see General Butler and some troops going out upon another expedition, with his purpose a profound secret, but which proved to be one of the most important movements of the first year and a half of the war. It was the expedition against New Orleans.

We have seen[1] that so early as September, 1861, General Butler was commissioned by the Secretary of War to go to New England and "raise, arm, and uniform a volunteer force for the war," to be composed of six regiments. Unavoidable collision with the efforts of State authorities to raise men ensued, and at one time it seemed as if Butler's mission would be fruitless. To give him more efficiency, the six New England States were constituted a Military Department, and Major-General Butler was made its commander while engaged in recruiting his division. He worked to that end with untiring energy, in the face of opposition; and it was not long before his six thousand troops and more were ready for the field. The Government had then turned its attention to the posts on the Gulf of Mexico and its tributary waters, and the seizure of Mobile and New Orleans, and the occupation of Texas, formed parts of its capital plan of operations in that region. Butler was called upon to suggest the best rendezvous for an expedition against Mobile. He named Ship Island, off the coast of Mississippi,

[1] See page 108.

between Mobile Bay and Lake Borgne (a low sand-bar, lying just above low water, and averaging seven miles in length and three-fourths of a mile in width), as the most eligible point for operations against any part of the Gulf Coast. Thither some of his troops were sent, in the fine steamship *Constitution*, under General J. W. Phelps, whom Butler well knew, and honored as a commander at Fortress Monroe and vicinity. The *Constitution* returned, and two thousand more of the six thousand men embarked, when an electrograph said to Butler, in Boston, "*Don't sail. Disembark.*"

The Government was then trembling because of the seeming imminence of war with Great Britain, on account of the seizure of Mason and Slidell. They were in Fort Warren, and the British Government had demanded their surrender. This made the authorities at Washington pause in their aggressive policy, to wait for the development of events in that connection. But the tremor was only spasmodic, and soon ceased. The work against treason was renewed with increased vigor. Edwin M. Stanton, who was in Mr. Buchanan's Cabinet during the closing days of his administration[1]—a man possessed of great physical and mental energy, comprehensiveness of intellectual grasp, and great tenacity of will, had superseded Mr. Cameron as Secretary of War,[a] and a conference between him and General Butler resulted in a decision to make vigorous efforts to capture New Orleans, and hold the lower Mississippi.

[a] Jan. 13, 1862.

EDWIN M. STANTON.

When that decision was referred to General McClellan, the latter thought such an expedition was not feasible, for it would take fifty thousand men to give it a chance of success, and where were they to come from? He was unwilling to spare a single man of his more than two hundred thousand men then lying at ease around Washington City. His question was promptly answered. New England was all aglow with enthusiasm, and its sons were eagerly flocking to the standard of General Butler, who asked for only fifteen thousand men for the expedition. Already more than twelve thousand were ready for the field, under his leadership. Two thousand were at Ship Island; more than two thousand were on ship-board in Hampton Roads; and over eight thousand were ready for embarkation at Boston.

President Lincoln gave the project his sanction. The *Department of the Gulf* was created, and General Butler was placed in command of it. On the 23d of February[b] he received minute orders from General McClellan to co-operate with the navy, first in the capture of New Orleans and its approaches, and then in the reduction of Mobile, Galveston, and Baton Rouge, with the ultimate view of occupying Texas. To his New

[b] 1862.

[1] See page 146, volume I.

England troops were added three regiments, then at Baltimore, and orders were given for two others at Key West and one at Fort Pickens to join the expedition. On paper, the whole force was about eighteen thousand, but when they were all mustered on Ship Island they amounted to only thirteen thousand seven hundred. Of these, five hundred and eighty were artillery-men and two hundred and seventy-five were cavalry.

On the day after receiving his instructions, General Butler left Washington and hastened to Fortress Monroe. To Mr. Lincoln he said, "Good-bye, Mr. President; we shall take New Orleans or you'll never see me again;" and with the assurance of Secretary Stanton, that "The man who takes New Orleans is made a lieutenant-general,"[1] Butler embarked at Hampton Roads,[a] accompanied by his wife, his staff, and fourteen hundred troops, in the fine steamship *Mississippi*. Fearful perils were encountered on the North Carolina coast, and vexatious delay at Port Royal;[2] and it was thirty days after he left the capes of Virginia before he debarked at Ship Island.[b] There was no house upon that desolate sand-bar, and some charred boards were all the materials that could be had for the erection of a shanty for the accommodation of Mrs. Butler. The furniture for it was taken from a captured vessel.

[a] Feb. 25, 1862.

[b] March 25.

When the war broke out, there was an unfinished fort on Ship Island, to which, as we have observed, Floyd, the traitorous Secretary of War, had ordered heavy guns.[3] The insurgents of that region took possession of it in considerable force,[c] and, during their occupation of it for about two months, they made it strong and available for defense. They constructed eleven bomb-proof casemates, a magazine and barracks, mounted twenty heavy Dahlgren guns, and named it Fort Twiggs. When rumors of a heavy naval force approaching reached the garrison, they abandoned the fort,[d] burnt their barracks, and, with their cannon, fled to the main. On the following day, a small force was landed from the National gun-boat *Massachusetts*, and took possession of the place. They strengthened the fort by building two more casemates, adding Dahlgren and rifled cannon, and piling around its outer walls tiers of sand-bags, six feet in depth. Then they gave it the name of their vessel, and called it Fort Massachusetts.[4] The *Constitution* arrived there with General Phelps and his troops[5] on the 3d of December, and on the following day[e] he issued a proclamation to the loyal inhabitants of the south-western States, setting forth his views as to the political status of those

[c] July, 1861.

[d] Sept. 16.

[e] Dec. 4.

---

[1] Parton's *General Butler in New Orleans*, page 194.

[2] The captain of the *Mississippi* appears to have been utterly incompetent. On the night after leaving Hampton Roads, he ran his vessel on a shoal off Hatteras Inlet, and barely escaped wrecking. On the following day it struck a sunken rock, five miles from land, off the mouth of the Cape Fear, and an hour later, while leaking badly, it was hard fast on the Fryingpan Shoals, and partly submerged, when relief came in the gun-boat *Mount Vernon*, Commander O. S. Glisson, of the blockading squadron off Wilmington. The *Mississippi* was taken to Port Royal and repaired, and was again run aground while passing out of that harbor, when her commander was deposed.

[3] See page 123, volume I.

[4] This fort was on the extreme western end of the island. It was nearly circular in shape, and built of brick. The sand-bags made its walls bomb-proof. Outside of the fort was a redoubt, built of sand-bags, upon which a heavy Dahlgren gun was mounted, so as to command the channel leading into the really fine harbor, in which vessels might find shelter from the worst storms on the Gulf.

[5] These were the Twenty-sixth Massachusetts, Colonel Jones, Ninth Connecticut, Colonel Cahill, and Fourth Battery Massachusetts Artillery, Captain Manning.

States and the slave-system within their borders. It pointedly condemned that system, and declared that it was incompatible with a free government, incapable of forming an element of true nationality, and necessarily dangerous to the Republic, when assuming, as it then did, a political character. He pictured to them the blessings to be derived from the abolition of slavery,

FORT MASSACHUSETTS, ON SHIP ISLAND.

and declared that his motto and that of his troops coming among them was, FREE LABOR AND WORKING-MEN'S RIGHTS.

This proclamation astonished Phelps's troops, provoked the pro-slavery officers under his command, and highly excited the people to whom it was addressed, who heard it, and who used it effectually in "firing the Southern heart" against the "abolition Government" at Washington. It was too far in advance of public opinion and feeling at that time, and General Butler, whose views were coincident with the tenor of the proclamation, considering it premature, and therefore injudicious, said, in transmitting his brigadier's report of operations at Ship Island, that he had not authorized the issuing of any proclamation, "and most certainly not such an one." So General Phelps and those of his way of thinking were compelled to wait a year or two before they saw a public movement toward the abolition of slavery.

All winter Phelps and his troops remained on the dreary little island, unable, on account of great and small guns in the hands of the neighboring insurgents, to gain a footing on the adjacent shore, and waiting in painful anxiety, at the last, for the arrival of General Butler and the remainder of his command, who, at one time it was feared, had gone to the bottom of the sea. Their advent produced joy, for the troops well knew that the stagnation of the camp would soon give place to the bustle of preparations for the field. That expectation was heightened when, a few hours after he landed, Butler was seen in conference with Captains Farragut and Bailey, of the navy, who were there, in which his Chief of Staff, Major George C. Strong, and his Chief Engineer, Lieutenant Godfrey Weitzel (both graduates of West Point) participated. The latter had been engaged in the completion of the forts below New Orleans, and was well acquainted with all the region around the lower Mississippi.

At that conference, a plan of operation against the forts below New

Orleans and the city itself was adopted, and was substantially carried out a few weeks later.

While preparations for that movement were in progress, some minor expeditions were set on foot. One against Biloxi, a summer watering-place on the Mississippi Main, was incited by the conduct of some Confederates who violated the sanctity of a flag of truce, under circumstances of peculiar wickedness. A little girl, three years of age, the daughter of a physician and noted rebel of New Orleans, was cast upon the shore at Ship Island after a storm, in which it was supposed her father had perished. She was kindly cared for by Mrs. Butler; and, as the child knew the name of her grandfather in New Orleans, the General determined to send her there. For that purpose Major George C. Strong, General Butler's chief of staff, took her in a sloop, under a flag of truce, to Biloxi, with money to pay her expenses to New Orleans. There she was left to be sent on. The sloop grounded on her return in the evening, and, while in that condition, an attempt was made to capture her by men who had been witnesses of Major Strong's holy errand. By stratagem he kept the rebels at bay until a gun-boat came to his rescue.

On the following day, an avenging expedition, commanded by Major Strong, proceeded to Biloxi. It was composed of two gun-boats (*Jackson* and *New London*), and a transport with the Ninth Connecticut, Colonel Cahill, and Everett's battery on board. Fortunately for the Biloxians, they were quiet. Their place was captured without opposition, and the Mayor was compelled to make a humble apology in writing for the perfidy of his fellow-citizens in the matter of the flag of truce.

Leaving Biloxi, Major Strong went westward to Pass Christian. While his vessels lay at anchor there that night, they were attacked by three Confederate gun-boats, that stole out of Lake Borgne. The assailants were repulsed. Major Strong then landed his troops, and, making a forced march, surprised and captured a Confederate camp three miles distant. The soldiers had fled. The camp was destroyed, and the public stores in the town on the beach were seized and carried away. Major Strong also captured Mississippi City.

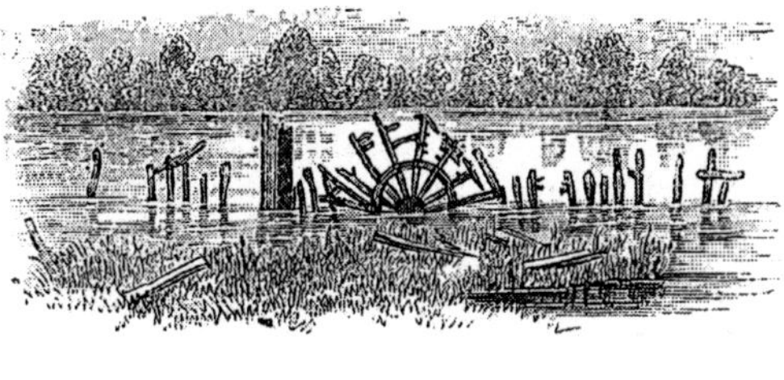

CHAPTER XIII.

THE CAPTURE OF NEW ORLEANS.

SHIP ISLAND was the place of rendezvous for the naval as well as the land portion of the forces destined for the capture of New Orleans. The naval force was placed under the command of Captain David G. Farragut, a loyal Tennesseean, who sailed from Hampton Roads in the National armed steamer *Hartford*, on the 2d of February, 1862, and arrived in the harbor of Ship Island on the 20th of the same month, having been detained by sickness at Key West. He had been instructed by the Secretary of the Navy[a] to proceed with all possible dispatch to the Gulf of Mexico, with orders for Flag-officer McKean, on duty there, to transfer to the former the command of the Western Gulf squadron. He was informed that a fleet of bomb-vessels, under Commander David D. Porter (with whose father Farragut had cruised in the *Essex* during the war of 1812), would be attached to his squadron, and these were to rendezvous at Key West. He was directed to proceed up the Mississippi so soon as the mortar-vessels were ready, with such others as might be spared from the blockade, reduce the defenses which guarded the approaches to New Orleans, and, taking possession of that city under the guns of his squadron, hoist the American flag in it, and hold possession until troops could be sent to him. If the Mississippi expedition from Cairo should then not have descended the river, he was to take advantage of the panic which his seizure of New Orleans would produce, and push a strong force up the stream, to take all their defenses in the rear. "Destroy the armed barriers which these deluded people have raised up against the power of the United States Government," said the Secretary, "and shoot down those who war against the Union; but cultivate with cordiality the first returning reason, which is sure to follow your success." With these instructions, and with plans of the known works on the lower Mississippi, furnished by General Barnard, who constructed Fort St. Philip, one of the chief of those works, Farragut proceeded to the performance of the duties required of him.

[a] Jan. 20, 1862.

Porter's mortar fleet had been for several months in preparation at the Navy Yard at Brooklyn, and had caused a great deal of speculation. It consisted of twenty-one schooners of from two hundred to three hundred tons each, made very strong, and constructed so as to draw as little water as possible. They were armed with mortars of eight and a half tons weight, that would throw a 15-inch shell, weighing, when filled, two hundred and twelve pounds. Each vessel also carried two 32-pounder rifled cannon. They rendezvoused at Key West; and when all were in readiness, it was arranged that the forts below New Orleans should be first attacked by Porter's fleet, Farragut and his larger and stronger vessels remaining in a reserve just outside of the range of the Confederate guns, until they should be silenced by the mortars. Failing in that, Farragut was to attempt to run by the forts. When this should be accomplished, he was to clear the river of the Confederate vessels and isolate the forts from their supplies and supports, when General Butler should land his troops in the rear of Fort St. Philip, the weaker fortification, and attempt to carry it by assault. If success should crown these efforts, the land and naval forces were to pass on toward New Orleans in such manner as might seem best. For these purposes, the combined forces were ready for action at the middle of April.

DAVID D. PORTER.

The Confederates had made the most ample provisions, as they thought, for the sure defense of New Orleans. The infamous General Twiggs,[1] whom the Louisiana insurgents had called to their command, had been superseded by Mansfield Lovell, formerly a politician and office-holder in the City of New York. He was assisted by General Ruggles, a man of considerable energy. Lovell everywhere saw evidences of Twiggs's imbecility; and, when he was informed of the gathering of National ships and soldiers in the Gulf, he perceived the necessity of strongly guarding every avenue of approach to New Orleans.[2]

Lovell's special efforts for defense were put forth on the banks of the Mississippi, between the city and its passes or mouths.[3] The principal of these were Forts Jackson and St. Philip, the former built by the Government, and the latter was an old Spanish fortress, which had figured somewhat in the war of 1812. These were at a bend of the Mississippi, about seventy-five miles above its passes. They occupied opposite sides of the stream, and were under the immediate command of Lieutenant-Colonel Edward Higgins, a Virginian. The general command of the river defenses was intrusted to General J. K. Duncan, formerly an office-holder in New York, who was regarded as one of the best artillerists in the Confederate service. The armament of the forts, for which they were prepared, was one hundred and fifty guns each. Between Fort Jackson, on the right bank of the river,

[1] See page 265, volume I.

[2] This was by far the largest and most important city within the bounds of the Confederacy. It is on the eastern side of the Mississippi River, about one hundred miles above its passes, or mouths, and has two extensive bodies of water lying to the north and east of it, named, respectively, Lake Pontchartrain and Lake Borgne. Its population was about 170,000 when the war began. Being at the outlet to the sea of the vast products of the region watered by the Mississippi and its tributaries, it had the largest export trade of any city in the world.

[3] The principal passes by which the waters of the Mississippi flow into the Gulf of Mexico, through vast morasses, are five in number, and named respectively, the Southwest, South, Southeast, and East Pass, and Pass à l'Outre. The seaward edge of these passes lies almost directly upon the arc of a circle with a radius of fifteen miles.

and the opposite shore, seven hundred yards distant, a heavy iron chain-cable was stretched upon buoys made of cypress logs, and covered by a battery at each end. Adjoining Fort Jackson a formidable water-battery was constructed; and under the guns of the forts lay a fleet composed of thirteen gun-boats, a powerful iron-clad floating battery called the *Louisiana*, and the ram *Manassas*, already mentioned.[1] Also numerous fire-rafts, prepared to send down to destroy the invading fleet.

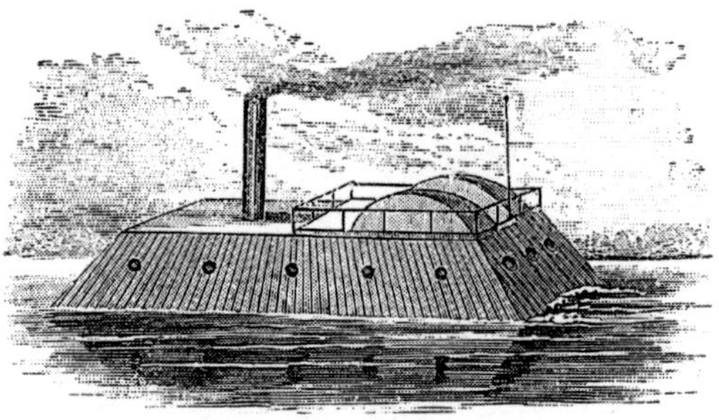

THE LOUISIANA.

In and around New Orleans was a force estimated at about ten thousand men, which the newspapers magnified, for the purpose of alarming the Nationals and strengthening the faith of the people.[2] That faith in the defenses of the city was very strong, for they believed them to be impregnable. Never doubting that impregnability, the citizens continued their occupations as usual. One of the journals boastingly said, "Our only fear is, that the northern invaders may not appear. We have made such extensive preparations to receive them, that it were vexatious if their invincible armada escapes the fate we have in store for it."[3] "The authorities at Richmond were so well assured of safety, by General Duncan, that they refused even to entertain the possibility of a penetration of the outer line of defenses, even when the mortar-fleet had begun its work."[4]

All things were in readiness for assault on the 17th of April. The fleets of Farragut and Porter[5] were in the river, and Butler, with about nine thousand troops,[6] was ready at the Southwest Pass, just below, to

---

[1] See page 113.

[2] The New Orleans *Picayune* of April 5 said, "We have 32,000 infantry, and as many more quartered in the neighborhood. In discipline and drill they are far superior to the Yankees. We have two very able and active generals, who possess our entire confidence—General Mansfield Lovell and Brigadier-General Ruggles. For Commodore, we have old Hollins—a Nelson in his way."

[3] New Orleans *Picayune*, April 5, 1862.

[4] Pollard's *First Year of the War*, page 310.

[5] These consisted of forty-seven armed vessels, eight of which were large and powerful steam sloops-of-war. Farragut's fleet was composed of the steamers *Hartford* (the flag-ship). Captain Wainright; sloops *Pensacola*, Captain Morris, and *Brooklyn*, Captain Craven, 24 guns each; *Richmond*, Captain Alden, 26; *Mississippi*, Captain M. Smith, 12; *Iroquois*, Commander De Camp, and *Oneida*, Commander S. P. Lee, 9 each; sailing sloop-of-war *Portsmouth*, 17; gun-boats *Varuna*, Captain Boggs, 12; *Cayuga*, Lieutenant Harrison, 5; *Winona*, Lieutenant Nichols, 4; *Katahdin*, Lieutenant Preble, 6; *Itaska*, Lieutenant Caldwell, 5; *Kineo*, Lieutenant Ransom, 5; *Wissahickon*, Lieutenant A. N. Smith, 5; *Pinola*, Lieutenant Crosby; *Kennebec*, Lieutenant Russell, 5; *Sciota*, Lieutenant Donalson, 6; schooner *Kittatinny*, Lieutenant Lamson, 9; *Miami*, Lieutenant Harroll, 6; *Clifton*, 5; and *Westfield*, Captain Renshaw, 6. There were twenty mortar-vessels, in three divisions, the first, or Red, of six vessels, under Lieutenant Watson Smith, in the *Norfolk Packet;* the second, or Blue, of seven vessels, commanded by Lieutenant Queen, in the *T. A. Ward;* and the third, or White, of seven vessels, commanded by Lieutenant Breese, in the *Horace Beales*. The names of the mortar-vessels were: *Norfolk Packet, Oliver H. Lee, Para, C. P. Williams, Orletta, William Bacon, T. A. Ward, Sidney C. Jones, Matthew Vassar, Jr., Maria J. Carlton, Orvetta, Adolphe Hugel, George Mangham, Horace Beales, John Griffith, Sarah Bruin, Racer, Sea Foam, Henry James, Dan Smith*, accompanied by the steamer *Harriet Lane*, 4 (Porter's flag-ship), and the gun-boat *Owasco*, Lieutenant Guest, 5. Some were only armed tugs, intended for the purpose of towing the mortar-schooners into position.

[6] Butler's troops, borne on five transports, consisted of the following regiments: On the *Mississippi*, the Commanding General and the Twenty-sixth Massachusetts, Colonel Jones; Thirty-first Massachusetts, Colonel Gooding, and Everett's Sixth Massachusetts battery. On the *Matanzas*, General Phelps, with the Ninth Con-

co-operate.[1] So early as the 28th of March, Fleet-captain Henry H. Bell had made a reconnoissance well up toward Fort Jackson, with two gun-boats, and found a thick wood covering the shores of the Mississippi for about four miles below it. This was favorable for the intended operations of the Nationals.

On the 8th of April, a detachment of the coast-survey party made a minute examination of the river-banks under the protection of the *Owasco;* and, on the 18th, two divisions (fourteen vessels) of Porter's flotilla were moored under cover of the wood, on the shores just below Fort Jackson. To prevent the discovery of his movement, Porter had daubed the hulls of his vessels with Mississippi mud, and clothed their masts and rigging with the boughs of trees, in such a way that they could not, at a distance, be distinguished from the forest. As when "Birnam wood" moved "toward Dunsinane," the strategy was successful, and his vessels were moored at desirable points without being discovered, the nearest one being two thousand eight hundred and fifty yards from Fort Jackson, and three thousand six hundred and eighty from Fort St. Philip. The remaining division (six vessels) was moored on the opposite side of the river, at a little greater distance from the forts, the hulls of the vessels screened by reeds and willows to conceal their character. The Mississippi was full to the brim. It was rising, and gradually submerging the adjacent country. The chain and its supports at Fort Jackson had been swept away by the flood, and only slight obstructions appeared in its place, composed of eight hulks and some of the cypress logs chained together.

MORTAR VESSELS DISGUISED.

The battle was begun before nine o'clock on the morning of the 18th, by a shot from Fort Jackson. As soon as Porter was ready, the *Owasco* opened fire, and the bombardment was commenced by the fourteen mortar-vessels, concealed by the woods, and the six in full view of the forts. Porter was in a position on the *Harriet Lane* to observe the effects of the shells, and he directed their range accordingly; and by ten o'clock the conflict was very warm. It was continued for several days with very little intermission, the gun-boats taking part by running up when the mortar-vessels needed relief, and firing heavy shells upon the forts.

Perceiving little chance for reducing the forts, Farragut prepared to execute another part of his instructions by running by them. On the 20th[a] he called a council of captains in the cabin of the *Hart-*

[a] April, 1862.

necticut, Colonel Cahill, and Holcomb's Second Vermont battery. On the *Great Republic*, General Williams, with the Twenty-first Indiana, Colonel McMillen; Fourth Wisconsin, Colonel Paine, and Sixth Michigan, Colonel Cortinas. On the *North America*, the Thirtieth Massachusetts, Colonel Dudley, and a company each of Reed's and Durivage's cavalry. On the *Will Farley*, the Twelfth Connecticut, Colonel Deming.

[1] On that day the Confederates sent down a "fire-ship"—a flat-boat filled with wood saturated with tar and turpentine—to burn the fleet. It came swiftly down the strong current, freighted with destruction; but it was quietly stopped in its career by some men in a small boat that went out from the *Iroquois*, who seized it with grappling irons, towed it to the shore, and there let it burn out in perfect harmlessness.

ford, when that measure was decided upon. General Butler, who had arrived with his staff, had been up in a tug to take a look at the obstructions, and had reported that they must be opened before any vessels could pass, especially when under fire. So, at ten o'clock that night, under cover of intense darkness, the wind blowing fiercely from the north, Commander Bell, with the *Pinola* and *Itaska*, supported by the *Iroquois*, *Kennebec*, and *Winona*, ran up to the boom. The *Pinola* ran to the hulk under the guns of Fort Jackson, and an attempt was made to destroy it by a petard, but failed. The *Itaska* was lashed to the next hulk, when a rocket thrown up from Fort Jackson revealed her presence, and a heavy fire from the fortress was opened upon her. The vigorous application of chisels, sledges, and saws for half an hour parted the boom of chains and logs, and the hulk to which the *Itaska* was lashed swung round and grounded the latter in the mud, in shallow water. The *Pinola* rescued her. Two hours afterward an immense fire-raft came roaring down the stream like a tornado, and, like its predecessors on similar errands, it was caught, and rendered harmless to the vessels it was intended to destroy.

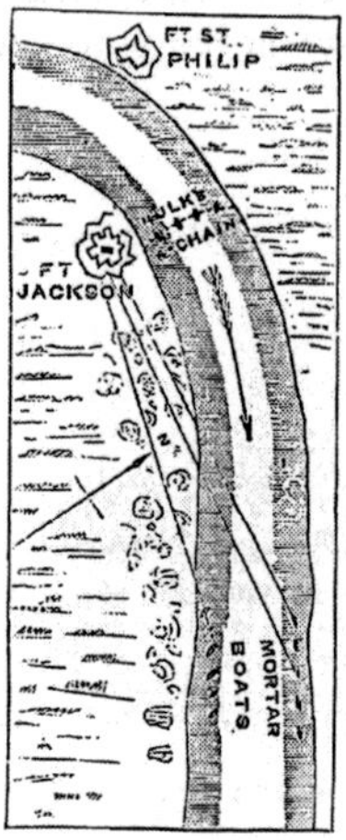

ATTACK ON THE FORTS.

Day after day the bombardment was continued, and night after night the fire-rafts were sent blazing down the stream. Fort Jackson, the principal object of attack, still held out. On the first day of the assault, its citadel was set on fire by Porter's shells and destroyed, with all the clothing and commissary stores, the garrison suffering severely for several hours from the intense heat of the conflagration. On the 19th, the mortar-schooner *Maria J. Carleton* was sunk by a rifle-shell from Fort Jackson, and, at the same time, the levee having been broken in scores of places by exploding shells, the waters of the Mississippi had flooded the parade-ground and casemates of the fort. For six days the bombardment continued, with such slight effect that Duncan reported that he had suffered very little, notwithstanding his *barbette* guns had been disabled at times, and that twenty-five thousand heavy shells had been hurled at him, of which one thousand had fallen within the fort.[1] "God is certainly protecting us," he said. "We are still cheerful, and have an abiding faith in our ultimate success."

[a] April, 1862.

At sunset on the 23d,[a] Farragut was ready for his perilous forward movement. The mortar-boats, keeping their position, were to cover the advance with their fire. Six gun-boats (*Harriet Lane*, *Westfield*, *Owasco*, *Clinton*, *Miami*, and *Jackson*, the last towing the *Portsmouth*) were to engage the water-battery below Fort Jackson, but not to make an attempt to pass it. Farragut, with his flag-ship *Hartford*, and the equally large ships *Richmond* and *Brooklyn*, that formed the first division, was to keep near the right bank of the river, and fight Fort Jackson, while Captain Theodorus Bailey, with the second division, composed of

[1] Duncan was not singular among Confederate officers in making other than the most exaggerated reports for the public. The number of shells thrown was about five thousand, and the number that entered the fort about three hundred.

the *Pensacola*, *Mississippi*, *Oneida*, *Varuna*, *Katahdin*, *Kineo*, *Wissahickon*, and *Portsmouth*, was to keep closely to the eastern bank, and fight Fort St. Philip. To Captain Bell was assigned the duty of attacking the Confederate fleet above the forts. He was to keep in the channel of the river with the *Sciota*, *Winona*, *Iroquois*, *Pinola*, *Itaska*, and *Kennebec*, and push right on to his assigned work without regard to the forts. General Butler and his staff went on board the *Saxon*, and at eleven o'clock at night a signal from the *Itaska*, that had run up to the boom, announced the channel clear of obstructions, excepting the hulks, which, with care, might be passed. The night was very dark, owing to a heavy fog; and the smoke from the steamers settled upon the waters, and shrouded every thing in almost impenetrable gloom.

THEODORUS BAILEY.

At one o'clock in the morning,[a] everybody was called to action. There was an ominous silence at the forts, which the inexperienced thought indicated their evacuation. It was not so. Energetic preparations for a more formidable assault were going on there. The fleet, now in command of Commodore Whittle, was summoned to a rendezvous near the fort; and other preparations indicated that a knowledge of the movement about to take place below had been communicated to the Confederate commanders.

[a] April 24, 1862.

The fleet moved at two o'clock, and at half-past three the divisions of Farragut and Bailey were going abreast up the swift stream, at the rate of four miles an hour. Then the mortars (the vessels still at their moorings), which were prepared for the most rapid firing, opened a terrible storm on Fort Jackson. Not less than half a dozen enormous shells were screaming through the thick night air, with their fiery trails, at the same moment. Steadily the fleet moved on, when the discovery of the *Cayuga*, Captain Bailey's ship, just as she had passed the opening in the boom, caused the forts to break their long silence, and bring heavy guns to bear upon her. She did not reply until she was close under those of Fort St. Philip, when she gave that work heavy broadsides of grape and canister as she passed by. The *Pensacola*, *Mississippi*, *Varuna*, and *Portsmouth* were following close in the wake of the *Cayuga*, and in all respects imitated her example; and the whole of Bailey's division passed the forts almost unharmed, excepting the sailing vessel *Portsmouth*, which, on firing a single broadside, lost her tow and drifted down the river.

Captain Bell was less fortunate. The *Sciota*, *Iroquois*, and *Pinola* passed the forts, but the *Itasca* was disabled by a storm of shot, one of which pierced her boiler, and she drifted helplessly down the river. From that storm the *Winona* recoiled, and the *Kennebec*, becoming entangled in the obstructions, lost her way in the intense darkness, and finally returned to her moorings below.

The waning moon was now just above the horizon, and the mist and smoke had become less dense. Farragut, in the fore-rigging of the *Hartford*, had been watching the movements of Bailey and Bell through his night-glass with the greatest interest, while the vessels under his immediate command were slowly approaching Fort Jackson. When he was within a mile and a quarter of it, the heavy guns of that fortress opened with a remarkable precision of aim, and the *Hartford* was struck several times. Farragut had mounted two guns upon the forecastle, and with these he promptly replied, at the same time pushing ahead directly for the fort. When he was within half a mile of it, he sheered off and gave the garrison such broadsides of grape and canister that they were driven from all their *barbette* guns. But the casemate guns were kept in full play, and the conflict became very severe. The *Richmond* soon joined in the fight; but the *Brooklyn* lagged behind, in consequence of becoming entangled with one of the hulks that bore up the great chain.

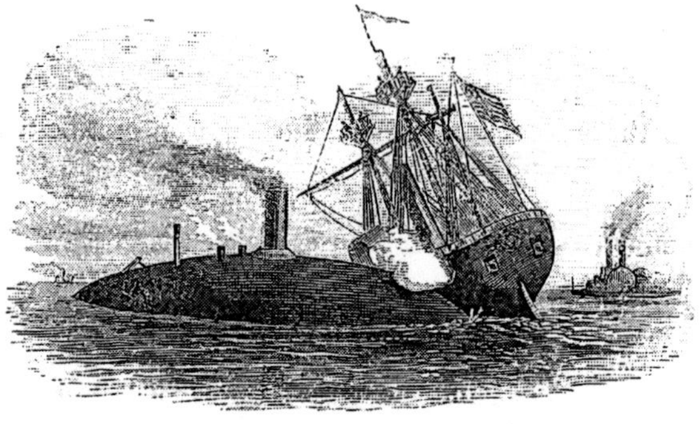

RAM MANASSAS ATTACKING THE BROOKLYN.

As soon as the *Brooklyn* was extricated and turned its bow up the river, the ram *Manassas* came down upon it furiously, and fired from its trap-door, when within about ten feet of the ship, a heavy bolt at the *Brooklyn's* smoke-stack, which fortunately lodged in some sand-bags that protected her steam-drum. The next moment the ram butted into the ship's starboard gang-way, but the chain armor that had been formed over the sides of the *Brooklyn* so protected it that the *Manassas* glanced off and disappeared in the gloom.

The *Brooklyn* had been exposed to a raking fire from Fort Jackson while entangled in the boom and encountering the *Manassas*. She had just escaped the latter, when a large Confederate steamer assailed her. She gave it a broadside that set it on fire and consigned it to swift destruction. Then pushing slowly on in the dark she suddenly found herself abreast Fort St. Philip, and very close to it. She was in a position to bring all her guns to bear upon it in the course of a few minutes. This was done with powerful effect. "I had the satisfaction," said Captain Craven in his report, "of completely silencing that work before I left it, my men in the tops witnessing, in the flashes of the bursting shrapnel,[1] the enemy running like sheep for more comfortable quarters."

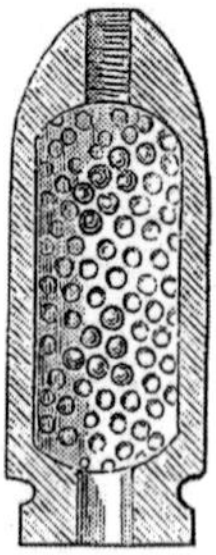

SHRAPNEL SHELL.

[1] A Shrapnel shell is sometimes spherical and sometimes conical, like that represented in section in the engraving. They are hollow spheres or cones of iron, filled with musket-balls or grape-shot, with sufficient gunpowder to explode them when ignited by a fuse. The balls are then scattered and are very destructive.

Commodore Farragut, in the mean time, "was having a rough time of it," as he said. While battling with the forts, a huge fire-raft, pushed by the *Manassas*, came suddenly upon him, all a-blaze. In trying to avoid this, the *Hartford* was run aground, and the incendiary came crashing alongside of her. "In a moment," said Farragut, "the ship was one blaze all along the port side, half way up to the main and mizzen tops. But thanks to the good organization of the fire department, by Lieutenant Thornton, the flames were extinguished, and at the same time we backed off and got clear of the raft. All this time we were pouring shells into the forts, and they into us, and now and then a rebel steamer would get under our fire and receive our salutation of a broadside."

THE HARTFORD.

Before the fleet had fairly passed the forts, the Confederate gunboats and rams appeared and took part in the battle, producing a scene at once awful and grand. The noise of twenty mortars and two hundred and sixty great guns, afloat and ashore, was terrific. The explosion of shells, sunken deep in the oozy earth in and around the forts, shook land and water like an earthquake; and the surface of the river was strewn with dead and helpless fishes stunned by the concussions. "Combine," said Major Bell, of Butler's staff, "all that you have ever heard of thunder, and add to it all you have ever seen of lightning, and you have perhaps a conception of the scene." And all this noise and destructive energy—the blazing fire-rafts, the floating volcanoes sending forth fire and smoke, and bolts of death, and the thundering forts, and the ponderous rams, were all crowded, in "the greatest darkness just before the dawn," within the space of a narrow river—"too narrow," said Farragut, "for more than two or three vessels to act to advantage. My greatest fear was that we should fire into each other; and Captain Wainwright and myself were hallooing ourselves hoarse at the men not to fire into our ships."

We have observed that the fleet had not fairly passed the river obstructions before the Confederate rams and gun-boats appeared.[1] The *Cayuga* encountered that flotilla as soon as she passed Fort St. Philip. The ram

[1] There were six rams, named *Warrior*, *Stonewall Jackson*, *Defiance*, *Resolute*, *Governor Moore*, and *General Quitman*, commanded respectively by Captains Stephenson, Philips, McCoy, Hooper, Kennon, and Grant. These were river steamers, made shot-proof by cotton bulk-heads, and furnished with iron prows for pushing. The ram *Manassas*, then commanded by Captain Warley, was an entirely different affair. She was thus described by an eye-witness: "She is about one hundred feet long and twenty feet beam, and draws from nine to twelve feet water. Her shape above water is nearly that of half a sharply pointed egg-shell, so that a shot will glance from her, no matter where it strikes. Her back is formed of twelve-inch oak, covered with one-and-a-half-inch bar iron. She has two chimneys, so arranged as to slide down in time of action. The pilot-

Manassas, the floating battery *Louisiana*, and sixteen other armed vessels, all under the command of Captain Mitchell of the *Louisiana*, were, for a few moments, intent upon her destruction. To stand and fight would have been madness in Captain Bailey, for no supporting friend appeared. So he exercised his skill in steering his vessel in a manner to escape the butting of the rams, and the attempts to board her. Thus he saved the *Cayuga*. He did more. In his maneuvers he was offensive as well as defensive, and compelled three of the Confederate gun-boats to surrender to him before the *Varuna*, Captain Boggs, and the *Oneida*, Captain Lee, came to his rescue. The *Cayuga* had been struck forty-two times during the struggle, and was so much damaged in masts and rigging that Captain Bailey thought it prudent to withdraw from the battle.

CHARLES BOGGS.

The *Varuna* was now the chief object of the wrath of the foe, and terribly its vials were poured upon her. Commander Boggs said, in his report, that immediately after passing the forts, he found himself "amid a nest of rebel steamers." His vessel rushed into their midst, and fired broadsides into each as he passed. The first one that received the *Varuna's* fire seemed to be crowded with troops. Her boiler was exploded by a shot, and she drifted ashore. Soon afterward the *Varuna* drove three other vessels (one a gun-boat) ashore, in flames, and all of them blew up. She was soon afterward furiously attacked by the ram *Governor Moore*, commanded by Beverly Kennon, who had abandoned his flag. It raked along the *Varuna's* port gangway, killing four and wounding nine of her crew. Boggs managed, he said, "to get a three-inch shell into her, abaft her armor, and also several shot from the after rifled gun, when she dropped out of action, partially disabled."

Meanwhile another ram, its iron prow under water, struck the *Varuna* a heavy blow in the port gangway. The *Varuna's* shot in return glanced harmlessly from the armored bow of her antagonist. Backing off a short distance, and then shooting forward, the ram gave the *Varuna* another blow at the same place, and crushed in her side. The ram, becoming entangled, was drawn around nearly to the side of the *Varuna*, when Boggs gave her five 8-inch shells abaft her armor from his port guns. "This settled her," said Boggs, "and drove her ashore in flames." Finding his own vessel sinking, he ran her into the bank, let go her anchor, and tied her bow up to the

---

house is in the stern of the boat. She is worked by a powerful propeller, but cannot stem a strong current. She carries only one gun, a 68-pounder, right in her bow.

"There is only one entrance to her, through a trap-door in her back. Her port-hole is furnished with a heavily plated trap, which springs up when the gun is run out, and falls down when it is run back. How the crew get their light and air, I cannot pretend to say."

trees. All that time her guns were at work crippling the *Moore*, and they did not cease until the water was over the gun-trucks, when Boggs turned his attention to getting the wounded and crew out of the vessel. Just then, the *Oneida*, Captain Lee, came to the rescue of the *Varuna*, but Boggs "waved him on" after the *Moore*, which was then in flames. The latter was surrendered to the *Oneida* by her second officer. She had lost fifty of her men, killed and maimed; and Kennon, her commander, had set her on fire and fled, leaving his wounded to the cruelty of the flames.[1]

Thus ended one of the most desperate combats recorded in the history of the war. It was "short, sharp, and decisive." Within the space of an hour and a half after the National vessels left their anchorage, the forts were passed, the struggle had occurred, and eleven of the Confederate vessels, or nearly the whole of their fleet, were destroyed. The National loss was thirty killed and not more than one hundred and twenty-five wounded.

When Captain Bailey withdrew with the crippled *Cayuga*, and left the

VIEW AT THE QUARANTINE GROUNDS.[2]

Varuna to continue the fight, he moved up the river to the Quarantine Station, a short distance above Fort St. Philip. On the west bank of the river opposite was a battery, in charge of several companies of Confederate sharpshooters of the Chalmette (Louisiana) regiment, commanded by Colonel Szymanski, a Pole. On the approach of the *Cayuga* they attempted to flee, but a volley of canister-shot from her guns made them halt, and they became

---

[1] Report of Captain Charles Boggs to Commodore Farragut, April 29th, 1862. In his report, Captain Boggs warmly commended a powder-boy named Oscar Peck, only thirteen years of age, whose coolness and bravery were remarkable. Seeing him pass quickly, Boggs inquired where he was going in such a hurry. "To get a passing-box, Sir," he replied: "the other was smashed by a ball." When the *Varuna* went down, the boy was missed. He had stood by one of the guns, and had been cast into the water. In a few minutes he was seen swimming toward the wreck. When he got on the part above water, on which Boggs was standing, he gave the usual salute and said, "All right, Sir; I report myself on board."

[2] This is a view of the quarantine grounds, its buildings, and a store-house, built of brick, belonging to the Government, and situated on the east or left bank of the Mississippi, just above the forts. This was the first Government property in Louisiana "repossessed" by the Government. The store-house is seen on the right. The next building was a hospital, and the small house next to it was General Butler's head-quarters when he took possession of the grounds.

prisoners of war. The battle was now over, and all of Farragut's ships, twelve in number, that had passed the forts joined the *Cayuga*. Then the dead were carried ashore and buried.

While this desperate battle was raging, the land troops, under General Butler, had been preparing for their part in the drama. They were in the transports at the Passes, and had distinctly heard the booming of the guns and mortars. The General and his staff, as we have observed, were on the *Saxon*. She followed close in the rear of Bailey's division, until the plunging of shells from the forts into the water around her warned the commanding General that he had gone far enough. So eager had been his interest in the scenes before him, that he had entered the arena of imminent danger without perceiving it. He ordered the *Saxon* to drop a little astern, to the great relief of her Captain, to whom a flaming shell would have been specially unwelcome, for his vessel was laden with eight hundred barrels of gunpowder. Almost at the same moment the *Manassas*, that had been terribly pounded by the *Mississippi*, and sent adrift in a helpless state, was seen moving down into the midst of Porter's mortar-fleet. Some of these opened fire upon her, but it was soon perceived that she was harmless. Her pipes were all twisted and riddled by shot, and her hull was well battered and pierced. Smoke was issuing from every opening, for she was on fire. In a few minutes her only gun went off, and the flames burst out from her bow-port and stern trap-door. Giving a plunge, like some huge monster, she went hissing to the bottom of the Mississippi.

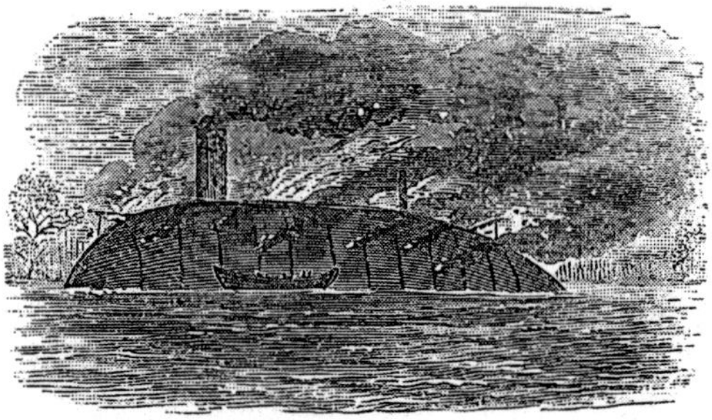

THE MANASSAS.

Farragut had now thirteen of his vessels in safety above the forts, and he prepared to move up to New Orleans, while Porter, with his mortar-fleet, was still below them, and they were yet firmly held by the Confederates. The time for Butler to act had arrived. Half an hour after Farragut had reached the Quarantine, he sent Captain Boggs in a small boat, through shallow bayous in the rear of Fort St. Philip with dispatches for Butler and Porter. The former had already procured the light-draft steamer *Miami* from Porter, and had hastened to his transports. These were taken to Sable Island, twelve miles in the rear of Fort St. Philip, and from that point the troops made their way in small boats through the narrow and shallow bayous with the greatest fatigue, under the general pilotage of Lieutenant Weitzel. Sometimes the boats were dragged by men waist deep in cold and muddy water; but the work was soon and well accomplished, and on the night of the 27th Butler was at the Quarantine, ready to begin the meditated assault on Fort St. Philip the next day. His troops were landed a short distance above the fort, under cover of the guns of the *Mississippi* and *Kineo.* A small force was sent across the river to a position not far above Fort Jackson.

In the mean time Porter had been pounding Fort Jackson terribly with the shells from his mortars. On the 26th, he sent a flag of truce with a demand for its surrender, and saying that he had information that Commodore Farragut was in possession of New Orleans. On the following morning, Colonel Higgins, the commander of the forts, replied that he had no official information of the surrender of New Orleans, and, until such should be received by him, no proposition for a surrender of the works under his command could be entertained for a moment. On the same day, General Duncan, then in Fort Jackson, issued an address to the soldiers, as the commander of the coast defenses, urging them to continue the contest, saying: "The safety of New Orleans and the cause of the Southern Confederacy—our homes, families, and every thing dear to man—yet depend upon our exertions. We are just as capable of repelling the enemy to-day as we were before the bombardment." But the soldiers did not all agree with him in opinion. They saw the blackened fragments of vessels and other property strewing the swift current of the Mississippi, and were satisfied that the rumors of the fall of New Orleans that had reached them were true. They had also heard of Butler's troops in the rear of Fort St. Philip. So that night a large portion of the garrison mutinied, spiked the guns bearing up the river, and the next day sallied out and surrendered themselves to Butler's pickets on that side of the river, saying they had been impressed, and would fight the Government no longer.

Colonel Higgins now saw that all was lost, and he hastened to accept the generous terms which Porter had offered. While these terms were being reduced to writing in the cabin of the *Harriet Lane*,[1] Mitchell towed his battery (the *Louisiana*), which lay above the forts, out into the strong current, set her on fire, and abandoned her, with her guns all shotted. He expected she would blow up in the midst of the mortar-fleet, but the explosion occurred when she was abreast of Fort St. Philip, when a flying fragment from her killed one of its garrison. She at once went to the bottom of the river, and the remaining Confederate steamers surrendered without resist-

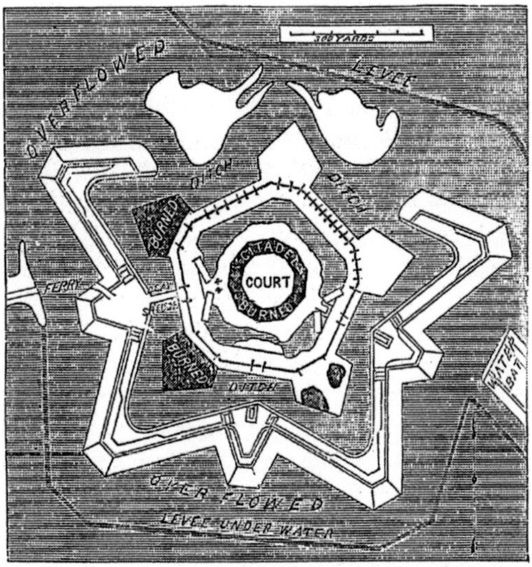

PLAN OF FORT JACKSON.

[1] The capitulation was signed on the part of the Nationals by Commanders David D. Porter and W. B Renshaw, and Lieutenant W. W. Wainright, commander of the *Harriet Lane;* and on the part of the Confederates by General J. K. Duncan, commander of the coast defenses, and Colonel Edwin Higgins, the commander of the forts. The writer was informed by an officer of the navy who was present at the surrender of Fort Jackson, that when the flag-officer of that work was asked for the garrison flag, which was not to be seen, he pretended to be ignorant of its whereabouts. He appeared to be unduly corpulent, and, on a personal examination, it was found that his obesity was caused by the flag, which was wrapped around his body.

ance.[1] Commodore Porter turned over the forts and all their contents to General Phelps. Fort Jackson was only injured in its interior works, and Fort St. Philip was as perfect as when the bombardment began.[2] No reliable report of the losses of the Confederates in killed and wounded was ever given. The number of prisoners surrendered, including those of the Chalmette regiment and on board of the gun-boats last taken, amounted to nearly one thousand. The entire loss of the Nationals, from the beginning of the contest until New Orleans was taken, was forty killed and one hundred and seventy-seven wounded.

MANSFIELD LOVELL.

Porter told Higgins the truth when he said Farragut was in possession of New Orleans. The city was really lost when the Commodore's thirteen armed vessels were lying in safety and in fair condition at the Quarantine.[a] Of this imminent peril of the city General Lovell had been impressed early that morning. He had come down in his steamer *Doubloon*, and arrived just as the National fleet was passing the forts. He came near being captured in the terrible mêlée on the river that ensued, and sought safety on shore. Then he hastened to New Orleans as fast as courier horses could take him, traveling chiefly along the levee, for much of the country was overflowed. He arrived there early in the afternoon, and confirmed the intelligence of disaster which had already reached the citizens. A fearful panic ensued. Drums were beating; soldiers were seen hurrying to and fro; merchants fled from their stores; women without bonnets and brandishing pistols were seen in the streets, crying, "Burn the city! Never mind us! Burn the city!" Military officers impressed vehicles into the service of carrying cotton to the levees to be burned. Specie, to the amount of four millions of dollars, was sent out of the city by railway; the consulates were crowded with foreigners deposit-

[a] April 24, 1862.

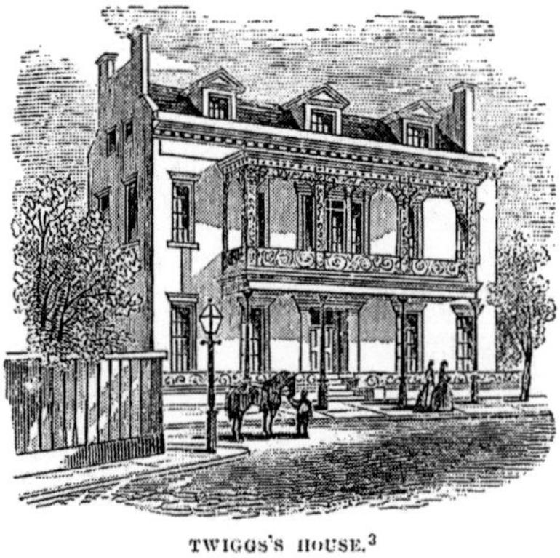

TWIGGS'S HOUSE.[3]

[1] There seems to have been no kindly co-operation between the forts and the Confederate fleet, and some very spicy correspondence occurred between General Duncan and Captain Mitchell. The former, in his official report, declared that the great disaster was "the sheer result of that lack of cheerful and hearty co-operation from the defenses afloat" which he had a right to expect.

[2] Over 1,800 shells fell inside of Fort Jackson, 170 in the water-battery, and about 3,000 in the ditches around the works. For minute particulars of the battle and its results, see the reports of Captains Farragut and Porter, and their subordinate commanders; of General Butler and those under his command; and of General Duncan and Colonel Higgins, of the Confederate forces.

[3] This was the appearance of Twiggs's residence when the writer visited it, in the spring of 1866. It was a

ing their money and other valuables for safety from the impending storm; and poor old Twiggs, the traitor, like his former master, Floyd, fearing the wrath of his injured Government, fled from his home, leaving in the care of a young woman the two swords which had been awarded him for his services in Mexico, to fall into the hands of the conquerors who speedily came.[1]

On his way to New Orleans, Lovell had ordered General Smith, who was in command of the river defenses below the town, known as the Chalmette batteries,[2] to make all possible resistance; and in the city he tried to raise a thousand volunteers, who should make a desperate attempt to board and capture the National vessels, but he found only one hundred men who evinced sufficient courage or desperation to undertake the perilous task. Lovell was satisfied himself, and he convinced the city authorities that the regular and volunteer troops under his immediate command were too few to make resistance, and he could not rely on the militia conscripts, nor a regiment of free colored men who had been pressed into the service, in the presence of foes that they might welcome as their friends. These considerations, and the fact that, on account of the height of the river surface at that time of flood, a gun-boat might pass up to Kenner's plantation, ten miles above the city, and command the narrow neck between the river and the swamp, across which the railway passes, and thus prevent the troops and supplies going out, or supplies and re-enforcements going into the town, made it absolutely necessary that they should escape as soon as possible. So Lovell prepared to abandon New Orleans. He disbanded the conscripts, and sent stores, munitions of war, and other valuable property up the country by steamboats and the railroad; and while a portion of the volunteers hastened to Camp Moore, on the Jackson and New Orleans

NEW ORLEANS AND ITS VICINITY.

large brick house, at the junction of Camp and Magazine Streets, and was then used by General Canby, the commander of the Department, as the quarters of his paymaster.

[1] Parton's *Butler in New Orleans*, page 264.

[2] These were on each side of the river. There were five 32-pounders on one side and nine on the other.

railway, seventy-eight miles distant, the regiment of colored troops refused to go.

With nine vessels Farragut proceeded up the river on the morning of the 25th, and when near the English Turn he met evidences of the abandonment of New Orleans by the Confederates in the form of blazing ships, loaded with cotton, that came floating down the stream. Soon afterward, he discovered the Chalmette batteries on both sides of the Mississippi, a few miles below the city, and at once made dispositions to attack them. The river was so full that his vessels completely commanded the Confederate works. Moving in two lines, they proceeded to the business of disabling them. The gallant Bailey, who had not noticed the signal for close order, was far ahead with the *Cayuga*, and for twenty minutes she sustained a heavy cross-fire alone. Farragut pressed forward with the *Hartford*, and, passing the *Cayuga*, gave the batteries such destructive broadsides of shell, grape, and shrapnel that at the first discharge the Confederates were driven from their guns. The *Pensacola* and the *Brooklyn*, and then the remainder of the fleet, followed the *Hartford's* example, and in the course of twenty minutes the batteries were silenced and their men were running for their lives.

The victors were now in the midst of a terrific scene. The river was strewn with fire rafts, burning steamers, and blazing cotton bales, and overhung by an awful canopy of black smoke, sent up by the great conflagration. As soon as it was known that the National vessels were approaching the city, another great panic prevailed, and the work of destruction of property commenced, by order of the Governor of Louisiana and General Lovell.[1] In a very short time a sheet of flame and pall of smoke, caused by burning cotton, sugar, and other staples of that region, were seen along the levee for the distance of five miles. Foolishly believing that the cotton which they regarded as king was the chief object of the Nationals, the infatuated people sent it in huge loads to the levee to be destroyed. In front of the various presses along the river front it was piled and fired, and in this way no less than fifteen thousand bales, valued at one million five hundred thousand dollars, were consumed. More than a dozen large ships, some of them laden with cotton, and as many magnificent steamboats, with unfinished gunboats and other vessels, were soon wrapped in flames and sent floating down the river, the Confederates hoping they might destroy the approaching

THE LEVEE AT NEW ORLEANS.

[1] Pollard, i. 316.

vessels.[1] But the latter all escaped, and at about one o'clock in the afternoon Farragut's squadron was anchored off the city, while a violent thunder-storm was raging.

New Orleans was now utterly defenseless. Lovell was there, but a greater portion of his troops had been sent away, with the concurrence of the civil authorities, who wished to spare the town the horrors of a bombardment. Captain Bailey was sent ashore with a flag, bearing a summons from Farragut for the surrender of the city, and a demand that the Confederate flag should be taken down and that of the Republic raised over the public buildings. Bailey made his way through a hooting, cursing crowd to the City Hall, escorted by sensible citizens. To the demand for surrender, Lovell returned an unqualified refusal, but saying, that as he was powerless to hold the city against great odds, and wishing to save it from destruction, he would withdraw his troops and turn it over to the civil authorities. At the same time he advised the Mayor not to surrender the city, nor allow the flags to be taken down by any of its people.

Acting upon this foolish advice, the Mayor (John T. Monroe), one of the most unworthy of the public men of the day, refused to surrender the city or take down the Louisiana flag from the City Hall. This refusal was in the form of a most ridiculous letter to Farragut, in which the Mayor declared that, while his people could not prevent the occupation of the city by the National forces, they would not transfer their allegiance to a government they had deliberately repudiated.[2] In the mean time a force had landed from the *Pensacola*, which was lying opposite Esplanade Street, and, unopposed, hoisted the National flag over the Government Mint; but as soon as they retired it was torn down and dragged in derision through the streets by young men belonging to the Pinckney Battalion, and a gambler named William B. Mumford.[3] This act was hailed with acclamation by the secessionists of New Orleans, and caused paragraphs of praise and exultation to appear in the public journals. It ended in a serious tragedy, as we shall observe presently.

In reply to the Mayor's absurd letter, the patient Farragut referred to the pulling down of the flag, the indignities to which it was subjected, and the insults offered to his officers, and said, with a meaning which the most obtuse might understand, "all of which go to show that the fire of this fleet may be drawn upon the city at any moment, and in such an event the levee would, in all probability, be cut by the shells, and an amount of distress ensue to the innocent population which I have heretofore endeavored to assure you that I desire by all means to avoid." He concluded by saying, "The election, therefore, is with you; but it becomes my duty to notify you to remove the women and children from the city within forty-eight hours, if I have rightly understood your determination."

---

[1] The shipyard at Algiers, opposite New Orleans, was burned, and with it an immense armored ram called *Mississippi*, which was considered the most important naval structure which the Confederates had yet undertaken.

[2] "As to the hoisting of any flag," he said, "than the flag of our own adoption and allegiance, let me say to you, Sir, that the man lives not in our midst whose hand and heart would not be palsied at the mere thought of such an act; nor could I find in my entire constituency so wretched and desperate a renegade as would dare to profane with his hand the sacred emblem of our aspirations."

[3] There was no guard left at the Mint to defend the flag, but a watch was set in the top of the *Pensacola*, from which a howitzer hurled grape-shot at the men who pulled down the flag, but without effect.

To this message the absurd Mayor returned a most ridiculous answer—as ridiculous, considering the circumstances, as the mock-heroic babble of a circus harlequin—in which he uttered nonsense about "murdering" women and children,[1] and charged Farragut with a desire to "humble and disgrace the people." After solemnly assuring the Commodore that such satisfaction he could not obtain, he said dramatically, "We will stand your bombardment, unarmed and undefended as we are. The civilized world will consign to indelible infamy the heart that will conceive the deed and the hand that will consummate it." The substance of the Mayor's letter was, as has been observed, "'Come on shore and hoist what flag you please. Don't ask *us* to do your flag-raising.' Slightly impudent, perhaps; but men who are talking from behind a bulwark of fifty thousand women and children *can* be impudent if they please."[2]

To the insolence of the Mayor was added the greater impertinence of the commander of a French ship-of-war which had just arrived, who wrote a note to Farragut that his Government had sent him to protect the persons and property of its thirty thousand subjects in New Orleans, and that he demanded sixty days, instead of forty-eight hours, as the time to be given for the evacuation of the city by the inhabitants. He concluded with a threat, saying, "If it is your resolution to bombard the city, do it; but I wish to state that you will have to account for the barbarous act to the power which I represent." The veteran commodore was sorely perplexed, and, while revolving in his mind what to do, he was relieved by the intelligence of the surrender of the forts below. He now felt that he could afford to wait, for the speedy possession of New Orleans by General Butler's troops was made an almost absolute certainty. Up to that moment it was believed by the citizens that the forts below could not be taken, and this was the chief reason for the defiant attitude of the public authorities there. Now their tone was changed, and, to appease Farragut, he was semi-officially informed, in a private manner, that the hauling down of the flag from the Mint was the "unauthorized act of the men who performed it."[3]

On the following day, Captain Bell landed with a hundred marines, put the National flag in the places of the ensigns of rebellion on the Mint and Custom House, locked the door of the latter, and returned with the key to his vessel. Those flags were undisturbed. The occupation of the "European Brigade," a military organization in New Orleans, ostensibly for the purpose of aiding the authorities in the protection of the citizens from unruly members, but really in the interests of the Confederates, composed of British, French, and Spanish aliens, was now almost at an end, and the English members of it, who admired the frequent displays of "British neutrality" elsewhere, now imitated it by voting at their armory, that, as they would have no further use for their weapons and accouterments,

---

[1] "Our women and children cannot escape from your shells, if it be your pleasure to murder them on a mere question of etiquette; but if they could, there are few among them who would consent to desert their families and their homes and the graves of their relatives in so awful a moment: they would bravely stand in sight of your shells, rolling over the bones of those who were dear to them, and would deem that they died not ingloriously by the side of the tombs erected by their piety to the memory of departed relatives."

[2] Parton's *Butler in New Orleans*, page 274.

[3] These were W. B. Mumford (who cut it loose from the flagstaff), Lieutenant Holmes, Sergeant Burns, and James Reed, all but Mumford members of the Pinckney Battalion of Volunteers.

they would send them to Beauregard's army at Corinth, as "a slight token of their affection for the Confederate States."

On the 30th,[a] Farragut informed the city authorities that he should hold no further intercourse with a body whose language was so offensive, and that, so soon as General Butler should arrive with his forces, he should turn over the charge of the city to him, and resume his naval duties.

[a] April, 1862.

Let us see what General Butler had been doing for the few preceding days.

A few hours after Mumford and his companions had pulled down the National flag, General Butler arrived and joined Farragut on the *Hartford;* and, in his report to the Secretary of War on the 29th, he foreshadowed his future act by saying: "This outrage will be punished in such manner as in my judgment will caution both the perpetrators and abettors of the act, so that they shall fear the *stripes* if they do not reverence the *stars* of our banner." He hastened back to his troops, and took measures for their immediate advance up the river. His transports were brought into the Mississippi, and these, bearing two thousand armed men, appeared off the levee in front of New Orleans on the first of May. The General and his staff, his wife, and fourteen hundred troops, were on the same vessel (*Mississippi*) in which they left Hampton Roads sixty-five days before. Preparations were made for landing forthwith. In his order for the movement, he forbade the plunder of all property, public or private, in the city; the absence of officers and soldiers from their stations without arms or alone; and held the commanders of regiments and companies responsible for the execution of the orders.

At four o'clock in the afternoon[b] the debarkation of a part of the troops at the city commenced, while others were sent over to occupy Algiers, opposite New Orleans. A company of the Thirty-first Massachusetts was the first to land. These were followed by the remainder of the regiment; also by the Fourth Wisconsin, Colonel Paine; and Everett's battery of heavy field-guns. These formed a procession and acted as an escort for General Butler and his staff, and General Williams and his staff; and to the tune of the "Star Spangled Banner" they marched through Poydras and St. Charles Streets to Canal Street, under the guidance of Lieutenant Weigel, of Baltimore, one of Butler's aids, who was familiar with the city. They took possession of the Custom House, whose principal entrance is on Canal Street, and there the Massachusetts regiment was quartered.

[b] May 1.

Strict directions had been given not to resent any insults that might be offered by the vast crowd that filled the side-walks, without orders; but if a shot should be fired from a house, to halt, arrest the inmates, and destroy the building. Every moment the crowd became greater and more boisterous, and the patience of the troops was much tried during that short march. Their ears were assailed by the most offensive epithets, vulgar and profane, applied to the General and his troops,[1] yet the consciousness of supporting power behind the pacific order caused them to march silently on to their

---

[1] Before the troops landed, voices from the crowd that covered the levee had been heard calling for "Picayune Butler," and asking him to show himself. The General was willing to have a practical joke, well satisfied

destination. Captain Everett posted his cannon around the Custom House, and comparative quiet prevailed in New Orleans that night. Colonel Deming's Twelfth Connecticut landed, and bivouacked on the levee by the side of Butler's head-quarters ship, the *Mississippi*, on board of which the commanding general spent the night. At an early hour in the evening, he had completed a proclamation to the inhabitants of New Orleans, in which his intentions, as the representative of the Government, were explicitly stated.[1]

General Butler had resolved to act with strictest justice toward the deluded people, and to be kind and lenient to all who showed a disposition to be peaceable. But his first trial of the temper of those with whom he had to deal was discouraging. He sent his proclamation to the office of the *True Delta* newspaper, to be printed as a hand-bill. The proprietor flatly refused to use his types in such an act of "submission to Federal rule." Two hours afterward an officer with a file of soldiers (half a dozen of whom were printers) had possession of the *True Delta* office, and the proclamation was soon issued in printed form. Meanwhile, Colonel Deming had encamped in Lafayette Square, and General Butler had taken possession of General Lovell's recent head-quarters in the St. Charles Hotel, not far distant, established his own there, and invited the city authorities to a conference. The silly Monroe told the General's messenger that the Mayor's place of business was at the City Hall. It was intimated to him that such a reply would not satisfy the commanding general; so the Mayor, taking counsel of prudence, waited upon General Butler at the St. Charles, with Pierre Soulé, formerly a representative in Congress, and some other friends. The interview was instructive to both parties. There appeared a wide difference of opinion as to the

---

that the real merriment would be on the side of himself and friends; so he requested the lively air of "Picayune Butler" to be played when they should debark. But none of the band-masters had the music, and the more appropriate National airs were the first that the citizens of New Orleans heard when the troops landed.

1 In that proclamation, General Butler called upon all who had taken up arms against their Government to lay them down, and directed all flags and devices indicative of rebellion to be taken down, and the American flag—the emblem of the Government—to be treated with the greatest respect. He told them that all well-disposed persons, natives or foreigners, should be protected in person and property, subject only to the laws of the United States; and he enjoined the inhabitants to continue in their usual avocations. He directed the keepers of all public property whatever, and all manufacturers of arms and munitions of war, to report to head-quarters. He directed that shops and places of amusement should be kept open as usual, and the services in the churches and religious houses to be held as in times of profound peace. Martial law was to be the governing power; and to the Provost-Marshal, keepers of public houses and drinking saloons were required to report and obtain license, before they were permitted to do business. He assured the inhabitants that a sufficient number of soldiers would be kept in the city to preserve order; and that the killing of any National soldier by a disorderly mob should be punished as murder. All acts interfering with the forces or laws of the United States were to be referred to a military court for adjudication and punishment. Civil causes were to be referred to the ordinary tribunals. The levy and collection of taxes, excepting those authorized by the United States, were forbidden, save those for keeping in repair and lighting the streets, for sanitary purposes. The use, in trade, of Confederate bonds or other evidences of debt was forbidden, excepting those in form of bank notes, which constituted the only circulating medium, and the use of the latter was to be allowed only until further orders. No seditious publications were to be allowed; and communications or editorials in newspapers, which should give accounts of the movements of the National soldiers, were not permitted to be circulated until the same had been submitted to a military censor. The same rule was to be applied to telegraphic dispatches. It was requested that any outrages committed by the National soldiers upon the persons or property of the citizens, should be reported to the provost-guard. Assemblages of persons in the streets were forbidden; and the municipal authority was to be continued, so far as the police of the city and its environs were concerned, until suspended. To assist in keeping order, the "European Brigade," which, as we have observed, had professedly been employed for that purpose, on the evacuation of the city by Lovell and his troops, were invited to co-operate with the military authorities. The General said, in conclusion: "All the requirements of martial law will be imposed, so long as, in the judgment of the United States authorities, it may be necessary; and while it is desired by these authorities to exercise this government mildly, and after the usages of the past, it must not be supposed that it will not be vigorously and firmly administered, as the occasion calls for it."

status of the inhabitants of New Orleans in relation to the General Government; and the dividing line was so distinctly seen at this interview, that there could be no question about it thereafter. Butler took the broad national ground that the inhabitants in general had been in rebellion against their lawful Government; that the authority of that Government, being supreme, rightfully demanded the allegiance of the people; and that no other authority, except that sanctioned by the Government, could be allowed in the management of the public affairs of the city. Soulé and his friends persisted in regarding Louisiana as an independent sovereignty, and the object of the primary allegiance of its citizens. They considered the National troops as invaders and intruders, and, as a sequence, the people as doing right in treating them with contempt and abhorrence, and fully justified in driving them from the city if they could.

An instant reply to this assumption was practically given. An immense mob had collected in the street in front of the St. Charles. They were exasperated by the seizure of that building by General Butler, and threatened violence. Cannon had been planted and a regiment had been posted for the protection of head-quarters, but, while the General and the city authorities had been in conference, the conduct of the populace had become so alarming, that General Williams sent word to Butler that he feared he could not control them. The General calmly replied: "Give my compliments to General Williams, and tell him, if he finds he cannot control the mob, to open upon them with artillery." The Mayor and his friends sprang to their feet in consternation. "Don't do that, General," exclaimed the terrified Monroe. "Why not, gentlemen?" said Butler. "The mob must be controlled. We can't have a disturbance in the street." The lunatic Mayor had partially recovered his senses in Butler's presence, and, going out to the balcony, he informed the mob of the General's orders, and advised them to disperse. That evening the inhabitants of New Orleans, who chose to listen, heard "The Star Spangled Banner" and other National airs, to which their ears had long been strangers, played by a band on the balcony of the St. Charles.[1]

Within twenty-four hours after this occurrence, the temper of the people and that of General Butler were mutually understood; and his proclamation, which was not issued until the 6th of May, was a rule for all loyal or disloyal citizens. It had been read at the conference at the St. Charles just mentioned, when Soulé declared that it would give great offense, and that the people, who were not conquered, and could not be expected to act as a conquered people, would never submit to its demands. "Withdraw your troops, General," said the distinguished and accomplished Frenchman, "and leave the city government to manage its own affairs. If the troops remain, there will certainly be trouble."

This threat, though uttered in smooth terms, brought a withering rebuke from the commanding general. "I did not expect to hear from Mr. Soulé a *threat* on this occasion," he said. "I have long been accustomed to hear threats from southern gentlemen in political conventions; but let me assure the gentlemen present that the time for tactics of that nature has passed, never to return. New Orleans *is* a conquered city. If not, why are we

---

[1] Parton's *Butler in New Orleans*, page 285.

here? How did we get here? Have you opened your arms and bid us welcome? Are we here by your consent? Would you or would you not expel us if you could? New Orleans has been conquered by the forces of the United States, and, by the laws of all nations, lies subject to the will of the conquerors."[1]

In accordance with this doctrine General Butler found it necessary to administer the affairs in the Department of the Gulf, of which he was the commander. In his interview with the Mayor and Soulé, he had generously offered to leave the municipal government of New Orleans to the free exercise of all its powers so long as it should act in consonance with true allegiance to the General Government, and that offer had been answered by a threat. He saw clearly that compromise was out of the question, and that rebellion must be treated as rebellion, and traitors as traitors. He accordingly commenced a most vigorous administration of public affairs. Major Joseph W. Bell was appointed Provost-Judge and Colonel Jonas H. French Provost-Marshal. At the same time an effort was made to remove all causes for unnecessary irritation, and to conciliate the people. The General left the St. Charles Hotel, and made his military head-quarters in the house of General Twiggs, and his private residence in the fine mansion of Dr. Campbell, on the corner of St. Charles and Julia Streets, which was afterward occupied by General Banks.

GENERAL BUTLER'S RESIDENCE.

The Common Council having accepted a generous proposition of the General, the civil city government was allowed to go on as usual. The troops were withdrawn from the vicinity of the City Hall, and camps on public squares were broken up. Quite a large number of the soldiers were sent to Carrolton, under General Phelps, where a permanent camp was formed. Others, under General Williams, went up the river with Commodore Farragut, to take possession of and hold Baton Rouge. Others were sent to points in the vicinity of New Orleans, and in the course of a few days the wish of Soulé was literally complied with, for the troops were all withdrawn from the city, excepting a sufficient number retained to act as an efficient provost-guard.

These concessions did not necessarily imply any relaxation of all proper authority. They were mistaken as such, however, and the rebellious spirit, which was made quiet only by compulsion, soon began to show itself. That spirit speedily learned that the commander of the Department was a real power within the sphere of his assigned duty, that must not be resisted. Sensible men also perceived that he was a power fraught with much good for the city, which had been ruled for years by vicious politicians of the Monroe school.[2] He established the most perfect order, and instituted a

---

[1] Parton's *Butler in New Orleans*, page 295.

[2] "For seven years past," said the *True Delta*, on the 6th of May, in commenting on Butler's proclamation, "the world knows that this city, in all its departments—judicial, legislative, and executive—had been at the

system of cleanliness for the promotion of the health of the citizens, before unknown to them, and which is yet in successful operation. On his arrival, ribald voices in the crowd on the levee had cried out, "Wait till Yellow Jack [yellow fever] comes, old Cock-eye! He'll make you fly!" But "Yellow Jack" was not allowed to come; and that terrible scourge has not appeared in New Orleans since General Butler made it clean, and taught the inhabitants to keep it so. Residents there declared to the author, when he visited that city in the spring of 1866, that gratitude for incalculable blessings should prompt the inhabitants to erect a statue of General Butler in one of the public squares, in testimony of their appreciation of a real benefactor.

General Butler organized plans for the alleviation of the distress among the inhabitants, and invited the civil authorities to unite with him in the merciful work. But they were deaf to the voice of righteousness. Withholding relief from their starving fellow-citizens, they sent provisions to the camps of the insurgents who had fled from the city.[1] In every possible way attempts were made to thwart the orders and wishes of General Butler while he was feeding the starving poor by thousands, and was working day and night to revive and restore the business of the city, that its wonted prosperity might return. Among his troops there was perfect order. No man had been injured, and no woman had been treated with the least disrespect. But the corrupt Mayor was surly and insolent. The newspapers were barely restrained from seditious teachings. The foreign consuls, and foreign population generally, sympathized with the spirit of resistance; and many of the women who claimed to be of the better sort, taking advantage of the wide latitude in speech and action allowed to their sex in American society, were particularly offensive in their manifestations of contempt for the General and his troops. When Union officers approached, they would leave the sidewalks, go round them in the middle of the street, and with upturned noses would utter some insulting words, often more vigorous than elegant. They would draw away their skirts when a private soldier passed them, and leave street cars and church pews when Union officers entered them. They wore secession colors on their bonnets; in feminine schools they kept the pupils singing rebel songs; groups on balconies turned their backs on passing soldiers, and played airs that were used with rebellious words; and in every conceivable way they insulted the troops. These things were patiently borne, as sensible men endure the acts of imbeciles or lunatics, notwithstanding they were indicative of the hellish spirit that was making war on the Government and the rights of man; and the follies of these deluded women were the subjects of much merriment among the troops. But when, at length, a woman of the "dominant class," with the low manners of the degraded of her sex, deliberately spat in the face of two officers, who were walking peacefully along the street, General Butler determined to arrest the growing evil at once, and on the 15th of May the town was startled by an order that struck the root of the iniquity, by placing such actors in their appropriate social position.

---

absolute disposal of the most godless, brutal, ignorant, and ruthless ruffianism the world has ever heard of since the days of the great Roman conspirators."

[1] See Butler's Order, May 9, 1862.

That order[1] was intended to work silently, peacefully, and effectually. And so it did. The grave offense was not repeated. Sensible and virtuous women did not indulge in such vulgarities, and were not touched by the order. The foolish women recovered their senses through its operation;[2] and so did the Mayor and his accomplices in crime, when the power of their outraged Government was felt by the former, by arrest and threatened imprisonment in Fort Jackson; by Soulé, the ablest of the instigators of treason in Louisiana, as a prisoner in Fort Warren; and by one of the leaders of the mob, when he stood a felon on the scaffold, in the midst of a vast number of his fellow-citizens, because of his overt act of treason in pulling down the National flag from the Government Mint.[3]

The Mayor had made the publication of the "Woman Order" the occasion of a most impudent and absurd letter to General Butler, saying, among other things, "Your officers and soldiers are permitted by the terms of this order to place any construction they may please upon the conduct of our wives and daughters, and upon such construction to offer them atrocious insults."[4] This letter was answered by the deposition and arrest of the

---

[1] The following is a copy of the document known as the "Woman Order," which the General himself framed from a similar one, and for a similar purpose, which he had read long before in a London newspaper:

"HEAD-QUARTERS, DEPARTMENT OF THE GULF,
NEW ORLEANS, May 15, 1862.

"*General Order No.* 28:

"As the officers and soldiers of the United States have been subject to repeated insults from the women (calling themselves ladies) of New Orleans, in return for the most scrupulous non-interference and courtesy on our part, it is ordered that hereafter, when any female shall, by word, gesture, or movement, insult or show contempt for any officer or soldier of the United States, she shall be regarded and held liable to be treated as a woman of the town plying her avocation.

"By command of
"MAJOR-GENERAL BUTLER.

"GEORGE C. STRONG, *Assistant Adjutant-General, Chief of Staff.*"

[2] Mr. Parton says that one of the women—"a very fine lady"—who lost her senses and behaved indiscreetly, and who, in sweeping her skirts away from possible contact with passing Union officers, lost her balance, fell in the gutter, and received the proffered aid of one of them, which she spurned, afterward declared that she really felt grateful to the officer at the time for his politeness, and added, "Order 28 [the 'Woman Order'] served the women right."

[3] See page 343.

[4] This willful perversion of the plain letter and spirit of the "Woman Order" was made the key-note of a cry of indignation that was heard in every part of the Confederacy, and was echoed by the friends of the conspirators in the North and in Europe. "Do not leave your women to the merciless foe," appealed "The daughters of New Orleans" to "every Southern soldier." . . . "Rather let us die with you, oh, our fathers! Rather, like Virginius, plunge your swords into our breasts, saying, 'This is all we can give our daughters.'" The Governor of Louisiana said: "It was reserved for a Federal general to invite his soldiers to the perpetration of outrages, at the mention of which the blood recoils with horror." A Georgian offered a reward of $10,000 "for the infamous Butler's head;" and "A Savannah Woman" suggested a contribution "from every woman in the Confederacy" "to triple the sum." Paul R. Hayne, the South Carolina poet, was again inspired to write nonsense (see page 104, volume I.), and said:—

"Yes! but there's *one who shall not die*
In battle harness! One for whom
Lurks in the darkness silently
Another and a sterner doom!
A warrior's end should crown the brave—
For *him*, swift cord! and felon grave!"

Lord Palmerston, the British premier, in the plenitude of his admiration for the insurgents, and remembering "how savages in red coats had been wont to conduct themselves in captured cities" on the Peninsula, and naturally supposed that "patriots in blue coats would follow their example," made himself appear exceedingly absurd before the world by mentioning the matter in Parliament, and saying, "An Englishman must blush to think that such an act has been committed by one belonging to the Anglo-Saxon race." Beauregard, whose wife and mother, living in the house of John Slidell, in New Orleans, were there treated in the most tender and respectful manner by the commanding general, first applied to that officer, it is said, the vulgar epithet of "Butler the Beast," and it was freely used by every enemy of the Government, South and North, until the end of the strife.

Mayor,[1] and the appointment of General G. F. Shepley, of Maine, as Military Governor of New Orleans, who at once organized an efficient police force and made the city a model of quiet and good order. This vigor was followed by the arrest of William B. Mumford, his trial and conviction by a military court, and his execution as a traitor in the presence of a vast multitude, who quietly dispersed to their homes, with the salutary reflection that the Government had indeed "repossessed" its property, and was exercising its rightful authority in the city of New Orleans.[2]

GEORGE F. SHEPLEY.

Of the details of General Butler's administration in the Department of the Gulf, until he was superseded by General Banks, at the middle of December following—how he dealt with representatives of foreign governments; with banks and bankers; with the holders of Confederate money and other property; and with disloyal men of every kind, from the small offender in the street to the greater offender in public positions and in the pulpit—it is not our province here to consider.[3] Suffice it to say, that it then seemed wise and salutary in the necessary assertion of the sovereign authority of his Government; and, to the candid student of events there, it yet seems to have been wise and salutary. Promptness and decision marked every step of his career.[4] Measures for the

---

[1] The terrified official hastened to explain his letter, when Butler agreed to release him from the penalty of imprisonment on condition that he should withdraw the letter and make an apology. This he did in the most humble manner.

[2] Mumford was a professional gambler, and consequently an enemy of society. He was about forty-two years of age. He was in the crowd in front of the St. Charles on the occasion of the General's conference with the Mayor and his friends, already alluded to, boasting of his exploit with the flag, inciting them to riot, and daring the National officers to arrest him. He continued his attitude of defiance, and became so dangerous to good order, as a leader of the turbulent spirits of New Orleans, that his arrest and punishment was a necessity. His overt act of treason was clear, and his execution had a most salutary effect. Mumford is the only man who, up to this time (1867), has been tried, condemned, and executed for treason since the foundations of the National Government were laid.

[3] In Mr. Parton's work, which has been so frequently referred to, and whose full title is, *General Butler in New Orleans: History of the Administration of the Department of the Gulf in the Year* 1862; *with an Account of the Capture of New Orleans*, may be found full details of that administration.

[4] So vigorous and efficient, so uncompromising with treason and rebellion, was Butler's administration of affairs in New Orleans, that the conspirators, and particularly the chief of the Confederacy, who had been his political associate a few years before, regarded him as an arch-enemy more to be dreaded than balls or bayonets. Their fears of him and personal hatred led them to the perpetration of the most foolish acts. At about the time when Butler left New Orleans, Jefferson Davis issued a notable proclamation,[a] for the purpose of "firing the Southern heart," in which he professed to review Butler's administration of affairs there. In connection with a recitation of Butler's alleged crimes, he pronounced him "to be a felon, deserving of capital punishment," and ordered that he should not be "treated simply as a public enemy of the Confederate States of America, but as an outlaw and common enemy of mankind; and that, in the event of his capture, the officer in command of the capturing force do cause him to be immediately executed by hanging." He also ordered that the same treatment should be awarded to all commissioned officers serving under Butler. In addition to these instructions, he ordered that all negro slaves captured in arms against the Confederacy, and all commissioned officers of the United States serving in company with them, who should be captured, should be delivered to the executive authorities of the respective States to which the negroes belonged, "to be dealt with according to the laws of said States."

[a] Dec. 23, 1862.

There is not, probably, any intelligent and candid man in the Union to-day, and especially among the residents of New Orleans at that time, who does not agree, in honest opinion, with the verdict of a competent

public good were continually planned and executed, and toward the close of summer he took the first step in the employment of negroes as soldiers, which the enemies of the Government had practised there. When General Banks arrived to take command of the Department, there were three regiments of these soldiers, with two batteries manned by them, well drilled for his use, under the common name of the Louisiana Native Guard.

LOUISIANA NATIVE GUARD.

The loss of New Orleans was the heaviest blow the Confederacy had yet received, and for a while it staggered under its infliction. "It annihilated us in Louisiana," said the Confederate historian of the war; "diminished our resources and supplies, by the loss of one of the greatest grain and cattle countries within the limits of the Confederacy; gave to the enemy the Mississippi River, with all its means of navigation, for a base of operations, and finally led, by plain and irresistible conclusion, to our virtual abandonment of the great and fruitful valley of the Mississippi."[1]

Let us now return to a consideration of the Army of the Potomac, which we left in a quiet condition after the little flurry at Drainsville, at near the close of the year.

---

historian (Parton), that "each of the paragraphs of Jefferson Davis's proclamation which relates to General Butler's conduct is the distinct utterance of a lie."

A few days after the proclamation was issued, Richard Yeadon, a prominent citizen of Charleston, publicly offered[a] a reward of $10,000 "for the capture and delivery of the said Benjamin F. Butler, dead or alive, to any proper Confederate authority." And "A Daughter of South Carolina," in a letter to the *Charleston Courier*, said, "I propose to spin the thread to make the cord to execute the order of our noble President, Davis, when old Butler is caught, and my daughter asks that she may be allowed to adjust it around his neck."

[a] Jan. 1, 1863.

[1] Pollard's *First Year of the War*, page 321.

CHAPTER XIV.

MOVEMENTS OF THE ARMY OF THE POTOMAC.—THE MONITOR AND MERRIMACK.

THE Grand Army of the Potomac had gained strength in numbers and discipline during the months it had been lying in comparatively quiet camps around the National Capital. The battles of Ball's Bluff and Drainsville, already mentioned, had kept it from rusting into absolute immobility; and the troops were made hopeful at times by promises of an immediate advance upon the Confederates at Manassas. But at the beginning of the year 1862, when that army numbered full two hundred thousand men, the prospect of an advance seemed more remote than ever, for the fine weather that had prevailed up to Christmas was succeeded by storms and frost, and the roads in many places soon became almost impassable. Very little preparation had been made for winter quarters, and much suffering and discontent was the consequence.[1] The people were exceedingly impatient, and were more disposed to censure the Secretary of War than the General-in-Chief, for they had faith in the latter. They were gratified when Mr. Cameron left the office, and they gave to the new incumbent, Mr. Stanton, their entire confidence.[2]

The President was much distressed by the inaction of the great army. He could get no satisfaction from the General-in-Chief, when he inquired why that army did not move. Finally, on the 10th of January, he summoned Generals McDowell and Franklin to a conference with himself and his Cabinet. Never, during the whole war, did he exhibit such despondency as at

[1] Various efforts were made by many officers to break the monotony of the camp and keep the soldiers cheerful. With this view, the musical "Hutchinson Family" were permitted, by Secretary Cameron, to visit the camps and sing their simple and stirring songs. They were diffusing sunshine through the army by delighting crowds of soldiers who listened to their voices, when their career of usefulness was suddenly arrested by the following order:

By direction of General McClellan, the permit given to the 'Hutchinson Family' to sing in the camp, and their pass to cross the Potomac, are revoked, and they will not be allowed to sing to the troops."

Why not? The answer was in the fact, that they had sung Whittier's stirring song, lately written, to the tune of Luther's Hymn, "Ein feste burg ist unser Gott," in which, among eight similar verses, was the following:—

"What gives the wheat-field blades of steel?
What points the rebel cannon?
What sets the roaring rabble's heel
On th' old star-spangled pennon?
What breaks the oath
Of th' men o' th' South?
What whets the knife
For the Union's life?
Hark to the answer: SLAVERY!"

[2] Edwin M. Stanton succeeded Simon Cameron, as Secretary of War, on the 13th of January, 1862.

that conference. He spoke of the exhausted condition of the treasury; of the loss of public credit; of the delicate condition of our foreign relations; the critical situation of National affairs in Missouri and Kentucky since Fremont left the *Western Department;* the lack of co-operation between Generals Halleck and Buell, and the illness of the General-in-Chief, which then, it was said, confined him to his house. He said he was in great distress under the burden of responsibility laid upon him. He had been to the house of the General-in-Chief, who did not ask to see him. He must talk to *somebody*, and he had sent for McDowell and Franklin to obtain a military opinion as to the probability of an early movement of the army. "If something is not soon done," he said in his simple way, "the bottom will be out of the whole affair; and, if General McClellan does not want to use the army, I would like to *borrow* it, provided I can see how it could be made to do something."[1]

The President, supported by public opinion, had resolved that something must be done by the army of the Potomac immediately, under the direction of General McClellan, or some other officer, and arrangements were in progress to that effect, when the General-in-Chief, who had been too ill to see the President on the 10th,[a] was out, and "looking quite well," on the following day. McDowell and Franklin, meanwhile, had been charged by the President with the duty of submitting a plan of a campaign. The former was decidedly in favor of an advance in heavy force upon the front and flanks of the Confederates at Manassas, whose numbers he was satisfied had been greatly exaggerated.[2] Such movement, if successful, would end the disgraceful blockade of the Potomac, and drive the army that was really besieging the National Capital back upon Richmond. General Franklin, who had been somewhat informed by General McClellan of his plans, was in favor of moving on Richmond by way of the Lower Chesapeake and the Virginia Peninsula. They consulted with Quartermaster-General Meigs (who agreed with McDowell), Colonel Kingsbury, the Chief of Ordnance of the Army of the Potomac, General Van Vliet, the Chief Quartermaster, and Major Shiras, the Commissary of Subsistence.

[a] Jan., 1862.

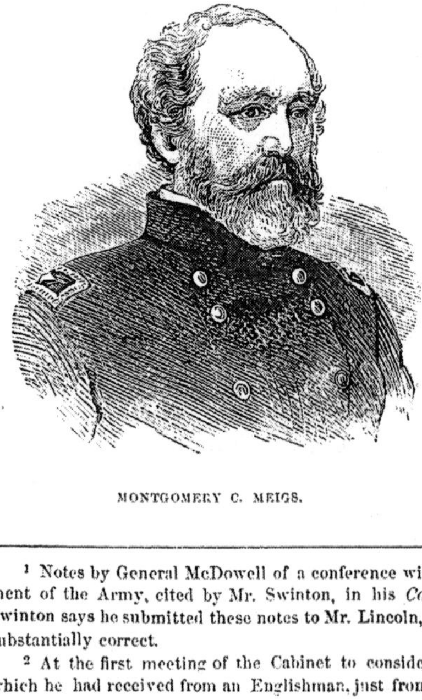

MONTGOMERY C. MEIGS.

The subject was discussed by these military officers and the President and his Cabinet on the same evening,[b] when McDowell and Franklin, being in general agreement as to the neces-

[b] Jan. 11.

[1] Notes by General McDowell of a conference with the President and others, on the subject of the movement of the Army, cited by Mr. Swinton, in his *Campaigns of the Army of the Potomac*, page 79 Mr. Swinton says he submitted these notes to Mr. Lincoln, during the summer of 1864, who declared that they were substantially correct.

[2] At the first meeting of the Cabinet to consider the subject, Mr. Seward stated, that from information which he had received from an Englishman, just from the Confederate lines, he was satisfied that they might

sity *now* of moving directly upon Manassas, recommended such movement. But there was a difference of opinion in the Cabinet.[1]

Two days afterward there was another meeting of those officers with the President and his Cabinet. General McClellan was present, but took no part in the discussion. He seemed offended; and in reply to some apologetic remarks from McDowell, in explanation of the position in which he and Franklin were placed, the General-in-Chief curtly remarked, "You are entitled to have any opinion you please." When the President asked McClellan "what and when any thing could be done, the latter replied, with more force than courtesy, that the case was so clear that a blind man could see it; and then spoke of the difficulty of ascertaining what force he could count upon; that he did not know whether he could let General Butler go to Ship Island,[2] or whether he could re-enforce Burnside."[3] To the direct question of the Secretary of the Treasury, to the effect as to what he intended doing with his army, and where he intended doing, McClellan answered, that the movements in Kentucky were to precede any from Washington.[4] This part of the plan of the General-in-Chief (the movements in the West) was soon gloriously carried out, as we have already observed; and before the Army of the Potomac had fairly inaugurated its campaign, in the spring of 1862, the active little army under Grant, and the forces of Buell and Pope, in connection with Foote's gun-boats and mortars, had captured Forts Henry and Donelson, Nashville and Columbus; had driven the Confederates out of Kentucky; had seized the Gibraltar of the Mississippi (Island Number Ten); and had penetrated to Northern Alabama, and fought the great battles and won a victory at Shiloh.[5]

At that conference, McClellan expressed his unwillingness to develop his plans, "always believing," he said, "that in military matters the fewer persons knowing them the better." He would tell them if he was *ordered* to do so. The President then asked him if he counted upon any particular time; he did not ask what time that was, but had he in his own mind any particular time fixed when a movement could be commenced. The General replied he had. "Then," rejoined the President, "I will adjourn this meeting."[6]

A few days after this conference, General McClellan, at the request of the President, laid before the latter a plan for moving against Richmond. It was to abandon his present base, and proceed toward the Confederate capital by way of the Lower Chesapeake. The President disapproved of the plan, because of the long time it would take to prepare for the move-

---

concentrate in front of the National army, at short notice, 103,000 men. General Wool, who had excellent means for obtaining correct information, had satisfied himself, and had so reported, that not one-half that number of Confederate soldiers were in all Virginia. It was afterward clearly shown that General Wool's estimate was not too low, and "that from October to March, Johnston never had an effective force of more than 40,000 under his orders, and that his preparations for an evacuation were begun as early as October, 1861; and that, after that time, he lay simply in observation." So declared W. H. Hurlburt, a public writer, who had many and rare facilities for knowing the strength of the Confederates.

[1] The Postmaster-General (Montgomery Blair) strongly urged McClellan's plans of moving at some future time by way of the Peninsula, because of the great obstacles of bad roads and immense forces to be encountered on the other route; to which the Secretary of the Treasury (Mr. Chase) replied that it was probable that, after losing much time and millions of money, there would be found as many obstacles to success on the newly proposed route. The Secretary of State (Mr. Seward) thought that a victory by the Army of the Potomac *somewhere* was desirable, it mattered not where.—McDowell's Notes.

[2] See page 324. [3] See page 315. [4] McDowell's Notes. [5] See Chapters VII., VIII., IX., and X.

[6] McDowell's Notes.

ment, and the importance of striking a blow immediately. He could no longer endure the delays of the General-in-Chief, and without consulting him, he, as commander-in-chief of the army and navy of the Republic, issued an order on the 27th of January,[a] known as General War Order No. 1, in which he directed the 22d of February following "to be the day for a general movement of the land and naval forces of the United States against the insurgent forces."[1] He also declared that the heads of executive departments, and especially the Secretary of War and of the Navy, with all their subordinates, as well as the General-in-Chief, with all commanders and subordinates of the land and naval forces, should "severally be held to their strict and full responsibilities for prompt execution of the order."

[a] 1862.

This proclamation sent a thrill of joy through every loyal heart. Four days later the President issued a special order to McClellan, directing him to form all the disposable force of the Army of the Potomac, after providing safely for the defense of Washington, into an expedition for the immediate object of seizing and occupying a point upon the railroad southwest of Manassas Junction, the details of the movement (which was to take place on or before the 22d of February) to be left to the discretion of the General-in-Chief. The object was to flank the insurgents at Manassas and Centreville, relieve Washington, threaten Richmond, and paralyze the main strength of the rebellion by destroying its most formidable army. Secretary Stanton at the same time urged McClellan to take immediate steps "to secure the reopening of the Baltimore and Ohio Railway, and free the banks of the lower Potomac from the rebel batteries which annoyed passing vessels."[2]

Instead of obeying the President's order, McClellan remonstrated against its execution. The patient Lincoln listened to all he had to say, and on the 3d of February wrote him a kind note, saying: "You and I have distinct and different plans for a movement of the Army of the Potomac; yours to be down by the Chesapeake, up the Rappahannock, to Urbana, and across land to the terminus of the railroad on the York River; mine to move directly to a point on the railway southwest of Manassas. If you will give satisfactory answers to the following questions, I shall gladly yield my plan to yours: 1st. Does not your plan involve a greatly larger expenditure of *time* and *money* than mine? 2d. Wherein is victory *more certain* by your plan than mine? 3d. Wherein is victory *more valuable* by your plan than mine? 4th. In fact, would it not be *less* valuable; in this, that it would break no great line of the enemy's communications, while mine would? 5th. In case of disaster, would not a retreat be more difficult by your plan than mine?"

McClellan did not reply to the President's kind note and important inquiries; but on the same day he sent a long letter to the Secretary of War, in which he recited a history of his connection with the Army of the

1 He specially ordered the army "at and around Fortress Monroe, the Army of the Potomac, the Army of Western Virginia, the army near Mumfordsville [Buell's] in Kentucky, the army and flotilla [Grant's and Foote's] at Cairo, and a naval force in the Gulf of Mexico [Farragut's and Porter's] to be ready to move on that day."

2 General McClellan's Report, page 42.

Potomac, and its organization; complained of the total absence of a general plan of operations under the administration of General Scott; and declared that it was his intention to gain, through the forces in the West, the control of the Eastern Tennessee Railroad, and then have attacks made simultaneously on Nashville and Richmond. He developed his plan for operations by the Army of the Potomac against Richmond by way of Chesapeake Bay, already mentioned, the base being Urbana, on the lower Rappahannock, and presented a long array of arguments in its favor. He arrayed against the President's plan the advantage possessed by the Confederates in holding a central defensive position; the uncertainties of the weather; the necessity of having long lines of communication, and the probable indecisiveness even of a victory. McClellan was so impressed with apprehensions of the sad fate that might befall his army by following the President's plan, that he declared he should "prefer to move from Fortress Monroe as a base, to an attack upon Manassas."

The President was not convinced by the General's arguments, but, in consequence of the latter's steady resistance and unwillingness to enter upon the execution of any other plan than his own,[1] he consented to submit the matter to a council of twelve officers, which was held at head-quarters on the 27th of February. The decision was made in favor of McClellan's plan, by a vote of eight against four.[2] The President acquiesced; and on the same day orders went out from the War Department for procuring transports, and preparations for the forward movement went rapidly on.

On the 8th of March the President, in a general order, directed the Army of the Potomac to be divided into four corps, and designated as their respective commanders Generals Keyes, Sumner, Heintzelman, and McDowell. Apprehending, because of some indications, that the General-in-Chief intended to take nearly the entire Army of the Potomac with him, the President, on the same day,[a] issued another order, directing that no change of the base of operation of that army should be made without leaving a competent force for the protection of Washington; that not more than fifty thousand troops should be moved toward the scene of intended operations, until the navigation of the Potomac from Washington to the Chesapeake should be "freed from the enemy's batteries and other obstructions;" that the new movement on Chesapeake Bay should begin as early as the 18th of March, and that the General-in-Chief should "be responsible that it so moves as early as that day;" and that "the army and navy co-operate in an immediate effort to capture the enemy's batteries upon the Potomac, between Washington and the Chesapeake Bay."

[a] March 8, 1862.

At this moment events were occurring that caused a material modification of the plans of the General-in-Chief. A new war-power had just been created, and was about to manifest its strength in Hampton Roads. The *Monitor*, whose exploits we shall consider presently, was on its way to those waters. At the same time a movement of the insurgents in front of Wash-

[1] See *Life, Public Services, and State Papers of Abraham Lincoln*, by Henry J. Raymond, page 267.

[2] The council was composed of Generals Fitz-John Porter, Franklin, W. F. Smith, M'Call, Blenker, Andrew Porter, Naglee, Keyes, McDowell, Sumner, Heintzelman, and Barnard. The first eight voted in favor of McClellan's plan, Keyes qualifying his vote by the condition that the army should not move until the rebels were driven from the Potomac.

ington was more immediately affecting the Army of the Potomac. On the day after the President's order just cited,[a] the General-in-Chief received information that the Confederates had abandoned Centreville and Manassas, and were falling back toward Richmond, by which McClellan's proposed flank movement by way of the lower Rappahannock was made unnecessary.

[a] March 9, 1862.

Preparations for this retirement had been commenced three weeks before by a quiet removal of the army stores and munitions, but the officers of McClellan's secret service seem to have been in profound ignorance of the fact, and by their reports were strengthening his belief that the number of the Confederates on his front was so great, that the utter discomfiture of his army would be risked by advancing against them at Manassas.[1] But from the statements of the Confederate commanders, and writers in the interest of the rebellion, it appears that Johnston had at no time during the winter intended to make a stand at Manassas, for his troops were too few in number and too scantily provided to make even a show of strong resistance. It was this weakness of his forces, and the order of the President for the forward movement of all the National armies on the 22d of February, and not a knowledge of McClellan's intended flank movement, as the latter afterward supposed, that caused Johnston to flee from Manassas.[2] The removal of his stores and war materials commenced a few days before the prescribed time for McClellan to advance upon his position. It was a masterly movement, and evinced that ability which has caused Johnston to be regarded by experts on both sides as by far the most able of the commanders of the Confederate armies.

[b] March 9.

On receiving information of the evacuation of Centreville and Manassas,[b] McClellan crossed the Potomac, and issued orders for the immediate advance of the whole army toward the abandoned posts, not, as he afterward explained in his report, for the purpose of pursuing the retiring Confederates, and pushing on toward Richmond, but to "get rid of superfluous baggage and other impediments which accumulate so easily around an army encamped for a long time in one locality," and to "give the troops some experience in the march and bivouac preparatory to the campaign."[3] His advance, composed of Colonel Averill's cavalry,

---

[1] On the day when Johnston's little army withdrew from Manassas, E. J Allen, the chief of McClellan's secret service corps, reported to his commander that the forces of the Confederates "at that date" were as follows: At Manassas, and within twenty miles of it, 98,000 men, at Leesburg and vicinity, 4,500; and in the Shenandoah Valley 13,500, making a total of 115,000. He also reported that they had about 300 field-guns, and from 26 to 30 siege-guns "in front of Washington." See General McClellan's Report, pages 56 and 57. At the same time General Wool at Fortress Monroe, and General Wadsworth, back of Arlington Heights, had the most reliable information that, ten days before the evacuation, not 50,000 troops were in front of the Army of the Potomac. Subsequent investigations and statements reduce that number below 40,000.

[2] In his report, made seventeen months after this occurrence, McClellan says: "The retirement of the enemy toward Richmond had been expected as the natural consequence of the movement to the Peninsula," and adds that "it was done immediately on ascertaining that such a movement was intended." See McClellan's Report, page 54. The evacuation was commenced almost a fortnight before the council of officers decided on the "movement to the Peninsula." That Johnston was ignorant of the intended flank movement at the time of the evacuation, is evident from a remark of an English officer then serving under him, who said, in speaking of the forces there: "In fact, McClellan was quietly maturing plans for the seizure of Centreville and Manassas, when Johnston suddenly gave orders for a general retreat, and all our army began to move rapidly southward."—See *Battle-fields of the South, from Bull Run to Fredericksburg; by an English Combatant, Lieutenant of Artillery on the Field Staff.*

[3] McClellan's Report, pages 54, 55.

reached Centreville on the 10th. The works there and at Manassas Junction were abandoned, and yet the Confederates were not far away for four days afterward.[a] General Stoneman, who had been sent out with a heavy force of cavalry to push their rear across the Rappahannock, saw them in large numbers at Warrenton Junction. On account of difficulty in procuring subsistence, heavy rains, and bad roads, Stoneman did not molest the retiring army, and the pursuit, if it may be so called, ended here. On the following day the main body of the Army of the Potomac, under the mask of a strong reconnoissance of the corps of Howard and Sumner toward the Rappahannock, moved back to Alexandria. Stoneman's advance retired at the same time, followed some distance, in spite of mud and weather, by the cavalry of Stuart and Ewell, a battery of artillery, and some infantry.[1] Then the Confederates moved leisurely on and encamped, first behind the Rappahannock, and then in a more eligible position beyond the Rapid Anna.[2]

[a] March 14, 1862.

GEORGE STONEMAN.

This "promenade" (as one of McClellan's aids, of the Orleans family, called it) of the Army of the Potomac disappointed the people, and confirmed the President's opinion, indicated in an order issued on the 11th, that the burden of managing that army in person, and, as general-in-chief, directing the movements of all the others, was too much for General McClellan to bear. By this order he kindly relieved that officer of a part of the burden.[3] To General Halleck was assigned the command of the National troops in the Valley of the Mississippi, and westward of the longitude of Knoxville in Tennessee; and a *Mountain Department*, consisting of the region between the commands of Halleck and McClellan, was created and placed under the command of General Fremont. The commanders of Departments were ordered to report directly to the Secretary of War.

The notable events in Hampton Roads, that modified McClellan's plans for marching on Richmond, occurred at this juncture. It was known that the Confederates were fashioning into a formidable iron-clad ram the fine steam-frigate *Merrimack*, which, as we have observed, was burned and sunk at Norfolk in the spring of 1861.[4] She had been raised; and, in accordance with a plan furnished by Lieutenant John M. Brooke, formerly

---

[1] Stoneman's report to General McClellan, March 16, 1862.

[2] This is the correct orthography of the name of one of three rivers in that part of Virginia, which has been generally written, in connection with the war, Rapidan. These small rivers are called, respectively, North Anna, South Anna, and Rapid Anna; the word Anna being frequently pronounced with brevity, Ann.

[3] "Major-General McClellan," said the order, "having personally taken the field at the head of the Army of the Potomac, until otherwise ordered, he is relieved from the command of the other Military Departments, he retaining the command of the *Department of the Potomac.*"

[4] See page 398, volume I.

of the National navy, she was transformed into a destructive implement of war, and named *Virginia.*[1] The world had never before seen a floating engine of war equal to this. From the spoils of the Norfolk Navy Yard she was completely equipped, and her commander was Captain Franklin Buchanan, an experienced officer of the National navy (who had been forty-five years in the service), assisted by Catesby Ap R. Jones, another traitor to his flag.

FRANKLIN BUCHANAN.

This terrible battery was completed at the beginning of March, and its appearance in Hampton Roads was then daily expected. Meanwhile another engine of destruction, of novel form and aspect, had been prepared at Green Point, Long Island, a short distance from New York, under the direction of its inventor, Captain John Ericsson, a scientific Swede, who had been a resident of the United States for twenty years. This vessel, almost a dwarf in appearance by the side of the *Merrimack*, presented to the eye, when afloat, a simple platform, sharp at both ends, and bearing a round revolving iron Martello tower, twenty feet in diameter and ten feet high, and forming a bomb-proof fort, in which two 11-inch Dahlgren cannon were mounted.[2]

---

[1] The *Merrimack* or *Virginia* appeared, when afloat, like a huge roof. This and her sides were composed of heavy oak timber, twenty-eight inches in thickness, covered six inches deep by railway iron bars and iron plates. A bulwark, or false bow, was added, and beyond this was a strong oak and iron beak, thirty-three feet long, after the fashion of those on the western waters, already mentioned. She was made apparently shot-proof; was propelled by two engines of great power, and carried on each side four 80-pounder rifled cannon, and at the bow and stern a gun that would hurl a 100-pound solid shot, or 120-pound shell. She was furnished with furnaces for heating shot, and apparatus for throwing hot water. Her engines and other apparatus were all below water-mark.

[2] The deck of the *Monitor* was only a few inches above water. The round revolving tower was twenty feet in diameter and ten feet in height above the deck. The smoke-stack was made with telescopic slides, so as to be lowered in action. The hull was sharp at both ends, the angle at the bow being about eighty degrees to the vertical line. It was only six feet six inches deep, with a flat bottom, and was 124 feet in length and 34 in width at the top. On this hull rested another, five feet in height, of the same form, that extended over the lower one three feet seven inches all around, excepting at the ends, where it projected twenty-five feet, by which protection was afforded to the anchor, propeller, and rudder. The whole was built of light three-inch iron, and was very buoyant. Its exposed parts were guarded by a wall of white oak, thirty inches in thickness, on which was laid iron armor six inches thick. A shot, to reach the lower hull, would have to pass through twenty-five feet of water, and then strike an inclined iron plane at an angle of about

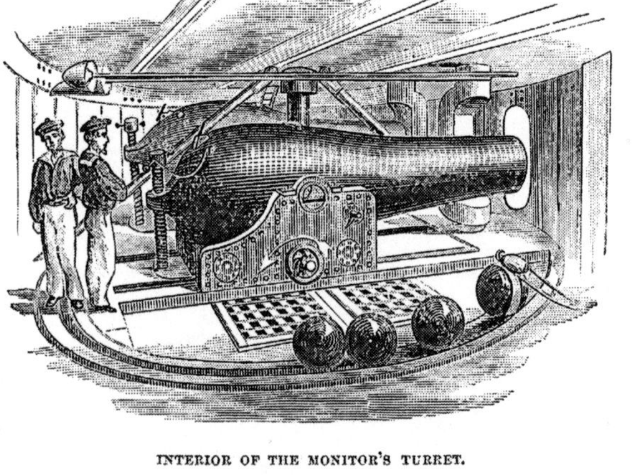

INTERIOR OF THE MONITOR'S TURRET.

This little vessel, full of the most destructive power, was called by the inventor *The Monitor.*[1] She too was completed at the beginning of March, and when General Wool, at Fortress Monroe, and Captain Marston, the commander of the squadron in Hampton Roads, informed the authorities at Washington that the *Merrimack* was ready for action, the *Monitor* was ordered to proceed to the expected scene of her performance.

At a little before noon on Saturday, the 8th of March,[a] the dreaded *Merrimack* was seen coming down the Elizabeth River toward Hampton Roads, accompanied by two ordinary gun-boats. At the same time, doubtless by pre-concert, two other Confederate gun-boats had come down from Richmond and made their appearance in the James River, a short distance above Newport-Newce. The sailing frigate *Congress*, commanded by Lieutenant Joseph B. Smith, and the sloop of war *Cumberland*, Lieutenant George M. Morris in temporary command, were lying in the mouth of the James River, off Newport-Newce.[2] Toward these the *Merrimack* moved. The flag-ship of the squadron (*Roanoke*), Captain John Marston, and the steam frigate *Minnesota*, Captain Van Brunt, were lying at Fortress Monroe, several miles distant. These were signaled to come to the assistance of the menaced vessels. They could not reach them in time to serve them much. The *Merrimack*, with her ports closed, paid no attention to the heavy shot from her intended victims, for they were turned away by her armor, as harmless as so many beans.

[a] 1862.

The *Merrimack* pushed right on in the face of the storm, and struck the *Cumberland* such a tremendous blow with her beak, under her starboard fore-channels, that a chasm was opened through which water flowed sufficient to drown the powder-magazine in thirty minutes. At the same time she opened her ports and delivered a most destructive fire. The *Cumberland* fought desperately in this death-grasp with the monster, and the conflict continued until half-past three o'clock, when the water had risen to her main hatchway, and she began to careen. Morris then gave the *Merrimack* a parting fire, and ordered his men to jump overboard and save themselves. The dead, and the sick and wounded, who could not be moved, to the number of about one hundred, were left on board, and these went down with her a little while afterward, in fifty-four feet of water. The top-mast of the *Cumber-*

---

ten degrees. The deck, lying flush with the sides of the upper hull, was also armored and made bomb-proof, and nothing was seen on it but the tower or citadel (turret, it is technically termed), the wheel-house, and a box covering the smoke-stack. The insurgents spoke of the vessel as a "Yankee cheese-box set on a plank."

The only entrance into the vessel that boarders of it could find was from the top of the turret, and then only one man at a time could descend. That turret was made of eight thicknesses of one-inch iron plate, so overlapped that at no spot was there more than one inch thickness of joint. The roof was of plate iron, perforated and shell proof, and placed on wrought iron beams six inches down the cylinder. In this was a sliding hatch to give light, and allow the employment of musketry if the vessel should be boarded. The turret was turned by a contrivance connected with the double-cylinder engine that propelled the vessel, and so placed that the governor could control its motion in taking aim. The two heavy guns, as seen in the engraving on the preceding page, moved on wrought iron slides across the base of the turret, on well-fitting carriages, and their muzzles were run out into the port-holes with ease. Such was the strange weapon of war destined to measure strength with the *Merrimack*.

[1] To Captain Fox, the Assistant-Secretary of the Navy, Ericsson wrote when proposing this name, that it would admonish the insurgents that their batteries on banks of rivers would no longer be barriers to the passage of the Union forces, and that it would prove a severe *monitor* to the leaders of the rebellion. He also said it would be a *monitor* that would suggest to the Lords of the English Admiralty the impropriety of completing their four steel-clad ships, then on the stocks, at the cost of three and a half millions of dollars apiece.

[2] The *Congress* carried fifty guns, and the *Cumberland* twenty-four guns of heavy caliber.

land remained a little above the water, with her flag flying from its peak.[1] The writer saw that spar, yet above the water, near Newport-Newce, in the spring of 1865, when on his way to Richmond, just after its evacuation by the Confederate troops.

While the *Merrimack* was destroying the *Cumberland*, her assistant gun-boats were assailing the *Congress*. That vessel fought her foes right gallantly until the *Cumberland* went down, when, with the help of the *Zouave*, she was run aground, under cover of the strong batteries at Newport-Newce. There the *Merrimack* also assailed her, sending raking shot through her, while the *Congress* could reply only with her stern guns, one of which was soon dismounted by the *Merrimack's* shot, and the other had the muzzle knocked off. The gallant Lieutenant Smith, Acting-Master Moore, and Pilot William Rhodes, with nearly half of her crew, were soon killed or wounded. Her hull was set on fire, and she had not a gun to bring to bear on her assailants. Further resistance would have been folly, and at half-past four Lieutenant Pendergrast hauled down her flag.[2] She was formally taken possession of by a Confederate officer, when a tug came alongside to take off the remainder of the crew, that she might be immediately burned. The batteries on shore drove off the tug, when the *Merrimack* again opened upon the battered vessel, notwithstanding a white flag was flying over her in token of surrender. After giving her a few shells, the ram proceeded to attack the *Minnesota*, that had come up, and, during this absence of the terrible monster, the crew of the ruined vessel escaped. The *Merrimack* returned at dark, and set the *Congress* on fire with hot shot. While burning, her guns went off one by one, and at midnight her magazine, containing five tons of powder, exploded with a terrible noise and utterly destroyed her. Only one-half of her crew of four hundred and thirty-four men responded to the call of their names next morning at Newport-Newce.[3]

We have noticed the attack on the *Minnesota*. Flag-Officer Marston had quickly responded to the signal for aid from the *Cumberland* and *Congress*. His own ship was disabled in its machinery, but, towed by two tugs, it was started for the expected scene of action. At the same time the *Minnesota* (steam frigate) was ordered to hasten in the same direction. Her main-mast was crippled by a shot sent from Sewell's Point when she was passing, and when within a mile and a half of Newport-Newce she ran aground. There

---

[1] Lieutenant Morris to Commander Radford, March 9, 1862. There were 376 souls on board the *Cumberland* when she went into action. Of these, 117 were lost and 23 were missing. The gallantry of her officers and crew was the theme of great praise, and painting and poetry celebrated their heroism. Lieutenant Morris, who was commanding in the absence of Captain Radford, was the recipient of special commendations from the Secretary of the Navy, in a letter to him on the 21st March. Just a week later, twelve citizens of Philadelphia, all personal strangers to him, presented to Lieutenant Morris, at the house of R. W. Leaming, an elegant sword, saying, in a letter to him, that it could have "no worthier recipient than the brave sailor who fought his ship while a plank floated, fired his last broadside in sinking, and went down with his flag flying at the peak." On the sword was the motto in Latin, "I sink, but never surrender." The citizens who presented the sword were Joseph R. Ingersoll, Charles D. Meigs, M. D., Horace Binney, Jr., J. S. Clark Hare, Thomas A. Biddle, J. Fisher Leaming, Ellwood Wilson, Lewis A. Scott, Clement Biddle, George W. Norris, J. Forsyth Meigs, Robert W. Leaming.

[2] McKean Buchanan, brother of the commander of the *Merrimack*, was an officer on board the *Congress*, and was in charge of the berth-deck during the terrible struggle. In a letter to the Secretary of War afterward, he said, "I thank God I did some service to my country."

[3] It is supposed that a capital object in this raid of the *Merrimack* was to destroy these two vessels, and seize the National camp at Newport-Newce. During the conflict, many shells were thrown into that camp. Aware of the danger that threatened it, General Wool had early forwarded re-enforcements, by land, from Fortress Monroe.

she was attacked by the *Merrimack* and two of the Confederate gun-boats, the *Jamestown* and *Patrick Henry*.[1] Fortunately, the water was so shallow that the *Merrimack* could not approach within a mile of her. She fought gallantly, and at dusk her assailants, considerably crippled, withdrew, and went up toward Norfolk.[2] Marston did not get up in time with the *Roanoke* to join in the fight. His vessel was grounded, and so was the frigate *St. Lawrence*, towed by the gun-boat *Cambridge*, that was trying to join in the conflict.[3]

The night after the battle[a] was one of greatest anxiety to the loyal men on the northern borders of Hampton Roads. It was expected the savage *Merrimack* would bear down upon the fast-grounded *Minnesota* in the morning, destroy her and perhaps others of the squadron, escape to sea, and appear like a besom of destruction in the harbors of the seaboard cities of the North. There seemed to be no competent human agency near to avert these threatened disasters, when, at a little past midnight, a mysterious thing came in from the sea between the capes of Virginia, lighted on its way by the burning *Congress*, and appearing to the wondering eyes of sentinels, who had no warning of its existence nor its expected advent, like a supernatural apparition. It was, indeed, a strange but substantial reality, for it was Ericsson's *Monitor*, on its trial trip to fulfil the stipulation of the contract with the Government, that she was not to be accepted until after a successful trial of her powers before the heaviest guns of the enemy, and at the shortest range. She was in command of Lieutenant John L. Worden, of the Navy,[4] and had been towed to the Roads by the steamer *Seth Low*, with two others as a convoy. Her sea-worthiness had been tested by a heavy gale and rolling sea, that had been encountered on her way from New York. Worden reported to the flag-officer in the Roads for orders on his arrival, and was immediately sent to aid the *Minnesota*. He was in conference with her commander (Captain Van Brunt) at two o'clock on Sunday morning.[b] The *Monitor* lay alongside of the grounded vessel, "when," said Van Brunt afterward, "all on

[a] March 8, 1862.

JOHN ERICSSON.

[b] March 9.

[1] The armed vessels that assisted the *Merrimack* in her raid, were the *Patrick Henry*, Commander Tucker, 6 guns; *Jamestown*, Lieutenant-Commanding Barney, 2 guns; and *Raleigh*, Lieutenant-Commanding Alexander; *Beaufort*, Lieutenant-Commanding Parker, and *Teazer*, Lieutenant-Commanding Webb, each one gun.

[2] Commodore Buchanan and several others on board the *Merrimack* were wounded. The Commander was so badly hurt that Captain Jones, his second in command, took charge of the vessels. Two of her guns were broken; her prow was twisted; some of her armor was damaged; her anchor and all the flag-staffs were shot away, and the smoke-stack and steam-pipe were riddled.—Report of Catesby Ap R. Jones to Flag-Officer F. Forest, March 8, 1862.

[3] Report of Flag-Officer John Marston to the Secretary of the Navy, March 9, 1862; also, of Lieutenants Morris and Pendergrast.

[4] See page 365, volume I.

board felt that we had a friend that would stand by us in an hour of trial."

That Sabbath morning dawned brightly. Before sunrise the dreaded *Merrimack*, with her attendants, was seen coming down the Elizabeth River again, to begin anew her savage work. The drums of the *Minnesota* beat to quarters, and the people hidden in the *Monitor* prepared for battle. As the *Merrimack* approached, the stern guns of the *Minnesota* were opened upon her, when the *Monitor*, to the astonishment of friend and foe, ran out and placed herself alongside the huge monster. She seemed like a pigmy at the foot of a giant. What she lacked in size she possessed in power, but it was power yet untried. It was immediately put forth. Her invulnerable citadel began to move, and from it her guns hurled ponderous shot in quick succession. These were answered by broadsides from her antagonist; and in this close and deadly encounter, in which the blazes of opposing guns met each other, these strange combatants struggled for some time, each thoroughly illustrating the wonderful resisting power of armored ships, which had just been manifested in a less degree on the Tennessee River. Neither of the mailed gladiators was damaged in the terrible onset.

The *Monitor* now withdrew a little, and each commenced maneuvering for advantage of position. The *Monitor* sought her antagonist's port-holes, or some vulnerable part of her armor, that she might send a shot through to her vitals,[1] while the *Merrimack* pounded her foe awfully with her heavy shot, some of them masses of iron weighing two hundred pounds each, and moving at the rate of two thousand feet in a second. They struck her deck and turret without bruising them, and many of the projectiles went over the little warrior that lay so close to the water's edge. Heavy round shot and conical bolts that struck the turret, glanced off as pebbles would fly from contact with solid granite, they receiving more harm than their intended victim.[2]

The *Merrimack* was wasting precious time in fighting an invulnerable and more agile antagonist; so she left the *Monitor*, and again made a furious assault on the grounded *Minnesota*. As she approached, Van Brunt opened upon her with all his broadside guns and a ten-inch pivot-gun,—"a broadside," he said, "which would have blown out of the water any timber-built

---

[1] The following description, by Captain Ericsson, will explain the way in which the guns of the *Monitor* were made to bear on her antagonist: "On one side of the turret there is a telescope, or reflector, the image being bent by a prism. The Sailing-Master, having nothing to do, was to turn the turret. He not only looked through the telescope, but, by means of a small wheel, turned the turret exactly where he liked. He did that to admiration, pointing exactly on the enemy. As the *Monitor* went round, the turret kept turning (it no doubt astonished Captain Buchanan), so that, wherever the *Monitor* was, in whatever position it was placed, the two bull-dogs kept looking at him all the time."

The *Monitor* had some wrought-iron shot, that were first forged into square blocks and then turned into spheres in a lathe, each weighing 184 pounds. These were not used, as the Dahlgren guns had not been tested with them. It was Ericsson's opinion that the armor of the *Merrimack* would have proved no defense against them.

MASHED BOLT.

[2] The annexed picture shows the effect produced upon a 100-pound solid iron bolt, now in the Naval Museum at Washington City, by its striking the turret. It was mashed like a piece of lead, while the turret was uninjured by it. The effect of such a blow, as we shall observe hereafter, was somewhat stunning to persons within the turret. "You were very correct," wrote Engineer Stimers to Captain Ericsson, "in your estimate of the effect of shot upon the man inside of the turret when it struck near him. Three men were knocked down, of whom I was one. The other two had to be carried below; but I was not disabled at all, and the others recovered before the battle was over."

ship in the world,"—but with very little effect. The *Merrimack* sent in return one of her terrible shells, that went crashing through the *Minnesota* to midships, exploding two charges of powder on its way, bursting in the boatswain's apartments, tearing four rooms all into one, and setting the ship on fire. The flames were soon extinguished. Another of her shells penetrated the boiler of the tug-boat *Dragon* and exploded it. Meanwhile at least fifty solid shot, from the *Minnesota*, had struck the *Merrimack* without the least effect, but her fiery little antagonist was bearing down upon her, and soon commanded her whole attention. The latter placed herself between the combatants, and compelled the *Merrimack* to change her position. In

BATTLE BETWEEN THE MONITOR AND MERRIMACK, IN HAMPTON ROADS.

so doing she grounded, when Van Brunt again brought all his guns to bear upon her. Her situation was a critical one, and as soon as she got afloat again she turned her prow toward Norfolk, when the *Monitor* gave chase. The monster suddenly turned upon its pursuer and ran with full speed upon the little warrior, its huge beak grating over the deck of the *Monitor.* It was more damaged by the contact than the vessel it assailed. This was instantly followed by the plunge of a heavy shot through the armor of the *Merrimack*, and the concentration of the guns of the latter on the turret and pilot-house of the *Monitor.* The encounter was desperate, but suddenly ceased, and the combatants withdrew; the *Monitor* making her way toward Fortress Monroe, and the *Merrimack* and her tenders toward Norfolk. The *Minnesota*, relieved of immediate danger, was lightened by throwing some heavy guns overboard, and was put afloat at two o'clock the next morning.[1]

During the combat, the gallant Captain Worden, whose record in the history of the Navy is without blemish as a man and a soldier, had suffered severely. He had stationed himself at the pilot-house, while Lieutenant Greene managed the guns, and Chief Engineer Alban C. Stimers, who was on board in the capacity of Government inspector, worked the turret. Nine

---

[1] Report of Captain G. J. Van Brunt to the Secretary of the Navy, March 10, 1862; Letter of Engineer A. C. Stimers to Captain Ericsson, March 9; oral statements to the author by Captain Worden, and various accounts by contemporaries and eye-witnesses; also, Report of Lieutenant Jones to the Confederate "Secretary of the Navy" at the close of the first day's engagement.

times that turret was struck by the *Merrimack's* projectiles. The side armor was hit eight times by them; three times they struck and glanced from the deck, and twice they gave the pilot-house—the most vulnerable point—a heavy blow. One of these struck fairly in front of the peep-hole, at which Worden was watching his foe. It shivered some cement, and cast it so violently in his face that it blinded him for several days, and so shocked him, that for a time he was insensible.[1] In the turret, Stimers and two others were knocked down by the concussion, when it was struck; but, with the exception of Worden, no one was very seriously injured on board the *Monitor*. He was taken to Washington City, where, for a few days, his life was in peril, but he recovered and performed other gallant exploits during the war. His courage in going out upon the Atlantic at that stormy season, in an untried vessel of strange fashion, and his bold fight with and glorious success against the most formidable warrior then afloat, belonging to the Confederates, won for him the most unbounded admiration. It was felt that he was the savior of his country at a most critical period; for had the *Merrimack* not been checked as she was, who shall say what conquering power she might not then, before the National navy was much clad in armor, have exerted in securing a triumph for the conspirators? Worden the warrior, and Ericsson the inventor, shared in the public gratitude. On the day of the battle, Chief Engineer Stimers wrote to the latter, saying, "I congratulate you upon your great success. Thousands have this day blessed you. I have heard whole crews cheer you. Every man feels that you have saved this place to the nation by furnishing us with the means to whip an iron-clad frigate, that was, until our arrival, having it all her own way with our most powerful vessels."

JOHN L. WORDEN.[2]

The *Merrimack*, whose exploits on Saturday had caused joy throughout the Confederacy,[3] was so much disabled on Sunday,[a] and had acquired such a wholesome respect for the *Monitor*, that

[a] March 9, 1862.

---

[1] Worden had no thought for himself. When he recovered from his insensibility, his first question was, "Is the *Minnesota* safe?" He had been ordered to her assistance, and that was his special duty. When informed that he had not only saved that ship, but driven off the *Merrimack*, he said, "I don't care, then, what becomes of *me*." While lying in a critical state at Washington, he received the most assiduous attentions from everybody that could administer them; and it is said that the tender-hearted President, when he first visited him, wept like a father over the blinded hero, to whom he felt extremely grateful for his inestimable services for the National cause.

[2] This is from a fine likeness of Captain Worden, taken before his injury on board the *Monitor*.

[3] "By this daring exploit," said the Norfolk *Day Book*, "we have raised the James River blockade without foreign assistance, and are likely, with the assistance of the *Virginia* [*Merrimack*], to keep open the communication." The Charleston *Mercury* said exultingly: "The iron-clad steamer *Virginia* cost $185,000 to fit her up, and in one day destroyed $1,000,000 worth of Yankee property." Even so late as the 11th, or two days after the *Monitor* had sent the *Merrimack* back to Norfolk a disheartened cripple, Jefferson Davis, in a message to the "Congress" at Richmond, claimed a triumph for the Confederates, saying, "The disparity of forces engaged did not justify the anticipation of so great a victory."

she did not again invite her little antagonist to combat,[1] and it was believed that the free navigation of the James River by the National gun-boats would speedily follow. Impressed with this idea, and influenced by the masterly movement of Johnston from Manassas, General McClellan somewhat changed his plan for moving on Richmond. He called a Council of War at Fairfax Court House,[a] by which it was decided to go down the Chesapeake and debark the army at Fortress Monroe, instead of Urbana or Mob-Jack Bay, and from that point, as a base of supplies, press toward the Confederate capital. This plan was approved by the President, on the condition that a sufficient force should be left for the perfect security of Washington City, and to hold Manassas Junction.[2]

[a] March 13.

Preparations for the new movement were immediately commenced. It was important for the security of Washington, to hold the Confederates in check in Western Virginia and in the Shenandoah Valley. Movements to this end had been made very soon after the close of the campaign in Western Virginia, recorded in Chapter IV. Early in January, the gallant and accomplished General Lander, who was suffering from a wound received in a skirmish at Edwards's Ferry, a few days after the battle of Ball's Bluff, in October, took command of a force to protect the Baltimore and Ohio Railway. He had a wily and energetic opponent in "Stonewall Jackson," who was endeavoring to gain what Floyd, and Wise, and Lee had lost, and to hold possession of the Shenandoah Valley. Lander, with a force of about four thousand men, made a series of rapid movements against him. With only four hundred horsemen, he dashed upon him in the night at Blooming Gap, in the middle of February,[b] captured seventeen of his commissioned officers and nearly sixty of his rank and file, and compelled him to retire. Lander also occupied Romney, but fell back on the approach of Jackson's superior force, when the latter took post at Winchester.

[b] Feb. 14.

FREDERICK W. LANDER.

Lander's career as an independent commander was short. His wound became painful from constant exertions, and this, with anxiety and exposure, brought on disease which assumed the form of a fatal congestion of the brain.

[1] The huge prow of the *Merrimack* was twisted by her collision with her foe; her flag-staff and anchor were shot away; her pipes for smoke and steam were riddled; and her commander (Buchanan) and seven of her crew were killed and wounded. Another Confederate gun-boat lost six men. The entire loss of the Nationals, during the two days of conflict, was not much short of 400 men, besides the fine frigates *Congress* and *Cumberland*, the tug *Dragon*, and damage inflicted on the *Minnesota*, and the property in the two vessels first named.

[2] General McClellan issued a stirring address to his soldiers, in the form of a General Order, in which he said: "For a long time I have kept you inactive, but not without a purpose. You were to be disciplined and instructed. The formidable artillery you now have had to be created. Other armies were to move and accomplish certain results. I have held you back that you might give the death-blow to the rebellion that has distracted our once happy country. . . . . The period of inaction has passed: I will bring you now face to face with the rebels, and only pray that God may defend the right."

He died on the 2d of March, when his country lost one of its ablest defenders. For his brief but valuable services in Western Virginia, the Secretary of War had publicly thanked him.[a] General Shields, another brave soldier, who had done good service in Mexico, was appointed Lander's successor in command of the troops of the latter.

[a] Feb. 17, 1862.

In the mean time General Banks, commanding the Fifth Corps, had sent a force under Colonel Geary to reoccupy Harper's Ferry,[1] as the first step toward seizing and holding the Shenandoah Valley. He took command there in person late in February, and with his forces occupied the heights near the ferry; also Charleston and Leesburg, and other important points on each side of the Blue Ridge. Jackson, who had occupied places directly in front of Banks, was pushed back to Winchester, where he was posted with his division of nearly eight thousand men, when, early in March, Johnston evacuated Manassas. That evacuation was followed by the retirement of Jackson up the Shenandoah Valley, on the approach of Union troops under Generals Hamilton and Williams.[b] He retreated to Mount Jackson, about forty miles above Winchester, where he was in direct communication with a force at Luray and another at Washington, on the eastern side of the mountain, not far from Thompson's Gap. Shields pursued[c] Jackson to his halting-place, creating the greatest consternation among the inhabitants. The secessionists fled southward, while their few slaves, suddenly relieved from bondage to their fugitive masters, took their departure, by every possible mode of conveyance, toward the National lines. Shields found his antagonist too strong to warrant an attack, and he fell back to Winchester, for the twofold purpose of safety and drawing Jackson from his supports. He was closely pursued by Jackson's cavalry, under Turner Ashby, one of the most dashing of the Confederate cavalry officers in that region.

NATHANIEL P. BANKS.

[b] March 11.

[c] March 19.

EXODUS OF SLAVES.

To Banks had been assigned the duty of covering the line of the Potomac and Washington City, after the movement agreed upon in council at Fairfax Court House had been conditionally sanctioned by the President, and he was ordered to place the bulk of his force at Manassas Junction and

[1] See page 138.

vicinity, and to repair the Manassas Gap Railway, so as to have a rapid and direct communication with the Shenandoah Valley. Accordingly, on the retirement of Jackson up the valley, he put the first division of his corps in motion for Centreville, under General Williams, leaving only the division of Shields and some Michigan cavalry in Winchester.

Spies informed Jackson of the weakening of Banks's army in the Valley, and he immediately moved down to attack him at Winchester. General Shields, who was in immediate command there, had a force of about six thousand infantry, seven hundred and fifty cavalry, and twenty-four guns, well posted on a ridge, so as to cover the roads entering Winchester from the south. This position was about half a mile north of the village of Kernstown, and two and a half south of Winchester.

Toward the evening of the 22d of March, Ashby's cavalry drove in Shields's pickets, when the latter moved a small force to oppose the assailants. While directing it in person, his arm was shattered above his elbow by the fragments of a shell, which also wounded his side. He was prostrated, but was able to make dispositions for a vigorous encounter with his foe the next day.[1] Under cover of the night he pushed forward the brigade of Colonel Kimball, of the Fourteenth Indiana, to Kernstown, supported by Daum's artillery, well posted. Colonel Sullivan's brigade was placed within supporting distance, as a reserve in Kimball's rear. In that order the troops reposed until morning, when a reconnoissance obtained no positive information of any Confederate force immediately in front, excepting Ashby's cavalry. General Banks believed General Jackson to be too weak or too prudent to attack Shields, and at ten o'clock that morning[a] he departed for Washington City by way of Harper's Ferry, in obedience to a summons from Head-quarters, leaving his staff-officers to start for Centreville in the afternoon. He was soon made to retrace his steps by the sounds of battle in his rear.

[a] March 22, 1862.

At the time when the National scouts saw nothing but Ashby's cavalry, Jackson's whole force was strongly posted in battle order, with artillery on each flank, in an eligible situation half a mile south of Kernstown, completely masked by woods, which were filled with his skirmishers; and within an hour after Banks left Winchester, Confederate cannon opened upon Kimball. Sullivan's brigade was immediately ordered forward to Kimball's support, and a severe action was commenced by artillery on both sides, but at too great distance to be very effective.

Jackson now took the initiative, and, with a considerable force of all arms, attempted to turn Kimball's left flank, when an active body of skirmishers, under Colonel Carroll, composed of his regiment (the Eighth Ohio) and three companies of the Sixty-seventh Ohio, were thrown forward on both sides of the Valley Turnpike, to oppose the movement. These were supported by four guns of Jenks's artillery. The Confederates were repulsed at all points, and Jackson abandoned his designs upon the National left, massed a heavy force on their right, and sent two additional batteries and his reserves to sup-

---

[1] Jackson had ten regiments of Virginia infantry, with 27 cannon and 290 cavalry. His force was, according to Pollard, "6000 men, with Captain McLaughlin's battery of artillery, and Colonel Ashby's Cavalry."—*First Year of the War*, 284.

port the movement. With this combined force he pressed forward to turn and crush his adversary's left. Daum's artillery could not check the movement, and imminent peril threatened the Union army. Informed of this, Shields, who from his bed was in a measure conducting the battle, ordered Colonel E. B. Tyler's brigade[1] to the support of Kimball, and directed the latter to employ all of his disposable infantry in an attempt to carry Jackson's batteries, and then to turn his left flank and hurl it back on its center. The execution of this important and perilous order was intrusted to the gallant Tyler and his fine brigade. The Confederates were pressed back to a stone fence, which gave them shelter, where a desperate struggle ensued with Jackson's famous "Stonewall brigade." For a little while the result was doubtful, when the Fifth and Sixty-second Ohio and Thirteenth Indiana, of Sullivan's brigade, and the Fourteenth Indiana, Eighty-fourth Pennsylvania, and parts of the Eighth and Sixty-seventh Ohio, of Kimball's brigade, hastened to the support of Tyler. The combined forces dashed on the Confederates, forced them back through the woods, and sent them in full retreat up the Valley, with a heavy loss,[2] but in good order, for their discipline was perfect. So ended the BATTLE OF KERNSTOWN.

JAMES SHIELDS.

The National troops bivouacked on the battle-field the night after the victory, and at an early hour in the morning began a vigorous pursuit of the Confederates toward Strasburg. Meanwhile, Shields, who was satisfied that re-enforcements for Jackson could not be far off, had sent an express after Williams's division, then far on its way toward Centreville. Banks, who was informed by telegraph of the battle, had already ordered it back. He also hastened to Winchester, took command in person, and followed the retreating Confederates up the valley almost to Mount Jackson. This demonstration of Jackson's, and information that he might instantly call re-enforcements to his aid, caused the retention of Banks's forces in the Shenandoah Valley, and the appointment of General James Wadsworth to the command of the troops left for the immediate defense of the National Capital. He was made military governor of the District of Columbia.

In the mean time General McClellan had been forwarding his forces to Fortress Monroe, preparatory to an advance on Richmond. He left Washington on the 1st of April, on which day he sent to the adjutant-general a

[1] The Seventh and Twenty-ninth Ohio, Seventh Indiana, First Virginia, and One Hundred and Tenth Pennsylvania.

[2] Jackson left behind 2 cannon, 4 caissons, many small arms, and about 300 prisoners. He reported his killed to be 80, and his wounded at 342. Shields reported 270 of the Confederate dead found on the battle-field after the conflict, and estimated Jackson's entire loss at nearly 1500. The National loss, according to his report, was nearly 600 men, of whom 103 were killed, and 441 were wounded. Among the slain was Colonel Murray, of the Eighty-fourth Pennsylvania.

statement of the number and intended disposition of the forces which he left behind: a part for the immediate defense of the Capital, and the remainder for other operations more remote, but whose chief business was to secure Washington City. The number left was a little more than seventy-three thousand.[1] A few days later, he had under his command, at Fortress Monroe, one hundred and twenty-one thousand men (exclusive of the forces of General Wool), which had been sent thither within a little more than thirty days, in transports furnished by the Assistant Secretary of War, John Tucker.[2]

The movements of "Stonewall" Jackson, General Ewell, and other active commanders in the Upper Valley of the Shenandoah and its vicinity, had made it important to strengthen Fremont in the Mountain Department, and for that purpose Blenker's division of ten thousand men was withdrawn from the Army of the Potomac before McClellan left Washington. A further reduction of the force under his command was made at this time, in consequence of a report of General Wadsworth, that the troops left for the immediate defense of Washington were insufficient.[3] This matter was referred to the Adjutant-General, (L. Thomas), and General E. A. Hitchcock, and, on their decision that the force was inadequate, the army corps of General McDowell was detached from McClellan's immediate command, and ordered to report directly to the Secretary of War. It was not withdrawn from active co-operation with McClellan. On the contrary, it was in a position, experts say, to perform the best service in such co-operation, while it would serve the other purpose of covering Washington, for it was to occupy a position to prevent Johnston turning back from the Rappahannock to sack the National Capital, and also to keep Confederate troops in that region and over the Blue Ridge from joining those at Richmond.

MAGRUDER'S HEAD-QUARTERS, YORKTOWN.[4]

[1] Of these 18,000 were to remain in garrison at and in front of Washington; 7,780 at Warrenton; 10,859 at Manassas; 35,467 in the Shenandoah Valley; and 1,350 on the Lower Potomac.—See McClellan's Report, page 66.

[2] Report of Assistant Secretary of War Tucker, April 5, 1862. Besides the soldiers, these transports, consisting of 13 steamers, 188 schooners, and 88 barges, conveyed 44 batteries, 14.592 beasts, 1,150 wagons, 74 ambulances, several pontoon bridges, telegraph materials, and an immense amount of equipage. The only loss sustained in this work of transportation consisted of 8 mules and 9 barges, the cargoes of the latter being saved.

[3] Wadsworth reported his force fit for duty at 19,022, nearly all of them new and imperfectly disciplined, and several of the regiments in a disorganized condition. At the same time he was under orders from McClellan to send three regiments to the Peninsula, one to Budd's Ferry, and 4000 men to Manassas and Warrenton. The absence of these would reduce the force in and around Washington to less than 15.000 men.

[4] This was the appearance of the old Court-House (which was Magruder's head-quarters in Yorktown), with the ruins of buildings near it, in 1863. It stands a short distance from the famous mansion of the Nelson family, which was bombarded during the siege of Yorktown in 1781.

At this time General J. B. Magruder, whom we have already met at Big Bethel and the burning of Hampton, was in command of eleven thousand men on the Virginia Peninsula, between the James and York rivers, with his head-quarters at Yorktown, which he had fortified. Magruder had intended to make his line of defense as far down the Peninsula as Big Bethel, at positions in front of Howard's and Young's Mills, and at Ship Point, on the York River. But when he perceived the strong force gathered at Fortress Monroe, he felt too weak to make a stand on his proposed line, and he prepared to receive McClellan on a second line, on Warwick River. He left a small body of troops on his first line and at Ship Point, and distributed his remaining force along a front of about thirteen miles. At Yorktown, on Gloucester Point opposite, and on Mulberry Island, on the James River,[1] he placed fixed garrisons, amounting in the aggregate to six thousand men, so that along a line of thirteen miles in front of McClellan's great army, there were only about five thousand Confederate soldiers behind incomplete earth-works. General McClellan estimated Magruder's force at from fifteen thousand to twenty thousand men, while the eight thousand troops under Huger at Norfolk, he supposed to be fifteen thousand in number.

When General McClellan arrived at Fortress Monroe, he found fifty-eight thousand men and one hundred cannon of his army there. Large numbers of troops were continually arriving. Perceiving the importance of marching upon Magruder before he could be re-enforced by Johnston, and hoping by rapid movements to drive or capture him and press on to Richmond, McClellan put his whole force then in readiness at Fortress Monroe in motion up the Peninsula, on the morning of the 3d of April. He had counted upon the co-operation of the remnant of the naval force in Hampton Roads in the reduction of the Confederate water-batteries on the York and James rivers, and Flag-officer Goldsborough had offered to extend such assistance in storming the works at Yorktown and Gloucester, provided the latter position should be first turned by the army. He was reluctant to weaken his force, for the *Merrimack* was hourly expected, with renewed strength, and the James River was blockaded by Confederate gun-boats on its bosom and Confederate batteries on its shore.

McClellan's invading force moved in two columns, one along the old Yorktown road and the other by the Warwick road. These were led respectively by Generals Heintzelman and Keyes. The former, on the right, led the divisions of Generals Fitz John Porter and Hamilton, of the Third Corps, and Sedgwick's division of the Second Corps; while Keyes led the divisions of Generals Couch and W. F. Smith, of the Fourth Corps. They pressed forward, and on the following day the right, accompanied by McClellan, was at Big Bethel, and the Commander-in-chief made his head-quarters at a house very near the spot where the gallant Greble fell, ten months

MCCLELLAN'S HEAD-QUARTERS.

[1] This was sometimes called Mulberry Point, for it is not actually an island now, the channel between it and the former main having been closed.

before.[1] The left was at the little village of Warwick Court House at the same time.

The army moved slowly on until the afternoon of the 5th, without any impediment excepting almost impassable mud, when the advance of each column was confronted and made to halt by Magruder's fortified lines, the right near Yorktown, on the York, the left near Winn's Mill, on the Warwick River. The latter stream heads within a mile of Yorktown, and, flowing across the Peninsula, falls into the James River. In front of these lines McClellan's continually augmenting army remained a month, engaged in the tedious operations of a regular siege, under the direction of General Fitz John Porter, casting up intrenchments, skirmishing frequently, and on one occasion making a reconnoissance in force, which resulted in an engagement disastrous to the Nationals. This was by the division of General Smith of the Fourth Corps, who attacked the Confederates at Dam No. 1, on the Warwick,[a] between the mills of Lee and Winn. The movement was gallantly made, but failed. The vanguard of the Nationals (composed of four Vermont companies, who had waded the stream, waist deep, under cover of the cannon of Ayre's battery, and who were re-enforced by eight other companies) was driven back across the river[3] with the loss of a hundred men, and was poorly compensated by inflicting upon the foe the loss of seventy-five men. This repulse confirmed McClellan in his belief that an immense force of Confederates was on his front, and Magruder (who had resorted to all sorts of tricks to mislead his antagonist) was enabled to write truly on the 3d of May, the day before he fled from Yorktown, "Thus, with five thousand men, exclusive of the garrison, we stopped and held in check over one hundred thousand of the enemy."[4]

SCENE AT WARWICK COURT-HOUSE.[2]

[a] April 16, 1862.

McClellan had reasons for being extremely cautious. His Government was evidently withholding from him its perfect confidence, and he began to fear that it might, in a degree, withhold its support also. The detachment of Blenker's division from his command disturbed him, but when McDowell's corps was also detached, and he was refused the control of the ten thousand

---

[1] See page 508, volume I.

[2] In this little sketch is seen the house, with two chimneys on the outside of the gable on the left, which was occupied by General Keyes on the night of the 4th of April.

[3] Among the really brave men who fell at this time was private William Scott, of the Third Vermont, who, a few months before, had been sentenced by McClellan to be shot for sleeping on his post. Secretary Cameron pardoned him, and no braver soldier was found in the ranks of the patriots. He was among the first who crossed the Warwick River in this movement.

[4] Magruder's report to Cooper, May 3, 1862. A British officer (Colonel Freemantle), who spent three months with the Confederate army, says Magruder told him "the different dodges he resorted to to blind and deceive McClellan as to his strength," and said he was greatly amused and relieved "when he saw that general with his magnificent army begin to break ground before miserable earth-works defended by only 8,000 men."—Freemantle's *Three Months in the Southern States.*

troops under General Wool at Fortress Monroe, he was alarmed. The use of all these troops formed a part of his plan of operations against Richmond. He knew the ability and energy of Johnston, and anticipated what really happened, namely, the movement toward Richmond of the bulk of the Confederate army when it was ascertained that the National army was in force on the Peninsula. He therefore, from his head-quarters before Yorktown, sent a remonstrance to the Government[a] against a further diminution of his force, declaring it to be his opinion that he would have to fight all the available troops of the Confederates not far from his position. "Do not force me to do so," he said, "with diminished numbers; but, whatever your decision may be, I will leave nothing undone to obtain success." He urgently requested Franklin's division of McDowell's corps to be sent to him, and it was done.

[a] May, 1862.

Two days later,[b] McClellan telegraphed to the War Department that it was clear that he would have the whole Confederate force on his hands, "probably not less than one hundred thousand men, and possibly more;" and in a dispatch to the President, on the same day, he assured him that his own force, fit for duty, did not exceed eighty-five thousand men. This statement astonished the President. McClellan had wearied him with complaints that he was not properly sustained, when the Government was doing all in its power for him compatible with its paramount duty to secure the capital. "Your dispatches," wrote the kind-hearted President,[c] "complaining that you are not properly sustained, while they do not offend me, do pain me very much." He then explained why Blenker's division was withdrawn, pointed to the necessity that held Banks in the Shenandoah Valley, and reminded the General that the explicit order that Washington should, "by the judgment of *all* the commanders of army corps, be left entirely secure," had been neglected, and that was the reason for detaining McDowell. "There is a curious mystery about the number of troops now with you," continued the President. "When I telegraphed you on the 6th, saying you had a hundred thousand with you, I had just obtained from the Secretary of War a statement taken, as he said, from your own returns, making one hundred and eight thousand then with you and *en route* to you. You now say you will have but eighty-five thousand men when all *en route* to you shall have reached you. How can the discrepancy of twenty-three thousand, be accounted for?"[1] The President then urged McClellan to strike a blow instantly. "By delay," he said, "the enemy will relatively gain upon you; that is, he will gain faster by fortifications and re-enforcements than you can by re-enforcements alone. And once more let me tell you," he said, "it is indispensable to *you* that you strike a blow. *I* am powerless to help this. You will do me the justice to remember, I always insisted that going down the Bay in search of a field, instead of fighting at or near Manassas, was only shifting and not surmounting a difficulty; that we would find the same enemy, and the same or equal intrenchments, at either place. The country will not fail to note—is now noting—that the present hesitation to move upon an intrenched enemy is but the story of Manassas repeated." The President

[b] April 7.

[c] August 9.

[1] This question was not answered then, nor has it been since. In his final report, McClellan gave the President's letter, but makes no comment on the significant question.

closed with an assurance that he never had a kinder feeling toward the General than he had then, nor a fuller purpose to sustain him, so far as in his most anxious judgment he consistently could. His last words were—"But you must act."

McClellan did not heed the closing injunction. Almost a month longer he hesitated in front of Magruder's feebly manned lines, digging parallels, forming batteries and redoubts, and preparing for an assault upon Yorktown with as much caution as did the American and French armies on the same field in 1781;[1] and at the close of April, when his preparations were almost completed, he reported the number of his entire army on the Peninsula, exclusive of General Wool's force at Fortress Monroe, which was fully co-operating with him,[2] at one hundred and thirty thousand three hundred and seventy-eight, whereof one hundred and twelve thousand three hundred and ninety-two were present and fit for duty. Franklin's division, which he so much desired, and with which he promised to invest and attack Gloucester Point immediately, as the preliminary to an assault on Yorktown, was promptly sent to him; but those troops, over twelve thousand strong, were kept in idleness about a fortnight on the transports in the York River, because, as McClellan alleged, his preparations for the attack were not completed when they arrived. He afterwards complained that the lack of McDowell's corps to perform the work he had promised to assign to Franklin, namely, the turning of Yorktown by an attack on Gloucester, was the cause of his failure to attack Yorktown, and "made rapid and brilliant operations impossible." Another and more restraining reason seems to have been the inability, during that fortnight, to decide whether to attempt to flank his foe or to make a direct attack upon him, until it was too late to do either.

In the mean time the Confederates had been active. Magruder, as we have observed, had made his five thousand men deceive McClellan with the appearance of an overwhelming force, and had kept him at bay; while Johnston, so soon as McClellan's movement was developed, put his army, then on the Rapid Anna, in motion for Richmond, and there kept it well in hand for the defense of the Confederate capital. General Robert E. Lee was then Jefferson Davis's Chief of Staff, and both he and Johnston considered the Peninsula, with the probability of the York and James rivers on each flank being opened to the National gun-boats, entirely untenable.

Soon after McClellan's arrival before Yorktown, Johnston visited and inspected the works there, and, being satisfied that its defenses were inadequate, urged the military authorities at Richmond to withdraw the troops, for he had no doubt that McClellan would (as he easily could have done) capture Yorktown, and with gun-boats and transports push rapidly to the head of the Peninsula. Johnston's desire was to concentrate all his forces around Richmond, and give the National troops a decisive battle there. He was overruled; and it was determined to hold the Peninsula, if possible,

---

[1] He established a depot of supplies at Ship Point, on the Poquosin River, an arm of Chesapeake Bay, near the mouth of the York River. His first parallel was opened at about a mile from Yorktown, and under its protection batteries were established along a curved line extending from the York River on the right to the head of the Warwick River on the left, with a cord about a mile in length. He constructed 14 batteries and 3 redoubts, and fully armed them with heavy siege-guns, some of them 100-pounders and 200-pounders.

[2] McClellan's dispatch to the President, April 7, 1862.

until Huger might dismantle the fortifications at Norfolk, destroy the naval establishment there, and evacuate the seaboard.[1] At that time the whole sea-coast below Norfolk to St. Augustine, excepting at Charleston and its immediate vicinity, was in possession of the National forces. For the purpose of holding the Peninsula temporarily, re-enforcements were sent down from Richmond when it was known that McClellan was intrenching,[2] and Johnston took command at Yorktown in person.

The spectacle was now exhibited of one party nervously hesitating to strike, while the other party was as nervously anxious to flee from the expected blow. And here began that series of tardy movements which distinguished McClellan's campaign on the Peninsula, in which disease consumed more brave men than the storms of battle swept away.[3]

---

[1] *Battle-fields of the South*, by an English Combatant, page 169. Mr. Swinton says (*Campaigns of the Army of the Potomac*, page 103) that this exposition of the views and wishes of the Confederate commander was given to him by Johnston himself.

[2] General Magruder, in his report, declared that he expected an attack immediately after the arrival of McClellan, and his troops slept in the trenches; "but," he said, "to my utter surprise, he permitted day after day to elapse without an assault." In a few days Magruder perceived earth-works rising in front of his, and took heart. "Re-enforcements," he said, "began to pour in, and each hour the army of the Peninsula grew stronger and stronger, until anxiety passed from my mind as to the result of an attack upon us."

[3] Twenty of the thirty days, during which the army lay before Yorktown, were stormy ones. Heavy thunder-showers followed each other in quick succession. The wearied and heated men who worked in the trenches, or who were on duty under arms, were compelled to rest on the damp ground at night, by which they were chilled. Fevers followed. "In a short time," says Dr. Marks, "the sick in our hospitals were numbered by thousands, and many died so suddenly that the disease had all the aspect of a plague."—*The Peninsula Campaign in Virginia*, by Rev. J. J. Marks, D. D., page 138.

General J. G. Barnard, McClellan's Engineer-in-Chief, in his report to his commander at the close of the campaign says, after speaking of the toils of the troops for a month in the trenches, or lying in the swamps of Warwick: "We lost few men by the siege, but disease took a fearful hold of the army; and toil and hardships, unredeemed by the excitement of combat, impaired their *morale*. We did not carry with us from Yorktown so good an army as we took there. Of the bitter fruits of that month gained by the enemy, we have tasted to our heart's content."

CHAPTER XV.

THE ARMY OF THE POTOMAC ON THE VIRGINIA PENINSULA.

GENERAL McCLELLAN'S batteries would all have been ready to open on the Confederate works on the morning of the 6th of May;[a] but there was then no occasion for their use, for those works were abandoned. So early as the 30th of April, Jefferson Davis and two of his so-called cabinet, and Generals Johnston, Lee, and Magruder, held a council at the Nelson House,[1] where, after exciting debates, it was determined to evacuate Yorktown and its dependencies. A wholesome fear of the heavy guns of the Nationals, whose missiles had already given a foretaste of their terrible power, and also an expectation that the National gun-boats would speedily ascend the two rivers flanking the Confederate Army, caused this prudent resolution. The *Merrimack* had been ordered to Yorktown, but it had so great a dread of the watchful little *Monitor* that it remained at Norfolk. Already some war-vessels, and a fleet of transports with Franklin's troops, as we have observed, were lying securely in Posquotin River, well up toward Yorktown. These considerations caused immediate action on the resolutions of the council. The sick, hospital stores, ammunition, and camp equipage were speedily sent to Richmond, and on the night of the 3d of May, the Confederate garrisons at Yorktown and Gloucester, and the troops along the line of the Warwick, fled toward Williamsburg. Early the next morning[b] General McClellan telegraphed to the Secretary of War that he was in possession of the abandoned

[a] 1862.

[b] May 4.

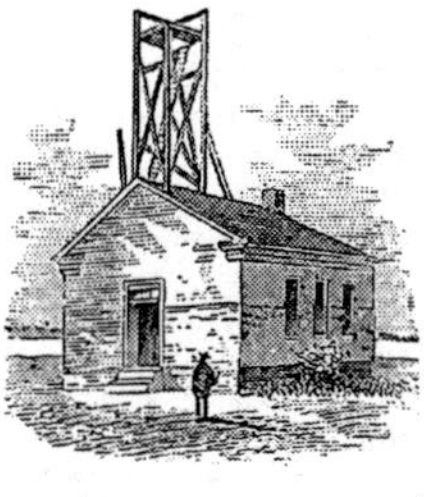

PARISH CHURCH IN 1866.

[1] This was a large brick house in Yorktown, which belonged to Governor Nelson, of Virginia, and was occupied by Cornwallis as head-quarters during a part of the period of the siege of that post in 1781, when, at the instance of the owner, who was in command of Virginia militia engaged in the siege, it was bombarded and the British General was driven out. When the writer visited Yorktown in 1848, the walls of that house exhibited scars made by the American shells and round shot on that occasion. When he was there in 1866 the house, which had survived two sieges more than eighty years apart, was still well preserved, and the scars made in the old War for Independence were yet visible. At his first visit he found the grave-yard attached to the old Parish Church in Yorktown, and not far from the Nelson House (in which two or three generations of the Nelson family were buried), in excellent condition, there being several fine monuments over the graves of leading members of that family; but at his last visit that cemetery was a desolation—those monuments were mutilated, and the place of the steeple of the Church (which the Confederates used for a quarter-master's depot, and whose walls and roof only were preserved) was occupied by a signal-tower, erected by Magruder. The Nelson house was used as a hospital by the Confederates.

post, and added: "No time shall be lost. I shall push the enemy to the wall."[1]

At that hour a vigorous pursuit of the fugitives had begun by the cavalry and horse-artillery under General Stoneman, followed along the Yorktown road by the divisions of Generals Joseph Hooker and Philip Kearney, and on the Winn's Mill road, which joins the former within two miles of Williamsburg, by the divisions of Generals W. F. Smith, Darius N. Couch, and Silas Casey. Those of Generals Israel B. Richardson, John Sedgwick, and Fitz-John Porter, were moved to the vicinity of Yorktown, to be ready to go forward as a supporting force, if required, or to follow Franklin's division, which was to be sent up the York River to West Point, to co-operate with the pursuing force on the flank of the fugitives, and to seize that terminus of the Richmond and York River railway. General Heintzelman was at first charged with the direction of the pursuit, but the General-in-Chief changed his mind, and directed General Edwin V. Sumner, his second in command, to go forward and conduct the operations of the pursuers. McClellan remained at Yorktown, to make arrangements for the dispatch of Franklin up the York.

EDWIN V. SUMNER.

The Confederates had, some months before, constructed a line of strong works, thirteen in number, across the gently rolling plateau on which Williamsburg stands. These were two miles in front of that city at the narrowest part of the Peninsula, the right resting on a deep ravine near the James River, and the left on Queen's Creek, near the York River. The principal work was Fort Magruder, close by the junction of the Yorktown and Winn's Mill roads. It was an earth-work with bastion front, its crest measuring nearly half a mile, surrounded by a wet ditch, and heavily armed. The others were redoubts, similar to those cast up around Washington City. At these works the retreating Confederates left a strong rear-guard to check the pursuers, while the main body should have time to place the Chickahominy River between it and the advancing Nationals.

---

[1] Yorktown presented to the victors evidences of great precipitation in the final departure of the troops, as well as deliberate preparation for a diabolical reception of the Nationals after the flight of the garrison. The Confederates left most of their heavy guns behind them, all of which were spiked. They also left their tents standing; and near wells and springs, magazines; in the telegraph office, in carpet bags and barrels of flour, and on grassy places, where soldiers might go for repose, they left buried torpedoes, so constructed and planted under bits of board, that the pressure of the foot of man or beast would explode them. By these infernal machines several men were killed, and others were fearfully wounded. Mr. Lathrop, Heintzelman's telegraph operator, had his foot blown off above the ankle. "The rebels," wrote General McClellan, "have been guilty of the most murderous and barbarous conduct in planting torpedoes here. I shall make the prisoners remove them at their peril." By his order some Confederate officers, who were prisoners, were compelled to search for and exhume them. They knew where they were planted, and it was a fitting work for such men to perform.

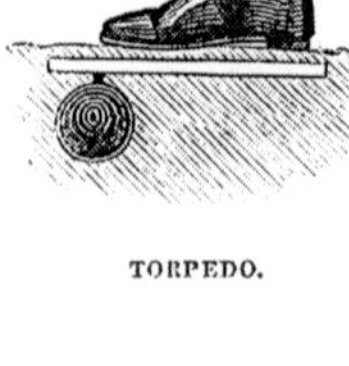

TORPEDO.

When Stoneman approached these lines he was met by Confederate cavalry, and these, with the guns of Fort Magruder and its immediate supporters, caused him to halt, fall back about four miles, and wait for the infantry. Hearing of this repulse, Hooker, who was not far in the rear of a brick church on the Yorktown road, was impatient to move forward, but the way was blocked by Smith's division. Therefore he sought and obtained leave of Heintzelman to throw his command on the Hampton or Warwick road; and in the mean time Sumner, with Smith's division, moved on to the point where Stoneman was halting, at five o'clock in the evening. These bivouacked for the night. Hooker pressed forward along the Hampton road, and took position on the left of Smith's at near midnight. Rain was then falling copiously, and the roads were rendered almost impassable. There all rested until dawn,[a] when Hooker again pressed forward, and at half-past five came in sight of the Confederate works, the spires of Williamsburg appearing in the distance across the open level land. Before the Nationals for nearly half a mile the way was obstructed by felled trees, and the open plain beyond was thickly dotted with rifle-pits.

[a] May 5, 1862.

Knowing that thirty thousand troops were within supporting distance of him, and the bulk of the Potomac Army within four hours' march, Hooker made an immediate advance upon the Confederate works, believing that he could sustain a conflict until aid might reach him, if needed. At half-past seven o'clock General Grover was directed to make the attack, by sending into the felled timber the First Massachusetts on the left, and the Second New Hampshire on the right, with orders to skirmish up to the verge of the open fields, to pick off the Confederate sharp-shooters and artillerists. At the same time the Eleventh Massachusetts and Twenty-sixth Pennsylvania were directed to form on the right of the New Hampshire regiment, and advance as skirmishers until they should reach the Yorktown road; while Weber's battery was pushed forward into the open field, within seven hundred yards of Fort Magruder. This drew the fire of the Confederates, which killed four of the artillerists and drove off the remainder. The battery was soon re-manned by volunteers from Osborn's, and with the assistance of Bramhall's, which was now brought into action, and also sharp-shooters, Fort Magruder was soon silenced, and the Confederates in sight on the plain were dispersed.

Patterson's brigade (Sixth, Seventh, and Eighth New Jersey) was charged with the support of these batteries, and was soon heavily engaged with Confederate infantry and sharp-shooters, who now appeared in great numbers. Hitherto the opponents of the Nationals were composed of only the Confederate rear-guard; now Longstreet's division, which had passed on through Williamsburg, had been sent back by Johnston to support that rear-guard, for the pressure of the pursuers was greater than the hitherto tardy movements of McClellan had given reason to expect. These were fresh and strong, and Hooker was compelled to send the First Massachusetts and Seventieth and Seventy-second New York (Excelsior Brigade), under Brigadier-general Grover, to the aid of Patterson. In the mean time the Eleventh Pennsylvania and Twenty-sixth Massachusetts had reached the Yorktown road, and Colonel Blaisdell, who led them, was directed to clear that way for the advance of the National forces, and form a connection with Heintzelman's corps.

EXCELSIOR BRIGADE.

Hooker was sorely pressed. The Confederates were heavily massed in front of Patterson and his supports. At half-past eleven o'clock he sent a note to Heintzelman, asking immediate assistance. That officer was absent, and Hooker was obliged to fight on unaided. At one o'clock the battle had assumed gigantic proportions, and Hooker's last regiments (Seventy-third and Seventy-fourth New York) had been sent into the fight. He was losing heavily and making no apparent head-way, for as the conflict progressed fresh Confederate troops under Pickett, Gholson, Pryor, and others hastened back from the direction of the Chickahominy to assist their struggling comrades, until a large portion of Johnston's army in that region were in the conflict. Three times the Confederates had made fierce charges on Hooker's center, with the hope of breaking his line, but were repulsed, and as often the places of the defeated ones were filled with fresh troops. Once a dash was made from the direction of Fort Magruder, which resulted in the capture of five of Weber's guns, and between two hundred and three hundred prisoners.

For almost nine consecutive hours Hooker's division fought the foe unaided,[1] excepting by the brigade of General J. J. Peck, of Couch's division, which arrived on the field early in the afternoon, and was posted on Hooker's right. There it acted as a continually repelling foil to the attacks of the Confederates, until near night, when it was relieved by two other of Couch's brigades. Finally the ammunition of some of Hooker's regiments, and also of the artillery, began to fail,[2] and no supply train had yet come up. The rain had made much of the road between Yorktown and Williamsburg an almost impassable slough, through which, and over the little wooded hills, whose trees the fugitives had cast in the way, and across miry ravines coursed by swollen brooks, cannon and wagons had to be dragged with almost a snail's pace. Hooker had called repeatedly on Sumner for help, but could get none, for that officer had ordered a large portion of the troops in hand to the right, under Hancock, to keep the Confederates in check in that direction, and to flank the works if possible.[3] So he fought on, maintaining his ground until between four and five o'clock, when the gallant and dashing Philip Kearney came up with his division, with orders

[1] Hooker found it impossible to use cavalry to advantage, and he was compelled to decline the proffered services of Brigadier-general Emory, and of Colonel Averill of the Third Pennsylvania cavalry, excepting for reconnoitering purposes. To Averill, and Lieutenant McAlister of the Engineers, Hooker publicly expressed his thanks; the latter having carefully reconnoitered such of the Confederate works as were concealed from view.

[2] Some of the shattered regiments were supplied with ammunition for a time only from the cartridge-boxes of their fallen comrades on the field.

[3] "History will not be believed," said Hooker, in his report of the battle (May 10, 1862), "when it is told that my division were permitted to carry on this unequal struggle from morning until night unaided, in the presence of more than 30,000 of their comrades with arms in their hands. Nevertheless it is true."

from Heintzelman (who with his staff had arrived on the ground early in the afternoon) to relieve Hooker's worn and fearfully thinned regiments. Kearney pressed to the front, and Hooker's troops withdrew from the fight and rested as a reserve. They had lost in the battle one thousand seven hundred of their companions.

Kearney deployed Berry's brigade to the left of the Williamsburg road, and Birney's to the right, and at the same time two companies of Poe's

ROAD BETWEEN YORKTOWN AND WILLIAMSBURG.

Second Michigan were pressed forward to cover the movement, and drive back Confederate skirmishers, who were almost silencing the National batteries. Thus Major Wainwright, Hooker's chief of artillery, was enabled to collect his gunners and re-open the fire from several quiet pieces. At that moment the fearfully shattered New Jersey Fifth went promptly to their support. The battle, which was lagging when Kearney arrived, was renewed with spirit, and the Nationals began to slowly push back their foe.

The heavy felled timber prevented all direct forward movement, and Kearney ordered the Thirty-eighth New York (Scott Life-guard), Colonel Hobart Ward, to charge down the road and take the rifle-pits in the center of the *abatis* by their flank. This duty was gallantly performed, with a loss to the regiment of nine of its nineteen officers. It did not quite accomplish Kearney's full desire, and he ordered the left wing of the Fortieth New York (Mozart), Colonel Riley, to charge up the open field and take the rifle-pits in reverse. Riley was hotly engaged in front, and the movement was performed under the lead of Captain Mindil, Birney's chief of staff, and the Confederates were driven out. By this time the rear brigade of the division had been brought up by General Jameson, and a second line was established under a severe fire. Disposition was at once made for further vigorous operations, when profound darkness fell upon the armies, the struggle ceased, and the wearied National soldiers rested on the soddened battle-field.

SITE OF THE DAM.[2]

Meanwhile Hancock had been successfully engaged in his flank movement. He had been dispatched by General Smith at an early hour, with about twenty-five hundred men,[1] to seize and hold an unoccupied redoubt at the extreme left of the Confederate position, which had been thrown up by Magruder, but was unknown to Johnston and his officers. It was upon a high bank above a ravine commanding a dam on Cub Dam Creek, a little tributary of Queen's Creek, about a mile and a half eastward of the Yorktown road. Hancock crossed the creek, took possession of the redoubt without opposition, and also of another one twelve hundred yards in advance of it, which was unoccupied. Two more redoubts stood between these and Fort Magruder, and a few shells and the bullets of sharp-shooters soon drove the Confederates from them. But Hancock's force was too small to make their occupation by it a prudent act, and he determined to wait for re-enforcements.

The occupation of the two redoubts on his extreme left by Hancock was the first intimation that Johnston had of their existence. He at once perceived the importance of the position, for it was on the flank and rear of the Confederate line of defense, and seriously menaced its integrity. He directed General Hill to send a sufficient force to drive back the Nationals, and to this duty General Jubal Early, with a force of Virginia and North Carolina troops, was assigned.

Hancock had earnestly called for re-enforcements, but they did not come. Twice General Smith had been ordered to send them, and each time the order was countermanded just as they were about to move, for Sumner was unwilling, he said, to risk the center by weakening it. So, instead of re-enforcements, Hancock received an order to fall back to his first position. He was slow to obey, for he felt the importance of his forward movement, but when, at about five o'clock, he saw the two redoubts nearest Fort Magruder

[1] These consisted of parts of his own, and of Davidson's brigade, which was then under his command. Of his own brigade he chose for this duty the Fifth Wisconsin, Forty-ninth Pennsylvania, and Sixth Maine; and from Davidson's, the Seventh Maine and Thirty-ninth New York Volunteers. These were accompanied by Lieutenant Crowen's New York battery of six guns, and Wheeler's battery.

[2] This is a sketch of the appearance of the site of the dam when the writer visited the spot in June, 1866. It is from a rude bridge then recently thrown across the stream. The redoubt was on the high bank directly over the little figure. Here the bank, as in many other places on the Peninsula, presented layers of perfect sea-shells (mostly escollop and oyster), the position of which is indicated in the sketch by the horizontal shaded lines near the figure. This dam was destroyed by Confederates while National troops were crossing the creek below, and the flood thus let loose drowned several soldiers.

re-occupied by Confederates, and a force moving on his front, and pressing forward with the war-cry of "Bull Run! Bull Run!" he retired beyond the crest of a ridge, not far from the dam, disputing the ground as he fell back, and there formed a line of battle and awaited Early's approach. When that force was within thirty paces of his line he ordered a general bayonet-charge. This was executed with the most determined spirit. The Confederates broke and fled with precipitation, with a loss of over five hundred men. Hancock held his position until Smith sent re-enforcements, by order of McClellan, who had arrived near the field of action, and soon afterward the contest ceased all along the line. So ended the BATTLE OF WILLIAMSBURG. That post was

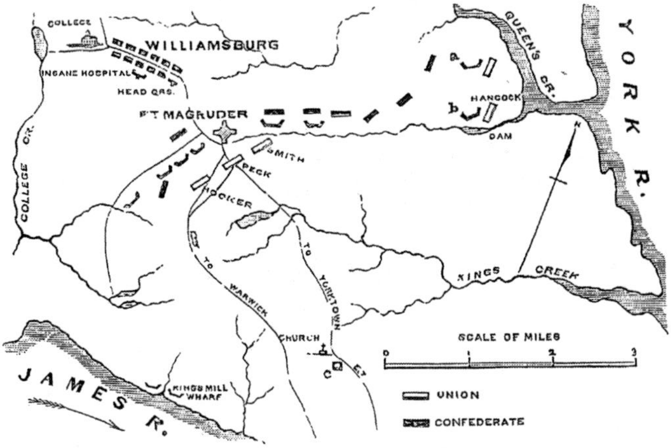

BATTLE OF WILLIAMSBURG.[1]

already won, for Hancock held the key of the position. McClellan reported the entire National loss in this battle at two thousand two hundred and twenty-eight, of whom four hundred and fifty-six were killed and fourteen hundred wounded.[2] That of the Confederates was, according to careful estimates, about one thousand.

This battle, in which so much of the precious blood of the young men of the country was shed,[3] appears to have been fought without any controlling mind in charge of the movement, or much previous knowledge of the locality and the Confederate works. The Commander-in-Chief was twelve

---

[1] In this plan, *a* and *b* indicate the two redoubts on the extreme left of the Confederates, taken by Hancock, and *c* the point to which Stoneman fell back to wait for re-enforcements.

[2] McClellan's report to the Secretary of War, August 4, 1863; reports of his division and brigade commanders engaged in the battle; reports of General Johnston and his subordinate officers, and oral and written statements to the author by actors in the struggle.

[3] No army in the world had ever exhibited an equal proportionate number of so many educated and highly respectable young men as this; and never did greater coolness or valor appear. Among the scores of young men who perished early in this campaign, and who were good examples of the best materials of that army, were Captain Henry Brooks O'Reilly, of the First Regiment, New York Excelsior Brigade, and Lieutenant William De Wolf, of Chicago, of the regular army, who had performed gallant service in the battles of Belmont and Fort Donelson. The former fell at the head of his company, while his regiment was maintaining the terrible contest in front of Fort Magruder, in the afternoon of the 5th of May. He had just given the words for an assault, "Boys, follow me! Forward, march!" when he fell, and soon expired. Lieutenant De Wolf was in charge of a battery of Gibson's Flying Artillery in the advance toward Williamsburg on the 4th, and in the encounter in which Stoneman and his followers were engaged with the Confederate cavalry on the day before the battle, and while valiantly doing his duty, he was severely wounded. Typhoid fever supervened, and he died a month later at Washington city. It would be a delightful task to record the names of all the brave who thus perished for their country, but we may only speak of one or two now and then as examples of true patriots and representatives of the Army of Liberty.

miles distant during most of the battle, and did not arrive near the field until near its close. A sudden change of commanders conducting the pursuit seems to have produced some confusion and misapprehension. When Kearney arrived on the field he ranked Hooker; and all day long there was uncertainty as to who was in command, each general appearing to fight as he considered best.[1] In consequence of this there was great confusion in the advance. The troops of different commands became mixed, and much delay ensued. So much was a head needed, and so tardy were re-enforcements, that while Hooker was heavily engaged, at noon, Governor Sprague and the Prince de Joinville rode in great haste to Yorktown, to urge McClellan to go immediately to the front. "I suppose those in front can attend to that little matter," was his short reply; but he was finally induced to mount his horse at two o'clock, and at five, when Kearney and Hancock were about giving the blow that won the victory, he approached the battle-field, ascertained that more than "a skirmish with the rebel rear-guard" was in progress, and gave some orders. The fighting soon afterward ceased, and he countermanded his order on leaving Yorktown for the divisions of Sedgwick and Richardson to advance, and directed them to accompany Franklin to West Point.

At ten o'clock that night, when Longstreet had commenced his flight from Williamsburg with such haste as to leave nearly eight hundred of his wounded men to become prisoners, and was following the more advanced of Johnston's army, in a rapid march toward the Chickahominy, McClellan telegraphed to the War Department, from "Bivouac in front of Williamsburg," that the Confederates were before him in force, probably greater than his own, and strongly intrenched. He assured the Secretary, however, that he should "run the risk of holding them in check there."[2] Experts on both sides (among them several of McClellan's Generals) declared their belief that, had the fugitives been promptly and vigorously pursued the next morning, the National army might easily have followed them right into Richmond;[3] but the Commanding General, in his report, made fifteen months afterward, declared that the mud was too adhesive to allow him to follow the retreating forces along the roads which the latter traveled with such celerity. They were safely encamped under the shelter of the fortifications around Richmond before he was ready to move forward from Williamsburg.

[a] May 6, 1862.

On the morning after the battle[a] the National troops took possession of Williamsburg, and General McClellan, from the house of Mr. Vest, Johnston's late head-quarters, telegraphed to the Secretary of War a brief account of the events of the previous day, and concluded with the prediction that was so terribly fulfilled—"We have other

---

1 Report of the Committee on the Conduct of the War, i. 20.

2 According to the Confederate official reports, the entire body of troops under Johnston, then below the Chickahominy, did not exceed 30,000 in number, while McClellan's "present and fit for duty" (within a distance of twelve miles of the battle-field) was about 100,000. The commanding General seems to have been singularly uninformed or misinformed concerning the country before him, during this campaign. He refused to receive information from the loyal negroes, preferring to take the testimony of Confederate prisoners. He officially declared that information concerning the forces and position of the enemy "was vague and untrustworthy," and when he commenced his march up the Peninsula, he did not know, he says, whether "so-called Mulberry Island was a real island," or which was "the true course of the Warwick River across the Peninsula," or that the Confederates had fortifications along that stream. See McClellan's Report, page 74.

3 See Report of the Committee on the Conduct of the War, i. 20.

battles to fight before reaching Richmond." At Williamsburg the pursuit really ended, and Johnston was permitted to place the Chickahominy and its malarious borders between himself and his tardy opponent.

The flank movement up the York was not commenced in time to perform its intended service as such. Franklin's long waiting division was not dispatched for that purpose until the day of the battle at Williamsburg, when it was debarked at Yorktown and re-embarked. It arrived at the head of York that night, and on the following morning[a] Newton's brigade landed and took position on a plain of a thousand acres of open land, on the right bank of the Pamunkey, one of the streams that form the York river.[1] Within twenty-fours hours afterward Franklin's whole division had encamped there, and gun-boats had quietly taken possession of West Point, between the two rivers, and the National flag was unfurled over that little village, from which every white person had fled. In the mean time General Dana had arrived with a part of Sedgwick's division, but remained on the transports. The divisions of Richardson and Porter soon followed.

a May 6, 1862.

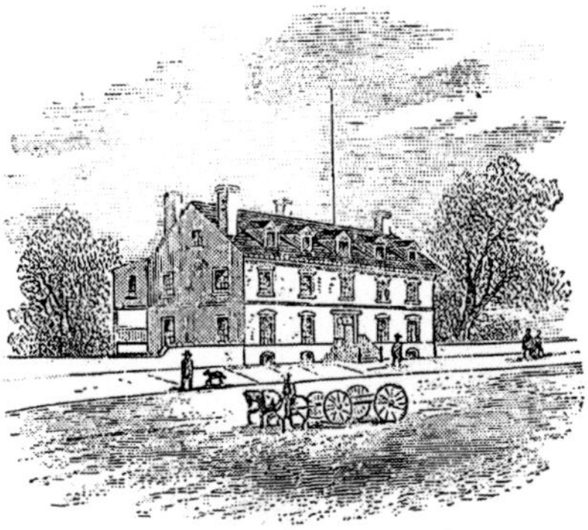

VEST'S HOUSE.[2]

No signs of Confederate troops appeared at first, but that night one of Franklin's vedettes was shot near the woods that bordered the edge of the plain. On the following morning a considerable force of Confederates was seen, when Dana landed, and the Sixteenth, Thirty-first, and Thirty-second New York, and the Ninety-fifth and Ninety-sixth Pennsylvania, were ordered to drive from the woods what was supposed to be a body of scouts lurking there in front of a few Confederate regiments. They pushed into the forest and were met by Whiting's division and other troops, forming the rear-guard of Johnston's retreating forces, when a spirited engagement began, chiefly by Hood's Texas brigade and Hampton's (South Carolina) Legion, on the part of the Confederates. The contest was continued for three or four hours, when the cannon on the gun-boats, and batteries that were speedily landed, drove the foe from their shelter in the woods, and kept them at bay. In this encounter the Nationals lost one hundred and ninety-four men, mostly of the Thirty-first and Thirty-Second New York. The loss of the Confederates was small. The National force now at the head of York was sufficient to hold it firmly, as a secure base of supplies for the Army of the Potomac.

As we have observed, McClellan's pursuit of Johnston nearly ended at Williamsburg, where his sick and wounded were placed in the buildings

---

[1] These are the Pamunkey and the Mattapony. Strictly speaking, these streams do not form the York River, for it is really a long estuary of Chesapeake Bay, and the two rivers are only its chief affluents.

[2] This was a large brick house, on the main street in Williamsburg, belonging to William M. Vest, and was used by the commanders of both armies. Its appearance in June, 1866, when the writer visited Williamsburg, is given in the above sketch.

of the venerable William and Mary College, and in portions of the Asylum for the Insane. While these were thus provided for, the men fit for duty were allowed to rest more than two days, until the main body of the army moving up from the direction of Yorktown should arrive. Then, on the 8th,[a] General Stoneman was sent forward with the advance to open a communication with Franklin, at the head of York, followed by Smith's division, on the most direct road to Richmond, by way of New Kent Court-House. The roads were left in a wretched condition by the fugitive Confederate Army, and the General-in-Chief, with the advance portion of his force, did not reach the vicinity of the White House,[1] at the head of the navigation of the Pamunkey, and about eighteen miles from Richmond, until the 16th. He arrived at Tunstall's Station, on the Richmond and York River railway, on the 18th, and on the 22d he made his head-quarters at Cool Arbor,[2] not far from the Chickahominy, and between eight and nine miles from Richmond. His advanced light troops had reached Bottom's bridge, on the Chickahominy, at the crossing of the New Kent road, two days before. The Confederates had destroyed the bridge, but left the point uncovered. Casey's division of Keyes's corps was thrown across,[b] and occupied the heights on the Richmond side of the stream, supported by Heintzelman.

[a] May, 1862.

[b] May 20.

THE MODERN "WHITE HOUSE."

[1] The "White House," as it was called, was the property of Mary Custis Lee, a great-granddaughter of Mrs. Washington, daughter of George W. P. Custis, the adopted son of Washington, and wife of the Confederate Commander, Robert E. Lee. It stood on or near the site of the dwelling known as "The White House," in which the widow Custis lived, and where the nuptial ceremonies of her marriage with Colonel George Washington were performed. That ancient house, then so honored, had been destroyed about thirty years before, and the one standing there in 1862 was only a modern structure bearing the ancient title. It was occupied, when the war broke out, by a son of Robert E. Lee. The wife and some of the family of Lee, who were there, fled from it on the approach of the National army, at the time we are considering. The first officer who entered the house found, on a piece of paper attached to the wall of the main passage, the following note:—

"Northern soldiers, who profess to revere Washington, forbear to desecrate the home of his first married life—the property of his wife—now owned by her descendant.

(Signed) "A GRANDDAUGHTER OF MRS. WASHINGTON."

See *The Siege of Richmond*, by Joel Cook, page 169.

This misrepresentation, made to save from injury property that was not in existence until more than thirty years after Washington's death, had the effect, for a while, to have it guarded, by order of the Commanding General, with as much care as if it had been the Tomb of the Father of his Country. Members of the Second regiment of cavalry, of which Robert E. Lee was Lieutenant-colonel when he abandoned his flag, were detailed to guard the house; and so sacred was it held to be, that the suffering sick soldiers, who greatly needed the shelter of its roof, were not allowed even to rest upon the dry ground around it. The false story of its history was soon exposed, and it was left to the fate that overtook the property of other rebellious Virginians.

[2] Cool Arbor derived its name from a tavern, at a delightful place of summer resort in the woods for the Richmond people, even so early as the time of the Revolution. The derivation of the name determines its orthography. It has been erroneously spelled Coal Harbor and Cold Harbor. The picture on the next page is a view of the house known as New Cool Arbor, not far from the site of the old one. It was yet standing when the writer visited the spot in June, 1866. It was on a level plain, and near it was a National cemetery into which the remains of the slain Union soldiers buried in the surrounding fields were then being collected and reinterred.

In the mean time a most important movement had been made in McClellan's rear by the Confederates at Norfolk, and by General Wool at Fortress Monroe. Wool, who saw the eminent advantage of the James River as a highway for the supplies of an army on the Peninsula, had, ever since McClellan decided to take that route to Richmond, urged the Government to allow him to attempt the capture of Norfolk, and thus make the breaking up of the blockade of the James an easy matter. But it was not until after the evacuation of Yorktown, when President Lincoln and Secretaries Chase and Stanton visited Fortress Monroe, that his suggestions were favorably considered. He then renewed his recommendations; and when, on the 8th,[a] he received positive information that Huger (who, with Burnside in his rear and McClellan on his flank, saw that his position was untenable) was preparing to evacuate that post, orders were given for an immediate attempt to seize Sewell's Point, and march on Norfolk. Arrangements were made with Commodore Goldsborough to co-operate; and a large number of troops were embarked on transports then lying in Hampton Roads. Goldsborough attacked the Confederate batteries on the point, which replied with spirit. The *Merrimack* came out to assist them, when the National vessels withdrew, and the troops were disembarked. The enterprise was abandoned for the time; but information that reached head-quarters a few hours later revived it.

[a] May, 1862.

M'CLELLAN'S HEAD-QUARTERS AT COOL ARBOR.

On the following day General Wool, with Colonel T. J. Cram (his Inspector-general, and an accomplished topographical engineer) and Secretary Chase, made a reconnoissance toward Willoughby's Point, and along the coast toward the sea, when it was decided to land five thousand troops at a summer watering-place called Ocean View, by which the works on Sewell's Point could be taken in reverse, and a direct route to Norfolk be opened. The troops were again embarked, and a bombardment was opened on Sewell's Point from Fort Wool, in the Rip Raps,[1] to deceive the Confederates with the appearance of a design to renew the attempt to land there.

At a little past midnight, the troops, artillery, infantry, and cavalry,[2] under the immediate command of Brigadier-general Max Weber, were in readiness for debarkation at Ocean View, and early in the morn-

---

[1] An unfinished fortification that commanded the entrance to Hampton Roads, in front of Fortress Monroe. It was at first called Fort Calhoun. Its name was changed to Wool, in honor of the veteran General.

[2] The troops composing the expedition consisted of the Tenth, Twentieth, and Ninety-ninth New York; Sixteenth Massachusetts; First Delaware; Fifty-eighth Pennsylvania; one hundred mounted riflemen; Follet's battery of light artillery, and Howard's battery.

ing[a] a landing was effected unopposed, under the direction of Colonel Cram. The water was so shallow that the troops were compelled to pass ashore on platforms laid on old canal barges. The entire movement was successful; and at eight o'clock in the morning General Wool, accompanied by the President and the two Secretaries, and Generals Mansfield and Viele, took command in person. The infantry were immediately pushed forward to secure the bridge over Tanner's Creek.[1] They found it on fire, and received shot from cannon on the opposite side of the stream. Supposing this to indicate intended opposition, the artillery was hurried forward, but on its arrival the foe had disappeared. The troops pushed forward, and at five o'clock in the afternoon reached the lines of the strongly intrenched camp of the Confederates, where they found twenty-

[a] May 10, 1862.

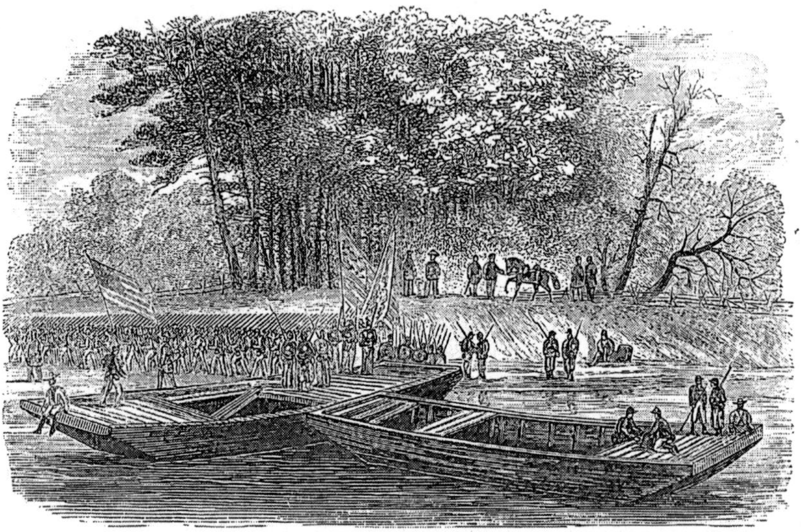

WOOL'S LANDING-PLACE AT OCEAN VIEW.

nine mounted cannon, but no troops. Onward they marched, and just before reaching the city they were met by a flag of truce, heralding the approach of the Mayor with a proposition to surrender the town. Huger had been instructed not to attempt to hold the city against any demonstration of National troops; and when he was informed that Wool had landed at Ocean View, he turned over Norfolk to the keeping of Mayor Lamb, and with his troops fled towards Richmond. Norfolk was formally surrendered to General Wool; and from the City Hall he issued an order announcing the fact, appointing General Viele Military Governor, and directing that all the rights and privileges of peaceable citizens should be carefully protected. The venerable commander then rode back to Ocean View (thus making a journey on horseback that day of thirty-five miles), and reached Fortress Monroe at near midnight with the pleasing intelligence of his success, for the anxious President and Secretary of War. On the following morning he

[1] By reference to the map on page 399, volume I., the reader will have an idea of the direction of the movement. Ocean View was on Willoughby's beach, about at the edge of the map, and the outward road was the one followed by the troops.

received publicly expressed thanks for his achievement.[1] At dawn the same morning a bright light was seen in the direction of Norfolk, and then an explosion was heard. The fleeing Confederates had set the *Merrimack*, other vessels, and the Navy Yard on fire, and by a slow match communicating with her magazine, the monster ram was blown into fragments.[2] Sewell's Point and Craney Island, both strongly fortified, were abandoned.[3] The Confederate gun-boats in the James River fled toward Richmond, and the navigation of that stream was opened to the National vessels.[4] The Confederates destroyed all they could by fire before they departed, but left about two hundred cannon in fair condition, to become spoils of victory. Two unfinished armored vessels were among those destroyed.

While the stirring events we have just considered were occurring in Southeastern Virginia, important military movements were seen in the Shenandoah Valley and the adjacent region on both sides of the Blue Ridge. There were three distinct Union armies in that region, acting independently of, but in co-operation with, the Army of the Potomac. One was in the Mountain Department, under Fremont; another in the Department of the Shenandoah, under Banks; and a third in the newly created Department of the Rappahannock, under McDowell. At about the time of the siege of Yorktown, early in April, General Fremont was at Franklin, in Pendleton County, over the mountains west of Harrisonburg, with fifteen thousand men; General Banks was at Strasburg, in the Valley, with about sixteen thousand; and General McDowell was at Fredericksburg, on the Rappahannock, with thirty thousand.

When the appearance of McClellan on the Peninsula drew Johnston's main body from the Rapid Anna to the defense of Richmond, Washington was relieved, and McDowell's corps was ordered forward to co-operate with the Army of the Potomac; and for this purpose Shields's division was detached from Banks's command and given to McDowell, making the force of the latter about forty-one thousand men and one hundred guns. Such was the disposition of the National forces in Virginia at the close of April, when "Stonewall Jackson," who, as we have observed, was driven up the Shenandoah Valley after his defeat by Shields at Kernstown, again commenced offensive operations.

Jackson remained a few days at Mount Jackson, after his flight from Winchester, and then took a position between the South Fork of the Shenan-

---

[1] "The skillful and gallant movements of Major-general John E. Wool, and the forces under his command," said Secretary Stanton, in an order issued by direction of the President, on the 11th, "which resulted in the surrender of Norfolk, and the evacuation of strong batteries erected by the rebels on Sewell's Point and Craney Island, and the destruction of the rebel iron-clad steamer *Merrimack*, are regarded by the President as among the most important successes of the present war; he therefore orders that his thanks, as Commander-in-Chief of the Army and Navy, be communicated by the War Department to Major-general John E. Wool, and the officers and soldiers of his command, for their gallantry and good conduct in the brilliant operations mentioned."

[2] The *Merrimack*, then in command of Commodore Tatnall, was at Craney Island, for the two-fold purpose of protecting Norfolk and guarding the mouth of the James River. The land troops had fled without informing Tatnall of the movement, and the unfortunate old man, seeing the Navy Yard in flames. and all the works abandoned, could do nothing better than to destroy his ship and fly, for with his best efforts he could not get her into the James River.

[3] Craney Island was much more strongly fortified now for the defense of Norfolk than it was in 1813. See *Lossing's Pictorial Field-Book of the War of* 1812. Captain Case, of the Navy, was the first man to land on the abandoned Island, and to pull down the ensign of rebellion and place the National flag there.

[4] Reports of Colonel T. J. Cram and Flag-officer Goldsborough; Narrative of Henry J. Raymond; Letter of General Wool to the author, May 23, 1862.

doah and Swift Run Gap, eastward of Harrisonburg, in Rockingham County. There he was joined[a] by the division of General R. S. Ewell, from Gordonsville, and also two brigades under Edward S. Johnson, who had an independent command in Southwestern Virginia. Jackson's entire force was now about fifteen thousand men, while General Banks was lying at Harrisonburg, not far away, his force reduced to about five thousand men by the withdrawal of Shields's division.

[a] April 30, 1862.

Jackson was watching Banks closely, with orders to hold him, while General Lee, with a strong column, should push beyond the Rappahannock to cut off the communication between Winchester and Alexandria,[1] when he was startled by the information that one of Fremont's brigades, under General Milroy, was approaching from the direction of Monterey, either to join Banks or to fall upon Staunton. He perceived that such a junction, or the occupation of Staunton, might give to the Nationals the possession of the Shenandoah Valley, and he took immediate measures to prevent the catastrophe. Leaving Ewell to watch Banks, he moved rapidly upon Staunton, and from that point sent Johnson, with five brigades, to attack Milroy. The latter, greatly outnumbered, fell back to the Bull Pasture Mountains and took post at McDowell, thirty-six miles west of Staunton, whither Schenck hastened with a part of his brigade to assist him. Jackson had also hurried from Staunton to assist Johnson, and on the 8th he appeared with a large force on a ridge overlooking the National camp, and commenced planting a battery there. Milroy led a force to dislodge him,[2] and for about five hours a battle, varying in intensity, was fought with great gallantry on both sides. Darkness put an end to the conflict. Schenck (who ranked Milroy) saw that the position of the Nationals was untenable, and by his direction the whole force retreated during the night to Franklin, having lost two hundred and fifty-six men, of whom one hundred and forty-five were only slightly wounded. Jackson reported a loss of four hundred and sixty-one, of whom three hundred and ninety were wounded. Among the latter was General Johnson. It was a fairly drawn fight, and yet Jackson, whose troops largely outnumbered the Nationals, and had every advantage of position, sent a trumpet-toned note to Ewell the next morning, saying, "Yesterday God gave us the victory at McDowell."

Jackson pursued the Nationals to Franklin, where he heard from Ewell that Banks was evidently preparing to fly from Harrisonburg. So he hastened back to McDowell, recrossed the Shenandoah mountains to Lebanon Sulphur Springs, rested a little, and then pressed forward to fall upon Banks. The latter had fled to Strasburg pursued by Ewell, and Jackson pushed on, joining the latter at New Market. Then he led the united forces into the Luray Valley, between the Massanutten Mountain and the Blue Ridge, and hastened toward Front Royal, to cut off Banks's retreat in that direction,

[1] On the 5th of May Lee wrote to Ewell that he had ordered North Carolina troops to report to him at Gordonsville, and said: "I desire that those troops shall not be drawn to Swift Run Gap unless your necessities require it, the object being to form a strong column for the purpose of moving beyond the Rappahannock, to cut off the enemy's communication between Winchester and Alexandria."—Autograph letter of Robert E. Lee. This was precisely such a movement as the Government anticipated, and which might have resulted in the capture of Washington, had not the corps of McDowell been left for its defense.

[2] These consisted of the Twenty-fifth, Thirty-second, Seventy-fifth, and Eighty-second Ohio and Third Virginia, with a 6-pounder of the Twelfth Ohio battery, under Lieutenant Bowen.

if he should attempt to join McDowell by way of the Manassas Gap railroad.

Ashby's cavalry so perfectly masked this movement that Banks was not aware of it, and almost without a warning Ewell fell[a] with crushing force on the little garrison of Front Royal, of about a thousand men, under Colonel Kenly.[1] That gallant Marylander[2] made a spirited resistance against the overwhelming force, ten times his own in

[a] May 23, 1862.

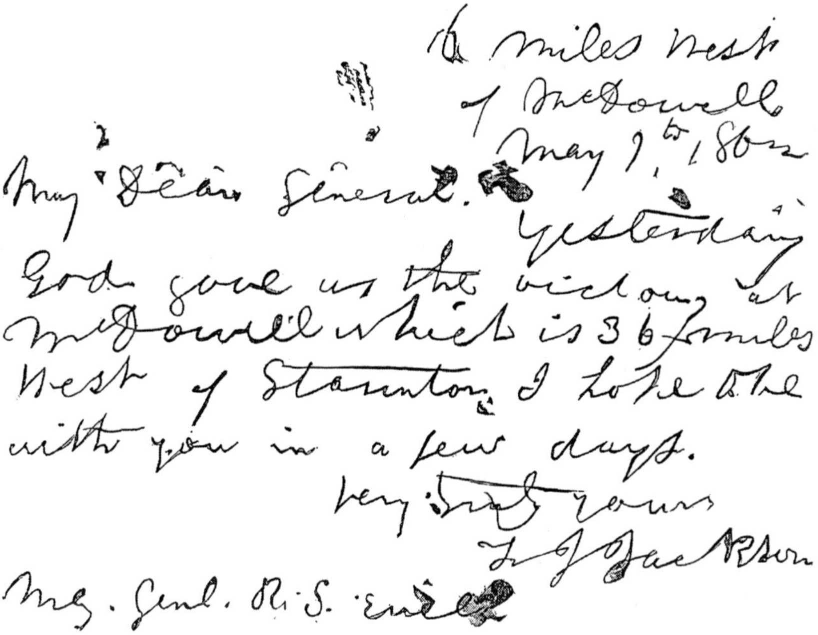
6 miles west of McDowell May 9th 1862

My Dear General.

Yesterday God gave us the victory at McDowell which is 36 miles west of Staunton. I hope to be with you in a few days.

Very truly yours
T. J. Jackson

Maj. Genl. R. S. Ewell

FAC-SIMILE OF JACKSON'S NOTE TO EWELL.[3]

number, but he was driven from the town. He made a stand on a ridge a mile distant, from which he was soon pushed across the river. He attempted to burn the bridge behind nim over the Shenandoah, but failed. His pursuers put out the flames, and he was soon overtaken by the cavalry of Ashby and Flournoy, when he again gave battle. In that encounter he was severely

---

[1] These were composed of two companies each of the Twenty-seventh Pennsylvania and Fifth New York cavalry, one company of Captain Mapes's Pioneers, and a section of Knapp's battery. Kenly was charged with the protection of the road and bridges between Front Royal and Strasburg. One company each of the Second Massachusetts, Third Wisconsin, and Twenty-seventh Indiana were posted along that road.

When the writer was at Nashville, early in May, 1866, he was permitted by General Ewell, then residing there, to peruse and make extracts from the manuscript records of his brigade, kept by his young adjutant. In it was the statement, that when Ewell's force was near Front Royal, a young woman was seen running toward them. She had "made a circuit to avoid the Yankees," and she sent word to General Jackson, by officers who went to meet her, "to push on—only one regiment in the town, and that might be completely surprised; if we pressed on we might get the whole." This "young lady" was the afterward notorious rebel spy, Belle Boyd, "who was to my eye," recorded the adjutant, "pleasant and lady-like in appearance, and certainly had neither 'freckled face, red hair and large mouth,' as the *New York Herald* said she had. She seemed embarrassed by the novelty of her position, and very anxious that we should push on."

[2] See page 553, volume I.

[3] This is an exact fac-simile of Jackson's entire note to Ewell, with all its blots, carefully copied from the original, kindly placed in the hands of the author by the late Frank Henry

wounded, and himself and seven hundred of his men, with a section of rifled 10-pounders and his entire supply-train, fell into the hands of the victors.[1]

Banks was at Strasburg, about fifteen miles distant, unsuspicious of great danger being so near, when, at evening, he was startled by intelligence of Kenly's disaster, and the more astounding news that Jackson, at the head of about twenty thousand men,[2] was rapidly making his way toward Winchester. It was Jackson's intention to cut Banks off from re-enforcements and capture or disperse his troops. Banks had perceived his danger too soon, and with his usual energy and skill he resumed his flight down the valley at nine o'clock the next morning,[a] his train in front, escorted by cavalry and infantry, and with a rear-guard or covering force of cavalry and six pieces of artillery, under the command of General John P. Hatch. The vanguard was led by Colonel Dudley Donnelly, and the center by Colonel George H. Gordon.

[a] May 24, 1862.

Just as the column had passed Cedar Creek, three miles from Strasburg, word came that the train had been attacked at Middletown, two miles farther on. The news was instantly followed by a host of frightened fugitives, refugees, and wagons, "which," says Banks, "came tumbling to the rear in wretched confusion." The column was instantly reorganized, with the train in the rear,[3] and Colonel Donnelly, pushing on to Middletown, encountered a small Confederate force there, which was easily driven back on the Front Royal road by Knipe's Forty-sixth Pennsylvania, supported by Cochran's New York Battery and the Twenty-eighth New York, Lieutenant-Colonel W. H. Brown. Broadhead's First Michigan cavalry now took the lead, and soon reported the road clear to Winchester, thirteen miles below Middletown; but before Banks's main body had all passed the latter village, the Confederates occupied it in large numbers. The rear-guard were compelled to fall back to Strasburg. Making a circuit to the Northward, Tompkins's First Vermont cavalry rejoined Banks at Winchester the next morning, and De Forest's Fifth New York cavalry made its way among the mountains of the Potomac with a train of thirty-two wagons and many stragglers, and joined Banks at Clear Spring. The main column meanwhile had moved on and encountered a Confederate force near Newton, eight miles from Winchester, which was repulsed by the Second Massachusetts, Twenty-eighth New York, and Twenty-seventh Indiana; and by midnight[b] the extraordinary race for Winchester was won by Banks, who had made a masterly retreat with very little loss, and had concentrated his infantry and artillery there. Broadhead's cavalry first entered the city.

[b] May 24.

---

[1] On the same day the Thirty-sixth and Forty-fourth Ohio, under Colonel George Crook, stationed at Lewisburg, in West Virginia, were furiously attacked by General Heth, with three Virginia regiments of Confederates. The assailants were soon repulsed, with a loss of arms, 400 prisoners, and about 100 killed and wounded besides. Colonel Crook, who was wounded in the foot, lost 11 killed and 51 wounded. Heth arrested pursuit by burning the bridge over the Greenbrier River.

[2] His force consisted of Ashby's cavalry, the brigades of Winder, Campbell, and Fulkerston, the command of General E. S. Johnson, and the division of General Ewell, composed of the brigades of Generals Elzy, Taylor, and Trimble, the Maryland line, consisting of the First Maryland and Brockenborough's battery, under General George H. Stewart, and the Second and Sixth Virginia cavalry, under Colonel Flournoy.

[3] In view of a possible necessity for a return to Strasburg, Banks sent Captain Abert, of the Topographical Engineers, to prepare the Cedar Creek bridge for the flames. Abert and the accompanying troops (Zouaves d'Afrique, Captain Collins) were cut off from the column, had a severe skirmish at Strasburg, and did not rejoin the army until it was at Williamsport, on the Potomac.

The retreating troops found very little time for rest. The Confederates, composed entirely of Ewell's corps, were closing around them in vast numbers compared to their own. Banks's force was less than seven thousand effective men, with ten Parrott guns and a battery of 6-pounders, smooth-bore cannon. The Confederate force was full twenty thousand in number. The leaders of the latter felt confident that on the morrow they would see the capture or destruction of their opponents. Yet they did not idly revel in these pleasing anticipations. Like a vigilant soldier, as he was, Ewell, who bivouacked within a mile and a half of Winchester, began operations to that end before the dawn. The equally vigilant Banks was on the alert, and at daylight his troops were in battle order. Colonel Gordon, commanding the right, was strongly posted on a ridge, a little south of the city, and Colonel Donnelly was in charge of the left. Near the center, the troops were well sheltered from their foes by stone walls. General Hatch (who was cut off at Middletown), with Tompkins's cavalry, had rejoined the army just in time to participate in the battle.

RICHARD S. EWELL.

The battle opened furiously in front of Winchester.[a] Ewell had placed a heavy body of troops on the Berryville road, to prevent re-enforcements reaching Banks from Harper's Ferry, and regiments were heavily massed on the National right, with the evident intention of turning it. This danger was so boldly and bravely met, that the Confederates were kept in check for five hours by a steady and most destructive fire.[1]

a May 25, 1862.

In the mean time Jackson's whole force had been ordered up,[2] and Banks's signal officers reported the apparition of regimental standards in sight that indicated a strength equal to twenty-five thousand men. The Union commander perceived that further resistance would be only a prelude to destruction. In anticipation of this contingency, his trains had been sent toward the Potomac, and now an order for retreat was given. Under a most galling fire of musketry the army broke into a column of march, and, covered by a rear-guard composed of the Second Massachusetts and Third Wisconsin, passed rapidly through Winchester, assailed in the streets by the secession-

[1] "One regiment," says Banks in his report, "is represented, by persons present during the action, and after the field was evacuated, as nearly destroyed."

[2] The battle thus far had been fought by Ewell without the aid of Jackson, and even without his knowledge of what was occurring in front of Winchester, for he was seven miles in the rear. So ignorant was he of the situation of affairs at the front, that at the moment when Banks was about to retreat, Colonel Crutchfield came to Ewell with orders from Jackson to fall back to Newton, seven miles distant, for the Nationals were being heavily re-enforced. Jackson supposed Ewell to be four or five miles from Winchester, when, as we have observed, he had encamped within a mile and a half of the city the evening before. It is evident from the manuscript daily record of Ewell's brigade, consulted by the writer, that to Ewell, and not to Jackson, is due the credit of driving Banks from Winchester.

ists of both sexes.[1] On leaving the city in some confusion (but finally in good order), it moved rapidly on toward Martinsburg, twenty-two miles distant, in three columns, and reached that point late in the afternoon. There the wearied and battle-worn soldiers rested less than two hours, and then, pressing on twelve miles farther, reached the Potomac, opposite Williamsport, in the course of the evening,[2] where soon afterward a thousand camp-fires were blazing on the hill-sides. Jackson had halted his infantry a short distance from Winchester, but George H. Stewart had followed the fugitives with cavalry to Martinsburg, where the pursuit was abandoned. Three days later a Confederate brigade of infantry drove a small Union force out of Charlestown.

Within the space of forty-eight hours after hearing of Kenly's disaster at Front Royal, Banks, with his little army, had marched fifty-three miles, with an overwhelming force on his flank and immediate rear a part of the way, and fought several skirmishes and a severe battle. Jackson attributed his failure to crush Banks to the misconduct of Ashby and his cavalry, who, stopping to pillage the abandoned wagons of Banks's train between Middletown and Newton, did not come up in time to pursue the fugitives after the battle at Winchester.[3]

After menacing Harper's Ferry, where General Rufus Saxton was in command, Jackson began[a] as hasty a retreat up the Valley as Banks had made down it, for he was threatened with immediate peril. General Shields, as we have observed, had been ordered to join McDowell in a movement toward Richmond, to co-operate with McClellan. He reached McDowell's camp with eleven thousand men on the day of the battle of Winchester.[b] On the following day the President and Secretary of War arrived there, when McDowell, whose army was then forty-one thousand strong, was ordered to move toward Richmond on the 26th. That order was countermanded a few hours later, for, on their return to Washington, the President and his War Minister were met by startling tidings from the Shenandoah Valley. The safety of the National capital seemed to be in great peril, and McDowell was ordered to push twenty thousand men into the Valley by way of the Manassas Gap Railroad, to intercept Jackson if he should retreat. At the same time Fremont was ordered by telegraph to hasten with his army over the Shenandoah Mountain to Harrisonburg for the same purpose, and with the hope that he and the troops from McDowell might join at Strasburg in time to head

[a] May 30, 1862.

[b] May 23.

HAND GRENADE.

[1] "My retreating column," said Banks, "suffered serious loss in the streets of Winchester. Males and females vied with each other in increasing the number of their victims, by firing from the houses, throwing hand-grenades, hot water, and missiles of every description."—Report to the Secretary of War, June, 1862.

Hand-grenades are usually small sheils, about two inches and a half in diameter, and are set on fire by a short fuse. They are sometimes made of other forms, with a percussion apparatus, as seen in the annexed illustration. This kind is used more on the water, and has a stem with guiding feathers, made of paper or parchment.

[2] Banks's loss during this masterly retreat, exclusive of Kenly's command, and the sick and wounded left in hospitals at Strasburg and Winchester, was 88 killed, 155 wounded, and 711 missing, making a total of 904. Only 55 of his 500 wagons were lost, and not a gun was left behind. A large amount of commissary and quarter-master's stores were destroyed. Jackson's reported loss, including that at Front Royal, was 68 killed and 329 wounded. He also reported that he captured 2 guns, 9,354 small arms, and about 3,050 prisoners, including 750 sick and wounded. The actual number of prisoners was a little less than 3,000.

[3] Jackson's Report to the Confederate "Secretary of War." "Never," he said, "have I seen an opportunity for cavalry to reap a richer harvest of the fruits of victory."

off Jackson. McDowell obeyed, but with a heavy heart, for, he said, "it is a crushing blow to us all."

Fremont's army made as rapid a march as possible over the mountain region, through drenching rains, and with five days' rations of hard bread. He took a more northerly road to the Valley than the one from Franklin to Harrisonburg, and reached Strasburg on the evening of the 1st of June, a little too late to intercept Jackson, for the latter had passed through that town a few hours before. Next morning Shields's vanguard of cavalry, under General Bayard, reached Strasburg, too late likewise for the intended service of interception. And now began a race up the Valley as exciting as the one down it ten days before. Shields marched vigorously up the South fork of the Shenandoah, between the Massanutten Mountains and the Blue Ridge, along the lateral Luray Valley, hoping to head his foe at some point above, while Fremont followed directly in his rear, up the North fork, along the great pike to Harrisonburg. The rains had swelled many of the little mountain tributaries of the Shenandoah into torrents too formidable to ford with safety, and Jackson destroyed all the bridges behind him, and sent cavalry through the Massanutten passes to break down or burn those in front of Shields. Thus he kept his prisoners at least a day in his rear, reaching Harrisonburg on the 5th of June.

Jackson now perceived that his only chance for escape was to cross the swollen Shenandoah at Port Republic, where there was a strong bridge; so, after a brief rest, he diverged to the southeast from the pike to Staunton, for that purpose. Another object in view was to prevent Shields, who was near at hand on the east side of the river, crossing the stream or forming a junction with Fremont, when the united forces would equal his own in numbers.

Jackson's rear was well covered with his cavalry (Second and Sixth Virginia), under General Turner Ashby. About two miles from Harrisonburg this rear-guard was attacked by a reconnoitering party of cavalry, under Colonel Percy Wyndham. A smart skirmish ensued, and at first the Nationals were repulsed, with the loss of that leader and sixty-three of his men, who were made prisoners.[1] General Bayard and Colonel Cluseret then pushed forward with cavalry and infantry, when Ashby, hard pressed, called for an infantry support. General Stewart's brigade was ordered up, and was soon engaged in a sharp fight, in which the little band of Kane's Pennsylvanians (Bucktail Rifles) performed uncommon deeds of valor. Kane was wounded and made prisoner, and lost fifty-five of his men. Ashby was killed. His death was a severe blow for the Confederates. They regarded his loss as equal to that of a regiment, for he was one of the most fearless and enterprising of their cavalry commanders.[2]

Fremont was so close upon the Confederates, that the latter were obliged to turn and fight before attempting the passage of the Shenandoah at Port Republic. Jackson left Ewell with three brigades (Elzy's, Trimble's, and

---

[1] The record of Ewell's Adjutant, mentioned in note 1, page 391, was kept in a blank book captured at this time, in which Colonel Wyndham had begun to enter copies of his military orders.

[2] A few minutes before his death, Ashby was riding a horse that belonged to Lieutenant Willis, his own very fine black English stallion being in the rear. Willis's horse was the same that was wounded under General Jackson at the battle of Bull's Run. He was now killed, and Ashby was on foot, just in front of the line of the Fifty-eighth Virginia, when he was shot through the body. He advanced a few paces and fell.

Stewart's) of the rear division of his army at Union Church, about seven miles from Harrisonburg, to keep back the Nationals and gain time, while he should throw forward his own division to cover the bridge at Port Republic, five miles farther on, and prevent Shields from crossing it.

A. ELZY.

Ewell strongly posted his force, about five thousand strong, on a ridge that crossed the road near the church, with his flanks well protected by woods. This excellent position was chosen by General Elzy. Trimble was a little in advance of the center; Stewart was on the right, and Elzy on the left. In that position he was attacked on Sunday morning, the 7th,[a] by Fremont, who had moved out of Harrisonburg at six o'clock, and at nine was ready for battle. Schenck was on the right,[1] Milroy in the center,[2] and General Stahl on the left,[3] forming a line about a mile and a half in length. Between Milroy's right and Schenck's left were the Sixtieth Ohio, Eighth Virginia, and the Garibaldi Guards of Blenker's division, commanded by Colonel Cluseret. Stahl's wing was supported by Bohlen's brigade, and the remainder of Blenker's division was held as a reserve. The Nationals moved steadily to the attack, down through a little valley and up a slope, in the face of a storm of shot and shell. At eleven o'clock the conflict was general and severe. It was specially so at the center, and continued several hours, Milroy and Schenck all the while gaining ground; the former with heavy loss. The brunt of the battle fell upon him and Stahl, and upon Trimble on the part of the Confederates. Stahl's troops finally gave way, and an order was given at about four o'clock for the whole line to fall back, at the moment when Milroy had penetrated Ewell's center, and was almost up to his guns. That daring soldier obeyed, but with the greatest reluctance, for he felt sure

[a] June, 1862.

UNION CHURCH AT CROSS KEYS.[4]

[1] With the Thirty-second, Fifty-fifth, Seventy-third, Seventy-fifth, and Eighty-second Ohio.

[2] With the Second, Third, and Fifth Virginia and Twenty-fifth Ohio.

[3] With the Eighth, Forty-first, and Forty-fifth New York and Twenty-seventh Pennsylvania, with the remnant of the brave Bucktails who survived the battle on the previous day.

[4] This little picture shows the appearance of the church when the writer sketched it, in October, 1866. It was built of brick, and stood in a grove of oaks, a short distance from the Port Republic road from Harrisonburg. Its interior was a ruin, and its walls showed many scars of heavy shot and shell. In front of it was a cemetery, in a substantial inclosure. Fremont used the church for a hospital.

of victory. The Confederates occupied the battle-field that night, and the Nationals rested where their first line was formed in the morning.[1] So ended the BATTLE OF CROSS KEYS.[2]

Ewell, whose position was an excellent one, intended to renew the battle with his repulsed enemy at dawn, but was called to aid Jackson in his operations at Port Republic. His troops slept on their arms, and just as day was breaking they silently moved toward the Shenandoah, carrying with them all of their wounded comrades excepting those who were mortally hurt. Fremont followed them closely[a] in battle order, with Milroy on the right, Blenker on the left, and Schenck in the center. The brigades of Stahl and Bayard formed the reserve.

[a] June 9, 1862.

In the mean time there had been stirring events at Port Republic. Jackson had crossed the Shenandoah, and was occupying the town when Fremont and Ewell were fighting at Cross Keys. The vanguard of Shields's force, under acting Brigadier-general Carroll, had been pressing up the eastern side of the Shenandoah from Conrad's Store, and a portion of it had arrived near Port Republic almost simultaneously with Jackson's advance. On Saturday, the 7th, Carroll had been ordered to hasten to that point, destroy the bridge, seize Jackson's train, and fall on his flank. With less than a thousand infantry, one hundred and fifty cavalry, and a battery of six guns, he went forward and halted that night within six miles of Port Republic. He was informed that Jackson's train was parked there, with a large drove of beef cattle. With the cavalry and five pieces of artillery he dashed into the town,[b] for the purpose of capturing the coveted prize; drove Jackson's cavalry-guard out, and took possession of the bridge. Had he burned that structure instantly he might have ruined Jackson, for he would have cut him off from Ewell, who was fighting Fremont a few miles distant. But he waited for his infantry to come up, and during that interval he was attacked by a superior force and driven out to a point two miles from the town, where in the afternoon he was joined by General E. B. Tyler and his brigade, two thousand strong, who had hastened to his assistance, and now took command.[3]

[b] June 8.

While awaiting orders from Shields, Tyler was informed that the Confederates were on his front in large force, endeavoring to outflank him on his left, and with all the approaches to the town and bridge covered by artillery. Ewell had escaped the pursuit of Fremont, and had crossed the bridge, and so strongly re-enforced Jackson that the latter justly felt almost invincible. Tyler quickly counteracted the flanking movement by employing nearly his whole force, which did not exceed three thousand men, in opposing it. With these, after being pushed back a little by the assailants, he drove into the woods about eight thousand Confederates, some

---

[1] The National loss in this battle was 664, of which two-thirds fell on Stahl's brigade. The losses were distributed as follows: Stahl's brigade, 427; Milroy's, 118; Bohlen's, 80; Cluseret's, 17; Schenck's, 14; Bucktail's, 8. Schenck's brigade inflicted a severe loss on the foe, chiefly by his artillery, while his own force suffered less than the others. One of the companies of the Bucktail Rifles lost all of its officers, commissioned and non-commissioned. Captain Nicholas Dunka, of Fremont's Staff, was killed.

[2] On the battle-ground was once a tavern, whose sign-board had the device of two keys crossed. Near it was a store and two or three dwellings, and a fourth of a mile distant the Union Church. This little settlement was known as the Cross Keys.

[3] The map on the opposite page shows the theater of events we have just been considering in this chapter, and of some a little later. It may be consulted with profit by the reader of succeeding chapters.

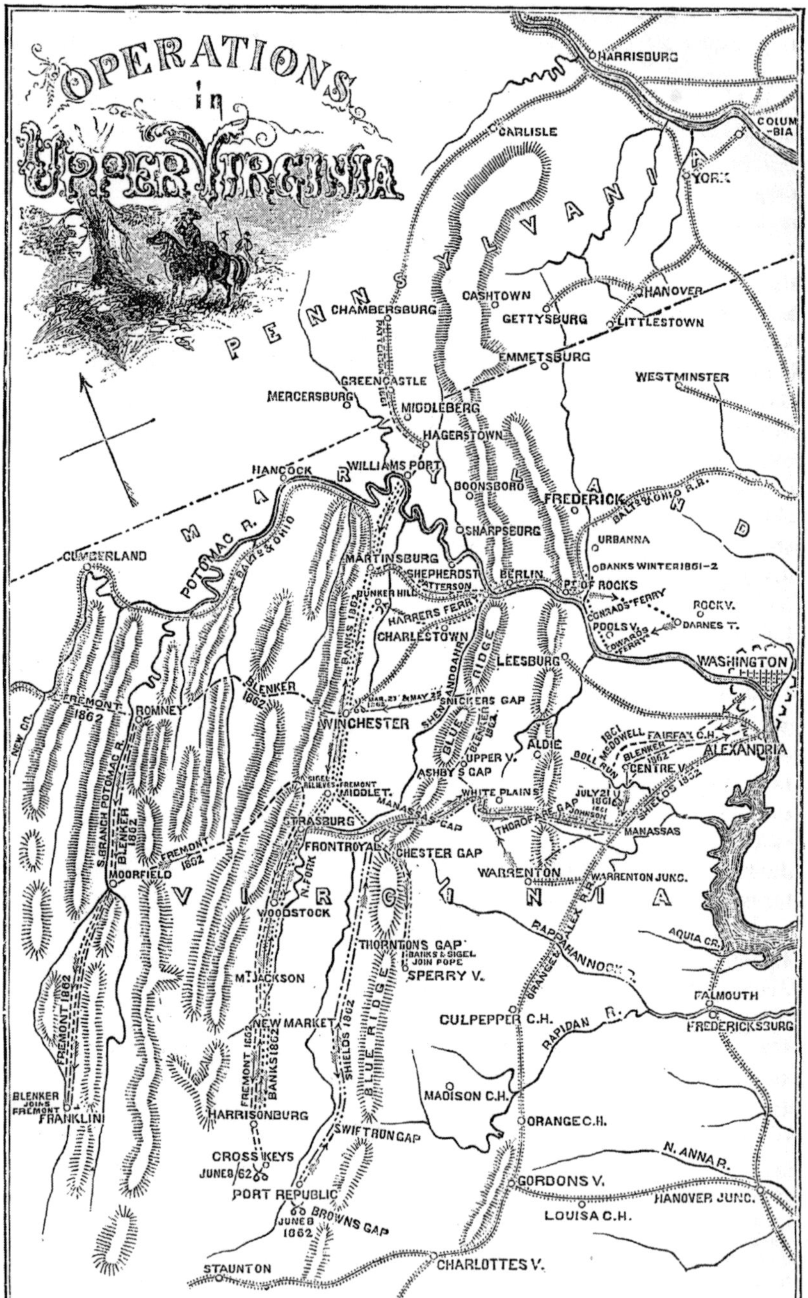
OPERATIONS
in
UPPER VIRGINIA
HARRISBURG
CARLISLE
COLUM-BIA
YORK
PENNSYLVANIA
CASHTOWN
HANOVER
CHAMBERSBURG
GETTYSBURG
LITTLESTOWN
EMMETSBURG
WESTMINSTER
GREENCASTLE
MERCERSBURG
MIDDLEBERG
HAGERSTOWN
HANCOCK
WILLIAMS PORT
MARYLAND
BOONSBORO
FREDERICK
SHARPSBURG
URBANNA
BANKS WINTER 1861-2
CUMBERLAND
POTOMAC R.
MARTINSBURG
SHEPHERDST.
BERLIN
PT OF ROCKS
PATTERSON
BUNKER HILL
CONRADS FERRY
ROCKV.
HARPERS FERRY
DARNES T.
CHARLESTOWN
POOLS V.
EDWARDS FERRY
LEESBURG
WASHINGTON
BLENKER 1862
FREMONT 1862
ROMNEY
SNICKERS GAP
WINCHESTER
SHENANDOAH R.
BLUE RIDGE
NEW CR.
ALDIE
FAIRFAX C.H.
MCDOWELL 1861
ALEXANDRIA
UPPER V.
ASHBY'S GAP
BULL RUN
CENTRE V.
WHITE PLAINS
MIDDLET.
STRASBURG
MANASSAS GAP
THOROFARE GAP
JOHNSON
MANASSAS
FRONTROYAL
CHESTER GAP
MOORFIELD
S. BRANCH POTOMAC R.
WARRENTON
WARRENTON JUNC.
VIRGINIA
N. FORK
WOODSTOCK
AQUIA CR.
RAPPAHANNOCK R.
THORNTONS GAP
BANKS & SIGEL JOIN POPE
SPERRY V.
MT JACKSON
FALMOUTH
NEW MARKET
CULPEPPER C.H.
RAPIDAN R.
FREDERICKSBURG
SHIELDS 1862
FREMONT 1862
BANKS 1862
MADISON C.H.
BLENKER JOINS FREMONT
FRANKLIN
HARRISONBURG
ORANGE C.H.
SWIFTRUN GAP
CROSS KEYS
JUNE 8/62
N. ANNA R.
PORT REPUBLIC
GORDONS V.
HANOVER JUNC.
JUNE 8 1862
BROWNS GAP
LOUISA C.H.
STAUNTON
CHARLOTTES V.
BANKS' ROUTE
FREMONT'S
SHIELDS'
BLENKERS
PATTERSON'S & McDOWELL'S
JOHNSON'S (REBEL)
SCALE OF MILES
0
10
20
30
40
50

of whom then crossed over and joined the regiments of General Winder, of Ewell's division, which was on Tyler's right, and where a battle had begun that soon became heavy. General Dick Taylor's Louisiana brigade, which had flanked and attacked General Tyler's left, but was driven back, now made a sudden dash through the woods that completely masked it, upon a battery of seven guns under Lieutenant-colonel Hayward, and captured it. With his own regiment (Sixty-sixth Ohio), and the Fifth and Seventh Ohio, Colonel Candy, who was in the rear of the battery, made a spirited counter-charge, and re-captured it with one of the Confederate guns, but the artillery horses having been killed, he was unable to take it off. Instead of the guns, he took with him, in falling back, sixty-seven of Taylor's men as prisoners.

So overwhelming was the number of Jackson's troops that Tyler was compelled to retreat. This was done in good order, "save the stampede of those who ran before the fight was fairly opened."[1] He was pursued about five miles, gallantly covered by Carroll and his cavalry. "Upon him I relied," said Tyler, "and was not disappointed."[2] In the engagement and retreat the Confederates captured four hundred and fifty prisoners, and eight hundred muskets. So ended THE BATTLE OF PORT REPUBLIC;[3] and Jackson telegraphed to Richmond, saying—"Through God's blessing the enemy near Port Republic was this day routed, with the loss of six pieces of his artillery." The battle was disastrous in its results, but glorious for the officers and men of the National army engaged in it. It was one of the brilliant battles of the war.[4]

Jackson kept Tyler in check until his main body crossed the bridge, when his rear-guard set it on fire. The sounds of battle and the sight of columns of smoke had hastened the march of Fremont. When he came near Port Republic he found the bridge in flames, the Shenandoah too deep to be forded anywhere, and his enemy beyond his immediate grasp. Here ended the pursuit—here ended the famous race of Fremont, Shields, and Jackson up the Shenandoah Valley, which was skillfully won by the latter. On the following morning[a] the National army began to retrace its steps, and, in the midst of a drenching rain, it reached Harrisonburg toward evening. Fremont fell back to Mount Jackson and Shields to New Market, when both commanders were called to Washington. Jackson re-crossed the Shenandoah and encamped at Weyer's Cave,[b] two miles from Port Republic, and on the 17th he was summoned, with a greater portion of his army, to assist in the defense of Richmond.

[a] June 9, 1862.

[b] June 12.

The writer, accompanied by two friends (S. M. Buckingham and H. L.

[1] Tyler's Report to Shields, June 12, 1862.

[2] Report of General Tyler to General Shields, June 12, 1862. The National troops employed in this struggle were the Seventh Indiana; Fifth, Seventh, and Twenty-ninth Ohio; and the First Virginia, with sections of Captains Clarke and Huntington's batteries, on the right; and the Eighty fourth and One Hundred and Tenth Pennsylvania; Sixty-sixth Ohio, and sections of Captains Clarke, Huntington, and Robinson's batteries, and a company each of the Fifth and Sixty-sixth Ohio, as skirmishers, on the left, which was the key of the position.

[3] Port Republic is a small village on the eastern bank of the south fork of the Shenandoah River, pleasantly situated on a plain. It is a post village of Rockingham County.

[4] General Ewell declared to the writer, that in that engagement the Confederate troops were three to one of the Nationals in number, and that it was a most gallant fight on the part of the latter.

Young), visited the theater of events recorded in this chapter early in October, 1866. Having explored places made famous by the exploits of Sheridan and others at a later period of the war, from Harper's Ferry to Winchester, and at Kernstown, Middletown, Cedar Creek, and Fisher's Hill, we left Strasburg for Harrisonburg at nine o'clock in the evening,[a] in an old-fashioned stage-coach, making three of nine passengers inside, with a remainder on the top. Our route lay along the great Valley Pike from Winchester to Staunton, a distance of fifty miles, and we were at breakfast in Harrisonburg the next morning at eight o'clock. An hour later we were on our way to the battle-fields of Cross Keys and Port Republic, in a well-worn and rusty pleasure-carriage belonging to a colored man, the proprietor of a livery-stable, who furnished us with an intelligent colored driver and a good team of horses. It was a very beautiful morning; and in the clear atmosphere the lofty hills of the Blue Ridge on the east, the Short Shenandoah Mountains on the west, and the Massanutten range northward, were perfectly defined. Our driver was a competent guide, being familiar with the events and the localities in that region, and we anticipated a day of pleasure and profit, and were not disappointed.

[a] Oct. 5, 1866.

A mile south of Harrisonburg we turned to the left up a rough, lane-like road, that skirted the field upon a ridge in which Ashby was killed. The place of his death was at the edge of a wood two hundred yards north of the road. The abrupt southern end of Massanutten Mountain, on which Jackson had a signal-station while Banks lay near him, arose like a huge buttress above the general level, seven miles to our left, while before us and to the right was a beautiful hill country, bordered by distant mountain ranges. We soon came to the battle-ground of Cross Keys, sketched the Union Church (see page 396), that was in the midst of the storm of conflict, and rode on to Port Republic, twelve miles from Harrisonburg, where we passed over a substantial new bridge on the site of the one fired by Ewell's rear-guard. After spending a little time there, we rode through the once pretty but then dreadfully dilapidated and half-deserted village, forded the Shenandoah (which was very shallow because of previously dry weather) a little above the town, and rode on two miles to the house of Abraham Mohler, the owner of Weyer's Cave near by, where we ordered dinner, and then proceeded with a guide to explore the famous cavern. Near it was the camping-ground of Jackson. We climbed a steep ridge, about one hundred and fifty feet above a tributary of the Shenandoah at its base, entered a rocky vestibule, each with a lighted tallow candle, and went down by rough paths and sometimes slippery acclivities far into the awful depths of the mountain, along a labyrinth of winding passages among the rocks. Chamber after chamber, recess after recess, passage after passage was visited until we were many hundred feet from the daylight. Here we were compelled to stoop because of the lowness of the roof; there its glittering stalactites were ninety feet above us; and everywhere we had the most strange and wonderful visions of cavern scenery. Nowhere did we find regularity of forms, nor abundant reasons for many of the fanciful names given to the localities, which Cooke's valuable little guide-book contains.

This is not the place nor the occasion to describe this really great wonder of nature—a wonder worthy of a voyage across oceans and continents to see;[1] so we will dismiss the consideration of it by saying that we ascended into upper air and the sunlight at a late hour in the afternoon, with appetites that gave a keen relish to a good dinner at Mohler's, for we had eaten nothing since breakfast. After dinner we rode on by a good highway, parallel with the Valley Pike, toward Staunton, passing the site of what is known as the Battle of Piedmont (to be mentioned hereafter) at sunset, and arrived at our destination at a late hour in the evening. We spent the next day (Sunday) in Staunton, and on Monday morning departed by railway for the scenes of strife eastward of the Blue Ridge, along the hollow of Rockfish Gap in that range, and through the great tunnel. Magnificent was the panorama seen on our right as we emerged from that dark artificial cavern in the mountains. Skirting the great hill-side along a terrace, we saw, a thousand feet below us, one of those beauteous and fertile valleys with which the mountain regions of Virginia abound. Others opened to our view as we descended gradually into the lower country. We passed the seat of Jefferson, near Charlottesville, at noon, dined at Gordonsville, and lodged that night at Culpepper Court-House. Our experience at the latter place will be considered hereafter.

[1] This cave is seventeen miles northeast from Staunton, in the northern extremity of Augusta County. It is on the eastern side of a high hill that runs parallel with the Blue Ridge, and a little more than two miles from it. It was accidentally discovered by a hunter—a German named Barnard Weyer—about the year 1804. A short distance from it, in the same hill, is Madison's Cave, so well described by Jefferson in his Notes on Virginia, at a time when this far greater cave was unknown.

CHAPTER XVI.

THE ARMY OF THE POTOMAC BEFORE RICHMOND.

E left the Army of the Potomac within a few miles of Richmond, its advance light troops at Bottom's Bridge, and the head-quarters of its commander at Cool Arbor.

When Huger fled from Norfolk, and the *Merrimack* was blown into fragments, the Confederate gun-boats in the James River retired to Richmond, closely followed by a flotilla of armed vessels under the command of Commodore John Rodgers, whose flag-ship was the iron-clad *Galena*. She was accompanied by the *Monitor*, *Aroostook*, *Port Royal*, and *Naugatuck*. They moved up the stream with great caution, for it was known that the Confederates had erected batteries on the shores at different points, and it was believed that guerrillas were abundant on the banks. From an armored look-out near the mast-head of the leading vessel, a vigilant watch for these was kept, but the squadron met with no serious impediment until it confronted a formidable battery on a bank nearly two hundred feet in height, called Drewry's Bluff, at a narrow place in the river, about eight miles from Richmond. Below this battery were two separate barriers, formed of spiles and sunken vessels, and the shores were lined with rifle-pits filled with sharp-shooters.

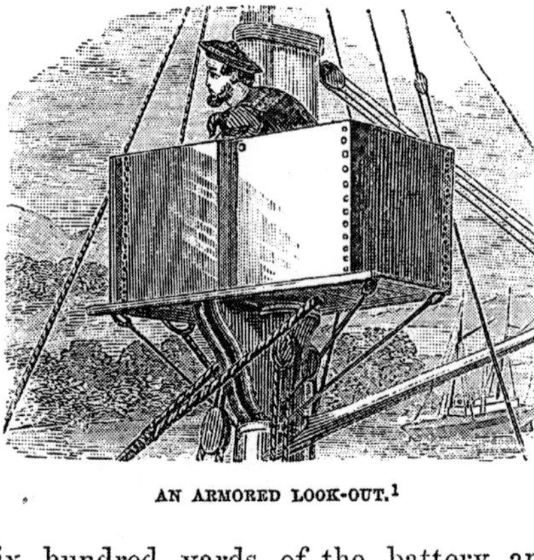

AN ARMORED LOOK-OUT.[1]

The *Galena* anchored within six hundred yards of the battery, and opened fire at near eight o'clock in the morning.[a] An hour later the *Monitor* ran above the *Galena*, but could not bring her guns to bear upon the elevated battery, and fell back. A sharp fight was kept up until after eleven o'clock, when the ammunition of the *Galena* was nearly expended. Then the flotilla withdrew. Rodgers lost in this attack twenty-seven men, and a 100-pounder rifled cannon that burst on board the *Naugatuck*, and disabled her. The commander of the battery,

[a] May 15, 1862.

---

[1] From a sketch by J. H. Schele.

Captain E. Farrand (once of the National Navy), reported his loss at fifteen. Rodgers fell back to City Point.[1]

The James and York rivers were now both offered as a highway for supplies for the Army of the Potomac, and General McClellan was left free to choose his base. He decided to continue it at the head of York until he should form a junction with McDowell's troops. The operations in the Shenandoah Valley, just recorded, speedily postponed that junction indefinitely, for, as we have seen, McDowell was necessarily detained to fight Jackson and Ewell, and to watch an active foe beyond the Rapid Anna River, who was then threatening Washington City.

SITE OF NEW BRIDGE.[2]

The two great armies were now in close proximity before Richmond, with the sluggish marsh-bordered Chickahominy between them. Their first collisions occurred on the 23d and 24th of May: one near New Bridge, a short distance from Cool Arbor, where the Fourth Michigan Cavalry, under Colonel Woodbury, waded the river,[3] and after a

[1] The appearance of this flotilla in the James, simultaneously with the advance of McClellan toward the Chickahominy, produced the greatest consternation in Richmond, especially among the conspirators. "General Johnston is falling back from the Peninsula," wrote a niece of the chief conspirator to her mother, "and Uncle Jeff. thinks we had better go to a safer place than Richmond. . . . . He is miserable. He tries to be cheerful and bear up against such a continuation of troubles: but oh, I fear he cannot live long, if he does not get some rest and quiet!" In this state of mind, the conspirator seems to have sought refuge in a Christian sanctuary. "Uncle Jeff.," wrote the pitying niece, "was confirmed last Tuesday, in St. Paul's Church, by Bishop Johns. He was baptized at home in the morning before church."—See Pollard's *Second Year of the War*, page 31.

There was a general expectation that Richmond would be in the hands of McClellan within a few days. Every preparation was made by the Confederate authorities to abandon it. The "archives of the Government" were sent to Columbia, in South Carolina, and to Lynchburg. The railway tracks over the bridges were covered with plank, to facilitate the passage of artillery. Mr. Randolph, the "Secretary of War," said to an attendant and relative, "You must go with my wife into the country, for to-morrow the enemy will be here." The Secretary of the Treasury had a special train, the steam of the locomotive continually up, ready for flight. —*A Rebel War Clerk's Diary*, ii. 126.

Disgusted and alarmed by the trepidation of the conspirators, the Legislature of Virginia, then in session, passed resolutions (May 14) calling upon the so-called "Government of the Confederate States" to defend Richmond at all hazards, and resolved, with a clearness that deprived the trembling Confederates of every excuse but fear, that "the President be assured that whatever destruction or loss of property of the State or individuals shall thereby result, will be cheerfully submitted to." This action was in accordance with the wishes of Johnston, and it is believed by his inspiration. But for this, the conspirators would have been seen in pale affright flying for personal safety to the Carolinas.

[2] This was the appearance of the rude bridge and the locality when the writer sketched it, at the close of May, 1866.

[3] In dry weather this stream is fordable at all points, but rains render it almost impassable for cavalry and artillery. The average width of the river in that vicinity is between forty and fifty feet. Heavily timbered bottoms spread out from it, from half a mile to a mile in width, and in some places it is bordered by extensive

smart skirmish captured thirty-seven of the Fifth Louisiana, then guarding that point, drove the remainder, and held the position. The other was at and near Mechanicsville, seven or eight miles from Richmond, when a part of McClellan's right wing was advancing toward the Chickahominy. At Ellison's Mill, about a mile from Mechanicsville, a part of Stoneman's command, with Davison's brigade of Franklin's corps, encountered[a] the Confederates in considerable force, infantry, cavalry, and artillery. A brisk skirmish ensued, and at sunset the Confederates fell back to Mechanicsville, from which they were driven across the Chickahominy the next morning. On this ground a battle was fought a month later.

[a] May 23, 1862.

This bold dash was followed the next day by an inspiriting general order from McClellan, that indicated an immediate advance of the whole army on Richmond.[1] Every thing was ready for such movement. The troops were

ELLISON'S MILL.[2]

rested; the material necessary for building bridges for crossing the Chickahominy had been prepared;[3] the weather was not very unfavorable, and nothing seemed to offer an excuse for an hour's delay. The Commander-in-

---

swamps, traversed by small streams, that are overflowed after rains. The river rises in the hill country northwest of Richmond, and is subject to a sudden increment of volume. With these features and condition, it formed a line of great difficulty between the contending armies.

[1] The order was read in all the camps. It directed the troops as they advanced beyond the Chickahominy to prepare for battle at a moment's notice, and to be entirely unencumbered, with the exception of ambulances; to carry three days' rations in their haversacks, and to leave their knapsacks with the wagons, that were parked on the left bank of the stream. After giving such directions, he told them "to bear in mind that the Army of the Potomac had *never yet been checked,*" and directed the soldiers to "preserve in battle perfect coolness and confidence, the sure forerunners of success." This seemed almost like cruel irony to the worn soldiers, who were painfully conscious that Magruder, with 5,000 men, had "checked" the Army of the Potomac for a whole month before Yorktown.

[2] This is a view of Ellison's Mill and the scene of the skirmish, and of a battle a little later, as it appeared when the writer sketched it, at the close of May, 1866. The Confederates were posted on the hills, on which the houses are seen beyond the stream, and the Nationals were on the heights near the Mill, up which the road to Gains's Mill passes.

[3] Johnston had caused all the bridges across the Chickahominy to be destroyed. General Barnard, McClellan's Chief Engineer, says in his report (page 21), that "so far as engineering operations were concerned, the army could have been thrown across the river as early as the 28th of May, when the Confederates near New Bridge could have been taken in the rear, and deprived of the power of making any formidable resistance to the passage of the right wing." In a review of the Peninsula campaign, Barnard says, "No very extensive work was anticipated, as the bottom lands were quite dry, and no inundation had yet occurred, or was anticipated. General McClellan was not waiting for the bridges, but the bridges were waiting for General McClellan."

Chief had been promptly informed[a] from Washington of the reasons and the necessity of countermanding the order for McDowell to move on from Fredericksburg to join him, and he had as usual sent back a complaining remonstrance, and charges of a withholding of troops from him. Nevertheless he issued that order of great promise.[b] He had said to the Secretary of War, ten days before, "I will fight the enemy, whatever their force may be, with whatever force we may have;" and the Secretary could see no reasons for a change now in the General's resolution, for, so long as the Confederate force that kept McDowell back was withheld from Richmond, McClellan was comparatively as strong in power to fight his enemy as if McDowell was with him, and Jackson and Ewell were confronting that soldier on the Chickahominy instead of on the Shenandoah or Rappahannock. The fact that McDowell could not then re-enforce him, imposed upon McClellan the obvious duty of acting with uncommon vigor before his enemy could be strengthened, for his was an offensive and not a defensive movement.

[a] May 24, 1862.

[b] May 25.

But McClellan seems not to have acted with the vigor that was expected, and the President evidently feared he would not, for, at about the time when the commander issued the order indicating a general advance, Mr. Lincoln, filled with just apprehensions for the safety of the capital, because of the movements in the Shenandoah Valley, telegraphed to him, saying—"I think the time is near when you must either attack Richmond, or give up the job and come to the defense of Washington." On the following day[c] he informed McClellan of the successful retreat of Banks, and asked him if he could not cut the railway between Richmond and Fredericksburg; and also what impression he had of the intrenched works for the defense of Richmond. The General replied that he did not think the Richmond works formidable, and that he had cut the Virginia Central railway in three places.[1] He also assured the President that he was "quietly closing in upon the enemy, preparatory to the last struggle," but thought it necessary to secure his flanks against "the greatly superior forces" in front of him.

[c] May 26.

For several days afterward, operations on the flank of the great army made the sum of its action. That army, fully prepared for an instant forward movement, and eager to perform it, not only lay passive, but was dangerously severed by the fickle Chickahominy,[2] whose power for mischief, when fed by rains, the commander was constantly setting forth. Instead of moving his whole force upon the works, which he did not consider formidable, he thought it best only to order a part of General Fitz-John Porter's corps (the Fifth) to Hanover Court-House, to secure his menaced right flank, and keep the way open for McDowell to join him. This detachment moved by way of Mecnanicsville, at three o'clock on the morning of the 27th, General W. H. Emory in the advance, with the Fifth and Sixth Regular Cavalry, and Benson's horse battery. These were followed by General Morell's division, composed of the brigades of Generals Martindale, But-

---

[1] This was done by cavalry under Stoneman.

[2] "I have two corps [Keyes's and Heintzelman's] across the Chickahominy, within six miles of Richmond; the others on this side [left] at other crossings within same distance, and ready to cross when bridges are completed."—McClellan's dispatch to the President, May 25, 1862.

terfield, and McQuade, with Berdan's sharp-shooters, and three batteries under Captain Griffin. Colonel G. K. Warren, with his provisional brigade,[1] moved along another road toward the same point, and for the same purpose.

FITZ-JOHN PORTER.

After marching fourteen miles through mud, caused by a heavy shower in the morning, and meeting a little resistance, Emory came upon the Confederates in force at noon, two miles from the Court-House, and was brought to a halt by the fire of artillery. He was speedily joined by the Twenty-fifth New York and Berdan's sharp-shooters, when a battle-line was formed, and skirmishing was kept up until the arrival of General Butterfield, with four of his regiments,[2] when a quick and furious charge was made upon the Confederates, which routed them after a contest of an hour, with a loss of one of their guns, captured by the Seventeenth New York. They were hotly pursued some distance, and in the mean time Martindale, with a part of his brigade, pushed on to Peake's Station, on the Virginia Central railway, encountered a Confederate force there, and drove it toward Ashland, upon the Richmond and Fredericksburg railroad, not far from the birthplace of Henry Clay.

While moving with a part of his brigade[3] toward Hanover Court-House, after this exploit, Martindale was attacked by a superior force that came up by railway from Richmond. He maintained his ground for an hour with great gallantry, until re-enforced by Porter, who was at the Court-House. On hearing of the attack on his rear, Porter at once faced his column about, recalled the cavalry sent in pursuit of the routed Confederates, and sent the Thirteenth and fourteenth New York, with Griffin's battery, directly to Martindale's assistance. The Ninth Massachusetts and Sixty-second Pennsylvania were sent to take the Confederates on the left flank, while Butterfield, with the Eighty-third Pennsylvania and Sixteenth Michigan, hastened through the woods still farther to the left of the foe. Warren, who had been delayed in repairing bridges, now came up, when the Confederates, outnumbered, fell rapidly back, keenly pursued. They lost seven hundred and thirty of their men made prisoners, and left two hundred dead on the field. They also lost one howitzer, a caisson, many small arms, two railway trains, and their camp at Hanover Court-House.[4] The National loss was three

---

[1] This was composed of the Fifth and Thirteenth New York, First Connecticut artillery, acting as infantry, Sixth Pennsylvania cavalry, and Weedon's Rhode Island Battery.

[2] Twelfth and Seventeenth New York, Eighty-third Pennsylvania, and Sixteenth Michigan.

[3] The Second Maine, the Twenty-fifth and a portion of the Forty-fourth New York, and a section of Martin's battery.

[4] The troops thus smitten were of the division of General L. O'B. Branch, composed chiefly of men from North Carolina and Georgia. These had been ordered to Virginia after Branch's defeat at New Berne, by Burnside.

hundred and fifty. At two o'clock the next morning[a] McClellan telegraphed to the Secretary of War that Porter had gained "a truly glorious victory" with his "magnificent division"—"not a defeat, but a complete rout"—and that he had "cut all but the Richmond and Fredericksburg Railroad." He expressed his belief that the Confederates were "concentrating every thing on Richmond," and that Washington was in no danger; and he told the War Minister that it was "the policy and duty of the Government" to send him "by water all the well-drilled troops available," as "the real issue" was "in the battle about to be fought in front of Richmond." He concluded by saying—"If any regiments of good troops remain unoccupied, it will be an irreparable fault committed."[1]

[a] May 28, 1862.

Having reason for believing that General Anderson, who was specially charged with confronting McDowell, was still at Ashland, McClellan ordered General Sykes's division of regulars to move on the 28th from New Bridge to Hanover Court-House, to be in a position to support General Porter; and, during that and the following day, expeditions went out in various directions to destroy railway and other bridges, for the purpose of obstructing the passage of re-enforcements and supplies to Johnston's army. The railway bridge over the South Anna was destroyed by a party under Major Williams, and the Richmond and Fredericksburg road was cut. A part of Emory's cavalry, under Captain Chambliss, drove the Confederates from Ashland, and destroyed a railway bridge and broke up the road and the telegraph in that vicinity. When these raids on the Confederate communications were accomplished, Porter withdrew to his camps with the main army, which was lying quietly on the Chickahominy, the extreme right being at Meadow Bridge. McClellan had again telegraphed to his superiors, telling of Porter's "complete victories," speaking of the greater force than he expected before him, and of the risk he was running in moving at all, and declaring—"I will do all that quick movements can accomplish, but you must send me all the troops you can, and leave to me full latitude as to choice of commanders."[2]

Three days afterward there were "quick movements" in the Army of the Potomac. The skillful and vigilant Johnston had observed with special satisfaction the perilous situation of that army, cut in twain by the Chickahominy, and its commander's almost timid caution, and he resolved, on the 30th,[b] to strike its portion lying on the Richmond side of the stream, and cut it off before it could be joined by troops on the other side. He ascertained that Casey's division of Keyes's corps held an advanced position on both sides of the Williamsburg road, half a mile

[b] May.

---

1 The patient President calmly rebuked the General for his forgetfulness of his own duty in assuming to teach the Government its business, and said—"I am very glad of General F. J. Porter's victory; still, if it was a total rout, I am puzzled to know why the Richmond and Fredericksburg railway was not seized again, as you say you have all the railroads but that. I am puzzled to see how, lacking that, you can have any excepting the scrap from Richmond to West Point. The scrap of the Virginia Central, from Richmond to Hanover Junction, without more, is simply nothing. That the whole of the enemy is concentrating on Richmond, I think cannot be certainly known to you. Saxton at Harper's Ferry informs us that large forces, supposed to be Jackson's and Ewell's, forced his advance from Charlestown to-day. General King telegraphs us from Fredericksburg, that contrabands give certain information that 15,000 left Hanover Junction Monday morning, to re-enforce Jackson. I am painfully impressed with the importance of the struggle before you, and shall aid you all I can, consistently with my view of due regard to all points."—Lincoln's dispatch to McClellan, May 28, 1862.

2 McClellan's dispatch to the Secretary of War, May 28, 1862.

beyond a point known as the Seven Pines,[1] six miles from Richmond;[2] that Couch's division of the same corps was at the Seven Pines, his right resting at Fair Oaks Station, on the Richmond and York River railway; that Kearney's division of Heintzelman's corps was on the same railway, three-fourths of a mile in advance of Savage's Station; and that the division of Hooker of the latter corps was guarding the approaches of the White Oak Swamp, that lay between these divisions and the Chickahominy.

SILAS CASEY.

The country thereabout is quite level, and was then mostly wooded and dotted with marshes. In that region the roads radiate from Richmond, and gave Johnston advantages of position for attack or retreat. In a degree they suggested the points of attack at the time in question, and it was arranged accordingly. General Longstreet was ordered to go out by the Williamsburg road, with his own and D. H. Hill's divisions, the latter in advance, to attack the Nationals in front, while General Huger should move down the Charles City road toward their left flank, and General G. W. Smith should follow the New Bridge road toward the "Old Tavern;" and then take the Nine Mile road toward their right at Fair Oaks Station. These columns were to move simultaneously at dawn,[a] but the rain had made the roads so soft, that it was ten o'clock before Hill's division began to move toward Keyes's front.

[a] May 31, 1862.

General Casey, who was in the advance, had intimations of an intended attack that day, and was vigilant.[3] He was busily engaged in constructing a redoubt, sinking rifle-pits, and forming an *abatis;* and when, about eleven o'clock, he was apprised of the approach of the Confederates in force, he ordered his men to take their arms. At the same time two hissing shells came heralding the enemy near, and made the soldiers quicken their abandonment of spades and axes for the weapons of war. They were none too soon in arms, for at a little past noon the Confederates came in heavy force. Casey's picket-line, with the One Hundred and third Pennsylvania, that had been sent to its support, was driven in, and Spratt's battery, with supporting troops under General Naglee,[4] who were in front of the works, were soon in

[1] This was the name of a country tavern near which were seven large pine trees. Only three were standing when the writer visited the spot, at the close of May, 1866.

[2] The advance to this position had been ordered by McClellan a few days before, contrary to the opinion and advice of both Keyes and Casey. See Report of the Committee on the Conduct of the War, i. 21.

[3] Casey's pickets had that morning captured Lieutenant Washington, one of Johnston's aids, and he was sent to Keyes. His conduct satisfied the National officers that an attack was about to be made. Besides, it had been reported that the rumbling of cars on the Richmond and York River railroad had been heard all night, indicating the transportation of troops and supplies.

[4] These were the One Hundred and fourth Pennsylvania, Colonel W. W. H. Davis; the Eleventh Maine, and Ninety-third and One Hundredth New York Volunteers.

fierce conflict with the foe. Bates's battery, under Lieutenant Hart, was in the unfinished redoubt. Wessel's brigade was in the rifle-pits, and Palmer's brigade was behind as a reserve. Naglee, with great persistence, kept the Confederates in check for some time by most gallant fighting, and then fell back to the remainder of the division in the rifle-pits, which had been strengthened by the Ninety-third Pennsylvania, of Peck's brigade.

The Confederates soon gained a position on Casey's flanks. Perceiving the peril of his artillery, that officer ordered a bayonet charge to save it. This was gallantly performed by the One Hundredth New York, One Hundred and Fourth Pennsylvania, and the Eleventh Maine, under the immediate direction of General Naglee. The troops sprang forward with a tremendous yell, and drove back the foe to the adjacent woods. From that cover the pursuers were assailed by a most murderous musket-fire, and out of it swarmed the Confederates in overwhelming numbers. The battle raged more furiously than ever, until about three o'clock, when General Rains had got in the rear of the redoubt, and the rifle-pits were nearly enveloped by the multitude of Confederates. Casey's position was no longer tenable, and he ordered his troops to fall back to the second line in possession of Couch. They did so, with the loss of six guns and many gallant officers and men.[1] The cannon in the redoubt were seized by General Rhodes, and turned upon the fugitives. Notwithstanding the great odds against them,[2] and the fearful enfilading fires to which they were exposed, Casey's men brought off three-fourths of their cannon.

HENRY M. NAGLEE.

Early in the action General Keyes had sent to Heintzelman for aid, but because of some unaccountable delay it did not arrive until it was almost too late. Seeing Casey's peril, he ordered forward several of Couch's regiments to his relief. On these (the Fifty-fifth New York, and Twenty-third, Sixty-first, and Ninety-third Pennsylvania) the tempest of battle fell most destructively. These were followed by the Seventh Massachusetts and Sixty-second New York; but all were pressed back to Fair Oaks Station, where they joined the First U. S. Chasseurs, under General John Cochran, and Thirty-first Pennsylvania, who were stationed there, and fought desperately under the orders of Generals Couch and Abercrombie. The embankments of the railway there formed a good breastwork for the Nationals.

[1] Among the officers killed was Colonel James M. Brown, of the One Hundredth New York, and Colonel G. D. Baily and Major Van Valkenburg, of the First New York Artillery. The gallant Colonel Davis, of the One Hundred and Fourth Pennsylvania, was severely wounded.

[2] Casey's division numbered only a little more than four thousand men. The number of the assailants was estimated at more than thirty thousand.

With the assistance of Generals Devens and Naglee, Keyes formed a line at the edge of the woods, composed of the First Long Island and Thirty-sixth New York.

In the mean time Heintzelman had pressed forward with re-enforcements, and at a little past four o'clock Kearney appeared with Berry and Jameson's brigades. At about the same time General Peck led the Ninety-third and One Hundred and Second Pennsylvania across an open space exposed to an awful shower of balls, to assist the terribly smitten right; and for an hour he sustained a sharp contest near the Seven Pines, when he was forced to fall back. The Tenth Massachusetts had also been led by Keyes to the assistance of the crumbling right, which was heavily pressed by the corps of General G. W. Smith. That officer, who was accompanied by General Johnston, had been held in check by the latter until four o'clock, the Confederate chief waiting to hear the muskets of Longstreet and Hill, which were to be the signal for the flank attack. These sounds did not reach him, but when informed of what his center had been doing, he immediately threw forward Smith's command, which fell upon the Nationals at Fair Oaks Station, and a terrible conflict ensued. The fresh Confederates severed Couch's command, turned his left, interposed between him and Heintzelman, and pushed Kearney back to the border of the flooded White Oak Swamp. It seemed for a time as if the whole Army of the Potomac on the Richmond side of the Chickahominy was doomed to destruction.

At that critical moment relief came. When Heintzelman was informed of the heavy attack on Casey, he sent an officer with the news to Generals

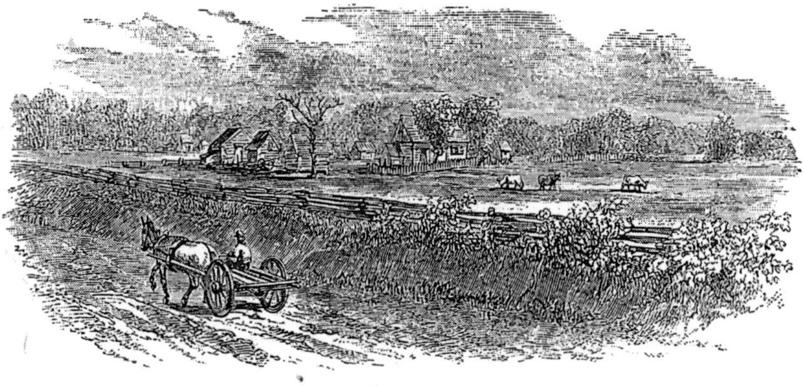

BATTLE-FIELD OF THE SEVEN PINES.[1]

McClellan and Sumner. The former was at New Bridge, and the latter was between the railway and Bottom's Bridge, at the head of the center of the army. The vigilant Sumner was so deeply impressed with the danger to which the left wing of the army across the Chickahominy would be exposed,

[1] This is a view on Sykes's farm, in front of the site of the Seven Pines tavern, where Casey's division fought so desperately after the charge of Naglee. This was the appearance of the farm-house and its surroundings when the writer sketched it, on the anniversary of the battle, 1866, from under a tree that was much scarred by the bullets.

in the event of a rain-storm, that, without orders from head-quarters, he had summoned Colonel E. E. Cross, of the Fifth New Hampshire,[1] so early as the 25th, to construct a bridge across the stream nearly in front of his position. Fortunately, it was completed on the evening of the 30th, when the river was high and rising. There was then no other bridge over which the army might cross, excepting Bottom's and the railway bridge; and this, known as the Grape-vine bridge, became an instrument of salvation for the Army of the Potomac.

Being satisfied that the attack on his left wing was serious, General McClellan ordered Sumner to prepare to move at a moment's warning. That officer had already done so, and when, at half-past two o'clock, a further order reached him to cross the stream, he was ready and moved immediately. By this readiness he saved at least an hour's time—an hour most precious, as we shall observe presently. The passage was difficult, owing to the flood.[2] Sedgwick's division crossed first, closely followed by Richardson's, and, with the former, Sumner reached the field at the moment when Couch and Heintzelman were separated, and all seemed lost. Had the precious hour just alluded to been spent in preparation, all might have been lost.

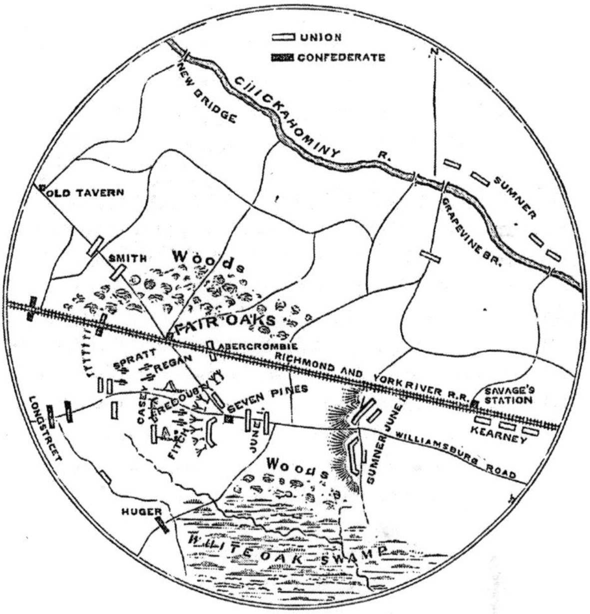

BATTLE OF SEVEN PINES AND FAIR OAKS.

Sumner now assumed the command. Sedgwick at once formed in line of battle, in the edge of a wood near Fair Oaks, with the First Minnesota on the right flank, and soon made the advancing Confederates recoil by hurling upon them a storm of canister from twenty-four guns. Then moving forward his whole line, he swept the field and recovered nearly all that Couch had lost. Meanwhile Gorman's brigade of Sedgwick's division had deployed in battle line on the crest of a gentle hill, in the rear of Fair Oaks, and swept

[1] This was one of the most useful and gallant regiments in the service. Cross was both skillful and brave, and his activity knew no rest. His men were noted for their skill in building, and had erected a signal-tower 100 feet high in front of Yorktown. They were so noted for their work as soldiers, also, that the regiment acquired the name of "the fighting Fifth." We shall meet it hereafter.

[2] The logs that formed the corduroy approaches to the bridge were all afloat, and were held only by the stumps of trees between which they lay; and the Grape-vine bridge was held to its place over the boiling flood only by ropes attached to trees.

down to the relief of Abercrombie, where Cochran's U. S. Chasseurs and Neill's Twenty-third Pennsylvania were fighting desperately. Then came heavy volleys of musketry enfilading the National right, when Sedgwick ordered the gallant General Burns to deploy the Sixty-ninth and Seventy-second Pennsylvania to the right, himself leading the Seventy-first and One Hundred and Sixth Pennsylvania in support of Gorman. The strife there was intense. For a moment the National line was bent and seemed ready to break, but the clear voice of Burns calling out—"Steady, men, steady!" gave them such inspiration that they broke into loud cheers, and held the position firmly. In the face of their terrible volleys the Confederates pressed on, and charged Brady's battery, whose murderous fire of canister, poured into their compact ranks, made fearful lanes, and sent them back in confusion to the woods in their rear. It was at about this time (sunset) that General Johnston, the Confederate Chief, was seriously wounded by the fragment of a shell, and was carried from the field, leaving that wing in charge of General G. W. Smith, who was also disabled soon afterward.

Undismayed by their repulse and the loss of their Chief, the Confederates again advanced, just as darkness came on, and endeavored to outflank Sumner's right, where General Dana had joined Gorman. After fighting heavily for some time, Sumner ordered a bayonet charge by five of his regiments.[1] This was bravely performed. The regiments leaped two fences between them and their foes, rushed upon the Confederate line and broke it into dire confusion. It was now eight o'clock in the evening, and the battle of Saturday, May 31, ceased. Richardson's division and Sumner's artillery, which had been mired near the Chickahominy, came up during the evening; and Kearney's brigades, that had been driven to the White Oak Swamp, also rejoined the army lying on the battle-field of Fair Oaks.

[a] June 1, 1862.

The conflict was renewed by the Confederates early in the morning[a] with Richardson's brigade. The latter was on the alert. His troops were prepared for battle when, at three o'clock, his foes drove in their pickets. He posted a battery of 10-pounder rifled Parrott guns, under Captain Hazard, so as to command an open field on his right front; and directly in front of his line he placed the brigade of General French, and a regiment of General O. O. Howard's brigade. The remaining regiments of Howard's brigade formed a second line, and the Irish brigade of General Thomas F. Meagher, with eighteen pieces of artillery, formed the third. The battle was now begun by General Pickett, supported by General Roger A. Pryor, with a part of Huger's division, which did not get up in time to join in the battle on the previous day. Pryor fell upon French, and Howard went to his support. Mahone came up to the aid of Pryor. Finally Meagher was ordered to the front, and after a desultory conflict of nearly three hours, in which a part of Hooker's command was engaged, and General Howard lost his right arm, the Confederates fell back, and did not renew the contest. They remained on the ground of Casey's camp during the day, as a cover

---

[1] Thirty-fourth and Eighty-second New-York, Fifteenth and Twentieth Massachusetts, and Seventh Michigan. The first three were of Gorman's brigade, and the two latter of Dana's brigade.

to the movement of their munitions of war and camp equipage to their lines at Richmond, and at evening they went in that direction themselves.

On the following morning Heintzelman sent Hooker with a strong reconnoitering party toward the Confederate capital. He went within four miles of the city without meeting any armed men, excepting a few pickets. On hearing of this temerity, McClellan ordered him back to Casey's camp,[1] where, at the house of George Turner, he established his head-quarters, and fortified it; and orders were given to throw up a line of strong intrenchments in front of Fair Oaks, to protect the army while building bridges over the Chickahominy.[3] Hooker established a hospital at a house near Fair Oaks Station, around which the tents of the sick and wounded were soon grouped. The losses in THE BATTLE OF FAIR OAKS OR THE SEVEN PINES[4] were very heavy, and about equal on both sides, amounting in the aggregate to about seven thousand each.[5] This was heavy, when it is considered that not more than fifteen thousand men on either side were engaged in the conflict. Casey's division, that so gallantly withstood the first shock of battle, lost one-third of its number.[6] The whole affair was managed on the part of the Nationals without any controlling end, for the Commander-in-Chief was

HOOKER'S HEAD-QUARTERS.[2]

[1] His order was—"General Hooker will return from his brilliant reconnoissance; we cannot afford to lose his division."

[2] This was the appearance of Hooker's head-quarters when the writer sketched it, at the close of May, 1866. In the foreground, on the right, is seen a part of the fortifications cast up there, and the trees in front of the two buildings, under which was Casey's tent.

[3] McClellan's Report, page 113. The General gave as a reason for recalling Hooker, that the bad state of the roads would not warrant an attempt to march on Richmond, or hold a position so near it. It was the opinion of several of his general officers that had Hooker been allowed to press on, with the supports at hand, he could have gone into Richmond, for the Confederates were disheartened by the loss of their chief, and demoralized by the events of the two preceding days. McClellan said on the same day, in a dispatch to the Secretary of War: "The *morale* of my troops is now such that I can venture much. I do not fear odds against me."

[4] Both titles are correct, and yet the use of them as synonyms in describing the battle would give an erroneous impression. In front of the place known as The Seven Pines, and at Fair Oaks Station—positions but a short distance apart—the heaviest engagements of the great battle were fought on the same day, and partly by the same troops.

[5] Among the National officers killed or disabled in this battle were Colonel Bailey and Major Van Valkenburg, of the artillery, and Colonels Riker, Brown, Ripley, and Miller, of the infantry. Among the wounded were Generals Naglee, Devens, Howard, and Wessels, and Colonel Cross, of the Fifth New Hampshire.

[6] This division, though composed in a large degree of raw troops, performed wonders of prowess, as we have seen; yet, in consequence of misinformation, it was exposed to severe public censure by McClellan's first dispatch to the Secretary of War, in which he said that it "gave way unaccountably and discreditably." Convinced of his error, the General so informed the Secretary a few days afterward, and, in a degree, made reparation for the injury.

not near the field, and scarcely knew what was going on there until all fighting had ceased on the second day.

For nearly a month after the battle just recorded, the Army of the Potomac lay along the line of the Chickahominy, a few miles from Richmond, in a very unhealthful situation,[1] quietly besieging the Confederate capital, and apparently preparing to take it by storm. In the mean time the Confederates concentrated their forces there for its defense. "Stonewall Jackson," having accomplished his purpose in the Shenandoah Valley, crossed the Blue Ridge, and, by a series of quick and inexplicable movements, made himself and his troops appear almost ubiquitous, and so puzzled the authorities at Washington and the Generals in the field, that it seemed to them that he was as likely to be then sweeping down the Shenandoah Valley as to be moving toward Richmond. That he was somewhere between the Rappahannock and Shenandoah, and the city of Richmond, with thirty or forty thousand troops, no one could doubt. "Neither McDowell, who is at Manassas, nor Banks and Fremont, who are at Middletown," the Secretary of War telegraphed to McClellan, so late as the 24th of June, "appear to have any accurate knowledge on the subject." The fact was, that on the 17th Jackson commenced a march of his main body toward Richmond, leaving a brigade of cavalry and a battery at Harrisonburg, to watch the movements of the Nationals in the Valley, and on the 25th he arrived at Ashland, sixteen miles from Richmond, with about thirty-five thousand men, preparatory to a blow on McClellan's right. Robert E. Lee had succeeded Joseph E. Johnston in command of the Army of Northern Virginia, and was now concentrating his troops to resist McClellan.

HOSPITAL AT FAIR OAKS.[2]

The position of the Army of the Potomac was now peculiar and unfortunate, and required great skill and caution in its management. So long as it was inactive, it was necessary to hold a large force behind the Chickahominy, for the protection of its line of communication with its supplies at the

[1] The troops on the Richmond side of the Chickahominy were soon strongly intrenched in the vicinity of Fair Oaks and the Seven Pines. Keyes was on the extreme flank, by the White Oak Swamp. On his right was Heintzelman, and still farther to the right Sumner occupied ground on both sides of the railway. Still farther to the right was the division of Franklin, that crossed on the 5th of June. The line presented nearly four miles of front. The line of intrenchments was at an average distance from Richmond, in a direct line, of about five miles. The country was mostly level. In wet weather a greater portion of it was a swamp, and in dry weather it was dotted with stagnant pools.

Fitz-John Porter's corps remained behind the Chickahominy, his right resting near Meadow Bridge, well up toward the Central Virginia railway-crossing, with Stoneman's cavalry scouting on his flank, to watch the approaches between him and the Pamunkey to the line of communication with the depot of supplies at the White House.

[2] In this picture a good representation is given of the army wagon, used by thousands during the war.

White House, on the Pamunkey. Had that base of supplies been changed to a point on the James River immediately after Rodgers drove the Confederate gun-boats to Richmond, and held that highway, it would doubtless have given a great advantage for maneuvering against that capital. Now, it was necessary, in order to move forward, either to thus change the base or to throw the entire army across the Chickahominy, vigorously attack the Confederate lines, and, if unsuccessful, then to make the base on the James, as was afterward done by compulsion. This was the alternative presented to the Commander-in-Chief, and his habitual indecision, which seemed chronic in his character, caused a delay until his foe would no longer permit him to consider.[1]

During the three weeks' siege of Richmond public expectation was kept constantly on the alert, by frequent assurances that the decisive battle would be fought "to-morrow." On the 2d of June, the day when Hooker looked into Richmond, the Commander said: "I only wait for the river to fall to cross with the rest of the force and make a general attack." Anxious to give him every possible support, the President ordered five regiments at Baltimore to join him; placed the disposable force at Fortress Monroe at his service, and notified him that McCall's division of McDowell's corps would be sent to him by water from Fredericksburg as speedily as possible. In reference to that notification the General said in a dispatch:[a] "I shall be in perfect readiness to move forward and take Richmond the moment McCall reaches here, and the ground will admit the passage of artillery."

[a] June 7, 1862.

The loyal people were delighted by this assurance; and when it was known that McCall's forces had arrived at the White House, a few days later,[b] they expected immediate intelligence of the fall of Richmond, for word had come that Jackson and Ewell had just been fighting Fremont and Shields near the upper Shenandoah,[2] so that these forces were yet withheld from Lee. But already McClellan had telegraphed[c] the dampening intelligence—"I am completely checked by the weather. The Chickahominy is in a dreadful state; we have another rain-storm on our hands." In the same dispatch there was a sentence ominous of an indefinite delay. It ran thus—"I present for your consideration the propriety of detaching largely from Halleck's army [in the Mississippi Valley] to strengthen this"—an operation that would require two or three weeks at least. The Secretary of War gave him cordial assurance of his desire to give him every possible aid, and informed him that preparations were made for sending to him the remainder of McDowell's corps, that officer being directed to co-operate fully with him. But the terms of that co-operation, which was simply that McDowell should retain an inde-

[b] June 12, 13.

[c] June 10.

---

[1] It seems proper here to remark that in his Report, made more than a year later, General McClellan says that a dispatch to him, received from the Secretary of War on the 18th of May, informing him that McDowell had been ordered to march to his assistance by the shortest route from Fredericksburg, rendered it impossible for him to use the James River as a line of operations. "It forced me," he said, "to establish our depots on the Pamunkey, and approach Richmond from the north." It was eleven days before that dispatch was sent that Rodgers went up to Drewry's Bluff; and General Barnard, the Chief Engineer of the Army of the Potomac, says that the decision to make "the depot of supplies on the Pamunkey, and approach Richmond from the north," was made at Roper's Church, on the 11th, or ten days before the receipt of the dispatch from the Secretary of War.

[2] See pages 396 and 397.

pendent command, were so offensive to McClellan that he answered—"If I cannot control all of his troops I want none of them, and would prefer to fight the battle with what I have, and let others be responsible for the result."[1]

This dispatch was written just after a most mortifying event had occurred. General J. E. B. Stuart, one of the most active of the Confederate cavalry officers, had on that and the previous day made a circuit entirely around the Army of the Potomac, with fifteen hundred cavalry and four pieces of horse artillery.[2] He attacked and dispersed two squadrons of the Fifth Regular Cavalry at Hanover Old Church, under Captain Royall, and sweeping around almost to the White House, by Tunstall's Station, seized and burned fourteen wagons and two schooners laden with forage at Garlick's Landing, above the White House, on the Pamunkey; captured and carried away one hundred and sixty-five prisoners, and two hundred and sixty mules and horses; rested three hours, and during the night crossed the Chickahominy, near the Forge Bridge, on hastily provided ones, and then leisurely returned to Richmond, on the morning of the 15th, by the Charles City road. This was the first of many similar but far more destructive raids, by both parties during the war. It produced great commotion in the Army of the Potomac, but on the night of the 14th, McClellan reported "all quiet in every direction."

J. E. B. STUART.

For ten days longer all was quiet on the Chickahominy; but during that time the Confederates were taking measures to strike a blow at the Army of the Potomac, which, when it was given, came near being a fatal one. Stuart's raid was more a reconnoissance for information than an expedition for destruction. It was determined to draw Jackson quietly from the Shenandoah Valley, and have him suddenly and unexpectedly strike the right flank of McClellan's army near Mechanicsville, and uncover the passage of that stream, when a heavy force would join him, sweep down the left side of the Chickahominy toward the York River, and seize the communications of the

---

1 Dispatch to the Secretary of War, June 14, 1862. In that angry dispatch he made an ungenerous insinuation of inordinate ambition on the part of a brother officer. McDowell had politely telegraphed to him his desire to have McCall's division of his own corps placed so as to join him immediately on his arrival. Because of this request, which was in accordance with orders from the War Department on the 8th, the angry General said—"I do not feel that, in such circumstances as these under which I am now placed, General McDowell should wish the general interest to be sacrificed for the purpose of increasing his command." Already loyal newspapers had intimated that it was possible that McDowell might take Richmond without waiting for McClellan, but there is no evidence that the former had any such intentions. Nor could the latter have been moved by such purely personal considerations, for in the same dispatch he said, "you know I have none."

2 Portions of the First, Fourth, and Ninth Virginia cavalry, and two squadrons of the Jeff. Davis Legion.

Army of the Potomac with the White House. To mask this movement, and to give the impression to both McClellan and his Government that more formidable operations were to be begun in the Shenandoah Valley, Lee sent Whiting's division in that direction, in a way that would be easily discovered by the National scouts. As we have observed, the movement was successful, and Jackson suddenly appeared at Ashland on the 25th of June.

McClellan had promptly informed the Secretary of War[a] of the rumored movement of Whiting, but on the same day, possessed of other information, he telegraphed to him that a general engagement might take place at any hour, and adding—"After to-morrow we shall fight the Rebel army as soon as Providence will permit." Two days later he informed the President that his defensive works would be completed the next day, and then expressed a desire to lay before the Executive his "views as to the present state of military affairs throughout the whole country," and also, he said, to "learn the disposition, as to numbers and positions, of the troops not under my command in Virginia and elsewhere." To this request, so extraordinary and inexplicable under the circumstances, the President kindly replied that he would be glad to have him give his views, if, he said, "it would not direct too much of your time and attention from the army under your immediate command;" but he thought it best not to communicate the information respecting the armies asked for, either by letter or telegraph, as it might reach the Confederates.[1]

[a] June 18, 1863.

And so the siege of Richmond went quietly on. Works had been thrown up, bridges built, re-enforcements called for, and abundant complaints uttered. Finally, on the 25th, General Heintzelman's corps, with a part of Keyes's and Sumner's, was ordered to move forward on the Williamsburg road, through a swampy wood, for the purpose, the commanding general said, "to ascertain the nature of the ground" beyond, "and to place Generals Heintzelman and Sumner in a position to support the attack intended to be made on the Old Tavern on the 26th or 27th, by General Franklin, by assailing that position in the rear." The movement was made, a fight ensued, in which the brigades of Sickles and Grover, of Hooker's division, bore the brunt, assisted by Kearney, and resulted in a loss to the Nationals of five hundred and sixteen men killed and wounded. This is called THE BATTLE OF OAK GROVE. General McClellan reported that the coveted point was gained with very little loss, and that "the enemy were driven from their camp."

SAMUEL P. HEINTZELMAN.

[1] McClellan's Report, page 118.

On returning from overlooking the affair at the Oak Grove, McClellan telegraphed to the Secretary of War, that "contrabands" had just informed him that Jackson was at or near Hanover Court-House, and that Beauregard had arrived in Richmond the day before, with re-enforcements. He said he was inclined to think Jackson would attack his right, and that if the reports were true, that the Confederate force was two hundred thousand in number, he would "have to contend against vastly superior odds." He gave the Government to understand that he considered himself "in no way responsible" for the inferiority of his numbers; and in seeming anticipation of defeat, he disclaimed all responsibility for that also.[1] More than a week previously[a] he had wisely prepared for a defeat, by making arrangements for a change of base from the Pamunkey to the James, in the event of disaster.[2]

[a] June 18.

Lee's preparations for striking McClellan a fatal blow, or to raise the siege of Richmond, were completed on the 25th of June, and on the following morning information that reached the latter of the advance of Jackson on his right, caused him to abandon all thought of moving toward the Confederate Capital. He at once took a defensive position, and prepared for a retreat to the James River.[3] He considered the positions of the troops on the Richmond side of the Chickahominy as reasonably secure, yet measures for a passage for their retreat through the White Oak Swamp were prudently taken. On the other side of the Chickahominy the right wing, consisting of the corps of Fitz-John Porter, about twenty-seven thousand strong, was also strongly posted. It was composed of the divisions of Morell, Sykes, and McCall, with a large portion of the cavalry reserve. Porter had ten heavy guns in a battery on the banks of the Chickahominy. McClellan says he was satisfied that he had to deal with double his own numbers, but, relying upon the character of his followers, he felt "contented calmly to await the bursting of the coming storm."[4]

He did not wait long. General Lee called a council of general officers on the 25th,[5] when it was resolved to begin the movement on McClellan's right, already mentioned, at three o'clock the next morning. Jackson was to advance, take with him Branch's troops, near Hanover Court-House, and turn the Beaver Dam Creek back of Mechanicsville. General A. P. Hill was to cross the Chickahominy at Meadow Bridge, and move on Mechanicsville;

---

1 "I will do all that a General can do with the splendid army I have the honor to command," he said, "and if it is destroyed by overwhelming numbers, can at least die with it and share its fate. But if the result of the action, which will probably occur to-morrow, or within a short time, is a disaster, the responsibility cannot be thrown on my shoulders; it must rest where it belongs." Dispatches to the Secretary of War, June 25, 1862, at six o'clock in the evening.

To this dispatch the President replied, that the General's suggestion that he might be overwhelmed by 200,000, and his talk as to whom the responsibility would belong, pained him very much. "I give you all I can," said Mr. Lincoln, "and act on the presumption that you will do the best you can with what you have; while you continue, ungenerously I think, to assume that I could give you more if I would, I have omitted, and shall omit, no opportunity to send you re-enforcements whenever I possibly can."

On the 20th General McClellan had reported the force under his command at 156,838, of whom only 115,102 were present or fit for duty; the remainder, 29,511, being absent on furlough, or sick, and under arrest. Lee's troops, it has been since ascertained, numbered about 75,000, and Jackson increased the number to about 110,000. Beauregard was not at Richmond.

2 Report to the Secretary of War, August 4, 1863, page 123.

3 Report, page 124.

4 Report, page 124.

5 Composed of Generals Lee, Baldwin, Jackson, A. P. Hill, D. H. Hill, Huger, Longstreet, Branch, Wise, Anderson, Whiting, Ripley, and Magruder.

and when the Mechanicsville bridge should be uncovered, Longstreet and D. H. Hill were to cross, and proceed to the support of the troops on the left side of the stream. This movement would leave only the divisions of Huger and Magruder between McClellan's left, at Fair Oaks, and Richmond.

The projected movement of the Confederates was delayed until the afternoon of the 26th, when, at about three o'clock, A. P. Hill crossed the Chickahominy, and drove a regiment and battery at Mechanicsville, back to the main line near Ellison's Mill. The movement had been discovered in time to call in all the pickets and prepare for the shock of battle. The Nationals were now strongly posted on the heights overlooking Beaver Dam Creek, near Ellison's Mill. There McCall's Pennsylvania Reserves, eight thousand five hundred strong, with five batteries, occupied a position commanding the stream below and the open fields beyond, over which the Confederates must approach. These, with two regiments of Meade's brigade as reserves, were well supported by Morell's division and Sykes's regulars. General Reynolds held the right, and General Seymour the left, and the brigades of Generals Martindale and Griffin were deployed on the right of McCall. The bridges over the creek had all been destroyed, and trees were felled along its margin.

MECHANICSVILLE BRIDGE OVER THE CHICKAHOMINY.[1]

In the face of these formidable obstacles, and a heavy fire of artillery and infantry, the leading brigades of Hill, followed by Longstreet's, moved to the attack. Then they massed on the National left to turn it, expecting Jackson to fall on its right at the same time; but the movement was foiled by Seymour, who stoutly opposed it. There was a terrific battle, and the Confederates were hurled back with fearful carnage. Night fell, and at nine o'clock THE BATTLE OF MECHANICSVILLE ceased.[2] The Nationals were

---

[1] This is a view of the bridge from the Mechanicsville side of the stream as it appeared when the writer sketched it, at the close of May, 1866. The Chickahominy was then "up," and overflowing the wooded bottom. In the distance toward Richmond is seen the edge of the high plain, along which was a line of heavy fortifications erected by the Confederates, and which commanded the Chickahominy for a long distance.

[2] This occurred on the same ground where the skirmish was fought on the 23d, and this battle-ground also is seen in the picture of Ellison's mill and vicinity on page 404. The road from Mechanicsville approaching the Beaver Dam Creek, runs along the foot of the distant eminences, almost parallel with the stream, and there the approaching Confederates presented a flank to the fire of their foes.

masters of the situation. Expecting a renewal of the fight in the morning, the gallant Reserves rested on their arms that night.[1]

Notwithstanding the Nationals gained a decided victory at Ellison's Mill, McClellan was satisfied that the time had come for him to fly to the James River. He ascertained that Jackson had passed the Beaver Dam Creek above, and was gaining his flank. Lee's intention to strike McClellan's communications with his base at the White House was clearly developed, and the latter was left to choose between a concentration of his whole army on the left bank of the Chickahominy, by means of the several bridges that now spanned it, and there give general battle to Lee's army; to concentrate his whole force on the right bank, and march directly on Richmond; or to transfer the right wing to that side of the stream, and with his supplies retreat to the James River. Experts say that a skillful and energetic commander would not have hesitated a moment at such juncture in concentrating his forces and marching on Richmond, whose defenses were manned by only about twenty-five thousand men. Thus he might have severed Lee from this force and his supplies, and turned upon and crushed him. Indeed, Magruder tremblingly expected this movement; and it was a theme of just wonder among many of the Confederate officers that it was not made, for Richmond was then really at the mercy of the Army of the Potomac.[2]

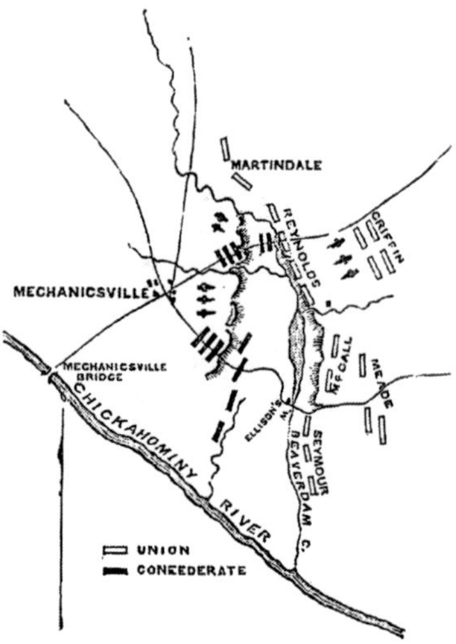

BATTLE OF MECHANICSVILLE.

McClellan chose the less hazardous course, and commenced a retreat toward the James River, for which, as we have observed, he had prepared several days before. "To that end," he said, "from the evening of the 26th every energy of the army was bent." He had already ordered Colonel Ingalls, the Quartermaster at the White House, to send the stores and munitions of war of every kind to Savage's Station, burn what he could not remove, and forward as many supplies as possible up the James. He also sent his wounded to Savage's Station, and prepared to cross the Chickahominy with the right wing for the flight, a perilous thing to do at that crisis, for Jackson and Ewell had crossed the Beaver Dam Creek above, cut

---

[1] The National loss was about four hundred. According to a statement made to Mr. Swinton (*Campaigns of the Army of the Potomac*, note, page 145) by General Longstreet, the Confederate loss was between three and four thousand.

[2] In his report (August 12, 1862) General Magruder said: "Had McClellan massed his whole force in column, and advanced it against any point of our line of battle, as was done at Austerlitz under similar circumstances by the greatest captain of any age, though the head of his column would have suffered greatly, its momentum would have insured him success, and the occupation of our works about Richmond, and consequently the city, might have been his reward. His failure to do so is the best evidence that our wise commander fully understood the character of his opponent."—Reports of the Operations of the Army of Northern Virginia, i. 191.

off Stoneman and his cavalry from the Army, and would doubtless fall upon Porter's flank in the morning, while the troops of Longstreet and the Hills would attack his front.

In order to save his heavy guns and supply-train, and keep Jackson from interfering with the removal of the public property at the White House, McClellan found it necessary to hold the Fifth Corps back for that purpose, and, as we have observed, the soldiers slept on their arms after the fight at Ellison's Mill. During the night most of the heavy guns and wagons were thrown across the river, and at a little before dawn[a] the troops were skillfully withdrawn to a strong position near Gaines's Mills, between Cool Arbor[1] and the Chickahominy. There, in line of battle, on the arc of a circle, and covering the approaches to the bridges (Woodbury's and Alexander's) over which the troops were to cross the river and join those on the Richmond side, the Fifth Corps awaited attack. A few of the siege-guns were yet in position there, and those which were passed over the stream were planted so as to cover the approaches to the bridges. Morell's division occupied the left, near a deep ravine traversed by a brook, and Sykes's division of Regulars and Duryea's Zouaves were on the right, extending toward Cool Arbor. McCall's division formed a second line, his left touching Butterfield's right; Seymour's brigade and the horse-batteries of Roberts and Tidball commanded the rear, and cavalry under General Philip St. George Cooke[2] were performing vedette and flanking-service near the Chickahominy. On that field, where Grant and Lee fought so desperately two years later, Porter was now preparing to give battle to a foe greatly his superior in numbers. It proved to be, before the conflict ended, thirty-five thousand against seventy thousand.

[a] June 27, 1862.

A. P. HILL.

Porter was attacked at two o'clock in the afternoon[b] by A. P. Hill, who led the advance of Lee's column, and had been waiting for Jackson, who was to form the left of the Confederate line, to come up.[3] Longstreet was held back for the same purpose. The brunt of the attack fell first upon Sykes, who threw the assailants back in great confusion, and with heavy loss. Many of these, so easily repulsed, were re-enforcements who had just come up from the sea-board, and had never been under fire before. Longstreet was at once ordered forward to their relief with his veterans. He was directed to make a feint on Porter's left, but was so promptly and stoutly met that he was compelled to make a real attack or

[b] June 27.

[1] A tavern called New Cool Arbor was nearer Dr. Gaines's than Old Cool Arbor, as will be observed by reference to the map.

[2] Five companies of the Fifth Regular Cavalry, two squadrons of the First Regular, and three squadrons of the Sixth Pennsylvania Cavalry.

[3] The divisions of A. P. Hill, Anderson, and Whiting, formed the center.

effect nothing. So he resolved to carry the heights by assault. While he was preparing to do so the corps of Jackson and D. H. Hill's division arrived, the former taking position on Longstreet's left, and the latter, after severe and successful fighting, gaining his destined point on the extreme left of the Confederate line. Ewell's division, in the mean time, came into action on Jackson's right, and two of the latter's brigades were sent to assist A. P. Hill.

The Confederate line was now in complete order, and made a general advance. Porter, hard pressed, sent to McClellan for aid, but the Commander-in-Chief, persuaded that the Confederates between himself and Richmond outnumbered his own forces, could spare only Slocum's division of Franklin's corps.[1] He was not aware that Magruder, who was making a great show and noise on his front, was repeating his successful game of deception practiced in the vicinity of Yorktown, and that he was at the head of only twenty-five thousand men, opposed to McClellan's sixty thousand, well intrenched, and was trembling for the safety of his army and the capital.[2]

Slocum's division crossed Alexander's bridge, and made Porter's force about thirty-five thousand strong. It reached him at half-past three o'clock, when the whole of Lee's army on that side of the river was in the action. So imminent was Porter's peril that the re-enforcements were divided, even to regiments, and hastily sent to weak points. The conflict was terrible, especially on the left, between the houses of Adams and Dr. Gaines. Indeed, the struggle along the whole line was fierce and persistent for hours, and the issue for a long time was extremely doubtful.

At five o'clock Porter again called for aid, and McClellan sent him the brigades of French and Meagher, of Richardson's division. They went forward at a quick pace, but before they could reach the river the Confederates, at about six o'clock, had rallied every available platoon in their ranks for a desperate effort to break or crush the National line. Brigade after brigade was hurled against the Union line, striking it here and there in rapid succession and tremendous force, where it appeared weak, hoping to break it. But for a long time it stood firm, though continually thinned and weakened by carnage. Finally, when Jackson, with the divisions of Longstreet and Whiting, made a furious assault upon the National left, Butterfield's gallant

---

[1] McClellan made inquiries from time to time of Heintzelman, Keyes, Franklin, and Sumner, about sparing men from their respective corps to send to Porter, and their reports were all discouraging, for Magruder, by great skill in his display of troops, made each believe that his particular position might be assailed at any time by an overwhelming force. See telegraphic correspondence between McClellan and these commanders, June 26 and 27, 1862, in McClellan's Report, pages 128, 129.

Magruder, as we have observed, managed with his inferior force to keep up a flurry of excitement all along the front of the National army during the whole day, threatening first one point and then another, and finally, at the middle of the afternoon, when Porter was most needing re-enforcements, he caused Burns's pickets to be attacked by a strong force. Burns sent word to Hancock to prepare for action. The messenger had just arrived when the latter was assailed with shot and shell from an unsuspected Confederate battery, followed by a furious attack of infantry. Burns on one side and Smith on the other supported Hancock with their Napoleon and Parrott guns, and very soon the latter repulsed his assailants. In this engagement, sometimes called The Second Battle of Fair Oaks, two Georgia regiments were dreadfully shattered, and the colonel of one of them was captured. He proved to be L. Q. C. Lamar, one of the most active men in the incipient stages of the rebellion in the South. See page 59, volume I.

[2] Alluding to this crisis, Magruder in his report (Reports of the Army of Northern Virginia, i. 191) says:—"I considered the situation of our army as extremely critical and perilous. The larger part of it was on the opposite side of the Chickahominy; the bridges had all been destroyed; but one was rebuilt, and there were but 25,000 men between his (McClellan's) army of 100,000 men and Richmond."

brigade, which had been repelling the heaviest of the attacks for more than an hour unassisted, now, sorely pressed on the front and flank, gave way and fell back toward the woods on the Chickahominy, leaving the batteries of Allen, Weedon, Hart, and Edwards, exposed. These made a desperate defense, but, being without support, fell back with a loss of several guns. Then the center bent, and, with the right, fell back in the same direction, toward Alexander's bridge. Seeing this, Porter called up all of his reserved and remaining artillery (about eighty guns in all), covered the retreat of his infantry, and for an instant checked the advance of the victors. Just at that moment General St. George Cooke, without orders, attacked their flank with his cavalry, which was repulsed and thrown into great disorder. The horses, terrified by the tremendous roar of nearly two hundred guns, and the rattle of thousands of muskets, rushed back through the Union batteries, giving the impression that it was a furious attack of Confederate cavalry. This made the artillerists recoil, and Porter's whole force was pressed back to the river. To this circumstance Porter attributed his failure to hold the field, and to take off all of his guns and wounded.

DANIEL. BUTTERFIELD.

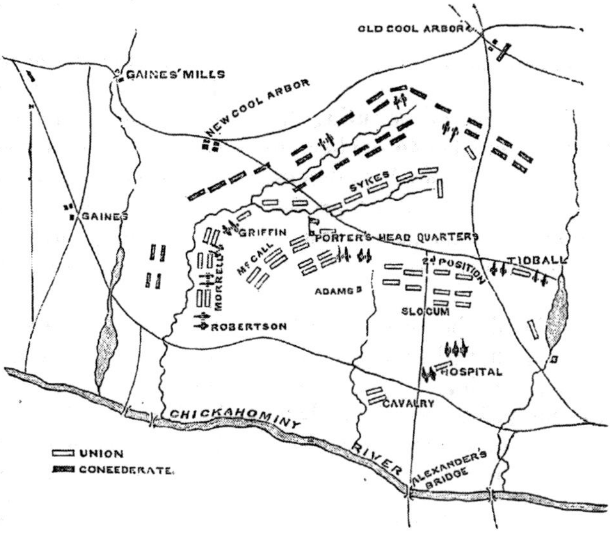

BATTLE OF GAINES'S FARM.

Porter's troops were now pressing toward the bridge, many of them in fearful disorder, and for a moment all seemed to be lost, for the Confederates were in crushing force just behind them. But relief for the fugitives was at hand. French and Meagher had just crossed the bridge, covered by the heavy guns in position on the Richmond side of the river, and, gathering up the vast multitude of stragglers, checked the flight. They advanced rapidly to the front, with cheers that thrilled with joy the fainting hearts of the

Unionists. Behind them the shattered brigades were speedily formed, while the batteries of Griffin and Martin poured a destructive storm of shot and shell upon the head of Lee's column. Seeing fresh troops on their front, and ignorant of their number, the Confederates fell back and rested upon the field they had won, at a fearful cost to themselves and their foes. Thus ended the sanguinary BATTLE OF GAINES'S FARM.[1]

During the night the thinned and exhausted regiments of Porter's corps were safely withdrawn to the other side of the river; the regular infantry forming the rear guard, and destroying the bridges after them. The cavalry of Stoneman and Emory, who had been cut off from Porter's force, proceeded to the White House, and thence to Yorktown, and rejoined the army on the James River. With this movement ended the siege of Richmond, for now McClellan abandoned all thoughts of capturing it, and studied only how he should transfer his army and supplies to the bank of the James. That evening he informed his General officers of his determination to fly and not to fight, and gave orders accordingly, directing Keyes to advance with his corps through the White Oak Swamp, across the creek that traverses it, and take position on the other side, so as to cover the passage of troops and trains.

RUINS OF GAINES'S MILLS.[2]

[a] June 28, 1862.

Before day-break the next morning[a] General McClellan went to Savage's Station, and remained there all day, superintending the movement, which was commenced at an early hour. By noon Keyes was in the prescribed position. During the day Porter's shattered division was moved across the swamp, and placed in positions covering the roads leading from Richmond toward White Oak Swamp and Long

[1] The Confederates in their reports called it *The Battle of the Chickahominy.* For full details see the reports of General McClellan, and of General Porter and his subordinates; also, of General Lee and his subordinates, contained in volume I. of the *Reports of the Army of Northern Virginia.* The losses on both sides may be given only in numbers derived from estimates, as McClellan says, "no general returns were made until we had arrived at Harrison's Landing," several days afterward. The estimates make the National loss in this battle about 8,000 men, of whom 6,000 were killed and wounded. Among those who were captured was General John F. Reynolds. The Confederate loss was probably about 5,000. Porter lost 22 guns, three of which ran off the bridge into the river.

[2] This is a view of the ruins of Dr. Gaines's mills, near which the battle was fought, as they appeared when the writer sketched the spot, at the close of May, 1866. The one in the foreground was a flouring-mill, built of brick; and the other, more distant, across the stream, of which only the flume and wheel remained, was a sawmill. The road seen on the slope is in the direction of Mechanicsville.

Bridge; and at night McCall's weakened division was also moved forward for a similar purpose. These were followed by a train of five thousand wagons laden with ammunition, provision, and baggage,[1] and a drove of twenty-five hundred beef cattle, all of which had to make the passage of the swamp along narrow causeways and defiles. Yet so perfectly was the movement masked from the Confederates, that they had no suspicion of it until the night of the 28th. To allow the trains and the cattle to get well forward, the corps of Sumner and Heintzelman, and Smith's division of Franklin's corps, were ordered to form an interior line, and remain on the Richmond side of the White Oak Swamp until dark of the 29th, in a position to cover the roads to Richmond, and also Savage's Station, on the railway, where Slocum's division was left as a reserve. Then they were to fall back across the swamp, and join the fugitive army. The left of this covering force rested on Keyes's old intrenchments, to the left of the Seven Pines, and the right so as to cover Savage's Station.

ERASMUS D. KEYES

There was a little flurry on the morning of the 28th, when Franklin's corps withdrew from Golding's farm in front of Woodbury's Bridge. The Confederates opened their artillery on Smith's division from Garnett's Hill, and from Porter's late position on Gaines's Hill, beyond the Chickahominy. This was followed by an attempt of two Georgia regiments to carry the works about to be abandoned, when they were driven back by the Twenty-third New York and Forty-ninth Pennsylvania, who were on picket duty with a section of Mott's battery. This repulse confirmed the Confederates in the belief that McClellan's army was all behind his intrenchments, preparing for another attack.

Lee was deceived. He supposed McClellan might at once throw his united force across the river, and give battle to preserve his communication with the White House; or else, if it was his intention to relinquish the siege of Richmond, that, having possession of the lower bridges of the Chickahominy, he would follow the way down the Peninsula which Johnston came up. So he kept the great bulk of his army on the northern side of the river, ready for battle if it should be offered, or to strike the retreating forces on flank and rear; and he sent Stuart and Ewell to seize the railway and cut McClellan's communication with the White House. They found that supply-station abandoned, a greater portion of the stores and munitions of war removed, and the remainder, with the White House itself, in flames.[2]

---

[1] Orders were given to the different commanders to load their wagons with ammunition and provisions, and only necessary baggage, and to destroy all property which could not be taken away.

[2] An order had been sent that morning to the commander at the White House to apply the torch to every thing there not already removed, so soon as indications of danger should appear. Warning thereof was quite

Lee was perplexed by these circumstances, for Huger and Magruder all that day reported the National fortifications in front of the Richmond lines to be fully manned. That night the amazing fact was disclosed to the Confederate commander that a greater portion of the Army of the Potomac had departed, not to give battle on the northern side of the Chickahominy, nor to retreat down the Peninsula; but to take a new position near the James River, with that stream as a highway for supplies, and a theater for the co-operation of a naval force, by which its offensive and defensive power would be wonderfully strengthened. He made instant preparations for a pursuit to crush that army before it could gain its destined goal.

McClellan left Savage's Station at an early hour on the morning of the

VIEW AT SAVAGE'S STATION IN 1866.[1]

29th, and moved across the White Oak Swamp toward the front of his retreating columns. He had issued the day before[a] two extraordinary documents. One was an order for the sick and wounded men who could not march, to be left at Savage's Station with surgeons, rations, and medical stores, to fall into the hands of the Confederates.[2] The other was a dispatch to the Secretary of War, which has no

[a] June 28, 1862.

early given, when the cars sent with supplies toward Savage's Station were turned back at Dispatch Station by reports that the Confederates were near. Before the close of the day an immense amount of provisions, stores, and munitions of war was there committed to the flames. The gallant Lieutenant George Sibbald Wilson, of Poughkeepsie (who gave his young life to his country in consequence of a wound received at Fredericksburg), who was among those detailed for that service, gave a graphic description of the scene in a letter to his mother, now before the writer. "Such quantities of elegant new tents," he said; "of nice beds for the sick; of fine liquors and wines, cordials and medicines, oranges, lemons, beef, corn, whiskey; immense quantities of hay; boxes on boxes of clothing, and every thing conceivable for use and comfort were committed to the flames."

The White House itself, as we have observed, was not spared. It was a small and common wooden structure (see page 386), surrounded by a field shaded by locust-trees. The patriotic impulses given by the written misrepresentation of its owner, which made McClellan say, officially, "I have taken every precaution to secure from injury this house, where Washington passed the first portion of his married life—I neither occupy it myself, nor permit others to occupy it, or the grounds in the immediate vicinity"—had been succeeded by feelings of contempt. At the time we are considering it was occupied by Roman Catholic Sisters of Charity, who accompanied the National army for the relief of distress.

[1] This is a view of Savage's Station as it appeared when the writer sketched it, at the close of May, 1866. In the foreground is seen the cellar and foundation wall of Savage's house, and between it and the site of the station on the left a pleasant grove, in which many of the wounded in the Battle of Gaines's Farm found grateful shelter from the hot sun. Savage's house was the general hospital at this place at the time considered in the text, and the out-buildings and about three hundred tents around them were filled with wounded men.

[2] The Commander ordered all the ambulances to depart empty, instead of carrying away the disabled; for "four or five thousand wounded and sick men would so embarrass the army, that its escape might be impossible."—*The Peninsula Campaign*, by J. J. Marks, D. D., page 239.

equal in history.[1] In a most unhappy state of mind he moved to the front with his staff, giving general orders to his commanders how to resist pursuit, and directing Keyes to move on to the James River, and occupy a defensive position near the high open ground of Malvern Hill. Porter was to follow him and prolong the line toward the right, and the trains were to be pushed forward to the James and placed under the protection of the gun-boats.

At about the hour when McClellan left Savage's Station, Lee put his troops in motion in pursuit.[a] Magruder and Huger were ordered to push along the Williamsburg and Charles City roads, to strike the fugitives on flank and rear; Longstreet and Hill to cross the Chickahominy at New Bridge, and move by flank routes so as to intercept the retreat; and Jackson was to cross at the Grape Vine Bridge and sweep with his usual celerity down the right bank of the Chickahominy.

[a] June 29, 1862.

McClellan had twenty-four hours the start in this exciting race, and his trains and a large part of his army were well on toward the James before the pursuit began. Yet that advantage did not secure his army immunity from a terrible struggle for life with its foe. It began on the extreme rear, on the morning of the 29th, when Magruder approached Savage's Station. Seeing this menace, Sumner, who had vacated his position at Fair Oaks early in the morning, and taken position on Allen's farm, near Orchard Station, moved his corps to Savage's, uniting there with Smith's division of Franklin's corps, and taking chief command. The divisions of Richardson and Sedgwick were formed on the right of the railway, fronting Richmond, the latter joining that of Heintzelman's left.

Magruder made a furious attack on Sedgwick's right at about nine o'clock,[b] but was easily repulsed. Supposing the Nationals to be advancing, he sent to Huger for aid. Two brigades were for-

[b] June 29.

---

[1] After reporting the battle of the previous day, he said: "Had I 20,000 or even 10,000 fresh troops to use to maneuver, I could take Richmond; but I have not a man in reserve, and shall be glad to cover my retreat and save the material and *personnel* of the army. If we have lost the day, we have yet preserved our honor, and no one need blush for the Army of the Potomac. I have lost this battle because my force was too small. I again repeat, that I am not responsible for this, and I say it with the earnestness of a general who feels in his heart the loss of every brave man who has been needlessly sacrificed." He told the Secretary that he hoped to retrieve the fortunes of the day, but to do it he must send "very large re-enforcements, and send them at once." Then, repeating the assertion that the Government must not hold him responsible for the result, he said: "I feel too earnestly to-night. I have seen too many dead and wounded comrades to feel otherwise than that the Government has not sustained this army. If you do not do so now the game is lost. If I save this army now I tell you plainly that I owe no thanks to you or any other persons in Washington. You have done your best to sacrifice this army."

Military history may be searched in vain for an instance where such language of an officer to his superior was not followed by arrest or instant dismissal from the service. It appears utterly inexcusable, judged by General McClellan's official report made more than a year afterward, in which it is repeated, and especially in the clear light of subsequent investigation. It was a precedent for the most mischievous insubordination throughout the army. Had General Casey, when, after the Battle of Seven Pines, he looked sadly upon one-third of his entire division killed or maimed, and felt keenly the injustice of his commander's stinging words of censure, sent a note to the Commander-in-Chief, saying (and with more reason): "Because of your wretched blunder in placing me in the position I was in, without adequate support, I lost the day, you and not I must be held responsible; if any of my division are saved, I tell you plainly I owe no thanks to you—you have done your best to sacrifice it," he would probably have been arrested on a just charge of most dangerous insubordination, and perhaps tried by a drum-head court-martial, and shot before sunset by the order of his chief, as an example to the army. The act would have been justified by military discipline and precedent. But the patient and forbearing President, who was specially insulted by the dispatch, only replied, after telling the irate general that re-enforcements should be sent to him as fast as possible: "If you have had a drawn battle or a repulse, it is the price we pay for the enemy not being in Washington. We protected Washington, and the enemy concentrated on you. Had we stripped Washington, he would have been upon us before the troops sent could have got to you. Less than a week ago, you notified us that re-enforcements were leaving Richmond to come in front of us. It is the nature of the case, and neither you nor the Government is to blame."

warded, but these were withdrawn when it was ascertained that the Nationals in their works were only a covering party for the retreating army. Magruder accordingly made dispositions to attack them. Unfortunately Heintzelman, on Sumner's left, who had been directed to hold the Williamsburg road, had mistaken the order and fallen back entirely across the White Oak Swamp, leaving a gap of three-fourths of a mile between Sumner and Franklin, and placing his own troops too distant to be of immediate service.

Magruder perceived this weakness, and at about four o'clock in the afternoon he fell upon his enemy with great violence. He was gallantly met and repulsed by the brigade of General Burns, supported by those of Brooke and Hancock. The Sixty-ninth New York also came up in support, while the batteries of Pettit, Osborn, and Bramhall took an effective part in the action. The conflict raged furiously until between eight and nine o'clock in the evening, when Magruder recoiled. He had expected aid from Jackson, but the latter had been too long delayed in re-building the Grape Vine bridge. Darkness put an end to the fight, and thus ended THE BATTLE OF SAVAGE'S STATION.[1] Covered by French's brigade as a rear-guard, the National troops all fell back to White Oak Swamp that night, according to McClellan's original order (now repeated), and by five o'clock on the following morning[a] they were beyond the creek, and the bridge over which almost the entire Army of the Potomac and its trains had passed was destroyed behind them. Twenty-five hundred wounded men had been left at Savage's Station, by order of the Commanding General. It was a sad necessity, for many of them were afterward intense sufferers in Confederate prisons.

[a] June 30, 1862.

On the morning of the 30th McClellan had reached Malvern Hills, which he considered the key to his contemplated new position, and made the mansion-house on the estate that covered their southern extremity his head-quarters.[2] There he made arrangements with Major Myer, the Chief of the Signal Corps, for instant communication with his army and the gunboats, and then went on board the *Galena*, to confer with Commodore Rodgers. By this time a greater part of the army had emerged from the White Oak Swamp into the high open region of Malvern Hills, well covered

---

[1] Speaking of this battle, an eye-witness said that, as usual, the Confederates had hurled heavy bodies of troops against the National line here and there, for the purpose of breaking it. Sometimes the troops would recoil, but "there was General Burns," said the narrator, "who, with clothes and hat pierced, and face covered with blood, still rallied and cheered his men." On one occasion, two exposed companies commenced to march off the field. "The General expostulated, entreated, commanded them, all in vain. At length, taking off his torn hat and throwing it down, he besought them not to disgrace themselves and their general. This last appeal was successful. They returned and fought more desperately, to wipe out the cowardice of a moment." The same writer says—"After the enemy was repulsed at Savage's Station, General Sumner sent to General McClellan for, as he expressed himself, 'orders to push the enemy into the Chickahominy.' The General's reply was, 'The rear-guard will follow the retreat of the main body of the army.' On the reception of this command, the greatest contternation and displeasure reigned among both officers and men. Many openly rebelled—they wished to sacrifice themselves in any way rather than by a disgraceful retreat."—Dr. Marks's *Peninsula Campaign*, page 254.

[2] The picture on page 429 shows the appearance of the house when the writer visited it, at the close of May, 1866. It was upon the southern extremity of the Malvern Hills, and from the lawn in front of it there was a comprehensive view of the lowlands and the James River, in the vicinity of Turkey Bend. The view southward was bounded by City Point in the distance. The old mansion was of brick, and had a modern addition of wood. During the old war for independence, the estate was owned by one of the Randolph family. It was the head-quarters of Lafayette while he was pursuing Cornwallis down the Peninsula. The writer has in his possession two autograph letters by the Marquis, dated at "Malvern Hills," in the year 1781.

in the movement by a rear-guard under Franklin, and very soon the van reached the vicinity of the river at Turkey Bend. The supply trains were pushed forward to Haxall's plantation, and the artillery parks were on Malvern Hills.

McCLELLAN'S HEAD-QUARTERS ON MALVERN HILLS.

This position had not been gained without a severe struggle. Franklin had been left with a rear-guard[1] to hold the passage of White Oak Swamp Bridge, and cover the withdrawal of the trains from that point. The pursuit was in two columns: one, composed of the corps of Longstreet and A. P. Hill, which was joined by Jackson's command, followed directly on the track of the fugitive army; the other, under Magruder and Huger, pushed along the Charles City road to the right of the retreating troops. Jackson had been ordered on the morning of the 30th to sweep around toward the Chickahominy, so as to gain their left and rear, but was checked by the destruction of a bridge; and when, at noon, he sought to cross the White Oak Swamp Bridge, he found it destroyed, and was there met by Smith, Richardson, and Naglee, and the batteries of Ayres and Hazard, who kept him at bay during the day and evening. Hazard was mortally wounded, and his force was so cut up that his battery was withdrawn. Ayres kept up a cannonade with great spirit all the afternoon. The Nationals retired during the night, leaving three hundred and fifty sick and wounded behind, and some disabled guns, as spoils for the Confederates next morning.

While this contest for the passage of the bridge was in progress, a very severe battle occurred at Glendale, or Nelson's Farm, about two miles distant. There, at the intersection of the Long Bridge road and the Quaker or Willis road, along which the Nationals had fled, and not far from Willis Church, McCall's division was posted, Meade's brigade on the right, Seymour's on the left, and

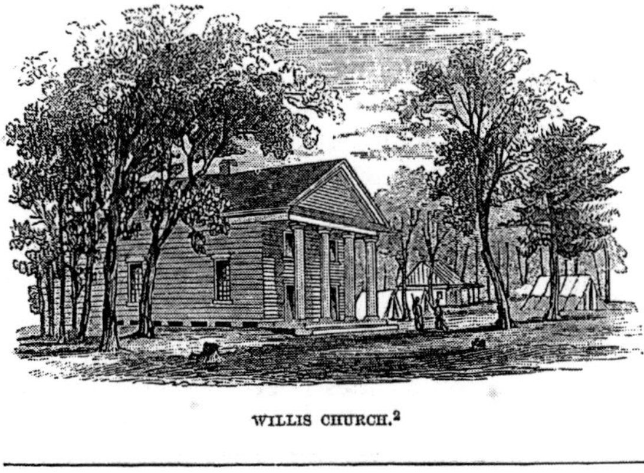

WILLIS CHURCH.[2]

---

[1] Composed of his own corps, the division of General Richardson, and Naglee's brigade. Slocum's division was on the right of the Charles City road.

[2] This was the appearance of the building and its surroundings when the writer sketched it, at the close of May, 1866. It is a few rods from the scene of the hottest of the battle of Glendale or Frazier's Farm, in a beautiful grove, where the tents of a burial-party were pitched. It was founded by "Father Willis" of the Methodist Church, and was built just before the war.

that of Reynolds (who was a prisoner), under Colonel S. G. Simmons, of the Fifth Pennsylvania, in reserve. The artillery was all in front of this line. Randall's regular battery was on the right, Cooper and Kerns's opposite the center, and Dietrich's and Kennerheim's (20-pounder Parrotts) on the left. Sumner was some distance to the left, with Sedgwick's division; Hooker was at Sumner's left, and Kearney was at the right of McCall.

Longstreet and Hill had hurried forward to gain this point before McClellan's army could pass it, hoping there to cut that army in two and destroy it. But they were a little too late. When Longstreet (who was accompanied by Lee and Jefferson Davis) found himself confronted there, he waited for Magruder to come up, and it was not until between three and four o'clock in the afternoon[a] that he began an attack. He fell heavily upon McCall, whose force (Pennsylvania Reserves), when he reached the Pamunkey, was ten thousand, but had been reduced by sickness, fatigue, and fighting, to six thousand. The Confederates attempted by the weight of their first blow to crush his left, but were repulsed by a charge of the Fifth, Eighth, Ninth, and Tenth Pennsylvania Reserves, led by Colonel Simmons, who captured two hundred of them and drove the remainder back to the woods. Then the fugitives turned, and by a murderous fire made the pursuers recoil, and flee to the forest in the rear of their first position. In that encounter the slaughter was dreadful. Simmons was mortally wounded, and the dead or maimed bodies of hundreds of his comrades strewed the field.

[a] June 30. 1862.

This first struggle was quickly followed by others. Backward and forward the contending lines were swayed by charges and counter-charges, for two hours. To break the National line and to capture its batteries seemed to be the chief object of the assailants. Cooper's battery, in the center, was taken, and then retaken, together with the standard of an Alabama regiment; and this was followed by the appearance of General Meagher, with his Irish brigade, who made a desperate charge across an open field, and drove the Confederates to the woods. By a gallant charge of a brigade (Fifty-fifth and Sixtieth Virginia), Randall's battery on the right was also captured, and the greater portion of its supporting regiment was driven back, when McCall and Meade rallied their infantry for its recapture. A terrible hand-to-hand fight ensued, and the reserves were repulsed, but they carried back with them their recovered guns. In this encounter, just at dark, Meade was severely wounded, and McCall, who had lost all of his brigadiers and was reconnoitering, was captured. Then the command devolved upon Seymour. The noise of battle had brought some of the troops of Hooker and Kearney to the field of action just at dark, and soon afterward the sound of cheering from the First New Jersey brigade (General Taylor) startled the wearied and broken Confederates, and they fell back to the woods. These fresh troops recovered a part of the ground lost by the Reserves. So ended THE BATTLE OF GLENDALE.[1]

[1] The Confederates call it the *Battle of Frazier's Farm*, it having been fought on a part of Frazier's and a part of Nelson's farms. The battle was fought desperately by both sides; on the part of the Nationals, in accordance with the judgment and discretion of the corps commanders, for the General-in-Chief was entirely ignorant of what was going on until "very late at night," as he said in his Report (page 138), when his aids returned to give him "the results of the day's fighting along the whole line, and the true position of affairs." He had been a part of the day on board of a gun-boat in the James River, according to his report, and another

While the Confederates were waiting for the dawn to renew the battle, the National troops were all silently withdrawn; and early the next day[a] the Army of the Potomac, united for the first time since the Chickahominy first divided it, was in a strong position on Malvern Hill, and its communication with a new base of supplies on the James assured. Terrible had been the experience of that army during the preceding seven days—terrible indeed had been its losses, and other afflictions. The high and dry land of Malvern Hills, and the sight of the James River, inspired the worn and wearied soldiers with gladness and hope; for they believed that they might now change front, repel their pursuers, rest a little, and then be called upon to march victoriously upon Richmond.

[a] July 1, 1862.

The troops were posted, under the direction of General Barnard, in a strong position, on the 1st of July.[b] Porter had reached Malvern Hills the day before, and placed his troops so as to command all the approaches to it from Richmond and the Swamp. The last of the trains and reserve of artillery arrived at about four o'clock in the afternoon, and at about that hour General Holmes, who had been summoned to Richmond from the south side of the James, and had marched down the river road with his brigade and a part of Wise's, appeared on the left of Porter (he having changed front, with his face toward Richmond), and opened fire upon him with artillery. Holmes soon found himself overmatched, for Porter had ample artillery at command, and withdrew so hastily that he left two of his guns behind. When the army had all arrived the next day, it was posted with its left and center resting on Malvern Hills, while the right curved backward through a wooded country, toward a point below Haxall's, on the James.

[b] 1862.

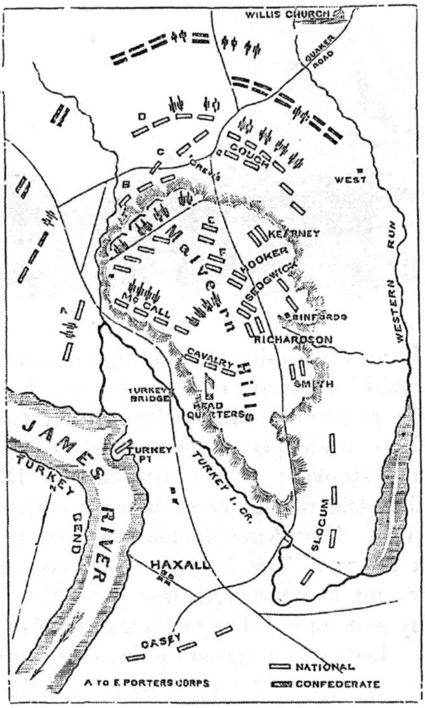

POSITION OF TROOPS ON MALVERN HILLS.

Malvern Hills form a high plateau, sloping toward Richmond from bold

---

part of the day at his quarters, only two or three miles from the scene of strife, the din of which, it would seem, was calculated to draw every interested soul into the vortex of the struggle, for it was a decisive point. The subordinate commanders well knew that if the army should be beaten there it would be ruined, and so they fought desperately for victory and won it, and then made arrangements, without the knowledge of the commanding General, to save it, by silently withdrawing during the night. All this had been accomplished before McClellan's aids (as he said) had informed him of "the true position of affairs." General Barnard, McClellan's Engineer-in-Chief, says, in speaking of this fact given in the General's Report: "It may well be doubted whether, in all recorded reports or dispatches of military commanders, a parallel to this extraordinary avowal can be found. We suppose it the especial business of a general to know at each moment 'the true position of affairs,' and to have some agency in ruling it."

banks toward the river, and bounded by deep ravines, making an excellent defensive position. Yet it was not considered a safe one for the army to halt, for it was too far separated from supplies. So, on the morning of the first, McClellan again went on board the *Galena*, to accompany Captain Rodgers, to "select the final location for the army and its depots." This was fixed at Harrison's Bar, a short distance down the river. While he was there a heavy cannonade was commenced on Malvern Hills.

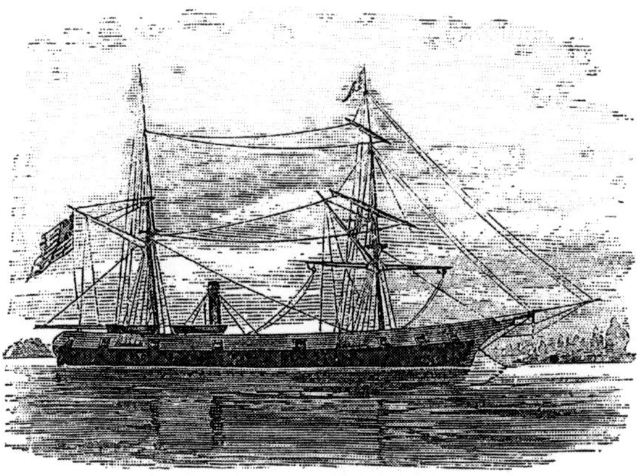

THE GALENA.

The National line of battle was formed with Porter's corps on the left, near Crew's house (with Sykes's division on the left and Morell's on the right), where the artillery of the reserve, under Colonel Hunt, was so disposed on high ground that a concentrated fire of sixty guns could be brought to bear on any point on his front or left; and on the highest point of the hill Colonel Tyler had ten siege-guns in position. Couch's division was placed on the right of Porter; next on the right were Kearney and Hooker; next Sedgwick and Richardson; next Smith and Slocum; then the remainder of Keyes's corps, extending in a curve nearly to the river. The Pennsylvania Reserves were in the rear of Porter and Couch, as a reserve. The left, where the weight of attack was expected, was very strong, and the right was strengthened by slashings,[1] and its flank covered by gun-boats. The map on page 431 shows the positions.

Lee concentrated his troops near Glendale on the morning of the 1st;[a] but owing to the nature of the country, and his lack of information concerning it, he did not get his line of battle formed and ready for attack until late in the afternoon, but had kept up an artillery fire here and there, after ten o'clock. He formed his line with the divisions of Jackson, Ewell, Whiting, and D. H. Hill, on the left (a large portion of Ewell's in reserve), and those of Magruder and Huger on the right, while A. P. Hill's and Longstreet's were held in reserve on the left, and took no part in the engagement that followed.

[a] July, 1862.

Lee resolved to carry Malvern Hills by storm, and for that purpose massed his troops on his right. He posted his artillery so that by a concentrated fire he expected to silence those of the Nationals, when Armistead's brigade of Huger's division was to advance with a shout and carry the battery immediately before it. That shout was to be the signal for a general advance with fixed bayonets to "drive the invaders into the James." This

---

[1] Trees cut so nearly off that they fall, but still adhere to the stump, and thus form a very strong kind of abatis.

movement was more easily planned than executed. Unforeseen contingencies arose; and when, between three and four o'clock in the afternoon, a heavy fire of artillery was opened upon Couch and Kearney, and D. H. Hill, believing that he heard the proposed signal-shout for a general advance, pushed forward upon Couch's front, he found his troops almost unsupported. "Instead of ordering up one or two hundred pieces of artillery to play on the Yankees," he said, "a single battery (Moorman's) was ordered up and knocked to pieces in a few minutes; one or two others shared the same fate of being beat in detail."[1] The Confederates were repulsed by cannon and musket, and driven back in confusion to the woods near the Quaker road. Then the National right, on the hills resting near Binford's, was advanced several hundred yards to a better position.

Meanwhile Magruder and Huger had made a furious attack on Porter at the left. The brigades of Kershaw and Semmes, of McLaw's division, charged through a dense wood nearly up to Porter's guns; and a similar dash was made by Wright, Mahone, and Anderson, farther to the right, and by Barksdale, nearer the center. But all were repulsed, and for a while fighting nearly ceased. It was only a lull in the storm. With a recklessness or desperation equaled only by his blunders in arrangements for the battle,[2]

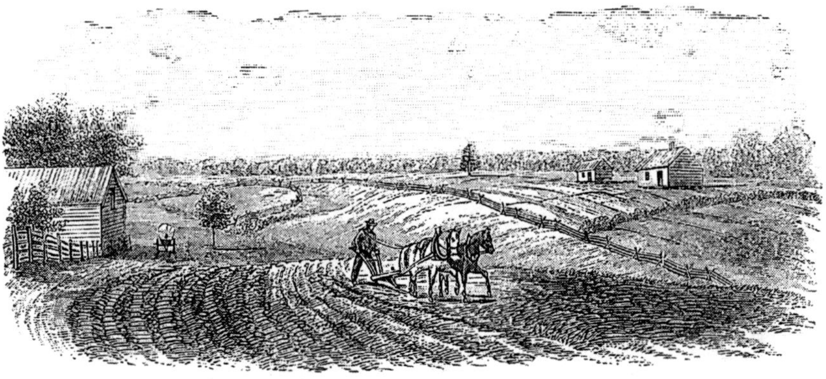

BATTLE-FIELD OF MALVERN HILLS.[3]

Lee ordered another assault on the "tier after tier of batteries grimly visible on the plateau, rising in the form of an amphitheater, one flank of the Yankees protected by Turkey Creek, and the other by gun-boats."[4] His shat-

[1] Reports of the Army of Northern Virginia, i. 186.

[2] There was much dissatisfaction felt in the Confederate Army with Lee's management of it, especially on the day of the battle of Malvern Hills. But Lee being a Virginian, with the prestige of an honorable family name and connections, and withal a special favorite of Jefferson Davis—whose will had now become law in the Confederacy, that commander's incompetency as the leader of a great army, which was apparent from time to time throughout the war, was hidden as much as possible, and no one was allowed to publicly find fault because of his military blunders, such as his invasions of Maryland and Pennsylvania. But on the occasion we are now considering, the outspoken D. H. Hill, in his report to the Assistant Adjutant-General, ventured to say—"Notwithstanding the tremendous odds against us, *and the blundering arrangements of the battle*, we inflicted heavy loss upon the Yankees." The odds were indeed against the Confederates, for the Nationals doubtless had more troops, and certainly a better position than they.

[3] This is a view from Crew's house, near which some of Porter's batteries were planted, overlooking the fields where the Confederates advanced to the charges on Porter and Couch. In the distance is seen the line of the dark pine-woods near Glendale, from which the assailing columns emerged. This was the appearance of the spot when the writer made the sketch, at the close of May, 1866.

[4] D. H. Hill's Report.

tered columns were re-formed in the dark pine-forest, not more than half a mile in front of the National line, and at about six o'clock in the evening he opened a general artillery fire upon Couch and Porter, and his infantry rushed from their covering at the double-quick, over the open undulating fields, to storm the batteries and carry the hill. They were met by a most withering fire of musketry and great guns; but as one brigade recoiled, another was pushed forward, with a culpable recklessness of human life, under the circumstances. Finally, at about seven o'clock, when a heavy mass of fresh troops, under the direction of Jackson, were charging Couch and Porter, and pressing them sorely, Sickles's brigade of Hooker's division, and Meagher's Irish brigade of Richardson's division, were ordered up to their support, and fought most gallantly. At the same time, the gun-boats in the river were hurling heavy shot and shell among the Confederates, with terrible effect, their range being directed by officers of the Signal corps stationed upon a small house a short distance from McClellan's quarters. The conflict was furious and destructive, and did not cease until almost nine o'clock in the evening, when the Confederates were driven to the shelter of ravines, and woods, and swamps, utterly broken and despairing.[1]

So ended THE BATTLE OF MALVERN HILLS.[2] The victory for the Nationals was decisive, and it was clear to every officer in the Army of the Potomac, that a vigorous movement toward Richmond in the morning (only about a day's march off) would not only lead to its immediate possession by that army, but the dispersion or capture of Lee's entire force. But other counsels prevailed. McClellan had been nearly all day on the *Galena*, and at times made somewhat anxious by the roar of battle.[3] He was sent for toward evening, and reached the right of the army while the battle was raging furiously on the left, at the time of the final struggle just recorded. Immediately after the repulse of the assailants, he issued an order for the victorious army to "fall back still farther"[4] to Harrison's Landing, a point

---

[1] According to the testimony of some of Lee's officers (see Reports of the Army of Northern Virginia, volume I.), the whole Confederate army was in the greatest disorder on the morning after the battle—"thousands of straggling men asking every passer-by for their regiment; ambulances, wagons, and artillery obstructed every road."

[2] Reports of General McClellan and his subordinate officers; also of General Lee and his subordinates; published narratives of eye-witnesses and participants in the battles, and oral and written statements to the author by officers and soldiers of the Potomac army.

The aggregate loss during the seven days' contest before Richmond, or from the battle at Mechanicsville until the posting of the army at Harrison's Bar, was reported by McClellan at 1,582 killed, 7,709 wounded, and 5,958 missing, making a total of 15,249. Lee's losses were never reported. He declared that he captured 10,000 prisoners, and took 52 pieces of cannon and 35,000 small arms.

[3] Dr. R. E. Van Grieson, Surgeon of the *Galena*, kept a diary of events at that time, in which he recorded that General McClellan went on board of that vessel at nine o'clock in the morning, and retired to the cabin "for a little sleep." They arrived at Harrison's Bar at noon, when Generals McClellan and Franklin went ashore and remained about an hour. On their return, the *Galena* started up the river. "As we pass up," says the diary, "we can hear heavy firing. After passing Carter's Landing, it increases to a perfect roar. McClellan, though quietly smoking a cigar on the quarter-deck, seems a little anxious, and looks now and then inquiringly at the signal officer, who is receiving a message from shore. After a while the signal officer reports, 'Heavy firing near Porter's division;' next came a message demanding his presence on shore. A boat is manned, and McClellan left." That message, according to Dr. Marks, was from Heintzelman, who sent him word that the troops "noticed his absence, and it was exerting a depressing influence over them, and he could not be answerable for the consequences if he longer held himself aloof from the scene of action and danger."—*The Peninsula Campaign in Virginia*, page 299. When asked by the "Committee on the Conduct of the War" (Report, i. 436) whether he was on board a gun-boat during any part of that day, McClellan replied: "I do not remember; it is possible I may have been, as my camp was directly on the river."

[4] General McClellan's Report, page 140.

on the James a few miles below, and then returned to the *Galena*.[1] This order produced consternation and the greatest dissatisfaction, for it seemed like snatching the palm of victory from the hand just opened to receive it.[2] However, it was obeyed, and by the evening of the 3d of July,[a] the Army of the Potomac was resting on the James; and on the 8th, what was left of Lee's Army of Northern Virginia was behind the defenses at Richmond. McClellan made his head-quarters in the mansion at Berkeley, the seat of the Harrison family, near Harrison's Landing,[3] and began calling loudly for re-enforcements, to enable him "to accomplish the great task of capturing Richmond and putting an end to the rebellion."[4] Thus ended the campaign against Richmond.

[a] 1862.

THE HARRISON MANSION.

The writer, accompanied by his two Philadelphia friends already alluded to, visited the theater of events recorded in this chapter at the close of May, 1866. After a delightful railway-journey of about two days from Greenville, in East Tennessee, stopping one night at Lynchburg, we arrived at Richmond on the 26th. When the object of our journey was made known

---

[1] Dr. Grieson's Diary, cited in Greeley's *American Conflict*, ii. 167.

[2] "Even Fitz-John Porter's devotion to his chief was temporarily shaken by this order, which elicited his most indignant protest."—Greeley's *American Conflict*, note 43, page 167. General Kearney said, in the presence of several officers—"I, Philip Kearney, an old soldier, enter my solemn protest against this order for a retreat. We ought, instead of retreating, to follow up the enemy and take Richmond; and in full view of all the responsibilities of such a declaration, I say to you all, such an order can only be prompted by cowardice or treason."—Dr. Marks's *Peninsula Campaign*, page 294.

[3] The picture above shows the appearance of the mansion at the time the writer was there, in the spring of 1865, when it was a signal-station. It was the residence of Dr. Starke when the war broke out. It is about five miles below City Point, on the opposite side of the river. There President Harrison was born. The estate was called Berkeley. A short distance below it, on the same side of the river, is the old family mansion of the Westover estate, that belonged to the Byrds in colonial times. It was famous as the center of a refined social circle on the Virginia Peninsula, and became noted in connection with Benedict Arnold's movements in Virginia, after he took up arms against his country. The annexed picture shows its appearance in the spring of 1865. It was then the property of John Seldon. Its landing, one of the best on the James, was made the chief depot of supplies while the Army of the Potomac lay between it and Berkeley, well sheltered by Herring Creek and a swamp.

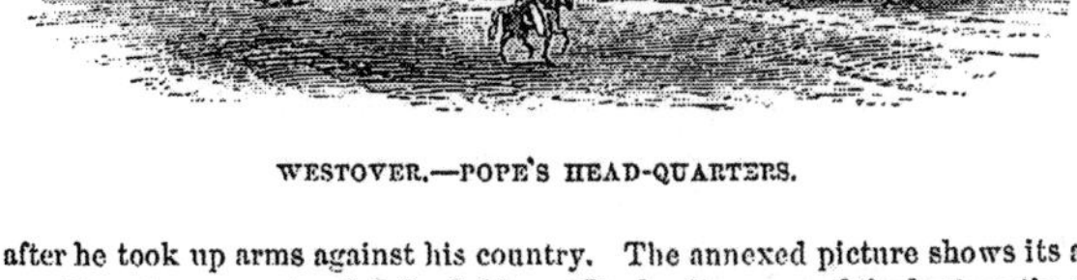

WESTOVER.—POPE'S HEAD-QUARTERS.

[4] On the morning of the battle of Malvern Hills, McClellan telegraphed to Washington for fresh troops, and saying he should fall back to the river, if possible. The President immediately replied, that if he had a million of men it would be impossible to get them to him in time for the emergency. He frankly informed McClellan that there were no men to send, and implored him to save his army, even if he should be compelled to fall back to Fortress Monroe, adding, with faith—"We still have strength enough in the country, and will bring it out." On the next day, McClellan telegraphed for fifty thousand fresh troops, when the President assured him that there were not at his disposal sufficient troops by 15,000 men to make the estimated sufficient

to Major-general Alfred H. Terry, then in command at Richmond, he kindly furnished us with every facility for an exploration of the battle-grounds in that vicinity. He placed his carriage and four horses at our disposal for several days; and we had competent guides as well as most genial companions in Colonels Martin, Graves, and Sullivan, of General Terry's Staff, who had participated in the stirring military events between Old Point Comfort and Richmond.

Our first trip was made on a wet day, which gave us a realizing sense of that "altogether abnormal" state of the season of which the commander of the Army of the Potomac wrote, four years before, when waiting for fairer skies and drier earth to permit him to take Richmond. We rode out to Mechanicsville, passing through the lines of heavy fortifications constructed by the Confederates along the brow of a declivity, on the verge of a plain that overlooked the Chickahominy. We passed that stream and the swamps that border

MECHANICSVILLE.

it (see picture on page 419) without difficulty, and were soon in Mechanicsville, a hamlet of a few houses, seated around a group of magnificent oak trees, which bear many scars of battle. At Mechanisville we turned in the direction of Cool Arbor, passing and sketching Ellison's Mill, and the battle-ground around it. A little farther on we came to a beautiful open wood, mostly of hickory trees, in which was the Walnut Grove Church, a neat wooden structure, painted white, wherein the wounded of both parties in the strifes in that vicinity had found shelter from sun and storm.

Soon after passing the ruins of Gaines's Mills (see picture on page 424), a little farther eastward, we found the country nearly level, and almost denuded of the forests that covered a large portion of it before the war. Now it had the desolate appearance of a moorland. Not a fence was visible over a space of many miles. As we approached the site of the New Cool Arbor tavern, we came to the heavy works thrown up by the Confederates at a later period of the war, and saw between these and others, constructed by the Nationals, a mile farther on, in the scarred and broken

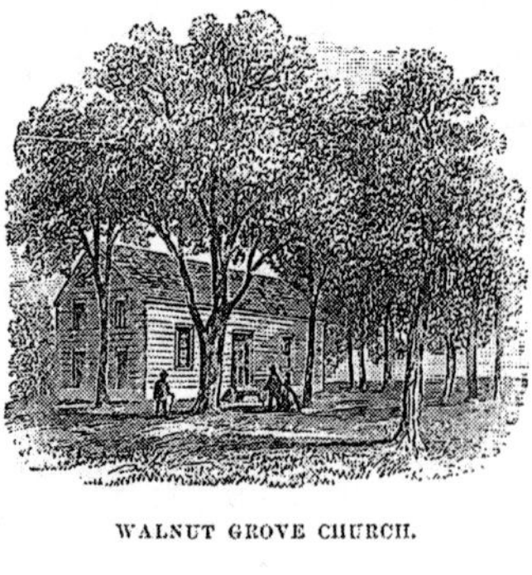

WALNUT GROVE CHURCH.

guard for the National Capital. He begged the General not to ask of him impossibilities, and told him that if he thought he was not strong enough to take Richmond, he did not ask him to do it then. Utterly unmindful of the kind and candid statements of the President, the General telegraphed on the 3d for 100,000 men, "more rather than less," with which to "take Richmond and end the rebellion;" and on the 4th he

trees, the evidences of the fierceness of the battle there between Grant and Lee, to be described hereafter. Over the plain between New and Old Cool Arbor (see map on page 423), where the deadly strife occurred, a National cemetery was laid out, and a burial party was there, gathering from the fields and forests around the remains of the Union soldiers, and interring them in this consecrated ground. The graves of fifteen hundred were already there. After thoroughly exploring the battle-ground, and sketching the remains of a general's head-quarters in a wood near Old Cool Arbor,[1] we turned our faces toward Richmond. We crossed the Chickahominy at New Bridge (see picture on page 403), and, after a stormy day, which made sketching and explorations difficult, reached the city at sunset, having journeyed about fourteen miles.

HEAD-QUARTERS NEAR COOL ARBOR.

On the following morning[a] we crossed the James River and drove down to Drewry's Bluff. That day's experience will be considered hereafter, when we come to the record of events on the south side of the James, at a later period of the war.

[a] May 30, 1866.

On the morning of the 31st we started for Malvern Hills, about fifteen miles distant. We went out on the Charles City road, stopping to sketch the small but now famous White's tavern, then kept by an Englishman and his wife. We crossed the borders of the White Oak Swamp, and near the junction of the Charles City, Long Bridge, and Quaker roads, followed a little miry by-way that brought us out to the field of the sanguinary battle of Glendale. In the woods, where the slain were laid in shallow graves, we saw the whitened bones of many of them; and on Frazier's Farm, where a portion of the battle in the open fields was fought, we observed another National cemetery, in which were scores of mounds already. The burial

WHITE'S TAVERN.

---

repeated that call. To these demands, which began to seem like studied annoyances, the patient President calmly replied as before, and told him that the governors of loyal States had offered him 300,000 men for the field; when McClellan, as if to give those annoyances more force, actually wrote a letter to Mr. Lincoln, advising him how he should conduct his administration, especially in regard to the matter of slavery, in which the conspirators and their friends were so deeply interested. After telling Mr. Lincoln what his duty was in regard to confiscations, military arrests, &c., he said that the military power should not be allowed to interfere with slavery, and gave it as his opinion, that, unless the principles of the Government on that point should be made known and approved, the effort to obtain requisite force to sustain the war would be almost hopeless. "A declaration of radical views," he said, "especially upon slavery, will rapidly disintegrate our present armies." Not agreeing with the General in this view, and believing it to be the duty of the latter to attend to the management of the army under his command rather than to that of the National Government, the President declined to discuss the matter.

[1] This was a delightful place for head-quarters. In an open wood a canopy of boughs was formed, under which the tents were pitched, and rude seats were constructed among them. Every thing but the tents remained. These have been inserted to give more reality to the picture, and to exhibit the usual forms of the tents.

party at work there had their tents pitched in the grove about Willis's Church (delineated on page 429).

We passed down the Quaker road through an almost level country, broken by ravines and water-courses for a mile or two, in the track of the fugitive Army of the Potomac, and at about one o'clock reached the beautiful open fields of Malvern Hills, where we had a pleasant reception at the old mansion—the head-quarters of McClellan (see picture on page 429)—by the family of Mr. Wyatt, the occupant. In a deep shaded ravine, on the southeastern slope of the hill, where a copious stream of pure spring water flows out of a bank composed of a mass of perfect sea-shells and coral,[1]

VIEW FROM MALVERN HILLS.[2]

beneath the roots of huge trees, we lunched; and at the small house, not far off, where Major Myer had his signal-station during the battle, we were furnished with rich buttermilk by a fat old colored woman, who said she was "skeered a' most to death" by the roar of the storm of battle. After sketching the charming view southward from the grove in front of the mansion, we proceeded to explore the battle-ground on which the hottest of the fight occurred. The theater of that conflict was on the farms of Cornelius

[1] There were immense escalop and ordinary sized oyster-shells closely imbedded, with small ammonites and clam shells. The coral was white, and in perfect preservation. This layer of marine shells and the spring are more than a hundred feet above the James River. Such layers occur throughout the region between Richmond and the sea, sometimes near the surface, and often many feet below it. On the battle-ground of the Seven Pines we saw many pieces of coral that had lain so near the surface that the plow had turned them up.

[2] This is one of the most extensive and charming views in all that region. The sketch comprehends the scenery around Turkey Bend, on the James River, looking southward from Malvern Hills mansion. From that position City Point (its place denoted by the three birds on the left) was visible, and the country up the Appomattox toward Petersburg. The two birds on the right denote the position of the gun-boats in the James that took part in the battle.

Crew, Dr. Turner, John W. West, E. H. Poindexter, James W. Binford, and L. H. Kemp. Crew's, near which the artillery of Porter and Couch was planted, had been a fine mansion, with pleasant grounds around it; but both mansion and grounds told the sad story of the desolation which had been brought to all that region by the scourge of war. Only two very aged women inhabited the shattered building, the garden was a waste, the shade-trees had disappeared, and only a single field was in preparation for culture. Late in the afternoon we left Malvern Hills, and returned to Richmond by the New Market or River road.

On the morning of the first of June, we rode out to the battle-grounds of the Seven Pines and Fair Oaks, and of Savage's Station. Our journey was on the Williamsburg road, as far as its junction with the Nine Mile road, when we followed the latter to Fair Oaks Station, seven miles from Richmond. There were no buildings visible there. We rode on to the site of the Seven Pines Tavern, where a burial party were filling a National cemetery with the remains of the Union dead; and crossing open fields beyond, we reached Savage's Station, about four miles from Fair Oaks, at noon. It was a warm, sunny day, and the shade of the grove there (see picture on page 426) was very grateful. There we lunched, and had a brief interview with Mr. Savage, who was living in a small house a few yards from the site of his mansion, which was destroyed by accident after the battle there. He was courteous, but outspoken concerning his hostility to his Government and his contempt for the Yankees, preferring to live in poverty in the midst of his eight hundred desolated acres, to allowing one of the despised "Northerners" to become his neighbor by a sale of a rood of his surplus land to him. We admired his pluck and pitied his folly. He was a fair example of that social dead-weight of pride and stupidity that denies activity and prosperity to Virginia.

We returned to Richmond before sunset, and early the following morning went down the river by steamer to visit Williamsburg and Yorktown. The weather was delightful, and the banks of the James were clad in richest verdure, hiding in a degree the deserted fortifications that line them all the way from Richmond to City Point. Water was flowing gently through the Dutch Gap Canal; and City Point, where a year before a hundred vessels might be seen at one time, now presented but a solitary schooner at its desolated wharf. At about noon we passed James Island, with its interesting tower of the ancient church in which the first settlers in Virginia worshiped, and near which we saw the battery erected and armed in the interest of the conspirators, at the expense of a wealthy planter named Allen,

BATTERY AND CHURCH-TOWER ON JAMESTOWN ISLAND.

whose vast domain was in that vicinity. Soon afterward we debarked at Grover's Landing, eight miles from Williamsburg, rode to that ancient capital of Virginia in an old ambulance, and during the afternoon visited Fort Magruder and its dependencies, and other localities connected with the battle there. We spent the evening pleasantly and profitably with the eminent Professor B. S. Ewell (brother of General R. S. Ewell), the President of William and Mary College, who was the Adjutant-General of Joseph E. Johnston until he was superseded in command by Hood, at Atlanta.

On the following morning we rode to Yorktown, twelve miles down the Peninsula, and spent the remainder of the day in visiting objects of interest in the vicinity. The old British line of circumvallation had been covered by the modern works; and the famous cave in the river-bank in which Cornwallis had his head-quarters, after he was driven out of the Nelson House, had been enlarged and converted into a magazine. The town appeared desolate indeed, the only house in it that seems not to have felt the ravages of war being that of Mrs. Anderson, of Williamsburg, in which McClellan and all of the Union commanders at Yorktown had their quarters. It was still used for the same purpose, there being a small military force there. We observed that the names of the few streets in Yorktown had been changed, and bore those of "McClellan," "Keyes," "Ellsworth," and others. The old "Swan Tavern," at which the writer was lodged in 1848, and the adjoining buildings, had been blown into fragments by the explosion of gunpowder during the war.

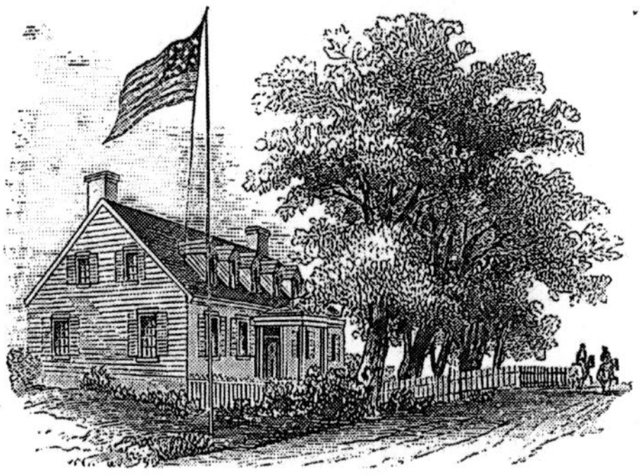

McCLELLAN'S HEAD-QUARTERS IN YORKTOWN.

On the morning of the 4th,[a] we left Yorktown for Grover's Landing, passing on the way the house of Mr. Eagle, a mile from the town, where General Johnston had his quarters and telegraph station just before the evacuation. We were again on the bosom of the James in a steamer at nine o'clock, and arrived at Richmond toward evening. Remaining there one day, we departed for the North, to visit the fields of strife between the South Anna and the Rappahannock.

[a] June, 1866.

CHAPTER XVII.

POPE'S CAMPAIGN IN VIRGINIA.

VERY grievous was the disappointment of the loyal people when they knew that the Grand Army of the Potomac had been driven from the front of Richmond, had abandoned the siege, and had intrenched itself in a defensive position in the malarious region of the James River, beneath the scorching sun of midsummer, where home-sickness and camp-sickness in every form were fearfully wasting it. They were perplexed by enigmas which they could not solve, and the addresses of General McClellan and of the Chief Conspirator at Richmond made these enigmas more profound; each claiming to have achieved victory, and promising abundant success to his followers.[1] And most astounding to the Government was the assurance of the commander of that army on the third day after the battle of Malvern Hills, when the shattered but victorious host was lying between Berkeley and Westover, that he had not "over 50,000 men left with their colors!"[2] What has become of the remainder of the one hundred and sixty thousand men who within a hundred days have gone to the Peninsula? was a problem very important for the Government to have solved, and the President went down to the head-

---

[1] On the 4th of July, General McClellan said, in a congratulatory address to his troops :—"SOLDIERS OF THE ARMY OF THE POTOMAC—Your achievements of the last ten days have illustrated the valor and endurance of the American soldier. *Attacked by superior forces, and without hope of re-enforcements*, you have succeeded in changing your base of operations by a flank movement, always regarded as the most hazardous of military expedients. You have saved all your material, all your trains, and all your guns except a few lost in battle, taking in return guns and colors from the enemy. Upon your march you have been assailed day after day with desperate fury, by men of the same race and nation, skillfully massed and led. Under every disadvantage of number, and necessarily of position also, you have in every conflict beaten back your foes with enormous slaughter. Your conduct ranks you among the celebrated armies of history. No one will now question that each of you may always with pride say, 'I belonged to the Army of the Potomac.' * * * On this our Nation's birth-day, we declare to our foes, who are rebels against the best interests of mankind, that this army shall enter the capital of the so-called Confederacy; that our National Constitution shall prevail, and that the Union, which can alone insure internal peace and external security to each State, 'must and shall be preserved,' cost what it may in time, treasure, and blood."

On the following day (July 5), Jefferson Davis issued an address to *his* soldiers, in which, after speaking of the "series of brilliant victories" they had won, he said : "Ten days ago an invading army, *vastly superior to you in numbers* and materials of war, closely beleaguered your capital, and vauntingly proclaimed its speedy conquest. * * * With well-directed movements and death-daring valor you charged upon him from field to field, over a distance of more than thirty-five miles, and, spite of his re-enforcements, compelled him to seek shelter under cover of his gun-boats, where he now lies cowering before the army he so lately derided and threatened with entire subjugation. Well may it be said of you, that you have done enough for glory; but duty to a suffering country and to the cause of constitutional liberty claims for you yet further efforts. Let it be your pride to relax in nothing which can promote your own future efficiency, your own great object being to drive the invaders from your soil, carrying your standard beyond the outer boundaries of the Confederacy, to wring from an unscrupulous foe the recognition which is the birthright of every independent community."

[2] Dispatch by telegraph to the Secretary of War, July 3, 1862.

quarters at Harrison's Landing[a] in search of that solution. There he found the remains of that splendid army greatly disheartened. Sadly

[a] July 8, 1862.

and wearily it had waded through the mud and been pelted by a pitiless storm while marching from the field of its victory on Malvern Hills to its present humiliating position, during the night succeeding the contest. It had been covered from an attack on its march by a rear-guard of all arms under Colonel Averill, and menaced continually by Stuart and his cavalry, and columns of infantry pushed forward by Lee. These found the National army too strongly posted to make a repetition of the blunder before Malvern Hills a safe experiment, and on the 8th Lee ceased pursuit and withdrew his army to Richmond, having lost, as nearly as now can be ascertained, since he took the command less than forty days before, about nineteen thousand men.

The President found the Army of the Potomac "present and fit for duty" nearly forty thousand souls stronger than its commander had reported on the 3d, and his hopes were revived to the point of belief that it might speedily march against Richmond. But he was unable then to get a reply to his question, Where are the seventy-five thousand men yet missing?[1] While he was there, the future movements of the Army of the Potomac was the subject of serious deliberation. It was known that the Confederates, aware of the weakness of the force left in defense of Washington, were gathering heavily in that direction; and the withdrawal of Lee's army to Richmond, on the day of the President's arrival at McClellan's head-quarters, indicated an abandonment of the pursuit, and a probable heavy movement northward. In view of the possible danger to the capital, and the fact that McClellan did not consider his army strong enough by "one hundred thousand men more, rather than less," to take Richmond, it was thought advisable by the President, and by several of the corps commanders of the Army of the Potomac, whose sad experience before the Confederate capital had shaken their confidence in their leader, to withdraw the army from the Peninsula and concentrate it in front of Washington. To this project McClellan was opposed, and at once took measures to defeat it.

Here we will leave the army on the Peninsula for a little while, and observe events nearer the National capital, with which its movements were intimately connected. To give more efficiency to the troops covering Washington, they were formed into an organization called the *Army of Virginia*, and placed under the command of Major-General John Pope, who was called from the West[b] for the purpose. The new army was arranged in three corps, to be commanded respectively by

[b] June 26.

---

[1] The President found about 86,000 men with McClellan, leaving 75,000 unaccounted for. This information perplexed him very much, and on the 13th, after his return to Washington, he wrote to the Chief of the Army of the Potomac, asking for an account of the missing numbers. The General replied on the 15th, in which he reported 88,665 "present and fit for duty;" absent by authority, 34,472; absent without authority, 3,778; sick, 16,619; making a total of 144,407. A week later the Adjutant-general's office reported the total of the Army of the Potomac, exclusive of General Wool's command, and a force under Burnside that had been ordered from North Carolina, 158,314, of whom 101,691 were present and fit for duty.

[a] July 20.

The Government was much disturbed by one fact in General McClellan's report of his numbers, namely, that over 34,000 men, or more than three-fifths of the entire number of the army which he had reported on the 3d, were absent on furloughs, granted by permission of the commanding General, when he was continually calling for re-enforcements, and holding the Government responsible for the weakness of his army. The President said, in reference to this extraordinary fact: "If you had these men with you, you could go into Richmond in the next three days."

Major-Generals Fremont, Banks, and McDowell. Pope having been Fremont's junior in Missouri, the latter was unwilling to serve under him, and he was permitted to relinquish his command, which was given to Major-General Sigel. In addition to those three corps was a force in process of organization at Alexandria, under Brigadier-General Sturgis; and the troops in the forts around Washington were placed under Pope's command. His force, exclusive of the latter, numbered about fifty thousand, of which nearly forty thousand were disposable for motion. The cavalry numbered about five thousand, but were poorly mounted, and not in good condition for service. These troops were posted from Fredericksburg to Winchester and Harper's Ferry in the Shenandoah Valley; and their commander was charged with the threefold duty of covering the National capital, guarding the Valley entrance to Maryland in the rear of Washington, and threatening Richmond from the north, as a diversion in favor of McClellan.

SAMUEL D. STURGIS.

Pope assumed command on the 28th of June, with Colonel George D. Ruggles as his efficient Chief-of-Staff. It was his intention to concentrate his troops eastward of the Blue Ridge, press on well toward Richmond, and there unite with McClellan in the operations of the siege, or strike an independent blow at the Confederate capital, as circumstances should dictate. But while he was gathering up his scattered forces, the retreat from before Richmond began, and all chances for McClellan to be re-enforced by land were thus destroyed. There was nothing better for Pope to do, then, than to place his army in front of any Confederate force whose face might be turned toward Washington, make a diversion in favor of the sorely smitten troops on the Peninsula, and enable them to withdraw from that unhealthful position without further loss. He accordingly withdrew Sigel and Banks from the Shenandoah Valley, and placed them at the eastward of the Blue Ridge, in position to watch the region they had left, the former taking post at Sperryville, near Thornton's Gap, and the latter a few miles eastward of him. General Ricketts, of McDowell's corps, was posted at Waterloo Bridge, on the Upper Rappahannock, between Warrenton and Sperryville; and General Rufus King, of the same corps, who was at Fredericksburg, was ordered to remain there, cover that city, and protect the railway between it and Aquia Creek, where there was a National depot of supplies.

Pope wrote a letter to General McClellan, cordially offering his co-operation with him, and asking for suggestions. The answer was cold in manner and vague in terms, and satisfied Pope that there could be no useful co-working between the Army of the Potomac and the Army of Virginia without a General-in-Chief, competent and authorized to control their movements. At his suggestion, it is said, a General-in-Chief was appointed. Halleck was called[a] from the West[1] to Washington to serve in that capacity, and entered upon the duties of that office on the 23d of July.

[a] July 11, 1862.

Let us turn back a moment, and observe events at Richmond and on the Peninsula, remembering that spies in the employment of the conspirators, and aided by persons out of the Confederacy who were in sympathy with them, were almost hourly giving information to Davis and Lee of the aspect of affairs in the National camps and in the National councils.

Immediately after his arrival at Washington, General Halleck visited General McClellan[b] at Harrison's Landing, to obtain exact information of the state and prospects of the army there. McClellan at first demanded of Halleck fifty thousand new troops to enable him to take Richmond, but finally agreed to make the attempt with an addition of twenty thousand. After consulting with a council of general officers, a majority of whom, upon learning the actual state of affairs, recommended the withdrawal of the army from the Peninsula, Halleck hastened back to Washington, and there received a dispatch from McClellan, saying that a re-enforcement of at least thirty-five thousand men must be sent.

[b] July 25.

It was now evident at the seat of Government that the Confederates were preparing to move in force northward, and that it was not safe to send any troops to the Peninsula. The only alternative was to withdraw those that were there, and unite them with Pope's in covering Washington City. Accordingly, on the 30th of July, Halleck telegraphed to McClellan to send away his sick (twelve thousand five hundred in number) as quickly as possible, preparatory to such movement; and on the third of August, when it was evident that Lee was preparing for a movement toward Washington in full force, Halleck ordered him to withdraw his army from the Peninsula immediately, and transfer it to Aquia Creek, on the Potomac. That this might be done with the expedition demanded by the exigency of the case, McClellan was authorized to assume control of all the vast fleets of war-vessels and transports on the James River and Chesapeake Bay. Already Burnside's army, which had been ordered from North Carolina, as we have observed,[2] and was at Newport-Newce, had been ordered[c] to Aquia Creek.[3]

[c] August 1.

Informed of these orders, the conspirators determined to attempt the capture of Washington before the junction of the two armies could be accomplished; and this would have been done but for the valor of the little force left for its defense, directed by energetic officers whose hearts were deeply

---

1 See page 296.

2 See page 315.

3 We have observed that when it was first proposed to withdraw the Army of the Potomac from the Peninsula, General McClellan placed himself in decided opposition to the measure. With every disposition compatible with the highest public good to give him an opportunity to recover what he had lost by disastrous slowness and indecision, the Government, when on the 17th he asked for Burnside's entire army in North Carolina to be sent to him, complied with his request. He "dreaded," he said, "the effect of any retreat on the *morale* of his men;" but it was evident that their courage was not easily broken, for he had just assured the Government that his army was "in fine spirits," after one of the most distressing series of retreats on record. So late as the 28th of July, he urged that he should be "at once re-enforced by all available troops;" and so earnest was he in insisting upon the wisdom of his own opinion, that he paid no attention to Halleck's order of the 30th, to remove the sick. When that order was repeated, on the 2d of August, he replied that, until he was informed what was to be done with his army, he could not decide what course to pursue with his sick, and added: "If I am kept longer in ignorance of what is to be effected, I cannot be expected to accomplish the

engaged in their country's cause, for it was more than twenty days after McClellan was ordered to transfer his army to Aquia Creek before that order was executed.

Satisfied that no further movements against Richmond would be made at that time, the conspirators, as we have observed, resolved to march northward in heavy force. A show of power had been kept up in the Shenandoah Valley and eastward of the Blue Ridge, to keep Pope from re-enforcing McClellan. It was determined in the conclave of conspirators at Richmond to repeat, on a grand scale, the exploit of Jackson in driving Banks out of the Shenandoah Valley;[1] and to arouse the people to action, and to swell the ranks of the Confederate Army, rumors were set afloat that efforts were about to be made, on a scale that promised entire success, to "drive the invaders from the soil" of the slave-labor States; to penetrate the regions beyond the Ohio and the Susquehanna, and to dictate terms of peace at the point of the bayonet in the cities of Cincinnati and Philadelphia. The people of the Confederate States were made to expect a speedy vision of Jefferson Davis in the chair of Dictatorship at Washington City, and Robert E. Lee, his cordial co-worker, laureled in state at his former home in Arlington House, in sight of the National capital.

These were dreams that were almost realized before the heats of summer had departed. Fortunately for the cause of Right, there were spies in Richmond also, who informed the Government of this scheme in time for it to take countervailing measures. It knew far better than the Commander of the Army of the Potomac, on the banks of the James, that the Army of Virginia, near the Rappahannock, was necessary for the defense of the National capital, and acted accordingly.

At this point we may properly resume the narrative of the movements of the Army of Virginia.

General Pope did not go to the field until near the close of July, but issued his orders from Washington City. He had determined to seize Gordonsville, if possible, and cut off railway communication between Richmond and the Shenandoah Valley, so as to impede the progress of any Confederate movement northward. For this purpose he directed General Rufus King, at Fredericksburg, to send forward detachments of cavalry to operate on the line of the Virginia Central railroad. These movements resulted in breaking up that road at several places. This being accomplished, General Banks was ordered forward with an infantry brigade, and all of his cavalry, to march upon and seize the village of Culpepper Court-House, on the Orange and Alex-

---

object in view." To this extraordinary dispatch Halleck simply answered, that it was expected that McClellan would have sent off his sick according to orders, "without waiting to know what were and would be the instructions of the Government respecting future movements;" and that the President expected him to carry out instructions given him with all possible dispatch and caution."—McClellan's Report, page 155.

Halleck's orders for the transfer of the army to Aquia Creek were met by a protest on the part of McClellan on the 4th. He informed the General-in-Chief, at the time when Stonewall Jackson, with a force greater than Pope's, was massing at Gordonsville, preparatory to a movement in heavy force on Washington, that Pope's army was "not necessary to maintain a strict defensive in front of Washington and Harper's Ferry," and that "the true defense of Washington" was "on the banks of the James, where the fate of the Union was to be decided." He asked his superior to rescind the order, and assured him that if he did not, he should obey it "with a sad heart."—McClellan's Report, page 154. Under the restraining influence of the kind-hearted President, Halleck wrote a long reply, rebutting McClellan's propositions and assertions, and adhering to his order to remove his troops as quickly as possible.

[1] See page 394.

andria railway. He did so, when he was further ordered[a] to send General Hatch, with all his cavalry, to seize Gordonsville, destroy the railway for several miles east of it in the direction of Richmond, and push on a detachment to Charlottesville at the same time, for the purpose of burning the bridges and breaking up the road. This movement was attempted, but it was so tardy that the advance of Jackson's corps, under Ewell, sent from Richmond, occupied Gordonsville the day before Hatch approached it. The latter was then ordered to go over the Blue Ridge, from Madison Court-House, with nearly two thousand picked horsemen, to a point whence he might easily fall upon and destroy the railway in the rear of Gordonsville, and, if successful there, to push on and demolish the tracks and bridges between Charlottesville and Lynchburg. This movement was also unsuccessful. Dissatisfied with Hatch, Pope relieved him of his command, and made General John Buford the chief of Banks's cavalry in his stead.[1]

[a] July 14, 1862.

Detachments sent out by General King from Fredericksburg made bold dashes toward Richmond. One composed of the Ira Harris Light Cavalry, under Colonel Davies, made a forced march on the 19th, and at dawn the following morning[b] they struck the Virginia Central railroad at Beaver Dam Creek, thirty-five miles from Richmond, destroyed it there, with the telegraph line, for several miles, and burned the railway depot, containing a considerable amount of provisions and munitions of war. This raid produced great consternation, and a second one, two days afterward, was equally successful and alarming. The rough riders met and defeated a troop of horse near Carmel Church, burning their camp and several car-loads of corn, and broke the telegraph between Richmond and Gordonsville. When returning they encountered Stuart's cavalry, drove them across the South Anna, and pursued them to within sight of Hanover Junction. All this was done in the space of twenty-nine hours, without the loss of a man on the part of the Nationals.

[b] July 20.

In the mean time General Pope had been making arrangements to take the field in person. On the 14th[c] he issued an address to his army calculated to increase the coldness of McClellan toward him,[2] and within a few days afterward he issued orders respecting the intended career of his army in Virginia which greatly stirred the Confederates, and caused Jefferson Davis to issue a countervailing manifesto in the form of a General Order, and in a characteristic letter he instructed Lee to "communicate it to the Commander-in-Chief of the armies of the United States."[3]

[c] July.

---

[1] General Pope's Report to General G. W. Cullum, January 27, 1863.

[2] Pope told his army that he had come from the West, where they had always "seen the backs of their enemies"—from an army who sought its adversary, and whose policy was "attack and not defense." He presumed he had been called to pursue the same system and vigor, and he said it was his purpose to do so. He wished them to forget certain phrases. He had heard constantly, he said, of "taking strong positions and holding them—of lines of retreat and bases of supplies." The strongest position a soldier should desire to occupy, he said, "is one from which he can most easily advance against the enemy. Let us study the probable lines of retreat of our opponents," he added, "and leave our own to take care of themselves. Let us look before and not behind." The disastrous retreats which General Pope was compelled to make after these declarations, gave keenness to many a sarcastic allusion to this famous address, which really reflected upon McClellan and his officers, though Pope disclaimed any intention to do so.

[3] In general orders on the 18th, he directed his troops to subsist upon the country in which they were operating as far as possible, the supplies to be taken by the officers in command. This was to prevent mere pillage.

Pope assumed the command of his army in the field in person on the 29th of July. The bulk of that army then lay between Fredericksburg, on the Rappahannock, and Culpepper Court-House, and preparations were made to drive Jackson from Gordonsville, which he had held since the 19th, preparatory to an advance toward the Rappahannock. Informed of Pope's strength, that daring officer was afraid to move forward without more troops. He called for re-enforcements, and they were speedily sent. Alarmed by recent raids that threatened his communications with his great source of near supplies, the Shenandoah Valley, and satisfied that he need not fear attack from McClellan, Lee sent the corps of A. P. Hill to Jackson, which made the force of the latter about twenty-five thousand—strong enough to attempt aggressive movements. Jackson sent heavy pickets toward the Rapid Anna, and the Seventh Virginia Cavalry, under General W. E. Jones, occupied Orange Court-House.

Both armies soon advanced in force. Pope's lay between Culpepper Court-House and Sperryville. A reconnoitering force under General S. W. Crawford went out from Culpepper, and drove the Confederates from Orange Court-House; and the Rapid Anna was picketed by the cavalry of Buford and Bayard from the foot of the Blue Ridge to the Raccoon Ford, eastward of the railway.

SAMUEL W. CRAWFORD.

On the morning of the 8th[a] Jackson had thrown his advance across the Rapid Anna, in the vicinity of Barnett's Ford, and driven the National cavalry back upon Culpepper just as Pope arrived there. Crawford was sent with his brigade to assist the cavalry in retarding the progress of Jackson, and, if possible, to ascertain his real intentions, for his movements were perplexing. Pope had been specially directed to preserve his

[a] August, 1862.

Vouchers for such property were to be given, stating on their face that they would be payable at the conclusion of the war, upon sufficient testimony that the owners had been loyal to the Government since the vouchers were given. He ordered trains to be dispensed with where it was known that the region to be traversed could furnish supplies.

On the same day Pope issued an order directing that no supply or baggage trains should accompany cavalry unless by special order, the men to carry two days' cooked rations, and contributions to be levied on villages and neighborhoods through which they should pass. On the same day another order was issued, declaring that the inhabitants along the lines of railways and telegraphs should be held responsible for any injury done to them, and for any attacks on trains or stragglers from the army by bands of guerrillas in the neighborhood; and that, in case of damage to roads, the citizens within five miles of it must be turned out *en masse* to repair them. In an earlier order it was also directed that if any soldiers, or legitimate followers of the army, should be fired upon from any house, the same should be razed to the ground. Another order directed all disloyal citizens within the lines of the army to be arrested, and those taking the oath of allegiance, or giving security for good behavior, to be allowed to remain; all others to be sent beyond the lines, and if found within them again, to be treated as spies. On the 13th, General Steinwehr issued an order for the arrest of five of the most prominent citizens of Page County, to be held as hostages, and to suffer death if any of the soldiers under his command should be killed by "bushwhackers," as lurking armed citizens were called.

These several orders had for their object the facile movements of the forces; the appropriation of supplies that would inevitably be given to the enemy if not so appropriated; and the suppression of that system of war-

communication with the Rappahannock at Fredericksburg at all hazards, and to that end he now made his movements conform. He could not determine, all day long, whether Jackson intended to strike Madison or Culpepper Court-House; so, as offering the greater safety to his communications, he drew his army still closer to the latter place, where he had his head-quarters, and on the morning of the 9th he sent Banks forward to Cedar Run with his whole corps, consisting of about eight thousand men, to join Crawford[1] near Cedar or Slaughter's Mountain, eight miles southward, take command of all the forces there, attack the enemy as soon as he should appear, and rely upon re-enforcements from head-quarters. Sigel was ordered to advance from Sperryville at the same time, to the support of Banks.

Jackson had now gained the commanding heights of Cedar Mountain. From that eminence he could look down upon the National camps and estimate the strength of his foe. The vision satisfied him that he had but little to fear, so he sent Ewell forward with his division under the thick mask of the forest. Early's brigade of that division was thrown upon the Culpepper road, and the remainder took position along the western slope of the mountain, and planted batteries at an altitude of two hundred feet above the common level below, so as to sweep the open cultivated country. Four guns, meanwhile, had been advanced to the front, and these, with the more elevated ones, opened fire on Crawford's batteries, while a part of Jackson's corps, under General Charles S. Winder, was thrown out to the left under the covering of the woods. Hill's division came up soon afterward; and when, at five o'clock in the afternoon, the Confederates threw out skirmishers, with a heavy body behind them ready to take the initiative, they had about twenty thousand veteran soldiers in line of battle, very strongly posted.

Against these odds Banks moved at five o'clock across the open fields and up gentle slopes, in the face of a fearful storm from artillery and infantry, and fell almost simultaneously upon Early on Jackson's right, and upon his left, commanded by General Taliaferro. The attacking force was composed of the divisions of General Augur, the advance led by General Geary,[2] and the division of General Williams, of which Crawford's gallant brigade was a part. The battle at once became general, and for an hour and a half a fierce

---

fare in which the citizens of that section of Virginia were almost universally engaged, known as "bushwhacking," which was cowardly and murderous in all its effects. These orders were justified by the common usages of war among civilized nations; and yet the crafty and malignant chief conspirator, who seems to have been ready at all times to *entertain propositions to assassinate, by the hand of secret murder, the officers of Government* at Washington,* issued an order for the purpose of "firing the Southern heart," declaring that the National authorities had "determined to violate all the rules and usages of war, and to convert the hostilities hitherto waged against armed forces into a campaign of robbery and murder against unarmed citizens and tillers of the soil." He ordered that Generals Pope and Steinwehr, and all commissioned officers under their respective commands, should not be considered as soldiers, but as out-laws; and in the event of their capture, to be held as hostages for the lives of bushwhackers or spies, one of each to be hung for every man executed under the orders above mentioned.

[1] Crawford's brigade was composed of the Forty-sixth Pennsylvania, Tenth Maine, Fifth Connecticut, and Twenty-eighth New York, with Best's battery of Regulars.

[2] Geary's brigade was composed of the Fifth, Seventh, and Twenty-ninth Ohio, and Twenty-eighth Pennsylvania, with Snapp's battery.

---

* See page 523, volume I. At about the time we are now considering, a Georgian named Burnham wrote to Jefferson Davis, proposing to organize a corps of five hundred assassins, to be distributed over the North, and sworn to murder President Lincoln, members of his cabinet, and leading Republican Senators, and other supporters of the Government. This proposition was made in writing, and was regularly filed in the "Confederate War Department," indorsed, "Respectfully referred to the Secretary of War, by order of the President," and signed "J. C. Ives." Other communications of similar tenor, "respectfully referred" by Jefferson Davis, were placed on file in that "War Department."

struggle was carried on, in which uncommon deeds of valor were performed by the respective combatants. "I have witnessed many battles during this war," wrote a newspaper correspondent, "but I have seen none where the tenacious obstinacy of the American character was so fully displayed."[1] The Nationals, outnumbered by more than two to one, and failing to receive re-enforcements in time,[2] were forced back by overwhelming weight, after incurring and inflicting a terrible loss of human life.[3] At dusk, Ricketts' division of McDowell's corps arrived on the field, and took position to relieve Banks and check the pursuit of the Confederates,[4] and artillery-firing was kept up until midnight. Late in the evening Sigel's corps began to arrive.[5] So ended the BATTLE OF CEDAR MOUNTAIN, or of Cedar Run, as the Confederates call it. None was more desperately fought during the war. A part of the sanguinary struggle was hand to hand, under the dark pall of smoke that obscured the moon.

These re-enforcements kept Jackson in check, who held fast to his mountain position until the night of the 11th,[a] when, informed of the approach of National troops from the Rappahannock, and alarmed for the safety of his communications with Richmond, he fled precipitately across the Rapid Anna, leaving a part of his dead unburied. He was pursued as far as that stream by Buford, with cavalry and artillery, and in the course of a day or two heavy rains placed almost impassable waters between the belligerents.[6] Pope made his head-quarters at the house of Robert Hudson, the proprietor of the Rose Hill estate, on which, and that of Mrs. Crittenden, nearer the foot of Cedar Mountain, the principal part of the battle was fought. On the verge of the battle-field, where both parties claimed to have achieved a victory, the wearied troops rested on their arms the night succeeding the day of conflict—a night remarkable for its brilliancy, the moon being at its full.

[a] Aug., 1862.

Generals Pope and Jackson were both re-enforced soon after the Battle of Cedar Mountain. The latter retired to Gordonsville, where he was joined by the van of Lee's army, composed of the divisions of Longstreet, two

---

1 *New York Herald*, August 10, 1862.

2 The battle was somewhat unexpected to Pope. The cannonading that opened late in the afternoon was so desultory, that Banks reported he did not expect an attack, and supposed that no great infantry force had come forward. The mask of the forest had completely concealed them, and the large number of the Confederates in his front was unsuspected by Banks. When, towards evening, the sounds of a heavy battle reached his ears, Pope ordered McDowell to send forward Ricketts' division, directed Sigel to bring his men upon the ground as quickly as possible, and then hastened to the front, where he arrived before the close of the action.

3 The dead bodies of both parties were found mingled in masses over the whole ground of the conflict. The National loss was about two thousand men killed and wounded, and that of the Confederates was about the same. General Crawford's brigade came out of that terrible fight a mere remnant. Some regiments, like those of the One Hundred and Ninth Pennsylvania and One Hundred and Second New York lost half of their number, dead or wounded. General Geary, with one Pennsylvania and five Ohio regiments, made one of the most desperate charges during the battle, and was severely wounded, with most of his officers. General Auger was also badly wounded; and General Prince, while passing from one part of his command to another, in the dark, was made prisoner. Lee, in his report (Reports of the Army of Northern Virginia, page 18), says he captured "400 prisoners, including a brigadier-general, 5,300 stand of small arms, one piece of artillery, several caissons, and three colors." Among Lee's officers who were slain was General C. S. Winder.

4 Lee says that Jackson made preparations to push on and "enter Culpepper Court-House before morning," but was detained by the knowledge of Banks's re-enforcements.

5 On receiving orders to move, Sigel sent to inquire which route he should take, and while waiting for an answer, the precious hours that might have taken him to the front and secured a victory were lost.

6 Reports of Generals Pope and Lee, and of their subordinates. Pope specially commended the brave conduct of General Banks in the fight, who, he said, "was in the front, and exposed as much as any man in his command." He also made special mention of the gallantry of Generals Augur, Geary, Williams, Gordon, Crawford, Prince, Green, and Roberts.

brigades under Hood, and Stuart's cavalry. Pope was joined by eight thousand of Burnside's soldiers under General Reno, and other troops under General King; and ten regiments under General Stevens, that had just come up from the South Carolina coast, had moved from Fredericksburg, and were within supporting distance. Pope was also authorized to call on General Cox for the greater portion of his troops in Western Virginia. Thus strengthened, he moved forward and formed a line with his right under Sigel, on Robertson's River, his left under Reno, at Raccoon Ford, and his center under McDowell, occupying the flanks of Cedar Mountain.

POPE'S HEAD-QUARTERS NEAR CEDAR MOUNTAIN.[1]

It was intended to hold this position until the Army of the Potomac should join the Army of Virginia, but before that was accomplished Pope found it necessary to fall back. Some Confederate cavalry were surprised and captured at Louisa Court-House, and from them positive information was obtained that Lee was about to throw his whole army with crushing force upon Pope, and to seize his communications with Fredericksburg and the capital.[2] Pope was immediately ordered to retire behind the North Fork of the Rappahannock,[3] which he did in good order[a] and without loss, taking position so that his left rested at Kelly's Ford and his right at Rappahannock Station, where the Orange and Alexandria railway crosses the North Fork. The Confederate cavalry had closely pursued, and on the 20th and 21st, Lee's army, in heavy force, reached the river, Longstreet, with Fitz-Hugh Lee's cavalry taking position opposite Pope's left, and Jackson, with Stuart's cavalry, posting themselves at Beverly Ford, above Rappahannock Station. There had been some brisk skirmishing between the cavalry of Bayard and Stuart all the way from Cedar Mountain, but no very severe fighting excepting near Brandy Station,[b] where the Nationals were worsted and driven across the Rappahannock.

[a] Aug. 18, 19, 20, 1862.

[b] August 20.

[1] This was the appearance of Mr. Hudson's house on Rose Hill when the writer visited and sketched it, in October, 1866. Mr. Hudson and his family were living there. He was then seventy-five years of age. They remained in the house during the battle. Several of Banks's cannon were planted near it, and several soldiers were killed in the yard in front and at the side of the house. Cedar Mountain, which is about a mile distant from Hudson's, is seen, in the sketch, between the two locust-trees on the right.

[2] Stuart was with the party, and narrowly escaped capture. His adjutant was not so fortunate. On his person was found an autograph letter from General Lee, dated the 15th, in which the intended movement was mentioned.—See Lee's Report accompanying the Reports of the Army of Northern Virginia, page 19.

[3] A few miles above Fredericksburg the Rappahannock forks, the more southern branch being the Rapid Anna, and the other the North Fork.

During the 20th and 21st there was an artillery conflict along the Rappahannock for seven or eight miles, the Confederates trying to force a passage of that stream in front of the Nationals, while the latter, well posted, continually repulsed them. On the second day it was clear to Lee and his officers that they could not succeed, so they began the more formidable movement of a march up the stream, to cross it above and flank Pope's army. This movement was masked by leaving a strong force at Beverly Ford under Longstreet. Pope had expected and dreaded this; for, being still under strict orders to keep up a communication with Fredericksburg, he was too weak in numbers to extend his right any farther up the stream. He telegraphed to Washington that he must either be re-enforced or retreat, and was assured[a] that if he could hold on two days longer he would be so strengthened by troops expected from the Peninsula that he would be able to resume the offensive. But on the morning of the 25th, the designated time, only seven thousand troops of that army had reached him.[1]

[a] August 21, 1862.

In the mean time Pope had determined to paralyze the dangerous flank movement, if possible, by the perilous one to himself of throwing his whole force across the Rappahannock, and falling furiously upon the flank and rear of the Confederates. He saw clearly that he must either do this or abandon the line of the Rappahannock and retire to Warrenton Junction, or retire to Fredericksburg and abandon the Orange and Alexandria railway, and thus leave open the direct approaches to Washington. Arrangements for the bold movement were made, when a heavy rain-storm set in and frustrated it. The river was raised several feet before morning, and the bridges were destroyed, and all the fords were drowned. At the same time Stuart was making a raid on Pope's rear, with a part of Robertson's and Lee's cavalry, and two guns, to cut the railway. He had crossed the river the previous day at Waterloo Bridge and vicinity, and under cover of intense darkness, the rain falling copiously, he pushed on unmolested to Warrenton, and around to Catlett's Station, at which Pope's army trains were then parked, and guarded by about fifteen hundred infantry and five companies of cavalry. Stuart fired a portion of the trains, but did not succeed in doing much damage, on account of the rain. He captured Pope's field quartermaster with

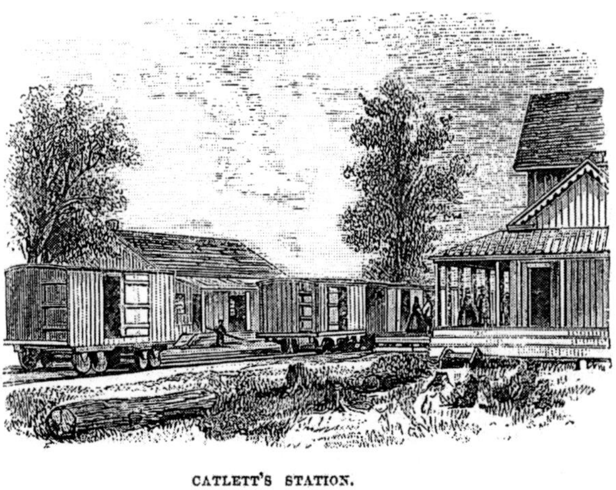

CATLETT'S STATION.

[1] These were 2,500 Pennsylvania Reserves, under General Reynolds, and the division of General Kearney, 4,500 strong, which on that day was at Warrenton Junction.

his papers, burned a few wagons, and carried off about two hundred prisoners, taken from the hospitals. The disgrace inflicted, it was thought, was more serious than the damage.[1] Stuart recrossed the Rappahannock at Warrenton Springs, after a little skirmishing.

The National capital was now in imminent danger, and slowly the Army of the Potomac was coming up to its relief.[2] Still it *was* coming, and Pope was made to believe that almost immediately he would be re-enforced by forty thousand or fifty thousand fresh troops, who had been resting for more than a month.[3] His own force had become much weakened by fighting and marching, and at this time its effective men did not exceed forty thousand in number.[4] But with the hope of immediate support, he massed his army in the neighborhood of Rappahannock Station,[a] for the purpose of falling upon the portion of the Confederates that had crossed the river above him, and was then supposed to be stretched between Waterloo Bridge, the Sulphur Springs, and Warrenton. He looked to the swollen river as a sufficient barrier to any attempt of the Confederates on its right bank to get between himself and Fredericksburg.

[a] August 23, 1862.

Sigel was directed to march his whole corps upon Sulphur Springs, supported by Banks and Reno, and McDowell (joined by the Pennsylvania Reserves, under Reynolds) was ordered, at the same time, to march directly upon Warrenton, that he might join with Sigel in pushing the Confederates back to Waterloo Bridge. General Halleck was requested to send Franklin's corps (which had arrived at Alexandria from the Peninsula) to Gainsville, on the Manassas Gap railway, eight miles west of the Junction. Sturgis, at Alexandria, had been ordered[b] to post strong guards along the railway between Manassas Junction and Catlett Station; and directions had been given to the commander at Manassas Junction, for

[b] August 22.

[1] Pope in his report says, the raid was "attended with but little damage," but "was most disgraceful to the force which had been left in charge of the trains."

[2] General Halleck had repeatedly urged General McClellan to hasten the departure of his army from the Peninsula. On the 9th, he informed him of the perils with which Pope's army and the capital were threatened, and said, "Considering the amount of transportation (an immense number of vessels in the James and at Hampton Roads) at your disposal, your delay is not satisfactory. You must move with all celerity." On the following day Halleck informed McClellan of the battle between Pope and Jackson, at Cedar Mountain, and said, "There must be no further delay in your movements; that which has already occurred was entirely unexpected, and must be satisfactorily explained." To these electrographs McClellan replied, that a lack of transportation was the cause of delay; and he assured the General-in-Chief that he was doing all in his power to carry out his orders. See McClellan's Report, pages 159–160.

[3] After the first few days succeeding the retreat to Harrison's Landing, Lee's army having fallen back to Richmond, with the exception of a brigade of cavalry left to watch the movements of the Army of the Potomac, there was very little service, excepting camp duty, for that army to perform. Immediately on its arrival upon the little peninsula formed by the James and Herring Creek, between Harrison's Point and Westover, the approaches to it were strongly fortified. It soon became evident that troops were gathering on the south side of the James, in the neighborhood of Petersburg. On the 30th of July, McClellan was informed from Washington that they were moving, when Hooker was ordered to advance with his division and Pleasanton's cavalry, and seize Malvern Hills as a menace of Richmond. He drove the Confederates from the Hills (Aug. 5), captured 100 of them, and pushed cavalry under Averill as far as White Oak Swamp Bridge, where they captured 28 men and horses of the Tenth Virginia cavalry. Hooker was satisfied that if he had been allowed to follow up this movement with any considerable number of troops, Richmond might have been taken with ease. McClellan had received a peremptory order to transfer his army to Acquia Creek, and it could not be done. Meanwhile General French, with a considerable Confederate force and 43 guns, had gone down the south side of the James to assail McClellan's camp. He appeared suddenly at Coggin's Point, before daylight on the morning of the first of August, and opened fire on the camp and vessels. So soon as McClellan's guns were brought to bear on him, he ceased firing and withdrew. McClellan sent a force across the James that drove the Confederates back to Petersburg, and strongly fortified Coggin's Point.

[4] Sigel's corps had become reduced to about 9,000 effectives; Banks's to 5,000; McDowells's, including Reynolds's division that had come from the Peninsula, was only 15,000; Reno's was 7,000; and the cavalry, greatly reduced in its equipment of horses and arms, did not exceed 4,000.

the first division of re-enforcements that should arrive to halt and take part in the works there, pushing forward its cavalry to Thoroughfare Gap.

Sigel with his supporters (Banks and Reno), moved slowly up the left side of the Rappahannock, and drove the Confederates from Great Run.[a] After re-building the bridge the latter had destroyed, he pushed forward, and, under the fire of artillery from the opposite side of the Rappahannock, took possession of Sulphur Springs the next morning, and went on toward Waterloo Bridge. The latter point was occupied by Buford's cavalry at noon,[b] and Sigel's advance under Milroy arrived there late in the afternoon.

[a] Aug. 23, 1862.

[b] Aug. 24.

Pope's army now faced westward, with Sigel's corps and Buford's cavalry near the Rappahannock, at Waterloo Bridge, and Banks just behind them. Reno was near Sulphur Springs; McDowell, with the divisions of Ricketts and King, was at Warrenton; and Heintzelman,[1] who had just arrived from the Peninsula, was at Warrenton Junction. Porter had been reported as near Bealton Station,[2] and it was expected that he would press forward and join Reno; while Franklin was expected to take post on Heintzelman's right. Sturgis and Cox were hourly expected at Warrenton Junction.

WM. B. FRANKLIN.

Such was the position of Pope's army, now about sixty thousand strong, on the 25th of August, the day on which Jackson, who led Lee's forces engaged in the great flank movement, crossed the Rappahannock at Hinson's Mill, four miles above Waterloo Bridge, passed through Orleans, bivouacked at Salem, and, moving with his accustomed celerity, the next day[c] crossed the Bull's Run Mountains at Thoroughfare Gap to Gainesville, where he was joined by Stuart with two cavalry brigades, and at twilight reached Bristow Station, on the Orange and Alexandria railway, in Pope's rear, and between him and Washington and Alexandria. This movement had been so thoroughly masked that Pope was completely deceived, and on the previous evening, when Jackson was reposing at Salem, between Thoroughfare and Manassas Gaps, he sent word to McDowell at Warrenton, that he believed "the whole force of the enemy had marched for the Shenandoah Valley, by way of Luray and Front Royal." From information received from an officer of the signal corps, at noon that day, Banks was of the same opinion. So little was Jackson expected at the rear of the army that two trains of cars ran up to Bristow Station, and were captured by him.

[c] Aug 26.

Jackson knew the peril of his position, and the necessity for quick

---

[1] Heintzelman was not well prepared for action at once. He had been sent forward by railway, without artillery, or wagons, or horses for his field officers, and only four rounds of ammunition to each man.

[2] Porter had but a small supply of provisions, and barely forty rounds of cartridges to each man.

action. He immediately dispatched Stuart with his cavalry, supported by two infantry regiments under General Trimble, to Manassas Junction, with general instructions to "throw his command between Washington City and the army of General Pope, and to break up his communications." This order was obeyed, and while Jackson was destroying Bristow Station, Stuart, before midnight, surprised the post at Manassas Junction, captured three hundred men, eight guns, and a large quantity of public property, and an immense amount of stores.[1] Some of the surprised party at the Junction fled to Union Mills, on Bull's Run, where Colonel Scammon, with the Eleventh and Twelfth Ohio, of General Cox's division, was stationed, and gave the alarm. Scammon immediately advanced upon the Junction, but after a severe skirmish at dawn, he was driven across Bull's Run, and made to retreat toward Alexandria by an overwhelming force, for Jackson had advanced with the rest of his command to the Junction, leaving General Ewell, with the Fifth Virginia cavalry, under Colonel Rosser, at Bristow Station. The Confederates, elated by their success, swept over the country along the line of the railway as far as Burke's Station, a few miles from Alexandria, and then around by Fairfax Court-House,[2] almost to Centreville. In the mean time Brigadier-General George W. Taylor, with the First, Second, Third, and Fourth New Jersey Infantry, of Franklin's division, had moved out from Alexandria by railway, to assist Scammon, and recover what was lost at the Junction; but the Confederates were too strong for him. His troops were soon routed, and in the conflict he lost a leg.

Pope and Lee were now both in a most critical position. The communications of the former with his re-enforcements and supplies were cut; and in the moving army of the latter, between Longstreet and Jackson, there was a gap of two marches, which Pope might occupy to Lee's mortal hurt. But Pope was not in a condition to take advantage of the occasion; yet he made a skillful use of the means at his command. He ordered[a] McDowell, with Sigel and Reynolds, to hasten to Gainesville that night, and there intercept Longstreet at the head of Lee's main column; and Reno was directed to move in parallel roads to Greenwich, followed by Kearney's division of Heintzelman's corps, with orders to communicate with, and support McDowell if necessary. Pope, in the mean time, had moved along the railway towards Manassas Junction, with Hooker's division of Heintzelman's corps. He directed Porter to remain at Warrenton Station until Banks should arrive there to hold it, and then to

[a] Aug. 27, 1862.

[1] They captured 175 horses, 200 new tents, 10 locomotives, 7 trains loaded with provisions and munitions of war, and a vast amount of commissary and quartermaster stores.

[2] This vicinity was the scene of many gallant deeds during the earlier part of the war, when the two armies were posted near it. We have already (page 487, vol. I.), noticed the gallant dash into the village of Fairfax Court-House, by Lieutenant C. H. Tompkins, with a handful of cavalry, at the beginning of the war: but one of the most brilliant feats in that neighborhood was performed at Burke's Station, by only fourteen members of the Lincoln (New York) cavalry, under Lieutenant Hidden, on the 9th of March, 1862, at about the time of the evacuation of Manassas. General Kearney had ordered the gallant Hidden to move forward cautiously with his little squad of men and "feel the enemy's position." They came suddenly upon 150 of the Confederate cavalry at Burke's Station. There was a strong temptation for a dash. The lieutenant and his men could not resist it, and that gallant young leader at their head fell upon the astounded foe with cheers and shouts. Some fled and others fought desperately. The victory finally rested with the Nationals, but at the cost of the life of Hidden. His comrades bore back his dead body, with eleven of the Virginia cavalry as prisoners. Kearney, who saw the whole movement, declared it to be one of the most brilliant he had ever seen, and took each man by the hand on his return, and complimented him for his bravery.

hasten forward to Gainesville, where it was expected the impending battle would be fought.

McDowell's movement was successfully accomplished without fighting. Hooker was not so fortunate. On approaching Bristow Station, late in the afternoon, he encountered Ewell. A sharp action ensued, by which each party lost about three hundred men. Ewell was driven away with a loss of part of his baggage, but he destroyed the bridge and railway track, and thus retarded pursuit, while he hastened to join Jackson at Manassas. Hooker's ammunition failed, and he could not pursue vigorously.

Pope now believed that by a vigorous movement in the morning he might "bag the whole crowd"[1] at Manassas Junction. For that purpose he ordered McDowell, at Gainesville, to move rapidly toward the Junction very early the next morning.[a] Reno was ordered to march at the same time from Greenwich to the Junction, and Kearney was directed to make his way to Bristow Station, for Jackson, hard pressed, might mass his troops and attempt to turn the National right at that point, seeking a way of escape. In order to make the right still further secure from a flank movement, Porter was ordered to move forward to Bristow Station at one o'clock in the morning. He did not obey, but waited until daylight before he moved, at which time Jackson had fortunately taken another direction, and "no serious consequences followed this disobedience of orders."[2] The Confederate leader had perceived his peril, and at three o'clock that morning had taken steps to evacuate Manassas, and seek a junction with Longstreet. He destroyed an immense amount of his captured stores, and as the way between himself and Longstreet, along the Manassas Gap railway, was blocked by National troops, he marched through Centreville, to gain, by a more circuitous route, a position where he might easily join Lee's main army, then approaching Thoroughfare Gap.

[a] Aug. 28, 1862.

THOROUGHFARE GAP.

This movement might have been thwarted, had Pope's orders been promptly carried out by all. Sigel, instead of advancing from Gainesville at dawn, as directed by McDowell, did not leave there until nearly three hours later, and Porter did not arrive at Bristow Station until after ten o'clock, when, instead of pushing forward with his fresh corps, he asked permission to remain there and rest his men.[3] In the mean time the

[1] Pope's order to McDowell, Aug. 27, 1862.

[2] Pope's Report to Halleck, January 27, 1863.

[3] Pope in his report says that the divisions of Sykes and Morell had been resting in camp all the day and night before, and that Porter's corps "was by far the freshest in the whole army," and was in better condition for service than any troops we had.

prompt Kearney, who had arrived at Bristow at eight o'clock in the morning, was sent forward in pursuit of Ewell, followed by Hooker, and, with the divisions of Kearney and Reno, Pope reached Manassas Junction at noon, just after Jackson with his rear-guard had left. He at once pushed all his available forces upon Centreville in pursuit, and ordered McDowell to march for that place, and Porter to come up to Manassas. Unfortunately McDowell had sent Ricketts' division toward Thoroughfare Gap, but with the remainder of his force he pushed on according to orders.

Kearney drove Jackson's rear-guard out of Centreville late in the afternoon,[a] and the main body of the Confederates fled by way of the Sudley Springs road and Warrenton turnpike,[1] destroying the bridges over the little streams behind them. Their faces were toward Thoroughfare Gap, from which was coming their help, and toward evening a strong force under Ewell and Taliaferro encamped on the wooded hills at the west side of the Warrenton pike, near the battle-ground of Bull's Run the year before.[b] King's division of McDowell's corps was in close pursuit, and when they had reached a point desired by the watching Confederates, the latter fell furiously upon their flank. A sanguinary battle ensued. The brunt of it, on the part of the Nationals, was borne by Gibbon's brigade, nobly supported by that of Doubleday's under its gallant commander. It continued until darkness interposed, when the advantage was with the Confederates. The losses on each side were very heavy. Taliaferro was badly wounded, and Ewell lost a leg.

a Aug. 28, 1862.

b July 21, 1861.

ABNER DOUBLEDAY.

Pope was now at Centreville; and, on hearing of this encounter, made immediate arrangements for crushing Jackson by circumambient pressure before he could form a junction with Longstreet. He directed McDowell and King to maintain their positions at all hazards; told Kearney to push forward from Centreville at one o'clock in the morning,[c] and follow Jackson closely along the Warrenton pike, to prevent his retreat northward toward Leesburg, and ordered Porter, whom he supposed to be at Manassas Junction, to move upon Centreville at dawn. But Longstreet's rapid march, quickened by a knowledge of Jackson's danger, defeated the plan. He had passed through Thoroughfare Gap before King's division was attacked, and near its entrance, between it and Haymarket, had encountered Ricketts' division, with the cavalry of Buford and Bayard, which had marched to confront him. An active engagement ensued, and ended only with the sunlight. The heaviest of the battle fell on the Eleventh Pennsyl-

c Aug. 29, 1862.

---

[1] See map on page 588, volume I.

vania, which lost about fifty men. Longstreet was held in check for a while; but when, from his superior force, he sent out flanking parties (a strong one to Hopewell Gap), Ricketts yielded to necessity and fled toward Gainesville, rapidly followed early the next morning[a] by his antagonist.

[a] Aug. 29, 1862.

Pope's advantage was lost on the morning of the 29th. His army was scattered and somewhat confused, while the chances for a junction of Jackson and Longstreet momentarily increased. King had been compelled to abandon the Warrenton pike, and had fallen back to Manassas Junction, to which point Ricketts had also hastened. This left the way open for a speedy embrace of the two Confederate leaders, and the advance of Lee's entire army. Pope perceived it, and endeavored to regain what was lost by ordering Sigel, supported by Reynolds, to advance from Groveton and attack Jackson in the wooded heights near, at dawn, while he should get the remainder of his force well in hand. He ordered Heintzelman to push forward from Centreville with the divisions of Hooker and Kearney toward Gainesville, to be followed by Reno, who was to attack promptly and heavily, while Porter, with his own corps and King's division, was to move upon the road to Gainesville from Manassas, for the purpose of turning Jackson's flank at the junction of that highway and the Warrenton pike, and to fall heavily upon his rear.

Jackson, who now commanded the Warrenton road, by which Lee was approaching, had determined to maintain his advantageous position at all hazards until relief should come. His troops were posted along the cut and grading of an unfinished railway, his right resting on the Warrenton pike, and his left near Sudley's Mill. The greater portion of his troops were under shelter of thick woods a little in the rear.

Sigel, with the division of Carl Schurz on his right, that of Schenck on his left, and Milroy in the center, advanced to attack at five o'clock in the morning,[b] and at seven a furious battle was begun. Until ten o'clock Sigel steadily gained ground, in the face of a destructive storm of missiles, when it became evident that Jackson had been re-enforced, and was assuming the offensive. It was so. Longstreet, with the vanguard of Lee's whole army, which had been streaming through Thoroughfare Gap all the morning, unopposed, had reached the field of action. Yet, against inevitably increasing odds, the Nationals maintained the sanguinary struggle until near noon, when Kearney's division arrived on the field by the Sudley Springs road, and took position on Sigel's right. At the same time Reno came up by the Gainesville road to the support of the center, and Reynolds, with the Pennsylvania Reserves, placed himself on the extreme left. Hooker arrived by the Sudley road at two in the afternoon, to the relief

[b] August 29.

PHILIP KEARNEY.

of Schurz and Milroy, who had been fighting since morning without tasting food, and had almost expended their ammunition.

At noon the Nationals outnumbered the Confederates, and from that time until half-past four o'clock the battle assumed the aspect of a series of severe skirmishes. Then Pope ordered Porter into action, with directions to attack and attempt to turn the Confederate right, which he supposed to be that of Jackson's troops; and soon afterward Heintzelman and Reno were ordered to assail their left and front in support of Porter's movement. But that movement was not made, in consequence, Porter says, of not receiving the order until dusk; so the brunt of battle fell upon Heintzelman and

MONUMENT AND BATTLE-GROUND NEAR GROVETON.[1]

Reno. It was desperate and gallant on both sides. Grover's brigade of Hooker's division penetrated two of Jackson's lines by a bayonet charge, and after a severe hand to hand struggle got possession of the railway embankment on the Confederate left, but at the cost of thirty per cent. of

---

[1] This is a view of the monument on the battle-field near Groveton, as it appeared when the writer visited and sketched it, early in June, 1866, with his traveling companions, Messrs. Dreer and Greble. We rode out from Manassas Junction in an ambulance early in the morning, and went over the battle-ground of Bull's Run, visiting the monument near the site of Mrs. Henry's house (see pages 594 and 603, volume I.), and, following the line of the retreat of the National troops, went down to the Warrenton turnpike, and westward to Groveton, a hamlet of a few dilapidated houses, on the slope of a hill. We passed through a lane near the ruins of Mrs. Henry Dogan's stone house, which remained as the shot and shell had left it after the battle. Pope's cannon were brought to bear upon it to drive out Confederate sharp-shooters. Ascending a hill through open fields, we soon reached the monument, from which we had a fine view of the country over which the battles of July 21, 1861, and the close of August, 1862, were fought. On the monument (which was built by the same hands, and of the same material as that near the site of the Henry house, see page 607, volume I.) was this inscription: "IN MEMORY OF THE PATRIOTS WHO FELL AT GROVETON, AUGUST 28, 29, AND 30, 1862." We are looking toward Manassas Junction, the place of which is indicated by the two birds. The single bird to the right indicates Groveton. Returning, we passed near Chinn's house, in which Colonel Broadhead, wounded in this vicinity, died; also the Pittsylvania house, and the store-house of Mr. Mathews, mentioned in the account of the battle of Bull's Run, in volume I. These were among the few houses in that region which had survived the war.

MRS. DOGAN'S HOUSE AT GROVETON.

its force. Kearney, meanwhile, had struck Jackson's left at the point occupied by A. P. Hill, doubled his flank upon his center, and assisted Hooker in holding the railway intrenchment for a time. This was a critical moment for the Confederates, for their ammunition was nearly exhausted, and Jackson's left had been driven back nearly a mile.

King's division of McDowell's corps had come into action about sunset, and boldly advanced beyond the general line of the Nationals, but was soon brought to a stand. Heavy re-enforcements, composed of a fresh division of Longstreet's corps, had come to the aid of Jackson. Among them was Hood's famous Texan brigade. By these and McLaws' Louisianians, Kearney's regiments, most in advance, were driven back with the loss of a gun, four flags, and one hundred men made prisoners; but soon afterward darkness put an end to the struggle. Porter, on receiving Pope's order at twilight, made a disposition for attack, but it was too late. So ended THE BATTLE OF GROVETON, with a loss of not less than seven thousand men on each side.[1]

Pope's entire army (excepting Banks's force at Bristow's Station) and a part of McClellan's was in the action just recorded. Fasting, sickness, and marches, and the casualties in battle, had greatly reduced the number of his effective men. It was estimated at only about forty thousand on the night of the battle of Groveton.[2] It had failed to accomplish the intentions of its commander in keeping Lee and Jackson apart and destroying the latter, and it was now decidedly the weaker party, for Lee's army had just become a powerful unit. Prudence counseled a retreat across Bull's Run, and even to the defenses of Washington, but Pope resolved to try the issue of another battle on the morrow, and so his troops rested on their arms that night. For this determination he had not sufficient warrant. He had received no re-enforcements or supplies since the 26th, and had no positive assurance that any would be sent. He confidently expected rations and forage from McClellan at Alexandria, who was to supply them, but it was not until the morning of the 30th, when it was too late to retreat and perilous to stand still, that he received the disheartening information, that seemed like a cruel mockery, that rations and forage would be "loaded into the available wagons

---

[1] Reports of Generals Pope and Lee, and their subordinate commanders. Pope, in his report, severely censured Porter, saying, "His force took no part whatever in the action; but were suffered by him to lie on their arms within sight and sound of the battle during the whole day. So far as I know," he said, "he made no effort whatever to comply with my orders, or to take any part in the action;" and declared that had he obeyed his orders, the whole or a greater part of Jackson's force might have been crushed or captured. "I believe," he said—"in fact I am positive—that at five o'clock on the afternoon of the 29th, General Porter had in his front no considerable force of the enemy." He said he believed at the time of the battle, and when he wrote his report (January, 1863), that it was an easy matter for Porter "to have turned the right flank of Jackson, and to have fallen in his rear," and that a decisive victory for the Nationals might have been gained before Jackson could have been joined by any of the forces of Longstreet.

In his report, Pope says that Longstreet did not reach the right of Jackson until about sunset, and he supposed Jackson's right to be the extreme of that wing of the Confederate Army. He was mistaken. According to fair inferences drawn from Lee's report (Reports of the Army of Northern Virginia, i. 23, 24), and the positive statements of other commanders of that army engaged in the action, contained in volume II., Longstreet had position on Jackson's right as early as noon that day, and if Porter had received the order at the time Pope thought he did, it is very doubtful whether he could have carried it out successfully. Porter says, as we have observed in the text, that he did not receive the order until dusk, when it was too late to execute it. Nearly the whole of Longstreet's corps had been directly in front of him for several hours when Pope's order reached him.

[2] His men were greatly fatigued by the intense labors of the fortnight preceding. For two days they had eaten but little. The cavalry and artillery horses had been ten days in harness and two days without food.

and cars" so soon as he should send a cavalry escort for the train!—a thing utterly impossible.[1]

Pope saw that he had no alternative. He must fight. So he put his line in V shape early the next morning, pivoting on the Warrenton pike. Reynolds occupied the left leg, Porter, Sigel, and Reno the right, and Heintzelman was posted on the extreme right. Pope had resolved to attack Lee's left, and at the same time the latter had made disposition during the night to attack Pope's left. Lee's movements for that purpose, in which he withdrew some of his troops from ground he had occupied the previous evening, gave Pope the impression that his foe was retreating along the Warrenton pike, and he was not undeceived until ten o'clock the next day. Meanwhile he had telegraphed to Washington the joyful tidings that the Confederates were "retreating to the mountains." Under this impression he ordered McDowell to follow with three corps, Porter's in the advance, along the Warrenton pike, and attack the fugitives, and Heintzelman and Reno, supported by Ricketts' division, were directed to assail and turn the Confederate left.

The attempt to execute this movement developed a fearful state of affairs for the National army. As Butterfield's division moved up the hill near Groveton, the eminence near the edge of the woods suddenly and unexpectedly swarmed with the Confederates, who, instead of retreating, had been massing under cover of the forest in preparation for an offensive movement. They at once opened a fierce fire of shot, shell, and bullet on the Nationals, and at the same time clouds of dust on the left indicated that the foe, in great numbers, were making a flank movement in that direction. To meet this peril McDowell ordered Reynolds to leave Porter's left, and hasten to the assistance of Schenck and Milroy, on whom the threatened blow seemed about to fall. This exposed Porter's key-point, when Colonel G. K. Warren, without orders, moved up with his little brigade of a thousand men and took Reynolds's place. Ricketts, in the mean time, had hastened to the left, and the battle soon became very severe. Porter's corps, which had been made to recoil by the force of the first unexpected blow, was rallied, and performed special good service, especially Warren's gallant little band of volunteers, and a brigade of regulars under Colonel Buchanan. For a while victory seemed to incline to the Nationals, for Jackson's advanced line was steadily pushed back until about five o'clock in the afternoon. Then Longstreet turned the tide. He found a commanding point on Jackson's right, and with four batteries he poured a most destructive raking artillery fire upon the Nationals. Line after line was swept away, and very soon the whole left was put to flight. Jackson immediately advanced, and Longstreet moved in support by pushing his heavy columns against Pope's center. Hood, with his two brigades, charged furiously upon Ricketts and Reynolds, followed by the divisions of Evans, R. H. Anderson, and Wilcox, supported by those of Kemper and Jones, and at the same time Lee's artillery was doing fearful execution on Pope's disordered infantry. Terrible was the struggle until dark, when it ceased. The National left had been pushed

---

[1] The letter was written by General Franklin by direction of General McClellan. "Such a letter," said Pope in his report, "when we were fighting the enemy, and Alexandria was swarming with troops, needs no comment."

back a considerable distance, but though confused, it was unbroken; and it still held the Warrenton turnpike, by which alone Pope's army might safely retreat.

Pope had now no alternative but to fall back toward Washington. He issued an order to that effect at eight o'clock in the evening.[a] The whole army was directed to withdraw during the night across Bull's Run to the heights of Centreville. This was done chiefly by way of the Stone Bridge;[1] the brigades of Meade and Seymour, and some other troops, covering the movement. The night was very dark, and Lee fortunately did not pursue; and in the morning[b] Bull's Run once again divided the two great armies. So ended THE SECOND BATTLE OF BULL'S RUN.

[a] Aug. 30, 1862.

[b] Aug. 31.

Pope was joined at Centreville by the corps of Franklin and Sumner, making his force a little more than sixty thousand, and fully equal to that of Lee. The 31st was passed by the Nationals in comparative quiet, but a severe struggle was had on the following day. Lee was not disposed to attack his foe in his strong position at Centreville, so he sent Jackson on another flanking enterprise at an early hour of the morning of the 31st. Jackson took with him his own and Ewell's divisions, and with instructions to turn and assail Pope's right, he crossed Bull's Run at Sudley Ford, and pushed on to the Little River turnpike. There, turning to the right the following day,[c] he marched down that highway toward Fairfax Court-House.

[c] Sept. 1.

Pope, in the mean time, suspecting this movement, had fallen back to positions covering Fairfax Court-House and Germantown, directed Sumner on the morning of the 1st of September to push forward two brigades toward the Little River pike, and ordered Hooker early in the afternoon to Fairfax Court-House, in support of Sumner.[2] Just before sunset Reno met Jackson's advance (Ewell and Hill) near Chantilly. A cold and drenching rain was falling, but it did not prevent an immediate engagement. Reno, with the remains of two divisions, was sharply attacked, when Hooker, McDowell, and Kearney came up to his assistance. The conflict was severe for a short time, when General Isaac J. Stevens, who was in command at the battle of Port Royal Ferry,[3] now leading Reno's second division, ordered a charge, which he led in person, and was shot dead. His command fell back in disorder, and to some extent put the remainder of Reno's force in confusion. Seeing this, General Kearney advanced with his division and renewed the action, sending Birney's brigade to the fore front. A furious thunderstorm was then raging, which made the use of ammunition difficult; but, unheeding this, Kearney brought forward a battery and planted it in position himself. Then, perceiving a gap caused by the retirement of Stevens's force yet remaining, he pushed forward to reconnoiter, and was killed just within the Confederate lines. He, too, was shot dead just at sun-

[1] See page 587, volume I.

[2] He ordered McDowell to move along the road to Fairfax Court-House as far as Difficult Creek, and connect with Hooker's left; Reno to Chantilly; Heintzelman to take post on the road between Centreville and Fairfax, in the rear of Reno; Franklin to take position on McDowell's left and rear; and Sigel and Porter to unite with the right of Sumner, who was on the left of Heintzelman. Banks, who, with the wagon-train, had come on from Bristow Station, was ordered to pursue the old Braddock road in the direction of Alexandria.

[3] See page 128.

set, and the command of his division devolved on the able Birney, who instantly ordered a bayonet charge by his own brigade, composed of the First, Thirty-eighth, and Fortieth New York. These, led by Colonel Egan, executed the orders with great bravery, and pushed back the Confederate advance some distance. Birney held the field that night, and the hours of darkness were spent in the sad task of burying the dead.[1] Precious were the lives on the Union side that were lost in this, THE BATTLE OF CHANTILLY,[2] a battle that ended the campaign of General Pope, and also his military career in the East.[3] He had labored hard under many difficulties, and he bitterly complained of a lack of co-operation with him in his later struggles by McClellan and some of his subordinates.[4]

By order of General Halleck, the broken and demoralized army was withdrawn within the fortifications around Washington the next day,[a] when it was allowed a brief rest. Pope now repeated with greater earnestness his request, made before he took the field, to be relieved of the command of the Army of Virginia, and allowed to return to the West, and it was granted. The Army of Virginia disappeared as a

[a] Sept. 2, 1862.

---

[1] By reference to the large Map of Operations in Upper Virginia, on page 398 of this volume, and to the smaller maps on pages 586, 588, 594, and 602 of volume I., the reader will have a fair idea of the region of Pope's campaign, and of the field of conflict in the vicinity of Manassas.

[2] Among them were Generals Kearney and Stevens, and Major Tilden, of the Thirty-eighth New York. Kearney was well known to General Lee, and that leader sent his body to Pope's head-quarters the next morning, with a flag of truce. Stevens led the attack at the head of the Seventy-ninth (Highlanders) New York, with the colors of that regiment, which had fallen from the hands of a wounded sergeant. In the Second Battle of Bull's Run, on the 30th, Colonel Fletcher Webster, son of Daniel Webster, fell; and, on the same day, Colonel George W. Pratt, of the Twentieth New York, son of the Honorable Zadock Pratt, was mortally wounded near Gainesville. On the same day Colonel Broadhead, of the regular army, received his death-wound on the Bull Run battle-ground; also Colonels O'Connor, Cantwell, and Brown. Among the wounded were Major-General Robert C. Schenck, and Colonel Hardin, of the Pennsylvania Reserves.

The National loss in Pope's campaign, from the Battle of Cedar Mountain to that of Chantilly, was never officially reported in full. The most careful estimates make it, including the immense number of stragglers who never returned to their regiments, almost 30,000. Lee's losses during that time amounted probably to 15,000. He claimed to have taken 7,000 prisoners, with 2,000 sick and wounded, thirty pieces of artillery, and 20,000 small arms.

[3] Reports of Generals Pope and Lee and their subordinates.

[4] According to Pope's Report, 20,500 men were all of the Army of the Potomac that joined him in active operations—"all," he said, "of the 91,000 veteran troops from Harrison's Landing which ever drew trigger under my command, or in any way took part in the campaign." . . . "Porter's corps," he said, "from unnecessary and unusual delays, and frequent and flagrant disregard for my orders, took no part whatever, except in the battle of the 30th of August." Pope afterward formally preferred charges against Porter of "misconduct before the enemy." Porter was tried by a court-martial, which, in January, 1863, pronounced a verdict of guilty, and he was sentenced to be "cashiered, and be forever disqualified from holding any office of trust or profit under the Government of the United States." At the request of the President the whole case was reviewed by Joseph Holt, then Judge Advocate-General, when the sentence was approved and executed.

Strenuous but ineffectual efforts were made by the President and the General-in-Chief to bring the Army of the Potomac to the aid of the Army of Virginia in confronting Lee, and through it to furnish Pope with supplies. The official electrographs that passed between the President and General Halleck and General McClellan exhibit the same indisposition on the part of the latter to promptly comply with the orders of his superiors that was shown while he was on the Peninsula. He seemed more disposed to give his advice than to obey commands; and while failing to afford the required aid to Pope, he affected to misunderstand explicit orders, and indicated his unwillingness to act under superior authority by saying in a dispatch to Halleck on the 27th of August: "I am not responsible for the past, and cannot be for the future, unless I receive authority to dispose of the available troops according to my judgment." After thwarting the efforts of the Government to get Franklin's corps to a position to give Pope greatly needed assistance on the 29th, and Halleck had telegraphed to him, saying, "I want Franklin's corps to go far enough to find out something about the enemy. . . . Our people must move more actively and find out where the enemy is; I am tired of guesses," McClellan telegraphed to the President, saying: "I am clear that one of two courses should be adopted. First, to concentrate all our available forces to open communication with Pope. Second, *to leave Pope to get out of his scrape*, and at once use all our means to make the Capital safe."—See McClellan's Report, page 175.

It was not until Pope was defeated and driven across Bull's Run to Centreville that the corps of Franklin and Sumner were permitted to take a position within supporting distance. It is clear to the comprehension of the writer, after a careful analysis of reports and dispatches, that had these corps and Porter's been allowed to give timely assistance to Pope, as they could have done, Lee's army might have been captured or dispersed, and

separate organization, and became a part of the Army of the Potomac; and General McClellan, in compliance with the wishes of a large majority of his surviving officers and men, was invested[a] with the command of all the troops for the defense of the capital.

[a] Sept. 2, 1862.

The sad results of Pope's campaign, and of that on the Peninsula, cast a pall of gloom over the spirits of the loyal people for a moment. But it was soon lifted; while the conspirators and their followers and friends were made jubilant and hopeful.[1]

---

perhaps a death-blow given to the rebellion. In view of all the testimony, and especially of that given in McClellan's Report, it does not seem to be a harsh judgment to believe that the commander of the Army of the Potomac and his friends were willing to see Pope defeated. "Pope's appointment to the command, and his address to his army on opening the campaign" (see page 446), says a careful writer, "had been understood by them as reflecting on the strategy of the Peninsula campaign; and this was their mode of resenting the indignity."—See Greeley's *American Conflict*, ii. 192.

[1] On the 2d of September Davis sent into the "Congress" at Richmond a message announcing news of complete triumph, from Lee, and said: "From these dispatches it will be seen that God has again extended his shield over our patriotic army, and has blessed the cause of the Confederacy with a second signal victory on the field [Bull's Run] already memorable by the gallant achievement of our troops."

The following are the names of the members of the so-called "Confederate Congress" at this time:—

"SENATE."

Alabama—*Clement C. Clay, *William L. Yancey *Arkansas*—*Robert W. Johnson, Charles B. Mitchell. *Florida*—James M. Baker, *Augustus E. Maxwell. *Georgia*—Benjamin H. Hill, *Robert Toombs. *Kentucky*—*Henry C. Burnett, *William E. Simms. *Louisiana*—Thomas J. Semmes, Edward Sparrow. *Mississippi*—*Albert G. Brown, James Phelan. *Missouri*—*John B. Clark, R. S. T. Peyton. *North Carolina*—George Davis, William T. Dortch. *South Carolina*—*Robert W. Barnwell, *James L. Orr. *Tennessee*—Langdon C. Haynes, Gustavus A. Henry. *Texas*—William S. Oldham, *Louis T. Wigfall. *Virginia*—*R. M. T. Hunter, *Wm. Ballard Preston.

"HOUSE OF REPRESENTATIVES."

Alabama—Thomas J. Foster, *William R. Smith, John P. Ralls, *J. L. M. Curry, *Francis S. Lyon, Wm. P. Chilton, *David Clopton, *James S. Pugh, *Edward L. Dargan. *Arkansas*—Felix L. Batson, Grandison D. Royston, Augustus H. Garland, Thomas B. Hanly. *Florida*—James B. Dawkins, Robert B. Hilton. *Georgia*—Julian Hartridge, C. J. Munnerlyn, Hines Holt, Augustus H. Kenan, David W. Lewis, William W. Clark, *Robert P. Frippe, *Lucius J. Gartrell, Hardy Strickland, *Augustus R. Wright. *Kentucky*—Alfred Boyd, John W. Crockett, H. E. Read, Geo. W. Ewing, *James S. Chrisman, T. L. Burnett, H. W. Bruce, S. S. Scott, E. M. Bruce, J. W. Moore, Robert J. Breckenridge, John M. Elliott. *Louisiana*—Charles J. Villerè, *Charles M. Conrad, Duncan F. Kenner, Lucien J. Duprè, John F. Lewis, John Perkins, Jr. *Mississippi*—J. W. Clapp, *Reuben Davis, Israel Welch, H. C. Chambers, *O. R. Singleton, E. Barksdale, *John J. McRae. *Missouri*—W. M. Cook, Thomas A. Harris, Casper W. Bell, A. H. Conrow, George G. Vest, Thomas W. Freeman, John Hyer. *North Carolina*—*W. N. H. Smith, Robert R. Bridgers, Owen R. Keenan, T. D. McDowell, Thomas S. Ashe, Arch. H. Arrington, Robert McClean, William Lander, B. S Gaither, A. T. Davidson. *South Carolina*—*John McQueen, *W. Porcher Miles, L. M. Ayer, *Milledge L. Bonham. James Farrow, *William W. Boyce. *Tennessee*—Joseph T. Heiskell, William G. Swan, W. H. Tebbs, E. L. Gardenshire, *Henry S. Foote, *Meredith P. Gentry, *George W. Jones, Thomas Meneese, *J. D. C. Atkins, *John V. Wright, David M. Currin. *Texas*—*John A Wilcox, *C. C. Herbert, Peter W. Gray, B. F. Sexton, M. D. Graham, Wm. B. Wright. *Virginia*—*M. R. H. Garnett, John R. Chambliss. James Lyons, *Roger A. Pryor, *Thomas S. Bococke, John Goode, Jr., J. P. Holcombe, *D. C. De Jarnett, *William Smith, *A. R. Boteler, John R. Baldwin, Walter R. Staples, Walter Preston, Albert G. Jenkins, Robert Johnson, Charles W. Russell.

Those marked with the * had been members of the United States Congress.

CHAPTER XVIII.

LEE'S INVASION OF MARYLAND, AND HIS RETREAT TOWARD RICHMOND.

ONLY thirty days had passed by since Lee was in the attitude of a defender of the Confederate capital, with two large armies threatening it from different points, when he was seen in the position of an exultant victor, ready to take the offensive in a bold menace of the National capital. He sent troops to check Pope, and the effect was the withdrawal of the Army of the Potomac from the Peninsula. Relieved of all danger in the latter direction, he moved in heavy force and pushed the Army of Virginia across the Rappahannock before the other great army lent it any aid; and now, at the beginning of September, he saw both armies which had threatened him, shattered and disordered behind the strong fortifications of the National capital, where McClellan concentrated them to defend that capital from an expected assault. From Fortress Monroe to the head waters of the James and the Rappahannock, and far up the Potomac and the intervening country, as well as the whole valley of the Shenandoah to its northern entrance at Harper's Ferry, there were no National troops, and the harvests in all that region were poured into the Confederate granary.

The Republic now seemed to be in great peril, and the loyal people were very anxious. Long before the disastrous termination of the campaign on the Peninsula, thoughtful men were losing faith in the ability, and some in the patriotism of the commander of the Army of the Potomac; and it was clearly seen that if one hundred and fifty thousand to two hundred thousand men could not make more headway in the work of crushing the rebellion than they had done under his leadership during full ten months, more men must be called to the field at once, or all would be lost. Accordingly the loyal Governors of eighteen States signed a request that the President should immediately take measures for largely increasing the effective force in the field. He had already, by a call on the 1st of June, drawn forty thousand men, for three months, from Massachusetts, Rhode Island, New York, Pennsylvania, and Ohio. In compliance with a request of the governors, he called for three hundred thousand volunteers "for the war," on the 1st of July; and on the 9th of August, when Pope was struggling with Jackson near the Rapid Anna, he called for three hundred thousand men for nine months, with the understanding that an equal number of men would be drafted from the great body of the citizens who were over eighteen and less than forty-five years of age, if they did not appear as volunteers.

These calls met with a hearty response, and very soon men were seen flocking to the standard of the Republic by thousands. The Conspirators at Richmond well knew that such a response would be made, and while they were wickedly deceiving the people of the Confederacy with the idea that "the Lincoln government," as they said in derision, was bankrupt in men and money, they were trembling with fear because of its wealth in both, which they well comprehended. Therefore they instructed Lee to take immediate advantage of the fortunate situation in which McClellan's failure to sustain Pope had placed him, to act boldly, vigorously, and even desperately, if necessary.

Lee saw clearly that an assault on the fortified National capital would be foolish and disastrous, and he conceived the idea of throwing his army across the Potomac to the rear of Washington, when, perhaps, after sweeping victoriously on to the Susquehanna, he might return and seize Baltimore and the National city. He believed the people of "sovereign" Maryland were chafing under the domination of the Government, and were ready to give all the support in their power to the Confederate cause; and that the presence of his army would produce a general uprising in that State. The conspirators at Richmond were in accord with Lee in this view, and he made instant preparations for throwing his army across the Potomac.

Lee was joined on the 2d[a] by the fresh division of D. H. Hill, from Richmond, and this was immediately sent as a vanguard toward Leesburg. The whole Confederate army followed, and between the 4th and 7th it had crossed the Potomac by the fords in the vicinity of the Point of Rocks, and encamped not far from the city of Frederick, on the Monocacy River. There General Lee formally raised the standard of revolt, and issued a proclamation[b] in words intended to be as seductive to the people of that commonwealth as those of Randall's impassioned appeal, entitled "Maryland! my Maryland!"[1] Lee declared it was the wish "of the people of the South" to aid those of Maryland in throwing off the "foreign yoke" they were compelled to bear, that they might be able to "again enjoy the inalienable rights of freemen, and to restore the independence and sovereignty of their State;" and he assured them that his mission was to assist them with the power of arms "in regaining their rights," of which they had "been so unjustly despoiled."

[a] Sept. 1862.

[b] Sept. 8.

Lee discoursed as fluently and falsely of the "outrages" inflicted by the generous Government which he had solemnly sworn to protect, and against which he was waging war for the perpetuation of injustice and inhumanity,[2]

[1] See page 555, volume I.

[2] In a speech at the raising of the National flag over Columbia College, in New York, immediately after the attack on Fort Sumter, in April, 1861, Dr. Francis Lieber admirably defined the character of soldiers like Robert E. Lee, who professed to believe in the State supremacy, but who had served in the armies of the Republic and deserted their flag. "Men," he said, "who believed, or pretended to believe in State sovereignty alone, when secession broke out, went over with men and ships, abandoning the flag to which they had sworn fidelity; thus showing that all along they served the United States like Swiss hirelings and not as citizens, in their military service. They did more: not only did they desert the service of the United States, on the ground that their individual States, to whom they owed allegiance, had declared themselves out of the Union: but in many cases they took with them, or attempted to take with them, the men who owed no such allegiance, being either foreigners or natives of other American States. In other cases they actually called publicly on their former comrades to be equally faithless, and desert their ships or troops. The Swiss mercenaries used to act more nobly. Once having sold their services, and having taken the oath of fidelity, they used to remain faithful unto death."

as did Jefferson Davis, his coadjutor in the monstrous crime; but he soon found to his shame and confusion that the disloyal Marylanders like Bradley Johnson, who had joined the Confederate army, had deceived him by false representations, and that, with the exception of a large rebellious faction in the more Southern slaveholding counties, the people of that State looked upon the gigantic iniquity of the conspirators and their abettors with abhorrence. He was met with sullen scorn in the form of apparent indifference, and he was soon made to feel that under that passivity there was burning a spirit like that of the venerable and more demonstrative Barbara Frietchie, of Frederick, one of the true heroines of whom history too often fails to make honorable mention.[1] Lee lost more men in Maryland by desertion than he gained by his proclamation. Had there been nothing repulsive in the work to which they were invited, the filthy and wretched condition of Lee's troops would have made the citizens of Maryland scornful of such an "army of liberators."

BARBARA FRIETCHIE.

McClellan was informed of Lee's movement on the morning of the 3d, and immediately put his troops in motion to meet the threatened peril. His army was thrown into Maryland north of Washington, and on the 7th,

---

[1] Barbara Frietchie (who died in June, 1864) lived close to a bridge which spans the stream that courses through Frederick. When, in this invasion of Maryland, "Stonewall Jackson" marched through Frederick, his troops passed over that bridge. He had been informed that many National flags were flying in the city, and he gave orders for them all to be hauled down. Patriotic Barbara's was displayed from one of the dormer-windows, seen in the sketch of her house here given, from a drawing made by the writer in September, 1866, in which, just beyond it, the bridge is seen. *Her* flag was pulled down. The remainder of the story has been told in the following words of John G. Whittier:—

Up rose old Barbara Frietchie then,
Bowed with her fourscore years and ten;
Bravest of all in Frederick town,
She took up the flag the men hauled down;
In her attic window the staff she set,
To show that one heart was loyal yet.
Up the street came the rebel tread,
Stonewall Jackson riding ahead.
Under his slouched hat left and right
He glanced: the old flag met his sight.
"Halt!" the dust-brown ranks stood fast.
"Fire!" out blazed the rifle-blast.
It shivered the window, pane and sash;
It rent the banner with seam and gash.
Quick, as it fell from the broken staff,
Dame Barbara snatched the silken scarf;
She leaned far out on the window-sill,
And shook it forth with a royal will.

BARBARA FRIETCHIE'S HOUSE.

"Shoot," if you must, this old gray head,
But spare your country's flag," she said.
A shade of sadness, a blush of shame,
Over the face of the leader came;
The nobler nature within him stirred
To life at that woman's deed and word:
"Who touches a hair of yon gray head
Dies like a dog! March on!" he said.
All day long through Frederick street
Sounded the tread of marching feet.
All day long that free flag tost
Over the heads of the rebel host.

leaving General Banks in command at the National capital, he hastened to the field, making his head-quarters that night with the Sixth Corps at Rockville. His army, composed of his own and the forces of Pope and Burnside, numbered a little more than eighty-seven thousand effective men. It advanced slowly toward Frederick by five parallel roads, and was so disposed as to cover both Washington and Baltimore. The left rested on the Potomac, and the right on the Baltimore and Ohio railway.[1]

Great caution was necessary, for the real intentions of Lee were unknown. Fortunately, these were discovered on the 13th, when McClellan's advance entered Frederick, after a brisk skirmish with the Confederate rear-guard, and found there a copy of Lee's general order issued on the 9th. It revealed the fact that he was not to make a direct movement against Washington or Baltimore, so long as McClellan lay between him and the two cities; but so soon as he could draw him toward the Susquehanna by menacing Pennsylvania, and thus take him away from his supplies, he might attack and cripple him, and then march upon one or both of those cities. To accomplish this he designed to take possession of Harper's Ferry (which he believed would be evacuated on his crossing the Potomac) and establish communication with Richmond by way of the Shenandoah Valley; and then, marching up the Cumberland Valley, endeavor to draw McClellan toward the heart of Pennsylvania.

Lee's maneuvers for the end proposed were most hazardous in their character, under the circumstances. He ordered Jackson to go over the South Mountain[2] by way of Middletown, and then, passing by Sharpsburg to the Potomac, cross that river above Harper's Ferry, sever the Baltimore and Ohio railway, and intercept any troops that might attempt to escape from the Ferry. Longstreet was to follow the same road to Boonsborough, westward of the South Mountain; while McLaws, with his own and Anderson's division, was to march to Middletown, and then press on toward Harper's Ferry and possess himself of Maryland Heights, on the left bank of the Potomac, overlooking that post, and endeavor to capture it and its dependencies. General Walker was to cross the Potomac at Cheeks' ford, and, if practicable, take possession of Loudon Heights, on the right bank of the river, at the same time, and co-operate with Jackson and McLaws. D. H. Hill's division was to form the rear-guard of the main body, and Stuart's cavalry was to cover the whole. The troops ordered to Harper's Ferry were directed to join the main army at Hagerstown or Boonsborough after capturing that post.

---

[1] The right wing was composed of the First and Ninth Corps, under General Burnside; the center, of the Second and Twelfth Corps, under General Sumner, and the left, of the Sixth Corps, under General Franklin. The First Corps (McDowell's) was placed under General Hooker; the Ninth, of Burnside's command, was under General Reno; the Twelfth was Banks's, which was now under General Mansfield, who had not before taken the field. Porter's corps remained in Washington until the 12th, and did not join the army until it reached the vicinity of Sharpsburg. General Hunt was made Chief of Artillery, and General Pleasanton commanded the cavalry division.

[2] This is a continuation into Pennsylvania of the ranges of the Blue Ridge in Virginia, severed by the Potomac at Harper's Ferry and vicinity. A lower range, called the Catoctin or Kittoctan Mountains, passes near Frederick, and is a continuation north of the Potomac, of the Bull's Run Mountains. See map on page 586, Volume I. Several roads cross these ranges, the best being the old National road from Baltimore to Cumberland, passing through Frederick and Middletown, the latter being the most considerable village in the Kittoctan Valley. The principal passes or gaps in the South Mountain range made memorable by this invasion were Crampton's and Turner's, the former five miles from Harper's Ferry.

This bold design of separating his army, then far away from his supplies, by a river liable to be made impassable in a few hours by a heavy rain, and with a pursuing force in superior numbers close behind, marked Lee as a blunderer, unless, as he "fully understood the character of his opponent," as Magruder had lately said,[1] he counted upon his usual tardiness and indecision. McClellan's army had moved between six and seven miles a day since he entered Maryland, watching rather than pursuing, for reasons already alluded to, and Lee doubtless supposed that pace would be kept up.

When Lee's plan was discovered, on the day after he moved westward from Frederick,[a] the National army was in the vicinity of that city, excepting Franklin's corps of about seventeen thousand men, which was several miles nearer Harper's Ferry. Between him and that post was only the division of McLaws, not more than twenty thousand strong, while at the Ferry was a garrison of nine thousand men strongly posted, but unfortunately under Colonel D. H. Miles, who behaved so badly on the day of the first battle of Bull's Run.[2] There were twenty-five hundred troops under General White, engaged in outpost duty at Martinsburg and Winchester, and these, with the garrison at the Ferry, were under the direct control of General Halleck.

[a] Sept. 13, 1862.

McClellan now possessed the rare advantage of knowing his opponent's plans, and a divided army to operate against, and it was believed that he would order Franklin to push vigorously forward, followed by heavy supports, to crush McLaws and save Harper's Ferry. But this was not a part of his plan. When Lee crossed into Maryland, McClellan, like the Confederate leader, considered Harper's Ferry to be untenable, and before he left Washington he advised its evacuation, and the employment of its garrison in co-operation with his army. As on the Peninsula, he seems now to have been haunted with the specter of an overwhelming force on his front, and began calling for re-enforcements. Four days after he took the field he again advised Halleck to order Miles to leave Harper's Ferry and join his army; and on the same day, in a long letter to the General-in-Chief, he counseled the abandonment of Washington City to the rebels, if that should be necessary to re-enforce his army in Maryland, and then trust to luck for the recapture of it.[3]

The National army moved in pursuit, from Frederick, in two columns, the right and center toward Turner's Gap, in South Mountain, in front of Middletown, Burnside leading the advance; and the left, composed of Franklin's corps, toward Crampton's Gap, in the same range, in front of Burkittsville. Lee was so confident that McClellan would be tardy, that he ordered Longstreet to follow Jackson and take post at Hagerstown, with a great portion of his corps (leaving only D. H. Hill's division to guard Turner's Gap[4]), and

---

[1] See note 2, page 420.

[2] See page 606, volume I.

[3] To this portion of his extraordinary letter Halleck replied:—"You attach too little importance to the capital. I assure you that you are wrong. The capture of this place will throw us back six months, if it should not destroy us. Beware of the evils I now point out to you. You saw them when here, but you seem to forget them in the distance."—Letter to McClellan, September 13, 1862.

[4] Turner's Gap is a deep and rugged pass, about 400 feet above the base of the mountain, with a crest on each side, one of them rising 600 feet higher. A good turnpike crossed the mountain eastward of the pass or hollow, and a good road went over it just westward of the pass. Crampton's Gap was a similar pass, and opened into Pleasant Valley, back of Maryland Heights, a few miles from Harper's Ferry.

to send six brigades to assist McLaws (who was guarding Crampton's Gap) in his operations for seizing Maryland Heights and Harper's Ferry.

ALFRED PLEASANTON.

Lee was mistaken. The discovery of his plan had led to more vigorous action in the National army, and on the following day[a] a startling apparition met the eyes of the Confederates on South Mountain. Stuart had reported the previous evening that only two brigades were in pursuit, and Hill felt quite sure that he could defend the Gap with his five thousand troops, notwithstanding they were somewhat scattered; but at an early hour in the morning Pleasanton's cavalry, with a battery, was seen moving along the pike toward the Gap, followed by Cox's Kanawha division of Reno's command, while nearly the whole National army was streaming down the Kittoctan hills, and across that most lovely of all the valleys in Maryland in which Middletown is nestled.

[a] Sept. 14, 1862.

Pleasanton followed the Hagerstown pike. The First Brigade of Cox's division, Colonel E. P. Scammon, composed of the Twelfth, Twenty-third, and Thirtieth Ohio, and McMullin's Ohio battery, marched along the Boonesborough road to reconnoiter the crest at the south of the Gap, followed by the Second Brigade, Colonel Crook, consisting of the Eleventh, Twenty-eighth, and Thirty-sixth Ohio, Simmons's battery and Scambeck's cavalry in support. They soon ascertained that a considerable force held that part of the mountain, when Reno ordered an advance to an assault, promising the support of his whole corps. Wilcox, Rodman, and Sturgis were ordered forward, and at an early hour in the forenoon, after some skirmishing, Cox reached the borders of the Pass. Under cover of a portion of the guns of the two batteries, he pressed up the wooded and rocky acclivity. He was at first confronted by General Garland, whose division was soon so badly cut up, and so disheartened by the loss of its commander, who was killed early in the action, that it fell back in confusion, and its place was supplied by that of Anderson, supported by Rhodes and Ripley. These held the position firmly for a long time, but, finally, by hard and persistent fighting

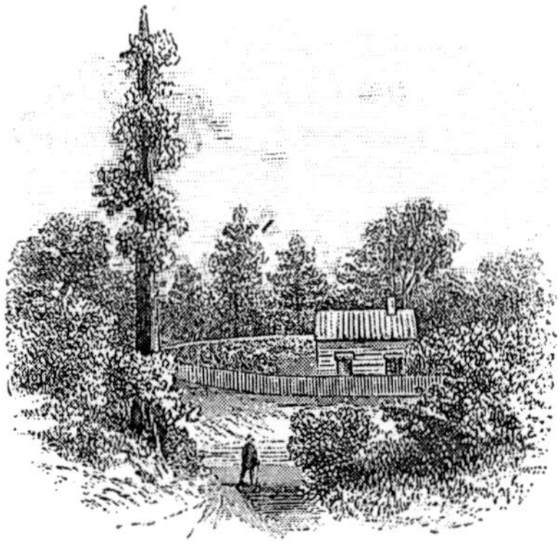

WISE'S HOUSE, SOUTH MOUNTAIN BATTLE-FIELD.[1]

[1] This is a view of Wise's house when the writer sketched it, at the beginning of October, 1866. It is on the Sharpsburg road, about a mile and a half south from Keedy's tavern, on the pike at Turner's Gap.

Cox gained a foothold on the crest, not far from the house of Daniel Wise, an earnest Union man.

It was now noon, and up to this time only the divisions of Cox and Hill had been engaged. Very soon the battle assumed far greater proportions. Hill had sent for Longstreet to come to his help, and between two and three o'clock two of his brigades arrived. These were soon followed by Longstreet himself with seven more brigades, making the Confederate force defending the two crests and the Gap, nearly thirty thousand strong. Meanwhile, during a partial lull of two hours in the contest, the divisions of Wilcox, Rodman, and Sturgis arrived and took position. Then at about two o'clock Hooker's corps came up, and at once moved to the right along the old Hagerstown road, to crush the Confederate left at the higher crest. An hour later a general battle-line was formed with Ricketts' division on the right, King's, commanded by General Hatch, in the center, and resting on the turnpike, and Reno's on the left. The Confederates had much the advantage of position, for the hillsides up which the Nationals toiled were steep and rocky, yet they nowhere faltered, and at four o'clock fighting was general along the whole line. The ground was contested at many points inch by inch. Hatch was wounded, when Doubleday took his command, his own passing to the care of Colonel Wainright, of the Seventy-sixth New York, who was soon disabled. Hooker had pressed steadily forward on the right, and at dusk had flanked and beaten the Confederate left.

BATTLE-FIELD ON SOUTH MOUNTAIN.[1]

The strife on the National left where Reno had gained a foot-hold on the mountain was very severe, and continued until dark. At about sunset the commanding general, who was at the head of his line, was killed in an open field in front of a thick wood while watching the movements of his foe. He died almost at the moment of victory, for at that time the position was fairly within the grasp of his friends. His command devolved on General Cox.

Meade had followed Hooker from the Kittoctan Creek, and went into

[1] This little picture shows the appearance of that portion of the battle-field on South Mountain, where General Reno was killed, as it appeared when the writer visited it, early in October, 1866. The field was dotted with evergreen shrubs. The place where Reno fell is marked by a stone set up by Daniel Wise, whose son owned the land. It is seen near the two figures. Not far from the spot was a chestnut tree, that bore the scars of many wounds made during the battle.

action with great gallantry on the right of Doubleday (Hatch's division) and fought heavily, his brigades being skillfully managed by General Seymour and Colonels Magilton and Gallagher. General Duryée, with his fine brigade of Ricketts' division, which had performed signal service under its gallant commander during the later struggles of Pope with Lee, was just coming up to the support of Meade, when the contest of that point ceased. Meanwhile the brigade of Gibbons and Hartsuff had pushed steadily up the turnpike along the Gap, fighting bravely and winning steadily, until almost nine o'clock in the evening, when, having reached a point near the summit of the Pass, their ammunition was exhausted. But the victory was secure. Gibbons and Hartsuff were relieved at midnight by the arrival of the divisions of Gorman and Williams, of Sumner's corps. Richardson's division had taken position in the rear of Hooker's resting soldiers; and Sykes's regulars and the artillery reserve were at Middletown. McClellan's right column was ready to resume the action in the morning, but Lee, who was with his troops toward evening, withdrew his forces during the night. So ended THE BATTLE OF SOUTH MOUNTAIN.[1]

While this contest was going on at Turner's Gap, Franklin was endeavoring to force his way over the mountain at Crampton's Gap, for the relief of Harper's Ferry. That pass was defended by three brigades of McLaws' force, who were commanded by the notorious Howell Cobb, Buchanan's treasonable Secretary of the Treasury.[2] In pursuance of McClellan's instructions, Franklin appeared at Burkittsville, before Crampton's Pass, at noon on the 14th,[a] on the road leading to Rohersville in Pleasant Valley, back of Maryland Heights, with a fine body of troops from New York, New Jersey, and Pennsylvania. He formed a line of battle with Slocum's division on the right of the road running through the Gap, and

[a] Sept. 1862.

[1] Reports of Generals McClellan and Lee, and their subordinate commanders. McClellan reported his loss at 312 killed, 1,234 wounded, and 22 missing; total, 1,568. The Confederate loss in killed and wounded was about the same, besides 1,500 prisoners, making the entire loss about 3,000.

[2] See page 44, volume I. Cobb was instructed to hold Crampton's Pass until the capture of Maryland Heights and Harper's Ferry should be completed, "even if he lost his last man in doing it." See McLaws' Report, ii. 165 of the Reports of the Army of Northern Virginia.

Howell Cobb and Robert Toombs, two of the leading traitors of Georgia, were now general officers in Lee's army. They had been chiefly instrumental in bringing the people of their State under the galling yoke of the despotism at Richmond, and were loud in their professions of willingness to "die for the cause of Southern independence." Their performances always fell short of their promises. They were ever ready "to spill the blood of all their relations," and to sacrifice the property of all their neighbors for the "holy cause," but on all occasions they were careful not to expose their own blood and property to waste. In an address to the people of Georgia, issued a few months earlier than the time we are considering, Cobb and Toombs, Cobb's brother Thomas, and M. J. Crawford, held the following language:—"The foot of the oppressor is on the soil of Georgia. He comes with lust in his eye, poverty in his purse, and hell in his heart. He comes a robber and a murderer. How shall you meet him? With the sword at the threshold! With death for him or for yourself! But, more than this—let every woman have a torch, every child a firebrand—let the loved homes of youth be made ashes, and the fields of our heritage be made desolate. Let blackness and ruin mark your departing steps, if depart you must, and let a desert more terrible than Sahara welcome the Vandals. Let every city be leveled by the flames, and every village be lost in ashes. Let your faithful slaves share your fortune and your crust. Trust wife and children to the sure refuge and protection of God, preferring even for these loved ones the charnel-house as a home, than loathsome vassalage to a nation already sunk below the contempt of the civilized world. This may be your terrible choice, and determine at once, without dissent, as honor and patriotism and duty to God require."

Most carefully did the demagogues who issued the grandiloquent manifesto, of which this is a fair specimen, avoid the funeral pile to which they invited their neighbors. With supreme contempt of the common sense of the people of their State, they attempted thus to "fire the Southern heart." It was a miserable failure, and those men who constituted themselves dictators of public opinion in Georgia, became objects of scorn and contempt. At the close of the war, Toombs, overrating his importance, fled in terror from the country. This act, and his boastings and cowardice throughout the war, won for him the just title given him by a distinguished rebel, of *The Humbug of the Confederacy.*

Smith's on the left. The brigades of Bartlett and Torbett, of Slocum's force, supported by Newton, advanced steadily upon Cobb at the base of the mountain, driving him from his stone-wall defenses up the acclivity. On the left, the brigades of Brooks and Irwin, of Smith's division, charged up the mountain in the same manner. After a struggle of several hours, in which the Nationals had much the superiority in numbers, the latter gained the crest of the Pass, and the Confederates fled down the western side of the mountain.[1]

Franklin was now only six miles from Harper's Ferry, and was competent to fly to its relief. Let us see what was the condition of affairs there at this critical juncture, and what happened.

The post at Harper's Ferry, as we have observed, was in command of Colonel D. H. Miles. A large amount of military stores had been collected there, which must be sacrificed if the garrison should be withdrawn. Halleck determined to hold it until McClellan should succor the garrison, and orders were given accordingly to the commander. McClellan advised another course; but on the day of the struggle at Turner's and Crampton's Gaps, he sent Miles word to "hold out to the last extremity," as he might "count on every effort" to relieve him. In the mean time Jackson, by quick movements, had crossed the Potomac at Williamsport[a] and marched rapidly upon Martinsburg. General Julius White, in command of troops there, fled with them to Harper's Ferry. He ranked Miles, but deferred to his position as an old army officer, and offered to serve under him. The junction of these forces, with some from Winchester, made the garrison over twelve thousand strong.

[a] Sept. 11, 1862.

At noon of the 13th Jackson was in full force in the rear of Harper's Ferry, and at once placed himself in communication with Walker and McLaws. The former was already on Loudon Heights, across the Shenandoah, and the latter was struggling for Maryland Heights, across the Potomac. The summits of these mountains are within cannon-shot of each other, and command Harper's Ferry below, into which plunging missiles of every kind might be hurled.

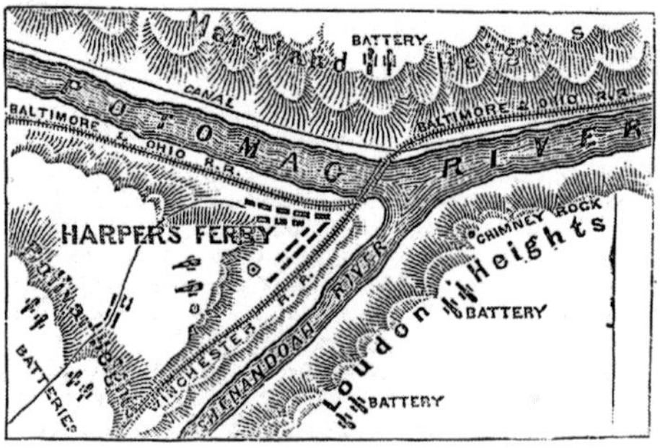

HARPER'S FERRY.

Heedless of the danger that might soon brood on those heights, Miles had done nothing worthy of a skillful or loyal commander to save his post and garrison below. He had placed a few troops under Colonel T. H. Ford, of the Thirty-second Ohio,[2] on Maryland Heights, but did not comply with that commander's requisition for intrenching tools, that he might fortify his position; so, on the 12th, when McLaws' advance appeared on the crest of the Elk

[1] Franklin's loss was 115 killed and 418 wounded; total, 533. His gain consisted of 400 prisoners, 1 caisson, and 700 small arms. Cobb's loss was upwards of 600.

[2] These were the Thirty-second Ohio, Thirty-ninth, One Hundred and Fifteenth, and One Hundred and Twenty-sixth New York, and part of a Maryland regiment.

Mountain, two or three miles northward, and soon commenced skirmishing,[1] Ford had only a slight breast-work of trees, with an *abatis* in front of it, near the crest, for defense. He repelled an assault in force at an early hour on the 13th, but when it was renewed a little later, by Kershaw, some of his troops gave way and fled in great confusion. They were rallied, but the Confederates had secured such vantage-ground that, under cover of darkness, at two o'clock the next morning, Ford, hopeless of aid from Miles, spiked his guns and withdrew to Harper's Ferry.

All was now lost, unless Miles could hold out until succor could come from Franklin. Harper's Ferry was completely invested early on the 14th, the great hills around it, excepting Bolivar Heights, on which the Nationals had batteries, being then in possession of the foe. From these commanding positions an artillery fire was opened in the afternoon. McLaws had pushed forward to the Potomac at Sandy Hook, and barred the way to escape down the river, and General Wright, with artillery, was well posted at the foot of Maryland Heights. "Hold out to the last extremity, Colonel Miles," said McClellan by messenger, "and, if possible, reoccupy Maryland Heights with your whole force. The Catoctin Valley is in our possession, and you can safely cross the river at Berlin." But Miles did no such thing. At nine o'clock that night he allowed his cavalry, two thousand strong, under Colonel Davis, to depart, and before morning eleven of Ewell's guns were taken across the Shenandoah, and so planted as to assail the National batteries on Bolivar Heights, in reverse. At dawn no less than nine batteries opened upon the garrison. The portion of it on Bolivar Heights was driven to the lower hill, near the town, and the certain destruction of all seemed impending. Miles soon displayed a white flag, and at eight o'clock terms of surrender had been agreed upon. Miles was then dead. His white flag had not been readily seen, and the firing had continued for thirty or forty minutes. A shot killed him, and the duty of surrendering devolved upon General White. Nearly twelve thousand men became prisoners of war, and a considerable amount of spoils fell into the hands of the victors.[2] The conduct of Miles was such, according to sworn testimony, that his loyalty to the cause of the Republic is suspected.[3]

Lee now possessed Maryland Heights and Harper's Ferry, but found himself in such peril that the victory seemed like a snare. Franklin's advent in Pleasant Valley on the morning of the 15th was a specter that appalled him. The severance of his army by his enemy was threatened, and he took measures to concentrate it. He withdrew his troops from South Mountain across Pleasant Valley and Elk Ridge, and took position in the Antietam

---

[1] McLaws and Anderson had evacuated Pleasant Valley on the day when Jackson captured Martinsburg. McLaws at once ordered Kershaw to take his own and Barksdale's brigades up a rough mountain road to the crest of the Elk Mountain, and to follow the ridge to Ford's position on Maryland Heights.

[2] The number of men surrendered was 11,583, half of them from New York, and the remainder from Ohio and Maryland. Most of them were raw levies, some of them being three months men, under the President's call of the first of June. The spoils were 73 cannon, 13,000 small arms, 200 wagons, and a large quantity of tents and camp equipage.

[3] A Commission appointed to investigate the matter showed that Miles had been ordered a month before the surrender to fortify Maryland Heights, but had neglected to do so; that he had refused to furnish Ford with intrenching tools; that two days before the surrender he had paroled sixteen Confederate prisoners and allowed them to pass into the Confederate lines, by which the foe might obtain full information; that he had held a private interview with a captured Confederate officer, and paroled him; that he allowed him to pass back into his own lines, and that he appeared among the first to reach the National camp as one of the victors.

Valley, in the vicinity of Sharpsburg. Jackson also, seeing the menacing peril, had left the matter of capitulation at Harper's Ferry to A. P. Hill, and with the remainder of his command recrossed the Potomac, and by swift marches rejoined Lee on the Antietam Creek. McLaws saw that his own force might be crushed by a vigorous movement on the part of Franklin, and as the surrender of Harper's Ferry seemed to give him leave to withdraw, he abandoned Maryland Heights, passed the Potomac at the Ferry, and made his way to Lee[a] by Shepherdstown. Walker had already abandoned Loudon Heights, and made his way by the same route toward the main army. By these quick movements Lee's forces became consolidated before McClellan was ready to strike him a serious blow. On the 16th of September the Confederate Army was well posted on the heights near Sharpsburg, on the western side of the Antietam Creek, which traverses a very beautiful valley, and falls into the Potomac six miles above Harper's Ferry.

[a] June 17, 1862.

When McClellan observed the Confederates retreating from South Mountain, on the morning of the 15th,[b] he ordered his whole army forward in pursuit. Lee's plans were thwarted, and he found himself compelled to fight; and with the troops in hand that morning he made as great a display of power as possible, that Jackson and his other leaders, who had been operating against Harper's Ferry, might bring up their forces. This stratagem was successful. McClellan was so impressed with the idea that overwhelming numbers were on his front, that he hesitated, and finally, as he says in his report (page 200), he "found that it was too late to attack that day." That hesitation and delay was fatal. At ten o'clock in the morning he had sent a thrill of joy through the country by announcing to the General-in-Chief the utter demoralization and decimation of the Confederates, and the assurance that he was "following as rapidly as the men could move;"[1] but sadness followed, for the hopes excited by that announcement were not realized.

[b] Sept.

There was some sharp skirmishing on the 15th; first with cavalry and then with artillery. McClellan's vanguard of horsemen overtook the covering cavalry of the Confederates at Boonsborough, charged upon them, killed and wounded a number, and captured two hundred and fifty men and two guns. And when the main body of the Nationals approached the Antietam Creek, on the Keedysville and Sharpsburg roads, the Confederates opened their artillery upon them, and received some sharp responses. This was the sum of the conflict on the 15th.

On the morning of the 16th[c] both armies were actively preparing for battle. The bulk of the Confederate forces, under Longstreet and D. H. Hill, stood along the range of heights between Sharpsburg and the Antietam, which flowed between the belligerents. Longstreet was on the right of the road between Sharpsburg and Boonsborough, and Hill on the left. Hood's division was posted between Hill and the Hagerstown road, north of Miller's farm, so as to oppose an expected flank move-

[c] Sept.

[1] See McClellan's dispatches. He erroneously supposed his troops had been fighting the whole of Lee's army, and he reported accordingly. "It is stated," he said, "Lee gives his loss at 15,000," and added, "We are following as rapidly as the men can move." This announcement on the morning of the 15th caused the President to telegraph to McClellan, saying, "God bless you and all with you; destroy the rebel army if possible."

ment in that direction; and near that point, in the rear, Jackson's exhausted troops were posted in reserve, his line stretching from the Hagerstown road toward the Potomac, and protected by Stuart with cavalry and artillery. Walker was posted on Longstreet's right with two brigades a little south of Sharpsburg, near Shaveley's farm. General Lee had his quarters in a tent, as usual, on the hill close by Sharpsburg, where the National cemetery now is, and from that point he overlooked much of the country that was made a battle-field the next day.

Along the line of the Confederate Army, the Antietam (a sluggish stream with few fords) was spanned by four stone bridges[1] of like architecture, three of which were strongly guarded. McClellan made his head-quarters at the fine brick mansion of Philip Pry, about two miles northeast of Sharpsburg, east of the Antietam, and on each side of him in front his army was posted. On the right, near Keedysville, and on both sides of the Sharpsburg pike, stood the corps of Sumner and Hooker. In advance, on the right of the turnpike and near the Antietam, General Richardson's division of Sumner's corps was posted. In line with this, on the left of that road, was Sykes's regular division of Porter's corps, protecting bridge No. 2. Farther down the stream, on the left, and not far from No. 3, Burnside's corps was posted. Upon a ridge of the first line of hills east of Antietam, between the turnpike and Pry's house, and in front of Sumner and Hooker, batteries of 24-pounder Parrott guns, commanded by Captains Taft, Langner, and Von Kleizer, and Lieutenant Weaver, were planted. On the crest of the hill, above bridge No. 3, were batteries under Captain Weed and Lieutenant Benjamin. Franklin's corps and Couch's division were farther down in Pleasant Valley, near Brownsville, and Morrell's division of Porter's corps was approaching from Boonsborough, and Humphrey's from Frederick. A detachment of the Signal Corps, under Major Myer, had a station on Red Ridge, a spur of South Mountain, which overlooked the entire field of operations, and from that

McCLELLAN'S HEAD-QUARTERS.

SIGNAL-STATION ON RED HILLS.

[1] The upper, or No. 1, was at the crossing of the Keedysville and Williamsport road; No. 2 was on the Keedysville and Sharpsburg turnpike, two miles below; No. 3 was about a mile below this and Sharpsburg, on the Rohersville and Sharpsburg road; and No. 4 near the mouth of the creek, on the Sharpsburg and Harper's Ferry road.

point it performed very important service. Such was the general position of the contending armies on the 16th of September.

The Confederates opened an artillery fire on the Nationals at dawn, but it was afternoon before McClellan was ready to put his troops in position for attack, the morning having been spent in reconnoitering, finding fords, and other preparations required by prudence. There was found to be a lack of ammunition and rations, and these had to be supplied from tardily approaching supply-trains. Finally he was in readiness, and at two o'clock in the afternoon Hooker was ordered to cross the Antietam at and near bridge No. 1, with the divisions of Ricketts, Meade, and Doubleday, and attack and turn the Confederate left. Sumner was directed to throw over the stream during the night General Mansfield's corps (Twelfth), and to hold his own (Second) ready to cross early the next morning. Hooker's movement was successful. Advancing through the woods he struck Hood, and after a sharp contest, commenced with Meade's Pennsylvania Reserves, near the house of D. Miller, and which lasted until dark, the Confederates were driven back. Hooker's men rested that night on their arms upon the ground they had won from their foe. Mansfield's corps (divisions of Williams and Greene) crossed the Antietam during the evening in Hooker's track, and bivouacked on Poffenberger's farm, a mile in his rear.

JOSEPH K. F. MANSFIELD.

The night of the 16th was passed by both armies with the expectation of a heavy battle in the morning. Few officers found relief from anxiety, for it was believed by many that it might be a turning-point in the war. Only the Commander-in-Chief of the National army seems to have had a lofty faith that all would be well. He retired to his room at a little past ten o'clock, and did not leave it until eight o'clock the next morning, when the surrounding hills had been echoing the sounds of battle which had been raging within a mile of head-quarters for three hours. Then, with some of his aids, he walked to a beautiful grove on the brow of a declivity near Pry's, overlooking the Antietam, and watched the battle on the right for about two hours, when he mounted his horse and rode away to Porter's position, on the right, where he was greeted, as usual, by the hearty cheers of his admiring soldiers.[1]

The contest was opened at dawn[a] by Hooker, with about eighteen thousand men. He made a vigorous attack on the Confederate left, commanded by Jackson. Doubleday was on his right, Meade on his left, and Ricketts in the center. His first object was to push the Confederates back through a line of woods, and seize the Hagers-

[a] Sept. 17, 1862.

[1] Oral statement to the author, by Mr. and Mrs. Pry.

town road and the woods beyond it in the vicinity of the Dunker Church, where Jackson's line lay. The contest was obstinate and severe. The National batteries on the east side of the Antietam poured an enfilading fire on Jackson that galled him very much, and it was not long before the Confederates were driven with heavy loss beyond the first line of woods, and across an open field, which was covered thickly in the morning with standing corn.[1]

DUNKER CHURCH.

Hooker now advanced his center under Meade to seize the Hagerstown road and the woods beyond. They were met by a murderous fire from Jackson, who had just been re-enforced by Hood's refreshed troops, and had brought up his reserves. These issued in great numbers from the woods, and fell heavily upon Meade in the cornfield. Hooker called upon Doubleday for aid, and a brigade under the gallant General Hartsuff was instantly forwarded at the double-quick, and passed across the cornfield in the face of a terrible storm of shot and shell. It fought desperately for half an hour unsupported, when its leader fell severely wounded.

In the mean time Mansfield's corps had been ordered up to the support of Hooker, and while the divisions of Williams and Greene, of that corps, were deploying, the veteran commander was mortally wounded. The charge of his corps then devolved on General Williams, who left his division to the care of General Crawford. The latter, with his own and Gordon's brigade, pushed across the open field and seized a part of the woods on the Hagerstown road. At the same time Green's division took position to the left of the Dunker Church.

Hooker had lost heavily by battle and straggling, yet he was contending manfully for victory. Doubleday's guns had silenced a Confederate battery on the extreme right, and Ricketts was struggling against a foe constantly increasing, but was bravely holding his ground without power to advance. The fight was very severe, and at length the National line began to waver and give way. Hooker, while in the van, was so severely wounded in the foot that he was taken from the field at nine o'clock, and to McClellan's head-quarters at Pry's, leaving his command to Sumner, who had just arrived on the field with his own corps. Up to this time the battle had been fought much in detail, both lines advancing and falling back as each received re-enforcements.

Sumner at once sent General Sedgwick to the support of Crawford and

---

[1] Hood had been withdrawn during the night, and his troops had been replaced by the brigades of Lawton and Trimble, of Ewell's corps, with Jackson's "Stonewall Brigade" under D. R. Jones, supported by the remaining brigades of Ewell. Jackson, surrounded by the remnant of his old command, was in charge of the Confederate left. That remnant, according to his report, was not more than 4,000 strong, it having been almost decimated by fighting from the Rapid Anna to the Potomac, and by straggling in Maryland.

In this encounter the Confederate leaders Lawton and Jones were wounded, and Early took the place of the former in command.

Gordon, and Richardson and French bore down upon the foe more to the left, when the corn-field, already won and lost by both parties, was regained by the Nationals, who held the ground around the Dunker Church. Victory seemed certain for the latter, for Jackson and Hood had commenced retiring, when fresh troops under McLaws and Walker came to Jackson's support, seconded by Early on their left. These pressed desperately forward, penetrated the National line at a Gap between Sumner's right and center, and the Unionists were driven back to the first line of woods east of the Hagerstown road, when the victors, heavily smitten by the National artillery, and

VIEW OF THE ANTIETAM BATTLE-GROUND.[1]

menaced by unflinching Doubleday, withdrew to their original position near the church. Sedgwick, twice wounded, was carried from the field, when the command of his division devolved on General O. O. Howard. Generals Crawford and Dana were also wounded.

It was now about noon, and fighting had been going on since dawn. The wearied right needed immediate support. It came at a timely moment. Franklin had come up from below, and McClellan, who remained on the east side of the Antietam, sent him over to assist the hard-pressed right. He formed on Howard's left, and at once sent Slocum with his division toward the center. At the same time General Smith was ordered to retake

[1] This was the appearance of the scene when the author sketched it, at the beginning of October, 1866. The view is from the grove, mentioned in the text, from which McClellan watched the battle, according to the statement of Mr. Pry, who accompanied him. The birds in the picture are over certain localities. The single bird on the left is over Alfred Cort's barn, whose house is seen in the middle ground. The two birds are over the Dunker Church; the three birds denote the place of Mumma's house; the four birds indicate the position of a burying-ground, and the five birds are over the spot at the edge of the woods, in the extreme distance, where General Mansfield was killed.

the ground over which there had been so much contention and bloodshed. Within fifteen minutes after the order was given it was executed. The Confederates were driven from the open field and beyond the Hagerstown road by gallant charges, accompanied by loud cheers, first by Franklin's Third Brigade, under Colonel Irwin, and then by the Seventh Maine. Inspired by this success, Franklin desired to push forward and seize a rough wooded position of importance; but Sumner thought the movement would be too hazardous, and he was restrained.

Meanwhile the divisions of French and Richardson had been busy. The former, with the brigades of Weber, Kimball, and Morris (the latter raw troops), pushed on toward the center, Weber leading; and while he was fighting hotly, French received orders from Sumner to press on vigorously and make a diversion in favor of the right. After a severe contest with the brigades of Hill (Colquitt's, Ripley's, and McRae's) not engaged with Jackson, the Confederates were pressed back to a sunken road in much disorder. In the mean time the division of Richardson, composed of the brigades of Meagher, Caldwell, and Brooks, which crossed the Antietam between nine and ten o'clock, moved forward to the attack on French's left. Right gallantly did Meagher fight his way up to the crest of a hill overlooking the Confederates at the sunken road, suffering dreadfully from a tempest of bullets; and when his ammunition was almost exhausted, Caldwell, aided by a part of Brooks's brigade, as gallantly came to his support and relief.

Hill was now re-enforced by about four thousand men, under R. H. Anderson, and the struggle was fierce for a while, the Confederates trying to seize a ridge on the National left for the purpose of turning that flank. This was frustrated by a quick and skillful movement by Colonel Cross with his "Fighting Fifth"[1] New Hampshire. He and the Confederates had a race for the ridge along parallel lines, fighting as they ran. Cross won it, and being re-enforced by the Eighty-first Pennsylvania, the Confederates were driven back with a heavy loss in men, and the colors of the Fourth North Carolina. An effort to flank the right at the same time was checked by French, Brooks, and a part of Caldwell's force,[2] and a charge of the Confederates directly on Richardson's front was quickly repulsed. The National line was steadily advanced until the foe was pushed back to Dr. Piper's house, near the Sharpsburg road, which formed a sort of citadel for them, and there they made an obstinate stand. Richardson's artillery was now brought up, and while that brave leader was directing the fire of Captain Graham's battery, he was felled by a ball that proved fatal.[3] General W. S. Hancock succeeded him in command, when a charge was made that drove the Confederates from Piper's in the utmost confusion, and only the skillful show of strength by a few of his fresh troops prevented a fatal severance of

---

1 See note 2, page 410.

2 Colonel Francis C. Barlow performed eminent service at this point in the struggle. With the Sixty-first and Sixty-fourth New York he attacked the flank of the Confederate force that was trying to enfilade the National line, and captured three hundred of the men and three flags. With these two regiments, assisted by Kimball's brigade, he so gallantly charged the Confederates on the right of Caldwell, that they were repulsed and scattered in great confusion.

3 General Richardson was taken to McClellan's head-quarters (Pry's), where he died after suffering seven weeks.

Lee's line.[1] The Nationals were deceived, and did not profit by the advantage gained. Night soon closed the action on the right and center, the Unionists holding the ground they had acquired. In the struggle near the center, the gallant General Meagher was wounded and carried from the field, and his command devolved on Colonel Burke, of the New York Sixty-third.

WINFIELD S. HANCOCK.

During the severe conflicts of the day, until late in the afternoon, Porter's corps, with artillery, and Pleasanton's cavalry, had remained on the east side of the Antietam as a reserve, and in holding the road from Sharpsburg to Middletown and Boonsborough. Then McClellan sent two brigades to support the wearied right, and six battalions of Sykes's regulars were thrown across bridge No. 2, on the Sharpsburg road, to drive away the Confederate sharp-shooters, who were seriously interfering with Pleasanton's horse batteries there. Warren's brigade was sent more to the left, on the right and rear of Burnside, who held the extreme left of the National line. This brings us to a notice of the operations of the day under the directions of Burnside.

The left was resting on the slopes opposite bridge No. 3, at Rohrback's farm, a little below Sharpsburg, which was held on the morning of the 17th by the brigade of Toombs (Second and Twentieth Georgia), supported by sharp-shooters and batteries on Longstreet's right wing, commanded by D. R. Jones. Burnside was directed, at eight o'clock in the morning, to cross that bridge, attack the foe, carry the heights on the opposite bank of the Antietam, and advance along their crest upon Sharpsburg. It was a task

THE BURNSIDE BRIDGE.

[1] D. H. Hill, in his report, speaking of the struggle at this point, declared that "affairs looked very critical," for the Nationals were within a few hundred yards of the hill which commanded Sharpsburg and the Confederate

of greatest difficulty, for the approaches to the bridge were in the nature of a defile, exposed to a raking fire from the Confederate batteries, and an enfilading one from their sharp-shooters. In several attempts to cross the bridge Burnside was repulsed. Finally, at about one o'clock in the afternoon, the Fifty-first New York and Fifty-first Pennsylvania charged across and drove its defenders to the heights. Gathering strength at the bridge by the crossing of the divisions of Sturgis, Wilcox, and Rodman, and Scammon's brigade, with the batteries of Durell, Clark, Cook, and Simmons, Burnside charged up the hill, and drove the Confederates almost to Sharpsburg, the Ninth New York capturing one of their batteries. Just then A. P. Hill's division, which had been hastening up from Harper's Ferry, came upon the ground, and under a heavy fire of artillery charged upon Burnside's extreme left, and after severe fighting, in which General Rodman was mortally wounded, drove him back almost to the bridge. In that charge General L. O'B. Branch, of North Carolina, was killed. The pursuit was checked by the National artillery on the eastern side of the stream, under whose fire the reserves led by Sturgis advanced, and the Confederates did not attempt to retake the bridge. Darkness closed the conflict here, as it did all along the line.

Hill came up just in time, apparently, to save Lee's army from capture or destruction. Experts say that if Burnside had accomplished the passage of the bridge and the advance movement an hour earlier, or had Porter been sent a few hours sooner to the support of the hard-struggling right, that result would doubtless have ensued. It is easy to conjecture what might have been. We have to do only with what occurred. Looking upon the event from that stand-point, we see darkness ending one of the most memorable days of the war because of its great and apparently useless carnage, for the result was only hurtful in the extreme to both parties.[1] With the gloom of that night also ended the conflict known as THE BATTLE OF ANTIETAM, in which McClellan said (erroneously as to the number of troops) "nearly two hundred thousand men and five hundred pieces of artillery were for fourteen hours engaged.[2] Our soldiers slept that night," he said, "conquerors on a field won by their valor, and covered by the dead and wounded of the enemy."

When the morning of the 18th dawned, both parties seemed willing not

---

rear. He rallied two hundred men, and made attacks with surprising effect. "The Yankees were completely deceived by this boldness," said Hill in his report (Reports of the Army of Northern Virginia, ii. 117), "and induced to believe that there was a large force in our center."

[1] For details of the *Battle of Antietam* (which the Confederates call the battle of Sharpsburg), see the reports of Generals McClellan and Lee, and their subordinate commanders. From these sources, and from written and oral statements from actors in the scene, the author has constructed the foregoing outline narrative.

The losses in that battle were very severe. From careful estimates, made after consulting the most reliable statements, it appears that McClellan's army was in round numbers 87,000 men, and that of Lee about 60,000. Couch's division of 5,000 men was too far away from the battle on that day to be available, having been sent, for some purpose, toward Harper's Ferry. McClellan reported his entire loss on that day at 12,469 men, of whom 2,010 were killed. He estimated the loss of Lee as much greater. No reliable official statement seems to have been made by the Confederate commander. The losses of the Unionists fell heavily upon particular brigades at particular points in the battle. That of the gallant Duryée, for example, returned from the field with not more than twenty men and four colors.—Statement to the author by General Duryée. See also *History of Duryée's Brigade*, by Franklin B. Hough, page 19. The carnage on the other side also fell on particular brigades. Jackson, in his report, says "more than half of the brigades of Lawton and Hays were either killed or wounded, and more than a third of Trimble's; and all the regimental commanders in those brigades, except two, were killed or wounded."

[2] McClellan's Report, page 210.

to renew the strife. Lee was really in a sad plight, for he could not easily call to his aid any re-enforcements; his supplies were nearly exhausted, and his army was terribly shattered and disorganized.[1] A careful estimate has made his losses at that time, since he commenced the invasion of Maryland, a fortnight before, nearly thirty thousand men.[2] McClellan's army was also

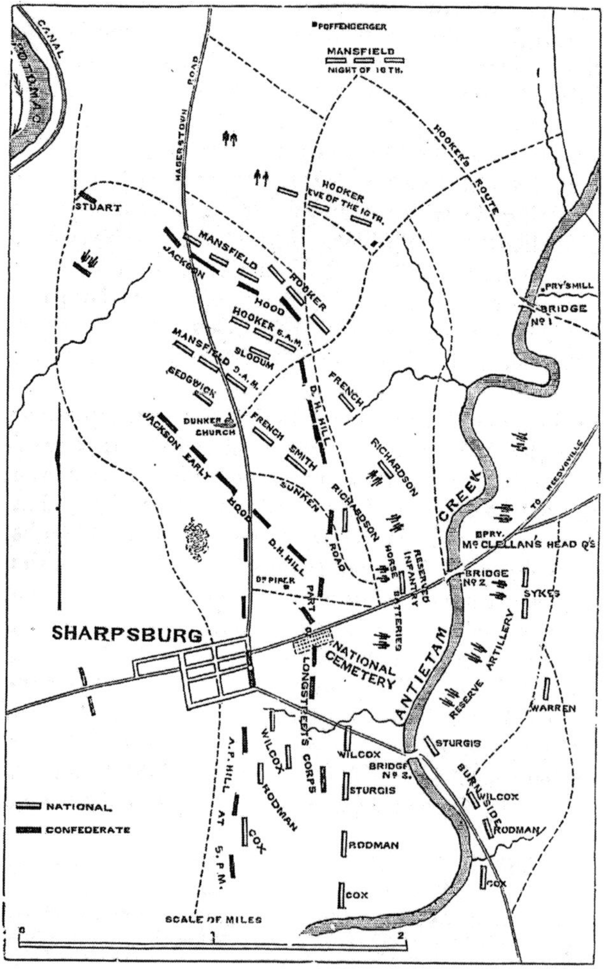

BATTLE OF ANTIETAM.

greatly shattered; but on the morning after the battle he was joined by fourteen thousand fresh troops under Couch and Humphrey. It is certain now that with these, and the effective remains of his army, he might easily have captured or ruined Lee's army that day. But there were grave considerations to be heeded. McClellan afterward said, "Virginia was lost, Washington menaced, Maryland invaded—the National cause could afford no risks of defeat."[3] He therefore hesitated, and finally, in opposition to the advice of Franklin and others, he deferred a renewal of the battle until the next morning. When that morning dawned, and he sent his cavalry to reconnoiter, the National army had no foe to fight, for Lee, with his shattered legions, had recrossed the Potomac under cover of darkness,

---

[1] We have before remarked that Lee lost more by desertion than he gained by recruits in Maryland. In his report of the Maryland campaign, he says the privations of rest and food, and general lack of supplies, "compelled thousands of brave men to absent themselves, *and many more had done so from unworthy motives.* This great battle was fought by less than 40,000 men on our side."

[2] He lost 6,000 made prisoners; also 15,000 small arms, 13 cannon, and 39 battle-flags.

[3] McClellan's Report, page 211.

and was on the soil of his native Virginia, with eight batteries under Pendleton on the river-bluffs, menacing pursuers.

That evening[a] at dusk General Porter ordered General Griffin, with his own and Barnes's brigade, to cross the Potomac to carry Lee's batteries. It was done, and four of their guns were captured. On the following morning,[b] a part of Porter's division made a reconnoissance in force. When a mile from the ford they were surprised by A. P. Hill, who lay in ambush, and they were driven back into and across the river in great disorder, with the loss of two hundred men made prisoners. The Confederates held the Virginia bank of the stream all that day, and on the next, Lee moved leisurely toward Martinsburg, destroying the Baltimore and Ohio railroad much of the way, with Stuart lingering on his rear to cover that retreat, and to deceive McClellan by a show of numbers and vigor. Stuart recrossed the river at Williamsport on the same day, when he was driven back by General Couch with a heavy force of all arms. McClellan then sent General Williams to retake Maryland Heights; and two days later[c] General Sumner occupied Harper's Ferry, and threw pontoon bridges across the Potomac and Shenandoah rivers at that place.

[a] Sept. 19, 1862.

[b] Sept. 20.

[c] Sept. 22.

Lee rested a few days, and then moved leisurely up the Shenandoah Valley to the vicinity of Bunker's Hill and Winchester, breaking up the railway much of the distance between the latter place and Harper's Ferry. McClellan, meanwhile, had begun to call for re-enforcements and supplies, as prerequisites to a pursuit. His disorganized army needed re-organization. His cavalry force was greatly weakened by casualties in battle, fatigues, and a distemper which disabled four thousand horses; and clothing, shoes, and camp equipage, were greatly needed. On the 27th[d] he renewed an application made on the 23d for re-enforcements, and then informed the Government that he intended to hold his army where it was, and "attack the enemy should he attempt to recross into Maryland." The Government was astounded by this declaration, and the loyal people, remembering the fatal restraints which had for months been holding the gallant Army of the Potomac from substantial victories, were very impatient. The President hastened to that army[e] to find out its actual condition by personal observation. He was so well satisfied that it was competent to move at once in pursuit of Lee, that on the 6th he instructed McClellan to "cross the Potomac and give battle to the enemy, or drive him South. Your army must now move," he said, "while the roads are good."

[d] Sept. 1862.

[e] Oct. 1.

Twenty days were spent in correspondence between the commander of the Army of the Potomac and the National authorities before that order was obeyed, the former calling for and receiving re-enforcements and supplies, and complaining of a lack of both to make it safe to move forward.[1] At length, when the beautiful month of October, during which the roads were perfect, had nearly passed by, and Lee's army was thoroughly rested, sup-

[1] McClellan complained of a want of horses, of shoes, of clothing, and of transportation, when the record shows that not a single requisition was left unanswered by immediate and full supply. His quartermaster-general declared before the army crossed the Potomac that complaints concerning clothing, particularly, were "groundless," and that every requisition was promptly met. See General Halleck's letter to the Secretary of War, October 28th, 1862. In reading the correspondence and the testimony concerning the delay in moving the Army of the Potomac, and the commander's continual complaints of a lack of men and supplies to make pursuit

plied, re-enforced, and his communications with Richmond were re-established, McClellan's advance began to cross the Potomac, on a pontoon-bridge at Berlin,[a] and on the 2d of November he announced that his whole army was once more in Virginia, prepared to move southward on the east side of the Blue Ridge, instead of pursuing Lee up the Shenandoah Valley, on its western side.

[a] Oct. 26, 1862.

Meanwhile Stuart, with eighteen hundred cavalry, had recrossed the river at Williamsport, and made once again a complete circuit of the Army of the Potomac without loss. He pushed on as far as Chambersburg, in Pennsylvania, where he destroyed a large amount of property,[1] and captured and paroled nearly three hundred sick and wounded soldiers found in the hospital there. Then he made a sweep around to the Potomac below McClellan's left, and recrossed into Virginia at White's Ford.

When the Army of the Potomac, now over one hundred thousand strong,[2] was ready to cross the river, Pleasanton, with his cavalry, led the way at Berlin. Burnside followed, leading an immense wagon-train, and others followed him. Perceiving this movement, the Confederates began retreating up the Shenandoah Valley, followed by Generals Sedgwick and Hancock a short distance. By the 4th,[b] the National army, re-enforced by the divisions of Generals Sigel and Sickles from Washington, occupied the whole region east of the Blue Ridge, with several of its gaps, from Harper's Ferry to Paris, on the road from Aldie to Winchester, and on the 6th McClellan's head-quarters were at Rectortown, near Front Royal. The Confederates, meanwhile, were falling back, and so, from the Potomac to Front Royal and Warrenton, the two great armies moved in parallel lines, with the lofty range of the Blue Ridge between them, and Richmond as the seeming objective.

[b] Nov.

That race was watched with the most intense anxiety. It was hoped that McClellan, with his superior force and equipment and ample supplies, might capture or disperse the army of his opponent by gaining its front, and striking it heavy blows on the flank through the mountain passes. But Lee was, as usual, too quick for his opponent. Anticipating this movement of

---

or fighting a safe operation, one is reminded of the famous letter of Napoleon to Marshal Augereau, on the 21st of February, 1814, which gives his idea of making war. The marshal had given excuses similar to those of McClellan for inaction. Napoleon said:—

"What! Six hours after receiving the first troops from Spain you are not yet in the field! Six hours' rest is quite enough for them. I conquered at Nangis with a brigade of dragoons coming from Spain, who from Bayonne had not drawn rein. Do you say that the six battalions from Nimes want clothes and equipage, and are uninstructed? Augereau, what miserable excuses! I have destroyed 80,000 enemies with battalions of conscripts, scarcely clothed, and without cartridge-boxes. The National Guard are pitiful. I have here 4,000 from Angers and Bretagne, in round hats, without cartridge-boxes, but with good weapons; and I have made them tell. There is no money, do you say? But where do you expect to get money but from the pockets of the enemy? You have no teams? Seize them! You have no magazines? Tut, tut, that is too ridiculous! I order you to put yourself in the field twelve hours after you receive this letter. If you are still the Augereau of Castiglione, keep your command. If your sixty years are too much for you, relinquish it to the oldest of your general officers. *The country is menaced and in danger. It can only be saved by daring and alacrity, and not by vain delays.* You must have a nucleus of 6,000 picked troops. I have not so many; yet I have destroyed three armies, captured 40,000 prisoners, taken 200 pieces of artillery, and thrice saved the capital. The enemy are in full flight upon Troyes? Be before them. Act no longer as of late. Resume the method and spirit of '93. When Frenchmen see your plume waving in the van, and you, first of all, exposed to the enemy's fire, you will do with them whatever you will."

[1] This consisted of a large quantity of military supplies, clothing, 5,000 muskets, the railway buildings, including station-house and machine-shops, and several trains of loaded cars.

[2] Lee reported his force then present at 86,583, of whom 73,554 were fit for duty. His entire army, present and absent, numbered 153,790.

his foe, he had pushed Longstreet rapidly forward, and on the day after McClellan's army had crossed the river, that able general had crossed the Blue Ridge, and was at Culpepper Court-House[a] in heavy force, between the Army of the Potomac and Richmond, ready to dispute [a] Nov. 3, 1862. the advance of the latter in its direct line of march toward the Confederate capital. Nothing but a quick and vigorous movement, by which Lee's army might be severed and destroyed in detail, could now secure a substantial victory for the Nationals. Would it be done? Experience shook its head ominously. The faith of the Government and of the loyal people in McClellan's ability or disposition to achieve a victory by such movement was exhausted, and on the 5th of November an order was issued from the War Department relieving him of his command, and putting General Burnside in his place. This order, borne by General Buckingham, was received by McClellan late in the evening of the 7th, at which time Burnside was in the tent of the chief.

Twice before, the command of that army had been offered to Burnside, who came from North Carolina with the prestige of a successful leader. He had modestly declined it, because he felt himself incompetent for the station. That modest estimate of his ability now made him shrink from the honor and the grave responsibilities; but duty at that critical moment, and the peremptory orders of his Government, compelled him to take both, and with the spirit of the assurance, "I'll try," he assumed the command on the 10th of November.[1]

Burnside's sense of the magnitude of his trust made him exceedingly cautious, and instead of going forward to the point of a great battle, to which McClellan's movements seemed tending, with promises of success,[2] he occupied about ten days getting the army, now one hundred and twenty thousand strong, well in mind and hand, and in reorganizing it.[3] He also adopted a new plan of operations, by which the capture of Richmond rather than the immediate destruction of Lee's army was made the objective. The National army was moving rapidly away from its base of supplies into an enemy's country, at a season when inclement weather might be expected; while the Confederate Army was continually nearing its base of supplies. Burnside therefore determined, with the acquiescence of the General-in-Chief, to make Aquia Creek, connected by railroad with Fredericksburg, his base, and to operate from that point by a nearer route to Richmond than Gor-

---

[1] At that time the Army of the Potomac was massed near Warrenton, as follows:—"The First, Second, and Fifth Corps, reserve artillery, and general head-quarters, at Warrenton; Ninth Corps on the line of the Rappahannock, in the vicinity of Waterloo; the Sixth Corps at New Baltimore; the Eleventh Corps at New Baltimore, Gainesville, and Thoroughfare Gap; Sickles's division of the Third Corps, on the Orange and Alexandria railroad, from Manassas Junction to Warrenton Junction; Pleasanton across the Rappahannock at Amisville, Jefferson, &c., with his pickets at Hazel River, facing Longstreet, six miles from Culpepper Court-House; and Bayard at Rappahannock Station."—See McClellan's Report, page 237.

[2] At that time Lee's army was in a perilous position. A great part of it, as we have observed, was under Longstreet, in the vicinity of the Rapid Anna; while Jackson, with a heavy force, was in the Shenandoah Valley, near Chester and Thornton's Gaps. A vigorous movement forward at this time must have fatally severed the two forces. To effect that object seems to have been McClellan's design. "I doubt," he said, "whether, during the whole period that I had the honor to command the Army of the Potomac, it was in such excellent condition to fight a great battle."

[3] He consolidated the six corps of the army into three grand divisions of two corps each. The Right Grand Division, commanded by General Sumner, was composed of the Second Corps, General Couch, and the Ninth Corps, General Wilcox. The Center Grand Division, under General Hooker, was composed of the Third Corps, General Stoneman, and the Fifth Corps, General Butterfield. The Left Grand Division, under General Franklin, was composed of the First Corps, under General Reynolds, and the Sixth Corps, under General W. F. Smith.

donsville. In accordance with this resolution, his forces began to move toward Fredericksburg on the 16th.[a] Meanwhile Jackson had been making some demonstration north and west of Winchester, for the purpose of detaching a part of Burnside's force in that direction, but failed; while Lee, with the great body of his troops, had retired to Gordonsville.

a Nov., 1862.

Sumner led the movement[b] down the left bank of the Rappahannock, toward Falmouth, opposite Fredericksburg, with the expectation of crossing the river at once, and taking possession of the city and the commanding heights in its rear. A feint was made toward Gordonsville, to mask this movement, but Lee penetrated it, and put in motion a countervailing force down the right bank of the river. The head of Sumner's column arrived at Falmouth on the 17th, and was assailed by a light battery already planted on the heights back of Fredericksburg. This was soon silenced by Petitt's battery, planted on the highest hill back of Falmouth, in the mansion on the summit of which, on his arrival toward evening, General Sumner made his quarters. He was anxious to cross over and seize those heights. The bridges were destroyed, but the stream was fordable just above Falmouth. The town was occupied by a regiment of Virginia cavalry and Barksdale's Mississippi brigade of sharp-shooters, their leader making his quarters where McDowell had made his, in the fine brick building of the Farmers' Bank, corner of George and Princess Streets. The city and those heights might then have been easily taken, but Burnside thought it best not to do so until his communications with Aquia Creek were established. Besides, expected pontoons had not arrived, and a sudden rain might cut off the occupying force from the main army, and expose it to capture by the rapidly approaching legions of Lee. So no attempt to cross was made.[1]

b Nov. 15.

SUMNER'S HEAD-QUARTERS.

FARMERS' BANK, FREDERICKSBURG.

Four days after his arrival, when a greater portion of the National army was near Falmouth, and its cannon commanded Fredericksburg, Sumner demanded the surrender of the city.[c] The authorities replied, that while it should not be

c Nov. 21.

[1] Without a shadow of truth, General Lee encouraged his troops and the deceived people by solemnly declaring in his official report that "the advance of General Sumner reached Falmouth on the afternoon of the 17th, and attempted to cross the Rappahannock, but was driven back by Colonel Ball with the Fifteenth Virginia cavalry, four companies of Mississippi infantry, and Lewis's light battery."

used for offensive operations against the National army, any attempt of that army to occupy it would be stoutly resisted. Expecting an immediate assault in response to this refusal, a greater portion of the inhabitants fled, and Barksdale's sharp-shooters were distributed throughout the town in ambush behind buildings.

Immediately after the arrival of the National army before Fredericksburg, a large force was detailed to repair the railway between that city and Aquia Creek, its base of supplies. The Confederates had destroyed all of the bridges and much of the track, but it was soon put in sufficient order for temporary purposes. The bridges were rebuilt rudely but strongly of wood, the most notable specimen of which was that over the Potomac Creek, that traversed a deep ravine. It was four hundred feet in length, and its top was ninety feet above the water.[1]

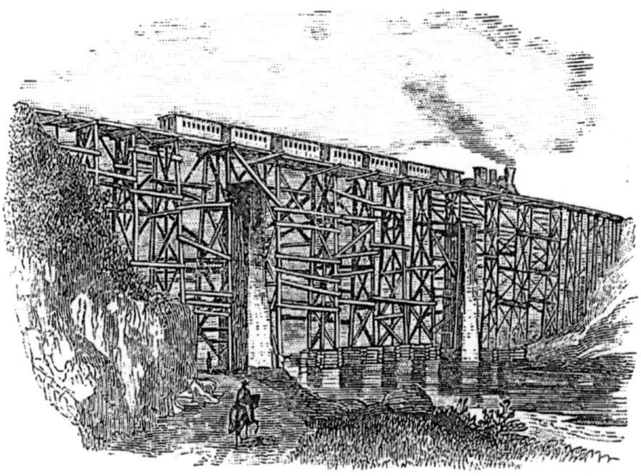

BRIDGE BUILT BY SOLDIERS OVER POTOMAC RUN.

Before this line of communication was established, the Confederates had made the seizure of Fredericksburg and the heights behind it impossible without a severe battle. Lee's army, eighty thousand strong, had pushed forward toward the Rappahannock as rapidly as possible, and at the close of November[a] it lay in a semicircle around Fredericksburg, each wing resting on the river; its right at Port Royal, below the city, and its left six miles above the city. Lee's engineers had been very busy, and had constructed two lines of fortifications along two concentric ridges a mile apart, extending from the river, a mile and a half above the city, to the Fredericksburg and Richmond railway, three miles below the town. These had grown without the possible interference of the Nationals, for not until the second week in December were pontoons, which had been ordered, ready for constructing bridges to cross the river. So formidable were their works then, that a direct attack in front, with Lee's main force behind them, would be almost like madness.

[a] 1862.

Arrangements were made to cross the river at Skenker's Neck, twelve miles below Falmouth, and turn the Confederate right. This was discovered, and Lee sent so heavy a force in that direction that the enterprise was abandoned. Yet those preparations had so engaged Lee's attention, that he kept a large force down the river to prevent such movement; and Burnside felt satisfied that he might successfully make a sudden crossing, and attack Lee's

[1] The picture shows the appearance of that structure. The two stone piers were the remains of the old bridge. A writer of the day said: "It is a precarious thing in appearance, the track simply propped up on trestle-work of round logs, and as the trains creep over the abyss, the impressions of the spectators are not, in the aggregate, comfortable."

front and fatally penetrate it, while his army was thus divided. Preparations for forcing the passage of the Rappahannock were made accordingly. The topgraphy of the river shores favored the enterprise, for Stafford Heights, where the Nationals lay, were close to its banks, and commanded the plain on which the city stands, while the heights on which Lee's batteries were planted were from three-fourths of a mile to a mile and a half from the banks. Such being the case, there seemed to be nothing to oppose the construction of the bridges but the Mississippi sharp-shooters in the city.

Every thing was in readiness on the 10th of December. During that night Stafford Heights, under the direction of General Hunt, chief of artillery, were dotted by twenty-nine batteries containing one hundred and forty-seven guns, so arranged that they commanded the space between the town and the heights back of it, and might protect the crossing of the troops. Burnside's head-quarters were at the house of Mr. Phillips, on the heights, a mile from the river, from which he could survey the whole field of operations. The Grand Divisions of Sumner and Hooker, sixty thousand strong, lay in front of the city, and that of Franklin, forty thousand strong, two miles below. It was arranged to throw five pontoon bridges across the Rappahannock for the passage of these troops—three of them opposite the city, and two where Franklin was to cross.

Before daylight on the morning of the 11th the engineers were quietly but vigorously at work making the bridges, covered by the Fifty-seventh and Sixty-sixth New York, of Zooks's brigade, Hancock's division, and concealed by a fog. They had one of the bridges about two-thirds completed, when they and their work were discovered. This drew upon them a shower of rifle-balls from the Mississippians concealed behind walls and houses on the city side of the stream. At the same time a signal-gun was fired to call the Confederate hosts to arms, for General Lee had expected this movement, and was prepared for an attack. The fire was so severe that the engineers were driven away. Several attempts to renew the work were foiled by the sharp-shooters. Nothing could be done while these remained in the town, and only artillery might effect their expulsion. So, at about ten o'clock in the morning, Burnside ordered the batteries on Stafford Heights to open upon the city, and batter it down, if necessary. The response to that order was terrific. More than a hundred guns fired fifty rounds each before the cannonade ceased, when the city was awfully shattered, and on fire in several places. Under cover of this cannonade a fresh attempt

THE PHILLIPS HOUSE ON FIRE.[1]

[1] This is a view of the Phillips House in flames, taken by the photographic process by Mr. Gardner, of Washington City, while it was burning.

was made to finish the bridges; but, strange to say, the sharp-shooters were there yet, and the effort failed. These must be dislodged. Volunteers were called for to cross the river in the open pontoon-boats, and drive them from their hiding-places, which cannon on the heights could not reach. The Seventh Michigan and Nineteenth and Twentieth Massachusetts, of Howard's division, offered their services for the perilous undertaking. These dashed across as rapidly as possible, and as soon as a sufficient number had landed, they rushed up the bank, drove the Mississippians from their shelter, captured nearly one hundred of them, and took possession of the river-front of the town.[1] The pontoon-bridges were soon completed; but at the loss, at this point and at Franklin's crossing-place, nearly two miles below, of three hundred men.[2]

PLACE OF FRANKLIN'S PASSAGE OF THE RAPPAHANNOCK.

That evening Howard's division of Couch's corps crossed the river, drove the Confederates (Seventeenth and Eighteenth Mississippi and Eighth Florida) out of Fredericksburg, and occupied the battered and smoking city.[3] Fortunately for the Nationals, there was another thick fog the next morning, and under its cover, and the wild firing in the mist from the Stafford Hills, the remainder of Sumner's Right Grand Division crossed to the city side of the Rappahannock. A large portion of Franklin's Left Grand Division crossed at the same time, while the Center Grand Division, under Hooker,[4] remained on the Falmouth side, in readiness,

---

[1] In this gallant exploit a drummer-boy of the Seventh Michigan, named Robert H. Hendershot, distinguished himself. It was his twelfth birthday, having been born on the 11th day of December, 1850. He volunteered to go, and with his drum slung to his back he jumped into one of the boats. His captain ordered him out, telling him he was too small for such business. "May I help push off the boat, Captain?" said the boy. "Yes," was the reply. He purposely let the boat drag him into the river, and, clinging to it, he so crossed the stream. A large number of the men in the boat were killed, and as the boy climbed up the bank his drum was torn in pieces by the fragment of a shell. He seized a musket belonging to one of his slain companions, and fought gallantly with the rest. His bravery was brought to the notice of Burnside, who warmly commended it. It was published abroad. The *Tribune* Association of New York presented him with an elegant new drum, and the proprietor of the Eastman Business College, at Poughkeepsie, offered to give him a home, a full support, and a thorough education, without charge; which generous offer the boy accepted, and he at once entered that institution.

[2] Franklin was opposed by sharp-shooters in rifle-pits in front of his bridges, near the mouth of Deep Run. These he soon dislodged, and by noon his bridges were ready for use. The above view of the place where Franklin's pontoons were laid is from a sketch made by the author in June, 1866, from the right bank of the river, and nearly opposite the site of the residence of Washington, when he was a boy. For a picture of that residence, see Lossing's *Field Book of the Revolution*, ii. 219. The river here is much wider than in front of the city.

[3] Eye-witnesses describe the scene in Fredericksburg after the bombardment on the 11th as sad in the extreme. Several buildings which had been set on fire were yet smoking, and very few had escaped wounds from the missiles. The streets were filled with furniture, carried out to be saved from the flames only to be destroyed by other causes. Fortunately, the few inhabitants who remained took refuge in cellars, and not one was killed. The picture in the text on the next page is from a sketch by Henry Lovie, made on the morning after the bombardment.

[4] See note 3, page 485.

if the movement succeeded, "to spring upon the enemy in their retreat." The entire day[a] was consumed in the crossing, and in reconnoitering the position of the Confederates, and that night the National troops lay on their arms, ready for the expected battle in the morning.

a Dec. 12, 1862.

The Confederates, with three hundred cannon well posted on the heights, were also ready for action; for Jackson's force, whose extreme right had been posted eighteen miles down the river, had been called in, and the whole of Lee's army, eighty thousand strong, was ready to oppose the Nationals.[1] Its left was composed of Longstreet's corps, with Anderson's division resting upon the river, and those of McLaws, Pickett, and Hood, extending to the right in the order named. Ransom's division supported the batteries on Marye's and Willis's Hills, at the foot of which Cobb's brigade and the Twenty-fourth North Carolina were stationed, protected by a stone wall.[2] The immediate care of this important point was intrusted to General Ransom. The Washington (New Orleans) Artillery, under Colonel Walton, occupied the redoubts on the crest of Marye's Hill, and those on the heights to the right and left were held by part of the Reserve artillery, Colonel E. P. Alexander's battalion, and the division batteries of Anderson, Ransom, and McLaws. A. P. Hill, of Jackson's corps, was posted between Hood's right and Hamilton's crossing on the railway, his front line under Pender, Lane, and Archer occupying the edge of a wood. Lieutenant Walker, with fourteen pieces of artillery, was posted near the right, supported by two Virginia regiments, under Colonel

SCENE IN FREDERICKSBURG ON THE MORNING OF THE 12TH.

[1] When Lee was satisfied that Burnside was moving on Fredericksburg, he ordered Jackson to cross the Blue Ridge and place himself in position to co-operate with Longstreet. A little later both he and Longstreet were ordered to Fredericksburg, when the division of D. H. Hill was sent to Port Royal to oppose the passage of gun-boats, which had appeared there. The rest of Jackson's division was disposed so as to support Hill. The cavalry brigade of General W. H. F. Lee was stationed near Port Royal, and the fords of the Rappahannock above Fredericksburg were closely watched. On the 28th of November, Wade Hampton crossed and made a reconnoissance as far as Dumfries and Occoquan, and captured two hundred Nationals and some wagons; and at about the same time a part of Beales's regiment of Lee's brigade dashed across the Rappahannock in boats, below Port Royal, and captured some prisoners. Hill and some of Stuart's horse-artillery had a skirmish with the gun-boats at Port Royal on the 5th of December, and compelled them to retire.—Lee's Report, volume I. of the Reports of the Army of Northern Virginia, pages 38 and 39.

[2] The little picture on page 491 shows the appearance at this point on a road at the foot of Marye's Hill, and just below his mansion, when the writer sketched it in June, 1866. The stone wall is on the city side of the road on which the Confederates were posted. The tents of a burial-party, encamped nearer the Rappahannock at the time, are seen in the distance.

Brockenborough. A projecting wood at the front of the general lines was held by Lane's brigade. Hill's reserve was composed of the brigades of Thomas and Gregg, with a part of Field's. The divisions of Early and Taliaferro composed Jackson's second line, and D. H. Hill's was his reserve. The cannon of the latter were well posted so as to command the open ground between the heights and the city. The plain on Jackson's right was occupied by Stuart, with two brigades of cavalry and his horse artillery, and his line extended to Massaponax Creek.[1]

WALL AT THE FOOT OF MARYE'S HEIGHTS.

A council of officers was held on the evening of the 12th, when Burnside submitted his plan of attack the next morning, which was for the whole force on the south bank of the Rappahannock to advance, and, by sudden assaults along the whole line, attempt to penetrate and carry the fortified heights occupied by the Confederates. The Right and Left Grand Divisions, under Sumner and Franklin, were to perform the perilous work; and, to give Franklin sufficient strength, two divisions from Hooker's command (his own and Kearney's) were sent to re-enforce him, making his whole number about fifty-five thousand men, or one-half of the effective force of the army.

It was expected that Franklin would make the main attack at dawn, and that upon its results would depend the movements of Sumner; but he did not receive his promised instructions until after sunrise, and then they were so open to misinterpretations that he was puzzled to know precisely how to act. They seemed, however, to demand that he should keep his whole command in position for a rapid movement on the old Richmond road, and to send out an armed reconnoissance, with a single division, to attack and seize some point of the heights. He accordingly threw forward Meade's division, supported by Gibbon's on its right, with Doubleday's in reserve. Meade had not proceeded far when he was confronted by a Confederate battery, placed by Stuart on the Port Royal road. This he silenced, and then pressed on, his skirmishers clearing the way, and his batteries shelling the woods in his front. All was silence on that front for a while, when a terrible storm of shell and canister, at near range, fell upon him. He pressed on, and three of his assailants' batteries were hastily withdrawn. He still pressed on. Jackson's advanced line, under A. P. Hill, was driven back with a loss of two hundred men made prisoners and several battle-flags. Meade still pressed on; crossed the railway and up to the crest of the hill, to a new military road, just constructed by Lee to connect his wings, where he encountered Gregg, with his South Carolina veterans, on Lee's second line. These gave Meade such a warm reception that he was obliged to halt, when Early's division swept forward at a double-quick, assailed his flanks, and compelled him to fall back with heavy loss.

---

[1] Lee's Report, March 6, 1863.

Gibbon now came up gallantly to Meade's support, but was repulsed, and when the shattered forces of both were made to fly in confusion, General Birney advanced with his division of Stoneman's corps in time to check the victorious pursuers, who pressed up to within fifty yards of his guns. But the Nationals were unable to advance, for Stuart's cavalry, on Lee's extreme right, strongly menaced the left. At length, when charge after charge had been repulsed, Reynolds, with re-enforcements, pushed the Confederates back to the Massaponax, where they kept up the contest with spirit until dark. The three divisions in the battle on the left that day composed Reynolds's corps, and by their gallantry, and that of the divisions of Birney and Sickles (the latter taking the place of Gibbon's), of Stoneman's corps, presented such a formidable front that Jackson did not hazard an advance against them that day, but stood on the defensive.[1] Smith's corps, twenty-one thousand strong, was near and fresh, and had not been much engaged in the battle throughout the day.[2]

Let us see what Sumner was doing while a part of Franklin's corps was struggling so fearfully on the left.

Sumner was to attack the Confederate front when Franklin should fairly inaugurate the battle with a prospect of success. The conditions were complied with. At eleven o'clock he and his staff repaired to the Lacey House, near the river opposite Fredericksburg, from which he could have a full view of the operations of his division. Couch's corps (Second) occupied the city, and Wilcox's (Ninth) the interval between Couch and Franklin's right. Upon Couch fell the honor of making the first attack. At noon he ordered out French's division, to be followed and supported by Hancock.[3] Kimball's

---

[1] Reynolds lost in the struggle full 4,000 men. Meade lost about forty per cent. of his whole command, and many valuable officers were slain or wounded. General C. F. Jackson was killed; and General George D. Bayard, who commanded the cavalry on the left, was mortally wounded by a shell, and died that night. He was only twenty-eight years of age, and was on the eve of marriage. His loss was widely felt. General Gibbon was wounded and taken from the field.

Bayard's brigade was famous for good deeds throughout the war. It was distinguished for gallantry in the following engagements before the death of its first leader:—Woodstock, Harrisonburg, Cross Keys, Cedar Mountain, Brandy Station, Rappahannock Station, Gainesville, Bull's Run, Warrenton, and Fredericksburg. After Bayard's death the brigade was formed into a division, under General Gregg, and served throughout the campaigns in Virginia under Stoneman, Pleasanton, and Sheridan. A portrait of the gallant Bayard, and a picture of the "Bayard Badge," will be found in the third volume of this work.

ARMY SIGNAL-TELEGRAPH.

[2] The army signal-telegraph was used with great effect on the left that day. Its lines extended from Burnside's head-quarters, at the Phillips house, across the Rappahannock to Franklin's quarters, a distance of about four miles. The wire was of copper, insulated, coiled on a drum or reel, and carried in a cart or by hand, as seen in the engraving, by the motion of which it was unwound. Each cart carried a series of reels, and each reel contained a mile of wire. The line was laid on light poles or on fences, and was operated upon wherever the cart or the men halted for the purpose, by a simple process. This telegraph was worked without batteries, and was so simple that it could be used, after one day's practice, by any soldier who could easily read and write. As we have observed, it was made useful on the day of the battle described in the text, when operations at various points were immediately made known by it at head-quarters. The cart or the men were often seen well up to the front of the battle, and exposed to all its consequences.

[3] French's was composed of the brigades of Kimball, Anderson, and Palmer. Hancock's was composed of the brigades of Zook, Meagher, and Caldwell.

brigade led, and the whole force, as it moved swiftly to the assault from the town, suffered greatly from the converging fire of the artillery on the heights, which swept the plain below. Those batteries could be but little affected by the National guns on the distant Stafford Hills.

On Marye's Hill, and behind a stone wall, on the road at its foot, near the town, already mentioned, Longstreet was posted, with heavy reserves behind him. Upon this formidable host, under the storm of iron from the heights which made great lanes through his ranks, French threw his columns, and was met by murderous volleys at short range from Barksdale's riflemen, who had been summoned to position behind the wall. The struggle was brief, and French was driven back shattered and broken by the loss of nearly half his command, while the victors shouted and yelled in wildest exultation. Hancock, who was close behind, now closed up, and with such portions of French's command as were still organized, advanced in the face of a like terrible tempest of bullet, ball, and shell. His brigades fought most gallantly, especially that of Meagher, composed of regiments of Irishmen,[1] which dashed itself time after time against the force at the stone wall, but without success, until the ground was strewn with two-thirds of its number.[2] After a struggle of only about fifteen minutes, Hancock was driven back with great slaughter. Of five thousand six hundred veterans, led by able and tried commanders, whom he took into action, two thousand and thirteen had fallen! Yet the struggle was maintained. Howard's division came to the aid of French and Hancock, and those of Sturgis and Getty, of the Ninth corps, made several attacks in support of the struggling Second, but still no advance could be made. Finally Burnside ordered Hooker across, with such of his force as he had in hand, saying, as he looked from the north bank of the river upon the smoking heights for which his troops had been unsuccessfully struggling for hours, "That crest must be carried to-night."[3]

THOMAS FRANCIS MEAGHER.

Hooker crossed with three divisions, but on surveying the ground and learning the situation of affairs, was so well satisfied of the hopelessness of the enterprise, that he hastened to Burnside and begged him to desist from further attacks. Burnside would not yield, so Humphrey's division, four thousand strong, was sent out from the city by Hooker with empty muskets, to use the bayonet only. They followed the track of French, Hancock, and Howard. When almost up to the fatal stone wall, which they intended

---

[1] The Sixty-third, Sixty-ninth, and Eighty-eighth New York, the Twenty-eighth Massachusetts, and One Hundred and Sixteenth Pennsylvania.

[2] In his official report General Meagher said: "Of the 1200 I led into action, only 280 appeared on parade the next morning!"

[3] Swinton's *Campaigns of the Army of the Potomac*, page 251.

to storm, these troops were hurled back by terrible volleys of rifle-balls, leaving seventeen hundred of their number prostrate on the field. Night soon closed the awful conflict,[a] when the Army of the Potomac had nearly fifteen thousand less effective men than when it began the battle on the previous day.[1] It was evident to the commanders engaged in the conflict that it would be useless to make any further attempt to carry the position by storm; but General Burnside, eager to achieve victory, prepared to hurl his old corps (the Ninth) on the following morning against the fatal barrier which had withstood French, Hancock, Howard, and Humphrey. He was dissuaded by the brave Sumner, who was supported in his opposition to the proposed movement by nearly every general officer; and it was finally determined to withdraw the troops to the north bank of the Rappahannock. For two days[b] they remained on the Fredericksburg side, while Lee, evidently ignorant of the real weakness and peril of his foe, fortunately maintained a defensive position, and was engaged during that time in strengthening his works in anticipation of another attack. On the morning of the 16th he was astonished by the apparition of a great army on the Stafford Hills, and seeing none in front of his line. During the night of the 15th Burnside had quietly withdrawn his entire force and all his guns, taken up his pontoon bridges, and offered Lee full permission to occupy Fredericksburg. The latter accepted the boon, and boasted of a great victory, in terms wholly irreconcilable with truth and candor.[2]

a Dec. 13, 1862.

b Dec. 14-15.

The disaster at Fredericksburg touched Burnside's reputation as a judicious leader very severely, and for a while he was under a cloud. Prompted by that noble generosity of his nature which made him always ready to award full honor to all in the hour of victory, he now assumed the entire responsibility of the measures which had caused a slaughter so terrible with a result so disastrous. That generosity blunted the weapons of vituperation which the friends of the late commander of the Army of the Potomac and the enemies of the Government were too ready to use.[3]

Although it was plain that his officers and men distrusted his ability, yet Burnside did not stop to offer excuses,[4] but, eager to do what he might to

---

[1] Hooker reported the loss in his Grand Division at 3,548; Franklin in his at 4,679, and Sumner in his at 5,494, making a total, with a loss of 50 of the engineers, of 13,771. Of this number 1,152 had been killed, 9,101 wounded, and 3,234 missing. Many of the latter soon rejoined the army, while seventy per cent. of the wounded ranked as "slightly," and soon recovered.

Lee at first reported his loss at "about 1,800, killed, wounded, and missing," but the detailed reports of Longstreet and Jackson made the number 5,309, including some prisoners. The Confederate loss was probably about one-half that of the reported loss of the Nationals.

[2] In a General Order on the 21st, congratulating his troops on their success in repelling the National army, he said the latter had given battle "in its own time, and on ground of its own selection!" Also, that less than 20,000 Confederates had been engaged in the battle, and that those who "had advanced in full confidence of victory," made "their escape from entire destruction" their boast. His own report, given in March the following year, and those of his subordinates, refute these statements. Lee, as we shall observe from time to time, was adroit in the use of "pious frauds" of this kind, by which his own lack of that military genius which wins solid victories was artfully concealed from all but his more able subordinates.

[3] In his report to General Halleck on the 19th, he declared that he owed "every thing to the brave officers and soldiers who accomplished the feat of recrossing the river in the face of the enemy. For the failure in the attack," he continued, "*I* am responsible." Alluding to the fact that the plan of moving to Fredericksburg from Warrenton, instead of pursuing Lee toward the Rapid Anna, was not favorably considered by the authorities at Washington, and that the whole movement was left in his own hands, he said that fact made him "more responsible."

[4] Burnside and his subordinates concurred in the opinion, that had the pontoons arrived earlier, so that the army might have been transferred to the south side of the Rappahannock before Lee could concentrate his forces

crush out the rebellion, and knowing well the value of time at that critical moment, he planned and proposed to execute measures for an immediate advance on Richmond. His plan was to make a feint above Fredericksburg, but to cross about six miles below, at the Seddon Farm, with his main body, to turn the position of the Confederates. At the same time twenty-five thousand cavalry, with four guns, were to cross at Kelley's Ford, and sweep through the country in the rear of Lee's army, to cut its communications with Richmond, raiding along the line of the Virginia Central and Orange and Alexandria railways to Lynchburg, destroying tracks and bridges, and the locks of the James River Canal, as circumstances might allow, and then, turning eastward, strike the Richmond and Danville road, cross the Nottaway River, and after destroying important portions of the road between Weldon and Petersburg, join General Peck, then in command at Suffolk. At the same time other bodies of mounted men were to sweep over the country, to distract the Confederates and conceal the real object of the general movement.

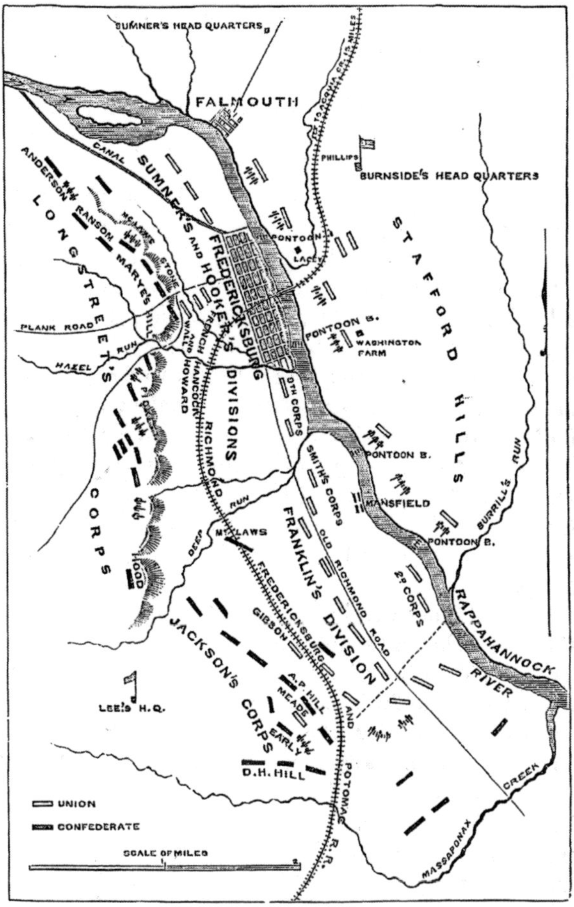

BATTLE OF FREDERICKSBURG.

These movements had just commenced when Burnside received a dispatch from the President,[a] directing him not to enter upon active operations without his knowledge. He was surprised, for the General-in-Chief had instructed him not to send any thing over the wires concerning his plans, but to act according to his own judgment. He had mentioned his plans to no one. His generals only knew that the passage of the river on the flank of the foe was to be attempted. The order was inexplicable. But Burnside instantly obeyed. He recalled the cavalry expedi-

[a] Dec. 30, 1862.

there, the success of Burnside's plans would doubtless have been secured. The delay in getting the pontoons earlier, or rather in the starting from Washington, appears to have been occasioned by a misunderstanding as to who should attend to the forwarding of them.

tion and hastened to Washington, to ask a reason for the interference. The President informed him that general officers of his army had declared that such was the feeling in that army against its commander, that its safety would be imperiled by a movement under his direction. Of these clandestine complaints to the President the General-in-Chief and the Secretary of War were ignorant, and they had nothing to say.

Never was the spirit of a man more sorely tried than was that of Burnside at this time. The country looked to him for acts that should retrieve the misfortunes at Fredericksburg, yet the General-in-Chief would not sanction any forward movement, and it was evident that there was a secret conspiracy among some of his general officers to effect his removal. His patriotism soared high above self, and he returned to the army with a determination to take the responsibility of doing something more for the salvation of his country. He ascertained that some of the details of his cavalry expedition had been communicated by traitors in his army to secessionists in Washington, and by them to Lee, and he abandoned that movement and proposed to cross the Rappahannock at Banks's and United States fords, above Fredericksburg, and endeavor to flank his foe and give him battle. For that purpose his army was speedily put in motion. The Grand Divisions of Franklin and Hooker ascended the river by parallel roads, while Couch's made a feint below the city. The reserve corps, now under Sigel, was ordered to guard the line of the river and the communications with the army.

Every thing was in readiness to cross the river stealthily on the night of the 20th, when a terrible storm of wind, snow, sleet, and rain came on, such as had seldom been known in that region, and for hours the troops who had approached the fords were hopelessly mired and almost immovable. They were discovered by the foe at dawn, and Lee was soon fully prepared to meet them. Even under these circumstances Burnside would have attempted to cross and give battle at an early hour, could he have gotten his bridges in position. This was impossible, and there that army remained until its three days' cooked provisions in haversacks were nearly exhausted, and the supply-trains could not come up. It was led back to its old camps as quickly as possible, and huts were at once built for the comfort of the troops. This was known in the army as the "Mud March."

APPEARANCE OF ARMY HUTS.

Burnside now proceeded to Washington, bearing a general order for instant dismissal from the service of the officers who, as he had ascertained, had made clandestine communications to the President concerning the defection of the troops toward their leader, and for other purposes. These he charged with "fomenting discontent in the army."[1] He was competent to issue the order on his own responsibility; but, in compliance with judicious advice, he submitted it to the President. Mr. Lincoln was perplexed. He appreciated the patriotism and soldierly qualities of Burnside, yet he could not consent to the suspension or dismissal of the officers named, even had there been greater personal provocation. He talked with Burnside as a friend and brother, and it was finally arranged that the General should be relieved of the command of the Army of the Potomac, and await orders for further service. This was done, and Major-General Hooker succeeded him in the command.[2] The arrangement made at that time, whereby the country might be best served, was highly creditable to the President and to General Burnside.

Here we will leave the Army of the Potomac in winter quarters on the Rappahannock, and consider the stirring events in the great Valley of the Mississippi since the siege of Corinth, and the capture of New Orleans and Memphis.

---

[1] In that order Generals Hooker, Brooks, and Newton were named for ignominious dismissal from the service, and Generals Franklin, W. F. Smith, Cochran, and Ferrero, and Lieutenant-Colonel J. H. Taylor, were to be relieved from duty in the Army of the Potomac. Generals Franklin and Smith, without the knowledge of Burnside, wrote a joint letter to the President on the 21st of December, expressing their belief that Burnside's plan of campaign could not succeed, and substantially recommending that of McClellan, by the James River and the country on its borders. The President replied that they were simply suggesting a plan fraught with "the old difficulty," and he appeared to be astonished, as Franklin had distinctly advised bringing the army away from the Peninsula.

[2] January 26, 1863. By the order relieving Burnside from the command, Franklin was also relieved. So also was General Sumner, at his own request. He soon afterward died, at Syracuse, New York.

CHAPTER XIX.

EVENTS IN KENTUCKY AND NORTHERN MISSISSIPPI.

WE left the Lower Mississippi, from its mouth to New Orleans, in possession of the forces under General Butler and Commodore Farragut, at the beginning of the summer of 1862;[1] and at the same time that river was held by the National forces from Memphis to St. Louis. General Thomas was at the head of a large force holding Southwestern Tennessee,[2] and Generals Buell and Mitchel were on the borders of East Tennessee, where the Confederates were disputing the passage of National troops farther southward and eastward than the line of the Tennessee River. Beauregard's army was at Tupelo and vicinity, under General Bragg.[3] Halleck had just been called to Washington to be General-in-Chief, and Mitchel was soon afterward transferred to the command of the Department of the South, with his head-quarters at Hilton Head.

Although the great armies of the Confederates had been driven from Kentucky and Tennessee, the absence of any considerable Union force excepting on the southern borders of the latter State, permitted a most distressing guerrilla warfare to be carried on within the borders of those commonwealths by mounted bands, who hung upon the rear and flanks of the National forces, or roamed at will over the country, plundering the Union inhabitants. The most famous of these guerrilla leaders was John H. Morgan, already mentioned.[4] He professed to be a leader of cavalry attached to the Confederate army, and so he was, but such license was given to him by the Confederate authorities, that he was as frequently a commissioned free-booter in practice as a leader of horsemen in legitimate warfare.

Morgan's first exploit of much consequence having the semblance of regularity was his invasion of Kentucky with about twelve hundred followers, under the conviction that large numbers of the young men of his native State would flock to his standard, and he might become the liberator of the commonwealth from the "hireling legions of Lincoln." He left Knoxville, in East Tennessee, on the 4th of July, crossed the Cumberland Mountains, and entered Kentucky on its southeastern border.

On the 9th of July, Morgan, assisted by Colonel Hunt, routed a detachment of Pennsylvania cavalry under Major Jordan, at Tompkinsville, in Monroe County, when the commander and nineteen others were made prisoners, and ten were killed or wounded. The assailants lost ten killed, inclu-

---

[1] See the latter part of chapter XIII. [2] See page 296. [3] See page 294. [4] See page 264.

ding Colonel Hunt. On the following day Morgan issued a characteristic proclamation to the citizens of Kentucky, declaring that he and his followers (who from the beginning to the end were mere guerrillas, in the fullest sense of that term) appeared as their liberators, and saying :—"Everywhere the cowardly foes have fled from my avenging arm. My brave army," he continued, "is stigmatized as a band of guerrillas and marauders. Believe it not. I point with pride to their deeds as a refutation of this foul assertion." He declared that the Confederate armies were rapidly advancing to their protection, and said :—"Greet them with the willing hands of fifty thousand of Kentucky's bravest sons. Their advance is already with you." Morgan's men, at that time, really formed the advance of the Confederate hosts, whose business was to terrify the Unionists of Kentucky, recruit from the ranks of the secessionists, and prepare the way for a formidable invasion by Bragg.

JOHN H. MORGAN.

Morgan's force was soon increased by several hundred recruits from the young men of Kentucky, and he roamed about the heart of the State, plundering and destroying with very little molestation. On the 12th[a] he attacked and defeated Unionists under Lieutenant-Colonel Johnston at Lebanon, Kentucky, the termination of the Lebanon branch of the Louisville and Nashville railway. He captured the place, and made the commander and twenty-six soldiers and Home Guards prisoners. His raid was so rapid and formidable that it produced intense excitement throughout the State. General Boyle, who was in command at Louisville, issued a proclamation[b] ordering every able-bodied man to "take arms, and aid in repelling the marauders;" and directed him, if he did not, to remain in his house forty-eight hours under the penalty of being shot if found out of it.

[a] July, 1862.

[b] July 8.

Morgan pressed on toward the Ohio. On the 14th he destroyed the long railway bridge between Cynthiana and Paris, and the next day he laid waste a portion of the track of the Lexington and Louisville railway, and the telegraph along its border. Two days afterward[c] he led his entire force[1] against three hundred and fifty Home Guards at Cynthiana, on the Covington and Cincinnati railway, under Lieutenant-Colonel Landrum. These maintained a severe fight with the guerrillas, but were overpowered and dispersed after losing thirteen killed and thirty-four wounded, and inflicting a loss on the assailants of twenty-four killed and seventy-eight wounded.

[c] July 17.

Cincinnati was now not far distant, and Morgan cast longing eyes toward its treasures of every kind. His approach had inspired it and its

[1] Morgan's force was now about 2,200 in number, and was composed of three regiments, comprising Kentuckians, Tennesseeans, Georgians, Mississippians, Texans, and South Carolinians.

neighbors on the Kentucky shore with terror, and its capture appeared to be probably an easy task. But Morgan went no farther northward at this time, for Green Clay Smith, of Kentucky, with a superior cavalry force, was on his track, and he retreated southward by way of Richmond, and rested at Clarksville, on the Cumberland,[1] which, with a large quantity of military stores, was captured a month later[a] by nine hundred roving Confederates under Colonel Woodward.[2] Morgan's band, on the retreat, was practically nothing but a marauding party, everywhere stealing horses and robbing stores, without inquiring whether their plunder belonged to friend or foe. Other marauding bands, mostly Kentuckians, were harassing the citizens of that commonwealth throughout its length and breadth,[3] and terror prevailed in all its borders.

[a] Aug. 19, 1862.

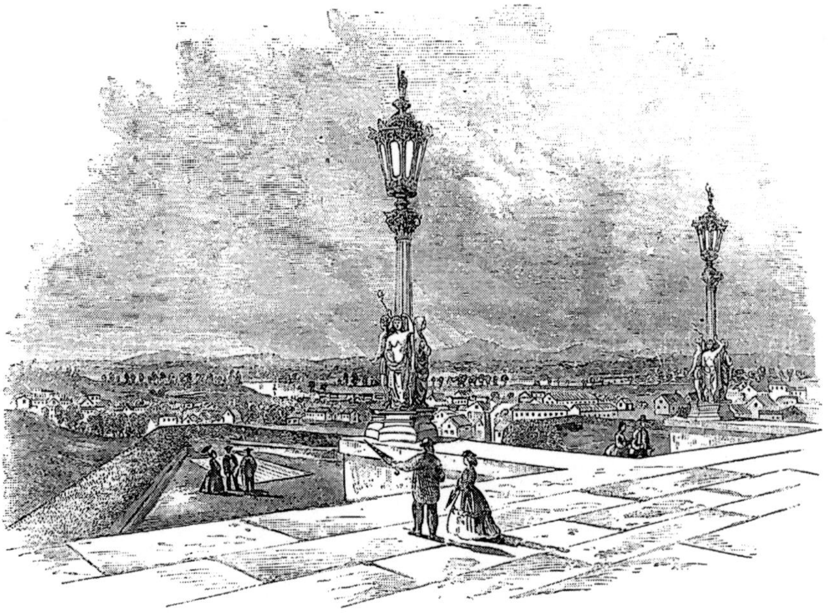

FORTIFICATIONS OF THE STATE-HOUSE AT NASHVILLE.[4]

Another bold leader of Confederate horsemen at this time was Brigadier-General N. B. Forrest,[5] who commanded the Second Brigade of cavalry.

[1] See page 232.

[2] The garrison consisted of a portion of the Seventy-first Ohio regiment, under Colonel Mason.

[3] At about this time guerrillas entered Henderson (July 15), on the Ohio below Louisville, and robbed the hospital there of its blankets and other supplies. Piloted by some Indiana traitors, the same party crossed the river, captured the hospital at the village of Newburg (July 21), paroled the sick found there, and carried away the supplies. A few days before, some guerrillas dashed into Memphis, captured the militia force stationed there, robbed the stores, and fled with their plunder.

[4] This picture shows the appearance of the front of the Capitol or State-House at Nashville, looking toward the Cumberland below the city. In the immediate foreground are seen the earth-works thrown up directly in front of the granite steps leading up to the entrance, and near the group of three persons is seen the platform for cannon at an angle of the works. The fine lamp-posts and lamps seen in the picture, which flank the steps at each of the four great entrances, are made of iron, the group of figures being life-size and beautifully modeled. A portion of the city is seen below, and the Cumberland and ranges of hills beyond in the distance. This was the appearance when the writer made the sketch, in May, 1866.

[5] See page 218.

While Morgan was spreading consternation in Kentucky, he was operating as boldly in the heart of Tennessee, and, like the former, was preparing the way for a more formidable invasion. On the morning of the 13th of July he suddenly appeared before Murfreesboro', below Nashville, with about three thousand men,[1] and attacked the smaller National force there under General T. L. Crittenden, and Colonel W. W. Duffield of the Ninth Michigan.[2] After a severe engagement in and near the town, the Nationals were defeated, and, with their leaders, were made prisoners. Forrest seized a quantity of valuable stores and decamped with his booty for other hostile operations.

Forrest's appearance so near Nashville produced much anxiety for the safety of that city, and the strengthening of the post by fortifications upon the surrounding hills was pushed on with great vigor by General Nelson, who was in command there. The State-House in the city was strongly fortified by casting up earth-works for cannon immediately around it, so that it became a powerful citadel overlooking the town and the surrounding country; and the most active preparations were made to meet an expected attack. At the same time the guerrillas were bold. They made raids to within sight of the city, and during the whole month of August it was seriously threatened. An attempt was also made[a] by some guerrillas, under Woodward, who captured Clarksville, to retake Fort Donelson, then held by a part of the Seventy-first Ohio, under Major J. H. Hart. Woodward had about seven hundred men, foot and horse. He demanded the surrender of the fort. Hart refused, and Woodward made an attack. He was soon repulsed with heavy loss, and fled; while the Nationals behind their intrenchments did not lose a man.

[a] Aug. 25, 1862.

While these raids were agitating Tennessee and Kentucky, Bragg was moving with a view to the recovery of these States. He and Buell had marched in nearly parallel lines eastward toward Chattanooga, the former on the north of the Tennessee River, and the latter south of it. Bragg moved with the greatest celerity, and won the race, and with full forty thousand men he turned his face toward the Ohio. His force was divided into three corps, commanded respectively by W. J. Hardee, Leonidas Polk, and E. Kirby Smith. The latter was sent to Knoxville, and the former two held Chattanooga and its vicinity. Buell disposed his army in a line stretching from Huntsville, in Alabama, to McMinnsville, in Warren County, Tennessee. His head-quarters, late in August, were at Huntsville, and General Thomas commanded the left wing at McMinnsville.

E. KIRBY SMITH

[1] Forrest's force was composed of one regiment each from Texas, Alabama, and Tennessee, and two from Georgia.

[2] The National force was composed of portions of the Ninth Michigan and Third Minnesota infantry regiments, companies of the Fourth Kentucky and Seventh Pennsylvania cavalry, and two companies of Hewitt's Kentucky battery; in all about 2,000 men.

So lay the opposing armies when E. Kirby Smith left Knoxville, and passing through Big Creek Gap of the Cumberland Mountains, with about six thousand men and a train of one hundred and fifty wagons, penetrated Kentucky by way of Knox County. By this movement he so completely outflanked and imperiled General G. W. Morgan, at Cumberland Gap,[1] that the latter blew up the works there and fled toward the Ohio, harassed nearly all the way by seven hundred of John Morgan's guerrillas.

Smith's troops marched rapidly with very little encumbrance, and subsisted most of the way over the mountain region upon green corn, with the anticipation of living on the fat of the land in the Blue Grass region of Kentucky, and perhaps reveling in the luxuries of Louisville and Cincinnati. His cavalry, under Colonel J. S. Scott, nine hundred strong, led the invasion, and scattered among the people a proclamation, telling them that good treatment would be the reward of good behavior, but hanging and destruction of property would be the fate of every man who should fire from the woods on the Confederate troops.

Smith's course was in the direction of Frankfort, at which point he might choose Louisville or Cincinnati as his grand objective in further movements. His invasion caused wide-spread alarm; and to Indiana and Ohio, where troops were in readiness for the field, all eyes were turned for power to roll back the fearful tide. Major-General Lewis Wallace had just been assisting Governor Morton in raising troops in Indiana. He offered to command a regiment for the crisis, and one was given him. He took with him to Louisville the Sixty-sixth Indiana, and offered his services to General Boyle, whom he ranked. They were accepted, and with the Sixty-sixth he hastened to Lexington, where he was put in command of all the troops there. But they were too few. He called for more from the region north of the Ohio, and they hastened to his standard in large numbers, for he was exceedingly popular. Leading men of Kentucky also flocked thither, and he was about to move forward to relieve Morgan at Cumberland Gap, and confront Smith with men full of the most glowing enthusiasm, when he was suddenly superseded in command by General William Nelson. The change dampened the ardor of the troops, especially those of Indiana.

Meanwhile Smith moved rapidly forward. His cavalry penetrated to Richmond, in Madison County, fighting and routing a battalion of Union cavalry at London, capturing one hundred and eleven of them, and repeating the exploit on a smaller scale at other places. The main body pushed on with celerity, and when approaching Richmond it was met by the force organized by Wallace and then commanded by General M. D. Manson, for Nelson had not arrived. That force was superior to Smith's in the number of its men and weapons; but it was largely composed of raw troops. Yet Manson pressed forward to meet the invader. They came in collision a little beyond Rogersville,[a] and a severe battle was fought for three hours, when Manson was driven back, fighting gallantly.

[a] Aug. 30, 1862.

At this juncture Nelson arrived and took command, and half an hour afterward his troops were utterly routed and scattered in all directions. Nelson was wounded, and Manson resumed command; but the day was

[1] See page 303.

lost. Smith's cavalry had gained the rear of the Nationals, and stood in the way of their wild flight. The disaster was terrible. General Manson, hurt by his horse falling on him, was made a prisoner: a fate shared by several hundred of his fellow-soldiers. The dispersion of his force was complete, and his losses very heavy.[1] Considering the rawness of the troops and their lack of discipline (some of them not over thirty days old as soldiers, and many who had not yet experienced a battalion-drill), the prowess displayed by them in THE BATTLE OF RICHMOND marked it as one of the most creditable engagements of the war on the part of the Nationals.

The elated victors pushed on to Lexington,[a] where they were warmly welcomed by the secessionists of that stronghold of slavery in Kentucky.[2] Their approach frightened the Legislature (then in session) from Frankfort. They adjourned to Louisville, whither the archives of the State and about a million of dollars in treasure from the banks of Richmond, Lexington, and Frankfort were carried. The movement was timely, for Smith tarried but little anywhere on his triumphal march. He did not then go farther toward Frankfort, however, but pushed on northward through Paris to Cynthiana, from which point he might at his option, as it appeared, strike Cincinnati or Louisville. The former city seemed to be more at his mercy, and he turned his face in that direction, confidently expecting to possess himself of its treasures of food, clothing, arms, and munitions of war in the course of a few days.

[a] Sept. 2, 1862.

The invader was confronted by an unexpected force near Cincinnati. When Wallace was deprived of his command at Lexington, he returned to that city. When intelligence of the disaster at Richmond reached there, he was ordered to Lexington by General Wright, then in Louisville, to resume command of the shattered forces. At Paris he was recalled to Cincinnati to provide for its defense, and half an hour after his arrival[b] in that city he issued a stirring proclamation, as commander of that and the cities of Covington and Newport opposite, in which he officially informed the inhabitants of the approach of the Confederates in strong force, and that the preservation of these towns from the consequences of war must be effected by the active co-operation of the citizens. He ordered all places of business to be closed, and the citizens of Cincinnati, under the direction of the mayor, to assemble an hour afterward in convenient public places, to be organized for work on intrenchments on the south side of the river.[3] He also ordered the ferry-boats to cease running, and proclaimed martial law in the three cities just named.

[b] Sept. 1.

This was a bold, startling, but necessary measure. In accordance with the principle expressed in his proclamation,—"Citizens for the labor—Sol-

---

[1] These have been estimated only. There were no full official returns made. It is supposed to have been about equal between the belligerents. The National loss was estimated at about 5,000, killed, wounded, and prisoners. Manson was well supported in the struggle by General Cruft, who, as we have seen, distinguished himself at the siege of Fort Donelson. See page 215.

[2] Encouraged by their friendly demonstrations, Smith issued a proclamation to the Kentuckians, assuring them that he came as a liberator, in the spirit of the State Supremacy Doctrine of the Resolutions of 1798. He had come, he said, to test the truth of what he believed to be a foul aspersion, that Kentuckians willingly joined in an attempt to subjugate their Southern brethren. Like all the other Confederate leaders, he talked about "the Northern hordes," who were treading the "sacred soil of the South."

[3] "This labor," said the proclamation, "ought to be that of love, and the undersigned trusts and believes it will be so. Anyhow, it must be done. The willing shall be properly credited; the unwilling promptly visited. The principle adopted is, Citizens for the labor—Soldiers for the battle."

diers for the battle,"—Wallace had demanded the services of all able-bodied men. The response was wonderful. In the course of a few hours he had at his command an army of workers and fighters forty thousand strong. While many did not believe that danger was so nigh,[1] all confided in the General, and the citizens and soldiers of Cincinnati, and Dickson's brigade of colored men, and the "Squirrel Hunters" from the rural districts of Ohio, streamed across a pontoon bridge that had been erected in a day under Wallace's

PONTOON BRIDGE AT CINCINNATI.[2]

directions, and swarmed upon the hills around Covington. There was a most stirring and picturesque night-march over that floating bridge, on which tons of supplies and many heavy cannon were also passing. Within three days after the proclamation was issued, a line of intrenchments, ten miles in length and semicircular in form, was thrown up, extending from the river bank above Cincinnati to the river bank below it, well armed and fully manned.[3] Steamers had been suddenly converted into gun-boats, and the river above and below the pontoon bridge was patroled by a large number of them.

The work for protection, so promptly commenced and vigorously carried forward, was scarcely completed when General Heath, with full fifteen thousand of Smith's invading troops (whose ranks had been swelled by volun-

[1] "If the enemy should not come, after all this fuss," said a doubting friend to the General, "you will be ruined."—"Very well," he responded; "but they will come, and if they do not, it will be because this same fuss has caused them to think better of it."

[2] This is a view of the passage of the troops over the pontoon bridge at Cincinnati on the night of the 3d of September, 1862. The bridge was laid along the line of the Suspension Bridge since erected. The unfinished piers of that bridge are seen on each side of the Ohio, in the picture.

[3] The principal work was named Fort Mitchel, in honor of the brave commander and philosopher then in the army.

teers from among the Kentucky secessionists), appeared. He was astounded and alarmed by the preparations to receive him, and retreated in haste[a] under cover of darkness and a heavy thunder-storm, dismayed and disheartened. When the danger was averted, Wallace led several of the volunteer companies back to Cincinnati, where he was greeted with the huzzas of thousands of citizens, who regarded him as their deliverer,[1] and he was the recipient of public honors suggested by a sense of gratitude.[2]

[a] Sept. 12, 1862.

Foiled in his attempt against Cincinnati, Smith turned his face toward Louisville. He took possession of Frankfort, the capital of Kentucky, on the day when Heath fled from before Wallace's lines.[b] There he organized a city government, and issued a proclamation, telling the inhabitants that they must join his standard or be considered his enemies. Here he awaited an opportunity to join his forces to those of Bragg, which for almost three weeks had been moving northward.

[b] Sept. 12.

Bragg crossed the Tennessee River at Harrison, just above Chattanooga, on the 21st of August, with thirty-six regiments of infantry, five of cavalry, and forty guns. Louisville was his destination. He pushed forward among the rugged mountains around the Sequatchee Valley, that lie well eastward of Nashville, and, sending out a strong cavalry force toward Buell's left at McMinnsville as a feint, had fairly flanked that leader's army, gained his rear, and was well on his way toward the Cumberland before the latter had fairly penetrated the Confederate general's designs.

The cavalry movement toward McMinnsville resulted in a serious fight near there. The horsemen were under General Forrest, who for several days had been hovering around Lebanon, Nashville, and Murfreesboro', and finally, on Saturday afternoon, the 30th of August, appeared a short distance from McMinnsville, making their way toward the road from that place to Murfreesboro', to cut off Buell's communications. Colonel E. P. Fyffe, of the Twenty-sixth Ohio, was ordered to take three regiments and prevent the threatened disaster. With his own regiment in advance, and the Seventeenth and Fifty-eighth Indiana following, he pressed forward five miles in sixty minutes, through woods, fields, and creeks, and soon afterward, when nine miles from his starting-place, encountered the foe, fifteen hundred strong. After a short struggle the Confederates were routed, and driven in such haste and confusion that they left every encumbrance behind them. Fyffe's troops were of General T. J. Wood's division, and were highly complimented by that commander in a general order.

Supposing Bragg was aiming at Nashville, Buell now took measures

---

1 Wallace issued an address to the citizens of Cincinnati, Covington, and Newport, commending their alacrity, fortitude, and bravery. "The most commercial of people," he said, "you submitted to a total suspension of business, and without a murmur adopted my principle—'Citizens for labor—Soldiers for battle.' In coming times, strangers viewing the works on the hills of Newport and Covington will ask, 'Who built those intrenchments?' You can answer, 'We built them.' If they ask, 'Who guarded them?' you can reply, 'We helped in thousands.' If they inquire the result, your answer will be, 'The enemy came and looked at them, and stole away in the night.'"

2 On the 17th of October following, the authorities of Cincinnati publicly expressed their gratitude to Wallace for his services rendered to the city in its hour of peril; and on the 14th of March, 1863, the Legislature of Ohio, by joint resolutions, thanked him for "the signal service he had rendered the country at large" in the Army of the Republic, and especially "for the promptness, energy, and skill exhibited by him in organizing the forces, planning the defense, and executing the movements of soldiers and citizens under his command at Cincinnati, which prevented the rebel forces under Kirby Smith from desecrating the free soil of our noble State."

accordingly. He pushed his army forward to Lebanon to cover it; but was soon satisfied, by an intercepted dispatch, that his opponent was pressing toward Louisville, and was threatening the main line of supplies for Buell's army, the Louisville and Nashville railway. At assailable points on this important highway he posted troops as soon as possible, and had strong stockades built for its protection.

A RAILWAY STOCKADE.

Bragg crossed the Cumberland at Carthage, eastward of Lebanon, entered Kentucky on the 5th of September, and made his headquarters at Glasgow, the capital of Barren County, where a railway connects with that between Nashville and Louisville. Breckenridge had been left in Tennessee with a large force of all arms, to retard Buell and invest Nashville, then garrisoned by the divisions of Thomas, Negley, and Palmer, under the command of General Thomas.

Bragg's advance under General J. R. Chalmers, about eight thousand strong, with seven guns, pushed on toward Louisville, and on the 14th,[a] two brigades[1] of the division of the Kentucky traitor, S. B. Buckner, under General Duncan, of Mississippi, encountered a little more than two thousand National troops, under Colonel T. J. Wilder,[2] at Mumfordsville, where the railway crosses the Green River, and where a stockade and strong earth-works had been hastily constructed on the south side of the stream and on each side of the road. Duncan arrived on Saturday evening, and demanded an unconditional surrender. It was refused, and at four o'clock the next morning[b] the Confederates drove in the National pickets. A battle began in earnest at dawn, and raged for about five hours, when four hundred of the Fiftieth Indiana, under Colonel C. L. Dunham, came to the aid of the garrison. The assailants were repulsed with heavy loss.[3]

[a] Sept. 1862.

[b] Sept. 14.

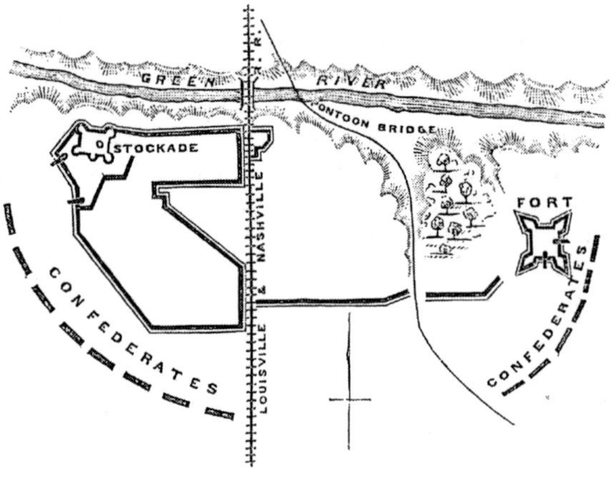

FORTIFICATIONS AT MUMFORDSVILLE.

Assured of final success, the Confederates remained quiet until the 16th,

[1] Composed of Mississippi, Georgia, and Alabama troops.

[2] These consisted of about 200 recruits of the Seventeenth Indiana, and Sixty-seventh and Eighty-ninth of the same State, and one company each of the Eighteenth Regulars, of cavalry, and of the Louisville Provost Guards. Their guns consisted of three 12-pounders and a 3-inch rifled cannon, under Lieutenant Mason. The Thirteenth Indiana and Thirty-third Kentucky batteries were also there and in position.

[3] The writer is indebted to Stephen Bowers, chaplain of the Sixty-seventh Indiana, for the above plan of the fortifications, and also for an interesting account of the affair we are considering.

when a large portion of Bragg's main body, under General (Bishop) Polk, appeared upon the hills on the north side of the river, overlooking the National camp, not less than twenty-five thousand strong. Wilder had been re-enforced by two regiments (Sixtieth and Eighty-fourth Indiana), but opposed the invaders with only four thousand effective men. He sustained a severe fight nearly all day, hoping Buell, then at Bowling Green, would send him promised relief. But relief did not come; and when, at sunset, the demand for a surrender was repeated, and Wilder counted forty-five cannon in position to attack his little force, he called a council of officers. It was agreed that further resistance would produce a useless sacrifice of life. At two o'clock in the morning[a] Wilder surrendered, and his troops marched out at six o'clock with all the honors of war.[1]

[a] Sept. 17, 1862.

Bragg was greatly elated by this event, and, counting largely on the usual tardiness of Buell, as Lee had done on that of McClellan, he felt assured of soon making his head-quarters in Louisville, or, at least, of plundering rich Kentucky as much as he desired. On the 18th he issued a proclamation from Glasgow, in which he repeated the declarations of his subordinates, that the Confederate Army had come as the liberators of Kentuckians "from the tyranny of a despotic ruler," and "not as conquerors or despoilers. Your gallant Buckner," he said, "leads the van; Marshall [Humphrey] is on the right; while Breckenridge, dear to us as to you, is advancing with Kentucky's valiant sons to receive the honor and applause due to their heroism." He told them that he must have supplies for his army, but that they should be fairly paid for;[2] and he appealed to the women of Kentucky for encouragement, assuring them that he had come as a chivalrous knight-errant to succor them from "fear of loathsome prisons or insulting visitations" thereafter. "Let your enthusiasm have free rein," he said. "Buckle on the armor of your kindred—your husbands, sons, and brothers—and scoff with shame him who would prove recreant in his duty to you, his country, and his God."

From Mumfordsville Bragg's troops moved northward without opposition, and, on the 1st of October, formed a junction with those of Kirby Smith, at Frankfort, where they performed the farce of making Richard Hawes, formerly a Congressman, "Provisional Governor of Kentucky."[b] At the same time Bragg's plundering bands were scouring the State under the "provisional" administration of bayonets, dashing up sometimes almost to Louisville, and driving away southward thousands of hogs and cattle, and numerous trains, bearing in the same direction bacon and breadstuffs of every kind. In every town the goods of merchants were taken, and worthless Confederate scrip given in exchange.[3]

[b] Oct. 4.

---

[1] Report of Colonel J. T. Wilder, September 18th, 1862. Wilder reported his entire loss during the siege at thirty-seven killed and wounded. "The enemy," he said, "admit a loss of 714 killed and wounded on Sunday alone."

[2] It is notorious that Bragg, who was a supple instrument of Jefferson Davis, and was his special favorite on that account, had not the means, nor manifested the least intention to pay for any thing. When, a little later, he retreated from Kentucky, he plundered the region through which he passed of cattle, horses, and supplies of every kind that came in his way, without inquiring whether he took from friends or foes, or offering even promises of remuneration. The invasions of Kirby Smith and Braxton Bragg were plundering raids, like John Morgan's, on a greater scale. It was the wealth of Kentucky, and Southern Ohio and Indiana, which they marched from the Tennessee River to secure, and not the hope of subjugation or permanent occupation.

[3] The *Lexington Observer*, in an article on the amount of plunder carried away by the marauders, says the *Richmond Examiner* was not far wrong when it said that "the wagon-train of supplies brought out of Ken-

Regarding Kentucky as a part of the Confederacy, for her professed representatives were in the "Congress" of the conspirators at Richmond, the conscription act was enforced there at the point of the bayonet. And so the insane policy of "neutrality," which had brought the war into Kentucky, yielded its fruit of wide-spread distress, until the whole people held out their hands imploringly to the National Government, which many of them had affected to despise, begging for deliverance from Buckner and Breckenridge, and other native and foreign "liberators."

To that cry for help Buell responded, but in a manner that seemed to the impatient loyalists and suffering Kentuckians almost as if he was in league with Bragg for the punishment of that Commonwealth. He left Nashville on the 15th of September, and made his way to Louisville, in an apparent race with Bragg for that city. He won it in the course of a fortnight, but all that time his opponent was gathering in the spoils he came for without hindrance. The Government was dissatisfied, and relieved Buell, but at the urgent request of his general officers he was reinstated, with the understanding that he should take immediate measures for driving the marauders from Kentucky. Buell's army was then about one hundred thousand strong, while Bragg had not more than sixty-five thousand, including Kirby Smith's troops.

Buell turned toward his opponent on the 1st of October. His army was arranged in three corps, commanded respectively by Generals Gilbert, Crittenden, and McCook. General George H. Thomas, who was Buell's second in command,[1] had charge of the right wing. It moved over a broad space, its right under the immediate command of Crittenden, marching by way of Shepherdsville toward Bardstown, to attack Bragg's main force, and the remainder moving more in the direction of Frankfort. The right soon began to feel the Confederates. Bragg fell slowly back to Springfield, impeding Buell as much as possible by skirmishing, that his supply-trains might get a good start toward Tennessee.

At Springfield Buell heard that Kirby Smith had evacuated Frankfort and crossed the Kentucky River, and that Bragg was moving to concentrate his forces at Harrodsburg or Perryville. He at once ordered the central division of his army, under Gilbert, to march on the latter place; and, toward the evening of the 7th,[a] the head of the column, under General R. B. Mitchell, fell in with a heavy force of Confederates within five miles of Perryville, drawn up in battle order. These were pressed back about three miles without fighting, when General Sheridan's division was ordered up to a position on heights near Doctor's Creek, and General Schoepff's was held in reserve. When these dispositions for battle were completed it was nightfall.

[a] Oct., 1862.

Buell was with Gilbert. Expecting a battle in the morning, he sent for

tucky by General Kirby Smith was 40 miles long, and brought a million of yards of jeans, with a large amount of clothing, boots and shoes, and two hundred wagon-loads of bacon, 6,000 barrels of pork, 1,500 mules and horses, and a large lot of swine." This was a very small portion of the property swept out of the State during this raid. Seventy-four thousand yards of jeans were stolen from one establishment in Frankfort, and one person in Lexington was plundered of jeans and linseys valued at $106,000. "For four weeks," said the *Observer*, "while the Confederates were in the vicinity of Lexington, a train of cars was running daily southward, carrying away property taken from the inhabitants, and at the same time huge wagon-trains were continually moving for the same purpose."

[1] Placed in that position on the 1st of September.

the flank corps of Crittenden and McCook to close up on his right and left, and, if possible, surround the foe. A great drouth was then prevailing, and the necessity for making a circuitous march to find water caused half a day's delay in the arrival of Crittenden. Meanwhile Bragg, perceiving the threatened peril, had begun to retreat. He was anxious to secure the exit of his plunder-trains from the State, and when informed of the delay of Crittenden, he resolved to give battle at once to the other corps, and, if successful, to fall upon the delayed one on its arrival, or retreat with his spoils. His troops then consisted of five divisions; two under Hardee, and one each under Anderson, Cheatham, and Buckner: the whole immediately commanded by Major-General Polk. Smith was retreating farther to the east, taking with him the "Provisional Government" in the person of poor "Governor" Hawes, and Withers had been sent to assist him.

There was a sharp engagement early in the morning of the 8th, when the Confederates attempted to repel the brigade of Colonel D. McCook,[1] of Sheridan's division, which Gilbert had ordered forward, accompanied by Barnett's battery and the Second Michigan cavalry, to occupy high ground, and to secure a watering-place. A desultory battle ensued, which lasted until nearly ten o'clock, when, just as General R. B. Mitchell's division was getting into line of battle on the right of the eminence occupied by McCook, the Second Missouri, of Pea Ridge fame,[2] with the Fifteenth Missouri as a support, came to McCook's aid. The Confederates were quickly repulsed and driven back into the woods, heavily smitten on the flank by the Second Minnesota battery. In this engagement a part of the Ninth Pennsylvania cavalry performed gallant service. Thus ended the preliminary battle of that eventful day.

Mitchell and Sheridan were ordered to advance and hold the ground until the two flank corps should arrive. The head of that of McCook, under General Rousseau, moving up from Macksville, on the Harrodsburg road, reached a designated point on Gilbert's left at ten o'clock in the morning. Only two of McCook's three divisions (Rousseau's and Jackson's) were present, that of Sill having been sent toward Frankfort. Rousseau advanced with his cavalry to secure the position, and the batteries of Loomis (Michigan) and Simonson (Indiana) were planted in commanding positions, when a reconnoissance was ordered to Chaplin's Creek, with the view of obtaining, if possible, a better position, where water for the troops might be had. This was done, and when McCook returned to his command, at about noon, his batteries were engaged in

LOVELL H. ROUSSEAU.

[1] Composed of the Eighty-fifth, Eighty-sixth, and One Hundred and Twenty-fifth Illinois, and Fifty-second Ohio.

[2] See page 256.

an ineffectual duel with those of the Confederates. He ordered their commanders to save their ammunition, and seeing no enemy in force, and having no apprehensions of a battle until he should offer one, he proceeded to the right of his line.

The foe was even then coming stealthily upon him. Cheatham's division, well masked, had stolen up to McCook's left, which was composed chiefly of raw troops, under General Terrell, of Major-General James S. Jackson's division, and fell suddenly upon them in flank, with horrid yells. By a bullet of their first volley Jackson was instantly killed,[1] and the raw and vastly outnumbered brigade of Terrell broke and fled in utter confusion, leaving most of the guns of Parsons's battery as trophies for the victors. In an attempt to rally his troops Terrell was mortally wounded, and died that night.

Fierce indeed was this charge, and when Terrell's force melted away the Confederates fell with equal fury upon Rousseau's division, standing ready and firmly at the foot of the hill to receive it. An attempt to flank and destroy Rousseau's left was gallantly met by Starkweather's brigade, and the batteries of Bush and Stone, who maintained the position for nearly three hours, until the ammunition of both infantry and artillery was nearly exhausted, and Bush's battery had lost thirty-five horses. The guns were drawn back a little, and the infantry, after retiring for a supply of ammunition, resumed their place in the line, not far from Russell's house.

Meanwhile Rousseau's center and right, held respectively by the brigades of Colonels L. A. Harris and W. H. Lytle, had fought stubbornly, repelling attack after attack led by Bragg in person, but losing ground a little, when the Confederates made a desperate charge upon Lytle's front, and hurled back his brigade with heavy loss. Lytle was wounded, as he supposed mortally, and refused to be carried from the field. This opened the way for the victors to Gilbert's flank, held by Mitchell and Sheridan, whose front had been for a short time engaged. And now the true mettle of Sheridan, so tried in many a hard-fought battle afterward, was proven. He held the key point of the Union position, and was determined to keep it. In the morning he had driven the foe out of sight, and had just repelled an assault on his front, when he was obliged to meet the triumphant force which had thrown back Rousseau's right. He quickly turned his guns upon them, and was fighting gallantly, when Mitchell pushed up Carlin's brigade to the support of Sheridan's right. This force charged at the double quick, broke the line of the Confederates, and drove them through Perryville to the protection of batteries on the bluffs beyond.[2]

In the mean time the brigade of Colonel Gooding had been sent to the aid of McCook. Forming on the extreme left of the National line, it fought with great persistence for two hours against odds, and losing full one-third of its number,[3] with its commander, whose horse was shot under him, made prisoner. It was not until about this time (four o'clock in the afternoon)

---

[1] General Jackson was a member of Congress from the Second Kentucky District, having been chosen by a very large majority over his secession opponent in 1861.

[2] In this charge the Nationals captured fifteen heavily loaded ammunition wagons, two caissons with their horses, and a train-guard of one hundred and forty men.

[3] The brigade numbered only 1,423, and lost 549, killed, wounded, and missing.

that Buell was aware that a battle of much account—really one of the most sanguinary battles of the war, in proportion to numbers engaged—had been in progress. It had been raging for several hours, when he received from McCook a request for re-enforcements.[1] Buell at once sent them, and also orders for Crittenden, who was approaching, to hurry forward. The latter was too late to engage decisively in the conflict,[2] which ended at dark, when the Confederates, who had chosen their position for battle, were repulsed at all points. So ended the destructive BATTLE OF PERRYVILLE, or Chaplin's Hills, as it is sometimes called.[3] Preparations were made by the Nationals for a renewal of the conflict in the morning. Gilbert and Crittenden moved early for that purpose, but during the night the Confederates had retired in haste to Harrodsburg, where Bragg was joined by Kirby Smith and General Withers, and all fled toward East Tennessee, leaving twelve hundred of their sick and wounded at Harrodsburg, and abandoning at various points about twenty-five thousand barrels of pork.[4] The retreat was conducted by General Polk, and covered by the cavalry of the active General Wheeler. They fled into East Tennessee by way of Danville, Stanford, Crab Orchard, and Mount Vernon, followed by a large portion of Buell's army to Rock Castle River, in Rock Castle County. A division of Crittenden's corps was pushed on as far as Wild Cat and London, and then returned to Columbia, when the main army was put in motion for Nashville, under General Thomas, and Buell went to Louisville.[5] The Government was so dissatisfied with the result of this campaign against Bragg[6] that Buell was relieved of command,[a] and Major-General Rosecrans, who had won substantial victories in Mississippi, was put in his place. Then the designation of the *Army of the Ohio*, which Buell had commanded, was changed to that of the *Army of the Cumberland*.

[a] Oct. 30, 1862.

JOSEPH WHEELER.

---

[1] See General Buell's Report to General Halleck, October 10, 1862.

[2] Wagner's brigade of Crittenden's corps went into action on Mitchell's right just at the close.

[3] Buell reported his effective force which advanced on Perryville, 58,000, of whom 22,000 were raw troops. He reported a loss in this battle of 4,348, of whom 916 were killed, 2,943 wounded, and 489 missing. Among the killed were Generals Jackson and Terrell, and Colonel George Webster, of the Ninety-eighth Ohio, who commanded a brigade. The Confederate loss is supposed to have been nearly the same as that of the Nationals in number. Bragg claimed to have captured fifteen guns and four hundred prisoners.

[4] So much property was abandoned on the way, or destroyed because of the inability of the Confederates to carry it with them, that it is probable they lost more in the way of outfit, waste of horses and mules, and the necessary expenses, than they gained by this great plundering raid.

[5] Reports of Generals Buell and Bragg, and their subordinate officers. Supplemental Report of the Committee on the Conduct of the War, volume II.

[6] The Confederates were equally disappointed, not because of any lack of effort on the part of Bragg, but because of the absence of demonstrations of a general feeling in Kentucky in favor of the conspirators. It was supposed that on the appearance of a large force like that of Kirby Smith, or the main army under

We have said that Rosecrans had won substantial victories in Mississippi. Let us look at the record.

When Halleck was called to Washington City, as we have observed, General Grant was left in command of his old army, and of the district of West Tennessee, with enlarged powers.[1] General Pope was called to Virginia, and General Rosecrans, who had gained fame in Western Virginia, was placed in command of that leader's forces, under Grant, to occupy Northern Mississippi and Alabama in the vicinity of Corinth, and eastward to Tuscumbia. His division was known as the *Army of the Mississippi*, with head-quarters at Corinth.

From June until September there were not many stirring military events in the region of Grant's command, excepting such as were connected with guerrilla operations, and he had an opportunity to reorganize and discipline his troops. So well had he disposed of his forces, and kept himself informed of the positions and numbers of the Confederates by continual cavalry reconnoissances, that he was able, without much danger to his district, to send troops, under orders from Washington, to Louisville, to the aid of Buell, while the latter was operating against Bragg and Smith, when moving toward Kentucky. This weakening of his forces tempted the Confederates in Mississippi, under Generals Price and Van Dorn,[2] to move toward the Tennessee River at the beginning of September; not, however, without the knowledge of the vigilant Grant, who was prepared to meet them.

When Bragg moved northward, supposing Rosecrans was crossing the Tennessee in pursuit, in conjunction with Buell, he ordered Price to follow. The latter, preparatory to such movement, first sent a heavy cavalry force, under General Armstrong, to cut Grant's communications and prepare the way for getting between him and Buell, and to operate on the latter's flank and rear while Bragg was moving into Kentucky. Armstrong advanced boldly, with over five thousand horsemen, to strike the Union forces at Bolivar, in Tennessee, and sever the railway there. He was repulsed[a] by less than one thousand men, under Colonel Leggett. On the following day he approached Jackson, and was again repulsed. This was repeated on the 1st of September at Britton's Lane, after a battle

[a] Aug. 30, 1862.

Bragg, there would be a general uprising in Kentucky that would swell the ranks of the invaders to a volume sufficient to enable them to sweep triumphantly the rich States of Ohio, Indiana, and Illinois, and bear back to the Tennessee, and beyond, food and clothing sufficient for the Confederate armies for a year. But with the exception of the great slaveholding region around Lexington, the people with whom the invaders came in contact were either generally passive or openly hostile; and so manifest was this feeling, that thousands of those who had joined the marauders dared not remain in the State, but fled with them, and became burdensome consumers of food. As in Maryland, so in Kentucky, the people generally refused to espouse the cause of the conspirators, who were confused and greatly disheartened by the disappointment of all their calculations of aid from these two powerful border States. Pollard, the Confederate historian, said (ii. 162) that "the South was bitterly disappointed in the manifestations of public sentiment in Kentucky," and that "the exhibitions of sympathy" were "meager and sentimental, and amounted to little practical aid" of the Confederate cause. "Indeed," he says, "no subject was at once more dispiriting and perplexing to the South than the cautious and unmanly reception given to our armies, both in Kentucky and in Maryland." He attributed it to a "dread of Yankee vengeance and a love of property," and expressed the belief that professions of attachment to the "Southern cause" in those States were made with no higher motive than "selfish calculation."

[1] See page 296.

[2] When about to march for Kentucky, Bragg informed[b] Van Dorn and Price of his movement, and that he should leave to them "the enemy in West Tennessee." Van Dorn had then established batteries at Port Hudson, secured the mouth of the Red River, and the navigation of the Mississippi to Vicksburg, and, being at liberty to devote more time to the northern portion of his department, he took position, accordingly, not far south of Grand Junction.

[b] Aug. 30.

of four hours with Illinois troops, under Colonel Dennis. Armstrong fled, leaving one hundred and seventy-nine dead and wounded on the field.

Grant promptly informed Rosecrans,[a] then at Tuscumbia, of this raid. The latter hastened to Iuka, a little village on the Memphis and Charleston railway, in Tishamingo County, Mississippi, a place of summer resort, on account of its healthfulness, the beauty of its surroundings, and especially for its fine mineral springs. There a large amount of stores had been gathered. Leaving the post in charge of Colonel R. C. Murphy, of the Eighth Wisconsin, with orders to remove the property to Corinth or destroy it, Rosecrans marched westward with Stanley's division to Clear Creek, seven miles east of Corinth, and encamped. Meanwhile the Missouri leader, Sterling Price, had moved northward from the vicinity of Tupelo, with about twelve thousand troops. He reached Jacinto on the 10th of September, when Murphy and his little force fled toward Corinth. Price moved forward, occupied Iuka, captured the National property there, and made his head-quarters at the fine mansion of Colonel J. L. Moore.

[a] Sept. 1, 1862.

IUKA SPRINGS.[1]

Grant had watched these movements in aid of Bragg with great interest, that he might penetrate the plans of the Confederates. The time had now come for him to act vigorously, and he put two columns in motion to crush the forces of the Missourian: one under General Rosecrans, to attack his flank and rear, and another under General Ord, to confront him. This combined movement began early in the morning of the 18th of September. General Ord, with about five thousand men, moved down to Burnsville, on the railway, seven miles west of Iuka, followed from Bolivar by as many troops under General Ross as Grant could

PRICE'S HEAD-QUARTERS.

[1] This is a view at the mineral springs in the village of Iuka, as it appeared when the writer sketched it late in April, 1866. There are two springs in a swale on the bank of Iuka Creek, a small stream that flows along the eastern border of the village. These were covered with neat pavilions. Close by the railway near by

spare. Rosecrans, meanwhile, moved with the separated divisions of Generals Stanley and C. S. Hamilton from Clear Spring with about nine thousand troops, through a drenching rain, and all bivouacked that night at Jacinto, on the Mobile and Ohio railway, nearly twenty miles southward from Iuka. On the morning of the 19th they pushed on in light marching order toward Iuka, with Mizner's cavalry, driving a Confederate guard from Barnett's Corners; and early in the afternoon Hamilton's division, moving cautiously, in expectation of hearing the co-operating guns of Ord, and skirmishing almost continually, was within two miles of Iuka, on densely wooded heights, at a cross-road connecting the highways running from the village to Jacinto and Fulton respectively. There Hamilton formed a line of battle and advanced his skirmishers, who found the Confederates in strong force and position along a deep ravine behind the crest of the hill. The skirmishers were driven back, and a severe battle was immediately begun.

VIEW ON THE IUKA BATTLE-GROUND.[1]

The ground, covered with underbrush, was difficult to operate upon; but, after much exertion, the Eleventh Ohio battery, under a heavy fire of grape, canister, and shell, was put in position on the crest of the hill, so as to command the road in front, with the Fifth Iowa, Colonel Matthias, and Twenty-sixth Missouri, Colonel Boomer, in support. At the same time Colonel Eddy, with the Forty-eighth Indiana, was holding ground under a terrible fire, a little in front of the battery to whose assistance the Fourth Minnesota, Captain Le Gro, and Sixteenth Iowa, Colonel Chambers, were speedily sent. The struggle of these few regiments against more than three times their number, led by General Price in person, was brave and unflinching, until Colonel Eddy was mortally wounded, and the remainder of his regiment was hurled back in disorder, leaving the battery (every horse of which had been killed, and seventy-two of the men, including nearly all of the officers, had been slain or wounded) to be seized by the Confederates. For the possession of these guns desperate charges and counter-charges were made, and they were repeatedly taken and retaken, until they were finally dragged from the field by the Confederates. The bravery of its commander, Lieutenant Sears, was specially commended.

While this struggle was going on, in which the movements were immediately directed by Brigadier-Generals Sanborn and Sullivan, Stanley's

---

was a very commodious public-house, well arranged for a pleasant summer residence, and called "Iuka Springs Hotel." When the writer was there a new proprietor was renovating it, the hotel and the grounds around the springs having been utterly neglected during the war. The house had been used as a hospital by both parties. Wearied and famished from excessive travel and lack of sleep and food, the author found absolute restoration by reposing there over night and part of a day, and making free use of the water. It must be a delightful place in summer, when the house and grounds are in order, for both invalids and pleasure-seekers.

[1] This little sketch shows the appearance of the battle-ground and the Jacinto road in front of the position of the Eleventh Ohio battery, looking toward Iuka. The largest tree with the immense wart was thickly dotted with the scars made by bullets and canister-shot, and those of the whole woods around it showed tokens of the battle.

division had come up, but the nature of the ground was such that more troops than were then engaged could not well be made useful, and only the Eleventh Missouri,[1] which was pushed to the front, and which gallantly assisted the Fifth Iowa and Twenty-sixth Missouri in driving the Confederates back to the ravine, participated in the battle. Stanley himself had been for some time at the front, assisting Hamilton and his officers. Colonel Perczel, with the Tenth Iowa and a section of Immell's battery, had foiled

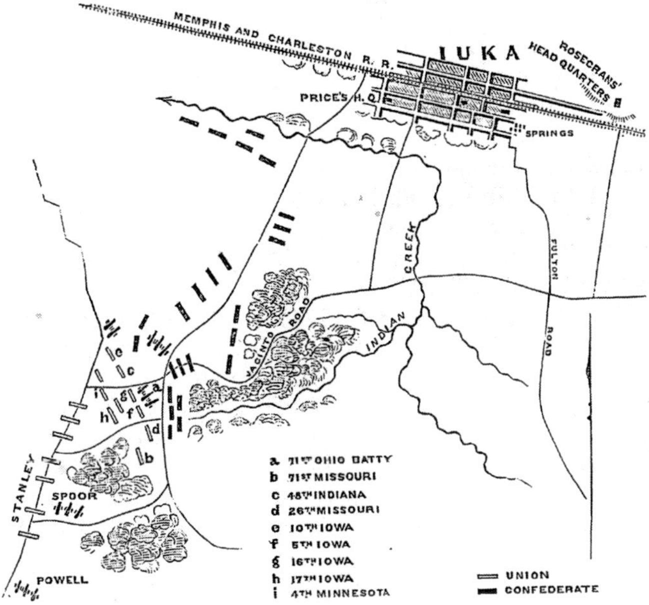

BATTLE OF IUKA.

the Confederates in an attempt to turn the National left, and soon afterward they were driven to the shelter of the hollows toward the town. Darkness came on, and THE BATTLE OF IUKA ended.

Where was Ord during the battle? He was expected to co-operate with Rosecrans, but did not. A greater portion of the day he had been watching the movements of a Confederate force upon Corinth, which proved to be only a feint. Leaving a portion of his force to strengthen the garrison at Corinth, he hastened to Burnsville, where he arrived at four o'clock, and found Ross waiting with about three thousand men. Grant ordered him immediately forward with about five thousand men, with directions to halt within four miles of Iuka, until he should hear Rosecrans's guns. A high wind from the northward prevented this, and there Ord lay in expectation of the summons until the next morning, when, hearing the sound of cannon, he pushed forward to Iuka, but not to find an enemy. Rosecrans and his victorious troops were there. They had rested on their arms during the

[1] This regiment, though organized in Missouri, was composed of citizens of Illinois, with the exception of about twenty men. For over half an hour it held its position in this battle without having a single round of ammunition.

night, expecting to renew the conflict in the morning; but when Stanley went forward at dawn for the purpose, he found that Price had fled southward along the Fulton road, under cover of the darkness, leaving behind him the guns of the Eleventh Ohio battery. A pursuit was immediately commenced that lasted all day, but Price had too much the start, and escaped. Marching to Ripley, in Mississippi, he joined[a] the larger force under Van Dorn, a detachment of which had been menacing Corinth, as we have seen, on the day of the battle at Iuka. Ord returned to Bolivar, and Rosecrans remained a few days in Iuka, making his head-quarters at the house of R. C. Brinkley, situated upon a hill a little eastward of the village.[1]

[a] Sept. 28, 1862.

ROSECRANS'S HEAD-QUARTERS.

The writer visited Iuka toward the close of April, 1866, and went over the battle-ground with Major George, a resident of the village, who had been one of the most active of the scouts of Forrest and Roddy in that region, and participated in the battle just described. We rode out in a carriage drawn by a span of spirited horses, driven by a colored boy only eight years and a half old, who managed them and the breaks of the vehicle, when going down steep hills and gullied ways, with all the skill of an experienced man. We passed along the Jacinto road to the crest of the hill on which the Eleventh Ohio battery was planted. It had been cleared of trees and underbrush, but a new growth nearly covered the ground, which at one place was white with the bleached bones of one hundred and fifty horses. Near by were the graves of the slain men of the Ohio battery, at the head

OUR COACHMAN.

[1] The disparity in numbers in this conflict was very great. "I say boldly," reported General Hamilton on the 23d of September, "that a force of not more than 2,800 men met and confronted a rebel force of 11,000 on a field chosen by Price and a position naturally very strong, and with its every advantage inuring to the enemy." In another part of his report he says: "My division marched nineteen miles, fought a desperate battle with seven regiments against a rebel force, under General Price, of not less than eighteen regiments, won a glorious victory, lying at night on their arms, and the following morning chased the fleeing enemy fifteen miles." In a general order, issued on the 26th, Rosecrans repeats this substantially, and told them that they might well be proud of the battle of Iuka. He reported his loss at 782, of whom 144 were killed, 598 were wounded, and forty were missing. Among the wounded was the gallant Colonel Boomer, of the Twenty-sixth Missouri. We have no official returns of the Confederate loss. Pollard says it was about 800; but Rosecrans estimates from various data, such as 265 of them buried by his troops and over 700 wounded left in the hospitals, their total loss at 1,438. He captured from them 1,629 stand of arms, 13,000 rounds of ammunition, and a large quantity of equipments and stores.

of many of which were rude boards, each bearing the name of the sleeper beneath.[1] The kind-hearted major showed much feeling, as he leaned on one of them and mused, while the writer was making the annexed sketch. "Poor fellows!" he said, "they fought bravely. The war is over, and we are now friends. If you meet with any of their relatives, tell them to write to Major George, and he will do every thing in his power to restore to them the remains of their friends." After visiting every part of the battle-field, and making the sketches herewith given, we returned to Iuka, and the next morning the writer journeyed toward Nashville.

Corinth, where stirring events occurred at the close of May,[2] became the theater of more stirring events early in October. Rosecrans arrived there from Iuka on the 26th of September, and prepared to meet an expected attack upon the post by the combined armies of Price and Van Dorn. Ord, as we have seen, returned to Bolivar. Grant made his head-quarters at Jackson, in Mississippi. Sherman was holding Memphis, and Rosecrans, with about twenty thousand men, was left to hold Corinth and the region around it. The earth-works constructed there by Beauregard and Halleck had been strengthened under the direction of General Cullum, but they were modified, and new ones were constructed by Major F. E. Prime, Grant's Chief-Engineer, which were better adapted for the use of a smaller force than occupied them in May. The new line was made especially strong westward of Corinth, from which direction the foe was expected, and was much nearer the town than the old ones.

GRAVES OF THE ELEVENTH OHIO BATTERY-MEN.

Immediately after their junction at Ripley, a point about half way between Jacinto and Holly Springs, Price and Van Dorn prepared to march upon Corinth, the key to the military possession of Tennessee and co-operation with Bragg. If Corinth could be taken, and the force there driven back on the Tennessee and cut off, Bolivar and Jackson would easily fall, and then, upon the arrival of the exchanged prisoners of war, West Tennessee might soon be in possession of the Confederates, and communication with Bragg be established through Middle Tennessee. So reasoned Van Dorn.[3] Regarding "the attack on Corinth as a military necessity," he moved forward[a] in command of the combined forces

[a] Sept. 29, 1862.

[1] Many of the boards had fallen down or been removed. Those standing, and seen in the picture, contained the following names:—Lieutenant R. Bauer, Sergeant M. V. B. Hall, Corporal S. C. Gilmore, Privates W. H Bolser, C. Schefteni, C. P. Olsen, W. Crawford, J. Ettle, J. W. Brewer, J. H. Ingersoll, J. T. Malson, J. Dean, J. Casey, J. Taylor.

[2] See page 293.

[3] See Van Dorn's Report, Oct. 20, 1862.

(he ranked Price), numbering about twenty-two thousand men, and struck the Memphis and Charleston railway at Pocahontas,[a] about half way between Corinth and Grand Junction. On the night of the 2d the Confederate Army bivouacked at Chewalla, only ten miles from Corinth. It was difficult for Rosecrans to determine whether Van Dorn's destination was Corinth, Bolivar, or Jackson. He was prepared for any emergency. His cavalry—"the eyes of the army," as Rosecrans called them—were on the alert in every direction, and troops were thrown out toward the foe, to meet his advance. Skirmishing ensued, but it was not until the morning of the 3d[b] that Rosecrans felt assured that Corinth was Van Dorn's objective. Then, before dawn, he disposed his troops to meet him. Hamilton's division formed the right, Davies's the center, and McKean's the left; and a brigade of three regiments, under Colonel Oliver, with a section of artillery, was thrown well forward beyond Beauregard's old works, on the Chewalla road, along which it was ascertained the Confederates were advancing. The cavalry was disposed so as to watch every highway radiating from Corinth, for the commanding general, being unable to find a map of the country, was illy informed concerning the northwesterly approaches to the town. Such was the position of Rosecrans's army for battle on the morning of the 3d.

[a] Oct. 1 1862.

[b] October.

Colonel Oliver felt the pressure of the advancing force early that morning.[c] It was their vanguard, under General Mansfield Lovell,[1] which at about half-past seven encountered Oliver, who was well posted on a hill, with orders to hold it so firmly that the strength of the foe might be developed. He was soon hard pressed, when General McArthur was sent to his support. McArthur found the foe numerous, and he, too, was soon heavily pushed, and the Confederates moving to outflank him; but he called up four regiments from McKean's division to his assistance. Meanwhile Rosecrans, informed that the foe was in strong force, had directed Davies to send up two regiments. By this time a skirmish that seemed to be a feint to make a more important movement was developing into a regular battle, when the Confederates made a desperate charge, drove the Nationals from the hill, and captured two guns.

[c] Oct. 3.

WILLIAM S. ROSECRANS.

It was now evident that the Confederates had come to recapture Corinth, with its immense stores, and that this was the beginning of the struggle. McKean's division was accordingly drawn back to the ridge next beyond the inner intrenchments, in front of the town, with orders to close with his right

---

[1] It consisted of the brigades of Villipigue, Bowen, and Rust. Van Dorn's army advanced in the following order:—Lovell's corps, with its left resting on the Memphis and Charleston railway; Price's corps, composed of the divisions of Maury and Hebert, with its right resting on the same road; and Armstrong's cavalry on the extreme left.

on Davies's left. Hamilton's division was moved so as to touch Davies's right, and Stanley took position in close *échelon* with McKean, near Corinth.

While these movements were going on, the Confederates were pressing heavily on the National center. Davies was pushed back. He called upon Stanley for aid. Colonel Mower was sent with a brigade, and had just arrived, and Hamilton was coming in through a thicket on Lovell's left, when darkness fell, and the struggle ceased. Many brave men of the National army had fallen. General Oglesby was severely wounded, and General Hackelman was killed. The Confederates, elated by seeming success, enveloped Rosecrans's front, and rested on their arms with assurance of victory in the morning. Van Dorn believed Corinth would be his before the rising of the sun. So early as three o'clock, when McKean fell back, he had sent a shout of triumph to Richmond by telegraph,[1] that was followed by a melancholy moan thirty hours later.

The battle was renewed before dawn the next morning.[a] Both parties had spent the night in preparing for it. Rosecrans and his staff were on the field all night. The National batteries around Corinth were well manned, and a new one, mounting five guns, and called Fort Richardson, was constructed during the dark hours by sappers and miners, composed of negro slaves, under Captain Gau, at the left of Hamilton's division.[2] The Confederates had also thrown up redoubts, one of which was not more than two hundred yards in front of Battery Robinett, that covered the Chewalla road northward from Corinth. It was that Confederate battery that opened the fight. Its shells fell in the streets of Corinth, producing great consternation among the non-combatants. It was not answered until daylight, when Captain Williams, from Battery Williams (which, with Robinett, protected Stanley's division), opened his 20-pounder Parrott guns upon it, and silenced it in three minutes. The Confederates fled with two of the guns, leaving a third as a trophy for the Nationals.

[a] Oct. 4, 1862.

FORT ROBINETT.[3]

This disconcerted the Confederate plan of attack, which was for Price on

[1] "Our troops," he said, "have driven the enemy from their position. We are within three-fourths of a mile of Corinth. The enemy are huddled together about the town. Some on the extreme left still trying to hold their position. So far all is glorious."

[2] The batteries of the new fortifications constructed by Major Prime extended from a point near the railway, close to the southern borders of Corinth, around west of it to a point due north from the starting-point. These were named Battery Madison, Lathrop, Tannrath, Phillips, Williams, Robinett, Powell, and Richardson. See map on page 522.

[3] This is a view of Fort Robinett and the ground in front of it, as it appeared on the morning after the battle, with the exception of the dead bodies of the Confederates which strewed the ground. It is from a photograph made that day by G. S. and C. T. Smith, of Jackson, Mississippi, who kindly gave the writer a copy of it when he was there in April, 1866.

their left to open a cannonade (as he did) to attract the attention of the Nationals and keep them employed in that direction, while Lovell, on the right in strong force, should storm the works on the National left. The sudden crushing out of Price's battery changed the plan. It was followed by the severe musket-firing of skirmishers in the thickets between the belligerents, and random thunderings of batteries. Finally, at a little after nine o'clock, the Confederates, in heavy masses, suddenly came out from cover northward of the railway, advanced rapidly along the Bolivar road, and in wedge form fell fiercely upon Davies and Fort Powell on the National right center, intending to penetrate Corinth. The struggle was very severe. Grape and canister shot made fearful lanes through the Confederate ranks, yet they pressed up most gallantly in the face of the storm.[1] A portion of Davies's division gave way, but was soon rallied. The sudden weakness encouraged the assailants, and they pressed forward, captured Fort Powell, and a score of them penetrated the town to the head-quarters of Rosecrans, on the public square, which they captured. Sheltered by its portico and angles, they fired upon the Nationals on the opposite side of the square. But their triumph was short lived. The column that had pushed Davies back was in turn assailed by a section of Immell's battery, supported by the Tenth Ohio and Fifteenth Minnesota, and driven toward the forest, when Sullivan coming to the aid of Davies, Fort Powell was retaken. This was accomplished by a charge of the Fifty-sixth Illinois. At the same time, the guns of Hamilton (who had fallen back with Davies) on the extreme right were making dreadful havoc in the Confederate ranks. The foe was

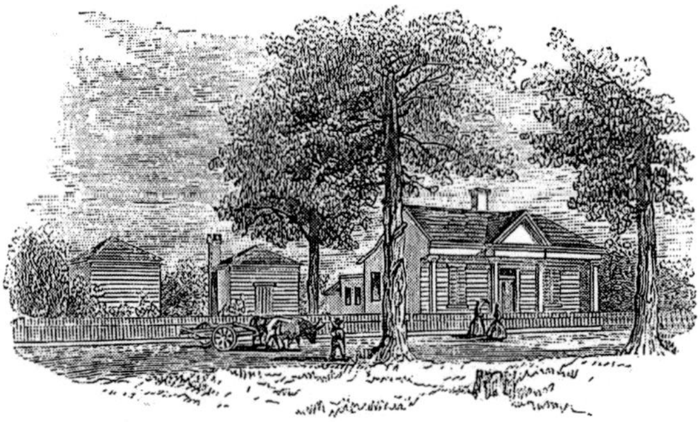

ROSECRANS'S HEAD-QUARTERS.[2]

[1] An eye-witness (correspondent of the *Cincinnati Commercial*) says the soldiers "marched steadily to death, *with their faces averted, like men striving to protect themselves against a driving storm of hail.*"

[2] This was the appearance of the house when the writer sketched it, late in April, 1866. It was the residence of Hampton Mark. During the battle, at the time mentioned in the text, it was much injured; but at the time of the writer's visit it was in good order. The correspondent of the *Cincinnati Commercial*, who was present, says, "Seven rebels were killed within the little inclosure in front of the General's cottage." Obliquely across the square was the public-house, known as the "Verandah Hotel," kept by Dr. Gibson, the post-master of Corinth, when the writer visited that place. This was the head-quarters of General Bragg at the time of the siege of Corinth, at the close of May, 1862, and was one of the few dwellings in that village that survived the storms of the war. It was used as a hospital, and bore many scars made by the conflict. During the occupation of Corinth by the Confederate Army, General A. S. Johnston's quarters were at the Tishamingo Hotel (which was burned), Polk's were at the house of the Widow Hayes, and Hardee's at the house of Dr. Stout.

BRAGG'S HEAD-QUARTERS.

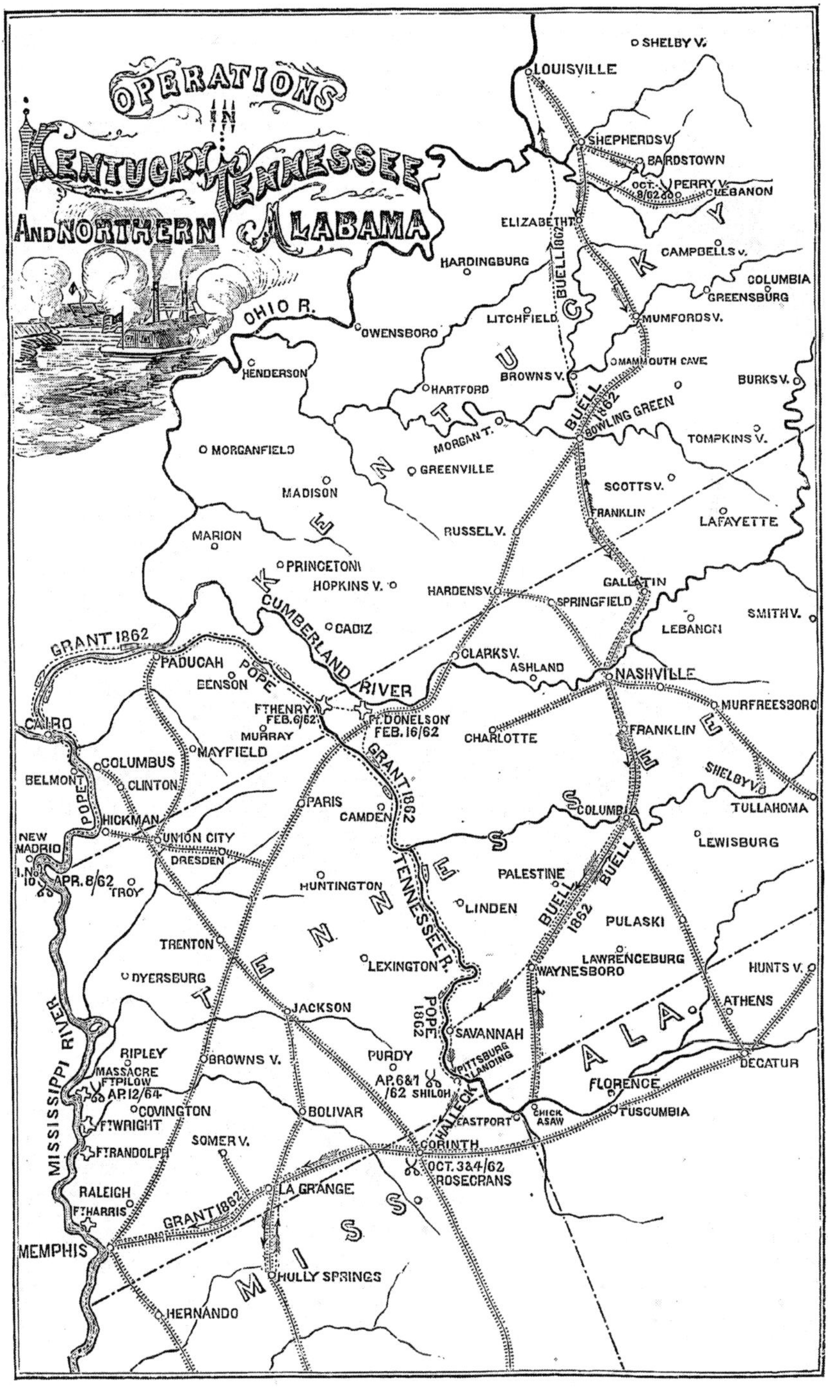
OPERATIONS IN KENTUCKY, TENNESSEE AND NORTHERN ALABAMA
SHELBY V.
LOUISVILLE
SHEPHERDSV.
BARDSTOWN
OCT. 8/62
PERRY V.
LEBANON
ELIZABETHT.
BUELL 1862
CAMPBELLS V.
HARDINGBURG
COLUMBIA
GREENSBURG
OHIO R.
OWENSBORO
LITCHFIELD
MUMFORDSV.
MAMMOUTH CAVE
HENDERSON
HARTFORD
BROWNS V.
BURKSV.
BUELL 1862
BOWLING GREEN
MORGANT.
TOMPKINS V.
MORGANFIELD
GREENVILLE
SCOTTSV.
MADISON
FRANKLIN
LAFAYETTE
RUSSELV.
MARION
PRINCETON
HOPKINS V.
HARDENSV.
GALLATIN
SPRINGFIELD
SMITHV.
LEBANON
CUMBERLAND RIVER
CADIZ
GRANT 1862
CLARKSV.
ASHLAND
NASHVILLE
PADUCAH
POPE
BENSON
RIVER
FT. HENRY FEB. 6/62
FT. DONELSON FEB. 16/62
MURFREESBORO
CAIRO
MURRAY
CHARLOTTE
FRANKLIN
MAYFIELD
COLUMBUS
BELMONT
CLINTON
POPE
SHELBYV.
GRANT 1862
PARIS
TULLAHOMA
HICKMAN
CAMDEN
COLUMBIA
NEW MADRID
UNION CITY
LEWISBURG
I. No. 10
DRESDEN
APR. 8/62
TROY
PALESTINE
BUELL
HUNTINGTON
TENNESSEE R.
LINDEN
BUELL 1862
PULASKI
TRENTON
LAWRENCEBURG
DYERSBURG
LEXINGTON
WAYNESBORO
HUNTS V.
JACKSON
POPE 1862
ATHENS
SAVANNAH
MISSISSIPPI RIVER
RIPLEY
PURDY
PITTSBURG LANDING
DECATUR
MASSACRE FT. PILOW AP. 12/64
BROWNS V.
AP. 6&7 /62 SHILOH
HALLECK
FLORENCE
COVINGTON
BOLIVAR
EASTPORT
CHICKASAW
TUSCUMBIA
FT. WRIGHT
CORINTH
FT. RANDOLPH
SOMER V.
OCT. 3&4/62 ROSECRANS
RALEIGH
LA GRANGE
FT. HARRIS
GRANT 1862
MEMPHIS
HOLLY SPRINGS
HERNANDO
KENTUCKY
TENNESSEE
MISS.
ALA.

speedily hurled back in great disorder, and casting away all incumbrances, fled to the woods, closely pursued by the victors with shouts of triumph.

In the mean time Lovell, whose attack on the National left was to have been simultaneous with that of Price on the right, had done his best. He sent forward a heavy skirmish-line, and with four columns of attack, composed chiefly of Texans and Mississippians, he pressed on in the face of the artillery fire from two batteries, and fell upon Fort Robinett and the adjacent lines. A bloody battle ensued, and great bravery was exhibited on both sides. Forts Robinett and Williams swept the approaching lines fearfully with grape and canister. Steadily those lines moved on and reached the ditch, where they paused for a moment—a fatal moment—before making the contemplated charge. Then Colonel Rogers, a brave acting-brigadier of Texas, with the new Confederate flag[1] in one hand, and a revolver in the other, leaped the ditch, scaled the parapet, and, with five companions, fell forward dead within the fort. There was

CONFEDERATE FLAG.

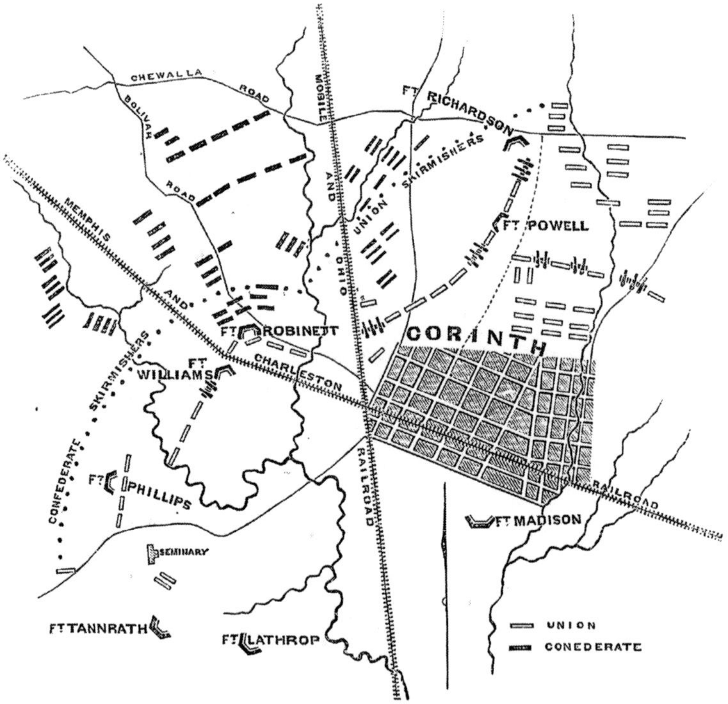

BATTLE OF CORINTH.

a power behind that parapet unsuspected by the Confederate leader. It was the Ohio brigade of Colonel Fuller,[2] which had lain prone until the foe was

[1] By a recent act of the "Congress" at Richmond the design of the Confederate flag had been changed. Instead of the "Stars and Bars" first adopted (see page 256, volume I.), it was a white flag, with the Union represented by stars on a blue field, arranged in the form of a cross. This was the style of the flag until the close of the war.

[2] Composed of the Twenty-seventh, Thirty-ninth, Forty-third, and Sixty-third Ohio, and Eleventh Missouri, Colonel Mower.

at the ditch, when portions suddenly rose and delivered such murderous volleys that the assailants recoiled. In a moment they rallied and came again to the encounter. The Eleventh Missouri and Twenty-seventh Ohio gave them fearful volleys, and then the word "Charge!" rang out along the line. The Nationals poured over the parapet, engaged in a terrible hand-to-hand fight with the assailants, and soon sent them flying in wildest confusion to the shelter of the forest. By noon THE BATTLE OF CORINTH was ended, and the whole Confederate force was retreating southward.

Rosecrans ordered five days' rations and a rest until the next morning for his gallant troops (who had been marching and fighting for forty-eight hours), preparatory to a vigorous pursuit. Just before sunset General McPherson arrived, with five fresh regiments sent by General Grant, and early in the morning he went forward as the advance of the pursuers, and followed the Confederates fifteen miles that day. In the mean time another division from Grant, under General Hurlbut, which had been pushed forward to attack the Confederate rear or intercept their retreat, had met the head of Van Dorn's column near Pocahontas, on the morning of the 5th, and was driving it back across the Hatchee, toward Corinth, at Davis's Bridge, when General Ord, who ranked Hurlbut, came up and took the command. There was severe fighting there, in what is known as THE BATTLE OF THE HATCHEE, where the Confederates lost two batteries, and three hundred men made prisoners. Ord had fallen severely wounded during the engagement, and Hurlbut resumed the command.[1] His force was inferior, and he did not pursue. The Confederates made a wide circuit, and crossed the Hatchee at Crown's bridge, a few miles farther south, burning it behind them. McPherson, coming up, rebuilt it, and on the following day[a] pushed on in pursuit. The greater portion of the National army followed the fugitives to Ripley, and their gallant leader, satisfied that he could soon overtake and capture or destroy Van Dorn's army, was anxious to continue the pursuit. Grant thought it best not to go farther, and Rosecrans was recalled. The fugitives had been followed forty miles by the main body of the victors, and sixty miles by the cavalry.[2]

[a] Oct. 6, 1862.

A few days after his return to Corinth, and while the country was ringing with his praises, Rosecrans was relieved from his command, and ordered to report at Cincinnati, where he found orders for him to supersede Buell in command of the Army of the Ohio, which, as we have observed, was now called the Army of the Cumberland.

---

[1] In this conflict General Veatch was also wounded. Ord's loss in that pursuit was heavier than that of the flying Confederates, who made a stand at three well-covered places, in succession.

[2] General Rosecrans reported his loss in the battle of Corinth and in the pursuit at 2,359, of whom 315 were killed, 1,812 wounded, and 232 missing. We have no official report of the loss of the Confederates. Rosecrans estimated it at 1,423 killed, 5,692 wounded, and 2,248 prisoners, making a total of 9,363. Pollard admits that their loss was more than 4,500. Among the trophies were 14 flags, 2 guns, and 3,300 small arms. Rosecrans says that, according to the Confederate authority, they had 38,000 men in the battle, and that his own force was less than 20,000. General Hackelman was among the loyal slain.

CHAPTER XX.

EVENTS WEST OF THE MISSISSIPPI AND IN MIDDLE TENNESSEE.

THE repulse of the Confederates at Corinth was followed by brief repose in the Department over which General Grant had command, and which, by a general order of the 16th of October, was much extended, and named the *Department of the Tennessee*,[1] with head-quarters at Jackson. He made a provisional division of it into four districts, commanded respectively by Generals W. T. Sherman, S. A. Hurlbut, C. S. Hamilton, and T. A. Davies—the first commanding the district of Memphis, the second that of Jackson, the third the district of Corinth, and the fourth the district of Columbus.

Vicksburg, a city of Mississippi, situated on a group of high eminences known as the Walnut Hills, on the eastern bank of the Mississippi River, at a bold turn of the stream, and a point of great military importance, had been fortified by the Confederates,[2] and was daily growing stronger. It was becoming a Gibraltar for them in opposing the grand scheme of the Nationals for gaining the command of the Great River, and thus severing important portions of the Confederacy. Toward the seizure of that point operations in the southwest were now tending. Vicksburg was not in General Grant's department, but its capture became his great objective, as well as that of others, and for that purpose a large portion of his forces had moved southward, and at the beginning of December had taken post between Holly Springs and Coldwater, on the two railways diverging from Grenada, in Mississippi, and the Tallahatchee River, behind which lay the Confederates in strength. There he was prepared to co-operate with the National forces westward of the Mississippi, and on the river below. That we may have a clear understanding of the relations of these co-operating forces, let us glance a moment at their antecedents, and especially their more recent movements. These forces, in other forms and numbers, we left, in former chapters, some under General Curtis, after the battle of Pea Ridge,[3] and others under General Butler[4] and Admiral Farragut.[5]

Let us first follow the fortunes of Curtis's army after the battle of Pea Ridge. We left it at Batesville, on the White River, in Arkansas, on the

[1] The newly organized Department included Cairo, Forts Henry and Donelson, Northern Mississippi, and those portions of Tennessee and Kentucky lying west of the Tennessee River.

[2] Here was the first blockade of the Mississippi. See page 164, volume I.

[3] See page 253. [4] See page 352. [5] See page 345.

6th of May,[1] where Curtis expected to find gun-boats and supplies, in charge of Colonel Fitch. The lowness of the water in the river had prevented their ascent, and one of the war-vessels had been destroyed by explosion in a struggle with a Confederate battery at St. Charles. This was a great disappointment to Curtis, for he had expected to advance on Little Rock, the capital of Arkansas. Being compelled to depend for his supplies by wagon-trains from Rolla, far up in Missouri, he did not feel warranted in making aggressive movements, and he remained at Batesville until the 24th of June, when he moved on toward the Mississippi, crossing the Big Black River on pontoon bridges, and traversing a dreary country, among a thin and hostile population, until he reached Clarendon, on the White River, a little below the mouth of the Cache River.

Curtis was joined at Jacksonport[a] by General C. C. Washburne, with the Third Wisconsin cavalry, which had made its way down from Springfield, in Missouri, without opposition. Southward the whole army moved, across the cypress swamps and canebrakes that line the Cache, and on the 7th of July the advance (Thirty-third Illinois), under Colonel A. P. Hovey, was attacked by about fifteen hundred Texas cavalry, led by General Albert Rust. Hovey halted until Lieutenant-Colonel Wood came up, with the First Indiana cavalry and two howitzers, when these re-enforcements made an impetuous charge, and put the foe to flight with heavy loss. They left one hundred and ten of their dead to be buried by the victors. The latter lost eight killed and forty-five wounded.

[a] June 25, 1862.

Curtis was again doomed to disappointment on reaching the White River at Clarendon, where he expected to meet gun-boats and supplies. These had gone down the river only twenty-four hours before his arrival. He was now short of provisions, and the people being intensely hostile, he felt compelled to go to the Mississippi by as short a journey as possible. After a most wearisome march of sixty-five miles, he reached Helena, in Phillips County, between the 11th and 13th of July. Washburne, with twenty-five hundred cavalry and five howitzers, had marched that distance in twenty-four hours. The infantry brought with them a few Arkansas volunteers, and a large number of negroes, who sought liberty and protection under the old flag.

Both the National and Confederate powers were weak in Arkansas at this time. Price and Van Dorn, with their armies, and a large number of the Arkansas troops, had been called to Corinth and vicinity, and when Governor Rector summoned militia to defend his capital when Curtis menaced it, the response was so feeble that he fled from the State, leaving the archives to be carried to Arkadelphia, more in the interior. Ten regiments had been drawn from Curtis to re-enforce the army in Tennessee about to attack Corinth, and he had not strength enough to seize the Arkansas capital. Rector's flight left the State without a civil head, and John S. Phelps, of Missouri, was appointed its military governor, but he could not take his seat in the capital, and his authority was nominal.

In the mean time National war-vessels had ascended the Mississippi to Vicksburg, and above, and exchanged greetings with others which had come down from Cairo. When New Orleans was fairly in the possession of the

---

[1] See page 260.

military power under Butler, Commodore Farragut sent a portion of his force up the river, for the purpose of reducing such posts on its banks as were held by the Confederates. Baton Rouge, the capital of Louisiana, was captured on the 7th of May without resistance. The Mayor refused to surrender it formally. So Commander Palmer, of the *Iroquois*, landed, and

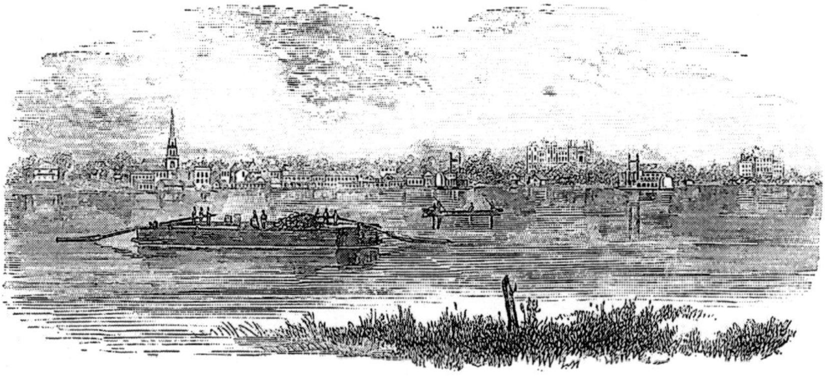

BATON ROUGE.

"repossessed" the National arsenal there.[1] Farragut arrived soon afterward, and the naval force moved on, with the advance under Commander S. P. Lee, on the *Oneida*, as far as Vicksburg,[a] without opposition. There the troops of Lovell, who fled from New Orleans, after having halted at different places, were now stationed. Lee summoned[b] the city to surrender, and was answered by a respectful refusal by the Mayor, and a preposterous note of defiance from "James L. Autry, Military Governor and Commandant Post."[2] M. L. Smith, the "Brigadier-General Commanding," also refused, and Lee prudently awaited the arrival of Farragut with the remainder of his squadron, a portion of Porter's mortar-fleet, and transports with four thousand land troops under General Thomas Williams. The latter were sent by General Butler to occupy and hold places that might be captured by the navy. It was expected that batteries would be found on the bluffs at Port Hudson, Elles's Cliffs, Natchez, and Grand Gulf, but no serious resistance was offered at those places. Williams landed below Elles's Cliffs, and made a circuit in the rear to capture a battery on their crown, but the troops had fled with their guns. There were no signs of opposition at Natchez, but fearing it at Grand Gulf, the troops landed, took possession of the town, and, in retaliation for being fired upon, they burned it before they left.

a May, 1862.

b May 18.

The whole force appeared off Vicksburg on the 26th of June, and that night the gun and mortar boats opened fire on the formidable Confederate batteries there. These were too elevated to be much damaged by the bombardment, and, after two days of almost ineffectual firing, Farragut deter-

[1] See notice of its capture by the insurgents on page 181, volume I. The large turreted building seen in the above picture, above al. the others, is the State-House of Louisiana.

[2] "I have to state," said Autry, "that Mississippians don't know, and refuse to learn, how to surrender to an enemy. If Commodore Farragut or Brigadier-General Butler can teach them, let them come and try."

mined to run by them. This he did without much harm,[1] at three o'clock on the morning of the 28th, with the flag-ship *Hartford* and six other vessels, leaving the mortar-fleet and transports below, and met the gun and mortar flotilla of Commodore Davis, and the steam-rams, under the younger Ellet

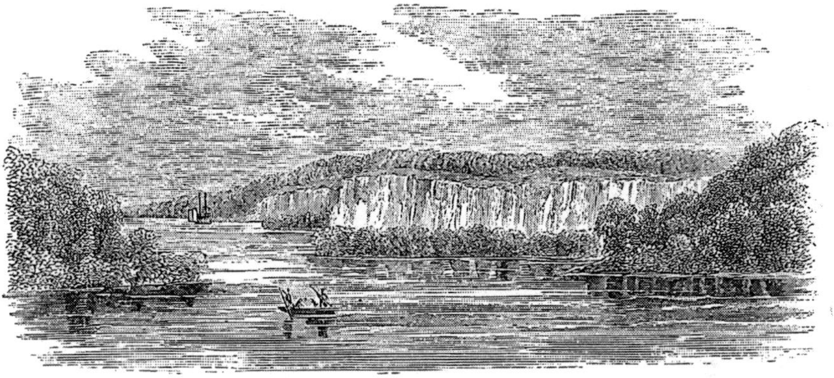

ELLES'S CLIFFS.[2]

(the elder having just died at Cairo), who had come down from Memphis. Williams, under the direction of Farragut, made an attempt, with twelve hundred negroes, to cut a canal across the peninsula opposite Vicksburg, through which his transports might pass in safety, but failed; and such was the result of a bombardment by the floating batteries above and below the town. So, in the course of a few days, the siege was temporarily abandoned.

A startling rumor now reached Farragut, to the effect that a formidable "ram" was lying in the Yazoo River, which empties into the Mississippi above Vicksburg. She had been commenced at Memphis, and two days before the evacuation of Fort Pillow[3] she was towed down the river with materials sufficient to finish her. She was now completed, with low-pressure engines possessing in the aggregate nine hundred horse-power, and was named *Arkansas*.[4] Farragut sent the gun-boats *Carondelet* and *Tyler*, and Ellet's ram, the *Queen of the West*, to reconnoiter her position. They passed cautiously up the Yazoo on the 15th, about six miles, when suddenly they encountered the formidable foe. A sharp contest ensued, in which the armored *Carondelet*, Captain Walke, bore the most con-

DAVID G. FARRAGUT.

[1] He lost by the fire of the batteries fifteen killed and thirty wounded.

[2] This is from a sketch of the Cliffs made by the writer from the steamer *Indiana*, in April, 1866. These cliffs, on the east bank of the river, are at a sharp turn in the stream, about eighteen miles below Natchez. They are of yellow clay, and rise from one hundred and fifty to two hundred feet above the water.

[3] See page 298.

[4] This was a sea-going steamer of 1,200 tons burden, and had a cutwater composed of a sharp, solid beak of

spicuous part. After a severe contest, in which the *Carondelet* was badly injured and lost fourteen men killed and wounded, and the *Arkansas* twenty-five killed and wounded, the latter, beating off and much damaging her antagonists, made her way down the Yazoo into the Mississippi, and took shelter under the batteries at Vicksburg.

Farragut now ran past the Vicksburg batteries again, and anchored below, and he and Davis abandoned the bombardment of that post. On the 22d[a] another attempt was made to capture or destroy the *Arkansas.* The *Essex*, Captain W. D. Porter, and Ellet's *Queen of the West* were employed for the purpose, while the gun-boats were bombarding the batteries above and below the town. The attempt was not successful, and, as the river was falling fast, and thus made naval operations less efficient, the siege of Vicksburg was abandoned, under instructions from Washington, and Farragut's fleet returned to New Orleans on the 28th. His transports having been annoyed by the firing upon them of a guerrilla band at Donaldsonville, on the left bank of the river, at the mouth of the Bayou

[a] July, 1862.

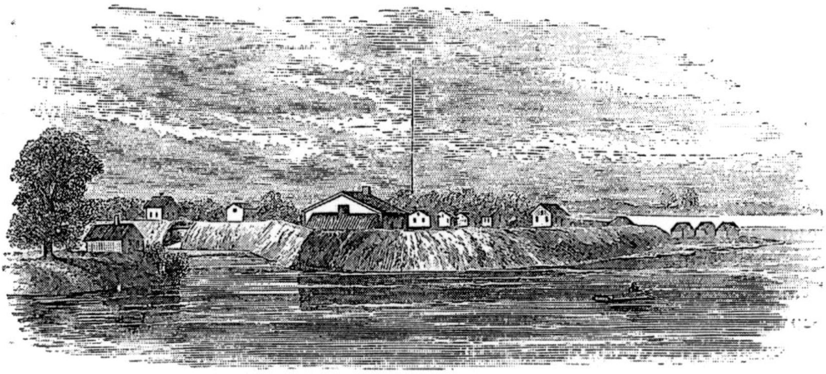

FORT BUTLER, AT DONALDSONVILLE.[1]

La Fourche, he ordered that village to be bombarded, after warning the inhabitants of his intention. Much of the town was destroyed.[b] It was afterward occupied by National troops, who built a strong earthwork there, and named it Fort Butler.

[b] Aug. 10.

When Farragut descended the river, General Williams and the land-troops debarked at Baton Rouge, for the purpose of permanently occupying it. Re-enforcements were sent to him, and Farragut took a position to give him aid in holding the place if necessary. Williams's troops were suffering severely from sickness, and this fact, in an exaggerated form, having been communicated to Van Dorn by resident secessionists, he organized an expedition to capture the post. It was composed of about five thousand men, under General J. C. Breckenridge, who expected to be aided by the ram

cast-iron, sixteen feet in length, covering the bow ten feet, and bolted through solid timber eight feet. She was covered with T-rail iron, with heavy thick timber bulwarks and cotton-pressed casemating, and was impervious to shot. She had a battery of ten 64-pounders and 32-pounders rifled, and was commanded by the best officers in the Confederate service.—Statement of Captain Walke.

[1] This was the appearance of Fort Butler and vicinity when the writer sketched it from the *Indiana*, just at the close of a bright April day, 1866. The mouth of the Bayou La Fourche is seen between the small building on the left and the fort.

Arkansas. He approached the city with General Daniel Ruggles, of Massachusetts, leading his left wing, and General Charles Clarke his right.[1] With his entire force moving along the two roads that enter Baton Rouge from the southwest, he made a vigorous attack at the early morning twilight of the 5th of August.

Williams was expecting an attack, and had well disposed his troops to meet it, both from land and water, as Confederate gun-boats had come out of the Red River, and the *Arkansas* was expected. His forces consisted of only about twenty-five hundred effective men. The regiments were very thin, on account of sickness. He posted the Fourth Wisconsin on Bayou Gros, on the extreme left, with a portion of Manning's battery in the Arsenal grounds on its left. On the right of that regiment was the Ninth Connecticut, with four of Manning's guns, in the Government cemetery. To the left of the Greenwell Springs road was the Fourteenth Maine; and next came the Twenty-first Indiana, posted in the woods in rear of the Magnolia Cemetery, with four guns of Everett's battery. Then the Sixth Michigan was posted across the country road on the right of the cemetery and the Clay Cut road, with two guns. In the rear of the two last-named regiments was the Seventh Vermont, near the Catholic Cemetery, and next the Thirtieth Massachusetts, forming the right, posted about half a mile in the rear of the State-House, and supporting Nim's battery.[2]

The first blow in the attack fell upon the Fourth Maine, Second Indiana, and Sixth Michigan. They were at first pushed back, when General Williams ordered up the Ninth Connecticut, Fourth Wisconsin, and a section of Manning's battery to the support of the left, and the Thirtieth Massachusetts and two sections of Nimm's battery to the support of the right. The battle raged fiercely for about two hours, and in the hottest of the fray the Twenty-first Indiana was grandly conspicuous. It lost all of its field-officers before the end of the action.[3] Seeing this, General Williams placed himself at its head, exclaiming, "Boys! your field-officers are all gone; I will lead you." They gave him hearty cheers, when a bullet passed through his breast, and he fell dead. He had just issued directions for the line to fall back, which it did in good order, with Colonel T. W. Cahill, of the Ninth Connecticut, in chief command. The Confederates, dreadfully smitten, also fell back, and then retreated. So ended THE BATTLE OF BATON ROUGE.[4]

The dreaded *Arkansas*, which was expected to sweep every National vessel from the Mississippi, and "drive the Yankees from New Orleans," did not appear in time for the fight. On the following morning, Porter, with the *Essex*, accompanied by the *Cayuga* and *Sumter*, went up the river to meet her. They found her five miles above Baton Rouge, when an engagement ensued. Owing to defects in her engines, the *Arkansas* became unmanageable, when she was headed to the river-bank, and set on fire. Her magazine exploded, and the monster was blown into fragments.

---

[1] Breckenridge's troops consisted of two Louisiana, two Mississippi, six Kentucky, and two Tennessee regiments, and one Alabama regiment, with thirteen guns and a considerable guerrilla force.

[2] Report of Lieutenant Godfrey Weitzel to General Butler, August 7, 1862.

[3] Lieutenant-colonel Keith and Major Hayes were severely wounded, and Adjutant Latham was killed.

[4] See reports of Colonels Cahill, Dudley, and others, and Lieutenant Weitzel. The National loss was reported eighty-two killed, two hundred and fifty-five wounded, and thirty-four missing. The Confederate loss is not known. The Nationals took about one hundred of them prisoners.

Soon after the repulse of the Confederates at Baton Rouge, that post was evacuated by the Nationals, and Porter ascended the river to reconnoiter batteries said to be in course of construction at Port Hudson. He passed up above to Bayou Sara to coal, where guerrillas fired upon him. The little town was destroyed in consequence. Because of the fiendish act of armed citizens of Natchez in firing on a boat's crew who went on shore to procure ice for sick men, that city was bombarded by the *Essex*, set on fire, and captured. The *Essex* then turned back, and on her passage down the river had a short and sharp contest[a] with the growing batteries at Port Hudson.

[a] Sept. 7, 1862.

General Butler was satisfied, at the beginning of September, that the Confederates had abandoned all idea of attempting to retake New Orleans, and he sent out some aggressive expeditions. The most important movement of this kind was to "repossess" the rich district of La Fourche, on the west side of the Mississippi, and for that purpose he sent the gallant Weitzel, then a brigadier-general, with a brigade of infantry, with artillery and Barnet's cavalry. Late in October, Weitzel landed at Donaldsonville, and traversed the region in its rear and south of it with very little difficulty, after a sharp fight near Labadieville on the 27th.[b] The Confederates, under McPheeters, were there on both sides of the Bayou La Fourche, with six pieces of artillery. Weitzel brought up his cannon and moved to the attack, with the Thirteenth Connecticut and Seventy-fifth New York in advance. A battle was soon opened, in which the Eighth New Hampshire and Twelfth Connecticut gallantly co-operated with the other two regiments. The batteries of Thompson and Carruth did eminent service. The Confederates were driven and pursued about four miles. Weitzel lost eighteen killed and seventy-four wounded. He captured two hundred and sixty-eight prisoners and one piece of artillery.

[b] October.

Weitzel now marched on through the country to open communication with the city by the bayou, and the railway connecting Brashear City with New Orleans. It was almost entirely abandoned by the white people, and the negroes received the victor joyfully as their deliverer. The industrial operations of the district were paralyzed, and General Butler thought it expedient, as a state policy and for the sake of humanity, to confiscate the entire property of the district. He did so, and he appointed a commission to take charge of it.[1] By that commission the negroes were employed and subsisted, and the crops were saved. Two Congressional districts in Louisiana were now recovered, and in December the loyal citizens of New Orleans elected to seats in Congress Benjamin F. Flanders and Michael Hahn, the number of Union votes in the city exceeding by a thousand the number of votes cast for secession.

General Butler was superseded in the command of the Department of the Gulf late in the autumn[c] by General Banks. The latter arrived at New Orleans on the 14th of December, and was received by the commanding general with great courtesy. Banks formally assumed his new duties on the 16th, and on the 24th, Butler, after issuing an admirable fare-

[c] Nov 9.

---

[1] This commission consisted of Major J. M. Bell, Lieutenant-colonel J. B. Kinsman, and Captain Fuller, of the Seventy-fifth New York Volunteers, the latter being made provost-marshal of the district.

well address to the citizens,[1] embarked in a steamer for New York. His administration had been marked by great vigor and justice, as the friend and defender of the loyal and the oppressed, and the uncompromising foe of the rebellious.[2] He took with him thirteen thousand seven hundred soldiers for the capture of New Orleans, and he turned over to his successor seventeen thousand eight hundred well-drilled and disciplined men, among whom, as we have observed, were regiments of colored troops.

In the mean time some active military operations had been in progress in Missouri and Arkansas. For some time General Curtis, whom we left at Helena,[3] was unable to do much more than menace Little Rock and watch and smite guerrilla bands, which, in conjunction with others in Missouri, soon crystallized into quite a formidable army, as we shall observe presently.

Since the autumn of 1861, General J. M. Schofield, Lyon's second at the battle of Wilson's Creek,[4] had been in command of the militia of Missouri, and in June, 1862, that State was erected into a separate military district, with Schofield at its head. He was vigilant and active; but when Curtis withdrew to the Mississippi, and left Arkansas and Southern Missouri open to the operations of guerrilla bands, then numerous in the western part of the former State, he found his forces inadequate to keep down the secessionists in his district. When Price crossed the Mississippi, early in May, he sent back large numbers of Missourians to recruit guerrilla bands for active service during the summer, and these, at the middle of July, were very numerous in the interior, and were preparing to seize important points in the State. To meet the danger, Schofield obtained authority from the Governor to organize all the militia of the State. This drew a sharp dividing line between the loyal and disloyal inhabitants. He soon had fifty thousand names on his rolls, of whom nearly twenty thousand were ready for effective service at the close of July, when the failure of the campaign against Richmond so encouraged the secessionists in Missouri, that it was very difficult to keep them in check.

Schofield's army of volunteers and militia was scattered over Missouri in six divisions,[5] and for two months a desperate and sanguinary guerrilla war-

[1] See Parton's *Butler in New Orleans*, page 603.

[2] General Butler found a large portion of the wealthier and more influential of the inhabitants of New Orleans, native and foreign, bitterly hostile to the Government. He also found that, in consequence of their rebellion, there was wide-spread distress among the poorer classes of the city, and he resolved to make the authors of their misery contribute largely to their relief. He discovered a list of contributors to the fund raised for the promotion of the rebellion, with the amount of their subscriptions, and he at once assessed them, for the relief of the poor, twenty-five per cent. of that amount. In various ways he made them play the part of benefactors of the poor. During the few months he was there, he collected, by fines, forfeitures, confiscations, taxation, and assessments, $1,088,000, all of which, as documentary evidence shows, he faithfully applied to the public service. He expended $525,000 in feeding the poor of New Orleans; he sent to the Government Treasury $345,000; and handed to the quartermaster and commissary of his successor about $200,000. He was cursed by the rebellious, and beloved by the loyal and oppressed.

In his farewell address General Butler said: "I saw that this rebellion was a war of the aristocrats against the middling men—of the rich against the poor: a war of the land-owner against the laborer; that it was a struggle for the retention of power in the hands of the few against the many; and I found no conclusion to it, save in the subjugation of the few and the disinthrallment of the many. I therefore felt no hesitation in taking the substance of the wealthy, who had caused the war, to feed the innocent poor who had suffered by the war. And I shall now leave you with the proud consciousness that I carry with me the blessings of the humble and loyal, under the roof of the cottage and in the cabin of the slave, and so am quite content to incur the sneers of the *salon* or the curses of the rich."

[3] See page 525.

[4] See page 50.

[5] Colonel John M. Neill, of the Missouri State Militia, commanded the northeastern part of the State; General Ben Loan the northwestern; General James Totten the central; General F. B. Brown the southwestern;

fare was carried on in the bosom of that Commonwealth, the chief theater being northward of the Missouri River, in McNeill's division, where insurgent bands under leaders like Poindexter, Porter, Cobb, and others, about five thousand strong, were very active. On the 6th of August,[a] McNeill, with one thousand cavalry and six guns, and Porter, with about twenty-five hundred men of all arms, had a desperate fight of four hours at Kirksville, in Adair County. Porter was defeated, with a loss of one hundred and eighty killed and about five hundred wounded, and several wagon-loads of arms. McNeill's loss was twenty-eight killed and sixty wounded. Four days later,[b] Colonel Odin Guitar, with six hundred horsemen and two guns, attacked and routed Poindexter's guerrillas, twelve hundred strong, while crossing the Chariton River in the night. Many of the guerrillas were driven into the river and were drowned. The survivors fled northward to join Porter, when they met Ben Loan, who forced them back and exposed them to another severe blow by Guitar. The forces of both guerrilla chiefs, as well as those of Cobb, were broken up and dispersed. From April until September, the loyal and disloyal warriors in Missouri were engaged in about one hundred combats.

[a] 1862.

[b] Aug. 10.

An attempt to aid the Missouri guerrillas was made by their more southern brethren early in August. Nearly eight hundred of these, under Colonel Hughes, attacked and captured[c] Independence, on the western border, with three hundred and twelve Missouri cavalry, under Lieutenant-colonel Buell; and, at about the same time, General Coffey, with fifteen hundred cavalry from Arkansas, invaded Southwestern Missouri, and pushed on rapidly northward to form a junction with Hughes and seize Lexington. He was followed by Colonel Clark Wright, with twelve hundred Missouri cavalry, and a combination was immediately formed to capture him, but failed.[1] The insurgent bands formed a junction, and in a combat at Lone Jack, in Jackson County, with Major Foster, who had sallied out of Lexington with eight hundred cavalry, they were successful. Foster was defeated, was wounded, and lost two of his guns. Coffey then pressed on with about four thousand five hundred men, when he was alarmed by intelligence that General James G. Blunt, then commanding in Kansas, was threatening his line of retreat with a strong force, while the commands of Loan and Wright were concentrating upon

[c] Aug. 11.

JAMES G. BLUNT.

Colonel J. M. Glover, of the Third Missouri cavalry, at Rolla; and Colonel Lewis Merrill, of the National Volunteer cavalry, at St. Louis.

[1] Totten was directed by Schofield to strike Hughes before he could join Coffey, while General Blunt, in Kansas, was requested to send a force from Fort Scott to co-operate in cutting off Coffey's retreat. At the same time Colonel Fitz-Henry Warren, with the First Iowa cavalry, was sent from Clinton with 1,500 men to effect a junction with Major Foster, whom Totten had sent out from Lexington in search of Hughes.

him. He suddenly turned his face southward, and, eluding Blunt while covered with darkness, he fled back into Arkansas with very little loss, hotly pursued to the borders of that State.

Missouri was now somewhat relieved, but the Confederates were gathering in force in Arkansas, where they were joined by conscripts from Southern Missouri, and a large number of troops from Texas. Their entire number was estimated to be fifty thousand at the middle of September, with General T. C. Hindman[1] in chief command, assisted by Generals Rains, Parsons, Cooper, McBride, and others. So threatening was this gathering, that Schofield took the field in person, and General Curtis succeeded him[a] in command of the District of Missouri.

[a] Sept. 24, 1862.

Schofield had at this time, at and near Springfield, over ten thousand troops, of whom eight thousand were available for active operations, after providing means for keeping open his communications. This was called the *Army of the Frontier*. Of these about five thousand were cavalry. He had also sixteen pieces of artillery, with a complement of men and horses. With these he moved toward Arkansas, with the knowledge that a considerable body of the foe was on his immediate front. General Salomon led the advance of over four thousand men. His vanguard was attacked at Newtonia,[b] when he moved forward with his whole force and joined in the struggle. After a contest which lasted all day, he was defeated, but with little loss, and retreated to Sarçoxie, covered by the brigade of Colonel Hall.

[b] Sept. 30.

Schofield pressed on to Sarcoxie, where he was joined by General Blunt, and the combined forces, ten thousand strong, pushed forward to attack the Confederates at Newtonia, whose number was estimated at about fifteen thousand. Blunt and Totten approached at different points, when the Confederates, who were illy equipped, fled without striking a blow, and were chased about thirty miles into Arkansas.

Schofield moved cautiously on, keeping his communications well guarded, and on the 17th of October he was on the old battle-ground of Pea Ridge. The Confederates were divided, a part, under General Cooper, having gone westward to Maysville, for the purpose of cutting the communications with Fort Scott, while the main body, under the immediate command of Rains, with about three thousand cavalry in the rear to mask the movement, were retreating toward Huntsville, in Madison County. Blunt was sent after Cooper, while Schofield, with his main army, made a forced march over the White River Mountains toward Huntsville, resting eight miles from that village, where Rains had encamped the day before.

Blunt made a hard night's march, and on the morning of the 22d of October[c] attacked Cooper at old Fort Wayne, near Maysville, captured his four guns, routed his men, and drove them in disorder toward Fort Gibson, in the Indian Territory. Schofield did not even get sight of the foe at Huntsville, for on his arrival there he found they were in full retreat over the mountains toward Ozark, with a determination to avoid a battle until expected re-enforcements should arrive. He pursued them some distance, when he turned northward, and marched to

[c] 1862.

---

[1] See page 191.

Cross Hollows and Osage Springs, near Pea Ridge.[1] There he learned that between three and four thousand Confederate cavalry were encamped on White River, eight miles from Fayetteville. He immediately ordered General Francis J. Herron to march with about a thousand cavalry to attack their rear, and General Totten to advance from Fayetteville and fall on their front. Herron first reached the foe. It was at the dawn of the 28th.[a] His attack was so vigorous that the Confederates fled to the mountains, leaving their camp equipage behind. Missouri was now comparatively secure from danger, and the importance of the services of Schofield was gratefully acknowledged by the loyalists of that State. Late in November he was compelled by sickness to resign his command, and leave it in charge of General Blunt.

FRANCIS J. HERRON.

[a] Oct., 1862.

General Hindman now prepared to strike a decisive blow for the recovery of his State. By a merciless conscription, and the concentration of scattered forces, he had collected in the western part of Arkansas over twenty thousand men at the close of November. Blunt, with the First division, was then at Lindsay's Prairie, fifteen miles south of Maysville, and on the 26th[b] was informed that Hindman's advance, consisting of a strong body of cavalry under Marmaduke, was at Cane Hill, about thirty miles south of him. On the following morning Blunt went forward with five thousand men, provisioned for four days, and thirty pieces of artillery, to attack Marmaduke. They marched twenty-seven miles that day, bivouacked at night, and at dawn the next morning his advance, composed of only two hundred of the Second Kansas cavalry, and his own staff and body-guard, with two mountain howitzers and Rabb's battery, were within half a mile of Marmaduke's camp before they met with resistance. The main body had been detained, and an artillery duel was kept up until their approach, when Marmaduke retreated to his reserves on the Boston Mountains, and took a good position on a height. Blunt, with his entire force, assailed him vigorously, and, by a charge of the Second Kansas cavalry, Third Cherokee Indians, and Eleventh Kansas infantry, he was driven away and compelled to retreat in the direction of Van Buren. Blunt then took position at Cane Hill. His loss in THE BATTLE OF BOSTON MOUNTAINS was four killed and thirty-six wounded. Marmaduke had seventy-five killed. The number of his wounded is not known.

[b] November.

Hindman now determined to crush Blunt, and on the 1st of December he crossed the Arkansas River at Van Buren with about eleven thousand men, including two thousand cavalry, and joined Marmaduke at a point fifteen miles northward. Informed of this, Blunt sent to Herron, then in Missouri,

---

[1] See map on page 258.

for assistance. That excellent officer was at Wilson's Creek when the message reached him, and within three hours afterward his divisions (Second and Third), which were fortunately much nearer the Arkansas border, were moving southward with guns and trains at the rate of twenty miles a day. They were at Elk Horn on the 5th,[a] when Herron sent forward his cavalry, three thousand strong, under Colonel Wickersham, for the immediate relief of Blunt, and, pressing on with the main army, he reached Fayetteville on the morning of the 7th, having marched all night. Resting there only one hour, he marched on for Cane Hill, and at the end of less than six miles he met a part of the cavalry he had dispatched from Elk Horn, who had been smitten and broken ten miles from Cane Hill by Marmaduke's horsemen.

[a] December, 1862.

Herron was now in a perilous position. For two days Blunt had been skirmishing with what he supposed to be the advance of Hindman's main army, when the fact was the Confederates had turned his left, were making for Blunt's trains, under the charge of General Salomons, at Rhea's Mill, and were interposing between him and Herron's infantry and artillery. This alarming fact he discovered on the 6th, and two hours afterward Wickersham, with four cavalry regiments,[1] arrived at Cane Hill, and reported that Herron would be at Fayetteville the next morning. Blunt tried to warn Herron of his danger, but failed, because of the vigilance of Marmaduke's cavalry; and that active and earnest officer was allowed to march on until he met the mounted vanguard of his enemy in force, at a little settlement on Illinois Creek, called Prairie Grove.

Herron was divested of his cavalry, and had only about four thousand men ready for action. He was in a strong position, and might have made a good defensive stand, but, unconscious of great danger near, and being intent on the relief of Blunt, he drove the Confederate cavalry across the Creek, when he was confronted by a force of infantry and artillery under Hindman, Parsons, and Frost, nearly twenty thousand strong. They were well posted on a wooded ridge, three-fourths of a mile from the ford, and so thoroughly masked that Herron did not suspect their real numbers. He pushed a light battery across to feel the foe. It was instantly driven back. Under cover of a feint of another advance, he pushed a battery (Murphy's) across the creek half a mile farther down, and opened partially on the flank of the foe. During the surprise and confusion which this occasioned, and which gave the impression that his force was much larger than it really was, he pushed three full batteries across the ford in his front, supported by three full regiments.[2] These, within sixty minutes, silenced the guns of their antagonists, and then, advancing across open fields, hurling before them a storm of grape and canister, they pushed up to within a hundred yards of the ridge. Then the Wisconsin and Iowa regiments were ordered to charge and capture the Confederate battery on their front. This was done in a few minutes, but they were unable to hold it, and fell back, when the foe, resolved on capturing Herron's batteries, dashed forward, but were repulsed in turn with heavy loss. Now two fresh regiments, under Colonel Houston (Twenty-sixth Indi-

[1] Second Wisconsin, First Iowa, Tenth Illinois, and Eighth Missouri.

[2] These were the batteries of Captain Backof, and Lieutenants Forest and Boeries. The supporting regiments were the Ninth Iowa, Twentieth Wisconsin, and Ninety-fourth Illinois.

ana and Thirty-seventh Illinois), came up gallantly, charged upon and recaptured the Confederate battery, but they too were compelled to fall back.

While Herron was thus struggling, at half-past two o'clock in the afternoon, Blunt came up and fell upon the Confederate left, where the troops had been massed to turn Herron's right. A severe battle ensued. Blunt brought three batteries to bear, which soon drove those of the Confederates and their supporters back into the woods, where Colonel Wier, with a heavy force,[1] charged upon them. Then ensued a musketry fight for three hours, the National artillery doing admirable service at the same time. Lieutenant Tenney, with six 10-pounder Parrotts, unsupported, repelled a heavy infantry attack, during which the Confederate General Stein, of Missouri, fell. At about the same time an attempt to capture the batteries of Rabb and Hopkins was repelled, to the great hurt of the assailants. Night ended the conflict, and the Nationals slept on their arms on the battle-field, expecting to renew the struggle in the morning. But the Confederates had no desire for more fighting, and retreated under cover of the darkness. Before the dawn, Hindman asked for a personal conference with Blunt concerning the burial of the dead. It was granted, but proved to be only a trick to keep back a pursuit of his flying army, which, as Blunt soon afterward learned, had commenced departing several hours before. The Confederates, having left their transportation south of the mountains, marched rapidly and escaped. Thus ended the sanguinary BATTLE OF PRAIRIE GROVE.[2]

While the war was thus progressing in the region of the lower Mississippi, on its western side, it was seen in many of its distressing aspects still farther west in Texas, the extreme southwestern State of the Republic. From the time when Twiggs betrayed it into the hands of the Confederates,[3] the loyal people of that State suffered intensely from the cruelties of the insurgents. In Western Texas, where there were few slave-holders, and consequently more patriotism, the Union element was very strong and pertinacious, and the inhabitants were both hated and feared by the banditti of the conspirators, who moved over the country with fire and rope to destroy property and strangle loyal citizens.

The sufferings of the Texan loyalists were intensified early in the summer of 1862, after the reverses of the Confederates in Tennessee, when Texas was placed under martial law, and a merciless conscription was enforced. The country was scoured by guerrilla bands, who committed the most atrocious crimes, robbing and murdering all who were even suspected of being friends of their country. Great numbers of the loyalists attempted to flee from the State to Mexico, singly and in small parties. The earlier fugitives escaped, but a greater portion were captured by the guerrillas and murdered. One of the organs of the conspirators (*San Antonio Herald*) said exultingly, "Their bones are bleaching on the soil of every county from Red River to the Rio Grande, and in the counties of Wise and Denton their bodies are suspended by scores from the Black Jacks."

[1] The Tenth and Thirteenth, and a part of the Second and Eleventh Kansas and Twentieth Iowa.

[2] Reports of Generals Blunt and Herron, and General Hindman. The National loss in this engagement was 1,148, of whom 167 were killed, 798 wounded, and 183 missing. A greater portion of the latter were captured by Marmaduke when he first attacked Herron's cavalry. General Blunt estimated the Confederate loss at about 3,000, as his command buried about 1,000 killed on the battle-field. Hindman reported his loss at 1,317, and claimed to have captured 275 prisoners, 5 flags, 23 wagons, and more than 500 small arms.

[3] See chapter XI., volume I.

A notable and representative instance of the treatment received by the Texan loyalists at the hands of their oppressors is found in the narrative of an attempt of about sixty of them, mostly young Germans belonging to the best families in Western Texas, to leave the country. They collected at Fredericksburg, on the frontier, intending to make their way to New Orleans by way of Mexico, and join the National army. On the night of the 9th of August they encamped on the edge of a cedar brake, on the Nueces River, about forty miles from the Rio Grande. They had moved with such secrecy that they scarcely felt any apprehension of danger from the guerrillas, who were scouring the country with orders to kill all Union men. But they were betrayed, and a leader named Duff sent over one hundred men to surprise and destroy them. At near daylight they approached the camp, and captured one of the party. His life was offered him as a reward if he would lead them to the camp of his companions. He refused, and was hanged. The guerrillas then fell upon the patriots who were sleeping. A desperate struggle ensued, and at length, opposed by overwhelming numbers and superior weapons, the Unionists were conquered, but not until two-thirds of their number were killed or wounded. The survivors fled toward the Rio Grande. Some escaped, and others were captured, tortured, and hung. The wounded, already in the hands of the insurgents, were murdered in the most barbarous manner by bullets, bayonets, bowie-knives, and hanging. Some, who were actually dying, were dragged to trees and hung by the fiends. The commander of the butchers, Lieutenant Lilley, afterward boasted that he killed several of the wounded with his own hands, "emptying two revolvers" in shooting them! The lives of forty of the sixty young men were sacrificed at an expense to the murderers of eight killed and fourteen wounded in the battle. When the banner of the Republic gave protection to the loyalists of Texas, three years later, measures were taken to collect the remains of the slain and bury them. This was accomplished, and a fine monument was erected to their memory.[1]

MONUMENT OF TEXAS MARTYRS.

Some attempts had been made to "repossess" important points in Texas, especially the city of Galveston. So early as the 17th of May,[a] Henry Eagle, commander of the war vessels in front of Galveston, summoned the town to surrender, under a threat of an attack from a land and larger naval force that would soon appear. "When the land and naval forces appear, we shall reply," was the answer; and so matters remained until the 8th of October following, when Galveston was formally surrendered by

[a] 1862.

[1] The writer is indebted to the Honorable Daniel Cleveland, the first Union Mayor of San Antonio after the close of the war, for the substance of the above narrative, and more in detail, both oral and written, and for a

its civil authorities to Commander Renshaw, of the National navy, the Confederate troops retiring on his approach with four steam-vessels of war. A small military force was placed in the city, and this, with the vessels, held possession until the close of the year.

We have now made note of the antecedents and position of the National troops westward of the Mississippi toward the close of the year 1862, destined to co-operate with the army of General Grant against Vicksburg. We left the latter encamped between Holly Springs and Coldwater, and the Tallahatchee River.[1] Let us leave this region for a while, and follow Rosecrans to his new field of operations after his splendid victory at Corinth.

Rosecrans found the Army of the Ohio, now the Army of the Cumberland, in a sad condition. It was greatly wasted in substance by marches and conflicts, and demoralized by lack of success—"its spirit broken, its confidence destroyed, its discipline relaxed, its courage weakened, and its hopes shattered."[2] It was showing in full measure the feeling of grievous disappointment which the loyal people were suffering because of the failure of Buell's campaign. With the exception of Nashville, then garrisoned by the small divisions of Negley and Palmer, and invested and threatened by a confident foe, there was little to show as the result of nine months' weary campaign by the Army of the Ohio. Its effective force was reduced from about one hundred thousand men to sixty-five thousand. About thirty-three thousand, or one-third of the whole army, were absent from their commands, ten thousand of them being in hospitals. Its cavalry was weak in number and equipment, and the rough-riders of Morgan and Forrest had so very little fear of or respect for it, that it was with the greatest difficulty that the communications of the army with its depot of supplies at Louisville could be kept open. Such was the condition and *morale* of the Army of the Cumberland (now known as the "Fourteenth Army Corps"), gathered at and around Bowling Green and Glasgow, when General Rosecrans assumed the command of it, on the 30th of October,[a] and proceeded to reorganize it.[3]

[a] 1862.

photograph of the monument, from which the above picture of it was made. "Upon the arrival of the United States troops at San Antonio, early in August, 1865," says Mr. Cleveland, "General Merrit furnished a small cavalry escort to the Hon. E. Degener (who had had two sons murdered in this battle), who, with other bereaved relatives, went to the battle-field and collected the remains of the murdered heroes, and brought them to the little town of Comfort, about fifty miles northwest of San Antonio, near which place most of them had lived, where, on the 10th day of August, the anniversary of the battle, they were buried. The funeral ceremony was peculiarly solemn and imposing. A little band, consisting of the survivors of the battle, the wives and children, parents and relations, of the deceased, had gathered from different portions of the State. Mr Degener delivered a short oration, a military salute was fired, and, midst the sobs and tears of the bereaved mourners, all that was mortal of the heroic dead was committed to its final resting-place. On the 10th of August, A. D. 1866, a stone monument was raised by their relatives over their graves with appropriate ceremonies. So died and were buried as noble a band of patriots as God ever inspired with sublime courage to do heroic deeds and die heroic deaths in the great cause of human freedom."

On one side of the monument are the words, FIDELITY TO THE UNION; and on the other the name s of those who perished.

[1] See page 524.

[2] *Annals of the Army of the Cumberland*, by John Fitch, the Provost-Judge of that army.

[3] The army was arranged in three grand divisions. The right, composed of the divisions of General J. W. Sill, Philip H. Sheridan, and Colonel W. E. Woodruff, was placed in charge of Major-General Alexander McD. McCook; the center, under Major-General George H. Thomas, composed of the divisions of General L. H. Rousseau, J. S. Negley, E. Dumont, and S. S. Fry; and the left, under T. L. Crittenden, composed of the divisions of Generals T J. Wood, H. P. Van Cleve, and W. S. Smith. Rosecrans placed the cavalry in charge of Major-General D. S. Stanley, of the Army of the Mississippi, and appointed the accomplished Julius P. Garesché his Chief of Staff. Captain J. St. Clair Morton was his Chief Engineer, and Colonel William Truesdail was appointed Chief of the Army Police. The services of the latter officer cannot be too highly estimated. He

When General Bragg perceived that the pursuit by the Nationals was relinquished after his army had crossed the Cumberland River, he halted his forces, and finally concentrated them, about forty thousand in number, at Murfreesboro', on the Nashville and Chattanooga railway, a little more than thirty miles southeast from Nashville, where he lay several weeks threatening the capital of Tennessee, but apparently without any fear or expectation of an attack from his opponent. He professed to be there to aid the Tennesseeans in "throwing off the yoke of the Lincoln despotism." Another object was to cover and defend the great cotton-producing regions of the Confederacy, and to hold the great lines of railway from those regions into the food-producing States of Tennessee and Kentucky.

BRAGG'S HEAD-QUARTERS AT MURFREESBORO'.[1]

While lying at Murfreesboro' with a feeling of absolute security, Bragg was visited by Jefferson Davis, who was his guest at his private residence in the fine mansion of Major Manning, within the suburbs of the town. That visit was made the occasion of festivities. Balls, parties, and lesser social gatherings at the houses of the secessionists in Murfreesboro', made the Confederate officers very happy. During that period Morgan, the guerrilla chief, was married to the daughter of Charles Ready, who was a member of the National Congress in 1853. Davis and the principal army officers were at the wedding. General (Bishop) Polk, assuming the cassock of the priest for the occasion,[2] performed the ceremony; and the party had the pleasure of dancing upon a floor carpeted with the flags of their country, which they took delight in thus dishonoring. But this season of joy and fancied security was short. Buell was no longer at the head of a tardily moved army. A loyal, earnest, and energetic soldier was its leader, and he soon disturbed the repose of his enemy.

Rosecrans perceived the peril that threatened Nashville, and took immediate steps to avert it. General McCook, with his grand division, moved in that direction on the morning of the 4th of November. His advance was not a moment too soon. On the next day[a] the Confederates made a demonstration against the city. Forrest, with about three thousand cavalry and some artillery, attacked the National picket line south of the town, between the Franklin and Lebanon Pikes, and

[a] Nov. 5, 1862.

---

gathered about him an army of spies and scouts, and designed a detective system of great perfection, by which the active friends of the Confederates of both sexes were found out, and their nefarious practices stopped. Nor were his services confined to the regulation of secret enemies. He made sutlers deal honestly as far as possible, and had a general police supervision over every department of army operations.

[1] This was the house of Mrs. Elliott, not far from the public square in Murfreesboro'. It was also the head-quarters of General Thomas when the National Army occupied Murfreesboro', early in 1863.

[2] Lieutenant-Colonel Freemantle, of the British Coldstream Guards, in giving an account of General Polk, says (*Three Months in the Southern States*, page 144) the latter explained to him the reasons "which had induced him temporarily to forsake the cassock." He did so with reluctance, he said, and intended, so soon as the war should cease, to resume his Episcopal functions, "in the same way as a man, finding his house on fire, would use every means in his power to extinguish the flames, and would then resume his ordinary pursuits." Colonel

caused the opening of the batteries of Forts Negley and Confiscation. The pickets, by order, fell back, so as to bring the Confederates under the guns of Fort Negley. The latter were too cautious to fall into the trap, and General Negley sallied out and drove them far toward Franklin, after an artillery fight for several hours. Almost at the same time Morgan, with twenty-five hundred men and one gun, made a dash on the Sixteenth Illinois Infantry, under Colonel Smith, on the north side of the river, with the evident intention of driving them and destroying the railway and pontoon bridges over the Cumberland at Nashville.[1] He was repulsed, with the loss of a regimental flag and twenty-four men. But the attempt to capture the city before Rosecrans's arrival was not abandoned; and when, on the afternoon of the 6th, McCook's vanguard reached Edgefield, opposite, their ears were saluted with the booming of Confederate cannon. General Sill entered the city on the following morning, when its safety was made secure, and the sentinel in his look-out at Fort Negley soon reported that no enemy was to be seen in any direction.

BRAGG'S PRIVATE RESIDENCE IN MURFREESBORO'.

The remainder of Rosecrans's force, excepting the main body of the center Division, which had arrived north of the Cumberland to protect the communications with Louisville, speedily arrived. The divisions were thrown out around the city southward, covering the roads in that direction; and for about six weeks he remained there collecting supplies of various kinds, preparatory to a movement in full force upon Bragg at Murfreesboro'. Late in November the latter was reported to be with a large part of his army within nineteen miles of Nashville, Morgan, with a heavy body of cavalry and mounted infantry, covering his right, and Forrest his left, while Wheeler was posted at Lavergne and Wharton at Nolensville. Bragg's right wing was commanded by E. Kirby Smith, his left by Hardee, and his center by Polk.

Freemantle said:—"He is very rich, and I am told he owns seven hundred negroes." The apprehended danger of these having their natural rights restored to them, in accordance with his Master's golden rule, was clearly the Bishop's incentive to take up arms against the rights of man. Those "seven hundred negroes," burning with a desire for freedom, was the Bishop's "house on fire."

[1] A correspondent of the Philadelphia *Press*, writing from Nashville on the sixth, says that for several days before, the secessionists of that city had been in fine spirits, and wagers were freely offered that the city would be in the hands of Bragg before Rosecrans could arrive. It was confidently predicted that the railway bridge would be destroyed before that time.

Bragg's superior cavalry force gave him great advantage, and Morgan was continually threatening and often striking the National supply-trains between Nashville and Mitchellsville until the railway was completed, toward the close of November.[a] Meanwhile Stanley had arrived and assumed command of the cavalry, and he very soon drove those raiders from the rear, and made them circumspect everywhere. He sent out detachments in many directions. Colonel John Kennett, acting chief of cavalry, captured a large quantity of Confederate stores, and drove Morgan across the Cumberland. A little later[b] he drove a Texan regiment fifteen miles down the Franklin pike. On the same day Wheeler was driven out of Lavergne by General E. N. Kirk, and wounded. Sheridan pushed the foe back on the Nolensville road, and Colonel Roberts, of the Forty-second Illinois, surprised and captured a squad of Morgan's men, under Captain Portch, on the Charlotte pike.

[a] Nov. 26 1862.

[b] Nov. 27.

LOOK-OUT AT FORT NEGLEY.[1]

These operations warned the Confederates that they had energetic men to oppose, and that warning was emphasized by the gallant act of Major Hill, who, with the Second Indiana, chased for about eighteen miles a Confederate force that had dashed across the Cumberland and captured a train and its escort taken from his command at Hartsville, forty-five miles northeast from Nashville. Hill recovered every thing, and killed about twenty of the foe. For this he was publicly thanked by Rosecrans, while some of his cowardly men of the escort, who had suffered themselves to be captured that they might be paroled and sent home, were severely punished.[2] A more permanent disaster to the Nationals occurred at Hartsville soon after this. General Thomas threw forward to this place from Castilian Springs, in front of Gallatin, about two thousand men of Dumont's division, who were placed in charge of Colonel A. B. Moore, of the One Hundred and Fourth Illinois. These were surprised, and fifteen hundred of them were captured by Morgan, with the same number of cavalry and mounted infantry, notwithstanding the remainder of Dumont's division was at Castilian Springs, nine miles distant. The surprise was at seven o'clock in the morning,[c] and seemed to be without excuse. Moore was severely censured, chiefly because of his alleged want of vigilance and preparation. He had neglected to fortify or intrench his camp, and his vedettes were few and careless. His captive men were hurried to Murfreesboro', stripped of their blankets and overcoats, and then taken to the National lines for exchange,

[c] Dec. 7.

[1] During the entire war large trees were used by both sides for the purposes of look-outs for sentinels or officers of the signal corps. A platform was constructed among the higher branches, which was reached by means of cleats on the trunks, and ladders among the limbs. The above sketch shows the appearance of one of two look-outs close to the ramparts of Fort Negley, at Nashville, and also a sentry-box at an angle of the stockade citadel within the fort. See sketch of the fort on page 265.

[2] This method of getting home without the danger attending desertion had become a great evil, and Rosecrans determined to put a stop to it. In the case here mentioned the crime was so clear that he ordered fifty of the delinquents to be paraded through the streets of Nashville, with ridiculous night-caps on their heads, preceded by a fife and drum playing the Rogue's March. They were sent in disgrace to the parole camp in Indiana. This severity lessened the evil.

contrary to an agreement between Rosecrans and Bragg. The former waived the matter for that time, and received his plundered men.[1]

The Battle of Hartsville was followed, two days later,[a] by a dash of Wheeler, with a heavy force of cavalry and mounted infantry, upon a National brigade[2] under Colonel Stanley Matthews, guarding a forage train at Dobbins's Ferry, on Mill Creek. After a short fight Wheeler was repulsed, and Matthews took his train to camp unharmed. Three days after this, General Stanley allowed his men to try the efficacy of two thousand revolving rifles, which he had just received. They pushed down the road toward Franklin, drove the Confederate vedettes from that village,[b] obtained some important information, and returned with a few prisoners.

[a] Dec. 9, 1862.

[b] Dec. 12.

Such were a few of the minor operations of the Army of the Cumberland, while its commander was preparing for more important movements. The hour for those movements had now arrived. On Christmas eve he had in store at Nashville thirty days' provisions and supplies. Bragg had no idea that Rosecrans would advance and undertake a winter campaign, and had sent a large portion of his cavalry to operate upon his antagonist's lines of communication and supply. The loyal people, worried by the tardiness and failure of Buell, had become exceedingly impatient of further delay; yet the commanding general was very properly deaf to the public clamor, for it is seldom an intelligent expression. But now, being fully supplied, and his army well in hand,[3] he determined to move upon Bragg.

At dawn on the morning of the 26th of December, a chilling rain falling copiously, the National army moved southward: McCook, with three divisions (fifteen thousand nine hundred and thirty-three men), along the Nolensville pike, toward Triune; Thomas, with two divisions (thirteen thousand three hundred and ninety-five men), by the Franklin and Wilson's pike; and Crittenden, with three divisions (thirteen thousand two hundred and eighty-eight men), on the Murfreesboro' pike, toward Lavergne. The brigade of engineers under Morton numbered seventeen hundred men. These covered all the roads leading southward from the city. It was intended that McCook, with Thomas's two divisions at Nolensville as a support, should attack Hardee at Triune, and if the latter should be beaten or should retreat, and the Confederates should meet the Nationals at Stewart's Creek, five miles south of Lavergne, Crittenden was to attack them. Thomas was to come in on the left flank, and McCook, in the event of Hardee's flight southward, was to move with the remainder of his force on his rear. Stanley was to cover these movements with his cavalry, which he disposed in good order.[4]

[1] The plunder of prisoners of war was a common occurrence in the army of Bragg, whose sense of honor seldom troubled his conscience in such matters. With the same lack of that soldierly quality that marked his conduct toward the gallant Worden, at the beginning of the strife (see page 369, volume I.), he now behaved toward his antagonist. Rosecrans complained of the robbery and violation of the agreement. Bragg wrote characteristic replies, and then, to "fire the Southern heart," he published his replies in the Confederate newspapers. He also permitted and justified the violations of flags of truce, and showed himself so perfidious that Rosecrans refused to have any further intercourse with him excepting by shot and shell.

[2] Fifty-first Ohio, Thirty-fifth Indiana, Eighth and Twenty-first Kentucky, and a section of Swallow's Seventh Indiana battery.

[3] The Army of the Cumberland now fit for duty numbered 46,910 men, of whom 41,421 were infantry, 2,223 artillery, with 150 guns, and 3,266 cavalry, the greater portion of the latter being raw recruits.

[4] Colonel Minty, with the First brigade, moved along the Murfreesboro' pike in advance of the left wing.

The Nationals had scarcely passed beyond their picket lines when they were heavily pressed by large bodies of cavalry, well supported by infantry and artillery. Sharp skirmishing ensued. The country, heavily wooded with oak forests and cedar thickets, grew rougher and rougher, and more difficult to traverse, and more easily defended. Yet McCook, his advance under Generals Davis and Sheridan skirmishing all the way, rested that night at Nolensville, and Crittenden, with the left, after considerable skirmishing, reposed near Lavergne. Long after dark, Rosecrans, with his staff, who left Nashville at noon, arrived at McCook's head-quarters.

Hardee was reported to be in heavy force at Triune, seven miles in front of McCook, and there it was expected he would give battle the next morning; but on McCook's advancing at mid-day, after a heavy fog had been lifted from the country, it was found that his foe had decamped, leaving a battery of six pieces, supported by cavalry, to dispute the crossing of Wilson's Creek. These were soon driven, and McCook rested at Triune that night.[a] Crittenden, in the mean time, had driven the Confederates out of Lavergne, and, in the face of continual opposition, advanced to Stewart's Creek, a deep stream with high banks, where Rosecrans expected the Confederates would make a stand. They did not, however, and their attempts to burn the bridge behind them failed, owing to a charge on their rear-guard by the Third Kentucky. After brisk skirmishing with portions of Hascall's brigade, the Confederates fell back in disorder.

[a] Dec. 27, 1862.

The following day was the Sabbath. The troops all rested, excepting Rousseau's division, which was ordered to move on to Stewartsburg, and Willich's brigade, which returned from a pursuit of Hardee as far as Riggs's Cross Roads, on his way to Murfreesboro'. On the following morning[b] McCook pushed on from Triune to Wilkinson's Cross Roads, six miles from Murfreesboro', with an advanced brigade at Overall's Creek, while Crittenden, moving on the Murfreesboro' pike, with Palmer in advance, followed by Negley, of Thomas's corps, skirmished to the West Fork of Stone's River, to within a short distance of Murfreesboro', when Palmer, deceived, erroneously signaled to head-quarters at Lavergne that the Confederates were evacuating the town. Crittenden was directed to send a division across the stream to occupy Murfreesboro.' General Harker was ordered to lead in that duty. His brigade crossed, drove the Confederates, and found Breckenridge in strong force on his front, whereupon Crittenden wisely took the responsibility of recalling him. Harker recrossed after dark without serious loss. On the following morning McCook moved toward Murfreesboro' from Wilkinson's Cross Roads, and fought his way almost to Stone's River, a little west of that town; and before evening nearly the whole of the National army was in an irregular line, more than three miles in length, in front of the Confederates, who were in strong position on the river before Murfreesboro.[1]

[b] Dec. 29.

The Second brigade, under Colonel Zahn, of the Third Ohio, moved along the Franklin road. The reserves, composed of nine regiments, and commanded by Stanley himself, preceded McCook's command on the Nolensville road. Colonel John Kennett commanded the left of the cavalry; and the Fourth regulars, under Captain Otis, was reserved for courier and escort duty.

[1] Bragg's army was disposed as follows:—The left wing in front of Stone's River, and the right wing in the rear of the stream. Polk's corps formed the left wing and Hardee's the right. Withers's division formed

Both armies prepared for battle on the night of the 30th. Rosecrans lay with Crittenden on the left, resting on Stone's River, Thomas in the center, and McCook on the right. These leaders met the commander at his quarters at nine o'clock that evening, when they received instructions for the morning. Rosecrans determined to throw his left and center heavily on Breckenridge at daybreak, crush him, wheel rapidly and attack with strong power the front and flank of the Confederate center, and then, sweeping through Murfreesboro', gain the rear of that center and their left, cut off their line of retreat, and destroy their army in detail. For this purpose McCook was to occupy the most advantageous position, taking every precaution to secure his right, and to receive and make an attack as circumstances might determine, and thus to hold all the force on his front for three hours, if possible. Thomas and Palmer were to open with skirmishing, and gain the Confederate center and left as far as the river, and Van Cleve's division of Crittenden's force was to fall upon Breckenridge and make the proposed sweep into Murfreesboro'.

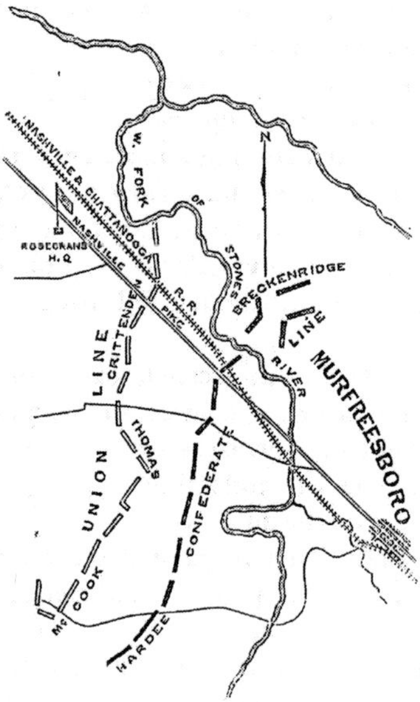

POSITION, DECEMBER 31ST.

The troops breakfasted at dawn of the 31st. Before sunrise Van Cleve crossed the river, and Wood was in readiness with his division to follow him in support. Meanwhile a counter-movement of the Confederates seriously interfered with Rosecrans's plan. Bragg had resolved to attack the National right at dawn, and for that purpose had massed his troops on his left under Hardee, in front of McCook. These in the dim morning twilight emerged suddenly and unexpectedly from thick woods —so unexpectedly that some of the battery horses had been unhitched and led to a stream to drink only a few minutes before. The four brigades under Cleburne led, and charged furiously upon McCook's extreme right before Van Cleve had moved. The divisions of Cheatham and McCown struck nearer the center, and at both points the National skirmishers were instantly thrown back upon their lines. Toward these the assailants pressed rapidly, in the face of a terrific storm of missiles, losing heavily every moment, but never faltering, and, falling with crushing force upon the brigades of Willich and Kirk, pressed them back in confusion. Kirk was severely wounded, and Willich, having his horse killed under him, was made prisoner. Edgarton's battery and a part of Goodspeed's were cap-

---

Polk's first line, and Cheatham's the second. Breckenridge's formed the first line of Hardee's, and Cleburn's the second. The two lines were eight hundred to one thousand yards apart. McCowan's division formed the reserve opposite the center, on high ground, and Jackson's brigade the reserve of the right flank, under the direction of Hardee. Bragg ordered the cavalry to fall back on the approach of the Nationals, Wheeler to form on the right and Wharton on the left, for the protection of the flanks of the line, and Pegram to go to the rear as a reserve. He ordered all supplies and baggage to be in readiness for an advance or a retreat, and, in the event of the latter, Polk's corps was to move on Shelbyville and Hardee's on the Manchester pike—trains in front, cavalry in the rear.

tured, and the guns were turned upon the fugitives. A large number of Johnson's scattered division was captured by the Confederates.

Following up this success, the victors fell with equal vigor upon McCook's left, composed of the divisions of Sheridan and J. C. Davis. They struck them on the flank. After a sharp struggle, Davis gave way. Sheridan fought longer and most desperately with the foe on his front, flank, and rear. Twice his gallant division changed front and drove back its assailants, but finally, outnumbered, and nearly surrounded, its ammunition exhausted, and every brigade commander killed or wounded,[1] it fell back in good order almost to the Nashville pike, with a loss of Houghtailing's battery and a part of Brush's. As these brigades fell back they fought gallantly, but the columns of the Confederates were too heavy to allow them to make serious resistance.

It was now eleven o'clock in the morning. The right wing, comprising full one-third of the army, was thoroughly broken up, and Bragg's cavalry were in Rosecrans's rear, destroying his trains and picking up his stragglers. McCook had early called for help, but it was not furnished, as the commander-in-chief supposed the right could hold its position until other contemplated movements should be made; but when Rosecrans (whose headquarters were not far from the site of the National cemetery since established there, a little more than two miles from Murfreesboro') was informed that the right wing was being driven, he directed General Thomas to give aid to Sheridan. Rousseau, then in reserve, was immediately sent with two brigades and a battery to Sheridan's right and rear, but it was too late. Crittenden had been ordered to suspend the operations of Van Cleve against Breckenridge, and to cover the crossing of the river with a brigade, and Wood was ordered to discontinue his preparations for following, and to hold Hascall in reserve.

When the right wing was broken up, it seemed as if the Nationals had lost the day. They had been driven from nearly one-half of the ground occupied by them at dawn, and hundreds of men had been lost. But there were able leaders and brave fighters left. They had hard work to perform. The Confederate batteries, in chosen positions, were playing fearfully upon the center, under the gallant Thomas, where Negley's division, in the cedar woods, was desperately fighting the victors over Sheridan and Davis. Negley's ammunition began to fail, his artillery horses became disabled, and a heavy column of the foe was crowding in between him and the remnant of the right wing. These circumstances compelled him to recoil, when Rousseau led his reserve division to the front, and sent a battalion of regulars, under Major Ring, to Negley's assistance. These made a successful charge, but with heavy loss, and caused the Confederates to fall back.

The brunt of the battle had now fallen upon Thomas, whose command was chiefly in and near the cedars. The assailants of Sheridan pressed farther toward the National rear, until they reached a position from which they poured a concentrated cross fire on Negley and Rousseau. This com-

[1] General J. W. Sill was killed early in the action, and at a later period Colonels Roberts and Schaeffer, each commanding a brigade, fell dead at the head of their troops.

pelled Thomas to withdraw from the cedar woods, and form a line on the open ground between them and the Nashville pike, his artillery taking a position on an elevation a little to the southwest of that highway. In this movement the brigade of regulars, under Lieutenant-Colonel Shepherd, were exposed to a terrible fire, and lost twenty-two officers and five hundred and two men in killed and wounded. It held its ground against overwhelming odds, with the assistance of the brigades of Beatty and Scribner, and the batteries of Loomis and Guenther.

The position now taken by Thomas was firmly held, and enabled Rosecrans to readjust the line of battle to the state of affairs. But the dreadful struggle was not over. Palmer's division, which held the right of the National left wing, and which had moved at eight o'clock in the morning to cover Negley's left, and successfully fought and repulsed an attack on his rear, was assailed with great fierceness on his front and right flank (which was exposed by Negley's retirement), while the new line was a forming. His right brigade, under Cruft, was forced back, when the assailants fell upon the flank of the Second, commanded by Acting Brigadier-General William B. Hazen, of the Forty-first Ohio Volunteers, who was posted on a gentle rise of ground—a cotton-field—between the Nashville pike and the Nashville and Chattanooga railway, now marked by the burial-ground of those of his command who fell on that occasion. He had but one regiment at first to protect this flank, but two battalions from the reserves soon came to its assistance. That brigade was the chief object in the way of complete victory for the Confederates, and in double lines, some in rear, some on flanks,

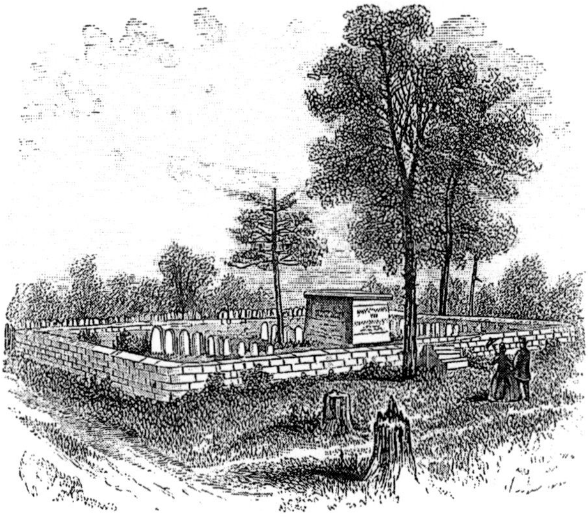

MONUMENT ERECTED BY HAZEN'S BRIGADE.[1]

[1] This was the appearance of the burial-ground and the monument on the battle-field of Murfreesboro', as it appeared when the writer sketched it, early in May, 1866. It is on the spot where Hazen's brigade had its struggle—the severest part of the battle on the 31st of December. The lot is oblong, forty by one hundred feet in size, surrounded by a substantial wall of limestone, found in the vicinity. In it are the graves of sixty-nine men of the brigade, buried there, and at the head of each grave is a stone, with the name of the occupant upon it. A substantial monument of the same kind of stone is within the inclosure. The wall and the monument were constructed by Hazen's men soon after the battle. The monument, which is seen at the left of the railway by travellers going toward Nashville, is ten feet square at the base, and about the same in height, and bears the following inscriptions:

West side.—"Hazen's Brigade. To the memory of its soldiers who fell at Stone River, December 31st, 1862. Their faces toward Heaven, their feet to the foe."

South side.—"The veterans of Shiloh have left a deathless heritage of fame upon the field of Stone River. Killed at Shiloh, April 7, 1862, Captain James Haughton, First Lieutenant and Adjutant T. Patton, and

and some in front, they made desperate attempts to demolish it. The gallant Hazen felt that his little band must decide the question of victory or defeat for the Nationals, and so at the cost of one-third of his brigade he beat back the foe, time and again, until Rosecrans was enabled to form his new line for vigorous action. To Hazen's brigade is freely given the honor of saving the day, and perhaps the Army of the Cumberland. Thirteen hundred men,[1] skillfully handled, had kept thousands at bay, by repelling them time after time, and stayed the tide of victory for the Confederates, which had been rolling steadily forward for hours.

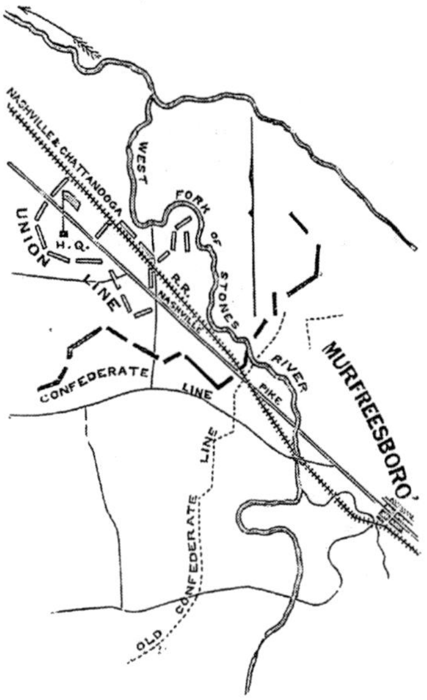

POSITION, NIGHT OF DECEMBER 31ST.

But the struggle was not yet over. Bragg's entire army, excepting a portion of Breckenridge's division across the river, was still pressing hard upon the Nationals, but in every attempt to break the newly-formed line they were repulsed with much slaughter. The gallant Wood, though severely wounded in the foot at ten o'clock in the morning, kept the saddle all day, and, with Van Cleve, skillfully fought the Confederate left under Breckenridge, and repulsed his charges. Wood's batteries had done nobly. Indeed, gallantry and skill were exhibited by both sides in every part of the field. The day closed, and darkness ended the battle, leaving the Nationals "masters of the original ground on their left, and the new line advantageously posted, with open ground in front, commanded at all points by their artillery."[2]

Rosecrans had lost heavily in men and guns,[3] yet he was not discouraged.

First Lieutenant Joseph Turner, Ninth Indiana Volunteers; First Lieutenant Franklin E. Pancoast and Second Lieutenant Chauncey H. Talcott, Forty-first Ohio Volunteers; Second Lieutenant Anton Hund, Sixth Kentucky Volunteers."

East side.—"Erected 1863, upon the ground where they fell, by their comrades, Forty-first Infantry, Ohio Volunteers, Lieutenant-Colonel A. Wiley; Sixth Infantry, Kentucky Volunteers, Colonel W. C. Whitaker; Ninth Infantry, Indiana Volunteers, Colonel W. H. Black; One Hundred and Tenth Infantry, Illinois Volunteers, Colonel T. S. Casey; Cockerill's Battery, Company F, First Artillery, Ohio Volunteers, Nineteenth Brigade Buell's Army of the Ohio, Colonel W. B. Hazen, Forty-first Infantry Ohio Volunteers Commanding."

North side.—"The blood of one-third of its soldiers, twice spilled in Tennessee, crimsons the battle-flag of the brigade, and inspires it to greater deeds. Killed at Stone's River, December 31, 1862, Lieutenant-Colonel George T. Colton and Captain Charles S. Todd, Sixth Kentucky Volunteers; Captain Isaac M. Pettit, Ninth Indiana Volunteers; First Lieutenant Calvin Hart and First Lieutenant I. T. Patchin, Forty-first Ohio Volunteers; Second Lieutenant Henry Kessler, Ninth Indiana Volunteers; Second Lieutenant Jesse G. Payne, One Hundred and Tenth Illinois Volunteers."

[1] These were comprised in four thin regiments, namely, Sixth Kentucky, Colonel W. C. Whittaker; Ninth Indiana, Colonel W. H. Blake; One Hundred and Tenth Illinois, Colonel T. S. Casey; and Forty-first Ohio, Colonel A. Wiley.

[2] Rosecrans's Report to Adjutant-General Thomas, February 12, 1863.

[3] More than 7,000 men were missing from the ranks at the close of the day. Several regiments had lost two-thirds of their officers. Johnson's ablest brigadiers, Willich and Kirk, were lost, the former being a prisoner, and the latter severely wounded. Sill, Schaeffer, and Roberts, Sheridan's brigadiers, were dead. Wood and Van Cleve were disabled by wounds, and no less than ten Colonels, ten Lieutenant-Colonels, and six Majors were missing. Sheridan alone had lost seventy-two officers. Nearly two-thirds of the battle-field was in the posses-

He established head-quarters that night[a] at a log hut near the Nashville pike, and there he called a council of general officers. These had seen his gallant bearing throughout the day, as he rode from point to point where danger to his troops was most apparent, and recognized the wisdom of his orders in the fact of success. He had been seen on every part of the field, directing the most important movements with perfect composure. When the head of the accomplished Garesché, his warm friend and his chief of staff, was shot off while he was riding by his commander's side, the General simply remarked, "I am very sorry, but we cannot help it;" and when it was erroneously reported to him that McCook was killed he made a similar reply, adding, "This battle must be won." With that determination he went into the council and said, "Gentlemen, we conquer or die right here." For his admiring officers his will was law. It was resolved to continue the fight,[1] and the Army of the Cumberland rested that night in full expectation of renewing the struggle the next morning.

[a] Dec. 31, 1862.

Bragg was confident of final victory. He sent a jubilant dispatch to Richmond, saying that, after ten hours' hard fighting, he had driven his foe from every position excepting his extreme left (held by Hazen), maintained the field, and had as trophies four thousand prisoners, two brigadier-generals, thirty-one pieces of artillery, and two hundred wagons and teams. He expected Rosecrans would attempt to fly toward Nashville during the night, and was greatly astonished in the morning to find his opponent's army not only present, but in battle order. He began to doubt his ability to conquer his foe, and moved more circumspectly. He attempted but little, and the sum of that day's operations was some heavy skirmishing and occasional artillery firing. That night both armies, alert and anxious, slept on their arms.

Friday morning[b] found Rosecrans with his army well in hand, and in an advantageous position. During the preceding evening Van Cleve's division of Crittenden's corps, then commanded by Colonel Beatty, of the Nineteenth Ohio, had been thrown across Stone's River, and occupied an eminence commanding the upper ford, nearly a mile below the bridge of the Nashville turnpike. Bragg, during the night, had stealthily planted four heavy batteries to sweep the National lines, and with these he suddenly opened a terrific fire at eight o'clock in the morning, to which Hascall's division was more immediately exposed, and made to suffer severely. Estep's battery was quickly disabled, but Bradley's, and the guns of Walker and Sheridan's divisions, soon silenced the cannon of the assailants. Then there was a partial lull until about three o'clock in the afternoon, yet it was evident from skirmishing along Beatty's front that the foe was massing in that direction.

[b] Jan. 2, 1863.

---

sion of the Confederates, and they had captured one-fifth of all of Rosecrans's artillery. Subsistence trains had been captured or destroyed; lines of communication were threatened by Confederate cavalry; artillery ammunition was not abundant; the obtaining of supplies was uncertain, and the wearied soldiers were resting fitfully on that cold and rainy December night without sufficient food or shelter.

[1] During the preceding evening Rosecrans had made a personal examination of the ground in the rear, as far as Overall's Creek, and had resolved to await the attack of his foe, while his provision train and a supply of ammunition should be brought up. On the arrival of these, should the Confederates not attack, the Nationals were to commence offensive operations.

Meanwhile Rosecrans, adhering to his plan of turning Bragg's right, and taking Murfreesboro', had strengthened Van Cleve's division with one of Palmer's brigades. He was examining the position in person, when suddenly a double line of Bragg's skirmishers, followed by three heavy columns of infantry and three batteries, emerged from the woods and fell heavily upon Van Cleve's force. The assailants were Breckenridge's entire corps, with ten Napoleon 12-pounders, commanded by Captain Robertson, and two thousand cavalry under Wharton and Pegram, aided by a heavy enfilading fire from Bishop Polk's artillery near the center. Beatty's (Van Cleve's) first line (Fifty-first Ohio, Eighth Kentucky, and Thirty-fifth and Seventy-eighth Indiana) checked the assailants for a moment, but by the sheer pressure of superior force it was compelled to give way. The reserve (Nineteenth Ohio, and Ninth and Eleventh Kentucky) then went forward and fought gallantly, but was soon compelled to fall back to avoid the conse-

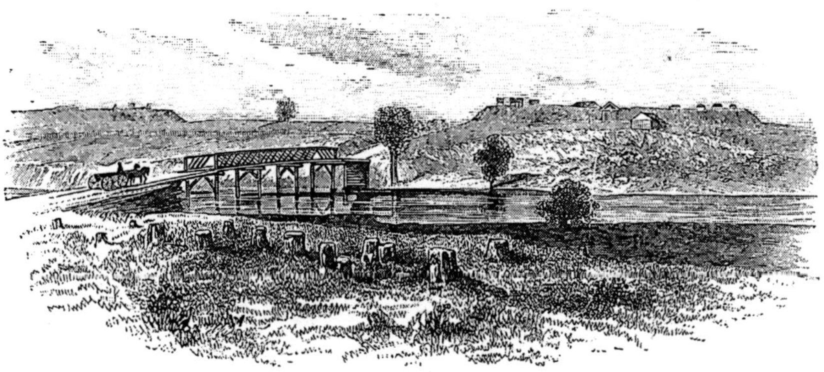

THE NASHVILLE PIKE BRIDGE OVER STONE'S RIVER.[1]

quences of a flank movement of the foe. The Nationals were speedily driven in confusion across the river, with heavy loss, closely followed by the increasing numbers of the Confederates—the entire right wing of Bragg's army—in three heavy lines of battle, who swept down the slopes to the edge of the stream.

In the mean time Crittenden's chief of artillery had massed his batteries along the rising ground on the opposite side of the river, so as to sweep and enfilade the foe with fifty-eight guns, while the remainder of the left wing was well prepared for action. These guns opened with murderous effect on the pursuers, cutting broad lanes through their ranks. At the same time the divisions of Negley and J. C. Davis, with St. Clair Morton's engineers, pushed forward to retrieve the disaster. A fierce battle ensued.

---

[1] This was the appearance of the locality when the writer sketched it, early in May, 1866, when fortifications thrown up by the Nationals were seen on both sides of the pike, on the Murfreesboro' side of the stream. The shores of the stream are rough with bowlders, and some have supposed that these gave the name to it, which is generally called Stone River. Its name was derived from a man named Stone, and its proper orthography is that given in the text. In the above picture Redoubt Brannon, named in honor of General Brannon, whom we met at Key West (see page 361, volume I.), is seen on the right of the pike. It was one of a series of redoubts which, with lines of intrenchments, the whole seven miles in extent, were erected by the Nationals and named Fort Rosecrans.

Both sides massed their batteries, and plied them with powerful effect. Both felt that the struggle would be decisive. And so it was. For a time it seemed as if mutual annihilation would be the result. Finally Stanley and Miller, with the Nineteenth Illinois, Eighteenth, Twenty-first, and Seventy-fourth Ohio, Seventy-eighth Pennsylvania, Eleventh Michigan, and Thirty-seventh Indiana, charged simultaneously, and drove the Confederates rapidly before them, capturing a battery and the flag of the Twenty-sixth Tennessee. The latter was a trophy of the Seventy-eighth Pennsylvania. This charge decided the day. In twenty minutes the Confederates lost two thousand men. At sunset the entire line had fallen back, leaving about four hundred men captives.

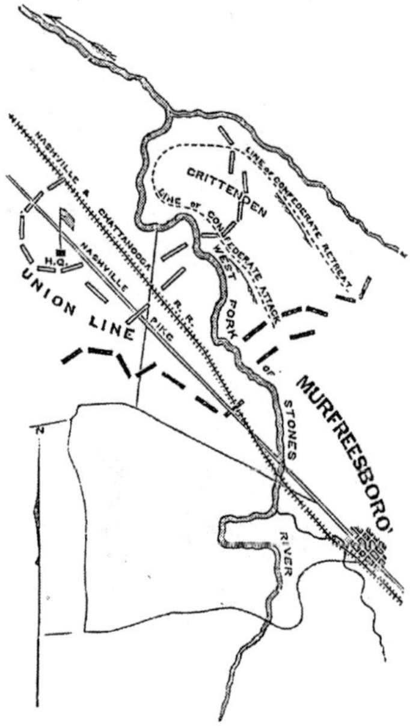

POSITION, JANUARY 2D.

So ended, in complete victory for the Nationals, THE BATTLE OF MURFREESBORO', one of the greater conflicts of the war. It shed great luster upon Rosecrans, who was seen in the last as well as in the first day's conflict, on various parts of the field, directing the fire of the batteries and the movements of the troops, and continually exposed to imminent personal danger. With forty-three thousand four hundred men, he had fought his foe, fully his equal in number,[1] on ground of the latter's choosing. He was highly commended for his persistence under the discouragements of early disasters and severe losses,[2] and the lips of the loyal were everywhere vocal with his praises.

When the Confederates gave way Rosecrans would have chased, but darkness was coming on, and rain was falling copiously. Crittenden's entire corps was thrown across the river, and before morning it was sufficiently intrenched to defy the foe. Rain fell heavily the next day, but it did not repress the ardor of the victorious Nationals. At ten o'clock a long-expected ammunition train came up. Batteries were constructed—some at points in range of Murfreesboro'—and preparations were made for another struggle. Thomas and Rousseau drove the Confederates from the cedar woods without much opposition, and at midnight Bragg stealthily retreated

[1] Reports of General Rosecrans and his subordinate commanders. Also the Reports of General Bragg and his subordinates. Rosecrans reported the number of his forces in battle at 43,400, and estimated those of Bragg at 62,720. To this he added, that the Confederates had at least fifteen per cent. the advantage in the choice of the ground and knowledge of the country. Bragg reported his force in the fight at the beginning at 35,000. He had 132 regiments of infantry, 20 regiments of cavalry, and 24 smaller organizations of horsemen. He also had 12 battalions of sharp-shooters and 23 batteries of artillery. These numbered over 60,000, at the lowest calculations of these regiments.

[2] Rosecrans officially reported his loss at nearly 12,000, while Bragg *estimated* it at 24,000. Rosecrans had 1,533 killed, 7,245 wounded, and about 3,000 made prisoners. Bragg claimed to have taken 6,273 prisoners. He admitted a loss on his part of 10,000, of whom 9,000 were killed and wounded. Among his killed were General G. J. Rains (see page 542, volume I.) and Roger W. Hanson, of Kentucky. Generals Chalmers and Adams were among his wounded.

through Murfreesboro' in the direction of Chattanooga. He had telegraphed cheerily to Richmond on the first,[a] saying in conclusion, "God has granted us a happy New Year." On the 5th he telegraphed from Tullahoma, saying: "Unable to dislodge the enemy from his intrenchments, and hearing of re-enforcements to him, I withdrew from his front night before last. He has not followed. My cavalry are close on his front."

[a] Jan., 1863.

Bragg's retreat was not known to Rosecrans until daylight, when he had too much the start to warrant a pursuit by the inferior cavalry force of the Nationals. He had fled so precipitately that he left about two thousand of his sick and wounded, with attendant surgeons, in his hospitals. The next day was Sunday, and all remained quiet. Early on Monday morning Thomas advanced into Murfreesboro', and drove the Confederate rear-guard of cavalry six or seven miles toward Manchester. Two divisions of the army followed and occupied the town that day, and Rosecrans made his head-quarters in the village, at the house of E. A. Keeble, a member of the Confederate "Congress."

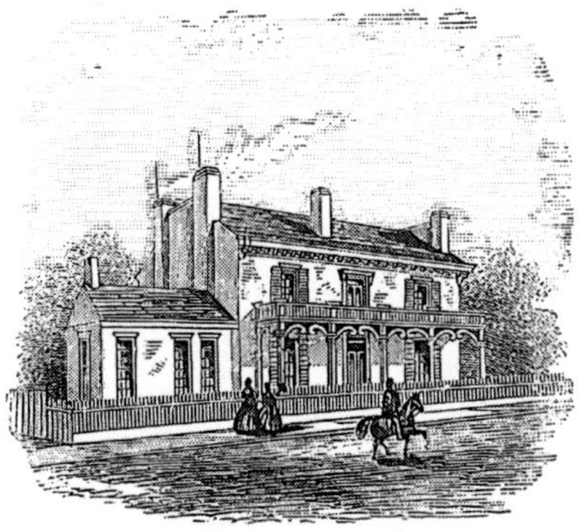

ROSECRANS'S HEAD-QUARTERS.

While the movements of Rosecrans and Bragg were tending to the great battle just recorded, the superior cavalry forces of the latter were busy in the rear of the former, as we have observed, in endeavors to destroy his communications and his trains. Forrest had been detached, with three thousand five hundred cavalry, to operate in West Tennessee upon the communications between Grant and Rosecrans, and between both and Louisville; and for a fortnight before the battle of Murfreesboro' he had been raiding through that region, much of the time with impunity, destroying railway tracks and bridges, attacking small National forces, and threatening and capturing posts. He crossed the Tennessee at Clifton, in the upper part of Wayne County, on the 13th of December, and, moving rapidly toward Jackson, seriously menaced that post. Sweeping northward, destroying tracks and bridges, he captured Humbolt, Trenton, and Union City, and menaced Columbus, the head-quarters of General Sullivan.

At Trenton Forrest captured and paroled seven hundred troops,[b] under Colonel Jacob Fry, making the number of his paroled prisoners since he crossed the river about one thousand. On his return he was struck at Parker's Cross Roads, between Huntington and Lexington, first by a force of sixteen hundred men, under Colonel C. L. Dunham, and then by General Sullivan,[c] who came suddenly upon the raiders with two fresh brigades under General Haynie[1] and Colonel Fuller,[2] just as Dunham's train was captured, his little band[3]

[b] Dec. 20, 1862.

[c] Dec. 31.

[1] One Hundred and Sixth and One Hundred and Nineteenth Illinois, Thirty-ninth Iowa, and Iowa Union Brigade of 200 men. In all, a little more than 1,200 men.

[2] Twenty-seventh, Thirty-ninth, and Sixty-third Ohio.

[3] Fiftieth Indiana, Thirty-ninth Iowa, One Hundred and Twenty-second Illinois, and Seventh Tennessee.

surrounded, and a second demand for a surrender had been made by Forrest and refused. Sullivan made a fierce onslaught on Forrest, whose troops were utterly routed, with a loss of fifty killed, one hundred and fifty wounded, and four hundred prisoners, including the latter. The Union loss was two hundred and twenty, of whom twenty-three were killed, one hundred and thirty-nine wounded, and fifty-eight missing. Forrest himself came very near being captured. His Adjutant (Strange) was made prisoner. Forrest fled eastward, recrossed the Tennessee at Clifton, and made his way to Bragg's army, below Murfreesboro'.

Morgan, the guerrilla, was raiding upon Rosecrans's left and rear, while Forrest was on his right. He suddenly appeared in the heart of Kentucky, where he was well known and feared by all parties. He dashed up toward Louisville along the line of the railway, and after skirmishing at Nolensville and other places, he suddenly appeared before Elizabethtown,[a] then garrisoned by five hundred men of the Ninety-first Illinois, under Lieutenant-Colonel Smith. They were too few to combat successfully Morgan's three thousand. These surrounded the town,[b] and, without warning to the inhabitants, fired over a hundred shot and shell into it. Smith had no artillery, and was compelled to surrender, when Morgan's men, as usual, commenced destroying property, stealing horses, and plundering the prisoners. They even robbed the sick soldiers in the hospital of blankets, provisions, and medicines.[1] After destroying the railway for several miles, Morgan made a raid to Bardstown, where he saw danger, and turning abruptly southward,[c] he made his way into Tennessee by way of Springfield and Campbellsville.

[a] Dec. 27, 1862.

[b] Dec. 28.

[c] Dec. 30.

A counter-raid was made at about this time, by a National force under Brigadier-General S. P. Carter, the object being the destruction of important railway bridges on the East Tennessee and Virginia railway, which connected Bragg's army with the Confederate forces in Virginia. Carter started from Winchester, in Kentucky, on the 20th of December, and crossed the mountains to Blountsville, in East Tennessee, where he captured one hundred and fifty North Carolinians, under Major McDowell, with seven hundred small arms, and a considerable amount of stores. He destroyed the great bridge, seven hundred and twenty feet long, that spanned the Holston there. He then pushed on toward Jonesboro', and destroyed a railway bridge over the Watauga, at Clinch's Station, where, in a skirmish, he captured seventy-five men. He menaced Bristol, but went no farther east at that time. Then he recrossed the mountains and returned to Winchester, after a ride of seven hundred miles, having lost but twenty men, most of them made prisoners, and inflicted a loss on the Confederates of five hundred men and much property.

The writer visited the battle-ground of Murfreesboro' early in May, 1866. He went down from Nashville by railway, on the morning of the 9th,[d] with Messrs. Dreer and Greble, and soon after their arrival they called at the house of the Post Chaplain, the Reverend Mr. Earnshaw, of the Methodist denomination, whom the writer had met in Washington City a few months before. He was actively engaged in the work of estab-

[d] May, 1866.

---

[1] See *Morgan and his Captors*, by Rev. F. Senour, page 85.

lishing a National Cemetery on the Murfreesboro' battle-ground, and collecting therein the remains of the slain Union soldiers in that vicinity. He would be absent on that duty until noon, so we went to the quarters of Captain Whitman, the energetic quartermaster, then absent on duty, under the direction of General Thomas, in visiting the battle-fields of the West, and looking up the graves of Union soldiers, preparatory to their removal to National cemeteries at different places. His son, an earnest, patriotic young man, kindly furnished us with an ambulance and horses, and accompanied us to places of interest around and within Murfreesboro'. We were hospitably entertained at dinner by his mother and sister, after which we were joined by Chaplain Earnshaw, and all rode out on the Nashville pike to the battle-field, passing on the way the heavy earth-works cast up in the vicinity of the village by the National troops. After crossing Stone's River we saw marks of the battle everywhere upon trees that had survived the storm. Especially prominent were these evidences around the monument on the spot where Hazen's brigade fought, and in the cedar woods few trees had escaped being wounded. The few surviving trees near the monument were terribly scarred, and one, seen in the picture on page 546, beyond the wall, had its top cut off by a passing shell.

The National Cemetery at Murfreesboro' is on the battle-ground between the railway and the Nashville pike. It was partly inclosed when we were there by a fine cut-stone wall, of material from limestone quarries near by. It is at nearly the center of the field of conflict, and covers the slope, on the crest of which Loomis's battery was planted during a part of the struggle there, supported by the Eighth Wisconsin. The cemetery includes sixteen acres of ground, well laid out, with a large square in the center, on which it is designed to rear a monument. Mr. Earnshaw was indefatigable in his labors in the holy work of collecting there, in consecrated ground, the remains of the defenders of their country, and erecting a suitable monument to their memory. Already he had gathered there the remains of six thousand of the patriots who died that the Republic might live.

Having completed our explorations and sketches during the day, we supped with Chaplain Earnshaw and his interesting family, and left for Chattanooga with the next morning's train. To that earnest patriot and zealous Christian minister, and to the equally earnest and patriotic Captain Whitman, the writer is indebted for many kind attentions and much valuable information, while at Murfreesboro' and since.

CHAPTER XXI.

SLAVERY AND EMANCIPATION.—AFFAIRS IN THE SOUTHWEST.

THE Army of the Cumberland was compelled by absolute necessity to remain at Murfreesboro' until late in 1863. That necessity was found in the fact that its supplies had to be chiefly drawn from Louisville, over a single line of railway, passing through a country a greater portion of whose inhabitants were hostile to the Government. This line had to be protected at many points by heavy guards, for Bragg's cavalry force continued to be far superior to that of Rosecrans, and menaced his communications most seriously. But during that time the Army of the Cumberland was not wholly idle. From it went out important expeditions in various directions, which we shall consider hereafter.

We have now taken note of the most important military operations of the war to the close of 1862, excepting some along the Atlantic coast after the capture of Fort Pulaski, the land and naval expedition down the coasts of Georgia and Florida, in the spring of 1862, and the departure of Burnside from North Carolina in July following, to join the Army of the Potomac.[1] The immediately succeeding events along that coast were so intimately connected with the long siege of Charleston, that it seems proper to consider them as a part of that memorable event.

Let us now take a brief view of civil affairs having connection with military events, and observe what the Confederate armed vessels were doing in the mean time.

The second session of the Thirty-seventh Congress commenced on the 2d of December, 1861. It was a most important period in the history of the country. A civil war of unparalleled magnitude and energy was raging in nearly every slave-labor State of the Republic, waged on the part of the insurgents for the destruction of the old Union, that the slave system might be extended and perpetuated; and on the part of the Government for the preservation of the life of the Republic and the maintenance of its constitutional powers. The people and the lawgivers had been much instructed by current events during the few months since the adjournment of

[a] Aug., 1861.

Congress,[a] and when that body now met both were satisfied that, in order to save the Republic, Slavery, the great corrupter of private and public morals, and the fuel of the fiery furnace in which the nation was then suffering, must be destroyed. Therefore much of the legislation of the

[1] See chapter XII.

session then commenced was upon the subject of that terrible evil, for it was resolved to bring all the powers of the Government to bear upon it, positively and negatively: positively, in the form of actual emancipation, under certain conditions and certain forms, such as confiscation; and negatively, by withholding all restraints upon the slave. Introductory to this legislation was a notice of Senator Trumbull, of Illinois, given as soon as Congress was organized, that he should ask leave to introduce "a bill for the confiscation of the property of rebels, and giving freedom to persons they hold in slavery." Such bill was accordingly introduced on the 5th of December, when the conspirators and the opposition immediately sounded the alarum-bell of "*unconstitutionality*," so often heard during the struggle, and warned the people of the designs of the Government party to destroy their liberties by revolution and despotism. The enlightened people, perfectly comprehending the alarmists, calmly responded by their acts, "*We will trust them.*" They agreed with Madison, one of the founders of the Republic, and called "the Father of the Constitution," that in a time of public danger such as then existed, the power conferred upon the National Legislature by the grant of the Constitution for the common defense had *no limitation* upon it, express or implied, save the public necessity. They remembered his wise words: "It is in vain to oppose constitutional barriers to the impulse of self-preservation: it is worse than vain," and acted accordingly.

For a long time the public mind had been much excited by the common practice of many of the commanding officers of the army of capturing and returning fugitive slaves to their masters. The bondsmen generally had the idea that the Union army was to be their liberator, and with that faith they flocked to it, when it was in camp and on its marches,[1] and it seemed specially cruel to deny them the kindness of hospitality. But that denial was a rule, and so early as the 9th of July, at the extraordinary session of Congress, Mr. Lovejoy, of Illinois, had called the attention of the House of Representatives to the subject, in a resolution which was passed by a vote of ninety-three yeas against fifty-five nays, that it was "no part of the duty of soldiers of the United States to capture and return fugitive slaves." On the 4th of December following he introduced a bill, making it a penal offense for any officer or private of the army or navy to capture or return, or aid in the capture or return, of fugitive slaves. On the same day, Mr. Wilson of Massachusetts gave notice in the Senate of his intention to introduce a bill for a similar purpose.[2]

---

[1] That faith has been alluded to on page 124, and illustrated in note 1, page 125. It was almost universal, and had been engendered unwittingly by the slave-holders themselves. As a rule, there was very little attention paid to the presence of a slave during conversation, it seeming to be the practical idea that they understood but little more than a horse or a dog. When the Republican party was formed, in 1856, the slave-holders everywhere, when they met, agreed that the election of Fremont to the Presidency might lead to the abolition of slavery. This was said at the tables, in the presence of waiting-servants. These repeated it to those of the kitchen, and they, in turn, to those of the plantations. It was also vehemently avowed at political gatherings, where the colored people were generally numerous. Such opinion was more positively stated when Mr. Lincoln was elected, and the story, on the authority of the masters, that slavery was now to be abolished, went from lip to lip throughout the domain of the slave-labor States. The bondmen believed it, and they regarded Mr. Lincoln as their temporary Messiah, and the armies that came in his name as the power that was to make them free. Such was the visible origin of their wonderful faith. That faith was finally justified by events, and the consequence is, that the freedmen are universally loyal to the Government that asserts their manhood.

[2] Perceiving the general lack of knowledge of the laws of war, particularly as touching the subject of the slaves of the country, Dr. Francis Lieber, the eminent publicist, suggested to General Halleck when he became General-in-Chief, in July, 1862, the propriety of issuing, in some form, a code or set of instructions on inter-

It is not the province of this work to record in detail the legislation upon this important subject.[1] Suffice it here to say, that measures, having a tendency to the great act of final emancipation, offered more as necessary means for suppressing the rebellion than as acts of justice and righteousness, were pressed with earnestness by the party in Congress known as *Republicans*, and were as earnestly opposed by the party in that body known as *Democrats.* The former, having a majority, usually carried their favorite measures; while the President, wise, cautious, and conciliatory, although sympathizing with the Republicans, stood as a balance between the two extremes. He saw clearly that the people were not yet educated up to the lofty point of justice which demanded, on moral as well as political grounds, the instant and universal emancipation of the slaves, and he therefore interposed objections to extreme measures, and proposed partial and gradual emancipation, in forms that would conciliate the slave-holders of the border slave-labor States. With this spirit he recommended Congress to pass a joint resolution that the Government, in order to co-operate with any State whose inhabitants might adopt measures for emancipation, should give to such State pecuniary aid, to be used by it at its discretion, to compensate it for the inconvenience, public and private, produced by such change of system. It was also proposed to colonize the freedmen somewhere on the American continent.

This emancipation proposition was commended to Congress more as a test of the temper of the slave-holders, and especially of those of the border States, and to offer them a way in which they might escape from the evils and embarrassments which emancipation without compensation (a result now seen to be inevitable, without the plan proposed) would produce, rather than as a fixed policy to be enforced, excepting with the strong approval of the people. A joint resolution in accordance with the President's views was passed by both houses,[2] and was approved by the Executive on the 10th of April; but the conspirators, their followers, and friends everywhere rejected this olive-branch of peace, while the more strenuous advocates of Confiscation and Universal Emancipation did not give it their approval. In the mean time Congress had taken an important practical step forward in the path of justice by abolishing slavery in the District of Columbia, over whose territory it had undisputed control.[3]

---

national rules of war, for the use of officers of the army. Dr. Lieber had already issued an important pamphlet on the subject of Guerrilla Warfare, which had attracted much attention. Halleck pondered the suggestion, and finally summoned its author to Washington City, when Secretary Stanton, by a general order, appointed a commission for the purpose, of which Dr. Lieber was chairman. Their labor resulted in the production of the celebrated code written by the chairman, which was published in April, 1863, by the War Department, as "General Order No. 100." It was a new thing in literature, and suggested to an eminent European jurist, Dr. Bluntschli, the idea of codifying, in a similar manner, the whole law of nations. In the portion of his work on the Modern Law of War, soon afterward published, nearly the whole of this American code found a place.

[1] A comprehensive view, in succinct detail, of measures concerning this subject, may be found in a volume entitled *Anti-Slavery Measures in Congress*, by Henry Wilson, of the National Senate.

[2] This bill was passed by a vote in the House of eighty-nine yeas against thirty-one nays, and in the Senate by thirty-two yeas against ten nays. The President resolved to give the experiment a fair trial. As indicative of that determination, when General Hunter, in command of the Department of the South, issued an order, on the 9th of May following, declaring all the slaves within that department to be thenceforth and forever free, without any apparent military necessity for such an act, the President issued a proclamation reversing the order, and declaring that he reserved to himself the power proposed to be exercised by a commander in the field by such proclamation. This manifesto silenced a great clamor which Hunter's proclamation had raised, and demonstrated the good faith of the Executive toward the slave-holders.

[3] The bill for this purpose was passed by a vote of ninety-two yeas against thirty-eight nays in the House

Mr. Lincoln believed his proposition to pay for emancipated slaves would detach the border slave-labor States from an interest in the Confederacy, and thus speedily put an end to the war. Anxious to consummate it, he invited the Congressmen of those States to meet him in conference in the Executive Chamber. They did so,[a] and he presented to them a carefully prepared address on the subject. But he was forcibly taught by that conference, and its results, that the policy which had been so long tried, of withholding vigorous blows from the rebellion out of deference to the border slave-labor States, was worse than useless. A majority of the Congressmen submitted a dissenting reply, and told the President plainly that they considered it his duty "to avoid all interference, direct or indirect, with slavery in the Southern States." A minority report concurred in the President's views; but their slave-holding constituents, generally, scouted the proposition with scorn, and the authorities of not one of the States whose inhabitants were thus appealed to responded to him. And a draft of a bill which he sent into Congress on the day of the conference[b] was not acted upon by that body. It was evident that the majority of the people, and their representatives in the National Legislature, were not in a mood to make any further compromise with the great enemy of the Republic, or concessions to its supporters.

[a] July 12, 1862.

[b] July 12.

Meanwhile a bill providing for the confiscation of the property of rebels, which involved the emancipation of slaves, had been passed by Congress and approved by the President,[c] entitled "An Act to make an Additional Article of War," to take effect from and after its passage. It prohibited all officers or persons in the military or naval service of the Republic from using any force under their commands for the purpose of restoring fugitive slaves to their alleged masters, on penalty of instant dismissal from the service. Congress had also recently passed "An Act to Suppress Insurrection, to Punish Treason and Rebellion, to Seize and Confiscate Property of Rebels, and for other purposes," which the President approved on the 16th of July, and which declared the absolute freedom of the slaves of rebels under certain operations of war therein defined.[1]

[c] March 13.

This gave the President a wide field for the exercise of Executive power, not only in freeing a large portion of the slaves in the country, but in employing them against their former masters in the suppression of the rebellion; and he was vehemently importuned to use it immediately and vigorously. The patient President held back, hoping the wiser men among

---

of Representatives, and in the Senate by twenty-nine yeas against fourteen nays. It was approved by the President on the 16th of April, 1862.

[1] It provided that all persons, after the passage of the bill, who should commit treason against the Republic should suffer death, and all his slaves, if he had any, should be free; or suffer a fine of $10,000, with the loss of his slaves: that any person found guilty of aiding treason should be subject to a fine of $10,000 and the loss of his slaves by their being made free; and that both classes of traitors should be forever excluded from office under the Government: that it should be the duty of the President to seize the property of all office-holders, civil and military, in the so-called "Confederate States," or persons who, having property in the loyal States, should aid the rebellion: that all persons who, engaged in the rebellion, should not, within sixty days after the President should duly proclaim the law, desist from their crimes, their property of every kind should be confiscated: that all fugitive slaves from rebellious masters, or persons who should give aid and comfort to rebels, and all slaves captured from such persons, or who had deserted from the rebel army, or from any territory deserted by the rebels, should be deemed captives of war, and should be forever free: that the President should have authority to employ such freedmen, with their own consent, for the suppression of the rebellion, and to make provision for colonizing them; and that he should be authorized to extend a pardon and amnesty to such rebels as, in his judgment, should be worthy of mercy.

the insurgents might heed the threats contained in the muttering thunders of Congress, in which were concentrated the tremendous energies of the people against these cherished interests. This hesitancy produced great disquietude in the public mind. The more impatient of the loyal people began to accuse the President of not only faint-heartedness, but whole-heartedness in the cause of freedom, and charged him with remissness of duty.[1] Finally a committee, composed of a deputation from a Convention of Christians of all of the denominations of Chicago, waited upon him,[a] and presented
[a] Sept. 13, 1862.
him with a memorial, requesting him at once to issue a proclamation of Universal Emancipation. The President, believing that the time had not yet come (though rapidly approaching) when such a proclamation would be proper, made an earnest and argumentative reply; saying, in allusion to the then discouraging aspect of military affairs under the administration of McClellan in the East and Buell in the West, "What good would a proclamation of emancipation from me do, especially as we are now situated? I do not want to issue a document that the whole world would see must necessarily be inoperative, like the Pope's bull against the Comet! Would my word free the slaves, when I cannot even enforce the Constitution in the rebel States?" He concluded by saying:—"I view this matter as a practical war measure,[2] to be decided on according to the advantages or disadvantages it may offer to the suppression of the rebellion." But before the departure of the Committee the President assured them of his sympathy with their views. "I have not decided against a proclamation of liberty to the slaves," he said, "but hold the matter under advisement. And I can assure you that the subject is on my mind, by day and night, more than any other. Whatever shall appear to be God's will, I will do."[3]

The President prayerfully considered the matter, and within a week after the battle of Antietam he issued[b] a preliminary procla-
[b] Sept. 23.
mation of emancipation, in which he declared it to be his purpose, at the next meeting of Congress, to again recommend pecuniary aid in

---

[1] On the 9th of August Horace Greeley addressed an able letter to the President on the subject, through his journal, the *New York Tribune*, to which Mr. Lincoln made a reply, it giving him a good opportunity to define his position. In that reply he declared it to be his "*paramount object to save the Union, and not either to save or destroy slavery.*" "If I could save the Union without freeing a slave, I would do it," he said. "If I could save it by freeing all the slaves, I would do it; and if I could do it by freeing some and leaving others alone, I would also do that. What I do about slavery and the colored race, I do because I believe it helps to save the Union; and what I forbear, I forbear because I do not believe it would help to save the Union."

[2] While there was great doubt and perplexity in the minds of all as to what were the real powers of the Government, and especially of the President, under the Constitution, and the ablest jurists disagreed in opinion, Mr. William Whiting, a lawyer in extensive practice in Boston, wrote a most lucid and conclusive treatise on the subject, entitled, "*The War Powers of the President and the Legislative Powers of Congress in relation to Rebellion, Treason, and Slavery,*" which was accepted as sound and conclusive. It was principally written in the Spring of 1862, with the exception of the chapter on the operation of the Confiscation Act of July 17, 1862. This able treatise caused Mr. Whiting to be called into the service of the Government, as Solicitor to the War Department. It is proper to add that Mr. Whiting, whose sole desire in preparing the treatise and in responding to the call to Washington was to serve his country, remained there until the close of the war, steadily refusing all compensation for his services, or even the reimbursement of his expenses. His treatise and his name will ever hold a deservedly conspicuous place in the annals of the war; the first as an unanswerable argument in defense of the acts of the President and Congress in saving the Republic, and the latter as that of an unselfish patriot.

[3] It has been the popular belief that Mr. Lincoln's preliminary proclamation was forced from him by outside pressure, and especially by the delegation from Chicago. The late Owen Lovejoy, M. C., has left on record the following statement, the substance of which he had from the President's own lips:—"He had written the proclamation in the summer, as early as June, I think, and called his Cabinet together, and informed them that he had written it, and he meant to make it; but wanted to read it to them for any criticism or remarks as to its features or details. After having done so, Seward suggested whether it would not be well to withhold its pub-

the work of emancipation and colonization to the inhabitants in States not in rebellion. He then declared that on the first of January next ensuing, the slaves within every State, or designated part of a State, the people whereof should then be in rebellion, should be declared "thenceforward and forever free;" such freedom to be maintained by the whole force of the Government, which should not, at the same time, repress any efforts the slaves might make for their actual freedom. He also declared that any State in which rebellion had existed that should have in Congress at that time[a] representatives chosen in good faith, at a legal election, by the qualified voters of such State, should have the benefit of such conclusive evidence of its loyalty, and be exempted from the operations of the threatened proclamation. He called their attention to the acts of Congress approved March 13, 1862, and July 16, 1862, bearing upon the subject, as his warrant for the warning.

[a] Jan. 1, 1863.

It seemed as if this preliminary proclamation would indeed be as "inoperative as the Pope's bull against the Comet." It was made instrumental in "firing the Southern heart" and intensifying the rebellious feeling, for it was pointed to by the conspirators, and their followers and friends in all parts of the Republic, as positive evidence that the war was waged, not for the restoration of the Union, but for the destruction of slavery, and the plunder of the inhabitants of the slave-labor States. This was vehemently asserted, notwithstanding the clear and evidently sincere assurances of the President to the contrary—notwithstanding the document itself opened with the solemn declaration, "that hereafter, as heretofore, the war will be prosecuted for the object of practically restoring the constitutional relation between the United States and each of the States, and the people thereof."

During the hundred days which intervened between the issuing of this proclamation and the first of January—this kindly, considerate, and warning proclamation, which gave to the conspirators and their associates in crime ample time for reflection and calm decision—millions of hearts in both hemispheres were stirred with emotions of greatest anxiety. Philanthropists and lovers of righteousness, whose aspirations rose above the considerations of temporary expedients, and the vast multitude of the slaves, who were all deeply interested in the decision, trembled with a fear that the liberal terms of reconciliation might be accepted, and thereby the great act of justice be delayed. And when it was seen that the rebels were still more rebellious, and waged war upon the Government more vigorously and malignantly than ever, the question was upon every lip, Will the President be firm? He answered that question on the appointed day by issuing the following

PROCLAMATION.

Whereas, On the 22d day of September, in the year of our Lord one thousand eight hundred and sixty-two, a proclamation was issued by the President of the United States, containing, among other things, the following, to wit:

lication until after we had gained some substantial advantage in the field, as at that time we had met with many reverses, and it might be considered a cry of despair. He told me he thought the suggestion a wise one, and so held over the Proclamation until after the battle of Antietam."—Letter to William Lloyd Garrison, February 22, 1864.

"That on the first day of January, in the year of our Lord one thousand eight hundred and sixty-three, all persons held as slaves within any State or designated part of a State, the people whereof shall then be in rebellion against the United States, shall be then, thenceforward, and forever free; and the Executive Government of the United States, including the military and naval authority thereof, will recognize and maintain the freedom of such persons, and will do no act or acts to repress such persons, or any of them, in any efforts they may make for their actual freedom.

"That the Executive will, on the first day of January aforesaid, by proclamation, designate the States and parts of States, if any, in which the people thereof, respectively, shall then be in rebellion against the United States: and the fact that any State, or the people thereof, shall on that day be in good faith represented in the Congress of the United States, by members chosen thereto at elections wherein a majority of the qualified voters of such State shall have participated, shall, in the absence of strong countervailing testimony, be deemed conclusive evidence that such State, and the people thereof, are not then in rebellion against the United States."

Now, therefore, I, Abraham Lincoln, President of the United States, by virtue of the power in me vested as Commander-in-Chief of the Army and Navy of the United States in time of actual armed rebellion against the authority and Government of the United States, and as a fit and necessary war measure for suppressing said rebellion, do, on this first day of January, in the year of our Lord one thousand eight hundred and sixty-three, and in accordance with my purpose so to do, publicly proclaimed for the full period of one hundred days from the day first above mentioned, order and designate, as the States and parts of States wherein the people thereof, respectively, are this day in rebellion against the United States, the following, to wit:

Arkansas, Texas, Louisiana (except the parishes of St. Bernard, Plaquemines, Jefferson, St. John, St. Charles, St. James, Ascension, Assumption, Terre Bonne, Lafourche, Ste. Marie, St. Martin, and Orleans, including the city of New Orleans), Mississippi, Alabama, Florida, Georgia, South Carolina, North Carolina, and Virginia (except the forty-eight counties designated as West Virginia, and also the counties of Berkley, Accomac, Northampton, Elizabeth City, York, Princess Anne, and Norfolk, including the cities of Norfolk and Portsmouth), and which excepted parts are, for the present, left precisely as if this proclamation were not issued.

And by virtue of the power and for the purpose aforesaid, I do order and declare that all persons held as slaves within said designated States and parts of States are, and henceforward shall be free; and that the Executive Government of the United States, including the military and naval authorities thereof, will recognize and maintain the freedom of said persons.

And I hereby enjoin upon the people so declared to be free to abstain from all violence, unless in necessary self-defense; and I recommend to them that, in all cases when allowed, they labor faithfully for reasonable wages.

And I further declare and make known that such persons, of suitable condition, will be received into the armed service of the United States, to garrison forts, positions, stations, and other places, and to man vessels of all sorts in said service.

And upon this act, sincerely believed to be an act of justice, warranted by the Constitution, upon military necessity, I invoke the considerate judgment of mankind, and the gracious favor of Almighty God.

In testimony whereof I have hereunto set my name, and caused the seal of the United States to be affixed.

[L. S.] Done at the City of Washington, this first day of January, in the year of our Lord one thousand eight hundred and sixty-three, and of the Independence of the United States the eighty-seventh.

ABRAHAM LINCOLN.

By the President.

WILLIAM H. SEWARD, *Secretary of State.*

Whereas, on the twentysecond day of September, in the year of our Lord one thousand eight hundred and sixtytwo, a proclamation was issued by the President of the United States, containing, among other things, the following, towit:

"That on the first day of January, in the year of our Lord one thousand eight hundred and sixty-three, all persons held as slaves within any State or designated part of a State, the people whereof shall then be in rebellion against the United States, shall be then, thenceforward, and forever free; and the Executive Government of the United States, including the military and naval authority thereof, will recognize and maintain the freedom of such persons, and will do no act or acts to repress such persons, or any of them, in any efforts they may make for their actual freedom.

"That the Executive will, on the first day of January aforesaid, by proclamation, designate the States and parts of States, if any, in which the people thereof, respectively, shall then be in rebellion against the United States; and the fact that any State, or the people thereof, shall on that day be in good faith represented in the Congress of the United States, by members chosen thereto at elections wherein a majority of the qualified voters of such State shall have participated, shall, in the absence of strong countervailing testimony, be deemed conclusive evidence that such State, and the people thereof, are not then in rebellion against the United States."

Now, therefore I, Abraham Lincoln, President of the United States, by virtue of the power in me vested as Commander-in-Chief, of the Army and Navy of the United States in time of actual armed rebellion against authority and government of the United States, and as a fit and necessary war measure for suppressing said rebellion, do, on this first day of January, in the year of our Lord one thousand eight hundred and sixtythree, and in accordance with my purpose so to do publicly proclaimed for the full period of one hundred days, from the day first above mentioned, order and designate as the States and parts of States wherein the people thereof respectively, are this day in rebellion against the United States, the following, towit:

Arkansas, Texas, Louisiana, (except the Parishes of St. Bernard, Plaquemines, Jefferson, St. John, St. Charles, St. James Ascension, Assumption, Terrebonne, Lafourche, St. Mary, St. Martin, and Orleans, including the City of New-Orleans) Mississippi, Alabama, Florida, Georgia, South-Carolina, North-Carolina, and Virginia, (except the fortyeight counties designated as West Virginia, and also the counties of Berkley, Accomac, Northampton, Elizabeth-City, York, Princess Ann, and Norfolk, including the cities of Norfolk & Portsmouth; and which excepted parts are, for the present, left precisely as if this proclamation were not issued.

And by virtue of the power, and for the purpose aforesaid, I do order and declare that all persons held as slaves within said designated States, and parts of States, are, and henceforward shall be free; and that the Executive government of the United States, including the military and naval authorities thereof, will recognize and maintain the freedom of said perso

And I hereby enjoin upon the people so declared to be free to abstain from all violence, unless in necessary self-defence; and I recommend to them that, in all cases when allowed, they labor faithfully for reasonable wages.

And I further declare and make known, that such persons of suitable condition, will be received into the armed service of the United States to garrison forts, positions, stations, and other places, and to man vessels of all sorts in said service.

And upon this act, sincerely believed to be an act of justice, warranted by the Constitution, upon military necessity, I invoke the considerate judgment of mankind, and the gracious favor of Almighty God.

In witness whereof I have hereunto set my hand and caused the seal of the United States to be affixed.

Done at the city of Washington, this first day of January, in the year of our Lord one thousand eight hundred and sixty three, and of the

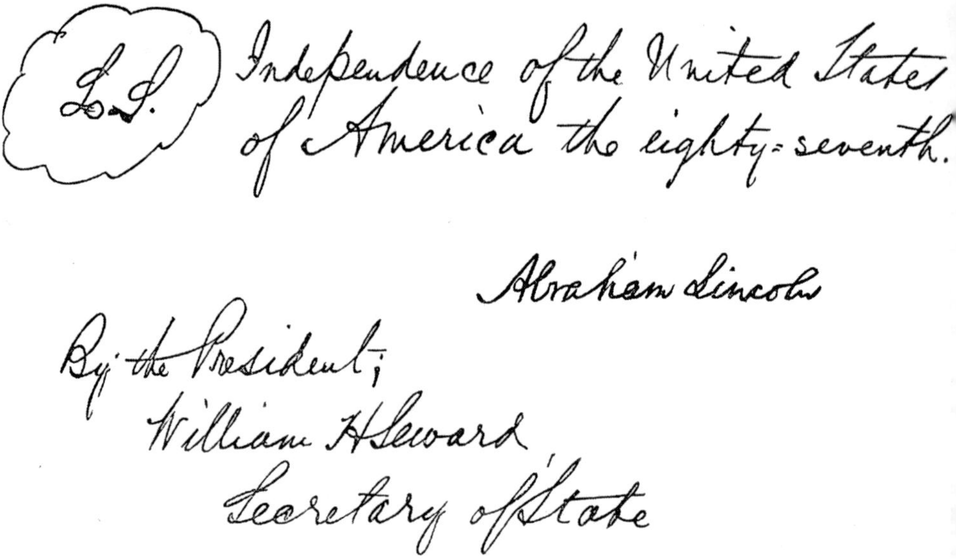
L. S. Independence of the United States of America the eighty-seventh.

Abraham Lincoln

By the President;
William H Seward
Secretary of State

THE PRESIDENT'S PEN.[1]

This Proclamation, considered in all its relations, was one of the most important public documents ever issued by the hand of man. And as time passes on, adding century to century of human history, it will be regarded with more and more reverence, as a consummation of the labors of the Fathers of the Republic, who declared the great truth, that "*all* men are created equal." With that belief, the writer has inserted, for the gratification of the present generation and of posterity, the form of the proclamation as it came from the hand of the President, and of the pen with which it was written.

Unlike the preliminary proclamation, it was wonderfully potential. The loyal portion of the nation was ready for the great act, and hailed it with

---

[1] This is a picture of the pen with which President Lincoln wrote the original draft of his Proclamation, a fac-simile of which is given on this and the three pages preceding. The pen was given to Senator Sumner by the President, at the request of the former, and by him presented to the late George Livermore, of Boston, from whom the writer received a photograph and a pencil drawing of it. It is a steel pen, known as the "Washington," with a common cedar handle—all as plain and unostentatious as the President himself.

The original draft of the Proclamation is on four pages of foolscap paper, from which a perfect fac-simile was made for the author of this work by the Government photographer, a few days after it was written, by permission of the President, and under the direction of his Private Secretary, John G. Nicolay. In speaking of it to the author the President said:—"I wish to make an explanation of the cause of the last formal paragraphs being in another's hand-writing, and the appearance of a tremulousness of hand when I signed the paper. It was on New Year's day. Before I had quite completed the proclamation, the people began to call upon me to present the compliments of the season. For two or three hours I shook hands with them, and when I went back to the desk, I could hardly hold a pen in the hand that had been so employed. So I used the hand of my private secretary in writing the closing paragraphs, having nothing more to add to the proclamation. I then signed it, with a tremulous hand, as you will perceive, made so, not from the agitation caused by the act, but from the reception of my visitors."

The fac-simile here given was made a little smaller than the original, to adapt it to the size of the page, but is perfect in every part. The original was presented by the President to the managers of a Sanitary Fair in Chicago, for the benefit of the soldiers, who sold it to T. B. Bryan, Esq., of that city, for the sum of $3,000.

joy, while the disloyal portion, and especially the conspirators, were struck with dismay, for it was a blow fatal to their hopes. It dissipated the charming vision of a magnificent empire within the Golden Circle,[1] founded on human slavery, which the conspirators had presented to the imaginations of their cruelly deceived dupes. It touched with mighty power a chord of sympathy among the aspirants for genuine freedom in the old world; and from the hour when that proclamation was promulgated, the prayers of true men in all civilized lands went to the throne of God in supplication for the success of the armies of the Republic against its enemies. And from the moment when the head of the nation proclaimed that act of justice, the power of the rebellion began to wane. Already freedmen by thousands had

LIVE-OAK GROVE AT SMITH'S PLANTATION, PORT ROYAL.

entered the public service, and large numbers were enrolled soldiers in the army of the Republic; and the first utterance of tidings by the mouth of man to freedmen of the Proclamation of Emancipation, was made to a regiment of them in arms beneath the shadows of a magnificent live-oak grove near Beaufort, in South Carolina, within bugle-sound of the place where many of the earlier treasonable movements in that State were planned. In Beaufort district, the stronghold of slavery, the first regiment of colored troops, under the provisions of the act of Congress, was organized, and it was to these that a public servant of the Republic announced the glad tidings.[2]

---

[1] See page 187, volume I.

[2] When the writer visited the village of Beaufort, in South Carolina, early in April, 1866, he spent an evening with Dr. Brisbane, the Government Tax-Collector of the District. He was born in South Carolina, but had been

While a large portion of the time of Congress, during the session of 1861-'62, was consumed in the consideration of military measures, and especially the subjects of slavery, confiscation, and emancipation, the financial affairs of the country, and public interests of every kind, were attended to with great assiduity. The financial measures and their operations and results will be considered hereafter. Let us now turn for a moment, and see what the Conspirators were doing at Richmond while their armies were in the field.

The Confederate "Congress," so called, reassembled in Richmond on the 18th of November, 1861, and continued in session, with closed doors most of the time, until the 18th of February, 1862, when its term as a "Provisional Congress," made up of men chosen by conventions of politicians and legislatures of States, expired. On the same day a Congress, profes-

---

driven from the State more than twenty years before, because he emancipated his slaves. He was residing in Wisconsin when the rebellion began. When Beaufort came into the permanent possession of the National forces, he was appointed tax-collector of the district from which he had been driven. In that district the first regiment of colored troops for the National army was organized. They were stationed on Smith's plantation (see map on page 126), about a mile and a half from Beaufort, near the ruins of the old Spanish fort Carolina, which gave the name to the State; and there, in a magnificent oak-grove near the water, Dr. Brisbane addressed them and a large concourse of people, white and colored, on the 1st of January, 1863. There he who had been driven from that, his native soil, because he emancipated a little more than *thirty* slaves, announced that on that day the President of the United States had proclaimed freedom for over *three millions* of slaves! What changes time and circumstances bring! When the writer had visited and sketched that grove, and strolled over the remains of the Spanish fort, and through the desolation of the once beautiful garden in front of the Smith mansion, hedged in by palmettos, his attention was called to a huge oak, on the gentle bank of Beaufort River, with double stems, between which were seats. On one of them, overlooking the harbor of Beaufort and Lady's Island, a Massachusetts Doctor of Divinity sat and wrote, a few years before, a large portion of a book devoted to a *Defense of Negro Slavery!*

LIVE OAK AT SMITH'S PLANTATION.

Dr. Brisbane was living in the fine old mansion of Edmond Rhett, one of the most violent of the South Carolina secessionists, in which it is said the treasonable "Southern Association" held its meetings (see note 1, page 91, volume I.), and where the form of the South Carolina Ordinance of Secession, afterward offered by Inglis in the Convention, was discussed. Beaufort was the summer resort of the aristocracy, so called, of South Carolina, and in its churchyards lie the remains of many distinguished persons. In that of the Episcopal church, and not far from the new-made grave of General Elliott, the writer saw and sketched a white marble monument in the form of a palmetto-stem, on the recumbent slab at the foot of which was the following suggestive inscription: "Sacred to the memory of Hugh Toland, son of Melvin and Eliza Sams. Born December 31st, 1846. Died July 29th, 1860. A youthful son of South Carolina, he sought to serve her, even while preparing for her better future service, and entered the State Military Academy in his seventeenth year. Carrying with him the impress of his childhood's training, he exhibited to his Alma Mater a respectful devotion akin to that which animated him as a son. His courteous bearing, high-toned sentiments, and exemplary conduct for nearly four years secured for him the high esteem of his professors and affectionate regards of his fellow-cadets. All grieve for their loss. This tribute is paid by his commanding officer. 'What I do, thou knowest not now, but thou shalt know hereafter.' John xiii. 17."

MONUMENT IN CHURCHYARD AT BEAUFORT.

sedly elected by the people,[1] commenced its session under the "Permanent Constitution of the Confederate States." In this assembly all of the slave-labor States were represented excepting Maryland and Delaware.[2] The oath to support the Constitution of the Confederate States was administered to the "Senators" by R. M. T. Hunter, of Virginia, and to the "Representatives" by Howell Cobb, of Georgia. Thomas Bocock, of Virginia, was elected "Speaker." On the following day the votes for "President" of the Confederacy were counted, and were found to be one hundred and nine in number, all of which were cast for Jefferson Davis.[3] Three days afterward[a] he was inaugurated President for six years. He chose for his "Cabinet" Judah P. Benjamin, of Louisiana, as "Secretary of State;" George W. Randolph, of Virginia, "Secretary of War;" S. R. Mallory, of Florida, "Secretary of the Navy;" C. G. Memminger, of South Carolina, "Secretary of the Treasury;" and Thomas H. Watts, of Alabama, "Attorney-General." Randolph resigned in the autumn of 1862, when James A. Seddon, a wealthy citizen of Richmond, who figured conspicuously in the Peace Convention at Washington,[4] was chosen to fill his place.

[a] Feb. 22, 1862.

JAMES A. SEDDON.

The Confederate "Congress" passed strong resolutions in favor of prosecuting the war more vigorously than ever, and declared, by joint resolution, that it was the unalterable determination of the people of the Confederate States "to suffer all the calamities of the most protracted war," and that they would never, "on any terms, politically affiliate with a people who were guilty of an invasion of their soil and the butchery of their citizens." With this spirit they did prosecute the war on land, and by the aid of some of the British aristocracy, merchants, and shipbuilders they kept afloat piratical craft on the ocean, that for a time drove most of the carrying trade between the United States and Europe to British vessels.

We have already noticed the commissioning of so-called "privateers" by the Confederate "Government,"[5] and some of their piratical operations

---

[1] In most instances these elections were as much the voice of the people as was that held in Virginia, in accordance with the following proposition of a leading paper in Richmond in the interest of the conspirators:—"It being necessary to form a ticket of electors, and the time being too short to call a Convention of the people, it was suggested that the Richmond editors should prepare a ticket, thus relieving the people of the trouble of making selections. The ticket thus formed has been presented. Among the names we find those of Wm. L. Goggin, of Bedford, and R. T. Daniel, of Richmond; E. H. Fitzhugh, of Ohio County; John R. Edmunds, of Halifax, and C. W. Newton, of Norfolk City. Every district in the State is embraced in this editorial report."

[2] For a list of the members of the "Provisional Congress" see page 463.

[3] The votes were as follows:—Alabama, 11; Arkansas, 6; Florida, 4; Georgia, 12; Louisiana, 8; Mississippi 9; North Carolina, 12; South Carolina, 8; Tennessee, 13; Texas, 8; Virginia, 18.

[4] See chapter X.. volume I.

[5] See page 372, volume I.

in the spring and summer of 1861.[1] Before the close of July, more than twenty of those depredators were afloat, and had captured millions of property belonging to American citizens. The most formidable and notorious of the sea-going ships of this character, were the *Nashville*, Captain R. B. Pegram, a Virginian, who had abandoned his flag, and the *Sumter*, Captain Raphael Semmes. The former was a side-wheel steamer, carried a crew of eighty men, and was armed with two long 12-pounder rifled cannon. Her career was short, but quite successful. She was finally destroyed by the *Montauk*, Captain Worden,[a] in the Ogeechee River.[2] The career of the *Sumter*, which had been a New Orleans and Havana packet steamer, named *Marquis de Habana*, was also short, but much more active and destructive. She had a crew of sixty-five men and twenty-five marines, and was heavily armed. She ran the blockade at the mouth of the Mississippi River on the 30th of June,[b] and was pursued some distance by the *Brooklyn*. She ran among the West India islands and on the Spanish Main, and soon made prizes of many vessels bearing the American flag. She was everywhere received in British colonial ports with great favor, and was afforded every facility for her piratical operations. She became the terror of the American merchant service, and everywhere eluded National vessels of war sent out in pursuit of her. At length she crossed the ocean, and at the close of 1861 was compelled to seek shelter under British guns at Gibraltar, where she was watched by the *Tuscarora*. Early in the year 1862 she was sold, and thus ended her piratical career.

[a] Feb. 28, 1862.

[b] 1861.

PIRATE SHIP SUMTER.

Encouraged by the practical friendship of the British evinced for these corsairs, and the substantial aid they were receiving from British subjects in various ways, especially through blockade-runners, the conspirators determined to procure from those friends some powerful piratical craft, and made arrangements for the purchase and construction of vessels for that purpose. Mr. Laird, a ship-builder at Liverpool and member of the British Parliament, was the largest contractor in the business, and, in defiance of every obstacle, succeeded in getting pirate ships to sea.

The first of these ships that went to sea was the *Oreto*, ostensibly built for a house in Palermo, Sicily. Mr. Adams, the American minister in London, was so well satisfied from information received that she was designed for the Confederates, that he called the attention of the British Government to the matter so early as the 18th of February, 1862. But nothing effective was done, and she was completed and allowed to depart from British waters. She went first to Nassau, and on the 4th of September suddenly appeared

[1] See pages 555 to 558, inclusive, volume I.

[2] The appearance of the remains of the *Nashville* in the Ogeechee River is seen in the tail-piece on page 327.

off Mobile harbor, flying the British flag and pennants. The blockading squadron there was in charge of Commander George H. Preble, who had been specially instructed not to give offense to foreign nations while enforcing the blockade. He believed the *Oreto* to be a British vessel, and while deliberating a few minutes as to what he should do, she passed out of range of his guns, and entered the harbor with a rich freight. For his seeming remissness Commander Preble was summarily dismissed from the service without a hearing—an act which subsequent events seemed to show was cruel injustice. Late in December the *Oreto* escaped from Mobile, fully armed for a piratical cruise, under the command of John Newland Maffit, son of a celebrated Irish Methodist preacher of that name. Maffit had been in the naval service of the Republic, but had abandoned his flag, and now went out to plunder his countrymen on the high seas "without authority."[1] The name of the *Oreto* was changed to that of *Florida*. Her career will be noticed hereafter.

JOHN NEWLAND MAFFIT.

The most famous of all these pirate ships built in England for the conspirators was the *Alabama*, made for the use of Semmes, the commander of the *Sumter*. As in the case of the *Oreto*, Mr. Adams called the attention of the British Government to the matter, but every effort to induce it to interpose its authority, in accordance with the letter and spirit of the Queen's proclamation of neutrality,[2] was fruitless. The *Tuscarora* watched her, but in vain. She was allowed to depart, with ample assistance, and under false pretenses she was supplied with cannon and other materials of war by an English merchant vessel, in a Portuguese harbor of the Western Islands. When all was in readiness, Captain Semmes and other officers of the *Sumter* were brought to her by a British steamer, and she left for Cardiff, to coal. Semmes took formal command, mustered his crew, and read his commission, duly signed and sealed by the Confederate "Secretary of the Navy." A copy of that commission, in blank, is given on the following page.[4]

RAPHAEL SEMMES.[3]

---

[1] See note 1, page 556, volume I.

[2] See page 567, volume I.

[3] This is from a photograph by Ferranti, of Liverpool, taken in the summer of 1864.

[4] That copy is a perfect fac-simile of the original, a little less than one-third the size. The original was engraved n England, and printed on elegant vellum, and it was much superior in material and execution to the commissions issued by our own Navy Department. The space within the wreath, on the trophy vignette at the bottom, was the place of the seal.

With orders from the Conspirators "to sink, burn, and destroy every thing which flies the ensign of the so-called United States of America," Semmes went forth on the ocean in the *Alabama* to achieve fame as one of

President of the Confederate States of America

TO ALL WHO SHALL SEE THESE PRESENTS,

GREETING

Know Ye that reposing special Trust and Confidence in the Patriotism, Valour, Fidelity and Abilities of ______ I do appoint him ______ in the Marine Corps of the CONFEDERATE STATES to rank as such from the ______ day of ______ 18__ He is therefore carefully and diligently to discharge the Duties of ______ by doing and performing all Manner of Things thereto belonging. And I do strictly charge and require all Officers Seamen and Marines under his Command to be obedient to his Orders as ______ And he is to observe and follow such Orders and Directions from time to time as he shall receive from me or the future PRESIDENT of the Confederate States of America or his Superior Officer set over him according to the Rules and Discipline of the Marine Corps.

Given under my Hand at ______ this ______ day of ______ in the Year of our Lord One Thousand Eight Hundred and ______

BY THE PRESIDENT

Secretary of the Navy

Registered No.

CONFEDERATE NAVAL COMMISSION.

the most eminent sea-robbers noted in history, and succeeded. His vessel had neither register nor record, no regular ship's papers, no evidence of transfer; and no vessel captured by her was ever sent into any port for adjudication. All the forms of law of civilized nations for the protection of private rights, and all the regulations of public justice which discriminate the legalized naval vessel from the pirate, were disregarded. Although she was a British vessel, manned chiefly by British subjects from a British port, armed with British cannon, and provided with coal and other supplies from British soil, she had no acknowledged flag nor recognized nationality, nor any accessible port to which she might send her prizes, nor any legal tribunal to adjudge her captures. She was an outlaw, roving the seas as an enemy of mankind, for plunder and destruction, and her commander was a pirate, whose career as such was as cowardly as it was criminal. For a year and a half, while carefully avoiding contact with our National vessels of war, he illuminated the seas with blazing merchant-ships. During the last ninety days of 1862, he destroyed by fire no less than twenty-eight helpless vessels. The subsequent career of the *Alabama* will be considered hereafter.

THE ALABAMA.

While this British ship was upon the sea, commissioned for destruction, a notable American ship was also on the sea, but for a widely different purpose. The blockade caused a lack of the cotton supply in England, and the greatly advanced price of that article made the manufacturers either run their mills only a part of each day, or shut them up altogether. This caused wide-spread distress among the poorly remunerated operatives in those mills, on which, in Lancashire alone, nearly a million of stomachs depended for food. Starvation invaded that region, and a most pitiful cry of distress came over the sea. The just indignation of the loyal Americans, because of the conduct of the ruling classes of Great Britain, and especially because of the conduct of the Government in the matter of the pirate-ships, was quenched by the emotions of common humanity, and the citizens of New York alone, whose merchants suffered most by the piracies, contributed more than one hundred thousand dollars for the relief of starving English families. They loaded the ship *George Griswold* with food, and sent her out on an errand of mercy, while at the same time they were compelled to send with her a Government war-vessel to protect her from the torch of the pirate, which had been lighted at the altar of mammon by British hands! The loyal

THE GEORGE GRISWOLD.[1]

[1] This was the appearance of the ship while she was a-loading at her wharf on the East River. High up on her rigging was a piece of canvas, on which were the words, "CONTRIBUTIONS FOR LANCASHIRE. FREIGHT FREE."

Americans forgive their British brethren for their unkindness in the hour of trial, but all the waters of the Atlantic cannot wash out the stain.

Let us now turn again to a consideration of military events, whose theater of action, at the close of 1862, was nearly coextensive with the area of the slave-labor States. Up to that time the loyal States had furnished for the war, wholly by volunteering, more than one million two hundred thousand men, of whom, on the 1st of January, 1863, about seven hundred thousand were in the service. Sickness, casualties in the field, the expiration of terms of enlistment, discharges for physical disability, and desertions, had greatly thinned the original regiments.[1]

The most important movement at the close of 1862 was that of the beginning of the second siege of Vicksburg, which resulted in its capture at the following midsummer, and which engaged the services of nearly all the troops westward of the Alleghanies, directly or indirectly, during several months. Though a city of only between four and five thousand inhabitants when the war broke out, the position of Vicksburg soon became one of the most important on the Mississippi River in a military point of view, while its peculiar topography made its conversion into a strong defensive post an easy matter. Port Hudson below (about twenty-five miles above Baton Rouge), another position of great natural strength, was now quite heavily fortified, and growing in defensive power every day. Between these fortified places, only, the Mississippi was free from the patrol of National war-vessels. Here was now the only connecting link between the portions of the Confederacy separated by the Mississippi, and here alone could the vast supplies of the grain and cattle growing regions of Western Louisiana and Texas be passed safely over the great river to Confederate armies, which, with those of the Nationals, were exhausting the regions eastward, between it and the mountain ranges that project into Georgia and Alabama. The importance of holding this connecting link firmly was felt by the Confederates, and when, in the autumn of 1862, Jefferson Davis visited his home within the bounds of that link, and was returning, he declared in a speech at Jackson that Vicksburg and Port Hudson must be held at all hazards. The Nationals, equally impressed with the importance of destroying that link, now bent all their energies to effect

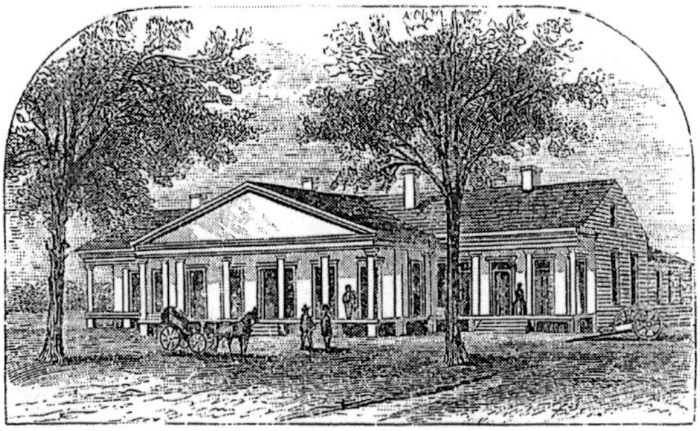

JEFFERSON DAVIS'S RESIDENCE.[2]

---

[1] The fearful waste of an army may be comprehended by considering the statement made by General Meade, in a reply to an address of welcome from the Mayor of Philadelphia, that from March, 1862, when the Army of the Potomac left its lines in front of Washington, to the close of 1863, not less than 100,000 men of that army had been killed or wounded.

[2] This is a view of Davis's mansion on his estate below Vicksburg, from a photograph by Joslyn, of that city. When it was taken, the front of the house over the colonnade bore the words, in large black letters, "The House Jeff. Built." The region was then in possession of the National forces, and Union soldiers occupied

it. At that time the Confederate forces at and near Vicksburg were under the command of General John C. Pemberton, a Pennsylvanian, who had lately been commissioned a lieutenant-general, and ranked both Van Dorn and Lovell.

We left the main forces of General Grant confronting the Confederates on the Tallahatcheé.[1] Grant's plan was for General Sherman, then at Memphis, to descend the river with troops in transports from that city, and from Helena, in Arkansas, and, with a gun-boat fleet, make an attack on Vicksburg. At the same time, General McClernand was to go down with troops from Cairo and re-enforce Sherman soon after his attack. Grant himself was to advance rapidly in the mean time upon the main body of the Confederate troops under Van Dorn, north and eastward of Vicksburg, and, if they should retreat to that place, follow them, and assist Sherman in the reduction of the post.

On the 4th of November Grant transferred his head-quarters from Jackson (Tennessee) to La Grange, a few miles west of Grand Junction, on the Memphis and Charleston railway. He had concentrated his forces for a vigorous movement in the direction of Vicksburg. On the 8th he sent out McPherson, with ten thousand infantry, and fifteen hundred cavalry under Colonel A. L. Lee, to drive a large body of Confederate cavalry from Lamar, on the railway southward of him. It was accomplished, and the Confederates were gradually pushed back to Holly Springs, on the same railway.

It was now evident that the Confederates intended to hold the line of the Tallahatchee River, for there Pemberton had concentrated his forces and cast up fortifications. Grant at once prepared to dislodge them, and on the 20th of November he moved toward Holly Springs with his main body, Hamilton's division in the advance. In the mean time Generals A. P. Hovey and C. C. Washburne had crossed the Mississippi[a] from Helena, landed at Delta, and moved in the direction of Grant's army. Their cavalry was distributed. That of Washburne pushed rapidly eastward to the Cold Water River, where they captured a Confederate camp. Moving swiftly down that stream and the Tallahatchee, they made a sweep by way of Preston, and struck the railway at Garner's Station, just north of Grenada, where the railways from Memphis and Grand Junction meet, and destroyed the road and bridges there. They then went northward to Oakland and Panola, on the Memphis road, and then struck across the country southeast to Coffeeville, on the Grand Junction road.

[a] Nov. 20, 1862.

---

the mansion and the plantation. Davis was the owner of a large number of slaves, and on his estate were found every implement employed in slave-labor and its management in that rich cotton district. Among other things found there was a lash for beating the slaves, represented in the engraving, which Colonel James Grant Wilson, of General Banks's staff, sent to his home in Poughkeepsie. It is a terrible instrument for punishment. The lash is twenty-five inches in length and a little more than two inches in width, composed of five thicknesses of heavy leather, sewed together with saddler's thread in seven rows, making the whole half an inch thick. This lash is inserted in a handle made of hickory, a little more than a foot long, and fastened by three screws on each side. Sometimes these lashes had holes in them, an inch in diameter, into which the flesh of the victim would rise when the blow was inflicted. Such was the kind of scepter with which Capital was to rule Labor in the horrid empire of injustice within "The Golden Circle" projected by Davis and his fellow-conspirators, and for the establishment of which they attempted to destroy the Republic.

SLAVE-LASH.

[1] See page 524.

Having accomplished the object of their expedition, Hovey and Washburne returned to the Mississippi.

This raid, in which the railways on which the Confederates depended were severely damaged, and the rolling stock destroyed, while Grant was pressing in front, disconcerted Pemberton, and he fell back to Grenada, and by the 1st of December Grant held a strong position south of Holly Springs, and commanding nearly parallel railways in that region, as we have observed on page 524. He pushed on to Oxford, the capital of Lafayette County, Mississippi, and sent forward two thousand cavalry, under Colonels Lee and T. L. Dickey, to press the rear of Van Dorn's retreating column. At Coffeeville, several miles southward, these encountered[a] a superior force of Van Dorn's infantry and some artillery, and, after a sharp struggle, were driven back several miles, with a loss of one hundred men, killed, wounded, and missing.

[a] Dec. 5, 1862.

Grant, with his main army, remained at Oxford.[1] The railway had been put in running order as far southward as Holly Springs, and there he had made his temporary depot of arms and supplies of every kind, valued, late in December, at nearly four millions of dollars. That very important post was placed in charge of Colonel R. C. Murphy, with one thousand men, who, as we have seen, abandoned a large quantity of stores at Iuka on the approach of the Confederates.[2] He now permitted a far greater disaster to befall the National cause. His treasures were a powerful temptation to Van Dorn, and Grant was so satisfied that he would attempt to seize them, that he had enjoined Murphy to be extremely vigilant. On the night of the 19th he had warned him of immediate danger, and sent four thousand men to make the security of the stores absolutely certain; but Murphy seems not to have heeded it. He made no preparations, by barricading the streets or otherwise, for defense. When, at daybreak the next morning,[b] Van Dorn and his cavalry burst into the town like an overwhelming avalanche, he was met by very little resistance. He captured Murphy and a greater portion of his men, gathered what plunder his troops wanted for personal use, and burned all the other public property, not sparing even a large hospital, filled with sick and wounded soldiers. The Second Illinois cavalry refused to surrender, and gallantly fought their way out with a loss of only seven men. Murphy accepted a parole, with his soldiers; and on the 9th of January[c] General Grant, in a severe order, "to take effect," he said, "from December 20th, the date of his cowardly and disgraceful conduct," dismissed Murphy from the army.[3]

[b] Dec. 20.

[c] 1863.

After remaining at Holly Springs ten hours, engaged in pillaging and

[1] Grant had a very efficient staff. Among the principal and most active officers were Brigadier-General J. D. Webster, a most skillful artillery officer, and then superintendent of military roads. Lieutenant-Colonel J. A. Rawlins was his chief of staff, and Captain T. S. Bowers was his most trusted aid-de-camp. The two latter remained on his staff throughout the entire war.

[2] See page 513.

[3] In an order on the 23d of December, General Grant spoke of the surrender as "disgraceful," and declared that with "all the cotton, public stores, and substantial buildings about the depot," Murphy might easily have kept the assailants at bay until relief arrived. He pointedly condemned the acceptance of a parole by Murphy for himself and men, a cartel having been agreed to, by which each party was bound to take care of its own prisoners. Had Murphy refused parole for himself and men, Van Dorn would have been "compelled," Grant said, "to have released them unconditionally, or to have abandoned all further aggressive movements for the time being."

destroying, blowing up the arsenal, and burning the public property,[1] Van Dorn's men departed at five o'clock in the evening, highly elated, and immediately afterward assailed in rapid succession the National troops at Coldwater, Davis's Mills, Middleburg, and even Bolivar, but without other success than the effect produced upon Grant by a serious menace of his communications.[2] Two hours after they had left Holly Springs, the four thousand troops which Grant had dispatched by railway to re-enforce Murphy arrived. They had been detained by accident on the way, or they might have reached the place in time to have saved the property. Its loss was a paralyzing blow to the expedition, for Grant was compelled to fall back to Grand Junction, to save his army from the most imminent peril, and perhaps from destruction. This left General Pemberton at liberty to concentrate his forces at Vicksburg for its defense.

In the mean time General Sherman had been preparing for his descent upon Vicksburg. While in command of the right wing of the Army of the Tennessee, with his head-quarters at Memphis, he had thoroughly drilled his troops, and put that important post in the most complete defensive state. In Fort Pickering he had constructed one of the finest of the numerous look-outs that were so extensively used by both parties during the war, from which, on several occasions, notice of the approach of guerrillas was given in time to save the place from pillage.

LOOK-OUT.

Sherman left Memphis with a little more than twenty thousand troops in transports, on the day of the sad disaster at Holly Springs,[a] leaving as a guard to the city a strong force of infantry and cavalry, and the siege-guns in place with a complement of artillerists. He proceeded to Friar's Point, a little below where Hovey landed, where he was joined by Admiral D. D. Porter (whose naval force was at the mouth of the Yazoo River) in his flag-ship *Black Hawk*, and with the gun-boats *Marmora* and *Conestoga* to act as a convoy. On the same evening the troops at Helena embarked, and joined Sherman at Friar's Point, and made his entire force full thirty thousand strong. Arrangements for future action were completed the following morning[b] by the two commanders. The army and navy moved down the stream, and were all at the mouth of the Yazoo River, about twelve miles above Vicksburg, on the 25th.[3] The plan was to make an attack upon Vicksburg in the rear, with a strong force, and for that purpose

[a] Dec. 20, 1862.

[b] Dec. 22.

---

[1] The kind and value of the public property destroyed was as follows:—1,809,000 fixed cartridges and other ordnance stores, including 5,000 rifles and 2,000 revolvers, $1,500,000; 100,000 suits of clothing and other quartermasters' stores, $500,000; 5,000 barrels of flour and other commissary stores, $500,000; medical stores, $1,000,000; 1,000 bales of cotton and $600,000 worth of sutlers' stores.

[2] It was at about this time, as we have observed (page 551), that Forrest was making his raid in West Tennessee.

[3] The fleet consisted of more than sixty transports, besides a number of gun-boats (some of them armored), and some mortar-boats.

the fleet and army passed up the Yazoo (which, in a great bend, sweeps round within a few miles of Vicksburg[1]) twelve miles, to Johnston's Landing, the troops debarking[a] at points in that vicinity along the space of three miles, without opposition.

[a] Dec. 26, 1862.

To understand the difficulties in Sherman's way, we must consider, for a moment, the topography of his field of intended operations. The bluffs or hills on which Vicksburg stands rise a little below the city, and extend northeast twelve or fifteen miles to the Yazoo River, where they terminate in Haines's Bluff. In the rear of the city the ground is high and broken, falling off gradually toward the Big Black River, twelve miles distant. This range of hills, fronting the Mississippi and the Yazoo, was fortified along its entire length, and the only approach to Vicksburg by land was up their steep faces, through which roads were cut in a manner indicated by the engraving. At the base of these bluffs were rifle-pits. To render the approach still more difficult, there is a deep natural ditch, called Chickasaw Bayou, extending from the Yazoo, below Haines's Bluff, passing along near the base of the bluffs for some distance, and emptying into the Mississippi. Added to this is a deep slough, whose bottom is quicksand, and supposed to have once been a lake which stretched along the foot of the bluffs, and entered the bayou where the latter approached them. These formed a natural moat in front of the fortifications, while on the plain over which Sherman had to approach the bluffs the cypress forests were felled in places, and formed a difficult *abatis*.

THE BLACK HAWK.

UPPER ENTRANCE TO VICKSBURG.[2]

Sherman's army was organized in four divisions, commanded respectively by Brigadier-Generals G. W. Morgan, Morgan L. Smith, A. J. Smith, and Frederick Steele. The first three divisions had three brigades each, and the fourth one (Steele's), four. In the plan of attack Steele was assigned to the

[1] The Yazoo River is a deep and narrow stream formed by the Tallahatchee and Yallobusha Rivers, which unite in Carroll County, Mississippi. It runs through an extremely fertile alluvial plain.

[2] This is a view on what is called the Valley road, the one entering Vicksburg from the north, nearest the river. At the point where this little sketch was taken was a strong palisade, and near it was a block-house, both of which were well preserved when the writer visited Vicksburg, in April, 1866.

command of the extreme left, Morgan the left center, M. L. Smith the right center, and A. J. Smith the extreme right. The latter division not having arrived from Milliken's Bend (where it had remained as a support to a force under Colonel Wright, sent to cut the railway on the west side of the Mississippi, that connects Vicksburg with Shreveport) when Sherman was ready to advance, General Frank P. Blair, of Steele's division, was placed in command on the extreme right. All of these divisions were to converge toward the point of attack on the bluffs at or near Barfield's plantation, where only, it had been ascertained, the bayou could be crossed at two points—one at a sand-bar, and the other at a narrow levee. Both were commanded by Confederate batteries and rifle-pits. The battery at the levee was on an ancient Indian mound,[1] near the bank of the bayou, and could sweep nearly the whole ground over which the Nationals must advance. Everywhere on that advance the ground was so soft that causeways had to be built for the passage of the troops and cannon. Difficulties were found to be much greater and more numerous than was anticipated.

ANCIENT MOUND, CHICKASAW BAYOU.

The army was ready to move on the 27th,[a] and the center divisions, including Blair's, marched slowly toward the bluffs, driving the Confederate pickets, silencing a battery on the left where Steele was to join the forward movement, and cheered by the confidence of the commanding general that full success would crown their endeavors. Alas! he did not then know of the disaster at Holly Springs, the recoil of Grant from Oxford, and the heavy re-enforcements which Pemberton had been sending to Vicksburg. He knew that the line that he was to attack was fifteen miles in length, and supposed there were only fifteen thousand men to man it, and he believed that, with his superior force concentrated at some point, he might break through the line, demolish it in detail, and march triumphantly into Vicksburg. He knew the position to be assailed was a strong one, but he was not aware of the ample preparations, by rifle-pits rising tier above tier upon the slopes, and batteries crowning every hill, to enfilade his troops at every point, and make success almost an impossibility. In ignorance of the strength before him, and expecting Grant's co-operation on the morrow, Sherman reposed on the night of the 27th, his army bivouacking in the cold air without fires.

[a] Dec., 1862.

The army pressed forward on Sunday morning, the 28th, driving the pickets of the Confederates across the bayou. Steele, moving on the extreme left, was soon checked by a slough and cypress swamp, across which there was no passage excepting by a corduroy causeway, enfiladed by the Confederate batteries and rifle-pits. Meanwhile Morgan had advanced under cover of a heavy fog and the fire of his artillery against the Confederate center. He pressed on to a point at the bayou where it approaches

[1] The little sketch above shows the appearance of the ancient mound when the writer visited it, in 1866. It was about twenty-five feet in height.

nearest the bluffs, and where it was impassable. He held his ground there throughout the day and the following night. At the same time M. L. Smith had advanced far to the right, and before noon was disabled by a sharpshooter's ball wounding his hip, when his command devolved on General David Stuart. A. J. Smith pushed forward on the extreme right until his pickets reached a point from which Vicksburg was in full view.

Steele's division was brought around that night to a point a little below the junction of the bayou with the Yazoo, and on the morning of the 29th, General Sherman, aware that the force of the Confederates on his front was rapidly increasing, ordered a general advance of his whole army. Morgan, being nearest the bayou and the bluffs, was expected to cross early and carry the batteries and heights on his front; but at the dawn the Confederates opened a heavy cannonade upon him, and it was almost noon before he thought it prudent to move forward. Meanwhile detachments had been constructing bridges over the bayou, for the purpose of crossing to assail the foe on the bluffs, and when Morgan was ready to move, Blair had come up with his brigade and was ready to go into the fight, with Thayer, of Steele's division, as a support.

Blair had moved forward between the divisions of Smith and Morgan, and obliquing to the left, which exposed him to a severe flank fire, in which Colonel J. B. Wyman, of the Thirteenth Illinois, was killed, he crossed Morgan's track, and there detached two regiments to the support of that commander. With the remainder he worked his way to the front of Morgan's left, near the house of Mrs. Lake, and at the van of Steele he crossed the bayou over a bridge his men had built, and advanced to the slough, whose bottom was a quicksand, and its banks were covered with a snarl of felled trees. Over this they passed, Blair leaving his horse floundering in the shallow water with its unstable bed. Dashing through the *abatis*, and followed by Thayer, with only a single regiment (Fourth Iowa) of his brigade then in hand, he pressed across a sloping plateau, captured two lines of rifle-pits, and fought desperately to gain the crest of the hill before him, while De Courcy's brigade of Morgan's command, which had crossed the bayou, charged on his right. But the effort was vain. The assailants

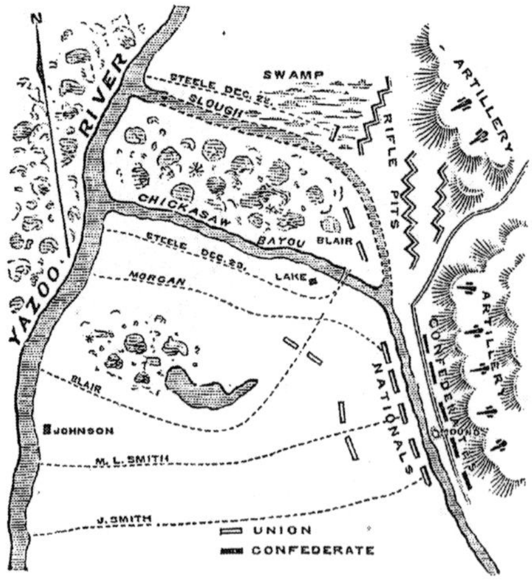

THE BATTLE OF CHICKASAW BAYOU.

suffered terribly, for the hills were swarming with men, bristling with weapons, and ablaze with the fire of murderous guns. It was a struggle of three thousand in open fields below with ten thousand behind intrenchments above. Pemberton, who had arrived and was in command, had been re-enforced by three brigades from Grenada, released by Grant's retrograde movement, and he defied Sherman. Blair and his companions were compelled to retreat. He had lost one-third of his brigade, and De Courcy, by a flank charge by the Seventeenth and Twenty-sixth Louisiana, lost four flags, three hundred and thirty-two men made prisoners, and about five hundred small arms.[1] So heavy and active was the force on the bluffs, that all attempts to construct bridges were frustrated, and they were abandoned. General A. J. Smith's advance (Sixth Missouri) had crossed the bayou at a narrow sand-bar on the extreme right, but could not advance because of the cloud of sharp-shooters that confronted them. So they lay below the bank until night, and then withdrew. Darkness closed the struggle, when Sherman had lost nearly two thousand men, and his foe only two hundred and seven. Thus ended The Battle of Chickasaw Bayou.

General Sherman was loth to relinquish his effort against Vicksburg. He had ordered another attack on the left after Blair was repulsed, but

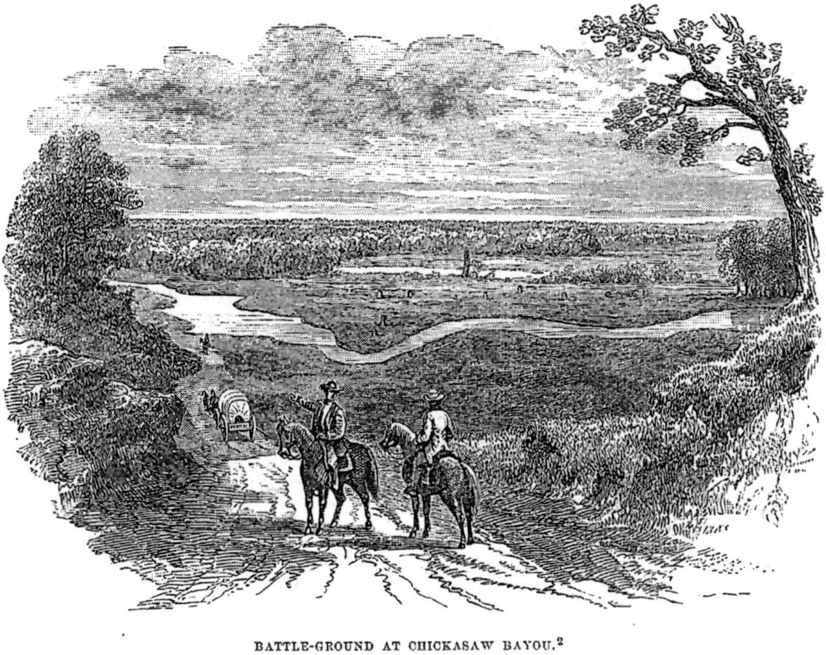

BATTLE-GROUND AT CHICKASAW BAYOU.[2]

wisely countermanded it; but that night, while rain was falling copiously, he caused his men to rest on their arms without fire, preparatory to another struggle in the morning. During the night he visited Admiral Porter on board his flag-ship, and concerted a fresh plan of attack, but on the following day,[a] after a careful estimate of his chances for success, and despairing of any co-operation on the part of Grant, he concluded to abandon the attempt to penetrate the Confederate lines, but to try and turn them. He proposed to go stealthily up the Yazoo

[a] Dec. 29, 1862.

[1] In this attack Lieutenant-Colonel Dister, of the Fifty-eighth Ohio, and Major Jaensen, of the Thirty-first Missouri, were killed. Colonel T. C. Fletcher, of the latter regiment, who is now (1867) Governor of Missouri, and his Lieutenant-Colonel, Simpson, were wounded. Fletcher was made a prisoner.

[2] This was the appearance of the battle-ground of Chickasaw Bayou when the writer sketched it, just at evening of a warm day in April, 1866. The view is taken from the road (see map on page 578), on the slope of

with the land and naval forces, and attack and carry Haines's bluff, on their extreme right, while by some diversion on the bayou the Confederates should be prevented from sending re-enforcements there in time to oppose the National army in securing a firm footing. The latter was then to take the remaining Confederate fortifications in flank and reverse, and fight its way to Vicksburg.

Preparations were made for this flank movement to begin at midnight of the 31st.[a] A dense fog interposed. The enterprise became known to Pemberton, and it was abandoned. Rumors of Grant's retreat to Grand Junction had reached Sherman, and he resolved to return to Milliken's Bend on the Mississippi. The troops were all re-embarked, and ready for departure from the Yazoo, when the arrival of General McClernand, Sherman's senior in rank, was announced.[b] On the 4th of January that officer assumed the chief command, and the army and navy proceeded to Milliken's Bend. The title of Sherman's force was changed to that of the Army of the Mississippi, and was divided into two corps, one of which was placed under the command of General Morgan, and the other under General Sherman.

[a] Dec., 1862.

[b] Jan. 2, 1863.

Before McClernand's arrival Sherman and Porter had agreed upon a plan for attacking Fort Hindman, or Arkansas Post, on the left bank, and at a sharp bend of the Arkansas River,[1] fifty miles from the Mississippi, while Grant was moving his army to Memphis, preparatory to a descent of the river, to join in the further prosecution of the siege of Vicksburg. McClernand approved of the plan, and the forces moved up the Mississippi to Montgomery Point, opposite the mouth of White River. On the 9th the combined force proceeded up that river fifteen miles, and, passing through a canal into the Arkansas, reached Notrib's farm, three miles below Fort Hindman, at four o'clock in the afternoon, when preparations were made for landing the troops. This was accomplished by noon the next day,[c] when about twenty-five thousand men, under McClernand, Sherman, Morgan, Stewart, Steele, A. J. Smith, and Osterhaus, were ready, with a strong flotilla of armored and unarmored gun-boats, under the immediate command of Admiral Porter, to assail the fort, garrisoned by only five thousand men, under General T. J. Churchill, who had received orders from General T. H. Holmes at Little Rock, then commanding in Arkansas, to "hold on until help should arrive or all were dead." The gun-boats moved slowly on, shelling the Confederates out of their rifle-pits along the levee, and driving every soldier into the fort,[2] and in the mean time the land troops pressed forward over swamps and bayous, and bivouacked that night around Fort Hindman, without tents or fires, prepared for an assault in the morning.

[c] Jan. 10, 1863.

the bluff which Blair attempted to carry. The Chickasaw Bayou is seen winding through the plain in the foreground. The solitary stem of a tree in the middle marks the place where there was an encounter on the 27th, when some Confederate pickets were captured, and all were driven back. The belt of trees in the distance marks the line of the Yazoo. The Indian mound is not far beyond the most distant point seen in the bayou, on the extreme left.

[1] This point is the first high land on the Arkansas, after leaving the Mississippi. There the French had a trading post and a settlement as early as 1685, and gave it the name which it yet bears. The Confederates had strongly fortified it, and named the principal work Fort Hindman, in honor of the Arkansas general. It was a regular square, bastioned and casemated work, with a ditch twenty feet wide and eight deep, and was armed with twelve guns.

[2] The vessels engaged in this bombardment were the iron-clads *Cincinnati*, *De Kalb*, and *Louisville*.

At about noon on the 11th, McClernand notified Porter that the army was ready to move upon the fort. The gun-boats opened fire at one o'clock, and soon afterward the brigades of Hovey, Thayer, Giles A. Smith, and T. Kilby Smith, pushed forward at the double-quick, finding temporary shelter in woods and ravines with which the ground was diversified. In a belt of woods, three hundred yards from the Confederate rifle-pits, they were brought to a halt by a very severe fire of musketry and artillery, but they soon resumed their advance with the support of Blair's brigade, and pushed up to some ravines fringed with bushes and fallen timber, within musket range of the fort. Morgan's artillery and the gun-boats had covered this advance by a rapid fire, and, with the batteries of Hoffman, Wood, and Barrett, had nearly silenced the Confederate guns. Parrott guns (10 and 20-pounders), under Lieutenants Webster and Blount, had performed excellent service in dismounting cannon that most annoyed the gun-boats. In this movement Hovey had been wounded by a fragment of a shell, and the horse of Thayer had been shot under him.

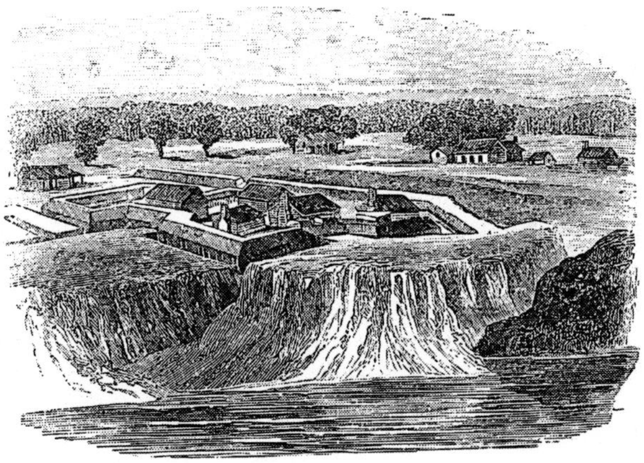

FORT HINDMAN.

General A. J. Smith now deployed nine regiments of Burbridge's and Landrum's brigades, supported by three more regiments in reserve, and drove the Confederate advance on the right, back behind a cluster of cabins, from which shelter they were dislodged by a charge of the Twenty-third Wisconsin, Colonel Guppy. Smith, meanwhile, pushed on his division until it was not more than two hundred yards from the fort, while Colonel Sheldon, of Osterhaus's division, had sent Cooley's battery, supported by the One Hundred and Eighteenth and One Hundred and Twentieth Ohio, and Sixty-ninth Indiana, to within two hundred yards of another face of the fort. They cleared the rifle-pits before them, and the One Hundred and Twentieth Ohio attempted to scale and carry by assault the eastern side of the fort, but were prevented by a deep ravine in addition to the ditch.

At a little past three o'clock, the guns of the fort having been silenced, and Sherman's right strengthened by the Twenty-third Wisconsin, Nineteenth Kentucky, and Ninety-seventh Illinois, of Smith's division, McClernand ordered an assault, when the troops dashed forward under a dreadful fire, Burbridge's brigade, two regiments of Landrum's, and the One Hundred and Twentieth Ohio, bearing the brunt. The Confederates saw that all was lost, and raised a white flag just as the One Hundred and Twentieth Ohio, followed by the Eighty-third Ohio and Sixteenth Indiana, under Burbridge, were pouring over the intrenchments on the east, while the troops of Sherman and Steele, which had stormed the works farther to the north and west, were also swarming over the works. General Burbridge had the honor of planting the standard of the Republic on the fort, which General Smith had placed in his hands in acknowledgment of his bravery. The garrison flag was captured by Captain Ennes, one of General Smith's aids. So ended THE BATTLE OF ARKANSAS POST, in which the army and navy won equal renown.[1]

After dismantling and blowing up Fort Hindman, burning a hundred wagons and other property that he could not take away, embarking his prisoners for St. Louis, and sending an expedition in light-draft steamers, under General Gorman and Lieutenant Commanding J. G. Walker,[a] up the White River to capture Des Arc and Duval's Bluff,[2] McClernand, by order of General Grant, withdrew with his troops and the fleet to Napoleon, on the Mississippi, at the mouth of the Arkansas River. Grant had come down the river from Memphis in a swift steamer, and at Napoleon he and the other military commanders, with Admiral Porter, made arrangements for the prosecution of the campaign against Vicksburg.

[a] Jan. 13, 1862.

[1] See Reports of General McClernand and his subordinates; Admiral Porter, and General Churchill. McClernand reported his loss at 977, of whom 129 were killed, 831 wounded, and 17 missing. The fleet lost three killed and twenty-six wounded. Churchill reported his loss at not exceeding 60 killed and 80 wounded, but McClernand saw evidences of a much greater number hurt. The spoils of victory were about 5,000 prisoners, 17 cannon, 3,000 small arms, and a large quantity of ordnance and commissary stores.

[2] The expedition was successful. Both places were captured without much trouble. Des Arc was quite a thriving commercial town on the White River, in Prairie County, Arkansas, about fifty miles northeast of Little Rock. Duval's Bluff was the station of a Confederate camp and an earth-work, on an elevated position, a little below Duval's Bluff. With some prisoners and a few guns, this expedition joined the main forces at Napoleon on the 19th. A post at the little village of St. Charles, just above Fort Hindman, was captured at about the same time.

CHAPTER XXII.

THE SIEGE OF VICKSBURG.

"VICKSBURG MUST BE TAKEN," was the fiat of General Grant, in obedience to the will of the loyal people, and he made instant preparations for the great work on his return to Memphis from the conference at Napoleon. The Government was fully alive to the importance and difficulties of the undertaking, and had sent him re-enforcements for the purpose. He had already adopted an important measure for the promotion of the efficiency of his army, by organizing it[a] into four corps, known as the Thirteenth, Fifteenth, Sixteenth, and Seventeenth Army Corps.[1] By this arrangement the Commander-in-chief was relieved of much official drudgery, and the generals under him commanding corps had a wider field in which to display their own powers.

[a] Dec. 22, 1862.

General Grant was fully sensible of the importance of the acts of Congress, and the proclamation of the President authorizing the enlistment and use of colored troops; and being a soldier and not a politician, and a manly citizen, who loved justice more than popularity, heartily approved of those measures, and, in orders, said:—"It is expected that all commanders will especially exert themselves in carrying out the policy of the administration, not only in organizing colored troops, and rendering them efficient, but also in removing prejudices against them." "As the servant of a great Republic," says an accomplished writer on military affairs, "he left to the Departments of the Government their specific duties, while he performed his own."[2]

It was evident that a direct assault upon the defenses of Vicksburg by the army and navy would result in failure, and Grant determined to move upon them in reverse or rear. How to get a base for such operations was a

---

[1] By a General Order issued on the 22d of December, 1862, in which the new organization was announced, the command of the *Thirteenth Corps* was assigned to Major-General John A. McClernand. It was composed of the Ninth Division, General G. W. Morgan; Tenth Division, General A. J. Smith, and "all other troops operating on the Mississippi River below Memphis, not included in the Fifteenth Army Corps." The command of the *Fifteenth Corps* was assigned to Major-General W. T. Sherman. It was composed of the Fifth Division, General Morgan L. Smith; the division from Helena, Arkansas, General F. Steele, and the forces in the "District of Memphis." The command of the *Sixteenth Corps* was assigned to Major-General S. A. Hurlbut. It was composed of the Sixth Division, General J. McArthur; the Seventh Division, General I. F. Quimby; Eighth Division, General L. F. Ross; Second Brigade of Cavalry, A. L. Lee; and the troops in the "District of Columbus," commanded by General Davies, and those in the "District of Jackson," under General Sullivan. The command of the *Seventeenth Corps* was assigned to Major-General J. B. McPherson. It was composed of the First Division, General J. W. Denver; Third Division, General John A. Logan; Fourth Division, General J. G. Lauman; First Brigade of Cavalry, Colonel B. H. Grierson; and the forces in the "District of Corinth," commanded by General G. M. Dodge.

[2] *Grant and his Campaigns*, by Henry Coppée, page 152.

vital question, and his attention was turned alternately to the Canal that General Williams attempted to cut,[1] Milliken's Bend, Lake Providence, the Yazoo Pass, and Steele's Bayou. All of these routes were tried, as we shall observe, before in another way he achieved the desired end.

It was determined first to complete Williams's canal across the peninsula opposite Vicksburg, which was traversed by the Shreveport and Vicksburg railroad—the great highway over which large quantities of supplies for the Confederates were transported from Western Louisiana. That cut-off was five or six miles from Vicksburg. By it, when completed, that city would be isolated, and through it troops and supplies might be safely transported out of reach of the Vicksburg batteries to a new base of supplies below that town. It also seemed probable that it would make a new channel for the Mississippi, and leave Vicksburg on the borders of a bayou only.

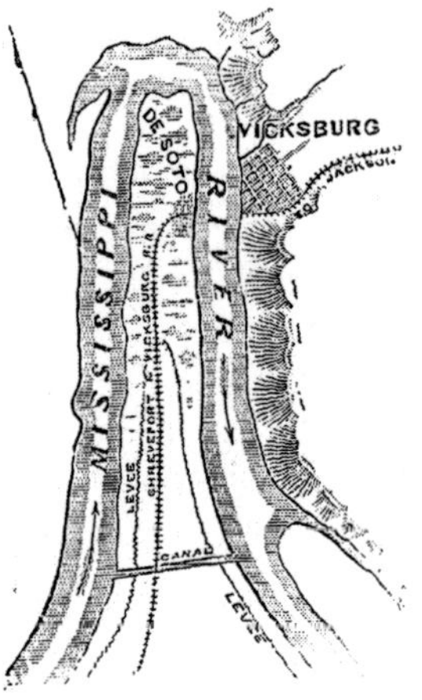

PENINSULA OPPOSITE VICKSBURG.

For the prosecution of this work McClernand, by order of Grant, moved with his army down the Mississippi on the day after the conference at Napoleon.[a] In consequence of detention by a storm, it did not reach its destination at Young's Point, on the right bank of the river, nearly opposite the mouth of the Yazoo, until late on the 21st. On the following day the troops landed, and took post a little farther down the river, so as to protect the

[a] Jan. 9, 1863.

VIEW SHOWING THE SITE OF THE CANAL.[2]

line of the canal. There also Porter's fleet, strengthened by the addition of several armored vessels, such as the *Chillicothe*, *Indianola*, *Lafayette*, *East-*

[1] See page 527.

[2] This is a view of the peninsula opposite Vicksburg, and the site of the canal, from a sketch by the author, taken from "Battery Castle," in the southern portion of the city, looking southwest. In making this sketch the writer stood upon the top of a mound in "Battery Castle," in which was mounted a 32-pounder rifled cannon, known as "Whistling Dick." It had belonged to the Confederates, and from the hill near the marine hospital it had been one of the most destructive enemies of the National gun-boats during the siege. The Confederates gave it the significant name. Its projectile was a short pointed solid shot, whose straight lines would form

port, and other gun-boats rendezvoused, and immense power was immediately brought to bear on the cutting of the canal, and other operations of a vigorous siege.

General Grant, as we have observed, hastened back to Memphis after the conference at Napoleon, and immediately commenced moving his troops, which had been gathered there after the disaster at Holly Springs, down the Mississippi, to assist in the siege of Vicksburg. These troops had been pushed to Memphis from Grand Junction as rapidly as possible, and were now reorganized and in readiness for other work. All these veterans of the Army of the Tennessee, excepting detachments left to hold posts in that State, and the divisions of Logan, were there, and with ample provisions and other supplies, they were now borne swiftly, on more than a hundred transports, upon the rapid current of the rising Mississippi, and were before Vicksburg at the beginning of February. Grant himself arrived at Young's Point on the 2d,[a] and assumed command in person. Already the work on the canal (which was only a mile in length) had been vigorously prosecuted by the soldiers with their picks and shovels, and by the powerful dredge *Samson*, with its immense and never-tiring iron scoop. The earth was cast up on the western side of the canal, on which the troops were encamped, to form a levee for protection against overflow in that direction. Day after day the great ditch grew deeper and longer, and day after day the waters of the Mississippi arose higher and higher, until their surface was full eight feet above the bottom of the canal. The river threatened a destructive overflow, and its menaces were met by piling up a great bulkhead at the upper end of the ditch. But the river was too powerful for puny man. On the 8th of March it broke through the barrier, drove the workmen to the levee, filled the ditch, submerged thousands of implements of labor, and flooded the camps. The river refused to make this canal its main channel, or more than a bayou, nearly dry at low water, and it was evident to the Commander-in-Chief that the canal project was a failure.

[a] Feb., 1863.

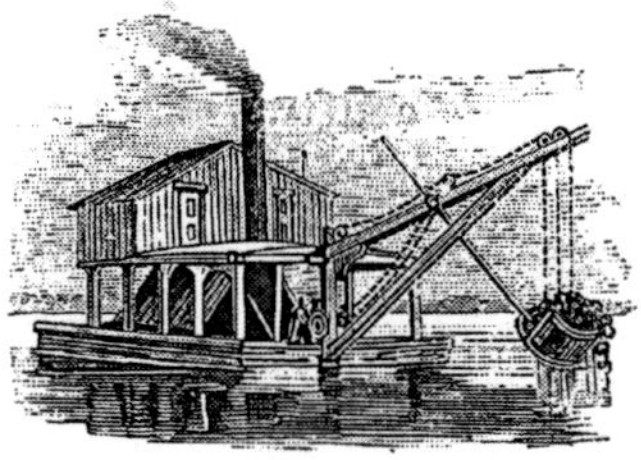

THE SAMSON.

In the mean time General Grant had employed others of his now redun-

almost a right-angled triangle. In the picture the Mississippi is seen sweeping sharply around the peninsula, and approaching itself within a mile where the canal was cut. The canal is indicated by the broad white line beyond the trees on the peninsula. Its terminus below the city was at a point hidden by the tree near the house on the left of the picture. There was a little hamlet on the peninsula, at the terminus of the railway opposite Vicksburg, called De Soto. The river was full, and the peninsula was partially submerged when the sketch was made.

The fortification from which this view was taken was named "Battery Castle," because it was on the site of a fine castellated building, the property and residence of Armistead Burwell, a leading lawyer of Vicksburg, who, on account of his stanch patriotism in adhering to his Government, was driven from his house by the traitors of Mississippi. He remained an exile at St. Louis until after the capture of the city by the Nationals. After that event, and when Grant had a new line of fortifications constructed for the defense of the post, Mr. Burwell's house was demolished to make room for a battery. The writer met this unselfish loyalist at the headquarters of General T. J. Wood, in April, 1866, and was deeply impressed by the purity and zeal of his devotion to his country. Notwithstanding he had been ruined pecuniarily by the war, he refused to apply to the Government for compensation for the loss of his mansion taken for the public use. When the writer remarked that it would be clearly a rightful claim, he replied:—"No, it will only lead the way to a host of dishonest claims upon my Government, and I will not ask it." The Government should *seek* to reimburse such men for their losses, without waiting for them to submit claims.

dant troops in preparing another way to reach the vitals of the Vicksburg defenses. It was by cutting a channel from the western shore of the Mississippi, forty or fifty miles above Vicksburg, across a narrow neck of land into Lake Providence, from which there was a continuous water communication to the great river, far below the city to be assailed, through bayous Baxter and Macon, and the Tensas River, as also into the Washita and Red rivers. This would be a long and tedious way by which to reach the Mississippi, and the chief object to be gained in opening it was the establishment of a communication with General Banks, in command of the Department of the Gulf, to whom had been assigned the duty of reducing Port Hudson, below. Another side cut was attempted from Milliken's Bend into bayous that connected with the eastern branch of the Tensas, and so through other bayous with the Mississippi, near New Carthage. At the same time other troops were employed in the more promising labor of opening a way for light-draft gun-boats and transports with troops from the Mississippi, near Milliken's Bend, through Moon Lake into Yazoo Pass, the Cold Water and Tallahatchee rivers, and so into the Yazoo, or River of Death,[1] which is formed by the Tallahatchee and Yallobusha rivers. Grant hoped to have his troops reach the Yazoo safely, and make another attempt, in connection with the gun-boats, to carry Haines's Bluff and press on to Vicksburg, as Sherman had desired to do. It was reported that the Confederates were building gun-boats and transports on those two chief affluents of the Yazoo, and the destruction of these was an important object of the proposed expedition.

About five thousand men were assigned to the Yazoo expedition. It was led by General L. F. Ross, with a division of McClernand's corps, and the Twelfth and Seventeenth Missouri, of Sherman's corps; and with it went the large gun-boats *Chillicothe* and *De Kalb*, five smaller ones, and nearly twenty transports, under the control of Lieutenant Watson Smith. These vessels passed out of the Mississippi on a swift current, through a broad cut in the levee, at the mouth of the tortuous bayou leading to Moon Lake, and a fearful voyage they had until the power of the redundant waters was modified by diffusion over the swamps. They swept among lofty and overhanging forest-trees, that demolished smoke-stacks and nearly all besides above the decks; and everywhere fallen and submerged trees, and sharp and difficult turns in the channel, were encountered. Three days were consumed in making their way twelve miles to the Cold Water, and they were constantly exposed to Confederate sharp-shooters on the shores. While rudders and wheels were badly wounded, the vessels were not seriously injured.

At the mouth of the Cold Water two mortar-boats joined the expedition,[a] and the whole flotilla moved cautiously down the Tallahatchee, when, just as it approached a sharp bend in the stream, near the little village of Greenwood, ten miles from its confluence with the Yallobusha, it encountered[b] a strong fortification called Fort Pemberton, in command of Major-General W. W. Loring. Near it a raft, with a sunken steamboat, had been placed to obstruct the Tallahatchee. The fort consisted of a line of breast-works thrown across the narrow neck a mile in width, where the two rivers approach

[a] March 2, 1863.

[b] March 11, 1863.

[1] Yazoo is the Choctaw word for River of Death. This stream was so named by the Indians, because of the fatal malarious fevers that brooded along its borders.

each other within that distance two or three miles above their junction. Its best guns were placed so as to sweep the Tallahatchee. In front of it was a slough that formed an excellent substitute for a ditch, and near the rivers it was flanked by low, oozy earth. It was a formidable barrier to the further progress of the expedition. The *Chillicothe*, heavily mailed, attempted to run by, but was made to recoil by a blow from a 32-pound shell, when she backed around the point at the sharp bend in the stream, and opened upon the fort with a heavy bow gun. After fighting for an hour in this half-sheltered position, she withdrew, when the *De Kalb* came forward, fought two hours, and in turn gave up the contest.

A BOW GUN.

On the following day[a] General Ross, under cover of a forest, erected a land battery in front of the Confederate works, and at ten o'clock on the morning of the 13th, its guns and those of both war-vessels opened simultaneously upon Fort Pemberton. The attack was kept up during the day, with considerable damage to the fort, but this was repaired that night, and the fire of the Nationals the next morning was returned with great spirit. After a short time the struggle ceased, and was not renewed until the morning of the 16th, when the gun-boats opened fire on the fort. The *Chillicothe* was soon hulled by an 18-pound Whitworth shot, which entered one of her port-holes, and struck and exploded a shell, by which three of her men were killed and fourteen were wounded. The *Chillicothe* then withdrew, but the *De Kalb* and the land batteries kept up the contest until sunset.

[a] March 12, 1863.

Ross was now satisfied that the fort could not be taken with the force at his command, and he retreated by the route he came. On the way he was met by General Quinby,[b] of McPherson's corps, with some troops, who ranked Ross, and took command. He returned to the front of Fort Pemberton, and was about to assail it, when he received orders[c] to return to the Mississippi.

[b] March 21.

[c] March 23.

There was still another effort made at this time to gain a footing in the rear of Vicksburg. Admiral Porter, whose zeal, energy, and skill in thridding the creeks and bayous of that strange region with his gun-boats were most remarkable, had thoroughly reconnoitered Steele's bayou from Swan Lake to the Yazoo. He was informed by the negroes that there was a channel to be found at that high-water period leading from the bayou into the Sunflower Creek, and so into the Yazoo, between Haines's Bluff and Yazoo City, of sufficient depth for the lighter iron-clads. At the latter place

"Commodore" Lynch, of Elizabeth City fame,[1] had a ship-yard, where he completed the *Arkansas*; and there, and in the Yallobusha, between Greenwood and Grenada, were moored for safety about thirty steamers and other vessels, which escaped from New Orleans when Farragut approached that city the year before. The destruction of these, and a lodgment behind Vicksburg, were advantages to be gained by a successful movement to the Yazoo, and Grant determined to attempt it. He accompanied Porter in person[a] up Steele's Bayou in the ram *Price*, preceded by several armored gun-boats, and, turning into the Black Fork, that led to Deer Creek and the Sunflower through the Rolling Fork, found it greatly obstructed by the overhanging and interlacing boughs, and the fallen trunks of trees.

[a] March 15, 1863.

Porter's boats were now in a perilous position, for the Confederates, apprised of the expedition and its progress, were gathering in strength in that direction, to capture or destroy the fleet. Grant hastened back to Young's Point, and ordered a pioneer force and a division of Sherman's corps to push across Eagle Bend to Steele's Bayou (there only a mile from the Mississippi), to the relief of Porter, and to assist in the labors of the expedition.

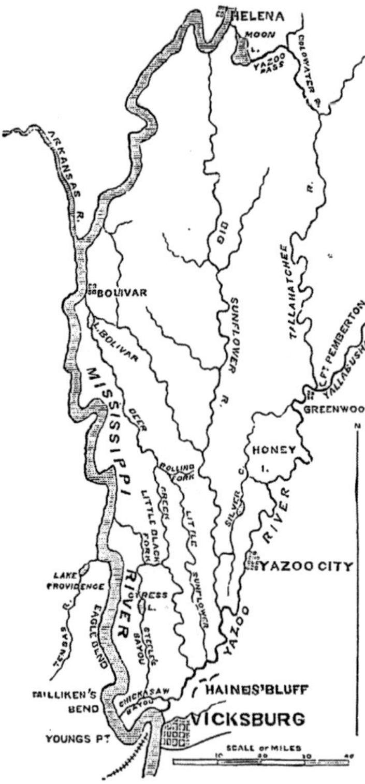

THE YAZOO REGION.

While these were slowly progressing against great difficulties, the Confederates, advised of the movement, were making ample preparations for the reception of the fleet in the Yazoo. The expedition was withdrawn just as the difficulties of the passage were overcome, for General Grant had planned new schemes for accomplishing his great object. A record in detail of the naval and military operations in the Yazoo region, during a part of the winter and early spring of 1863, would fill a volume with narratives more wonderful than romance affords.

While these events were occurring among the network of bayous in that region, there were some stirring scenes on the Mississippi. It was known that Confederate transports were in the river below Vicksburg, supplying the troops at that place and at Port Hudson with necessaries, and it was determined to destroy them. The ram *Queen of the West*, commanded by Colonel C. L. Ellet, was prepared to run by the batteries at Vicksburg. She was armed with a 30-pounder Parrott as a bow gun on her main deck, and

[1] See page 176.

one 20-pounder and three 12-pounder brass cannon on her gun-deck. She was manned by a good crew, well armed, and was accompanied by a squad of soldiers; and her machinery was protected by three hundred bales of cotton. Thus prepared, she went down the river before dawn on the morning of the 2d of February (the day Grant arrived at Young's Point), first to attack and destroy the steamer *City of Vicksburg*, that lay under the guns of the batteries at the city, and then to push farther down the river. After receiving a terrible cannonade while attacking the steamer, she passed on down, and just below Natchez destroyed three others. She ran a few miles up Red River, and, returning, repassed the Vicksburg batteries.

On the 10th of February[a] she was started on another raid down the river, to capture Confederate transports, pass the Port Hudson batteries, if possible, and effect a junction with the fleet of Farragut below that point. Accompanied by the gun-boat *De Soto* and a coal-barge, she again ran by Vicksburg, went up the Red River to the Atchafalaya, and, entering that stream, captured[b] a train of army-wagons; and at Simmsport, a little farther on, a quantity of stores. Returning to the Red River, she went up that stream also, and, a little above the mouth of the Black River, captured the small steamer *Era*, laden with corn and other supplies, and bearing a few Texan soldiers. These were paroled, and the *Era* was left in charge of a guard.

[a] 1863.

[b] Feb. 12.

The *Queen of the West* pushed on about twenty miles farther, toward a battery on the river called Fort Taylor, making the captured pilot of the *Era* ply his vocation on the ram. When turning a point near the fort the fellow ran her aground, when the Confederate guns opened upon her so severely and accurately that she was soon utterly disabled, and Ellet and his crew were compelled to leave her as a prize and retreat on floating bales of cotton. The *De Soto*, lying just below, picked them up. Going down the river, that vessel was also run into the bank by the treacherous pilot, and lost her rudder, when she and the coal-barge were scuttled and sunk.

The *Era* was now Ellet's last refuge. Throwing her corn overboard, she was made to go down the stream as rapidly and lightly as possible, the rebel pilot, strange to say, still at the helm, when he ran her ashore just after reaching the Mississippi. Four armed boats were then in close chase, the leader being the powerful iron-clad ram *Webb*, which had been lying at Alexandria, about sixty miles up the Red River. After much exertion the *Era* was loosed, and went slowly up the river, when she met the powerful iron-clad *Indianola*, just above Elles's Cliffs,[2] coming down in a fog. When

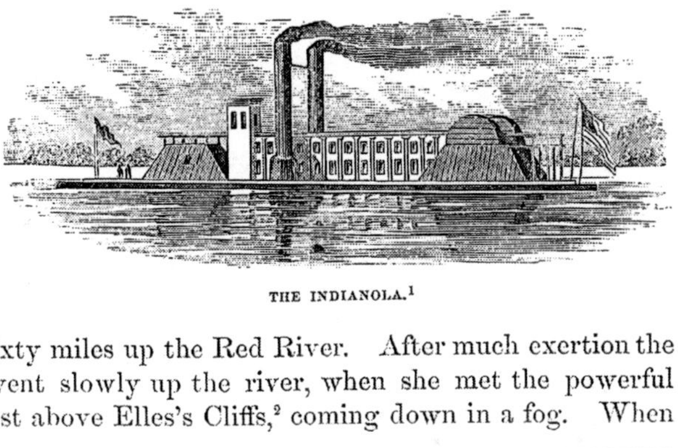

THE INDIANOLA.[1]

[1] The *Indianola* was a new vessel, seventy-four feet in length, fifty feet beam, and every way one of the finest in Porter's fleet. She was heavily armored all round, excepting some temporary rooms on deck. She was propelled by seven engines, and was armed with 9 and 11-inch Dahlgren guns.

[2] See page 527.

the mist dispersed the *Webb* in chase was in sight. She turned and fled, and was pursued a short distance, when the chase was relinquished, and the *Era* went safely up to a point below Vicksburg, notwithstanding she was fired at from Confederate batteries at Grand Gulf.

The appearance of the *Indianola* (Lieutenant-commanding Brown) was very opportune. She had left her anchorage at the mouth of the Yazoo on the night of the 13th of February, and silently drifted by Vicksburg undiscovered, until she had nearly passed the lower batteries. These opened upon her, but without serious effect, and were followed by others quite as harmless. She rescued Ellet, as we have seen, and then went on down the Mississippi, expecting to sweep it of all Confederate craft. She blockaded the mouth of the Red River a few days, and then turned her prow up the Mississippi, intending to go up the Big Black River, if possible, as far as the bridge of the Vicksburg and Jackson railway, which was one of the objects of her voyage. When, at half-past nine o'clock in the evening of the 24th,[a] she was nearly abreast of Grand Gulf, she was suddenly assailed by the ram *Webb*, the captured *Queen of the West*, which the Confederates had repaired, and two smaller gun-boats, which, without the knowledge of Lieutenant Brown, had gone up the Mississippi. The attack was so furious and skillful that the *Indianola* was soon disabled. Seven times the ram had struck her, and at last stove in her stern. Finding her in a sinking condition, her commander surrendered her, and she was immediately run ashore. And now the Confederates had nothing to fear on the Mississippi between Vicksburg and New Orleans, for at that time (near the close of February) Farragut and his fleet were on the Gulf coast.

[a] Feb., 1863.

The Confederates immediately began to repair the *Indianola*, with the expectation of holding sway with her and their other craft over the Mississippi, between Vicksburg and Port Hudson at least, when, by a trick fatal to their schemes, their hopes were blasted. Porter fitted up a worthless flat-boat in imitation of a ram, with smoke-stacks made of pork-barrels, and set it afloat one night on the current of the river, without a man on board. It was believed by the Confederates, when they discovered it, to be a most terrible iron-clad monster, and as it passed sullenly by in the darkness it drew a tremendous fire from the Vicksburg batteries. On it went, appearing more terrible as it seemed to defy shot and shell. Word was hastily sent to the *Queen of the West*, at Warrenton, to beware of the impending danger, whereupon she fled for her life. Orders were also sent for the *Indianola* to be instantly destroyed, to prevent her being captured by the awful ram. The trick was soon discovered, and other orders were sent to save the *Indianola;* but it was too late. Lighted gunpowder had blown her into fragments, and her cannon had gone to the bottom of the great river.

When General Grant withdrew his forces from the bayous he determined to send troops down the west side of the Mississippi by land, and make a lodgment at New Carthage, the first point below Vicksburg that could be reached in that way while the river was so full. General McClernand, with the Thirteenth Army Corps, moved in that direction on the 29th of March, and the Fifteenth and Seventeenth Corps were ordered to follow him as speedily as supplies of food and ordnance stores could be afforded them. The roads were heavy and the movements slow, and when the head of

McClernand's column reached a point only two miles from Carthage, it was found that breaches in the Bayou Vidal had caused that town and its neighborhood to be made an island, by the submerging of the country around it. The army was compelled to make a circuitous march of twelve miles further, around Bayou Vidal, and so the work was accomplished after overcoming great difficulties.

In the mean time measures had been in preparation for another and more daring experiment. It was no less than the passage of Porter's fleet, with transports and barges, by the heavy batteries at Vicksburg. The object was to afford means for carrying the troops across the Mississippi from Carthage, and to have gun-boats to cover the movement and the landing. Porter was ready for the attempt on the 16th of April. The gun-boats selected for the purpose were the *Benton*, Captain Green; *Lafayette*, Captain Walke; *Price*, Captain Woodworth; *Louisville*, Commander Owen; *Carondelet*, Lieutenant Murphy; *Pittsburg*, Lieutenant Hoel; *Tuscumbia*, Lieutenant Shirk; and *Mound City*, Lieutenant Wilson. All of these were iron-clad excepting the *Price*. They were laden with supplies for the army below, and were well fortified against missiles from the batteries by various overlayings, such as iron chains, timbers, and bales of cotton and hay. The transports chosen for the ordeal were the *Forest Queen*, *Henry Clay*, and *Silver Wave*. These, too, were laden with supplies for the army, with their machinery protected by baled hay and cotton. It was arranged for the iron-clads to pass down after dark in single file, a few hundred yards apart, each engaging the batteries as it passed, so that the transports might go by under cover of the smoke.

At dark of the 16th[a] every thing was ready for the perilous enterprise. Silently the armored vessels moved down the river, the *Benton* leading, followed by the *Lafayette*, with the gun-boat *Price* and a coal-barge in tow, and the other vessels in the prescribed order. All was silent and dark at Vicksburg, until, at nearly eleven o'clock, the ten vessels were abreast the city and its defenses, when suddenly the heights seemed all ablaze with lightning and the air fearfully resonant with thunder, as the batteries opened on the fleet. Their fire was returned with spirit, and under cover of the curtain of smoke the transports hastened down the river. The *Silver Wave* passed unhurt; the *Forest Queen* was so badly wounded that she had to be towed, and the *Henry Clay* was set on fire, and, being deserted by her people, went flaming and roaring down the river until she was burned to the water's edge and sunk. Of all the men who passed down with the fleet only one was killed and two were wounded. They were on the *Benton*. The affair was eminently successful, and Grant at once ordered six more transports,[1] similarly prepared, to run by the batteries. They did so on the night of the 22d of April, with the loss of only one of them (the *Tigress*), which was struck below water-mark, and sunk on the Louisiana shore, some distance below. The others were injured, but were soon made ready for use again.

[a] April, 1863.

Grant now prepared for vigorous operations against Vicksburg from the line of the Big Black, on its left flank and rear Awaiting this movement, let us see what was occurring in the Department of the Gulf, under the com-

[1] These were the *Tigress*, *Anglo-Saxon*, *Cheeseman*, *Empire City*, *Horizona*, and *Moderator*.

mand of General Banks, having reference to and bearing upon the grand object of opening the Mississippi and severing the Confederacy.

General Banks, as we have observed,[1] assumed command of the Department of the Gulf on the 16th of December. He found the disloyal inhabitants restive under the restraints imposed by General Butler, and tried the policy of conciliation. It was not received in the gentle and honorable spirit with which it was given, and arrogance, defiance, open contempt for the National power, and revived hopes of the speedy expulsion of the "Yankees" from New Orleans, were soon the visible results. His mild policy was a failure, and he was compelled to use the strong arm, as his predecessor had done.[2]

The destination and special object of an expedition under General Banks, fitted out in the north during the autumn of 1862, was the subject of much speculation. Banks succeeded better than most others in keeping that destination a secret, and the curiosity of the public mind was about as much satisfied by inquiries, as was that of one of the General's staff officers, who, anxious to know where they were going, adroitly inquired, "Shall I take thick or thin clothing with me, General?" Banks more adroitly answered, "You had better take both." By the time the expedition sailed it was generally believed that Texas was its destination. General Andrew J. Hamilton, the newly appointed Provisional Governor of Texas, was in New Orleans, anxiously awaiting its arrival, with that expectation; and the loyal people of Texas were stretching forth their hands toward the Government in piteous petitions for relief from one of the most terrible despotisms the world had ever experienced.

When Banks arrived in New Orleans, he found there, as we have observed, seventeen thousand five hundred well-disciplined men, whom his predecessor turned over to him. These, with the troops that accompanied him, made an army at his command of about thirty thousand men, with the designation of the Nineteenth Army Corps. With these he was expected to co-operate with Grant in opening the Mississippi, and in taking possession of the Red River region, and expelling the Confederates from Louisiana, with a view to the speedy restoration of the National authority in Texas. The task before him, as we shall observe, was much greater than was anticipated, and for a long time afterward Texas remained bound in chains. Even the important positions of Sabine Pass and Galveston, which the Government had "repossessed," were wrested from it within a month after Banks's arrival. Let us see how it happened.

We have observed how Galveston was surrendered to Commodore Renshaw without resistance,[3] when the civil and military authorities retired to the main land. To make the possession of the city and island[4] more secure,

---

[1] See page 530.

[2] "These Southern people," remarked an English writer who went to New Orleans with General Banks, "with their oriental civilization and institutions, cherish something of the eastern impression, that kindness and conciliation imply weakness, originating in a fear of inflicting punishment. They hated Butler, and feared him; now the more foolish sort hope for a certain amount of impunity to the treason yet latent among them."

[3] See page 538.

[4] The City of Galveston is at the northeastern end of Galveston Island, an extensive sand-spit near the entrance to Galveston Bay, into which empty the rivers San Jacinto and Trinity. The island, at the time we are considering, was connected with the main land by a wooden bridge about two miles in length. Its harbor is one of the few on that cheerless coast of the Gulf of Mexico that may fairly claim the dignity of that title.

General Banks, at the request of Renshaw, sent thither from New Orleans the Forty-second Massachusetts, Colonel Burrill. Three companies (two hundred and sixty men) of that regiment arrived there at near the close of December, and were landed[a] and encamped on the wharf. In front of the town lay the gun-boats *Westfield*, *Clifton*, *Harriet Lane*, *Owasco*, *Coryphæus*, and *Sachem*, under the command of Commodore Renshaw, whose relations with the Confederate leaders were so cordial that he enjoyed perfect quiet.

[a] Dec. 28, 1862.

General John B. McGruder had been sent to Texas from Virginia, and was then in chief command in that Department. He had so high an opinion of Renshaw's courtesy and conciliatory spirit, that he went from Houston to Virginia Point, opposite Galveston, and passed over one night with eighty men, and inspected the defenses of the city He found the long wooden bridge connecting that island with the mainland in good order and unprotected, and in view of other evidences of a feeling of perfect security, he was satisfied that he might make an easy conquest of the city with a few troops. But could he hold it? Probably not; so he took four steamboats from the adjacent rivers, put guns on them, and fortified them with cotton-bales. At the same time he collected all the available Confederate troops, volunteers, and arms, in his power, and with this land and naval force, such as it was, he proceeded to attack the National land and naval force at Galveston before dawn on the morning of the first of January, 1863.

The secessionists of Galveston were in such high spirits on the previous day, and there were so many enigmatical assurances of a speedy change of affairs there, that it was easy to perceive that mischief for the National forces was impending. Renshaw, who was in command of these forces on land and water, was warned that an attack was contemplated, yet no extraordinary preparations for resistance were made. Under his direction the handful of Massachusetts troops had been encamped on the wharf, their only protection from an assault from the city being an open space of water, made by taking up the wharf planks, and a barricade formed of them.

At about midnight, while the moon was shining brightly, Magruder crossed the long bridge on a train of cars, with his troops and field-pieces, and, proceeding to within two squares of the camp of the Massachusetts soldiers, planted his artillery there so as to bear upon Renshaw's squadron. In the mean time the armed Confederate steamers were seen in the bay, approaching. These were tardy, and Magruder became nervous, for he was anxious to attack before daylight. The moon went down at four o'clock, and, under cover of the darkness, a storming party five hundred strong and a battalion of sharp-shooters attacked the Massachusetts troops. At the same time Magruder's cannon opened on the gun-boats. The storming party were repulsed and the assailing field-pieces were silenced, and all appeared to be going well for the Nationals, when the Confederate steamers came up, amply manned by a portion of Sibley's brigade, who, we have seen, were driven out of New Mexico.[1] Two of the steamers (*Bayou City* and *Neptune*) fell at once upon the *Harriet Lane*, Captain Wainwright, sweeping her decks with a murderous fire of small arms. She gave the *Neptune* a

---

[1] See page 188.

blow in return, which sent her to the bottom of the harbor. The only cannon on the *Bayou City* (a 68-pounder) had bursted, and it seemed as if she, too, must speedily succumb, when, by a quick maneuver, she ran her bow into the wheel of the *Harriet Lane*, held her fast, careened her so that she could not bring her guns to bear, and allowed Sibley's soldiers to swarm over on her deck. A brief resistance by an inferior force followed, and when Captain Wainwright was killed, and Lieutenant-commanding Lee was mortally wounded, she was captured. The *Owasco*, coming up to her assistance, was kept at bay by the sharp-shooters and the fear of the *Lane's* captured cannon, now in the custody of the Confederates, and she withdrew to a safe distance.

Meanwhile the *Westfield*, Renshaw's flag-ship, which went out to meet the Confederate steamers in Bolivar Channel, had run hard aground at high tide, and signaled for assistance, when the *Clifton* hastened to her relief. During the absence of the latter the attack began. Observing this, Renshaw ordered her back. She opened upon Fort Point batteries, and drove the Confederates up the beach; and at about sunrise a flag of truce came to her commander, Lieutenant Law, with a demand for a surrender of the fleet. Law refused, and time was given to communicate with Renshaw, on the *Westfield*. He, too, rejected the proposal, ordered the National vessels and troops to escape, and, as he could not get his own ship off, he resolved to blow it up, and with officers and crew escape to two of the transports. The firing of the magazine was done prematurely by a drunkard, it was said, and Commodore Renshaw, Lieutenant Zimmerman, Engineer Green, and about a dozen of the crew, perished by the explosion. Nearly as many officers and men were killed in the Commodore's gig, lying by the side of the *Westfield*.

In the mean time, while flags of truce were flying on the vessels and on shore, the Massachusetts troops, with artillery (which they had not) bearing upon them, were treacherously summoned to surrender by General R. Scurry.[1] Resistance would have been vain, and they complied,[2] satisfied that when the *Harriet Lane* should be relieved from contact with the *Bayou City*, she would be too much for the *Clifton* or the *Owasco*. Law fled in the latter, with the remains of the fleet, to New Orleans. Before the *Harriet Lane* could be repaired and got out to sea as a Confederate pirate ship, Farragut sent a competent force to re-establish the blockade of Galveston, and Magruder's victory was made almost a barren one.[3] Just as that blockade was re-established under Commodore Bell, with the *Brooklyn* as

---

[1] Richardson Scurry was a native of Tennessee, and was a representative in Congress from Texas from 1851 to 1853.

[2] Report of Captains James S. Palmer and Melancthon Smith, and Lieutenant-commanding L. A. Kimberly (who composed a court of inquiry appointed by Admiral Farragut), dated January 12, 1863. The Confederates acknowledged the bad faith on their part. An eye-witness, in a communication in the *Houston Telegraph*, January 6, 1863, declared that the flag of truce was only a trick of the Confederates to gain time. It was evident, he said, that if the *Harriet Lane* could not be speedily disengaged, the Nationals would escape, and the flag was to make a delay. "A truce of three hours was agreed upon," said the writer. "During the truce with the vessels, the unconditional surrender of the Massachusetts troops was demanded and complied with." Magruder, in his official report, declared that Renshaw had "agreed to surrender." If that be true, the conviction is forced upon us that Renshaw was a traitor, and was acting in concert with Magruder.

[3] Magruder's spoils were only the *Harriet Lane* and her property, the 260 officers and men of the Forty-second Massachusetts, and about 120 on board of the *Harriet Lane*, made prisoners. His loss he reported at 26 killed and 117 wounded, and the steamer *Neptune*.

his flag-ship, a strange sail appeared in the distance,[a] when the gun-boat *Hatteras* was sent to make her acquaintance. At first the stranger moved off slowly, and Lieutenant Blake, commanding the *Hatteras*, gave chase and prepared for action. He overtook the tardy and even waiting fugitive, and on hailing her was informed that she was the British ship *Vixen*. Blake was about to send a boat aboard, when the craft was revealed as the pirate ship *Alabama*. A hot fight ensued, which ended in the destruction of the *Hatteras*. Her heaviest guns were 32's, while the *Alabama* had a 150-pounder on a pivot, and a 68-pounder. There was a vast disparity in their power. The *Hatteras* was sunk, but her crew were saved, and the *Alabama* went into the friendly British port of Kingston, Jamaica, for repairs.

[a] Jan. 11, 1863.

Ten days later two National gun-boats (*Morning Light* and *Velocity*), blockading the Sabine Pass, were attacked by two Confederate steamers (*John Bell* and *Uncle Ben*) that came down the Sabine. They were driven out to sea and captured, with guns, prisoners, and a large amount of stores. And so when Grant was beginning the siege of Vicksburg in earnest, not a rood of Texas soil was "repossessed" by the National authority.

General Banks began offensive operations immediately after his arrival. On the 18th of December he sent General Cuvier Grover with ten thousand men to reoccupy Baton Rouge, preparatory to an advance on Port Hudson. This was done without serious opposition, but the advance was delayed, because the Confederate force there was stronger than any Banks could then march against it. So he turned his attention to the rich sugar and cotton districts of Louisiana west of the Mississippi, for the purpose of weakening or destroying the Confederate forces there, for they might give him much trouble on his flank and rear, and seriously menace New Orleans. Already National troops had overrun a portion of the territory between the railway from New Orleans to Brashear City, and the Gulf, but between that road and the Red River National troops had not penetrated, excepting in La Fourche district,[1] and the inhabitants were mostly disloyal.

The country in which Banks proposed to operate is a remarkable one. It is composed of large and fertile plantations, extensive forests, sluggish lagoons and bayous, passable and impassable swamps, made dark with umbrageous cypress-trees draped with Spanish moss and festooned with interlacing vines, the earth matted and miry, and the waters abounding in alligators. At that season the country was almost half submerged by the superabundant waters of the Mississippi and its tributaries, and the great bayous. A single railway (New Orleans, Opelousas, and Great Western railroad) then penetrated that region, extending from New Orleans to Brashear City, on the Atchafalaya, a distance of eighty miles, at which point the waters of the great Bayou Tèche meet those of the Atchafalaya, and others that flow through the region between there and the Red River. The latter gather in Chestimachee or Grand Lake, and find a common outlet into the Gulf of Mexico at Atchafalaya Bay.

These waters formed a curious mixture of lake, bayou, canal, and river at Brashear City, and presented many difficulties for an invading army.

[1] See page 530.

These difficulties were enhanced by obstructions placed in the streams, and fortifications at important points. Near Pattersonville, on the Tèche, was an earthwork called Fort Bisland, with revetments; and well up the Atchafalaya, at Butte à la Rose, was another. There was also an armed steamer called the *J. A. Cotton* on the Bayou Tèche. These were intended to dispute the passage of those important waters by National gun-boats from Red River, or forces by land from New Orleans.

A LOUISIANA SWAMP.

Some operations by National forces had already been made on the Tèche, and it was now determined to drive the Confederates from their strong places in the vicinity of Brashear City, and to destroy their gun-boat. An expedition for that purpose was led by General Weitzel, accompanied by a squadron of gun-boats under Commodore McKean Buchanan, who fought his traitor brother so bravely on the *Congress* in Hampton Roads.[1] Weitzel left Thibodeaux on the 11th of January,[a] and placing his infantry on the gun-boats at Brashear City, he sent his cavalry and artillery by land.[2] All moved slowly up the Bayou to Pattersonville, and at Carney's Bridge, just above, they encountered the first formidable obstacles. These consisted of the piles of the demolished Bridge, against which lay a sunken old steamboat laden with brick, and in the bayou below, some torpedoes. Just above these was the very formidable steamer *Cotton*, ready for battle, and batteries (one of them Fort Bisland) were planted on each side of the bayou, and defended by the Twenty-eighth Louisiana and artillerymen, in all about eleven hundred men.

[a] 1863.

Buchanan proceeded to attack the obstructions and the batteries on the morning of the 15th,[b] when, after a short engagement, the stern of the *Kinsman* was lifted fearfully but not fatally by a torpedo that exploded under it. Just then a negro, who had escaped from the *Cotton* for the purpose, warned them of another torpedo just ahead.[3] Without

[b] Jan.

---

[1] See note 2, page 362. His squadron consisted of the gun-boats *Calhoun* (flag-ship), *Kinsman*, *Estrella*, and *Diana*.

[2] Weitzel's force consisted of the Eighth Vermont, Seventy-fifth and One Hundred and Sixtieth New York, Twelfth Connecticut, Twenty-first Indiana, Sixth Michigan, a company of the First Louisiana Union cavalry, and artillery under Lieutenants Bradley, Carruth, and Briggs. A portion of the Seventy-fifth New York, under Captain Fitch, volunteered as sharp-shooters.

[3] A correspondent of the *New York Times*, with the expedition, wrote that one of the torpedoes fished up bore the name of a New York firm who manufactured them, and remarked, concerning the good offices of the

heeding the warning, Buchanan passed on in the *Calhoun*, standing on her bow with his spy-glass in his hand, in the face of a fierce cannonade from the vessel and the batteries, and prominently exposed to the sharp-shooters of the foe. Presently his acting chief-engineer, standing near him, was wounded in the thigh by a spent ball from a rifle-pit, and the Commodore said, "Ah, you've got it!" The next moment a ball passed through the brave and beloved commander's head, and he fell dead.

The Eighth Vermont was now in the rear of the Confederates, and clearing the rifle-pits, while the batteries of the Fourth Maine and Sixth Massachusetts (Lieutenants Bradley's and Carruth's), supported by Fitch's sharp-shooters and the One Hundred and Sixtieth New York, had flanked the defenses on the south side of the bayou, and were raking the *Cotton* with a terrible enfilading fire. She and the Confederate land forces soon retreated, the latter leaving forty of their number prisoners. Two or three times the *Cotton* returned to the fight and retired, and finally, at two o'clock on the morning of the 16th, she was seen unmanned, and floating sullenly on the bayou, as the nucleus of a vast sheet of flame. Having destroyed this monster and driven the Confederates from their works, the expedition went no farther, but returned to Brashear City, with a loss of seven killed and twenty-seven wounded. The latter were placed upon a raft, and towed down the bayou by a steamer in the night of the 15th, after the battle had ceased. The air was very mild and soft, and in the pale light of the moon, which rose at a little past midnight, the sufferers had a more comfortable voyage than they could have had in the close air of a steamer.

RAFT WITH WOUNDED SOLDIERS ON BAYOU TÈCHE.

Ineffectual efforts to open the Bayou Plaquemine so as to capture Butte à la Rose followed the expedition to the Tèche, when the enterprise was abandoned, and General Banks concentrated his forces (about twelve thousand strong) at Baton Rouge, for operations in conjunction with Admiral Farragut, then on the Lower Mississippi. The latter, on hearing of the loss of the *Queen of the West* and the *De Soto*,[1] determined to run by the batteries at Port Hudson with his fleet, and recover the control of the river from that point to Vicksburg.[2] For this purpose he gathered his fleet at Prophet's Island, a few miles below Port Hudson, on the 13th of March,[a] and on the same day Banks sent forward about twelve thousand men to divert the attention of the foe while the fleet should perform the proposed perilous act. These drove in the pickets before them, while the

a 1863.

fugitive slave who warned them of their danger,—"While people in the North are enriching themselves by manufacturing these hellish things to blow our brave men to atoms, a poor black 'animal' down here has friendship and humanity enough to come and warn them off from their terrible doom."

1 See page 589.

2 His fleet consisted of the frigates *Hartford* (flag-ship), *Mississippi*, *Richardson*, and *Monongahela*; the gun-boats *Essex*, *Albatross*, *Kineo*, *Genesee*, and *Sachem*, and six mortar-boats.

gun-boats *Essex* and *Sabine*, and the mortars, bombarded the Confederate works.

Farragut intended to pass the batteries the next morning, under cover of a vigorous attack by the troops; but the night being very dark, he concluded not to wait until morning, but as silently as possible glide up the river in the gloom. The fleet moved accordingly, at a little past nine in the evening. The *Hartford*, Captain Palmer, led, with the Admiral on board, and the gun-boat *Albatross* lashed to her side. The other frigates followed, each with a gun-boat attached. But the darkness was not sufficiently profound for the quick vision of the vigilant sentinels, who had equally quick ears. The approach of the fleet was discovered, and soon rockets and other signal-lights were streaming in the air. Then an immense bonfire suddenly blazed out in front of one of the heaviest batteries, lighting up the scene for several miles around, and fully revealing the approaching fleet. Still the vessels moved on, when a heavy gun from the west side of the river fired on

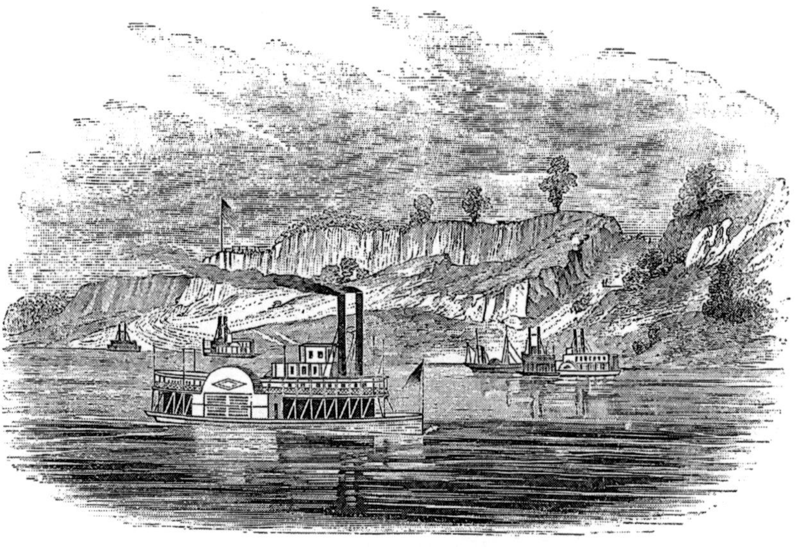

LANDING-PLACE AT PORT HUDSON.[1]

the *Hartford*. She replied, and instantly the batteries along the Port Hudson bluff opened their thunders. The mortar-boats responded; and as the frigates and their gun-boats severally came within range of the batteries, as they moved slowly up the stream, gave them broadside after broadside, while the howitzers on their tops and their heavy pivot bow-guns were very active. Several of the batteries were so high and well managed that the fleet could not harm them,[2] and the advantage was all on the side of the Confederates.

---

[1] This is a view of the river-front of the high bluff whereon the little village of Port Hudson stood, and the Confederate works were constructed. No place on the river, excepting Vicksburg, was better adapted for defense than this. The landing-place (known as Hickey's) at the foot of the bluff is a very difficult one, owing to the strong eddies, and the high banks extend a long distance from this point.

[2] The guns in the works on the edge of the high bluff would be pointed downward at the proper angle to strike the vessels, run out, discharged, and instantly run back out of the way of harm from shot from below

The air soon became thick with sulphurous smoke, and when the bonfire was a smoldering heap the darkness was most profound. Still the fight went on, and grape, canister, and shrapnel shot, and the bullets of sharp-shooters, swept murderously over the decks as the vessels went nearer the bluff, and when, at one o'clock in the morning,[a] after a contest of an hour and a half, the firing ceased, only the *Hartford* and her consort, the *Albatross*, had passed by. The *Mississippi* had run aground abreast the central heaviest battery, where her commander (Melancthon Smith) fought her under the concentrated fire of many large guns for half an hour, when he abandoned her and set her on fire. Lightened by the consumption of the flames, she floated down the river with her fine armament of twenty-one heavy guns and two howitzers, and was blown into fragments several miles below by the explosion of her magazine. The other vessels of the fleet, badly bruised, returned to their anchorage near Prophet's Island, and General Banks, whose force was too light to attempt the capture of Port Hudson at that time, whose garrison was reported to be sixteen thousand effective men, returned to Baton Rouge; not, however, with the intention of abandoning the enterprise.

[a] March 14, 1863.

Banks now sent a large portion of his movable troops again into the Louisiana region west of the Mississippi. He concentrated his forces at Brashear City, on the Atchafalaya, when, on the 10th of April,[b] General Weitzel crossed over to Berwick without opposition, but discovered that the Confederates were in considerable force on his front, under General Richard Taylor, one of the most active of the trans-Mississippi Confederate leaders. General Emory's division crossed on the 12th, and all moved toward Franklin, driving the foe before them until he reached Fort Bisland and his other works near Pattersonville, where he made a stand. On the same day Banks sent General Grover with his division, on transports and four gun-boats,[1] up the Atchafalaya and Lake Chestimachee to Irish Bend, a short distance from Franklin, and on the flank of the Confederates, with the intention of gaining their rear and cutting off their retreat, should they be driven from Fort Bisland. It was a most difficult landing-place, and besides the delay in getting ashore, Grover was compelled to withstand a vigorous attack. He repelled the assailants, but the time consumed in the struggle enabled Taylor to abandon Fort Bisland and escape. Taylor burned several steamboats at Franklin and fled toward Opelousas, destroying the bridges behind him, and making a stand at Vermilion Bayou. He had been followed rapidly by cavalry, artillery, and Weitzel's brigade, with a part of

[b] 1863.

RICHARD TAYLOR.

[1] These were the *Calhoun*, *Clifton*, *Estrella*, and *Arizona*.

Emory's division, under Colonel Ingraham, as a support. So close was the pursuit, that Taylor could not get five transports, laden with commissary stores and ammunition at New Liberia, out of harm's way, and these, with an incomplete iron-clad gun-boat, were destroyed.

Emory came up with Taylor at Vermilion Bayou on the 17th. The latter was driven after a sharp contest, burning the bridges behind him; and on the 20th Banks entered Opelousas in triumph, and sent cavalry to Washington, six miles farther on. During this retreat the *Queen of the West*, which, as we have seen, was captured in the Red River by the Confederates,[1] and had come down the Atchafalaya to Lake Chestimachee, was assailed by the National gun-boats and destroyed, and her crew were made prisoners of war. And on the day when Banks entered Opelousas,[a] the gun-boats, under Lieutenant-commanding A. P. Cooke, captured Butte à la Rose, with its garrison of sixty men, two heavy guns, and a large quantity of ammunition, and opened the way through the Atchafalaya to the Red River, the *Arizona* passing through and reaching Admiral Farragut above Port Hudson, on the 2d of May.

[a] April 20, 1863.

On the 22d of April Banks moved on from Opelousas toward Alexandria, General William Dwight, of Grover's division, with detachments of cavalry and artillery, leading. Taylor retreated before these to Fort De Russey. That post he also abandoned as Banks came rapidly on, and fled through Alexandria toward Shreveport.[2] Admiral Porter had ascended the Red River with a fleet of gun-boats, and seized Alexandria on the 6th of May, and on that evening the advance of Banks's column, under General Dwight, entered the town. Weitzel was pressed forward in pursuit of Taylor nearly to Grande Ecore, beyond Natchitoches, when the fugitive force had so diminished that it was of little account, and the chase was abandoned. The most considerable and by far the most fertile region of Louisiana was now in the possession of the Government forces, and on the 7th of May[b] Banks wrote officially: "We have destroyed the enemy's army and navy, and made their reorganization impossible by destroying or removing the material. We hold the key of the position. Among the evidences of our victory are two thousand prisoners, two transports, and twenty guns taken, and three gun-boats and eight transports destroyed."[3]

[b] 1863.

Banks's attention was now turned again to the Mississippi, for it was many weeks before General Taylor was able to organize a respectable force of Confederates in Louisiana. Banks had been informed by Farragut, while he was at Brashear City, that Grant would send him twenty thousand men from his large army near Vicksburg, to assist in the capture of Port Hudson, with the intention of then employing the combined forces in the capture of

---

[1] See page 589.

[2] On the march a letter from Governor Moore, of Louisiana, to General Taylor, fell into the hands of General Banks. It contained an order from the Governor for Taylor to retreat slowly to Alexandria, and, if pressed, to retire to Texas. An intercepted letter showed that on the day before the advance of Banks's army from the vicinity of Brashear City, Taylor had intended to attack that post.

[3] At Opelousas Banks issued an order (May 1st, 1863) announcing his purpose of organizing "a corps d'armée" of colored troops, to be designated as the "Corps d'Afrique," to consist, ultimately, of eighteen regiments, infantry, cavalry, and artillery. He expressed a desire to detail, for temporary or permanent duty, the best officers of the army for the organization, discipline, and instruction of that corps, with the conviction that it would render important service to the Government. The prejudices and opinions of men, he said, were in no way involved in the transaction, and he significantly inquired, "Why should not the negro contribute whatever is in his power for the cause in which he is as deeply interested as other men?"

the former place. Banks was preparing for these movements, when, on the 12th of May, he received a letter from Grant, dated two days before, informing him that he had crossed the Mississippi in force, and had entered on the campaign along the line of the Big Black River, which resulted so gloriously. He asked Banks to join him in this new movement against Vicksburg; but the latter, wanting sufficient transportation on the Red River, and unwilling to leave New Orleans and the "repossessed" territory of Louisiana at the mercy of the strong garrison at Port Hudson, and the possible force General Taylor might gather, declined. He sent General Dwight to Grant with satisfactory proof of the wisdom of his decision, and on the 14th and 15th of May he put his army in motion at Alexandria for an investment of Port Hudson. Grant having sent word back by Dwight that he would endeavor to spare Banks five thousand men for an effort to capture that stronghold, all the transports at hand were laden with troops, and the remainder were marched to Simm's Port. There they crossed the Atchafalaya, and moved down the west side of the Mississippi to a point opposite Bayou Sara, where they crossed on the night of the 23d, and proceeded to invest Port Hudson from the north on the following day.[a] At the same time General C. C. Auger, marching up from Baton Rouge, invested it on the south with three thousand five hundred men.

[a] May 24, 1863.

Here we will leave General Banks for a while, and follow General Grant in his campaign on the flank and rear of Vicksburg.

C. C. AUGER.

We left Grant late in April, with troops, transports, and gun-boats, below Vicksburg, prepared to cross and open a new series of operations against that stronghold. At that time some of his cavalry which had been left in Tennessee were engaged in a most extensive and destructive raid through Mississippi, spreading terror everywhere in the region of its track. The story may be thus briefly told, though in its details it presents one of the most remarkable events on record. On the 17th of April, Colonel Benjamin H. Grierson, of the Sixth Illinois cavalry, left La Grange, Tennessee, with his own regiment, and the Seventh Illinois and Second Iowa, the latter commanded respectively by Colonels Edward Prince and Edward Hatch, marched southward, sweeping rapidly through Ripley, New Albany, Pontatoc, Houston, Clear Spring, Starkville, and Louisville, to Newton, in the heart of the rich western portion of Mississippi, and behind all of the Confederate forces with which Grant had to contend. These horsemen were scattered in detachments, as much as prudence would allow, striking the Confederate forces which had been hastily gathered here and there to oppose them, breaking up railways and bridges, severing telegraph-wires, wasting public property, and, as much as possible, diminishing the means of transportation of the Confederates in their efforts to aid the army at Vicksburg. Their marches were long and very severe each day, often through tangled swamps, dark and rough forests, and across swollen streams and submerged plains. At Newton, being below Jackson, they turned sharply to the southwest toward Raleigh, and pushed rapidly through that town to Westfield and Hazelhurst. They halted at Gallatin, where they captured a 32-pounder rifled Parrott gun, with fourteen hundred pounds of gunpowder, on the way to Grand Gulf. They pushed on to Union Church, a little behind Natchez, where they had a skirmish, when, turning back, they struck the New Orleans and Jackson railway a little north of Brookhaven, and proceeded to burn the station-house, cars, and bridges at the latter place. Then they went to Bogue Chitto with a similar result, and pressing southward to Greensburg, in Louisiana, they marched rapidly westward on the Osyka and Clinton road to Clinton, fighting Confederates that lay in ambush at Amite River, and losing Lieutenant-Colonel Blackburn, of the Seventh Illinois, who was mortally wounded.

BENJAMIN H. GRIERSON.

The 2d of May was the last day of the great raid. They marched early, burned a Confederate camp at Sandy Creek Bridge, and, a little later, captured Colonel Stewart and forty-two of his cavalry on Comite River. This was the crowning act of their expedition, and at noon on that day[a] the troops that remained with Grierson, wearied and worn, and their horses almost exhausted, entered Baton Rouge, in the midst of the plaudits of Banks's troops stationed there.

[a] May 2, 1863.

Grierson had sent back the Second Iowa and about one hundred and seventy-five men of other regiments, and with a little less than one thousand men he made the raid, one of the most remarkable on record. In the space of sixteen days they had ridden six hundred miles in a succession of forced marches, often in drenching rain, and sometimes without rest for two days, through a hostile country, over ways most difficult to travel, fighting men and destroying property. They killed and wounded about one hundred of the foe, captured and paroled full five hundred, destroyed three thousand stand of arms, and inflicted a loss on the Confederates of property valued at about six millions of dollars. Grierson's loss was twenty-seven men and a number of horses. Twenty-five horses were drowned in crossing an overflowed swamp, eight miles wide, on the Okanoxubee River. The smallness of his loss of men and horses was remarkable, considering the hazards, fatigues, and privations they had encountered. Detachments sent out here and there to destroy were chased and attacked by some of the thousands sent for the purpose from Vicksburg and Jackson, and sometimes they would be compelled to ride sixty miles in a day, over blind, rough, and miry roads, in order to regain the main body. During the twenty-eight hours preceding their arrival at Baton Rouge, the whole body had traveled seventy-six miles, engaged in four skirmishes, and forded the Comite River, in which many of the horses were compelled to swim. Grierson's experience caused him to declare that the Confederacy was but "a shell," and subsequent events justified the opinion.

Grant's first movement toward the Big Black region was to direct Porter to make a naval attack on the batteries of Grand Gulf. This was done on the morning of the 29th of April,[a] and after a contest of five hours and a half the lower batteries were silenced. The upper ones were too high to be much affected. The Confederates had field-batteries that were moved from point to point, and the sharp-shooters who filled the rifle-pits on the hill-sides were extremely mischievous to the people on the gun-boats. It was evident that the post could not be taken; so at a little past noon Grant ordered a cessation of the battle, and directed Porter to run by the batteries with gun-boats and transports, as he had done at Vicksburg and Warrenton, while the army should move down to a point opposite Rodney, where it might cross without much opposition. At six o'clock that evening Porter again attacked the batteries, and under cover of the fire all the transports passed by in good condition. Three of Porter's gun-boats were much injured in the fight and in the passage of the batteries, and he lost twenty-four men killed and fifty-six wounded. The injured vessels were soon repaired and made ready for active service..

[a] 1863.

GRIERSON'S RAID.

Informed by a negro that there was a good road from Bruinsburg (half-way between Grand Gulf and Rodney) to Port Gibson or the Bayou Pierre, in rear of Grand Gulf, Grant decided to cross at that point. At daylight the next morning the gun-boats and transports commenced ferrying the troops. So soon as the Thirteenth corps, under McClernand, was landed, it was pushed forward toward Port Gibson with three days' rations, followed by the Seventeenth corps under McPherson, which had lately come down from beautiful Lake Providence,[1] as fast as it crossed the river. The advance was met by a Confederate force the next morning[b] at two o'clock, eight miles from Bruinsburg, where the foe was pressed back, but was not pursued until daylight. McClernand then pushed on

[b] May 1.

[1] The picture on page 604, giving a view of a portion of the shore of Lake Providence, a little west of the Mississippi, in Upper Louisiana, is from the pencil of Henri Lovie. The fine building in the foreground was the head-quarters of General McPherson during the time his troops were encamped on the lake. It was the residence of Dr. Sellers.

to the parting of roads, four miles from Port Gibson, each running along a ridge with deep hollows on each side. There he was confronted by a strong force from Vicksburg, under General John Bowen, with troops advantageously posted on the two roads and the broken ridges around them.

McClernand's troops were divided for the occasion. On his right were the divisions of Generals Hovey, Carr, and Smith, and on his left that of General Osterhaus. The former, superior in numbers pressed the foe on its front steadily back to Port Gibson, while the latter was unable to move forward until he was re-enforced by a brigade of General Logan's division of the advance of McPherson's corps. Another brigade of the same division was sent to the help of McClernand, and after a long and severe struggle the Confederates were repulsed, late in the afternoon, with heavy loss, and pursued to Port Gibson. Night coming on, the Nationals halted and rested on their arms, expecting to renew the contest in the morning. But the Confederates had fled across Bayou Pierre during the night, burned the bridges over the two forks of the bayou behind them, and retreated toward Vicksburg. So ended THE BATTLE OF PORT GIBSON.

VIEW ON LAKE PROVIDENCE.

The bridges were rebuilt and the pursuit of the Confederates was continued. Meanwhile Porter was directed to assail Grand Gulf again, but on approaching it, on the 3d of May, he found it deserted. The Confederates there, flanked by the Nationals at Port Gibson, had joined with the defeated troops in their flight toward Vicksburg. The Nationals followed them closely to Hankinson's Ferry, on the Big Black, skirmishing and taking prisoners on the way.[1] Grant at once made arrangements for a change of his base of supplies from Bruinsburg to Grand Gulf.

In the mean time General Sherman, with the Fifteenth corps, had been operating on the Yazoo again. He had been left above Vicksburg, with the expectation of soon following McClernand and McPherson down the west side of the Mississippi. On the 28th of April Grant sent him word that he intended to attack Grand Gulf the next day, and suggested that he should make a feint simultaneously on Haines's Bluff. Sherman was quick to act, and at ten o'clock on the morning of the 29th he started from Milliken's Bend for the mouth of the Yazoo, with Blair's division, in ten steamers. There he found three iron-clads[2] and several unarmed gun-boats, under Cap-

[1] The National loss in the Battle of Port Gibson (called by some the Battle of Thompson's Hill) was 840 men, of whom 130 were killed and the remainder wounded. They captured three guns, four flags, and 580 prisoners.

[2] *Black Hawk*, *DeKalb*, and *Choctaw*.

tain Breese, in readiness to go forward. They passed up the river and spent the night at the mouth of the Chickasaw Bayou. Early the next morning[a] they went within range of the batteries at Haines's Bluff, and for four hours the armored gun-boats and the Tyler assailed the fortifications there. Then there was a lull in the fight until toward evening, when Blair's brigade was landed on the south side of the Yazoo, as if to attack. The bombardment was resumed and kept up until dark, when the troops were quietly re-embarked. The assault and menace, with reconnoissances, were repeated the next day, when Sherman received an order from Grant to hasten with his troops down the west side of the river to Grand Gulf. Sherman kept up his menaces until evening, when he quietly withdrew his whole force to Young's Point, whence Blair's division was sent to Milliken's Bend, there to remain until other troops, expected from above, should arrive. The divisions of Tuttle and Steele marched rapidly down the west side of the Mississippi to Hard Times, crossed the river there, and on the following day[b] joined Grant's troops at Hankinson's Ferry, on the Big Black. Sherman's feint was entirely successful in keeping re-enforcements from the Confederates at Port Gibson.

[a] May 6, 1863.

[b] May 8

Grant, as we have observed, had expected to send troops down the river to assist Banks in operations against Port Hudson, intending, in the mean time, to remain at Grand Gulf, and collect there ample supplies of every kind. Circumstances compelled him to change his purpose, and on the 7th of May he moved his army forward on two nearly parallel roads on the eastern side of the Big Black River. These columns were led respectively by Generals McClernand and McPherson, and each was followed by portions of Sherman's corps, which had been divided for the purpose. The immediate destination of the army was the important railway that connects Vicksburg with Jackson, the capital of the State of Mississippi, and also that capital itself, immediately in the rear of Vicksburg. Grant intended to have McClernand and Sherman strike the railway between the stations of Bolton and Edwards, while McPherson, bending his course more to the east, should march rapidly upon Jackson by way of Raymond and Clinton, destroy the railway and telegraph lines, seize the capital, commit the public property there to the flames, and then push westward and rejoin the main force.

Very little serious opposition to the Nationals was experienced until the morning of the 12th of May, when the van of each column was approaching the railway. On the previous evening Grant had telegraphed to Halleck that he was doubtless on the verge of a general engagement; that he should communicate with Grand Gulf no more, unless it should be necessary to send a train with a heavy escort, and that he might not hear from him again in several weeks. He and his army were now committed to the perilous but extremely important task of capturing Vicksburg. That night McClernand's corps was on and near the Baldwin's Ferry road, and not far from the Big Black River; Sherman's, in the center of the forming line, and accompanied by General Grant, was at and beyond Auburn; and McPherson's was eight miles to the right, a little in advance of Utica, in the direction of Raymond.

When, early in the morning of the 12th, the troops moved forward, they began to encounter stout resistance. The most formidable opposition was in front of McPherson, who, two or three miles from Raymond, the capital of Hinds County, Mississippi, encountered two Confederate brigades about six thousand strong, under Generals Gregg and Walker (commanded by the former), well posted near Farnden's Creek, with infantry on a range of hills, in timber and in ravines, and two batteries commanding the roads over which the Nationals were approaching. Logan was in the advance, and not only received the first heavy blow at about ten o'clock, but bore the brunt of the battle that ensued. Brisk skirmishing had begun sometime before with the advance cavalry, under Captain Foster It speedily developed into a severe though short struggle.

The Confederates were mostly concealed in the woods, but their fire was soon drawn by Logan's Second brigade,[1] which advanced toward their covering. Soon afterward De Golyer's (Eighth Michigan) battery was ordered forward to assist in dislodging the foe, when for the first time the latter opened their batteries. Finding it impossible to silence the Michigan guns, the Confederates dashed forward to capture them, when they were repulsed with heavy loss by two shells that burst among their advancing troops. They fled beyond the creek and rallied.

McPherson now ordered an advance upon the new position of the Confederates. The movement was led by General Dennis's brigade, supported by General Smith's. A very severe conflict ensued, in which the Twentieth Ohio, Twentieth Illinois, and Twenty-third Indiana, lost heavily. The Confederates were pushed back a little, yet they maintained an unbroken front, when the Eighth Illinois, Colonel Sturgis, charged furiously upon them with fixed bayonets, broke the line into fragments, and drove them from the creek in wild disorder. So ended THE BATTLE OF RAYMOND. It had lasted about three hours.

The Confederates rallied and retreated in fair order though Raymond toward Jackson, followed cautiously by Logan, who occupied the town an hour after the fight,[2] and found there Jackson newspapers of the day before, announcing, in grandiloquent style, that the "Yankees had been whipped at Grand Gulf and Port Gibson, and were falling back to seek the protection of their gun-boats.[3]" During the engagement McPherson and Logan were seen riding along the lines directing the battle, and exposed to death every moment. This conduct greatly inspirited their troops.

McClernand and Sherman had skirmished pretty heavily while McPherson was struggling at Raymond, and when the result of that struggle was known to Grant, he ordered the other corps to move toward Jackson. He had learned that General Joseph E. Johnston, the ablest of the Confederate leaders, was hourly expected at Jackson, to take the command of the Confederate troops in that region in person. Perhaps he was already there. "I therefore determined," Grant said in his report, "to make sure of that place, and leave no enemy in my rear."

---

[1] Composed of the Twentieth, Sixty-eighth and Seventy-eighth Ohio, and Thirteenth Illinois.

[2] The Union loss in this battle was 442, of whom 69 were killed, 341 wounded, and 32 missing. The loss of the Confederates was 823, of whom 103 were killed, and 720 were wounded and made prisoners. In this engagement the Eighth Illinois and Seventh Texas, which faced each other at Fort Donelson, now had a fierce encounter. "The Eighth Missouri (Union) and Tenth Tennessee (Confederate), both Irish regiments, here met, and," the correspondent of the *Cincinnati Commercial* said, "exchanged compliments with genuine Hibernian accent."

[3] Correspondent of the *Cincinnati Commercial*, May 13, 1863.

On the morning of the 13th,[a] McPherson pushed on to Clinton, which he entered unopposed at two o'clock in the afternoon, and began tearing up the railway between that town and Jackson. Sherman was marching at the same time on the direct road from Raymond to Jackson, while McClernand was moving to a point near Raymond. That night was a tempestuous one. The rain fell heavily, and made wretched roads. But the troops under Grant were never overcome by mud, and early the next morning[b] Sherman and McPherson pushed on toward Jackson.

[a] May, 1863.

[b] May 14.

McPherson moved at five o'clock, with General Crocker's division (late Quinby's) in advance. At nine these encountered and drove in the Confederate pickets, five miles from Jackson; and two and a half miles from that city they were confronted by a heavy Confederate force, consisting chiefly of Georgia and South Carolina troops, which had arrived the previous evening, under General W. H. T. Walker. These were discovered by Crocker when he gained the brow of a gentle hill, arranged in battle order along the crest of a ridge over which the road to Jackson passed, and in a shallow ravine at its foot. Their artillery was chiefly on their right, near the road, and between the two armies were broad open fields.

Crocker disposed his forces in battle order while a heavy shower of rain was falling, and at eleven o'clock they moved to the attack slowly and cau-

BATTLE-GROUND NEAR JACKSON.[1]

tiously, preceded by a line of skirmishers. The First Missouri battery had been placed near a cotton-gin in the open field, and Crocker now threw out two brigades (Colonel Sanborn's and Colonel Holmes's) on the right and left of it, supported by Colonel Boomer's. His skirmishers were soon met by such volleys from the infantry in the hollow, that they were recalled. Crocker saw that the foe in that hollow as well as on the crest of the hill, must be dislodged, or the National troops must retire; so he ordered a charge by his whole line, with loaded muskets and fixed bayonets. Instantly

[1] This is a view on the principal battle-ground near Jackson, as it appeared when the writer sketched it, late in April, 1866. It was taken from the open field over which Crocker's troops advanced to the charge. In the middle ground traversed by a fence is seen the ravine out of which the Confederates were driven, and on the crest of the hill, where they broke and fled, are seen the chimneys of the ruined mansion of O. P. Wright, on whose farm the battle was fought. The brow of the hill on the left, where the road passes over, is the place where the Confederate cannon were planted.

the troops moved steadily forward with, banners flying, unchecked by heavy volleys of musketry, and pushed the Confederates out of the ravine, and up the slopes to the crest where their artillery was planted. Still onward Crocker pressed, when the astonished Confederates broke and fled toward the city, closely chased for a mile and a half to the earthworks which formed the inner defenses of Jackson. There the batteries of McMurray and Dillon poured a storm of grape and canister upon the swarming Confederates, and under its cover the Nationals were halted and re-formed, with the intention of immediately assailing the works. But there was no occasion. They were empty. The garrison had fled. Sherman had come up and shelled them out of their works at another point, and now troops and civil officers and leading secessionists had evacuated the city and fled northward, the Governor carrying away as many State papers as possible, and the State Treasurer bearing away the public funds. McPherson and Sherman entered Jackson in triumph, finding there seventeen cannon which the Confederates had abandoned; and standing around the Deaf and Dumb Institute, which was used as a hospital, were tents enough to shelter an entire division. They found the commissary and quartermaster stores in flames.

So ended The Battle of Jackson, in the capture of the city, and the unfurling of the National flag over the State House of Mississippi by the Fifty-ninth Indiana. General Grant entered the town that night, and learned that General Johnston had arrived, taken command of the Department, and ordered Pemberton to move out immediately from Vicksburg, cross the Big Black River, and fall upon the National rear. The reason of the flight of the troops northward from Jackson now seemed plain. No doubt Johnston intended to have them form a junction with Pemberton, and crush Grant by the weight of superior numbers. Grant perceived the menacing peril, and instantly took measures for striking Pemberton before such junction should be effected. For this purpose he gave orders for a concentration of his forces in the direction of Edwards's Station, which was about two miles from the railway bridge over the Big Black River. McPherson was directed to retrace his steps to Clinton the next morning,[a] and McClernand's scattered divisions[1] were ordered to march simultaneously toward Bolton's Station and concentrate, while Sherman was directed to remain in Jackson only long enough to cause a thorough destruction of the railways, military factories, arsenal, bridges, a large cotton factory, stores, and other public property, and then to rejoin the main army.

[a] May 15, 1863.

JOHN C. PEMBERTON.

[1] One division of McClernand's troops was then in Clinton, another at Mississippi Springs, a third at Raymond, and a fourth, with Blair's division of Sherman's corps, with a wagon train between Raymond and Utica.

Early on the morning of the 16th General Grant was pretty accurately informed, by two persons who had been employed on the railway, and who had come through Pemberton's lines, of the position, strength, and intentions of that commander, who had been for two or three days near Edwards's Station. They informed him that Pemberton's force was about twenty-five thousand strong, composed of eighty regiments, with ten batteries of artillery, and that he was moving forward with the intention of attacking the National rear. This was confirmatory of information already received, and Grant resolved to strike first. Blair was ordered to push forward with his division toward Edwards's Station, and McClernand and Osterhaus were directed to follow immediately, while McPherson was ordered to keep up communication with McClernand on another road. In order to prevent any miscarriage, Grant sent Lieutenant-Colonel Wilson, of his staff, to McClernand, to explain the situation, and urge him to move promptly. Then the Commander-in-Chief hastened to the front, to have a personal direction of the movements there.

Pemberton, who appears to have been a rather tardy and timid leader, had advanced a few miles eastward from his fortifications near Edwards's Station. On the day of the battle at Jackson,[a] he had received a dispatch from Johnston at that place, "suggesting, not ordering," he afterward said, a combined attack on McPherson at Clinton, when Pemberton called a council, and, pursuant to its decision, prepared to attack the next morning, quite unconscious that his chief had already been made a fugitive by the very troops he was about to fall upon.

[a] May 14, 1863.

A branch of Baker's Creek was so swollen by the rains that he was delayed until the afternoon, when he advanced four or five miles to a strong position on broken ground, near the railway, and not far from Baker's Creek, known as the Champion Hills, where he received a note from Johnston directing him to move northward, so as to form a junction with that officer's shattered forces. Pemberton at once sent his trains back to the Big Black, and was about to follow with his troops, when he found Grant close upon him, and he felt compelled to remain and fight. He was posted across the main Vicksburg dirt road that led to Edwards's Station, with a high undulating hill on the left, crowned with a dense forest. General W. W. Loring commanded

CHAMPION HILLS BATTLE-GROUND.

his right. General John Bowen, who had been driven from Port Gibson, led his center, and General Carter L. Stevenson commanded his left. To reach Pemberton's line from the road the Nationals had to cross two open fields, and ascend a steep slope dotted with stumps of trees, exposed to the fire of the foe in thick woods.

General Hovey's division held the advance in front of Pemberton, and when Grant arrived[a] his skirmishers were close to the pickets of his foe, and his troops were coming rapidly into line. McPherson's corps (excepting Ransom's brigade), which soon came up, was thrown to the right of the road, and threatened Pemberton's rear. There were promises of immediate success in case of a strife, but Grant, unwilling to risk a battle without evidently sufficient numbers to gain a victory, forbade an attack until McClernand's corps should be near. That corps was advancing from Bolton's Station, and Grant sent an urgent messenger for its commander to hasten forward. Then he listened anxiously, but in vain, for McClernand's guns. He knew the belligerents were too close together to allow much delay. At length firing commenced, and at eleven o'clock a battle had fairly begun. Hovey's division, composed of Ohio, Indiana, Iowa, and Wisconsin troops, was bearing the brunt. His first brigade, mostly Indiana troops, under General McGinnis, opened the battle gallantly. The Confederates brought two batteries of four guns each to bear upon them from a ridge. One of these was charged upon and captured by the Eleventh Indiana[1] and Twenty-ninth Wisconsin, and the other by the Forty-sixth Indiana. But after a severe struggle for an hour and a half, against constantly increasing numbers (for Pemberton massed his troops on his right so as to crush and turn Grant's left), Hovey's infantry were compelled to fall back half a mile, to the position of his artillery, leaving behind them the captured guns. There Hovey was re-enforced by a portion of Crocker's (late Quinby's) division, when he re-formed, and, massing his artillery, which was strengthened by the addition of Dillon's Wisconsin battery, he renewed the fight with great spirit.

[a] May 16, 1863.

In the mean time Logan's division of McPherson's corps (its second brigade, under General M. D. Legget, forming on the right of Hovey) had fallen upon Stevenson, on Pemberton's left. Seeing this, Pemberton sent two of Bowen's brigades to assist Stevenson, and ordered General Loring to join Bowen and the remainder of his division, in further attempts to crush and turn Grant's left. Loring refused obedience, and seemed like a man demented. The battle went on without him, with varied fortunes, until late in the afternoon, when Stevenson's line, which had fought most gallantly, began to bend under Logan's severe pressure, and at five o'clock broke and fell back in confusion. Meanwhile the divisions of Osterhaus and Carr, of McClernand's corps, had come up, but did not engage very severely in the battle.

With that demolition of Pemberton's left, the Confederates became so confused and disheartened that nothing better seemed left for them than flight. Loring, with his troops sharing the panic of their leader, had

[1] This was the famous regiment of Zouaves, first organized by Colonel (afterward Major-General) Lewis Wallace. See page 517, volume I.

already moved from the field, leaving his artillery behind, and a large number of his men as prisoners, and was making his way to Johnston's camp at Canton. Seeing this, Pemberton ordered his whole army to retreat toward the Big Black, when Grant, who had been on the field directing his troops in battle, ordered the fresh brigades of Osterhaus and Carr to follow with all speed to that river, and to cross it if possible. In his flight, and in this instant pursuit, Pemberton lost many of his troops made prisoners. Thus ended THE BATTLE OF CHAMPION HILLS, or Baker's Creek, as it is sometimes called, it having been fought near that stream. It was "fought mainly," Grant said in his report, "by General Hovey's division of McClernand's corps, and Generals Logan and Quinby's divisions (the latter commanded by General M. M. Crocker) of McPherson's corps."[1]

The Confederates were pursued until after dark that night, with a loss of some men, and a train of cars loaded with provisions and ordnance stores captured, and a large quantity of similar and other stores which they themselves burned. McClernand accompanied the pursuing party, with whom he bivouacked that night on the hill overlooking Edwards's Station, and the broad and fertile plain between it and the Big Black. Early the following morning—a beautiful Sabbath morning in May[a]—the pursuit was resumed, but not continued long, for it was found that the Confederates were well posted on both sides of the Big Black at the railway bridge, and were strongly fortified. On the bottom, near the eastern bank of the stream, they had a line of well-armed works, in front of which, and about a mile from the river, was a bayou that formed an efficient ditch, with a line of rifle-pits behind it. On the opposite side of the river the bank was steep and covered with works, well armed with heavy guns; and back of these, at a little distance, was a forest. Behind the defenses on the eastern side of the river, to meet the first onset of the pursuers, were the brigades of Green, Villepigue, and Cockrell. Just above the railway bridge, Pemberton had constructed a passage-way for troops, composed of steamboat hulks.

[a] May 7, 1863.

General Carr's division occupied the extreme advance of the pursuing columns. A heavy line of skirmishers, supported by two brigades of his division, were deployed in the woods on the right of the road, while Osterhaus's division was similarly posted on the left of it. Very soon Carr's skirmishers were hotly engaged with those of the foe, which had come out to meet them, and speedily a severe battle was raging between the two armies in the thick forest. This continued for about three hours, when General Lawler, commanding Carr's extreme right, discovered a good opportunity for a charge. He gave the order, and right gallantly his brigade, composed

---

[1] The National loss in the battle, as reported by Grant, was 2,457, of whom 426 were killed, 1,842 wounded, and 189 missing. Hovey's division alone lost 1,202, or one-third of its entire number. The Confederate loss is unknown, as no official account was given. It was estimated in killed and wounded as quite equal to that of the National forces, besides almost 2,000 prisoners, 18 guns, and a large quantity of small arms. Among their killed was General Loyd Tighlman, who was captured at Fort Henry the previous year. He was killed by a shell from one of the guns of the Chicago Mercantile battery. Indiana was more largely represented in the desperate battle of Champion Hills than any other State.

The Twenty-fourth Iowa was called the "Methodist regiment," its principal officers and a large portion of its men being of that denomination. They fought most gallantly, and at evening, after the battle was over, they held a religious meeting, and made the hills resound with the grand air and stirring words of "Old Hundred."

of the Twenty-first, Twenty-second, and Twenty-third Iowa, and Eleventh Wisconsin, sprang forward with cheers, and drove the foe to his intrenchments; not, however, without suffering fearfully from an enfilading fire from a curtain of the Confederate breast-works, which prostrated one hundred and fifty of their number. Undismayed, they waded the bayou, pressed forward, delivered and received heavy volleys of bullets, and rushed upon the foe with fixed bayonets before the latter had time to reload. Meanwhile many of the Confederates within the intrenchments fled to the other side of the river, and communicated to the troops there their own irrepressible panic.

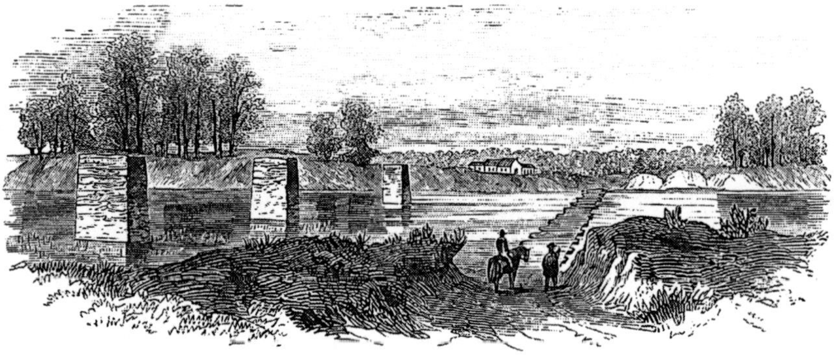

THE PASSAGE OF THE BIG BLACK RIVER.[1]

They expected the Nationals would immediately cross the river and assail them, and so they burned the two bridges, cut off the retreat of their comrades who were yet fighting, and fled pell-mell toward the safer region of the defenses around Vicksburg, making the inhabitants of that city pale with affright, and forebodings of the greatest calamities impending. Pemberton and his staff, it is said, tried to prevent the incendiarism and stop the flight. but in vain. The assailed garrison, about fifteen hundred strong, were captured, with seventeen guns (a part of them taken from Grant the day before), several thousand stand of arms, and a large quantity of commissary stores, and losing, besides, twenty killed and two hundred and forty-two wounded. Thus ended The Battle of the Big Black River, in which Osterhaus was wounded, when his command devolved temporarily upon Brigadier-General A. L. Lee.

McClernand could not immediately follow the fugitives toward Vicksburg. Their retreat was covered by the batteries and sharp-shooters on the high western bank of the river, who for hours kept the Nationals from constructing floating bridges. Grant's only pontoon train was with Sherman, who, under his chief's orders, and while the events we have just been considering were occurring, had been making his way from Jackson to Bridgeport, on the Big Black, a few miles above the railway bridge. He arrived there

---

[1] This was the appearance at the passage of the railway travel between Jackson and Vicksburg, over the Big Black River, as it appeared to the writer when he made the sketch, in April, 1866, from the eastern side of the stream, while on his way from Vicksburg to Jackson. The passengers had crossed the river on the pontoon bridge seen in the sketch, and while waiting for the cars to start, the drawing was made. On the left are seen the piers of the railroad bridge destroyed by the Confederates, and beyond the stream are the high banks, with the forest near, on which the Confederate batteries were planted.

during the afternoon of the 17th, and prepared to cross the stream in the morning. The Confederates at the railway bridge, finding themselves flanked, fled to Vicksburg. Then McClernand's men constructed a floating bridge there and just above, over which his and McPherson's corps crossed the next morning at about eight o'clock. Sherman crossed at the same hour,[a] and all pressed on over the wooded and broken country toward Vicksburg. Three miles and a half from that city Sherman turned to the right and took possession of the Walnut Hills, near the Chickasaw Bayou,[1] without opposition, and cutting off the Confederates at Haines's Bluff. McPherson followed Sherman's track some distance to the point where he turned to the right, and halted, while McClernand, advancing on the line of the retreat of the Confederates, on the direct highway from Jackson to Vicksburg, bent his course a little to the left, and took position at Mount Albans, so as to cover the roads leading out of Vicksburg on the southeast. So, on the morning of the 19th of May, Grant's army, which for more than a fortnight had subsisted off the country in which it was moving, completely invested Vicksburg on the land side, and, by a successful movement of Admiral Porter, his base of supplies was changed from Grand Gulf to the Yazoo.

[a] May 18, 1863.

Let us see what Porter did. On the morning of the 16th[b] he went to the Yazoo. He left several of his iron-clad steamers below Vicksburg, while others in the Yazoo were ready for co-operation with Grant. When on the 18th he heard the booming of guns in the rear of the city, he knew that the army was approaching, and very soon he saw through his glass National troops on the Walnut Hills. These were Sherman's men. Porter immediately sent Lieutenant-Commander Breese up the Yazoo with the *De Kalb*, *Choctaw*, *Romeo*, and *Forest Rose*, to open communication with the army, which was accomplished in the course of a few hours. The *De Kalb* then pushed on toward Haines's Bluff, which the Confederates had already commenced to evacuate. The latter fled precipitately, leaving everything behind them, such as stores, ammunition, gun-carriages, and an admirably constructed camp. All these Porter destroyed, and the next day he sent Lieutenant Walker, with five gun-boats, to Yazoo City. Walker found the navy yard and vessels in flames, and the citizens ready to surrender the town, with fifteen hundred sick soldiers in the hospital. Other public property which the Confederates had not destroyed Walker burned,[3] and then

[b] May.

PEMBERTON'S HEAD-QUARTERS IN VICKSBURG.[2]

[1] See map on page 578.

[2] This is a view of the fine residence of C. A. Manlove, on Cherry Street, Vicksburg, when the writer sketched it, in 1866, which was occupied by General Pemberton as his head-quarters during the siege of Vicksburg. It is a brick building, stuccoed, with a pleasant garden in front of it.

[3] Among the vessels on the stocks at Yazoo City was the *Republic*, a ram three hundred and ten feet in length and seventy-five in width. Also another called the *Mobile*, which was ready for plating. The navy-yard was well supplied with machinery and workshops, and such as were not on fire when he arrived, Walker committed to the flames.

returned without opposition, excepting by some ambushed riflemen and a battery at Liverpool Landing, where he was fired upon, and lost one killed and eight wounded. Before Walker's return Porter had forwarded to Grant's army much needed supplies.

Now, with nothing to fear on rear or flank, excepting the troops under General Johnston, beyond the Big Black, Grant closely invested Vicksburg, and commenced the siege proper, with Sherman occupying the right of his line, McPherson the center, and McClernand the left. Pemberton had reorganized his shattered army within his defenses, with General Martin L. Smith on his left, General Forney in the center, General Stevenson on the right, and General Bowen in reserve. He had received a letter from Johnston, written on the 17th, saying:—"If Haines's Bluff be untenable, Vicksburg is of no value and cannot be held. . . . . If it be not too late, evacuate Vicksburg and its dependencies, and march to the northeast."

It was indeed "too late," and Pemberton, perplexed by conflicting orders from General Johnston and Jefferson Davis,[1] was compelled to remain and see the commencement of a close siege of his position, when he had only sixty days' rations for his troops.

[1] Davis appears to have been exceedingly anxious to keep the horrors of war from his own State, without regard to the sufferings of others. He had sent Johnston to Tennessee in November previous, with full powers to control the armies under Bragg, E. Kirby Smith, and Pemberton, and yet he was continually interfering with his plans of campaign, and making every thing bend to the defense of his own State of Mississippi. When Bragg, menaced by Rosecrans in December, needed strengthening, he ordered Stevenson's brigade of ten thousand men to be detached from Bragg's command, and sent, without sufficient transportation, six hundred miles, to re-enforce Pemberton. Johnston had earnestly protested against the measure, but in vain, and Davis, stimulated by his inordinate conceit, and reveling in power, treated Johnston's opinions almost with contempt. And now, when Johnston was more intent upon saving Pemberton's army than Vicksburg or Port Hudson, and directed him to unite his forces and beat Grant, saying, "Success will win back all you will abandon to gain it," Davis, without Johnston's knowledge, telegraphed to Pemberton (May 7, 1863) to hold both Vicksburg and Port Hudson. It was this order that made Pemberton so weak that he could not avoid being finally shut up in Vicksburg by Grant.

CHAPTER XXIII.

SIEGE AND CAPTURE OF VICKSBURG AND PORT HUDSON.

AN immediate assault upon the defenses of Vicksburg seemed to Grant an imperative necessity. His army was not strong enough to invest the post so absolutely as to make a sortie by Pemberton, for the purpose of joining his forces with Johnston, in Grant's rear, an impossibility. He was holding a line almost twenty miles in extent, from the Yazoo to the Mississippi at Warrenton, and so thin on its extreme left that it was little more than a series of pickets. Johnston was at Canton, receiving re-enforcements from Bragg's army, in Tennessee, for his five thousand troops with whom he fled from Jackson.[1] He was making every exertion in his power to collect a force sufficient to warrant him in falling upon Grant's rear, and endeavoring to compel him to raise the siege. That danger was imminent, and there seemed but one way to avert it, and that was by a speedy capture of the post and garrison. If Grant could possess himself of Vicksburg immediately, he might turn upon Johnston and drive him from the State of Mississippi, and, holding all of the railroads, and practical military highways, effectually secure to the Nationals all territory west of the Tombigbee River, thereby saving the Government the sending of re-enforcements to him which were so much needed elsewhere. In view of impending danger, and of the importance of the immediate capture of Vicksburg, and with the belief that in the then demoralized state of Pemberton's army, because

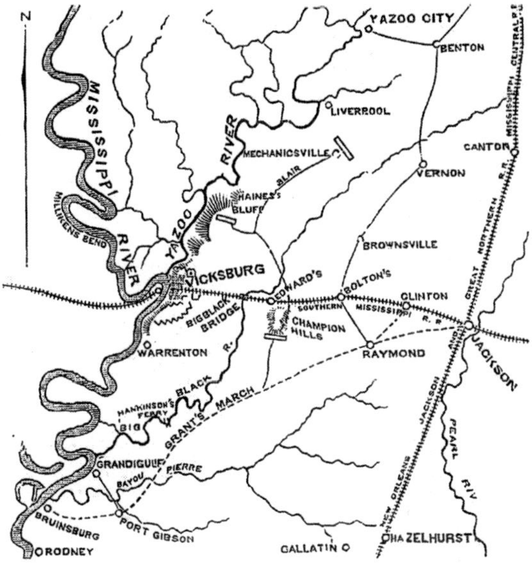

MILITARY OPERATIONS AROUND VICKSBURG.

---

[1] See page 608.

of recent reverses, the task would be comparatively easy, Grant resolved to attempt it. His troops were impatient to possess the object of their toils for months, and he was satisfied that, if an immediate assault should end in failure, they would work better in the trenches while prosecuting a regular siege, than they would do if denied an opportunity to capture the post by direct assault. Grant therefore prepared to storm the Confederate works on the day after the arrival of his troops before them, which had occurred on the anniversary of Farragut's advent there the year before. He made his head-quarters in his tent, pitched in a canebrake near an immense tree, in the edge of a wood on the farm of E. B. Willis, about three miles northeast from Vicksburg, and there he issued his orders for assault.

Grant ordered the attack to be commenced at two o'clock in the afternoon of the 19th.[a] It was begun by Sherman's corps, which was nearest the works on the northeastern side of the city, which lay on both sides of the old Jackson road, the one on the right, in approaching the town, known as Fort Hill, and the one on the left as Fort Beauregard. The attack was directed upon the former. Blair's division took the lead, followed by Tuttle's as a support. As it moved, it occupied both sides of the road. The ground was very rough, and was cleft by deep chasms, in which were trees standing and trees felled; and along the entire front of the Confederate works was such a tangle of hills and obstacles that the approach was excessively difficult and perilous.

[a] May, 1863.

GRANT'S HEAD-QUARTERS AT VICKSBURG.[1]

There had been artillery skirmishing and sharp-shooting all the morning: now there was to be close work. Both parties were nerved for the task. Steadily Blair's regiments moved on, and their first blow was given to General Schoup's Louisiana brigade, which struck back powerfully and manfully. After a slight recoil, Blair's troops moved on across the ditch to the exterior slope of the works, where the Thirteenth Regulars, of General Giles Smith's brigade, planted the flag of the Republic, but at the cost of seventy-seven of its two hundred and fifty men, its leader, Captain Washington, being among the fatally wounded. The Eighty-third Indiana and One Hundred and Twenty-seventh Illinois also gallantly gained the slope, but all were unable

[1] This is a view of the place of Grant's head-quarters, as it appeared when the writer sketched it, on the 19th of April, 1866. He was accompanied to the spot by Captain White, of General T. J. Wood's staff, who was on the staff of General Legget during the siege, and was very often at head-quarters. There they found the insulator of Grant's telegraph, seen in the picture on the sapling between the large tree and the tent. The position and form of Grant's tent and its veranda, composed of a rude frame-work covered with cane-leaves, were given to the writer by Captain White, and a delineation of it, which he pronounced correct, was added to the sketch, and so restores the appearance of the head-quarters at the time of the siege.

to enter, in the face of the most determined resistance. Perceiving that they were exposed to destruction in detail, Sherman recalled them at dark to places of safety behind the hills, and the assault was abandoned. The other corps succeeded in getting into good positions nearer the Confederate works while this struggle was going on at the right, but did not participate much in the contest of the day.

Two days succeeding this attack were occupied in heavy skirmishing, in bringing up from the Yazoo and distributing supplies to the army, making roads, planting cannon, and otherwise preparing for another assault. Grant informed Admiral Porter of his intentions, and requested him to engage the batteries on the river front, on the night of the 21st,[a] as a diversion, as he intended to storm their works on the land side with his entire army the following morning. Porter opened fire accordingly, and all night long he kept six mortars playing upon the town and the works, and sent the *Benton*, *Mound City*, and *Carondelet* to shell the water batteries and other places where troops might be resting. It was a fearful night in Vicksburg, but the next day was more fearful still. It dawned gloriously. The sky was unclouded, and the troops and citizens within the circumvallating lines of the Confederates were so encouraged by the failure of the assault on the 19th, that they had no doubt that the garrison could hold out until succor should arrive.

[a] May, 1863.

Grant ordered an assault by his whole line at ten o'clock on the morning of the 22d. That there might be perfect concert of action, the corps commanders set their watches by his, and at a proper time the chief took position near McPherson's front, where he might overlook much of the field of strife. At the appointed hour the storming columns all moved forward, while Porter's mortars and the cannon of his gun-boats were pelting the batteries and the city furiously with shot and shell, and receiving in return many a crushing reply from the mouths of "Whistling Dick," on the main fort,[1] and other heavy guns.

As on the 19th, so now, Blair's division formed the advance of Sherman's column, its van being the brigade of General Hugh S. Ewing, of the Thirtieth Ohio, with those of Giles Smith and T. Kilby Smith following in support. In the advance sharp-shooters were actively skirmishing, and with them was a small party carrying materials for bridging the ditches. At the same time five batteries (Wood's, Barrett's, Waterhouse's, Spoor's, and Hart's) were concentrating their fire upon Fort Hill, or the northeast bastion of the works at the designated point of attack.

Onward the van moved, with no signs of a foe on their front until they reached the salient of the bastion, and were near the sally-port, when there sprang up before them on the parapet, as if from the bosom of the earth, two rows of sharp-shooters, whose terrible volleys swept down the first line near them in an instant. The rear of the column then attempted to push on, but was repulsed with severe loss. Bending their course a little to the right, Ewing's braves crossed the ditch on the left face of the bastion, and, climbing the slope, planted the National flag near the top of the parapet, and there sheltered themselves from the sharp-shooters on their flank, in holes which

---

[1] See note 2, page 584.

they burrowed in the bank for the purpose. Meanwhile Giles Smith's brigade had taken a position where it seriously menaced the parapet at another point, and that of T. Kilby Smith, deployed on an off slope of the spur of a hill, assisted Ewing in keeping the Confederates quiet within the works by firing at every head seen above the parapet. The storming party held their ground under cover of the artillery, but when, finally, the brigades of Giles Smith, in connection with that of Ransom, of McPherson's corps, attempted to carry the parapet by assault, they were repulsed with heavy loss.

While this struggle was occurring, Steele's division had been fighting at the Grave-Yard Bastion, half a mile farther to the right of Fort Hill, as desperately, and without gaining any visible advantage. It had pushed across deep chasms and ravines, and made its way up to the parapet in the face of a heavy fire. It failed to carry it, but held the hillside until dark, when it too was withdrawn. But while these struggles were going on, between twelve and one o'clock, Grant was encouraged by a dispatch from McClernand on the left, "stating positively and unequivocally that he was in possession of, and still held, two of the enemy's forts; that the American flag waved over them," and asking him "to have Sherman and McPherson make a diversion in his favor."[1] On the strength of this assurance, Sherman renewed the assault on his left front, by sending Tuttle forward. Mower's brigade charged up to the position from which Ewing had been repulsed, and the colors of his leading regiment (Eleventh Missouri) were soon planted by the side of those of Blair's storming party, which remained there. After heavy loss and no substantial advantage gained, this second storming party was withdrawn under cover of darkness.

Turning farther toward the left, we find McPherson's corps in the center, vying with Sherman's in the spirit of its attacks, and sharing with it the calamities of heavy losses and the mortifications of defeat. It is believed that McPherson lost ten men to one of the assailed party, in his endeavors to carry the main fort, near the Vicksburg and Jackson railway. He gained some ground, but most of it was abandoned in the evening.

On the left McClernand assailed the works most gallantly, but with less positive success than he seems to have supposed. Precisely at the appointed hour his storming party, composed of the brigades of Lawler and Landrum, rushed impetuously upon the works southeast of the city, and within the space of fifteen minutes carried the ditch, slope, and bastion of the redoubt immediately on their front. Sergeant Griffith and eleven privates of the Twenty-second Iowa entered it as conquerors, but all were prostrated within it but Griffith, who escaped, and took with him thirteen prisoners. Meanwhile the colors of the Forty-eighth Ohio and Seventy-seventh Illinois had been raised on the bastion, and the brigades of Benton and Burbridge, inspirited by the success of Lawler and Landrum, had carried the ditch and slope of another strong earthwork, and planted their colors there. At the same time a gun of the fort had been disabled by shot from a piece of the Chicago Mercantile battery, which Captain White had dragged by hand to the ditch, and fired into an embrasure.

---

[1] See General Grant's Report, July 6, 1863.

Believing his winnings thus far to be permanent, McClernand sent the dispatch to Grant already mentioned, to which the latter replied by telling him to order up McArthur, of his own (McClernand's) corps, to his assistance. Before receiving this order McClernand had sent another dispatch similar to the first, and this was soon followed by a third, in which he said, "We have gained the enemy's intrenchments at several points, but are brought to a stand;" and in a postscript informed Grant that his troops were all engaged, and he could not "withdraw any to re-enforce others." Grant, who was in a commanding position, "could not see his possession of the forts," he said, "nor the necessity for re-enforcements, as represented in his dispatches," and expressed to both Sherman and McPherson his doubts of their correctness; yet, unwilling to allow any opportunity to capture the post to escape, he ordered Quinby's division of McPherson's corps to report to McClernand. He also made the diversion in his favor already mentioned, which, Grant said, "resulted in the increase of our mortality list full fifty per cent., without advancing our position or giving us other advantages."[1] Two hours later, McClernand informed Grant that he had lost no ground; that some of his men were in two of the forts, which were commanded by the rifle-pits in the rear, and that he was hard pressed. He had really gained no substantial advantage. He attributed his failure to do so to a lack of proper support, McArthur being some miles distant when Grant's order came to call him up, and Quinby not arriving until twilight.[2] Meanwhile Osterhaus and Hovey, on the left of McClernand, had been unsuccessful in their assaults. Porter had joined in the fight from the river with his mortars and gun-boats, increasing the horrors of the day in the city.[3] Night closed in with positive defeat and heavy loss to the National

---

[1] See Grant's Report, July 6, 1863.

[2] In a congratulatory address to his troops, General McClernand reflected upon General Grant and the disposition of his troops at the time of the assault. The commanding-general, perceiving in this great danger to the harmony and efficiency of the army, and unwilling to allow such a phase of insubordination to become a precedent, relieved General McClernand from command, on the 15th of June, and assigned it to General E. O. C. Ord.

[3] Grant had requested Porter to shell the hill batteries at Vicksburg on the morning of the assault, from half-past nine until half-past ten o'clock, to annoy the garrison while the army should attack. Accordingly, in the morning the *Mound City*, *Benton*, *Tuscumbia*, and *Carondelet* were sent down the river, and made an attack at the prescribed time on the hill batteries, opposite the canal, and soon silenced them. Porter then pushed three of them up to the water batteries, leaving the *Tuscumbia* to keep the hill batteries still. They had a furious fight with the water batteries, and were repulsed after receiving several wounds. "This," said the Admiral, "was the hottest fight the gun-boats had ever been under, the water batteries being more on a level with them than usual." Yet he did not have a man killed, and only a few were wounded. His vessels, fighting bow on, were not much damaged.—Report of Admiral Porter to the Secretary of the Navy, May 23, 1863.

We have remarked that the day of the assault was a terrible one in Vicksburg. The following notice of it, from the diary of a citizen during the siege, from the 17th of May to the 4th of July, gives a vivid picture of those horrors: "*Friday, May* 22.—The morning of this day opened in the same manner as the previous one had closed. There had been no lull in the shelling all night, and as daylight approached, it grew more rapid and furious. Early in the morning, too, the battle began to rage in the rear. A terrible onslaught was made on the center first, and then extended farther to the left, where a terrific struggle took place, resulting in the repulse of the attacking party. Four gun-boats also came up to engage the batteries. At this time the scene presented an awfully sublime and terrific spectacle—three points being attacked at once, to wit, the rifle-pits, by the army in the rear; the city, by the mortars opposite; and the batteries, by the gun-boats. Such cannonading and shelling has perhaps scarcely ever been equaled, and the city was entirely untenable, though women and children were on the streets. It was not safe from behind or before, and every part of the city was alike within range of the Federal guns. The gun-boats withdrew after a short engagement, but the mortars kept up shelling, and the armies continued fighting all day. Several desperate charges were made in force against the lines, without accomplishing their object. It would require the pen of a poet to depict the awful sublimity of this day's work. The incessant booming of cannon, and the bang of small arms, intermingled with the howling of shells and the whistling of Minié balls, made the day truly most hideous."

army,[1] and at eight o'clock in the evening the troops were recalled from the more advanced and exposed positions, leaving pickets to hold the ground which had been absolutely gained.

"After the failure of the 22d," Grant said in his report, "I determined upon a regular siege." The post was completely invested. The Nationals held military possession of the peninsula opposite Vicksburg, and Admiral Porter, with his fleet and floating batteries (scows bearing 13-inch mortars and 100-pounder Parrott guns, moored under the banks securely, where they could throw shells into the city), firmly held the water in front of the town. The beleaguered garrison was composed of only about fifteen thousand effective men, out of about thirty thousand within the lines, as Grant was officially informed five days after the assault, with short rations for only a month, and their commander calling earnestly on Johnston for aid.[2] But the latter was almost powerless to help. "I am too weak to save Vicksburg," he wrote to Pemberton on the 29th,[a] in reply to a dispatch that reached him. "Can do no more than attempt to save you and your garrison." General Frank K. Gardner, at Port Hudson, to whom, so early as the 19th, Johnston had sent orders to evacuate that place and join Pemberton, was now also calling for help,[b] and telling his chief that National troops were about to cross the Mississippi at Bayou Sara, above him, and that the whole of Banks's force at Baton Rouge was on his front. Johnston could only repeat his orders for the evacuation, and say, "You cannot be re-enforced. Do not allow yourself to be invested. At every risk save the troops, and if practicable move in this direction." This did not reach Gardner, for before he could receive it Port Hudson was invested, and the sad fruits of Jefferson Davis's interference with Johnston's orders were fast ripening. And all that Johnston could do for Pemberton, at that time, was to send him, by smugglers, about forty thousand percussion caps.[3]

[a] May, 1863.

[b] May 21.

FRANK K. GARDNER.

When the victory at Champion Hills was won, Grant declared that the capture of Vicksburg was then secured. Yet he relaxed no vigilance or efforts. Now, when he felt certain that the post must soon fall into his

[1] The National loss was almost 3,000 men.

[2] On the 27th of May Pemberton sent out a courier with a dispatch to Johnston, in which he said:—"I have 15,000 men in Vicksburg, and rations for thirty days—one meal a day.* Come to my aid with 30,000 men. If you cannot do this within ten days, you had better retreat. Ammunition is almost exhausted, especially percussion caps." The courier (Douglas, of Illinois, who was tired of the Confederate service) carried this dispatch to Grant, by which the poverty and weakness of his antagonist were revealed.

[3] General Joseph E. Johnston's Report to S. Cooper, November 1, 1863.

* In the Diary of a Confederate in Pemberton's army, then in the city, quoted in the *Rebellion Record*, the writer said, May 26th:—"We have been on half rations of coarse corn bread and poor beef for ten days." On the 1st of June he wrote:—"We are now eating bean bread, and half rations of that." He recorded that the beef gave out on the 10th of June, and that they were "drawing a quarter of a pound of bacon to the man."

hands, he made that event doubly sure by calling re-enforcements to his army. His effective men, after the assault, did not exceed twenty thousand in number, but to these were very soon added the divisions of General Lauman and four regiments from Memphis, with the divisions of Generals A. J. Smith and Kimball, of the Sixteenth corps. These were assigned to the command of General Washburne. On the 11th of June General Herron arrived with his division from the Department of Missouri, and on the 14th two divisions of the Ninth corps came, under General Parke. Now the investment of Vicksburg was made absolute, with Sherman's corps on the extreme right, McPherson's next, and extending to the railway, and Ord's (late McClernand's) on the left, the investment in that direction being made complete by the divisions of Herron and Lauman, the latter lying across Stout's Bayou, and touching the bluffs on the river. Parke's corps, and the divisions of Smith and Kimball, were sent to Haines's Bluff, where fortifications commanding the land side had been erected to confront any attempt that Johnston might make in that direction.

Meanwhile Admiral Porter had made complete and ample arrangements for the most efficient co-operation on the river, and his skill and zeal were felt throughout the siege. While his heavier vessels and the mortars and great Parrott guns on the scows already mentioned were doing effective work in the immediate operations of the siege,[1] his smaller vessels were patrolling the river, to keep its banks clear of guerrillas, who were gathering in strength on the western side, and to prevent supplies reaching Vicksburg. And so skillfully were his vessels handled during the close siege, that only one of them was badly disabled,[2] and, with the exception of the casualties on that vessel, he lost only six or seven men killed and wounded.[3]

For a month General Grant closely invested Vicksburg. Day after day he drew his lines nearer and nearer, crowning hill after hill with batteries, and mining assiduously in the direction of the stronger works of his foe, with the intention of blowing them high in air. Day and night, with only slight intermissions, his heavy guns and those of Porter were hurling shot and shell with fearful effect into the city, and its suburbs within the lines,

---

[1] For forty-two days the mortar-boats were at work without intermission. During that time they fired 7,000 mortar shells, and the gun-boats fired 4,500 shells.—Porter's Report.

[2] The *Cincinnati*, Lieutenant George M. Bache commanding. She had been prepared with bales of hay and cotton, and sent to assist in silencing a troublesome water battery. After being fired at several times by "Whistling Dick," as she moved down without being hit, she went on with a full head of steam toward the position assigned her, under the fire of all the river batteries. At length a ball entered her magazine, and caused it to be drowned, and she began to sink. Shortly afterward her starboard tiller was carried away. Her commander ran her ashore at the peninsula, where she sunk. In attempting to swim ashore from her, about fifteen of her people were drowned. Twenty-five were killed and wounded. The *Cincinnati* went down with her colors nailed to the stump of her mast She was afterward raised.

[3] Report of Admiral D. D. Porter, dated "Black Hawk, July 4, 1863." The printing-press on board the flag-ship was employed for other than official business. To while away the tedious hours of the officers and men, a journal was printed on a broad-side, entitled, *The Black Hawk Chronicle*, and contained notices of the events of the siege on land and water as it progressed, often in a strain of wit and humor that must have been agreeable to the readers. The first number, issued on the 8th of June, is before the writer. It is well printed on dull yellow paper, in two columns. "Terms, 2,000 dollars per annum in Confederate notes, or equal weight in cord-wood." It informed the public, "that no special reporter belonged to the establishment," and therefore nothing but the truth might be expected. The contents were composed generally of short items. In noticing the disaster to the *Cincinnati*, the editor said:—"On the morning of May 27, the gun-boat 'Cincinnati,' packed with all kinds of fenders, went down to co-operate with General Sherman in an attack on a water battery and rifle-pits. Said battery, having grown during the night, sent some ugly customers after our gun-boat, which vessel retired on finding the place too hot for her, having first received three or four shots in her bottom. Not wishing to be annoyed by the enemy, she wisely sunk in three fathoms of water, out of reach of the enemy's shot, when the officers and crew coolly went in to bathe."

making it hell for the inhabitants, and the soldiers too, who sought shelter for limb and life in caves dug in the steep banks where streets passed through the hills. In these the women and children of whole families, free and bond, found protection from the iron hail that perforated the houses, plowed the streets, and even penetrated to these subterranean habitations, where gentle

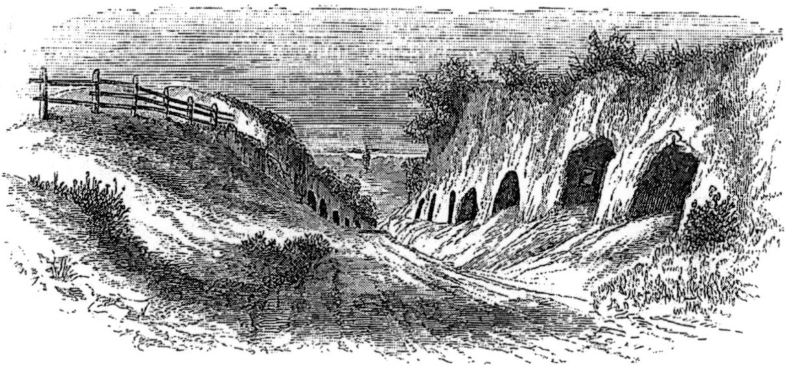

CAVES NEAR VICKSBURG.

women were waiting and praying for deliverance, and where children were born.[1] It was a terrible ordeal, and yet during that long siege very few persons, not in the army, lost their lives.

Pemberton's only hope for deliverance was in the ability of Johnston to compel Grant to raise the siege. With that hope he held out against a mul-

[1] The streets of Vicksburg are cut through the hills, and houses are often seen far above the street passengers. In the perpendicular banks formed by these cuttings, and composed of clay, caves were dug at the beginning of the siege, some of them sufficiently large to accommodate whole families, and in some instances communicating with each other by corridors. Such was the character of some made on Main Street, opposite the house of Colonel Lyman J. Strong, for the use of his family and others, and of which the writer made the accompanying sketch, in April, 1866. The caves were then in a partially ruined state, as were most of them in and around Vicksburg, for rains had washed the banks away, or had caused the filling of the caves. In this picture the appearance of the caves in their best estate is delineated, with furniture, in accordance with descriptions given to the writer by the inhabitants.

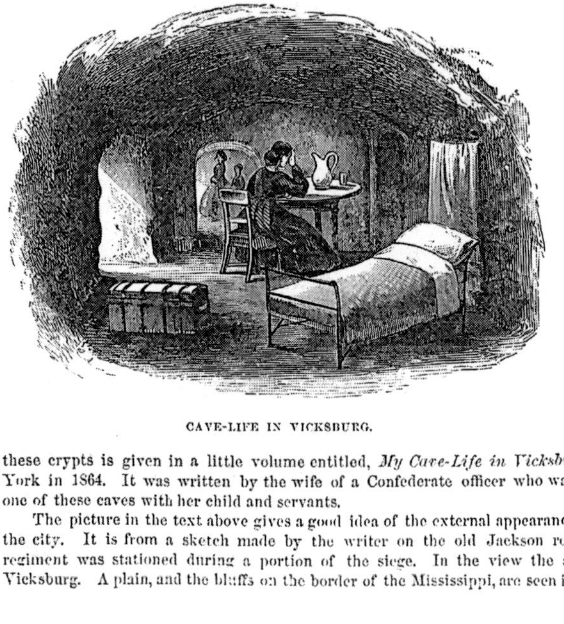

CAVE-LIFE IN VICKSBURG.

A graphic account of events in these crypts is given in a little volume entitled, *My Cave-Life in Vicksburg, by a Lady*, published in New York in 1864. It was written by the wife of a Confederate officer who was in the besieged city, and lived in one of these caves with her child and servants.

The picture in the text above gives a good idea of the external appearance of these caves, in the suburbs of the city. It is from a sketch made by the writer on the old Jackson road, where the Second Mississippi regiment was stationed during a portion of the siege. In the view the spectator is looking down toward Vicksburg. A plain, and the bluffs on the border of the Mississippi, are seen in the distance.

titude of temptations to yield.[1] On the 14th[a] Johnston sent him word that all he could attempt to do was to save the garrison, and suggested, as a mode of extrication and conjunction, a simultaneous attack upon Grant's line at a given point by his own troops without, and Pemberton's within. He asked the latter to designate the point of attack, north of the railroad (nearer Johnston's communications); and he then informed him that General Taylor (whom Banks, as we have seen,[2] had driven from the heart of Louisiana, and who was gathering forces there again) would endeavor, with eight thousand men from Richmond, in that State, to open communication with him from the west side of the river. Already that commander had sent between two and three thousand troops, under General Henry McCulloch (brother of Ben., who was killed at Pea Ridge), to strike a blow. It was leveled at a little force, chiefly of colored troops, called the "African brigade," stationed at Milliken's Bend, under General Elias S. Dennis, composed of about fourteen hundred[3] effective men, of whom all but one hundred and sixty (the Twenty-third Iowa) were negroes.

[a] June, 1863.

McCulloch's blow fell first, though lightly, on the Ninth Louisiana (colored), commanded by Colonel H. Lieb, who went out on a reconnoissance from Milliken's Bend toward Richmond, on the 6th of June,[b] preceded by two companies of the Tenth Illinois cavalry, Captain Anderson. Lieb went within three miles of Richmond, where he encountered Taylor's pickets, and fell slowly back at first. It was evident that a heavy force was in his front. Very soon some of the cavalry came dashing back, hotly pursued, when Lieb formed his troops in battle order, and with one volley dispersed the pursuers. He continued to fall back, and the Confederates, in strong number, horse and foot, pursued nearly up to the earthworks at the Bend.

[b] 1863.

H. LIEB.

It was now night, and the Confederates lay on their arms, expecting to make an easy conquest of Dennis's force in the morning. The latter was on the alert, and when, at three o'clock,[c] the Con-

[c] June 7.

[1] The misfortunes of Pemberton, before he was driven into Vicksburg by Grant, had been construed by some into crimes. He was even accused of treasonable intentions—of "selling Vicksburg." These charges reached him. Stung by them, he took a public occasion to repel them. After the failure of Grant's assault on the 22d, he made a speech to the citizens and soldiers. "You have heard," he said, "that I am incompetent and a traitor, and that it was my intention to sell Vicksburg. Follow me, and you will see the cost at which I will sell Vicksburg. When the last pound of beef, bacon, and flour—the last grain of corn, the last cow and hog, and horse and dog, shall have been consumed, and the last man shall have perished in the trenches, then, and only then, will I sell Vicksburg."

[2] See page 600.

[3] These were the Twenty-third Iowa, white; and Ninth and Eleventh Louisiana and First Mississippi, colored.

federates rushed to the assault, with the cry of "No quarter!"[1] they were met by a volley that made them recoil for a moment, but before the inexperienced blacks could fire more than another volley, they had rushed over the intrenchments. Then occurred a most sanguinary hand-to-hand fight for several minutes, with bayonets and clubbed muskets, the colored troops contesting every inch of ground with the greatest obstinacy, and answering the question often asked, "Will the negroes fight?" with a distinct affirmative, and in repetition of what had been done a few days before at Port Hudson.[2] Combatants were found after the struggle close together, mutually transfixed, the white and the black face—the master and the slave—close together and equal in death.

The Confederates drove the Nationals from their works to the levée, where a sharp contest was kept up until noon. Fortunately for the Nationals, Porter had received word the night before of the investment of Milliken's Bend, and had ordered the gun-boats *Choctaw* and *Lexington* to the aid of the garrison. This order was obeyed. They joined the troops in the struggle, and at meridian the Confederates were repulsed, and were pursued a short distance, with a loss estimated at one hundred and fifty killed and three hundred wounded. The National loss was one hundred and twenty-seven killed, two hundred and eighty-seven wounded, and about three hundred missing.[3] A week later, the Confederates were driven out of Richmond by an expedition from Young's Point, composed of the command of General Mowry, and the marine brigade under General R. W. Ellet.

Grant pressed the siege with vigor as June wore away. Johnston was beyond the Big Black, chafing with impatience to do something to save the beleaguered garrison, but in vain, for he could not collect troops sufficient for the purpose, while Pemberton, still hoping for succor, fought on, and suffered with the heart-sickness of hope deferred. Finally, on the 21st[a], he sent a messenger to Johnston, who had moved out from Canton as far as Vernon, near the Big Black, recommending him to move north of the railroad toward Vicksburg, to keep the attention of the Nationals attracted to that side, while the garrison should move down the Warrenton road at the proper time, break through the investing line, and, crossing the Big Black at Hankinson's Ferry, escape. Evidently doubting the success of his proposed movement, Pemberton suggested to Johnston, the next day, the propriety of abandoning Vicksburg, and proposing to Grant the passing out of all the troops "with their arms and equipage." Johnston declined taking this step, because he said it would be a confession of weak-

[a] June, 1863.

---

[1] It is asserted, upon what seems good authority, that orders went out from the chief conspirators at Richmond, after the promulgation of the President's Proclamation of Emancipation, to give no quarter to colored troops, and the officers commanding them. That certainly was the practice in several instances. In the fight here just recorded, the Confederates seem to have made it their special business to kill the officers commanding the colored troops. The casualties among them showed this.

[2] Up to about this time there had been no good opportunity to try the mettle of the negroes in open battle Those upon whom this first trial fell were, like all the others, inexperienced and raw recruits, having had very little time for discipline or drill. The valor with which they fought here, and at Port Hudson a few days before, satisfied the loyal public, and the Confederates, that the negro henceforth would be a power in military operations. The writer met Colonel Lieb at Vicksburg in April, 1866, who informed him that his experience at Milliken's Bend at the time we are considering, and ever afterward, with negro troops, satisfied him that there is no better material for soldiers than they. Colonel Lieb had held distinguished rank in military service in Europe, and had much experience in the discipline of troops.

[3] See Report of General Elias S. Dennis to J. A. Rawlins, Assistant Adjutant-General, June 16, 1863.

ness on his part, but told Pemberton that when it should become necessary to make terms, they might be considered as made under his authority. As Pemberton had assured him that he had sufficient supplies of short rations to last until the first week in July, Johnston hoped something might yet occur by which the garrison might be saved.

We have observed that Johnston moved out to Vernon. This was noticed by Grant's vigilant scouts, when he ordered Sherman[a] to proceed with five brigades and oppose his further advance. With these, and some re-enforcements, Sherman constructed defenses from Haines's Bluff to the Big Black that defied Johnston, and he was obliged to look for another approach to Vicksburg to co-operate with Pemberton in an effort on the part of the latter to escape. He took position between Brownsville and the river, and on the night of the third of July he sent a messenger with a note to Pemberton, informing him that a diversion would be made to enable the latter to cut his way out. The message was intercepted by General Ewing,[1] and two days afterward such news reached Johnston from Vicksburg that he fell back in haste to Jackson.

[a] June 22, 1863.

Toward the close of June the most important of Grant's mines was completed. It extended under Fort Hill Bastion, on the right of the old Jackson road, in front of McPherson, under whose direction it was constructed. The trench had been excavated in the usual zig-zag way, by workmen behind an immense gabion, which was rolled before as a protection, with a movable redoubt formed of gabions behind them, armed with a cannon, and manned by artillerists and sharp-shooters to keep the garrison behind their parapets. Mining and counter-mining had been going on for some time, but this was the first that was ready for destructive work. Between four and five o'clock in the afternoon of the 25th[b] it was fired. The explosion was terrific. The garrison, expecting the event, were partly removed, and but few were injured. But a great breach was made. A part of the face of the fort was thrown

McPHERSON'S SAPPERS AT FORT HILL.[2]

[b] June.

[1] This message (the original), written on a small piece of paper, was, until lately, in possession of the writer. It was found on the person of the spy, folded into a small space, and concealed between the cloth and the lining of the breast of his coat.

[2] This little picture illustrates the manner of approach to the fort by the sappers and miners. The ground is given as it appeared when the writer visited the spot, in April, 1866, and made a sketch from the ditch. The men and their implements have been introduced to illustrate the subject. To the reader, uninformed in military terms, it may be proper to say that gabion is a French name given to cylindrical baskets of various sizes, made of small branches of trees, open at both ends, and used to revet the interior slopes of batteries, the cheeks of embrasures, and to form the parapet of trenches. The baskets, when used, are filled with earth. For an illustration, see the tail-piece on page 376 of this volume.

down, and a bloody struggle ensued when the Nationals attempted to go in and the Confederates sought to keep them out. Hand to hand they fought, and backward and forward over the ramparts went murderous hand-grenades. Three days later,[a] another face of Fort Hill Bastion was blown away, and another struggle ensued. Other mines were ready for infernal work, and Grant was preparing for another general assault. The long, gaunt fingers of Famine were busier than ever with the life-tissues of the beleaguered. Fourteen ounces of food had become the allowance for each person for twenty-four hours, and the flesh of mules had become a savory dish![1]

[a] June 28, 1863.

Pemberton had now lost hope. For forty-five days he had been engaged in a fearful struggle, and he saw nothing but final submission. Reason and humanity demanded a cessation of hopeless strife, and so, at about eight o'clock on the morning of the 3d of July, he caused a white flag to be displayed on the crest of a hill above the camp of General Burbridge, of A. J. Smith's corps. It was borne by Major-General Bowen and Colonel Montgomery, of Pemberton's staff, who conveyed a letter from their chief to General Grant, in which he proposed the appointment of three commissioners on each side, to arrange terms for the capitulation of the post. "I make this proposition," he said, "to save the further effusion of blood, which must otherwise be shed to a frightful extent, feeling myself fully able to maintain my position a yet indefinite period." To this note General Grant replied, saying: "The effusion of blood you propose stopping by this course can be ended at any time you may choose, by an unconditional surrender of the city and gar-

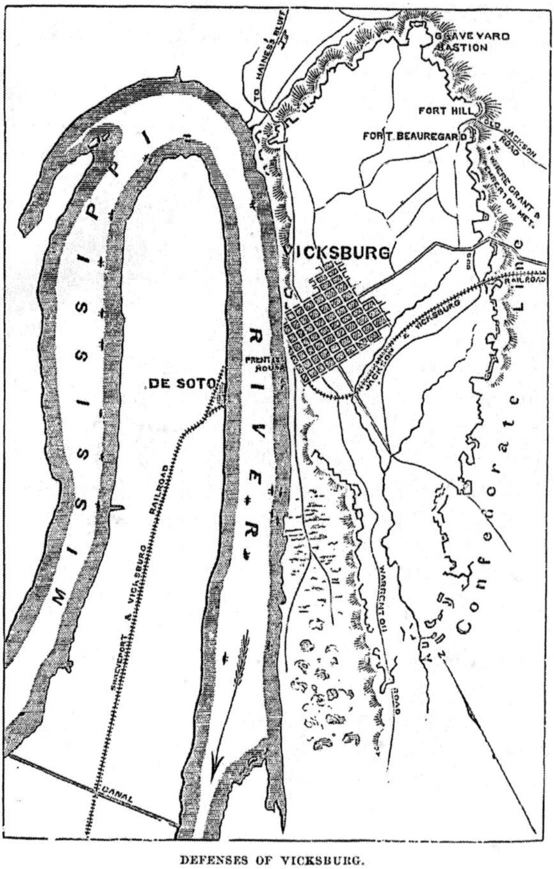

DEFENSES OF VICKSBURG.

1 "This day," wrote a citizen of Vicksburg in his diary, under date of June 30, "we heard of the first mule-meat being eaten. Some of the officers, disgusted with the salt junk, proposed to slaughter some of the fat mules as an experiment; as, if the siege lasted, we must soon come to that diet. The soup from it was quite rich in taste and appearance. Some of the ladies ate of it without knowing the difference."

rison. Men who have shown so much endurance and courage as those now in Vicksburg, will always challenge the respect of an adversary, and I can assure you will be treated with all the respect due them as prisoners of war. I do not favor the proposition of appointing commissioners to arrange terms of capitulation, because I have no other terms than those indicated above."

General Bowen expressed to General Smith a strong desire to converse with General Grant. The latter declined this, but consented to meet General Pemberton between the lines in McPherson's front at any hour that afternoon which the Confederate commander might choose. The hour of three was appointed. The moment when the leaders approached the place of meeting was announced by a signal-gun fired by the Nationals, which was answered by the Confederates. Grant was accompanied by Generals McPherson, Ord, Logan, and A. J. Smith; Pemberton, by General Bowen and Colonel Montgomery. They met on the southern slope of Fort Hill, to the left of the old Jackson road; and after introductions and a few minutes conversation, the two chiefs withdrew to the shade of a live-oak tree, where they sat down on the grass and held a private conference.[1] It ended by Grant promising to send Pemberton a proposition in writing before night, and both agreeing that hostilities should cease while the subject was under discussion.

MONUMENT AT VICKSBURG.

Toward evening Grant sent General Logan and Lieutenant-Colonel Wilson, of his staff, with a letter to Pemberton, in which he proposed that, on the acceptance of his terms, he should march in one division as a guard and take possession the next morning at eight o'clock; that as soon as paroles could be prepared and signed, the vanquished should march out of the National lines, the officers taking with them their regimental clothing—the staff, field, and cavalry officers one

[1] The live-oak tree under which Grant and Pemberton held their private conference was very soon afterward hewn down, and converted into the forms of canes and other objects by the officers and soldiers, as mementoes, and on its site a handsome commemorative monument was erected, which is delineated in the above engraving, as it and its surroundings appeared when the writer sketched it. in April, 1866. The monument was of white veined marble, about twelve feet in height, composed of an obelisk and base, and surmounted by a sphere. It was very much mutilated by having pieces knocked off of every edge, and also of the devices, by relic-seekers, and the lettering obliterated by the rebellious, it is said. It was difficult to determine the character of the devices on it, or decipher the inscription. I was informed that they were as follows: On one side of the obelisk was an eagle bearing the Goddess of Liberty on its wings, as it hovered over a group of implements of war, and holding in its talons a shield, and in its beak a ribbon, with the National motto, E PLURIBUS UNUM. The monument bore the inscription, "To the Memory of the Surrender of Vicksburg, by Lieutenant-General J. G. Pemberton, to Major-General U. S. Grant, U. S. A., on the 4th of July, 1863."

It was evident that no monument of stone could long endure the vandalism of relic-seekers, so the mutilated one was removed toward the close of 1866, and a new and appropriate one erected on its base, which will forever defy the destructive hand. It is an immense iron cannon, of very nearly the proportions of the marble obelisk, and is surmounted by a huge shell, which takes the place of the sphere.

horse each, and the rank and file to be allowed to take all their clothing, but no other property. He consented to their taking from their own stores any amount of rations necessary, and cooking utensils for preparing them; also, thirty wagons (counting two two-horse or mule teams as one) for transportation.

At three o'clock on the morning of the 4th,[a] General Legget, quartered at Fort Hill, received Pemberton's reply to Grant, and immediately forwarded it to his chief's head-quarters by Captain W. J. White, of his staff. Colonel Bowers received it and read it to the General. Pemberton accepted the terms proposed, in the main, but wished to amend, "in justice," he said, "to the honor and spirit of his troops," by having permission granted for them to march out with their colors and arms, and to stack them in front of the Confederate lines; also, that the officers should "retain their side-arms and personal property, and the rights and property of citizens be respected." Grant instantly wrote a reply, refusing to accede to Pemberton's amendments in full. He declined subjection to any restraint concerning the citizens, at the same time giving assurances that they should not suffer undue annoyances. He consented to the marching out of the brigades, at ten o'clock in the morning, to the front of their respective positions, when, after stacking their arms, they should retire inside, and remain prisoners of war until paroled. Unwilling to suffer any further delay, he gave Pemberton to understand that if these modified terms were not accepted he should open fire upon him at nine o'clock.

[a] July, 1863.

Pemberton accepted the terms. McPherson's corps was immediately placed under arms as a guard during the ceremonies of surrender. At ten o'clock on that ever-memorable holiday of the nation,[b] the brigades began to march out. In the course of three hours their arms were stacked, and they were again within their intrenchments.

[b] July 4.

McPherson had been commissioned to formally receive the stipulated surrender from Pemberton. When the work was finished, he was joined by Grant and Logan, and the three leaders, with their respective staff officers, and, accompanied by Pemberton and his staff, rode into the city in triumph at a little past noon. Already the National flag had been raised on the Court-House, while the joyous soldiers were singing the stirring song beginning—

"Yes, we'll rally 'round the flag, boys, we'll rally once again,
Shouting the battle-cry of Freedom!
We'll rally from the hill-side, we'll gather from the plain,
Shouting the battle-cry of Freedom!"

By three o'clock the possession of the post was absolute, and Porter's powerful fleet and the flotilla of transports were lying quietly at the levée. That evening, in commemoration of the National birthday, the soldiers regaled the citizens of Vicksburg with fire-works more harmless than those which, for more than forty nights, had coursed the heavens above them like malignant meteors, heralding war, pestilence, and famine. McPherson made his head-quarters at the fine mansion of Dr. Balfour, on the corner of Crawford and Cherry Streets, whence he issued a stirring congratulatory address to his soldiers, and Grant returned to his modest tent in the distant cane-

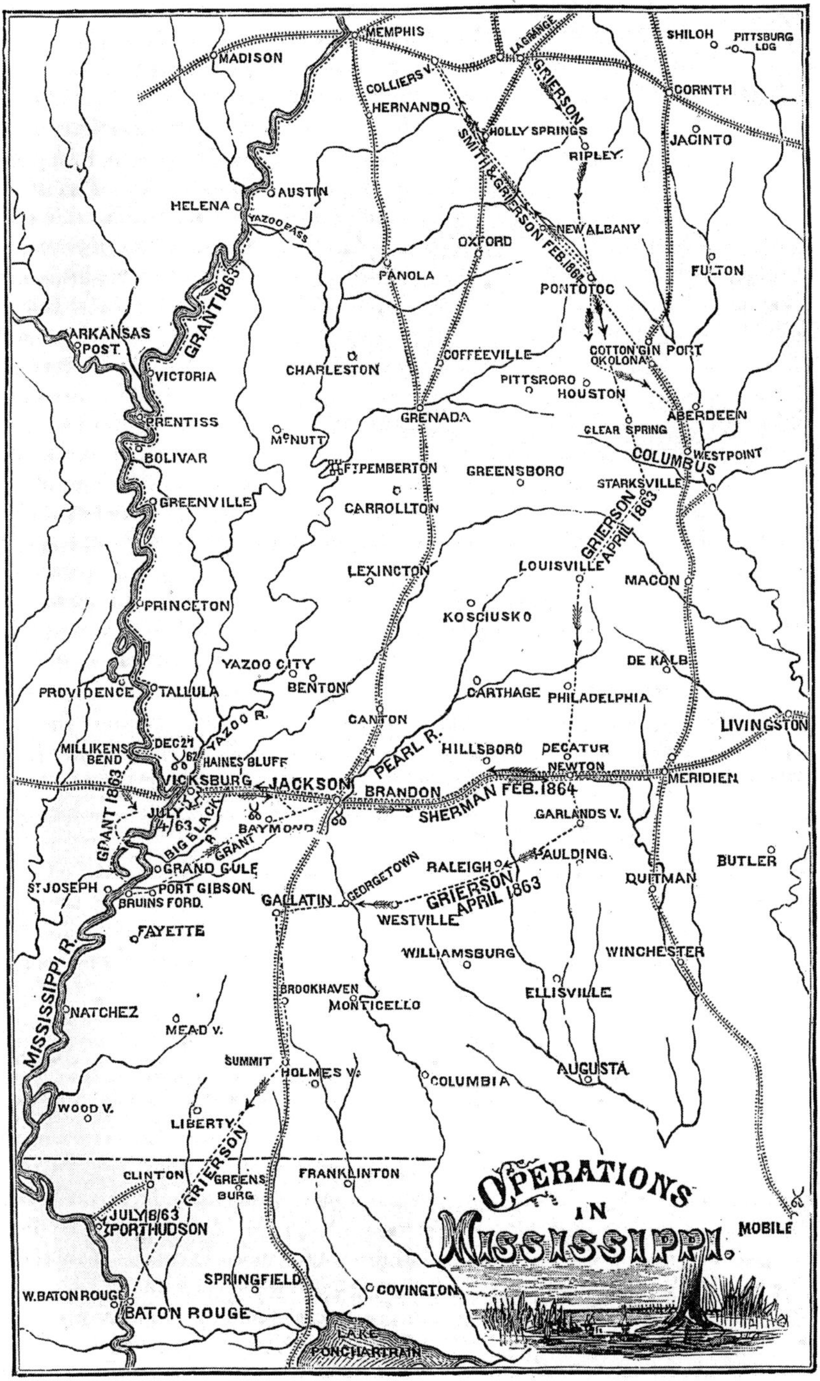
OPERATIONS IN MISSISSIPPI.
MEMPHIS
MADISON
LAGRANGE
SHILOH
PITTSBURG LDG
CORINTH
COLLIERS V.
HERNANDO
GRIERSON
HOLLY SPRINGS
JACINTO
RIPLEY
SMITH & GRIERSON FEB. 1864
AUSTIN
HELENA
YAZOO PASS
NEW ALBANY
OXFORD
FULTON
PANOLA
PONTOTOC
GRANT 1863
ARKANSAS POST
COFFEEVILLE
COTTON GIN PORT
OKOLONA
VICTORIA
CHARLESTON
PITTSBORO
HOUSTON
PRENTISS
GRENADA
ABERDEEN
CLEAR SPRING
McNUTT
BOLIVAR
COLUMBUS
WESTPOINT
FT PEMBERTON
GREENSBORO
STARKSVILLE
GREENVILLE
CARROLLTON
GRIERSON APRIL 1863
LEXINGTON
LOUISVILLE
MACON
PRINCETON
KOSCIUSKO
YAZOO CITY
DE KALB
BENTON
PROVIDENCE
TALLULA
CARTHAGE
PHILADELPHIA
YAZOO R.
CANTON
LIVINGSTON
MILLIKENS BEND
DEC 27 62
PEARL R.
HILLSBORO
DECATUR
HAINES BLUFF
NEWTON
VICKSBURG
JACKSON
BRANDON
MERIDIEN
JULY 4/63
SHERMAN FEB. 1864
GRANT 1863
GARLANDS V.
BIG BLACK R.
BAYMOND
GRANT
RALEIGH
PAULDING
BUTLER
GRAND GULF
GEORGETOWN
QUITMAN
ST JOSEPH
PORT GIBSON
GRIERSON APRIL 1863
BRUINS FORD.
GALLATIN
WESTVILLE
FAYETTE
WILLIAMSBURG
WINCHESTER
MISSISSIPPI R.
BROOKHAVEN
ELLISVILLE
MONTICELLO
NATCHEZ
MEAD V.
SUMMIT
HOLMES V.
AUGUSTA
COLUMBIA
WOOD V.
LIBERTY
GRIERSON
CLINTON
GREENSBURG
FRANKLINTON
JULY 8/63
PORT HUDSON
MOBILE
SPRINGFIELD
COVINGTON
W. BATON ROUGE
BATON ROUGE
LAKE PONCHARTRAIN

brake[1] for the night, the greatest conqueror of the war thus far. After they were duly paroled, and were supplied with three days' rations, the vanquished soldiers were escorted[a] across the Big Black River, and sent on their way rejoicing to Johnston at Jackson.

[a] July 11, 1863.

The spoils of the great victory were more important in character and number than any that had yet been won during the war.[2] Its effect, in connection with the great National victory at Gettysburg, in Pennsylvania, won simultaneously, and which we shall consider presently, was most disastrous to the cause of the Conspirators.[3] The Fourth of July, 1863, marked the turning-point in the war, and thenceforth the star of the Republic was evidently in the ascendant.

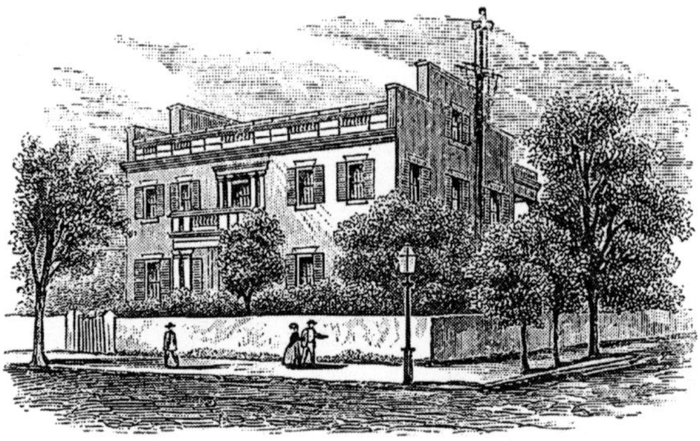

McPHERSON'S HEAD-QUARTERS.

Notwithstanding his troops were much exhausted by forced marches, battles, and the long siege, and he had reported that they absolutely required a rest of several weeks before they would be fit for another campaign, Grant

---

[1] See page 616.

[2] General Grant thus stated the result of the operations of his army from Port Gibson to Vicksburg:—"The result of this campaign has been the defeat of the enemy in five battles outside of Vicksburg; the occupation of Jackson, the capital of the State of Mississippi, and the capture of Vicksburg and its garrison, and munitions of war; a loss to the enemy of thirty-seven thousand (37,000) prisoners, among whom were fifteen general officers; at least ten thousand killed and wounded, and among the killed Generals Tracy, Tilghman, and Green, and hundreds, and perhaps thousands, of stragglers, who can never be collected and reorganized. Arms and munitions of war for an army of sixty thousand men have fallen into our hands, besides a large amount of other public property, consisting of railroads, locomotives, cars, steamboats, cotton, &c., and much was destroyed to prevent our capturing it."

He summed up his loss, in the series of battles known as Port Gibson, Fourteen Mile Creek (skirmish), Raymond, Jackson, Champion Hills, Big Black railroad bridge, and Vicksburg, at 9,855, of whom 1,223 were killed, 7,095 wounded, and 537 missing. "Of the wounded," he said, "many were but slightly wounded, and continued on duty; many more required but a few days or weeks for their recovery. Not more than one-half of the wounded were permanently disabled."—General Grant's *Report*, July 6, 1863.

The 37,000 prisoners were not all captured at Vicksburg. The number there paroled, including 6,000 of the sick and wounded in the hospitals, was 27,000, of whom only 15,000 were reported fit for duty. The generous terms of surrender, and the paroling of the prisoners, was complained of. Of this Grant said, in his report: "These terms I regard more favorable to the Government than an unconditional surrender. It saved us the transportation of them North, which at that time would have been very difficult, owing to the limited amount of river transportation on hand, and the expense of subsisting them. It left our army free to operate against Johnston, who was threatening us from the direction of Jackson; and our river transportation to be used for the movement of troops to any point the exigency of the service might require."

[3] The blow was unexpected to the Conspirators. They knew how strong Vicksburg was, and were confident that the accomplished soldier, General Johnston, would compel Grant to raise the siege. Even the *Daily Citizen*, a paper printed in Vicksburg, only two days before the surrender (July 2) talked as boastfully as if perfectly confident of success. In a copy before the writer, printed on wall-paper, the editor said: "The great Ulysses—the Yankee generalissimo surnamed Grant—has expressed his intention of dining in Vicksburg on Saturday next, and celebrating the Fourth of July by a grand dinner, and so forth. When asked if he would invite General Joe Johnston to join him, he said, 'No! for fear there will be a row at the table.' *Ulysses* must get into the city before he dines in it. The way to cook a rabbit is, 'first catch the rabbit,' &c." In another paragraph, the *Citizen* eulogized the luxury of mule-meat and fricasseed kitten.

When the National troops entered the city, they found the forms of this issue of the *Citizen* standing, when some soldier-printers, taking out a paragraph at the bottom of the fourth column, inserted the following in its stead, and printed a few copies on the wall-paper found in the office: "Two days bring about great

found it necessary to take immediate measures for driving Johnston from his rear, and for that purpose he dispatched Sherman, with a large force. The result will be noticed hereafter. He also prepared to send an expedition under General Herron to assist Banks in the reduction of Port Hudson, when he received intelligence of events at that stronghold which made the expedition unnecessary. Let us observe what those events were.

We left General Banks investing Port Hudson, or Hickey's Landing,[1] late in May. His troops were commanded by Generals Weitzel, Auger, Grover, Dwight, and T. W. Sherman, and the beleaguered garrison were under the command of General Frank K. Gardner, as we have observed.[2] The troops with which Banks crossed the river at Bayou Sara formed a junction on the 23d[a] with those which came up from Baton Rouge under Auger and Sherman, and the National line on that day occupied the Bayou Sara road, about five miles from Port Hudson. At Port Hudson Plains, Auger, on his march, encountered and repulsed a force of Confederates under Colonel Miles, the latter losing one hundred and fifty men; and on the day of the investment[b] the Confederates were driven within their outer line of intrenchments. Weitzel, who had covered

[a] May, 1863.

[b] May 24.

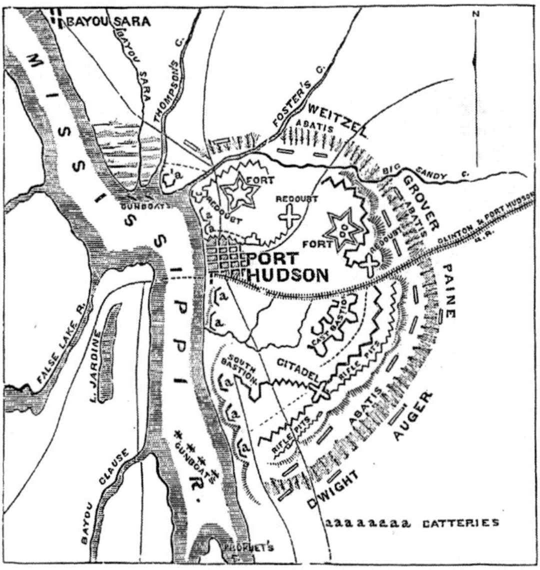

THE DEFENSES OF PORT HUDSON.

---

changes. The banner of the Union floats over Vicksburg. General Grant has 'caught the rabbit,' he has dined in Vicksburg; and he did bring his dinner with him. The 'Citizen' lives to see it. For the last time it appears on wall-paper. No more will it eulogize mule-meat and fricasseed kitten—urge Southern warriors to such diet never more. This is the last wall-paper edition, and is, excepting this note, from the types as we find them."

Johnston sent the astounding news of the surrender of Vicksburg to the Conspirators on the 7th. It was a staggering blow, and Jefferson Davis and his friends endeavored to blind the people to the fact that the disaster was mainly due to his incompetence to direct, and his mischievous interference with the military movements in Mississippi, by trying to cast the blame on Johnston, who was not only unable, on account of his wounds, to perform active service in the field, but was denied sufficient troops to act efficiently, and was trammeled with the orders of his incompetent official superior in Richmond. "The news of the fall of Vicksburg," wrote John R. Thompson from Richmond to the *Atlanta Appeal*, "has awakened here the bitterest sorrow, not unmingled with surprise. . . . . The *Sentinel*, the Government organ, holds General Johnston mainly responsible for the result, and the immediate representatives of the Administration are said to blame him in unmeasured terms."

[1] See page 598. We have before observed that Port Hudson was on a high bank or bluff, on the east side of the Mississippi, at a sharp bend. Its fortifications were well arranged for defense. Below the landing known as Hickey's, the first batteries were on a bluff about forty feet above high-water mark. There three series of batteries extended along the river above Port Hudson to a point on Thompson's Creek, the whole continuous line being about three miles in length. Above the creek was an impassable marsh, making an excellent flank defense. From the lower battery began a line of land fortifications of a general semicircular form, about ten miles in extent, and terminating at Thompson's Creek. The guns with which these works were armed were very heavy, and there were light batteries that might be moved to strengthen any part of the line.

[2] See page 620.

Banks's march from Alexandria, had arrived and made the investment of the fort complete, for Admiral Farragut, with the *Hartford*, *Albatross*, and one or two other gunboats above Port Hudson, and the *Monongahela*, *Richmond*, *Essex*, and *Genesee*, with mortar-boats under Commander C. H. B. Caldwell, below, held the river, and were shelling the Confederate works at intervals, day and night.

Banks was informed that the Confederates were withdrawing from the post, and on the 26th was told that very few were behind the works. The defenses were thoroughly reconnoitered without gaining positive information concerning the strength of the garrison, and he determined to develop it by a general assault. Orders were given accordingly, and on the morning of the 27th[a] his artillery opened upon them with spirit, and continued firing during nearly the whole day. It was intended for the infantry to assail the works at the same time at all points, under the fire of the great guns, but unfortunately there was a miscarriage. At about ten o'clock, while the batteries were zealously at work, Generals Weitzel, Grover, and Payne, on Banks's right, made a vigorous attack, but it was long past noon before Auger in the center, and Sherman on the left, were fairly at work. The navy was fully up to time, and from the *Hartford* and *Albatross* above, and the *Monongahela*, *Richmond*, *Essex*, and *Genesee* below, and the mortar-boats, Farragut poured a continuous stream of shells upon the garrison (which was still in full force) with marked effect. Already his shells had driven them from their first battery on the river below, and now, by taking their landward batteries in reverse, while they were hotly engaged with the troops, several of the heavy guns were dismounted by the naval missiles. The battle was furious, and never did men fight with greater determination than Banks's little force against the odds of an equal number behind strong intrenchments, which were defended in front by rifle-pits, and approached only through thick *abatis*, over which swept, like a besom of destruction, the shells from Confederate guns.

[a] May, 1863.

On the National right the struggle was most severe; the First and Second Louisiana colored troops vying with their white companions-in-arms in deeds of valor, and in fortitude under heavy pressure. These made three desperate charges upon the batteries, losing heavily each time, and justifying by their courage and deeds the hopes of their commander, and winning his special commendation.[1] The Nationals gained ground continually, as hour after hour wore away. They crossed Big Sandy Creek, and, at four o'clock, drove the Confederates through woods to their fortifications. On the left and center there was equal bravery; and along the whole line, at sunset, the Confederates, who had fought gallantly, were behind the shelter of their works. The Nationals moved close up to these, and they and their antagonists held opposite sides of the parapet. The troops on the right continued to hold this position, but those on the left, exposed to a flank fire, withdrew to a belt of woods not far off. So ended the first general assault upon Port

[1] This first important trial of the mettle of negro troops, repeated a few days later at Milliken's Bend (see page 624), produced a profound impression in the army and throughout the country. "The position occupied by these troops," said General Banks in his report, "was one of importance, and called for the utmost steadiness and bravery in those to whom it was confided. It gives me pleasure to report that they answered every expecta-

Hudson, in which many a brave man passed away.[1] The National loss was two hundred and ninety-three killed and fifteen hundred and forty-nine wounded. The Confederate loss did not exceed three hundred in killed and wounded.

DESTRUCTION IN THE WORKS AT PORT HUDSON.

Banks was not disheartened by this disastrous failure. He occupied the next day in burying his dead, under the protection of a truce, and then he went to work with a determination to reduce the post by a regular siege. Bravely his men worked in the hot June sun, exposed every moment to the bullets of the expert sharp-shooters of the foe. Day after day his cannon and Farragut's great guns shelled the works, disabling many of their guns, and giving the interior of their fortifications the sad aspect of almost universal destruction. They disturbed the repose of the garrison

---

tion. In many respects their conduct was heroic. No troops could be more determined or more daring. They made, during the day, three charges upon the batteries of the enemy, suffering very heavy losses, and holding their position at nightfall with the other troops on the right of our line."

The Confederates and their friends in the Free-labor States had sneered so much and so persistently at the idea of negroes fighting, or being disciplined into efficient troops, that the intelligence of these tests was received by the loyal people with the most generous enthusiasm.

"Niggers won't fight," ah, ha!
"Niggers won't fight," ah, ha!
"They are no good for war,
One in a hundred."
Let Mississippi's shore,
Flooded with negro gore,
Echo back evermore—
"See *our* six hundred!"

said a writer in the Albany *Evening Journal*, in imitation of Tennyson's "Charge of the Six Hundred" at Balaklava; and George H. Boker, of Philadelphia, wrote that noble tribute to the valor of the Second Louisiana, which closes with:—

"Hundreds on hundreds fell;
But they are resting well.
Scourges and shackles strong
Never shall do them wrong.
O, to the living few,
Soldiers, be just and true!
Hail them as comrades tried,
Fight with them side by side;
Never, in field or tent,
Scorn the black regiment."

[1] Among the slain were Colonels Clark, of the Sixth Michigan, D. S. Cowles, of the One Hundred and Twenty-eighth New York, Payne, of the Second Louisiana, and Chapin, of the Thirtieth Massachusetts. Gene-

incessantly, day and night, and wore them down with fatigue and watching; while their provisions were becoming scarce, their medical stores exhausted, and famine was threatened. They were completely hemmed in, and could receive nothing from the outer world but pure air, the sunlight, and the messengers of death from their foes. Banks's little army, then not exceeding twelve thousand effective men, was also closely hemmed in by a cordon of intensely hostile inhabitants; and since the raid of Grierson and his troop, Confederate cavalry had been concentrating in his rear, while General Taylor was gathering a new army in the regions of Louisiana, which the National troops had almost abandoned for the purpose of completing the task of opening the Mississippi. These might be joined by a force from Texas sufficient to capture New Orleans, while General Johnston might sweep down in the rear of Grant and fall upon Banks at any moment.

There was peril before and peril behind, and Banks felt the necessity of a speedy reduction of Port Hudson. He accordingly planned another assault, and on the 11th of June[a] he attempted to establish a new line within easy attacking distance of the Confederate works, so as to avoid the dangers of a movement on their front over a broad space of ground. Under a heavy fire of his artillery the troops advanced at three o'clock in the morning, and made their way through the *abatis*, when the movement was promptly met by the garrison, and a severe struggle ensued. At first some of the Confederates were driven within their works, and the Nationals, under General Birge, attempted to scale them, but were repulsed. The only soldier who reached the parapet was the gallant young Connecticut officer, Lieutenant Stanton Allyn, who gave his life to his country not long afterward, when his body was buried in the soil of Louisiana.[1] His men, accustomed to his courage and skill, followed him willingly in the desperate struggle; but the terrible fire from the works hurled them back, and the entire attacking force was driven beyond the *abatis* with heavy loss, a considerable number having been made prisoners.

[a] 1863.

This failure was followed three days later[b] by an attempt to carry the works by storm. At that time Banks's army lay mostly in two lines, forming a right angle, with a right and left, but no center. The division of Grover, on the upper side of the post, extended nearly three miles, from near the mouth of Thompson's Creek into the interior, within supporting distance of General Auger's division, which extended from near that point about the same distance to the river below Port Hudson, and within hailing distance of the fleet. When the final disposition for assault was made, General Gardner was entreated to surrender and stop the effusion of blood,[2] but refused, hoping, like General Pemberton

[b] June 14.

---

ral T. W. Sherman was very seriously wounded, but finally recovered with the loss of a leg, and General Neal Dow, of Maine, was slightly wounded. Colonel Cowles, of Hudson, New York, one of the noblest men in the army, was wounded in the thickest of the fight by a bayonet thrust, and died half an hour afterward.

[1] It was afterward removed to his native State.

[2] Banks sent a note to General Gardner on Saturday, the 13th, demanding an unconditional surrender of the post. He complimented the commander and his garrison for their courage and fortitude, and demanded the surrender in the name of humanity. He assured him of the overwhelming force of the Nationals in men and cannon, and that Gardner's dispatch to Johnston, telling of his straits and the dangers of starvation, had been intercepted, and the weakness of the post made known.

at Vicksburg, even while shot and shell were spreading death and destruction all around him,[1] that Johnston would come to his rescue.

It was arranged for the main attack to be made by Grover and Weitzel on the extreme northeasterly angle of the Confederate works, while Generals Auger and Dwight should make a feint or a real attack, as circumstances might determine, on the right of the works. He was directed to press up stealthily through a ravine, and rush over the defenses simultaneously with the attack on their left.

On the National right two regiments were detailed as sharp-shooters (Seventy-fifth New York and Twelfth Connecticut), to creep up and lie on the exterior slope of the breastworks, followed by another regiment (the Ninety-first New York), each man carrying his musket and a five-pound hand-grenade, to throw over the parapet. A third regiment (Twenty-fourth Connecticut) was detailed to carry sand-bags full of cotton, with which to fill the ditch in front of the breastworks, and enable the storming party to pass easily. These were to be followed by the regiments of Weitzel's brigade, under Colonel Smith, of the One Hundred and Fourteenth New York, to be supported by the brigades of Colonels Kimball and Morgan, under the general command of General Birge, the whole forming the storming party on the right. In conjunction with these, and on their left, moved a separate column under General Paine, composed of the old division of General Emory. Both parties were under the command of General Grover, who planned the attack. Acting Brigadier-General Dudley's brigade, of Auger's division, was held in reserve. It was intended to have Weitzel's command[2] effect a lodgment inside of the Confederate works, and thus prepare the way for the operation of Paine's division.[3]

This movement commenced just at dawn[a] (first along a covered way to within three hundred yards of the works), and was met by a most determined resistance by the Confederates, who, informed of it, were massed at the point of attack. The skirmishers, making their way over rough and vine-tangled ground, in the face of an incessant fire in the front, reached the ditch, where they were terribly smitten by an enfilading one, that drove them back; and even the hand-grenades were made to plague their bearers, for they were caught up by the besieged and

[a] June 14, 1863.

---

[1] It appears from the diary of a captured Confederate soldier (J. A. Kennedy, of the First Alabama), that one of Banks's heavy guns had been named by the besieged, as we have observed one of the Confederate cannon at Vicksburg was—"Whistling Dick," and that it was the means of great destruction Under date of "June 9," he wrote: "Whistling Dick is at work to-day, tearing our camps all to pieces. Our sick have been removed to the ravine. It is difficult to get something to eat. The Yankee artillery is playing upon us all round. . . . . The Hessians burned our commissary with a shell to-day."

[2] Weitzel's command was composed of his own brigade (Eighth Vermont, Twelfth Connecticut, and Seventy-fifth and One Hundred and Fourteenth New York), and the Twenty-fourth Connecticut and Fifty-second Massachusetts, of Grover's division. The Seventy-fifth New York and Twelfth Connecticut, forming a separate command under Colonel Babcock, of the first-named regiment, were detailed as skirmishers.

[3] Paine's column advanced to the assault in the following order: In the advance, as skirmishers, the Eighth New Hampshire and Fourth Wisconsin. Behind these were five companies of the Fourth Massachusetts, One Hundred and Tenth New York, and four companies of the Third Brigade. Closely upon these followed the Third Brigade, under Colonel Gooding, composed of the Thirty-first, Thirty-eighth, and Fifty-third Massachusetts, and One Hundred and Fifty-sixth and One Hundred and Seventy-fifth New York. Then a part of the Second Brigade, under Colonel Fearing, composed of the One Hundred and Thirty-third and One Hundred and Seventy third New York, the remainder of the brigade being detailed as skirmishers. After the Second Brigade followed the First, under Colonel Ferris, composed of the Twenty-eighth Connecticut (his own), Fourth Massachusetts, and four companies of the One Hundred and Tenth New York. Nimm's battery and pioneers accompanied the column.

sent back to explode among the assailants. Yet steadily the assaulting column moved up and made a series of vigorous attacks, but effected little, so heavily were the works manned at the point of the blow. Meanwhile, Dwight was fighting desperately on the left, but without effecting an entrance into the works, and Auger was as gallantly struggling, but to as little purpose. Success was with the Confederates. The Nationals were repulsed at all points, and at eleven o'clock in the morning the struggle ceased. Banks had lost in this assault about seven hundred men, and General Paine, whose division had borne the brunt of the battle, was among the wounded. Yet he had gained a decided advantage by the operation. Paine and Weitzel on the right had advanced much nearer to the Confederate works than they were before, where their men intrenched and began the erection of new batteries, while on the left General Dwight carried and held a hill which commanded the "citadel"—a vital point of the intrenchments—and he was thereby enabled a few days later to seize and hold another point on the same ridge with the "citadel," within ten yards of the Confederate line.

Now again the siege went on in the usual way. There was mining and counter-mining. The shells from the army and navy poured upon the garrison, and fearfully increased the miseries of the worn and half-starving troops. Gun after gun on the Confederate works was disabled, until at length only fifteen effective ones remained on the landward side; only twenty rounds to each man of the ammunition for small arms was left, and the garrison were beginning to subsist on mule-meat, and even fricasseed rats.[1] At the same time, Banks had nearly completed a mine, by which thirty barrels of gunpowder would have been exploded under the "citadel." The beleaguered garrison could have held out but a few days longer. Their gallant leader had begun to despair of aid from Johnston, and was at his wit's end, when he and his troops were suddenly startled by the thunder of cannon and loud cheering along the whole National line[a] and upon the river squadron, followed by the shouts of pickets—"Vicksburg has surrendered!" This was the knell to Gardner's hopes. At midnight he sent a note by a flag to General Banks, inquiring if the report were true, and if so, asking for a cessation of hostilities, with a view to the consideration of terms for surrendering the position. Banks assured Gardner that he had an official dispatch from General Grant to that effect, dated on the 4th instant, but he refused his consent to a cessation of hostilities for the purpose named. Gardner then called a council of officers, composed of General Beale, Colonels Steadman, Miles, Lyle, and Shelby, and Lieutenant-Colonel M. J. Smith, when it was agreed to surrender, and the commander proposed to Banks the appointment of joint commissioners to arrange the terms. This was agreed to, and General Charles P. Stone, Colonel Henry W. Birge, and Lieutenant-Colonel Richard B. Irwin were chosen for the purpose on the part of Banks. The terms agreed upon were the surrender of the post and its appurtenances, the officers and privates to receive the treatment due prisoners of war, and

[a] July 7, 1863.

[1] The garrison's supply of meat gave out on the 30th of June, when Gardner ordered mules to be slain for food. "Many of the men, as if in mockery of famine, caught rats and ate them, declaring that they were better than squirrels."—Narrative of a Confederate writer, dated Mobile, July 20, 1863.

to retain their private property; the garrison to stack their arms and colors in submission on the following day. The surrender was duly completed early in the morning of the 9th,[a] when six thousand four hundred and eight men, including four hundred and fifty-five officers, became prisoners of war, and the National troops took possession of the post.[1] The little hamlet of Port Hudson, within the lines, composed of a few houses and a small church, was in ruins. General Banks found comfortable quarters at the farm-house of Riley's plantation, not far distant, which had survived the storm of war. Farragut, with the veteran *Hartford* and the *Albatross*, moved down to Port Hudson, and received the cordial greetings of the troops.

[a] July, 1863.

BANKS'S HEAD-QUARTERS, PORT HUDSON.

Banks's loss in men during the siege of forty-five days was about three thousand, and that of Gardner about eight hundred. The spoils of victory were the important post, two steamers, fifty-one pieces of artillery, five thousand small arms, and a large quantity of fixed ammunition for the latter and for cannon. Banks stated that his winnings for the campaign which then ended so gloriously for the National arms, amounted to ten thousand five hundred and eighty-four prisoners, seventy-three guns, six thousand small arms, three gun-boats, eight transports, and a large quantity of cotton, cattle, and other property of immense value.

This conquest gave the final blow in the removal of the obstructions to the free navigation of the Mississippi River by Confederate batteries, for which Fremont planned and worked so earnestly in the first year of the war, and for which the Western troops fought so gallantly and persistently. The first of these obstructions, as we have seen, was erected at Vicksburg,[2] and there the finishing blow was really given, for the fall of Port Hudson was but a consequence of the siege and surrender of Vicksburg. The Mississippi was now open to the passage of vessels upon its bosom, from St. Louis to New Orleans, and its waters, as the President said, unobstructed by batteries or other impediments, now "went unvexed to the sea." On the 16th of July the steamer *Imperial*, from St. Louis, arrived at New Orleans, making the first communication of the kind between those cities for two years. On the 28th of the same month she returned to her wharf at St. Louis, announcing the fact that the great highway of the commerce of the Mississippi Valley was again open, and was hailed with the welcoming shouts of thousands of citizens.

The capture of Vicksburg and Port Hudson, by which powerful portions of the Confederacy were severed and weakened, was hailed with the most

[1] General Banks deputed General George L. Andrews to receive the surrender. To him General Gardner offered his sword. Andrews received it, but immediately returned it to the general, complimenting him for maintaining the defense of the post so gallantly.

[2] See page 164, volume I.

profound satisfaction by the loyal people of the Republic. Occurring at the moment when the aggressive power of the Confederates was fatally smitten at Gettysburg, it gave assurances of the final triumph of the Government over its enemies. It dismayed the conspirators, and destroyed the hopes of the ruling classes abroad, who, until that time, had believed they would speedily see an ignominious ending of the great experiment of republican government in America. It utterly confounded those prophets among the political leaders in the Free-labor States who sympathized with the conspirators, and who, at that very moment, as we shall observe hereafter, were prophesying, in apparent accordance with their own wishes, the speedy triumph of Jefferson Davis and his legions, civil and military. In the blindness of partisan zeal, they were unable to discover the great lights of eternal principles that were illuminating the pathways of those who were contending for the life of a great Nation and the Rights of Man. They and the conspirators seemed to forget that there is a God whose throne is established upon JUSTICE and MERCY, whose ear is ever open to the cry of the oppressed, and whose arm is ever bared in the defense of the righteous.

The writer visited the theater of events described in this and the preceding chapter in April, 1866. He had spent a few days in New Orleans, where he had experienced the kind courtesies of Generals Sheridan and Hartsuff, and held interviews with several Confederate leaders, mostly temporary visitors there. Among these was General Frank K. Gardner, the commander at Port Hudson, who was residing in the city, and pursuing the business of a civil engineer, and from him the writer received interesting facts then, and afterward by letter, concerning the siege of Port Hudson, and also of Mobile, where Gardner was in command at a later period of the war.

The writer left New Orleans on the fine river steamer *Indiana*, on the afternoon of the 16th,[a] intending to stop at Port Hudson that night. The weather was fine, and the Mississippi was full to the brim with the spring flood, so that from the main deck we had a perfect view of the country on both sides of the great river. Among the passengers was a short, stout man, a little past sixty years of age, who happened to be the first one whom the writer addressed. When the former found that the latter was from the North, he began to curse the "Yankees" furiously. Remembering the wisdom uttered by the sacred sage, that "a soft answer turneth away wrath," the author soon allayed the passions of his elder, and during the remainder of the voyage they journeyed pleasantly together. The wrathful man had been a major in Forrest's cavalry, and was a citizen of Vicksburg. He imparted to the author a great deal of information concerning the interior of the Confederate cavalry service, in which he was largely engaged, and of the leading men in that service. He said Forrest expressed his principles of action in that service by saying, "War means fight, and fight means kill—*we want but few prisoners.*" This major had been an imprisoned spy in Sherman's camp at Vicksburg, under sentence of death by hanging the next morning. He was confined in a shanty. A heavy rain-storm came up in the evening, and while the guard was engaged for a moment in taking measures to keep out the water, the prisoner sprang into the black night, and, being well acquainted with the region, escaped.

[a] April, 1866.

We passed Baton Rouge early in the evening, and just afterward we glided by the roaring mouth of an immense crevasse, or breach in the levée, out of which a flood was pouring into the lower ground on the western side of the river, and submerging rich plantations over an area of hundreds of square miles. Informed that Port Hudson was a desolation, and then without a lodging-place, and that we should pass it at midnight, the writer concluded to omit his intended visit there, feeling little regret, for the kind hands of friends, the photographic art, and official records, had already given him more information concerning things and events there than he could possibly have learned by personal observation. Toward morning we passed the mouth of the Red River, and at sunrise were abreast the bluff, on the east side of the Mississippi, on which Fort Adams stood, a little north of the boundary-line between the States of Mississippi and Louisiana.

To the writer, who was a voyager on the Mississippi for the first time, the scenery was most strange. On each side were wide clearings, on which now were the ruins of many rich plantations, bordered by swamps covered with cypress-trees, and lying lower than the river, for the Mississippi, like the Nile, is now running upon a ridge, the ground sloping gently to these morasses. Here and there an alluvial bluff was seen, breaking the monotony, and everywhere at that high-water season the green points that project into the river, and shores covered with cotton-wood, shrubs, and larger trees, were crumbling and disappearing in the flood. After a detention of some hours, because of an accident to our steamer, we passed up the river, and, at near midnight, landed at Vicksburg.

During the writer's visit at Vicksburg he was the recipient of the kindest courtesies from Major-General T. J. Wood (then the commander of the Department of the Mississippi) and his family, and from members of his staff, and other officers stationed there. General Wood offered the services of an ambulance, horses, and driver, and the company of one of his staff, in visiting the places of historic interest about Vicksburg. Fortunately for the writer, that companion was Captain W. J. White, who, as has been already observed, was a member of General Legget's staff during the siege and at the time of the surrender. We visited together every place and object of interest in the city and along the lines, from below the railway, on the Warrenton road, to Chickasaw Bayou, and finding here and there Union people, who had suffered much "in mind, body, and estate." Among these was the family of Mr. Shirley, who was a leading lawyer of Vicksburg. His house was on the old Jackson road, not far from Fort Hill, and was occupied by General Logan as his head-quarters. Being on a lofty eminence, overlooking much of the field of operations, it was the frequent resort of General Grant

THE SHIRLEY HOUSE.

and other commanders during the siege. It was also a target for Confederate shot and shell, by which it was much shattered. It was still in a dilapidated state when we visited it, and dined with Mrs. Shirley and her daughter. The husband and father, who was quite aged, had sunk under the operations of anxiety, privations, and exposure in the woods, ravines, and caves during the siege, and died soon after the city was occupied by the National troops. The accomplished daughter kept a diary during the siege, each day's record closing with a prediction that success would crown the efforts of the Unionists. "The wish was father to the thought," and her patriotism was rewarded with the possession of the heart and hand of the gallant Colonel (afterward General) Eaton, of the National army. At the time of our visit she was a young bride.

From Mrs. Shirley's we rode to the head-quarters of General Grant, in the cane-brake, and then over the rough Walnut Hills to Chickasaw Bayou, passing on the way the house of Dr. Smith, who acted as guide to General S. D. Lee, in the fight with Sherman. He accompanied us to the theater of strife, and pointed out the various localities of interest connected with that conflict. After making a drawing of the battle-ground on the bayou, delineated on page 579, in the presence of the doctor, we left him and passed on to the Valley road, along the bottom, between the hills and the bayou, sketching the Indian Mound (see page 577) on the way, and rode into Vicksburg from the north through the deep cuts in the hills, just as a thunder-storm, which had been gathering for some time, fell upon the city. On the following morning the writer departed by railway for Jackson, and the region of Sherman's destructive march toward Alabama as far as Meridian, the stirring events of which will be considered presently.

END OF VOLUME II.

CPSIA information can be obtained at www.ICGtesting.com
Printed in the USA
BVOW071445310812

299346BV00001B/13/P

9 781429 020329